Learning Microsoft® Office 2007: Advanced Skills

Suzanne Weixel

Faithe Wempen

Catherine Skintik

PEARSON

Boston, Massachusetts
Chandler, Arizona
Glenview, Illinois
Upper Saddle River, New Jersey

ISBN-13: 978-0-13-369153-5
ISBN-10: 0-13-369153-5

PEARSON

3 4 5 6 7 8 9 10   12 11 10 09

Contents

Access 2007

Lesson 1
Managing Tables
and Data 437

PowerPoint 2007

Challenge Exercises

Introduction

Microsoft Office 2007 is Microsoft's suite of application software. The Standard version includes Word, Excel, Outlook, and PowerPoint. Other editions may also include Access, Publisher, OneNote, and InfoPath. This book covers Word (the word processing tool), Excel (the spreadsheet tool), PowerPoint (the presentation tool), and Access (the database tool). Because Microsoft Office is an integrated suite, the components can all be used separately or together to create professional-looking documents and to manage data. This book covers some of the advanced features of Microsoft Office

HOW THE BOOK IS ORGANIZED

Learning Microsoft Office 2007: Advanced Skills is made up of five Lessons. Lessons are comprised of short exercises designed for using Microsoft Office 2007 in real-life business settings. Each exercise is made up of seven key elements:

- **Software Skills.** Each exercise starts with a brief overview of the Microsoft Office tools that you'll be working with in the exercise.

- **Application Skills.** The objectives are then put into context by setting a scenario.

- **Terms.** Key terms are included and defined at the start of each exercise, so you can quickly refer back to them. The terms are then highlighted in the text.

- **Notes.** Concise notes for learning the computer concepts.

- **Procedures.** Hands-on mouse and keyboard procedures teach all necessary skills.

- **Application Exercise.** Step-by-step instructions put your skills to work.

- **On Your Own.** Each exercise concludes with a critical thinking activity that you can work through on your own. In many of these exercises you need to create your own data. The On Your Own sections can be used as additional reinforcement, for practice, or to test skill proficiency.

Each lesson ends with a **Critical Thinking Exercise**. As with the On Your Own sections, you need to rely on your own skills to complete the task, and a **Curriculum Integration Exercise**, which incorporates Language Arts, Math, Science, or Social Studies content.

A **Business Connection** appears in each lesson. These activities involve research on a topic and then using that data in a Microsoft Office application.

WORKING WITH DATA AND SOLUTION FILES

As you work through the exercises in this book, you'll be creating, opening, and saving files. You should keep the following instructions in mind:

- For many of the exercises, you can use the data files provided on the CD-ROM that comes with this book. The data files are used so that you can focus on the skills being introduced—not on keyboarding lengthy documents. The files are organized by application in the **Datafiles** folders on the CD-ROM.

- When the application exercise includes a file name and a CD icon ⊙ , you can open the file provided on CD.

- If the exercise includes a CD icon ⊙ and a keyboard icon ⌨ , you can choose to work off of either the data file or a file that you created in an earlier exercise.

- Unless the book instructs otherwise, use the default settings for text size, margin size, and so on when creating a file. If someone has changed the default software settings for the computer you're using, your exercise files may not look the same as those shown in this book. In addition, the appearance of your files may look different if the system is set to a screen resolution other than 800×600.

- All the exercises instruct you to save the files created or to save the exercise files under a new name.

- When you see **_xx** in any instructions in this book, it means that you should type an underscore followed by your own initials—not the actual text "_xx". This will help your instructor identify your work.

- You should verify the name of the hard disk or network folder to which files should be saved.

WHAT'S ON THE CD ⊙

The CD contains the following:

- **Data Files** for many of the exercises. This way you don't have to type lengthy documents from scratch.

- **Technology Applications Student Worktext.** This Student Worktext provides a complete foundation for essential computer concepts. Seventeen chapters of beautifully illustrated, full-color lessons covering everything students need for a comprehensive understanding of information technology, including end-of-chapter assessment activities.

To Access the Files Included on CD

1. Insert the *Learning Microsoft Office 2007: Advanced Skills* CD in the CD-ROM drive.
2. Navigate to your CD-ROM drive; right-click **start** / ⊙ and choose Explore from the shortcut menu.
3. Navigate to your CD-ROM drive.
4. Right-click the folder that you wish to copy.
5. Navigate to the location where you wish to place the folder.
6. Right-click and choose Paste from the Shortcut menu.

Lesson | 1

Advanced Formatting

Skills Covered

- ■ **Design Documents for Publication**
- ■ **Set Paper Size**
- ■ **Adjust Character Spacing**
- ■ **Control Text Flow**
- ■ **Insert a Blank Page or a Cover Page**
- ■ **Set Up an Employment Portfolio**

Software Skills Word's desktop publishing features let you improve the appearance of a published document and make the content easier to read. You can adjust the amount of space around and between text and control the way text flows from the bottom of one page to the top of the next. Specifically, you can set character spacing to make words easier to read, control text line and page breaks, and set a paper size. You can also insert a blank page anywhere in a document, or select a preformatted cover page design from a gallery to insert at the beginning of your document.

Application Skills Liberty Blooms, a flower shop, has asked you to prepare a brochure about roses and how to select them. They want the brochure to be professional and eye-catching. They plan to print the brochure on custom-sized paper and make it available as a handout to customers in the shop. In this exercise, you will select a paper size, adjust character spacing, select options to control the text flow, and insert a cover page.

TERMS

Balance A basic principle of design that describes the visual weight of objects on a page, and the way the objects are arranged in relation to each other.

Baseline The bottom of a line of text.

Commercial printer A business that provides printing, copying, and publishing services.

Consistency The use of repetition to create a uniform and predictable design or layout.

Content control A feature of Word 2007 that acts as a placeholder for information.

Contrast A basic principle of design that describes the visual weight of objects on a page and the way the objects are arranged in relation to each other. Also, the degree of separation of color values within a picture.

Cover page The first page of a document that usually displays such information as the document title and subtitle, the author's name, and the date.

Desktop publishing The process of designing and printing a document using a desktop computer and printer.

Employment portfolio A collection of documents that illustrates the qualities and abilities of a job candidate.

Kerning Spacing between pairs of characters.

Orphan The first line of a paragraph printed alone at the bottom of a page.

Page layout The way text, graphics, and space are organized on a document page.

Page size The dimensions of a finished document page.

Paper size The dimensions of the sheet of paper on which a document is printed. Also called sheet size.

Publish Output a document so it can be distributed to readers.

Widow The last line of a paragraph printed alone at the top of a page.

NOTES

Design Documents for Publication

- **Desktop publishing** refers to designing and producing documents using a publishing system that includes appropriate software and a personal computer.

- You **publish** the finished product to make it available to readers.

- Documents may be published using a variety of methods:
  - You may print a document on a desktop printer.
  - You may post a document on the Internet or World Wide Web.
  - If you have complex publishing requirements such as color matching or binding, you may be able to design the document on your own equipment, but you may need to use a **commercial printer** to produce the final product.
  - You may transmit the document to a copy shop for reproduction.

- Both basic and advanced desktop publishing features are built into most word-processing programs, such as Microsoft Office Word 2007.

- For example, you can use Microsoft Office Word 2007 to create simple reports, or complex documents such as instructional manuals, employment portfolios, multiple-page newsletters, and business brochures.

- You can also use Microsoft Office Word 2007 to design and produce documents for publishing on the Internet or World Wide Web.

- Desktop publishing programs, such as Microsoft Office Publisher 2007, offer more sophisticated features for designing documents for publication.

- Some Web page design programs offer features specifically for creating and publishing document on-line.

- When selecting a publishing system, you should take into consideration the types of documents you plan to publish, the features you will need available in the software program, and the cost of the equipment.

- When designing documents for publication, you should use established standards and styles of publishing in order to create a professional-looking product.

- For example, you should use the basic principles of design, which include **contrast**, **balance**, and **consistency**.

- You should make use of effective **page layout** techniques including newsletter columns, tables, borders, alignment, graphics, and spacing to highlight the content and capture the reader's attention.

- You should also use care when selecting fonts and colors in order to enhance the appearance of the document without detracting from the content.

Set Paper Size

- The default **paper size** in Word 2007 is Letter, which is 8.5 inches by 11 inches.

- You can select from a list of different sizes such as A5 which is 5.83 inches by 8.27 inches, B5, which is 7.17 inches by 10.12 inches, or Legal, which is 8.5 inches by 14 inches,

- You can also set your own custom size using the options on the Paper tab of the Page Setup dialog box.

  ✓ *Note that although the term **page size** is often used interchangeably with the term paper size, they are not exactly the same. Page size is the dimensions of a finished document page, while paper size is the dimensions of the sheet of paper on which the document is printed.*

Paper tab of the Page Setup dialog box

Adjust Character Spacing

- Use character spacing to improve the readability of the text, as well as to control the amount of text that fits on a line or on a page.

- In Word, the amount of space between characters is determined by the current font set.

- When certain characters that are wider than other characters in a font set are next to each other, they may appear to run together.

- Set the **kerning** to automatically adjust the space between selected characters, when the characters are larger than a particular point size.

- You can also adjust spacing between characters by changing the scale, the spacing, or the position.

  - Set the scale to stretch or compress selected text based on a percentage. For example, set the character spacing scale above 100% to stretch the text, or below 100% to compress the text.

  - Set the spacing to expand or condense the spacing between all selected characters by a specific number of points.

  - Set the position to raise or lower characters relative to the text **baseline** by a specific number of points.

Character Spacing tab of the Font dialog box

Control Text Flow

- Use text flow options to control the way Word breaks paragraphs and lines at the end of a page. For example, you can control whether or not a heading stays on the same page as the paragraph that follows it.

- The following text flow options are available on the Line and Page Breaks tab of the Paragraph dialog box:

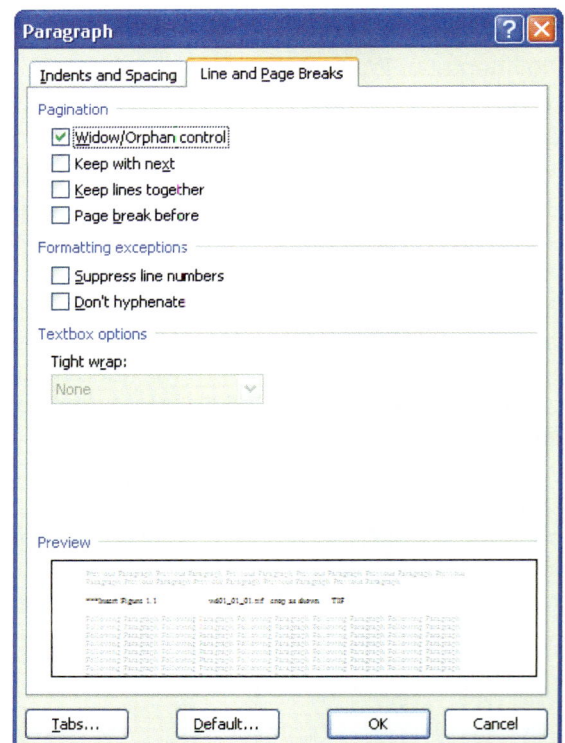

  - **Widow/Orphan** control. Select this option to prevent either the first or last line of a paragraph from printing on a different page from the rest of the paragraph.

  - Keep with next. Select this option to prevent a page break between the current paragraph and the following paragraph.

  - Keep lines together. Select this option to prevent a page break within a paragraph.

  - Page break before. Select this option to force a page break before the current paragraph.

- You can also press `Shift`+`Enter` to manually insert a hard line break.

- A hard line break forces Word to wrap text before reaching the right margin.

  ✓ *To see hard line breaks on-screen, display nonprinting characters.*

Line and Page Breaks tab of the Paragraph dialog box

Insert a Blank Page or a Cover Page

- You can insert a blank page anywhere in a document by selecting Blank Page in the Pages group on the Insert tab of the Ribbon.

- When you insert a blank page, Word inserts hard page breaks before and after the new page.

- You can insert a **cover page** by selecting Cover Page in the Pages group on the Insert tab of the Ribbon.

- Word includes a gallery of preformatted cover pages that include page layout and design features as well as placeholders—called **content controls**—for standard text, such as the document title and the author's name.

- You replace the sample text by typing new text or by selecting data from the content control's drop-down list.

Set Up an Employment Portfolio

- Set up an employment portfolio to organize information about yourself that you can use as a reference while looking for a job.

- An employment portfolio is usually a binder in which you store documents that demonstrate your qualifications for employment.

- Most employment portfolios include a resume, transcripts, letters of application, lists of references, copies of certifications, and examples of achievement that illustrate your capabilities.

- For example, if you are looking for a position as an executive assistant, you should include examples of business letters that you have typed.

- If you are looking for a position in an accounting department, you might include examples of a financial spreadsheet you have created.

- If you are looking for a position in a marketing department, you should include examples of presentations you have created.

- If you are looking for a teaching position, you should include examples of lesson plans.

- Employment portfolios may also include information frequently requested on employment applications, such as the names of schools and graduation dates, as well as the names and addresses of current or former employers and the dates of employment.

- The documents should be placed in the binder in plastic sleeves for protection and to maintain a professional appearance.

- In addition, you should organize the documents by category or type. For example, store all letters of recommendation together, all certifications together, and examples of achievement together.

- In some cases, the portfolio may be posted on-line and filled with electronic documents. However, you should always maintain hard copy printouts of the contents of a portfolio that you can bring with you to interviews.

- Throughout your career, you should maintain and update your employment portfolio so that it is always ready if you need it.

PROCEDURES

Set Paper Size

1. Click **Page Layout** tab . . . . Alt + P

   Page Setup Group

2. Click **Size** button 🗔 . . . . S, Z

3. Click desired size in gallery . . . . ↑/↓, Enter

   OR

   a. Click **More Paper Sizes** . . . A

   b. Click **Paper size** drop-down arrow . . . . Alt + R

   c. Click desired size . . . . ↑/↓, Enter

✓ *To insert a continuous section break and format only the section following the insertion point location, click the Apply to drop-down arrow and click This point forward.*

   d. Click **OK** . . . . Enter

Set a Custom Paper Size

1. Click **Page Layout** tab . . . . Alt + P

   Page Setup Group

2. Click **Size** button 🗔 . . . . S, Z

3. Click **More Paper Sizes** . . . . . . A

4. Click **Width** box . . . . Alt + W

5. Key paper width.

6. Click **Height** box . . . . Alt + E

7. Key paper height.

   ✓ *To insert a continuous section break and format only the section following the insertion point location, click the Apply to drop-down arrow and click This point forward.*

8. Click **OK** . . . . Enter

Adjust Character Spacing

To set automatic kerning:

1. Select text to format.
2. Click **Home** tab . . . . Alt +H

   Font Group

3. Click **Font** group dialog box launcher ⊡ . . . . F , N
4. Click **Character Spacing** tab . . . . Alt +R
5. Click to select **Kerning for fonts**: check box, if it is not already selected . . . . . Alt +K
6. Click in **Points and above** box . . . . Alt +O
7. Key font size above which you wish to kern (in points).
8. Click **OK** . . . . Enter

To set scale:

1. Select text to format.
2. Click **Home** tab . . . . Alt +H

   Font Group

3. Click **Font** group dialog box launcher ⊡ . . . . F , N
4. Click **Character Spacing** tab . . . . Alt +R
5. Click **Scale** drop-down arrow . . . . Alt +C
6. Select desired percentage . . . . ↑ / ↓ , Enter

   OR

   Key custom percentage.
7. Click **OK** . . . . Enter

To set spacing:

1. Select text to format.
2. Click **Home** tab . . . . Alt +H

   Font Group

3. Click **Font** group dialog box launcher ⊡ . . . . F , N
4. Click **Character Spacing** tab . . . . Alt +R
5. Click **Spacing** drop-down arrow . . . . Alt +S
6. Select desired option: ↑ / ↓ , Enter
   - **Normal**, to use default spacing.
   - **Expanded**, to increase spacing.
   - **Condensed**, to decrease spacing.
7. Click **By** box . . . . Alt +B
8. Key spacing to apply (in points).
9. Click **OK** . . . . Enter

To set position:

1. Select text to format.
2. Click **Home** tab . . . . Alt +H

   Font Group

3. Click **Font** group dialog box launcher ⊡ . . . . F , N
4. Click **Character Spacing** tab . . . . Alt +R
5. Click **Position** drop-down arrow . . . . Alt +P
6. Select desired option: ↑ / ↓ , Enter
   - **Normal**, to use default position.
   - **Raised**, to move text above baseline.
   - **Lowered**, to move text below baseline.
7. Click **By** box . . . . Alt +Y
8. Key spacing to apply (in points).
9. Click **OK** . . . . Enter

Control Text Flow

1. Click **Home** tab . . . . Alt +H

   Paragraph Group

2. Click **Paragraph** group dialog box launcher ⊡ . . . . P , G
3. Click **Line and Page Breaks** tab . . . . Alt +P
4. Select or deselect desired option(s):
   - **Widow/Orphan control** . . . . Alt +W
   - **Keep with next** . . . . . Alt +X
   - **Keep lines together** . . Alt +K
   - **Page break before** . . . Alt +B
5. Click **OK** . . . . Enter

Insert a Blank Page

1. Position insertion point where you want to insert blank page.
2. Click **Insert** tab . . . . Alt +N

   Pages Group

3. Click **Blank Page** button ▯ . . . . N , P

Insert a Cover Page

1. Position insertion point anywhere in document.
2. Click **Insert** tab . . . . Alt +N

   Pages Group

3. Click **Cover Page** button ▤ V
4. Click desired cover page in gallery . . . . ↑ / ↓ / ← / →
5. Click text to replace.
6. Key new text.

EXERCISE DIRECTIONS

1. Start Word, if necessary, open the document 🔘 **01HANDOUT**, and save it as **01HANDOUT_xx**.

2. Set the paper size to 6.5 inches wide by 6.5 inches high.

3. Select the title heading and expand the character spacing by 1 point.

4. Scale the text in both bulleted lists to 90% of their original spacing.

5. Scroll down and position the insertion point in the orphan line of text at the bottom of page 2.

6. Select to use Widow/Orphan control. The line should move to the top of page 3.

7. Scroll down and select the second paragraph under the heading *Judging Rose Quality*.

8. Select the Keep lines together option. The entire paragraph should move to the top of page 4.

9. Scroll down and position the insertion point in the heading at the bottom of page 4.

10. Select the Keep with next option. The heading should move to the top of page 5.

11. Justify all body text paragraphs except the bulleted lists.

12. Insert the Cubicles cover page.

13. On the cover page, click the Type the Company Name placeholder and type **Liberty Blooms**.

14. Select the text in the Title placeholder and type **Selecting Roses**.

15. Click the Subtitle placeholder and type **A Buyer's Guide**.

16. Click the Author placeholder and type your name.

17. Click the Year placeholder and type the current year.

18. Check the spelling and grammar in the document.

19. Display the cover page in Print Preview. It should look similar to Illustration A.

20. Close Print Preview and print the document.

21. Close the document, saving all changes, and exit Word.

Illustration A

Liberty Blooms

Selecting Roses
A Buyer's Guide
Student's Name

08

ON YOUR OWN

1. Organize an employment portfolio that you can use to help in a job search.

2. Start by purchasing the actual binder that you will use, as well as the plastic sleeves for protecting the documents that you add to the portfolio.

3. Start Word, create a new document, and save the document as OWD01_xx.

4. Select a paper size and set margins as necessary. Keep in mind that you will be placing the pages into your portfolio.

5. Perform a self-evaluation to determine the type of position you would like, what you have to offer an employer, and what qualities make you a suitable candidate. It is important to be honest with yourself. The information will be useful as you build the portfolio and contact employers.

6. Type the information in the document. You may type the information in several essays, lists, or articles. You should include a description of yourself and your accomplishments, as well as what you are looking for in an employer. Use headings to identify each section.

7. On a second page, make a list of the actual documents you would like to include in the portfolio. You do not have to have all of the documents available right now. Remember to include a resume, cover letters, list of references, and examples of achievement in the list.

8. Insert a cover page. Select a professional-looking page that would be suitable to show to a prospective employer. Replace the sample text by typing new text, and delete any content controls that you do not need.

9. Preview the document and use character spacing and text flow options to adjust the spacing and position of text and paragraphs.

10. Preview the document again, and then print it. Ask a classmate to review the document and offer comments or suggestions.

11. Incorporate the comments and suggestions into the document, check and correct the spelling and grammar, and then print it again.

12. Close the document, saving all changes, and exit Word.

13. Place the document pages in the plastic sleeves, and then add them to your portfolio binder.

Skills Covered

- **Reveal Style Formatting**
- **Keep Track of Formatting**

- **Mark Formatting Inconsistencies**

Software Skills   Consistent formatting insures that your documents look professional and are easy to read. Microsoft Office Word 2007 includes tools that help you monitor and track inconsistent formatting. You can use the Style Inspector to reveal details about paragraph and character formatting, and you can track and mark formatting inconsistencies as you work. Once you identify inconsistencies, you can use tools such as styles, themes, and direct formatting to correct them.

Application Skills   You are preparing a document for the Liberty Blooms flower shop that lists classes the shop is offering in the coming months. However, the document does not appear to be formatted consistently. In this exercise, you will turn on the check formatting and mark formatting features, and you will reveal style formatting in order to identify and correct formatting inconsistencies.

TERMS

Character style   A collection of formatting settings that can be applied all at once to a single character or multiple characters.

Direct formatting   Individual font or paragraph formatting settings applied directly to text, as opposed to a collection of settings applied with a style.

Paragraph style   A collection of formatting settings that can be applied all at once to a single paragraph or multiple paragraphs.

NOTES

Reveal Style Formatting

- Use Word's Style Inspector and Reveal Formatting task panes to display specific information about formatting applied to the current text.
- The Style Inspector displays the name of the current **paragraph style** and/or **character style**, as well as any **direct formatting** that has been manually applied.

Style Inspector task pane

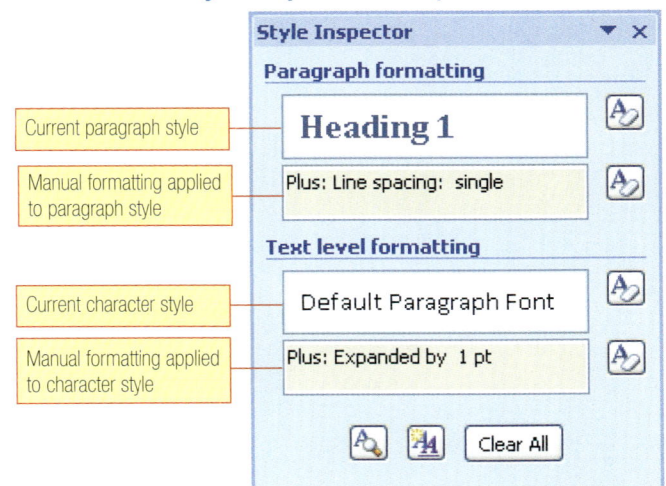

Current paragraph style

Manual formatting applied to paragraph style

Current character style

Manual formatting applied to character style

Style Inspector

Paragraph formatting

Heading 1

Plus: Line spacing: single

Text level formatting

Default Paragraph Font

Plus: Expanded by 1 pt

Clear All

- In the Reveal Formatting task pane, you can view specific details about font formatting, paragraph formatting, and page setup.

Reveal Formatting task pane

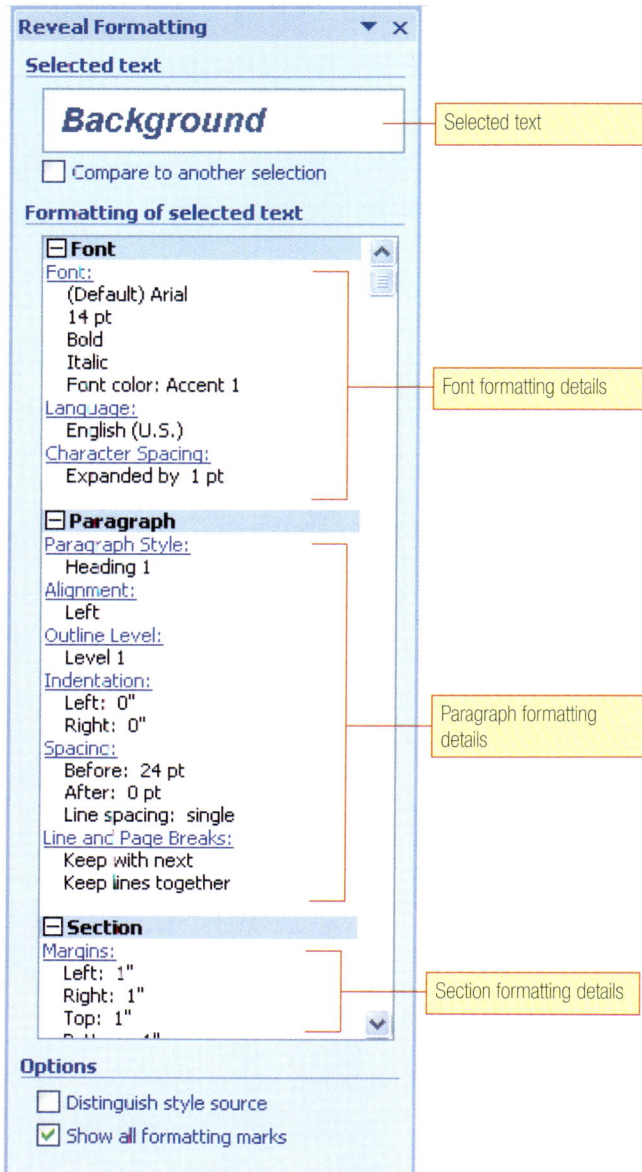

Reveal Formatting

Selected text

Background — Selected text

☐ Compare to another selection

Formatting of selected text

⊟ **Font**
Font:
   (Default) Arial
   14 pt
   Bold
   Italic
   Font color: Accent 1 — Font formatting details
Language:
   English (U.S.)
Character Spacing:
   Expanded by 1 pt

⊟ **Paragraph**
Paragraph Style:
   Heading 1
Alignment:
   Left
Outline Level:
   Level 1
Indentation:
   Left: 0"
   Right: 0" — Paragraph formatting details
Spacing:
   Before: 24 pt
   After: 0 pt
   Line spacing: single
Line and Page Breaks:
   Keep with next
   Keep lines together

⊟ **Section**
Margins:
   Left: 1"
   Right: 1" — Section formatting details
   Top: 1"

Options
☐ Distinguish style source
☑ Show all formatting marks

Keep Track of Formatting

- Word 2007 keeps track of direct formatting that you apply manually.
- You can turn the feature off by selecting it on the Advanced tab of the Word Options dialog box.
- You can also customize the feature in the Style Pane Options dialog box to keep track of paragraph level formatting, font formatting, and/or bullet and numbering formatting.

Mark Formatting Inconsistencies

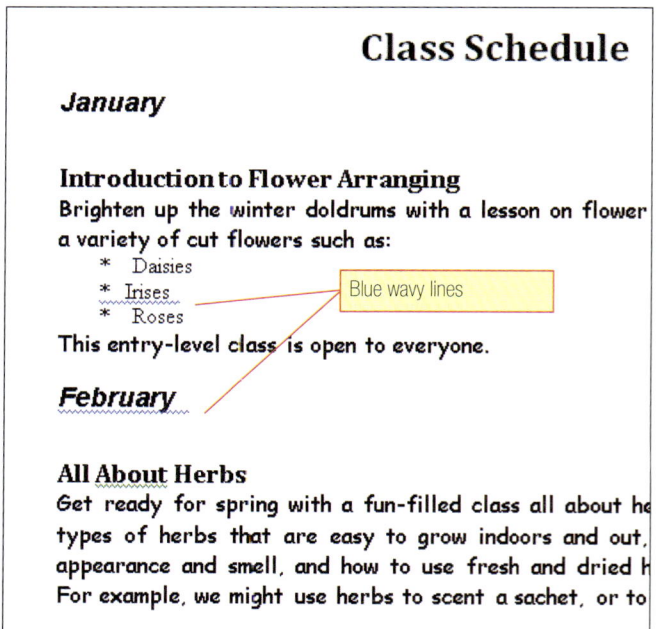

- You can set Word to check formatting while you work in much the same way that it checks spelling and grammar.
- If Word identifies a formatting inconsistency, it marks it with a wavy blue underline.
- For example, if you apply direct formatting instead of a style, Word would identify the formatting as inconsistent.
- You can ignore the blue lines and keep typing, or you can use a shortcut menu to correct the formatting error.
- The automatic format checker is off by default; you must turn it on to use it.

   ✓ *You must have Keep Track of Formatting enabled in order to check formatting while you type.*

Mark formatting inconsistencies

Class Schedule

January

Introduction to Flower Arranging
Brighten up the winter doldrums with a lesson on flower a variety of cut flowers such as:
   * Daisies
   * Irises — Blue wavy lines
   * Roses
This entry-level class is open to everyone.

February

All About Herbs
Get ready for spring with a fun-filled class all about he types of herbs that are easy to grow indoors and out, appearance and smell, and how to use fresh and dried h For example, we might use herbs to scent a sachet, or to

PROCEDURES

Reveal Formatting in the Style Inspector

1. Position insertion point in formatted text.

   OR

   Select formatted text.
2. Click **Home** tab . . . . [Alt]+[H]

   Styles Group

3. Click **Styles** group dialog box launcher [⌐] . . . . [F], [Y]
4. Click **Style Inspector** button [⚐] . . . . . . [F6], [⇆] *nx*, [Enter]

   ✓ *You can move the insertion point with the Style Inspector open in order to reveal formatting for different text.*

Reveal Formatting in the Reveal Formatting Task Pane

1. Position insertion point in text.

   OR

   Select formatted text.
2. Display Style Inspector.
3. Click **Reveal Formatting** button [⚐].

Turn Keep Track of Formatting Off or On

1. Click **Office Button** [⚐] . . . [Alt]+[F]
2. Click **Word Options** . . . . [I]
3. Click **Advanced** . . . . [A]
4. Click to select or deselect the **Keep track of formatting** check box . . . . [Alt]+[E], [E], [Spacebar]

   ✓ *A check mark in the check box indicates the option is selected.*

5. Click **OK**. . . . . [Enter]

Select Type of Formatting to Track

1. Turn on Keep Track of Formatting.
2. Click **Home** tab . . . . [Alt]+[H]

   Styles Group

3. Click **Styles** group dialog box launcher [⌐] . . . . [F], [Y]
4. Click **Options** . . . . . . [⇆] *7x*, [Enter]
5. Click to select/deselect formatting to show as styles:
   - **Paragraph level formatting** . . . . [Alt]+[P]
   - **Font formatting** . . . . . [Alt]+[O]
   - **Bullet and numbering formatting** . . . . [Alt]+[B]

   ✓ *If the Select formatting to show as styles options are not available, the Keep Track of Formatting feature is off.*

6. Click **OK**. . . . . [Enter]

Turn on Automatic Format Checking

1. Click **Office Button** [⚐] . . . [Alt]+[F]
2. Click **Word Options** . . . . [I]
3. Click **Advanced** . . . . [A]
4. Click to select the **Keep track of formatting** check box . . . . . . [Alt]+[E], [E], [Spacebar]

   ✓ *A check mark in the check box indicates the option is selected.*

5. Click to select the **Mark formatting inconsistencies** check box . . . . . . [Alt]+[F], [Spacebar]

   ✓ *A check mark in the check box indicates the option is selected.*

6. Click **OK**. . . . . [Enter]

Check Formatting as You Type

1. Right-click formatting inconsistency marked with blue, wavy underline.
2. Click desired correct formatting option on shortcut menu.

   OR

   Click **Ignore Once** to hide this occurrence . . . . [I]

   OR

   Click **Ignore Rule** to hide all occurrences. . . . . [U]

EXERCISE DIRECTIONS

1. Start Word, if necessary open the document 02CLASSES, and save it as 02CLASSES_xx.

2. Set Word to keep track of formatting and to mark formatting inconsistencies.

3. Notice that Word identifies a formatting inconsistency in the bulleted list and marks it with a wavy blue underline.

4. Click on the underlined word—*Irises*—and then display the Style Inspector. Note that there are no styles applied to the text.

5. Keeping the Style Inspector open, click on the first bulleted item—*Daisies*. Note in the Style Inspector that it is formatted with the List Paragraph style.

6. Click on the third bulleted item—*Roses*. Note that it, too, is formatted with the List Paragraph style.

7. Delete the asterisk character and the following tab preceding the text *Irises* in the second bulleted item.

8. Use the Format Painter to copy the formatting from the first bulleted item to the second bulleted item—*Irises*. Note that now all three items have consistent formatting, and the blue wavy underline no longer displays.

9. Select the text *February* and format it in 14-point Arial bold italic.

10. Copy the formatting to the text *March*. Note that both words are now marked with blue wavy underlines.

11. Display the Reveal Formatting task pane, and then close the Style Inspector.

12. Examine the formatting for the text *March*.

13. Click in the text *February* in the document, and then examine its formatting in the Reveal Formatting task pane.

14. Right-click the text *February* in the document and click Replace direct formatting with style Heading 2 on the shortcut menu.

15. Right-click the text *March* in the document and click Replace direct formatting with style Heading 2 on the shortcut menu.

16. Examine the formatting in the Reveal Formatting task pane again. All three month headings should now be the same.

17. Check the spelling and grammar in the document.

18. Preview the document. It should look similar to Illustration A on the following page.

19. Print the document.

20. Set Word to track formatting, but deselect all options under Select formatting to show as styles in the Style Pane Options dialog box.

21. Turn off the Mark formatting inconsistencies feature.

22. Close the document, saving all changes.

ON YOUR OWN

1. Start Word, open 02NEWS and save it as OWD02_xx.

2. Set Word to track formatting and to mark formatting inconsistencies.

3. If Word identifies formatting inconsistencies, use the Style Inspector or the Reveal Formatting task pane to review the formatting to determine the problems.

4. Correct the problems so that the formatting is consistent throughout the document.

   ✓ *If Word does not identify any inconsistencies, you might try to apply direct formatting in place of headings to see if Word marks the inconsistency.*

5. Check the spelling and grammar in the document.

6. Save changes and then print the document.

7. Ask a classmate to review the document and offer comments and suggestions.

8. Incorporate the suggestions into the document.

9. Set Word to track formatting but not to mark formatting inconsistencies.

10. Close the document, saving all changes.

Liberty Blooms

345 Chestnut Street, Philadelphia, PA 19106

Class Schedule

January

Introduction to Flower Arranging
Brighten up the winter doldrums with a lesson on flower arranging! We'll work with a variety of cut flowers such as:
* Daisies
* Irises
* Roses

This entry-level class is open to everyone.

February

All About Herbs
Get ready for spring with a fun-filled class all about herbs! We'll learn about the types of herbs that are easy to grow indoors and out, how to identify herbs by appearance and smell, and how to use fresh and dried herbs in a variety of ways. For example, we might use herbs to scent a sachet, or to flavor a pot of stew.

March

Perennial Garden Design
A successful perennial garden enhances blooms all season long, year after year. This seminar will cover the basics of planning a perennial garden. Learn how to determine the amount of space you need, how to lay out the garden, and how to select the right types of plants. Time permitting, we will discuss soil composition and planting techniques.

Space is limited for all classes and seminars. For more information or to register, call 215-555-2837 or visit our Web site www.libertyblooms.net.

Skills Covered

- **Set a Default Theme and Style Set**
- **Restore a Template Theme**
- **Save a Custom Theme**
- **About Ergonomic Design**

Software Skills   Word comes with templates to help you create consistent documents efficiently. Most templates have a default theme that includes page setup and formatting settings to insure that new documents will be uniform. In many cases, they include standard text and graphics as well. You can set a default theme for documents and templates, and you can restore a template theme to its original settings. You can also save a customized theme for future use.

Application Skills   Marilyn Stewart, an account manager at Restoration Architecture, a building design firm, has been researching the requirements for an ergonomically-sound work environment so that the information can be used to improve employee health and productivity. She wants to prepare and distribute a brief report summarizing the information. In this exercise, you will use a template to create the report document. You will customize the theme and style set and set the new options as the defaults. You will save the settings as a custom theme. You will fill in the information to create the report, then you will restore the template to its original settings and delete the custom theme.

TERMS

Ergonomic   Designed to reduce injuries and increase productivity. Usually used to refer to furniture and equipment.

Style set   A group of coordinated styles designed for formatting common document elements, such as headings, titles, and lists.

Template   A sample or model document on which new documents are based. Templates include formatting settings, text, and graphics used to create the new documents.

Theme   A set of coordinated colors, fonts, and effects that can be applied to Office 2007 documents.

NOTES

Set a Default Theme and Style Set

- Most **templates** have a built-in default **theme** and **style set**.
- You can select a different theme and style set for a template, and set them as the default.
- If you change the default, new documents based on the template are created using the new default theme and style set.
- Take care when modifying the theme and style set associated with the Normal template, as the changes will affect all new, blank documents.

Restore a Template Theme

- If you modify the theme associated with a template, you can restore it by resetting the original template theme.
- Likewise, you can reset the style set associated with a template.
- If you change the default theme associated with a template, and then decide you want to go back to the original default theme, you can select the original settings, and then set them as the new default.

Save a Custom Theme

- You can save a theme for which you have customized the colors, fonts, or effects.
- You give the theme a name, and Word stores it in the Document Themes folder.
- A saved custom theme displays at the top of the Themes Gallery under the heading Custom so that you can apply it to any document.
- You can delete a custom theme that you no longer need.

About Ergonomic Design

- **Ergonomic** refers to the science of designing products to reduce injury and increase productivity.
- Businesses that implement ergonomics usually see fewer worker injuries, less absenteeism, fewer errors, and higher productivity.
- Ergonomically-designed products include chairs that help reduce back problems and ergonomic keyboards that help reduce carpal-tunnel syndrome.

PROCEDURES

Set a Default Theme and Style Set

1. Create a new document.

   ✓ *Use the template for which you want to change the theme and style set.*

2. Click **Page Layout** tab . . . `Alt`+`P`

   Themes Group

3. Click **Themes** button 🅰 . . . . `T`, `H`
4. Click theme to apply . . . . `↑`/`↓`/`←`/`→`, `Enter`
5. Click **Home** tab . . . . `Alt`+`H`

   Styles Group

6. Click **Change Styles** button 🅰🅰 . . . . `G`
7. Click **Style Set** . . . . `Y`

8. Click name of style set to apply . . . . `↑`/`↓`, `Enter`
9. Click **Change Styles** button 🅰🅰 . . . . `Alt`+`H`, `G`
10. Click **Set as Default** . . . . `S`
11. Close the document . . . . `Alt`+`F`, `C`
12. Click **Yes** to save the file . . . . . `Y`

    OR

    Click **No** to close the file without saving . . . . `N`
13. Click **Yes** to save the changes to the template . . . . . `Y`

    ✓ *Note that all new documents created with the template will use the new default theme and style set.*

Restore a Template Theme

1. Click **Page Layout** tab . . . `Alt`+`P`

   Themes Group

2. Click **Themes** button 🅰 . . . . `T`, `H`
3. Click **Reset to Theme from Template** . . . . `R`

Restore a Style Set

1. Click **Home** tab . . . . `Alt`+`H`

   Styles Group

2. Click **Change Styles** button 🅰🅰 . . . . `G`
3. Click **Style Set** . . . . `Y`
4. Click **Reset to Quick Styles from Template** . . . . `R`

Restore the Default Normal Template Theme and Style Set

1. Create a new blank document.
2. Click **Page Layout** tab . . . `Alt`+`P`

3. Click **Themes**
   button `Aa` . . . . `T`, `H`
4. Click **Office** . . . `↑`/`↓`/`←`/`→`, `Enter`
5. Click **Themes**
   button `Aa` . . . . . `Alt`+`P`, `T`, `H`
6. Click **Reset to Theme
   from Template** . . . . `R`
7. Click **Home** tab . . . . `Alt`+`H`

8. Click **Change Styles**
   button `AA` . . . . `G`
9. Click **Style Set** . . . . `Y`
10. Click **Word 2007** . . . . `↑`/`↓`, `Enter`
11. Click **Change Styles**
    button `AA` . . . . `Alt`+`H`, `G`
12. Click **Style Set** . . . . `Y`
13. Click **Reset to Quick Styles
    from Template** . . . . `R`
14. Click **Change Styles**
    button `AA` . . . . `Alt`+`H`, `G`
15. Click **Set as Default** . . . . `S`

Save a Custom Theme

1. Apply theme to current document.
2. Customize the theme colors:
   a. Click **Page Layout**
      tab . . . . `Alt`+`P`

   b. Click **Theme Colors**
      button `▦▾` . . . . `T`, `C`
   c. Click color scheme
      to apply . . . . `↑`/`↓`, `Enter`
3. Customize the theme fonts:
   a. Click **Page Layout**
      tab . . . . `Alt`+`P`

   b. Click **Theme Fonts**
      button `A▾` . . . . `T`, `F`
   c. Click font scheme
      to apply . . . . `↑`/`↓`, `Enter`
4. Customize the theme effects:
   a. Click **Page Layout**
      tab . . . . `Alt`+`P`

   b. Click **Theme Effects**
      button `◉▾` . . . . `T`, `E`
   c. Click effects scheme
      to apply . . . . `↑`/`↓`, `Enter`

5. Click **Page Layout**
   tab . . . . `Alt`+`P`

6. Click **Themes**
   button `Aa` . . . . . `Alt`+`P`, `T`, `H`
7. Click **Save Current Theme** . . . `A`
8. Type name for custom theme.
9. Click **Save** . . . . `Alt`+`S`

Delete a Custom Theme

1. Click **Page Layout** tab . . . `Alt`+`P`

2. Click **Themes**
   button `Aa` . . . . . `Alt`+`P`, `T`, `H`
3. Right-click the customized theme
   to delete.
4. Click **Delete** . . . . `Alt`+`D`
5. Click **Yes** . . . . `Enter`

EXERCISE DIRECTIONS

1. Create a new document based on the Urban Report template.
2. Change the theme color scheme to Metro.
3. Change the theme font scheme to Origin.
4. Change the style set to Modern.
5. Set the new options as the defaults for the Urban Report template.
6. Save the current theme as a custom theme with the name **RA_Report**.
7. Close the document without saving changes, but save the changes to the Urban Report template.
8. Create a new document based on the Urban Report template, and save it as **03REPORT_xx**.

9. Insert the following information in the content controls on the cover page:
   - Date: **Today's date**
   - Document Title: **Ergonomic Design**
   - Document Subtitle: **An Overview**
   - Author: **Marilyn Stewart**
10. On page 2, replace the sample text in the body of the report with the text shown in Illustration A on page 18. Use the formatting shown in the illustration:
    a. Apply the Heading 1 style to all headings from *What is Ergonomic Design?* down.
    b. Use the No Spacing style for the body text, increase the font size to 12 points, and apply a first-line indent.
    c. Use the default bullet list style for the lists, but remove the spacing before and after each paragraph, and use single line spacing.

11. Check the spelling and grammar in the document.

12. Display the document in Print Preview. Page 2 should look similar to the one in Illustration A on the following page.

13. Print the document.

14. Close the document, saving all changes.

15. Create a new blank document based on the Urban Report template.

16. Change the theme color scheme to Urban.

17. Change the theme font scheme to Urban.

18. Set the new options as the defaults for the Urban Report template.

19. Delete the custom theme RA_Report.

20. Close the document without saving changes, but save the changes to the Urban Report template.

ON YOUR OWN

1. Word includes templates for a wide variety of documents, including publications such as manuals and brochures. In this exercise, think of a task for which you could create an instruction manual. The task might be school or class related, or it might be extracurricular. For example, you might create a manual about how to fill out a course registration form, throw a shot put, prepare a science fair exhibit, or use a self-serve gas pump.

2. Once you select a task, gather all of the information you need. Decide how many chapters or sections you will need, what the titles will be, and map out the precise steps the reader will have to follow to complete the task.

3. When you are ready, start Word and use the Manual template to create a new document.

   ✓ *You should be able to find the Manual template by selecting More categories under Microsoft Office Online in the New dialog box, and then searching for Manual. If you cannot locate the Manual template, use the file* 📀 **03MANUAL** *provided with this book. In the New Document dialog box, click New from existing, locate and select* **03MANUAL**, *and then click Create New.*

4. Save the document as **OWD03_xx**.

5. Scroll through the document to see the components of the manual. Note that the Manual template creates a complex document that includes a table of contents, an index, and a lot of sample text and instructions. As you work, you can delete the sections, text, and graphics you don't need and retain those that you want to use.

6. Replace the sample text, headings, and graphics with your own information. Simply type your text and insert graphics or symbols to illustrate the document.

7. Save your document frequently so that you do not accidentally lose information.

8. When you have entered all of the text and graphics and have deleted the sample information that you don't need, check the spelling and grammar in the document.

9. Print the document.

10. Ask a classmate to review the manual and offer suggestions and comments on both the content and the design.

11. Incorporate the suggestions into the document.

12. Assess the document and decide if you want to include it in your employment portfolio as an example of your achievements with Microsoft Office Word. If so, print it again, insert the pages into sleeves, and add them to the portfolio folder.

13. Close the documents, saving all changes.

Business Connection

What's a Resume?

A resume may be the most important document you will ever create. It introduces you to prospective employers, highlights your strengths, and provides insight into your past experiences—all in a single page of bulleted lists! A resume must be neat, eye-catching, and to-the-point. It should contain all of the fundamental information and absolutely no errors. Once you develop a resume, you can fine-tune it for different job opportunities, and keep it up-to-date so you can use it if you need it.

Prepare Your Resume

Start by looking at sample resumes online, in your library, or career center. Take note of the type of information included on each resume, such as name, address, and contact info, education history, employment history, and honors, awards, and special skills. Pay attention to the wording used to emphasize points, and the way attention is drawn to specific skills. Compare page layouts to decide which one is the easiest to read and the most appealing. When you are ready, use Word to create a resume document. You can start with a blank document and lay out the resume using a table or tabbed columns, or base the document on one of Word's built-in resume templates. Enter all of the information in the proper order, and check it for errors. Print the document and exchange it with a classmate. Proofread each other's resumes, and note problems with spelling, grammar, punctuation, and content. Reclaim your own resume and make the corrections as necessary. Print a clean copy and show it to a career counselor or teacher.

Marilyn Stewart

ERGONOMIC DESIGN

AN OVERVIEW

Heading 1

WHAT IS ERGONOMIC DESIGN?

Normal

According to SafeComputingTips.com, ergonomics is the applied science of equipment design, specifically for the workplace, intended to maximize productivity by reducing operator fatigue and discomfort. Practitioners, called *ergonomists*, are responsible for such varied tasks as performing job performance analysis and for designing products, workspaces, and environments.

Heading 1

FINANCIAL BENEFITS

Normal

When ergonomically designed products are properly implemented in the workplace, they can return numerous financial benefits. Specifically, benefits are realized by the following:

Bullet list

- A decrease in the number of days employees are absent.
- A decrease in the number of errors by employees.
- An increase in the efficiency of each employee.
- A shorter learning curve, so employees are productive faster.
- An increase in employee satisfaction.

Heading 1

REQUIREMENTS FOR AN ERGONOMICALLY-SOUND OFFICE

Normal

An ergonomically-sound workplace is designed to maximize the health, safety, and productivity of the employee. In an office, ergonomics are chiefly affected by lighting, glare, and ventilation. Other workplace environments may be affected by different factors. For example, working in laboratory hoods or biological safety cabinets, may force lab workers to stand or sit in awkward positions, which may result in back or neck injuries.

To insure an ergonomically-sound environment, glare from overhead lights, desk lamps and windows should be reduced to a minimum, air should circulate effectively throughout the office, furniture should be adjustable, and designed for maximum comfort. In addition, workers should be able to change positions in order to avoid repetitive stress disorders.

Heading 1

RESOURCES

Bullet list

- Cornell University Ergonomics Web, http://ergo.human.cornell.edu/.
- SafeComputing.tips.com, http://www.safecomputingtips.com/.
- Centers for Disease Control and Prevention, http://www.cdc.gov/od/ohs/Ergonomics/ergohome.htm.

Exercise | 4

Skills Covered

- **Insert a Field from Quick Parts**
- **Set Field Display Options**

- **About Employment Packages**

Software Skills   Insert a field into a document as a placeholder for data that might change, such as a date, results of a calculation, or page number. Access the available fields using Word's Quick Parts menu to quickly locate the field, enter field options, and insert the field at the desired location.

Application Skills   As an administrative assistant at Executive Recruitment Resources, Inc., a job search and recruitment agency, you want to show that you are resourceful. In this exercise, you will design a letterhead that you will save as a building block. You can then insert it in a newsletter explaining types of benefits often included in employment packages. You will also insert fields from Quick Parts for the date and time and set field display options.

TERMS

Employment package   Compensation offered to employees by an employer, usually including salary, insurance, and other benefits.

Field   A placeholder used to insert information that changes, such as the date, the time, a page number, or the results of a calculation.

Field code   A code that represents the data that Word will display in a document.

Field value   The data displayed in a field.

NOTES

Insert a Field from Quick Parts

- Use Word's **Quick Parts** menu to access a list of all **fields** available for insertion in Word 2007 documents.

- The available fields are listed alphabetically on the left side of the Field dialog box.

- Properties and options for the selected field display on the right side of the dialog box.

- By default, all fields are listed; you can select a category from the Categories drop-down list to display only the fields in that category.

- Available categories include:
  - Date and Time
  - Document Automation
  - Document Information
  - Equations and Formulas
  - Index and Tables
  - Links and References
  - Mail Merge
  - Numbering
  - User Information

- Most of the fields can also be inserted using other Word features and commands.

- For example, you can insert the date and time using the Date and Time dialog box, which can be opened from the Text group on the Insert tab of the Ribbon.

Properties of the selected field

Categories drop-down list

List of fields

Options for the selected field

Field

Please choose a field

Categories:
(All)

Field names:
AutoNumOut
AutoText
AutoTextList
BarCode
Bibliography
BidiOutline
Citation
Comments
Compare
CreateDate
Database
Date
DocProperty
DocVariable
EditTime
Eq
FileName
FileSize

Field properties

Date formats:
7/1/08

7/1/08
Tuesday, July 01, 2008
July 1, 2008
7/1/2008
2008-07-01
1-Jul-08
7.1.08
Jul. 1, 08
1 July 2008
July 08
Jul-08
7/1/08 10:53 AM
7/1/08 10:53:16 AM
10:53 AM
10:53:16 AM
10:53
10:53:16

Field options

☐ Use the Hijri/Lunar calendar

☐ Insert the date in last used format from Insert tab

☐ Use the Saka Era calendar

☑ Preserve formatting during updates

Description:
Today's date

[Field Codes] [OK] [Cancel]

■ Some fields have a content control placeholder, which displays when the field is selected.

■ Use the Update button on the placeholder or press F9 to update the field.

Set Field Display Options

■ On the Advanced tab of the Word Options dialog box, you can select options for how fields display in a document.

■ You can select to display **field codes** instead of **field values**.

■ You can select to display shading when a field is selected, always, or never.

About Employment Packages

■ Most businesses offer new hires an **employment package** that includes benefits as well as salary.

■ Most employment packages include some level of health insurance as well as a pension or retirement plan. They usually include vacation time, holidays, and sick/personal days.

■ Other benefits that may be offered include:
  ● Life insurance
  ● Disability insurance
  ● Transportation assistance
  ● Cafeteria plan
  ● Tax-sheltered annuities
  ● Fitness assistance
  ● Tuition reimbursement
  ● Dependent care

■ Benefits have value, and prospective employees should consider the entire package when evaluating whether or not to accept a position.

■ When evaluating an employment package, prospective employees should consider factors such as:
  ● The value of the offered benefits.
  ● The amount the employee must contribute for benefits and whether the contribution is deducted "pre-tax."
  ● Whether the benefits cover family members.
  ● Whether benefits are available immediately, or if there is a waiting period.
  ● Whether there is flexibility in selecting or changing benefit coverage.

PROCEDURES

Insert a Field from Quick Parts

1. Position the insertion point where you want field inserted.
2. Click **Insert** tab . . . . [Alt]+[N]

   [Text Group]

3. Click **Quick Parts** button 📋 . . [Q]
4. Click **F**ield . . . . [F]
5. Click field to insert . . . . [↓]/[↑]

   OR

   a. Click **C**ategories drop-down arrow . . . . [Alt]+[C]
   b. Click category . . . . [↓]/[↑], [Enter]
   c. Click field to insert . . . . [↓]/[↑]

6. Select field properties as necessary.
7. Select field options as necessary.
8. Click **OK** . . . . [Enter]

Set Field Display Options
To show/hide field codes

1. Click **Office Button** 📋 . . [Alt]+[F]
2. Click **Word Options** . . . . [I]
3. Click **Advanced** . . . . [A]
4. Click to select or deselect the **Show field codes instead of their values** check box . . . . [Alt]+[F], [F], [F], [Spacebar]
5. Click **OK** . . . . [Enter]

To set field shading

1. Click **Office Button** 📋 . . [Alt]+[F]
2. Click **Word Opt**i**ons** . . . . [I]
3. Click **Advanced** . . . . [A]
4. Click the **Field sh**a**ding** drop-down arrow . . . . [Alt]+[H], [H], [↓]
5. Click one of the following:
   ■ **Never** . . . . [↓]/[↑]
   ■ **Always** . . . . [↓]/[↑]
   ■ **When selected** . . . . . . [↓]/[↑]
6. Click **OK** . . . . [Enter]

EXERCISE DIRECTIONS

Create a Building Block

1. Start Word, and create a new document.
2. Design the letterhead shown in Illustration A as follows.
   a. Apply the No Spacing Quick Style.
   b. Type the company name in a 22-point serif font (Garamond is used in the illustration), small caps, flush left.
   c. Type the address in the same font in 14 points, using Wingdings symbol #118 as a separator. Do not use small caps.
   d. Type the phone, fax, and Web site information in the same font in 11 points, using the same symbol as a separator.
   e. Select all paragraphs and apply a gray pattern style fill of 12.5%.
   f. Position the insertion point in the last line and apply a 3-point border line of your choosing in a dark blue color below the paragraph.

3. Save the letterhead as a building block with the name ERR_Letterhead, in the Quick Parts gallery.
   a. Press [Ctrl]+[A] to select everything in the document.
   b. Click the Quick Parts button on the Insert tab and click Save Selection to Quick Parts Gallery.
   c. Type the name **ERR_Letterhead**.
   d. Use the default Gallery, Save in, and Options settings.
   e. Type the description **Letterhead for Executive Recruitment Resources**.
   f. Click OK.
4. Close the document without saving any changes.

Create a Newsletter and Insert a Building Block

1. Create a new document and save it as **04PACK_*xx***.
2. Set the page margins to .75 inch on all sides.
3. Insert the ERR_Letterhead building block from the Quick Parts gallery.

EXECUTIVE RECRUITMENT RESOURCES, INC.
8921 Thunderbird Road ❖ Phoenix ❖ Arizona ❖ 85022
Phone: 602-555-6325 ❖ Fax: 602-555-6425 ❖ www.restorationarc.net

What Is an Employment Package?

An employment package—which is sometimes called a benefits package—is all of the compensation that an employer provides for an employee. It includes monetary compensation, such as salary, overtime, and commissions, as well as other benefits, such as insurance coverage.

Benefits and non-monetary compensation have value. Therefore, it is important that everyone who is looking for employment, or who is considering accepting a new position, understands the concept of an employment package. It is also important to know how to evaluate and compare different packages.

An overview of the standard employment package should be discussed during the interview process. A prospective employer should provide a complete, written explanation of the employment package at the time he or she makes a job offer to the prospective employee. It is also advisable for the prospective employee to sit down and discuss the package with a human resources professional or recruitment counselor. The HR professional should be able to answer all questions, and explain the package in detail.

Evaluating an Employment Package

Medical Insurance: Consider the type of plan, what is covered, the amount of the deductibles, co-payments, exclusions, and whether it includes coverage for family members. Also, consider whether there is separate coverage for dental and orthodontic care, as well as for vision and eye care.

Life Insurance: Consider the amount and type of coverage, and whether it is possible to purchase additional coverage.

401(k) plan: A 401 (k) is a tax-deferred retired account. Many companies are replacing pension plans with 401 (k) plans. Consider the maximum amount you can contribute, whether the employer matches your contributions, and conditions for transferring the account if you change employers.

Pension plan: Some organizations, particularly government agencies, still offer pension plans for retirement savings. Consider the length of time it takes to become eligible, how the account is managed, and the age at which you can start claiming benefits.

Vacation/holiday/sick/personal days: Consider the number of days for each, when you become eligible, and whether you are paid your full salary for time off. Some companies allow you to carry over unused days from one year to the next.

Other benefits to consider include cafeteria plans which subsidize meals, transportation assistance which subsidizes mileage or public transportation costs incurred while traveling to and from work, and tuition reimbursement for work-related education.

Prepared by: Student's Name   Date: July 1, 2008   Time: 16:11

---

4. Insert a continuous section break, and then format the second section into two columns of equal width.

5. Apply the Heading 1 style and type **What Is an Employment Package?**

6. On a new line, type the following paragraphs:

An employment package—which is sometimes called a benefits package—is all of the compensation that an employer provides for an employee. It includes monetary compensation, such as salary, overtime, and commissions, as well as other benefits, such as insurance coverage.

Benefits and non-monetary compensation have value. Therefore, it is important that everyone who is looking for employment, or who is considering accepting a new position, understands the concept of an employment package. It is also important to know how to evaluate and compare different packages.

An overview of the standard employment package should be discussed during the interview process. A prospective employer should provide a complete, written explanation of the employment package at the time he or she makes a job offer to the prospective

employee. It is also advisable for the prospective employee to sit down and discuss the package with a human resources professional or recruitment counselor. The HR professional should be able to answer all questions, and explain the package in detail.

7. On a new line, insert a clip art picture relating to the keyword *question*.

   ✓ *If you cannot find a suitable clip, insert the bitmap picture file* 💿 **04CLIP** *supplied with this book.*

8. Resize the width of the picture to approximately 1.75 inches. The height should adjust automatically.

9. Start a new paragraph and insert a column break.

10. Apply the Heading 1 style and type **Evaluating an Employment Package**.

11. On a new line, type the following paragraphs:

    Medical Insurance: Consider the type of plan, what is covered, the amount of the deductibles, co-payments, exclusions, and whether it includes coverage for family members. Also, consider whether there is separate coverage for dental and orthodontic care, as well as for vision and eye care.

    Life Insurance: Consider the amount and type of coverage, and whether it is possible to purchase additional coverage.

    401(k) plan: A 401(k) is a tax-deferred retired account. Many companies are replacing pension plans with 401(k) plans. Consider the maximum amount you can contribute, whether the employer matches your contributions, and conditions for transferring the account if you change employers.

    Pension plan: Some organizations, particularly government agencies, still offer pension plans for retirement savings. Consider the length of time it takes to become eligible, how the account is managed, and the age at which you can start claiming benefits.

Vacation/holiday/sick/personal days: Consider the number of days for each, when you become eligible, and whether you are paid your full salary for time off. Some companies allow you to carry over unused days from one year to the next.

Other benefits to consider include cafeteria plans which subsidize meals, transportation assistance which subsidizes mileage or public transportation costs incurred while traveling to and from work, and tuition reimbursement for work-related education.

Insert Fields from Quick Parts

1. Insert a continuous section break and change the formatting in the new section to one column.

2. Type **Prepared by:** and then type your own name.

3. Press Tab three times and then type **Date:**.

4. Use Quick Parts to display the Field dialog box, and then insert a date field using the MMMM, d, yyyy format.

5. Press Tab four times, and then type **Time:**.

6. Use Quick Parts to display the Field dialog box, and then insert a time field using the HH:mm format.

7. Check the spelling and grammar in the document.

8. Set Word to display field shading all of the time.

9. Set Word to display field codes instead of values.

10. Display the document in Print Preview. Notice that the fields are not shaded, and that the values display. The document should look similar to the one in Illustration A.

11. Print the document.

12. Set Word to display field values instead of codes.

13. Set Word to display field shading only when a field is selected.

14. Delete the ERR_Letterhead building block.

15. Close the file, saving all changes.

ON YOUR OWN

1. Start Word and create a new document.
2. Design a letterhead for yourself. Use character and paragraph formatting to make it look professional.
3. Save the letterhead as a building block in the Quick Parts gallery, with a descriptive name, such as MYLETTERHEAD.
4. Close the document without saving the changes.
5. Create a new document and save it as OWD04_xx.
6. Set page margins and select a theme and style set, if necessary.
7. Insert your letterhead at the top of the page.
8. Insert a date field in the appropriate place for a business letter.
9. Type a cover letter, or letter of application, that you could send to a prospective employer expressing your interest in a particular position. The letter should include at least three paragraphs: one introducing yourself and explaining why you are writing, one describing your qualifications, and a third describing why you believe a position at that particular company would be a good match for you. You may also want to include information specifying your salary requirements, including benefits and other components that might be part of an employment package.
10. Check the spelling and grammar in the letter.
11. Display the document in Print Preview.
12. Print the document.
13. Ask a classmate to review the letter and offer comments and suggestions.
14. Incorporate the suggestions into the document.
15. Assess the letter and decide if you want to include it in your employment portfolio. If so, print it again, insert the page into a sleeve, and add it to the portfolio folder. (Note that when you create and send actual letters of application to actual employers, you should always store a copy in your portfolio. This will help you keep track of the places you apply, when you apply, and the names of the people you contacted.)
16. Close the document, saving all changes.

Critical Thinking

Application Skills Ms. George, the Director of Training at Executive Recruitment Resources, Inc., wants to increase enrollment in technology training classes. She has asked you to design a one-page flyer that describes the importance of ongoing training to keep pace with changing technology, and includes information about the company's class offerings and tuition reimbursement benefit. She has supplied you with a file containing the information she wants included in the flyer. In this exercise, you will open the file, set a paper size, and set a default theme and style set. You will also insert fields from Quick Parts. You will enhance the flyer by using newsletter columns and graphics.

EXERCISE DIRECTIONS

1. Start Word, if necessary, open the file ◎ **05FLYER**, and save it as **05FLYER_xx**.
2. Set the paper size to 8.5 inches by 11 inches.
3. Select the Technic theme and the Traditional style set.
4. Customize the theme by changing the colors to Foundry and the fonts to Flow
5. Set the new theme and style set as the default.
6. Move the insertion point to the beginning of the line *Climb the Ladder to Success* and insert a continuous section break.
7. Format the second section into two columns of equal width.
8. Apply the Heading 1 style to the three main headlines (refer to Illustration A).
9. Create a bulleted list from the three items in the first article beginning with the word Increase.
10. Format the first letter in each of the three main articles as a dropped capital.
11. Insert a new line after the last paragraph in the flyer and then insert a clip art picture related to training, like the one shown in Illustration A.

    ✓ *If you cannot find a suitable clip, insert the bitmap picture file* ◎ **05CLIP** *provided with this book.*

12. Resize the picture to approximately 2 inches high by 2.5 inches wide.
13. Insert a continuous section break after the picture.
14. Change the formatting for the last section to one column.
15. Set paragraph spacing for the first line in the new section to leave 18 points of space before.
16. Type **Prepared by:** and then type your own name.
17. Press Tab three times and then type **Date:**.
18. Use Quick Parts to display the Field dialog box, and then insert a date field using the M, d, yy format.
19. Press Tab twice times, and then type **Time:**.
20. Use Quick Parts to display the Field dialog box, and then insert a time field using the HH:mm:ss AM/PM format.
21. Check the spelling and grammar in the document.
22. Display the document in Print Preview. Notice that two lines display at the top of the right column.
23. Select the three bulleted items and change the left indent to .25 inches.
24. Change the spacing before the headline *In-House Training* to 12 points.
25. Display the document in Print Preview again. It should look similar to the one in Illustration A.

26. Print the document, and then close it, saving all changes.

27. Create a new blank document and restore the default Office theme and style set settings.

28. Close the document without saving changes.

EXECUTIVE RECRUITMENT RESOURCES, INC.

8921 Thunderbird Road ❖ Phoenix ❖ Arizona ❖ 85022
Phone: 602-555-6325 ❖ Fax: 602-555-6425 ❖ www.restorationarc.net

Climb the Ladder to Success

Technology evolves quickly. Hardware and software that we consider state-of-the-art today may be outdated by tomorrow. Keeping pace with the rapid changes in technology is vital to your success in the workplace. If you want to get ahead, you must know how to use the latest programs and devices. Continuing your education and training will provide immediate benefits. In addition to learning new skills, you will also:

- Increase your productivity.
- Increase your value to the company.
- Increase your chances for promotion.

In-House Training

Executive Recruitment Resources understands the value of on-going training. That is why we offer a wide variety of in-house training courses designed to improve your skills with current technology, and provide you with the opportunity to learn about cutting edge technological developments.

We know that the skills you need today may not be the same as the ones you relied on yesterday. That's why we regularly evaluate our courses to keep them up to date. Courses range from introductory word processing to advanced database management to financial and accounting systems. Courses are offered at intervals throughout the year at different locations, insuring that all employees have access. Check out our current schedule on the company Web site, or stop by the training department for more information.

We Pay for You to Learn

Did you know that Executive Recruitment Resources offers a tuition reimbursement benefit? If we do not offer an in-house training course that meets your needs, we will pay for you to attend that class at an approved facility. We offer 100% reimbursement for up to three courses per calendar year. Approved facilities include the local community college and continuing education programs. In the past, employees have been reimbursed for classes in computer-aided design, software programming, database design, marketing, and even foreign language training.

The process requires that you obtain approval before registering for the class. Upon successful completing of the class, Executive Recruitment Resources will repay you for the entire cost of tuition. The necessary forms are available online, and in the Human Resources department. For more information, call 602-555-6425, extension 343.

Prepared by: Student's Name

Date: 7/22/08   Time: 4:33:37 PM

Curriculum Integration

Application Skills   For your science class, use the skills you have learned in Lesson 1 to create a multipage newsletter about computer technology. Specifically, the topics you should cover include: employment opportunities in the field of computer information systems, emerging information systems tools and operating systems, tools available to facilitate worldwide telecommunications (such as cyberpals, global surveys, and research), and security controls for information systems. You can work alone, but it is suggested that you work in teams to complete the assignment. As a team, you can set goals, prioritize tasks, and develop a schedule. You can assign each team member a different responsibility and topic, and work cooperatively to complete the project. Refer to Illustration A to see page 1 of a sample newsletter.

EXERCISE DIRECTIONS

Start the project by developing a schedule, allocating assignments, and setting goals. Assign each team member the responsibility of writing at least one article for the newsletter.

Research the topics listed in the Application Skills paragraph above to gather the information you will need to write your articles. Take notes and record source information.

Work cooperatively to develop and edit the articles. Meet as a team to read and discuss each other's work, offering and accepting constructive criticism.

When the articles are finished, or close to finished, start Word, if necessary, and create a new document. Save it as **06SCIENCE_xx**.

Display elements that might help you while you work, such as the rulers, nonprinting characters, and text boundaries, and make sure all the features you want to use are enabled, such as AutoCorrect and AutoFormat as You Type.

Select a theme, style set, and colors for the document, or create and save a custom theme. Set an appropriate paper size. Design the newsletter to include a title, headlines, body text, columns, and sections.

Type and format the text you want to include in the newsletter, or insert files submitted by each team member. Insert section breaks so you can apply different page layout settings. For example, you probably want the newsletter title in one column, but the articles in two or three columns. Adjust spacing to control text flow and make the text easier to read.

Use dropped capitals and borders and shading to enhance the appearance of the document, and insert graphics as appropriate. Remember to include page numbers.

Check the spelling and grammar in the newsletter, and use a thesaurus to replace common or boring words. Track formatting to identify and correct inconsistencies.

Ask a classmate who was not part of your team to review the document and make suggestions for how you might improve it. Incorporate your classmate's suggestions into the document, and save it. Print the newsletter and distribute it to your classmates.

Assess the newsletter and decide whether you want to include it in your employment portfolio. If so, print a clean copy, insert the pages in sleeves, and add it to the portfolio.

Close all files, saving all changes.

Illustration A

COMPUTER TECHNOLOGY REPORT

A Guide to Emerging Technologies and Careers Opportunities

Published by Mrs. Smith's Third Period Science Class | **Spring**

What's New?

Emerging technologies are developments for which the science is understood, but the potential is unfulfilled. (http://www.bitpipe.com/tlist/Emerging-Technologies.html).

In computer technology some of the exciting developments to watch include solar powered laptops, touch screen displays, solid state drives, cloud computing, and ambient data streaming. Following is an overview of a few specific areas where emerging technology may impact our lives in the not-too-distant future.

Information Systems

Emerging technologies in information systems are tools for managing vast amounts of data and information stored in complex networks and databases.

Operating Systems

A real time operating system (RTOS) controls a real time computer system, which is one that responds to input signals fast enough to keep an operation moving at its required speed.

Security

According to Samuel Greengard, in an article written for Microsoft.com, five emerging technologies that will impact computer and data security are: universal serial bus (USB) tokens, built-in biometrics, self-aware Web applications, encrypted hard drives, and built-in mobile device protection. (http://www.microsoft.com/midsizebusiness/security/technologies.mspx)

Communicate Much?

Communications tools have made it possible to communicate with people around the world, at any time, from almost any location. Most people are familiar with e-mail, instant messaging, telephones, and text messaging. Some have even used video conferencing and Web cameras. Here is an overview of some other communications technologies:

Social networking groups such as Cyberpals let people with similar interests find each other and share information, no matter where they live or work.

Businesses and organizations make use of global surveys conducted via the Internet to learn what people around the world are thinking, doing, buying, and more.

Search engines are evolving rapidly into specialized research tools. They quickly plow through the vast array of data stored online to locate and retrieve the exact bit of information someone is looking for.

Life is easier and more interesting because people can communicate across time and distance.

Did You Know...

...that according to the Bureau of Labor and Statistics, Database Managers can earn up to $116,000 per year?

See page two for an overview of careers in the Information Technology industry.

Lesson | 2

References and Automation

Exercise | 7

Skills Covered

- **About Word Options**
- **Customize the Quick Access Toolbar**
- **Set a Default Save Location**
- **Personalize Your User Name and Initials**
- **Customize the View for Opening E-Mail Attachments**

Software Skills Microsoft Office Word 2007 is designed to provide quick access to the tools and features that you will need most often. In addition, you can customize the Quick Access Toolbar to display buttons you want to have available at all times. You can also specify a storage location where new documents will be saved by default, and you can personalize the user name and initials that Microsoft Office Word uses to identify you as the author of documents that you create.

Application Skills You would like to customize and personalize Microsoft Office Word 2007 for your own use. In this exercise, you will practice customizing the Quick Access Toolbar by adding and removing buttons, you will specify a default location for storing documents, you will learn how to personalize your user name and initials, and you will learn how to customize the view for opening e-mail attachments.

TERMS

User name A name assigned to someone who uses a computer system or program that identifies the user to the system.

NOTES

About Word Options

- You can modify the way Word 2007 executes certain commands and features by customizing settings in the Word Options dialog box.
- The settings in the Word Options dialog box are organized into groups according to the type of command.
- For example, settings that affect the way documents and commands appear on-screen or when printed are in the Display group, and settings that affect the way documents are saved are in the Save group.
- The groups display in a pane on the left side of the Word Options dialog box; you click a group name to display the settings in that group.

Display settings in the Word Options dialog box

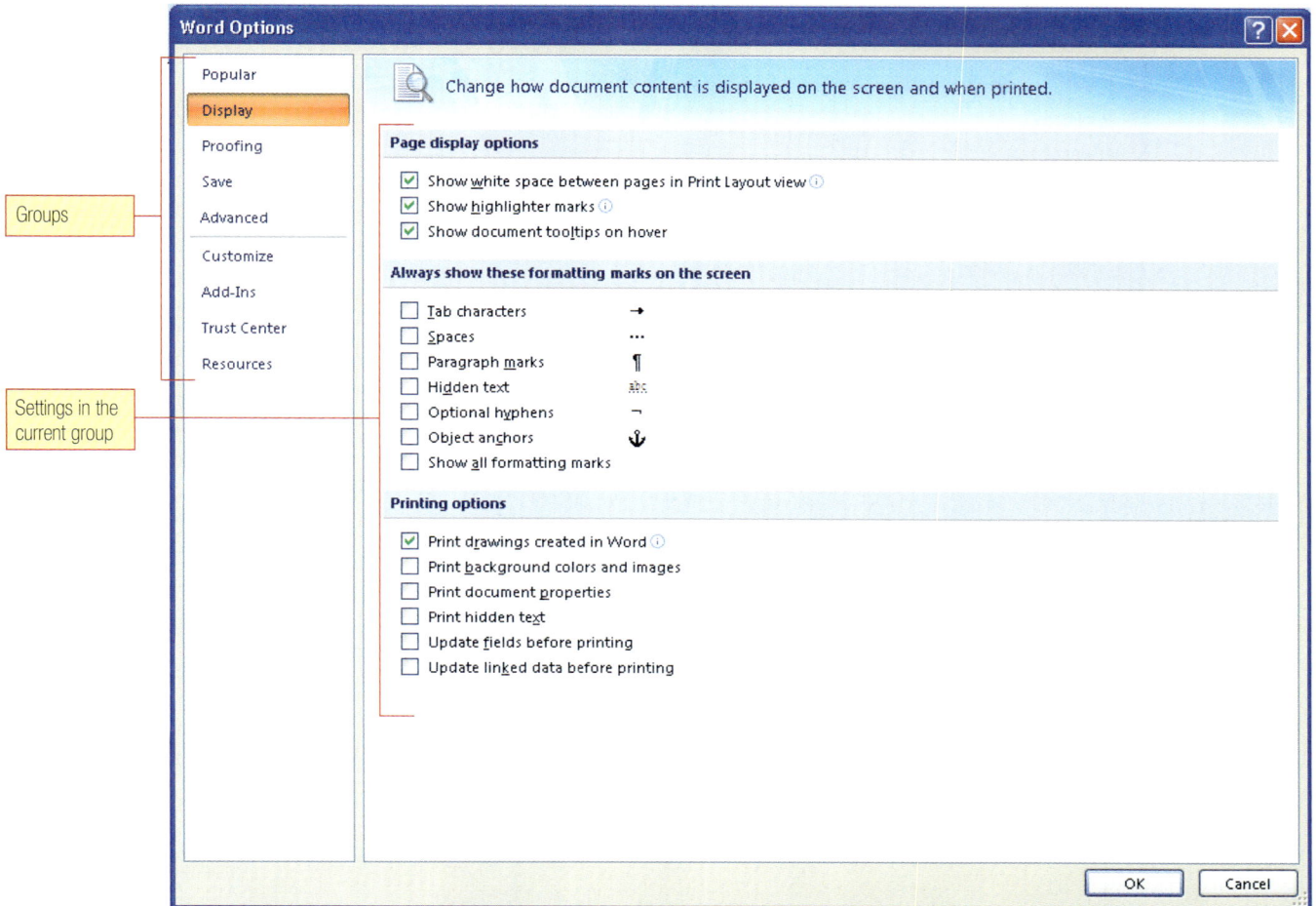

Customize the Quick Access Toolbar

■ By default, the Save, Undo, and Repeat buttons display on the Quick Access Toolbar in the upper-left corner of the program window, no matter which tab displays on the Ribbon.

■ You can customize the Quick Access Toolbar by adding and removing buttons for other commands.

■ For example, if you frequently print documents using the default Print settings, you can add the Quick Print button to the Quick Access Toolbar.

■ Some common buttons display on a menu when you click the Customize Quick Access Toolbar button.

■ You simply click a button on the menu to add it to the Quick Access Toolbar.

■ If the button does not display in the menu, you can locate it on its Ribbon tab, right-click it, and select the command to add it to the Quick Access Toolbar.

■ Alternatively, you can select it from a list of all available commands using the Customize group in the Word Options dialog box.

■ You can also rearrange the order of buttons on the Quick Access Toolbar, and you can reset the Quick Access Toolbar to its default configuration.

■ Finally, you can choose to display the Quick Access Toolbar below the Ribbon.

Customize settings in the Word Options dialog box

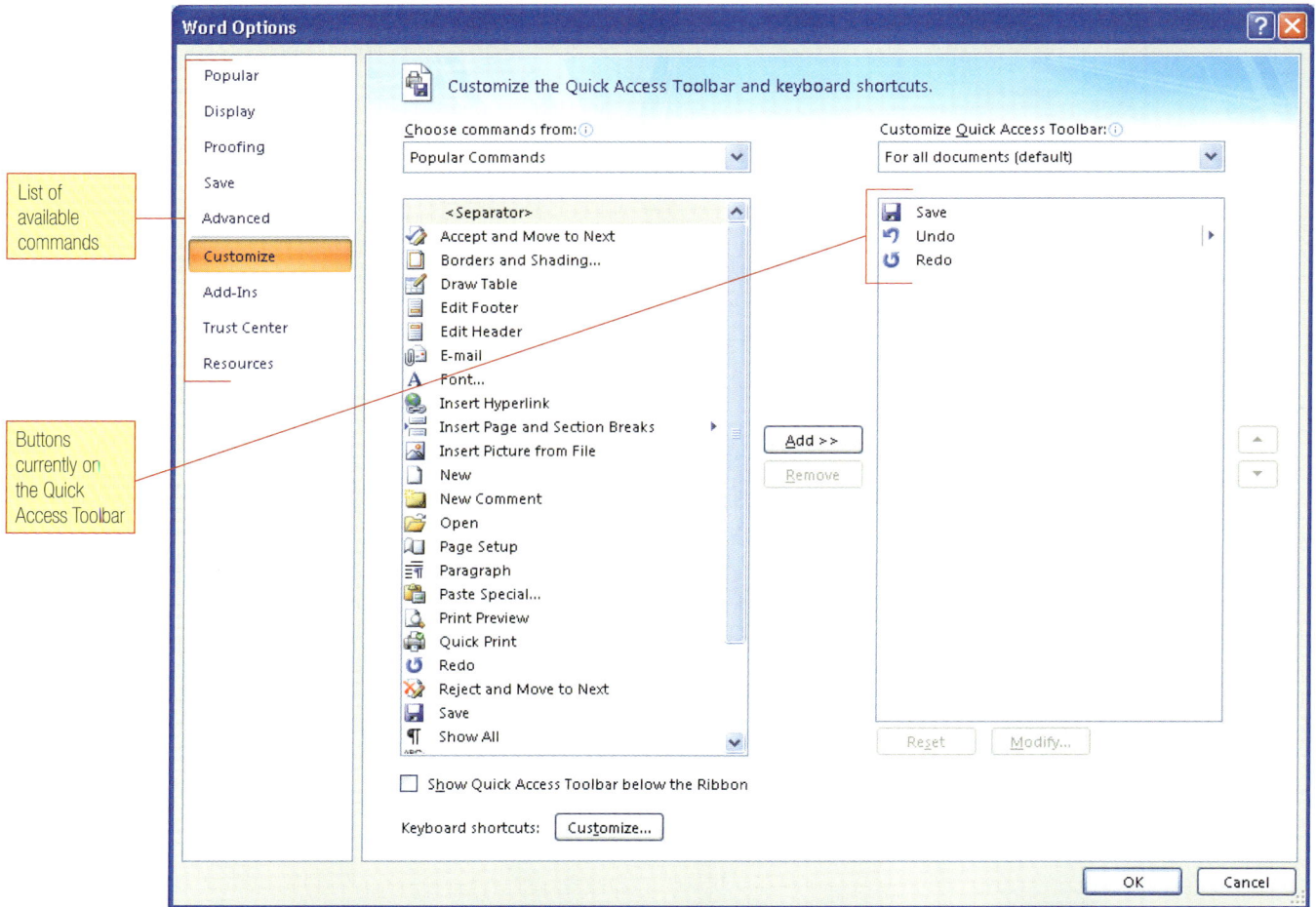

Word Options

Popular
Display
Proofing
Save
Advanced
Customize
Add-Ins
Trust Center
Resources

Customize the Quick Access Toolbar and keyboard shortcuts.

Choose commands from: ⓘ

Popular Commands ▼

Customize Quick Access Toolbar: ⓘ

For all documents (default) ▼

<Separator>
Accept and Move to Next
Borders and Shading...
Draw Table
Edit Footer
Edit Header
E-mail
Font...
Insert Hyperlink
Insert Page and Section Breaks ▶
Insert Picture from File
New
New Comment
Open
Page Setup
Paragraph
Paste Special...
Print Preview
Quick Print
Redo
Reject and Move to Next
Save
Show All

Save
Undo
Redo

Add >>

Remove

Reset   Modify...

☐ Show Quick Access Toolbar below the Ribbon

Keyboard shortcuts: Customize...

OK   Cancel

List of available commands

Buttons currently on the Quick Access Toolbar

Set a Default Save Location

- By default, Word 2007 saves documents in the My Documents folder if you are using the Windows XP operating system, or the Documents folder if you are using the Windows Vista operating system.

- You can change the default storage location to a different folder or drive using options in the Save group in the Word Options dialog box.

- Your system may have been customized to use a different default save location. For example, files may be saved on a network.

Personalize Your User Name and Initials

- When you set up Microsoft Word 2007 on your computer, you enter a **user name** and initials.

- Word uses this information to identify you as the author of new documents that you create and save, and as the editor of existing documents that you open, modify, and save.

- In addition, your user name is associated with revisions that you make when you use the Track Changes features, and the initials are associated with comments that you insert.

- You can change the user name and initials using options in the Popular group in the Word Options dialog box.

Customize the View for Opening E-Mail Attachments

- By default, when you open a document that you receive as an attachment to an e-mail message, it displays in Full Screen Reading view.

- You can use the Word Options dialog box to disable the feature so that the document opens in Print Layout view.

Save settings in the Word Options dialog box

Word Options

Popular
Display
Proofing
Save
Advanced
Customize
Add-Ins
Trust Center
Resources

Save group

Current Save location

Customize how documents are saved.

Save documents

Save files in this format: Word Document (*.docx)

☑ Save AutoRecover information every 10 minutes

AutoRecover file location: C:\Documents and Settings\Student 1.MAINXP\Application Data\Microsoft\Word Browse...

Default file location: C:\Documents and Settings\My Documents\ Browse...

Offline editing options for document management server files

Save checked-out files to: ⓘ
● The server drafts location on this computer
○ The web server

Server drafts location: C:\Documents and Settings\Student 1.MAINXP\My Documents\SharePoint Drafts\ Browse...

Preserve fidelity when sharing this document: 📄 Document1

☐ Embed fonts in the file ⓘ
☐ Embed only the characters used in the document (best for reducing file size)
☐ Do not embed common system fonts

Popular settings in the Word Options dialog box

Word Options

Popular
Display
Proofing
Save
Advanced
Customize
Add-Ins
Trust Center
Resources

Popular group

Current user name

Current initials

Change the most popular options in Word.

Top options for working with Word

☑ Show Mini Toolbar on selection ⓘ
☑ Enable Live Preview ⓘ
☐ Show Developer tab in the Ribbon ⓘ
☐ Always use ClearType
☑ Open e-mail attachments in Full Screen Reading view ⓘ

Color scheme: Blue

ScreenTip style: Show feature descriptions in ScreenTips

Personalize your copy of Microsoft Office

User name: Suzanne Weixel

Initials: SW

Choose the languages you want to use with Microsoft Office: Language Settings...

PROCEDURES

Add a Command Button to the Quick Access Toolbar

1. Click **Customize Quick Access Toolbar** button
   ⏷ . . . . `Alt`, `H`, `↑`, `→`, `→`, `Enter`
2. Click command to add . . . `↓`, `Enter`

   ✓ *A check mark next to command name indicates it is already on the Quick Access Toolbar.*

   OR

1. Right-click command button to add on Ribbon.
2. Click **A**dd to Quick Access Toolbar . . . . `A`

   OR

1. Click **Customize Quick Access Toolbar** button
   ⏷ . . . . `Alt`, `H`, `↑`, `→`, `→`, `Enter`
2. Click **M**ore Commands . . . . . . `M`
3. Click **C**hoose commands from drop-down arrow . . . `Alt`+`C`
4. Click category of commands . . . . `↓`, `Enter`

   ✓ *Click All Commands to display all available commands.*

5. Click command to add . . . `⇤`, `↓`
6. Click **A**dd . . . . `Alt`+`A`
7. Click **OK** . . . . `Enter`

Remove a Command Button from the Quick Access Toolbar

1. Click **Customize Quick Access Toolbar** button
   ⏷ . . . . `Alt`, `H`, `↑`, `→`, `→`, `Enter`
2. Click command to remove . . . . `↓`, `Enter`

   ✓ *No check mark next to command name indicates it is not displayed on the Quick Access Toolbar.*

   OR

1. Right-click command button to remove on Quick Access Toolbar.
2. Click **R**emove from Quick Access Toolbar . . . . `R`

OR

1. Click **Customize Quick Access Toolbar** button
   ⏷ . . . . `Alt`, `H`, `↑`, `→`, `→`, `Enter`
2. Click **M**ore Commands . . . . . . `M`
3. Click the button to remove in the list on the right side of the dialog box . . . . `Alt`+`Q`, `⇤`, `↓`
4. Click **R**emove . . . . `Alt`+`R`
5. Click **OK** . . . . `Enter`

Rearrange Buttons on the Quick Access Toolbar

1. Click **Customize Quick Access Toolbar** button
   ⏷ . . . . `Alt`, `H`, `↑`, `→`, `→`, `Enter`
2. Click **M**ore Commands . . . . . . `M`
3. Click the button to move in the list on the right side of the dialog box . . . . `Alt`+`Q`, `⇤`, `↓`
4. Click **Move Up** button `▲` to move button up list.

   ✓ *Moving a button up the list moves it to the left on the Quick Access Toolbar.*

   OR

   Click **Move Down** button `▼` to move button down list.

   ✓ *Moving a button down the list moves it to the right on the Quick Access Toolbar.*

5. Click **OK** . . . . `Enter`

Reset the Default Quick Access Toolbar

1. Click **Customize Quick Access Toolbar** button
   ⏷ . . . . `Alt`, `H`, `↑`, `→`, `→`, `Enter`
2. Click **M**ore Commands . . . . . . `M`
3. Click **R**e**s**et . . . . `Alt`+`S`

Change the Location of the Quick Access Toolbar

1. Click **Customize Quick Access Toolbar** button
   ⏷ . . . . `Alt`, `H`, `↑`, `→`, `→`, `Enter`
2. Click **S**how Below the Ribbon . . . . `S`

OR

Click **S**how Above the Ribbon . . . . `S`

Set a Default Save Location

1. Click **Office Button** 🔘 . . `Alt`+`F`
2. Click Word Opt**i**ons . . . . `I`
3. Click **S**ave . . . . `S`
4. Click **D**efault file location . . . . `Alt`+`I`
5. Key path to new storage location.

   OR

   a. Click **B**rowse button . . . . `⇤`, `Enter`
   b. Navigate to new storage location.
   c. Click **OK** . . . . `Enter`

6. Click **OK** . . . . `Enter`

Personalize Your User Name and Initials

1. Click **Office Button** 🔘 . . `Alt`+`F`
2. Click Word Opt**i**ons . . . . `I`
3. Click **U**ser name . . . . `Alt`+`U`
4. Key new user name.
5. Click **I**nitials . . . . `Alt`+`I`
6. Key new initials.
7. Click **OK** . . . . `Enter`

Customize the View for Opening E-Mail Attachments

1. Open a document.
2. Click **Office Button** 🔘 . . `Alt`+`F`
3. Click Word Opt**i**ons . . . . `I`
4. Click to deselect **Open e-mail attachments in Full Screen Reading view** check box . . . . `Alt`+`F`

   ✓ *Select the check box to open e-mail attachments in Full Screen Reading view.*

5. Click **OK** . . . . `Enter`

EXERCISE DIRECTIONS

1. Start Word, if necessary.
2. Click the Customize Quick Access Toolbar button and add the Quick Print button to the Quick Access Toolbar.
3. Click the Customize Quick Access Toolbar button and add the Print Preview button to the Quick Access Toolbar.
4. Click the Customize Quick Access Toolbar button and then click More Commands to open the Word Options dialog box with the Customize group settings displayed.
5. Display all available commands.
6. Add the Open button to the Quick Access Toolbar.
7. Remove the Quick Print button from the Quick Access Toolbar.
8. Rearrange the buttons on the Quick Access Toolbar into the following order, from left to right: Open, Print Preview, Undo, Redo, Save.
9. Click OK to apply the changes and close the Word Options dialog box.
10. Select to display the Quick Access Toolbar below the Ribbon. The window should look similar to Illustration A.
11. With your instructor's permission, set the default save location to a network drive or folder.
12. With your instructor's permission, set the default save location to your desktop.
13. Change the default save location back to its previous setting.
14. With your instructor's permission, change your user name to **User1** and your initials to **U1**.
15. With your instructor's permission, deselect the option for opening e-mail attachments in Full Screen Reading view.
16. Change the user name and initials back to their previous settings.
17. Reset the Quick Access Toolbar to its default configuration.
18. Select to display the Quick Access Toolbar above the Ribbon.
19. Select to open e-mail attachments in Full Screen Reading view.
20. Exit Word. Do not save the document.

Illustration A

ON YOUR OWN

1. Start Word and open the Word Options dialog box.
2. Explore the settings available in each group listed in the left pane.
3. Select the Customize group.
4. Click the Choose commands from drop-down arrow and review the available command tabs.
5. Select any tab and review the available commands.
6. Select a different tab and review the available commands.
7. Add at least two buttons to the Quick Access Toolbar.
8. Rearrange the order of the buttons on the Quick Access Toolbar.
9. Reset the Quick Access Toolbar to its default configuration.
10. Change the default view for opening e-mail attachments.
11. Set the view for opening e-mail attachments to Full Screen Reading.
12. With your instructor's permission, set the default save location to a network drive or folder.
13. In the document file, type a brief explanation or list of reasons why you might need or want to save a document to a network storage location.
14. Save the document to the default save location, with the name OWD07_xx.
15. Check the spelling and grammar in the document, and then print it, using a network printer, if there is one available.
16. Change the default save location back to its original setting.
17. Close the document, saving all changes, and exit Word.

Skills Covered

- **Insert a Cross-Reference**
- **Insert a Caption**

- **Create an Index**
- **Modify an Index**

Software Skills   Sometimes it may be difficult for readers to locate the specific information they need in long or complex documents. To quickly refer a reader from one location to another related location, you can create a cross-reference. To help readers identify illustrations such as tables or figures, you can insert captions. To help readers find the page containing specific information, you can create an index in which topics and subtopics are listed; Word automatically fills in the correct page number.

Application Skills   The Liberty Blooms flower shop has hired you to prepare a report about roses to publish in its monthly newsletter. The report is almost complete but would benefit from features that will help readers find the information they need. In this exercise, you will create cross-references in the report and insert captions. You will also generate an index to help readers locate specific topics in the document quickly and easily.

TERMS

Caption   A text label that identifies an illustration such as a figure, table, or picture.

Cross-reference   Text that refers a reader to a different location in a document.

Cross-reference text   The information entered in a document to introduce a cross-reference.

Cross-reference type   The type of object that is being referred to, such as a bookmark or heading.

Index   An alphabetical list of topics and/or subtopics in a document along with the page numbers where they appear.

Tab leaders   Characters inserted to the left of text aligned with a tab stop, such as page numbers in an index.

NOTES

Insert a Cross-Reference

- A **cross-reference** is text that directs a reader to another location in the same document for more information. For example, "*For more information, see page 22*" is a cross-reference.

- You can create cross-references to existing headings, footnotes, bookmarks, captions, numbered paragraphs, tables, and figures, as well as to endnotes and equations.

- When you create a cross-reference with Word, you enter the **cross-reference text**, and then select the **cross-reference type**.

- After you select the reference type, you select whether you want Word to reference the item by page number, text, or paragraph. This is the information Word will automatically insert in the document.

- Word enters the reference as a field, so it can be updated if necessary. This means that if you reference a heading and then move the heading to another location in the document, you can update the cross-reference to reflect the change.

- By default, Word inserts a cross-reference as a hyperlink. When you are viewing a document on-screen, Ctrl + click the cross-reference to jump to the specified destination.

- You can change the setting if you do not want the cross-reference inserted as a hyperlink.

- If the cross-reference field code is displayed in your document instead of the field value, you must deselect the Show field codes instead of their values option in the Advanced group in the Word Options dialog box.

Cross-reference dialog box

Insert a Caption

- Insert a **caption** to label an item.

- Each caption includes a text label and a number field.

- By default, Word comes with labels for tables, figures, and equations.

- You can create new labels for other items or to use different label text. For example, you might want to label a figure as an Illustration.

- By default, Word uses Arabic numbers and positions the captions below the item. You can customize the number format and select to position the caption above the item.

- Word automatically updates the numbers for each caption entered; however, if you delete or move a caption, you must manually update the remaining captions.

- You can insert a caption manually or set Word to automatically insert captions.

Caption dialog box

Create an Index

- An **index** lists topics and subtopics contained in a document, along with the page numbers where they appear.

- Word automatically generates an alphabetical index based on index entries you mark in the document text.

- Word comes with a selection of index formats.

- Other index layout options include the number of columns in the index and whether subtopics should be run in on the same line or if each subtopic should be indented. The default setting is for two columns and indented subtopics.

■ You can also choose to right-align page numbers and to precede page numbers with **tab leaders**.

Index dialog box

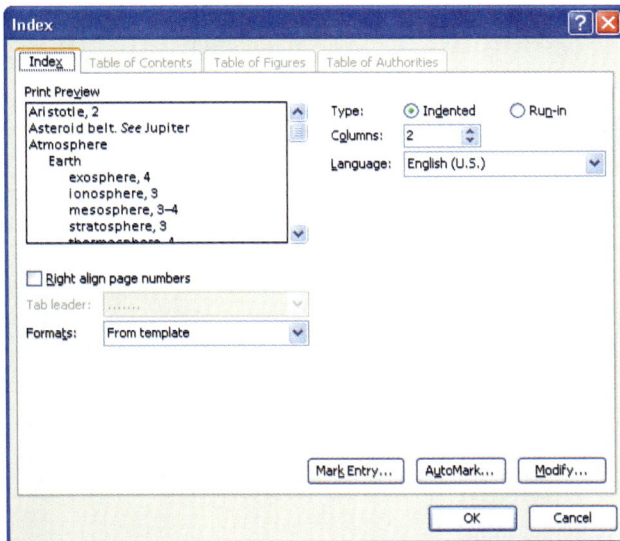

■ You can index a single character, a word, a phrase, or a topic that spans multiple pages.

■ You can mark all occurrences of the same text, or mark a single occurrence. Keep in mind that Word only marks all occurrences of *exactly* the same text. That means that the formatting, capitalization, tense, etc., must be exactly the same.

■ Index entries can cross-reference a different index entry. For example, *Cats, see Pets* is a cross-referenced index entry.

■ If you index many subtopics, you can use a multilevel index. For example, *Pets* may be the main index topic, with *Cats, Dogs*, and *Goldfish* as subtopics.

■ To mark entries for an index, you enter the text you want to display in the index in the Mark Index Entry dialog box.

■ If you select the text in the document, it is automatically entered in the Mark Index Entry dialog box. Alternatively, you can type the entry.

■ You can type the entry text using any formatting; it does not have to match the selected text in the document. However, if you are marking all items, only the items that appear exactly as the *selected text* will be marked. It doesn't matter what you type in the Main entry text box.

■ If the selected item is exactly as you want it to appear in the index, you do not have to retype the entry text.

■ If the entry is for a subtopic, you type the main entry topic under which the subtopic should be listed, then the subentry text as you want it displayed.

■ Word automatically inserts an Index Entry field in the document following the selected item.

✓ *If hidden text is displayed, you see the Index Entry fields in the document. This makes the document appear longer than it will be when printed. To see the document as it will print, hide hidden text or change to Print Preview.*

Mark Index Entry dialog box

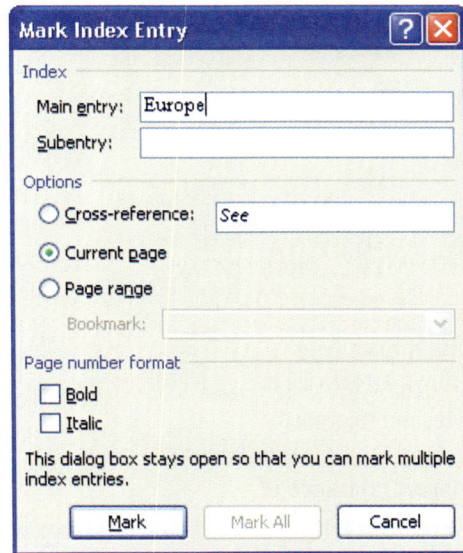

Modify an Index

■ You can edit existing index entries by editing the text in the Index Entry field.

■ If you add, delete, or move indexed items in the document, you must update the index so that Word changes the page numbers.

PROCEDURES

Insert a Cross-Reference

✓ *Before inserting a cross-reference, make sure that the item which is being referenced—such as the heading, bookmark, or footnote—already exists.*

1. Position insertion point where you want cross-reference to appear.
2. Type cross-reference text, followed by a space and any necessary punctuation.

   ✓ *For example, type the text: For more information see.*

3. Click **References** tab . . . . `Alt` + `S`

   Captions Group

4. Click **Cross-reference** button

   . . . . `R`, `F`

   ✓ *You can also click the Cross-reference button in the Links group on the Insert tab.*

5. Click **Reference type** drop-down arrow . . . . `Alt` + `T`
6. Click desired reference type . . . . `↑`/`↓`, `Enter`
7. Click **Insert reference to** drop-down arrow . . . . `Alt` + `R`
8. Click desired reference option . . . . `↑`/`↓`, `Enter`
9. Select specific item in **For which** list. . . `Alt` + `W`, `↑`/`↓`

   ✓ *If you do not want cross-reference inserted as a hyperlink, deselect the **Insert as hyperlink** check box.*

10. Click **Insert** . . . . `Alt` + `I`
11. Click **Close** . . . . `Esc`

Update a Cross-reference

1. Select cross-reference to update.
2. Press `F9`.

   OR

   a. Right-click cross-reference to update.
   b. Click **Update Field** . . . . `U`

Insert a Caption Manually

1. Select item to caption.
2. Click **References** tab. . . . `Alt` + `S`

   Captions Group

3. Click **Insert Caption** button

   . . . . `P`

4. Click **Label** drop-down arrow . . . . `Alt` + `L`
5. Select desired label.

   OR

   a. Click **New Label** . . . . . `Alt` + `N`
   b. Type label name.
   c. Click **OK** . . . . `Enter`

6. Click **Position** . . . . `Alt` + `P`
7. Select either **Below selected item** (default) or **Above selected item**.
8. To customize number format, click **Numbering** . . . . `Alt` + `U`
9. Click **Format** drop-down arrow. . . . . `F`
10. Click format to use.
11. Click **OK** . . . . `Enter`
12. Click **OK** . . . . `Enter`

Insert a Caption Automatically

1. Click **References** tab. . . . `Alt` + `S`

   Captions Group

2. Click **Insert Caption** button

   . . . . `P`

3. Click **AutoCaption** . . . . . . `Alt` + `A`
4. In **Add caption when inserting** list, click check box(es) for item(s) you want to label . . . . . `↑`/`↓`, `Spacebar`
5. Click **Use label** . . . . `Alt` + `L`
6. Click desired label.

   OR

   a. Click **New Label** . . . . . `Alt` + `N`
   b. Type label name.
   c. Click **OK** . . . . `Enter`

7. Click **Position** . . . . `Alt` + `P`
8. Click desired position.
9. To customize number format, click **Numbering** . . . . `Alt` + `U`
10. Click **Format** drop-down arrow. . . . . `F`
11. Click format to use.
12. Click **OK** . . . . `Enter`
13. Click **OK** . . . . `Enter`

Create an Index

To mark index entries:

1. Click **References** tab. . . . `Alt` + `S`

   Index Group

2. Click **Mark Entry** button

   . . . . `N`

3. In document, select text to mark.

   ✓ *Mark Entry dialog box remains open while you select text to mark. If necessary, move Mark Entry dialog box out of the way.*

   OR

   Position insertion point after text to mark, or where you want to place the index code.

4. Click **Main entry** text box, if necessary . . . . `Alt` + `E`
5. Type or edit main index entry text.
6. Click **Subentry** text box . . . . `Alt` + `S`
7. Type subentry text if necessary.
8. Do one of the following:

   ■ Click **Mark** to mark selected occurrence only . . . . . `Alt` + `M`

   OR

   ■ Click **Mark All** to mark all occurrences of selected text in document. . . . . `Alt` + `A`

9. Repeat steps 3–8 until all entries are marked.
10. Click **Close** . . . . `Enter`

To mark a cross-referenced entry:

1. Click **References** tab . . . . Alt + S

   Index Group

2. Click **Mark Entry** button

   . . . . N

3. In document, select text to mark.

   ✓ *Mark Entry dialog box remains open while you select text to mark. If necessary, move Mark Entry dialog box out of the way.*

   OR

   Position insertion point after text to mark, or where you want to place the index code.

4. Click **Main entry** text box, if necessary . . . . Alt + E

5. Type main index entry text.

6. Click **Cross-reference** option button . . . . Alt + C

7. In Cross-reference text box, following the word *See*, type referenced main entry.

8. Click **Mark** . . . . Alt + M

9. Repeat steps 3–8 until all entries are marked.

10. Click **Close** . . . . Enter

To generate index:

1. Position insertion point in document where you want index displayed.

2. Click **References** tab . . . . Alt + S

   Index Group

3. Click **Insert Index** button

   X

4. Click **Formats** drop-down arrow . . . . Alt + T

5. Click desired format . . ↑ / ↓ , Enter

6. Select any other desired options.

7. Click **OK** . . . . Enter

To update index:

1. Click **References** tab . . . . Alt + S

   Index Group

2. Click **Update Index** button

   . . . . D

   OR

   a. Click in index.

   b. Press F9 .

   OR

   a. Right-click index.

   b. Click **Update Field** . . . . U

EXERCISE DIRECTIONS

1. Start Word, if necessary, open the document
   08ROSES, and save it as **08ROSES_xx**.

2. Replace the text *Student's Name* in the header with your own name.

3. Replace the text *Today's Date* in the header with the current date.

Insert Captions

1. Select the first table in the document.

2. Insert a caption to label the table. Use the label text **Table**, the default numbering scheme, and position the caption above the table.

3. Insert a page break before the caption to move Table 1 to the top of page 3.

4. Select the second table in the document.

5. Insert a caption to label the table, using the same options that you used to create the first caption. Table 2 should display at the top of page 4. If it does not, insert a page break before the Table 2 caption.

Insert Cross References

1. Position the insertion point at the end of the first paragraph under the heading *History*.

   ✓ *You may want to use the Document Map to navigate through the document.*

2. Type the following cross-reference text: **(For information on types of roses, refer to the section .)** Be sure to leave a space between the last word and the period.

3. Position the insertion point to the left of the period you just typed, and insert a hyperlinked cross-reference to the heading *Types of Roses*.

4. Scroll down to the heading *Types of Roses* on page 2 (or use the cross-reference hyperlink you inserted in step 3).

5. At the end of the paragraph under the heading *Types of Roses*, type the following cross-reference text: **For a description of common types of roses, refer to**

6. Position the insertion point to the right of the space after the word *to*, and insert a hyperlinked cross-reference to the entire caption for Table 1.

7. Position the insertion point after the cross-reference field and type a space followed by the text **on page .**

8. Position the insertion point to the left of the period and then insert a hyperlinked cross-reference to Table 1, referencing the page number on which it is located.

9. Ctrl + click the page number to go to the table.

10. In the document, move the insertion point to the end of the sentence under the heading *Grafted Roses* and type the following cross-reference text: **For information about the grading system, refer to**

11. Position the insertion point to the right of the space after the word *to*, and insert a hyperlinked cross-reference to the entire caption for Table 2.

12. Position the insertion point after the cross-reference field and type a space followed by the text **on page .**

13. Position the insertion point to the left of the period and then insert a hyperlinked cross-reference to the page number on which Table 2 is located.

14. Close the Cross-reference dialog box and then check the spelling and grammar in the document.

15. Display the document in Print Preview. Page 3 should look similar to Illustration A.

> ✓ *If you have the Field shading option set to Always in the Advanced group of the Word Options dialog box, the table number and cross-reference text will be shaded with gray.*

Create an Index

1. Close Print Preview and then press Ctrl + Home to move the insertion point to the beginning of the document.

2. Mark entries for an index as follows:

> ✓ *Note that to help you identify the text to mark in the following steps, it is formatted in italics. However, the text in the document is formatted according to the current and appropriate paragraph formatting.*

> ✓ *You might want to use the Find command to locate the specified text.*

   a. Select the text *roses* in the first sentence of the introduction, open the Mark Index Entry dialog box and mark all entries of the text.

   b. Select the text *symbol*, and mark all entries.

   c. Mark all entries of the text *cultivation, types, varieties,* and *hybrids.*

   d. Mark the name *Cleopatra.*

   e. Mark the phrases *bare-root plants* and *potted plants*, editing the main entry text so there are no initial capital letters.

   f. Select the text *ornamental decorations* in the first sentence under the heading *The Rose in Use*. Edit the text in the Main entry box to **usage**, and then type **ornamental decoration** in the Subentry box. Mark the entry.

   g. Select the text *confetti*, edit the main entry text to **usage**, and then type the text **confetti** in the Subentry box. Mark the entry.

   h. Continue entering the following as subentries for the main entry *usage*: **Egyptian mummies**, **perfume**, **medicine**, and **currency**.

   i. Select the text *white rose* under the heading *The Rose as Symbol*. Type **York** as the Subentry text. Select the Cross-reference option button, and type **symbol** after the word *See* in the Cross-reference box, then mark the entry.

   j. Select the text *red rose*. Type **Lancaster** as the Subentry text. Select the Cross-reference option button and type **symbol** after the word *See* in the Cross-reference box, then mark the entry.

   k. Mark the phrase *Wars of the Roses.*

   l. Mark the phrase *American Nursery Standards.*

   m. Mark all occurrences of the following words: *diseases, quality,* and *insects.* If necessary, edit the main entry text so there are no initial capital letters.

   n. Mark the first occurrence of the word *pests* and add a cross-reference to insects.

3. When you have finished marking the necessary entries, close the Mark Index Entry dialog box.

4. Press Ctrl + End to move the insertion point to the end of the document.

5. Press Enter to move the insertion point to a new line. It should display at the top of a new page (page 7). If necessary, insert a page break.

6. At the top of the new page, type **Index**, and format it with the Heading 1 style.

7. Press Enter.

8. Generate the index as follows:

   a. Select the Classic style.

   b. Right-align page numbers.

   c. Use a dotted tab leader.

   d. Use two columns.

   e. Indent the subtopics.

9. When the index is inserted in the document, save the changes.

10. Preview the document.

11. Close Print Preview and mark all occurrences of the text *rose water* as a main index entry.

12. Update the index to reflect the change.

13. Preview the index page. It should look similar to Illustration B.

14. Close the document, saving all changes.

Illustration A

Student's Name

Today's Date

Table 1

Species Roses	These are uncultivated varieties. They are Usually hardy and disease resistant. They come in a wide variety of types and colors.
Old European Garden Roses	These are the oldest group of cultivated roses. They are hybrid groups common in European gardens prior to the 18th century. They usually have a strong fragrance and can withstand cold winters, but are susceptible to heat, drought, and disease.
Hardy Repeat-Blooming Old Roses	These plants are similar to the Old European Garden Roses but they will bloom more than once each season.
Modern Roses	These include the varieties developed after the 18th century.
Miniature Roses	Small plants that are extremely useful for small gardens and container planting.
Shrub Roses	Plants that are noted for their rounded shape, winter hardiness and disease resistance. Shrub roses tend to be free-flowering, which means they provide blooms all season long, and are suitable for using as hedges and in border gardens.

Judging Rose Quality

The quality of rose plants varies depending on the vendor. Ask for references before purchasing to make sure that other customers have been satisfied with the plants. You can order plants by mail or on-line, but unless you are completely certain that you are dealing with a reputable vendor, you may prefer purchasing plants locally, so you can see them before you buy, and so that you can return them if necessary.

Grafted Roses

Grafted roses are rated based on an American Nursery Standards grading system. For information about the grading system, refer to Table 2 on page 4.

3

Illustration B

Student's Name   Today's Date

Index

5

ON YOUR OWN

1. Plan a research report on a topic of your choice. Prepare a list of three to five possible topics, and then ask your instructor to approve one of them. Select a topic based on something you are currently learning at school, or something new you would like to learn more about. For example, for a business class, you might select a topic about marketing, how to identify business trends, business ethics, or even how to project a professional attitude in the workplace. For a technology class, you might select a topic such as types of networking systems.

2. Conduct preliminary research that will help you organize your report. Use books, magazines, or the Internet to locate useful information. Remember to keep track of all source information to use in a bibliography or for footnote references.

3. Start Word and create a new document.

4. Save the document as OWD08_*xx*.

5. Select a professional-looking theme and style set, and set appropriate margins and line spacing.

6. Using the preliminary research, create a first draft. You might want to start with an outline, or just organize the report using headings. Try to include at least four main headings, along with the necessary subheadings.

7. Review the first draft and make improvements by expanding the content and rearranging it, if necessary. Insert footnotes or endnotes, as necessary.

8. If you have not already done so, create one or two tables to illustrate the text, and then insert captions for the tables.

9. Insert cross-references in the document. Try using different cross-reference types. For example, select a heading for one cross-reference and a footnote or table for another.

10. Create an index for the document. Mark main entries and subentries, and cross-references, if necessary.

11. Insert the index on a new page at the end of the document. Try different formatting options, such as the Fancy format with dotted tab leaders.

12. Preview the document and insert page breaks as necessary.

13. Update the index and the cross-references if necessary.

14. Print the document. Ask a classmate to review the document and offer comments or suggestions.

15. Incorporate the comments and suggestions into the document.

16. Close the document, saving all changes, and exit Word.

Exercise | 9

Skills Covered

- Create a Table of Contents
- Create a Table of Figures
- Create a Bibliography
- Manage Sources
- Create a Table of Authorities
- Update a Table

Software Skills   Professional documents and reports use tables to present lists to help readers locate and understand information. A table of contents helps readers locate information they need in a long document by listing headings and the page numbers where each heading starts. Likewise, a table of figures lists the page numbers where tables are located. A table of authorities is used specifically in a legal document to list references such as cases, statutes, and rules. A bibliography lists sources of information used to develop and create the document. Use Word to automatically generate a table of contents, table of figures, table of authorities, or bibliography. If the page numbers or information change, you can update the table.

Application Skills   You have just about completed the document about roses for Liberty Blooms. The final touch is to add a table of contents and table of figures to help readers locate the information they need, and then to create a bibliography. In this exercise, you will generate the table of figures. You will check that all topics you want included in the table of contents are formatted with heading styles. Then, you will generate the table of contents. You will insert citations for a bibliography and then generate the bibliography. Finally, you will make some editing changes to the report and update the tables to reflect the changes.

TERMS

Bibliography   A list of sources of information used to develop and create a document.

Bibliography citation style   The style used to organize and format source information in a bibliography. Some common styles include Chicago and MLA.

Citation   A reference to a source of information. In legal documents, it is a reference to previous court decisions or authoritative writings.

Passim   A word used in citations of cases, articles, or books in a legal document to indicate that the reference is found in many places within the work.

Table of authorities   A list of citations in a legal document, usually accompanied by the page numbers where the references occur.

Table of contents   A list of topics and subtopics in a document, usually accompanied by the page numbers where the topics begin and placed before the main body of the document.

Table of figures   A list of figures in a document, usually accompanied by the page numbers where the figures are located.

NOTES

Create a Table of Contents

- Word generates a **table of contents** based on paragraphs formatted with the built-in heading styles.

- You can select from a list of built-in preformatted styles, or you can create a customized table using the options in the Table of Contents dialog box.

- If you create a customized table of contents, you can use as many levels as you want, depending on how many levels of headings are used in the document.

- You do not have to include all heading levels in the table of contents. For example, you may have paragraphs formatted with up to four heading levels, but select to include only two heading levels in the table of contents.

- Paragraphs formatted with the same level of heading style will be listed at the same level in the table of contents.

- Word comes with a selection of table of contents formats that you can preview in the Table of Contents dialog box.

- You can also select whether to include page numbers and whether to right-align them.

- If you right-align page numbers, you can select a tab leader.

- By default, Word formats the headings in a table of contents as hyperlinks. Ctrl + click the heading in the table to jump to the destination.

- If you don't want to use hyperlinks in your table of contents, deselect the Use hyperlinks instead of page numbers check box in the Table of Contents dialog box.

Table of Contents dialog box

Create a Table of Figures

- A **table of figures** includes a list of the captions used to identify items in a document.

- To create the table, specify the captions you want to include.

- Word sorts the captions by number and displays them in the table of figures.

  ✓ *For information on inserting captions, refer to Exercise 8.*

Table of Figures dialog box

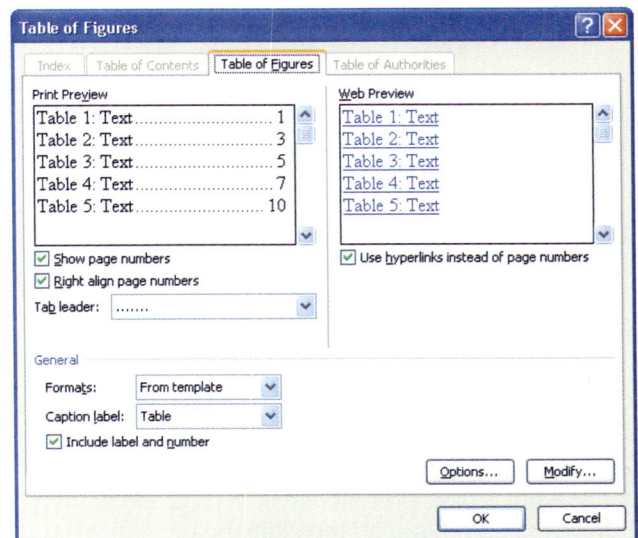

Create a Bibliography

- Create a **bibliography** to list the sources you use to find information included in a document or report.

- Word creates a bibliography by compiling a list of all **citations** you insert in the document.

- You insert a citation at the location where you include information you obtained from the source.

- For each citation, you enter source information in bibliography fields such as the type of source, the author, the publisher, and the publication date.

- The bibliography fields depend on the type of source. For example, a Web site source type includes fields for URL and date accessed. An article in a periodical source type includes fields for article title, periodical title, and pages.

  ✓ *You can select to display all bibliography fields, if you want.*

Create Source dialog box

Create Source

Type of Source: Book

Bibliography Fields for MLA

Author: _____ Edit

☐ Corporate Author _____

Title: _____

Year: _____

City: _____

Publisher: _____

☐ Show All Bibliography Fields

Tag name
Placeholder1

OK   Cancel

- The citation displays inline at the insertion point location; the format depends on the selected **bibliography citation style**.
- For example, in MLA style, the author's last name displays in parentheses.
- Alternatively, you can insert a citation placeholder that displays as a question mark in the document, reminding you to fill in the source information at a later time.
- You can also quickly insert a citation using information already entered for a source.
- After entering the citations, you can automatically generate a bibliography that lists all of the source information entered in the citations.
- The bibliography is formatted in the selected bibliography citation style.
- If you add or edit sources, you can update the bibliography.

Manage Sources

- Bibliography source information is stored in the Source Manager. (See illustration on the following page.)
- The Source Manager displays a list of sources in the current document and a master list of all sources you have entered for all documents.
- You can use the Source Manager to edit and delete sources, to fill in information for a placeholder source, and to add a source from the master list to the current document.
- You can also preview sources in the current bibliography citation style.

Create a Table of Authorities

- Create a **table of authorities** to list citations in a legal document, along with the page numbers where the references are located.
- If a citation appears on five or more pages, you may select to substitute the word **passim** for the page numbers.
- Word comes with built-in categories of common citations, such as cases, statutes, regulations, and rules. You can create new categories if you want.
- Use the Mark Citation dialog box to mark each citation in the document with a table of authorities field code.

  ✓ *This process is similar to marking items for an index. For information on creating an index, refer to Exercise 8.*

- You can mark each occurrence manually, or automatically mark all occurrences.
- You can also specify a short version of a citation to mark automatically along with the long version.

  ✓ *As with index entries, you see the field codes in the document if you have hidden text displayed. To see the document as it will print, hide hidden text or change to Print Preview.*

- Word can automatically search through a document to find citations, or you can scroll through manually. To find citations, Word searches for the text **v**.
- When all items are marked, use the Table of Authorities dialog box to select options and generate the table.
- Word sorts the citations by category.

Source Manager

Source Manager

Search: [   ]   Sort by Title [v]

Sources available in: Browse...   Current List
Master List

Master list of all sources →
Easy Roses for North American Gardeners (1999), Christopher, Tom
History of the Rose (2007), Unknown
Rose History (2007), The Santa Barbara Rose Society
Source for All Info (2009), Smith, Joe
The History of Roses (2007), Stack, Greg

Copy ->
Delete
Edit...
New...

✔ Easy Roses for North American Gardeners (1999), Christopher, Tom
✔ History of the Rose (2007), Unknown
✔ Rose History (2007), The Santa Barbara Rose Society
✔ The History of Roses (2007), Stack, Greg

List of sources in current document →

✔   cited source
?   placeholder source

Preview (Chicago):

Preview →

Citation: (Christopher 1999)

Bibliography Entry:
Christopher, Tom. *Easy Roses for North American Gardeners*. New York: Putnam Pub Group, 1999.

Close

Table of Authorities dialog box

Table of Authorities

| Index | Table of Contents | Table of Figures | Table of Authorities |

Print Preview

Cases
Baldwin v. Alberti,
    58 Wn. 2d 243 (1961)......5, 6
Dravo Corp. v. Metro. Seattle,
    79 Wn. 2d 214 (1971)..passim
Forrester v. Craddock,

☑ Use passim
☑ Keep original formatting
Tab leader: [.......   v]
Formats: [From template   v]

Category:
All
Cases
Statutes
Other Authorities
Rules
Treatises
Regulations
Constitutional Provisions
8

Mark Citation...   Modify...

OK   Cancel

Update a Table

■ If the page numbers where items in a table are located change, you can automatically update the table.

■ Likewise, you can update heading text in a table of contents, caption text in a table of figures, citation text in a table of authorities, or source information in a bibliography.

■ In a table of contents or table of figures, you can select to update the entire table or page numbers only.

PROCEDURES

Insert a Built-in Table of Contents

1. Apply heading styles to all paragraphs you want in table of contents.
2. Position insertion point where you want table of contents to display.
3. Click **References** tab .... `Alt`+`S`

   Table of Contents Group

4. Click **Table of Contents** button
   .... `T`
5. Click a table of contents in the gallery of built-in styles.............. `↓`/`↑`,`Enter`

Create a Table of Contents

1. Apply heading styles to all paragraphs you want in table of contents.
2. Position insertion point where you want table of contents to display.
3. Click **References** tab .... `Alt`+`S`

   Table of Contents Group

4. Click **Table of Contents** button
   .... `T`
5. Click **Insert Table of Contents**. .... `I`
6. Click **Formats** list box .... `Alt`+`T`
7. Select desired format .... `↑`/`↓`,`Enter`
8. Click **Show levels** box .... `Alt`+`L`
9. Enter number of heading levels to include.
10. Select or deselect **Show page numbers** .... `Alt`+`S`
11. Select or deselect **Right align page numbers** .... `Alt`+`R`

    ✓ *If you select to right-align page numbers, select a tab leader option from **Tab leader** drop-down list.*

12. Select or deselect **Use hyperlinks instead of page numbers** .... `Alt`+`H`
13. Click **OK**.

Update a Table of Contents

1. Position insertion point anywhere in table.
2. Click **References** tab .... `Alt`+`S`

   Table of Contents Group

3. Click **Update Table** button
   .... `U`
4. Click **Update page numbers only** .... `Alt`+`P`

   OR

   Click **Update entire table** .... `Alt`+`E`
5. Click **OK**. .... `Enter`

   OR

1. Position insertion point anywhere in table.
2. Press `F9`.

   OR

   a. Right-click anywhere in table.
   b. Click **Update Field** .... `U`
3. Click **Update page numbers only**. .... `Alt`+`P`

   OR

   Click **Update entire table** .... `Alt`+`E`
4. Click **OK**. .... `Enter`

Create a Table of Figures

1. Insert captions as desired.

   ✓ *Refer to Exercise 8 for information on inserting captions.*

2. Position insertion point where you want table to display.
3. Click **References** tab .... `Alt`+`S`

   Captions Group

4. Click **Insert Table of Figures** button .... `G`
5. Click **Formats** list box ... `Alt`+`T`
6. Select desired format .... `↑`/`↓`,`Enter`
7. Click **Caption label** list box .... `Alt`+`L`

8. Select label to include. .... `↑`/`↓`,`Enter`
9. Select or deselect **Include label and number** ...... `Alt`+`N`
10. Select or deselect **Show page numbers**. .... `Alt`+`S`
11. Select or deselect **Right align page numbers** .... `Alt`+`R`

    ✓ *If you select to right-align page numbers, select a tab leader option from **Tab leader** drop-down list.*

12. Select or deselect **Use hyperlinks instead of page numbers**. .... `Alt`+`H`
13. Click **OK**.

Update a Table of Figures

1. Position insertion point anywhere in table.
2. Click **References** tab .... `Alt`+`S`

   Captions Group

3. Click **Update Table** button
   .... `V`
4. Click **Update page numbers only**. .... `Alt`+`P`

   OR

   Click **Update entire table** .... `Alt`+`E`
5. Click **OK**. .... `Enter`

   OR

1. Position insertion point anywhere in table.
2. Press `F9`.

   OR

   a. Right-click anywhere in table.
   b. Click **Update Field** .... `U`
3. Click **Update page numbers only** .... `Alt`+`P`

   OR

   Click **Update entire table** .... `Alt`+`E`
4. Click **OK**. .... `Enter`

Create a Bibliography

To select a citation style:

1. Click **References** tab. . . . `Alt`+`S`

   Citations & Bibliography Group

2. Click **Style** button drop-down arrow

   `Style: MLA` . . . . `L`, `↓`

3. Click desired style . . . . `↑`/`↓`, `Enter`

To insert a citation by adding a new source:

1. Position insertion point after the text you want to cite.

2. Click **References** tab. . . . `Alt`+`S`

   Citations & Bibliography Group

3. Click **Insert Citation** button

   . . . . `C`

4. Click **Add New Source**. . . . . . `S`

   ✓ *To insert a placeholder, click **Add New Placeholder**. Edit the source to fill in the citation information.*

5. Click **Type of Source** drop-down arrow. . . . . . . `Alt`+`S`

6. Select source type . . . . `↑`/`↓`, `Enter`

7. Press `⇥` to move insertion point to first field.

8. Type information.

9. Press `⇥` to move insert point to next field.

10. Repeat steps 8 and 9 to fill in fields as necessary.

    ✓ *Click to select **Show All Bibliography Fields** check box to display all available fields.*

11. Click **OK**.

To insert a citation using an existing source:

1. Position insertion point after the text you want to cite.

2. Click **References** tab. . . . `Alt`+`S`

   Citations & Bibliography Group

3. Click **Insert Citation** button

   . . . . `C`

4. Click source to insert . . `↑`/`↓`, `Enter`

To generate a bibliography:

1. Insert citations as necessary.

2. Position insertion point where you want bibliography to display.

3. Click **References** tab. . . . `Alt`+`S`

   Citations & Bibliography Group

4. Click **Bibliography** button

   . . . . `B`

5. Click a bibliography in the gallery of built-in styles. . . . . `↓`/`↑`, `Enter`

   OR

   Click **Insert Bibliography** . . . . `B`

Update a Bibliography

1. Position insertion point anywhere in table.

2. Press `F9`.

   OR

   a. Right-click anywhere in table.

   b. Click **Update Field** . . . . `U`

Manage Sources

To edit a source:

1. Click **References** tab. . . . `Alt`+`S`

   Citations & Bibliography Group

2. Click **Manage Sources** button

   . . . . `M`

3. Click source to edit . . . . . . `↑`/`↓`

   ✓ *To change to Current list, press* `Alt`+`U`.

4. Click **Edit** . . . . `Alt`+`E`

5. Edit information as necessary.

6. Click **OK**. . . . . `Enter`

7. Click **Yes** to update source . . . `Y`

To delete a source:

1. Click **References** tab. . . . `Alt`+`S`

   Citations & Bibliography Group

2. Click **Manage Sources** button

   . . . . `M`

3. Click source to delete . . . . `↑`/`↓`

   ✓ *To change to Current list, press* `Alt`+`U`.

4. Click **Delete** . . . . `Alt`+`D`

To find a source in the Master List:

1. Click **References** tab. . . . `Alt`+`S`

   Citations & Bibliography Group

2. Click **Manage Sources** button

   . . . . `M`

3. Click in **Search** text box . . . . `Alt`+`S`

4. Type the title or author of the source.

To copy a source from the Master List to the Current List or vice versa:

1. Click **References** tab. . . . `Alt`+`S`

   Citations & Bibliography Group

2. Click **Manage Sources** button

   . . . . `M`

3. Click source to copy . . . . . `↑`/`↓`

   ✓ *To change to Current list, press* `Alt`+`U`.

4. Click **Copy** . . . . `Alt`+`C`

To sort sources:

1. Click **References** tab. . . . `Alt`+`S`

   Citations & Bibliography Group

2. Click **Manage Sources** button

   . . . . `M`

3. Click **Sort by** list box . . . . `Alt`+`S`, `⇥`, `↓`

4. Select sort type . . . . `↑`/`↓`

To create a new source:

1. Click **References** tab. . . . `Alt`+`S`

   Citations & Bibliography Group

2. Click **Manage Sources** button

   . . . . `M`

3. Click **New** . . . . `Alt`+`N`

4. Click **Type of Source** drop-down arrow. . . . . `Alt`+`S`

5. Select source type . . . . `↑`/`↓`, `Enter`

6. Press `⇥` to move insertion point to first field.

7. Type information.

8. Press `⇥` to move insertion point to next field.

9. Repeat steps 7 and 8 to fill in fields as necessary.

   ✓ Click to select *Show All Bibliography Fields* check box to display all available fields.

10. Click **OK**.

Create a Table of Authorities
To mark entries:

1. Click **References** tab . . . . `Alt`+`S`

   Table of Authorities Group

2. Click **Mark Citation** button
   . . . . `I`

3. In document, select text to mark.

   ✓ *Mark Citation dialog box remains open while you select text to mark. If necessary, move dialog box out of the way.*

4. Click **Category** drop-down arrow . . . . `Alt`+`C`

5. Selected desired category . . . . `↑`/`↓`,`Enter`

6. Click **Short citation** box . . . . `Alt`+`S`

7. Type short version of citation, if necessary.

8. If necessary, click **Selected text** box and edit or format text . . . . `Alt`+`T`

9. Do one of the following:

   ■ Click **Mark** to mark selected occurrence only . . . . . `Alt`+`M`

   OR

   ■ Click **Mark All** to mark all occurrences of selected text in document . . . . `Alt`+`A`

10. Repeat steps 3–9 until all entries are marked.

   ✓ *To search for the next citation in the document, click the **Next Citation** button.*

11. Click **Close** . . . . `Enter`

To generate table:

1. Position insertion point in document where you want table displayed.

2. Click **References** tab . . . . `Alt`+`S`

   Table of Authorities Group

3. Click **Insert Table of Authorities** button . . . . `R`, `T`

4. Click **Category** list . . . . . . `Alt`+`G`

5. Click category to include . . `↑`/`↓`

   ✓ *Click All to include all citations.*

6. Click **Formats** drop-down arrow . . . . `Alt`+`T`

7. Click desired format . . . . `↑`/`↓`,`Enter`

8. Select or deselect **Use passim** . . . . `Alt`+`P`

9. Select or deselect **Keep original formatting** . . . . . `Alt`+`R`

10. Click **Tab leader** drop-down arrow . . . . `Alt`+`B`

11. Click desired tab leader . . . . `↑`/`↓`,`Enter`

12. Click **OK**.

Update a Table of Authorities

1. Position insertion point anywhere in table.

2. Click **References** tab . . . . `Alt`+`S`

   Table of Authorities Group

3. Click **Update Table** button
   . . . . `R`, `U`

   OR

1. Position insertion point anywhere in table.

2. Press `F9`.

   OR

   a. Right-click anywhere in table.

   b. Click **Update Field** . . . . `U`

EXERCISE DIRECTIONS

1. Start Word, if necessary, and open the document **09ROSES**, a version of the report you used in the previous exercise. Save it as **09ROSES_xx**.

2. Replace the text *Student's Name* in the header with your own name.

3. Replace the text *Today's Date* in the header with the current date.

Generate a Table of Figures

1. Position the insertion point at the end of the second paragraph under the heading *Diseases and Insects* (the last paragraph of text in the document).

2. Press Enter to insert a blank line.

   ✓ *Display paragraph marks, if necessary. However, be aware that displayed hidden text such as marked index entries affects the position of text in the document.*

3. Using the Heading 1 style, type **Table of Figures**.

4. Press Enter to move the insertion point to a new blank line.

5. Generate a table of figures using the following options:

   a. Distinctive format.

   b. Caption label: Table.

   c. Include label and number.

   d. Show page numbers.

   e. Right-align page numbers.

   f. Use a dot tab leader.

   g. Do not use hyperlinks.

6. Save the changes.

Generate a Table of Contents

1. Press Ctrl + Home to move the insertion point to the beginning of the document.
2. Scroll through the document to verify that all headings are formatted with heading styles.
3. Press Ctrl + Home again to move the insertion point to the beginning of the document.
4. Insert two blank lines after the title.
5. Clear all formatting from the new blank lines.
6. On the first blank line, type **Table of Contents** in 20-point Calibri, centered.

7. Position the insertion point on the second blank line.
8. Create a table of contents using the following options:
   a. Distinctive format.
   b. 3 heading levels.
   c. Right-aligned page numbers.
   d. Dot tab leader.
   e. Use page numbers, not hyperlinks.
9. Preview the first page of the document. It should look similar to Illustration A.
10. Close Print Preview.

Illustration A

Student's Name   Today's Date

Roses

Table of Contents

Throughout history, roses have been considered a symbol of love and beauty. Did you know they have also been a symbol of war and death? In the following pages you will learn the story of the rose as well how to select and care for these beautiful flowers.

History

Fossil evidence shows that there were roses on earth more than 35 million years ago. Roses are believed to have grown wild throughout most of the world. The earliest roses were all red, or shades of red. In fact, the genus name, *Rosa*, means red in Latin. The first cultivation probably began 5,000 years ago in China. Human beings have been captivated by the flower ever since. They have worked hard to nurture and develop these wondrous blooms so that now there are hundreds of types, varieties, and hybrids. (For information about types of roses, refer to the section Types of Roses.)

1

Add Sources

1. Select the MLA bibliography citation style.
2. Position the insertion point after the first sentence under the heading *History* and insert a new bibliography citation.
3. Add a new source and enter the following source information:
   a. Type of source: **Web site**
   b. Author: **The Santa Barbara Rose Society**. Click to select the Corporate Author check box.
   c. Name of Web Page: **Rose History**
   d. Year: **2007**
   e. Year Accessed: **2008**
   f. Month Accessed: **May**
   g. Day Accessed: **15**
   h. URL: **http://www.sbrose.org/rosehistory.htm**
4. Click OK to add the source to the document.
5. Position the insertion point after the fourth sentence under the heading *History* and insert a new bibliography citation.
6. Add a new source and enter the following source information:
   a. Type of source: **Web site**
   b. Author: **Greg Stack**
   c. Name of Web Page: **The History of Roses**
   d. Year: **2007**
   e. Year Accessed: **2008**
   f. Month Accessed: **May**
   g. Day Accessed: **15**
   h. URL: **http://www.urbanext.uiuc.edu/roses/history.html**
7. Click OK to add the source to the document.
8. Position the insertion point after the first paragraph under the heading *The Rose in Use*, and insert a citation referencing the Stack source.
9. Position the insertion point after the second paragraph under the heading *The Rose in Use*, and insert a citation referencing the Santa Barbara Rose Society source.
10. Position the insertion point after the paragraph under the heading *The Rose as Symbol* and insert a new bibliography citation.
11. Add a new source and enter the following source information:
    a. Type of source: **Web site**
    b. Author: **Unknown**
    c. Name of Web Page: **History of the Rose**
    d. Year: **2007**
    e. Year Accessed: **2008**
    f. Month Accessed: **May**
    g. Day Accessed: **15**
    h. URL: **http://www.herbs2000.com/flowers/r_history.htm**
12. Position the insertion point after the paragraph under the heading *Types of Roses* and insert a new bibliography citation.
13. Add a new source and enter the following source information:
    a. Type of source: **Book**
    b. Author: **Tom Christopher**
    c. Title: **Easy Roses for North American Gardens**
    d. Year: **1999**
    e. City: **New York**
    f. Publisher: **Putnam Pub Group**
14. Position the insertion point after the paragraph under the heading *Grafted Roses*, and insert a citation referencing the Stack source.
15. Position the insertion point after the first paragraph under the heading *Diseases and Insects*, and insert a citation referencing the Christopher source.
16. Save the changes to the document.

Generate the Bibliography

1. Press Ctrl + End to move the insertion point to the end of the document, and insert a page break.
2. Using the Heading 1 style, type **Bibliography** and then press Enter to insert a blank line.
3. Insert a bibliography.
4. Change the Bibliography citation style to Chicago. Note that the bibliography updates automatically. It should look similar to Illustration B.

Complete the Document

1. Preview all pages of the document. If necessary, add or remove page breaks, or adjust spacing to improve the appearance and text flow in the document. For example, you might change the spacing before all Heading 1 paragraphs to 12 points, delete the hard page break and extra blank line before Table 1, and insert page breaks before the headings *Judging Rose Quality* and *Table of Figures*.
2. Update the page numbers and headings in the table of contents.
3. Update the page numbers in the table of figures.
4. Update the page numbers in the index.
5. Check the spelling and grammar in the document.
6. Print the document.
7. Close the document, saving all changes.

Illustration B

Student's Name   Today's Date

Bibliography

Christopher, Tom. *Easy Roses for North American Gardens.* New York: Putnam Pub Group, 1999.

Stack, Greg. *The History of Roses.* 2007. http://www.urbanext.uiuc.edu/roses/history.html (accessed May 15, 2008).

The Santa Barbara Rose Society. *Rose History.* 2007. http://www.sbrose.org/rosehistory.htm (accessed May 15, 2008).

Unknown. *History of the Rose.* 2007. http://www.herbs2000.com/flowers/r_history.htm (accessed May 15, 2008).

7

Business Connection

Glitches, Crashes, and Keyboard Malfunctions

Would you know what to do if your keyboard stopped working, or if your computer display went blank? Computers are machines, and like all machines, they can break. Every minute you spend unable to work because your computer is broken costs your employer money. You can minimize your downtime and be back up and running quickly if you know how to use problem-solving skills to diagnose common computer errors and solutions.

Troubleshooting Challenge

Brainstorm four or five common computer problems you might encounter at work. You may choose to use the Internet or other research sources to look up the information. In a Word document, list each problem along with a paragraph describing a scenario in which the problem occurs. Include the symptoms of the problem, but do not mention the cause. Exchange the first document with a classmate. Read each scenario and use problem-solving skills to determine the problem, its cause, and the best solution. Write your response to each scenario in a separate Word document.

ON YOUR OWN

1. Start Word and open OWD08_*xx*, the research report you have been working on.
2. Save the document as OWD09_*xx*.
3. Complete the research project.
4. Finish adding and editing content as necessary.
5. Insert source citations as necessary.
6. Create a table of figures if appropriate.
7. Create a table of authorities if appropriate.
8. Create a table of contents.
9. Create a bibliography.
10. Preview the document.
11. Adjust page breaks as necessary.
12. Update all tables.
13. Check the spelling and grammar.
14. Ask a classmate to review the report and make comments and suggestions.
15. Incorporate the comments and suggestions.
16. Adjust page formatting and update tables as necessary.
17. Print the report.
18. Close the document, saving all changes, and exit Word.

Skills Covered

- **Convert a Table to Text**
- **Convert Text to a Table**

Software Skills   You can quickly use Word commands to convert existing text into a table or an existing table into document text. These features can be particularly helpful for exchanging data with Excel, because you can make Excel data more readable by converting it to text, and make Word data easier to copy to a worksheet by converting it to a table.

Application Skills   You have been working with the president of the Horticultural Shop Owners Association to select a location for a national meeting. You have information about different cities stored in an Excel worksheet. In this exercise, you will copy the Excel data to a Word document and convert it to paragraph text. You will also convert into a table a list of association members who have volunteered to help.

TERMS

Separator character   A character such as a comma or a tab used to delineate the location where text should be divided into columns and/or rows.

NOTES

Convert a Table to Text

- Convert an entire table or selected table rows into regular document text.
- Word inserts the specified separator character into the text at the end of each column.
- Word starts a new paragraph at the end of each row.
- If document text is set to wrap around a table, when you convert the table to text Word inserts the text in a text box.

Convert Table To Text dialog box

Convert Text to a Table

- You can easily convert existing document text into a table format.
- Word automatically divides text into columns based on the location of a specified **separator character** such as a comma or tab.
- Word starts a new row at each paragraph mark.
- When you convert the text into a table, you can specify a column width or an AutoFit behavior.
- For example, you can AutoFit the table to its contents, which adjusts the column width to accommodate the widest content, or you can AutoFit the table to the window, which adjusts the column width to fit within the current window size.

Convert Text to Table dialog box

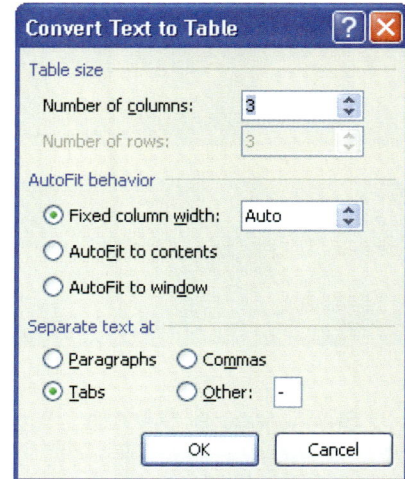

Convert Text to Table	? X
Table size	
Number of <u>c</u>olumns:	3
Number of rows:	3
AutoFit behavior	
⦿ Fixed column <u>w</u>idth:	Auto
◯ Auto<u>F</u>it to contents	
◯ AutoFit to win<u>d</u>ow	
Separate text at	
◯ <u>P</u>aragraphs	◯ <u>C</u>ommas
⦿ <u>T</u>abs	◯ <u>O</u>ther: -
OK	Cancel

PROCEDURES

Convert a Table to Text

1. Select table to convert.

    OR

    Select rows to convert.

2. Click **Table Tools Layout** tab . . . . [Alt]+[J], [L]

    Data Group

3. Click **Convert to Text** button

    ☷ . . . . [V]

4. Click separator character to insert:

    - **Paragraph marks** . . . [Alt]+[P]
    - **Tabs** . . . . [Alt]+[T]
    - **Commas** . . . . [Alt]+[M]
    - **Other** . . . . [Alt]+[O],
      type character

5. Click **OK** . . . . [Enter]

Convert Text to a Table

1. If necessary, insert separator characters in text where you want new columns to begin.

2. Select text to convert.

3. Click **Insert** tab . . . . [Alt]+[N]

    Tables Group

4. Click **Table** button ▦ . . . . . . [T]

5. Click **Con<u>v</u>ert Text to Table** . . . [V]

6. If necessary, enter the number of columns to create . . . . [Alt]+[C], *type number*

7. Select AutoFit behavior:

    - **Fixed column <u>w</u>idth** . . [Alt]+[W]
    - **Auto<u>F</u>it to contents** . . [Alt]+[F]
    - **AutoFit to win<u>d</u>ow** . . . [Alt]+[D]

8. Select separator character used in selected text:

    - **Paragraphs** . . . . [Alt]+[P]
    - **Tabs** . . . . [Alt]+[T]
    - **Commas** . . . . [Alt]+[M]
    - **Other** . . . . [Alt]+[O],
      type character

9. Click **OK** . . . . [Enter]

EXERCISE DIRECTIONS

1. Start Word, if necessary, and open the Word document ⊙ **10MEMO**. Save the document as **10MEMO_*xx***.

2. Replace the sample text *Your Name* with your own name, and the sample text *Today's date* with the current date.

3. Open the Excel workbook ⊙ **10DATA**.

4. Select the data in cells B3:B13 and copy it to the Clipboard.

> ✓ *To select the data, click cell B3, press and hold Shift, and then click cell B13.*

5. Close the Excel workbook and exit Excel.

6. Make the **10MEMO_*xx*** document active, and position the insertion point on the second blank line after the first paragraph in the body of the memo.

7. Paste the data from the Clipboard into the document. It is pasted as a table.

8. Select the table, and convert it to text, using paragraph marks as the separator.

9. Select the list of volunteers at the end of the document.

10. Convert the text to a table, selecting to AutoFit the table to the contents, and separating the text at the commas.

11. Apply the Table Contemporary table style to the table.

12. Remove the bold from the first row in the table.

13. Center the table horizontally on the page.

14. Check the spelling and grammar in the document.

15. Preview the document. It should look similar to Illustration A.

16. Print the document.

17. Close the document, saving all changes.

Illustration A

Horticultural Shop Owners Association

452 Cathedral Street ❀ Baltimore, MD 21201

MEMORANDUM

Date:	Today's date
To:	Ms. Knowlton
From:	Student's Name
Subject:	Regional Meetings

Following is a list of potential sites for the national meeting. Let me know if you have a preference.

Cleveland, Ohio
Rock and Roll Hall of Fame
No trip to Cleveland would be complete without paying a visit to the Rock Hall! See exhibits and maybe catch a concert!

Philadelphia, Pennsylvania
Independence Hall
A World Heritage Site where both the Declaration of Independence and the U.S. Constitution were created.

Phoenix, Arizona
The Desert Botanical Garden
Combines desert plants with desert wildlife that can both be seen from short trails that are well marked.

Here is the contact information for the association members who have volunteered to help plan the national meeting:

Alyssa Jenkins	Volunteer	410-555-5678	Mid West
Stephen Knight	Volunteer Coordinator	410-555-7890	Southeast
Jessie Samsonov	Marketing Director	410-555-4321	Mid West
Debra Whist	Public Relations	410-555-7654	Mid Atlantic
Justin Bachman	Fundraising	410-555-6534	Mid Atlantic

ON YOUR OWN

1. There are many types of resources you can use to find employment opportunities: classified advertisements in newspapers, magazines, and online; career centers at schools and other organizations; employment agencies; and company Web sites or newsletters. In this exercise, create a directory list of resources someone could use to find job openings in your area. The list should include at least ten items, with three bits of information about each item. For example, the list might include a name along with an e-mail address, phone number, and area of employment.

2. Start Word, create a new document and save the document as OWD10_*xx*.

3. Type the directory using tabs to separate each item of information.

4. In the same document, create a table in which you can type information in paragraph form about the directory. For example, the first row might include the name of the resource, the second row might include a sample job opening, and the third might include a description of the job requirements.

5. When the document is complete, check the spelling and grammar.

6. Exchange the document with a classmate.

7. Working in the document created by your classmate, convert the tabbed directory into a table and the table to paragraph text.

8. AutoFit the table columns to fit the contents.

9. Adjust spacing and formatting as necessary. For example, center the table horizontally, and use shrink to fit to make the document fit on one page.

10. Preview the document and print it.

11. Give it back to the author.

12. In your original document, make changes or corrections that you think are necessary. Sort the list into alphabetical order.

13. Save the document, close it, and exit Word.

Exercise | 11

Skills Covered

- **Use the Research Tool**
- **Print a Web Page**

- **Copy Data from a Web Page into a Word Document**

Software Skills Use Word's Research tool to locate information about a specific topic. You can select a reference source or search all available sources, including the Internet. When a Web page is displayed on your computer, print it for future reference or to pass along to someone else. If you don't need to print the entire page, you can copy the data you need into a Word document to save or print for future use.

Application Skills The Horticultural Shop Owners Association has selected Cleveland, Ohio, as the location for a national meeting. In this exercise, you will use Word's Research tool to look up information about the Rock and Roll Hall of Fame, which you will copy into a Word document.

TERMS

Plagiarism The unauthorized use of another person's ideas or creative work without giving credit to that person.

Reputable Trustworthy, honest, and reliable.

NOTES

Use the Research Tool

- Use the Research task pane in Office 2007 programs such as Word to search through online reference sources, such as dictionaries, encyclopedias, and translation services.
- You can search for a keyword, term, or phrase.
- You can locate information such as definitions, synonyms, encyclopedia entries, and even links to relevant Web pages.
- You can select the specific reference tool or service to search from a list of available sources.
- Alternatively, you can select to search all available sources of a particular type, such as all reference books, or all research sites.

- The results of the search are displayed in the Research task pane.
- Some results also display a link to a relevant Web page; click a link to go to the destination.
- You can determine which reference sources are available in the Research task pane by adding or removing items from the Services list in the Research Options dialog box. (See illustration on the following page.)
- You can also add new services to the list, remove services, and update current services.
- Note that some research services require that you sign up for a subscription.
- You can also view the properties for each available service. The properties include a description of the services, copyright information, the provider's name, and the path to the site.

Research task pane

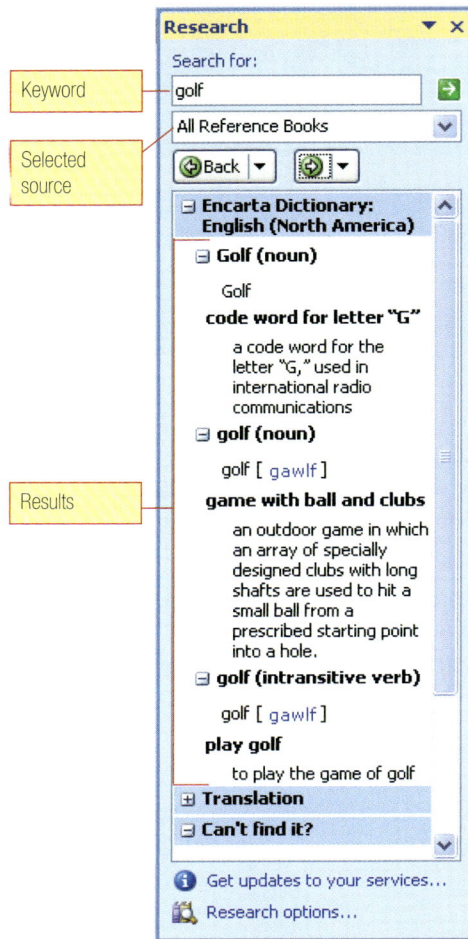

Keyword

Selected source

Results

Research Options dialog box

Research Options

To activate a service for searching, select the check box associated with that service.

Services:

Reference Books
- ☑ Encarta Dictionary: English (North America)
- ☐ Encarta Dictionary: English (U.K.)
- ☐ Encarta Dictionary: French
- ☐ Foreign Word Spelling Look Up (Korean)
- ☐ Hangul Word Romanization (Korean)
- ☐ Local Address Search (Korean)
- ☐ Thesaurus: English (Australia)
- ☐ Thesaurus: English (U.K.)
- ☑ Thesaurus: English (U.S.)
- ☐ Thesaurus: French (Canada)
- ☑ Thesaurus: French (France)
- ☑ Thesaurus: Spanish (International Sort)
- ☑ Translation

Properties...

Add Services...   Update/Remove...   Parental Control...

OK   Cancel

Print a Web Page

- You can use your browser's Print command to print a Web page.

- The commands for printing a Web page are similar to printing a Word document; you select the command and then select the printer and print options you want to use.

- In order to print, your computer must be correctly connected to a printer and set up for use with the printer.

- Paper must be loaded in the printer, and the printer must be turned on.

- Keep in mind that many Web pages are longer than standard document pages, which means you might end up printing on more sheets of paper than you expect, or tying up the printer for a long time.

- If you use Web page data in a report or other project, you must cite the source in a footnote, bibliography, or other list of sources.

- If you include a direct quote in your document, you can format it to stand out from the surrounding text using a double indent and single line spacing.

- It is also important to know whether or not the source is **reputable** before you select to use the information.

- Some ways to identify whether or not a source is reputable include the following:
  - The domain is .gov or .edu.
  - You can find at least two additional sites that support, verify, or confirm the information.
  - There is an actual author credited on the site, and he or she has the qualifications to write about the topic.
  - If there are misspellings or other errors on the page, the content may be inaccurate as well.

Copy Data from a Web Page into a Word Document

- You can use the Copy and Paste commands to copy data from a Web page into a Word document.

- You can copy a URL from an Address bar and paste it into a Word document or directly into the Source Manager. This is useful for recording a Web page address that you will need to use in a footnote or bibliography.

- Remember that copying someone else's work and using it without attribution is **plagiarism**.

PROCEDURES

Use the Research Tool

1. Click **Review** tab . . . . Alt + R

   Proofing Group

2. Click **Research** button . . . R

   ✓ *The Research task pane opens.*

3. Type keyword or topic in Search for box.

4. Click the reference source drop-down arrow. . . →, →, ↓

5. Click research tool or reference service to search . . . . ↓/↑

6. Click **Start searching** button .

7. Click link in Research task pane to display information.

Display Results of a Previous Search

1. Click **Review** tab . . . . Alt + R

   Proofing Group

2. Click **Research** button . . . R

   ✓ *The Research task pane opens.*

3. Click **Previous search** button Back to display results of previous search.

   OR

   a. Click **Previous search** drop-down arrow Back ▼ .

   b. Click previous search to display . . . . ↑/↓, Enter

   OR

   ■ Click **Next search** button to display results of search displayed prior to the selected previous search.

OR

a. Click **Next search** drop-down arrow ▼ .

b. Click search to display . . . . ↑/↓, Enter

Select Research Services to Use

1. Click **Review** tab . . . . Alt + R

   Proofing Group

2. Click **Research** button . . . R

   ✓ *The Research task pane opens.*

3. Click **Research options** link.

4. Click to select or deselect services to use . . . . ↓/↑, Spacebar

5. Click **OK** . . . . Enter

View Research Services Properties

1. Click **Review** tab . . . . Alt + R

   Proofing Group

2. Click **Research** button . . . R

   ✓ *The Research task pane opens.*

3. Click **Research options** link.

4. Click service to view . . . . . ↓/↑

5. Click **Properti̲es** . . . . Alt + E

6. Click **Close** . . . . Enter

7. Click **OK**.

Add a Research Service to the Services List

1. Click **Review** tab . . . . Alt + R

   Proofing Group

2. Click **Research** button . . . R

   ✓ *The Research task pane opens.*

3. Click **Research options** link.

4. Click **A̲dd Services** . . . . . Alt + A

5. Type URL address of service to add.

6. Click **A̲dd** . . . . Alt + D

7. Repeat steps 5 and 6 to add additional services.

8. Click **Close** . . . . Esc

9. Click **OK**.

Update or Remove a Research Service

1. Click **Review** tab . . . . Alt + R

   Proofing Group

2. Click **Research** button . . . R

   ✓ *The Research task pane opens.*

3. Click **Research options** link.

4. Click **U̲pdate/Remove** . . . Alt + U

5. Select service or group to update or remove . . . . ↓/↑

6. Click **U̲pdate** . . . . Alt + U

   OR

   Click **R̲emove** . . . . Alt + R

7. Follow instructions to update or remove selected service or group.

8. Click **Close** . . . . Esc

9. Click **OK**.

Print a Web page *(Ctrl + P)*

1. Open the Web page in your browser.

2. Click **Print** button on the browser's toolbar.

   ✓ *The Print dialog box displays.*

3. Select print options.

4. Click **Print**.

Copy Data from a Web Page into a Word Document *(Ctrl + C/Ctrl + V)*

To use shortcut menus:

1. Display the Web page in your Web browser.
2. Select data to copy.
3. Right-click selection.
4. Click **Copy** C
5. Open Word document.
6. Right-click position where you want to paste the data.
7. Click **Paste** . . . . P , Enter

To use menu commands:

1. Display the Web page in your Web browser.
2. Select data to copy.
3. Click **Edit** on your browser's menu bar . . . . Alt + E
4. Click **Copy** C
5. Open Word document.

6. Position insertion point where you want to paste the data.
7. Click **Home** tab . . . . Alt + H

   Clipboard Group

8. Click **Paste** button

   . . . . V , P

EXERCISE DIRECTIONS

Set Research Options

1. Start Word, if necessary, open the document 💿 **11INVITE**, and save the file as **11INVITE_xx**.
2. Display the Research task pane.
3. Click the Research options link to display the Research Options dialog box.
4. Verify that the Encarta Dictionary: English (North America) source is selected. If not, select it.
5. Verify that at least one Research Site, such as Live Search, is selected. If not, select it.
6. With the Live Search site selected, click the Properties button to review the site's properties.
7. Close the Service Properties dialog box, and then click OK to close the dialog box.

Search for Information

1. In the Research task pane, type the phrase **Rock Music** in the Search for text box.
2. Select to search the dictionary, and then start the search. The first item in the results list should be a definition of rock music.
3. Click in the Search for text box and type **Rock and Roll Hall of Fame**.
4. Select to search using an available research site, such as Live Search or MSN Search. The first item in the results list should include a link to the Rock and Roll Hall of Fame's Web site.
5. Click the link. Your Web browser should start and display the home page of the Rock and Roll Hall of Fame.

   ✓ If you cannot locate the link using the Research tool, or if it will not display the Web page, start your Web browser and go to the URL http://www.rockhall.com.

6. Click the Visitor Info link in the links bar on the Web page.
7. Scroll down to view the address information under the heading Directions.
8. Select the five lines of text starting with the line Directions and copy the selection to the Clipboard.
9. Exit your Web browser.
10. Make the **11INVITE_xx** document active.
11. Position the insertion point on the blank line in the middle of the page (before the quotation) and paste the selection from the Clipboard. Use the Paste Options button to select to Keep Source Formatting.
12. Close the Research task pane. Edit the pasted heading *Directions* to **Location**.

Format the Quotation

1. Select the entire quotation and the name of the speaker (Billy Joel).
2. Format the paragraphs to apply a 1-inch indent from both the left and the right, and leave no space after the paragraph.
3. Justify the selection.
4. Position the insertion point at the beginning of the name of the speaker, and then set a left tab stop at 4 inches on the horizontal ruler.
5. Tab in to the new tab stop.
6. Check the spelling and grammar in the document.
7. Display the document in Print Preview. It should look similar to Illustration A.
8. Print the document.
9. Close the document, saving all changes, and exit Word.

Illustration A

Horticultural Shop Owners Association

452 Cathedral Street ⊕ Baltimore, MD 21201

Horticultural Shop Owners Association Annual Meeting

Opening Reception

Rock and Roll Hall of Fame

Join fellow members of the association to start the annual meeting in style.

When: Friday, 6:30 p.m.

Dress: Casual

Tours will be available throughout the evening.

Location

The Rock and Roll Hall of Fame and Museum
751 Erieside Ave
Cleveland, Ohio 44114
(East Ninth Street at Lake Erie)

"You can't go home with the Rock and Roll Hall of Fame. You don't sleep with the Rock and Roll Hall of Fame. You don't get hugged by the Rock and Roll Hall of Fame, and you don't have children with the Rock and Roll Hall of Fame. I want what everybody else wants: to love and to be loved, and to have a family. Being in love has always been the most important thing in my life."

Billy Joel

ON YOUR OWN

1. Start Word, if necessary, create a new document, and save it with the name OWD11_*xx*.

2. Write a brief paragraph about a place in the world you would like to visit. It may be a city, a country, a landmark, a historic site, or a vacation destination.

3. Use the Research task pane to look up information in an encyclopedia about the place.

4. Use the Research task pane to search for links to Web sites about the destination.

5. Copy at least one paragraph of information about the destination to the Word document.

6. Record the source information and add it to your document.

7. Apply formatting as necessary. If there are any quotes in the content, format them with a double indent, justified.

8. Ask a classmate to review the document and make comments or suggestions.

9. Incorporate the comments and suggestions into the document.

10. Close the document, saving all changes.

11. Exit your Web browser.

Critical Thinking

Application Skills As the owner of an eye care clinic, you are concerned about eye health for your clients and also about how to increase business. Your plan is to educate clients and potential clients about the importance of eye care, which you believe will result in an increase in business. In this exercise, you will modify and format a multipage document about eye care for seniors. You will use the find and replace feature; create headers, and footers; and insert captions. You will insert page breaks, control text flow as necessary, and insert cross-references. You will also create a table of figures, an index, a table of contents, and a bibliography.

EXERCISE DIRECTIONS

Use Find and Replace

1. Start Word, if necessary.
2. Open the 12SENIORS document and save it as 12SENIORS_xx.
3. Replace the text *Student's Name* with your own name.
4. Find and replace all occurrences of the text *the elderly* with the text **seniors**. Use the match case option.
5. Find and replace all occurrences of the text *the Elderly* with the text **Seniors**. Use the match case option.

Edit the Document

1. Go to the heading *Eyesight and Medication*.
2. Under the heading *Eyesight and Medication*, move the paragraph beginning with the text *The U.S. Department of Agriculture* and the list that follows it to the end of the Nutrition section.
3. Go to the section *Common Eye Ailments*.
4. Save the changes to the document.

Convert Text to Tables and a Table to Text

1. In the section on common eye ailments, select the six lines of text after the first paragraph (beginning with *Common Eye Ailments* and ending with *Macular Degeneration*).

2. Convert the selection to a table. Create two columns, and separate the text at the tabs.
3. Apply the Table Grid 8 style to the table, and then apply bold to the text in the second row.
4. Select the table under the heading *Glaucoma* and convert it to text, separating the text with paragraph marks.
5. Apply the default bullet list formatting to the selected lines.
6. Under the heading *Macular Degeneration*, select the 12 lines of text after the first paragraph (beginning with *Some Symptoms of Common Eye Ailments*).
7. Convert the selection to a table. Create two columns, and separate the text at the tabs.
8. Apply the Table Grid 8 style to the table, and then apply bold to the text in the second row.

Use the Research Tool

1. Position the insertion point in the first blank cell in the new table—column 1, row 6—and then display the Research task pane.
2. Check the Research Options to verify that the Encarta Encyclopedia and Live Search are active. If necessary, make them active.
3. Search for information on symptoms of cataracts.
4. Scroll down the list to see the links under Live Search.

5. Use the link to the WebMD Web site to display the page. If it is not available, use a different link.

6. Read the article to identify five symptoms of cataracts.

7. Fill in the blank table cells with the following symptoms: **Cloudy vision**, **Glare from lamps or sun**, **Difficulty driving at night**, **Frequent changes in eyeglass prescription**, **Double vision**.

8. Close your Web browser, and then close the Research task pane.

9. Save the changes to the document.

Insert Captions and Cross-References

1. Insert the caption **Table 1** for the first table in the document, using the default settings.

2. Insert the caption **Table 2** for the second table in the document, using the default settings.

3. In the second column of Table 1, insert hyperlinked cross-references to the page numbers where the reader can find the corresponding heading.

4. At the end of the text in the Presbyopia, Cataracts, and Macular Degeneration sections, insert the cross-reference text, **For a list of symptoms, refer to**, and insert a cross-reference to Table 2. Insert the same cross-reference before the last sentence in the Glaucoma section.

5. Save the changes to the document.

Create a Bibliography

1. Select the MLA style of bibliography citations.

2. Position the insertion point after the first sentence under the heading *Common Eye Ailments*, and insert the following bibliography citation:
   a. Type of source: **Web site**
   b. Author: **American Academy of Ophthalmology**
   c. Select the Corporate Author check box.
   d. Name of Web Page: **EyeSmart**
   e. Year: **2007**
   f. Year Accessed: **2008**
   g. Month: **May**
   h. Day: **20**
   i. URL: **http://www.geteyesmart.org/**

3. Position the insertion point after the last sentence under the heading *Common Eye Ailments*, and insert the following bibliography citation:
   a. Type of source: **Web site**
   b. Author: **Family Vision Care Center**
   c. Select the Corporate Author check box.
   d. Name of Web Page: **Senior Eye Care**

   e. Year: **2007**
   f. Year Accessed: **2008**
   g. Month Accessed: **May**
   h. Day Accessed: **20**
   i. URL: **http://www.saratogasight.com/Seniors.htm**

4. Position the insertion point after the first sentence under the heading *Cataracts*, and insert the following bibliography citation:
   a. Type of source: **Web site**
   b. Author: **Burcham Eyecare Center**
   c. Select the Corporate Author check box.
   d. Name of Web Page: **Helpful Eye Health Information**
   e. Year: **2007**
   f. Year Accessed: **2008**
   g. Month Accessed: **May**
   h. Day Accessed: **20**
   i. URL: **http://www.denver-eye.com/eye-health.htm#Cataracts**

5. Position the insertion point after the text under the heading *Cataracts*, and insert the following bibliography citation:
   a. Type of source: **Web site**
   b. Author: **WebMD, Inc.**
   c. Select the Corporate Author check box.
   d. Name of Web Page: **Cataracts – Symptoms**
   e. Year: **2005**
   f. Month: **November**
   g. Day: **15**
   h. Year Accessed: **2008**
   i. Month Accessed: **May**
   j. Day Accessed: **20**
   k. URL: **http://www.webmd.com/eye-health/cataracts/cataracts-symptoms**

6. Position the insertion point at the end of the last bullet item under the heading *Glaucoma*, and insert the following bibliography citation:
   a. Type of source: **Document from Web site**
   b. Author: **University of Illinois Eye & Ear Infirmary**
   c. Select the Corporate Author check box.
   d. Name of Web Page: **Glaucoma causes Optic Nerve Cupping (atrophy) and Vision Loss**
   e. Name of Web site: **The Eye Digest**
   f. Year: **2007**

g. Month: **June**

h. Day: **16**

i. Year Accessed: **2008**

j. Month Accessed: **May**

k. Day Accessed: **20**

l. URL: **http://www.agingeye.net/glaucoma/ glaucomainformation.php**

7. Position the insertion point after the first sentence under the heading *Eyesiight and Medication*, and insert the following bibliography citation:

a. Type of source: **Web site**

b. Author: **Transitions Optical, Inc.**

c. Select the Corporate Author check box.

d. Name of Web Page: **Medications**

e. Year: **2007**

f. Year Accessed: **2008**

g. Month Accessed: **May**

h. Day Accessed: **20**

i. URL: **http://www.eyeglassguide.com/ visiting/Medications.aspx**

8. Position the insertion point at the end of the second sentence under the heading *Lifestyle Choices*, and insert the following bibliography citation:

a. Type of source: **Document from Web site**

b. Author: **George L. Schmidt, O.D.**

c. Name of Web Page: **Preventing Eye Disease and Blindness**

d. Name of Web site: **The Eye Site**

e. Year Accessed: **2008**

f. Month Accessed: **May**

g. Day Accessed: **20**

h. URL: **http://www.i-care.net/eyereport.html**

9. Position the insertion point at the end of the first sentence under the heading *Nutrition* and insert the University of Illinois bibliography citation.

10. Insert a page break at the end of the document.

11. At the top of the last page, type the heading **Bibliography** using the Heading 1 style, centered.

12. Below the new heading, insert the bibliography.

13. Select all lines in the bibliography and insert 6 points of space before each paragraph.

14. Save the changes to the document.

Create an Index, Table of Figures, and a Table of Contents

1. Insert another page break after the Conclusion section and before the bibliography.

2. At the top of the new page, type the heading **Table of Figures** using the Heading 1 style, centered.

3. On a new line below the heading, insert a table of figures, using the Classic format, with page numbers right-aligned, using dot tab leaders, with no hyperlinks.

4. Leave a blank line and then type the heading **Index** using the Heading 1 style, centered.

5. Mark items to create an index for the document. Use your judgment as to which words to include. Include at least ten words. Include at least two cross-references. Include at least three subentries.

6. When all items are marked, move the insertion point to a blank line below the heading *Index*, and create the index. Use the Classic format, with page numbers right-aligned, using dot tab leaders, indented in two columns.

7. Insert a blank line before the heading *Overview* near the beginning of the document, and clear all formatting from it.

8. Generate a table of contents in the Classic format, with page numbers right-aligned, using dot tab leaders, with no hyperlinks.

9. Save the changes to the document.

Complete the Document

1. Insert a page break between the table of contents and the heading *Overview*.

2. Insert a header on all but the first page that has your name flush left and the date flush right.

✓ *Adjust the right tab stop if necessary.*

3. Insert a footer on all pages that has the page number in the format of **Page X of N** centered.

✓ *Adjust the tab stops if necessary.*

4. Preview all pages of the document and check the overall layout and formatting.

5. Insert a page break after the paragraph under the heading *Macular Degeneration* to move Table 2 to the next page.

6. Update the page numbers in cross-references, the table of contents, the table of figures, and the index.

7. Check the spelling and grammar in the document.

8. Display the document in Print Preview again. With two pages displayed at a time, it should look similar to the following illustrations.

9. If necessary, make adjustments and corrections.

10. Print the document. Decide if you want to include the document in your employment portfolio as an example of your achievement. If so, print a copy to add to your portfolio.

11. Close the document, saving all changes.

Illustration A, Pages 1 and 2

Eye Care for Seniors

How Aging Affects the Health of Our Eyes
Prepared by
Student's Name

Overview

As people age, their bodies change in many ways. One feature that may be overlooked is the effects of aging on eyesight. And yet, good vision may have a positive impact on a senior's ability to enjoy life to its fullest, while poor vision can lead to an inability to function in society, which in turn may lead to depression and lost quality of life.

This report takes a look at some of the unique eye care challenges facing seniors, as well as actions they and their caregivers can take to insure proper eye health.

Common Eye Ailments

According to the American Academy of Ophthalmology, most Americans begin experiencing some form of vision loss starting at age forty. (American Academy of Ophthalmology) Many seniors are afraid to admit they are experiencing vision problems, because they think it will be seen as a sign that they cannot continue to live independently. However, most of the common eye ailments can be prevented, cured, or treated successfully. The most common eye ailments affecting seniors are listed in Table 1. (Family Vision Care Center)

Table 1

Common Eye Ailments	
Ailment	For more information, refer to:
Presbyopia	2
Cataracts	3
Glaucoma	3
Macular degeneration	3

Presbyopia

Presbyopia is the gradual decline in the ability to focus on close objects, or to see small print. It is the result of a normal process of aging in which the lens of the eye becomes thicker, which causes it to lose its ability to properly focus light. This condition can easily be corrected by proper eyeglasses. For a list of symptoms, refer to Table 2.

Illustration B, Pages 3 and 4

Cataracts

The leading cause of reversible blindness in the United States is cataracts. (Burcham Eyecare Center) Cataracts cloud the eye's normally clear, transparent lens, resulting in blurred vision. This is one of the most common and most treatable eye conditions among seniors. Vision can usually be restored by eye surgery, usually done on an outpatient basis. For a list of symptoms, refer to Table 2. (WebMD, Inc.)

Glaucoma

Glaucoma is caused by a progressive increase of pressure within the eye. It can lead to irreversible damage to the optic nerve, which is responsible for carrying images to the brain. In the early stages it may have no symptoms, but it can be diagnosed during an eye exam. When caught early, glaucoma can be treated so that vision loss can be prevented. For a list of symptoms, refer to Table 2. Anyone can get glaucoma, but those at higher risk include:

- African-Americans over the age of forty.
- Anyone over the age of sixty.
- People with a family history of glaucoma. (University of Illinois Eye & Ear Infirmary)

Macular Degeneration

Macular degeneration occurs when the macula, or central point of focus on the retina, is damaged. This may occur naturally with aging, as the macula becomes thin. It reduces the ability of the eye to see fine detail, and may eventually lead to blindness. It affects as many as 15 million people over the age of fifty. There is no proven treatment, but many people believe that nutrition may play a role. For a list of symptoms, refer to Table 2.

Table 2

Some Symptoms of Common Eye Ailments	
Symptom	Ailment
Straining to read newsprint	Presbyopia
Confusing similar numerals	Presbyopia
Difficulty focusing on price tags	Presbyopia
Cloudy vision	Cataracts
Glare from lamps or sun	Cataracts
Difficulty driving at night	Cataracts
Frequent changes in eyeglass prescription	Cataracts
Double vision	Cataracts
Reduced ability to see fine detail	Macular degeneration
General loss of vision	Glaucoma

Maintaining Eye Health

In addition to annual eye exams, many people consider that eye health, like general body health, can be affected by lifestyle choices and diet. As such, seniors can take steps to maintain their vision.

Nutrition

It is generally accepted that food choices can help reduce the risk for chronic diseases such as heart disease, cancers, diabetes, stroke, and osteoporosis. (University of Illinois Eye & Ear Infirmary) However, few people stop to consider that diet and nutrition can also play a role in reducing eye ailments and vision problems.

The U.S Department of Agriculture states that the basic checklist for insuring proper nutrition is the same for all people, no matter what their age:

- Eat a variety of foods.
- Choose a diet high in grain products, vegetables, and fruits.
- Choose a diet low in fat, saturated fat, and cholesterol.
- Choose a diet moderate in sugars.
- Choose a diet moderate in salt and sodium.
- Drink alcohol only in moderation.
- Drink plenty of water.

Illustration C, Pages 5 and 6

Student's Name   Today's Date

Lifestyle Choices

The single most important step anyone can take to improve health is to stop smoking. Smoking increases your risk of developing macular degeneration by up to 600%, and more than doubles your risk for cataracts. (George L. Schmidt) Other factors that impact eye health include physical fitness, family and social networks, intellectual activity, and economics.

Eyesight and Medication

Both prescription and over-the-counter medications can affect vision. (Transitions Optical, Inc.) Some side effects of medications may be only temporary, but others can cause long-term changes in your eyes. Combining medications can also cause visual side effects, so seniors must be sure doctors know what drugs they are already taking before prescribing new drugs. Also, it is important to let optometrists know about any medications. Medications affect each person differently, but some common side effects include:

- Blurry vision
- Poor night vision
- Dry eyes
- Double vision
- Increased pupil dilation
- Sensitivity to light
- Excessive tearing.

Conclusion

Maintaining eye health and proper vision is important for seniors because as people age, nervous system response time slows. Proper vision helps insure seniors will function correctly in situations where response time matters, such as while driving, biking, or even walking on city streets. They will also enjoy life more.

Student's Name   Today's Date

Table of Figures

Index

Illustration D, Page 7

Student's Name   Today's Date

Bibliography

American Academy of Ophthamology. EyeSmart. 2007. 20 May 2008 <http://www.geteyesmart.org/>.

Burcham Eyecare Center. Helpful Eye Health Information. 2007. 20 May 2008 <http://www.denver-eye.com/eye-health.htm#Cataracts>.

Family Vision Care Center. Senior Eye Care. 2007. 20 May 2008 <http://www.saratogasight.com/Seniors.htm>.

George L. Schmidt, O.D. "Preventing Eye Disease and Blindness." The Eye Site. 20 May 2008 <http://www.i-care.net/eyereport.html>.

Transitions Optical, Inc. Medications. 2007. 20 May 2008 <http://www.eyeglassguide.com/visiting/Medications.aspx>.

University of Illinois Eye & Ear Infirmary. "Glaucoma causes Optic Nerve Cupping (atrophy) and Vision Loss." 16 June 2007. The Eye Digest. 20 May 2008 <http://www.agingeye.net/glaucoma/glaucomainformation.php>.

WebMD, Inc. Cataracts -- Symptoms. 15 November 2005. 20 May 2008 <http://www.webmd.com/eye-health/cataracts/cataracts-symptoms>.

Curriculum Integration

Application Skills   A new business depends on many people. Usually, someone must make decisions about how to spend money to make the business grow and succeed. For your social studies class, imagine you are responsible for selecting the computer system and other technology for a new business. Working alone or in a team, select a type of business and then conduct research to determine the systems you need. Start with the basics, such as the type of hardware and software. Also consider the operating system, networking tools, data storage, and security options. Compare the available options, including features and cost, and make a decision about the technology you would purchase. Keep track of your sources. When you have completed your research, use the skills you have learned in this lesson to create a report detailing what you have learned, what purchasing decision you recommend, and why. Present the report orally to your class.

EXERCISE DIRECTIONS

Start the project by selecting a business.

Develop a schedule and set goals for completing the assignment. If you are working in a group, assign each team member specific responsibilities.

Research the type of business you select to determine how it uses technology. From this information, you can decide the types of technology you would need to purchase.

Continue your research to learn about the technology, including the names of manufacturers, what platforms are available, and so on. Take notes and record source information.

When the research is complete, start Word, if necessary, and create a new document. Save it as **13TECH_xx**.

Select to display elements that might help you while you work, such as the rulers, nonprinting characters, and text boundaries, and make sure all the features you want to use are enabled, such as AutoCorrect and AutoFormat as You Type.

Select a theme, style set, and colors for the document, or create and save a custom theme.

Create a first draft of the report, organizing the information into a logical order. Use headings to identify key sections of the text.

Proofread the first draft and make improvements. Determine if you need to conduct additional research or if you have all of the information you need.

If you are working as a team, cooperate to revise and improve the content.

Prepare a second draft of the report. Include tables, headers, footers, and other features that make the document easier to read. Use cross-references if necessary, and insert citations according to the format requested by your instructor. Create a title or cover page, as shown in Illustration A.

Again, proofread the document and make improvements. Check the spelling and the layout.

When you are satisfied with the report, create an index and a bibliography. If you have included figures, create a table of figures as well. Insert a table of contents at the beginning of the report.

Proofread and preview the document and make final corrections and improvements, as necessary.

Check the spelling and grammar, and use a thesaurus to replace common or boring words.

Ask a classmate who was not part of your team to review the document and make suggestions for how you might improve it.

Incorporate your classmate's suggestions into the document, and save it.

Print the report and distribute it to your classmates.

You may want to develop a visual aid to show during the presentation, such as a chart comparing systems or a list of costs. Deliver an oral presentation to the class, explaining and defending your recommendation.

Assess the document and decide whether you want to include it in your employment portfolio. If so, print a clean copy, insert the pages in sleeves, and add it to the portfolio.

Close all files, saving all changes.

Illustration A

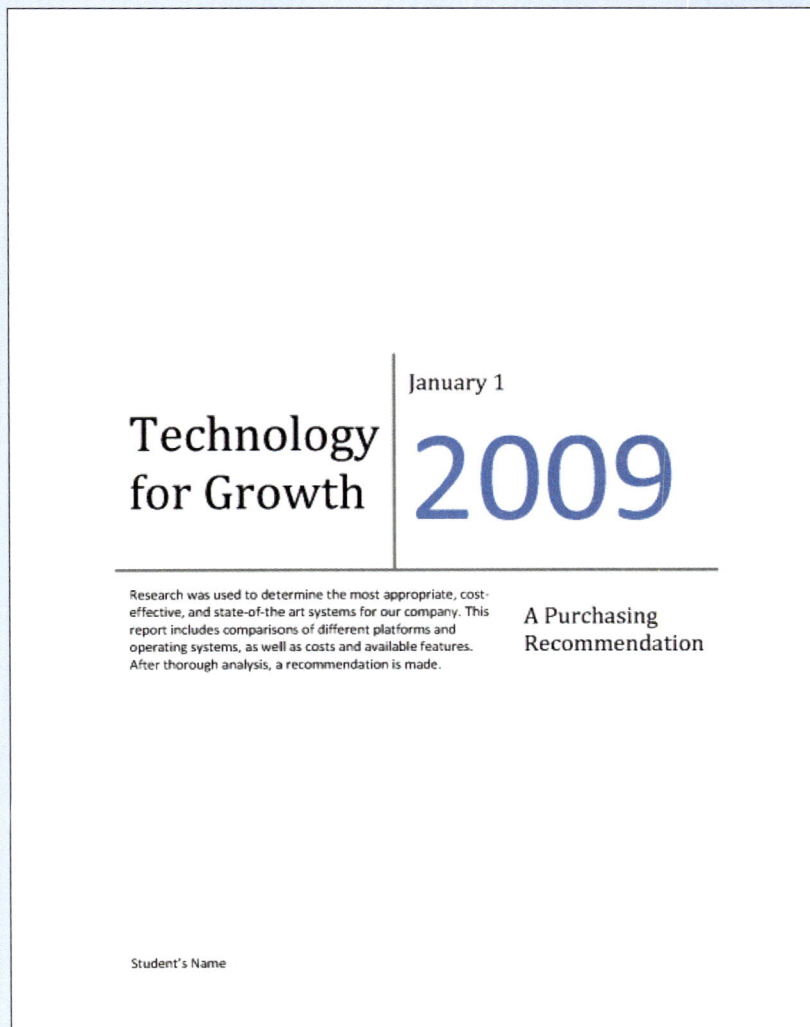

January 1

Technology for Growth

2009

Research was used to determine the most appropriate, cost-effective, and state-of-the art systems for our company. This report includes comparisons of different platforms and operating systems, as well as costs and available features. After thorough analysis, a recommendation is made.

A Purchasing Recommendation

Student's Name

Lesson | 3

Advanced Graphics

Skills Covered

- **About Advanced Graphics**
- **Resize Objects**
- **Set Text Wrap Options**
- **Position an Object**

Software Skills Using Word 2007's advanced graphics options, you can integrate graphics objects with text and white space on the page to create professional-looking documents. You can apply precise settings for sizing and positioning objects, and you can adjust the text wrap style to make the document easier to read and more interesting for the reader.

Application Skills Business owners and managers must continually look for ways to bring in customers, improve products, and develop opportunities. In this exercise, you will enhance a newsletter for the Liberty Blooms flower shop by incorporating graphics.

TERMS

Anchor An element in a document, such as the margin or the page itself, relative to which you can position an object.

Aspect ratio The relative horizontal and vertical sizes of an object, or the ratio of height to width.

Clip art Files, such as pictures, sounds, and video, that you can insert into an Office document.

Drawing object A shape or line created in Word and saved as part of the Word document.

Floating object An object that is positioned independently from the document text.

In line Positioned on a line of text, like a typed character.

Object A graphic, picture, chart, shape, text box, or other element that can be inserted into a document.

Picture object A graphics object created using a different application and then inserted into a Word document.

Scale Adjust the size of an object based on a percentage of its original size.

Shapes Pre-drawn objects that come with Office 2007.

Sizing handles Rectangular boxes around the edges of a selected object that you use to resize the object.

Text box A rectangular drawing object in which text or graphics images can be inserted and positioned anywhere on a page.

Wrapping style The way objects are integrated with text and white space on a page.

NOTES

About Advanced Graphics

- You can insert many types of graphics **objects** into a Word document, including **drawing objects** and **picture objects**.

- Common types of drawing objects include **shapes** and **text boxes**.

- Common types of pictures include photographs and **clip art**.

   ✓ *Charts, WordArt, and Smart Art diagrams are also types of objects.*

- Use the Insert tab to insert graphic objects.
   - Click the appropriate button within the Illustrations group to insert Shapes, pictures, and clip art.
   - Click the Text Box button in the Text group to insert a text box.

- When you select an object, a Format tab becomes available on the Ribbon.

- The options available for formatting all types of objects are similar. For example, you can change the size and position of the object, or apply effects.

- Some options vary depending on the type of object. For example, you can apply Quick Styles to shapes and text boxes. You can adjust the contrast and brightness of pictures, but not of shapes and text boxes.

- Note that although the commands are similar, the access keys for selecting a command vary, depending on the type of object. For example, to make the Format tab available when working with a picture, press [Alt]+[J]+[P]. To make the Format tab available when working with a text box, press [Alt]+[J]+[X]. To make the Format tab available when working with a shape, press [Alt]+[J]+[D].

Resize Objects

- The easiest way to resize an object is to drag a **sizing handle** with the mouse.

- To set advanced sizing options, click the dialog box launcher in the Size group on the Format tab of the Ribbon.

- You can set a precise, or absolute, size for an object by specifying values for the height and width.

- For shapes and text boxes, you can set a size relative to the height or width of the page or margin.

   ✓ *You cannot set a relative size for pictures.*

- When an object's **aspect ratio** is locked, you can resize the object evenly so the height and width remain proportional.

Size tab of the Format AutoShape dialog box

Drawing Tools Format tab

- Unlock the aspect ratio if you want to resize the object unevenly, distorting the image.
- You can **scale** an object to resize it based on a percentage of its original size. For example, scale it to 200% to double its size, or scale it to 50% to shrink it to half its original size.

Set Text Wrap Options

- By default, Word inserts shapes as **floating objects** so they can be positioned anywhere on a page, and it inserts pictures **in line** with text.
- You can change an object's **wrapping style** to affect the way the object is integrated into the document text.
- Select from seven wrapping options:
  - In Line with Text: Object is positioned on a line with text characters.
  - Square: Text is wrapped on all four sides of the object's bounding box.
  - Tight: Text is wrapped to the contours of the image.
  - Behind Text: Text continues in lines over the object, obscuring the object.
  - In Front of Text: Text continues in lines behind the object, which may obscure the text.
  - Top and Bottom: Text is displayed above and below object but not on left or right sides.
  - Through: Text runs through object.

**Text Wrapping tab of the
Advanced Layout dialog box**

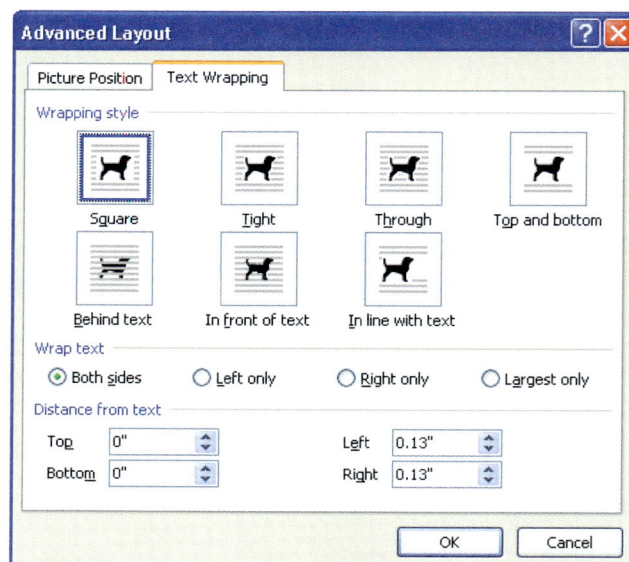

- You can set advanced text wrapping options on the Text Wrapping tab of the Advanced Layout dialog box.
- For example, you can select to wrap text only at the left or right side of the object, and you can specify the distance that you want to leave between the object and the text.

Position an Object

- The easiest way to move an object is to drag it to a new location.
- You can also select a built-in position from the Position gallery, including in line with the text, or left, right, or centered relative to the top, bottom, or center of the page.
- To position an object precisely, use the options on the Picture Position tab of the Advanced Layout dialog box.
- On the Picture Position tab, you can select from four horizontal alignment options and three vertical alignment options. Each option has its own set of parameters:
- For horizontal alignment, select:
  - *Alignment* to align the object left, right, or centered relative to the selected **anchor** (margin, page, column, or character).
  - *Book layout* to align the object on the inside or outside of the anchor (margin or page).
  - *Absolute position* to specify the precise distance (in inches or points) that you want to leave between the left edge of the object and the anchor (margin, page, column, or character).
  - *Relative position* to specify the distance that you want to leave between the left edge of the object and the anchor (margin or page) as a percentage.
- For vertical alignment, select:
  - *Alignment* to align the object on the top, bottom, inside, outside, or centered relative to the anchor (margin, page, or line).
  - *Absolute position* to specify the precise distance (in inches or points) that you want to leave between the top edge of the object and the anchor (margin, page, paragraph, or line).
  - *Relative position* to specify the distance that you want to leave between the top edge of the object and the anchor (margin or page) as a percentage.

**Picture Position tab of the
Advanced Layout dialog box**

Advanced Layout

Picture Position | Text Wrapping

Horizontal
- ○ Alignment — Left — relative to — Column
- ○ Book layout — Inside — of — Margin
- ● Absolute position — 0.83" — to the right of — Column
- ○ Relative position — relative to — Page

Vertical
- ○ Alignment — Top — relative to — Page
- ● Absolute position — 0.14" — below — Paragraph
- ○ Relative position — relative to — Page

Options
- ☐ Move object with text   ☑ Allow overlap
- ☐ Lock anchor   ☑ Layout in table cell

OK   Cancel

- Note that when nonprinting characters are displayed, an anchor icon indicates the location of an object's anchor.
- By default, the object moves with the anchor if you insert or delete text, graphics, or white space in the document.
- You can set Word so the object stays in place even if the surrounding content moves, and you can lock the anchor to keep the object in its same position relative to the page, even if it moves to a different page.

PROCEDURES

Resize an Object Using the Mouse

1. Click object to select it.
2. Drag a corner sizing handle to resize both height and width.

   ✓ *Press and hold Shift while dragging a corner hander to resize proportionally.*

   OR

   Drag a side sizing handle to resize height or width only.

Display the Format Tab for Different Types of Objects

1. Click object to select it.
2. Click Format tab:
   - ■ **Drawing Tools Format** tab . . . . [Alt]+[J], [D]
   - ■ **Text Box Tools Format** tab . . . . [Alt]+[J], [X]
   - ■ **Picture Tools Format** tab . . . . [Alt]+[J], [P]
   - ■ **WordArt Tools Format** tab . . . . [Alt]+[J], [W]

Lock an Object's Aspect Ratio

1. Click object to select it.
2. Click **Format** tab.

   Size Group

3. Click **Size** dialog box launcher . . . . [S], [Z]
4. Click **Lock aspect ratio** check box . . . . [Alt]+[A]
5. Click **OK** or **Close** . . . . [Enter]

Resize an Object Precisely

1. Click object to select it.
2. Click **Format** tab:

   Size Group

3. Click **Height** box

   1.51" . . . . [H]
4. Type height in inches . . . . *type height*, [Enter]

   OR

   Click increment arrows to enter height.

5. Click **Width** box

   1.43" . . . . . . [Alt], [J], [D], [W]
6. Type width in inches . . . . *type width*, [Enter]

   OR

   Click increment arrows to enter width.

Scale an Object

1. Click object to select it.
2. Click **Format** tab.

   Size Group

3. Click **Size** dialog box launcher . . . . [S], [Z]
4. Click **Height** box . . . . [Alt]+[H]
5. Type height as a percentage of original height . . . *type percentage*

   OR

   Click increment arrows to enter percentage.

6. Click **Width** box . . . . [Alt]+[W]

7. Type width as a percentage of original width. . . . *type percentage*

   OR

   Click increment arrows to enter percentage.

8. Click **OK** or **Close** . . . . [Enter]

Set a Relative Size for an Object

1. Click object to select it.
2. Click **Format** tab:
   - **Drawing Tools Format** tab . . . . [Alt]+[J], [D]
   - **Text Box Tools Format** tab . . . . [Alt]+[J], [X]
   - **WordArt Tools Format** tab . . . . [Alt]+[J], [W]

   ✓ *Relative sizes are not available for pictures.*

   Size Group

3. Click **Size** dialog box launcher 🔲 . . . . [S], [Z]
4. Click **Relative** option button . . . . [Alt]+[L]
5. Click **Relative** box and type height as a percentage. . . . . [⇤],

   type percentage

   OR

   Click increment arrows to enter percentage.

6. Click **relative to** drop-down arrow. . . . . [Alt]+[T]
7. Click comparative item.
8. Click **Relative** option button . . . . [Alt]+[I]
9. Click **Relative** box and type width as a percentage. . . . . [⇤],

   type percentage

   OR

   Click increment arrows to enter percentage.

10. Click **relative to** drop-down arrow. . . . . [Alt]+[E]
11. Click comparative item.
12. Click **OK**. . . . . [Enter]

Set Text Wrap Options

1. Click object to select it.
2. Click **Format** tab.

   Arrange Group

3. Click **Text Wrapping** button 🔲 . . . . [T], [W]
4. Click desired option:
   - **In Line With Text** . . . . [I]
   - **Square** . . . . [S]
   - **Tight** . . . . [T]
   - **Behind Text** . . . . [D]
   - **In Front of Text** . . . . [N]
   - **Top and Bottom** . . . . [O]
   - **Through** . . . . [H]

Set Advanced Text Wrap Options

1. Click object to select it.
2. Click **Format** tab.

   Arrange Group

3. Click **Text Wrapping** button 🔲 . . . . [T], [W]
4. Click **More Layout Options** . . . [L]
5. Click **Text Wrapping** tab, if necessary . . . . [Ctrl]+[⇤]
6. Select desired text wrapping style:
   - **Square** . . . . [Alt]+[Q]
   - **Tight** . . . . [Alt]+[T]
   - **Through** . . . . [Alt]+[H]
   - **Top and bottom** . . . . . [Alt]+[O]
   - **Behind text** . . . . [Alt]+[B]
   - **In front of text** . . . . . [Alt]+[F]
   - **In line with text** . . . . [Alt]+[I]
7. For Square, Tight, and Through styles, select desired text wrapping options:
   - **Both sides** . . . . [Alt]+[S]
   - **Left only** . . . . [Alt]+[L]
   - **Right only** . . . . [Alt]+[R]
   - **Largest only** . . . . [Alt]+[A]

8. For Square, Tight, Through, and Top and bottom styles, set distance from text, as follows:
   a. Click **Top** . . . . [Alt]+[F]
   b. Type distance to leave between text and top of object.
   c. Click **Bottom** . . . . [Alt]+[M]
   d. Type distance to leave between text and bottom of object.
   e. Click **Left** . . . . [Alt]+[E]
   f. Type distance to leave between text and left of object.
   g. Click **Right** . . . . [Alt]+[G]
   h. Type distance to leave between text and right of object.

   ✓ *Not all distance options will be available for all styles.*

9. Click **OK**. . . . . [Enter]

Move an Object

1. Select object.
2. Position the mouse pointer over object until pointer changes to a four-headed arrow ✛.
3. Drag object to new location.
4. Release mouse button.

To move horizontally or vertically only:

1. Select object.
2. Position the mouse pointer over object until pointer changes to a four-headed arrow ✛.
3. Press and hold [Shift].
4. Drag object to new location.
5. Release mouse button.

To move in small increments:

1. Select object.
2. Press an arrow key:
   - [↑] to move up 1 pixel.
   - [↓] to move down 1 pixel.
   - [←] to move left 1 pixel.
   - [→] to move right 1 pixel.
3. Repeat step 2 until object is positioned as desired.

Position an Object

1. Click object to select it.
2. Click **Format** tab.

   Arrange Group

3. Click **Position** button
   .... P, O
4. Click position to
   apply .... ↓/←/→/↑, Enter

Position an Object Precisely

1. Click object to select it.
2. Click **Format** tab.

   Arrange Group

3. Click **Position** button
   .... P, O
4. Click **More Layout Options** ... L

5. Click **Picture Position**
   tab .... Ctrl + ⇄
6. Do one of the following to set
   horizontal position:

   a. Click **Alignment** drop-down
      arrow ..... Alt + A, ⇄, ↓
   b. Click desired
      alignment .... ↓/↑, Enter
   c. Click **relative to** drop-down
      arrow .... Alt + R
   d. Click desired
      anchor .... ↓/↑, Enter

      OR

   a. Click **Book layout** drop-down
      arrow ..... Alt + B, ⇄, ↓

   b. Click desired
      position .... ↓/↑, Enter
   c. Click **of** drop-down
      arrow .... Alt + F
   d. Click desired
      anchor .... ↓/↑, Enter

      OR

   a. Click **Absolute position**
      box .... Alt + P, ⇄
   b. Type amount of space to leave.
   c. Click **to the right of** drop-down
      arrow .... Alt + T
   d. Click desired
      anchor .... ↓/↑, Enter

      OR

   a. Click **Relative position**
      box .... Alt + R, ⇄
   b. Type percentage to leave.
   c. Click **relative to** drop-down
      arrow .... Alt + E
   d. Click desired
      anchor .... ↓/↑, Enter

   ✓ *Relative positioning is not available for pictures.*

7. Do one of the following to set
   vertical position:

   a. Click **Alignment** drop-down
      arrow ..... Alt + G, ⇄, ↓
   b. Click desired
      alignment .... ↓/↑, Enter
   c. Click **relative to** drop-down
      arrow .... Alt + E
   d. Click desired
      anchor .... ↓/↑, Enter

      OR

   a. Click **Absolute position**
      box .... Alt + S, ⇄
   b. Type amount of space to leave.
   c. Click **below** drop-down
      arrow .... Alt + W
   d. Click desired
      anchor .... ↓/↑, Enter

      OR

   a. Click **Relative position**
      box .... Alt + I, ⇄
   b. Type percentage to leave.
   c. Click **relative to** drop-down
      arrow .... Alt + O
   d. Click desired
      anchor .... ↓/↑, Enter

   ✓ *Relative positioning is not available for pictures.*

8. Select check box options as
   necessary:

   ■ **Move object with
      text** .... Alt + M
   ■ **Lock anchor** ...... Alt + L
   ■ **Allow overlap** ...... Alt + V
   ■ **Layout in table
      cell** .... Alt + C
9. Click **OK** .... Enter

Delete an Object

1. Click the object to select it.
2. Press Delete.

EXERCISE DIRECTIONS

1. Start Word, if necessary.

2. Open ⊙ **14BLOOMS**, and save the file as **14BLOOMS_xx**.

3. Insert a Sun shape from the Basic Shapes palette.

4. Unlock the shape's aspect ratio, if necessary, and then resize it to 1.5 inches high by 1 inch wide.

5. Position the shape centered horizontally and vertically on the page.

6. Set the text wrapping to Tight.

7. Insert a clip art picture of a rose. If you cannot find a suitable picture, insert the .gif graphics file ⊙ **14ROSE** supplied with this book.

8. Set the text wrapping for the picture to Square, and size it to 1.5 by 1.5 inches.

9. Position the picture horizontally on the left, relative to the margin, and vertically 1 inch below the top margin.

10. If necessary, set the text to wrap only on the right side of the object, and set the distance between the right side of the object and the text to .5 inch.

11. Select the sun shape and lock its aspect ratio.

12. Scale the size of the shape by 200%.

13. Change the text wrapping style for the shape to Behind Text.

14. Preview the document. It should look similar to Illustration A.

15. Check the spelling and grammar in the document.

16. Print the document.

17. Close the file, saving all changes.

Illustration A

Liberty Blooms News

Published by the Liberty Blooms Flower Shop
345 Chestnut Street, Philadelphia, PA 19106

Welcome

Welcome to the first issue of *Liberty Blooms News*, a monthly newsletter for people who visit the Liberty Blooms Flower Shop. The primary goal of this publication is to provide you with news about activities and events that you might find of interest. In addition, we intend to publish class schedules, gardening tips, and general information about related topics.

Liberty Blooms News will be mailed directly to everyone who has registered at our Chestnut Street store. Please contact us with questions and suggestions. We will do our best to address your comments in future issues.

Recipe Showcase

Chicken with Tomatoes and Herbs   *Yield: Four Servings*

Ingredients

8 boneless chicken pieces
1 tablespoon olive oil
10 ½ oz. tomatoes, drained
¾ cup chicken stock
2 teaspoons mixed herbs, chopped
1 ½ oz. black olives, chopped
1 teaspoon sugar
Fresh basil to garnish

Classes and Seminars

If you are a frequent visitor to Liberty Blooms, you know there is always something going on at 345 Chestnut Street. From flower arranging to cooking with herbs, we try to fill the calendar with interesting and informative activities that the whole family will enjoy.

The following events are scheduled for the coming months. Some events require registration, so please call ahead for more information.

Edible Gardens   May 13
Flower Arranging   May 21
Water Gardens   June 3
Potpourri Designs   June 11

Directions

1. Heat oil in large skillet.
2. Add chicken pieces and cook until browned on all sides.
3. Add the tomatoes, stock and mixed herbs and simmer for 30 minutes or until chicken is cooked through.
4. Add the olives and sugar and simmer for an additional 5 minutes.
5. Garnish with fresh basil and serve with rice or pasta.

ON YOUR OWN

1. Start Word, if necessary, create a new blank document, and save the file as OWD14_*xx*.

2. Create a newsletter for a club or organization. Use desktop publishing and word processing skills to make the document interesting, professional, and easy to read.

3. Write at least three articles for the newsletter. You may want to write more and use multiple pages.

4. Enhance the document using columns, borders, and shading.

5. Insert at least four objects of varying types in the newsletter document, such as a picture in the newsletter title, a text box in the body of the document, and a shape.

6. Size and position the objects for the best effect.

7. Try different text wrapping options, such as Behind Text, Tight, or Top and Bottom.

8. Check spelling and grammar in the document.

9. Preview the document.

10. If necessary, adjust paragraph and font formatting as well as column breaks so that the text flows on the page and the document looks professional.

11. Print the document.

12. Ask a classmate to review the document and offer comments and suggestions, particularly about the layout and design, and the use of graphics.

13. Incorporate the suggestions into the document.

14. Assess the newsletter and decide whether you want to include it in your employment portfolio. If so, print a clean copy, insert the pages in sleeves, and add it to the portfolio.

15. Close the document, saving all changes.

Business Connection

Dressing the Part

Different occupations have different standards when it comes to how employees should dress. Some—like banking—require business suits, some—like nurse—might require a uniform, while others—like repair technician—might fall somewhere in between. When you show up dressed and groomed appropriately for work, you send a positive message to your employer. You indicate that you care about your appearance, and you understand how to fit in.

You're Invited!

Working alone or in small teams, research the standards of dress and grooming for a variety of occupations. Then, use Word's desktop publishing tools, or a digital design software program such as Publisher, to design and create an invitation to a fashion show of workplace attire. Use an invitation template to create the document, and insert text and graphics to detail the date, time, and location of the event. Include information and pictures about the specific occupations, workplace environments, and clothing that will be featured. When you have completed the invitation, print it. If possible, as a class organize and present an actual fashion show demonstrating standards of dress and grooming for a variety of workplace environments.

Skills Covered

- **Link Text Boxes**
- **Align Drawing Objects**
- **Copy Objects**

Software Skills   Using text boxes makes it possible to position and format text independently from the rest of the document. You can link the text boxes so that the text flows from one to another. Align objects to improve the appearance of the document. Copy objects to save time and to insure consistency between similar objects in a document.

Application Skills   New Media Designs, a Web site design and management company, wants to inspire local students to pursue careers in computer information systems and technology. It is sponsoring an essay-writing contest for students in grades 1 through 12 to encourage them to learn more about the available opportunities. In this exercise, you will open an existing flyer advertising the contest and edit it. You will use text boxes and shapes to make the flyer interesting.

TERMS

Link   Establish a connection between text boxes so that text which does not fit within the borders of the first text box flows into the next, linked text box.

NOTES

Link Text Boxes

- You can **link** text boxes in a document so that text which does not fit within the first text box automatically flows into the next linked text box.

- To link one text box with another, select the first text box, click the Create Link button in the Text group on the Text Box Tools Format tab of the Ribbon, then click the next text box.

- The second text box must not contain text when you establish the link.

- A series of linked text boxes is called a *text box chain*.

- Text flows through the chain in the order in which you link the text boxes, not in the order in which the text boxes appear in the document, or in the order in which the text boxes were created.

- Use the Break Link button to break the link and move all text into the first text box.

Align Drawing Objects

- You can align an object horizontally or vertically relative to the page or to the margins.

- You can also align selected objects relative to each other.

- You can display gridlines to help you align objects if you want.

Copy Objects

- Duplicate an object by using the standard Copy and Paste commands.
- For example, you can use the Copy and Paste buttons on the Home tab of the Ribbon, or you can use the commands on a shortcut menu.

- Duplicating is useful for creating an exact copy of an object, which you can then edit or format.
- When you duplicate a floating object, you cannot control where Word will insert the new copy; drag the copy to move it to its new location.

PROCEDURES

Link Text Boxes

1. Insert text boxes.
2. Select first text box.
3. Click **Text Box Tools Format** tab . . . . Alt +J , X

   Text Group

4. Click **Create Link** button 🔗 . . C

   ✓ *The mouse pointer changes to display:*

   a pouring pitcher . . . .
   when it is over a text box

   or an upright pitcher . . . .
   when it is over anything other than a text box.

5. Click the next text box.
6. Repeat steps 3–5 to link additional text boxes.

Break a Text Box Link

1. Select a linked text box.
2. Click **Text Box Tools Format** tab . . . . Alt +J , X

   Text Group

3. Click **Break Link** button
   ⧉
   . . . . B

Align an Object on the Page

1. Click object to select it.
2. Click **Format** tab:
   - **Drawing Tools Format** tab . . . . Alt +J , D
   - **Text Box Tools Format** tab . . . . Alt +J , X
   - **Picture Tools Format** tab . . . . Alt +J , P
   - **WordArt Tools Format** tab . . . . Alt +J , W

   Arrange Group

3. Click **Align** button 📐 . . . A , A
4. Click alignment option:
   - **Align Left** L
   - **Align Center** C
   - **Align Right** . . . . R
   - **Align Top** . . . . T
   - **Align Middle** . . . . M
   - **Align Bottom** . . . . B

To select to align to the page or the margin:

1. Click object to select it.
2. Click **Format** tab.

   Arrange Group

3. Click **Align** button 📐 . . . A , A
4. Click one of the following:
   - **Align to Page** to align object with the page . . . . P
   - **Align to Margin** to align object with the margins . . . . A

Align an Object with Another Object

1. Select objects to align.

   ✓ *You may select different types of objects, such as shapes and text boxes.*

2. Click **Format** tab.

   Arrange Group

3. Click **Align** button 📐 . . . A , A
4. Click **Align Selected Objects** . . . . O
5. Click **Align** button
   📐 . . . . . . Alt , J , D , A , A

   OR

   Click **Align** button
   📐 . . . . . . Alt , J , X , A , A

6. Click alignment option:
   - **Align Left** L
   - **Align Center** C
   - **Align Right** . . . . R
   - **Align Top** . . . . T
   - **Align Middle** . . . . M
   - **Align Bottom** . . . . B

Display or Hide Gridlines

1. Click object to select it.
2. Click **Format** tab.

   Arrange Group

3. Click **Align** button 📐 . . . A , A
4. Click **View Gridlines** . . . . S

Copy an Object

1. Right-click object to copy.
2. Click **Copy** C
3. Right-click blank area of document.
4. Click **Paste** . . . . P , Enter
5. Position copy as necessary.

   OR

1. Select object to copy.
2. Click **Home** tab . . . . Alt +H

   Clipboard Group

3. Click **Copy** button 📋 C
4. Position insertion point.

   OR

   Deselect selected object.

5. Click **Home** tab . . . . Alt +H

   Clipboard Group

6. Click **Paste** button 📋 . . . V , P

EXERCISE DIRECTIONS

Insert Shapes

1. Start Word, if necessary, open 💿 **15ESSAY**, and save the file as **15ESSAY_xx**.

2. Insert the Explosion 1 shape from the Stars and Banners palette.

3. Resize the shape to 2.25 inches high by 2.75 inches wide.

4. Align the shape left horizontally relative to the margin.

5. Position the shape vertically .5 inch below the page.

6. Copy the object and align the copy on the right horizontally, relative to the margin.

7. Select both shapes and align the tops to each other.

8. Set the text wrapping to Behind Text.

9. Save the document.

Insert Text Boxes

1. Position the insertion point anywhere on the tenth line of the document (within the text *Blogs. Good or Bad?*).

   ✓ *This positions the object's anchor.*

2. Insert a blank text box approximately .75 inch high and 1.75 inches wide.

3. Position the text box horizontally aligned on the left, relative to the margin, and vertically aligned .5 inch below the line where the anchor is located. (Lock the anchor so it does not move.)

   ✓ *If necessary, display hidden characters to see the anchor.*

4. Set the text wrapping for the text box to Top and Bottom.

5. Copy the text box; position the copy centered horizontally relative to the margin and vertically aligned .5 inch below the line.

6. Copy the text box again; position the third copy horizontally aligned on the right, relative to the margin and vertically aligned .5 inch below the line.

7. In first text box—on the left—type the following lines of text in 16-point Arial, centered. Press Enter at the end of each line, and do not worry if you cannot view all of the text within the text box.

   Junior Division

   Grades 1–4

   Middle Division

   Grades 5–9

   Senior Division

   Grades 10–12

   ✓ *Some of the text will not display within the boundaries of the text box.*

8. Link the text box on the left to the text box in the center, and then link the text box in the center to the text box on the right.

9. Save the changes.

Insert a Shape with Added Text

1. Insert the 5-Point Star shape from the Stars and Banners palette.

2. Resize it to 2.75 inches high by 3 inches wide.

3. Center the shape horizontally relative to the page, and position it vertically 4.5 inches below the margin.

4. Set the text wrapping to Top and Bottom.

5. Add the following text to the shape, using 14-point Arial in bold and centered: **Winners will be announced June 1!**

   ✓ *The text should wrap within the shape.*

6. Save the document.

7. Check the spelling and grammar.

8. Display the document in Print Preview. It should look similar to Illustration A.

9. Print the document.

10. Close the file, saving all changes.

Illustration A

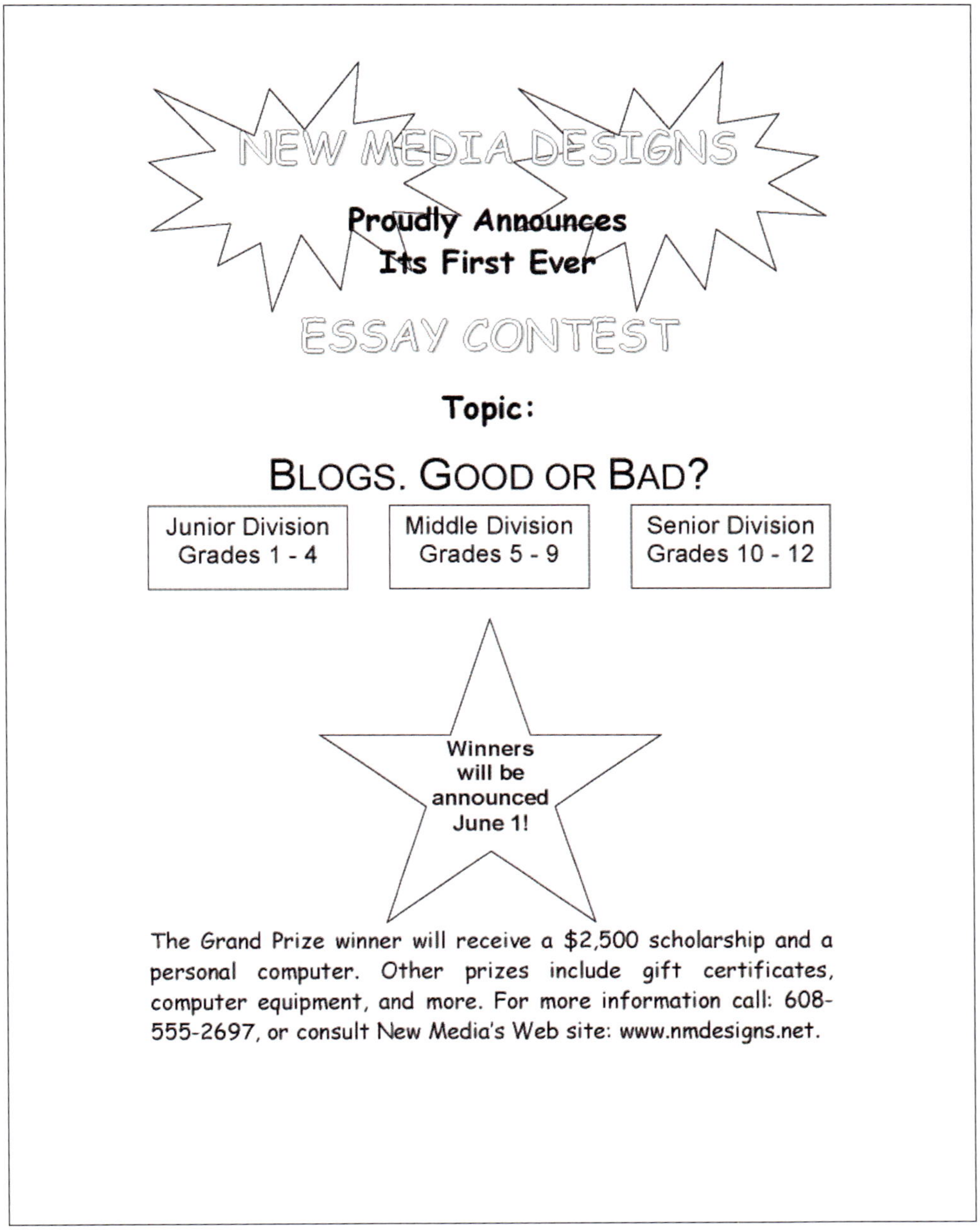

NEW MEDIA DESIGNS

Proudly Announces
Its First Ever

ESSAY CONTEST

Topic:

BLOGS. GOOD OR BAD?

Junior Division	Middle Division	Senior Division
Grades 1 - 4	Grades 5 - 9	Grades 10 - 12

Winners
will be
announced
June 1!

The Grand Prize winner will receive a $2,500 scholarship and a personal computer. Other prizes include gift certificates, computer equipment, and more. For more information call: 608-555-2697, or consult New Media's Web site: www.nmdesigns.net.

ON YOUR OWN

1. Open ⌨ **OWD14_*xx***, the newsletter document you used in the On Your Own section of Exercise 14, or open ◉ **15NEWS**. Save the file as **OWD15_*xx***.

2. Insert at least two linked text boxes in the document, and use them to position and display multiple lines of text. You may want to create a new text box and enter new text, insert a text box around existing text, or use a text box that you already have entered in the document.

3. Position and align the text box(es) for the best visual effect.

4. Copy a shape and position the copy somewhere else in the document.

5. Check spelling and grammar in the document.

6. Preview the document.

7. Adjust column breaks, balance columns, adjust paragraph spacing, and otherwise edit or reformat the document as necessary to make it look professional and appealing.

8. Print the document.

9. Ask a classmate to review the document and make comments and suggestions, paying particular attention to layout and design.

10. Incorporate the suggestions as necessary.

11. Close the document, saving all changes.

Skills Covered

- **Apply Quick Styles to Objects**
- **Format the Shape Outline**
- **Format the Shape Fill**
- **Apply Shadows and 3-D Effects**

Software Skills   Use color and special effects with drawing objects to create professional-looking graphics and pictures. You can change the color and style of the lines used to draw both closed shapes and lines, and you can enhance closed shapes by filling them with color or patterns. Shadows behind an object give a document the appearance of depth, while 3-D effects give depth to the object itself.

Application Skills   In this exercise, you will modify the graphics objects that you used in the flyer announcing the essay contest for New Media Designs. You will change the line color, style, and fill color of one shape, apply shadows to the text boxes, and apply a 3-D effect to the star.

TERMS

3-D effect   An effect applied to an object to make it appear three dimensional.

Fill   Color or patterns used to fill a closed shape.

Line style   The width and appearance of a line used to draw an object.

Outline   The line or border around a shape, text box, or other graphics object.

Shadow   An effect applied to an object to make it appear to be casting a shadow.

NOTES

Apply Quick Styles to Objects

- Most objects have a Styles gallery on their Format tab from which you can select a Quick Style.

- Each Quick Style includes a coordinated set of formatting options, such as fill, outline, shadows, and 3-D effects.

- For pictures, Quick Styles also include the picture shape.

  ✓ *For more on formatting pictures, see Exercise 17.*

- You can modify the Quick Style formatting if you want.

Picture Tools Format tab

Document3 - Microsoft Word — Text Box Tools

Home | Insert | Page Layout | References | Mailings | Review | View | Format

Draw Text Box | Text Direction | Create Link | Break Link — **Text**

Shape Fill | Shape Outline | Change Shape — **Text Box Styles**

Shadow Effects — **Shadow Effects**

3-D Effects — **3-D Effects**

Position | Bring to Front | Send to Back | Text Wrapping | Align | Group | Rotate — **Arrange**

1.74" | 2.39" — **Size**

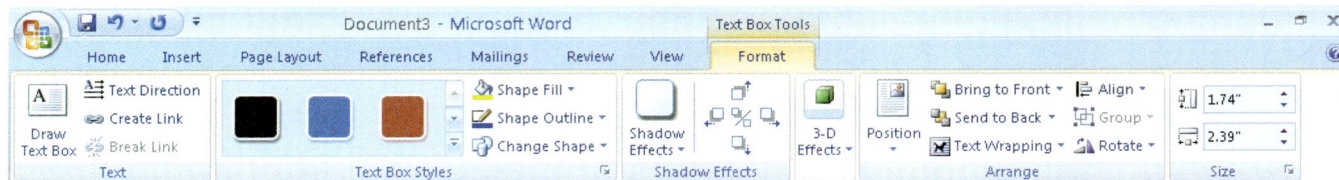

Format the Shape Outline

- By default, drawing objects have a solid single-line border on all sides.

- You can format the **outline** by changing the **line style** and/or color.

- The outline options are similar to those used for tables and paragraphs. For example, you can select a 3 point turquoise dashed border.

- You can modify the outline of a picture by changing the color, style, and weight of its border.

Format the Shape Fill

- You can apply a shape **fill** to fill an object with color, texture, a gradient, or a pattern.

- Fill color options are similar to those available for table cells and paragraphs. For example, you can fill an object with a color or gray shading.

- Remember that color and textures are best used in documents designed to be viewed on-screen, such as Web pages, or documents that will be printed on a color printer.

- You cannot modify the fill of a picture.

Apply Shadows and 3-D Effects

- **Shadows** and **3-D effects** can be applied to any object.

- You can select from a gallery of built-in effects, or you can customize the effects.

- For example, you can customize a shadow effect by changing the shadow color and/or by adjusting the position of the shadow.

- You can customize the 3-D effect by changing the color, lighting, depth, direction, angle, and/or surface of the object.

PROCEDURES

Apply a Quick Style to an Object

1. Click object to select it.
2. Click **Format** tab:
   - **Drawing Tools Format** tab . . . . Alt + J, D
   - **Text Box Tools Format** tab . . . . Alt + J, X
   - **WordArt Tools Format** tab . . . . Alt + J, W

   Shape/Text Box/WordArt Styles Group

3. Click style to apply.

   ✓ If necessary, use scroll arrows to scroll the gallery

   OR

   a. Click **More** button ⊽ . . . . K
   b. Click style to apply . . . . . $←$/$→$/$↑$/$↓$, $Enter$

Apply a Fill

1. Click object to select it.
2. Click **Format** tab.

   Shape/Text Box/WordArt Styles Group

3. Click **Shape Fill** button drop-down arrow . . . . . . S, F

   ✓ To quickly apply color displayed on button, click button instead of drop-down arrow.

4. Click color to apply . . . . $←$/$→$/$↑$/$↓$, $Enter$

   OR

   Click one of the following:
   - **No Fill** to remove current fill. . . . . N
   - **More Fill Colors** to select a custom color . . . . M
   - **Picture** to select options for a picture fill . . . . P
   - **Gradient** to select a gradient fill. . . . . G
   - **Texture** to select a texture fill. . . . . T
   - **Pattern** to select options for a pattern fill . . . . A

Format the Outline

1. Click object to select it.
2. Click **Format** tab.

   Shape/Text Box/WordArt Styles Group

3. Click **Shape Outline** button drop-down arrow . . . S, O

   ✓ To quickly apply color displayed on button, click button instead of drop-down arrow.

4. Click color to
apply . . . . [←]/[→]/[↑]/[↓], [Enter]

OR

Click one of the following:

- ■ **No Outline** to remove
  current outline . . . . [N]
- ■ **More Outline Colors** to
  select a custom color. . . . . [M]
- ■ **Weight** to select a line
  weight . . . . [W]
- ■ **Dashes** to select a dash
  style. . . . . [S]
- ■ **Arrows** to select an arrow
  style. . . . . [R]

✓ *Arrows is only available if you select an
arrow or line shape.*

- ■ **Pattern** to select options
  for a patterned line. . . . . . [A]

Apply Shadows

To turn shadow effect off or on:

1. Click object to select it.
2. Click **Format** tab.

Shadow Effects Group

3. Click **Shadow On/Off**
button ■ . . . . [O]

To apply a shadow effect:

1. Click object to select it.
2. Click **Format** tab.

Shadow Effects Group

3. Click **Shadow Effects**
button ▢ . . . . [V]
4. Click effect to
apply . . . . [←]/[→]/[↑]/[↓], [Enter]

✓ *Click **Shadow Color** to select a color
and/or transparency for the shadow.*

To increase or decrease the width of a shadow:

1. Click object to select it.
2. Click **Format** tab.

Shadow Effects Group

3. Click one of the following:

- ■ **Nudge shadow up** ▣ . . . . [!/1]
- ■ **Nudge shadow left** ▣ . . . [@/2]
- ■ **Nudge shadow right**
  ▣ . . . . [#/3]
- ■ **Nudge shadow down**
  ▣ . . . . [$/4]

Apply 3-D Effects

To turn 3-D effects off or on:

1. Click shape to select it.
2. Click **Drawing Tools Format**
tab . . . . [Alt]+[J], [D]

3-D Effects Group

✓ *If necessary, click **3-D Effects** group
button to display additional commands.*

3. Click **3-D On/Off** button ▣ . . . [O]

To adjust position of 3-D effect:

1. Click shape to select it.
2. Click **Drawing Tools Format**
tab . . . . [Alt]+[J], [D]

3-D Effects Group

✓ *If necessary, click **3-D Effects** group
button to display additional commands.*

3. Click one of the following:

- ■ **Tilt Up** ▣ . . . . [%/5]
- ■ **Tilt Right** ▣ . . . . [&/7]
- ■ **Tilt Left** ▣ . . . . [^/6]
- ■ **Tilt Down** ▣ . . . . [*/8]

To apply a 3-D effect:

1. Click shape to select it.
2. Click **Drawing Tools Format**
tab . . . . [Alt]+[J], [D]

3-D Effects Group

✓ *If necessary, click **3-D Effects** group
button to display additional commands.*

3. Click **3-D Effects** button
▢ . . . . [U]
4. Click effect to
apply . . . . [←]/[→]/[↑]/[↓], [Enter]

EXERCISE DIRECTIONS

1. Start Word, if necessary, and open 📧 **15ESSAY_xx** or open 💿 **16ESSAY**. Save the document as **16ESSAY_xx**.
2. Select the explosion shape in the upper-left corner.
3. Apply the Linear Up Gradient – Accent 1 Quick Style to the shape.
4. Change the outline weight to 3 pt.
5. Select the explosion shape in the upper-right corner.
6. Apply the Linear Up Gradient – Accent 2 Quick Style to the shape.
7. Change the outline weight to 3 pt.
8. Select all three text boxes.

   ✓ *Select the first box, press and hold Shift, then select the other two boxes.*

9. Apply the Drop Shadow Style 4 effect to the selected text boxes.
10. Change the shadow color to the theme color, Blue, Accent 1.
11. Select the star shape.
12. Change the fill color to the theme color Orange, Accent 6, Lighter 60%.
13. Apply the 3-D Style 2.
14. Customize the 3-D effect by clicking the Tilt Right button three times and the Tilt Up button twice.
15. Preview the document. It should look similar to the one in Illustration A.
16. Print the document.
17. Close the document, saving all changes.

Illustration A

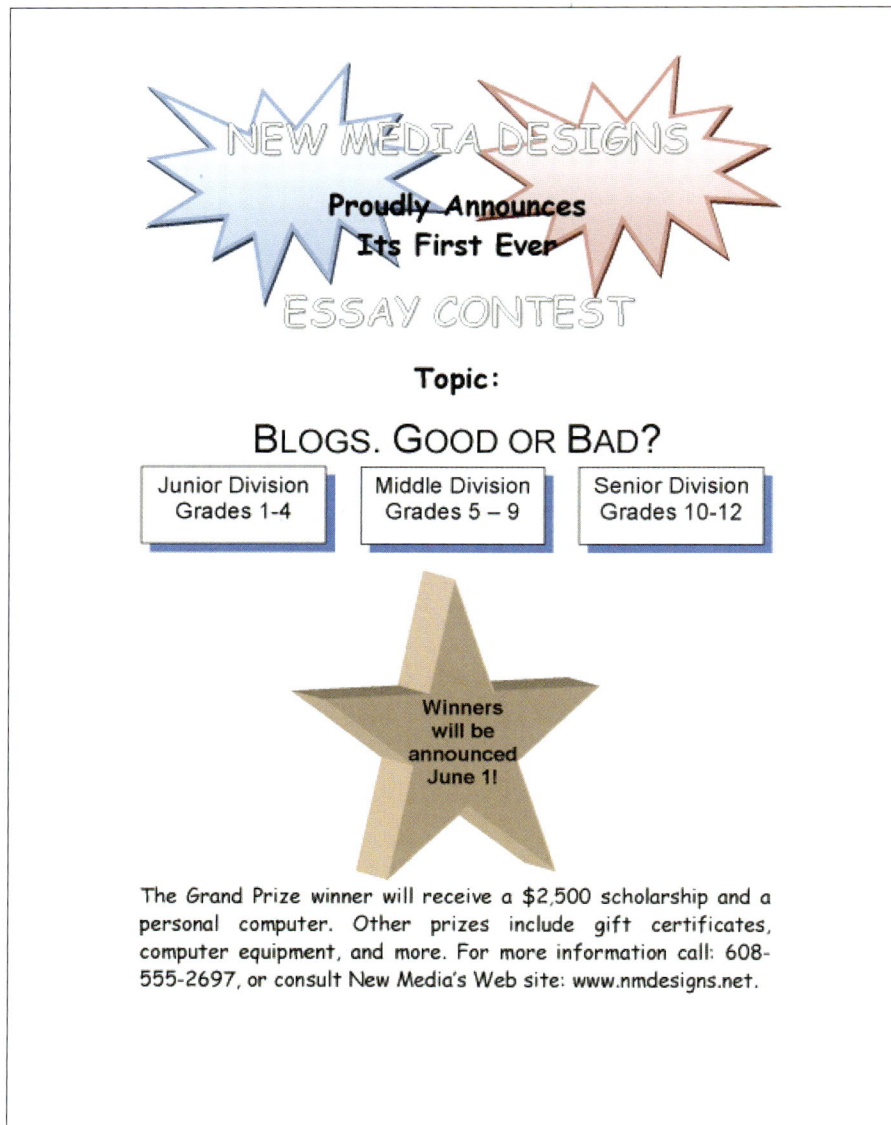

ON YOUR OWN

1. Start Word, and create a new blank document.
2. Save the document as OWD16_*xx*.
3. Type an announcement for an event such as a meeting, birthday, graduation, or performance.
4. Insert graphics objects such as shapes and text boxes.
5. Format the objects using line colors, styles, fills, and effects.
6. Resize and position the objects as necessary.
7. Set text wrapping options.
8. When you achieve the look you want, print the document.
9. Ask a classmate to review the document and offer comments and suggestions.
10. Incorporate the suggestions into the document as necessary.
11. Close the document, saving all changes, and exit Word.

Skills Covered

- **Format Pictures**
- **Compress a Picture**

Software Skills Pictures bring life and reality to a document or publication. Although many commands for formatting and enhancing pictures are the same as for other objects, you can also apply certain types of effects to pictures that you cannot apply to shapes or text boxes. For example, you can adjust the brightness and contrast of pictures, change the picture shape, and compress pictures so they take up less storage space.

Application Skills In this exercise, you use pictures to improve a newsletter for the Liberty Blooms flower shop.

TERMS

Brightness The amount of white or black added to a color. Sometimes called tint.

Compress To reduce the size of something, such as a file.

Contrast The difference between the color values of different parts of an image.

NOTES

Format Pictures

- You can use the buttons in the Adjust group on the Picture Tools Format tab of the Ribbon to change the **brightness** and **contrast** of colors in a picture object.
- You can also adjust the transparency of one color in a picture, or recolor all colors.
- You can use Picture Styles, which are Quick Styles for picture objects, to format a picture with coordinated settings.
- You can also apply a border, shadows, and 3-D effects to a picture.
- You can even change the shape of a picture.
- If you are not happy with the changes, you can reset the picture to its original formatting.

Compress a Picture

- Picture files may be large and therefore take up a lot of disk space or take a long time to transmit electronically.
- You can **compress** a picture to make its file size smaller.
- Compressing reduces the color format of the image, which makes the color take up fewer bits per pixel.
- You can select options to control the final resolution of the compressed picture. For example, if you plan to print the picture, you can select a higher resolution than if you plan to display the picture on-screen or send the picture by e-mail.
- You can compress the selected picture or all pictures in the document.

PROCEDURES

Adjust Brightness

1. Click picture to select it.
2. Click **Picture Tools Format**
   tab . . . . `Alt`+`J`, `P`

   Adjust Group

3. Click **Brightness** button ☀ . . . `B`
4. Click desired
   brightness . . . . `↓`/`↑`, `Enter`

Adjust Contrast

1. Click picture to select it.
2. Click **Picture Tools Format**
   tab . . . . `Alt`+`J`, `P`

   Adjust Group

3. Click **Contrast** button ◑ . . . . . `N`
4. Click desired
   contrast . . . . `↓`/`↑`, `Enter`

Recolor a Picture

1. Click picture to select it.
2. Click **Picture Tools Format**
   tab . . . . `Alt`+`J`, `P`

   Adjust Group

3. Click **Recolor** button 🖼 . . . . . `E`
4. Click desired color
   effect . . . . `↓`/`↑`/`←`/`→`, `Enter`

Set the Transparency of One Color

1. Click picture to select it.
2. Click **Picture Tools Format**
   tab . . . . `Alt`+`J`, `P`

   Adjust Group

3. Click **Recolor** button 🖼 . . . . . `E`
4. Click **Set Transparent Color** . . `S`

   ✓ The mouse pointer changes
   to display the pickup color tool ✎ .

5. In the picture, click the color you
   want to make transparent.

Reset a Picture

1. Click picture to select it.
2. Click **Picture Tools Format**
   tab . . . . `Alt`+`J`, `P`

   Adjust Group

3. Click **Reset Picture** button
   🖼 . . . . `Q`

Compress Pictures

To compress all pictures in the document:

1. Click any picture to select it.
2. Click **Picture Tools Format**
   tab . . . . `Alt`+`J`, `P`

   Adjust Group

3. Click **Compress Pictures** button
   🖼 . . . . `M`
4. Click **OK**. . . . . `Enter`

To compress only the selected picture:

1. Click picture to select it.
2. Click **Picture Tools Format**
   tab . . . . `Alt`+`J`, `P`

   Adjust Group

3. Click **Compress Pictures** button
   🖼 . . . . `M`
4. Click to select **Apply to
   selected pictures only**
   check box . . . . `Alt`+`A`
5. Click **OK**. . . . . `Enter`

To select compression options:

1. Click picture to select it.
2. Click **Picture Tools Format**
   tab . . . . `Alt`+`J`, `P`

   Adjust Group

3. Click **Compress Pictures** button
   🖼 . . . . `M`
4. Click **Options** . . . . `Alt`+`O`

5. Select or deselect compression
   options:
   - **Automatically perform
     basic compression on
     save** . . . . `Alt`+`A`
   - **Delete cropped areas
     of pictures** . . . . `Alt`+`D`
6. Select desired target output
   resolution:
   - **Print (220 ppi)** . . . . . . `Alt`+`P`
   - **Screen (150 ppi)** . . . . `Alt`+`S`
   - **E-mail (96 ppi)** . . . . . `Alt`+`E`
7. Click **OK**. . . . . `Enter`

Apply a Picture Style

1. Click picture to select it.
2. Click **Picture Tools Format**
   tab . . . . `Alt`+`J`, `P`

   Picture Styles Group

3. Click style to apply.

   ✓ If necessary, use scroll arrows to scroll
   the gallery.

   OR

   a. Click **More** button ▼ . . . . `K`
   b. Click style to
      apply . . . . . `←`/`→`/`↑`/`↓`, `Enter`

Format the Picture Border

1. Click picture to select it.
2. Click **Picture Tools Format**
   tab . . . . `Alt`+`J`, `P`

   Picture Styles Group

3. Click **Picture Border** button 🖌▾
   drop-down arrow. . . . . . . `S`, `O`

   ✓ To quickly apply color displayed on
   button, click button instead of drop-
   down arrow.

4. Click color to
apply . . . .⌨←/→/↑/↓, ⌨Enter

OR

Click one of the following:

- **No Outline** to remove current
  outline . . . . ⌨N
- **More Outline Colors** to select
  a custom color . . . . ⌨M
- **Weight** to select a line
  weight . . . . ⌨W
- **Dashes** to select a dash
  style . . . . ⌨S

Apply Picture Effects

1. Click picture to select it.

2. Click **Picture Tools Format**
tab . . . . ⌨Alt+⌨J, ⌨P

Picture Styles Group

3. Click **Picture Effects** button
. . . . ⌨F

4. Click desired category of
effect . . . . ⌨↓/↑, ⌨→

5. Click desired
effect . . . . ⌨↓/↑/←/→, ⌨Enter

Modify the Picture Shape

1. Click picture to select it.

2. Click **Picture Tools Format**
tab . . . . ⌨Alt+⌨J, ⌨P

Picture Styles Group

3. Click **Picture Shape** button
drop-down arrow . . . . ⌨I

4. Click shape to
apply . . . . ⌨↓/↑/←/→

EXERCISE DIRECTIONS

1. Start Word, if necessary, open 🔘 **17BLOOMS**, and save the file as **17BLOOMS_xx**.

2. Position the insertion point in the last section of the document, at the end of the word *Directions*.

3. Use the Clip Art task pane to search for clips with the keyword **Tomato**.

4. Insert the clip shown in Illustration A, and then close the Clip Art task pane.

✓ *If you cannot locate the same clip, select a different clip, or insert the picture file* 🔘 **17FOOD** *supplied with this book.*

5. Set the text wrapping to Square.

6. Lock the anchor for the picture, and position the picture horizontally on the right, relative to the column, and vertically even with the line

7. Resize the picture to approximately 1 inch high (the width should adjust automatically).

✓ *Refer to Illustration A to see the position of the picture.*

8. Increase the contrast by 10%.

9. Apply the Bevel Perspective Picture Style.

10. Select the picture in the top left corner of the page.

11. Apply a 3 point Red, Accent 2 border around the picture.

12. Recolor the picture by applying the Accent color 6 Light color variation.

13. Increase the brightness of the picture by 10%.

14. Compress all of the pictures in the document, using the default settings.

15. Check the spelling and grammar in the document.

16. Display the document in Print Preview. It should look similar to the one in Illustration A.

17. Print the document.

18. Close the file, saving all changes.

Liberty Blooms News

Published by the Liberty Blooms Flower Shop
345 Chestnut Street, Philadelphia, PA 19106

Welcome

Welcome to the first issue of *Liberty Blooms News*, a monthly newsletter for people who visit the Liberty Blooms Flower Shop. The primary goal of this publication is to provide you with news about activities and events that you might find of interest. In addition, we intend to publish class schedules, gardening tips, and general information about related topics.

Liberty Blooms News will be mailed directly to everyone who has registered at our Chestnut Street store. Please contact us with questions and suggestions. We will do our best to address your comments in future issues.

Classes and Seminars

If you are a frequent visitor to Liberty Blooms, you know there is always something going on at 345 Chestnut Street. From flower arranging to cooking with herbs, we try to fill the calendar with interesting and informative activities that the whole family will enjoy.

The following events are scheduled for the coming months. Some events require registration, so please call ahead for more information.

Edible Gardens	May 13
Flower Arranging	May 21
Water Gardens	June 3
Potpourri Designs	June 11

Recipe Showcase

Chicken with Tomatoes and Herbs   *Yield: Four Servings*

Ingredients

8 boneless chicken pieces
1 tablespoon olive oil
10 ½ oz. tomatoes, drained
¾ cup chicken stock
2 teaspoons mixed herbs, chopped
1 ½ oz. black olives, chopped
1 teaspoon sugar
Fresh basil to garnish

Directions

1. Heat oil in large skillet.
2. Add chicken pieces and cook until browned on all sides.
3. Add the tomatoes, stock and mixed herbs and simmer for 30 minutes or until chicken is cooked through.
4. Add the olives and sugar and simmer for an additional 5 minutes.
5. Garnish with fresh basil and serve with rice or pasta.

ON YOUR OWN

1. Start Word and open ⌨ **OWD15_xx**, the newsletter you last worked on in Exercise 15, or open 💿 **17NEWS**. Save the document as **OWD17_xx**.

2. Use formatting to enhance the objects in the newsletter.

3. If there are no pictures in the document, insert at least one new picture.

4. Try different styles, outlines, fills, effects, and picture shapes.

5. Test color, brightness, and contrast options on pictures.

6. Size and position the objects to enhance the document.

7. Select text wrapping that integrates the graphics effectively with the document text. For example, try sending the object behind the text.

8. Preview the document.

9. Adjust breaks and formatting as necessary.

10. Check the spelling and grammar in the document.

11. Preview the document again.

12. Print the document.

13. Ask a classmate to review the report, offering comments and suggestions.

14. Incorporate the suggestions into the document.

15. Close the document, saving all changes.

Skills Covered

- **Adjust Objects**
- **Rotate and Flip Objects**

- **Crop a Picture**

Software Skills   You can manipulate objects to make sure they are positioned the way you want in a document. You can rotate objects around an axis and flip them horizontally or vertically. Many drawing objects have adjustment handles, which you can use to alter the most prominent feature of the object. For example, you can change the mouth on a smiley face from a smile to a frown.

Application Skills   You've been hired to design a logo for Long Shot, Inc., a company that manufactures golf products. The company president wants the logo suitable for use on everything from the letterhead and business cards to golf shirts and umbrellas. In this exercise, you will use text and two graphics objects—one Shape and one clip art picture—to create the logo. You will resize, adjust, and rotate the AutoShape, and you will resize, crop, and flip the clip art picture.

TERMS

Adjustment handle   A small yellow diamond used to alter the most prominent feature of an AutoShape. The mouse pointer is an arrowhead when resting on an adjustment handle.

Crop   Trim or hide one or more edges of a picture.

Flip   Reverse the position of an object.

Outcrop   Use the cropping tool to add a margin around an object.

Rotate   Shift the position of an object in a circular motion around its axis, or center point.

Rotation handle   A small, green circle used to rotate an object on its axis. The mouse pointer looks like a circular arrow when resting on a rotation handle.

NOTES

Adjust Objects

- Some—but not all—AutoShapes have one or more **adjustment handles** that look like a small yellow diamond.

- You can drag the adjustment handle to alter the most prominent feature of the shape.

- For example, you can drag an adjustment handle on a block arrow AutoShape to change the width of the arrow body or the length of the arrowhead.

- When the mouse pointer touches an adjustment handle, it looks like an arrowhead.

Some shapes have adjustment handles and/or rotation handles

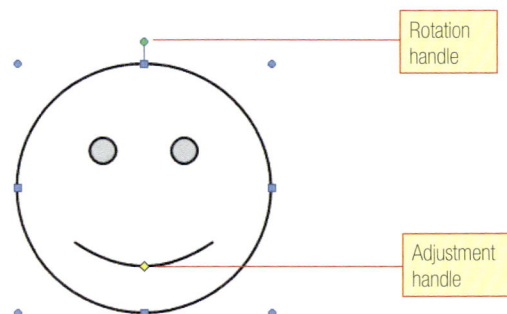

Rotation handle

Adjustment handle

Rotate and Flip Objects

- You can **rotate** an object to the left or right around its center point, or axis.

- If a selected object has a green **rotation handle**, you can drag the handle to freely rotate the object in either direction.

    ✓ *Hold down the Shift key while you drag to rotate in 15 degree increments.*

- When the mouse pointer touches the rotation handle, it looks like a circular arrow.

- Alternatively, use commands in the Arrange group to rotate the object left or right by 90 degrees.

- You can also use the Size dialog box or Size tab in the Format *object* dialog box to set a precise rotation amount for the selected object, relative to its original position.

    - For example, enter 90 to rotate the object 90 degrees—or ¼ turn—to the right; enter 270 to rotate the object 270 degrees—or ¾ turn.

    - Enter negative values to rotate the object to the left. For example, -90 rotates the object to the same position as 270.

- **Flip** an object to reverse it, or create a mirror image.

- You can flip an object horizontally or vertically.

- You cannot rotate or flip a text box.

Crop a Picture

- **Crop** a picture to remove or trim one or more of the edges.

- You can crop from the left, right, top, and/or bottom.

- Cropping hides the edges, but does not permanently delete them.

    ✓ *You can permanently delete cropped edges when you compress a picture. Select the Delete cropped areas of pictures check box in the Compression Options dialog box.*

- You can reset a cropped picture to its original appearance.

- If you want to add a margin around a picture, you can **outcrop** it.

PROCEDURES

Adjust an Object

1. Click object to select it.
2. Position the mouse pointer over yellow adjustment handle.

    ✓ *When pointer is positioned correctly, it resembles the outline of an arrowhead* ▷.

3. Drag handle as necessary to change the shape of the object.
4. Release mouse button when object is adjusted as desired.

Rotate an Object by Dragging

1. Click object to select it.
2. Position the mouse pointer over green rotation handle.

    ✓ *When pointer is positioned correctly, it resembles a circular arrow* 🔄.

3. Drag handle clockwise or counter-clockwise.
4. Release mouse button when object is positioned as desired.

Rotate or Flip an Object

1. Click object to select it.
2. Click **Format** tab:
    - **Drawing Tools Format** tab . . . . Alt + J , D
    - Click **Picture Tools Format** tab . . . . Alt + J , P
    - **WordArt Tools Format** tab . . . . Alt + J , W

    Arrange Group

3. Click **Rotate** button ⬒ ▾ . . . . A , Y
4. Click desired option:
    - **Rotate Right 90°** . . . . R
    - **Rotate Left 90°** L
    - **Flip Vertical** V
    - **Flip Horizontal** . . . . H

Rotate or Flip an Object Precisely

1. Click object to select it.
2. Click **Format** tab.

    Arrange Group

3. Click **Rotate** button ⬒ ▾ . . . . A , Y
4. Click **More Rotation Options** . . . . M
5. Click **Rotation** increment box . . . . Alt + T
6. Enter rotation amount.

    ✓ *Enter a positive value to rotate to the right; enter a negative value to rotate to the left.*

7. Click **OK** . . . . Enter

Reset a Picture Object

1. Click picture to select it.
2. Click **Picture Tools Format**
   tab . . . . Alt + J , P

   Arrange Group

3. Click **Rotate** button
   |⟁ ▾| . . . . A , Y
4. Click **More Rotation**
   Options . . . . M
5. Click **Reset** . . . . Alt + S
6. Click **OK** . . . . Enter

Crop a Picture

1. Click picture to select it.
2. Click **Picture Tools Format**
   tab . . . . Alt + J , P

   Size Group

3. Click **Crop** button 🖼 C

   ✓ *Crop handles display on side and corners of picture.*

4. Drag a crop handle in to crop picture.

   OR

   Drag a crop handle out to outcrop picture.

5. Click **Crop** button 🖼 to turn
   the feature off C

   OR

   Click outside the picture object.

EXERCISE DIRECTIONS

1. Start Word, if necessary, create a new document, and save it as **18LOGO_xx**.
2. Press Enter twice to insert blank lines.
3. Using a sans serif font in a large font size in Dark Blue, Text 2 (72-point Arial Rounded MT is used in the illustration), type **LSI**.
4. Insert the 8-Point Star AutoShape from the Stars and Banners palette.
5. Resize the star so it is .75 inch high and wide.
6. Drag the adjustment handle toward the center of the star to make the points thinner (refer to the illustration).
7. Rotate the star 25 degrees to the right.
8. Position the star above the *I* in *LSI* as shown in the illustration.

   ✓ *The absolute position shown in the illustration is 1.07 inch to the right of the column and -.01 inch below the paragraph.*

9. Apply the Center Gradient – Accent 1 style to the shape.
10. Open the Clip Art task pane and search for pictures related to golf.
11. Locate the picture of the golf ball and club head shown in the illustration.

    ✓ *If you cannot locate the picture as shown, insert the file*
    💿 **18GOLF** *supplied with this book.*

12. Insert the clip into the **18LOGO_xx** document.
13. Flip the picture horizontally.
14. Resize the picture so it is 1.5 inches high (the width will adjust automatically).
15. Crop the picture about .5 inch from the left side only, just far enough to remove the tee and ball (refer to the illustration).
16. Recolor the picture using the Accent color 1 Light variation.
17. Adjust the brightness of the picture to +20%.
18. Set the text wrapping for the picture to Behind Text.
19. Position the picture so the bottom half of the *S* in *LSI* is sitting in the flat part of the club head.

    ✓ *The absolute position shown is .26 inch to the right of the column and .3 inch below the paragraph.*

20. Preview the document. It should look similar to the one in Illustration A.
21. Make any adjustments necessary to the size and position of the objects.
22. Print the document.
23. Close the document, saving all changes.

Illustration A

ON YOUR OWN

1. Start Word and create a new document. Save the document as OWD18_xx.

2. Use graphics objects and text to design a logo for yourself, a club, or an organization.

3. Adjust, rotate, and flip the objects as necessary.

4. Resize and position the objects as necessary.

5. Preview the document and then print it.

6. Ask a classmate to review the document and offer suggestions and comments.

7. Incorporate the suggestions and comments into the logo as necessary.

8. Close the document, saving all changes, and exit Word.

Skills Covered

- **Group and Ungroup Objects**
- **Layer Objects with Other Objects or Text**

Software Skills   Integrate drawing objects with text to illustrate and enhance documents. Objects can be layered with each other and with text to create different effects. For example, you can design a letterhead with text layered on top of a logo created from drawing objects. You can group objects together to create one complete picture, and ungroup objects to edit them individually.

Application Skills   In this exercise, create a version of the logo for Long Shot, Inc. that does not include a picture, by layering a text box and a shape and then grouping them together. You will then copy the entire logo into a memo document.

TERMS

Group   Select multiple objects and combine them into a single object.

Layer   Position objects and/or text so they overlap on the page.

Regroup   Group objects that have been separated again.

Ungroup   Separate a grouped object into individual objects.

NOTES

Group and Ungroup Objects

- **Group** objects together to create a single unified object.
- Sizing handles are displayed around the entire grouped object, not around the individual objects.
- The entire group has a single rotation handle.
- All changes are made to the entire group.
- You can group shapes with other shapes, text boxes with other text boxes, or text boxes with shapes.
- You cannot include a picture object in a group.
- You can **ungroup** the objects in order to edit them individually.
- After you ungroup objects that have been grouped, you can use the **Regroup** command to group them again without having to select them all again.

Group multiple objects into a single unit

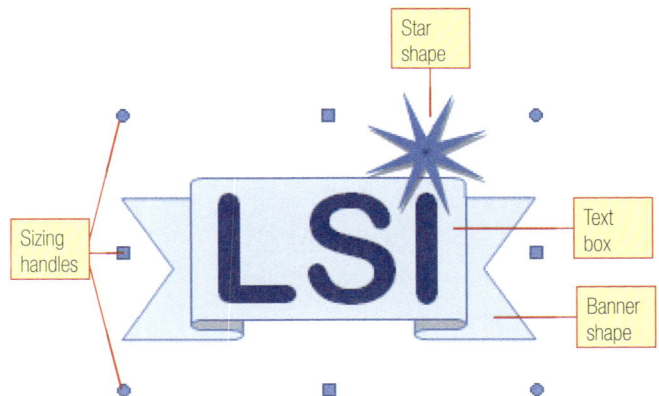

Star shape

Text box

Banner shape

Sizing handles

103

Layer Objects with Other Objects or Text

- **Layer** drawing objects with other objects or with document text to control the order in which text and objects overlap in a document.

- Elements layered in front of other elements appear to be on the top; elements layered behind—or in back of—other elements appear to be on the bottom.

- All text is always in the same layer. However, you can layer objects in front of or behind the text layer.

  - Layering an object in front of text is the same as setting the text wrapping for the object to the In Front of Text setting.

  - Layering an object behind text is the same as setting the text wrapping for the object to the Behind Text setting.

- Objects in layers can be rearranged layer by layer using the Bring Forward command to move an object forward one layer at a time or the Send Backward command to move an object backward one layer at a time.

- The Send to Back command lets you move the selected object in back of all other objects.

- The Bring to Front command lets you bring an object in front of all other objects.

- Use the Send Behind Text or Bring in Front of Text commands to layer objects that combine text and graphics, such as text boxes and AutoShapes that have added text.

PROCEDURES

Group Objects

1. Click first object to select.
2. Press and hold [Shift].
3. Click next object to select.
4. Repeat step 3 to select additional objects.
5. Release [Shift].
6. Click **Format** tab:
   - **Drawing Tools Format** tab . . . . [Alt]+[J], [D]
   - **Text Box Tools Format** tab . . . . [Alt]+[J], [X]
   - **WordArt Tools Format** tab . . . . [Alt]+[J], [W]

   ✓ *If you select a combination of objects, all Format tabs become available.*

   Arrange Group

7. Click **Group** button 📷▾ . . . . [A], [G]
8. Click **Group** . . . . [G]

Ungroup Objects

1. Click to select grouped objects.
2. Click **Format** tab.

   Arrange Group

3. Click **Group** button 📷▾ . . . . [A], [G]
4. Click **Ungroup** . . . . [U]

Layer Objects with Other Objects or Text

1. Click object to select it.
2. Click **Format** tab.

   Arrange Group

3. Click **Bring to Front** button drop-down arrow 📑 . . . . [A], [F]
4. Click one of the following:
   - **Bring to Front** . . . . [R]
   - **Bring Forward** . . . . [F]
   - **Bring in Front of Text** . . . . [T]

   ✓ *To quickly move the selected object to the front layer, click the **Bring to Front** button 📑 .*

OR

5. Click **Send to Back** button drop-down arrow 📑 . . . . [A], [E]
6. Click one of the following:
   - **Send to Back** . . . . [K]
   - **Send Backward** . . . . [B]
   - **Send Behind Text** . . . . [H]

   ✓ *To quickly move the selected object to the back layer, click the **Send to Back** button 📑 .*

EXERCISE DIRECTIONS

1. Start Word, if necessary, open ⊙ **19LOGO**, and save the document as **19LOGO_*xx***. The document contains a text box and two shapes that you will use to create the logo.

2. Select the text box and set it to have no outline and no fill.

3. Select the star shape and position it above the *I* in *LSI* by setting the absolute position to 1.44 inches to the right of the column and 0 inches below the paragraph.

4. Select the banner shape and send it behind the text.

5. Set the position for the banner shape behind the text box, as shown in Illustration A.

   ✓ *In the illustration, the absolute position is .91 inch to the right of the page and .42 inch below the paragraph.*

6. Select the banner and the text box and group them together.

   ✓ *If you have trouble selecting objects, use the Select Objects tool in the Editing group on the Home tab of the Ribbon: Click the Home tab, click the Select button, then click Select Objects.*

7. Send the group—the banner shape and the text box—behind the star shape.

8. Select the group and then select the star shape, and group them together.

9. Position the object in the top center relative to the margins. The page should look similar to Illustration A.

10. Select the grouped object and copy it to the Clipboard.

11. Open ⊙ **19MEMO**.

12. Save the file as **19MEMO_*xx***.

13. Paste the logo object into the document.

14. Position the object in the bottom center of the page, relative to the margins.

15. Preview the memo document. It should look similar to the one in Illustration B.

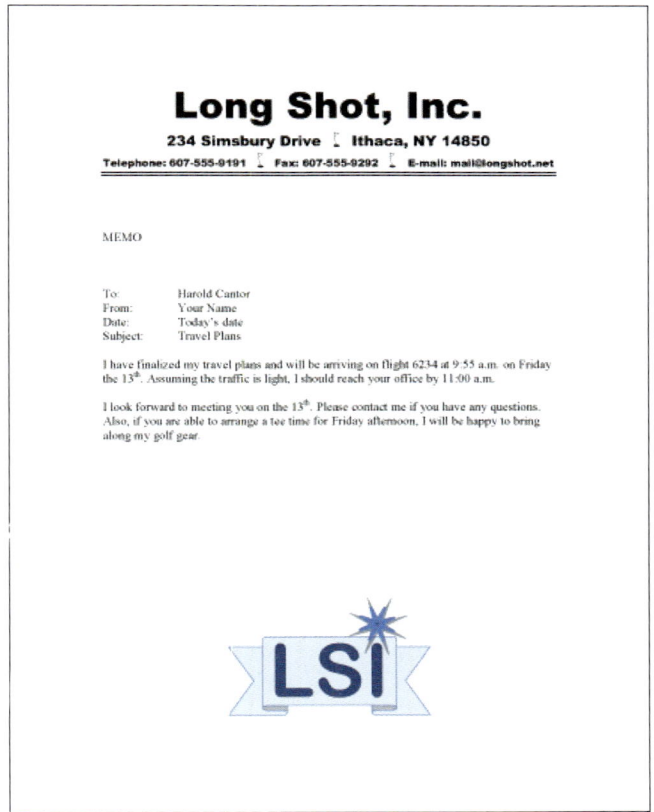

16. If necessary, make adjustments to the position of the logo.

17. Print the document.

18. Close all open documents, saving all changes.

Illustration A

Illustration B

ON YOUR OWN

1. Start Word if necessary and create a new document.
2. Save the file as OWD19_*xx*.
3. Design a letterhead or logo for a club, business, or organization. Create the graphic by layering objects and text.
4. Make use of line styles, colors, fills, and effects to achieve the look you want. Group objects to apply formatting to all of them.
5. If necessary, rotate, flip, and adjust objects so they look good on the page.
6. When you are satisfied with the document, print it.
7. Ask a classmate to review the document and make comments and suggestions.
8. Incorporate the comments and suggestions as necessary.
9. Assess the graphic and decide whether or not you want to include it in your employment portfolio as an example of achievement. If so, print a copy and add it to the portfolio.
10. Close the document, saving all changes, and exit Word.

Skills Covered

- **Create WordArt**
- **WordArt Text**

- **WordArt Shapes and Formatting**

Software Skills   Use WordArt to transform text into artwork for letterheads, logos, brochures, and other documents. WordArt lets you create special effects using any text that you type. You can stretch characters, rotate them, reverse direction, and even arrange the text in shapes such as circles, waves, or arcs.

Application Skills   Liberty Blooms is opening a new store. In this exercise, you will design a flyer announcing the grand opening.

TERMS

WordArt   A feature of Word used to transform text into a drawing object.

NOTES

Create WordArt

- **WordArt** is an Office feature that you use to transform text into a drawing object.
- By default, WordArt objects are inserted in line with text, but you can change the text wrapping to make them float.

- The WordArt Gallery includes a selection of styles you can quickly apply to any text
- You can customize WordArt objects to achieve the specific results you want.

WordArt Gallery

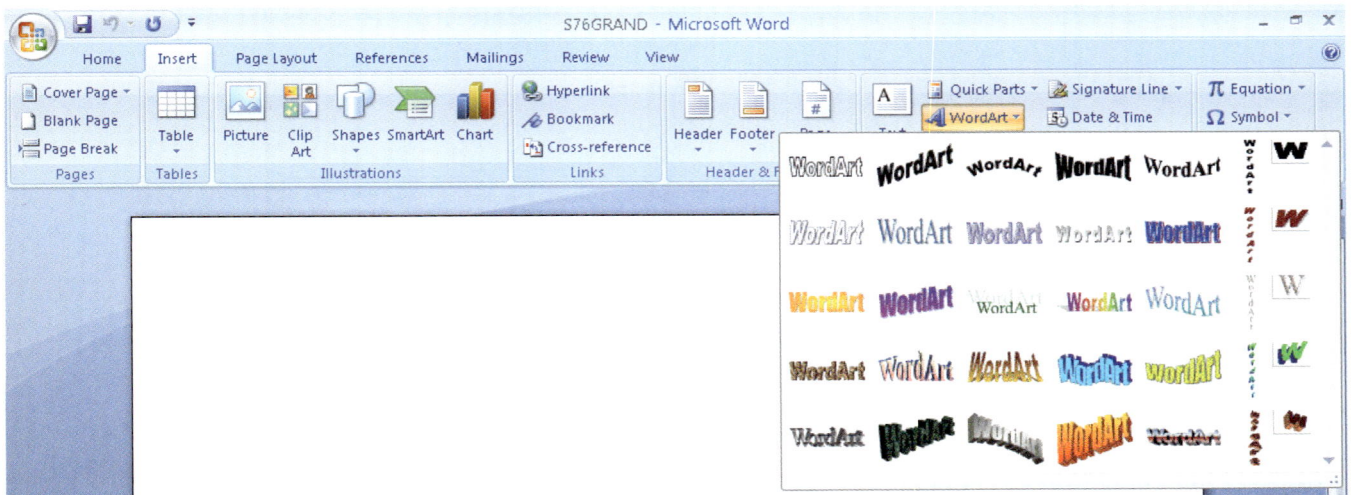

WordArt Text

- You enter WordArt text when you create the Word-Art object.

- The placeholder text is *Your Text Here,* which is replaced by any text you type.

- You can select text already typed in the document to use as the WordArt text.

- You can edit the text displayed in a WordArt object at any time.

- You can change the font, font size, and font style used for WordArt text.

WordArt Shapes and Formatting

- The WordArt styles in the WordArt Gallery include shape and formatting characteristics.

- When you select a WordArt object, the WordArt Tools Format tab displays on the Ribbon, so you can edit and format the object.

- You can quickly apply a set of formatting characteristics to the WordArt object by selecting a style from the WordArt Styles gallery.

- Alternatively, you can manually format the WordArt object.

- Many of the formatting commands are similar to those used to format other objects, such as shapes and text boxes.

- For example, you can set text wrapping; resize, position, and align the WordArt object; or change the outline or fill. You can also rotate and adjust a WordArt object or apply shadows and 3-D effects.

- Some formatting commands are unique to Word-Art. For example, you can change the shape of a WordArt object by selecting a different shape from the WordArt Change Shape palette.

- You can also format the text in the WordArt object using buttons in the Text group on the Format tab.
  - You can make all characters the same height.
  - You can align WordArt text vertically.
  - You can align WordArt text horizontally.
  - You can adjust the spacing between characters in a WordArt object.

Enter WordArt Text

PROCEDURES

Create WordArt

1. Click **Insert** tab . . . . [Alt]+[N]

   [Text Group]

2. Click **WordArt** button drop-down arrow ⬛ WordArt ▾ . . . . [W]
3. Click desired WordArt style . . . . [↑]/[↓]/[←]/[→], [Enter]
4. Type WordArt text.
5. Click **OK**.

WordArt Text

To edit WordArt text:

1. Click object to select it.
2. **WordArt Tools Format** tab . . . . [Alt]+[J], [W]

   [Text Group]

3. Click **Edit Text** button ✐ABC . . [E]
4. Type new text.
5. Click **OK**.

To format WordArt text:

1. Click object to select it.
2. **WordArt Tools Format** tab . . . . [Alt]+[J], [W]

   [Text Group]

3. Click **Edit Text** button ✐ABC . . [E]
4. Click **Font** drop-down arrow . . . . [Alt]+[F]
5. Click desired font . . . . . [↑]/[↓], [Enter]
6. Click **Size** drop-down arrow . . . . [Alt]+[S]
7. Click desired size . . . . . [↑]/[↓], [Enter]
8. Click Font style buttons as necessary:

   - **Bold** [B] . . . . [Alt]+[B]
   - **Italic** [I] . . . . [Alt]+[I]

9. Click **OK**.

Change WordArt Shape

1. Click object to select it.
2. **WordArt Tools Format** tab . . . . [Alt]+[J], [W]

   [WordArt Styles Group]

3. Click **Change Shape** button A▾ . . . . [I]
4. Click shape to apply . . . . [←]/[→]/[↑]/[↓], [Enter]

Set Even Character Height

1. Click object to select it.
2. **WordArt Tools Format** tab . . . . [Alt]+[J], [W]

   [Text Group]

3. Click **Even Height** button Aa . . . . [A], [H]

   ✓ *Repeat to return text to normal height.*

Align WordArt Text Vertically

1. Click object to select it.
2. **WordArt Tools Format** tab . . . . [Alt]+[J], [W]

   [Text Group]

3. Click **WordArt Vertical Text** button ꜟ . . . . [A], [V]

   ✓ *Repeat to return text to normal height.*

Adjust Character Spacing

1. Click object to select it.
2. **WordArt Tools Format** tab . . . . [Alt]+[J], [W]

   [Text Group]

3. Click **Spacing** button AV . . . . [A], [S]
4. Click one of the following options:

   - **Very Tight** . . . . [I]
   - **Tight** . . . . [T]
   - **Normal** . . . . [N]
   - **Loose** . . . . [L]
   - **Very Loose** . . . . [V]
   - **Kern Character Pairs** . . . . . [K]

Align WordArt Text Horizontally

1. Click object to select it.
2. **WordArt Tools Format** tab . . . . [Alt]+[J], [W]

   [Text Group]

3. Click **Align Text** button ≡▾ . . . . [A], [L]
4. Click one of the following options:

   - **Left Align** . . . . [L]
   - **Center** . . . . [C]
   - **Right Align** . . . . [R]
   - **Word Justify** . . . . [W]
   - **Letter Justify** . . . . [T]
   - **Stretch Justify** . . . . [S]

EXERCISE DIRECTIONS

Enter Document Text

1. Start Word, if necessary, create a new document, and save the document as **20GRAND_*xx***.

2. Using a 36-point script or handwriting font, such as Freestyle Script, type the following five lines of text:

   Announces
   The
   Grand Opening
   of a
   New Store

3. Center the five lines of text horizontally, and change the spacing to leave only 6 points of space after each line.

Insert WordArt

1. Make sure there is no text selected in the document and then insert a WordArt object.

2. Select the WordArt style 20, which is in the fourth row of the second column (refer to Illustration A).

3. Using a 40-point sans serif font, such as Tahoma, enter the WordArt text **Liberty Blooms**, and then click OK to create the object.

4. Set Text Wrapping to Top and Bottom.

5. Resize the WordArt object to approximately 1 inch high and 5.5 inches wide.

6. Set the character spacing to Very Tight.

7. Center-align the object horizontally, relative to the margins.

8. Position the object vertically .5 inch below the margin.

9. Set paragraph formatting to leave 54 points of space before the first line of the text *Announces*.

10. Create another WordArt object using the arc style that is in the first row of the third column.

11. Using a 28-point serif font, such as Times New Roman, type the following address and URL information on three separate lines, and then click OK to insert the object into the document:

    345 Chestnut Street
    Philadelphia, PA
    http://www.libertyblooms.net

12. Change the text wrapping to Top and Bottom.

13. Change the WordArt object shape to Button (Curve).
    a. Select the object.
    b. Click the Change Shape button in the WordArt Styles group.
    c. Click the Button (Curve) shape.

    ✓ *Use ScreenTips to identify the names of the shapes.*

14. Set the size of the WordArt object to approximately 2.5 by 3.25 inches.

15. Position the object in the bottom center of the page.

Insert a Shape and Clip Art

1. Insert the Explosion 1 AutoShape from the Stars and Banners palette.

2. Resize the shape to approximately 1.75 by 1.75 inches, and position it in the upper-left corner of the page.

3. Apply the Linear Up Gradient – Accent 6 style to the shape, and set the text wrapping to Behind Text.

4. Search for clip art images of roses.

5. Locate the image shown in Illustration A and insert it into the document.

    ✓ *If you cannot locate the image, select a comparable image, or use the* 🔘 **20ROSE** *file provided with this book.*

6. Resize the picture height to approximately 2.0 inches— the width should adjust automatically—and set the text wrap for the picture to Behind Text.

7. Align the picture on the left horizontally, relative to the margins, and 4 inches below the margin vertically.

8. Create a copy of the picture, or insert a second copy.

9. Flip the copy horizontally.

10. Align the copy on the right horizontally, relative to the margins, and 4 inches below the margin vertically.

11. Apply an art page border of flowers around the page.

12. Preview the document. It should look similar to Illustration A.

13. If necessary, make adjustments to the size and position of all objects in the document.

14. Print the document.

15. Close the document, saving all changes.

Illustration A

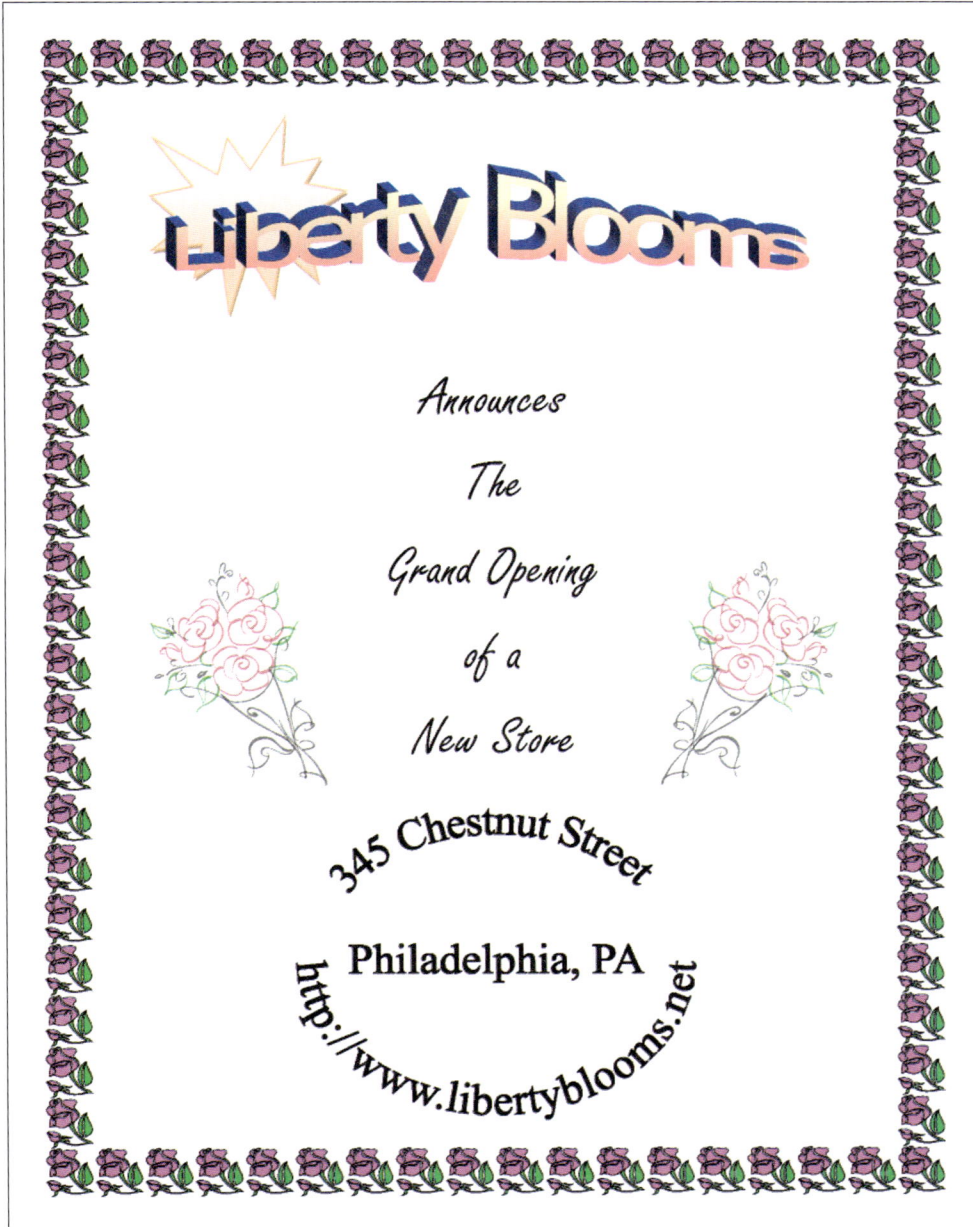

Liberty Blooms

Announces

The

Grand Opening

of a

New Store

345 Chestnut Street

Philadelphia, PA

http://www.libertyblooms.net

ON YOUR OWN

1. Start Word and create a new document.
2. Save the document as OWD20_*xx*.
3. Use WordArt to create a logo for a business, club, or organization to which you belong.
4. Try different WordArt Shapes.
5. Try different formatting such as Even Height, Character Spacing, or Vertical Text.
6. Try applying effects such as 3-D or Shadows to the WordArt object.
7. See how rotating or adjusting the WordArt object affects its appearance.
8. When you are satisfied with the result, print the document.
9. Ask a classmate to review the document and offer comments and suggestions.
10. Incorporate the comments and suggestions into the document as necessary.
11. Close the document, saving all changes, and exit Word.

Exercise | 21

Skills Covered

- **Watermarks**

Software Skills   Place a watermark on almost any document to make an impression on readers, convey an idea, or provide a consistent theme. For example, a watermark on corporate stationery can create a corporate identity. Watermarks can be fun or serious, barely noticeable or strikingly bold. You can save a watermark as part of a template and use it on new documents.

Application Skills   Long Shot, Inc. is growing by leaps and bounds. To fill job vacancies, it is hosting an open house and career fair. In this exercise, you will create a notice announcing the event. You use a picture to create a watermark on the document.

TERMS

Watermark   A pale or semitransparent graphic object positioned behind text in a document.

NOTES

Watermarks

- Insert text or graphics objects as a **watermark** to provide a background image for text-based documents.

- In Word 2007, you can select a watermark from the Watermark gallery in the Page Background group on the Page Layout tab.

- You can also create a custom watermark using the options in the Printed Watermark dialog box.

- A watermark may be a graphics object, such as clip art, a text box, WordArt, or a shape.

- You can also create a watermark from text.

- To achieve a watermark effect, the inserted object should be centered horizontally and vertically on the page, and its color should be adjusted to make it appear faded, or washed out.

- Watermarks are usually inserted into the document header so that they automatically appear on every page, and so that they are not affected by changes made to the document content.

- To view or edit the watermark, use Print Preview, Full Screen Reading View, or display headers and footers.

- When you use the Printed Watermark dialog box, Word 2007 automatically sizes, formats, and positions the object.

- If you manually create a watermark, you must size, position, and format it yourself.

- Watermarks are a nice feature to add to a template because every document based on the template will display the same watermark.

PROCEDURES

Insert a Built-In Watermark

1. Click **Page Layout** tab . . . <kbd>Alt</kbd>+<kbd>P</kbd>

   Page Background Group

2. Click **Watermark** button
   . . . . <kbd>P</kbd>, <kbd>W</kbd>

3. Click built-in watermark to insert . . . . <kbd>↑</kbd>/<kbd>↓</kbd>/<kbd>←</kbd>/<kbd>→</kbd>

Automatically Create a Watermark from a Picture File

1. Click **Page Layout** tab . . . <kbd>Alt</kbd>+<kbd>P</kbd>

   Page Background Group

2. Click **Watermark** button
   . . . . <kbd>P</kbd>, <kbd>W</kbd>

3. Click **Custom Watermark** . . . . <kbd>W</kbd>

4. Click **Picture watermark** option button . . . . <kbd>I</kbd>

5. Click **Select Picture** . . . . . <kbd>Alt</kbd>+<kbd>P</kbd>

6. Locate and select desired picture file.

7. Click **Insert** . . . . <kbd>Alt</kbd>+<kbd>S</kbd>

8. Click **Scale** drop-down arrow . . . . <kbd>Alt</kbd>+<kbd>L</kbd>

9. Select size as a percentage of the original picture size . . . . <kbd>↑</kbd>/<kbd>↓</kbd>, <kbd>Enter</kbd>

   ✓ *Select Auto (the default) to have Word automatically size the object to fit on the page.*

10. Click to select **Washout** check box . . . . <kbd>Alt</kbd>+<kbd>W</kbd>

    ✓ *A check mark indicates the option is already selected.*

11. Click **OK** . . . . <kbd>Enter</kbd>

Automatically Create a Watermark from Text

1. Click **Page Layout** tab . . . <kbd>Alt</kbd>+<kbd>P</kbd>

   Page Background Group

2. Click **Watermark** button
   . . . . <kbd>P</kbd>, <kbd>W</kbd>

3. Click **Custom Watermark** . . . . <kbd>W</kbd>

4. Click **Text watermark** option button . . . . <kbd>X</kbd>

5. Click **Text** drop-down arrow . . . . <kbd>Alt</kbd>+<kbd>T</kbd>

6. Select built-in text option . . . . <kbd>↑</kbd>/<kbd>↓</kbd>, <kbd>Enter</kbd>

   OR

   a. Type desired text.

   b. Press **Enter** . . . . <kbd>Enter</kbd>

7. Click **Font** drop-down arrow . . . . <kbd>Alt</kbd>+<kbd>F</kbd>

8. Select font . . . . <kbd>↑</kbd>/<kbd>↓</kbd>, <kbd>Enter</kbd>

9. Click **Size** drop-down arrow . . . . <kbd>Alt</kbd>+<kbd>S</kbd>

10. Select font size . . . . . . <kbd>↑</kbd>/<kbd>↓</kbd>, <kbd>Enter</kbd>

11. Click **Color** drop-down arrow . . . . <kbd>Alt</kbd>+<kbd>C</kbd>

12. Select color . . . <kbd>↑</kbd>/<kbd>↓</kbd>/<kbd>→</kbd>/<kbd>←</kbd>, <kbd>Enter</kbd>

13. Click one of the following layout options:

    - **Diagonal** . . . . <kbd>Alt</kbd>+<kbd>D</kbd>
    - **Horizontal** . . . . <kbd>Alt</kbd>+<kbd>H</kbd>

14. Click **OK**.

Remove an Automatic Watermark

1. Click **Page Layout** tab . . . <kbd>Alt</kbd>+<kbd>P</kbd>

   Page Background Group

2. Click **Watermark** button
   . . . . <kbd>P</kbd>, <kbd>W</kbd>

3. Click **Remove Watermark** . . . . <kbd>R</kbd>

Manually Create a Watermark from a Picture

1. Click **Insert** tab . . . . <kbd>Alt</kbd>+<kbd>N</kbd>

   Header & Footer Group

2. Click **Header** button . . . . . <kbd>H</kbd>

3. Click **Edit Header** . . . . <kbd>E</kbd>

4. Click **Insert** tab . . . . <kbd>Alt</kbd>+<kbd>N</kbd>

   Illustrations Group

5. Click **Picture** button . . . . . <kbd>P</kbd>

   ✓ *The Insert Picture dialog box displays.*

6. Navigate to location where picture file is stored.

7. Click picture to insert.

8. Click **Insert** . . . . <kbd>Alt</kbd>+<kbd>S</kbd>

9. Position and size picture as desired.

10. Click **Picture Tools Format** tab . . . . <kbd>Alt</kbd>+<kbd>J</kbd>, <kbd>P</kbd>

    Adjust Group

11. Click **Recolor** button . . . . . <kbd>E</kbd>

12. Under Color Modes, click **Washout** . . . . <kbd>↓</kbd>, <kbd>←</kbd>, <kbd>←</kbd>, <kbd>Enter</kbd>

13. Click **Picture Tools Format** tab . . . . <kbd>Alt</kbd>+<kbd>J</kbd>, <kbd>P</kbd>

    Arrange Group

14. Click **Text Wrapping** button
    . . . . <kbd>T</kbd>, <kbd>W</kbd>

15. Click **Behind Text** . . . . <kbd>D</kbd>

16. Click **Header and Footer Tools Design** tab . . . . <kbd>Alt</kbd>+<kbd>J</kbd>, <kbd>H</kbd>

    Close Group

17. Click **Close Header and Footer** button . . . . <kbd>C</kbd>

Manually Create a Watermark from a Graphics Object

1. Click **Insert** tab . . . . ⌊Alt⌋+⌊N⌋

    Header & Footer Group

2. Click **Header** button 📄 . . . . ⌊H⌋
3. Click **Edit Header** . . . . ⌊E⌋
4. Click **Insert** tab . . . . ⌊Alt⌋+⌊N⌋

    Illustrations Group

5. Insert desired object.

    ✓ *For example, insert a shape, a text box, or WordArt.*

6. Format object fill and outline using light colors or gray shading.
7. Size and position object, as desired.
8. Layer object behind text.
9. Click **Header and Footer Tools Design** tab . . . . ⌊Alt⌋+⌊J⌋, ⌊H⌋

    Close Group

10. Click **Close Header and Footer** button ❌ . . . . ⌊C⌋

Remove a Manual Watermark

1. Click **Insert** tab . . . . ⌊Alt⌋+⌊N⌋

    Header & Footer Group

2. Click **Header** button 📄 . . . . . ⌊H⌋
3. Click **Edit Header** . . . . ⌊E⌋
4. Click to select watermark object.
5. Press ⌊Delete⌋.
6. Click **Header and Footer Tools Design** tab . . . . ⌊Alt⌋+⌊J⌋, ⌊H⌋

    Close Group

7. Click **Close Header and Footer** button ❌ . . . . ⌊C⌋

EXERCISE DIRECTIONS

1. Start Word, if necessary, open 💿 **21JOBFAIR**, and save the file as **21JOBFAIR_xx**.
2. Create a printed watermark using the picture file 💿 **21SOAR** supplied with this book.

    ✓ *Alternatively, select a picture of an eagle or other soaring bird from the Clip Organizer.*

3. Select to edit the header and then select the picture object.
4. Rotate the object approximately 70 degrees.
5. Resize the picture so the width is 10 inches (the height should adjust automatically).
6. Close the header and footer.
7. Check the spelling and grammar in the document.
8. Preview the document. It should look similar to the one in Illustration A.
9. Print the document.
10. Close the document, saving all changes.

Illustration A

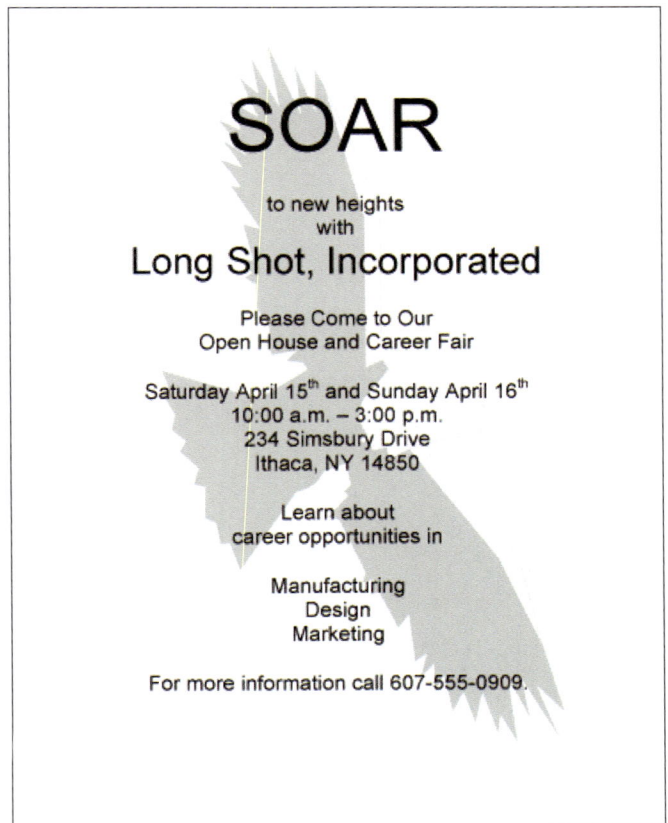

SOAR

to new heights
with

Long Shot, Incorporated

Please Come to Our
Open House and Career Fair

Saturday April 15th and Sunday April 16th
10:00 a.m. – 3:00 p.m.
234 Simsbury Drive
Ithaca, NY 14850

Learn about
career opportunities in

Manufacturing
Design
Marketing

For more information call 607-555-0909.

ON YOUR OWN

1. Start Word, create a new document, and save it as a document template with the name OWD21-1_xx.

2. Locate a clip art picture or create your own object to use as a watermark on the template. Select a watermark that is professional or that reflects your personality.

3. Insert and format the watermark. Make sure the watermark is correctly sized and positioned on the page.

4. You may also want to set up a letterhead in the template.

5. Check the spelling and grammar in the template, and then preview the template with the watermark.

6. Print the template.

7. Ask a classmate to review the document and offer comments and suggestions. Incorporate the changes, and then save the template and close it.

8. Create a new document based on the template and save it as OWD21-2_xx.

9. Using full block formatting, type a letter thanking someone for meeting with you to discuss a job opening, or for giving you a job interview. In the letter, refer specifically to the date and time you met and the position you discussed. Also mention why you want the position, and why you are qualified.

10. Check the spelling and grammar in the letter.

11. Ask a classmate to review the document and offer comments and suggestions.

12. Incorporate the changes, and then save and print the document.

13. Add the document to your employment portfolio as an example of a thank you letter.

14. Close the document, saving all changes, and exit Word.

Critical Thinking

Application Skills   You've been asked to design an invitation to a luncheon honoring the judges of New Media Designs' Essay contest. The invitation will be printed on custom-sized paper. It will integrate a text box, an AutoShape, WordArt, and a watermark created from a clip art picture to create an effective, eye-catching document.

EXERCISE DIRECTIONS

1. Start Word, if necessary, create a new document, and save it as **22INVITE_xx**.
2. Set the paper size to 5 inches wide by 7 inches high, and set the margins to 1 inch on all sides.
3. Make sure that the Office theme and Office 2007 styles set are selected.

Create a Text Box

1. Using no line and paragraph spacing, in a 12-point script font, type the following lines of text (Brush Script MT is used in Illustration A):

   You are cordially invited

   To attend a luncheon

   In honor of

   the Essay Contest Judges

   Friday, October 19

   12:30 in the afternoon

   New Media Designs

   Highway 73

   Cambridge, WI 53523

   RSVP (608) 555-2697

2. Insert a text box around the text.
3. Set text wrap for the text box to Behind Text.
4. Center the text in the text box and then center the text box horizontally and vertically, relative to the margins.
5. Remove the fill and the outline from the text box.
6. Save the document.

Create WordArt

1. Create a WordArt object as follows:
   a. Select the style in the first row of the third column.
   b. Use a sans serif font in 40 points (Arial Black is used in the illustration).
   c. For the WordArt text, type **New Media Designs**.
2. Size the WordArt object to approximately 1 inch high by 3.5 inches wide.
3. Set text wrapping to Top and Bottom.
4. Position the object in the top center of the page.
5. Using the Standard Colors palette, set the outline color to Dark Blue and the fill color to Light Blue.
6. Create a second WordArt object as follows:
   a. Select the style in the second row of the fourth column.
   b. Use a serif font in 28 points (Garamond is used in Illustration A).
   c. Type **Contest Judges** as the WordArt text.
7. Size the new WordArt object to approximately .5 inch high by 2 inches wide.
8. Set the text wrapping for the object to Square.
9. Center the object horizontally on the page, and position it vertically 1.5 inches below the page.
10. Change the outline color of the WordArt object to Light Blue.
11. Change the shadow color of the WordArt object to Dark Blue.

Insert a Shape

1. Insert the Down Ribbon AutoShape from the Stars and Banners palette.

2. Size it to 1.25 inches high by 3.75 inches wide.

3. Position the object in the bottom center of the page, with Square text wrapping.

4. Select to add text to the AutoShape, select the No Spacing style, and change the font size to 12 points.

5. Type the text **Honorees**.

6. Start a new line, change the font size to 10 points, set the horizontally alignment to Center, and type the following names, using the Wingdings symbol 171 as the separator:

   ★ Alex Gogan ★ Mikel Arroyo
   ★ Sharon Zide ★ Jackie Wirth
   ★ Bob Sanchez ★ Liz Ching

   ✓ *Do not leave extra space between the lines. Also, the word wrap should break each line after the second name. Only insert paragraph marks if necessary.*

7. Fill the AutoShape with any light blue color.

8. Save the changes.

Create a Watermark

1. Create a watermark using the 22QUILL picture file supplied with this book. Or, select an appropriate clip.

2. Check the spelling and grammar in the document.

3. Preview the document. It should look similar to the one in Illustration A.

4. Print the document.

5. Close the document, saving all changes.

Illustration A

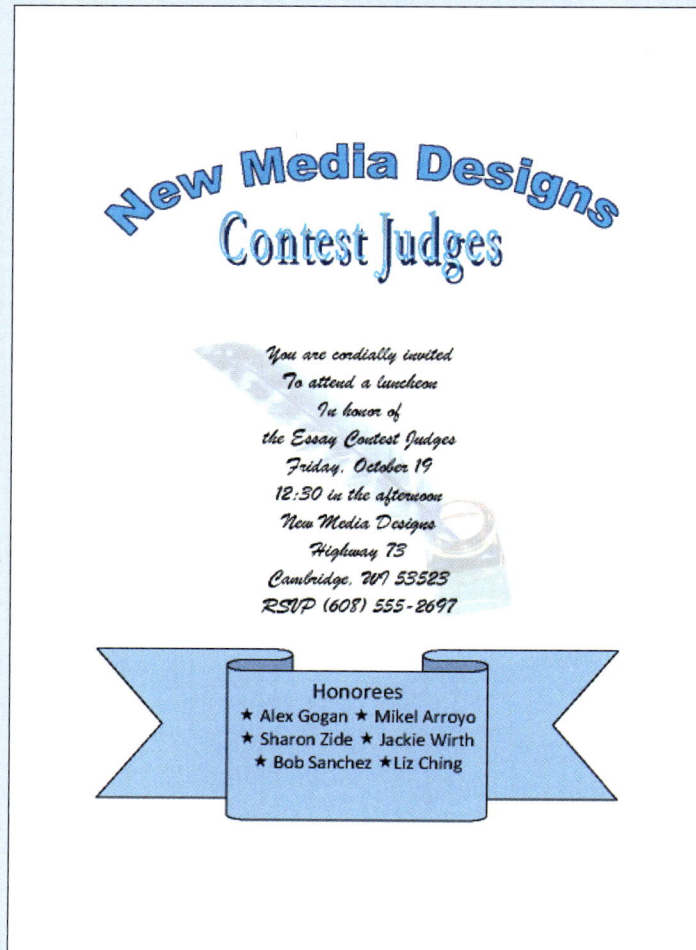

New Media Designs
Contest Judges

You are cordially invited
To attend a luncheon
In honor of
the Essay Contest Judges
Friday, October 19
12:30 in the afternoon
New Media Designs
Highway 73
Cambridge, WI 53523
RSVP (608) 555-2697

Honorees
★ Alex Gogan ★ Mikel Arroyo
★ Sharon Zide ★ Jackie Wirth
★ Bob Sanchez ★ Liz Ching

Curriculum Integration

Application Skills   For your mathematics class, use the skills you have learned in Lesson 3 to design and create a poster illustrating a concept you have learned about this year. For example, you might illustrate geometric shapes or curves, or you might use graphics objects to create a picture about a mathematician. Refer to Illustration A to see a sample of a poster. When you are finished, print the poster and distribute it to your classmates.

EXERCISE DIRECTIONS

Start Word, if necessary, and create a new document. Save it as **23MATH_*xx***.

Select to display elements that might help you while you work, such as the rulers, nonprinting characters, and gridlines.

Select a theme, style set, and colors for the document. You may want to use a page background, as well.

Set the paper size, and set margins.

Insert the objects and pictures you want to include on the poster, sizing and positioning them as appropriate. Include shapes, WordArt, and clip art, if appropriate. Apply formatting to enhance the poster, such as 3-D effects, borders, and fills.

Use text boxes to add text labels to objects, and remember to set text wrapping and layering. Group objects, if necessary, so they stay together when you move them.

Check the spelling and grammar in the poster.

Ask a classmate to review the document and make suggestions for how you might improve it.

Incorporate your classmate's suggestions into the document, and save it.

Print the poster and distribute it to your classmates.

Close all files, saving all changes.

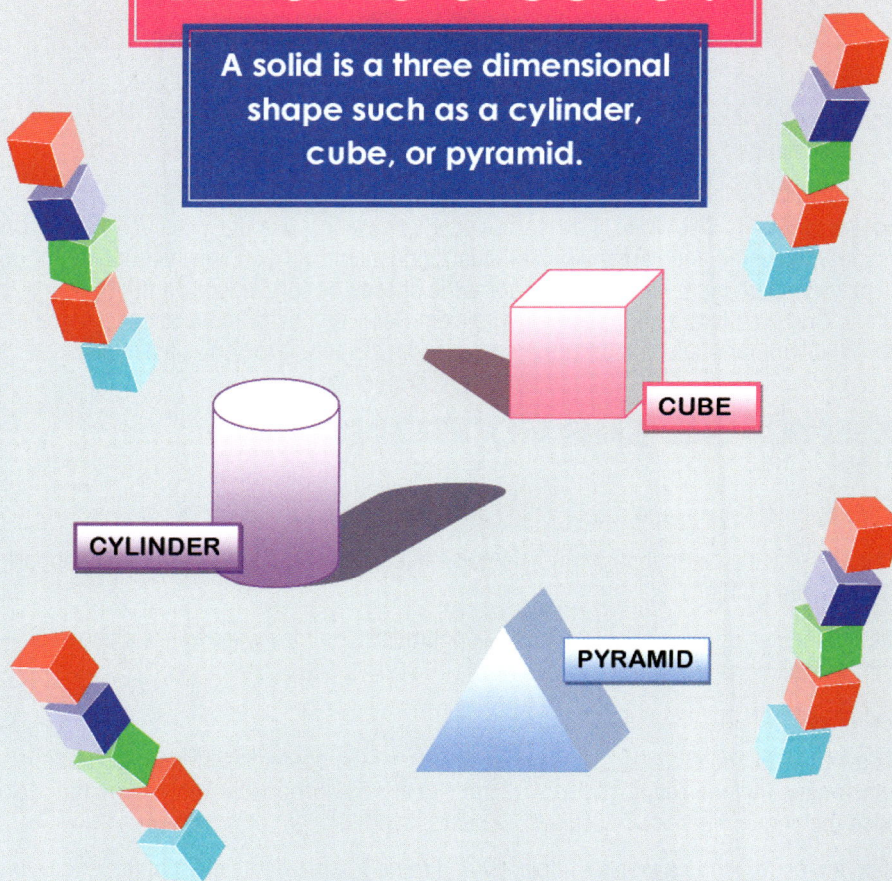

What is a Solid?

A solid is a three dimensional shape such as a cylinder, cube, or pyramid.

CUBE

CYLINDER

PYRAMID

GEOMETRY

Lesson | 4

Securing Documents

Skills Covered

- **Protect a Document**
- **Set Protection Exceptions**
- **Apply Password Protection**

- **About Codes of Conduct**
- **Computer Ethics**

Software Skills With Word, you can protect documents that you do not want others to change. You can set password protection to limit unauthorized access to a document, and you can set different levels of access to allow others to read but not edit or format a document, or to require the track changes feature to mark all edits.

Application Skills The research and development department at Long Shot, Inc. is working on an exciting new product. It is important that all information related to the product remain confidential and out of the hands of business competitors. The department manager has asked you to generate a memo to all team members explaining the importance of confidentiality with regard to this project, and what problems might arise from a breach of confidentiality. In this exercise, you will create the document and then protect it so that it cannot be edited.

TERMS

Code of conduct A policy that defines the behavior expected of all employees.

Confidentiality A legal and ethical principle that prevents the disclosure of secret information to unauthorized parties.

Digital signature An electronic, encryption-based, secure stamp of authentication on a macro or document.

Encryption Scrambling so as to be indecipherable.

Ethical Conforming to accepted standards of social or professional behavior.

Integrity Adherence to a strict moral or ethical code.

Password A string of characters used to authenticate the identity of a user, and to limit unauthorized access.

Unethical Not conforming to accepted standards of social or professional behavior.

Workgroup A group of individuals who work together on the same projects, usually connected via a network.

NOTES

Protect a Document

- You can restrict others from editing or formatting a document, or parts of a document.
- To protect a document from formatting changes, you limit the ability of others to modify selected styles and apply direct formatting.
- To protect a document from editing changes, you may select from four options:
  - Tracked changes. Use this option to automatically display changes to a document with revision marks.
  - Comments. Use this option to allow **workgroup** members to enter comments without being able to edit document text.
  - Filling in forms. Use this option to allow changes in form fields only.
  - No changes (Read only). Use this option when you do not want to allow any changes at all.
- The options for protecting a document are found in the Restrict Formatting and Editing task pane, which you can access using the Protect Document button on the Review tab of the Ribbon.
- When you open a protected document, the Protect Document task pane displays information about the changes you may or may not make to the document.
- You can remove the protection to enable unlimited editing.

Set Protection Exceptions

- By default, an entire document is protected from changes made by all users.
- If you set formatting, read only, or comments protection, you may specify exceptions by allowing some people or groups access to all or parts of the document.
- To add a person to the exceptions list, you must know his or her e-mail address or Microsoft Windows user account name.
- After assigning an exception, you can select the specific part or parts of the document that a person or group may access, or you may allow access to the entire document.

Restrict Formatting and Editing task pane

Apply Password Protection and Encryption

- To ensure that users cannot remove or change document protection, you can assign **password** protection. Only someone who enters the assigned password can change the document protection settings.
- You can also assign a password to prohibit unauthorized users from opening or modifying a file by using the **Encryption** options in the General Options dialog box.
- Encryption increases the security of the document, because only authenticated owners of the document can remove the protection.

  ✓ *Authenticity is based on use of a valid **digital signature**. Digital signatures are covered in Exercise 27.*

- You can also use the Encrypt Document command to apply a more stringent password to prevent an unauthorized user from opening the file.

- Always create a strong password, which is one that cannot easily be guessed by unauthorized personnel.

- According to Microsoft, a strong password combines upper- and lowercase letters, numbers, and symbols, and is more than 8 characters long.

- Take care when assigning passwords. If you forget the password, you will not be able to access the document.

General Options dialog box

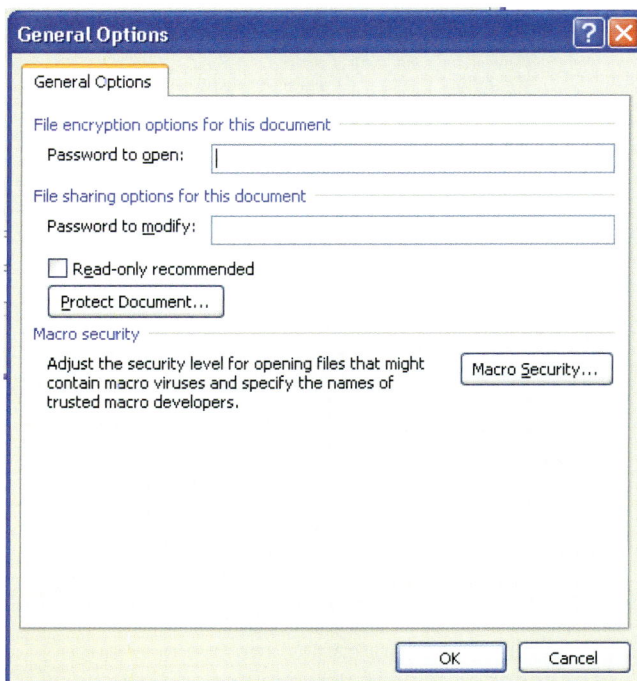

```
General Options                              [?][X]
 ┌─────────────┐
 │General Options│
 └─────────────┘
 File encryption options for this document
   Password to open:    [                    ]

 File sharing options for this document
   Password to modify:  [                    ]

   ☐ Read-only recommended
   [ Protect Document... ]
 Macro security
   Adjust the security level for opening files that might   [ Macro Security... ]
   contain macro viruses and specify the names of
   trusted macro developers.




                              [    OK    ] [  Cancel  ]
```

About Codes of Conduct

- Employers expect employees to have **integrity** and to conduct themselves in a professional and **ethical** manner.

- Most employers have a written policy called a **code of conduct** that specifies the rights and responsibilities of employees.

- The codes vary depending on the organization. Most list the types of behavior that are considered acceptable, as well as behavior that is considered unacceptable.

- Some typical expectations include:
  - Reporting **unethical** or illegal behavior in others.
  - Respecting the **confidentiality** of clients, co-workers, and employers.
  - Arriving and leaving on time.
  - Wearing professional attire in the workplace.

- Most codes also specify the consequences of failing to meet the standards.

- For a first or minor infraction, the punishment might be a warning letter placed in an employment file.

- For a severe or repeated infraction, the punishment might be dismissal.

Computer Ethics

- In general, the ethics for computer use should follow the same basic code of ethics for all business and personal conduct.

- In other words, employees and employers should conduct themselves with honesty and integrity, according to legal and corporate policies.

- Most companies and organizations establish corporate computer application policies or rules, as well as policies for using the Internet and e-mail.

- These policies address the legal and social aspects of computer use and are designed to protect privacy while respecting personal and corporate values and adhering to federal and local laws.

- Some topics typically covered by corporate computer application policies include:
  - The type of language allowed in documents and messages.
  - Permissions for accessing documents and data.
  - The amount of time allowed for personal Internet and e-mail use.
  - The types of Web sites that may be accessed from corporate computers.
  - Storage policies for documents and e-mail.
  - The types of programs that may be used on corporate computers.

PROCEDURES

Protect a Document from Formatting Changes

1. Open the document to protect.
2. Click **Review** tab . . . . Alt + R

   Protect Group

3. Click **Protect Document** button
   . . . . P , R
4. Click **Restrict Formatting and Editing**, if necessary . . . . F
5. Click **Limit formatting to a selection of styles** check box . . . . Spacebar
6. Click **Settings** link.
7. Deselect the check boxes beside the styles which you want to restrict . . . . ↓ , Spacebar

   ✓ *Selected styles may be modified.*

   OR

   Click one of the following:
   - **All** . . . . Alt + L
   - **Recommended Minimum** . . . . Alt + R
   - **None** . . . . Alt + N

8. Select Formatting options as desired:
   - **Allow AutoFormat to override formatting restrictions** . . . . Alt + A
   - **Block Theme or Scheme switching** . . . . Alt + W
   - **Block Quick Style Set switching** . . . . Alt + K

9. Click **OK**.

   ✓ *If the document contains styles that you have deselected, Word may ask if you want to remove them from the document. Click Yes to remove the formatting or click No to preserve the existing formatting.*

10. Click **Yes, Start Enforcing Protection**.
11. Click **OK** . . . . Enter

    OR

    Set password protection as described below.

Protect a Document from Editing Changes

1. Open the document to protect.
2. Click **Review** tab . . . . Alt + R

   Protect Group

3. Click **Protect Document** button
   . . . . P , R
4. Click **Allow only this type of editing in the document** check box . . . . ↓ , ↓ , Spacebar
5. Click **Editing restrictions** drop-down arrow . . . . ⇆ , ↓
6. Select restriction to apply: . . . . ↓ /↑ , Enter
   - **Tracked changes**
   - **Comments**
   - **Filling in forms**
   - **No changes (Read only)**
7. Click **Yes, Start Enforcing Protection**.
8. Click **OK** . . . . Enter

   OR

   Set password protection as described below.

Set Protection Exceptions

1. Open the document to protect.
2. Click **Review** tab . . . . Alt + R

   Protect Group

3. Click **Protect Document** button
   . . . . P , R
4. Click to select **Allow only this type of editing in the document** check box . . . . ↓ , ↓ , Spacebar
5. Click **Editing restrictions** drop-down arrow . . . . ⇆ , ↓
6. Click **No changes (Read only)** . . . . ↓ , ↓ , ↓ , Enter
7. If necessary, select parts of the document that may be edited.

   ✓ *Use standard selection techniques to select paragraphs, pages, or sections in the document.*

8. Click the check box beside each individual or group who may edit the selected sections.

   OR

   a. Click **More users** link.
   b. Type user account names or e-mail addresses, separated by semicolons.
   c. Click **OK** . . . . Enter

9. Click **Yes, Start Enforcing Protection**.
10. Click **OK** . . . . Enter

    OR

    Set password protection as described below.

Add Password Protection for Editing Restrictions

1. Open the document to protect.
2. Click **Review** tab . . . . Alt + R

   Protect Group

3. Click **Protect Document** button
   . . . . P , R
4. Select desired type of protection.
5. Click **Yes, Start Enforcing Protection**.
6. Click **Enter new password** text box . . . . Alt + E
7. Type password.
8. Click **Reenter password to confirm** text box . . . . Alt + P
9. Type password.
10. Click **OK** . . . . Enter

Edit a Protected Document

1. Open the document to edit.
2. In the Restrict Formatting and Editing task pane, click **Find Next Region I Can Edit**.

   OR

   Click **Show All Regions I Can Edit**.
3. Edit document as usual.

Remove Document Protection

1. Open the document to protect.
2. Click **Review** tab . . . . `Alt`+`R`

   Protect Group

3. Click **Protect Document** button
   🔒 . . . . `P`, `R`
4. Click **Stop Protection**.

   ✓ *If password protection has been applied, Word will prompt you to enter the correct password and then click OK.*

5. Deselect protection options as necessary.
6. Close the Restrict Formatting and Editing task pane.

Require a Password to Open and/or Modify a File

1. Open the document to protect.
2. Click **Office Button** 🔘 . . . `Alt`+`F`
3. Click **Save As** . . . . `A`
4. Click **Tools** drop-down
   arrow . . . . `Alt`+`L`
5. Click **General Options** . . . . `G`
6. Click **Password to open** text
   box . . . . `Alt`+`O`
7. Type password.
6. Click **Password to modify** text
   box . . . . `Alt`+`M`
7. Type password.

   ✓ *You may set a password to open or to modify. You do not have to set both. If you only set one, only one password confirmation dialog will display.*

8. Click **OK**. . . . . `Enter`
9. Click **Reenter password to open**
   text box . . . . `Alt`+`P`
10. Type password.
11. Click **OK**. . . . . `Enter`
12. Click **Reenter password to modify**
    text box . . . . `Alt`+`P`
13. Type password.
14. Click **OK**. . . . . `Enter`
15. Select options and save file as usual.

Add Encryption Protection for Opening a File

1. Open the document to protect.
2. Click **Office Button** 🔘 . . . `Alt`+`F`
3. Point to **Prepare** . . . . `E`
4. Click **Encrypt Document** . . . . . `E`
5. Click **Password** text
   box . . . . `Alt`+`R`
6. Type password.
7. Click **OK**. . . . . `Enter`
8. Click **Reenter password** text
   box . . . . `Alt`+`R`
9. Type password.
10. Click **OK**. . . . . `Enter`

EXERCISE DIRECTIONS

1. Start Word, if necessary, create a new document, and save the document as **24SECURE_xx**.
2. Make sure that the document is formatted with the Office theme and Office 2007 style set.
3. Type the memo shown in Illustration A, using the styles as marked, replacing the text *Student's Name* with your own name and *Today's Date* with the current date.
4. Check the spelling and grammar in the document.
5. Preview the document. It should look similar to the one in Illustration A.
6. Protect the document from all changes by everyone, and apply the password **LSIxx01**.
7. Save the document and close it.
8. Open the document.
9. Try to delete the last line in the document.

   ✓ *You will not be able to edit the document.*

10. Remove document protection. When prompted, type the password **LSIxx01**.
11. Delete the last line.
12. Close the document, saving all changes, and exit Word.

Title style

MEMO

No spacing style

Date: Today's Date
To: Team Members
From: Student's Name
Re: Confidentiality

Blank line with
Title style

Normal style

As you all know, we are working on a new and exciting product which the company expects to completely revolutionize the golf equipment industry. This memo is simply a reminder of the Long Shot, Inc. corporate policy on confidentiality and ethical behavior.

Confidentiality in business refers to the protection of proprietary and secret information. In some businesses, the information belongs to a client, and it is the responsibility of the business to make sure no one else can access the information. For example, in health care, providers may not share information about patients with unauthorized personnel. Such a breach in confidentiality could impact a patient's access to insurance, job security, and privacy.

In our case, the information belongs to the corporation, and it is our responsibility to make sure no one outside the company gains access. Breaching confidentiality by sharing corporate secrets gives our competitors an advantage they would not otherwise have, and puts our investment at risk. In the past, our competitors have tried many illegal and unethical tactics to try to gain access to our confidential information. They have tried hacking into our computer system, posing as customers and vendors, and even offering bribes to employees.

Please remember that you have all signed confidentiality agreements which state that you will not share your knowledge of this product with anyone outside the development team. The confidentiality agreement is a binding, legal contract. If you breach the agreement, we will prosecute you to the fullest extent of the law.

Thank you all for your consideration in this important matter. We are in the process of a technological breakthrough of which we can all be very proud. I am confident that every member of our team will respect and honor Long Shot's code of conduct and confidentiality. For a complete copy of the policy, please consult the human resources department.

ON YOUR OWN

1. Many companies request that employees sign a confidentiality agreement when leaving the company, as well as when they are working with private information. Think about why confidentiality agreements are important. Consider how ethical behavior impacts a business and the effects that a breach of confidentiality might have. You might want to research the topic using books, magazines, or the Internet.

2. Start Word, create a new document, and save the document as OWD24_*xx*.

3. Using formatting appropriate for a one-page report, write an essay that analyzes ethical practices in business and the risks of breach of confidentiality. Include a thesis that states your opinion, and then back it up with facts. You should have at least three paragraphs in the essay. Include a header with your name and the date.

4. When the essay is complete, check the spelling and save the changes.

5. Protect the document so that only comments may be entered.

6. Exchange files with a classmate.

7. Read your classmate's document and insert at least two comments.

8. Change the protection to allow tracked changes.

9. Exchange files with another classmate.

10. Make editing and formatting changes to the document, and then save it.

11. Return the file to the original author. You should now have your original document back.

12. Remove all protection from the document.

13. Review the comments and changes.

14. Accept or reject the changes, and respond to the comments as necessary.

15. Protect the document from all additional changes. Do not apply a password.

16. Close the document, saving all changes, and exit Word.

Business Connection

Snail Mail

Even is this day and age of e-mail, text messaging, and social networking, writing a proper letter may be the key to obtaining a job. At a minimum, you should be prepared to write three types of letters to communicate with a potential employer: a letter of inquiry to ask about job opportunities, a cover letter to accompany your resume, and a thank you letter to follow up an interview. These letters provide you with the chance to introduce yourself; highlight a skill, experience, or qualification that you think will help you catch the employer's attention; and prove that you can be a professional. While you may be able to deliver the letter as an attachment to an e-mail message instead of through the U.S. Postal Service, you must still follow proper business letter style and formatting.

Write Letters

First, look up samples of the three types of letters online, in your library, or in your career center. Next, use the classified ads or other job listings to select a position for which you would like to apply. Use Word to create a block or modified-block business letter of inquiry asking for more information about the position, or other similar positions at the company. Then, create a block or modified-block business cover letter to accompany your resume. Customize the letter for the specific position. Finally, assume you interviewed for the position, and write a block or modified-block business letter thanking the employer for taking the time to meet with you. Be sure to proofread each letter for correct spelling and grammar as well as for proper layout and formatting. Ask a classmate to review your letters and provide you with feedback that will help you improve the documents.

Exercise | 25

Skills Covered

- Use the Document Inspector
- Use the Compatibility Checker

Software Skills   Use the Document Inspector to remove personal or confidential information from your Word documents. Use the Compatibility Checker to identify features that might not be compatible with earlier versions of Microsoft Office Word.

Application Skills   Long Shot, Inc. has been working on a new mission statement. An edited version of the document—including revision marks—is being distributed to all department managers for review. In this exercise, you will use the Document Inspector to locate and remove any personal or confidential information that might be part of the document. Also, because you know some managers are using previous versions of Word, you will use the Compatibility Checker to identify and modify any incompatible features.

TERMS

No new terms in this exercise.

NOTES

Use the Document Inspector

- Document properties frequently include personal or confidential information, such as the names of people who reviewed the document and comments made by reviewers.
- Releasing such information might result in a breach of confidentiality.
- Run the Document Inspector to remove personal or confidential information from your Word documents.
- For example, you might want to delete comments before passing a file on to another reviewer.

- When you start the Document Inspector, you can select to check for the following types of information:
  - Comments, revisions, versions, and annotations.
  - Document properties and personal information.
  - Custom XML data.
  - Headers, footers, and watermarks.
  - Text formatted as Hidden.

Select information to find using the Document Inspector

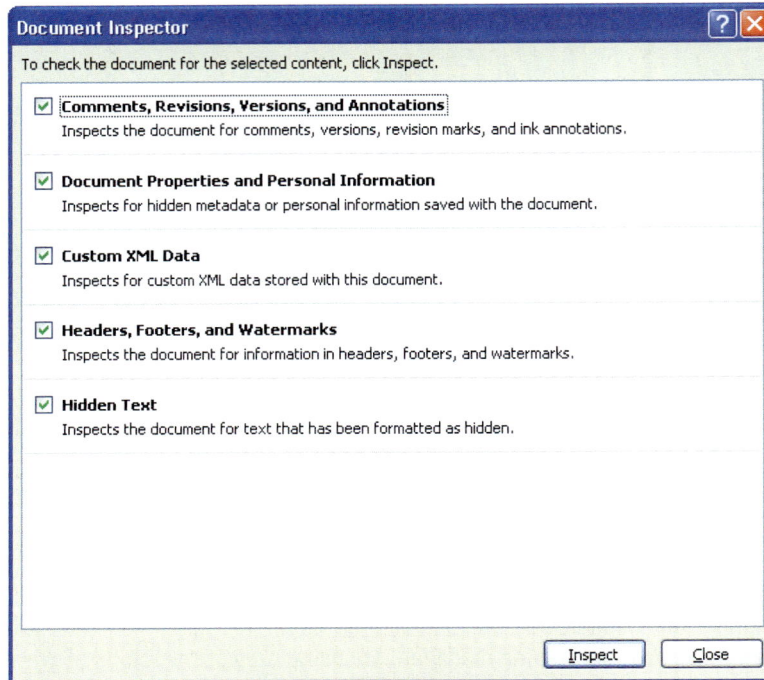

Document Inspector

To check the document for the selected content, click Inspect.

☑ **Comments, Revisions, Versions, and Annotations**
Inspects the document for comments, versions, revision marks, and ink annotations.

☑ **Document Properties and Personal Information**
Inspects for hidden metadata or personal information saved with the document.

☑ **Custom XML Data**
Inspects for custom XML data stored with this document.

☑ **Headers, Footers, and Watermarks**
Inspects the document for information in headers, footers, and watermarks.

☑ **Hidden Text**
Inspects the document for text that has been formatted as hidden.

[Inspect] [Close]

■ After inspecting the document, Document Inspector displays a list of found items.

■ You have the option of leaving the found items in the document or removing them.

■ You can reinspect the document to verify that all items have been removed.

■ It is a good idea to save a copy of the document before removing information with the Document Inspector, because you may not be able to undo the action.

Select whether to remove information

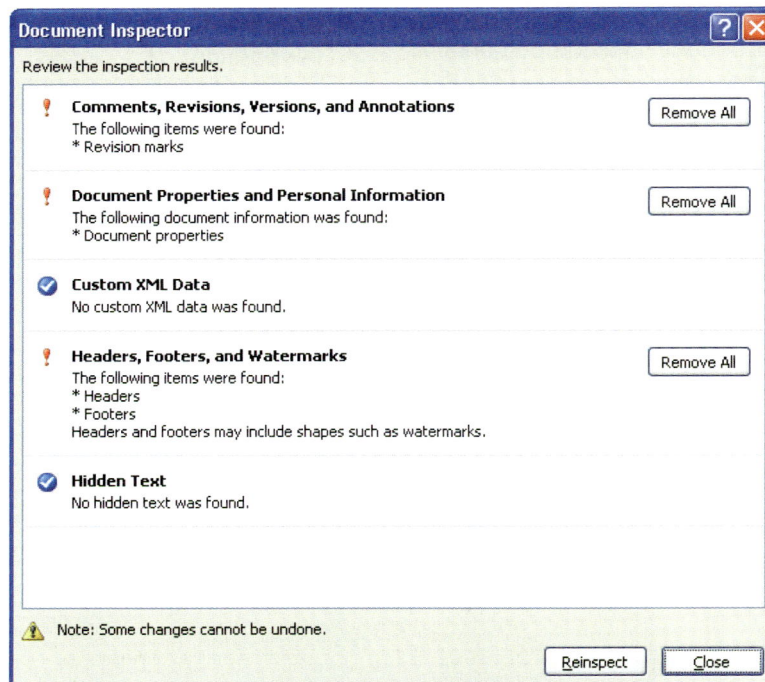

Document Inspector

Review the inspection results.

❗ **Comments, Revisions, Versions, and Annotations**
The following items were found:
* Revision marks
[Remove All]

❗ **Document Properties and Personal Information**
The following document information was found:
* Document properties
[Remove All]

✔ **Custom XML Data**
No custom XML data was found.

❗ **Headers, Footers, and Watermarks**
The following items were found:
* Headers
* Footers
Headers and footers may include shapes such as watermarks.
[Remove All]

✔ **Hidden Text**
No hidden text was found.

⚠ Note: Some changes cannot be undone.

[Reinspect] [Close]

Use the Compatibility Checker

- The Compatibility Checker checks a document created with Word 2007 to identify features that might not be supported by earlier versions of Word.

- By default, the Compatibility Checker runs automatically when you use the Save As command to save a document in Word 97-2003 format.

- You can run the Compatibility Checker at any time to check the document by opening the Office menu and then selecting the Run Compatibility Checker command from the Prepare submenu.

- After checking the document, Word 2007 displays a summary list of incompatible features.

- The summary list includes the number of times the feature is used and explains the action Word 2007 will take to resolve the incompatibility issue when the document is saved in Word 97-2003 format.

- For example, if the Word 2007 document contains a content control, such as a date in a header, the control is converted to text when the file is saved in Word 97-2003 format.

- The changes are made only in the documents saved in Word 97-2003 format; the original Word 2007 documents remain unchanged.

- Alternatively, you can edit the document to remove the incompatible features manually, or to replace them with features that are compatible with previous versions of Word.

Compatibility Checker summary list

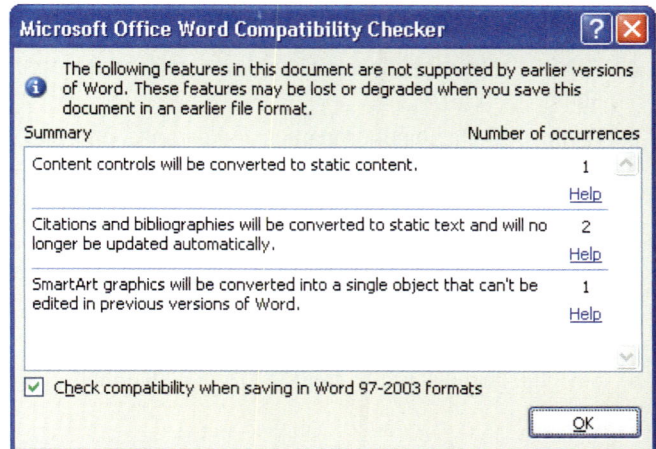

Microsoft Office Word Compatibility Checker

The following features in this document are not supported by earlier versions of Word. These features may be lost or degraded when you save this document in an earlier file format.

Summary	Number of occurrences
Content controls will be converted to static content. Help	1
Citations and bibliographies will be converted to static text and will no longer be updated automatically. Help	2
SmartArt graphics will be converted into a single object that can't be edited in previous versions of Word. Help	1

☑ Check compatibility when saving in Word 97-2003 formats

OK

PROCEDURES

Use the Document Inspector

1. Open the document to inspect.
2. Click **Office Button** [icon] . . . Alt + F
3. Point to **Prepare** . . . . E
4. Click **Inspect Document** I

   ✓ *If necessary, click Yes in the dialog box that displays to save document and continue.*

5. Click to select or deselect desired items . . . . ↓ / ↑ , Spacebar

   - **Comments, Revisions, Versions, and Annotations**
   - **Document Properties and Personal Information**
   - **Custom XML Data**
   - **Headers, Footers, and Watermarks**
   - **Hidden Text**

   ✓ *Word checks for the selected items; a check mark indicates an item is selected.*

6. Click **Inspect** I
7. For first set of found items, do one of the following
   - Click **Remove All** . . . . ←⏎ , Enter
   - Take no action.
8. Repeat step 7 for each set of found items.
9. Click **Close** . . . . Alt + C

   OR

   a. Click **Reinspect** . . . . . Alt + R
   b. Repeat steps 7–9.

Use the Compatibility Checker

1. Open the document to check.
2. Click **Office Button** [icon] . . . Alt + F
3. Point to **Prepare** . . . . E
4. Click **Run Compatibility Checker** C
5. Review found items.
6. Click **OK** . . . . Enter

To toggle the automatic Check compatibility when saving in Word 97-2003 formats feature off or on:

1. Open the document to inspect.
2. Click **Office Button** [icon] . . . Alt + F
3. Point to **Prepare** . . . . E
4. Click **Run Compatibility Checker** C
5. Click to select or deselect **Check compatibility when saving in Word 97-2003 formats** check box . . . . H

   ✓ *A check mark indicates the option is on.*

6. Click **OK** . . . . Enter

EXERCISE DIRECTIONS

1. Start Word, if necessary, open the file 💿 **25MISSION**, and save it as **25MISSION_xx**.

2. Start the Document Inspector.

3. Select to look for all possible information, and then inspect the document.

4. Remove all comments, revisions, versions, and annotations.

5. Remove all document properties and personal information.

6. Do not remove all headers, footers, and watermarks, hidden text, or custom xml data.

7. Reinspect the document to make sure the data you selected to remove has been removed, and then close the Document Inspector.

8. Save the changes to the **25MISSION_xx** document.

9. Run the Compatibility Checker, review the incompatible features, and then close the Compatibility Checker.

10. Delete the SmartArt graphic object below the text by clicking it and pressing [Delete].

11. Save the document in Word 97-2003 format, with the file name **25MISSIONa_xx**.

12. When the Compatibility Checker displays, click Continue to convert the incompatible features to compatible features.

   ✓ *The document will display in Compatibility Mode.*

13. Display the **25MISSIONa_xx** document in Print Preview. It should look similar to Illustration A.

14. Print the document.

15. Close the document, saving all changes, and exit Word.

Illustration A

LSI

Long Shot, Inc. Mission Statement

Customer Satisfaction

Long Shot, Inc. is committed to providing quality service to all of our clients at every level of our organization. Our ultimate goal is to hear our clients say, "Thank you. That is just what we wanted."

Employee Well-Being

Second only to customer satisfaction is the happiness and well-being of our employees. The employees at Long Shot, Inc. are encouraged to set personal and professional goals. We respect all employees as individuals and believe that fostering a strong community within the workplace strengthens our position in the marketplace.

Conclusion

At Long Shot, Inc. we vow to maintain the highest standards, pursue the extraordinary, and guarantee customer satisfaction. We are confident that our commitment to quality will make us leaders in our industry.

Today's Date

ON YOUR OWN

1. Start Word and open the document ⌨ **OWD24_xx**, the document you worked with in the On Your Own section of Exercise 24, or open 💿 **25INSPECT**.

2. Save the document as **OWD25-1_xx**, and stop all editing and formatting protection.

3. Click the Office button, Prepare, and then Properties to view the document's properties. If necessary, insert document properties such as a title, author, and subject, or other properties that may not already be entered in the document.

4. Insert a footer from the gallery that includes a content control for the page number.

5. Insert the CONFIDENTIAL 1 watermark from the gallery of watermarks.

6. Run the Document Inspector, saving the document as prompted.

7. Remove all properties, but keep the header, footer, and watermark.

8. Save the document in Word 97-2003 format, with the name **OWD25-2_xx**.

9. In the Compatibility Checker dialog box, review the changes that Word will make, and then click Continue to save the document.

10. Print the document.

11. Close the document, saving all changes, and exit Word.

Skills Covered

- **Mark a Document as Final**
- **Recover a Document**

- **About System Protection and Recovery**
- **About Computer Security**

Software Skills Mark a document as final to indicate to others that they are viewing a completed or final version of a document, and to prevent others from making unauthorized or inadvertent changes to the document. Recover a document that may have been damaged or closed before changes were saved. Learn how to protect your computer system from disasters, accidents, and malicious intent.

Application Skills Now that everyone has seen, read, and approved of the new mission statement for Long Shot, Inc., you will mark the document as final.

TERMS

AutoRecover A feature in Microsoft Office that automatically saves open documents at a set interval so that in the event of a system failure, the files may be recovered.

Firewall Software or hardware that monitors information as it passes from a network to your computer in order to detect and prohibit the transfer of malicious programs.

Malware (Malicious Software) Software designed to infiltrate or do damage to a computer system.

Phishing A method of tricking computer users into divulging private or confidential information over the Internet.

Virus A malicious computer program designed to cause damage to a computer system.

Worm A self-replicating program designed to cause damage to a computer system.

NOTES

Mark a Document as Final

- You can select the Mark as Final command from the Prepare submenu when you plan to share a completed document with others.

- The Mark as Final command changes the status of the document to Final and sets the document to open in Read-only mode.

- Typing, editing commands, and track changes commands are not available in a document marked as final, so that no changes can be made to the document.

- A document marked as final has a Marked as Final icon in the status bar.

- You can remove the marked as final status from the document at any time.

- Alternatively, you can save a copy of the document so you can edit it.

- The Mark as Final command is not compatible with previous versions of Word, so when you open a Word 2007 document in a previous version it can be edited.

Marked as Final icon in status bar

| Page: 2 of 2 | Words: 130 | 🔖 | | | | 📄📖📄📄📄 110% ⊖ ── ⊕ |

Icon

Recover a Document

- By default Microsoft Office Word is set to save **AutoRecover** information every ten minutes.

  ✓ *You can change the AutoRecover interval—or turn it off—using options in the Save group in the Word Options dialog box.*

- In the event of a system failure, Word will attempt to recover your files based on the most recently saved AutoRecover information.

- If any damage was done to the file data during the crash, Word will attempt to repair it.

- When you open the program again, the Document Recovery task pane displays, listing original files, recovered files (if any), and repaired files (if any).

- Click the drop-down arrow beside a file name to display a list of options for opening the file, saving it with a new name, deleting it, or showing repairs.

- In addition, in the event of a program crash Word will ask if you want to send a report to Microsoft. If you agree to send a report, your computer will log on to the Internet and transmit the information.

Document Recovery task pane

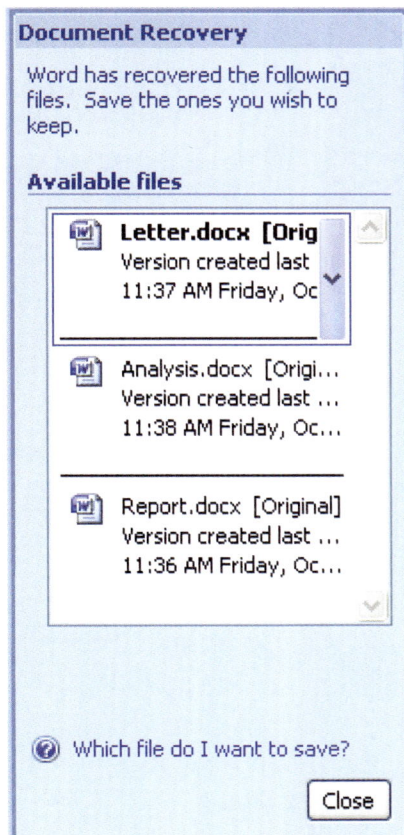

Document Recovery

Word has recovered the following files. Save the ones you wish to keep.

Available files

📄 **Letter.docx [Orig**
Version created last
11:37 AM Friday, Oc

📄 Analysis.docx [Origi...
Version created last ...
11:38 AM Friday, Oc...

📄 Report.docx [Original]
Version created last ...
11:36 AM Friday, Oc...

❔ Which file do I want to save?

[Close]

About System Protection and Recovery

- Many situations can put your computer information at risk.

  - Disasters such as a flood or fire might make a hard disk unusable.

  - Accidentally knocking out a power cord might delete unsaved changes to a file.

  - A thief might steal your notebook computer or external hard drive.

  - Malicious software such as a **virus** or **worm** might corrupt your data.

  - A **phishing** Web site might capture private information such as passwords and financial data.

- Some steps you can take to safeguard your data include saving frequently, backing up to a remote location on a regular basis, and storing backup data in a fire- and flood-proof safe.

- You should activate a **firewall** to prevent unauthorized programs from accessing your system via a network.

- You should use a malicious software detector tool, such as Windows Defender, to monitor and protect your system from **malware** such as worms.

- You should use a virus protection program to prohibit, detect, and remove computer viruses.

- You should also learn about the features and tools that your operating system has for preventing data loss:

  - You can use System Restore to revert to a restore point to undo changes.

  - You can use system recovery tools such as Startup Repair or Memory Diagnostics.

About Computer Security

- Maintaining the security of computer systems is a vital part of any business.

- Computer system security usually includes hardware and software devices as well as managerial procedures that work together to protect the system from unauthorized access, to make sure the data is available when needed, and to maintain the integrity of the data.

- Types of security devices include firewalls, virus detection programs, passwords, and data encryption.

- A breach in security compromises data stored on the system, resulting in lost revenues.

- In addition, there are laws governing computer security, which means businesses may be legally responsible for a breach.

PROCEDURES

Mark a Document as Final

1. Open the document to inspect.
2. Click **Office Button** 📇 . . . `Alt` + `F`
3. Point to **Prepare** . . . . `E`
4. Click **Mark as Final** . . . . `F`
5. Click **OK** . . . . `Enter`
6. If a second confirmation dialog box displays, click **OK** . . . . `Enter`

Remove the Mark a Document as Final Status

1. Open the document to inspect.
2. Click **Office Button** 📇 . . . `Alt` + `F`
3. Point to **Prepare** . . . . `E`
4. Click **Mark as Final** . . . . `F`

Recover a File

1. Click drop-down arrow beside desired file in Document Recovery task pane.
2. Click desired option to open, save, or delete file.

   ✓ *If you save a repaired file, Word will prompt you to review the repairs before continuing.*

EXERCISE DIRECTIONS

1. Start Word, if necessary, open the file 💿 **26MISSION** and save it as **26MISSION_*xx*.**
2. Mark the document as final.
3. Try to edit the document.
4. Display the document in Print Preview. Your screen should look similar to Illustration A, with the Marked as Final icon in the Status bar.
5. Print the document.
6. Close the document, saving all changes.

Illustration A

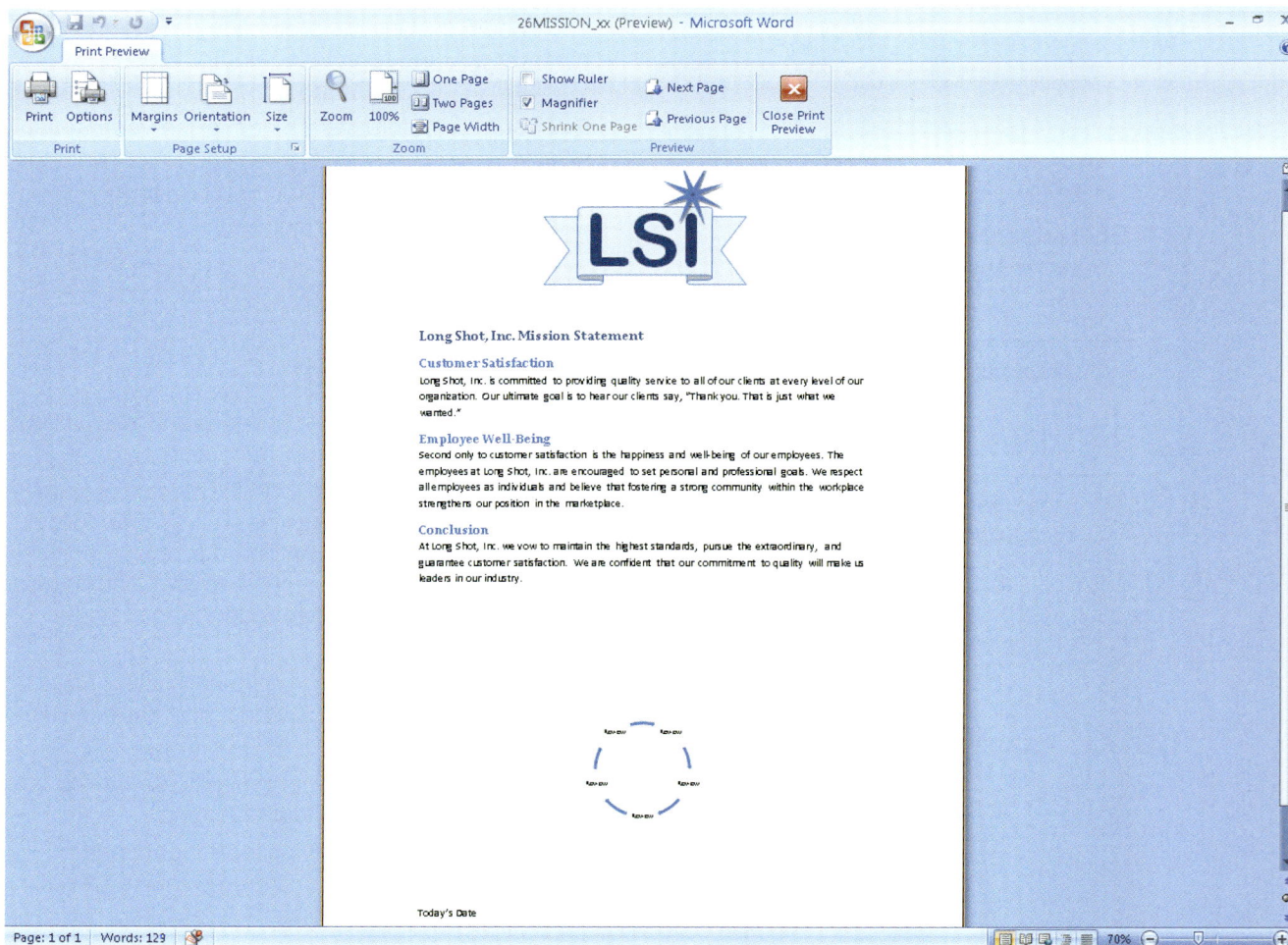

ON YOUR OWN

1. Start Word, create a new document, and save it as OWD26_*xx*.

2. Use books, magazines, or the Internet to research your state's laws and legislation concerning computer security and computer security breaches. Try to find the most up-to-date information that you can. You may also want to research federal laws and legislation. You might want to focus on a specific case.

3. Write a summary of the information that you find. Include your source(s).

4. Check the spelling and grammar in the document.

5. Ask a classmate to read it and offer comments and suggestions.

6. Edit the document as necessary.

7. Save the changes to the document.

8. Mark the document as final.

9. Print the document.

10. Close the document, saving all changes, and exit Word.

Skills Covered

- **About Digital Signatures**
- **Use a Visible Digital Signature**
- **Use an Invisible Digital Signature**
- **Verify a Digital Signature**

Software Skills   Use a visible or invisible digital signature to verify the authenticity of a document. Once you add a digital signature, the document is automatically marked as final and cannot be edited.

Application Skills   Unauthorized versions of the confidentiality memo have been circulating through the corporate offices. In this exercise, you will add an invisible digital signature to the authorized document. You will then save a copy of the memo document and add a visible digital signature line which you will sign.

TERMS

Digital certificate   An attachment for a file, macro, project, or e-mail message that vouches for its authenticity, provides secure encryption, or supplies a verifiable signature.

Invisible digital signature   A digital signature that is attached to a document but does not display in the document.

Signature line   A graphics object inserted in a document, on which a person can insert, type, or handwrite a digital signature.

Visible digital signature   A digital signature that displays on a signature line in a document.

NOTES

About Digital Signatures

- A digital signature can be used like a written signature to verity the authenticity of information.
- A digital signature indicates the following:
  - The signer is who he or she claims to be.
  - The content has not changed since the digital signature was applied.
  - The signer read and approved the document.
- A digital signature is created using a **digital certificate**, which can be obtained from an authorized vendor or from the internal security administrator responsible for your computer system.
- Windows usually creates a personal digital certificate—called a digital ID—for each user account.

- If you attempt to add a digital signature to a document, but you do not have a digital certificate, Word will display the Get a Digital ID dialog box, from which you can create your own personal digital certificate.
- A personal digital certificate is authorized only on the computer on which it is created.
- Once a digital signature is added, the document becomes read-only, and the Signatures icon displays in the status bar.
- With Word 2007, you can either apply a **visible digital signature** or an **invisible digital signature** to a document.

Use a Visible Digital Signature

- A visible signature is similar to a standard signature line on a contract or other type of agreement.
- When you add a visible signature, Word inserts a **signature line** into the document.
- You can use the options in the Signature Setup dialog box to add information about the signer, such as a name and a title, as well as instructions for the signer on how to add a digital signature.
- To sign the document, the signer opens the Sign dialog box in which he or she may type a signature or insert a digital image of the signature.

  ✓ *If the signer has a Tablet PC, he or she may use the Inking feature to sign the document.*

Signature Setup dialog box

Sign dialog box

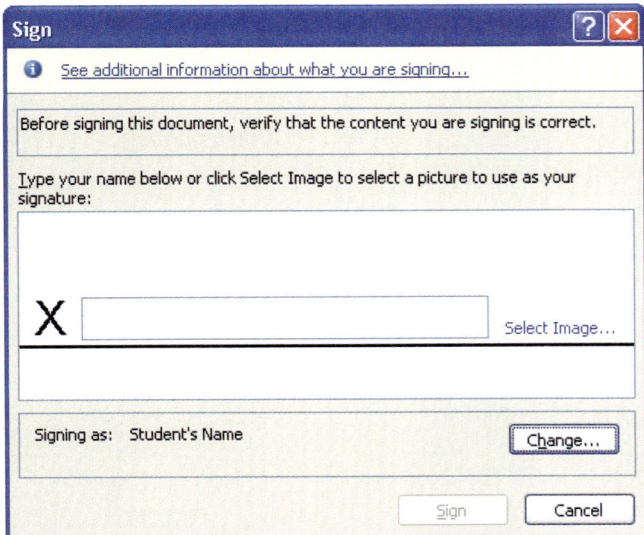

Use an Invisible Digital Signature

- An invisible digital signature is attached to the document but does not display as an actual signature in the document.
- You can verify that the document has been signed by viewing the document's digital signature(s) in the Signatures task pane.

Verify a Digital Signature

- An authorized digital signature is listed as having a valid digital certificate.
- If the certificate is not valid, it is listed as Invalid.
- If the status of a certificate cannot be verified, the signature is listed as having certificate issues.
- Some factors that might cause an invalid certificate or certificate issues include:
  - The content of the document has been changed since the signature was applied.
  - The digital signature has a time limit, which has expired.
  - The certificate associated with the signature is unauthorized.
- You can manually change a certificate from invalid to valid in the Signature Details dialog box, by adding it to a list of trusted certificates.

Signatures listed in the Signatures task pane

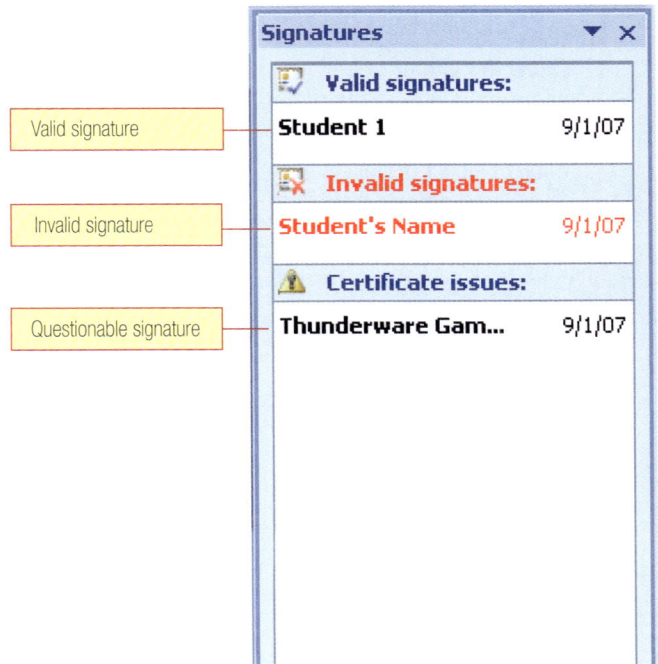

PROCEDURES

Insert a Signature Line for a Visible Digital Signature

1. Position the insertion point where you want the signature to display.
2. Click **Insert** tab . . . . `Alt`+`N`

   Text Group

3. Click **Signature Line** button
   . . . . `G`, `Enter`
4. If a confirmation dialog box displays, click **OK**.
5. If desired, do the following:
   a. Click **Suggested signer** text box . . . . `Alt`+`S`
   b. Type the signer's name.
   c. Click **Suggested signer's title** text box . . . . `Alt`+`T`
   d. Type the signer's title.
   e. Click **Suggested signer's e-mail address** text box. . . . . `Alt`+`E`
   f. Type the signer's e-mail address.
   g. Click **Instructions to the signer** text box. . . . . . `Alt`+`I`
   h. Type instructions.
   i. Click to select or deselect **Allow the signer to add comments in the Sign dialog** check box . . . . `Alt`+`C`
   j. Click to select or deselect **Show sign date in signature line** check box . . . . . . `Alt`+`D`
6. Click **OK**. . . . . `Enter`

Attach a Visible Digital Signature

1. Open the document.
2. Double-click the signature line.

   OR

   a. Right-click the signature line.
   b. Click **Sign** . . . . `S`
3. Click **OK**.

   ✓ At this point, if you do not already have a digital ID, Word may prompt you to get one. See the steps **Create a Digital ID** for more information.

4. Do one of the following:
   a. Click in **Type your name below** text box . . . . `Alt`+`T`
   b. Type your signature.

      OR

   a. Click **Select Image**.
   b. Locate and select digital signature image.
   c. Click **Select** . . . . `Alt`+`S`

      OR

   a. Click **Change** . . . . `Alt`+`H`
   b. Select digital certificate . . . . `↑`/`↓`
   c. Click **OK** . . . . `Enter`
5. Click **Sign** . . . . `Alt`+`S`
6. Click **OK**. . . . . `Enter`

Attach an Invisible Digital Signature

1. Click **Office Button** . . . `Alt`+`F`
2. Point to **Prepare** . . . . `E`
3. Click **Add a Digital Signature** . . . . `S`
4. If a confirmation dialog box displays, click **OK**.
5. Click **Purpose for signing this document** text box . . . . . `Alt`+`P`
6. Type reason why you are attaching the digital signature.

   ✓ Steps 5 and 6 are optional.

7. Click **Sign** . . . . `Alt`+`S`

   OR

   a. Click **Change** . . . . `Alt`+`H`
   b. Click digital certificate to use. . . . . `↑`/`↓`
   c. Click **OK** . . . . `Enter`
   d. Click **Sign** . . . . `Alt`+`S`
8. Click **OK**. . . . . `Enter`

Create a Digital ID

1. Position the insertion point where you want the signature to display.
2. Click **Office Button** . . . `Alt`+`F`
3. Point to **Prepare** . . . . `E`
4. Click **Add a Digital Signature** . . . . `S`

   ✓ If you do not have a digital certificate, the Create a Digital ID dialog box displays.

5. Type your name in the Name box.
6. Type your e-mail address in the E-mail address box.
7. Type your company or organization name in the Organization box.
8. Type your geographic location in the Locate box.
9. Click **Create**. . . . . `Enter`

View Digital Signatures Attached to a Document

- Click **Signatures** icon on status bar.

   OR

   a. Click **Office Button** . . . . `Alt`+`F`
   b. Point to **Prepare** . . . . `E`
   c. Click **View Signatures** . . . . `W`

View/Change Status of Digital Signature

1. Click **Signatures** icon 🧑 on status bar.

   OR

   a. Click **Office Button** 🖼️ . . . . Alt + F
   b. Point to **Pr<u>e</u>pare** . . . . E
   c. Click **Vie<u>w</u> Signatures** . . . . W

2. Click a signature's drop-down arrow.

3. Click **Signature Details** . . . . . . G

4. Click **Click here to trust this user's identity**, to make signature valid.

View Digital Certificate Associated with a Digital Signature

1. Click **Signatures** icon 🧑 on status bar.

   OR

   a. Click **Office Button** 🖼️ . . . . Alt + F
   b. Point to **Pr<u>e</u>pare** . . . . E
   c. Click **Vie<u>w</u> Signatures** . . . . W

2. Click a signature's drop-down arrow.

3. Click **Signature Details** . . . . . . G

4. Click **<u>V</u>iew** V

5. Click **OK** . . . . Enter

6. Click **Close** . . . . Esc

Remove a Digital Signature

1. Right-click the visible digital signature line.

   OR

   a. Open the document.
   b. Click **Office Button** 🖼️ . . . . Alt + F
   c. Point to **Pr<u>e</u>pare** . . . . E
   d. Click **Vie<u>w</u> Signatures** . . . . W
   e. Click signature's drop-down arrow.

2. Click **Remove Sig<u>n</u>ature** . . . . . N

3. Click **Yes** . . . . Y

4. If a confirmation dialog box displays, click **OK** . . . . Enter

EXERCISE DIRECTIONS

1. Start Word, if necessary.

2. Open the file 💿 **27SIGNED**.

3. Save the document as **27SIGNED_xx**.

4. Select to attach an invisible digital signature to the document.

5. In the Purpose for signing this document text box, type **Verify the authentic memo**.

6. Use the default digital certificate to sign the document.

   ✓ *If necessary, create a digital ID.*

7. Save a copy of the **27SIGNED_xx** document as **27SIGNEDa_xx**.

8. Check the details of the signature, and then remove it from the document.

9. Press Ctrl + End to move the insertion point to the end of the document and insert a new blank line.

10. Insert a visible signature line using your own name and the title Team Leader. Leave the e-mail address information blank, and use the default instructions.

11. Sign the document by typing your name.

12. If the signature is marked as invalid, display the signature details and select to trust the user's identity.

13. Close the Signatures task pane.

14. Display the document in Print Preview. It should look similar to Illustration A.

   ✓ *Your complete name may not fit within the signature line object.*

15. Print the document.

16. Close the document and exit Word.

MEMO

Date: Today's Date
To: Team Members
From: Student's Name
Re: Confidentiality

As you all know, we are working on a new and exciting product which the company expects to completely revolutionize the golf equipment industry. This memo is simply a reminder of the Long Shot, Inc. corporate policy on confidentiality and ethical behavior.

Confidentiality in business refers to the protection of proprietary and secret information. In some businesses, the information belongs to a client, and it is the responsibility of the business to make sure no one else can access the information. For example, in health care, providers may not share information about patients with unauthorized personnel. Such a breach in confidentiality could impact a patient's access to insurance, job security, and privacy.

In our case, the information belongs to the corporation, and it is our responsibility to make sure no one outside the company gains access. Breaching confidentiality by sharing corporate secrets gives our competitors an advantage they would not otherwise have, and puts our investment at risk. In the past, our competitors have tried many illegal and unethical tactics to try to gain access to our confidential information. They have tried hacking into our computer system, posing as customers and vendors, and even offering bribes to employees.

Please remember that you have all signed confidentiality agreements which state that you will not share your knowledge of this product with anyone outside the development team. The confidentiality agreement is a binding, legal contract. If you breach the agreement, we will prosecute you to the fullest extent of the law.

Thank you all for your consideration in this important matter. We are in the process of a technological breakthrough of which we can all be very proud. I am confident that every member of our team will respect and honor Long Shot's code of conduct and confidentiality. For a complete copy of the policy, please consult the human resources department.

7/18/08

X Student's Name
Student's Name
Team Leader

ON YOUR OWN

1. Start Word.

2. Open ⌨ **OWD25-1_xx**, the essay document you worked with in the On Your Own section of Exercise 25, or open 💿 **27ESSAY**.

3. If there is a watermark in the document, delete it.

4. Save the document as **OWD27-1_xx**.

5. Add an invisible digital signature to the document.

6. Save a copy of the **OWD27-1_xx** document as **OWD27-2_xx**.

7. Remove the invalid signature from the document.

8. Stop protection, if necessary.

9. Insert a signature line at the bottom of the document. Set it up for a classmate's signature, and have the classmate set his or her document up for your signature.

10. Save the changes and close the document.

11. Exchange documents with the classmate.

12. Sign the document.

13. Print the document.

14. Close the document and exit Word.

Skills Covered

- **Create a Form**
- **Insert Content Controls and Form Fields**
- **Set Content Control and Form Field Properties**
- **Fill Out a Form**
- **About Surveys**
- **About Legal Documents**

Software Skills Use forms to collect information such as names and addresses for product registrations, data for surveys, or products and pricing for invoices or purchase orders. With Word, you can create forms that can be printed and filled out manually. You can also store forms on a computer so they can be filled out on-screen.

Application Skills As the Manager of in-house training at Long Shot, Inc., you recognize that changes to the business environment affect all departments, including training. You would like to survey employees to learn how to use developing technology to provide the best in-house training to the most people. In this exercise, you will create a form that employees can fill out indicating their attitudes towards different types of teaching methods. You will print the form, and, finally, you will test the form by filling it out on the computer.

TERMS

Form   A document used to collect and organize information.

Form field   A field inserted in a form document, where users can enter variable information.

NOTES

Create a Form

- A **form** is useful for collecting information that can be stored, analyzed, and used for different purposes.

- For example, a marketing department might use a form to collect and store customers' opinions about a product. Or, a human resources department might use a form to collect and store employee information.

- In Word, you can create a form by combining content controls and instructional text in a template file.

- You can also use **form fields**.

- To use the form, you create a document based on the template.

- Forms are protected so that users can enter data in the content controls or form fields but cannot change any other parts of the document.

- You can protect the entire form, or you can protect individual content controls.

  ✓ *If you protect only the content controls, users may be able to edit the other content in the form document.*

- You can print the document and fill out the form on paper, or you can fill out the form on your computer and store it on a disk.

- If you plan to print the form, you should use form fields instead of content controls, because content controls are designed to be used on-screen in Word.

- You can save a new Word document as a form, or you can save an existing Word document as a form.

- In some ways, Word forms are similar to mail merge documents. They contain standard text and graphics that appear the same on every document, and they contain content controls and/or form fields where users can enter variable data.

Insert Content Controls and Form Fields

- Use the buttons in the Controls group on the Developer tab of the Ribbon to insert content controls or form fields.

- The Developer tab does not display by default; you must set options to make it available.

- Content controls, which are suitable for forms that you intend to fill out on-screen, include:
  - Rich Text
  - Text
  - Combo Box
  - Drop-Down List

- Form fields, which are suitable for forms that you intend to print to fill out on paper or fill out on-screen, include:
  - Text Form Field
  - Check Box Form Field
  - Drop-Down Form Field

- Instructional text automatically displays in each content control that you insert.

- For example, if you insert a Text control, it displays *Click here to enter text*. If you enter a Drop-Down List control, it displays *Choose an item*.

- Form fields do not include instructional text.

- When inserting content controls and form fields, give some consideration to the form layout. You may want to use a table or tab stops to be sure items are aligned to look good on the page and so that it will be easy for users to fill out the form.

- Also, it is important to keep in mind that when a user fills out a form on-screen using the Tab key to move from field to field, Word moves the insertion point based on the order in which fields and controls are inserted in the document.

- To ensure a logical order for users filling out the form, you should give some thought to the order in which you insert the form fields and controls.

- You can use both content controls and form fields in the same form document.

Set Content Control and Form Field Properties

- By default, Word inserts content controls and form fields using basic settings. For example, text form fields are set to allow users to enter an unlimited number of text characters.

- You can customize the content control and form field options in the item's Properties dialog box.

- For example, you can set text form field options to limit users to entering valid dates, or no more than ten characters, and you can assign a style to text entered in a plain text content control.

- You can also change the instructional text that displays in a content control.

- You must set properties for drop-down form fields or content controls in order to enter the drop-down list items.

Fill Out a Form

- To fill out a form manually, simply print it.

- To fill out a form on-screen, create a new document based on the form template, enter data in the form fields, then save the document.

- Use the Tab key to move from one field to the next when you are filling out a form on-screen.

- You can leave form fields blank.

About Surveys

- A survey lets you collect information that you can use to analyze trends and changes.

- Watching and analyzing trends can help managers make informed business decisions.

- For example, retailers watch for trends in the colors and products customers are buying so they know what items to stock in stores.

- A well-designed survey makes it easier to identify trends. It usually includes a plan for who to survey and the questions to ask, as well as a form for entering the answers to the survey questions.

About Legal Documents

- Legal documents are used to insure the legal rights of people, groups, or organizations.

- Legal documents may be as simple as a handwritten note that is signed by all concerned parties and witnessed by a third party.

- Alternatively, legal documents may be long, complex, and written using legal terms and language.

- Many legal documents are forms that combine text and blank spaces or form fields where you may enter customized information.

- Other legal documents are reports, case studies, or opinions that include references to legal authorities.

  ✓ *Creating a table of authorities is covered in Exercise 9.*

- Some common legal forms include the following:
  - Bill of Sale
  - Last Will and Testament
  - Rental Agreement
  - General Release
  - Living Will
- The laws governing legal documents vary from state to state.
- You may be able to find legal document forms on the Internet.

PROCEDURES

Display the Developer Tab on the Ribbon

1. Click **Office Button** 🗐 . . . Alt + F
2. Click **Word Options** I
3. Click **Popular**, if necessary . . . . P, P
4. Click to select **Show Developer tab in the Ribbon** check box . . . . Alt + D

   ✓ A check mark in the check box indicates the option is selected.

5. Click **OK**. . . . . Enter

Create a Form Template

1. Create a new Word document.

   OR

   Open an existing document.
2. Click **Office Button** 🗐 . . . Alt + F
3. Point to **Save As** . . . . A
4. Click **Word Template** . . . . . . T
5. Type template file name.
6. Select location where you want form template stored.
7. Click **Save** . . . . Enter
8. In the document, type standard text that will display on all forms.
9. If necessary, delete variable text that you do not want to display on forms.
10. Insert content controls and form fields as necessary.

    ✓ Refer to **Insert Content Controls** and **Insert Form Fields** procedures for step-by-step instructions on inserting form fields.

11. Click **Developer** tab . . . . . Alt + L

    Protect Group

12. Click **Protect Document** button 🗐 . . . . P, R
13. Click to select **Allow only this type of editing in the document** check box . . . . ↓, ↓, Spacebar
14. Click Editing restrictions drop-down arrow. . . . . . . ⇥, ↓
15. Click **Filling in forms**. . . . . ↓, ↓, Enter
16. Click **Yes, Start Enforcing Protection**.
17. Click **OK**. . . . . Enter

    OR

    Set password protection, as desired.

    ✓ For information on protecting documents and setting exceptions, refer to Exercise 24.

18. Close the template file . . . . Alt + F, C

Open Form Template for Editing

1. Open form template document.
2. Click **Developer** tab . . . . . Alt + L

   Protect Group

3. Click **Protect Document** button 🗐 . . . . P, R
4. Click **Stop Protection**.

Insert Content Controls

1. Open form template for editing.
2. Click **Developer** tab . . . . . Alt + L

   Controls Group

3. Click **Design Mode** button 🖉 . . . . D + M
4. Position insertion point where you want to insert content control.
5. Click **Developer** tab . . . . . Alt + L

   Controls Group

6. Click button for content control to insert:
   - **Rich Text** Aa . . . . Q
   - **Text** Aa . . . . E
   - **Picture** 🖼 I
   - **Combo Box** 🗐 . . . . C, O
   - **Drop-Down List** 🗐 . . . . . O
   - **Date Picker** 🗐 . . . . K
   - **Building Block Gallery** 🗐 . . . . B
7. Repeat steps 4–6 to insert additional content controls.

   ✓ You may combine content controls and form fields in the same form.

8. Click **Developer** tab . . . . . Alt + L

   Controls Group

9. Click **Design Mode** button 🖉 . . . . D + M
10. Protect, save, and close form template document.

Remove Content Control

1. Right-click content control.
2. Click **Remove Content Control** . . . . E

Insert Form Fields

1. Open form template for editing.
2. Position insertion point where you want to insert form field.
3. Click **Developer** tab . . . . . Alt + L

   Controls Group

4. Click **Legacy Tools** button

   . . . . N
5. Click form field to insert:

   ■ **Text Form Field** ab| . . . . . E
   ■ **Check Box Form Field**

   . . . . H
   ■ **Drop-Down Form Field**

   C
6. Repeat steps to insert additional form fields.

   ✓ *You may combine content controls and form fields in the same form.*

   ✓ *To toggle form field shading off or on, click the **Form Field Shading** button in the Legacy Tools gallery.*

7. Protect, save, and close form template document:

Set Content Control Properties

1. Click content control.
2. Click **Developer** tab . . . . . Alt + L

   Controls Group

3. Click **Properties** button

   L
4. Select options as desired.
5. Click **OK**. . . . . Enter

Set Form Field Properties

Text form fields:

1. Click text form field.
2. Click **Developer** tab . . . . . Alt + L

   Controls Group

3. Click **Properties** button

   L
4. Select options as follows:

   ■ Click **Type** drop-down list and select type of text allowed . . . . Alt + P,

   ↓ /↑ , Enter
   ■ Click **Default text** text box and enter default text to display . . . . Alt + E
   ■ Click **Maximum length** text box and enter number of characters allowed . . . Alt + M
   ■ Select format from **Text format** drop-down list . . . . . . Alt + F

   ✓ *Name of format box changes depending on the type of text selected from **Type** drop-down list.*

5. Click **OK**. . . . . Enter

Check box form fields:

1. Click check box form field.
2. Click **Developer** tab . . . . . Alt + L

   Controls Group

3. Click **Properties** button

   L
4. Set size options as follows:

   ■ Select **Auto** option button to set size according to current font size . . . . . Alt + A
   ■ Select **Exactly** option button to type specific size in points. . . . . Alt + E
5. Set default value options as follows:

   ■ Select **Not checked** to display check box not checked by default . . . . Alt + K

■ Select **Checked** to display check box checked by default . . . . Alt + D

6. Click **OK**. . . . . Enter

Drop-down form fields:

1. Click drop-down form field.
2. Click **Developer** tab . . . . . Alt + L

   Controls Group

3. Click **Properties** button

   L
4. Click **Drop-down item** text box . . . . Alt + D
5. Type first option you want displayed in drop-down list.
6. Click **Add** . . . . Alt + A
7. Repeat steps 4–6 until all drop-down options are entered.
8. Click **OK**. . . . . Enter

Fill Out a Form On-Screen

1. Start Word.
2. Create a new document based on the form template.
3. To enter data, use the action appropriate for the different types of form fields or content controls as follows:

   ■ Click content control and type text.
   ■ Click content control drop-down arrow and select option.
   ■ Type text in text form field.
   ■ Click check box form field to select or deselect check box.
   ■ Click drop-down form field arrow, then click desired option.
4. Press ⇥ to move to next form field.

   ✓ *You do not have to enter data in every field.*

5. Save and name document.

EXERCISE DIRECTIONS

Design the Form Template

1. Start Word, if necessary.

2. Open ⊙ **28LSI**.

3. Save the document as a template with the name **28LSI_xx**.

   ✓ *Ask your instructor where to store the new template file.*

4. Draw a table in the document as shown in Illustration A. Keep gridlines displayed, but do not use any borders.

   ✓ *Cell measurements are approximate.*

5. Using a 16-point serif font, type the text in the table shown in Illustration A.

6. Center the words *Yes*, *No*, and *Maybe* in their cells.

7. Check the spelling and grammar in the document.

8. Preview the document. It should look similar to Illustration A.

   ✓ *Gridlines are displayed in the illustration so you can see the size of columns and rows; they will not display in Print Preview.*

9. Print the document.

Illustration A

Insert Content Controls and Form Fields

1. If necessary, display the Developer tab in the Ribbon.

2. In row 1, column 2, insert a Text content control using default properties.

3. In row 2, column 2, insert another Text content control, using default properties.

4. In row 3, column 2, insert a Date Picker content control, using the default properties.

5. In rows 5 and 6, insert check box form fields with the default properties under the text *Yes* and *No* in columns 2 and 3.

   ✓ *Position the insertion point at the end of the text and press Enter to position the insertion point centered on the next line in the cell.*

6. In row 7, column 2, insert a Text content control, using the default properties.

7. In row 8, insert check box form fields under the text *Yes*, *No*, and *Maybe* in columns 2, 3, and 4.

8. In row 9, column 2, insert a Drop-Down List content control.

9. Customize the properties to enter the following three drop-down list items: **Live instructor, Online classroom, Individual training workstation**.

   a. Select the content control and click Properties.

   b. Click Add.

   c. Type the first list item, **Live instructor**.

   d. Click OK.

   e. Follow steps 9b through 9d to add the **Online classroom** and **Individual training workstation** list items.

   f. Click OK.

10. In row 10, column 2, insert a Text content control.

11. Form protect the template.

12. Preview the document. It should look similar to the one in Illustration B.

13. Close the template document, saving all changes.

Fill Out the Form

1. Create a new document based on the **28LSI_*xx*** form template.

2. Save the document as **28SURVEY_*xx***.

3. Fill out the form as follows:

   a. Enter your name in the first Text content control.

   b. Enter *Marketing* in the second Text content control.

   c. Select the current date from the Date Picker content control.

   d. Select *Yes* for whether or not you have attended in-house training classes.

   e. Select *No* for whether or not you were satisfied.

   f. For the reason why you were not satisfied, type that you thought the course was not challenging enough.

   g. Select *Maybe* for whether or not you are interested in future classes.

   h. Select *Online classroom* as the location you would prefer.

   i. Enter any comments you would like in the final text content control.

4. Print the document.

5. Close the document, saving all changes.

Long Shot, Inc.

234 Simsbury Drive   Ithaca, NY 14850

Telephone: 607-555-9191   Fax: 607-555-9292   E-mail: mail@longshot.net

Name: Click here to enter text.

Department: Click here to enter text.

Date: Click here to enter a date.

	Yes	No
Have you attended in-house training classes in the past?	☐	☐
If so, were you satisfied with the class?	☐	☐

If you were not satisfied, why not?   Click here to enter text.

	Yes	No	Maybe
Are you interested in attending in-house training classes in the future?	☐	☐	☐

Which training method would you prefer?   Choose an item.

Comments: Click here to enter text.

ON YOUR OWN

1. Plan a form that could be used as a legal document for a club or organization to which you belong. For example, a field trip permission slip is a legal form. If the organization rents or loans equipment, you might create a rental form. Decide the content controls and/or form fields you would need on the form, as well as the standard text. Plan the layout and design of the form.

2. Start Word and create a new document.

3. Save the document as a template with the name OWD28-1_*xx*.

4. Enter all of the standard text you want on your form. Use a table if it helps you line up the information neatly on the page.

5. Insert the content controls and form fields you will need on your form. Remember to enter them in the order in which you want users to fill them out.

6. Check the spelling and grammar in the document.

7. Form protect the document.

8. Print the document.

9. Ask a classmate to review the document and offer comments and suggestions.

10. Incorporate the comments and suggestions into the form template.

11. Save the template and close it.

12. Create a new document based on the OWD28-1_*xx* template.

13. Save the document as OWD28-2_*xx*.

14. Fill out the form on the screen, or print it and fill it out manually.

15. Save the form, close it, and exit Word.

Critical Thinking

Application Skills   In this exercise, you will create a registration form that New Media Designs employees can use to offer their services as contest judges. You will test the registration form by filling it out on-screen, and you will attach a digital signature to the completed form.

EXERCISE DIRECTIONS

1. Create a new blank document and save it as a template with the name **29FORM_xx**.

2. Type and format the document shown in Illustration A, using a table to arrange the content.

3. Insert content controls and form fields as follows:

   ■ First Name: Text content control with default properties.

   ■ Last Name: Text content control with default properties.

   ■ Department: Drop-Down List content control with options for **Administration**, **Art**, **Editorial**, **Human Resources**, **Information Systems**, **Marketing**, **Other**.

   ■ Phone Extension: Text content control with default properties.

   ■ Email Address: Text content control with default properties.

   ■ Contest for which you would like to be a judge: Drop-Down List content control with options for **Art**, **Contest Ideas**, **Essay**, **Games**.

   ■ Yes: Check box form field.

   ■ No: Check box form field.

   ■ Comments: Text field with default properties.

4. Check the spelling and grammar.

5. Form protect the document.

6. Preview the document. It should look similar to Illustration A.

   ✓ *If there are border lines in your document, remove them.*

7. Print the form.

8. Close the document, saving all changes.

9. Create a new document based on the **29FORM_xx** template.

10. Save the document as **29REGISTER_xx**.

11. Fill out the form.

12. Print the document and then save it.

13. Attach your digital signature to the form.

14. Close the document and exit Word.

New Media Designs
Contest Judge Registration Form

First Name:	Click here to enter text.
Last Name:	Click here to enter text.
Department:	Choose an item.
Phone Extension:	Click here to enter text.
Email Address:	Click here to enter text.

Contest for which you would like to be a judge:	Choose an item.	
Have you ever been a New Media Designs contest judge before?	Yes ☐	No ☐
Comments:	Click here to enter text.	

Curriculum Integration

Application Skills A survey is an effective method of collecting information that can help you identify business trends and changes. Once you collect the data, you can analyze it so that you can use the information to make business decisions. For your social studies class, use the skills you have learned in Lesson 4 to design and create a form that you can use to survey classmates to collect information about a change or trend. For example, you might survey classmates about changes in cafeteria food purchases, how they spend their money on the weekends, or what color clothes they like to buy. When you are finished, ask your classmates to fill out the form on-screen or in print. You can use the results of the survey to create a chart or table, or to write a newspaper article analyzing the data. Refer to Illustration A to see a sample of a survey form.

EXERCISE DIRECTIONS

Pick a topic that you want to use for your survey. The topic should relate to a business trend.

Plan a form that can be used to collect responses to your survey. Consider the type of content controls and forms you will need, the standard text, and how you want to design the form so that it is easy to fill out. Also, think about whether you want the responses to be anonymous.

Start Word, if necessary, and create a new document. Save it as a Word template with the name **30SURVEY_xx**.

Select to display elements that might help you while you work, such as the rulers, nonprinting characters, and gridlines.

Enter all of the standard text you want on your form. You can insert graphics as well, such as a clip art picture, or shapes. Use a table if it helps you line up the information neatly on the page. Alternatively, you might want to use text boxes.

Insert the content controls and form fields you will need on your form. Remember to enter them in the order in which you want users to fill them out.

Check the spelling and grammar in the document.

Form protect the document, and then print it.

Ask a classmate to review the document and offer comments and suggestions.

Incorporate the comments and suggestions into the form template.

Save the template and close it.

Ask your classmates to fill out the form as a printed hard copy or on-screen.

Collect the results and analyze them. Create a chart, graph, or table illustrating the results, or write an article explaining them.

Assess the survey form, data, and analysis to decide if you want to include it in your employment portfolio as an example of achievement. If so, print the material and add it to the portfolio.

Illustration A

Social Studies

Please take the time to complete this survey. The results are strictly confidential.

Age: Click here to enter text.

Gender: Male   Female
                            ☐   ☐

Date: Click here to enter a date.

How many movies do you see a month?   Choose an item.

How much money do you spend at the   Choose an item.
concession stand each time?

Do you think you are   More   Less   Not Sure
spending more or less   ☐   ☐   ☐
on movies and
concessions than you
did last year?

Comments: Click here to enter text.

Lesson | 5

Integration

Skills Covered

- Microsoft Office 2007
- Run Multiple Programs at the Same Time
- Arrange Multiple Program Windows
- Switch Among Open Programs
- Copy and Move Data from One Office Document to Another
- About Acceptable Use Policies

Software Skills   If you use Microsoft Office 2007, you may find it necessary to work with more than one application at a time. For example, you might want to create a report detailing your department's decreased costs by combining a Word document with an Excel spreadsheet. Or, you might want to illustrate a Word letter using an Excel chart. Using your operating system commands, you can open multiple applications at the same time and easily switch among them. You can also arrange the open applications on the screen so you can quickly find the information you need.

Application Skills   The owners of Fresh Food Fair, a small chain of organic grocery stores, are thinking about starting a home delivery service. You have been asked to coordinate a feasibility study, and the owners have sent you information prepared in Word, Excel, and PowerPoint. In this exercise, you will start Word and open a memo document. You will then start the other Office programs, open the other program files, arrange the windows on-screen, and switch among the open windows. You will also copy data from an Excel worksheet into a Word document.

TERMS

Acceptable use policy   A set of rules governing how a network or the Internet may be used.

Active window   The window in which you are currently working.

Cascade   Arrange open windows on-screen so they overlap, with the active window displayed on top.

Destination file   The file where the data is pasted.

Group button   A taskbar button that represents all open windows for one application.

Software suite   A group of software applications sold as a single unit. Usually, the applications have common features that make it easy to integrate and share data among documents.

Source file   The file that contains the data to be copied.

Tile   Arrange open windows on-screen so they do not overlap.

NOTES

Microsoft Office 2007

- Microsoft Office 2007 is a version of the popular Microsoft Office **software suite**.

- Different editions of the suite are available to suit the needs of different people and businesses.

- Most editions include the following core Microsoft Office System programs:
  - Word, a word processing program.
  - Excel, a spreadsheet program.
  - PowerPoint, a presentation graphics program.
  - Outlook, a personal information manager and communications program.

- Some editions may include the following additional programs:
  - Access, a database application.
  - Publisher, a desktop publishing program.
  - OneNote, a note-taking and management program.
  - InfoPath, an information gathering and management program.

- The programs in the Microsoft Office 2007 suite are designed for integration, which means it is possible to share data created in one program with other programs.

- For example, you can copy and paste data from Excel to Word, or from Word to PowerPoint, and so on.

- Sharing information saves time, because you do not have to reenter the same data more than once, and it also helps insure accuracy.

- Many of the commands and features are common to all of the programs, making it easy to transfer your knowledge of one program to the others.

- In addition, Microsoft provides tools to help you apply consistent formatting to your files, no matter which program you are using.

- For example, you can apply the same theme to a Word document as to a PowerPoint presentation.

- Microsoft Office 2007 can run with either the Microsoft Windows XP or the Microsoft Windows Vista operating system.

- Microsoft Office 2007 programs are fully compatible with files created with previous versions.

Run Multiple Programs at the Same Time

- You can open multiple program windows at the same time. This is useful for comparing the data in different files, as well as for exchanging data between files.

- Use Windows to start an Office program.
  - You can select the program you want to start from the Microsoft Office folder accessed from the Windows All Programs menu.
  - If the program has been used recently, or pinned to the Windows Start menu, you can select it directly from the Windows Start menu.
  - You can double-click a program shortcut icon on the Windows desktop, if available.

Arrange Multiple Program Windows

- Use Windows commands to arrange open program windows on your screen.

- Each open window is represented by a button on the Windows taskbar.

- If there is not room on the taskbar to display buttons for each open window, Windows displays a **group button**.

  > ✓ *The taskbar may not be visible on-screen if Windows is set to hide the taskbar, or to display windows on top of the taskbar. To see the taskbar, move the mouse pointer to the edge of the screen where it usually displays, or press* Ctrl + Esc .

- You can **tile** windows if you want to see all of them at the same time. Tiled windows do not overlap.

- You can tile windows horizontally—stacked—or vertically—side by side.

- The more windows you have open, the smaller they display when tiled.
  - If necessary in smaller windows, the program may hide common screen elements such as the Office Button, Quick Access Toolbar, and Ribbon and display only a program icon on the left end of the title bar.
  - You can click the program icon to display a shortcut menu of commands including Maximize, Minimize, and Close.

- You can **cascade** windows if you want to see the active window in its entirety, with the title bars of all open windows displayed behind it.

Cascading windows

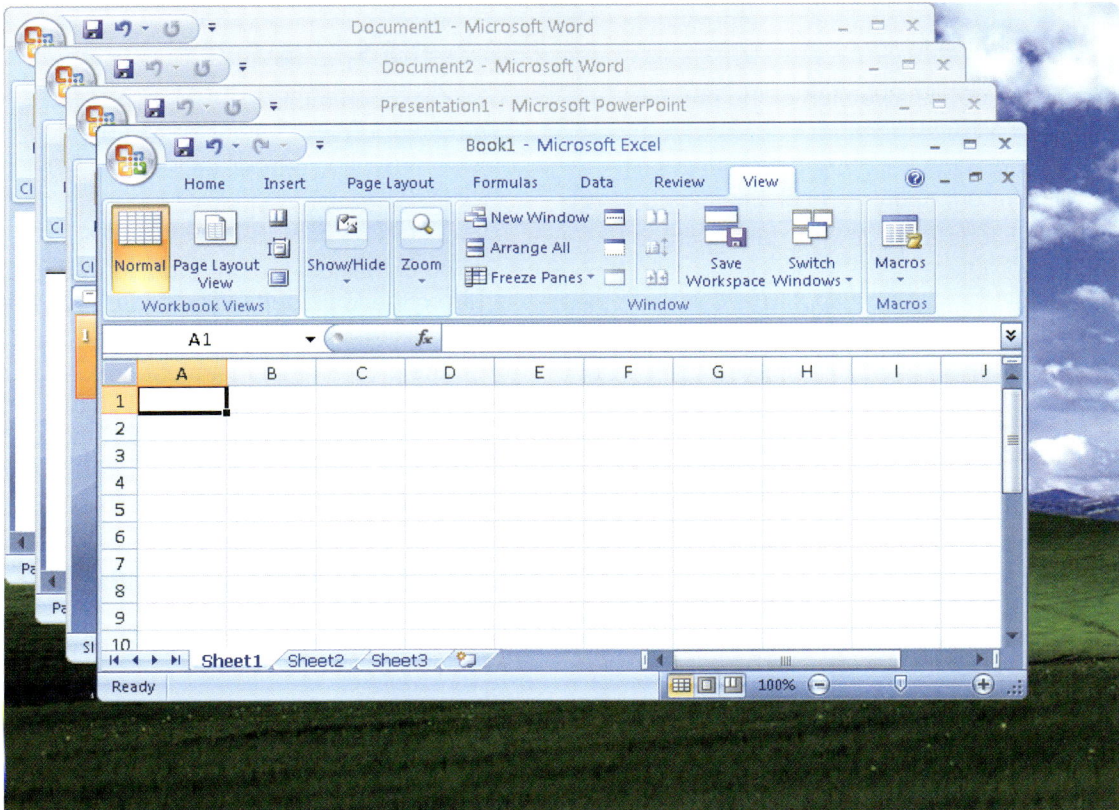

Tiled windows

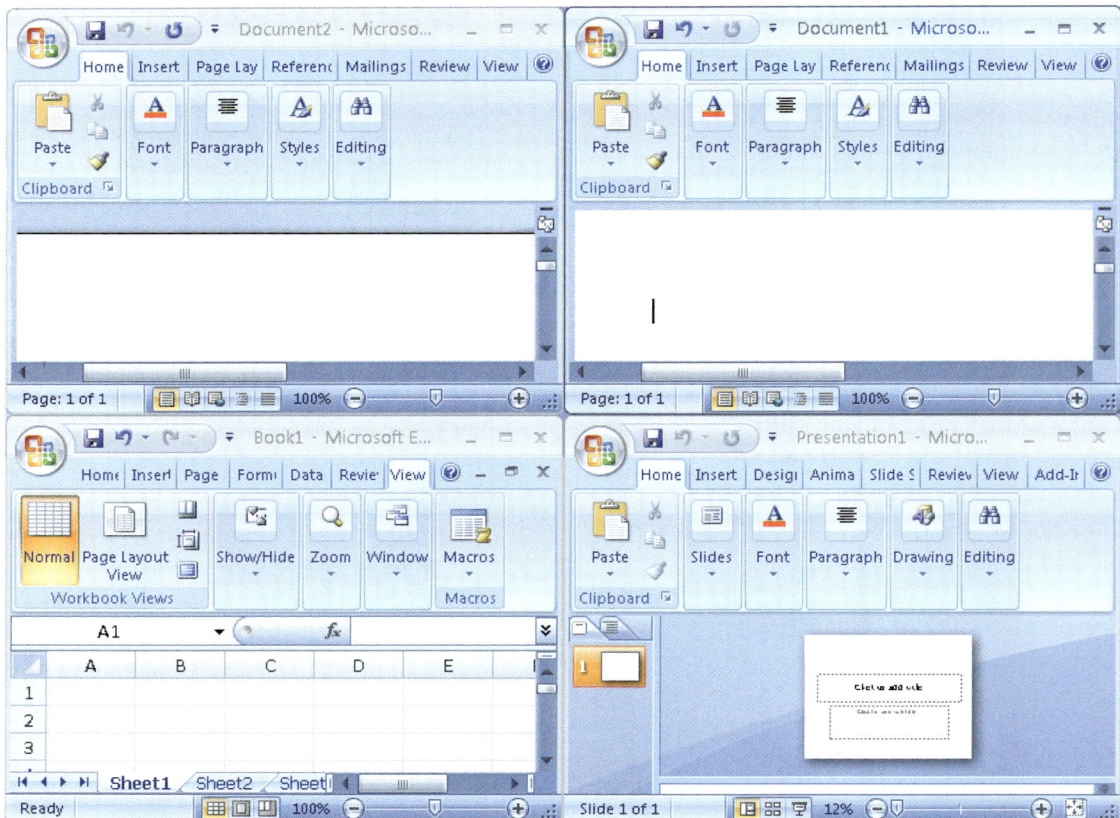

Switch Among Open Programs

- Only one window can be active—or current—at a time.
- The **active window** displays on top of other open windows. Its title bar is darker than the title bars of other open windows, and its taskbar button appears pressed in.
- You can use Windows commands to switch among open windows to make a different window active.

Copy and Move Data from One Office Document to Another

- Use the Windows Clipboard or drag-and-drop editing to copy or move data from one Office document to another.
- The **source file** contains the original data and the **destination file** is where the data is pasted.
- Data pasted into a destination file becomes part of the destination file. There is no link to the source file.
- Word may automatically format pasted data. For example, Excel data pasted into a Word document is displayed as a table, and a PowerPoint slide pasted into a Word document is formatted as a picture.
- You edit pasted data using standard commands for the destination application.

About Acceptable Use Policies

- Most businesses and organizations have an **acceptable use policy** (AUP) that specifies rules for using the corporate network or the Internet.
- Usually, a person must sign the policy before he or she is allowed access.
- Typically, an AUP describes the most important aspects of what a person may or may not do when using the network, and what the punishments for breaking the rules will be.
- The AUP may reference a more detailed policy document.
- The AUP may vary, depending on the type of business or organization.
- Some rules that are typically found on an AUP cover issues such as the following:
  - Use of appropriate language while online.
  - Participation in illegal activities.
  - Disruption of others' work.
  - Release of personal information.
  - Dissemination of obscene or defamatory material.
  - Plagiarism and other copyright infringements.

PROCEDURES

Start an Office Program

1. Click **Start** button
   / start . . . . Ctrl + Esc
2. Click **All Programs** . . . . . P , Enter
   - ✓ *If you are using Windows Vista, the keystrokes to open the All Programs menu are ↑ , Enter .*
3. Point to **Microsoft Office** folder icon . . . . ↓ , →
4. Click name of the Office program . . . . ↓ , Enter

   OR

1. Click **Start** button
   / start . . . . Ctrl + Esc
2. Click name of the Office program in the list of recently used programs. . . . . ↓ , Enter

   OR

3. Double-click a program shortcut icon on the desktop:
   - Word shortcut icon to start Word.
   - Excel shortcut icon to start Excel.
   - PowerPoint shortcut icon to start PowerPoint.
   - Access shortcut icon to start Access.
   - Outlook shortcut icon to start Outlook.
   - Publisher shortcut icon to start Publisher.

Exit an Office Program

- Click **Program Close** button ✗ at the right end of the program's title bar.
  - ✓ *If you are using Windows Vista, the Program Close button may look different.*

  OR

1. Click **Office Button** . . . Alt + F
2. Click **Exit** *program name*. X
3. Click **Yes** to save open documents . . . . Y

   OR

   Click **No** to exit without saving . . . . N

Arrange Program Windows

In Windows XP:

1. Right-click on blank area of Windows taskbar.
2. Select desired option:
   - **Cascade Windows**.... $\boxed{S}$, $\boxed{\text{Enter}}$
   - **Tile Windows Horizontally**........... $\boxed{H}$
   - **Tile Windows Vertically**............. $\boxed{E}$

   ✓ *Maximize active window to display active window only.*

In Windows Vista:

1. Right-click on blank area of Windows taskbar.
2. Select desired option:
   - **Cascade Windows**........ $\boxed{\uparrow}$/$\boxed{\downarrow}$, $\boxed{\text{Enter}}$
   - **Show Windows Stacked**........ $\boxed{\uparrow}$/$\boxed{\downarrow}$, $\boxed{\text{Enter}}$
   - **Show Windows Side by Side**........... $\boxed{\uparrow}$/$\boxed{\downarrow}$, $\boxed{\text{Enter}}$

   ✓ *Maximize active window to display active window only.*

Switch Between Open Windows

- Click taskbar button of desired window.

   OR

- Click in desired window.

   OR

1. Click group taskbar button.
2. Click name of window.

   OR

1. Press and hold $\boxed{\text{Alt}}$.
2. Press $\boxed{\leftrightarrows}$ to cycle through open windows.
3. Release both keys when desired window is selected.

Copy Data from One Office Document to Another (Ctrl+C, Ctrl+V)

To use the Clipboard:

1. Start programs.
2. Open source file.
3. Open destination file.

4. Select data to copy in source file.
5. Click **Home** tab in source.............. $\boxed{\text{Alt}}$+$\boxed{H}$

   Clipboard Group

6. Click **Copy** button 🗐 .... $\boxed{C}$

   OR

   a. Right-click selection.
   b. Click **Copy** .... $\boxed{C}$

7. Make destination file active.
8. Position insertion point in new location.
9. Click **Home** tab in destination........... $\boxed{\text{Alt}}$+$\boxed{H}$

   Clipboard Group

10. Click **Paste** button 📋 ... $\boxed{V}$, $\boxed{P}$

   OR

   a. Right-click insertion point location.
   b. Click **Paste**.......... $\boxed{P}$, $\boxed{\text{Enter}}$

To use drag-and-drop editing:

1. Start programs.
2. Open source file.
3. Open destination file.
4. Right-click on blank area of Windows taskbar.
5. Select **Tile Windows Vertically** .... $\boxed{E}$

   ✓ *In Windows Vista, select Show Windows Side by Side.*

6. Select data to copy in source document.
7. Scroll in destination document to display desired new location.
8. Move pointer to edge of selection.
9. Press and hold down $\boxed{\text{Ctrl}}$.
10. Drag selected data to correct position in destination file.

   ✓ *A gray vertical bar indicates location where selection will be dropped.*

11. Release mouse button.
12. Release $\boxed{\text{Ctrl}}$.

Move Data from One Office Document to Another (Ctrl+X, Ctrl+V)

To use the Clipboard:

1. Start programs.
2. Open source file.
3. Open destination file.
4. Select data to move in source file.
5. Click **Home** tab in source.............. $\boxed{\text{Alt}}$+$\boxed{H}$

   Clipboard Group

6. Click **Cut** button 📑 .... $\boxed{X}$

   OR

   a. Right-click selection.
   b. Click **Cut** .... $\boxed{T}$, $\boxed{\text{Enter}}$

7. Make destination file active.
8. Position insertion point in new location.
9. Click **Home** tab in destination........... $\boxed{\text{Alt}}$+$\boxed{H}$

   Clipboard Group

10. Click **Paste** button 📋 ... $\boxed{V}$, $\boxed{P}$

   OR

   a. Right-click insertion point location.
   b. Click **Paste**.......... $\boxed{P}$, $\boxed{\text{Enter}}$

To use drag-and-drop editing:

1. Start programs.
2. Open source file.
3. Open destination file.
4. Right-click on blank area of Windows taskbar.
5. Select **Tile Windows Vertically** .... $\boxed{E}$

   ✓ *In Windows Vista, select Show Windows Side by Side.*

6. Select data to move in source document.
7. Scroll in destination document to display desired new location.
8. Move pointer to edge of selection.
9. Drag selected data to correct position in destination file.

   ✓ *A gray vertical bar indicates location where selection will be dropped.*

10. Release mouse button.

EXERCISE DIRECTIONS

✓ *This exercise assumes you know how to locate and select data in an Excel worksheet. If you do not, ask your instructor for more information.*

Start and Arrange Multiple Program Windows

1. Start Word, if necessary, and open the document 31MEMO. Save the file as **31MEMO_xx**.

2. Start Excel and open the workbook 31DATA. You do not have to save the workbook file with a new name.

3. Start PowerPoint and open the presentation 31PRES. You do not have to save the presentation file with a new name.

4. Tile the windows vertically—side by side—on-screen. They should look similar to Illustration A, although the order may vary.

5. Make the file **31MEMO_xx** active.

6. Tile the windows horizontally—stacked.

7. Make the file **31DATA** active.

8. Cascade the windows.

9. Make the file **31PRES** active and maximize the Power-Point window.

10. Exit PowerPoint without saving any changes.

Copy Data from One Program to Another

1. Make the file **31MEMO_xx** active and maximize the window.

2. Replace the text *Your Name* with your own name.

3. Replace the text *Today's date* with the current date.

4. Position the insertion point on the blank line at the end of the document.

5. Make the **31DATA** file active, and maximize the window.

Illustration A

6. Select cells A4 through B9.

   a. Click the cell in the fourth row of the first column (it contains the text *Initial Investment*).

   b. Press and hold Shift.

   c. Click the cell in the ninth row of the second column (it contains the value *$243,500.00*).

7. Copy the selected range of cells to the last line of the **31MEMO_xx** document.

   a. Click the Copy button on the Home tab of the Ribbon.

   b. Switch to the **31MEMO_xx** document.

   c. Make sure the insertion point is on the last line.

   d. Click the Paste button on the Home tab of the Ribbon.

8. Select the table and apply the Table Grid 8 table style.

9. Center the table horizontally on the page.

10. Check the spelling and grammar in the document.

11. Preview the **31MEMO_xx** document. It should look similar to Illustration B.

12. Print the document.

13. Close the **31DATA** workbook file and exit Excel without saving any changes.

14. Close **31MEMO_xx**, saving all changes, and exit Word.

Illustration B

Fresh Food Fair
Route 117, Bolton, MA 01740

MEMO

To: Kimberly and Jack Thomson
From: Student's Name
Date: Today's date
Subject: Home Delivery Service

I believe the research bears out the need for a home delivery service. The data indicates we could be profitable within six months. Please review the information and let me know how you want to proceed.

Initial Investment	
Trucks	$100,000.00
Equipment	$55,000.00
Supplies	$52,000.00
Training	$36,500.00
Total	$243,500.00

ON YOUR OWN

1. In this exercise, use Word and Excel to begin developing your own set of guidelines controlling the acceptable use of online services.

2. Start Word, create a new document, and save the document as **OWD31-1_xx**.

3. Type a letter to your instructor, your parents, or someone else explaining that you are working on an acceptable use policy and that you are starting by compiling a list of Internet sites and online services that should be governed by the policy. Ask them to review the list and offer suggestions for other sites and services that should be included.

4. Start Excel and create a new workbook, or open the workbook ⊙ **31ONLINE**. Save the file as **OWD31-2_xx**.

5. Create a worksheet listing the online service, a description, and the URL. If you are using the existing workbook, you may want to add or change some of the entries.

6. Select the Excel worksheet data and copy it to the Word document.

7. Format the data in the Word document to improve its appearance and make it easier to read.

8. Check the spelling and grammar in the document.

9. Print the document.

10. Ask a classmate to review the document and make comments or suggestions.

11. Incorporate the comments and suggestions into the document.

12. Close all files and programs, saving all changes.

Business Connection

Changing Jobs

Statistics indicate that most people will change jobs many times during their working careers. There are many reasons for changing jobs: promotion, dissatisfaction, relocation, and layoff, just to name a few. Different employers have different procedures for changing jobs. Usually, employers include information about leaving in the employee handbook. Typical procedures might include writing a letter of resignation, providing two weeks' notice, and participating in an exit interview during which you explain your reasons for leaving. For all employees, it is important to maintain a professional attitude, and display courtesy and honesty. Remember, you might return to work at the same place in the future, or need a reference from your old manager.

A Letter of Resignation

Imagine you are ready to leave your current place of employment. At this time, the reasons do not really matter. You simply have to inform your employer that you are resigning. Create a new Word document and write a block or modified-block business letter to the employer. Include the specific details of your resignation, such as the date that will be your last on the job. You should be polite but direct, and thank the employer for time you had on the job, the opportunities, and the experience you have gained. Remember to proofread the letter for correct spelling, grammar, layout, and formatting. Ask a classmate to review your letter and provide you with feedback that will help you improve the document.

Skills Covered

- **Link Files**
- **Edit a Linked Object**

- **Update Links**

Software Skills Link files when you have existing data in one file that you want to use in one or more other files. Whenever the original data is changed, the link ensures that it will be updated in all other files. Linking lets you maintain data in a single file location, yet use it in other files as well.

Application Skills As the new training director at Long Shot, Inc., you have been asked to submit the department's expenses for the first quarter to the Director of Human Resources. However, you only have preliminary data available. In this exercise, you will link the preliminary data stored in an Excel worksheet into a Word memo. You will then change the data to reflect actual expenses, and update the link to update the data in the Word document.

TERMS

Link To insert an object in a destination file. When the source file is edited, the linked object in the destination file is updated to reflect the change.

NOTES

Link Files

- **Link** data to create a dynamic connection between two files. Linking enables you to keep files that include the same data up to date, without having to edit the data in every file.

- The source file contains the original data and the destination file contains the linked object.

- Source data can be linked to many destination files. For example, data in an Excel worksheet can be linked to multiple Word documents and to a Power-Point slide.

- When you edit the source file, the linked object in the destination file(s) changes as well.

- Use the Paste Special command with the Paste Link option enabled to link files.

- In the Paste Special dialog box, you can also select how you want to format the selected object. The choices depend on the source program.

- A description of the selected format displays in the Result area of the dialog box.

Paste Special dialog box

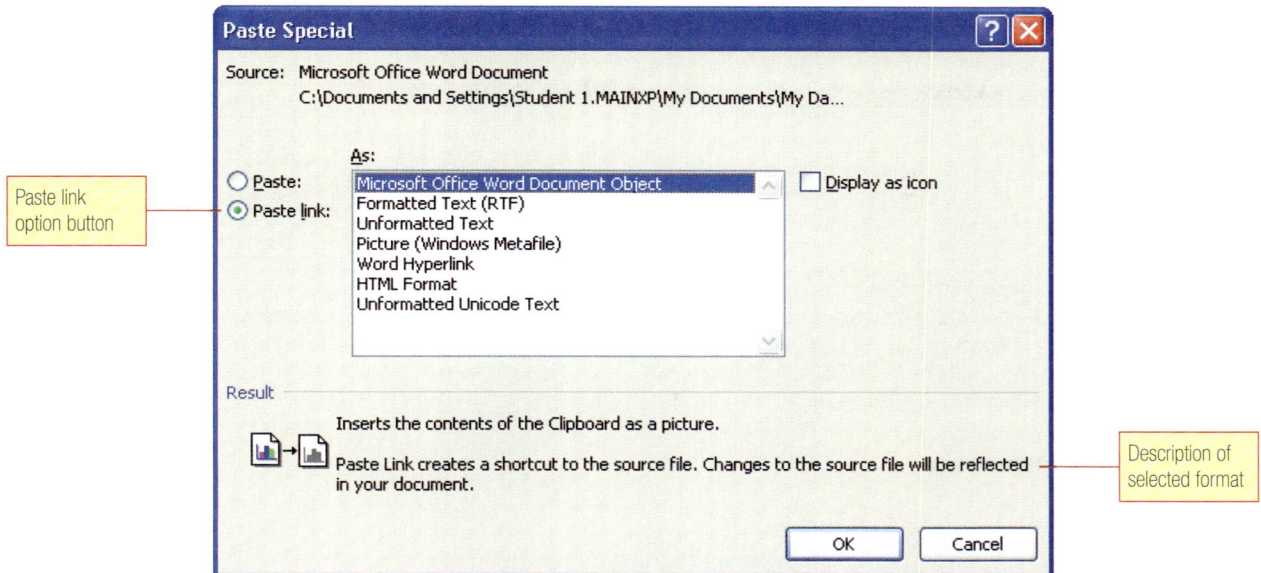

Paste link
option button

Description of
selected format

Edit a Linked Object

- To make sure that the original data is always up-to-date, you use the source program to edit a linked object.

- For example, if you have a linked Excel object in a Word memo, you must use Excel to edit the object in the memo.

- When you double-click a linked object, the source program and file open so you can access the appropriate commands.

- Changes made to the original source file are reflected in the linked object when the link is updated.

- Although you cannot edit a linked object using the destination program, linked objects can be formatted, moved, and resized using many techniques you use to work with graphics objects.

Update Links

- By default, links update automatically.

- When both the source and destination files are open, the linked object must be selected for the update to occur.

- When only the source file is open, the linked object is updated when you open the destination file.

- If there are many links in a file, automatic updating can slow down your system.

- You can turn off automatic updates and manually update links.

- When you open a document that contains linked objects, Word prompts you to update the document with data from the linked files.

- If Word cannot locate the source file (for example, if it has been deleted, renamed, or moved), it will display a warning message telling you that it cannot update the link. You can use the Links dialog box to break the link or to change the location of the source file.

- Breaking the link leaves the object in the destination document without a link to a source document or program.

- Changing the source file in the Links dialog box links the object to a different source file.

- You can lock a link to prevent it from being updated.

- You can set Word options so that no links in any Word document will be updated.

Links dialog box

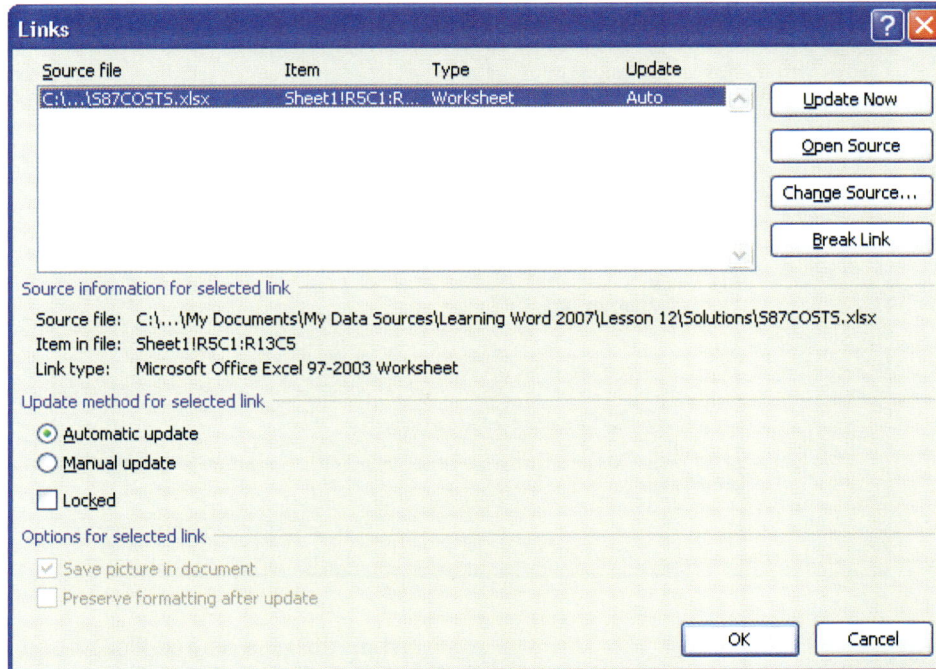

PROCEDURES

Link Files

1. Open source and destination files.
2. Select data to be linked in source file.
3. Click **Home** tab in source . . . . `Alt`+`H`

   `Clipboard Group`

4. Click **Copy** button 🗐 . . . . `C`

   OR

   a. Right-click selection.
   b. Click **Copy** . . . . `C`
5. Make destination file active.
6. Position insertion point in the desired location.
7. Click **Home** tab in destination. . . . . `Alt`+`H`

   `Clipboard Group`

8. Click **Paste** button drop-down arrow 📋 . . . . `V`
9. Click **Paste Special** . . . . `S`

10. Click **Paste link** option button . . . . `Alt`+`L`
11. Click **As** box, if necessary . . . . `Alt`+`A`
12. Click format to use . . . . . . `↓`/`↑`
13. Click **OK**. . . . . `Enter`

Edit a Linked Object

1. Open file containing linked object.
2. Double-click linked object.

   ✓ *Source program and file open.*

3. Edit source file.
4. Close source program and file, saving all changes.

Turn Off Automatic Updating

1. Open the document.
2. Click **Office Button** 🔘 . . . `Alt`+`F`
3. Point to **Prepare** . . . . `E`
4. Click **Edit Links to Files** . . . . . `L`

   ✓ *If there are multiple links in the file, click the specific link in the Source file list.*

5. Click **Manual update** option button . . . . `Alt`+`M`
6. Click **OK**. . . . . `Enter`

Update a Link Manually

1. Open the document.
2. Click **Office Button** 🔘 . . . `Alt`+`F`
3. Click **Prepare**. . . . . `E`
4. Click **Edit Links to Files** . . . . . `L`

   ✓ *If there are multiple links in the file, click the specific link in the Source file list.*

5. Click **Update Now** . . . . . . `Alt`+`U`
6. Click **OK**. . . . . `Enter`

   OR

1. Open the document.
2. Right-click object.
3. Click **Update Link** . . . . `D`

Turn On Automatic Updating

1. Open the document.
2. Click **Office Button** ... `Alt`+`F`
3. Click **Pr**e**pare** . . . . `E`
4. Click **Edit Links to Files** . . . . . `L`

   ✓ *If there are multiple links in the file, click the specific link in the Source file list.*

5. Click **Automatic update** option button. . . . . `Alt`+`A`
6. Click **OK**. . . . . `Enter`

Lock a Link *(Ctrl+F11)*

1. Open the document.
2. Click **Office Button** ... `Alt`+`F`
3. Click **Pr**e**pare** . . . . `E`
4. Click **Edit Links to Files** . . . . . `L`

   ✓ *If there are multiple links in the file, click the specific link in the Source file list.*

5. Click to select **Locked** check box . . . . `Alt`+`K`
6. Click **OK**. . . . . `Enter`

Unlock a Link *(Ctrl+Shift+F11)*

1. Open the document.
2. Click **Office Button** ... `Alt`+`F`
3. Click **Pr**e**pare** . . . . `E`
4. Click **Edit Links to Files** . . . . . `L`

   ✓ *If there are multiple links in the file, click the specific link in the Source file list.*

5. Click to deselect **Locked** check box . . . . `Alt`+`K`
6. Click **OK**. . . . . `Enter`

Prevent All Links in All Documents from Updating

1. Open the document.
2. Click **Office Button** ... `Alt`+`F`
3. Click **Word Options** . . . . `I`
4. Click **Advanced** . . . . `A`
5. Under General, click to deselect **Update automatic links at open** check box . . . . `Alt`+`U`, `U`, `U`, `Spacebar`

   ✓ *Select the check box to allow links to update.*

6. Click **OK**. . . . . `Enter`

Break a Link *(Ctrl+Shift+F9)*

1. Open the document.
2. Click **Office Button** ... `Alt`+`F`
3. Click **Pr**e**pare** . . . . `E`
4. Click **Edit Links to Files** . . . . . `L`

   ✓ *If there are multiple links in the file, click the specific link in the Source file list.*

5. Click **Break Link** . . . . `Alt`+`B`
6. Click **Yes** to break the link . . . . `Y`

   OR

   Click **No** to leave the link in place . . . . `N`
7. Click **OK**. . . . . `Enter`

Change a Link's Source

1. Open the document.
2. Click **Office Button** ... `Alt`+`F`
3. Click **Pr**e**pare** . . . . `E`
4. Click **Edit Links to Files** . . . . . `L`

   ✓ *If there are multiple links in the file, click the specific link in the Source file list.*

5. Click **Change Source** . . . . `Alt`+`N`
6. Locate and select new source file.
7. Click **Open** . . . . `Alt`+`O`
8. Click **OK**. . . . . `Enter`

EXERCISE DIRECTIONS

✓ *The steps in this exercise assume you know how to select and enter data in an Excel worksheet. If necessary, ask your instructor for more information.*

Link Data from Excel to Word

1. Start Word, if necessary, open 💿 **32MEMO**, and save the document as **32MEMO_xx**.
2. Replace the sample text *Your Name* with your own name, and the sample text *Today's date* with the current date.
3. Position the insertion point on the blank line at the end of the document.
4. Start Excel, open the worksheet file 💿 **32COSTS**, and save the file as **32COSTS_xx**.

5. Select the cell range A5:E13, copy the range to the Clipboard, and then use Paste Special to link the Excel worksheet data onto the blank line at the end of the **32MEMO_xx** document.
6. In the memo document, center the linked object horizontally on the page.

   ✓ *Click the object to select it, then click the Center button in the Paragraph group on the Home tab of the Ribbon.*

7. Save the changes to the Word document.

Edit the Data and Update the Link

1. Double-click the linked object in the Word document.

   ✓ *Excel displays the 32COSTS_xx workbook.*

2. Press `Esc` to cancel the selection marquee.

3. In cell C9—February Facility rentals (the empty cell)—type **1,500** and then press [Enter].

✓ *Excel is set to automatically format the data as currency.*

4. Close the worksheet, saving the changes, and exit Excel.

5. Switch to the **32MEMO_xx** document.

6. Manually update the link.

7. Double-click the Excel object in the Word memo.

✓ *Excel starts and opens the **32COSTS_xx** workbook.*

8. Click cell D12—March Miscellaneous expenses—and type **150** to edit the entry. Press [Enter] to enter the data in the cell.

9. Close the worksheet, saving the changes, and exit Excel.

10. Manually update the link in Word.

11. Preview the **32MEMO_xx** document. It should look similar to Illustration A.

12. Print the document.

13. Close the document, saving all changes, and exit Word.

Illustration A

Long Shot, Inc.

INTERDEPARTMENTAL MEMORANDUM

To: Director of Human Resources
From: Student's Name
Date: Today's date
Re: Training Department Expenses

Per your request, here are the preliminary expense figures for the training department for the first quarter of the year. I will update the figures as soon as I receive the actual amounts.

	January	February	March	Total
Salaries	$135,000.00	$135,000.00	$135,000.00	$405,000.00
Overtime	$30,000.00	$32,000.00	$29,000.00	$91,000.00
Entertainment	$1,500.00	$1,750.00	$1,200.00	$4,450.00
Facility rentals	$2,000.00	$1,500.00	$1,500.00	$5,000.00
Books	$500.00	$250.00	$500.00	$1,250.00
Supplies	$250.00	$150.00	$375.00	$775.00
Miscellaneous	$200.00	$175.00	$150.00	$525.00
Total	$169,450.00	$170,825.00	$167,725.00	$508,000.00

ON YOUR OWN

1. Start Word and open ⌨ OWD31-1_*xx*, the letter you created in the On Your Own section of Exercise 31, or open ⊙ 32REQUEST.

2. Save the document as OWD32-1_*xx*.

3. Delete the table from the document.

4. Start Excel and open ⌨ OWD31-2_*xx*, the workbook containing the list of online sites and services you created in the On Your Own section of Exercise 31, or open ⊙ 32ONLINE.

5. Save the workbook as OWD32-2_*xx*.

6. Link the worksheet data to the Word document.

7. Change some of the data in the Excel worksheet.

8. Make sure the data updates in the Word document. Manually update the link, if necessary.

9. Close the Excel workbook, saving all changes, and exit Excel.

10. Close the Word document, saving all changes, and exit Word.

Exercise | 33

Skills Covered

■ **Embed Objects**   ■ **Edit Embedded Objects**

Software Skills Embed data when you do not want a link between the source data and the embedded object. You can edit embedded data without the changes affecting the source. This is useful for illustrating changes that might occur, or for submitting information that might vary depending on the recipient, such as a proposal bid or a contract.

Application Skills As the new training director at Long Shot, Inc., you are planning a weekend training retreat for upper-level management. The Director of Human Resources has asked you to submit a preliminary budget for the event. In this exercise, you will embed an existing budget in a Word memo. You will then edit and format the object using Excel.

TERMS

Embed To insert an object in a file. The embedded object is not linked to a source file, but it is linked to the source application. You edit the object using the source application, but changes do not affect the source file data.

NOTES

Embed Objects

■ **Embed** an object to insert it into a destination file.

■ There is no link between the original data in the source file and the embedded object; however, you can use all of the source program's commands to edit, format, and manipulate the embedded object.

■ Use the Paste Special command to create an embedded object from existing data.

■ Use the Object button in the Text group on the Insert tab of the Ribbon to create a new embedded object.

■ Embedding an object uses more disk space than linking an object, because the same data is stored in both the source and destination files.

Edit Embedded Objects

■ Edit and format embedded objects using the source program.

■ When you edit embedded objects in Word, the source application commands display in the Word window.

■ Changes you make to the embedded object do not affect the original file.

Edit an embedded Excel worksheet object in Word

Word title bar

Excel formula bar

Word document window

Excel Ribbon

Worksheet frame

Word status bar

S88RETREAT - Microsoft Word

File   Window

Home   Insert   Page Layout   Formulas   Data   Review   View   Developer

Arial   10   General

A3   Spring Training Retreat Budget

To: Director of Human Resources
From: Student's Name
Date: Today's date
Re: Training Department Expenses

Per your request, here are the preliminary budget figures for the training retreat planned for September. I based the figures on the last training retreat. We can easily use Excel to update and format the data as necessary.

	A	B	C
3	Spring Training Retreat Budget		
4			
5		Planned	Actual
6	Travel	$ 1,500.00	$ 1,500.00
7	Accommodations	$ 6,350.00	$ 6,350.00
8	Meals	$ 1,200.00	$ 1,375.00
9	Facility rentals	$ 2,500.00	$ 2,500.00
10	Books	$ 875.00	$ 875.00
11	Supplies	$ 500.00	$ 465.00
12	Miscellaneous	$ 1,000.00	$ 800.00
13	**Total**	$13,925.00	$13,865.00

Sheet1   Sheet2   Shee

Page: 1 of 1   Words: 58   117%

PROCEDURES

Embed Selected Data

1. Open source file.
2. Select data to be copied.
3. Click **Home** tab in source . . . . Alt +H

Clipboard Group

4. Click **Copy** button C

   OR

   a. Right-click selection.
   b. Click **Copy** C
5. Make destination file active.
6. Position insertion point in the desired location.
7. Click **Home** tab in destination. . . . . Alt +H

Clipboard Group

8. Click **Paste** button drop-down arrow V
9. Click **Paste Special** . . . . S
10. Click **As** box, if necessary . . . . Alt +A
11. Click format to use . . . . . . ↓/↑
12. Click **Paste** option button . . . . Alt +P
13. Click **OK**. . . . . Enter

Embed a New Object

1. Open destination file.
2. Position insertion point.
3. Click **Insert** tab . . . . Alt +N

Text Group

4. Click **Object** button . . . . J, J
5. Click **Create New** tab . . . . Alt +C
6. Click **Object type** list box . . . . Alt +O
7. Select object type. . . . . . . ↓/↑
8. Click **OK**. . . . . Enter

   ✓ *Selected application opens.*

9. Enter, edit, and format data to create object.
10. Click outside of object to close source application and display object in destination file.

Embed Entire File

1. Open destination file.
2. Position insertion point.
3. Click **Insert** tab . . . . ⌐Alt⌐+⌐N⌐

   Text Group

4. Click **Object** button

   🖼▾ . . . . ⌐J⌐, ⌐J⌐
5. Click **Create from File**

   tab . . . . ⌐Alt⌐+⌐F⌐

6. Click **Browse** . . . . ⌐Alt⌐+⌐B⌐
7. Locate and select file.
8. Click **Insert** . . . . ⌐Alt⌐+⌐S⌐
9. Click **OK**. . . . . ⌐Enter⌐

Edit Embedded Object

1. Open file containing embedded object.
2. Double-click embedded object.

   ✓ *Source application commands display within destination application.*

3. Edit embedded data using source application commands.
4. Click outside embedded object to close source application.

EXERCISE DIRECTIONS

Embed an Excel Object in a Word Document

1. Start Word, open 💿 **33RETREAT**, and save the document as **33RETREAT_xx**.
2. Replace the sample text *Your Name* with your name and the sample text *Today's date* with the current date.
3. Position the insertion point on the blank line at the end of the document.
4. Start Excel and open the workbook file 💿 **33BUDGET**.
5. Save the file as **33BUDGET_xx**.
6. Embed the cells A3:C13 as a Microsoft Office Excel Worksheet Object on the last line of the Word document.
7. Close the **33BUDGET_xx** file and exit Excel.

Edit and Format the Embedded Object

1. Double-click the Excel object in the Word document.

   ✓ *Excel commands become available in Word.*

2. Edit the worksheet title from *Spring Training Retreat Budget* to **Fall Training Retreat Budget.**
3. Delete all of the data from the *Actual* column.
4. Apply the 20% - Accent1 cell style to cell A3.
   a. Select cell A3.
   b. Click the Cell Styles button drop-down arrow in the Styles group on the Home tab of the Ribbon.
   c. Click the 20% - Accent1 style in the gallery.

5. Apply the 60% - Accent1 cell style to cells A5:A13.
6. Increase the font size of the data in cells A3:C13 to 12 points, and make the text bold.
7. If necessary, adjust the widths of columns A and B so all data is visible.

   ✓ *Drag borders between columns, or double-click borders between columns on worksheet frame.*

8. Click outside the embedded object to close Excel.
9. Center the embedded object horizontally on the page.
10. Check the spelling and grammar in the document.
11. Save the document and preview it. It should look similar to the one in Illustration A.
12. Print the document.
13. Start Excel and open the worksheet **33BUDGET_xx**. Notice that the changes you made to the object in Word did not affect the original worksheet.
14. Close the worksheet and exit Excel.
15. Close the **33RETREAT_xx** document, saving all changes.

Long Shot, Inc.

INTERDEPARTMENTAL MEMORANDUM

To: Director of Human Resources
From: Student's Name
Date: Today's date
Re: Training Department Expenses

Per your request, here are the preliminary budget figures for the training retreat planned for September. I based the figures on the last training retreat. We can easily use Excel to update and format the data when this year's numbers become available.

Fall Training Retreat Budget

	Planned
Travel	$1,500.00
Accommodations	$6,350.00
Meals	$1,200.00
Facility rentals	$2,500.00
Books	$875.00
Supplies	$500.00
Miscellaneous	$1,000.00
Total	$13,925.00

ON YOUR OWN

1. Start Word and open ⌨ **OWD32-1**, the letter you modified in the On Your Own section of Exercise 32, or open 💿 **33REQUEST**.

   ✓ *If Word prompts you to update links, click No.*

2. Save the document as **OWD33-1_xx**, and then delete the linked object from the document.

3. Start Excel and open ⌨ **OWD32-2**, the worksheet containing the list of online sites and services, or open 💿 **33ONLINE**. Save the file as **OWD33-2_xx**.

4. Embed the worksheet data into the Word document, and then close the Excel worksheet and exit Excel.

5. Use Excel to edit the data in the embedded object in the Word document.

6. Apply formatting to the embedded object.

7. If you want, check to see that the original data has not changed in Excel.

8. Print the Word document, then close it, saving all changes, and exit Word.

Exercise | 34

Skills Covered

■ **Insert SmartArt**
■ **Insert a Chart**

■ **Enter Chart Data**
■ **Modify a Chart**

Software Skills   Charts are an effective way to illustrate numeric data and trends. For example, you can use charts to plot sales over time, compare projected income to actual income, or to show a breakdown in revenue sources. You can use Word's SmartArt tool to create many types of diagrams in any Word document.

Application Skills   As the person in charge of researching the feasibility of the home delivery service for Fresh Food Fair, you have recently completed two surveys of people in your target areas. The first survey asked a group of 100 people how likely they were to use a grocery home delivery service. The second asked groups in each of four target areas whether they would be more likely to use a grocery home delivery service for produce, packaged goods, dairy products, or meat. In this exercise, you will create charts detailing this information and include them in a memo to the company owner. You will also include an organization chart SmartArt diagram for the project.

TERMS

Chart object   A chart embedded in a Word document.

Chart title   The name of the chart.

Data axis   The scale used to measure the data in the chart. The Y axis shows the vertical scale, and the X axis shows the horizontal scale.

Data label   Text that identifies the units plotted on the chart, such as months or dollar values.

Data range   A range of cells in which you may enter data.

Data series   A range of values plotted in a chart.

Diagram   A graphic used to illustrate a concept or describe the relationship of parts to a whole.

Legend   The key that identifies what each color or symbol in the chart represents.

Organization chart   A diagram that depicts hierarchical relationships, such as a family tree or corporate management.

NOTES

Insert SmartArt

- The SmartArt graphic feature, new in Office 2007, makes it easy to create **diagrams** in a document.

- SmartArt diagrams are organized into categories, and each category contains a selection of layouts.

- The categories include: List, Process, Cycle, Hierarchy, Relationship, Matrix, and Pyramid.

- Use SmartArt graphics to illustrate information, concepts, and ideas such as the relationship between employees in an **organization chart**, or the steps in a procedure.

- To insert SmartArt, click the SmartArt button in the Illustrations group on the Insert tab of the Ribbon.

- You then use the Choose a SmartArt Graphic dialog box to select a category and a specific layout to insert.

- To add text to the diagram, you can type in the Text pane that displays when you create the object, or directly in the SmartArt layout's shapes.

- To format the diagram, use the commands on the SmartArt Tools Design tab on the Ribbon.

- Many of the formatting commands are the same as those for formatting pictures, shapes, and text boxes. For example, you can resize the diagram, apply styles, set text wrapping, and position the object on the page.

- You can also change design elements of the diagram using the SmartArt Tools Design tab on the Ribbon.

Choose a SmartArt Graphic dialog box

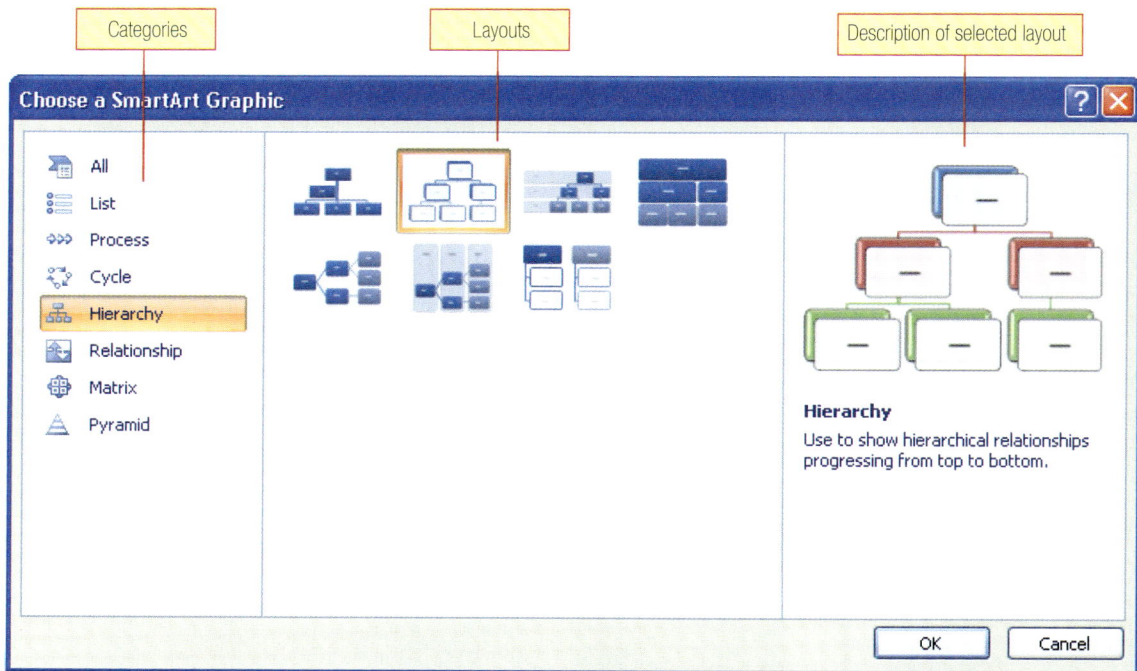

Insert a Chart

- Word comes with a Chart tool that lets you use Microsoft Excel charting features to embed **chart objects** in Word documents.

- To create the chart, you click the Chart button in the Illustrations group on the Insert tab of the Ribbon to open the Insert Chart dialog box.

- In the Insert Chart dialog box, you choose from a wide selection of chart types and subtypes, which you can use to plot your data.

Insert Chart dialog box

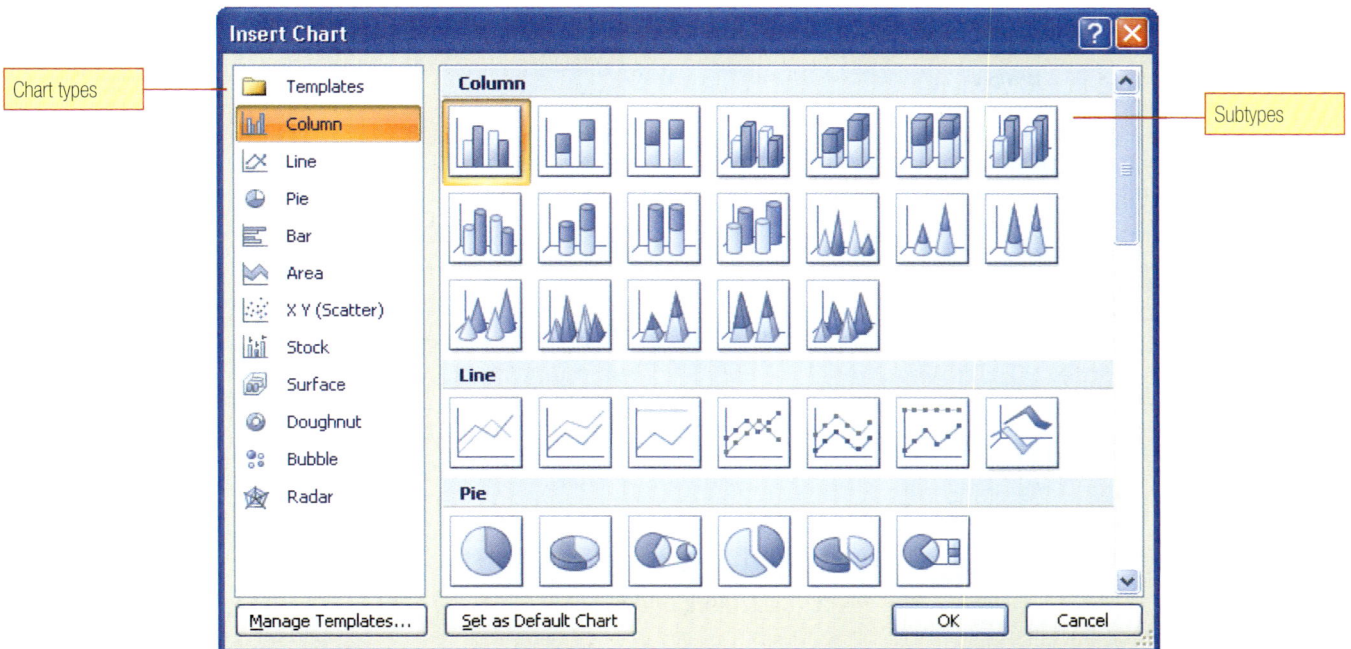

- Some of the chart types available include the following:
  - Column: Compares values across categories in vertical columns.
  - Line: Displays trends over time or categories.
  - Pie: Displays the contributions of each value to a total value. Often used to show percentages of a whole.
  - Bar: Compares values across categories in horizontal bars.
  - Area: Displays trends over time or categories by showing the contribution of each value to the whole.
  - XY (Scatter): Compares pairs of values.
- Additional chart types include Stock, Surface, Doughnut, Bubble, and Radar.

Enter Chart Data

- When you select to insert a chart, Word creates the chart object in the document, and then displays an Excel worksheet where you enter the chart data.
- When you insert a chart with Word, Excel opens with sample data entered in a **data range** in the worksheet.
- The data is organized for the type of chart you selected.

- For example, if you select to create a Column chart, the top row in the worksheet displays sample **data labels** for three columns: *Series 1, Series 2,* and *Series 3*.
- The left column displays sample **data series** labels for four rows: *Category 1, Category 2, Category 3,* and *Category 4*.
- To create your own chart, you replace the sample data in the worksheet cells. Excel automatically generates the chart.
- You can resize the data range by dragging its lower right corner, if necessary.
- You can use the Windows Clipboard to copy existing data from a Word table, an Excel worksheet, or an Access table into a chart's Excel worksheet.

Modify a Chart

- Charts are linked to the data you enter in the Excel worksheet, so when you edit the worksheet, the chart changes, too.
- To open the Excel worksheet to edit a chart, click the Edit Data button in the Data group on the Chart Tools Design tab of the Ribbon.
- You can change the chart type by selecting a different type in the Change Chart Type dialog box.

- You can resize and position a chart object the same way you do other graphics objects in a Word document.

  ✓ *For more information on working with graphics objects, see Lesson 3.*

- You can apply a chart layout, which controls the way chart elements are positioned in the chart.

- You can also apply a chart style to quickly format the chart elements with color and effects.

- Alternatively, you can select to display and format different elements of the chart, including the **chart titles**, the **data axis** names, the **legend**, gridlines, and the data labels.

PROCEDURES

Insert SmartArt

1. Click **Insert** tab . . . . [Alt]+[N]

   Illustrations Group

2. Click **SmartArt** button . . . [M]

   ✓ *The Choose a SmartArt Graphic dialog box displays.*

3. Click a category in the left pane . . . . [↓]/[↑]

4. Click a layout in the center pane . . . . [⇆], [↓]/[↑]/[←]/[→]

5. Click **OK** . . . . [Enter]

6. Type text and apply formatting as necessary.

Add a Shape to a Diagram

1. Click shape to which you want to add a new shape.

2. Click **SmartArt Tools Design** tab . . . . [Alt]+[J], [S]

   Create Graphic Group

3. Click **Add Shape** button drop-down arrow . . . . [O]

4. Click one of the following:
   - **Add Shape After** . . . . [A]
   - **Add Shape Before** . . . . [B]
   - **Add Shape Above** . . . . [V]
   - **Add Shape Below** . . . . [W]
   - **Add Assistant** . . . . [T]

5. Type text and apply formatting as necessary.

Apply a SmartArt Style

1. Click diagram to select it.

2. Click **SmartArt Tools Design** tab . . . . [Alt]+[J], [S]

   SmartArt Styles Group

3. Click Quick Style to apply in gallery.

   ✓ *If necessary, use scroll arrows to scroll the gallery.*

   OR

   a. Click **More** button ▾ . . . . [S], [S]

   b. Click Quick style to apply . . . . . [←]/[→]/[↑]/[↓], [Enter]

Resize the Object Precisely

1. Click object to select it.

2. Click **SmartArt Tools Format** tab . . . . [Alt]+[J], [O]

3. Click **Size Group** button [▱] . . . . [Z], [Z]

   Size Group

4. Click **Shape Height** box [1.51"] . . . . [H]

5. Type height in inches . . . . *type height*, [Enter]

   OR

   Click increment arrows to enter height.

6. Click **Shape Width** box [1.43"] . . . . [Alt]+[J], [O], [Z], [Z], [W]

7. Type width in inches . . . . *type width*, [Enter]

   OR

   Click increment arrows to enter width.

Delete an Object in a Diagram

1. Click object to select it.

2. Press [Delete].

Create a Chart

1. Position insertion point in document.

2. Click **Insert** tab . . . . [Alt]+[N]

   Illustrations Group

3. Click **Chart** button . . . . . . [C]

4. Click chart type . . . . [↓]/[↑]

5. Click chart subtype . . . . . [⇆], [↓]/[↑]/[←]/[→]

6. Click **OK** . . . . [Enter]

   ✓ *Chart is created with sample data entered in worksheet.*

To enter data in worksheet:

1. Click in worksheet cell.

2. Type new data.

3. Press [⇆] to move to cell to right.

   ✓ *Use the arrow keys to move to other cells in the worksheet.*

4. Type new data.

5. Repeat steps 3 and 4 until data is entered.

To change size of chart data range:

- Drag lower-right corner of current range to new position.

To edit data in worksheet:

1. Select chart object.

2. Click **Chart Tools Design** tab . . . . [Alt]+[J], [C]

Data Group

3. Click **Edit Data** button ▦ . . . `D`
4. Click in worksheet cell.
5. Type new data.

Copy Data into a Chart's Worksheet

1. Select table or worksheet data to copy in source file.
2. Click **Home** tab . . . . `Alt`+`H`

Clipboard Group

3. Click **Copy** button ▢ . . . . . . `C`

   OR

   a. Right-click selection.
   b. Click **Copy** . . . . `C`
4. Open Word document and select chart object.
5. Click **Chart Tools Design** tab . . . . `Alt`+`J`, `C`

Data Group

6. Click **Edit Data** button ▦ . . . `D`
7. Click cell in datasheet where inserted data should start.
8. Click **Home** tab in Excel . . . . `Alt`+`H`

Clipboard Group

9. Click **Paste** button ▢ . . . `V`, `P`

   OR

   a. Right-click insertion point location.
   b. Click **Paste** . . . . `P`, `Enter`

Change Chart Type

1. Open Word document and select chart object.
2. Click **Chart Tools Design** tab . . . . `Alt`+`J`, `C`

Type Group

3. Click **Change Chart Type** button ▦ . . . . `C`
4. Click chart type . . . . `↓`/`↑`
5. Click chart subtype . . . . . `⇆`, `↓`/`↑`/`←`/`→`
6. Click **OK** . . . . `Enter`

Switch the Display of Rows and Columns

1. Open Word document and select chart object.
2. Click **Chart Tools Design** tab . . . . `Alt`+`J`, `C`

Data Group

3. Click **Switch Row/Column** button ▦ . . . . `W`

Display Chart Elements

To display chart title:

1. Open Word document and select chart object.
2. Click **Chart Tools Layout** tab . . . . `Alt`+`J`, `A`

Labels Group

3. Click **Chart Title** button ▦ . . . `T`
4. Click chart title option to apply . . . . `↓`/`↑`, `Enter`

✓ *Click More Title Options to display additional options for positioning and formatting titles.*

To display legend:

1. Open Word document and select chart object.
2. Click **Chart Tools Layout** tab . . . . `Alt`+`J`, `A`

Labels Group

3. Click **Legend** button ▦ . . . . `L`
4. Click legend option to apply . . . . `↓`/`↑`, `Enter`

✓ *Click More Legend Options to display additional options for positioning and formatting legend.*

To display data labels:

1. Open Word document and select chart object.
2. Click **Chart Tools Layout** tab . . . . `Alt`+`J`, `A`

Labels Group

3. Click **Data Labels** button ▦ . . . . `B`

4. Click data label option to apply . . . . `↓`/`↑`, `Enter`

✓ *Click More Data Label Options to display additional options for positioning and formatting data labels.*

Edit Text Labels

1. Open Word document and select chart object.
2. Click element to edit.
3. Type new text.

Format Chart

To resize the chart precisely:

1. Click chart to select it.
2. Click **Chart Tools Format** tab . . . . `Alt`+`J`, `O`
3. Click **Size Group** button, if necessary ▦ . . . . `Z`, `Z`

Size Group

4. Click **Shape Height** box ▦ 1.51" . . . . `H`
5. Type height in inches . . . . *type height*, `Enter`

   OR

   Click increment arrows to enter height.
6. Click **Shape Width** box ▦ 1.43" . . . . `Alt`+`J`, `O`, `Z`, `Z`, `W`
7. Type width in inches . . . . *type width*, `Enter`

   OR

   Click increment arrows to enter width.

To delete a chart:

1. Click chart to select it.
2. Press `Delete`.

Format Chart Elements

1. Right-click element in chart.
2. Select **Format** *element name* from shortcut menu.
3. Select desired formatting options.
4. Click **OK** . . . . `Enter`

EXERCISE DIRECTIONS

Create Chart 1

1. Start Word, if necessary, open 🔘 **34CHARTS**, and save the document as **34CHARTS_xx**.

2. Position the insertion point on the blank line at the end of the document.

3. Insert a Clustered Column chart object.

4. Replace the sample data in the worksheet with the following survey results:

	No	Maybe	Yes	Don't Know
Responses	10	38	49	3

5. Delete the sample data not replaced by new data in rows 2 and 3 as follows:

   a. Click the row number in the worksheet frame.

   b. Press [Delete].

6. Resize the data range to include only the cells that contain data (A1:E2).

   ✓ *Drag the lower-right corner of the data range up to the lower right corner of cell E2.*

7. Minimize the worksheet.

8. Change the chart type to Pie in 3-D.

9. Switch the display of rows and columns to change the data series.

10. Edit the title to **Likely to Purchase Home Delivery** and change the font size to 12 points.

11. Hide the chart legend.

12. Display data labels on the outside end, and format them to display category names and percentages, with leader lines.

   a. Right-click a data label.

   b. Click Format Data Labels.

   c. Select the check boxes for Category Name, Percentage, Show Leader Lines, and Outside End.

   d. Deselect all other check boxes.

   e. Click Close.

13. Display the worksheet and change the number of responses for *Maybe* to **36** and the number for *Yes* to **51**. Notice the changes in the chart.

14. Resize the chart object to 2 inches high by 3.5 inches wide.

15. Drag the data labels to position them so they can be seen clearly.

16. Center the chart horizontally on the page.

Create Chart 2

1. Insert a new blank line at the end of the document and insert a Clustered Column chart.

2. In Excel, open the workbook file 🔘 **34SURVEY**.

3. Copy the data in cells A4:E8 to the Clipboard.

   ✓ *Click cell A4, press and hold Shift, then click cell E8. Click the Copy button.*

4. Switch to the chart's worksheet in Excel.

5. Position the insertion point in the upper-left cell of the worksheet.

6. Paste the data from the Clipboard into the worksheet.

7. Minimize the worksheet.

8. Resize the chart to about 2.5 inches high by 3.75 inches wide.

9. Overlay the title **Product Preference by Area**, centered on the chart, using a 12-point font.

10. If necessary, center the chart horizontally on the page.

11. Preview the document. It should look similar to Illustration A.

   ✓ *If necessary, adjust the vertical position of the chart objects.*

12. Close all open worksheets and exit Excel.

Create SmartArt Diagram

1. Move the insertion point to the end of the Word document and insert a page break.

2. On the new page, type the following using the Title Quick Style:

   Home Delivery Service Organization Chart

3. Change the font size to 22 points and center the text horizontally.

4. Start a new line and then insert a SmartArt Organization Chart graphic from the Hierarchy category.

5. Fill in the default shapes as follows:

   - Top: **Director of Services**
   - Third row left: **Driver Manager**
   - Third row middle: **Inventory Manager**
   - Third row right: **Customer Service Manager**

6. Delete the shape on the second row.

7. Add a shape below the Driver Manager shape, and key the text **Two Drivers**.

8. Add a shape below the Customer Service Manage shape, and key the text **Two Customer Service Representatives**.

9. Apply the Intense Effect SmartArt style to the object.

10. Insert a plain page number centered on the bottom of both pages in the document.

11. Check the grammar and spelling in the document.

12. Preview the document. Page 2 should look similar to Illustration B.

13. Print both pages of the document.

14. Close the document, saving all changes, and exit Word.

Illustration A

Fresh Food Fair
Route 117, Bolton, MA 01740

MEMO

To: Kimberly and Jack Thomson
From: Student's Name
Date: Today's date
Subject: Home Delivery Service

Here are some charts showing the results of two surveys of our target market, as well as the organization chart you requested. Call me if you have questions.

Likely to Purchase Home Delivery

Don't Know 3%
No 10%
Maybe 36%
Yes 51%

Product Preference by Area

- Produce
- Packaged Goods
- Dairy
- Meat

Area 1   Area 2   Area 3   Area 4

1

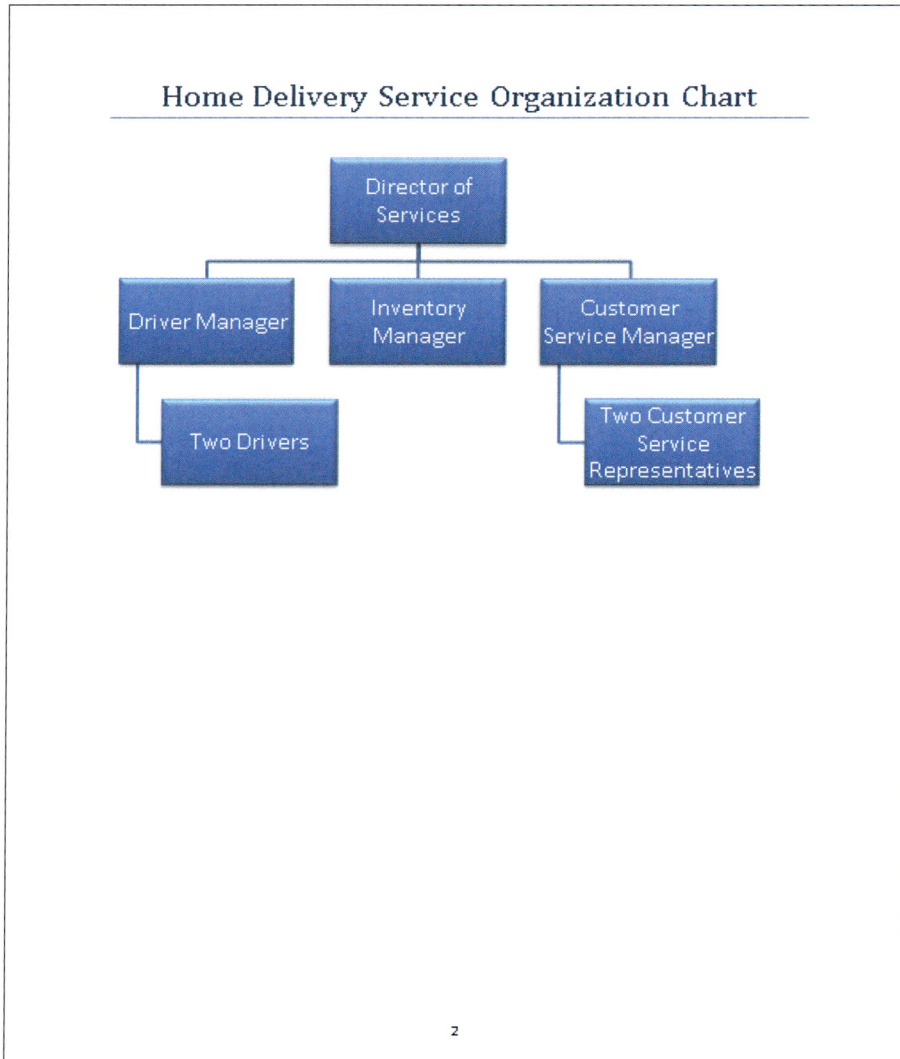

Home Delivery Service Organization Chart

ON YOUR OWN

1. Design a survey that you can use to solicit input from your classmates, instructors, and administrators for the acceptable use policy. For example, you might want them to give their opinion about certain rules and guidelines, rank the level of importance of guidelines, provide reaction to AUPs in general, or even rank the types of punishments that should be imposed for breaking the terms. You might want to create a form in Word, or just write down the questions to ask. Survey at least 20 people, and compile the results.

2. Start Word, create a new document, and save the document as OWD34_*xx*.

3. Type a letter to your instructor, parent, or someone else describing the survey and its purpose, and explaining the results.

4. Insert a chart in the letter to illustrate the results of your survey.

5. Enter the data from your survey in the datasheet; add a title and any necessary labels.

6. Select the chart type that best illustrates your data. For example, use a pie chart to show percentages of a whole, or a line chart to show values over time.

7. Save the document and preview it. If necessary, change the formatting of the chart to make it easier to read.

8. Print the document.

9. Ask a classmate to review the document and make comments or suggestions.

10. Incorporate the comments and suggestions into the document.

11. Close the document, saving all changes.

Skills Covered

■ **Use Smart Tags**

Software Skills Use smart tags to perform actions in Word that you would otherwise have to open a different program to accomplish. For example, you can use a smart tag to look up an address in an Outlook contact list and then automatically enter the address into a letter in Word, or access the Internet to find stock quotes or street maps.

Application Skills Long Shot, Inc. has signed an agreement to sponsor a golf tournament at a golf course in Myrtle Beach, South Carolina. You need to add the golf course manager to your contacts list. In this exercise, you will make sure all of your smart tags options are enabled. You will then open an existing letter to the golf course manager and use a smart tag to add his information to your Outlook Contacts folder. You will then open another letter and use the smart tag to automatically insert the address.

TERMS

Smart tag   A type of data that Word (and other Microsoft Office 2007 programs) recognizes and labels as available for use with other programs.

Recognizer   A type of data that Word identifies as a smart tag.

NOTES

Use Smart Tags

■ **Smart tags** are a feature of Office 2007 that you can use to automatically integrate data entered in one program with another program.

■ For example, you can use smart tags to integrate Outlook contact information with your Word documents:

  • If you type a person's name into a Word document, you can use a smart tag to add the person to your Outlook Contacts list, or to insert the person's address from your Contacts list into the letter.

■ Word comes with a set of **recognizers** used to identify and label Addresses, Financial Symbols, Dates, Names, Places, Telephone Numbers, and Times.

■ On the Smart Tags tab of the AutoCorrect dialog box, you can select which of the recognizers you want Word to mark as smart tags in your documents.

■ You can download additional smart tags from Microsoft and other vendors.

■ Word marks smart tags in a document using a purple dotted underline.

■ When you rest the mouse pointer over the smart tag, the Smart Tag Actions button displays.

■ Move the mouse pointer over the button to display a drop-down arrow. Click the arrow to display a menu of available actions.

Smart Tags tab of the AutoCorrect dialog box

AutoCorrect `[?][X]`

AutoCorrect	Math AutoCorrect	AutoFormat As You Type
AutoFormat		Smart Tags

Word can recognize certain types of data in your document. For each recognized type, you can perform actions with that data.

☑ Label text with smart tags

Recognizers:

☑ Address (English)
☑ Canadian Financial Symbol Dummy File (Smart tag lists)
☑ Date (Smart tag lists)
☑ Financial Symbol (Smart tag lists)
☑ Measurement Converter (Measurement Converter)
☑ Person Name (English)
☑ Person Name (Outlook e-mail recipients)
☑ Place (English)
☑ Telephone Number (Smart tag lists)
☑ Time (Smart tag lists)
☑ UK Financial Symbol Dummy File (Smart tag lists)

[Properties...]

[Recheck Document]   [More Smart Tags...]

[Remove Smart Tags]

☑ Show Smart Tag Actions buttons

[OK]   [Cancel]

Smart tag on a name

Dear Mr. McLaughlin,

Smart Tag Actions button
Mouse pointer
Purple dotted underline

Smart Tag Actions menu

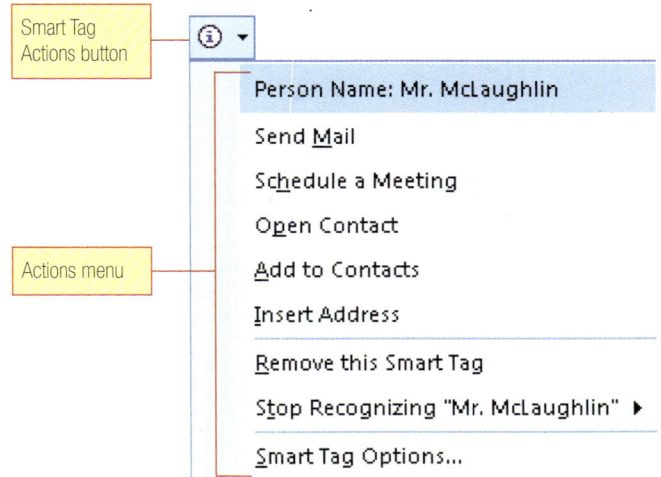

Smart Tag Actions button

ⓘ ▾

Actions menu

Person Name: Mr. McLaughlin

Send **M**ail

Sc**h**edule a Meeting

Open Contact

Add to Contacts

Insert Address

Remove this Smart Tag

S**t**op Recognizing "Mr. McLaughlin" ▸

Smart Tag Options...

- The types of actions available on the menu depend on the type of recognizer.
- Smart tags are on by default, but you can turn them off on the Smart Tags tab of the AutoCorrect dialog box.
- If you want to use smart tags but do not want to see the smart tag purple underlines, you can use the Advanced page of the Word Options dialog box to hide the underlines.
- You can hide the Smart Tags Actions buttons as well.
- You can save smart tags with your documents if you want to retain a link between the data in your Word document and the source data.
- If you don't need the link, you don't need to save the smart tag—the data remains saved in the document.
- If you don't need all of the smart tags in a document, you can select the specific smart tags you want to retain and the ones you want to discard.
- Saving smart tags with your document increases document size.
- If you want to use smart tags on Web pages created with Word, you must set Word to save the smart tags in XML format.

PROCEDURES

Turn Smart Tags Off or On

1. Open a document.
2. Click **Office Button** 🔲 . . . `Alt`+`F`
3. Click **Word Opt_ions** . . . . `I`
4. Click **Proofing** . . . . `P`
5. Click **AutoCorrect Options** . . . . `Alt`+`A`
6. Click **Smart Tags** tab . . . `Ctrl`+`⇥`
7. Click to select **Label text with smart tags** check box . . . `Alt`+`L`

   ✓ *A check mark in the check box indicates the option is on.*

8. Click **OK**. . . . . `Enter`
9. Click **OK**.

Turn Display of Smart Tags Underlines Off or On

1. Open a document.
2. Click **Office Button** 🔲 . . . `Alt`+`F`
3. Click **Word Opt_ions** . . . . `I`
4. Click **Advanced** . . . . `A`
5. Click to deselect or select the **Show Smart Tags** check box . . . . `Alt`+`A`, `A`, `Spacebar`

   ✓ *A check mark in the check box indicates the option is on.*

6. Click **OK**. . . . . `Enter`

Select Smart Tag Recognizer(s)

1. Open a document.
2. Click **Office Button** 🔲 . . . `Alt`+`F`
3. Click **Word Opt_ions** . . . . `I`
4. Click **Proofing** . . . . `P`
5. Click **AutoCorrect Options** . . . . `Alt`+`A`
6. Click **Smart Tags** tab . . . `Ctrl`+`⇥`
7. Click to select recognizer to display. . . . . `↓`/`↑`, `Spacebar`

   ✓ *A check mark in the check box indicates that Word is set to recognize that smart tag type.*

8. Repeat step 7 to select or deselect additional recognizers.
9. Click **OK**. . . . . `Enter`
10. Click **OK**.

Use a Smart Tag

1. Rest mouse pointer over smart tag in document.

   ✓ *Word displays the Smart Tag Actions button.*

2. Click **Smart Tag Actions** button.
3. Click desired action.

Show/Hide Smart Tags Actions Buttons

1. Open a document.
2. Click **Office Button** 🔲 . . . `Alt`+`F`
3. Click **Word Opt_ions** . . . . `I`
4. Click **Proofing** . . . . `P`
5. Click **AutoCorrect Options** . . . . `Alt`+`A`
6. Click **Smart Tags** tab . . . `Ctrl`+`⇥`
7. Click to select or deselect the **Show Smart Tag Actions buttons** check box . . . . `Alt`+`B`

   ✓ *A check mark in the check box indicates that the option is selected.*

8. Click **OK**. . . . . `Enter`
9. Click **OK**.

Save Smart Tags with Document

1. Open a document.
2. Click **Office Button** 🔲 . . . `Alt`+`F`
3. Click **Word Opt_ions** . . . . `I`
4. Click **Advanced** . . . . `A`
5. Click to select the **Embed s_mart tags** check box . . . . `Alt`+`M`, `Alt`+`M`, `Alt`+`M`, `Spacebar`

   ✓ *A check mark in the check box indicates the option is on.*

6. Click **OK**. . . . . `Enter`

Save Smart Tags as XML in Web Pages

1. Open a document.
2. Click **Office Button** 🔲 . . . `Alt`+`F`
3. Click **Word Opt_ions** . . . . `I`
4. Click **Advanced** . . . . `A`
5. Click to select the **Sa_ve smart tags as XML properties in Web pages** check box . . . . `Alt`+`V`, `V`, `Spacebar`

   ✓ *A check mark in the check box indicates the option is on.*

6. Click **OK**. . . . . `Enter`

Remove a Smart Tag from a Document

1. Rest mouse pointer over smart tag in document.

   ✓ *Word displays the Smart Tag Actions button.*

2. Click **Smart Tag Actions** button.
3. Click **Remove this Smart Tag** . . . . `R`

Remove all Smart Tags

1. Open a document.
2. Click **Office Button** 🔲 . . . `Alt`+`F`
3. Click **Word Opt_ions** . . . . `I`
4. Click **Proofing** . . . . `P`
5. Click **AutoCorrect Options** . . . . `Alt`+`A`
6. Click **Smart Tags** tab . . . `Ctrl`+`⇥`
7. Click **Remove Smart Tags** . . . . `Alt`+`R`
8. Click **OK**. . . . . `Enter`
9. Click **OK**.

EXERCISE DIRECTIONS

✓ *This exercise assumes you have Outlook 2007 installed.*

1. Start Word, if necessary, open the document ⊙ **35CONFIRM**, and save it as **35CONFIRM_xx**.

2. Open the Word Options dialog box and set Word to display smart tag underlines.

3. Open the AutoCorrect dialog box and display the Smart Tags tab.

4. Enable smart tags, select all available recognizers, and select to display the Smart Tag Actions button.

5. Close the AutoCorrect dialog box and the Word Options dialog box, and then check the document.

6. Move the mouse pointer over the smart tag under the recipient's name in the **35CONFIRM_xx** document.

7. Click the Smart Tags Actions button and select Add to Contacts.

8. Word displays a Contact card from your Outlook Contacts folder. Note that the name is already filled in.

9. Fill in the following information for Hugh McLaughlin:

✓ *You can use the Copy and Paste commands to copy data from the Word document into the fields in the Contact card. You do not have to fill in every field on the card.*

Full Name:	**Mr. Hugh McLaughlin**
Job Title:	**Manager**
E-mail address:	**hugh@hideaway.net**
Business phone:	**(843) 555-5432**
Business fax:	**(843) 555-5434**
Business address:	**Hideaway Golf Club and Resort**
	2242 Ocean Boulevard
	Myrtle Beach, SC 29577

10. When you are done, close the Contact card, saving the changes.

11. Close the **35CONFIRM_xx** document, saving all changes.

12. Open the ⊙ **35THANKS** document and save it as **35THANKS_xx**.

13. Replace the sample text *Today's date* with the current date, and then press ⏎ twice to insert a blank line.

14. Type **Mr. Hugh McLaughlin** and press ⏎. After a moment or two, Word should recognize the name as a smart tag.

15. Rest the mouse pointer on the smart tag to display the Smart Tag Actions button, click the button's drop-down arrow, and then click Insert Address. Word should insert the address that you entered on the Outlook Contact card.

16. If necessary, delete the extra blank line between the address and the salutation.

17. Check the spelling and grammar in the document.

18. Display the document in Print Preview. It should look similar to Illustration A.

19. Print the document.

20. Disable smart tags.

21. Close the document, saving all changes, and exit Word.

Today's date

Mr. Hugh McLaughlin
Hideaway Golf Club and Resort
2242 Ocean Boulevard
Myrtle Beach, SC 29577

Dear Hugh,

It was a pleasure meeting you yesterday to discuss the tournament. I know this will be a wonderful opportunity for both of our organizations.

Thank you very much for your time. I look forward to a successful partnership.

Sincerely,

Jason Hadid
Marketing Director
Long Shot, Inc.
234 Simsbury Drive
Ithaca, NY 14850

JH/yo

Copy to: M. Whitman

ON YOUR OWN

1. Enter the name and address of an employer you have interviewed with in your Outlook Contact list. If you have not had any interviews, enter the name and address of someone you would like to interview with.

   ✓ *If necessary, consult your instructor for more information on using the Outlook Contact list.*

2. Start Word, create a new document, and save the document as OWD35_*xx*.

3. Set Word to display smart tag underlines.

4. Enable smart tags, and select all available recognizers.

5. Type a thank you letter for an interview, or type a letter requesting an interview to someone whose name is entered in your Outlook Contacts list.

6. Use smart tags to insert the address.

7. When the letter is complete, check the spelling and grammar.

8. Preview the letter and print it. Assess the document to determine if you should include it in your employment portfolio. If so, print a clean copy and add it to the portfolio.

9. Try using a different Smart Tag feature, such as looking up a map of an address, or sending an e-mail message.

10. Disable smart tags.

11. Close all open documents and exit all programs.

Skills Covered

- **Merge a Word Document with an Access Database**

Software Skills   Creating a new data source document in Word for a mail merge is unnecessary if you already have a database stored in a database application, such as Microsoft Access. You can easily merge the Access data with a Word main document.

Application Skills   As the manager of in-house training at Long Shot, Inc., you want to send a letter to everyone who attended the Word 1 class last session to invite them to take the Word 2 class next session. The information for each student is already entered in an Access database. In this exercise, you will create a memo document in Word and then merge it with data in the Access database.

TERMS

Database   A file used to store records of data.
Query   An object containing a subset of records in an Access database.

Table   An object in an Access database that organizes and stores data in rows and columns.

NOTES

Merge a Word Document with an Access Database

- If you have an existing Access **database** file, you can use it as a data source for a mail merge in Word.
- You set up the merge document the same way you would if you were using a Word data source document.
- The only difference is that you select the Access file as the data source.

- If there is more than one **table** or **query** in the database file, you are prompted to select the one you want to use.
- You can sort and filter records in the Access data source file using the same methods you use when you create the data source using Word.
- You cannot edit the records using Word. To make changes, open the database file in Access.

Select the table or query to use as the data source

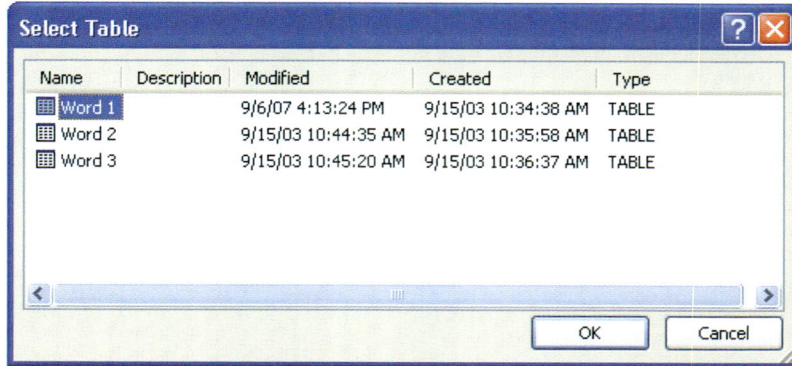

Name	Description	Modified	Created	Type
Word 1		9/6/07 4:13:24 PM	9/15/03 10:34:38 AM	TABLE
Word 2		9/15/03 10:44:35 AM	9/15/03 10:35:58 AM	TABLE
Word 3		9/15/03 10:45:20 AM	9/15/03 10:36:37 AM	TABLE

OK   Cancel

PROCEDURES

Use an Access Database as a Data Source File for a Mail Merge

1. Open a new blank document.

   OR

   Open an existing letter document.

2. Click **Mailings** tab . . . . . . `Alt`+`M`

   Start Mail Merge Group

3. Click **Start Mail Merge** button
   . . . . `S`

4. Click a document type:
   - **Letters** . . . . `L`
   - **E-Mail Messages** . . . . . . `E`
   - **Envelopes** . . . . `V`
   - **Labels** . . . . `A`
   - **Directory** . . . . `D`

5. Click **Select Recipients** button
   . . . . `Alt`+`M`, `R`

6. Click **Use Existing List** . . . . . . `E`

   ✓ *The Select Data Source dialog box displays.*

7. Locate and select the Access database file.

8. Click **Open** . . . . `Alt`+`O`

   ✓ *If there is more than one table or query, Word displays the Select Table dialog box.*

9. If necessary, click desired table or query . . . . `↓`/`↑`

10. Click **OK** . . . . `Enter`

11. Continue with the steps for setting up and merging the selected document type.

To set up a form letter for a merge:

1. Complete steps 1 through 10 above.

2. In the main document, begin typing the letter, including all text and formatting as you want it to appear on each merge document. For example, type the date and move the insertion point down four lines.

3. Position the insertion point at the location where you want to insert a field.

4. Click **Mailings** tab . . . . . . `Alt`+`M`

   Write & Insert Fields Group

5. Do one of the following:
   a. Click **Address block** button
      . . . . `A`

   ✓ *Word displays the Insert Address Block dialog box.*

   b. Select desired options for formatting address.

   c. Click **OK** . . . . `Enter`

   OR

   a. Click the **Greeting Line** button
      . . . . `G`

   ✓ *Word displays the Greeting Line dialog box.*

   b. Select desired options for formatting greeting line.

   c. Click **OK** . . . . `Enter`

   OR

   a. Click **Insert Merge Field** button
      . . . . `I`

   b. Click field to insert . . . . `↓`/`↑`

6. Continue typing and formatting letter, repeating steps to insert merge fields or merge blocks at desired location(s).

7. Save the document.

To preview merge documents:

1. Click **Mailings** tab . . . . . . `Alt`+`M`

   Preview Results Group

2. Click **Preview Results** button
   . . . . `P`

3. Click **Next record** button
   . . . . `Alt`+`M`, `X`

OR

Click **First record** button

◀◀ . . . . $\boxed{\text{Alt}}$+$\boxed{\text{M}}$, $\boxed{\text{Q}}$

OR

Click **Previous record** button

◀ . . . . $\boxed{\text{Alt}}$+$\boxed{\text{M}}$, $\boxed{\text{M}}$

OR

Click **Last record** button

▶▶ . . . . $\boxed{\text{Alt}}$+$\boxed{\text{M}}$, $\boxed{\text{V}}$

To complete the merge:

1. Click **Mailings** tab . . . . . . $\boxed{\text{Alt}}$+$\boxed{\text{M}}$

   Finish Group

2. Click **Finish & Merge** button

   . . . . $\boxed{\text{F}}$

3. Do one of the following:

   a. Click **Print Documents** . . . . $\boxed{\text{P}}$

   ✓ *Word displays the Merge to Printer dialog box.*

   b. Specify records to print.

   c. Click **OK** . . . . $\boxed{\text{Enter}}$

   ✓ *Word displays the Print dialog box.*

d. Select print options.

e. Click **OK** . . . . $\boxed{\text{Enter}}$

   OR

a. Click **Edit Individual Documents** . . . . $\boxed{\text{E}}$

✓ *Word displays the Merge to New Document dialog box.*

b. Specify records to include in new document.

c. Click **OK** . . . . $\boxed{\text{Enter}}$

✓ *You can make changes to individual letters, and/or save the entire merge document to print later.*

EXERCISE DIRECTIONS

1. Open the Access database file 💿 **36STUDENTS**, and save a copy as **36STUDENTS_xx**.

2. Start Word, and open 💿 **36MEMO**. Save the document as **36MEMO_xx**.

3. Replace the sample text *Your Name* with your own name, and *Today's Date* with the current date.

4. Start Mail Merge and select to create letters, using the current document.

5. Locate and select **36STUDENTS_xx** as the data source file, and select to use the Word 1 table as the data source table.

6. Use all records in the table.

7. Insert merge fields as shown in Illustration A.

8. Check the spelling and grammar in the document, make any necessary corrections, and then preview the merge documents.

9. Complete the merge by merging all records to a new document, and save the document as **36MERGE_xx**.

10. Print the merge documents.

11. Close all open files, saving all changes.

Long Shot, Inc.

INTERDEPARTMENTAL MEMORANDUM

To: «First_Name» «Last_Name», «Department»
From: Student's Name
Date: Today's Date
Subject: In-house training

I hope you enjoyed participating in the «Course» class last session. The instructor told me that everyone who attended is now ready to move on to the next level. With that in mind, «First_Name», I want to let you know that we are planning to offer the Word 2 class on Thursday evenings starting in January. The course will run for eight weeks, and will cover the intermediate aspects of the software program. Please contact the training department to enroll for next session.

Best regards,

Student's Name

P.S. Tell everyone in «Department» how much you learned from in-house training. We'd love them to sign up as well!

ON YOUR OWN

1. Create an Access database file named **OWD36-1_xx** that includes a table listing the names and addresses of the people you surveyed in the On Your Own section of Exercise 34. Alternatively, open the Access database file ⦿ **36LIST** and save a copy as **OWD36-1_xx**.

2. Start Word, create a new document, and save it as **OWD36-2_xx**. Write a one-page draft of an acceptable use policy, focusing on guidelines for using online services. You may want to research AUPs online to learn what to include, and to see examples of one or two written by others. Spend time editing, proofreading, and improving the document. When you are satisfied with the draft, save the changes.

3. Insert a blank page at the beginning of the document, and type a form letter main document asking the people you interviewed for your survey to read the AUP draft and provide feedback to help you improve it.

4. Use the table in the **OWD36-1_xx** database file as the data source for the **OWD36-2_xx** form letter. Insert the appropriate merge fields and merge blocks into the letter.

5. Preview the merge results and make changes if necessary.

6. Merge the letters to a new document named **OWD36-3_xx**.

7. Save and close all open files, and exit all open applications.

Skills Covered

- **Embed a PowerPoint Slide in a Word Document**
- **Export PowerPoint Slides and Notes to a Word Document**
- **Export PowerPoint Text to a Word Document**

Software Skills Share information between two applications to save yourself work and to provide consistency between documents. If you have a PowerPoint presentation, for example, you can use the presentation information in a Word document. You can embed Power-Point slides in a Word document as graphics objects, and you can export text and graphics from a PowerPoint presentation into a Word document.

Application Skills You have been asked to present information about the Fresh Food Fair home delivery service at a company meeting. You already have a PowerPoint presentation about the study. You can use pieces of the presentation to create documents to distribute as a package at the meeting. In this exercise, you will create a cover page for the package using a slide from the PowerPoint presentation. You will then export the entire presentation to a Word document to use as a handout, leaving blank lines for writing notes. Finally, you will export the text from the presentation as an outline to use as a table of contents for the handout package.

TERMS

Export To send text or data from one application to another application. The original data remains intact.

NOTES

Embed a PowerPoint Slide in a Word Document

- You can embed a slide in a Word document.
- The slide displays in the Word document in full color with graphics and text.
- Embedding a slide is similar to embedding an Excel object in a Word document.

  ✓ *See Exercise 33 for information on embedding an Excel object in a Word document.*

Export PowerPoint Slides and Notes to a Word Document

- You can **export** PowerPoint slides and notes to a Word document.
- When you export slides, miniatures of your slides are inserted in a table in the Word document.
- You can print slide notes with the slides, or leave blank lines for entering handwritten notes or comments.
- You can link the slides in the Word document to the source presentation so when you change the source presentation the linked document in Word updates automatically.

Export PowerPoint Text to a Word Document

- You can export PowerPoint text to a Word document.

- Text will be saved in Rich Text Format (.rtf).

- The text will be formatted using Outline heading levels.

- When you open the .rtf file in Word, you can save it as a Word file.

PROCEDURES

Embed a PowerPoint Slide in Word

1. Open presentation in PowerPoint.
2. Select slide to copy.
3. Click **Home** tab . . . . `Alt`+`H`

   Clipboard Group

4. Click **Copy** button . . . . `C`

   OR

   a. Right-click selection.
   b. Click **Copy** . . . . `C`
5. Make destination file active.
6. Position insertion point in the desired location.
7. Click **Home** tab . . . . `Alt`+`H`

   Clipboard Group

8. Click **Paste** button drop-down arrow . . . . `V`
9. Click **Paste Special** . . . . `S`
10. Click **As** box, if necessary . . . . `Alt`+`A`
11. Click Microsoft Office PowerPoint Slide Object . . . . `↓`/`↑`
12. Click **Paste** option button . . . . `Alt`+`P`
13. Click **OK** . . . . `Enter`

Export PowerPoint Slides and Notes to Word

1. Open the presentation.
2. Click **Office Button** . . . `Alt`+`F`
3. Point to **Publish** . . . . `U`
4. Click **Create Handouts in Microsoft Office Word** . . . . `H`
5. Select option for page layout in Word:
   - **Notes next to slides** . . . . . `N`
   - **Blank lines next to slides** . . . . `A`
   - **Notes below slides** . . . . . . `B`
   - **Blank lines below slides** . . . . `K`
   - **Outline only** . . . . `O`
6. Select one of the following:
   - **Paste** . . . . `P`
   - **Paste link** . . . . `I`
7. Click **OK** . . . . `Enter`

Export PowerPoint Text to Word

1. Open the presentation.
2. Click **Office Button** . . . `Alt`+`F`
3. Click **Save As** . . . . `A`
4. Key file name.
5. Select storage location.
6. Click **Save as type** drop-down arrow . . . . `Alt`+`T`
7. Select **Outline/RTF** . . `↓`/`↑`, `Enter`
8. Click **Save** . . . . `Alt`+`S`

Open RTF File in Word

1. Start Word.
2. Click **Office Button** . . . `Alt`+`F`
3. Click **Open** . . . . `O`
4. Click **Files of type** drop-down arrow . . . . `Alt`+`T`
5. Select **All Files** . . . . . `↓`/`↑`, `Enter`
6. Select storage location.
7. Select file to open.
8. Click **Open** . . . . `Alt`+`O`

EXERCISE DIRECTIONS

✓ *The steps in this exercise assume you know how to use a PowerPoint presentation file. If you do not, ask your instructor for more information.*

Embed a Slide in a Word Document

1. Start Word, if necessary, open 🔘 **37COVER**, and save the document as **37COVER_xx**.
2. Replace the sample text *Today's Date* with the current date.
3. Replace the sample text *Your Name* with your own name.
4. Start PowerPoint, open 🔘 **37PRES**, and save it as **37PRES_xx**.
5. Select slide 1 and copy it to the Clipboard.
6. Switch to the **37COVER_xx** document in Word.
7. Embed the slide from the Clipboard onto the last blank line at the end of the document.
8. Center the picture object horizontally on the page.
9. Change the theme of the **37COVER_xx** document to Module to match the theme of the presentation slide.
10. Check the spelling and grammar in the document.
12. Preview the document. It should look similar to Illustration A.
13. Close the document, saving all changes.

Illustration A

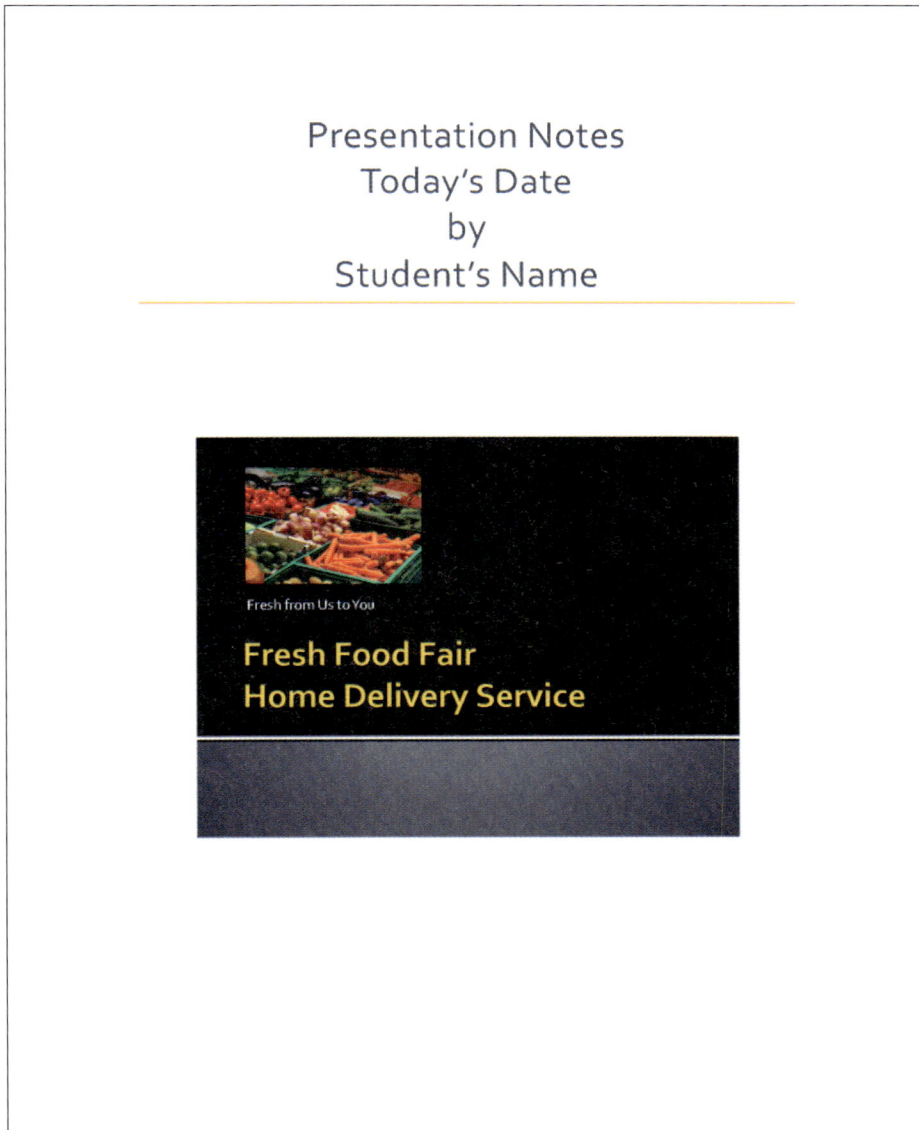

Export PowerPoint Data to Word

1. Switch back to the **37PRES_xx** PowerPoint presentation, and select to export the slides to a new Word document, selecting the Blank lines next to slides layout, and pasting the data.

2. Save the document as **37HANDOUT_xx**, and apply the Module theme.

3. Preview both pages of the document. They should look similar to Illustration B.

4. Close the document, saving all changes.

Illustration B

5. Switch back to the **37PRES_xx** PowerPoint presentation.

6. Save the file in Outline/RTF format with the name **37OUT_xx**.

7. Close the **37PRES_xx** presentation file and exit PowerPoint. Do not save any changes.

8. Switch to Word and open the **37OUT_xx** file.

9. Change to Outline view.

10. Deselect the Show Text Formatting check box in the Outline Tools group on the Outlining tab of the Ribbon. The document should look similar to the one in Illustration C.

11. Close the document, saving all changes.

Illustration C

Fresh Food Fair
Home Delivery Service
   Fresh from Us to You

Our Target Area
   ■ Young families
   ■ Middle to high income
   ■ Long distance between markets
   ■ Families always too busy
What Are the Benefits?
   ■ Reach customers where they live
   ■ Create new profit center
   ■ Opens market for new products
   ■ Generates good will
Estimated Startup Costs
Estimated Monthly Expenses
Conclusion
   ■ There is a market for this service
   ■ It creates a new profit center
   ■ It generates good-will

ON YOUR OWN

1. Create a PowerPoint presentation about yourself or about a club or organization to which you belong, or open the presentation 37MYLIFE, and save the presentation with the name OWD37-1_*xx*.

2. Create handouts in Word by exporting the entire presentation to a new document. Include notes if there are any, or leave blank lines for hand writing notes.

3. Save the Word document with the name OWD37-2_*xx*.

4. Apply the same theme to the Word document that you used for the PowerPoint presentation.

5. Insert a blank page at the beginning of the document, and then enter and format text for a report title on the new first page.

6. Embed a slide from the presentation to illustrate the report cover.

7. Check the spelling and grammar in the document.

8. Print the document.

9. Ask a classmate to review the document and offer comments and suggestions.

10. Incorporate the suggestions and comments into the document.

11. Close all open documents, saving all changes.

12. Present the report along with the slide show to your class.

Critical Thinking

Application Skills The Horticultural Shop Owners' Association is sponsoring a trip to tour the Botanical Gardens in Montreal, Canada. The president of the association has asked you to create an information packet to send to members. She has sent you an Excel worksheet with financial information, a PowerPoint presentation about the trip, and an Access database that includes the names and addresses of the members. In this exercise, you will export the PowerPoint presentation to create a Word document. You will add a cover page to the document on which you will create a chart showing the satisfaction level of people who went on the trip last year, and you will add another page to the document on which you will embed financial information as an Excel worksheet object. Finally, you will use the Access database as a data source to create mailing labels so you can mail the packets to the members.

EXERCISE DIRECTIONS

✓ *The steps in this exercise assume you know how to use Excel, Access, and PowerPoint files. If you do not, ask your instructor for more information.*

Export a PowerPoint Presentation to Word

1. Start PowerPoint and open the presentation file
   ◎ **38MONTREAL**.
2. Publish the file as handouts in Word, pasting the slides and using the layout that leaves blank lines next to each slide.
3. Save the Word document as **38PACKET_xx**, and apply the Median theme, which is the theme used for the **38MONTREAL** presentation.

Create and Format a Graph Object

1. Insert a blank page at the beginning of the document to create a cover page.
2. Move the insertion point to the beginning of the document and type the title **Tour the Botanical Gardens of Montreal**, formatted with the Title Quick Style.
3. Press ⏎ to start a new line, and apply the No Spacing Quick Style. Set the formatting to leave 108 points (1.5 inches) of space before and type the following:

   Join the Horticultural Shop Owners' Association on an exciting four-day trip to the Botanical Gardens in Montreal, Canada. Last year, twenty members of the association joined a

similar tour. When asked whether they were pleased with the experience, the overwhelming majority answered with a resounding "YES!"

4. Insert two blank lines in the Normal style, and then insert a new Clustered Column chart object.
5. Enter the following data in the worksheet:

Responses	
Happy	8
Unhappy	3
Ecstatic	14

6. Delete any remaining sample data from the worksheet (you cannot delete the default column labels), resize the data range to fit the data, and minimize the worksheet.
7. Change the chart type to Exploded Pie in 3-D and resize it to approximately 3.5 inches high by 5.5 inches wide.
8. Hide the chart title and the legend.
9. Display data labels and format them to show the category name, percentages, and leader lines. Apply bold to the data label text, and position the data labels so you can read them clearly.
10. Remove the outline border from around the chart object.
11. Set text wrapping for the chart to Top and Bottom, center it horizontally relative to the page, and set it vertically 4.5 inches below the margin (about 2 inches above the bottom of the page).
12. Save the changes.

Embed Excel Worksheet Data

1. Move the insertion point to the end of the document and insert a page break.

2. On the new last page of the document, type the following title in the Title Quick Style:

   Breakdown of Costs for Montreal Trip

3. Press ⏎ to insert a new line and set paragraph formatting to leave 108 points (1.5 inches) of space before.

4. Open the file 💿 **38COSTS** in Excel

5. Select cells A4:D8 and copy the selection to the Clipboard.

6. Switch back to **38PACKET_***xx* and embed the data as a Microsoft Office Excel Worksheet object on the last line of the document.

7. Double-click the object in Word to make the Excel commands available.

8. Apply the 40% - Accent1 cell format to cells A4:C8 and the 20% - Accent1 cell format to cells D4:D8.

9. Increase the font size of the entire range—A4:D8—to 12 points and make it bold, and apply an Ice Blue, Accent 1, solid line border around the outside of the selection.

10. Click outside the object to make the Word commands available again.

11. Center the object on the page.

12. Insert page numbers centered in the footer of all pages in the **38PACKET_***xx* document.

13. Check the spelling and grammar in the document.

14. Preview the document, two pages at a time. Pages 1 and 2 should look similar to Illustration A, and page 3 should look similar to Illustration B.

15. Print the document.

16. Close the document, saving all changes, and then close the **38COSTS** workbook without saving changes, and exit Excel.

Merge with an Access Database

1. Create a new blank Word document and save it as **38SETUP_***xx*. Apply the Median theme.

2. Use mail merge to generate mailing labels.

3. Select the Avery US Letter label number 5663.

4. Use the 💿 **38MEMBERS** Access database file as the data source.

5. Insert the Address Block field on the first label, apply the No Spacing style to the field, and then update the labels.

6. Merge the labels to a new document.

7. Save the merge document as **38LABELS_***xx*.

8. Print the document.

9. Close all open documents, saving all changes.

10. Exit all open applications.

Illustration A

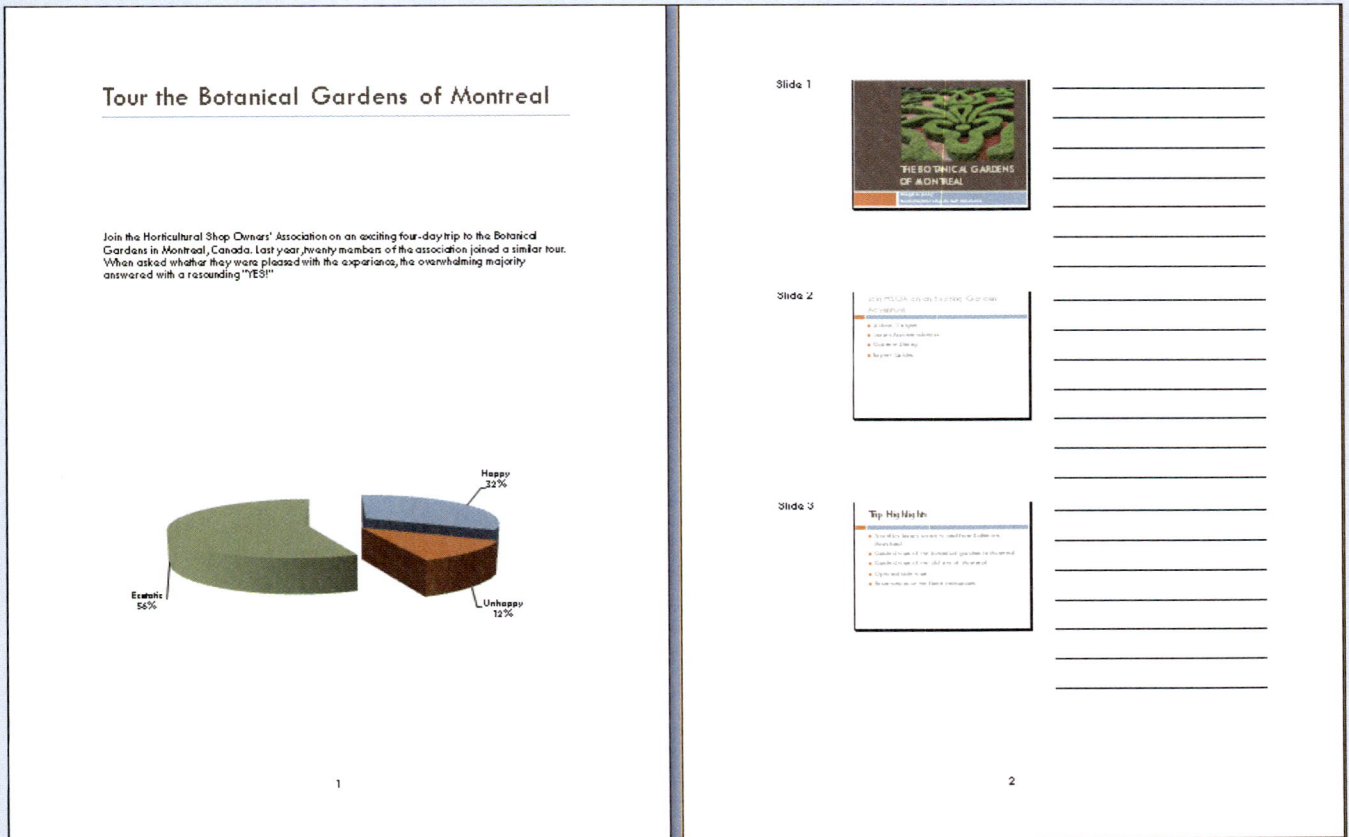

Breakdown of Costs for Montreal Trip

Transportation	350
Lodging	925
Meals	195
Guides	250
Total	1720

3

Exercise | 39

Curriculum Integration

Application Skills   For your language arts class, use the skills you have learned in this lesson to create a multimedia presentation about a work of literature or an author. You can use the Research tool to locate information, pictures, and even sound. You can use the information you find to create a presentation. You can export the presentation to Word to create handouts for your class. If there is data that is suitable for charting, you can create a graph or chart, or use SmartArt to create a flowchart that illustrates plot development or a timeline of an author's life. Deliver your presentation to your class. Refer to Illustration A to see a sample of a SmartArt graphic you might include in your work.

EXERCISE DIRECTIONS

Pick a work of literature or an author that you have studied in class or at home, and research the topic to find out more about it. You can look up definitions, encyclopedia entries, or Web pages that contain relevant information.

Take notes about the topic, or copy the information from the sources into a Word document. Always remember to record the source information so you can include it in a bibliography, footnotes, or a list of works cited.

When you have completed your research, use PowerPoint to create a presentation about the topic. Include text, graphics, and sound, if available. Make the presentation interesting and exciting as well as informative. Save the presentation with a name such as **39PRES_xx**, and apply an appropriate theme

Test and proofread your presentation. Ask a classmate to view it and offer suggestions for how to improve it.

When you are satisfied with your presentation, export it to Word to create handouts. Save the handout document as **39HANDOUT_xx**, and apply the same theme you used for the presentation. Add one or more pages to the handout to create a cover page, a bibliography or list of works cited, and to add a SmartArt graphic or chart, if applicable.

Check the spelling and grammar in the document, and ask a classmate to review it. After making the final edits, print the document.

Save the document and close it. Exit all applications.

Pass out the handouts and deliver the presentation to your class.

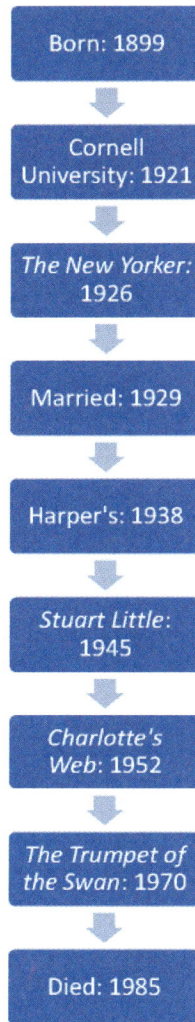

2

Lesson | 1
More on Entering Data, Saving, and Printing

Exercise 1
- Use Go To
- Use Name Box

Exercise 2
- Enter Labels on Multiple Lines
- Enter Fractions and Mixed Numbers
- Smart Tags
- Insert and Delete Selected Cells
- Copy or Move Data with the Office Clipboard

Exercise 3
- Convert Text to Columns

Exercise 4
- Link Documents with Hyperlinks
- Add a Hyperlink to a Worksheet

Exercise 5
- Hide Data Temporarily
- Hide Worksheet Gridlines
- Hide Row and Columns Headings
- Custom Views

Exercise 6
- More Alignment Options
- Format Dates and Times
- Create Custom Number Formats
- Adjust Row Height
- Delete (Clear) a Cell's Formats

Exercise 7
- Change Cell Borders
- Fill Cells with Pattern
- Modify and Save a Theme
- Conditional Formatting
- Add a Watermark
- Format Worksheet Background

Exercise 8
- Save a Workbook in a Different Format
- Use Compatibility Checker
- Create a New Folder for Saving Workbooks
- Enable Macros in a Workbook
- Create Original Templates

Exercise 9
- E-mail a File
- Display and Print Formulas
- Set Precise Margins for Printing

END OF LESSON PROJECTS

Exercise 10
- Critical Thinking

Exercise 11
- Curriculum Integration

Skills Covered

- **Use Go To**
- **Use Name Box**

Software Skills   You can click any visible cell to make it active, but you can also use the Go To command and the Name box to change the active cell even more quickly.

Application Skills   You've been doing a great job at your new job at Intellidata, but the worksheets they use are typically very large, so you need to practice some techniques for moving around Excel quickly and easily.

TERMS

Name box   The box located at the left end of the Formula bar. The Name box displays the location of the current (active) cell.

NOTES

Use Go To

- Go To is a feature that allows you to tell Excel the exact address of the cell that you want to be the current active cell.
- Using Go To changes the location of the active cell.

Use Name Box

- The **Name box** displays the location or address of the active cell.
- Like Go To, the Name box can be used to change the location of the active cell.

PROCEDURES

Change Active Cell Using Go To (Ctrl+G)

1. Click **Home** tab . . . . `Alt`, `H`

   Editing Group

2. Click **Find & Select** button ⚲ . . . . `F`, `D`

3. Click **Go To** . . . . `G`

   OR

   Press **F5** . . . . `F5`

   ✓ *The Go to list box displays the last four addresses to which you went with Go To.*

4. Type cell reference in **Reference** text box . . . . `Alt`+`R`

5. Click **OK** . . . . `Enter`

   ✓ *If you want to select a group of related cells using Go To, click the Special button in the Go To dialog box; then choose the type of cells you want to select and click OK.*

Change Active Cell Using Name Box

1. Click in the **Name** box.
2. Type the cell reference.
3. Press **Enter** . . . . `Enter`

EXERCISE DIRECTIONS

1. Start Excel.
2. Move the cell pointer to cell I8 using the arrow keys.

   ✓ *Notice that the cell reference is displayed in the Name box and that the related column and row heading are highlighted.*

3. With the mouse, make cell F12 active.
4. Using the keyboard, perform the following tasks:

   a. Scroll using the arrow keys so you can see cell BH76, and make it the active cell.

   b. Scroll to cell J32 and make it active.

   c. Use Go To to jump to cell Q81.

   d. Return to cell A1.

   e. Use the Name box to make cell K112 the active cell.

5. Type your first name in cell K112 and press Enter.
6. With the keyboard, return to cell A1.
7. With the mouse, perform the following tasks:

   a. Scroll so you can see cell Z94.

   b. Scroll to cell C21.

   c. Scroll to cell H4.

   d. Scroll back to cell K112.

8. Exit Excel.

   ✓ *Do not save the workbook.*

ON YOUR OWN

1. Start Excel.

2. Using Go To, move the active cell to the following:
   Q201
   C96
   HH4302

3. Using the Name box, move the active cell to the following:
   CQ102
   P33
   M5937

4. Using Go To, move the active cell back to C96.

   ✓ Note that your four previous Go To destinations are also displayed in the Go To box.

5. Type the following in the indicated cells:
   a. C96: **Blue**
   b. O116: **Green**
   c. K21: **Red**

6. Zoom to 75%.

7. Using the mouse, change the active cell to the following:
   A10
   K21
   R32
   J106

8. Zoom to 100%.

9. Repeat step 7 to change the active cell.

   ✓ Notice that you need to scroll more, since less of the worksheet is displayed at any given time.

10. Repeat step 7 with a custom percentage of your choice, such as 65%.

   ✓ How low can you go in terms of zoom percentage and still be comfortable reading your data?

11. Move the active cell to A1.

12. Drag the scroll box on the vertical scroll bar and watch the ScreenTip change as it displays the row numbers.

13. Repeat step 12 with the horizontal scroll bar.

14. Exit Excel.

   ✓ Do not save the workbook.

Skills Covered

- **Enter Labels on Multiple Lines**
- **Enter Fractions and Mixed Numbers**
- **Smart Tags**

- **Insert and Delete Selected Cells**
- **Copy or Move Data with the Office Clipboard**

Software Skills When entering labels, especially long ones, you may want to display them on more than one line so the column will not need to be as wide. Entering fractions, on the other hand, requires a special technique so they display properly. In order to shorten the time it takes to enter data, Excel displays smart tags that provide quick access to related commands. After you create a worksheet, you may want to rearrange data by moving or copying it, or by adding new cells between existing data.

Application Skills As Junior Manager for a local PhotoTown store, you have been asked to create some way to track weekly sales for individual sales clerks. Your plan is to start with an existing daily sales worksheet, and to use it to create a weekly sales tracker.

TERMS

Format To apply attributes to cell data to change the appearance of the worksheet.

Line break A code inserted into text that forces it to display on two different lines.

Smart tags Buttons that appear after you take particular actions, or enter certain kinds of data. The smart tag button provides convenient access to related actions.

NOTES

Enter Labels on Multiple Lines

- If you have long column labels, you can adjust the column width to fit them.
  - This doesn't always look pleasing, however, especially when the column label is much longer than the data in the column.
  - For example, the two columns shown here are much larger than their data:

Unit Number	Total Annual Sales
2	$125,365.97

- One of the easiest ways to fix this problem is to enter the column label with **line breaks**.

- Entering line breaks between words in a cell enables you to place several lines of text in the same cell, like this next example.

Unit Number	Total Annual Sales
2	$125,365.97

- The height of the row adjusts automatically to accommodate the multiple-line column label.

Enter Fractions and Mixed Numbers

- If you type the value 1/3 into a cell, Excel thinks that it's a date (in this case, January 3rd).

- To enter a fraction, you must precede it with a zero (0) and a space, which tells Excel that the data is a number. For example, to enter 1/3, type 0 1/3.

- A fraction appears as a decimal value in the Formula bar. The fraction 1/3 appears as 0.333333333333333 in the Formula bar.

- You don't need to add the preceding zero when you're entering a mixed number (a number and a fraction, as in 4 1/2).

- To enter a mixed fraction, simply type it: Type 4, a space, then the fraction, 1/2. For example, 4 1/2.

- You can **format** existing data to look like fractions. To do this, use the Format Cells command.

Smart Tags

- Excel has the ability to recognize certain types of data and particular actions, and to display a **smart tag**.

- Smart tags may be turned on by default on the system you're using. See the procedures to turn them off.

- Smart tags are indicator triangles that appear in cells. Point to an indicator to display a button that you can click to see a menu of related actions.

- Smart tags appear when you enter particular types of data:

  - If you enter the name of someone in your Outlook contacts list to whom you've recently sent an e-mail message, the smart tag will allow you to send another message, schedule a meeting, display the contact information, and so on.

  - If you enter any person's name, you can add that person to the Outlook contact list.

  - If you enter a date into a cell, you can use the smart tag to check your calendar in Outlook for meetings and appointments scheduled that day.

  - If you type a stock symbol, the smart tag allows you to download current information about that stock from the Internet, and copy it directly into the worksheet.

- Microsoft's Web site offers additional smart tags you can add to Excel to expand its functionality.

Insert and Delete Selected Cells

- You can insert or delete a selected group of cells within your worksheet data.

- You might do this if you've entered some data into the wrong columns or rows accidentally, and you simply want to shift the data over.

- When you insert cells, surrounding cells can be shifted either down or to the right in order to make room.

- Likewise, if you delete a selected group of cells, the surrounding cells can be shifted up or to the left to fill the gap.

Copy or Move Data with the Office Clipboard

- When you cut (or copy) data, it's temporarily stored on the Clipboard.

- Actually, the data is stored on two Clipboards—the Windows Clipboard and the Office Clipboard.

Office Clipboard task pane

- The Windows Clipboard stores the last item you cut or copy.

- The Office Clipboard stores the last item as well as previously cut or copied items (up to a total of 24) so you can cut or copy multiple items with ease.

■ The Office Clipboard is only accessible within Office programs, so you can use its enhanced capabilities to collect multiple items and paste them throughout any of your Office documents.

■ In order to collect multiple items, you must display the Office Clipboard first, before you start copying and cutting.

■ You can display the Office Clipboard manually from the Clipboard group on the Home tab, or you can set an option to have it appear automatically under certain conditions.

■ If you set the Office Clipboard to appear automatically, then the task pane appears after you either:

  ● Copy or cut two different items in succession, in the same program.

  ● Copy and paste an item, then copy another item in the same program.

■ Data is stored on the Windows Clipboard until you copy or cut something else, which then replaces it.

■ Data is not replaced on the Office Clipboard until you cut or copy the twenty-fifth item.

■ When you quit all Office programs, the Office Clipboard is automatically cleared.

■ You can paste any item you want from the Office Clipboard—multiple times, if you like.

■ Items appear in the Clipboard list in the order in which they were copied there—newest items at the top.

■ Each item in the list is identified with the program icon of its source.

■ You can clear the Office Clipboard of all items.

■ The Windows Clipboard is cleared as well.

PROCEDURES

Enter Line Breaks in a Cell Entry

1. Type first line of label.
2. Press **Alt+Enter** . . . . `Alt`+`Enter`
3. Type second line of label.
4. Repeat steps 2 and 3 as needed.
5. Press **Enter** . . . . `Enter`

Enter a Number as a Fraction

1. Select the cell.
2. Type **zero**.
3. Press the **Spacebar** . . . . . . `Spacebar`
4. Type a fraction.

   ✓ *Example: 0 1/5*

5. Press **Enter** . . . . `Enter`

Enter Mixed Numbers

1. Select the cell.
2. Type a whole number.
3. Press the **Spacebar** . . . . . . `Spacebar`
4. Type the fraction.

   ✓ *Example: 3 1/3*

5. Press **Enter** . . . . `Enter`

Turn on Smart Tags

✓ *To display smart tags when you enter certain data such as stock symbols, you must turn on the smart tags feature.*

1. Click **Office Button** . . . `Alt`+`F`
2. Click **Excel Options** . . . . `I`
3. Click **Proofing** . . . . `↑`/`↓`
4. Click **AutoCorrect Options** . . . . `Alt`+`A`
5. Click **Smart Tags** tab . . . `Ctrl`+`⇆`
6. Select **Label data with smart tags**. . . . . `L`
7. Select items you want Smart Tags to recognize from the **Recognizers** list . . . . `E`, `→`/`←`/`↑`/`↓`

To check the workbook for existing smart tags:

■ Click **Check Workbook** . . . . . . `C`

To download new smart tags from the Internet:

■ Click **More Smart Tags** . . . . . . `M`

To control how smart tags appear:

a. Click down arrow to open **Show smart tags as** list . . . `S`
b. Click a view option in the list that appears.

To save smart tags with a workbook:

■ Click **Embed smart tags in this workbook** . . . . `B`
8. Click **OK** twice . . . . `Enter`, `Enter`

Use Smart Tags

1. Excel's smart tags option buttons appear automatically when you first enter text recognized as a smart tag in a cell. To display the smart tags option button at a later time, move the mouse pointer over a purple triangle indicator.
2. Click the down arrow on the button.
3. Click an option on the list that appears.

Insert Cells

1. Select the range where you want to insert new cells.
2. Click **Home** tab . . . . [Alt], [H]

3. Click **Insert** button arrow 📥 . . . . [I]
4. Click **I**nsert Cells . . . . [I]
5. Click **Shift cells ri**ght . . . . [I]

   OR

   Click **Shift cells **down . . . . [D]
6. Click **OK** . . . . [Enter]

Remove Cells

1. Select the range you want to remove.
2. Click **Home** tab . . . . [Alt], [H]

3. Click **Delete** button arrow 📥 . . . . [D]
4. Click **D**elete Cells . . . . [D]
5. Click **Shift cells **left . . . . [L]

   OR

   Click **Shift cells **up . . . . [U]
6. Click **OK** . . . . [Enter]

Display the Office Clipboard

1. Click **Home** tab . . . . [Alt], [H]

2. Click **Clipboard** dialog box launcher ⬜ . . . . [F], [O]

   ✓ If the Office Clipboard is open in a different Office program, such as Word, you can display the Clipboard task pane In Excel by double-clicking the Clipboard icon 📋 in the notification or icons area of the Windows taskbar (if present).

Use the Office Clipboard

- To copy a selected item, click the **Copy** button 📋 on the Home tab.
- To paste an item from the Clipboard, click its name in the Clipboard list.
- To paste all the items from the Clipboard, click the **Paste All** button 📋 Paste All.
- To remove a single item from the Clipboard, open the item's menu, and then click **Delete**.
- To clear the Clipboard, click the **Clear All** button 📋 Clear All.

Set Office Clipboard Options

1. Click **Options** button Options ▼ on Office Clipboard task pane.
2. Select desired option:
   - **O**ffice Clipboard **Automatically** . . . . [A]

   ✓ Displays the Office Clipboard task pane as soon as you start copying or cutting.

   - **Show Office Clipboard when Ctrl+C Pressed Twice** . . . . [P]

   ✓ Displays the Office Clipboard when you press the key sequence.

   - **C**ollect Without Showing Office Clipboard . . . . [C]

   ✓ Starts to collect copied or cut data automatically, without displaying the Office Clipboard task pane.

   - **Show Office Clipboard Icon on **Taskbar . . . . [T]

   ✓ Displays the Office Clipboard icon on the Windows taskbar, so you can quickly display the Clipboard in another program, and monitor its contents.

   - **Show **Status Near Taskbar When Copying . . . . [S]

   ✓ Displays the message X items of XX near the task bar when copying or moving data to the Office Clipboard.

EXERCISE DIRECTIONS

1. Start Excel, if necessary.
2. Open 🔵 **02WeeklyProductTracker**.
3. Save the file as **02WeeklyProductTracker_xx**.
4. Open the Office Clipboard so you can collect the employee names for pasting in various locations later on:
   a. Display the Office Clipboard.
   b. Click Clear All to clear the Clipboard.
   c. Click cell A7 and click Copy.
   d. Click A8 and click Copy.
   e. Repeat, copying the employee names in cells A9 and A12 one at a time, to the Office Clipboard.

5. Collect the product names by selecting the data in cells B7, B8, B10, B12, and B13:
   a. Click each of these cells, one at a time, and click Copy to copy each item to the Clipboard.
   b. Paste the *T-shirts* label into cell A24.
   c. Paste the label *Photo books* into cell A25; *Mugs* into cell A26; *Greeting cards* into cell A27; and *3-D photos* into cell A28.
6. Select the range, A21: I29 and copy it to the Clipboard as well:
   a. Paste the weekly product sales data to the range beginning with cell A30.
   b. Repeat this process two more times, pasting the same data to the ranges beginning with cell A39 and A48.

7. You should now have four empty data areas for recording weekly product sales by employee. Use the Office Clipboard to paste some data:

   a. Click cell A22.

   b. Click the first employee name in the Clipboard task pane to paste it.

   c. Click the Paste Options smart tag that appears, and choose Match Destination Formatting.

   d. Repeat this process, pasting each of the remaining three employee names, one each in cells A31, A40, and A49. (See Illustration A.)

   e. Clear the Office Clipboard, then close the task pane.

8. You need to add a column to the daily tracker, in order to record the sizes of the t-shirts being sold, but you don't want to insert a column in the weekly product sales sheets below:

   a. Select the range C6:C15.

   b. Insert new cells into the selection, shifting the existing cells to the right.

   c. Type the label **T-Shirt Size** on two lines in cell C6. Center the label.

   d. Type **10 1/2** in cell C7.

   e. Type **8** in cell C11.

9. Copy the format of cell E6 to the ranges E1:E5 and E16:E19.

10. Copy the format of cell C16 to the range D16:D17.

11. Adjust column widths as needed.

12. Spell check the worksheet.

13. Print the worksheet.

14. Close the workbook, saving all changes.

Illustration A

ON YOUR OWN

1. Start Excel, if necessary.
2. Open ⊙ **02ORDER**.
3. Save the file as **OXL02_xx**.
4. Type the date in cell C3.
5. Insert two columns between B and C.

   ✓ *Use the Insert Options button to copy the formatting from the right.*

6. Use Cut and Paste to move the date back from cell E3 to cell C3.
7. Enter the labels Cartons Ordered, Price per Carton, and Product Total Sale in cells C7:E7.

   ✓ *Use two-line column labels.*

8. Enter prices for each of the products:

Klean Kan Industrial Cleaner	$27.00
Klean Kan Carpet	$23.00
Klean Kan Windows	$19.50
Toilet Sanitizer	$18.50
Paper Towels	$11.00

9. Create formulas to compute the total sale per product.
10. Create a grand total as well and enter a label for it in cell D13.
11. Adjust column widths as needed.
12. Display the Office Clipboard, and use it to copy the entire order form. Paste the form onto Sheet 2 and Sheet 3.

    a. Use the Paste Options button to copy the source column widths as well.

    b. Clear the Clipboard, and then close the task pane.

13. Enter some sales data in the form on Sheet 1.

    a. Enter your name in the Salesperson cell (C5).

    b. Enter a customer number in cell C4.

    c. Use fractions and mixed numbers to order half-cartons of cleaning supplies.

14. Adjust column widths again as needed.
15. Spell check the worksheet.
16. Print the worksheet.
17. Close the workbook, saving all changes.

Business Connection

Finding Job Opportunities

A source of employment is any business, organization, or individual that hires and pays someone to perform a job. Usually, when employers need new employees, they advertise. They might run an ad in the classified section of a newspaper, magazine, or Web site, or display a Help Wanted sign in a store window. There are many ways they get the word out; your responsibility as a job seeker is to find the advertisement, wherever it might be.

Tracking Employment Ads

Use Excel to set up a worksheet in which you can store information about different sources of employment. You can list the name of the source, the type, and other information such as a contact name and Web page link. You can expand the worksheet to include data that might help you spot a trend, such as how many job listings are posted by that source on a regular basis, or the average amount of time a job is listed. Use Excel features such as fill cells to fill the same data into adjacent cells, or fill series to fill a series of data such as dates or numbers into adjacent cells. If the worksheet is very long, freeze the column and row headings so you can see them even when you scroll down or right.

→

- **Convert Text to Columns**

Software Skills   Occasionally, you won't create problems in Excel, but *inherit* them. For example, someone might have created a long list of important data, such as client names and e-mail addresses. Maybe you've been given the job of using this list to send out automated e-mail newsletters, coupons, and other incentives. The problem is, certain fields that should have been kept separated (such as first and last names) are located in the same column, making it impossible to perform simple maintenance tasks such as sorting by last name. Luckily, Excel allows you to split such cells into their component parts, and to put each part (such as the first name and last name) into its own cell.

Application Skills   Your boss at The Little Toy Shoppe wants you to create a newsletter to inform clients of new products and to entice them to return to the store on special sales days. Luckily, Rob the intern has been keeping track of customer names and addresses in a new worksheet. Unfortunately, Rob doesn't know the first thing about creating a workable database. With the help you'll find in this exercise however, you'll be able to easily fix Rob's mistakes without resorting to reentering the data.

TERMS

No new terms in this exercise.

NOTES

Convert Text to Columns

- When working with large amounts of text data in Excel, pre-planning is often critical.
  - For example, when creating a long list of customers, it's useful to place first names in one column, and last names in another. That way, you can sort on the single column, Last Names, and arrange the customer list alphabetically by last name.
  - It might also be useful to separate out the parts of a customer's address into different columns—one each for street address, city, state, and ZIP Code—so the customer list can be sorted by state or ZIP Code if you like.

- If such a customer list was not set up properly, you can easily fix it by having Excel split the contents of a cell across several cells.
  - For example, if you had entered a customer's first and last name into the same cell, you could have Excel split the contents of that cell into two cells—one for the first name and another for the last.
  - To make such a conversion easier, you can select the entire column of customer names, and have Excel split their data into two columns in one step.
- Excel can split the contents of a single cell, a range, or an entire column in one step.

PROCEDURES

Convert Delimited Text to Columns

1. Select the cell, column, or range whose contents you wish to split.
2. Click **Data** tab . . . . `Alt`, `A`

   Data Tools Group

3. Click **Text to Columns** button . . . . `E`

   ✓ *The Convert Text to Columns Wizard appears.*

4. Click **D̲elimited** . . . . `D`
5. Click **Next** . . . . `Enter`
6. Select how fields are separated (delimited):

   ✓ *After selecting the correct deliminator, the fields in the selected cell, range, or column will appear in the Data preview pane, separated by vertical lines.*

   - **T̲ab** . . . . `T`
   - **Se̲micolon** . . . . `M`
   - **C̲omma** . . . . `C`
   - **S̲pace** . . . . `S`

     OR

   a. **O̲ther** . . . . `O`
   b. Enter the delimiter for other.

7. To skip empty columns, click **T̲reat consecutive delimiters as one** . . . . `R`
8. Click **Next** . . . . `Enter`

9. Select the formats to apply:

   a. Click column in the **Data p̲review section** . . . . . `Alt`+`P`
   b. Select column data format:

      - **General** . . . . `Alt`+`G`
      - **T̲ext** . . . . `Alt`+`T`
      - **D̲ate** . . . . `Alt`+`D`

        OR

      - **Do not i̲mport column (skip)** . . . . `Alt`+`I`

10. Repeat step 9 for each column.
11. Select a destination for the split data:

    a. Click in **D̲estination** text box . . . . `Alt`+`E`
    b. Type destination cell, range, or column.

    ✓ *You can also click the Collapse Dialog button and select the destination cell, range, or column.*

12. Click **F̲inish** . . . . `Alt`+`F`

Convert Fixed Text to Columns

1. Select the cell, column, or range whose contents you wish to split.
2. Click **Data** tab . . . . `Alt`, `A`

   Data Tools Group

3. Click **Text to Columns** button . . . . `E`

   ✓ *The Convert Text to Columns Wizard appears.*

4. Click **Fixed w̲idth** . . . . `W`

5. Click **Next** . . . . `Enter`
6. Select how fields are separated:

   - Click ruler at the desired position to create a break (separation) there
   - To delete a break, double-click it.
   - To adjust where a break occurs, drag it.

   ✓ *After placing the deliminators correctly, the fields in the selected cell, range, or column will appear in the Data preview pane, separated by vertical lines.*

7. Click **Next** . . . . `Enter`
8. Select the formats to apply:

   a. Click column in the **Data p̲review section** . . . . . `Alt`+`P`
   b. Select column data format:

      - **General** . . . . `Alt`+`G`
      - **T̲ext** . . . . `Alt`+`T`
      - **D̲ate** . . . . `Alt`+`D`

        OR

      - **Do not i̲mport column (skip)** . . . . `Alt`+`I`

9. Select a destination for the split data:

   a. Click in **D̲estination** text box . . . . `Alt`+`E`
   b. Type destination cell, range, or column.

   ✓ *You can also click the Collapse Dialog button and select the destination cell, range, or column.*

10. Click **F̲inish** . . . . `Alt`+`F`

EXERCISE DIRECTIONS

1. Start Excel if necessary.
2. Open ⊙ **03Customers**.
3. Save the file as **03Customers_*xx***.
4. Insert two columns between columns B and C.
5. Type **First Name** in cell B5; type **Last Name** in cell C5.
6. Split the names in column B into three columns (some of the first names are two part, and result in two columns of data):
   a. Select the range B6:B57.
   b. Display the Convert Text to Columns Wizard.
   c. Select the Delimited option and Space as the delimiter used.
   d. Select Text as the format for all three columns.
   e. Place the result in the range beginning with cell B6, and answer OK when asked if you want to replace data.
7. A few of the names use all three columns; those names have two part first names which should appear together in column B. You can easily correct this situation, however, and get rid of the third column you don't really need.
   a. Type **Mary Jane** in cell B11 and **Brink** in cell C11.
   b. Type **Chu Gi** in cell B34 and **Nguyen** in cell C34.
   c. Delete column D.
8. Insert two columns between columns E and F.
9. Type **City** in cell E5, **State** in cell F5, and **Zip Code** in cell G5.

10. Split the addresses in column E into three columns:
    a. Select the range E6:E57.
    b. Display the Convert Text to Columns Wizard.
    c. Select the Delimited option, and Comma as the delimiter used.

    ✓ *You'll notice that the data is split into only two columns; this is OK since you will easily fix this by using the Convert Text to Columns Wizard a second time.*

    d. Select Text as the format for first column.
    e. Place the result in the range beginning with cell E6, and answer OK when asked if you want to replace data.
11. Repeat this process to split the state and zip codes in column F into two columns:
    a. Select the range F6:F57.
    b. Display the Convert Text to Columns Wizard.
    c. Select the Delimited option and Space as the delimiter used.
    d. Do not import the first column.
    e. Select Text as the format for second column, and General for the third column.
    f. Place the result in the range beginning with cell F6, and answer OK when asked if you want to replace data.
12. Adjust column widths as needed. (See Illustration A.)
13. Spell check the worksheet.
14. Print the worksheet.
15. Close the workbook, saving all changes.

S03Customers - Microsoft Excel

The Little Toy Shoppe
Customer Database

Title	First Name	Last Name	Address	City	State	Zip Code	Phone
Mrs.	Barbara	Adamson	7770 Dean Road	Cincinnati	OH	33240	844-1589
Mr.	Carlos	Altare	4125 Fairlinks Ave.	Carmel	IN	46231	298-1212
Mrs.	Diana	Bond	10208 E. Ridgefield Drive	Indian Blade	IN	46236	899-1712
Mrs.	Jan	Borough	7556 Hilltop Way	Cincinnati	OH	33254	291-3678
Mr.	Adam	Bounds	4943 Windridge Drive	Indianapolis	IN	42626	542-8151
Mrs.	Mary Jane	Brink	704 Fairway Drive	Cincinnati	OH	33250	255-1655
Mr.	Shakur	Brown	5648 Hydcort	Indianapolis	IN	46250	842-8819
Mrs.	Rafiquil	Damir	14559 Senator Way	Indianapolis	IN	46226	844-9977
Mrs.	Diana	Dogwood	6311 Douglas Road	Wayne's Town	OH	33502	251-9052
Mrs.	Lucy	Fan	5784 N. Central	Indianapolis	IN	46268	255-6479
Mr.	Joshua	Fedor	1889 E. 72nd Street	Indian Blade	IN	46003	251-4796
Mrs.	Michele	Floyd	3203 Wander Wood Ct	Indianapolis	IN	46220	291-2510
Mrs.	Jennifer	Flynn	9876 Wilshire Ave.	Cincinnati	OH	33240	975-0909
Ms.	Katerina	Flynn	4984 Wander Wood Lane	Indianapolis	IN	42626	542-0021
Mr.	Eram	Hassan	8123 Maple Ave.	Cincinnati	OH	33250	722-1487
Mrs.	Betty	High	7543 Newport Bay Drive	Cincinnati	OH	33250	722-1043
Mrs.	Addie	Howard	7960 Susan Drive, S.	Westland	IN	46215	849-3557
Mr.	Tyrell	Johnson	11794 Southland Ave.	Wayne's Town	OH	33505	846-9812
Mr.	Michael	Jordain	4897 Kessler Ave.	Indianapolis	IN	46220	255-1133
Mrs.	Ashley	Kay	8738 Log Run Drive, S.	Carmel	IN	46234	299-6136
Mrs.	Rhoda	Kuntz	567 W. 72nd Street	Indian Blade	IN	46003	251-6539
Ms.	Verna	Latinz	14903 Senator Way	Indianapolis	IN	46226	844-4333
Mr.	Wu	Lee	6467 Riverside Drive	Carmel	IN	46220	257-1253
Mr.	Chu	Lee	5821 Wilshire Ave.	Cincinnati	OH	33240	975-0484
Mr.	Shamir	Lewis	11684 Bay Colony Drive	Plainsville	IN	46234	297-1894
Mrs.	Martha	Luck	4131 Brown Road	Cincinnati	OH	33454	547-7430
Mrs.	Maria	Navarro	3847 Shipshore Drive	Indianapolis	IN	46032	873-9664
Mr.	Tony	Navarro	7998 Maple Ave.	Westland	IN	46215	849-1515
Mr.	Chu Gi	Nguyen	8794 Dean Road	Cincinnati	OH	33240	853-1277

Sheet1 / Sheet2 / Sheet3

ON YOUR OWN

1. Start Excel if necessary.
2. Open ◉ **03JewelryCustomers**.
3. Save the file as **OXL03_*xx***.
4. Split the contents of the range I5:I56 into three columns:
   a. Label column I **Color**, column J **Cut**, and column K **Clarity**.
   b. Choose Comma as the delimiter.
   c. Select Text as the format for all three columns.
   d. Place the result in the range beginning with cell I5, and answer OK when asked if you want to replace data.
5. Apply additional formatting to the worksheet as desired.
6. Adjust column widths as needed.
7. Spell check the worksheet.
8. Print the worksheet.
9. Close the workbook, saving all changes.

Skills Covered

- **Link Documents with Hyperlinks**
- **Add a Hyperlink to a Worksheet**

Software Skills A hyperlink can connect a worksheet to specific locations within any worksheet in any workbook, or to information on the Internet or the company intranet. Using a hyperlink is a convenient way to provide quick access to related information. For example, in a sales worksheet, you could provide a hyperlink to an area in the workbook (or in another workbook) that provides product costs or other revenues.

Application Skills You've been put in charge of tracking patient services at Wood Hills Animal Clinic. You've put together a patient worksheet listing the various pets that have recently visited the clinic and a separate worksheet listing owner information. Before you get too far on your project, you want to test out its usability, adding hyperlinks that connect each pet with its owner's personal data. Finally, you want to link from a pet's name to its patient history, which is stored in a third worksheet.

TERMS

HTML Short for Hypertext Markup Language, the language used to display information on a Web page.

Hyperlink Text or graphics linked to related information in the same workbook, another workbook, or another file.

Internet A global collection of interconnected networks.

Intranet A private Internet-like network, typically used to link the various parts of a company.

MHTML A modified version of HTML, in which graphics, animations, and other accessory objects are stored in a single Web page file, rather than as separate files linked to the HTML file.

URL Short for Uniform Resource Locator. The address or location of the page or file on the Internet.

Web pages Documents (frequently including multimedia elements) that can be accessed with a Web browser.

NOTES

Link Documents with Hyperlinks

- A **hyperlink** is text or a graphic that, when clicked, displays related information elsewhere in the worksheet or in another file.
  - Text hyperlinks are typically formatted in blue and underlined.
  - You can link to information in the same worksheet, another worksheet in the same workbook, another workbook, or anywhere on the Internet.

- You can also link to any other file, such as a Word document, sound file, graphic image, movie, and so on.
- These files may be located on your hard disk, the company network, the **Internet** or an **intranet**.
- You can link to your e-mail address, to help the user send you an e-mail message.
- You can also create a new workbook to link to.

■ Documents on the Internet that use **HTML/MHTML** format are called **Web pages**.

  ● Web pages frequently have multimedia capabilities such as sound, movies, animations, and so on, as well as controls such as forms, dialog boxes, and buttons.

  ● Web pages are connected to each other and to various files such as sound and movie files, through hyperlinks similar to those you can insert into Excel workbooks.

■ When you move the mouse pointer over a hyperlink, it changes to a pointing hand 🖑.

  ● This change helps you distinguish hyperlinks from regular text, and hyperlink graphics from regular pictures.

  ● Because the mouse pointer changes to a hand when over a hyperlink, you must use special techniques to select the link for editing.

■ Also, when a mouse pointer moves over a hyperlink, a ScreenTip appears, displaying the URL of the linked file or e-mail address.

  ● You can override this default ScreenTip with a short description of the linked file or e-mail address.

■ A hyperlink can also be represented by a graphic image.

■ Usually, when a hyperlink is represented as text, that text appears in a blue underlined font.

  ✓ *You can change the default color of hyperlink text.*

  ● When you click a text hyperlink and then later return to it, you'll probably notice that it has changed to purple underlined text.

  ● This change helps you quickly identify the links you've used (and those you haven't).

■ Clicking a hyperlink moves you to the associated location.

  ● If the hyperlink involves another file, that file is opened automatically.

  ● If you want the user to move to a particular place within a worksheet, you might want to create a range name so that you can use that name in the link. Clicking the hyperlink takes the user to that range within the worksheet.

  ✓ *If you don't want to create a range name, you can still link to a specific place within a worksheet by typing its cell address.*

■ You can create hyperlinks that connect a user to data in the current workbook or workbooks located on a company intranet.

■ You can also connect to data on the Internet.

  ● You can connect to Excel files or to HTML/MHTML files, since Excel can display either.

  ● This capability allows you to include links to related Web pages (since they're coded in HTML or MHTML) within your worksheets.

■ You can include hyperlinks in ordinary Excel worksheets.

  ● You can also include hyperlinks in workbooks that you have converted to HTML format.

Add a Hyperlink to a Worksheet

■ If you want to create a hyperlink from text, enter the text before you follow the steps to create the hyperlink.

■ Likewise, if you want to create a hyperlink from a graphic image, insert the image into the worksheet first.

Insert Hyperlink dialog box

- Normally, you insert a hyperlink using the Insert Hyperlink dialog box.
- If you want to create a hyperlink to a Web page or an intranet document, you can bypass the Insert Hyperlink dialog box and simply type the Web page address (URL) or intranet location into a cell.
  - Excel will instantly recognize the address as a URL, and create a hyperlink from it automatically.

- A Web address might look like this: http://www.fakeco.com/augsales.html
- With your Internet or intranet connection, you can include a hyperlink to an e-mail address within a worksheet.
  - When a user clicks this type of hyperlink, an e-mail message is automatically created, with the recipient's address included.

PROCEDURES

Insert a Hyperlink to a File

1. Select the text or graphic you want to use for the link.
2. Click **Insert** tab . . . . $\boxed{\text{Alt}}$, $\boxed{\text{N}}$

   Links Group

3. Click **Hyperlink** button 🌐 . . . . $\boxed{\text{I}}$
4. Click the **Existing File or Web Page** in the Link to bar . . . . $\boxed{\text{Alt}}$ + $\boxed{\text{X}}$
5. Enter the path to the file in the **Address** text box . . . . $\boxed{\text{Alt}}$ + $\boxed{\text{E}}$

   OR

   a. Select drive and/or folder from **Look in** list . . . . $\boxed{\text{Alt}}$ + $\boxed{\text{L}}$
   b. Select file . . . . $\boxed{\uparrow}$/$\boxed{\downarrow}$

   OR

   a. Click **Recent Files** . . . $\boxed{\text{Alt}}$ + $\boxed{\text{C}}$
   b. Select a file you've used recently from those listed . . . . $\boxed{\uparrow}$/$\boxed{\downarrow}$

6. To link to a specific location within the file:

   a. Click **Bookmark** . . . . . $\boxed{\text{Alt}}$ + $\boxed{\text{O}}$
   b. Select the name from those listed . . . . $\boxed{\uparrow}$/$\boxed{\downarrow}$

   ✓ If you're linking to an Excel workbook, you can link to a specific range, or you can select a sheet from those listed and type a cell address.

7. Click **OK** . . . . $\boxed{\text{Enter}}$

8. To change the ScreenTip that appears when the mouse pointer rests on the hyperlink:

   a. Click **ScreenTip** button . . . . $\boxed{\text{Alt}}$ + $\boxed{\text{P}}$
   b. Enter the description you want to display.
   c. Click **OK** . . . . $\boxed{\text{Enter}}$
9. Click **OK** . . . . $\boxed{\text{Enter}}$

Insert a Hyperlink to a Web Page

1. Select the text or graphic you want to use for the link.
2. Click **Insert** tab . . . . $\boxed{\text{Alt}}$, $\boxed{\text{N}}$

   Links Group

3. Click **Hyperlink** button 🌐 . . . . $\boxed{\text{I}}$
4. Click the **Existing File or Web Page** in the Link to bar . . . . $\boxed{\text{Alt}}$ + $\boxed{\text{X}}$
5. Enter the path to the file in the **Address** text box . . . . $\boxed{\text{Alt}}$ + $\boxed{\text{E}}$
6. Enter the address of the Web page in the **Address** text box . . . . $\boxed{\text{Alt}}$ + $\boxed{\text{E}}$

   OR

   a. Click the **Browse the Web** button 🌐.
   b. Using your Web browser, change to the page you want.
   c. Switch back to Excel.

OR

   a. Click **Browsed Pages** button . . . . $\boxed{\text{Alt}}$ + $\boxed{\text{B}}$
   b. Select a page you've visited recently from those listed . . . . $\boxed{\leftrightarrows}$, $\boxed{\uparrow}$/$\boxed{\downarrow}$

7. To link to a specific location within the page:

   a. Click **Bookmark** button . . . . $\boxed{\text{Alt}}$ + $\boxed{\text{O}}$
   b. Select the name from those listed . . . . $\boxed{\uparrow}$/$\boxed{\downarrow}$

8. To change the ScreenTip that appears when the mouse pointer rests on the hyperlink:

   a. Click **ScreenTip** button . . . . $\boxed{\text{Alt}}$ + $\boxed{\text{P}}$
   b. Enter the description you want to display.
   c. Click **OK** . . . . $\boxed{\text{Enter}}$
9. Click **OK** . . . . $\boxed{\text{Enter}}$

Insert a Hyperlink to a Location in the Current Workbook

1. Select the text or graphic you want to use for the link.
2. Click **Insert** tab . . . . $\boxed{\text{Alt}}$, $\boxed{\text{N}}$

   Links Group

3. Click **Hyperlink** button 🌐 . . . . $\boxed{\text{I}}$
4. Click the **Place in This Document** in the Link to bar . . . . $\boxed{\text{Alt}}$ + $\boxed{\text{A}}$

5. Enter the cell address in the **Type the ce̲ll reference** text box . . . . `Alt`+`E`

   OR

   Select a location from the **Or select a pla̲ce in this document** list . . . . `Alt`+`C`, `↑`/`↓`

6. To change the ScreenTip that appears when the mouse pointer rests on the hyperlink:

   a. Click **ScreenTip̲** button . . . . `Alt`+`P`

   b. Enter the description you want to display.

   c. Click **OK** . . . . `Enter`

7. Click **OK** . . . . `Enter`

Insert a Hyperlink to a New Workbook

1. Select the text or graphic you want to use for the link.

2. Click **Insert** tab . . . . `Alt`, `N`

   Links Group

3. Click **Hyperlink** button 🌐 . . . . `I`

4. Click the **Create N̲ew Document** in the Link to bar . . . . `Alt`+`N`

5. Type a name for the new workbook in the **Name of new d̲ocument** text box . . . . `Alt`+`D`

6. If necessary, change the drive and folder in which you want the new workbook saved:

   a. Click **Change** . . . . `Alt`+`C`

   b. Select drive and/or folder from **Save in** list. . . . . `Alt`+`I`

   c. Click **OK** . . . . `Enter`

7. Indicate when you want to edit the new workbook:

   ■ **Edit the new document later** . . . . `Alt`+`L`

     OR

   ■ **Edit the new document now̲** . . . . `Alt`+`W`

8. To change the ScreenTip that appears when the mouse pointer rests on the hyperlink:

   a. Click **ScreenTip** button . . . . `Alt`+`P`

   b. Enter the description you want to display.

   c. Click **OK** . . . . `Enter`

9. Click **OK** . . . . `Enter`

Insert a Hyperlink to an E-mail Address

✓ *This type of link will open an e-mail form with the recipient's e-mail address included.*

1. Select the text or graphic you want to use for the link.

2. Click **Insert** tab . . . . `Alt`, `N`

   Links Group

3. Click **Hyperlink** button 🌐 . . . . `I`

4. Click **E-m̲ail Address** in the Link to bar. . . . . `Alt`+`M`

5. Enter the address for e-mail messages in the **E-mail address** text box . . . . `Alt`+`E`

   OR

   Select an address from the **Re̲cently used e-mail addresses** list . . . . `Alt`+`C`, `↑`/`↓`

6. Type a description for the messages in the **Su̲bject** box . . . . `Alt`+`U`

7. To change the ScreenTip that appears when the mouse pointer rests on the hyperlink:

   a. Click **ScreenTip** button . . . . `Alt`+`P`

   b. Enter the description you want to display.

   c. Click **OK** . . . . `Enter`

8. Click **OK** . . . . `Enter`

Activate a Hyperlink

■ Click the hyperlink to display the related file.

Edit Data of Cell Containing Hyperlink

1. Use arrow keys to select the cell.

   OR

   Press **Ctrl** and click cell.

2. Edit as usual.

3. Press **Enter** . . . . `Enter`

Edit a Hyperlink

1. Move cursor to cell containing the hyperlink you want to edit.

2. Click **Insert** tab . . . . `Alt`, `N`

   Links Group

3. Click **Hyperlink** button 🌐 . . . . `I`

4. Make your changes.

5. Click **OK** . . . . `Enter`

Remove a Hyperlink

1. Move cursor to cell containing the hyperlink you want to remove.

2. Click **Insert** tab . . . . `Alt`, `N`

   Links Group

3. Click **Hyperlink** button 🌐 . . . `I`

4. Click **Remove Link** . . . . . `Alt`+`R`

EXERCISE DIRECTIONS

1. Start Excel, if necessary.

2. Open 🔘 **04Patients**.

3. Save the workbook as **04Patients_xx**.

4. Create a link to Akemi's medical history:

   a. With cell A6 selected, click the Hyperlink button on the Insert tab.

   b. Click the Existing File or Web Page button on the Link to bar.

   c. Select the Datafiles folder from the Look in list.

   ✓ *If you've copied the files out of the Datafiles folder, browse to the proper location.*

   d. Select the file 🔘 **04AkemiHistory** from the list.

   e. Create a ScreenTip that reads **Akemi's medical history**.

   f. Click OK to create the hyperlink.

5. Create a hyperlink to information about Akemi's owner:

   a. Click cell E6.

   b. Click the Hyperlink button.

   c. Click the Existing file or Web Page button on the Link to bar.

d. Change to the Data folder and select the file 🔘 **04Owners** from the list.

e. Create a ScreenTip that says **View owner information**.

f. Click the Bookmark button.

g. Select the range name woo_daniel.

h. Click OK.

i. Click OK again to create the hyperlink.

6. Test both links by clicking them one by one. See Illustration A. (The linked workbook has been arranged on-screen with **04Patients_xx**, so you can see how they are linked—when you click a link, only the linked workbook appears on the screen, unless you too arrange the view so you can see both.)

7. Close both workbooks (**04AkemiHistory** and **04Owners**) after testing the links.

8. Widen columns in **04Patients_xx** as needed.

9. Spell check the worksheet.

10. Print the worksheet.

11. Close the workbook, saving all changes.

Illustration A

ON YOUR OWN

1. Start Excel, if necessary.
2. Open 04Toys.
3. Save the workbook as OXL04_*xx*.
4. Create a similar workbook listing January sales figures, then close OXL04_*xx*, saving all changes.
5. Save this new workbook as OXL04A_*xx*.

   a. To make this new workbook look like the original, apply the Concourse theme.

   b. Apply the Metro color set.

6. In OXL04A_*xx*, create a hyperlink to the December workbook, OXL04.
7. Create a graphical hyperlink to the company's Web site, www.sillytoy.com.
8. Format the links as you like, and then test each one.
9. Widen columns as needed.
10. Spell check the worksheet.
11. Print the worksheet.
12. Close the workbook, saving all changes.

Skills Covered

- Hide Data Temporarily
- Hide Worksheet Gridlines
- Hide Row and Column Headings
- Custom Views

Software Skills   If you have data that's considered confidential or is needed strictly as supporting information, you can hide it from view. This helps you keep the displayed information to just the relevant data, and prevents you from accidentally printing private data.

Application Skills   As the bookkeeper for Intellidata Database Services, your job is to produce three versions of one Web traffic statistics report, each of which is distributed to a different office.

TERMS

Gridlines   A light gray outline that surrounds each cell on the screen. Gridlines don't normally print; they're there to help you enter your data into the cells of the worksheet.

Headings   Markers that appear at the top of each column in Excel (such as A, B, and IX) and to the left of each row (such as 1, 2, and 1145).

Hide   To prevent Excel from displaying or printing certain data. You can hide the contents of individual cells, whole rows or columns, and even worksheets or workbooks.

Unhide   To redisplay hidden data, worksheets, or workbooks.

View   A saved arrangement of the Excel display and print settings that you can restore at any time.

NOTES

Hide Data Temporarily

- To prevent data from displaying or printing in a workbook, you can **hide** the data.

- You can hide the contents of individual cells, whole rows or columns, and even whole worksheets or workbooks.

  ✓ Hiding data is useful for keeping important supporting or confidential information out of sight, but it won't prevent those who know Excel from exposing that data if they can get access to the workbook. If you need to keep data away from prying eyes, password-protect the workbook as described in Exercise 37.

- You can hide multiple cells, rows, columns, and worksheets.

- When a row or column is hidden, the row number or column letter is missing from the worksheet frame. Hiding row 12, for example, leaves the row headings showing 11, 13, 14, and so on.

- Hiding a worksheet makes its tab disappear. If worksheets use a sequential numbering or naming scheme (such as Sheet1, Sheet2, Sheet3), the fact that a worksheet is hidden may be obvious.

- If you hide the contents of a cell, the cell appears to contain nothing, but the cell itself doesn't disappear from the worksheet.

- Even if a cell's contents are hidden, you can still display the contents in the Formula bar by selecting the cell.

  ✓ To prevent the data from displaying in the Formula bar, you can protect the worksheet, as described in Exercise 37.

■ You can also hide all the zeros in a worksheet, displaying blank cells instead.

■ If you hide a workbook, its contents aren't displayed even when the workbook is open. This feature is useful for storing macros that you want to have available but not necessarily in view. (See Lesson 12 for more on Excel macros.)

■ If you copy or move hidden data, it remains hidden.

■ Hidden data doesn't print.

■ Because the data in hidden columns or rows doesn't print, you can use this feature to print noncontiguous columns or rows as if they were contiguous.

■ To edit, format, or redisplay the contents of hidden rows, columns, or worksheets, **unhide** the rows, columns, or worksheet.

Hide Worksheet Gridlines

■ When presenting Excel data on-screen to a client, you might prefer to present it cleanly, without various on-screen elements such as gridlines.

■ To turn off gridlines on-screen, you select that option from the View tab.

■ As you might already know, whether or not cell **gridlines** appear on the screen, they don't print unless you select the Gridlines - Print check box in the Sheet Options group of the Page Layout tab on the Ribbon.

Select the Print option if you want to print gridlines with the worksheet data

Hide Row and Column Headings

■ When presenting Excel data on-screen to a client, your boss, or a group of fellow employees, you might prefer to present it without the distraction of various Excel screen elements.

  ● In the previous section, you learned that you can turn off the gridlines so they do not display on-screen.

  ● In Full Screen view all Excel elements such as the Ribbon and the Formula bar are removed from the screen so more of the worksheet can be displayed.

■ Even in Full Screen view, the column **headings** that display the letter assigned to each column (such as A, B, and IX) still display.

■ The row headings (1, 2, 3, and so on) display as well.

■ You can turn off row and column headings whenever you want, although you might not want to turn them off if you're still entering data, since the headings make it easier for you to perform certain tasks.

■ You can turn off the headings in any view; you don't have to be in Full Screen view to turn them off.

Hide row and column headings and gridlines when desired

Custom Views

■ You can set up the display of a workbook as you like, then save that setup in a custom **view** so you can switch back to it when needed.

■ For example, you could save one view of the worksheet with all cells displayed, another view with certain rows or columns hidden, and so on.

■ Before creating a view, set up the screen exactly as you want it to appear in the view.

■ Settings in a view include any selected cells, current column widths, how the screen is split or frozen, window arrangements and sizes, filter settings, print setup, and defined print area (if any).

■ When creating a view, you can specify whether to save the settings for hidden columns and rows (hidden worksheets are always hidden in the view), and/or the print settings.

■ Because custom views can control print settings, you can create the same arrangement of printed data each time you print from that view (for example, printing just the tax deductible expenses from a monthly expense workbook).

■ The current view is saved with the workbook.

PROCEDURES

Hide Cell Contents

1. Select cell(s) containing data to hide.
2. Click **Home** tab . . . . `Alt`, `H`

3. Click **Format Cells Number** dialog box launcher ⬚ . . . . `F`, `M`
4. Click the **Category** list box . . . . `Alt`+`C`
5. Select **Custom** . . . . `↑`/`↓`
6. Click the **Type:** text box . . . . `Alt`+`T`
7. Replace the contents with ;;; (three semicolons). . . . . `;`, `;`, `;`
8. Click **OK**. . . . . `Enter`

Redisplay Hidden Cell

> ✓ To redisplay the data in a hidden range, simply apply a different number format.

1. Select cell(s) to format.
2. Click **Home** tab . . . . `Alt`, `H`

3. Click arrow on **Number Format** button `General ▾` . . . `N`
4. Select a number format . . . . `↑`/`↓`, `Enter`

Hide All Zeros for Current Worksheet

1. Click **Office Button** ⬚ . . . `Alt`+`F`
2. Click **Excel Options** . . . . `I`
3. Click **Advanced** . . . . `↑`/`↓`

   > ✓ Under Display options for this worksheet section:

4. Turn off **Show a zero in cells that have zero value** . . . . `Alt`+`Z`
5. Click **OK**. . . . . `Enter`

Hide Columns

1. Select the columns to hide.
2. Click **Home** tab . . . . `Alt`, `H`

3. Click **Format** button ⬚ . . . . . . `O`
4. Click **Hide & Unhide** . . . . `U`
5. Click **Hide Columns**. . . . . `C`

   > ✓ A thick border appears in the worksheet frame where a column is hidden.

Unhide Hidden Column(s)

1. Select the columns bordering the columns you want to unhide.
2. Click **Home** tab . . . . `Alt`, `H`

3. Click **Format** button ⬚ . . . . . . `O`
4. Click **Hide & Unhide** . . . . `U`
5. Click **Unhide Columns**. . . . . . . `L`

Hide Columns by Dragging

1. Select columns to hide.
2. Point to the right border of column heading.

   > ✓ The pointer becomes ✛.

3. Drag ✛ left to column's left border.

   > ✓ A thick border appears in the worksheet frame where a column is hidden.

Unhide a Hidden Column by Dragging

1. Point just right of column heading border.

   > ✓ The pointer becomes ✛.

2. Drag ✛ right.

Hide Rows

1. Select the columns to hide.
2. Click **Home** tab . . . . `Alt`, `H`

3. Click **Format** button ⬚ . . . . . . `O`
4. Click **Hide & Unhide** . . . . `U`
5. Click **Hide Rows** . . . . `R`

   > ✓ A thick border appears in the worksheet frame where a row is hidden.

Unhide Hidden Row(s)

1. Select the rows bordering the rows you want to unhide.
2. Click **Home** tab . . . . `Alt`, `H`

3. Click **Format** button ⬚ . . . . . . `O`
4. Click **Hide & Unhide** . . . . `U`
5. Click **Unhide Rows** . . . . `O`

Hide Rows by Dragging

1. Select rows to hide.
2. Point to the bottom border of row heading.

   > ✓ The pointer becomes ✚.

3. Drag ✚ up to row's top border.

   > ✓ A thick border appears in the worksheet frame where a row is hidden.

Unhide a Hidden Row by Dragging

1. Point just below row heading border.

   > ✓ The pointer becomes ✚.

2. Drag ✚ down.

Hide a Workbook Window

1. Open workbook you wish to hide.
2. Click **View** tab . . . . Alt , W

   Window Group

3. Click **Hide** button ▭ . . . . . . H
4. If asked, click **Yes** to save the workbook when you close Excel.

Unhide a Workbook

1. Open workbook(s) you wish to unhide.
2. Click **View** tab . . . . Alt , W

   Window Group

3. Click **Unhide** button ▭ . . . . . U
4. Select workbook(s) you want to unhide . . . . ↑ /↓
5. Click **OK** . . . . Enter

Hide Worksheet

1. Select the sheet(s) you wish to hide.
2. Click **Home** tab . . . . Alt , H

   Cells Group

3. Click **Format** button ▥ . . . . . O
4. Click **Hide & Unhide** . . . . U
5. Click **Hide Sheet** . . . . S

Unhide Worksheet

1. Select the sheets to unhide.
2. Click **Home** tab . . . . Alt , H

   Cells Group

3. Click **Format** button ▥ . . . . . O
4. Click **Hide & Unhide** . . . . U
5. Click **Unhide Sheet** . . . . H
6. Select sheet(s) you want to unhide . . . . ↑ /↓
7. Click **OK** . . . . Enter

Hide Worksheet Gridlines in Current Worksheet

1. Click **View** tab . . . . Alt , W

   Show/Hide Group

2. Click **Gridlines** check box . . . . V , G

Hide Row and Column Headings for Current Worksheet

1. Click **View** tab . . . . Alt , W

   Show/Hide Group

2. Click **Headings** check box . . . . V , H

Create Custom View

1. Set up the screen the way you want it to appear in the custom view. If desired, set up the print settings as well.
2. Click **View** tab . . . . Alt , W

   Workbook Views Group

3. Click **Custom Views** button ▣ C
4. Click **Add** . . . . Alt + A
5. Type a name for the view.
6. Change options, if desired.
7. Click **OK** . . . . Enter

Display a Custom View

1. Set up the screen the way you want it to appear in the custom view. If desired, set up the print settings as well.
2. Click **View** tab . . . . Alt , W

   Workbook Views Group

3. Click **Custom Views** button ▣ C
4. In the **Views** list, select view to display . . . . Alt + W , ↑ /↓
5. Click **Show** . . . . Alt + S

   ✓ *When you save the workbook, the view that's currently in effect is also saved. The next time you open the workbook, that view will still be in effect.*

Delete a View

1. Set up the screen the way you want it to appear in the custom view. If desired, set up the print settings as well.
2. Click **View** tab . . . . Alt , W

   Workbook Views Group

3. Click **Custom Views** button ▣ C
4. In the **Views** list, click the view you want to delete . . . . Alt + W , ↑ /↓
5. Click **Delete** . . . . Alt + D
6. Click **Yes** to confirm the deletion . . . . Enter
7. Click **Close** . . . . Alt + C

EXERCISE DIRECTIONS

1. Start Excel, if necessary.
2. Open ◉ **05UsageStats**.
3. Save the workbook as **05UsageStats_xx**.
4. Hide gridlines on the *Usage statistics 0704* worksheet.
5. Create a custom view of the *Usage statistics 0704* worksheet that includes only the rows for the North office and the totals:
   a. Select just the rows that are labeled in column B with South and Central.

   ✓ *Hold down Ctrl while clicking all ten row headers.*

   b. Hide the selected rows.
   c. Hide row and columns headings.
   d. Create a custom view called **North**.
   e. Check the boxes for Print settings and Hidden rows, columns, and filter settings.
   f. Click OK.
6. Unhide the hidden rows:
   a. Select the data rows 6 through 26. (Redisplay the row and column headings if needed.)
   b. Unhide the selected rows.

7. Repeat this process to create two new custom views for the South and Central offices.

   ✓ *If you redisplayed the row and column headings so you could select the rows to hide, be sure to rehide the headings prior to creating each view.*

   ✓ *Perhaps you've noticed the one problem with creating views this way: Since the division labels appear next to "North" for each group, they disappear in the views for the South and Central offices. This is the kind of problem we'll address in Exercise 22.*

8. Spell check the worksheet.
9. With all rows unhidden, test switching to a custom view by showing the North view. See Illustration A.
10. Adjust columns widths if needed.
11. Print the worksheet.
12. Repeat steps 9–11 to print the data for the other two offices.
13. Unhide all rows and redisplay the row and column headings again.
14. Close the workbook, saving all changes.

Illustration A

S05UsageStats - Microsoft Excel									
Intellidata Hosting · Management · Warehousing		**Usage statistics** Giant Frog Supermarkets - District # 0855 Period of 4 July - 31 July 2008							
		4 Jul				11 Jul			18 J
Department	Region	Avg. Bandwidth *Kb/sec*	Data In *Mb*	Data Out *Mb*	Transactions	Avg. Bandwidth *Kb/sec*	Data In *Mb*	Data Out *Mb*	Transactions	Avg. Ban *Kb/s*
Merchandising	North	56.5	518	3106	10312	53.4	494	3066	9981
	Total	**156.6**	**1419**	**8723**	**27928**	**153.1**	**1345**	**8456**	**27226**
Purchasing	North	110.4	1304	6103	35406	108.5	1206	6055	32854
	Total	**259.3**	**3332**	**14815**	**90001**	**253.2**	**3030**	**13848**	**80693**
Distribution	North	38.6	1551	2064	9102	36.1	1642	1794	9012
	Total	**67.4**	**3101**	**4650**	**21683**	**59.3**	**3087**	**4174**	**20911**
Accounting	North	114.5	2601	12359	64135	106.4	2564	11643	62164
	Total	**413.8**	**7454**	**43487**	**192300**	**400.5**	**7382**	**41605**	**188363**
Point of sale	North	213.9	3164	26492	103454	212.3	3121	25945	101354
	Total	**507.8**	**7787**	**61689**	**247590**	**473.4**	**7456**	**57877**	**238592**

ON YOUR OWN

1. Start Excel, if necessary.

2. Open the file ⊚ **05PetesEEList**.

3. Save the file as **OXL05_xx**.

4. Hide gridlines on the current worksheet.

5. Save the current view with the name **Employee List**.

6. Hide information not directly related to the raise, such as Social Security number, address, phone number, and the like.

7. Hide row and column headings.

8. Save this view with the name **EE Rates**, and print it.

9. Redisplay the row and column headings temporarily so you can work.

10. Create another view that includes only the employee name, address, and phone number. Be sure to rehide the row and column headings and then save the view with the name **Emergency List**.

11. Spell check the worksheet.

12. Adjust columns widths if needed.

13. Print this new view.

14. Change back to the Employee List view. Redisplay gridlines.

15. Save the workbook and exit Excel.

Skills Covered

- **More Alignment Options**
- **Format Dates and Times**
- **Create Custom Number Formats**
- **Adjust Row Height**
- **Delete (Clear) a Cell's Formats**

Software Skills Sometimes, in order to accommodate the various kinds of data in a worksheet, you have to apply various formatting techniques that you might not ordinarily use, such as adjusting the row heights, merging cells, and slanting column labels. Other refinements you may need to make include applying the proper format to data—even if that means removing existing formats and creating your own.

Application Skills As the owner of Giancarlo Franchetti's Go-Cart Speedrome, you're interested in using Excel to help you manage your growing business. You've created a worksheet for tracking daily admissions and receipts, and you want to use your knowledge of Excel formatting to make the worksheet more attractive.

TERMS

No new terms in this exercise.

NOTES

More Alignment Options

- As you already know, Excel offers many standard alignment options for formatting data, such as centering and aligning to the right.

- You can also change a cell's alignment vertically—such as aligning data at the top of a cell.

- There are other alignment options you may not know about that you might want to apply occasionally. For example, you can:
  - Change the orientation (rotation) of data.
  - Wrap paragraphs of text between a cell's borders.
  - Justify data (add spaces between characters in a paragraph in order to place the left and right edges of each line in a paragraph except for the last one against the borders of the cell).
  - Vertically justify data by adding blank lines between lines of text so the text is placed against the top and bottom edges of the cell.
  - Distribute data (justify all the lines in a paragraph, including the last one, against either the borders of the cell or the indented left and right margins).
  - Fill data (repeat data to fill a cell completely).
  - You can shrink the size of data to fit the cell even if that cell is resized.

Alignment tab, Format Cells dialog box

Format Dates and Times

- You can change the way a date or time is displayed by formatting a cell or cells before or after entering the date/time.

- There are several standard date and time formats you can apply, the most common ones located on the Number Format list on the Home tab of the Ribbon.

- Other standard date and time formats are applied through the Format Cells dialog box.

- You can also customize the way you want dates displayed, by creating a custom number format.

Create Custom Number Formats

- When a number format doesn't fit your needs, you can create a custom number format.

  - Typically, you use a custom number format to preformat a column or row, prior to data entry. The custom format speeds the data entry process.

  - For example, if you want to type account numbers into a column, and the format is similar to AB-2342-CO, you can create a format that will display the dashes in the correct spots, without you actually typing them. And if all the account numbers end in -CO, you can build that into the custom format as well, and only enter AB2342 into the cell to display AB-2342-CO.

- You create a custom number format by typing a series of special codes.

  ✓ *To speed the process, select an existing format and customize it.*

- You can specify format codes for positive numbers, negative numbers, zeros, and text.

  - If you wish to specify all four formats, you must type the codes in the order listed above.

  - If you specify only two formats, you must type a code for positive numbers and zeros first, and a code for negative numbers second.

  - If you specify only one format, all numbers in the row or column will use that format.

  - To separate the formats, use a semicolon, as in the following custom number format: $#,##0.00;[red]($#,##0.00);"ZERO";[blue].

  - This format displays positive numbers as $0,000.00, negative numbers in red and parentheses, a zero as the word ZERO, and text in blue.

- Standard colors you can use by typing the name in brackets include: red, black, blue, white, green, yellow, cyan, and magenta.

- The following table shows examples of codes you can use in creating a format:

#	Digit placeholder
0	Zero placeholder
?	Digit placeholder
@	Text placeholder
.	Decimal point (period)
%	Percent
,	Thousands separator (comma)
$	Dollar sign
-	Negative sign
+	Plus sign
( )	Parentheses
:	Colon
_	Underscore (skips one character width)
[*color*]	Type the name of one of the eight colors previously mentioned.

- Examples of formats you can create:

To display:	Use this code:
5.56 as 5.5600	#.0000
5641 as $5,641	$#,##0
5641 as $5,641 and -5641 as ($5,641) in red	$#,##0;[red]($#,##0)
5641 as $5,641.00 and -5641 as ($5,641.00) in red	$#,###0.00;[red]($#,##0.00)

- Custom number formats are saved with the worksheet.

  - To use a number format you've created in another worksheet, copy the format from a cell in the worksheet to a cell in the other worksheet manually.

Adjust Row Height

- You usually don't need to adjust row height, since Excel automatically adjusts row height to fit the font size of your data.

  - If you increase the size of data, then the row height is automatically made larger.

  - If you decrease the size of data, the row height is automatically made smaller.

- You can adjust the row height manually if you like.
  - For example, you might increase the row height of a title to make it stand out from the regular data.
  - After you specify a row height, Excel won't adjust the height of that row automatically.
- You can adjust a single row, or adjust multiple rows at one time.

Delete (Clear) a Cell's Formats

- Earlier, you learned how to delete the contents of a cell.
- Sometimes, you want to keep the data, but remove the formatting you've applied.
- Excel allows you to clear just the format of a cell, without clearing its contents.

PROCEDURES

Align Data Horizontally Using Format Dialog Box

1. Select cell(s) to format.
2. Click **Home** tab . . . . [Alt], [H]

   Alignment Group

3. Click **Format Cells: Alignment** dialog box launcher [⬚] . . [F], [A]
4. Click **Horizontal** . . . . [Alt]+[H]
5. Select an option from the list . . . . [↑]/[↓], [Enter]
   - **General**
   - **Left (indent)**
   - **Center**
   - **Right (indent)**
   - **Fill**
   - **Justify**
   - **Center Across Selection**
   - **Distributed (Indent)**
6. Add **Indent** if applicable . . . . . [Alt]+[I], [↑]/[↓]
7. Select additional options:
   - **Wrap text** . . . . [Alt]+[W]
   - **Shrink to fit** . . . . [Alt]+[K]
   - **Merge cells** . . . . [Alt]+[M]
8. Click **OK** . . . . [Enter]

Align Data Vertically Using Format Dialog Box

1. Select cell(s) to format.
2. Click **Home** tab . . . . [Alt], [H]

   Alignment Group

3. Click **Format Cells: Alignment** dialog box launcher [⬚] . . [F], [A]

4. Click **Vertical** . . . . [Alt]+[V]
5. Select an option from the list . . . . [↑]/[↓], [Enter]
   - **Top**
   - **Center**
   - **Bottom**
   - **Justify**
   - **Distributed**
6. Click **OK** . . . . [Enter]

Change Orientation of Data

1. Select cell(s) to format.
2. Click **Home** tab . . . . [Alt], [H]

   Alignment Group

3. Click **Orientation** button [⬚] . . . . [F], [Q]
4. Select option:
   - **Angle Counterclockwise** . . [O]
   - **Angle Clockwise** . . . . [L]
   - **Vertical Text** . . . . [V]
   - **Rotate Text Up** . . . . [U]
   - **Rotate Text Down** . . . . . . [D]

Change Orientation of Data Precisely

1. Select cell(s) to format.
2. Click **Home** tab . . . . [Alt], [H]

   Alignment Group

3. Click **Format Cells: Alignment** dialog box launcher [⬚] . . [F], [A]
4. Click **Degrees** . . [Alt]+[D], [↑]/[↓]

5. Click in Orientation pane to set angle desired.

   ✓ *Click the left Orientation pane to display text vertically in a cell, reading from top to bottom. Click on the semicircle in the right Orientation pane to select an angle to display text.*

6. Click **OK** . . . . [Enter]

Format Date or Time with Standard Format

1. Select cells to format.
2. Click **Home** tab . . . . [Alt], [H]

   Number Group

3. Click arrow on **Number Format** list

   General ▼ . . . . [N]

4. Select a date or time format from those listed list . . . . [↑]/[↓], [Enter]

Format Dates

1. Select cells to format.
2. Click **Home** tab . . . . [Alt], [H]

   Number Group

3. Click **Format Cells: Number** dialog box launcher [⬚] . . . . [F], [M]
4. Click **Date** in **Category** list . . . . [Alt]+[C], [↑]/[↓]
5. Select a date **Type** . . . . [Alt]+[T], [↑]/[↓]
6. Click **OK** . . . . [Enter]

Customize Date Format

1. Select cell(s) containing date(s) to format.
2. Click **Home** tab . . . . Alt , H

   Number Group

3. Click **Format Cells Number** dialog box launcher 🔲 . . . . F , M
4. In the **Category** list box, click **Custom** . . . . Alt + C , ↑ / ↓
5. In the **Type** box, type or select the desired format . . . . Alt + T , ↑ / ↓

   ✓ Example: yyyy-mm-dd or yyyy/mmm dd.

6. Click **OK**. . . . . Enter

Format Times

1. Select cells to format.
2. Click **Home** tab . . . . Alt , H

   Number Group

3. Click **Format Cells: Number** dialog box launcher 🔲 . . . . F , M
4. Click **Time** in **Category** list . . . . Alt + C , ↑ / ↓
5. Select a time **Type** . . . . Alt + T , ↑ / ↓
6. Click **OK**. . . . . Enter

Create Custom Number Format

1. Select cell(s) to format.
2. Click **Home** tab . . . . Alt , H

   Number Group

3. Click **Format Cells Number** dialog box launcher 🔲 . . . . F , M
4. In the **Category** list box, click **Custom** . . . . Alt + C , ↑ / ↓
5. Type the format you want to use in the **Type** box. . . . . Alt + T

   ✓ It's usually easier to select a format from those listed in the **Type** box and then customize it.

6. Click **OK**. . . . . Enter

Adjust Row Height

✓ To adjust multiple rows at once, drag over the headings for the rows you wish to change.

1. Select the row(s) to size.
2. Click **Home** tab . . . . Alt , H

   Cells Group

3. Click **Format** button 📋 . . . . . . O
4. Click **Row Height**. . . . . H
5. Type a number (0-409) in the **Row height** text box . . . . . R

   ✓ This number represents the height of the row in points.

6. Click **OK**. . . . . Enter

Change Row Height Using the Mouse

✓ To adjust multiple rows at once, drag over the headings for the rows you wish to change.

1. Point to the bottom border of the row heading.

   ✓ The pointer becomes ╋.

2. Drag up or down.

   ✓ Excel displays the row height in a ScreenTip while row is being sized.

Clear a Cell's Formatting

1. Select the cell's to clear.
2. Click **Home** tab . . . . Alt , H

   Editing Group

3. Click **Clear** button 🧹 . . . . . . E
4. Click **Clear Formats** . . . . F

Set the Row Height to Fit the Tallest Entry

✓ To adjust multiple rows at once, drag over the headings for the rows you wish to change.

■ Double-click the bottom border of the row heading(s).

   ✓ For example, if row 3 was accidentally adjusted so that it was a lot taller than the tallest data, you could double-click the bottom border of the row 3 header, and the row would adjust to the exact height of the tallest data item in that row.

EXERCISE DIRECTIONS

1. Start Excel, if necessary.
2. Open 💿 **06DailyAdmissions**.
3. Save the workbook as **06DailyAdmissions_xx**.
4. Format the column labels:
   a. Select the range C8:H8.
   b. Apply the Angle Counterclockwise orientation.
5. Format the times of each session:
   a. Select the range C9:D20.
   b. Using the Format Cells dialog box, apply the Time format: 1:30 PM.
6. Apply the Rotate Text Up orientation to cell A9:
   a. Select the range A9:A20.
   b. Merge the cells.
   c. Apply center alignment both horizontally and verti-cally.
   d. Apply the Rotate Text Up alignment.
   e. Change the font size of the selected range to 24 point.
   f. Apply Turquoise, Accent 4, Lighter 60% fill.
7. Apply a custom number format to the Session Number column.
   a. Select the range, E9:E20.
   b. Display the Format Cells dialog box, click the Number tab, and select Custom format.
   c. Replace the contents of the Type box with this:
      00-00-"Session "0

d. Enter the session numbers, without the dashes, and let the format do the work:

E9	**10051**
E10	**10052**
E11	**10081**
E12	**10091**
E13	**10101**
E14	**10102**
E15	**10103**
E16	**10111**
E17	**10112**
E18	**10113**
E19	**10121**
E20	**10122**

8. Remove the formatting in the title area and start over (see Illustration A):
   a. Select the range A1:J7.
   b. Clear the formats in the selected range.
   c. Apply 40% Accent4 cell style to the selection.
   d. Apply bold formatting to the selection.
   e. Change the point size of cell C3 to 24 point.
   f. Adjust the height of row 3 to 65.
9. Spell check the worksheet.
10. Adjust columns widths if needed.
11. Print the worksheet.
12. Close the workbook, saving all changes.

Illustration A

ON YOUR OWN

1. Start Excel, if necessary.
2. Open the file ⊙ **06SalesComp**.
3. Save the file as **OXL06_xx**.
4. The formatting of the worksheet is a mess, so you'll start by removing all formats.

   a. Choose a theme, then apply cell styles you like.

   b. Apply an appropriate number format for the data, selecting or creating a custom format for the Increase/Decrease in Sales that emphasizes negative sales so they are easy to spot.

   c. Merge cells B4:B9, then display the text using Vertical orientation. Change the font size to 9 point.

   d. Adjust the height of row 4 so the entire *Division* label displays.

   e. Wrap the text in cell F4 and then make that column narrower.

5. Format the date in cell C3 using whatever date format you prefer.
6. Spell check the worksheet.
7. Adjust columns widths if needed.
8. Print this new view.
9. Save the workbook and exit Excel.

Skills Covered

- ■ **Change Cell Borders**
- ■ **Fill Cells with Pattern**
- ■ **Modify and Save a Theme**

- ■ **Conditional Formatting**
- ■ **Add a Watermark**
- ■ **Format Worksheet Background**

Software Skills Each worksheet tells a story—of lost profits, increased costs, or skyrocketing sales. To help your worksheet tell its "story," you can add shading, borders, or conditional formatting to highlight or separate important information in a complex worksheet. To make a worksheet look more professional, you might want to customize the standard themes Excel provides by choosing company-style fonts and colors, adding a watermark, or applying a custom worksheet background.

Application Skills The worksheet you designed to track accessories sold each day at your PhotoTown store has proven very helpful, and the corporate headquarters may adopt it throughout the company. Before you send it off for their review, you want to add some professional formatting touches.

TERMS

Border An outline applied to the sides of a cell.

Conditional formatting Formatting that Excel automatically applies to cells when specified conditions are met.

Pattern A cell can be filled with a plain color and/or a pattern. A pattern is laid on top of the cell in your choice of layouts, such as a vertical stripe or a thin crosshatch. You can also select a pattern of dots, which has the effect of muting the fill color so that it's less intense.

Reverse type Normal type is typically black on a light background; reverse type is white text on a black or dark background.

Watermark A faint image embedded in paper that identifies its maker. This faint image appears behind text when it's printed on the page.

NOTES

Change Cell Borders

- ■ To outline or separate data, you can include a variety of line styles that **border** the edge (top, bottom, left, or right) of a cell or range of cells.

- ■ Borders can be set with the Border tab in the Format Cells dialog box or by using the Borders button on the Formatting toolbar.

  ✓ *You can vary the border line style and color as well.*

- ■ If you prefer, you can "draw" borders along cell edges rather than selecting a pattern from a list or dialog box.

Fill Cells with Pattern

- ■ Cells in a worksheet can be filled with a background color and/or **pattern**.

  ✓ *Even if you're using a black-and-white printer, you can still achieve an interesting look by applying a fill color to the cells. Depending on the color you choose, the cell may appear light, medium, or dark gray when printed.*

- ■ To apply a solid fill color, select one from the Fill Color palette, located on the Home tab.

- If you want to apply a color using a pattern (such as stripes), use the Fill tab of the Format Cells dialog box.

- You can also combine solid colors to create a new color using the Fill tab of the Format Cells dialog box.

    - To do this, you select a main color from the Background Color palette, choose a % Gray pattern such as 25% Gray in the Pattern Style list, and then choose a pattern color in the Pattern Color list.

    - For example, if you choose an aqua from the Background Color palette and yellow from the Pattern Color palette, then open the Pattern Style list and select the 25% Gray pattern style, you would end up with a light green with just a hint of yellow—the result of blending 75% aqua with 25% yellow.

    - If you switched to a 75% Gray pattern, the result color would look more yellow, since the ratio would then be 25% aqua and 75% yellow.

Blend colors together on the Fill Tab of the Format Cells dialog box

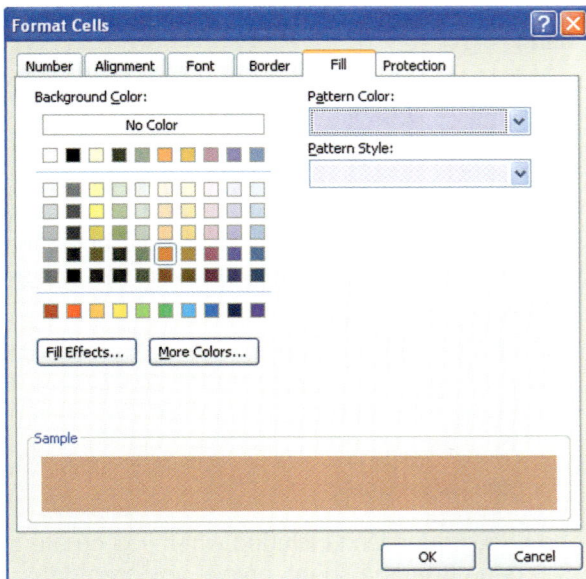

- When changing the fill color of a cell, you may also wish to change the font color of the data inside.

- It's possible to display and print data in white against a black (or dark colored) background. This is sometimes called **reverse type**.

Modify and Save a Theme

- A theme is a collection of fonts, colors, and effects, saved as a collection that can be applied in a single click.

- Effects include line and fill effects such as special borders and shadows.

- You can select a different set of existing fonts, colors, and effects, save these new choices together in a new theme.

- You can also create your own custom set of colors or fonts for use with a theme.

- Themes you create are automatically added to the Themes list on the Page Layout tab.

Conditional Formatting

- To call attention to particular values, apply **conditional formatting**.

- Excel provides a set of conditional formats that allows you to easily identify particular values, such as:

    - Numbers greater or less than a certain value

    - The top ten or bottom ten values in a selected range

    - Text that contains a particular set of characters

    - A certain date

- Using conditional formatting, you can display data bars, color sliders, or special icons throughout a selected range, based on their values.

    - Data bars vary in size, visually representing the size of each value within the selected range of values. For example, a comparatively small value in the range would display a short data bar.

    - Color sliders display various colors that represent each cell's value. For example, large numbers might display a red color bar, while small values appear with a blue color bar.

    - Special icon sets include one icon for each type of value—for example, greater than or equal to 67, less than 67 but greater than or equal to 33, or less than 33.

- With certain kinds of conditional formats (Highlight Cell Rules and Top/Bottom Rules), a dialog box appears where you can select the type of formatting you want applied when cells meet the associated condition.

The Greater Than, Highlight Cell Rules dialog box

- For example, you could highlight expenses over $15,000 by adding a Blue fill, a Red text color, or both.
  - The formatting you choose is applied only to cells that meet the conditions you select.
  - Any formatting that's applied is added to existing formatting in the cell.
- You can copy conditional formatting with the Format Painter button, just as you would any other formatting.
- A cell can have multiple conditional formats applied.
  - Typically, based on the value in the cell, the formatting for any rule that qualifies is then applied.
  - Rules are evaluated in the order in which they are applied to a cell. You can control the order in which specific rules are evaluated and applied by using the Conditional Formatting Rules Manager.

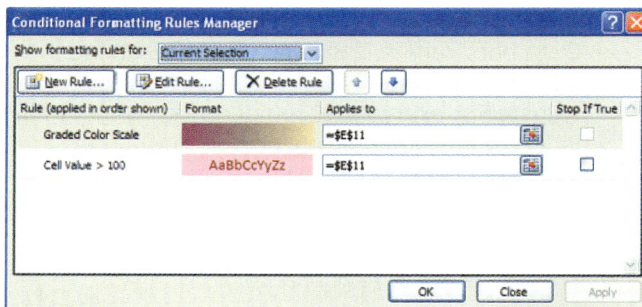

Conditional Formatting Rules Manager

- By changing the order in which rules are evaluated, you can stop the processing of rules when the first rule evaluates as true.

Add a Watermark

- You can recreate the look of a **watermark** by placing a graphic behind your Excel data.
  - You add the watermark graphic to either the header or footer of every page.
  - This graphic begins within either the header or footer area, and depending on its size, extends into the data area to act as a watermark.
  - After inserting the graphic, you can adjust its size so that it fills the page.
  - You can also adjust the inserted graphic's brightness and contrast in order to make the worksheet data (which appears on top of the watermark) easier to read.
- Watermarks appear only on the worksheet on which they were added, and not every worksheet within the workbook.

Format Worksheet Background

- You can add a graphic to the background of the worksheet, behind the data.
- Such a background is used for on-screen display purposes only, and does not print (unlike a watermark).
  - You might want to add a worksheet background graphic to enhance a worksheet you know will only be used in on-screen presentations.
  - Because you won't be able to adjust the brightness or contrast of your image after it's inserted, for the best effect, be sure to use a graphic that's very light in color, so that your data can still be read.

  ✓ *After inserting a graphic for use as a worksheet background, if you have trouble reading your data, you can apply a fill color to just the data cells so that the data can be read more easily.*

  ✓ *You can also hide gridlines to make the worksheet data more readable; see Exercise 5.*

- The background isn't included when you create a Web page from the sheet, unless you create the Web page from the whole workbook.

PROCEDURES

Change Borders Using Standard Formats

1. Select cell(s) to format.
2. Click **Home** tab . . . . [Alt], [H]

   [Font Group]

3. Select the border you want:
   - Click the **Borders** button [⊞▾] to apply the displayed border.

     OR

   a. Click the arrow on the **Borders** button [⊞▾] . . . . [B]
   b. Click desired border . . . . [↑]/[↓], [Enter]

Change Borders with the Format Cells Dialog Box

1. Select cell(s) to format.
2. Click **Home** tab . . . . [Alt], [H]

   [Font Group]

3. Click **Format Cells: Font** dialog box launcher [⌐] . . . . [F], [N]
4. Click **Border** tab. . . . . . . [Ctrl]+[⇤]
5. Select a **Style** . . . . [Alt]+[S], [↑]/[↓]
6. Select a **Color** . . . . . . [Alt]+[C], [↑]/[↓], [Enter]
7. Select a border setting:
   - **None** . . . . [Alt]+[N]
   - **Outline**. . . . . [Alt]+[O]
   - **Inside** . . . . [Alt]+[I]

   ✓ Inside borders are not available if only a single cell is selected.

   ✓ You can create a custom border by clicking one of the other preset designs, or by clicking inside the preview box at the point(s) where you would like to add a border line.

8. Click **OK**. . . . . [Enter]

Draw Borders

1. Select cell(s) to format.
2. Click **Home** tab . . . . [Alt], [H]

   [Font Group]

3. Click the arrow on the **Borders** button [⊞▾]. . . . . [B]
4. To draw borders around a range, click **Draw Border** . . . . [W]

   OR

   To draw borders around a range of cells, and gridlines within that range, click **Draw Border Grid** . . . . [G]
5. Set line style:
   a. Click **Home** tab . . . . . [Alt], [H]

   [Font Group]

   b. Click the arrow on the **Borders** button [⊞▾]. . . . . [B]
   c. Click **Line Style** . . . . [Y]
   d. Choose a line style. . . . . [↑]/[↓], [Enter]
6. Set line color:
   a. Click **Home** tab . . . . . [Alt], [H]

   [Font Group]

   b. Click the arrow on the **Borders** button [⊞▾] . . . . . [B]
   c. Click **Line Color**. . . . . [I]
   d. Choose a line color . . . . . [→]/[←]/[↑]/[↓], [Enter]
7. Drag over a range of cells to draw the border.

   ✓ You can click at the edge of a cell to draw a single border.

8. If needed, erase any undesired borders:
   a. Click **Home** tab . . . . . [Alt], [H]

   [Font Group]

   b. Click the arrow on the **Borders** button [⊞▾]. . . . . [B]
   c. Click **Erase Border**. . . . . . [E]
   d. Click the border to remove.

Remove All Borders from Cells

1. Select cell(s).
2. Click **Home** tab . . . . [Alt], [H]

   [Font Group]

3. Click the arrow on the **Borders** button [⊞▾]. . . . . [B]
4. Click **No Border**. . . . . [N]

   ✓ You can also select the range, then press Ctrl+Shift+- (hyphen).

Change Cell Fill Color

1. Select cell(s) to format.

   ✓ To apply the same fill color to all cells in a worksheet, click the Select All button, located in the upper left-hand corner of the worksheet.

2. Click **Home** tab . . . . [Alt], [H]

   [Font Group]

3. Select the fill color you want:
   - Click the **Fill Color** button [▨▾] to apply the displayed color

     OR

   a. Click the arrow on the **Fill Color** button [▨▾] . . . . [H]
   b. Click desired color . . . . . [→]/[←]/[↑]/[↓], [Enter]

Apply Fill Color and Pattern

1. Select cell(s) to format.
2. Click **Home** tab . . . . [Alt], [H]

   [Font Group]

3. Click **Format Cells: Font** dialog box launcher [⌐] . . . . [F], [N]
4. Click **Fill** tab . . . . [Ctrl]+[⇤]
5. Select **Background Color** . . . [Alt]+[C], [→]/[←]/[↑]/[↓]

   ✓ To select a color not included in the worksheet theme color set, click *More Colors*.

6. Select a pattern if desired:

   a. Select a **Pattern Color** . . . . `Alt`+`A`, `→`/`←`/`↑`/`↓`, `Enter`

   b. Select a **Pattern Style** . . . . `Alt`+`P`, `→`/`←`/`↑`/`↓`, `Enter`

7. Click **OK** . . . . `Enter`

Apply Gradient Fill

1. Select cell(s) to format.
2. Click **Home** tab . . . . `Alt`, `H`

   Font Group

3. Click **Format Cells: Font** dialog box launcher 🔲 . . . . `F`, `N`
4. Click **Fill** tab . . . . `Ctrl`+`⇥`
5. Click **Fill Effects** . . . . `Alt`+`I`
6. Select **Color 1** . . . . `Alt`+`!`, `→`/`←`/`↑`/`↓`, `Enter`
7. Select **Color 2** . . . . `Alt`+`@₂`, `→`/`←`/`↑`/`↓`, `Enter`
8. Select a shading style:

   - **Horizontal** . . . . `Alt`+`Z`
   - **Vertical** . . . . `Alt`+`V`
   - **Diagonal up** . . . . `Alt`+`U`
   - **Diagonal down** . . . . . `Alt`+`D`
   - **From corner** . . . . `Alt`+`F`
   - **From center** . . . . `Alt`+`M`

9. Select one of the **Variants** . . . . `Alt`+`A`, `→`/`←`/`↑`/`↓`
10. Click **OK** . . . . `Enter`
11. Click **OK** . . . . `Enter`

Modify an Existing Set of Theme Colors

1. Click **Page Layout** tab . . . `Alt`, `P`

   Themes Group

2. Click **Colors** button 🔳 . . `T`, `C`
3. Click **Create New Theme Colors** . . . . `C`
4. Click the arrow on the button for the color type you wish to choose:

   - **Text/Background – Dark 1** . . . . `Alt`+`T`
   - **Text/Background – Light 1** . . . . `Alt`+`B`
   - **Text/Background – Dark 2** . . . . `Alt`+`D`
   - **Text/Background – Light 2** . . . . `Alt`+`L`
   - **Accent 1** . . . . `Alt`+`!`
   - **Accent 2** . . . . `Alt`+`@₂`
   - **Accent 3** . . . . `Alt`+`#₃`
   - **Accent 4** . . . . `Alt`+`$₄`
   - **Accent 5** . . . . `Alt`+`%₅`
   - **Accent 6** . . . . `Alt`+`^₆`
   - **Hyperlink** . . . . `Alt`+`H`
   - **Followed Hyperlink** . . `Alt`+`F`

5. Select a color . . . . `→`/`←`/`↑`/`↓`, `Enter`
6. Type a name for this set of theme colors . . . . `Alt`+`N`, *name*
7. Click **Save** . . . . `Enter`

   ✓ If you don't want to save this new set of colors, click **Reset** to reset them to the original theme colors.

Modify an Existing Set of Theme Fonts

1. Click **Page Layout** tab . . . `Alt`, `P`

   Themes Group

2. Click **Fonts** button 🅰 . . . `T`, `F`
3. Click **Create New Theme Fonts** . . . . `C`
4. Open the **Heading font** list . . . . `Alt`+`H`
5. Select new heading font . . . . `↑`/`↓`, `Enter`
6. Open the **Body font** list . . . . `Alt`+`B`
7. Select new body font . . . . `↑`/`↓`, `Enter`
8. Type a name for this set of theme fonts . . . . `Alt`+`N`, *name*
9. Click **Save** . . . . `Enter`

Save a New Theme

1. Select the existing theme you wish to use as a starting point.
2. Choose a different set of colors, fonts, or effects, as desired.

   ✓ You can create a new set of colors or fonts to use if you like; see the procedures in this section for help.

3. Click **Page Layout** tab . . . `Alt`, `P`

   Themes Group

4. Click **Themes** button 🅰 . . . . `T`, `H`
5. Click **Save Current Theme** . . . `A`
6. Type name for theme in **File name** box . . . . . . `Alt`+`N`, *name*
7. Click **Save** . . . . `Enter`

Apply Standard Conditional Formatting

1. Select the cell or range to which you want to apply conditional formatting.
2. Click **Home** tab . . . . `Alt`, `H`

   Font Group

3. Click **Conditional Formatting** button 🔳 . . . . `L`
4. Choose a category:

   - **Highlight Cells Rules** . . . . `H`
   - **Top/Bottom Rules** . . . . `T`
   - **Data Bars** . . . . `D`
   - **Color Scales** . . . . `S`
   - **Icon Sets** . . . . `I`

5. If you choose Highlight Cells Rules or Top/Bottom Rules in step 4:

   a. In the box on the left, type a value to base the conditional formatting on, or select a cell to use as a sample.

   b. In the box on the right, select the formatting you want to apply when the condition is true.

   c. Click **OK** . . . . `Enter`

   OR

   If you choose Data Bars, Color Scales, or Icon Sets in step 4, choose an option off the palette that appears . . . . . . `→`/`←`/`↑`/`↓`. `Enter`

Create Your Own Conditional Formatting Rule

1. Select the cell or range to which you want to apply conditional formatting.
2. Click **Home** tab . . . . `Alt`, `H`

   Font Group
3. Click **Conditional Formatting** button . . . . `L`
4. Click **New Rule** . . . . `N`
5. Select a rule type . . . . `Alt`+`S`, `↑`/`↓`
6. Select the formats you want to associate with the rule.

   ✓ *Depending on the rule type you choose in step 5, a different dialog box appears, but generally, you need to specify what values you want to format, and the type of formats you want to apply when a cell contains the appropriate value.*

7. Click **OK**. . . . . `Enter`

Manage the Conditional Formatting Rules

1. To manage the rules associated with a particular cell, click that cell.
2. Click **Home** tab . . . . `Alt`, `H`

   Font Group
3. Click **Conditional Formatting** button . . . . `L`
4. Click **Manage Rules** . . . . `R`
5. Select which rules to show:
   a. Open **Show formatting rules for** list . . . . `Alt`+`S`
   b. Select the type of rules you want to manage . . . . `↑`/`↓`, `Enter`

   ✓ *Rules of the type you selected appear in the Rule list.*

6. Click a rule in the list.

7. To delete the rule, click **Delete Rule**. . . . . `Alt`+`D`
8. To change the values or formatting associated with the rule:
   a. Click **Edit Rule** . . . . . . `Alt`+`E`
   b. Change the value and/or formatting as desired.
   c. Click **OK**. . . . . `Enter`
9. Change how multiple rules work together:

   ✓ *Rules are processed in the order in which they appear. Unless the Stop If True option is on, each rule is evaluated in turn, and all formatting that matches the value in the cell is applied.*

   a. To make the currently selected rule the most important, click the up arrow until the rule is above other rules in the listing.
   b. To make the currently selected rule less important, click the down arrow until the rule is below other rules in the listing.
   c. To stop the processing of rules later in the listing if the current rule is true for a cell, click **Stop If True**.

Clear All Conditional Formatting

1. To remove conditional formatting from only a selected range, select it.
2. Click **Home** tab . . . . `Alt`, `H`

   Font Group
3. Click **Conditional Formatting** button . . . . `L`
4. Click **Clear Rules** . . . . `C`
5. Choose which rules to clear:
   a. **Clear Rules From Selected Cells** . . . . `S`
   b. **Clear Rules From Entire Sheet**. . . . . `E`

Find All Cells That Have Conditional Formatting

1. Click **Home** tab . . . . `Alt`, `H`

   Editing Group
2. Click **Find & Select** button . . . . `F`, `D`
3. Click **Conditional Formatting** . . . . `C`

Find Cells with the Same Conditional Formatting

1. Click a cell with the type of conditional formatting you want to find.
2. Click **Home** tab . . . . `Alt`, `H`

   Editing Group
3. Click **Find & Select** button . . . . `F`, `D`
4. Click **Go to Special** . . . . `S`
5. Click **Conditional formats** . . . . `T`
6. Click **Same** . . . . `E`
7. Click **OK**. . . . . `Enter`

Add a Watermark

1. Change to the sheet on which you want to add a watermark.
2. Click **Insert** tab . . . . `Alt`, `N`

   Text Group
3. Click **Header & Footer** button . . . . `H`
4. Click in the Left, Center, or Right section of the header or footer.
5. Click **Design** tab . . . `Alt`, `J`, `H`

   Header & Footer Elements Group
6. Click **Picture** button . . . . . . `I`
7. Change to the folder containing the image you want to use as a watermark.
8. Select the watermark image.
9. Click **Insert** . . . . `Enter`

Format a Watermark

1. Click in the section of the header or footer where you added the watermark.
2. Click **Design** tab . . . ⌨Alt⌨, ⌨J⌨, ⌨H⌨

   Header & Footer Elements Group

3. Click **Format Picture** button 🖼 . . . . ⌨C⌨
4. If desired, turn on Lock aspect ratio to retain the image's current ratio of height to width by clicking **Lock aspect ratio** . . . . . ⌨Alt⌨+⌨A⌨
5. If desired, turn on Relative to original picture size to retain the image's original aspect ratio by clicking **Relative to original picture size** . . . . ⌨Alt⌨+⌨R⌨
6. Adjust image size:
   a. Adjust **Height** . . . . . . ⌨Alt⌨+⌨E⌨, ⌨↑⌨/⌨↓⌨
   b. Adjust **Width** . . . . ⌨Alt⌨+⌨D⌨, ⌨↑⌨/⌨↓⌨

   OR

   a. Adjust scale **Height** . . . . . . ⌨Alt⌨+⌨H⌨, ⌨↑⌨/⌨↓⌨
   b. Adjust scale **Width** . . . . ⌨Alt⌨+⌨W⌨, ⌨↑⌨/⌨↓⌨

7. Change to **Picture** tab . . . . ⌨Ctrl⌨, ⌨⇆⌨
8. Crop watermark if desired:
   - Crop from **Left** . . . . ⌨Alt⌨+⌨L⌨, ⌨↑⌨/⌨↓⌨
   - Crop from **Right** . . . . . . ⌨Alt⌨+⌨R⌨, ⌨↑⌨/⌨↓⌨
   - Crop from **Top** . . . . ⌨Alt⌨+⌨T⌨, ⌨↑⌨/⌨↓⌨
   - Crop from **Bottom** . . . . . . ⌨Alt⌨+⌨B⌨, ⌨↑⌨/⌨↓⌨
9. Adjust brightness and contrast so data that appears on top of the watermark can be easily read:
   a. Open **Color** list. . . . . . ⌨Alt⌨+⌨C⌨
   b. Select **Washout** . . . . ⌨↑⌨/⌨↓⌨, ⌨Enter⌨

   OR

   a. Increase **Brightness** . . . ⌨Alt⌨+⌨H⌨, ⌨↑⌨/⌨↓⌨
   b. Decrease **Contrast** . . . . . ⌨Alt⌨+⌨N⌨, ⌨↑⌨/⌨↓⌨
10. Click **OK** . . . . ⌨Enter⌨

Format Worksheet Background

1. Change to the sheet whose background you want to change.
2. Click **Page Layout** tab . . . ⌨Alt⌨, ⌨P⌨

   Page Setup Group

3. Click **Background** button 🖼 . . ⌨G⌨
4. Select the file you want to use as a background.

   ✓ *The graphic will be tiled to fill the worksheet.*

5. Click **Insert** . . . . ⌨Enter⌨

Remove Worksheet Background

1. Change to the sheet whose background you want to change.
2. Click **Page Layout** tab . . . ⌨Alt⌨, ⌨P⌨

   Page Setup Group

3. Click **Delete Background** button 🖼 . . . . ⌨G⌨

EXERCISE DIRECTIONS

1. Start Excel, if necessary.
2. Open 💿 **07ProdSold**.
3. Save the file as **07ProdSold_xx**.
4. Insert the graphic 💿 **07phototownbackground.jpg** as the background on the July 22 sheet.
5. Hide the worksheet gridlines.
6. Apply a color fill to the range A6:C14:
   a. Change to the Home tab and click the Format Cells: Font dialog box launcher.
   b. Click the Fill tab.
   c. Select Light Yellow, Background 2, Darker 25%, from the Background Color list (third from the left in row three).
   d. Open the Pattern Style list and select the pattern style, 50% Gray.

   e. Open the Pattern Color list and select Brown, Accent 2, Lighter 40% (sixth from the left in the fourth last row).

   ✓ *You can point to a color on the Pattern Color list, and a ScreenTip will appear, displaying the color name. This does not happen when you point to a color in the Background Color list.*

   f. Click OK.
7. Add borders below the column labels:
   a. Select the range A6:C6.
   b. Change to the Home tab.
   c. Click the arrow on the Border button and select Top and Double Bottom Border.
8. Add a watermark:
   a. Change to the July 23 sheet.
   b. Change to the Insert tab, and click Header & Footer.

c. Click in the middle section of the header, then click the Picture button.

d. Select and insert 🔘 **07phototownbackground.jpg**.

e. Click the Format Picture button.

f. On the Size tab, with the Lock aspect ratio check box selected, set the Scale Height to 75%. (The Scale Width will automatically change to 75%.)

g. Change to the Picture tab, set the Brightness to 75%, set the Contrast to 25%, and click OK.

9. Apply conditional formatting (see Illustration A):

a. Select the range C6:C16.

b. Change to the Home tab and click the Conditional Formatting button.

c. Choose Highlight Cell Rules, Between.

d. Type 3 in the first value cell, 20 in the second value cell, choose Light Yellow Fill with Dark Yellow Text, and click OK.

10. Save some new colors:

a. Change to the Page Layout tab, click the Colors button and choose Create New Theme Colors.

b. Select Accent 5 to change it, and click More Colors.

c. Set Red to 224, Green to 183, and Blue to 119 and click OK.

d. Select Accent 6 to change it, and click More Colors.

e. Change Red to 160, Green to 113, and Blue to 255 and click OK.

f. Type Photo Town in the Name box, and click Save to save the new color set.

11. Try out the new color set:

a. Select the range A5:C5.

b. Change to the Home tab, click the Fill Color button, and choose Light Orange, Accent 5, Lighter 40%.

c. Click the Font Color button and choose Light Blue, Accent 6, Darker 25%.

12. Save the theme with its new colors:

a. Change to the Page Layout tab and click the Themes button.

b. Click Save Current Theme.

c. Type Photo Town in the File name box and click Save.

13. Widen columns as needed on each worksheet.

14. Spell check each worksheet.

15. Print each worksheet.

16. Close the workbook, saving all changes.

Illustration A

ON YOUR OWN

1. Start Excel, if necessary.
2. Start a new workbook and save it as **OXL07_xx**.
3. Type **Pete's Pets** at the top of the worksheet.

   ✓ *Because you'll be using a graphic for your worksheet in a later step, you might want to place the title and the data a few rows down and a few columns over.*

4. Create columns for each day of the week. (The store is closed on Mondays, but open Saturday and Sunday.) Add a **Totals** column.
5. Create rows labeled Birds, Dogs, Cats, Fish, and Other.
6. Type in some made-up sales data, depicting the number of items sold each day.

   ✓ *For example, you might have sold 10 dogs on Tuesday.*

7. Create formulas that calculate the total number of each item sold.

8. Format the title, column, and row labels:
   a. Choose a theme.
   b. Customize the color set as you like, and save it as **PPets**.
   c. Customize the font set too, choosing a new heading font. Save the result as **PPets**.
   d. Save your choices in a new theme called **PPets**.
   e. Use your custom colors to apply fills and cell borders to the worksheet.
   f. Apply your custom heading font to the worksheet title, Pete's Pets.
   g. Draw some borders, either around the data, or just under the title and/or headings.
   h. Apply other formats as desired, such as alignments, fonts, and font sizes.
9. Format the sheet background using the graphic **07bwdogandcat.gif**.
10. Hide the worksheet gridlines.
11. Close the workbook, saving all changes.

Skills Covered

- **Save a Workbook in a Different Format**
- **Use Compatibility Checker**
- **Create a New Folder for Saving Workbooks**
- **Enable Macros in a Workbook**
- **Create Original Templates**

Software Skills   If you share Excel data, you can easily save that data in a format that's compatible with the program someone else is using, such as an older version of Excel. Sometimes you want to share not the data, but the format and formulas in a workbook in a reusable format called a *template*. With a template, you can create as many similar workbooks as you like, with only a minimum of effort. Using macros are also easy, since they are designed to save you time by automating repetitive tasks.

Application Skills   Since you first started keeping records for Holy Habañero, you've learned quite a lot about using Excel, and so you feel pretty confident in using macros and creating reusable templates, so you'd like to give it a try with a new produce log a colleague has developed. You also need to convert the worksheet to Excel 2003 format, which is being used by the manager of a different restaurant location.

TERMS

Macro   A series of recorded actions that can be replayed when needed. The recorded actions are carried out automatically for the user.

PDF Format   A format that preserves the layout of text and graphics, and any special text formatting in a workbook, so that when it's viewed by someone else, the workbook looks the same as it did on yours, even if the user's computer is different. In addition, a PDF document cannot be easily changed, so it preserves your data.

Play a macro   Execute the macro commands.

Template   A workbook designed for a specific purpose, complete with formatting, formulas, text, and row and column labels that you can customize.

Trusted publisher   You can designate which macro publishers (designers) you trust, and together they form a list of "trusted publishers" for your computer.

NOTES

Save a Workbook in a Different Format

- Although many programs can open Excel files, you may occasionally need to save your workbook in a different format.

- For example, you might need to save a workbook in Excel 2003 format so that a colleague using an older version of Excel can open it.

- Besides converting a workbook to an earlier version of Excel, you can also convert your data to popular formats such as text with tabs, CSV, DIF, PDF format, and XPS format.

- You can also save a workbook as a template for creating new workbooks (see later in this exercise).

- When needed, you can save Excel data as a Web page for posting to the Internet.

- In order to view a workbook saved in PDF format, you need Adobe Reader. To view a worksheet saved in XPS format, you need an XPS viewer, available free from Microsoft.
  - To make changes to a workbook saved as PDF, you can use Adobe Acrobat, or simply open the original file in Excel, make your changes, and then resave the file in PDF format.
  - To make changes to a workbook saved in XPS, open the original file in Excel, make your changes, and resave the file.
  - To save a workbook in PDF or XPS format, you need to install the PDF/XPS add-in, located on Microsoft's Web site at **http://www.microsoft.com/downloads**.

Use Compatibility Checker

- Sometimes saving your workbook in a different format will result in a loss of some data—typically formatting changes.
- You can see which features might be lost before resaving a workbook in an older version of Excel by running the Compatibility Checker first.

Compatibility Checker

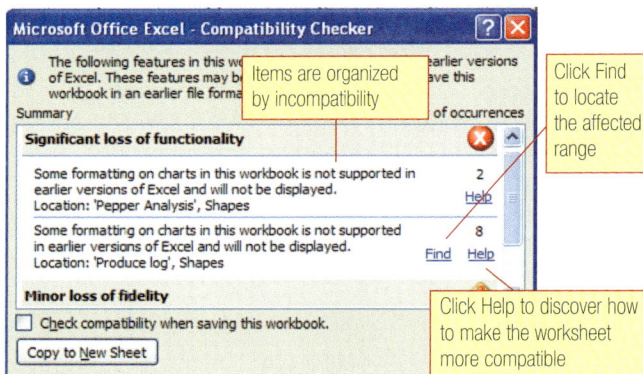

Microsoft Office Excel - Compatibility Checker

The following features in this workbook are not supported by earlier versions of Excel. These features may be lost or degraded when you save this workbook in an earlier file format.

Items are organized by incompatibility

Summary | of occurrences

Significant loss of functionality

Some formatting on charts in this workbook is not supported in earlier versions of Excel and will not be displayed. Location: 'Pepper Analysis', Shapes — 2 Help

Click Find to locate the affected range

Some formatting on charts in this workbook is not supported in earlier versions of Excel and will not be displayed. Location: 'Produce log', Shapes — 8 Find Help

Minor loss of fidelity

☐ Check compatibility when saving this workbook.

Copy to New Sheet

Click Help to discover how to make the worksheet more compatible

- The Compatibility Checker scans the workbook and lists any incompatibilities, and the number of occurrences of that incompatibility.
  - Incompatibilities are grouped by severity.
  - You can copy this list of incompatibilities to a sheet in the workbook for further review if you want.

Create a New Folder for Saving Workbooks

- Whether you're saving a workbook for the first time, or simply saving it under a new name or in a new location, you can create a new folder in which to save it.
- When you create a folder, you must give that folder a name.
  - ✓ The name can contain spaces and numbers.
- The new folder automatically appears in the Save As dialog box.
  - ✓ This makes it easy for you to save your file in the new folder.
- Although you can create folders anywhere on your own computer, you might want to place your new folders within the My Documents or Documents folder, since Excel uses that folder by default.
- You may not be able to create new folders on network drives unless you have specific permission to do so. See your network administrator for help.

Enable Macros in a Workbook

- A macro is a series of actions that are recorded and saved in a file.
  - ✓ You might record a series of actions you perform routinely, such as searching for an item in a worksheet, copying or moving data, entering company or personal information, inserting common formulas, and so on.
- When you play a macro, the recorded actions are performed automatically, without any intervention from you.
- If you've created a macro and you'd like to save it with a workbook, you must use a special file format called Excel Macro-Enabled Workbook.
- If you want to open and then use a workbook that includes macros, you need to enable them first.
- In order to protect you from macros that may perform commands that are harmful to your system (many computer viruses are created as macros), Excel uses its Trust Center to examine macros to see if they might be malicious. The macro is checked to see if:
  - The macro is digitally signed by the person who created it, and the signature is valid (the signature is registered with an online digital certification database and has not expired.)
  - The person who signed the macro is a **trusted publisher**.
  - ✓ Learn how to digitally sign a workbook so it can be authenticated by turning to Exercise 40.

■ Normally, all macros are disabled automatically when you open a workbook, although you can change this level of security to allow certain workbook/macros to be enabled automatically.

■ With the default security settings turned on, if the Trust Center detects a workbook with a macro, a message appears on the Message Bar warning you.

- All macros within the workbook are disabled, and the workbook is opened.

- You can click the Options button on the Message Bar, learn more about the macros contained within the workbook (for instance, are the macros digitally signed, but not by a trusted publisher?), and enable the macro(s) if you trust the source of the workbook.

The Message Bar displays a warning

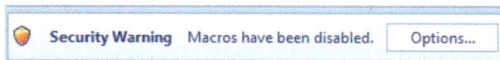

> 🛡 **Security Warning** Macros have been disabled. [Options...]

■ You can change the macro security settings if you want, although it's typically best to let Excel pre-screen workbooks with embedded macros for you.

- *Disable all macros without notification*—This option disables all macros in all workbooks, and does not display a warning message on the Message Bar.

- *Disable all macros with notification*—This is the normal setting, in which all macros are disabled, and a notice appears whenever a workbook is opened which contains a macro.

- *Disable all macros except digitally signed macros*—This option disables macros in workbooks that are not digitally signed, and macros in workbooks signed, but not by a trusted publisher. A warning appears only if the macros are signed but not trusted. In such a case, you can opt to enable the macros anyway.

- *Enable all macros*—This option is not recommended because it basically disables all macro security. With this option turned on, all macros within any workbook are enabled.

Create Original Templates

■ If you create workbooks with a lot of similar elements—a company name and logo, similar column and row labels, and so on—create one workbook and save it as a template.

- You can create a new workbook based on any existing workbook without creating a template from it first.

- However, if you often base new workbooks on a particular workbook, you can save time by creating a template.

- For example, with a template, you won't have to delete the data from the copied workbook before you can enter new data.

Create your own templates and use them to create workbooks

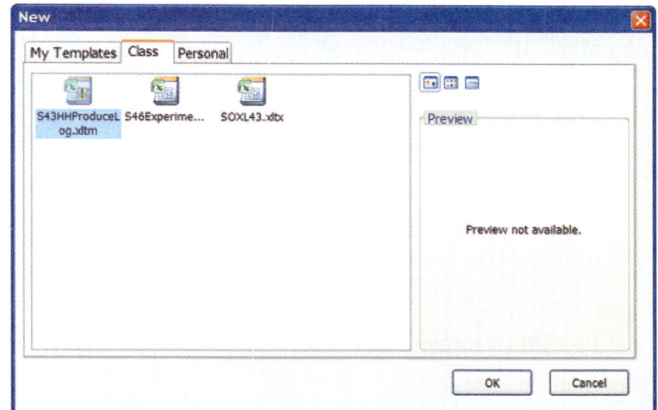

■ With a template, you can quickly create new documents that contain the same elements.

■ In the New dialog box, you can browse through the templates you've created.

■ By default, templates are saved in the Templates folder, and then appear on the My Templates tab of the New dialog box.

- You can create a subfolder off this Templates folder, and organize your personal templates by category, if you like.

- If you create a subfolder off the Templates folder, that subfolder will appear as its own tab in the New dialog box, like the Personal tab shown in the previous illustration.

■ You can edit and modify templates that you create as well as any existing templates.

- When saving a template, you can save it as read-only to prevent any accidental changes.

✓ *Template files have .XLTX file name extensions.*

PROCEDURES

Save in a Different Format

1. Click **Office Button** [Alt]+[F]
2. Point to **Save As** [F]
3. Click **Other Formats** [O]
4. Select desired format from **Save as file type** list [Alt]+[T], [↑]/[↓], [Enter]
5. If desired, click in **File name** text box [Alt]+[N]

   ✓ *Since selecting a different file type automatically changes the file extension, you don't need to use a different file name in order to protect your original Excel file. It will not be replaced.*

6. Type new file name.
7. Select drive and folder in which to save the tile.
8. Click **Save** [Enter]

Save in a PDF or XPS Format

   ✓ *To save a workbook in PDF or XPS format, you need to first install the add-in, Microsoft Save as PDF or XPS.*

1. Click **Office Button** [Alt]+[F]
2. Point to **Save As** [F]
3. Click **PDF or XPS** [P]
4. Select desired format from **Save as file type** list [Alt]+[T], [↑]/[↓], [Enter]
5. If desired, click in **File name** text box [Alt]+[N]
6. Type new file name.
7. To display a PDF file immediately in Adobe Reader, choose **Open file after publishing** [←], [Spacebar]
8. Select how to optimize:
   a. **Standard (publishing online and printing)** [Alt]+[A]
   b. **Minimum size (publishing online)** [Alt]+[M]

9. Click **Options** [Alt]+[O]
   a. Select desired **Page range** options:
      - All [A]
      - Page(s) [G], ##, [←], ##
   b. Select desired **Publish what** options:
      - **Selection** [S]
      - **Entire workbook** [E]
      - **Active sheet(s)** [V]
      - **Ignore print areas** [O]
   c. Select desired **Include nonprinting information** options:
      - **Document properties** [R]
      - **Document structure tags for accessibility** [M]
   d. Select desired **PDF options:**
      - ISO 19005-1 compliant (PDF/A) [Alt]+[¡]
   e. Click **OK** [Enter]
10. Click **Publish** [Enter]

Use Compatibility Checker

1. Click **Office Button** [Alt]+[F]
2. Point to **Prepare** [E]
3. Click **Run Compatibility Checker** [C]

   ✓ *If you do not understand why a particular feature is incompatible, and what may happen if you save the workbook in an older version of Excel anyway, click the **Help** link next to that particular feature in the list.*

   ✓ *If the incompatibility has to do with data outside the range compatible with older versions of Excel, you can click **Find** to have Excel locate the out-of-range data for you.*

4. To check compatibility again, automatically, when this workbook is resaved, click **Check compatibility when saving this workbook** [H]

5. To copy the incompatibility list to a worksheet, click **Copy to New Sheet** [Alt]+[N]

   ✓ *A new worksheet, Compatibility Issues, is added to the workbook behind existing worksheets.*

6. Click **OK** [Enter]

Create a New Folder to Save the File

1. In the Save As dialog box, click **Create New Folder** button.
2. Type the name of the folder in the **Name** box in the New Folder dialog box
3. Click **OK** [Enter]

Save a Macro Enabled Workbook

1. Click **Office Button** [Alt]+[F]
2. Point to **Save As** [F]
3. Click **Excel Macro-Enabled Workbook** [M]
4. If desired, click in **File name** text box [Alt]+[N]

   ✓ *Since selecting a different file type automatically changes the file extension, you don't need to use a different file name in order to protect your original Excel file. It will not be replaced.*

5. Type new file name.
6. Select drive and folder in which to save the tile.

   ✓ *You can skip steps 5 and 6 and click a folder on the Places bar, such as My Documents.*

7. Click **Save** [Enter]

Enable Macros in an Open Workbook

1. Click **Options** button on Message Bar.
2. Click **Enable this content** . . . . `Alt`+`E`

   OR

   Click **Trust all documents from the publisher** . . . . `Alt`+`T`
3. Click **OK**. . . . . `Enter`

Change Trust Center Macro Settings

1. Click **Office Button** . . . `Alt`+`F`
2. Click **Excel Options** . . . . `I`
3. Click **Trust Center** . . . . `↑`/`↓`
4. Click **Trust Center Settings**. . . . . `Alt`+`T`
5. Click **Macro Settings**. . . . . `↑`/`↓`
6. Select the desired macro settings:
   - **Disable all macros without notification** . . . . `Alt`+`L`
   - **Disable all macros with notification** . . . . `Alt`+`D`
   - **Disable all macros except digitally signed macros** . . . . `Alt`+`G`
   - **Enable all macros**. . . `Alt`+`E`
7. Click **OK**. . . . . `Enter`

Create a Template from a Workbook

1. Click **Office Button** . . . `Alt`+`F`
2. Point to **Save As** . . . . `F`
3. Click **Other Formats** . . . . `O`
4. Open **Save as file type** list . . . . `Alt`+`T`
5. Select **Excel Template** or **Excel Macro-Enabled Template** from the list . . . . `↑`/`↓`, `Enter`

   ✓ *The Templates folder is displayed. If you want to create a subfolder for your own templates, click the Create New Folder button* □ *in the Save As dialog box, type a folder name, and click OK.*

6. Select the file name in **File name** text box . . . . `Alt`+`N`
7. Type new file name.
8. Click **Save** . . . . `Enter`

Save File as a Template with Read-Only Recommendation

1. Click **Office Button** . . . `Alt`+`F`
2. Point to **Save As** . . . . `F`
3. Click **Other Formats** . . . . `O`
4. Open **Save as file type** list . . . . `Alt`+`T`

5. Select **Excel Template** or **Excel Macro-Enabled Template** from the list . . . . `↑`/`↓`, `Enter`

   ✓ *The Templates folder is displayed. If you want to create a subfolder for your own templates, click the Create New Folder button* □ *in the Save As dialog box, type a folder name, and click OK.*

6. Select the file name in **File name** text box . . . . `Alt`+`N`
7. Type new file name.
8. Click the **Tools** button

   [Tools ▼] . . . . `Alt`+`L`, `↓`
9. Click **General Options** . . . . `G`
10. Click **Read-only recommended**. . . . . `Alt`+`R`
11. Click **OK**. . . . . `Enter`
12. Click **Save** . . . . `Enter`

Edit an Original Template

1. Click **Office Button** . . . `Alt`+`F`
2. Click **Open**. . . . . `O`
3. Change to the folder that contains the template you wish to edit.
4. Select the template and click **Open** . . . . `Enter`
5. If needed, click **Enable Macros** . . . . `E`
6. Make changes to the template.
7. Click **Office Button** . . . `Alt`+`F`
8. Click **Close** . . . . `C`
9. Click **Yes** to save changes . . . . `Y`

EXERCISE DIRECTIONS

1. Start Excel, if necessary.
2. Open ◎ **08HHProduceLog0214**.
3. The macros in the workbook are not enabled:
   a. On the Message Bar, click Options.
   b. Click Enable this content and click OK.
4. Save the file as a macro-enabled workbook called **08HHProduceLog0214_xx**:
   a. Click the Office Button.
   b. Point to Save As, and then select Excel Macro-Enabled Workbook.

5. There's a macro in the workbook that creates a chart for you automatically. Run the chart macro by pressing Ctrl+Shift+R. Change the chart title to **Pepper Analysis**.
6. Save the workbook again so your changes are preserved.
7. Create a template from the workbook:
   a. Change to the Produce log sheet, and select the range B20:J21 and press Delete. See Illustration A.
   b. Delete the chart sheet, Pepper Analysis.
   c. Click the Office Button, point to Save As, and then select Other Formats.

d. Choose Excel Macro-Enabled Template from the Save as file type list.

e. Click the Create New Folder button, and create a folder for your templates within the normal Templates folder. Call the folder Class.

f. Type **08HHProduceLog_xx** in the File name box and click Save.

g. Close the template.

8. Create a new workbook, using the template:

a. Click the Office Button and select New.

b. Click My templates.

c. Change to the Class tab, and select the **08HHProduceLog_xx** template and click OK.

d. Enable macros.

e. Save the new workbook as **08HHProduceLog0221_xx**, using the Excel Macro-Enabled Workbook format.

f. Type **Week of February 21** in cell D4.

9. Use the Compatibility Checker to see if any features are incompatible with Excel 2003 format:

a. Click the Office button, point to Prepare, and then select Run Compatibility Checker.

b. Looks like some of the formatting (themes) are not compatible with the older version of Excel. Click OK.

✓ Despite the warning, this formatting issue is not really a big concern, and the worksheet will function properly in Excel 2003. But it's always best to test the converted workbook to make sure that it looks and works as you want it to before you send it to your colleague.

c. Resave the workbook in Excel 97-2003 format, using the filename **08HHProduceLog0221_OF_xx** (old format).

d. The Compatibility Checker pops up again; click Continue.

10. Spell check the workbook.

11. Print the workbook.

12. Close the workbook, saving all changes.

Illustration A

	A	B	C	D	E	F	G	H	I
6		Bushels required							
7		Habanero	Serrano	Red Amazon	Japone	Chile de Arbol	Jalapeno	Chipotle	Pasilla
8	Dragon's Cauldron	4		2					
9	Belly of the Beast	2	4		3				
10	Magma Core	2		4				3	
11	Typhoon Warning		2			3	6		
12	Uranium 235			5	2				
13	Szechuan Singe				3	4			
14	Wasabi Fusion			2			2		
15	Sorrento Serrano		6						
16	Yucatan Bomb				2		4	3	
17	Toast Jammer						2		5
18	Calculations								
19	Total bushels required	8	12	13	10	7	14	6	5
20	Bushels in stock								
21	Garden on hand								
22	No. of bushels to reorder	8	12	13	10	7	14	6	5
23	Costs								
24	Valparaiso price/bushel	$ 8.50	$ 8.20	$ 10.50	$ 7.20	$ 9.35	$ 6.75	$ 9.25	$ 9.75
25	Guadalajara price/bushel	$ 8.40	$ 8.75	$ 10.95	$ 7.50	$ 9.50	$ 5.75	$ 9.80	$ 9.70
26	Reorder cost	$ 67.20	$ 98.40	$ 136.50	$ 72.00	$ 65.45	$ 80.50	$ 55.50	48.50
27									
28	Total reorder cost	$ 640.55							
29									
30									

S08HHProduceLog0214 - Microsoft Excel

Pepper Analysis   Produce log

254

ON YOUR OWN

1. Start Excel, if necessary.

2. Create a template for tracking a day's worth of sales at Country Crazy Antiques.

3. Save the template in the Class folder as **OXL08_*xx*.xlt**.

4. You need to keep track of the salesperson who took the order, item number, description, quantity purchased, price per item, and the total amount of the sale. You might also want to keep track of how the item was purchased (check, credit card, or cash), and the customer's name and phone number. Typical items include dressers, tables, chairs, bed frames, mirrors, and accessories.

5. Create totals for the day's sales.

6. Format the template however you like.

7. Save the template and close it.

8. Open the template again and make several formatting changes to the template. For example you might want to remove the extra worksheets you don't need. Save your edits to the template.

9. Create a new workbook based on the template, and enter today's sales.

10. Save the workbook in XML format as **OXL08_*xx*.xml**. Click Yes when asked if you want to continue.

11. Spell check the worksheet.

12. Print the worksheet.

13. Close the workbook, saving all changes.

Exercise | 9

Skills Covered

- **E-mail a File**
- **Display and Print Formulas**
- **Set Precise Margins for Printing**

Software Skills   In today's fast-paced office environment, instant communication is the key to success, and so is sharing information and resources. These goals merge beautifully with the sharing of Excel data via e-mail. Of course, another way in which you can share Excel data is by printing it out. As non-technical as that might seem, sometimes data speaks more loudly in your hand than it does on a tiny computer screen. Prior to printing, you may want to adjust the margins in order to reduce the number of pages or to produce a nicer looking printout. And prior to sharing printed data, you'll want to proofread it, and one effective way to do that is to display your formulas for review.

Application Skills   There has been a lot of upper-management interest in the new produce log you've developed, and so you want to proofread it carefully for errors before printing out a copy for local management and e-mailing a copy to managers in another location. After displaying and printing formulas, you'll adjust the print margins to reduce page count, and then print and e-mail the result.

TERMS

E-mail   Short for electronic mail. E-mail is a message sent via modem or network cable to another computer.

Margins   The distance between worksheet data and the top, bottom, left, and right edges of the paper in a printout.

NOTES

E-mail a File

- Worksheets and entire workbook files may be sent electronically via **e-mail.**
- You can perform this task if you're on a network or on the Internet and you have e-mail capability.
- You have two options when sending Excel data via e-mail.
  - The workbook can be sent as an attachment to the e-mail message.
  - The workbook data can be embedded within the message area, and sent within the e-mail.
  - ✓ *To use this second option, you need to add a special command to the Quick Access Toolbar. Only one worksheet (the current one) can be sent in this manner.*

Display and Print Formulas

- When you type a formula into a cell and press Enter or otherwise confirm the entry, the result of that formula is displayed in the cell.
- In other words, formulas do not normally appear in the worksheet—but the results of formulas do.
- If you have a complicated worksheet with lots of formulas, you might want to display them temporarily.
  - Displaying formulas allows you to check them visually for errors.
  - You can also print the formulas while they are displayed, and review them that way.

Set Precise Margins for Printing

- There are various ways in which you can prepare your worksheet for printing, including the setting of margins.

- You can choose from a set of standard margin options, located on the Page Layout tab.

- To set more precise margins, you need to use the Margins tab of the Page Setup dialog box.
  - Increase or decrease the Top, Bottom, Left, or Right margins to control the distance between your data and the edge of the paper.
  - Increase or decrease the Header or Footer margins to specify the distance between the top or bottom of the page and the header/footer.

Margins tab of Page Setup dialog box

PROCEDURES

Send a Workbook as an E-mail Attachment

1. Click **Office Button** . . . Alt + F
2. Point to **Send** . . . . D
3. Click **E-mail** . . . . E
4. Type the e-mail address in the **To** box.
5. The file name of the workbook serves as the Subject; type a new **Subject** if you want
6. Type a message in the message area.
7. Click **Send** . . . . Alt + S

Add Send to Mail Recipient Button to the Quick Access Toolbar

1. Click **Office Button** . . . Alt + F
2. Click **Excel Options** I
3. Click **Customize** . . . . ↑ / ↓
4. Choose **All Commands** from the **Choose command from** list . . . . Alt + C, ↑ / ↓, Enter

5. Choose **Send to Mail Recipient** from the list on the left . . . ↑ / ↓
6. Click **Add** . . . . Alt + A
7. Click **OK** . . . . Enter

Send a Worksheet as Text in an E-mail Message

✓ *Add the Send to Mail Recipient button to the Quick Access Toolbar before attempting this procedure.*

1. Click the **Send to Mail Recipient** button .
2. Click **Send the current sheet as the message body** . . . . . Alt + B
3. Click **OK** . . . . Enter
4. Type the e-mail address in the **To** box.
5. The filename of the workbook serves as the Subject; type a new **Subject** if you want.
6. Type a message in the **Introduction** box.
7. Click **Send this Sheet** . . . Alt + S

Display or Hide Formulas

1. Display all the formulas In a worksheet . . . . Ctrl + `
2. Hide all the formulas and display results again . . . . Ctrl + `

Set Margins Precisely

1. Click **Page Layout** tab . . . Alt , P

   Page Setup Group

2. Click **Margins** button . . . . . M
3. Click **Custom Margins** . . . . A
4. Adjust margins precisely:
   - **Top** . . . . Alt + T, ↑ / ↓
   - **Bottom** . . . . . . Alt + B, ↑ / ↓
   - **Left** . . . . Alt + L, ↑ / ↓
   - **Right** . . . . Alt + R, ↑ / ↓
   - **Header** . . . . . . Alt + A, ↑ / ↓
   - **Footer** . . . . . Alt + F, ↑ / ↓
5. If desired, center the data on the printed page:
   - **Horizontally** . . . . Alt + Z
   - **Vertically** . . . . Alt + V
6. Click **OK** . . . . Enter

EXERCISE DIRECTIONS

1. Start Excel, if necessary.
2. Open 08HHProduceLog0221_*xx* that you created in Exercise 8, or open 09HHProduceLog0221. Enable Macros.
3. Save the file as 09HHProduceLog0221_*xx*.
4. Display formulas by pressing Ctrl+`. See Illustration A.
5. Prepare to print the worksheet:
   a. Click the Orientation button on the Page Layout tab and click Landscape.
   b. Select the range A1:J26, click the Print Area button on the Page Layout tab, and choose Set Print Area. Hint: Use the Name box to make the selection if you have trouble with the image in cell A1.
   c. Change the Top, Bottom, Left, and Right margins to .50 inch.
6. Spell check the workbook.
7. Print the workbook.
8. Hide formulas again by pressing Ctrl+`.
9. E-mail the workbook to your instructor:
   a. Click the Office Button and choose Send, E-Mail.
   b. Address the e-mail and write a short note.
   c. Click Send to send the e-mail with the workbook attached.
10. Close the workbook, saving all changes.

Illustration A

	A	B (Habanero)	C (Serrano)
6		Bushels required	
7			
8	Dragon's Cauldron	4	2
9	Belly of the Beast	2	4
10	Magma Core	2	4
11	Typhoon Warning		2
12	Uranium 235		5
13	Szechuan Singe		
14	Wasabi Fusion		2
15	Sorrento Serrano		6
16	Yucatan Bomb		
17	Toast Jammer		
18		Calculations	
19	Total bushels required	=SUM(B8:B17)	=SUM(C8:C17) =SUM(D8:
20	Bushels in stock		
21	Garden on hand		
22	No. of bushels to reorder	=IF(B19-(B20+B21)<0,0,B1	=IF(C19-(C20+C21)<0,0,C =IF(D19-(I
23		Costs	
24	Valparaiso price/bushel	8.5	8.2 10.5
25	Guadalajara price/bushel	8.4	8.75 10.95
26	Reorder cost	=IF(B24<B25,B24*B22,B25	=IF(C24<C25,C24*C22,C =IF(D24<[
27			
28	Total reorder cost	=SUM(B26:J26)	
29			
30			

Produce log

ON YOUR OWN

1. Start Excel, if necessary.

2. Open the file [⌨] **OXL06_xx**, created in the On Your Own section of Exercise 6, or open [◎] **09SalesComp**. Save the file as **OXL09_xx**.

3. Display the formulas.

4. Preview the worksheet, then adjust the orientation and margins as needed to produce a nice-looking printout.

5. Center the data both horizontally and vertically on the page.

6. Spell check the worksheet.

7. Print the worksheet.

8. E-mail the worksheet to your instructor.

9. Close the workbook, saving all changes.

Critical Thinking

Application Skills You are the payroll clerk at PhotoTown, and you've been calculating payroll checks manually ever since you were hired a month ago. Now that you're familiar with Excel, however, you want to use it to complete this weekly task more easily.

EXERCISE DIRECTIONS

1. Start Excel, if necessary.

2. Open ◎ **10PhotoTownPayroll**.

3. Save the file as **10PhotoTownPayroll_xx**.

4. Type several two-line column labels:

   a. In cell A7, type **Check Number** (enter the column label on two lines).

   b. In cell B7, type **Employee ID Number** on two lines.

   c. In cell E7, type **Hours Worked** on two lines.

   d. Adjust column widths as needed.

5. Separate the Name column into First Name and Last Name:

   a. Insert a column to the right of column D.

   b. After selecting the range D8:D37, click the Text to Columns button on the Data tab.

   c. Choose the Delimited, Space options.

   d. Format both columns as text, and save the result in the range beginning in cell D8.

   e. Type **First Name** in cell D7 and **Last Name** in cell E7.

   f. Correct the one error by typing **Chu Gi** in cell D26, and **Nguyen** in cell E26.

6. Enter the hours everyone has worked as mixed fractions, as shown in Illustration A.

7. Use Go To to jump to the cell that displays the total cost of the payroll this week:

   a. Click the Find & Select button on the Home tab, and choose Go To.

   b. Choose *Payroll_Total* from the list, and click OK to jump to cell L41.

8. Enter today's date in cell H3, and apply the Short Date format.

9. Type **Click here to view employee tax data** in cell G2:

   a. Select the range G2:H2, and apply Merge cells, Wrap text, centered Horizontal, and centered Vertical alignment format.

   b. Use this text to create a hyperlink to ◎ **10PhotoTownEE**, located in the Data folder.

   c. Use the ScreenTip **Employee Database**.

   d. Change the point size of the hyperlink text to 11 point.

10. Fill all cells in the worksheet with the color, Light Blue, Accent 6, Lighter 60% (see Illustration A):

    a. Select rows 1-6, and fill them with Light Yellow, Background 2, Darker 10%.

    b. Select A7:L7, and apply a pattern: Background Color Brown, Accent 3, Darker 25% (5th row, 6th column), Pattern Color Light Blue, Accent 6, Lighter 80% (last column, 2nd row), and Pattern Style 50% Gray.

    c. Apply conditional formatting to the Net Pay column to highlight any net pay value greater than $100 using Light Red Fill with Dark Red Text.

11. Create two custom views:

   a. Save the current view with the name **Full View**.

   b. Hide columns B-G, and call that view **Payroll Checks**.

   c. Adjust columns as needed, then spell check and print the worksheet.

12. Change back to Full View.

13. Widen columns as needed.

14. Spell check the worksheet.

15. E-mail the workbook to your instructor.

16. Close the workbook, saving all changes.

Illustration A

S10PhotoTownPayroll - Microsoft Excel

PhotoTown
Miller Rd
Unit #2166

Click here to view employee tax data

Date 8/28/2008

Check Number	Employee ID Number	Title	First Name	Last Name	Hours Worked	Rate	Gross Pay	Fed	SS	State	Net Pay
41289	63778	Mr.	Carlos	Altare	12	$6.30	$75.60	$14.36	$5.86	$4.16	$51.22
41290	31524	Mrs.	Jan	Borough	22	$6.50	$143.00	$27.17	$11.08	$7.87	$96.88
41291	18946	Mr.	Shakur	Brown	40	$7.00	$280.00	$53.20	$21.70	$15.40	$189.70
41292	71335	Mr.	Taneed	Black	38 1/2	$7.00	$269.50	$51.21	$20.89	$14.82	$182.59
41293	22415	Mr.	Jairo	Campos	21 3/4	$7.20	$156.60	$29.75	$12.14	$8.61	$106.10
41294	20965	Mrs.	Rafiquil	Damir	10 1/2	$6.15	$64.58	$12.27	$5.00	$3.55	$43.75
41295	64121	Mrs.	Diana	Dogwood	19 3/4	$6.20	$122.45	$23.27	$9.49	$6.73	$82.96
41296	30388	Mrs.	Lucy	Fan	31 1/4	$6.55	$204.69	$38.89	$15.86	$11.26	$138.68
41297	44185	Mrs.	Jennifer	Flynn	30	$7.00	$210.00	$39.90	$16.28	$11.55	$142.28
41298	32152	Ms.	Katerina	Flynn	30	$7.10	$213.00	$40.47	$16.51	$11.72	$144.31
41299	31885	Ms.	Kere	Freed	32 1/2	$7.10	$230.75	$43.84	$17.88	$12.69	$156.33
41300	33785	Mr.	Eram	Hassan	27 1/2	$6.85	$188.38	$35.79	$14.60	$10.36	$127.62
41301	55648	Mr.	Tyrell	Johnson	22	$6.50	$143.00	$27.17	$11.08	$7.87	$96.88
41302	60219	Ms.	Verna	Latinz	12 1/2	$6.30	$78.75	$14.96	$6.10	$4.33	$53.35
41303	28645	Mr.	Wu	Lee	10 3/4	$7.00	$75.25	$14.30	$5.83	$4.14	$50.98
41304	67415	Mr.	Shamir	Lewis	20	$7.10	$142.00	$26.98	$11.01	$7.81	$96.21
41305	27995	Mrs.	Maria	Navarro	20	$6.30	$126.00	$23.94	$9.77	$6.93	$85.37
41306	32151	Mr.	Tony	Navarro	18 3/4	$6.35	$119.06	$22.62	$9.23	$6.55	$80.66
41307	28499	Mr.	Chu Gi	Nguyen	23 1/2	$6.85	$160.98	$30.59	$12.48	$8.85	$109.06
41308	17564	Mr.	Juan	Nuniez	39 1/4	$7.00	$274.75	$52.20	$21.29	$15.11	$186.14
41309	14558	Mr.	Akira	Ota	14 1/2	$7.25	$105.13	$19.97	$8.15	$5.78	$71.22
41310	31022	Mrs.	Meghan	Ryan	31 3/4	$7.00	$222.25	$42.23	$17.22	$12.22	$150.57
41311	41885	Mrs.	Kate	Scott	23	$6.85	$157.55	$29.93	$12.21	$8.67	$106.74
41312	25448	Mr.	Jyoti	Shaw	32 1/4	$6.50	$209.63	$39.83	$16.25	$11.53	$142.02
41313	23151	Ms.	Jewel	Vidito	35	$6.55	$229.25	$43.56	$17.77	$12.61	$155.32
41314	37785	Mrs.	Corrine	Walters	35 1/2	$6.65	$236.08	$44.85	$18.30	$12.98	$159.94
41315	58945	Mrs.	Antonia	Whitney	21 1/4	$6.75	$143.44	$27.25	$11.12	$7.89	$97.18
41316	57445	Mr.	Shale	Wilson	35 3/4	$7.00	$250.25	$47.55	$19.39	$13.76	$169.54
41317	36684	Mrs.	Shiree	Wilson	39	$7.10	$276.90	$52.61	$21.46	$15.23	$187.60
41318	55412	Mrs.	Su	Yamaguchi	27 1/4	$6.30	$171.68	$32.62	$13.30	$9.44	$116.31

Payroll

Curriculum Integration

Application Skills Your science class is going to be doing several in-classroom experiments. Your teacher wants you to take careful notes, recording each day's changes. You've decided to create a worksheet to record information, and to save it as a reusable template.

EXERCISE DIRECTIONS

Start Excel, if necessary, and begin a new, blank workbook. Save the file with an appropriate filename, such as **11Experiment_*xx***. Type a title for your worksheet in row 1, and your name in row 2. In the next row, type **Experiment Details**.

Set up an area to record the Experiment Description, your Prediction, and the actual Result. Create a box into which you can type the related text, and format each box so that the text wraps within a large range of merged cells. You might want to center the text vertically as shown in Illustration A.

Add a Timeline section as shown, applying counter-clockwise orientation and adding borders. Create a custom theme, and use it to format the rest of the worksheet. Add a watermark or special worksheet background to dress up the sheet.

Create several views—All, Experiment Details Only, and Timeline Only. Adjust column widths as needed to display data and check spelling in the workbook. Print each view after making adjustments to the margins and print orientation as needed to produce a nice looking printout.

Redisplay all data and save the workbook. Resave it again as a template (in your Solutions folder), but only after deleting any sample data you may have added to aid in formatting. Close the workbook.

Illustration A

S11Experiment - Microsoft Excel

Science Class Experiments

Name: Jennifer Fulton

Experiment Details

Experiment Description

I submerged an egg in vinegar for four days, and then placed it in syrup for four more.

Prediction

The shell will dissolve and the egg will rot

Result

The shell remained intact and became enlarged, filled with the vinegar. When placed in syrup, the shell dissolved and the white evaporated. Instead, the inner membrane became hard, and the egg remained solid, even without its shell. The egg did not rot--there was no smell except the smell of vinegar.

Timeline

Visual Analysis

	Egg is intact and submerged in vinegar	A few bubbles have appeared on the surface of the shell	Egg shell appears more "bubbly"	The shell has cracked and is still bubbling	Egg is removed from vinegar and placed in syrup	The shell appears to be disappearing	I can see the inner, transparent membrane and it is hard	The white has disappeared, and only the yolk remains.
Date	10/5	10/6	10/7	10/8	10/9	10/10	10/11	10/12

Sheet1 / Sheet2 / Sheet3

Lesson | 2
Getting Tricky with Formulas and Graphics

Skills Covered

- **Conditional Sum Wizard**

- **Conditionally Summarize Data with AVERAGEIF and AVERAGEIFS**

Software Skills   With the Conditional Sum Wizard, you can quickly create a formula that totals only certain cells in a range, such as those cells that contain sales amounts for Indiana. The Conditional Sum Wizard takes the guesswork out of trying to use the IF function to perform the same task. On the other hand, sometimes a simple IF function is just what you need, as in the case of the AVERAGEIF and AVERAGEIFS functions.

Application Skills   Your boss at Wood Hills Animal Clinic has asked you to modify the monthly sales report and create an analysis of sales based on several factors such as animal type (cat versus dog, for example) and purpose (ear infection versus flea control for example).

TERMS

Add-in   An Excel feature that's not installed initially, but which you can easily add to the program when needed.

Conditional Sum Wizard   A series of dialog boxes that help you create an IF formula to total a given range, provided that the cells meet the criteria you set.

IF function   A special function that performs a calculation only if the cell meets given criteria.

NOTES

Conditional Sum Wizard

- Using the **Conditional Sum Wizard**, you can create a formula that uses the **IF function** to total a given range of cells that meet the criteria you specify.

  - For example, if you have a list of sales totals, you can use the Conditional Sum Wizard to total all sales over $10,000.

- The Conditional Sum Wizard is an **add-in** that's not initially installed; it needs to be loaded on first use.

- You can apply multiple conditions to the IF formula.

  - For example, you could tell the Conditional Sum Wizard to total only those sales that are $10,000 or more for stores in Boston.

Conditional Sum Wizard

Conditionally Summarize Data with AVERAGEIF and AVERAGEIFS

■ AVERAGEIF is a Statistical function that uses criteria you specify to calculate the average (the mean) of the values in a range.

■ If the value in a cell matches the criteria, then the associated value is added to a running average; if it doesn't match, then the value is skipped.

■ The format for an AVERAGEIF statement is =AVERAGEIF(*range, criteria, average_range*).

■ The *range* is the range of cells you want to test.

✓ *This can be any range—even one that contains text.*

■ The *criteria* is an expression that is either true or false, that defines which cells should be included.

✓ *The criteria is written using the special symbols listed in this section. You must enclose the criteria in quotation marks " ".*

■ The *average_range* is the range of cells whose values you want to average.

✓ *This can be the same range as the range specified earlier (in which case, you can omit the argument), or a completely different range altogether.*

■ For example, if you had a worksheet listing sales for several different products, you could average the total sales for products selling for $100 or more only by using this formula: =AVERAGEIF(D2:D55,">=100",G2:G55)

● Assume here that column D contains the price of the product being sold, and that column G contains the total sales amount for that sale.

● If column D contains a value equal to or greater than 100, then that record is added to the running average of sales.

✓ *Remember that you must enclose the criteria in quotation marks (" ").*

■ When entering the criteria, you can use any of the following conditional operators:

=	Equals	<>	Not equal to
>	Greater than	>=	Greater than or equal to
<	Less than	<=	Less than or equal to
&	Used for joining text		

■ If you do not use an operator when specifying criteria, then an equals sign is implied.

✓ *For example, if you want to average all the Widget products, you could specify "=Widget" or simply "Widget".*

■ AVERAGEIFS() is a function similar to AVERAGEIF() except that it allows you to enter multiple qualifying criteria.

■ The syntax for an AVERAGEIFS statement is =AVERAGEIFS(*average_range,criteria_range1,criteria1,etc.*)

● The *average_range* is the range of cells whose values you want to average.

● The *criteria_range1* is the range of cells you want to test.

● The *criteria1* is an expression that is either true or false, that defines which cells should be counted.

● You can add additional criteria_range and criteria arguments as needed. You can specify the same criteria_range or use a different one.

● All specified ranges must all be the same shape and size.

■ Using the earlier example, if you wanted to calculate the average all Widget sales with a value over $10,000, you could use a formula such as: =AVERAGEIFS(G2:G55,D2:D55,"Widget", G2:G55,">10000")

✓ *Again, column D contains the name of the product being sold, and column G contains the total amount for that sale.*

■ Like any other function, you can enter an AVERAGEIF or AVERAGEIFS function manually, use AutoComplete, or use the Insert Function and/or the Function Arguments dialog boxes to help you.

PROCEDURES

Install the Conditional Sum Wizard

1. Click **Office Button** 🏢 . . . [Alt], [F]
2. Click **Excel Options** . . . . [I]
3. Click **Add-ins** . . . . [↑][↑]/[↓]
4. Select Excel Add-ins from the **Manage** list
5. Click **Go** . . . . [Alt]+[G]
6. Click Conditional Sum Wizard . . . . [↑][↑]/[↓], [Spacebar]
7. Click **OK** . . . . [Enter]
8. Click **Yes** . . . . [Enter]

Use the Conditional Sum Wizard

1. Click inside the data range.

   ✓ *The data range is the range that contains the worksheet data, and column row labels.*

2. Click **Formulas** tab . . . . . [Alt], [M]

   Solutions Group

3. Click **Conditional Sum** button 🗙 . . . . [Y]
4. Verify the selected range and click **Next** . . . . [Enter]

   ✓ *The proper data range should be selected automatically—if it's wrong, click the Collapse Dialog button and select the range yourself before clicking **Next**.*

5. Select the **Column to sum**, if it's not already correct . . . . . . [Alt]+[S], [↑][↑]/[↓]
6. Select the **Column** to be checked for conditional values . . . . . . [Alt]+[C], [↑][↑]/[↓]
7. Select the **Is** condition operator . . . . [Alt]+[I], [↑][↑]/[↓]
8. Select **This value** and select a label . . . . [Alt]+[T], [↑][↑]/[↓]
9. Click **Add Condition** . . . . . [Alt]+[A]

   ✓ *You can repeat steps 6 to 9 to add additional conditions.*

10. Click **Next** . . . . [Enter]
11. Specify how you want to copy the formula to the worksheet:

    ■ **Copy just the formula to a single cell** . . . . [Alt]+[C]

    OR

    ■ **Copy the formula and conditional values** . . . [Alt]+[O]

12. Click **Next** . . . . [Enter]
13. Enter the cell location for the formula in the **Type or select a cell and then click Finish** box . . . . [Alt]+[T]

    OR

    Use the Collapse Dialog button to select the cell.

    ✓ *If you're copying the formula and the conditional values, specify a cell where you want to place each conditional value and click **Next**. Then specify the cell where you want to copy the formula.*

14. Click **Finish** . . . . [Enter]

    ✓ *The formulas created by the Conditional Sum Wizard are array formulas, and they work a little differently—if you edit an array formula, you must press Ctrl+Shift+Enter when you are done to lock in any changes you make.*

Enter AVERAGEIF Function

1. Click cell where result should display . . . . [→]/[←][↑][↑]/[↓]
2. Click **Formulas** tab . . . . . [Alt], [M]

   Function Library Group

3. Click **More Functions** button 📦 . . . . [Q]
4. Click **Statistical** . . . . [S]
5. Click **AVERAGEIF** . . . . . . [↑][↑]/[↓], [Enter]

   ✓ *The Function Arguments dialog box appears.*

6. Click **Range** text box.
7. Type the range to test.

   ✓ *You can select the range instead of typing it.*

8. Click **Criteria** text box . . . . . . [⇥]
9. Type condition.

   ✓ *Excel will automatically place the condition you type in quotations " ".*

10. Click **Average_range** text box.
11. Type the range to calculate.
12. Click **OK** . . . . [Enter]

Enter AVERAGEIFS Function

1. Click cell where result should display . . . . [→]/[←][↑][↑]/[↓]
2. Click **Formulas** tab . . . . . [Alt], [M]

   Function Library Group

3. Click **More Functions** button 📦 . . . . [Q]
4. Click **Statistical** . . . . [S]
5. Click **AVERAGEIFS** . . . . . [↑][↑]/[↓], [Enter]

   ✓ *The Function Arguments dialog box appears.*

6. Click **Average_range** text box.

   ✓ *You can select the range instead of typing it.*

7. Type the range to calculate.
8. Click **Criteria_range1** text box.
9. Type the range to test.
10. Click **Criteria1** box . . . . [⇥]
11. Type condition.

    ✓ *Excel will automatically place the condition you type in quotations " ".*

12. Click **Criteria_range2** text box . . . . [⇥]

13. Type the range to test against this new condition.

✓ *You can select the range instead of typing it. This range must be the same size and shape as the one in step 7.*

✓ *You can select the same range as used in step 7, or use a different range.*

14. Click **Criteria2** box . . . . 🔲

15. Type condition.

✓ *Excel will automatically place the condition you type in quotations " ".*

16. Repeat steps 12–15 to add additional conditions and ranges to test.

✓ *As you add criteria, they are individually numbered. Thus, the next criteria would be Criteria3.*

17. Click **OK**. . . . . 🔲

EXERCISE DIRECTIONS

1. Start Excel, if necessary.

2. Open 💿 **12AugDrugSales**.

3. Save the workbook as **12AugDrugSales_xx**.

4. In cell D99, enter a formula to compute the total sales revenues.

5. Use the Conditional Sum Wizard to create a formula that totals the revenues for dog care products only:

✓ *The Conditional Sum Wizard must be installed to complete this step. See the Procedures section for help.*

  a. Click a cell in the list such as A8, and click the Conditional Sum button on the Formulas tab.

  b. Make sure the range A7:K94 is selected, and then click Next.

  c. Select Total Sales from the *Column to sum* list, then choose To treat from the *Column* list, = from the *Is* list, and Dog from the *This* value list.

  d. Click Add Condition, then click Next.

  e. Choose Copy just the formula to a single cell, and choose Next.

  f. Choose cell D100, then click Finish.

6. Repeat these steps with the Conditional Sum Wizard to create formulas that total the sales for cat only, flea, flea and tick, and heartworm products. (See Illustration A.)

  • To calculate the "Other Sales," create a formula that subtracts the sales of flea, flea and tick, and heartworm products from the total sales in cell D99.

7. In cell D108, enter a formula to compute the total average sales.

8. In cell D109, use AVERAGEIF to create a formula that calculates the average revenues for dog care products only:

  a. Click the More Functions button on the Formulas tab, and choose Statistical, AVERAGEIF.

  b. Enter the Range C8:C94.

  c. Type **Dog** in the Criteria box.

  d. Enter the Average_range K8:K94.

9. Repeat these steps to create formulas that calculate the average sales for cat only, flea, flea and tick, and heartworm products. (See Illustration A.)

✓ *For the flea, flea and tick, and heartworm calculations, enter the Range B8:B94.*

10. To calculate the average of other sales (cell D115), you need to use AVERAGEIFS, and apply multiple conditions.

  a. Enter the Average_range K8:K94.

  b. Enter the Criteria_range1 B8:B94.

  c. Enter the Criteria1 <>Flea

  d. Enter the Criteria_range2 B8:B94.

  e. Enter the Criteria2 <>Flea and TIck

  f. Enter the Criteria_range3 B8:B94.

  g. Enter the Criteria3 <>Heartworm.

11. Apply the Accounting format with two decimal places to the range D99:D115.

12. Adjust column widths as needed.

13. Spell check the worksheet.

14. Print the worksheet.

15. Close the workbook, saving all changes.

	A	B	C	D	E	F
	S12AugDrugSales - Microsoft Excel					
98	**Sales Analysis**					
99		Total Sales		$ 263,465.96		
100		Sales of dog only products		$ 157,691.75		
101		Sales of cat only products		$ 24,091.11		
102						
103		Sales of flea products		$ 18,630.10		
104		Sales of flea and tick products		$ 1,748.85		
105		Sales of heartworm products		$ 70,944.70		
106		Other sales		$ 172,142.31		
107						
108		Average Sales		$ 3,028.34		
109		Average sales of dog only products		$ 3,583.90		
110		Average sales of cat only products		$ 1,853.16		
111						
112		Average sales of flea products		$ 1,693.65		
113		Average sales of flea and tick products		$ 874.43		
114		Average sales of heartworm products		$ 7,094.47		
115		Average of other sales		$ 2,689.72		
116						
117						
118						

ON YOUR OWN

1. Start Excel, if necessary.
2. Open ⊙ **12PetStoreSales**.
3. Save the file as **OXL12_*xx***.
4. The owner would like to analyze the sale of fish and accessories, the two highest profit items in the store.

   a. Use the Conditional Sum Wizard to compute the total sales for each sales person and record the results in cells D62:D63.

   b. Use AVERAGEIF to compute the average sales for each sales person and record the results in cells E62:E63.

   c. Use the Conditional Sum Wizard and two criteria to compute the total fish sales for each sales person and record the results in cells D66:D67.

   d. Use the Conditional Sum Wizard to compute the total accessories for each sales person and record the results in cell E66:E67.

   e. Use AVERAGEIFS to calculate the average fish sales for each sales person, and record the results in cells D70:D71.

   f. Use AVERAGEIFS to calculate the average accessories for each sales person, and record the results in cells E70:E71.

5. Apply Accounting format, 2 decimal places to all the results.
6. Adjust column widths as needed.
7. Spell check the worksheet.
8. Print the worksheet.
9. Close the workbook, saving all changes.

Business Connection

Skills for Success

Most employers expect employees to exhibit certain characteristics while on the job. These characteristics include basic courtesy, professionalism, and a positive attitude. Someone with a positive attitude is happier, easier to work with, and more productive. He or she is likely to look for a solution instead of dwelling on a problem, use compromise and cooperation to get along with others, and be willing to help out as needed. These are all qualities that make a better, successful employee.

Track Your Attitude

Do you have a positive attitude? Use Excel to track your outlook by recording daily events or occurrences to which you react either positively or negatively. For example, you might react negatively to a homework assignment but positively to a friend's invitation to work on the assignment together. Set up a worksheet in which you can record the number of positive and negative reactions you have each day. At the end of a week, you can determine whether you have a positive or a negative attitude. Write a brief essay explaining the results. Include information about why you think it is important to have a positive attitude in school and at work. Then, if your attitude tends toward the negative, work to change your reactions to be more positive.

Skills Covered

- **Format Text with Formulas**
- **Replace Text**

Software Skills   Using a series of simple text functions, such as PROPER, UPPER, LOWER, and SUBSTITUTE, you can quickly effect changes to text that's been entered incorrectly. For example, with the UPPER function, you can change the text in a cell to all uppercase.

Application Skills   As the new Human Resources Manager for PhotoTown, you've been busy getting familiar with their various employee and benefit related worksheets. It's just been brought to your attention that the Employee Listing has several problems, all text related. It's your hope that you can make the necessary corrections using Excel's vast array of text functions, avoiding the need to retype data.

TERMS

No new terms in this exercise.

NOTES

Format Text with Formulas

- If you enter your own text into a worksheet, chances are that you entered it correctly. For example, every sentence probably begins with a capital letter.

- If you're using text from another source, however, it may or may not be properly capitalized. Excel provides some functions that might be able to solve such a problem:
  - PROPER (*text*)—Capitalizes the first letter at the beginning of each word, plus any letters that follow any character that's not a letter, such as a number or a punctuation mark.
  - UPPER (*text*)—Changes all letters to uppercase.
  - LOWER (*text*)—Changes all letters to lowercase.

Replace Text

- Sometimes, all an old worksheet needs in order to be useful again is an update.

- One way in which you can update data (such as department names, cost codes, or old dates) is to substitute good text for the outdated text.
  - SUBSTITUTE(*text,old_text,new_text, instance_num*)—Replaces *old_text* with *new_text* in the cell you specify with the *text* argument. If you specify a particular *instance* of *old_text*, such as instance 3, then SUBSTITUTE replaces only that specific instance—the third instance—of *old_text* and not all of them.
  - REPLACE(*old_text,start_num,num_chars, new_text*)—Replaces *old_text* with *new_text*, beginning at the position (*start_num*) you specify. The argument *num_chars* tells Excel how many characters to replace. This allows you to replace 4 characters with only 2 if you want.

PROCEDURES

Enter PROPER Function

1. Click cell where result should
   display. . . . . →/←/↑/↓
2. Click **Formulas** tab . . . . . Alt, M

   Function Library Group

3. Click **Text** button 🅰 . . . . T
4. Click **PROPER** . . . . . . ↑/↓, Enter

   ✓ *The Function Arguments dialog box
   appears.*

5. Click **Text** text box.
6. Type a cell address, text (enclosed
   in quotations), or some formula
   that returns text as a result.

   ✓ *You can select the range instead of
   typing it.*

7. Click **OK**. . . . . Enter

Enter UPPER Function

1. Click cell where result should
   display. . . . . →/←/↑/↓
2. Click **Formulas** tab . . . . . Alt, M

   Function Library Group

3. Click **Text** button 🅰 . . . . T
4. Click **UPPER** . . . . ↑/↓, Enter

   ✓ *The Function Arguments dialog box
   appears.*

5. Click **Text** text box.
6. Type a cell address, text (enclosed
   in quotations), or some formula
   that returns text as a result.

   ✓ *You can select the range instead of
   typing it.*

7. Click **OK**. . . . . Enter

Enter LOWER Function

1. Click cell where result should
   display. . . . . →/←/↑/↓
2. Click **Formulas** tab . . . . . Alt, M

   Function Library Group

3. Click **Text** button 🅰 . . . . T
4. Click **LOWER** . . . . ↑/↓, Enter

   ✓ *The Function Arguments dialog box
   appears.*

5. Click **Text** text box.
6. Type a cell address, text (enclosed
   in quotations), or some formula
   that returns text as a result.

   ✓ *You can select the range instead of
   typing it.*

7. Click **OK**. . . . . Enter

Enter SUBSTITUTE Function

1. Click cell where result should
   display. . . . . →/←/↑/↓
2. Click **Formulas** tab . . . . . Alt, M

   Function Library Group

3. Click **Text** button 🅰 . . . . T
4. Click
   SUBSTITUTE . . . . ↑/↓, Enter

   ✓ *The Function Arguments dialog box
   appears.*

5. Click **Text** text box.
6. Type a cell address, text (enclosed
   in quotations), or some formula
   that returns text as a result.

   ✓ *You can select the range instead of
   typing it.*

7. Click **Old_text** text box.
8. Type the text you want to replace.
9. Click **New_text** text box.
10. Type the replacement text.
11. If desired, click **Instance_num**
    box.

12. Type the number of the specific
    instance you want to replace.

    ✓ *If you don't specify an Instance_num,
    then all instances of the Old_text are
    replaced with New_text.*

13. Click **OK**. . . . . Enter

Enter REPLACE Function

1. Click cell where result should
   display. . . . . →/←/↑/↓
2. Click **Formulas** tab . . . . . Alt, M

   Function Library Group

3. Click **Text** button 🅰 . . . . T
4. Click **REPLACE** . . . . . ↑/↓, Enter

   ✓ *The Function Arguments dialog box
   appears.*

5. Click **Old_text** text box.
6. Type a cell address, text (enclosed
   in quotations), or some formula
   that returns text as a result.

   ✓ *You can select the range instead of
   typing it.*

7. Click **Start_num** text box.
8. Type the position of the character where you want to begin the
   replacement.

   ✓ *For example, to begin replacing at
   the first two numbers in the text
   Emp200401, type 4.*

9. Click **Num_chars**.
10. Type the number of characters you
    want replaced, beginning with the
    starting position you specified in
    step 8.

    ✓ *For example, to replace the first two
    digits (20) in the text Emp200401,
    then type 2.*

11. Click **New_text** text box.
12. Type the replacement text.
13. Click **OK**. . . . . Enter

EXERCISE DIRECTIONS

1. Start Excel, if necessary.

2. Open 💿 **13PhotoTownEEListing**.

3. Save the workbook as **13PhotoTownEEListing_xx**.

4. The letters at the end of each department number should be capitalized; correct this by using UPPER:

   a. Click cell J8, then click the Text button on the Formulas bar and choose UPPER.

   b. In the Text box, type **E8** and click OK.

   c. Copy this formula down the range J9:J37.

   d. Copy the range J8:J37.

   e. Click cell E8, and paste only the values.

   ✓ *Use Paste Special to paste values only.*

5. The department names should be capitalized as well. You can correct this problem using PROPER:

   a. Click cell J8, and press Delete to clear its contents, then click the Text button on the Formulas bar and choose PROPER.

   b. In the Text box, type **F8** and click OK.

   c. Copy this formula down the range J9:J37.

   d. Copy the range J8:J37.

   e. Click cell F8, and paste only the values.

6. All the department numbers beginning with a 6 must be changed so they begin with a 9 instead. You'll make this change using SUBSTITUTE:

   a. Click cell J8, and press Delete to clear its contents, then click the Text button on the Formulas bar and choose SUBSTITUTE.

   b. In the Text box, type **E8**.

   c. In the Old_text box, type **6**.

   d. In the New_text box, type **9**.

   e. In the Instance_num box, type **1** and click OK.

   f. Copy this formula down the range J9:J37.

   g. Copy the range J8:J37.

   h. Click cell E8, and paste only the values. See Illustration A.

7. Delete the data in the range J8:J37.

8. Adjust column widths as needed.

9. Spell check the worksheet.

10. Print the worksheet.

11. Close the workbook, saving all changes.

Illustration A

	Employee ID	Title	First Name	Last Name	Department Number	Department Name	Rate	Soc Sec No.
8	63778	Mr.	Carlos	Altare	910412PR	Processing	$6.30	504-12-3131
9	71335	Mr.	Taneed	Black	218975AM	Asst. Manager	$7.00	775-15-1315
10	31524	Mrs.	Jan	Borough	911748QC	Quality Control	$6.50	727-25-6981
11	18946	Mr.	Shakur	Brown	482178CA	Cashier	$7.00	505-43-9587
12	22415	Mr.	Jairo	Campos	914522IN	Inker	$7.20	110-56-2897
13	20965	Mrs.	Rafiquil	Damir	911748QC	Quality Control	$6.15	102-33-5656
14	64121	Mrs.	Diana	Dogwood	918796SO	Special Orders	$6.20	821-55-3262
15	30388	Mrs.	Lucy	Fan	910412PR	Processing	$6.55	334-25-6959
16	44185	Mrs.	Jennifer	Flynn	482178CA	Cashier	$7.00	221-32-9585
17	32152	Ms.	Katerina	Flynn	271858KC	Kiosk Control	$7.10	107-45-9111
18	31885	Ms.	Kere	Freed	910412PR	Processing	$7.10	222-15-9484
19	33785	Mr.	Eram	Hassan	271858KC	Kiosk Control	$6.85	203-25-6984
20	55648	Mr.	Tyrell	Johnson	218975AM	Asst. Manager	$6.50	468-25-9684
21	60219	Ms.	Verna	Latinz	911748QC	Quality Control	$6.30	705-85-6352
22	28645	Mr.	Wu	Lee	918796SO	Special Orders	$7.00	255-41-9784
23	67415	Mr.	Shamir	Lewis	910412PR	Processing	$7.10	112-42-7897
24	27995	Mrs.	Maria	Navarro	910412PR	Processing	$6.30	302-42-8465
25	32151	Mr.	Tony	Navarro	271858KC	Kiosk Control	$6.35	401-78-9855
26	28499	Mr.	Chu Gi	Nguyen	911748QC	Quality Control	$6.85	823-55-6487
27	17564	Mr.	Juan	Nuniez	914522IN	Inker	$7.00	208-65-4932
28	14558	Mr.	Akira	Ota	911748QC	Quality Control	$7.25	285-68-9853
29	31022	Mrs.	Meghan	Ryan	910412PR	Processing	$7.00	421-85-6452
30	41885	Mrs.	Kate	Scott	482178CA	Cashier	$6.85	489-55-4862
31	25448	Mr.	Jyoti	Shaw	911748QC	Quality Control	$6.50	389-24-6567
32	23151	Ms.	Jewel	Vidito	911748QC	Quality Control	$6.55	885-63-7158
33	37785	Mrs.	Corrine	Walters	918796SO	Special Orders	$6.65	622-34-8891
34	58945	Mrs.	Antonia	Whitney	271858KC	Kiosk Control	$6.75	312-86-7141
35	57445	Mr.	Shale	Wilson	482178CA	Cashier	$7.00	375-86-3425
36	36684	Mrs.	Shiree	Wilson	482178CA	Cashier	$7.10	415-65-6658
37	55412	Mrs.	Su	Yamaguchi	910412PR	Processing	$6.30	324-75-8021

ON YOUR OWN

1. Start Excel, if necessary.

2. Open ⌨ **OXL05_xx**, created in the On Your Own section of Exercise 5 or open 💿 **13PetesEEList**.

3. Save the file as **OXL13_xx**.

4. Type **Adjusted Rate** in cell P9. Copy the format from cell O9.

5. The new rates you've just calculated for everyone need to be adjusted. The owner wants all the new rates to end in .50, regardless of whether that means an adjustment up or down.

   a. Using REPLACE, you can easily change the value after the decimal place in each new rate to .50.

   b. The only complication is that you'll need to use an IF statement. If a new rate is over 9.99, then you want to tell REPLACE to switch out the 4th and 5th digits with .50; otherwise, you want REPLACE to replace the 3rd and 4th digits with .50 instead.

   c. After entering the formula in cell P10, copy it down the column.

   d. Right-align the values in column P.

6. Adjust column widths as needed.

7. Spell check the worksheet.

8. Print the worksheet.

9. Close the workbook, saving all changes.

Skills Covered

- **Formula Error Checking**
- **Error Messages**
- **Audit Formulas**

- **Use the Watch Window**
- **Evaluate a Formula**
- **Suppress Errors While Printing**

Software Skills If you have a problem with formulas in a large or complex worksheet, working through each formula to locate the values in the cells it references and to verify that everything is all right can be a tedious, complex job unless you use Excel's error and formula auditing features.

Application Skills It looks like the sale of your old building and the purchase of a new headquarters for the Wood Hills Animal Clinic is going to go through. Before you can get final approval for your loan, however, you must prepare a balance sheet and a profit and loss statement. You've been working on the profit and loss statement, and there's just something wrong with the numbers. Your hope is that Excel's powerful formula auditing tools can help you sort out the problem.

TERMS

Dependents Formulas whose results depend on the value in a cell.

Evaluate View the intermediate results step-by-step, as Excel solves a formula.

Precedent A cell referenced in a formula.

Profit and loss statement A financial document that shows revenues, costs, and expenses incurred during a period of time.

Watch Window Special toolbar that allows you to watch the results of formulas change as you change data.

NOTES

Formula Error Checking

- As you enter formulas into a worksheet, Excel automatically checks them for various types of errors.

- If an error is found, that cell is highlighted with a small green triangle in its upper left-hand corner.

- When you click the arrow on the Error Options button, a list of options appears. Select one of these options (even the option, Ignore Error) to resolve the problem.

Error Options Menu

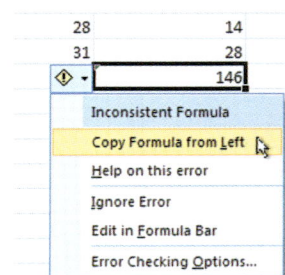

28	14
31	28
◇ ▾	146

Inconsistent Formula
Copy Formula from Left
Help on this error
Ignore Error
Edit in Formula Bar
Error Checking Options...

- You can redisplay errors that you ignored earlier if you like.
- You can also turn off automatic error checking, although that's usually not a good idea.
- Excel checks for the following errors:
  - Formulas that result in an error value, such as #DIV/0.

  ✓ *You'll learn more about error values and their cause in the section "Error Messages."*

  - Formulas containing a text date entered using a two-digit year, which might be misinterpreted, as in =YEAR("02/20/27"), which could refer to 02/20/2027 or 02/20/1927.
  - Numbers stored as text rather than actual numbers—these could cause sorting and other errors.
  - Formulas that are inconsistent with formulas in surrounding cells.

  ✓ *For example, if Excel notices the pattern =SUM(A2:A10), =SUM(B2:B10) in two adjacent cells, and then sees the formula =SUM(C2:C4) in another adjacent cell, it will flag it as a possible mistake because it doesn't fit the pattern of the other formulas.*

  - Formulas that omit adjacent cells.

  ✓ *For example, the formula =AVERAGE(C3:C10) would be flagged if cells C11, C12, and so on contain data which perhaps should be included in the range used in the formula.*

  - An unprotected formula.

  ✓ *If you turn on worksheet protection (which you'll learn about in Exercise 38), cells are typically all protected against changes. You can selectively "unprotect" the cells you want to allow others to enter data into. However, if you unprotect a cell with a formula, Excel will see that as a possible error, because it's unusual that you would want someone else to change your formulas.*

  - A formula that refers to empty cells.
  - Invalid data is entered in a cell.
  - Inconsistent formula in a calculated table column.
- When you find an error in a formula, one way in which you might need to correct it is to change the cell(s) that the formula references. For example, you might need to change the formula =SUM(D2:D10) so that it reads =SUM(D2:D12).
  - When you click a cell with a formula, and then click in the Formula bar, the cells referenced by the formula are outlined with colored borders.

- You can drag these colored borders and drop them on different cells, in order to change the cells used in the formula.
- You can also resize a colored border to make the formula reference more or less cells in that range.

Error Messages

- The following is a list of some error messages you might get if you enter data or formulas incorrectly:
  - **####**—The cell contains an entry that's wider than the cell can display. In most cases, you can just widen the column to correct the problem.
  - **#VALUE!**—The wrong type of data was used in a formula. Possible causes are entering text when a formula requires a number or logical value, or entering a range in a formula or function that requires a single value.
  - **#DIV/0!**—A formula is attempting to divide a value by zero. For example, if the value in cell B5 in the formula =A5/B5 is zero, or if cell B5 is empty, the result will be the #DIV/0! error.
  - **#NAME?**—Excel doesn't recognize text in the formula. Possible causes include a misspelling or using a nonexistent range name, using a label in a formula if the Accept labels in formulas option is turned off, or omitting a colon (:) in a range reference.
  - **#N/A**—No value is available to the formula or function. Possible causes include omitting a required argument in a formula or function or entering an invalid argument in a formula or function.
  - **#REF!**—A cell reference is invalid. Possible causes include deleting cells referred to by formulas.
  - **#NUM**—Indicates a problem with a number in a formula or function. Possible causes include using a nonnumeric argument in a function that requires a numeric argument, or entering a formula that produces a number too large or too small for Excel to represent.
  - **#NULL!**—The formula contains incorrect operators or cell references using ranges in formulas. For example, if you left the comma out of the following formula, a #NULL! error would occur: SUM(A1:A6,C1:C6).

- A circular reference is a special kind of error that's caused when a formula references itself. For example, if you're adding the values of a group of cells and include the cell that contains the formula, you are creating an endless loop, which generates a circular reference error.
  - When a circular reference occurs, an error message appears, followed by a Help screen filled with tips to help you correct the error.
  - Until you correct a circular reference, the status bar displays the word "Circular" and the address of the cell(s) with the Circular Reference error.
  - You can also locate any cell(s) that contain circular references by using the Circular References option on the Error Checking button on the Formulas toolbar.

Locate a circular reference

Audit Formulas

- If you're having a problem with a formula, you can check its result with the buttons in the Formula Auditing group on the Formulas tab.

Formula Auditing group

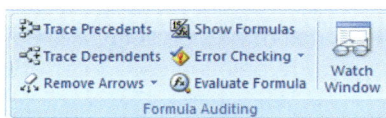

- Using the Error Checking option on the Error Checking button, you can check your formulas for errors. This allows you to review each cell marked by a green triangle and to select an option to resolve each error, one at a time.
- You can also change the conditions that flag an error and reset ignored errors from the Error Checking dialog box.
- With the Trace Precedents button, you can also trace a formula's **precedents**—cells referred to by the formula.
  - ✓ *For example, in the formula =C2/D4, cells C2 and D4 are precedents to the cell that contains the formula.*

- If you're worried about changing the value in a cell, you can trace its **dependents** with the Trace Dependents button.
  - A dependent is a cell whose value depends on the value in another cell.
  - ✓ *For example, suppose cell D5 contains the formula =C2/D4. If you traced the dependents of cell C2, Excel would point to cell D5, since that cell's value depends on the value in cell C2.*
- When you trace precedents or dependents, arrows point to the related cells.

Tracing the precedents of a formula

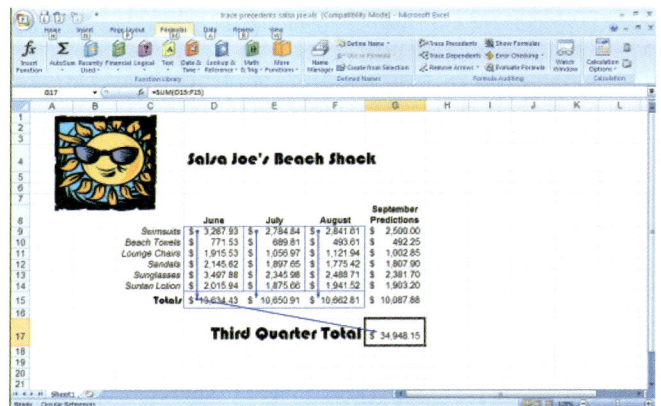

- If a formula contains an error, you can use the Trace Error option on the Error Checking button to trace the problem.

Use the Watch Window

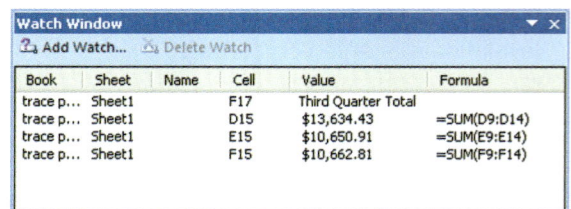

- One of the buttons in the Formula Auditing group displays the **Watch Window**.

The Watch Window

- Using the Watch Window, you can watch the results of your formulas change as you change other data, even if that formula is located in a cell that's out of view, on another worksheet, or located in another open workbook.
- You can watch multiple cells and their formulas if you like.
- Since the Watch Window is actually a task pane, you can dock it along any side of the workbook window, or float it in the middle.

Evaluate a Formula

- One way in which you can determine the problem with a formula is to **evaluate** it.
- When you evaluate a formula, you display each intermediate result, as Excel solves the formula step by step.

Evaluate a formula

Evaluate Formula dialog box

Reference:
Sheet1!$P$10 = IF(TRUE,REPLACE(O10,4,2,50),REPLACE(O10,3,2,50))

Sheet1!$O$10 = J10+N10

Sheet1!$J$10 = $11.25

The cell currently being evaluated contains a constant.

Evaluate | Step In | Step Out | Close

Suppress Errors While Printing

- You can control how errors appear when printing a worksheet.
- For example, instead of printing the error #DIV/0 in a cell, you can print #N/A, --, or nothing at all.

PROCEDURES

Trace Dependents

1. Select the cell containing data used by a formula.
2. Click **Formulas** tab . . . . . [Alt], [M]

   Formula Auditing Group

3. Click **Trace Dependents** button [icon] . . . . [D]
4. Repeat step 3 as needed to display all dependents for the selected cell.

Trace Precedents

1. Select cell containing formula.
2. Click **Formulas** tab . . . . . [Alt], [M]

   Formula Auditing Group

3. Click **Trace Precedents** button [icon] . . . . [P]
4. Repeat step 3 as needed to display all precedents for the selected cell.

Remove Tracer Arrows

1. Select the cell containing tracer arrows.
2. Click **Formulas** tab . . . . . [Alt], [M]

   Formula Auditing Group

3. Click **Remove Arrows** button [icon] . . . . [A]
4. Specify which arrows to remove:
   - **Remove Precedent Arrows** . . . . [P]
   - **Remove Dependent Arrows** . . . . [D]

Remove All Tracer Arrows

1. Select the cell containing tracer arrows.
2. Click **Formulas** tab . . . . . [Alt], [M]

   Formula Auditing Group

3. Click arrow on **Remove Arrows** button [icon] . . . . [A]
4. Click **Remove Arrows** . . . . [A]

Check for Errors

1. Click **Formulas** tab . . . . . [Alt], [M]

   Formula Auditing Group

2. Click **Error Checking** button [icon] . . . . [K]
3. Click **Error Checking** . . . . [K]
4. Click the appropriate button:

   ✓ *Buttons vary based on the error; buttons not listed here may appear.*

   - To ignore the error, click **Ignore Error** . . . . [I]
   - To get help, click **Help on this error** . . . . [I]
   - To step through the calculation, click **Show Calculation Steps** . . . . [C]
   - To correct the error manually, click **Edit in Formula Bar** . . . . [F]

5. If needed, click **Resume** . . . . . [S]
6. Click **Next** . . . . [N]
7. Click **OK** . . . . [Enter]

Trace an Error in a Formula

1. Select cell that contains a formula with an error message such as #NULL!
2. Click **Formulas** tab . . . . . Alt , M

   Formula Auditing Group

3. Click arrow on **Error Checking** button 🔷 . . . . K
4. Click **Trace Error** . . . . E

   ✓ *Precedent and dependent cells are indicated by arrows.*

Watch Formulas

1. Click **Formulas** tab . . . . . Alt , M

   Formula Auditing Group

2. Click **Watch Window** button 🔲 . . . . W
3. To add a cell to the Watch Window, click **Add Watch** button 🔲 Add Watch... .
4. Select the cell(s) whose value you wish to observe.
5. Click **Add** button

   Add . . . . Alt + A

6. Repeat steps 4 to 5 as needed to add additional cells to the Watch Window.

Remove a Watch

1. Select the watch to remove from the Watch Window.
2. Click **Delete Watch** button 🔲 Delete Watch .

Evaluate a Formula

1. Click the cell whose formula you wish to evaluate.
2. Click **Formulas** tab . . . . . Alt , M

   Formula Auditing Group

3. Click **Evaluating Formula** button 🔲 V
4. Click **Evaluate** to have Excel solve the underlined portion of the formula . . . . Alt + E

   OR

   a. Click **Step In** to display the exact address and value of the underlined cell . . . . Alt + I
   b. Click **Step Out** to continue to evaluate the formula . . . . Alt + O

5. Click **Evaluate** as needed to step-through the intermediate formula results until the formula is solved . . . . Alt + E
6. When the final result is displayed, select an option:

   ■ To review the formula again, click **Restart** button . . Alt + E

   OR

   ■ To close the Evaluate Formula window, click **Close** . . . . Alt + C

Suppress Errors While Printing

1. Click **Page Layout** tab . . . Alt , P

   Sheet Options Group

2. Click **Sheet Options dialog box launcher** button 🔲 . . . . . S , O
3. Select an option from the **Cell errors as** list . . . . Alt + E , ↓/↑ , Enter
4. Click **Print** . . . . Alt + P
5. Click **OK** . . . . Enter

EXERCISE DIRECTIONS

1. Start Excel, if necessary.
2. Open 💿 **14BalSheetP&L**.

   ✓ *Click Cancel when you see the notice about the circular reference error. You will correct that error and others in this exercise.*

3. Save the workbook as **14BalSheetP&L_xx**.
4. Change to the P&L worksheet.
5. Display the Watch Window by clicking the Watch Window button on the Formulas tab.
   a. Click the Add Watch button.
   b. Type or select cell E16 and click Add.
   c. Repeat steps a-b to add cells E23, E57, E61, E64.

6. List the dependents of the following cells:
   a. D28

      Dependent cell(s):_____
   b. E56

      Dependent cell(s):_____
   c. D60

      Dependent cell(s):_____
7. List the precedents of the following cells:
   a. E61

      Precedent cell(s):_____
   b. E43

      Precedent cell(s):_____
   c. E64

      Precedent cell(s):_____

8. Since the status bar tells you that cell E57 contains a circular reference, let's begin there.

   a. Click cell E57, and then click the Trace Precedents button three times to show all precedents.

   b. Even though the arrows do not show it very clearly, cell E57 is its own precedent, and that's what's causing the circular error.

   c. Clear the arrows.

   d. Click in the Formula bar.

   e. Edit the formula to read **=SUM(E32,E43,E56)**.

   f. Press Enter to complete the edit.

9. That's cleared off the circular reference error from the status bar, but it seems you still have problems. Go ahead and print the worksheet, replacing cell errors such as the one shown in cell E64 with a simple #N/A.

10. Now let's see if we can clear up that #DIV/0! error.

    a. Click cell E64 and click Error Checking button.

    b. Click Show Calculation Steps to evaluate the formula.

    ✓ *It looks like one of the precedent cells is set to zero, and when Excel tries to divide by zero, it gets an error.*

    c. Click Close to close the dialog box, then click the Close button on the Error Checking dialog box.

    d. Click the Error Checking button arrow, and then choose Trace Error.

    ✓ *Arrows appear, tracing the precedent cells.*

    e. There it is! The formula points to cell E62, and it's an empty cell. Change the formula in cell E64 to =E61/E63

    ✓ *You can retype the formula, or simply click in the formula bar and then drag the colored outline down to cell E63.*

11. There's still something wrong, because you know the net income is greater than zero:

    ✓ *Why is the cost of goods sold (the cost of selling pet medicines and supplies) a negative number? Let's evaluate it.*

    a. Click cell E16.

    b. Click the Trace Precedents button once.

    c. Cost of goods sold is equal to the cost of buying all that inventory, minus the value of any remaining inventory, so that's not the problem. Click the Trace Precedents button again.

    d. Why is the inventory value equal to zero? Click the Trace Precedents button again so you can see where that number is coming from.

✓ *A black arrow appears, with a worksheet icon at the end of it. This tells you that the cell being referenced is located on another worksheet, or in another workbook.*

   e. Double-click the black arrow (not the worksheet icon) so you can see the cell that's being addressed on some other worksheet.

✓ *You'll see the Go To dialog box. As long as the referenced worksheet or workbook is open, you can use it to display the referenced cell. If a workbook is being referenced and that workbook is not open, then following these next few steps will result in an "Invalid reference" error. Open the workbook and try these steps again, and Excel will automatically switch workbooks to display the referenced cell.*

   f. In the Go To dialog box, select the cell address in the listing, then click OK.

   g. It's referencing an empty cell on the BalanceSheet worksheet. It should reference cell C15.

   h. Change back to the P&L worksheet, and click cell D12.

   i. Type **=**, then change to the BalanceSheet worksheet and click cell C15.

   j. Press Enter to complete the formula.

   k. Click the Remove Arrows button.

12. That's better, but the Gross Profit should be higher than that, considering you had over 3 million dollars of patient revenue.

    a. Click cell E23.

    b. Click the Trace Precedents button.

    c. That's the problem. The formula doesn't include the patient income. Edit the formula to read **=E9-E16+E21**.

    d. The $2 earnings per share of stock seems about right, but it's not completely accurate since it's being rounded up. Increase the number of decimal places in cell E64 to 2.

13. Now that you've found all the errors, you can clear the Watch Window.

    a. Click the first entry in the Watch Window.

    b. Click Delete Watch.

    c. Select the remaining entries and click Delete Watch.

    d. Close the Watch Window.

14. Adjust column widths as necessary.

15. Spell check the worksheet.

16. Print the worksheet again.

17. Close the workbook, saving all changes.

ON YOUR OWN

1. Start Excel, if necessary.
2. Open 🔵 **14Earnings**.
3. Save the workbook as **OXL14_xx**.
4. Create formulas that calculate the commission and bonuses for each salesperson:
   a. Commissions are calculated by taking the sales amount times a percentage that varies from year to year.
   b. In the commission column, use an absolute reference when referring to cell B9, where you will later enter a commission rate.
   c. Bonuses, when applicable, are given as a flat dollar amount that also varies from year to year.
   d. In the bonus column, use an absolute reference when referring to cell B10, where you will later enter a bonus amount.
   e. Sales personnel receive a bonus only if their sales are over $40,000.
5. Create formulas that calculate the total earnings, which is the total of commissions and bonuses.

6. Click any cell in the commission column and trace the precedents. Remove the arrows.
7. Click any cell in the bonus column and trace the precedents. Remove the arrows.
8. Click any cell in the total earnings column and trace the precedents. Remove the arrows.
9. Type **0.06** in cell B9 and type **$200** in cell B10. Apply the Percentage format, zero decimal places, to cell B9. See Illustration A.
10. Click cell B9 and trace its dependents. Remove the arrows.
11. Click cell B10 and trace its dependents. Remove the arrows.
12. Click any cell in the sales column and trace its dependents. Remove the arrows.
13. Evaluate a formula in column E.
14. Adjust column widths as necessary.
15. Spell check the worksheet.
16. Print the worksheet.
17. Close the workbook, saving all changes.

Illustration A

SOXL14 - Microsoft Excel

	A	B	C	D	E	F	G	H	I
1	**Certificate of Deposit Income Evaluation**								
2	Present value	$5,000.00		Value at 3 years	$7,256.20				
3	Interest rate	2.50%		Value at 4 years	$8,046.62				
4	Term (in years)	5		Value at maturity	$8,857.03				
5	Contribution each month	$50.00							
6									
7	Month	Balance	Interest Earned	Contribution	New Balance (Balance+Interest+Contribution)				
8	1	5,000.00	10.42	50.00	5,060.42				
9	2	5,060.42	10.54	50.00	5,120.96				
10	3	5,120.96	10.67	50.00	5,181.63				
11	4	5,181.63	10.80	50.00	5,242.42				
12	5	5,242.42	10.92	50.00	5,303.34				
13	6	5,303.34	11.05	50.00	5,364.39				
14	7	5,364.39	11.18	50.00	5,425.57				
15	8	5,425.57	11.30	50.00	5,486.87				
16	9	5,486.87	11.43	50.00	5,548.30				
17	10	5,548.30	11.56	50.00	5,609.86				
18	11	5,609.86	11.69	50.00	5,671.55				
19	12	5,671.55	11.82	50.00	5,733.37				
20	13	5,733.37	11.94	50.00	5,795.31				
21	14	5,795.31	12.07	50.00	5,857.38				
22	15	5,857.38	12.20	50.00	5,919.59				
23	16	5,919.59	12.33	50.00	5,981.92				
24	17	5,981.92	12.46	50.00	6,044.38				
25	18	6,044.38	12.59	50.00	6,106.97				
26	19	6,106.97	12.72	50.00	6,169.70				
27	20	6,169.70	12.85	50.00	6,232.55				
28	21	6,232.55	12.98	50.00	6,295.53				
29	22	6,295.53	13.12	50.00	6,358.65				
30	23	6,358.65	13.25	50.00	6,421.90				
31	24	6,421.90	13.38	50.00	6,485.28				
32	25	6,485.28	13.51	50.00	6,548.79				
33	26	6,548.79	13.64	50.00	6,612.43				
34	27	6,612.43	13.78	50.00	6,676.21				
35	28	6,676.21	13.91	50.00	6,740.12				
36	29	6,740.12	14.04	50.00	6,804.16				
37	30	6,804.16	14.18	50.00	6,868.33				
38	31	6,868.33	14.31	50.00	6,932.64				
39	32	6,932.64	14.44	50.00	6,997.08				
40	33	6,997.08	14.58	50.00	7,061.66				

CD Income

Skills Covered

- **Draw Shapes**
- **Resize, Group, Align, and Arrange Shapes**

Software Skills After putting all that hard work into designing and entering data for a worksheet, of course you want it to look its best. You've learned how to add formatting, color, and borders to a worksheet to enhance its appeal. But to make your worksheet stand out from all the rest, you may need to do something "unexpected," such as adding your own art. You can insert predesigned shapes (such as stars or arrows) or combine them to create your own designs.

Application Skills You're the accountant at Wood Hills Animal Clinic, and you're going over the profit and loss statement. You notice that the cost of goods sold has gone down (caused by decreased inventory costs), so you want to create some shapes that help call attention to that for the presentation you'll be making at the next meeting.

TERMS

Adjustment handle A yellow diamond-shaped handle that appears with some objects. You can drag this handle to manipulate the shape of the object, such as the width of a wide arrow, or the tip of a speaking bubble's pointer.

Group Objects can be grouped together so they can act as a single object. Grouping makes it easier to move or resize a drawing that consists of several objects.

Handles Small white circles that appear around the perimeter of the active drawing object. You can resize an object by dragging one of these handles.

Order The position of an object with respect to other objects that are layered or in a stack.

Shape A predesigned object (such as a banner or star) that can be drawn with a single dragging motion.

Stack A group of drawing objects layered on top of one another, possibly partially overlapping. Use the Order command to change the position of a selected object within the stack.

NOTES

Draw Shapes

- With the Shapes button in the Illustrations group of the Insert tab, you can create many **shapes**.
- Add lines, arrows, starbursts, rectangles, and banners to highlight important information in your worksheet.
- You can also add a text box or a callout—a shape in which you can type your own text.

- A text box or callout, like other shapes, can be placed anywhere on the worksheet.

  ✓ *You'll learn how to add text boxes in Exercise 17.*

- The Shapes button presents you with a palette of shapes sorted by category that makes it easy for you to select the shape you want to insert.
- To insert a shape, simply select the shape you want, and then drag in a cell to create it—no actual "drawing" needed.

- After inserting a shape, you can format it as needed.

  ✓ *See Exercise 16.*

The Shapes palette

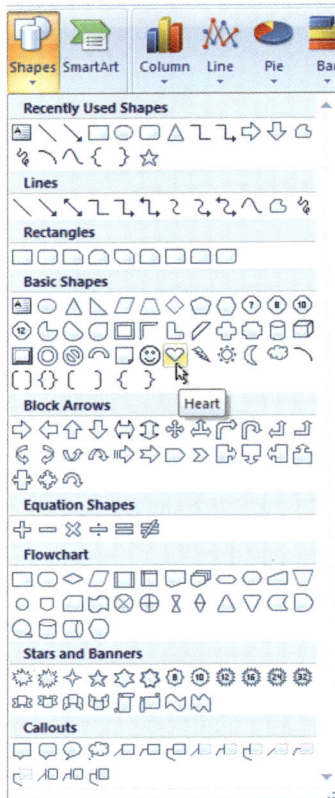

Resize, Group, Align, and Arrange Shapes

- A Shape can also be resized, moved, and copied, like any other object (such as clip art).
  - To resize an object, drag one of the selection **handles**.
  - To manipulate the shape of an object, drag the **adjustment handle** if one is available with that particular object.
- You can move shapes so that they partially cover other shapes.
  - To move a shape, drag it.
  - To position a shape more precisely, use Snap to Grid. When you drag a shape, it snaps automatically to the closest gridline or half-gridline.
  - The Snap to Shape command is similar, but it snaps a shape to the edge of a nearby shape when you drag the first shape close enough.

- Shapes can be aligned in relation to each other automatically.
  - For example, you might align objects so that their top edges line up.
  - Shapes can be aligned along their left, right, top, or bottom edges.
  - Shapes can also be aligned horizontally through their middles.
- When needed, you can change the **order** of objects that are layered (in a **stack**) so that a particular object appears "on top" or "behind" another.
- To select an object, you simply click it.
  - Sometimes, selecting one object in a stack is difficult because the objects overlap and even obscure other objects below them in the stack.
  - The Selection Pane makes it easy to select a specific object because all the objects on a worksheet appear in a list. To select one, click it.
  - The Selection Pane also makes it easy to rearrange objects in the stack.

Selection Pane

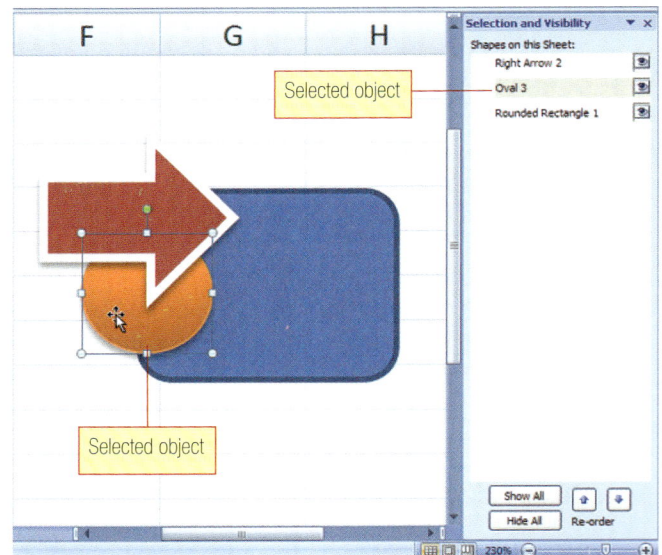

- You can **group** two or more objects together so they act as one object.

PROCEDURES

Draw a Shape

1. Click **Insert** tab . . . . `Alt`, `N`

   Illustrations Group

2. Click **Shapes** button
   . . . . `S`, `H`
3. Click the desired
   shape . . . . `→`/`←`/`↑`/`↓`, `Enter`
4. Click in the worksheet or chart where you want to draw the shape.
5. Drag to create the shape.

   ✓ Use the **Shift**, **Alt**, and **Ctrl** keys to affect the shapes as you draw. For example, hold down **Shift** while drawing a rectangle to draw a perfect square, or to size whatever you're drawing proportionally. If you press **Alt**, the shape is sized to fit the cells in which it's drawn. Press **Ctrl** and the shape is drawn outward from its center.

   ✓ If you're drawing a line or arrow, you can connect it to an existing shape by moving the mouse pointer over the shape and clicking the connection point to which you want to attach the line/arrow. After clicking, drag as normal to draw the line/arrow.

Draw a Scribble Line

1. Click **Insert** tab . . . . `Alt`, `N`

   Illustrations Group

2. Click **Shapes** button
   . . . . `S`, `H`
3. Click the **Scribble** line
   shape . . . . `→`/`←`/`↑`/`↓`, `Enter`
4. Drag in any direction to draw the scribble line.

Draw a Freeform Line

1. Click **Insert** tab . . . . `Alt`, `N`

   Illustrations Group

2. Click **Shapes** button
   . . . . `S`, `H`
3. Click the **Freeform** line
   shape . . . . `→`/`←`/`↑`/`↓`, `Enter`
4. Click in the worksheet or chart where you want to start the first line segment.
5. Drag to start the first segment of the line.
6. Click again to start a new segment.
7. Repeat step 6 to add as many line segments as you want.
8. Double-click to end the line.

Display Selection Pane

1. Click **Page Layout** tab . . . `Alt`, `P`

   Editing Group

2. Click **Selection Pane**
   button . . . . `A`, `P`
3. Click object's name in Selection
   Pane . . . . `↑`/`↓`, `Enter`

Select an Object

- Click an object.

   ✓ Press Ctrl and click to select multiple objects.

   ✓ After an object is selected, selection handles appear around its perimeter.

   OR

- Click the object's name in the Selection Pane.

   ✓ Press Ctrl and click to select multiple objects.

   ✓ After an object is selected, selection handles appear around its perimeter.

   OR

a. Click **Home** tab . . . . . `Alt`, `H`

Editing Group

b. Click **Find & Select**
   button . . . . `F`, `D`
c. Click **Select Objects** . . . . . `O`
d. Drag to draw an outline around the shape or shapes to select.

Change a Shape to a Different Shape

1. Select the shape you want to change.
2. Click **Format** tab . . . `Alt`, `J`, `D`

   Insert Shapes Group

3. Click **Edit Shape** button . . . `E`
4. Click the shape you want to
   use . . . . `→`/`←`/`↑`/`↓`, `Enter`

Resize Object

1. Click object to select it.
2. Position mouse pointer over a handle.

   - Click handle and drag outward to make the shape larger, or inward to make it smaller.
   - To resize the object proportionally, press `Shift` and drag a corner handle.
   - To resize the object in one direction, drag the handle in that direction.
   - To resize the object from the center outward, press `Ctrl` and drag a handle.
   - To resize the object proportionally from the center outward, press `Ctrl`+`Shift` and drag a corner handle.
   - If a yellow diamond-shaped adjustment handle appears with the object, you can drag it to manipulate the shape of the object.

3. Release mouse button.

Move Object

1. Click object to select it.
2. Position mouse pointer over shape.

   ✓ *Pointer changes to* 🔧.

3. Press and hold mouse button as you drag object.

   ✓ *You can position an object more precisely by choosing either Snap to Grid or Snap to Shape from the Align menu on the Format tab.*

4. Release mouse button.

Delete an Object

1. Select the object you want to remove.
2. Press . . . . `Delete`

Bring a Stacked Object to the Front

1. Select object in a group of objects that you wish to bring forward within the stack.
2. Click **Format** tab . . . `Alt`, `J`, `D`

   `Arrange Group`

3. Click arrow on **Bring to Front** button 🔳 . . . . `A`, `F`
4. Click **Bring to Front** . . . . `R`

   OR

   Click **Bring Forward** . . . . `F`

   ✓ *The **Bring Forward** button moves the object one place at a time in the stack. You may have to click this button repeatedly to move the object to the correct position.*

Send a Stacked Shape to the Back

1. Select object in a group of objects that you wish to send backward within the stack.
2. Click **Format** tab . . . `Alt`, `J`, `D`

   `Arrange Group`

3. Click arrow on **Send to Back** button 🔳 . . . . `A`, `E`
4. Click **Send to Back** . . . . `K`

   OR

   Click **Send Backward** . . . . `B`

   ✓ *The **Send Backward** button moves the object one place at a time in the stack. You may have to click this button repeatedly to move the object to the correct position.*

Group Objects

   ✓ *Grouped objects can be resized, formatted, copied, deleted, and moved as one object.*

1. Select the objects you want to group.
2. Click **Format** tab . . . `Alt`, `J`, `D`

   `Arrange Group`

3. Click **Group** button 🔳 . . . `A`, `G`
4. Click **Group** . . . . `G`

Ungroup Objects and Regroup Objects

1. Select the grouped objects.
2. Click **Format** tab . . . `Alt`, `J`, `D`

   `Arrange Group`

3. Click **Group** button 🔳 . . . `A`, `G`
4. Click **Ungroup** . . . . `U`
5. Leave ungrouped if you wish, or make adjustments and then:

   a. Reselect the previously grouped objects if needed.

   b. Click **Format** tab . . . . `Alt`, `J`, `D`

   `Arrange Group`

   c. Click **Group** button 🔳 . . . . `A`, `G`

   d. Click **Regroup** . . . . `E`

Align Objects

1. Select the objects to align.
2. Click **Format** tab . . . `Alt`, `J`, `D`

   `Arrange Group`

3. Click arrow on **Align** button 🔳 . . . . `A`, `A`
4. Select an option:

   ■ **Align Left** . . . . `L`
   ■ **Align Center** . . . . `C`
   ■ **Align Right** . . . . `R`
   ■ **Align Top** . . . . `T`
   ■ **Align Middle** . . . . `M`
   ■ **Align Bottom** . . . . `B`

EXERCISE DIRECTIONS

1. Start Excel, if necessary.

2. Open 🖮 **14BalSheetP&L** or ⊙ **15BalSheetP&L**.

3. Save the file as **15BalSheetP&L_xx**.

4. Add a rectangle to the right of the Cost of Goods Sold amount (E16):

   a. Click the Shapes button on the Insert tab.

   b. Select the Rounded Rectangle shape, in the Rectangles category.

   c. Click at the upper-left corner of cell F15, then drag downward to the lower-right corner of cell I18.

   ✓ All the shapes you'll draw in this exercise will appear in the default style and color; you'll change this in the next exercise and even add some text!

   d. Resize the rectangle as needed so it fills the range F15:I18 as shown in Illustration A.

5. Draw another rectangle:

   a. Click the Shapes button and select Rectangle from the Rectangles category.

   b. Click on the worksheet and draw the second rectangle as shown.

   c. Resize and move the rectangle as needed to position it correctly.

6. Draw an arrow:

   a. Click the Shapes button and select Right Arrow from the Block Arrows category.

   b. Click on the worksheet and draw the arrow as shown.

   c. Resize and move the arrow as needed to position it correctly.

7. Align the arrow and the smaller rectangle:

   a. Click the Selection Pane button on the Page Layout tab.

   b. Press Ctrl and the Right Arrow, Rectangle, and Rounded Rectangle shape names in the Selection Pane.

   ✓ Do not select Picture 5.

   c. Click the Align button on the Format tab.

   d. Choose Align Middle.

8. Group the shapes:

   a. With the shapes still selected, click the Group button on the Format tab.

   b. Click Group.

9. Close the Selection Pane.

10. Adjust column widths as necessary.

11. Spell check the worksheet.

12. Print the worksheet.

13. Close the workbook, saving all changes.

Illustration A

ON YOUR OWN

1. Start Excel, if necessary.
2. Open 15Antique.
3. Save the file as OXL15_*xx*.
4. Format the range A7:G10 however you like.
5. Add your choice banner using the Shapes button, and place it under the title, Country Crazy Antiques, in rows 4 and 5.

   ✓ *You'll format and add text to this banner in later exercises. You can try out various banner styles easily by selecting the original banner shape, clicking the Edit Shape button on the Format tab, selecting Change Shape, and selecting a new shape to try.*

6. Using various shapes, create a logo for Country Crazy Antiques:

   a. In the area below the table, create at least five objects, such as squares, rectangles, ovals, or other shapes of your choice.

   ✓ *You'll format these shapes in the next exercise, so what you're looking for here is a nice combination of shapes, sized to fit the area within the range A1:A6.*

   b. Move the objects so they overlap.
   c. Change the order of the objects and continue moving them until you get the effect you want for the logo.
   d. Group the objects.
   e. Move the finished logo to the area at the left of the Country Crazy Antiques title.
   f. Resize the logo, if necessary, to best fit the area.

7. Widen columns as necessary.
8. Spell check the worksheet.
9. Print the worksheet.
10. Close the workbook, saving all changes.

Exercise | 16

Skills Covered

- **Format Shapes**
- **Add Shape Effects**

Software Skills   When shapes such as rectangles, block arrows, and banners are added to a worksheet, they originally appear in the default style—a shape with a black outline, filled with the Accent 1 color. You can change both the color and the outline style of any shape easily. You can also add special effects such as shadows and soft edges.

Application Skills   You're the accountant at Wood Hills Animal Clinic, and you're preparing for an upcoming meeting in which you'll present the profit and loss statement. You've drawn some shapes to highlight an important improvement and now you want to format them.

TERMS

Effect   Special complex-looking formats that can be applied with a single click, such as shadows, reflections, glows, and beveled edges.

Format   The process of adding color, patterns, borders, or effects to an object.

Shape   A predesigned object (such as a banner or star) that can be drawn with a single dragging motion.

NOTES

Format Shapes

- When a **shape** is selected, the Format tab appears along the row of tabs.
- Click the Format tab to display it's buttons.
- With the buttons on the Format tab, you can **format** shapes and other objects.
- Since all new shapes appear in the default style (a black outline around the shape, which is filled with the Accent 1 color), you might want to apply a different shape style, fill, outline, or **effect**.

- Specifically, you can change:
  - *Shape Styles*—A set of formats that includes the outline color and style, edge style, and fill.
  - *Shape Fill*—The color, picture, gradient, or texture that fills a shape.

  ✓ *A line shape cannot be "filled"; the line's color is determined by the Shape Outline settings.*

  - *Shape Outline*—The color, weight, and style of the border that outlines a shape.

  ✓ *You can change the color, weight, and style of a line. You can also add arrows at one or both ends.*

  - *Shape Effects*—Complex formats applied with a single click. See the next section for more information.

- As mentioned earlier, you can fill a shape with a color, picture, gradient, or texture.
- Even if you fill a shape with a simple color, using the Colors dialog box, you can custom mix the exact color you want, and even add transparency if desired.

Colors dialog box

Select a color

Adjust lightness/brightness

Add Shape Effects

- Shape effects that you can apply to a selected shape include:
  - Shadows
  - Reflections
  - Glows
  - Soft edges
  - Beveled edges
  - 3-D rotations

  ✓ *You'll learn how to apply 3-D effects in Exercise 17.*

- Each shape effect style comes with options that allow you to customize the effect to get the look you want.
- The Preset category on the Shape Effects button displays a set of common effects, with the options already pre-selected for you.
- Choose one of the Preset effects to quickly change the look of a selected shape.

Preset effects save you time

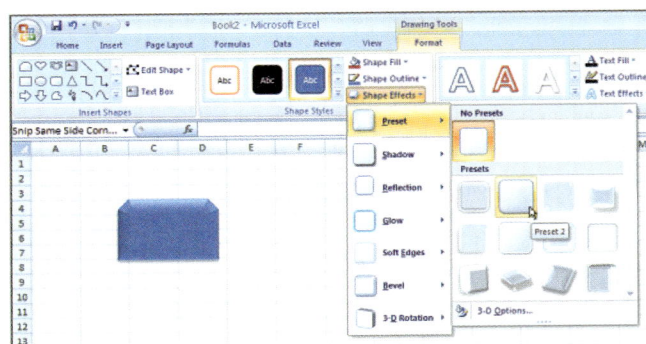

PROCEDURES

Apply Shape Style

1. Select shape(s) to format.
2. Click **Format** tab . . . Alt , J , D

   Shape Styles Group

3. Click **More** button ⊟ . . . S , S
4. Select a style . . . . ←/→/↑/↓ , Enter

Apply Shape Fill Color

1. Select shapes(s) to format.
2. Click **Format** tab . . . Alt , J , D

   Shape Styles Group

3. Select the fill color you want:
   - Click the **Shape Fill** button 🎨 ▾ to apply the displayed color.

OR
a. Click the arrow on the **Shape Fill** button 🎨 ▾ . . . . . . S , F
b. Click desired color from color palette . . . . →/←/↑/↓ , Enter

OR
a. Click **More Fill Colors** . . . . M
b. Click a standard color . . . . Alt + C , →/←/↑/↓

OR

a. Click the **Custom** tab . . . . `Ctrl`+`⇤`

b. Drag pointer on **Colors** palette to select a color.

c. Adjust the lightness/darkness of the selected color by dragging the pointer on the **right**.

✓ *You can choose an exact color by selecting a **Color model** (RGB or HSL) first, and then selecting the individual **Red**, **Green**, and **Blue**, or **Hue**, **Sat**, and **Lum** settings.*

d. Adjust the apparent **Transparency** of the shape by dragging the slider . . . . `Alt`+`T`, `↑`/`↓`

e. Click **OK** . . . . `Enter`

Apply Shape Fill Picture

1. Select shapes(s) to format.
2. Click **Format** tab . . . `Alt`, `J`, `D`

    Shape Styles Group

3. Click arrow on **Shape Fill** button 🎨▾ . . . . `S`, `F`
4. Click **Picture** . . . . `P`
5. If the picture you want to use is not listed in the current folder, perform one of the following:

    a. Click **Look in** . . . . `Alt`+`I`
    b. Select desired drive. . . . . `↑`/`↓`, `Enter`

    OR

    Double-click folder name . . . . `⇤`, `↑`/`↓`, `Enter`

    OR

    Click the appropriate button on the Places bar.

6. Click the picture you want to use to fill the select shape(s).
7. Click **Insert** . . . . `S`

Apply Gradient Shape Fill

1. Select shapes(s) to format.
2. Click **Format** tab . . . `Alt`, `J`, `D`

    Shape Styles Group

3. Click arrow on **Shape Fill** button 🎨▾ . . . . `S`, `F`
4. Point to **Gradient** . . . . `G`
5. Select a gradient from the palette that appears . . . . . . `→`/`←`/`↑`/`↓`, `Enter`

    OR

    a. Click **More gradients** . . . . . `M`
    b. Click **Gradient fill** . . . . `G`
    c. Select one of the **Preset colors** . . . `R`, `→`/`←`/`↑`/`↓`, `Enter`
    d. Select **Type** of gradient pattern . . . . . . `Y`, `↑`/`↓`, `Enter`
    e. Select gradient **Direction** . . . . `D`, `→`/`←`/`↑`/`↓`, `Enter`
    e. (If available) adjust gradient **Angle** . . . `E`, `→`/`←`/`↑`/`↓`, `Enter`

6. To rotate the gradient if the shape is rotated, select **Rotate with shape** . . . . `W`
7. Click **Close** . . . . `Enter`

    ✓ *You can create a custom gradient by selecting a stop (a point at which the gradient changes color), selecting a new color for that stop, and adjusting the color's transparency. You can add/remove existing stops as well.*

Apply Shape Fill Texture

1. Select shapes(s) to format.
2. Click **Format** tab . . . `Alt`, `J`, `D`

    Shape Styles Group

3. Click arrow on **Shape Fill** button 🎨▾ . . . . `S`, `F`
4. Point to **Texture** . . . . `T`
5. Select a texture from the palette that appears. . . `→`/`←`/`↑`/`↓`, `Enter`

Remove a Shape Fill

1. Select shapes(s) to format.
2. Click **Format** tab . . . `Alt`, `J`, `D`

    Shape Styles Group

3. Click arrow on **Shape Fill** button 🎨▾ . . . . `S`, `F`
4. Click **No Fill** . . . . `N`

Apply Shape Outline Color

1. Select shapes(s) to format.
2. Click **Format** tab . . . `Alt`, `J`, `D`

    Shape Styles Group

3. Select the outline color you want:

    ■ Click the **Shape Outline** button 🖊 to apply the displayed color.

    OR

    a. Click the arrow on the **Shape Outline** button 🖊 . . . . `S`, `O`
    b. Click desired color from color palette . . . . `→`/`←`/`↑`/`↓`, `Enter`

    OR

    a. Click **More Outline Colors** . . . . `M`
    b. Click the **Standard** tab . . . . `Ctrl`+`⇤`
    c. Click a standard color . . . . `Alt`+`C`, `→`/`←`/`↑`/`↓`

    OR

    a. Click the **Custom** tab . . . . `Ctrl`+`⇤`
    b. Drag pointer on **Colors** palette to select a color.
    c. Adjust the lightness/darkness of the selected color by dragging the pointer on the **right**.

    ✓ *You can choose an exact color by selecting a **Color model** (RGB or HSL) first, and then selecting the individual **Red**, **Green**, and **Blue**, or **Hue**, **Sat**, and **Lum** settings.*

d. Adjust the apparent **Transparency** of the shape by dragging the slider . . . . . . `Alt`+`T`, `↑`/`↓`

e. Click **OK** . . . . `Enter`

Apply Shape Outline Weight

1. Select shapes(s) to format.
2. Click **Format** tab . . . `Alt`, `J`, `D`

   Shape Styles Group

3. Click the **Shape Outline** button ⬚ . . . . `S`, `O`
4. Click **Weight** . . . . `W`
5. Select a weight from the list that appears . . . . `↑`/`↓`, `Enter`

   OR

   a. Click **More Lines** . . . . `L`
   b. Select border **Width** . . . . `W`, `↑`/`↓`, `Enter`
   c. Select line type (**Compound type**) . . . . `C`, `↑`/`↓`, `Enter`
   d. Select **Dash type** . . . . `D`, `↑`/`↓`, `Enter`
   e. Select the style for each end of the line from **Cap type** list . . . . . `A`, `↑`/`↓`, `Enter`
   f. Select the style where two lines connect from the **Join type** list . . . . . `J`, `↑`/`↓`, `Enter`
   g. (If applicable), select arrow **Begin type** . . `B`, `→`/`←`/`↑`/`↓`, `Enter`
   h. (If applicable), select arrow **End type** . . `E`, `→`/`←`/`↑`/`↓`, `Enter`
   g. (If applicable), select arrow **Begin size** . . `S`, `→`/`←`/`↑`/`↓`, `Enter`
   g. (If applicable), select arrow **End size** . . `N`, `→`/`←`/`↑`/`↓`, `Enter`
6. Click **Close** . . . . `Enter`

Apply Preset Shape Effect

1. Select shapes(s) to format.
2. Click **Format** tab . . . `Alt`, `J`, `D`

Shape Styles Group

3. Click the **Shape Effects** button ⬚ . . . . `S`, `E`
4. Point to **Preset** . . . . `P`
5. Select preset style . . . . `→`/`←`/`↑`/`↓`, `Enter`

Apply Shadow Shape Effect

1. Select shapes(s) to format.
2. Click **Format** tab . . . `Alt`, `J`, `D`

   Shape Styles Group

3. Click the **Shape Effects** button ⬚ . . . . `S`, `E`
4. Point to **Shadow** . . . . `S`
5. Select a shadow style from the palette that appears . . . . `↑`/`↓`, `Enter`

   OR

   a. Click **Shadow Options** . . . . `S`
   b. Select shadow **Color** . . . . `C`, `→`/`←` `↑`/`↓`, `Enter`
   c. Set the amount of shadow **Transparency** . . . . `T`, `↑`/`↓`, `Enter`
   d. Set shadow **Size** . . . . `S`, `↑`/`↓`, `Enter`
   e. Set degree of **Blur** . . . . `B`, `↑`/`↓`, `Enter`
   f. Set apparent **Distance** . . . . `D`, `↑`/`↓`, `Enter`
6. Click **Close** . . . . `Enter`

Apply Reflection Shape Effect

1. Select shapes(s) to format.
2. Click **Format** tab . . . `Alt`, `J`, `D`

Shape Styles Group

3. Click the **Shape Effects** button ⬚ . . . . `S`, `E`
4. Point to **Reflection** . . . . `R`
5. Select a reflection style from the palette that appears . . . . `↑`/`↓`, `Enter`

Apply Glow Shape Effect

1. Select shapes(s) to format.
2. Click **Format** tab . . . `Alt`, `J`, `D`

   Shape Styles Group

3. Click the **Shape Effects** button ⬚ . . . . `S`, `E`
4. Point to **Glow** . . . . `G`
5. Select a glow style from the palette that appears . . . . `↑`/`↓`, `Enter`

   OR

   a. Click **More Glow Colors** . . . `M`
   b. Select a glow color from the palette that appears . . . `→`/`←`/`↑`/`↓`, `Enter`

Apply Soft Edges Shape Effect

1. Select shapes(s) to format.
2. Click **Format** tab . . . `Alt`, `J`, `D`

   Shape Styles Group

3. Click the **Shape Effects** button ⬚ . . . . `S`, `E`
4. Point to **Soft Edges** . . . . `E`
5. Select a glow style from the list that appears . . . . `↑`/`↓`, `Enter`

Apply Bevel Shape Effect

1. Select shapes(s) to format.
2. Click **Format** tab . . . `Alt`, `J`, `D`

   Shape Styles Group

3. Click the **Shape Effects** button ⬚ . . . . `S`, `E`
4. Point to **Bevel** . . . . `B`
5. Select a bevel style from the list that appears . . . . `↑`/`↓`, `Enter`

   ✓ *The Bevel effect adds the look of a third dimension, depth. You can format this look further, adjusting the amount of apparent depth, the surface texture, and other options. See Exercise 17 for help.*

EXERCISE DIRECTIONS

1. Start Excel, if necessary.

2. Open [⌨] **15BalSheetP&L** or [💿] **16BalSheetP&L**.

3. Save the file as **16BalSheetP&L_xx**.

4. Display the Selection Pane by clicking the Selection Pane button on the Page Layout tab.

5. Format the smallest rectangle:
   a. In the Selection Pane, click Rectangle.
   b. Click the Format tab.
   c. Click the Shape Fill button and click Orange, Accent 6, Lighter 60% (last color, third row).
   d. Click the Shape Effects button, point to Bevel, and then click Circle.
   e. Click the Shape Outline button and choose Red, Accent 2, Lighter 60% (sixth color, third row).

6. Format the block arrow:
   a. In the Selection Pane, click Right Arrow.
   b. Click the Format tab.

   c. Click the Shape Fill button, point to Gradient, and then click More Gradients.
   d. Select Gradient fill, and from the Preset colors list, select Gold.
   e. Select the Linear Type, and the from the Direction list, choose the first option.
   f. Select the Line Color category.
   g. Click the Color button and then select Olive Green, Accent 3, Lighter 40% (seventh color, fourth row).

7. Format the outer rectangle (see Illustration A):
   a. In the Selection Pane, click Rounded Rectangle.
   b. Click the More button in the Shape Styles group, and select the Moderate Effect, Accent 2 style.
   c. Click the Shape Effects button, point to Reflection, and click Tight Reflection, 4 pt. Offset.

8. Spell check the worksheet.

9. Print the worksheet.

10. Close the workbook, saving all changes.

Illustration A

ON YOUR OWN

1. Start Excel, if necessary.

2. Open [⌨] **OXL15_xx**, created in the Cn Your Own section of Exercise 15, or open [◎] **16Antiques**.

3. Save the file as **OXL16_xx**.

4. Display the Selection Pane.

   a. Now that you know how to format shapes, apply various fill, outline, and effects styles to the individual parts of the logo you created in Exercise 15. See Illustration A.

   b. Use the Selection Pane as needed to select logo parts so you can format them.

5. Format the banner underneath the Country Crazy Antiques title.

6. Widen columns as necessary.

7. Spell check the worksheet.

8. Print the worksheet.

9. Close the workbook, saving all changes.

Illustration A

Column1	Beds	Dressers	Dining Tables	End Tables	China Cabinets	Chairs
Previous Balance	3	4	6	10	4	23
Ending Balance	2	2	5	5	2	12
Total Sold During Period	1	2	1	5	2	11

Skills Covered

- **Add Text to a Text Box, Callout, or Other Shape**
- **Add 3-D Effects**
- **Rotate Shapes**

Software Skills   If you need to place text in some spot within the worksheet that doesn't correspond to a specific cell, you can "float" the text over the cells by creating a text box or by adding a callout. A text box or callout can be placed anywhere in the worksheet, regardless of the cell gridlines. You might use a text box or callout to draw attention to some particularly important data in the worksheet. If you don't like the look of a plain text box or a balloon-like callout, you can add to any other shape you chose. Add 3-D effects or rotation to shapes to really make them stand out.

Application Skills   The financial review at Wood Hills Animal Clinic is fast approaching, and you still have a few more changes you want to make to the profit and loss statement. In this exercise, you'll add some text to the banner, insert a text box, and rotate the logo to finalize the look.

TERMS

Callout   Text that's placed in a special AutoShape balloon. A callout, like a text box, "floats" over the cells in a worksheet—so you can position a callout wherever you like.

Rotation handle   A green circular handle that appears just over the top of most objects when they are selected. Use this handle to rotate the object manually.

Text box   A small rectangle that "floats" over the cells in a worksheet, into which you can add text. A text box can be placed anywhere you want.

NOTES

Add Text to a Text Box, Callout, or Other Shape

- A **text box** is an independent object that contains text.
  - A text box can be resized, moved, copied, deleted, formatted, and manipulated independently of the data in the worksheet.
  - The text in the text box can be formatted in the same way in which you format worksheet text.

- You can use a text box to point out important information within a worksheet, or to add a comment that's displayed all the time.

  ✓ *By default, comments aren't visible until the mouse pointer rests on the cell that contains it.*

- A text box is created with the Text Box tool on the Insert tab.
  - When you create a text box, you drag with the mouse pointer to create the exact size you need.
  - You then type text into this box.

- A **callout** is a type of shape.
- A callout is basically a text box, shaped into something more interesting, such as a cartoon balloon.
- Callouts typically include an extension (such as a line) that points to the information you wish to write about.
  - When a callout shape is selected, a yellow diamond indicates this "extension point."
  - ✓ *On other shapes, this yellow diamond handle is called an adjustment handle, because it lets you adjust the outline of the shape itself.*
  - Drag this yellow extension point to make the callout point precisely to the data you wish to talk about.
  - Text boxes do not have these extensions, but you can easily add an arrow or line shape to a text box to accomplish the same thing.
- You can use a callout like a text box, to draw attention to important information, or to add a comment to a worksheet.
- You can actually add text to any shape, such as a rounded rectangle, or even a heart.
- The border of a selected shape changes to indicate whether you're editing the object itself (solid border) or the text in the object (dashed border).
  - To move, resize, copy, or delete the object, the border must be solid.

You can format any shape with a solid border

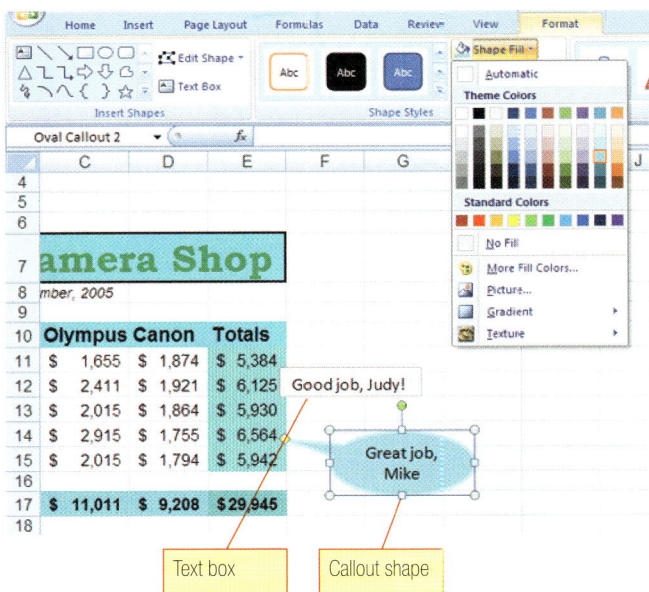

  - To edit or add text in a text box or shape, the border must be dashed.

You can add text to any shape with a dotted border

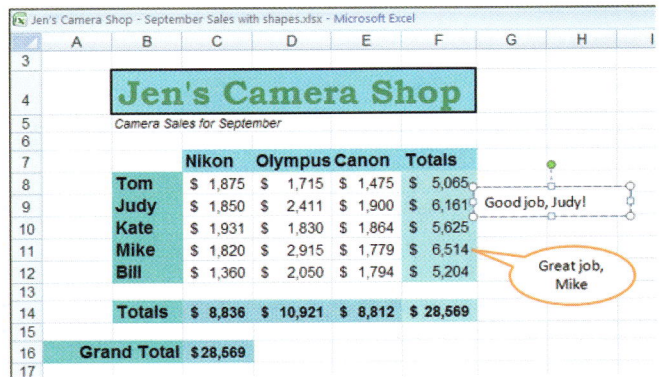

Add 3-D Effects

- When you add 3-D effects to an object, that object appears to have depth.
- You can add 3-D effects to any object, even grouped objects.
- Select the 3-D rotation style you want first, from the 3-D Rotation palette, located on the Shape Effects button.
  - If you choose 3-D Rotation Options instead, the Format Shape dialog box appears, where you can customize the settings.

Set 3-D rotation options first

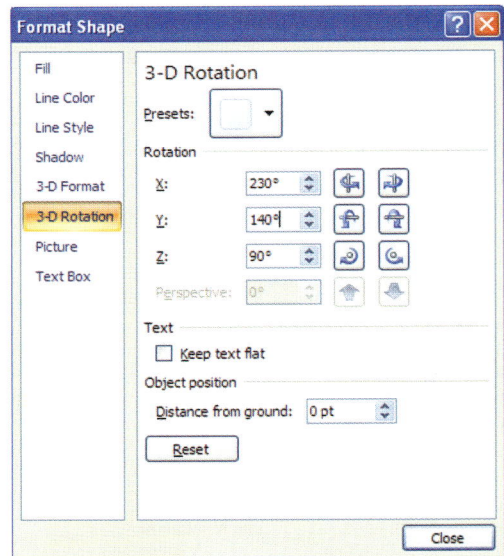

  - Here you can set the exact degree of rotation and other options such as whether you want the text in the shape (if any) to be rotated with the shape.
  - Objects are rotated along three axes—the X (horizontal), Y (vertical), and Z (depth dimension).

- In the Format Shape dialog box, you can also adjust the format of the 3-D shape, selecting its depth, surface texture, and other options.

Set 3-D format options next

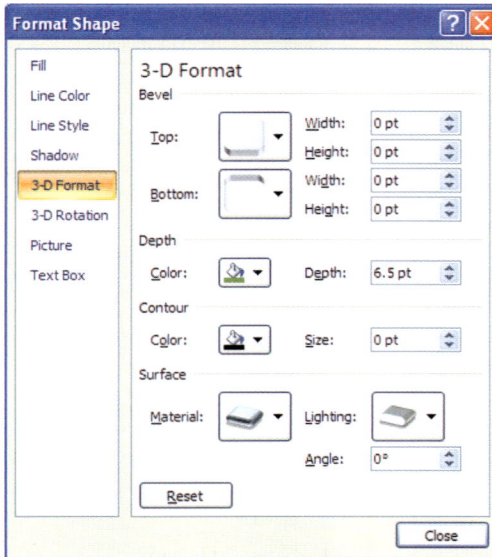

- Here, you can adjust the style of the edge of your 3-D shape. You can also change the color and contour of this third dimension.

- You can also select a surface texture—such as the apparent material used.

- You can also change how the surface is lit (both the color of the light and the angle at which it shines on the 3-D object).

Rotate Shapes

- A shape can be rotated around an invisible pin holding its center in place on the worksheet.
  - Using the Rotate button on the Format tab, you can quickly rotate a shape to the left or the right, by 90 degrees.
  - You can also rotate a shape by a custom amount.
  - Shapes can be manually rotated, using the **rotation handle**.
- A shape can also be flipped vertically (like falling over a horizontal pole) or flipped horizontally (like twisting around a vertical pole).

PROCEDURES

Create a Text Box

1. Click **Insert** tab . . . . $\boxed{\text{Alt}}$, $\boxed{\text{N}}$

2. Click **Text Box** button $\boxed{\text{A}}$ . . . . . $\boxed{\text{X}}$
3. Drag to create the text box.

To create a text box:

- Drag box outline until desired size is obtained.

To create a square text box:

- Press **Shift** and drag box outline until desired size is obtained.

To center the text box at the pointer position:

- Press **Ctrl** and drag box borders away from the center until desired size is obtained.

To create a text box that snaps to gridlines:

- Press **Alt** and drag box outline until desired size is obtained.

4. Type text as desired:
5. Click outside text box to return to normal operations.

Create a Callout

1. Click **Insert** tab . . . . $\boxed{\text{Alt}}$, $\boxed{\text{N}}$

2. Click **Shapes** button $\boxed{\text{}}$ . . . . $\boxed{\text{S}}$, $\boxed{\text{H}}$
3. Click the desired callout shape. . . . . . . $\boxed{\rightarrow}$ / $\boxed{\leftarrow}$ / $\boxed{\uparrow}$ / $\boxed{\downarrow}$, $\boxed{\text{Enter}}$

   ✓ You'll find the callout shapes in the Callout category on the palette.

4. Click and drag to create the callout.

   ✓ Use the **Shift**, **Alt**, and **Ctrl** keys to affect the shapes as you draw. For example, hold down **Shift** while drawing a rectangle to draw a perfect square, or to size whatever you're drawing proportionally. If you press **Alt**, the shape is sized to fit the cells in which it's drawn. Press **Ctrl** and the shape is drawn outward from its center.

5. Drag extension point/adjustment handle (yellow diamond), if necessary, to adjust the callout extension so it points to the data you're discussing in the text.

6. Type text as desired.
7. Click outside text box to return to normal operations.

Add Text to a Callout or Other Shape

1. Click the shape you wish to add text to.
2. Type the text for the shape.

   ✓ If the shape already contains text, the text you type will be added to the end of the existing text. You can replace text by selecting it first, then typing new text.

3. Click outside shape to return to normal operations.

Format Text in a Shape

1. Click the text box or shape to select it.
2. Click **Home** tab . . . . $\boxed{\text{Alt}}$, $\boxed{\text{H}}$

3. Apply the desired text formats, such as bold, center alignment, text color, font, or font size.

   ✓ Note that you do not need to select the text in the text box or shape in order to format it, unless you want to apply a format to only a portion of the text.

Format Text in a Text Box

1. Click the text box.
2. Select the text to format.
3. Click **Home** tab . . . . $\boxed{\text{Alt}}$, $\boxed{\text{H}}$

4. Apply the desired text formats, such as bold, center alignment, text color, font, or font size.

Adjust the Alignment of Text in a Text Box or Shape

1. Right-click the text box or shape to format.
2. Click **Format Shape**. . . . . $\boxed{\text{O}}$
3. Click **Text Box** . . . . $\boxed{\downarrow}$
4. Click **Vertical Alignment** arrow. . . . . $\boxed{\text{Alt}}$+$\boxed{\text{V}}$
5. Select desired alignment . . . . $\boxed{\uparrow}$/$\boxed{\downarrow}$, $\boxed{\text{Enter}}$
6. Click **Close** . . . . $\boxed{\text{Enter}}$

Adjust the Direction of Text in a Text Box or Shape

1. Right-click the text box or shape to format.
2. Click **Format Shape**. . . . . $\boxed{\text{O}}$
3. Click **Text Box** . . . . $\boxed{\downarrow}$
4. Click **Text direction** arrow. . . . . $\boxed{\text{Alt}}$+$\boxed{\text{X}}$
5. Select desired direction . . . . $\boxed{\uparrow}$/$\boxed{\downarrow}$, $\boxed{\text{Enter}}$
6. Click **Close** . . . . $\boxed{\text{Enter}}$

Make Text Adjust Automatically When Object is Resized

1. Right-click the text box or shape to format.
2. Click **Format Shape**. . . . . $\boxed{\text{O}}$
3. Click **Text Box** . . . . $\boxed{\downarrow}$
4. Select **Resize shape to fit text** . . . . $\boxed{\text{Alt}}$+$\boxed{\text{F}}$
5. Click **Close** . . . . $\boxed{\text{Enter}}$

Change Margins in a Text Box or Shape

1. Right-click the text box or shape to format.
2. Click **Format Shape** . . . . O
3. Click **Text Box** . . . . ↓
4. Adjust margins:
   - **Left** . . . . Alt +L, ↑ /↓
   - **Right** . . . . Alt +R, ↑ /↓
   - **Top** . . . . Alt +T, ↑ /↓
   - **Bottom** . . . . . Alt +B, ↑ /↓
5. Click **Close** . . . . Enter

Apply 3-D Rotation Style

1. Select shapes(s) to format.
2. Click **Format** tab . . . Alt , J , D

   Shape Styles Group

3. Click the **Shape Effects** button ▭ . . . . S , E
4. Point to **3-D Rotation** . . . . D
5. Select desired rotation from palette . . . . → /← /↑ /↓ , Enter
   OR
   a. Click **3-D Rotation Options** . . . . R
   b. Adjust **X**-axis rotation . . . . . Alt +X, ↑ /↓
   c. Adjust **Y**-axis rotation . . . . . Alt +Y, ↑ /↓
   d. Adjust **Z**-axis rotation . . . . . Alt +Z, ↑ /↓

6. To *not* rotate text with the object, select **Keep text flat** . . . . . Alt +K
7. Adjust object's apparent **Distance from ground** (distance from the worksheet) . . . . Alt +D, ↑ /↓
8. Click **Close** . . . . Enter

Adjust 3-D Format

1. Select shapes(s) to format.
2. Right click and choose **Format Shape** . . . . O
3. Click **3-D Format** . . . . ↑ /↓
4. Select edge **Color** . . . . . Alt +C, → /← /↑ /↓ , Enter
5. Adjust apparent **Depth** . . . . . Alt +D, ↑ /↓ , Enter
6. Select **Color** of edge curve (contour) . . . . Alt +O, → /← /↑ /↓ , Enter
7. Adjust **Size** of edge curve (contour) . . . . Alt +S, ↑ /↓ , Enter
8. Select surface **Material** . . . . Alt +M, → /← /↑ /↓ , Enter
9. Select **Lighting** type . . . Alt +L, → /← /↑ /↓ , Enter
10. Adjust lighting **Angle** . . . . . . Alt +A, ↑ /↓ , Enter
11. Click **Close** . . . . Enter

Rotate Shape

1. Select shapes(s) to rotate.
2. Click **Format** tab . . . Alt , J , D

   Arrange Group

3. Click the **Rotate** button ▣ . . . . A , Y
4. Select standard rotation:
   - **Rotate Right 90°** . . . . R
   - **Rotate Left 90°** L
   OR
   a. Click **More Rotation Options**
   b. Enter degree of **Rotation** . . . . . Alt +T, ↑ /↓

Rotate Shape Manually

1. Select shape to rotate.
2. Click rotation handle (green circle).
3. Drag handle left or right to rotate shape.

Flip Shape

1. Select shapes(s) to flip.
2. Click **Format** tab . . . Alt , J , D

   Arrange Group

3. Click the **Rotate** button ▣ . . . . A , Y
4. Select which direction to flip the shape:
   - **Flip Vertical** V
   - **Flip Horizontal** . . . . H

EXERCISE DIRECTIONS

1. Start Excel, if necessary.

2. Open 📼 **16BalSheetP&L_xx** or open 💿 **17BalSheetP&L**.

3. Save the workbook as **17BalSheetP&L_xx**.

4. Add text to grouped shape:

   a. Click the peach colored rectangle in the group shape twice to select it.

   b. Type **This cost is down because of better inventory management**.

   c. Change the font color to Red, Accent 2, Darker 25%.

   d. Change the font size to 9 point.

5. Create a callout:

   a. Click the Shapes button, and choose Rounded Rectangular Callout, located in the Callouts section.

   b. Draw a callout as shown in Illustration A.

   c. Type **Increases in A/R have increased patient income and the gross profit**.

   d. Click the More button in the Shape Styles group of the Format tab, and choose Moderate Effect - Accent 2 style.

   e. Change the text size to 9 point.

   f. Click the yellow extension point until the callout tip points to cell D20 as shown in Illustration A.

6. Add a text box:

   a. Click the Text Box button in the Text group on the Insert tab.

   b. Draw a text box as shown in Illustration B.

   c. Type **Next year's purchases should be much less than this**.

   d. Click the border of the text box.

   ✓ *This changes the selection from a dashed border to a solid border, indicating that you can now change its color.*

   f. Click the arrow on the Shape Fill button and choose Red, Accent 2, Darker 25%.

   g. Change the font color to White, Background 1.

   h. Change the font size to 9 point.

   i. Click the Shapes button and choose Arrow from the Lines category.

   j. Drag to draw the arrow from the text box to cell D38 as shown in Illustration B.

   k. Use the Shape Outline button to change the arrow color to Red, Accent 2, Darker 25%. Change the weight to 1 pt.

Illustration A

7. Add a 3-D effect:

  a. Click the text box created in step 6.

  b. Click Shape Effects, point to 3-D Rotation, and then select Off Axis 1 Right.

  c. Right-click the text box and choose Format Shape. Click 3-D Format

  d. Set the depth color to Red, Accent 2, Lighter 40%

  e. Set the depth to 4 pt.

  f. Set the contour color to Red, Accent 2, Lighter 40%.

  g. Set the contour size to 1.5 pt.

8. Add a text box:

  a. Click the Text Box button on the Format tab.

  b. Click and draw a text box to fit the range, F45:H47.

  c. Type **These expenses stayed more or less the same as last year**.

  d. Click the Rotate button and choose More Rotation Options.

  e. Set the rotation to 350 and click Close.

  f. Apply Red, Accent 2, Darker 25% shape fill color.

  g. Apply White, Background 1 font color, and change the font size to 9 pt.

  h. Drag the text box into place as shown in Illustration B.

9. Adjust column widths as necessary.

10. Spell check the worksheet.

11. Print the worksheet.

12. Close the workbook, saving all changes.

Illustration B

	A	B	C	D	E	F	G	H
30		Sales equipment purchases		$ 7,893				
31		Sales equipment depreciation		$ 4,858				
32		Total sales expenses			$ 111,885			
33	**Patient Care**							
34		Veterinary salaries		$ 428,175				
35		Non-Veterinary salaries		$ 158,410				
36		Charity or pro-bono work		$ 11,219				
37		Lab work		$ 41,876				
38		Examination room supplies		$ 178,145				
39		Examination room equipment purchases		$ 41,189				
40		Examination room equipment depreciation		$ 29,141				
41		Kennel equipment purchases		$ 13,789				
42		Kennel equipment depreciation		$ 10,897				
43		Total patient care expenses			$ 912,841			
44	**General and Administrative**							
45		Administrative salaries		$ 18,948				
46		Office supplies		$ 21,415				
47		Office equipment purchases		$ 16,296				
48		Office equipment depreciation		$ 2,184				
49		Payroll taxes		$ 451,164				
50		Employee benefits		$ 33,148				
51		Legal and accounting fees		$ 18,954				
52		Repairs expense		$ 19,215				
53		Utilities expense		$ 18,159				
54		Insurance expense		$ 10,284				
55		Interest expense		$ 10,189				
56		Total general and admistrative expenses			$ 619,957			
57		Total operating expenses			$ 1,644,683			
58								
59		Earnings before income tax			$ 2,718,851			
60		Income tax		$ 278,914				
61	**Net Income**				$ 2,439,937			
62								
63	Common stock shares outstanding				1,325,000			
64	Earnings per share of common stock				$ 1.84			
65								
66								

Next years purchases should be much less than this.

These expenses stayed more or less the same as last year.

ON YOUR OWN

1. Start Excel, if necessary.
2. Open ⌨ 16Antiques_xx, created in the On Your Own section of Exercise 16, or open 💿 17Antiques.
3. Save the workbook as OXL17_xx.
4. Add the text **Inventory as of 6/10/08** to the banner you created. Format the text as you like.
5. Add a text box to explain the large amount of end tables sold. Make up a reason.
   a. Format the callout as you like. See Illustration A.
   b. Apply a 3-D effect to the callout.
6. Rotate the logo you created.
7. Adjust column widths as necessary.
8. Spell check the worksheet.
9. Print the worksheet.
10. Close the workbook, saving all changes.

Illustration A

Column1	Beds	Dressers	Dining Tables	End Tables	China Cabinets	Chairs
Previous Balance	3	4	6	10	4	23
Ending Balance	2	2	5	5	2	12
Total Sold During Period	1	2		5	2	11

End table sale was held 6/1-6/3

Skills Covered

- ■ **Insert WordArt**

Software Skills   WordArt allows you to bend, stretch, and rotate text to create dynamic effects. With a simple piece of WordArt, you can add an element of surprise to an otherwise boring worksheet full of numbers. WordArt gives your worksheets a professional touch, enabling you to create a lasting impression with something that takes only minutes to create.

Application Skills   As the Chief Technician and Repairperson at Breakaway Bike Shop, you must detail each part and the amount of labor you put into any bike repair. You've repaired a customer's bike, and you want to make certain she's notified about the extent of the work you did. So you'll add text to the repair sheet that explains the charges.

TERMS

Transform   To bend, stretch, or twist small bits of text.

WordArt   A tool that allows you to twist, bend, and stretch text to create interesting effects.

NOTES

Insert WordArt

- ■ With **WordArt**, you can quickly create dynamic-looking text for use in your worksheets.
- ■ The WordArt palette provides the basic effects from which you can choose.
  - • After you choose an effect, you type the text you want to use in the WordArt.
  - • Basic WordArt text is graphic in design, but you can do more to it.
  - • For example, like any other shape, you can fill WordArt text with color, a picture, a gradient, or a texture.
  - • You can also change the outline of the WordArt text by adjusting its weight, style, and color.

WordArt palette

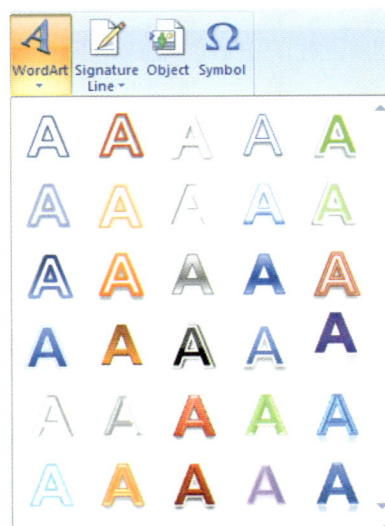

- To create an interesting look, however, you might want to **transform** your WordArt text.
  - When you transform text, you select a curve from a menu, and then the text is placed along that curve so that it twists and bends.
  - If you choose to transform the text in your Word-Art, you should limit it to only a few words for best results.
  - After selecting a transform style, you can adjust the curve along which your text runs by dragging the purple diamond adjustment handles.

- Besides transforming text, you can also add other text effects to WordArt:
  - ✓ *See Exercise 17 for help in applying these affects.*
  - Shadow
  - Reflection
  - Glow
  - Bevel
  - 3-D Rotation
- A WordArt object can be moved, resized, copied, and deleted, just like any other object.
- Rotate a WordArt object by dragging its green diamond-shaped handle.
- Because WordArt is an object, many of the procedures you learned with shapes work with WordArt as well, such as order, grouping, etc.

PROCEDURES

Insert WordArt Object

1. Click **Insert** tab . . . . `Alt`, `N`

   `Text Group`

2. Click **WordArt** button `🔷` . . . . . `W`
3. Select a WordArt design . . . . `→`/`←`/`↑`/`↓`, `Enter`
4. Type desired text.
5. Adjust the curve if needed by dragging a purple adjustment handle.

Change WordArt Text

1. Select the WordArt object you wish to change.
2. Drag over the text to change.
3. Type replacement text.

Change WordArt Style

1. Select the WordArt object you wish to change.
2. Click **Format** tab . . . `Alt`, `J`, `D`

   `WordArt Styles Group`

3. Click **More** button `▼` . . . . `K`
4. Select a WordArt style from the palette that appears . . . . . . `→`/`←`/`↑`/`↓`, `Enter`

Transform WordArt

1. Select the WordArt object you wish to transform.
2. Click **Format** tab . . . `Alt`, `J`, `D`

   `WordArt Styles Group`

3. Click **Text Effects** button `🅰` . . . . `T`, `X`
4. Click **Transform** . . . . `T`
5. Select a transform style from the palette that appears . . . . . . `→`/`←`/`↑`/`↓`, `Enter`
6. Adjust the curve if needed by dragging a purple adjustment handle.

Convert WordArt to Regular Text Box

1. Select the WordArt object you wish to convert.
2. Click **Format** tab . . . `Alt`, `J`, `D`

   `WordArt Styles Group`

3. Click **More** button `▼` . . . . `K`
4. Click **Clear WordArt** . . . . `C`

Convert Text Box to WordArt Object

1. Select text box you want to convert.
2. Click **Format** tab . . . `Alt`, `J`, `D`

   `WordArt Styles Group`

3. Click **More** button `▼` . . . . `K`
4. Select a WordArt design . . . . `→`/`←`/`↑`/`↓`, `Enter`

EXERCISE DIRECTIONS

1. Start Excel, if necessary.
2. Open 🔘 **18PartsReplacement**.
3. Save the file as **18PartsReplacement_xx**.
4. Delete the contents of cell B1, and replace it with WordArt:
   a. Click the WordArt button on the Insert tab.
   b. Select Gradient Fill – Accent 1 style from the palette.
   c. Type the text **Parts Replacement Detail**.
   d. Change the font size to 28 point.
5. Transform the WordArt:
   a. Click the Text Effects button on the Format tab.
   b. Point to Transform, and then select the Double Wave 1 style.

6. Apply a glow:
   a. Click the Text Effects button on the Format tab.
   b. Point to Glow, and then select Accent color 3, 5 pt glow.
7. Drag the WordArt object into the position shown in Illustration A. Resize the object as needed.
8. Adjust column widths as necessary.
9. Spell check the worksheet.
10. Print the worksheet.
11. Close the workbook, saving all changes.

Illustration A

ON YOUR OWN

1. Start Excel, if necessary.
2. Open ⊙ **18Cater**.
3. Save the file as **OXL18_xx**.
4. Format the tables in the worksheet however you like by choosing a theme, then applying fonts, font sizes, fills, and borders.
5. Replace the title, *Kat's Catering*, with WordArt of the same title.
6. Try out various transform styles on the WordArt, and experiment with the adjustment handle.
7. Experiment with different text effects.
8. Create a rectangle to house the WordArt title:
    a. Format the rectangle with colors and a border to go with the title design. See Illustration A.
    b. Place the title in the rectangle and size one or the other to fit.
    c. Group them together and move them to the location you prefer.
9. Adjust column widths as necessary.
10. Spell check the worksheet.
11. Print the worksheet.
12. Close the workbook, saving all changes.

Illustration A

Exercise | 19

Skills Covered

- **Insert Clips**
- **Insert Pictures**

- **Format Graphics**

Software Skills   Images and graphics help the mind comprehend what it's seeing. Even the slightest amount of aesthetics can make it easier for a reader to digest a page full of otherwise boring figures and statistics. In this exercise, you'll learn how to import pictures from image files and from clip art.

Application Skills   To add the finishing touch to the usage breakdown statement you designed for Intellidata Services, you need to add the corporate logo and some clip art from Microsoft's collection. Luckily, you've just learned how to search for clip art, insert, and resize it.

TERMS

Clip   A small file—clip art, photos, audio, or video—that can be inserted in a worksheet from the Clip art task pane.

Clip art   Images that you can insert into any Office program, including Excel.

Clip Art task pane   A task pane that displays clip art matching the keywords you enter.

Clip Organizer   A dialog box that displays clip art images by category.

Cropping handle   A corner or side bracket along the border of a picture, enabling you to crop edges off of the corresponding side or corner.

Picture   Personal clip art or photos that you can also add to a worksheet.

Shape   A predesigned object (such as a banner, rectangle, or star) that can be drawn with a single dragging motion.

NOTES

Insert Clips

- You can insert **clip art** and other graphic images into your worksheet to enhance its appearance.

- Typically, you search for clip art using the **Clip Art task pane**, and then insert it.

    - The task pane allows you to search for clip art by entering a keyword or phrase, such as "savings" or "goal."

- After displaying a list of matching clip art images, you can preview and then insert any clip you wish.

- You can also view the properties of a clip, search for clip art in a similar style and delete and copy the images.

- Like all task panes, the Clip Art task pane can be dragged into the work area where it might be more convenient to use.

- Initially, the Clip Art task pane displays all the **clips** that are currently available to you—including clips installed on your local system, as well as online through Microsoft if you have an active Internet connection. You can easily add your own clips to the collection.

Clip Art task pane

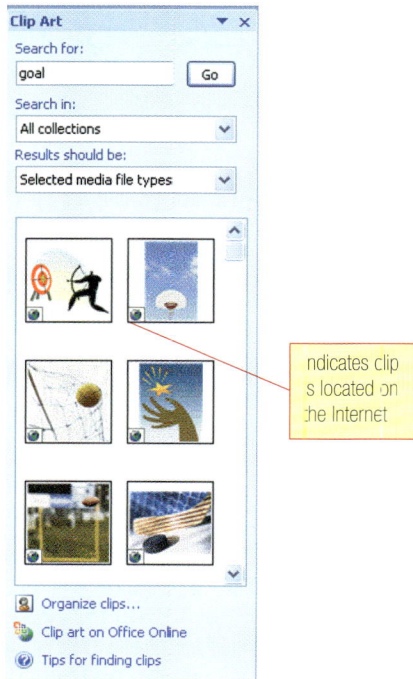

Indicates clip is located on the Internet

- To display clips by category, such as Business, open the **Clip Organizer**.
  - The clips in the Clip Organizer are organized into categories. Select the category you want, and then insert the desired clip.
  - Use the Clip Organizer (rather than the task pane) to organize your clips as you prefer.
- You can create new folders for organizing clips.
- Clips are organized in the Collections List in three main folders:
  - My Collections is a folder you can use to store your favorite clips and clips you haven't categorized yet.
  - Office Collections contains most of the clips that come with Microsoft Office, organized by category.

- Web Collections contains clips especially suitable for use on Web pages. These include buttons, page dividers, animated graphics, and so on.

Clip Organizer

- After inserting a clip, you can move and resize it as needed.
  - ✓ Audio and video files appear as icons when inserted in a worksheet, which can move and resize (to make smaller, for example) as desired.

Insert Pictures

- In addition to the clips stored in the Clip organizer, you can insert other graphics as well, such as your own photos or clip art.
- Excel calls personal graphics such as these **pictures**.
- You can move and resize pictures as you might other clips.

Format Graphics

- Once you've inserted clip art or a picture, you can adjust its appearance and other characteristics using the Format tab.
  - You can make a color picture grayscale, sepia, washed out, or black and white.
  - You can make overall adjustments to a picture's contrast and brightness.
  - You can crop a picture to any smaller size you need.
  - You can crop a picture to fit within the borders of a shape you select.
- You can also perform the same tasks on a clip that you can on a shape, such as resizing, moving, rotating, adding a border or effect, or applying a style.

  ✓ *See Exercises 15 and 16.*

- The changes to make to clip art or a picture in your worksheet (such as cropping) will *not* be reflected in the original version.
- To crop a picture, click the picture, click the Crop button, and then drag one of the **cropping handles** along the border in the direction of reduction.

Cropping handles

Corner cropping handle

Side cropping handle

PROCEDURES

Insert Clips with Clip Art Task Pane

1. Select cell where object will be inserted.
2. Click **Insert** tab . . . . Alt , N

   Illustrations Group

3. Click **Clip Art** button 🖼 . . . . . F
4. Type a few keywords in **Search for** box.
5. To limit the search to a particular collection of clips, choose a collection from the **Search in** list.
6. To limit the search to clips of a particular type (such as clip art and photos), choose that type from the **Results should be** list.
7. Click **Go** button Go .

   ✓ *A list of images matching the keyword(s) is displayed.*

8. Click clip to insert it.

   OR

   Click the arrow on clip thumbnail and select an option:

   ✓ *Some options are not available with all types of clips.*

- **Insert** Inserts the clip.
- **Copy** Copies the clip to the Clipboard, so you can use it with a different application.
- **Delete from Clip Organizer** Removes the clip from the collection.
- **Make Available offline** Copies the clip to your hard disk so you can use it even if you're not connected to the Internet.
- **Copy to Collection** If the clip has been copied to your hard disk (it does not display the global icon that indicates a clip from the Internet), this command copies the clip to another folder in the collection.
- **Move to Collection** Moves the clip to another folder in the collection.
- **Edit Keywords** Allows you to change the keywords associated with the clip.
- **Find Similar Style** Displays clips with a similar artistic style.

- **Preview/Properties** Displays the clip in a larger preview window, along with the clip's properties (file type and size).

Insert Clips with Clip Organizer

1. From the Clip Art task pane, click the **Organize clips** link.
2. Select the collection you wish to look in.
3. To insert a clip, drag and drop the clip on the worksheet.
4. Close the Clip Organizer.

Insert Picture

1. Select cell at upper left corner of where picture will be inserted.
2. Click **Insert** tab . . . . Alt , N

   Illustrations Group

3. Click **Picture** button 🖼 . . . . . . P
4. In the dialog box, choose the folder that contains the picture you want to use.

5. Click the file name.
6. Click **Insert** . . . . [Enter]
7. If asked to Convert File:
   a. Choose a file format.
   b. Click **OK**.

   ✓ *The picture will appear aligned against the upper-left corner of the active cell.*

Import Clip Art into the Clip Organizer

1. In the Microsoft Clip Organizer, click **File** . . . . [Alt]+[F]
2. Point to **Add Clips to Organizer** . . . . [A]
3. Click **On My Own** . . . . [O]
4. Select drive and folder that contains the clip art you wish to import.
5. Select clip art file(s).
6. Click **Add** to add to the current folder . . . . [Alt]+[A]

   ✓ *If you use Windows Vista, click **Open** instead.*

   OR
   a. Click **Add To** . . . . [Alt]+[D]
   b. Select a folder.

   ✓ *To create a new folder, click **New**, type a folder name, and click **OK**.*

   c. Click **OK** . . . . [Enter]
   d. Click **Add** . . . . [Alt]+[A]

   ✓ *If you use Windows Vista, click Open instead.*

Recolor Graphic

1. Click graphic to select it.
2. Click **Format** tab . . . [Alt], [J], [P]

   Adjust Group

3. Click **Recolor** button 🖼 . . . . . [E]
4. Select color . . . . [→]/[←]/[↑]/[↓], [Enter]
   OR
   a. Click **More Variations** . . . . [M]
   b. Click color to use . . . . [→]/[←]/[↑]/[↓], [Enter]

Make Part of Graphic Transparent

1. Click graphic to select it.
2. Click **Format** tab . . . [Alt], [J], [P]

   Adjust Group

3. Click **Recolor** button 🖼 . . . . . [E]
4. Click **Set Transparent Color** . . . . [S]
5. Click the color on the graphic you want to make transparent.

Adjust Brightness

1. Click graphic to select it.
2. Click **Format** tab . . . [Alt], [J], [P]

   Adjust Group

3. Click **Brightness** button 🔆 . . . [B]
4. Select brightness level . . . . [↑]/[↓] [Enter]

Adjust Contrast

1. Click graphic to select it.
2. Click **Format** tab . . . [Alt], [J], [P]

   Adjust Group

3. Click **Contrast** button ◑ . . . . . [N]
4. Select contrast level . . . . [↑]/[↓] [Enter]

Change One Picture for Another

1. Click picture to select it.
2. Click **Format** tab . . . [Alt], [J], [P]

   Adjust Group

3. Click **Change Picture** button 🖼 . . . . [G]
4. In the dialog box, choose the folder that contains the picture you want to use.
5. Click the file name.
6. Click **Insert** . . . . [Enter]
7. If asked to Convert File:
   a. Choose a file format.
   b. Click **OK**.

   ✓ *The picture will appear aligned against the upper-left corner of the active cell.*

Reset Graphic to Normal

1. Click graphic to select it.
2. Click **Format** tab . . . [Alt], [J], [P]

   Adjust Group

3. Click **Reset Picture** button 🖼 . . . . [Q]

Fit Graphic to a Shape

1. Click picture to select it.
2. Click **Format** tab . . . [Alt], [J], [P]

   Picture Styles Group

3. Click **Picture Shape** button 🔲 . . . . [I]
4. Select shape . . . . [→]/[←]/[↑]/[↓], [Enter]

Crop Graphic

1. Click graphic to select it.
2. Click **Format** tab . . . [Alt], [J], [P]

   Size Group

3. Click **Crop** button 🖼 . . . . [C]
4. Point to cropping handle.

   ✓ *Use a corner handle to crop from two sides.*

   ✓ *Use a side handle to crop from the corresponding side.*

5. Drag handle inward to reduce picture's size.
6. When you're done cropping, click **Format** tab . . . . [Alt], [J], [P]

   Size Group

7. Click **Crop** button . . . . [C]

EXERCISE DIRECTIONS

1. Start Excel, if necessary.

2. Open ⊙ **19MonUsage**.

3. Save the file as **19MonUsage_*xx***.

4. Insert a picture from your computer:
   a. Click cell A1.
   b. Click the Picture button on the Insert tab.
   c. Navigate to the drive and folder where your student data files are stored.
   d. Insert ⊙ **19Intellidata logo.gif**.

5. Crop extra space from the top and bottom of the picture:
   a. Click the Crop button on the Format tab.
   b. Grab the side cropping handle on the bottom edge, and drag it up to just below the "exclamation point" in the logo, as depicted in Illustration A.
   c. Grab the side cropping handle on the top edge, and drag it down to just above the blue "D" in the logo.
   d. Click the Crop button again to turn cropping off.

6. Move the picture into position:
   a. Click and hold anywhere in the middle of the picture.
   b. Drag up until the upper-left corner of the shadow marquee touches the upper- left corner of cell A1.
   c. Release the mouse button.

7. Resize the picture to fit:
   a. Hold down both Shift and Alt.
   b. Drag the lower-right corner handle of the picture until it snaps to the lower-right corner of cell B4.

8. Increase the height of row 3 to fit the logo as shown in Illustration A.

9. Copy the picture to the second panel of the worksheet:
   a. With the picture selected, click the Copy button on the Home tab.
   b. Click cell A17.
   c. Click the Paste button.
   d. Resize row 19 as you resized row 3.

10. Insert a clip art image:
    a. Click cell F1.
    b. Click the Clip Art button on the Insert tab.
    c. Type **computer** in the Search for text box.
    d. Click Go.
    e. Scroll down until you locate the image shown at the top of Illustration A. Or, select a similar image.
    f. Click the image to insert it.
    g. Resize the image as needed, so that it matches Illustration A.

11. Place the clip in a shape:
    a. Click the Picture Shape button on the Format tab.
    b. Click the Oval shape.

12. Recolor the clip:
    a. Click the Recolor button.
    b. Choose Accent Color 5 Dark.

13. Adjust column widths as necessary.

14. Spell check the worksheet.

15. Print the worksheet.

16. Close the workbook, saving all changes.

Intellidata — Hosting · Management · Warehousing

Monthly Usage Breakdown

Diaz Used Auto Sales

	James Murphy	Kenesha Stevens	Tai Ling Wong	Julie Jung	Yolanda Dickerson	Totals
Message Management	1,385.00	563.00	925.00	777.00	1,298.00	4,948.00
E-Mail Auto-Respond	483.00	177.00	341.00	488.00	399.00	1,888.00
Online Sales Reports	18.00	8.00	4.00	13.00	8.00	51.00
Wireless Lead Alerts	529.00	507.00	516.00	808.00	424.00	2,784.00

Intellidata — Hosting · Management · Warehousing

Monthly Usage Breakdown

Diaz Used Auto Sales

	Message Management	E-Mail Auto-Respond	Online Sales Reports	Wireless Lead Alerts		
James Murphy	1,385.00	483.00	18.00	529.00		
Kenesha Stevens	563.00	177.00	8.00	507.00		
Tai Ling Wong	925.00	341.00	4.00	516.00		
Julie Jung	777.00	488.00	13.00	808.00	Message Management	3,562.56
Yolanda Dickerson	1,298.00	399.00	8.00	424.00	E-Mail Auto-Respond	1,793.60
Totals	4,948.00	1,888.00	51.00	2,784.00	Online Sales Reports	63.75
Charge per item	0.72	0.95	1.25	1.10	Wireless Lead Alerts	3,062.40
Total charge	3,562.56	1,793.60	63.75	3,062.40	Total invoice	8,482.31

Sheet1 / Sheet2 / Sheet3

ON YOUR OWN

1. Create a sales workbook for Country Crazy Antiques.
2. Save the file as **OXL19_*xx*.**
3. List sales (in dollars) for beds, dressers, dining tables, end tables, china cabinets, and chairs sold each month for the last three months.

   ✓ *You might create a row for each type of furniture and a column for each month, or vice versa.*

4. Format the worksheet however you like.
5. Insert a piece of clip art as a logo.

   ✓ *Move and resize the object as needed.*

6. Apply a picture style to add a decorative border/edge. See Illustration A.
7. Recolor the clip to match the formatting in the worksheet.
8. Adjust column widths as necessary.
9. Spell check the worksheet.
10. Print the worksheet.
11. Close the workbook, saving all changes.

Illustration A

SOXL19 - Microsoft Excel

Country Crazy Antiques

	June	July	August
Beds	$ 21,895	$ 23,497	$ 25,141
Dressers	$ 15,978	$ 18,945	$ 19,174
Dining Tables	$ 25,145	$ 24,958	$ 21,345
End Tables	$ 11,689	$ 9,775	$ 10,858
China Cabinets	$ 32,187	$ 31,958	$ 27,458
Chairs	$ 15,449	$ 13,497	$ 16,478
Totals	$122,343	$122,630	$120,454

Exercise | 20

Critical Thinking

Application Skills You supervise the Customer Account Representatives at Intellidata, and it's their job to service the accounts for your 2,000 plus clients. You're anxious to stop the increasing number of clients who have been switching to rival BitBank, so you've made some changes in the department. You've also been tracking client numbers lately to see if your changes are making a difference. Your boss, the Chief Financial Officer, is interested, too, so you've created a report, which you need to spruce up a bit before printing it out for him.

EXERCISE DIRECTIONS

1. Start Excel, if necessary.
2. Open ⊙ **20ClientOutlook**.

   ✓ Click Cancel when you see the notice about the circular reference error. You will correct that error and others in this exercise.

3. Save the file as **20ClientOutlook_xx**.
4. There are problems with the two formulas. Let's figure out what's wrong:
   a. Click the smart tag in cell E24.
   b. That's the problem. The SUM function doesn't include all the cells it should. Click Update Formula to Include Cells.
   c. There's a circular reference notice on the status bar. Click the arrow on the Error Checking button on the Formulas tab and point to Circular Reference.
   d. Click the cell reference on the menu that appears. The offending cell (F24) is highlighted.

      True, you know which cell has the circular reference (its name appears on the status bar), so you could have just clicked cell F24 yourself, but why not have Excel select it for you? This is especially helpful when working with a large worksheet where the circular cell is out of view.
   e. The formula refers to cell F24; edit the formula so that the included range is F8:F23.

5. Import the logo into the Clip Organizer:
   a. Click the Clip Art button on the Insert tab.
   b. Click the Organize clips link.
   c. Choose File, Add Clips to Organizer, On My Own.
   d. Select the file ⊙ **20Intellidata logo.gif** located in the data files folder, and click Add To.
   e. Select the Favorites folder in the My Collections folder and click OK.
   f. Click Add.
   g. Close the Clip Organizer window.
   h. In the Clip Art task pane, type **logo** in the Search for text box.
   i. In the Search In list, select My Collections.
   j. Click Go.
   k. Insert the Intellidata logo, cropping the extra space along the top and bottom, then resizing and moving it as needed to fit it in the range A1:D5.
   l. Close the task pane.
6. Draw some shapes:
   a. Create a text box, and type the following text into it (using Calibri (Body), 11 point, italic font): **When we changed our campaign, our client retention improved.**
   b. Resize and move the text box as shown in Illustration A.

c. Apply shape style Subtle Effect – Accent 2.

d. Change the shadow options to: Color Red Accent 2 Darker 50%, Transparency 68%, Size 100%, Blur 3.15 pt, Angle 52°, Distance 7 pt.

e. Draw an arrow from the box to cell F24.

f. Change the weight of the arrow outline to 1 ½ pt.

g. Select both arrow and the text box, and group them together.

7. Add some WordArt:

a. Create a WordArt object using the text **Client Retention Analysis** and the style, Fill - Accent 2, Matte Bevel.

b. Change the point size to 32.

c. Click the Text Effects button on the Format tab, point to Transform, and select the Chevron Up transform efftect

d. Move the WordArt into place as shown in Illustration A.

8. Add some formulas:

a. Use the Conditional Sum Wizard to total the new, mid-sized clients for May, and place the result in cell D33.

b. Repeat this process, using the Conditional Sum Wizard to create totals for cells D34:D36, E33: E36.

c. Use AVERAGEIFS to create a formula that calculates the average of new, mid-sized clients for May, and place the result in cell F33.

d. Repeat this process, using AVERAGEIFS to create averages for cells F34:F36, G33:G36.

e. Apply Number format, 2 decimals to the range F33:G36.

9. Adjust column widths as needed.

10. Spell check the worksheet.

11. Print the worksheet.

12. Close the workbook, saving all changes.

Illustration A

Exercise | 21

Curriculum Integration

Application Skills   In a math class, you are working on complex formulas. As a real-world example, your instructor has compared the formulas for *simple interest*—where interest is paid on the original principle only—and *compound interest*—where the interest paid on the original principle plus previously-earned interest. To see how quickly interest can add up when it compounds, you'll add some advanced functions into a worksheet and then enter different values to take a "what if" look at how much you'd earn with different investment and interest amounts. You'll also create a macro that makes it easy to print each set of what-if values you enter.

EXERCISE DIRECTIONS

Start Excel, if necessary. Open the workbook file ⊙ **21CertificateofDeposit**, and save the file as **OXL21_***xx* in the Excel Macro-Enabled Workbook format. Once you complete the spreadsheet, it will enable you to calculate the future value of an investment in a Certificate of Deposit and to test what-if scenarios by entering various present value, interest rate, and contribution amounts. (This particular type of CD enables you to make a monthly contribution to increase the principle amount.)

In cell C8, enter a formula that calculates the interest for month 1 based on the amount in cell B8. Use the IPMT function, and be sure to divide rates by 12 and use absolute references as needed. Copy the formula from cell C8 down the column through cell B67.

In cells E2:E4, enter formulas that calculate the value of the CD at the 3 year, 4 year, and 5 year (maturity) marks. Use the FV (future value) function, and be sure to reference cells B2, B3, and B5 in the appropriate locations.

Hint: As the FV function results in negative values, you can multiply by -1 to convert the results to positive values.

Format the values in cells E2:E4 in the Currency number format, if needed.

Record and save a macro named PrintCDIncome that does the following:

- Sets the print area to A1:E67
- Scales the printout to 1 page tall by 1 page wide in Portrait orientation
- Prints the worksheet using the default printer.

Perform a what-if analysis by changing the values in cells B2, B3, and B5. (See Illustration A.) Use the PrintCDIncome macro to print at least three different what-if combinations so you can compare the projected income.

Note: Excel offers what-if analysis tools called Scenario Manager and Goal Seek in the Data Tools group of the Data tab. In this case, you could use Scenario Manager to save each different combination of values in B2:B5 as a separate scenario that you could then quickly redisplay via Scenario Manager.

When you finish printing, save the workbook and exit Excel.

Illustration A

	A	B	C	D	E
1	Certificate of Deposit Income Evaluation				
2	Present value	$5,000.00		Value at 3 years	$7,256.20
3	Interest rate	2.50%		Value at 4 years	$8,046.62
4	Term (in years)	5		Value at maturity	$8,857.03
5	Contribution each month	$50.00			
6					
7	Month	Balance	Interest Earned	Contribution	New Balance (Balance+Interest+Contribution)
8	1	5,000.00	10.42	50.00	5,060.42
9	2	5,060.42	10.54	50.00	5,120.96
10	3	5,120.96	10.67	50.00	5,181.63
11	4	5,181.63	10.80	50.00	5,242.42
12	5	5,242.42	10.92	50.00	5,303.34
13	6	5,303.34	11.05	50.00	5,364.39
14	7	5,364.39	11.18	50.00	5,425.57
15	8	5,425.57	11.30	50.00	5,486.87
16	9	5,486.87	11.43	50.00	5,548.30
17	10	5,548.30	11.56	50.00	5,609.86
18	11	5,609.86	11.69	50.00	5,671.55
19	12	5,671.55	11.82	50.00	5,733.37
20	13	5,733.37	11.94	50.00	5,795.31
21	14	5,795.31	12.07	50.00	5,857.38
22	15	5,857.38	12.20	50.00	5,919.59
23	16	5,919.59	12.33	50.00	5,981.92
24	17	5,981.92	12.46	50.00	6,044.38
25	18	6,044.38	12.59	50.00	6,106.97
26	19	6,106.97	12.72	50.00	6,169.70
27	20	6,169.70	12.85	50.00	6,232.55
28	21	6,232.55	12.98	50.00	6,295.53
29	22	6,295.53	13.12	50.00	6,358.65
30	23	6,358.65	13.25	50.00	6,421.90
31	24	6,421.90	13.38	50.00	6,485.28
32	25	6,485.28	13.51	50.00	6,548.79
33	26	6,548.79	13.64	50.00	6,612.43
34	27	6,612.43	13.78	50.00	6,676.21
35	28	6,676.21	13.91	50.00	6,740.12
36	29	6,740.12	14.04	50.00	6,804.16
37	30	6,804.16	14.18	50.00	6,868.33
38	31	6,868.33	14.31	50.00	6,932.64
39	32	6,932.64	14.44	50.00	6,997.08
40	33	6,997.08	14.58	50.00	7,061.66

CD Income

Lesson | 3

Performing Analyses

Skills Covered

- **Filter the Items in a Table**
- **Filter Items without Creating a Table**
- **Sum, Average, and Count the Items in a Filtered Table**

Software Skills   It doesn't take much time before a list gets too large to view completely on the screen without having to do a lot of scrolling. When you're looking for particular records, such as all the salespeople who work in the Grand Avenue office, you can use a filter to filter (reduce) the number of records to just the ones you want to view right now. With a regular filter, even large lists become manageable.

Application Skills   You're continuing to put together the inventory tracking sheet for Wood Hills Animal Clinic, and it's looking pretty good. It's your job now to make some sense of all this data. You plan to use filtering to organize the information and make printouts based on particular data the boss has requested.

TERMS

Calculated column   A special column that can be added to a table, in which a single formula is automatically applied to each row.

Excel table   Data arranged in columns and specially formatted with column headers that contain commands that allow you to sort, filter, and perform other functions on the table.

Filter   Reduce the total number of records displayed on the screen to a selected group.

List   A range of Excel data organized primarily by columns.

Total row   A row that can be displayed at the bottom of an Excel table, which provides functions for calculating the values in each column selectively.

NOTES

Filter the Items in a Table

- An **Excel table** allows you to reference a range of data in a formula more naturally as in this example: **=AVERAGE(Sales[June])**.
  - This formula averages the values in a column called June, which is located in a table named Sales.
  - In addition, sorting and **filtering** the data in a table is much easier than with ordinary Excel data.

- You create a table by applying a table style to selected data.
  - For best results, the data you wish to convert into an Excel table should be arranged in a **list**.
  - After creating the table, you can sort and filter its data as needed.

  ✓ *You'll learn about filtering in this exercise. See Exercise 24 for help in sorting it.*

- You can also filter a list without converting it to a table first, as you'll learn in the next section.

■ Whether you choose to create a table or not, you can use filtering to select which records (which rows of data) you wish to view.

✓ *Filtering a table or a list doesn't delete records or alter the work-sheet in any way—it simply hides the records you don't want to see, or that don't apply to the criteria you've specified.*

✓ *There are complex filters you can apply which do more than the filters discussed in this exercise; see Exercise 23 to learn about advanced filters.*

■ In the following example, filtering was used to display only the records for bookings on the *Kon Tiki I.*

Filtering example

Kon Tiki I was selected from the Ship list

April was selected from the Departure Date list

■ You use the down-arrow button at the top of a column to pull down a drop-down list of filter choices.

● Besides the sort options explained in Exercise 24, this drop-down list contains one instance of each entry in that column.

✓ *For example, if a list contains records of bookings for three ships, Kon Tiki I, Kon Tiki II, and Island Girl, the bottom of the drop-down list will contain one entry for each of these ships.*

■ To have an Excel table or list show only entries containing one particular entry in a column, open the drop-down list for that column and choose that entry.

✓ *For example, if you select Kon Tiki I from the Ship drop-down list, only rows with Kon Tiki I in that column will be shown.*

● After you make a selection for a column, the arrow button beside that column displays the Filter icon to remind you which column is controlling the filter.

● The row numbers of the filtered records also appear in blue.

✓ *This is to remind you that records between those blue-numbered rows may be hidden.*

■ Once a table or list has been filtered, the drop-down lists for the other columns will only contain choices from the filtered entries.

✓ *So if no bookings for the Kon Tiki I were made for 5/7/2008, that date would not appear in the drop-down list for the Departure Date column.*

● Choose (Select All) from the filter list menu to display all records again.

✓ *To redisplay all records in the database, select the (All) option from the list with the blue arrow.*

● The numbered columns in a filtered table or list provide you with the (Top 10…) option, which displays the top (or bottom) 10 records in that category.

✓ *Despite the name, you can select the actual number of items to display. The number must be between 1 and 500.*

● (Custom…) This option allows you to specify up to two conditions, such as records with sales greater than $1,000 or a sale date between 2/15/08 and 2/22/08.

● (Blanks) This option allows you to display only the records with no value in this column.

✓ *The Blanks option only appears in columns that contain at least one blank cell.*

✓ *Use the Blanks filter to locate and correct records with missing data.*

■ If conditional formatting (see Exercise 7) has been applied to a table or list, then a Filter by Color option appears on the menu.

● Use this option to select the fill color or the text color of the rows you want to display.

■ You can make selections from more than one filter list in order to create a small subset of records.

✓ *For example, you might select Ohio from the State list and then (Top 10) from the Sales list to display the top ten sales records in the Ohio region.*

✓ *If you select criteria from more than one filter list, only records that match both criteria are displayed.*

Filter Items without Creating a Table

■ As mentioned earlier, you do not need to convert a list into an Excel table in order to filter its data.

■ A table, however, does give you several advantages. With a table, you can:

- Create formulas that reference the columns in the table by their name.

- Format the table with a single click.

- Add a **total row** that allows you to select from a range of functions that sum, average, count, or perform other operations on the data in a column.

- Add a **calculated column** that allows you to enter a formula and have that formula copied instantly throughout the column.

Sum, Average, and Count the Items in a Filtered Table

■ Tables provide a lot of flexibility when it comes to managing columnar data.

■ For example, it's easy to add totals and perform other calculations on the columns in a table by simply adding a total row.

- Once a total row is added, click in the total row at the bottom of a column you want to calculate, and choose an available function such as SUM, AVERAGE, or MIN.

- You can select a different function for each column, or none at all.

- You can also enter text in the total row if needed.

■ You can temporarily hide the total row when needed.

A total row provides built-in functions

■ Another easy way to add calculations to a table is to use calculated columns.

- A calculated column can be located in a blank column inserted between existing table columns, or simply in the first blank column to the right of a table.

- To create a calculated column, just type a formula in the blank column you've inserted in the table, or in a blank column just to the right of the table.

- The formula is instantly copied down the column.

- If new rows are added to the table, the formula is copied to that new row automatically.

PROCEDURES

Formatting a Table

1. Click in table range.
2. Click **Home** tab . . . . [Alt], [H]

   Styles Group

3. Click **Format as Table** . . . . [T]
4. Click table style . . . . . [↑]/[↓], [Enter]
5. Confirm range, and
   click **OK** . . . . [Enter]

Filter a Table

1. Click any cell in the table.
2. Click the down-arrow button of the column you wish to filter.
3. Deselect the (Select All) option, then select the values you want to display.

   OR

   a. Point to **Text Filters** . . . . . . [F]
   b. Click a filter option from list
      on left . . . . . [←], [↑]/[↓], [Enter]
   c. Select an operator from the
      first list . . . . [Shift]+[←],
      [↑]/[↓], [Enter]

d. Select or type a value in the
   second list . . . [←], [↑]/[↓], [Enter]
e. To specify other criteria for the
   column:

   Select **And** . . . . [Alt]+[A]

   OR

   Select **Or** . . . . [Alt]+[O]

f. Select second
   operator . . . . . [←], [↑]/[↓], [Enter]

g. Select or type the second
   value . . . . [←], [↑]/[↓], [Enter]

h. Click **OK** . . . . [Enter]

   OR

a. Point to **Number Filters**. . . `F`

b. Click a filter
option . . . . `↑`/`↓`, `Enter`

c. Select an operator from the
first list . . . . `Shift`+`⇤`,
`↑`/`↓`, `Enter`

d. Select or type a value in the
second list . . . `⇤`, `↑`/`↓`, `Enter`

e. To specify other criteria for the
column:

Select **And** . . . . `Alt`+`A`

OR

Select **Or** . . . . `Alt`+`O`

f. Select second
operator . . . . . `⇤`, `↑`/`↓`, `Enter`

g. Select or type the second
value . . . . `⇤`, `↑`/`↓`, `Enter`

h. Click **OK** . . . . `Enter`

4. Repeat steps 2–3 to add filtering
to additional columns.

Filter a List without Creating a Table

1. Select any cell in list.
2. Click **Data** tab . . . . `Alt`, `A`

Sort & Filter Group

3. Click **Filter** button `▼` . . . . `T`

✓ *Arrow buttons appear next to each
column name.*

4. Click the down-arrow button of the
column you wish to filter.
5. Deselect the (Select All) option,
then select the values you want to
display.

OR

a. Point to **Text Filters** . . . . . . `F`

b. Click a filter
option . . . . `↑`/`↓`, `Enter`

c. Select an operator from the
first list . . . . `Shift`+`⇤`,
`↑`/`↓`, `Enter`

d. Select or type a value in the
second list . . . `⇤`, `↑`/`↓`, `Enter`

e. To specify other criteria for the
column:

Select **And** . . . . `Alt`+`A`

OR

Select **Or** . . . . `Alt`+`O`

f. Select second
operator . . . . . `⇤`, `↑`/`↓`, `Enter`

g. Select or type the second
value . . . . `⇤`, `↑`/`↓`, `Enter`

h. Click **OK** . . . . `Enter`

OR

a. Point to **Number Filters**. . . `F`

b. Click a filter
option . . . . `↑`/`↓`, `Enter`

c. Select an operator from the
first list . . . . `Shift`+`⇤`,
`↑`/`↓`, `Enter`

d. Select or type a value in the
second list . . . `⇤`, `↑`/`↓`, `Enter`

e. To specify other criteria for the
column:

Select **And** . . . . `Alt`+`A`

OR

Select **Or** . . . . `Alt`+`O`

f. Select second
operator . . . . . `⇤`, `↑`/`↓`, `Enter`

g. Select or type the second
value . . . . `⇤`, `↑`/`↓`, `Enter`

h. Click **OK** . . . . `Enter`

6. Repeat steps 3–4 to add filtering
to additional columns.

Display Greatest or Least Records Only

1. Select any cell in list.
2. Click the down-arrow button of the
column you wish to filter.
3. Point to **Number Filters** . . . . . `F`
4. Select **Top 10** . . . . `T`
5. Select **Top** or **Bottom** from the first
list . . . . . . `⇤`, `⇤`, `↑`/`↓`, `Enter`
6. Choose the number of records
(or percentage threshold)
to display in the second
list . . . . `⇤`, `↑`/`↓`, `Enter`
7. Choose whether to display the
chosen number of records, or the
chosen percentile of records, in
the third list . . . . `⇤`, `↑`/`↓`, `Enter`
8. Click **OK** . . . . `Enter`

✓ *Records may not be sorted.*

Display Above Average or Below Average Records Only

1. Select any cell in list.
2. Click the down-arrow button of the
column you wish to filter.
3. Point to **Number Filters** . . . . . `F`
4. Select **Above Average** . . . . `A`

OR

Select **Below Average** . . . . `O`

Display Items Based on Their Conditional Formatting

1. Select any cell in list.
2. Click the down-arrow button of the
column you wish to filter.
3. Point to **Filter by Color** . . . . . . `L`
4. Select a color from the palette that
appears . . . . `↑`/`↓`, `Enter`

Redisplay All Records in Table or List

1. Select any cell in a table or list.
2. Click **Data** tab . . . . `Alt`, `A`

Sort & Filter Group

3. Click **Clear** button `▼` . . . . . . `C`

✓ *You can also click each arrow with
a Filter icon and select (Select All) to
redisplay all records.*

Remove a Filter from a List

✓ *This process will redisplay all records
and remove the filter arrows from a
list, but not a table.*

1. Select any cell in list.
2. Click **Data** tab . . . . `Alt`, `A`

Sort & Filter Group

3. Click **Filter** button `▼` to
deselect it . . . . `T`

Add a Total Row to a Table

1. Select any cell in the table.
2. Click **Design** tab . . . `Alt`, `J`, `T`

Sort & Filter Group

3. Click **Total Row** option . . . . . . `T`

Add a Total Function to a Column in a Table

1. Select any cell in the table.
2. Click in the total row, at the bottom of the column you wish to calculate.
3. Click down arrow to display function list.
4. Select function to apply . . . . $\uparrow$/$\downarrow$, Enter

   ✓ Select **More Functions** to enter any function you want.

Remove a Total Row to a Table

1. Select any cell in the table.
2. Click **Design** tab . . . Alt, J, T

   Sort & Filter Group

3. Click **Total Row** option to deselect it . . . . T

Add a Calculated Column to a Table

1. Select any cell in a blank column in the table, or just to its right.
2. Type the formula you want copied down the column.

3. Press Enter . . . . Enter

   ✓ *If data exists in some of the cells in the calculated column, the AutoCorrect Options button appears. Click this button and choose **Overwrite all cells in this column with this formula**.*

   ✓ *If you edit the formula in any cell in a calculated column, the formula is automatically updated down the column.*

Remove a Calculated Column

1. Select any cell in the calculated column.
2. Click **Home** tab . . . . Alt, H

   Cells Group

3. Click **Delete** arrow. . . . . D
4. Click **Delete Table Columns** . . M

EXERCISE DIRECTIONS

1. Start Excel, if necessary.
2. Open ⌨12AugDrugSales or 💿 22AugDrugSales.
3. Save the file as **22AugDrugSales_xx**.
4. Convert the list to a table:
   a. Click a cell in the list.
   b. Click the Format as Table button on the Home tab, and select the Table Style Medium 21.
   c. Make sure the range A7:K94 is selected and the My table has headers option is on, then click OK.
5. Display only the heart medications:
   a. Click the arrow next to For use on in cell B7, deselect (Select All), select Heart, and click OK.
   b. Sort the records by price by clicking the arrow next to Item Cost, and choosing Sort Smallest to Largest.
6. Adjust column widths as needed.
7. Spell check the worksheet.
8. Print the worksheet.
9. Clear the filter by choosing the Clear button on the Data tab.

10. Display only items with 100 or more units remaining in inventory:
    a. Click the arrow next to Total Items2, and point to Number Filters.
    b. Select Greater Than Or Equal To from the list.
    c. Enter **100** in the box immediately to the right.
    d. Click OK.
11. Add a total row (see Illustration A):
    a. Click anywhere in the table, then select the Total Row option on the Design tab.
    b. Click at the bottom of the Total Items2 column, click the arrow, and choose Average.
    c. Click at the bottom of the Total Items column, click the arrow, and choose Sum.
12. Add a calculated column:
    a. In cell L7, type **Estimated Profit**.
    b. Since you make roughly 23% on each product, in cell L8, type **=K9*.23**.
    c. Press Enter and the formula is copied down the column.
13. Apply Accounting format, 2 decimal places to the Estimated Profit column.

14. Click the arrow in the Total Row at the bottom of the Estimated Profit column, and choose Sum.

15. Adjust column widths as needed.

16. Print the worksheet.

17. Display all items that start with "E":

   a. Clear the filter.

   b. Click the arrow next to Drug, point to Text Filters, and select Custom Filter.

   c. From the list on the left of the first row, choose begins with.

   d. In the box on the right of that row, enter **E**.

   e. Click OK.

18. Print the worksheet.

19. Display the top 15 selling items:

   a. Clear the filter.

   b. Click the arrow next to Total Sales, point to Number Filters, and choose Top 10.

   c. In the center box, choose 15, then click OK.

20. Close the workbook, saving all changes.

Illustration A

	A	B	C	D	E	F	G	H	I	J
5					Starting Inventory			Ending Inventory		
6										
7	Drug	For use on	To treat	No. of Case	Items per Case	Loose Item	Total Item	Total Items2	No. Sol	Item C
17	Droncit Tapeworme	De-wormer	Dog or Cat	6	100	88	688	432	256	$ 2
57	Enacard	Heart	Dog or Cat	10	30	14	314	158	156	$ 3
66	Anipryl	Endocrine	Dog	12	20	19	259	152	107	$ 5
68	Enacard	Heart	Dog or Cat	12	22	20	284	61	223	$ 2
73	Bomazeal Senior	Arthritis	Dog	14	50	42	742	382	360	$ 2
74	Enacard	Heart	Dog or Cat	14	30	3	423	222	201	$
79	Proin	Incontinence	Dog	15	35	33	558	390	168	$ 3
81	Tapazole	Hyperthyroidism	Cat	15	30	29	479	358	121	$ 4
83	Heartgard Plus Blue	Heartworm	Dog	18	75	42	1,392	968	424	$ 1
84	Soloxine	Hyperthyroidism	Dog or Cat	18	20	17	377	51	326	$ 3
88	Revolution	Heartworm	Dog	21	32	6	678	325	353	$ 2
89	Soloxine	Hyperthyroidism	Dog or Cat	21	20	4	424	186	238	$ 4
90	Advantage Green	Flea	Dog	22	25	14	564	268	296	$ 1
91	Heartgard Plus Green	Heartworm	Dog	22	75	36	1,686	1,296	390	$ 1
94	Heartgard Plus Brown	Heartworm	Dog	30	75	19	2,269	918	1,351	$ 2
95	Total						11,137	411		

Sales Analysis

Total Sales	$ 263,465.96
Sales of dog only products	$ 157,691.75
Sales of cat only products	$ 24,091.11
Sales of flea products	$ 18,630.10
Sales of flea and tick products	$ 1,748.85
Sales of heartworm products	$ 70,944.70
Other sales	$ 172,142.31
Average Sales	$ 3,028.34
Average sales of dog only products	$ 3,583.90
Average sales of cat only products	$ 1,853.16
Average sales of flea products	$ 1,693.65
Average sales of flea and tick products	$ 874.43
Average sales of heartworm products	$ 7,094.47
Average of other sales	$ 2,689.72

ON YOUR OWN

1. Start Excel, if necessary.

2. Open ⌨ **OXL12**, created in the On Your Own section of Exercise 12, or open 💿 **22PetStoreSales**.

3. Save the file as **OXL22_xx**.

4. Turn on filtering for the list.

5. Apply a filter to the Product Type column to display only Dog and Cat products.

6. Adjust column widths as necessary.

7. Spell check the worksheet.

8. Print the worksheet.

9. Convert the list to a table:

   a. Remove the filter.

   b. Select the list, and clear all formats.

   c. Format the list as a table, using Table Style Dark 2.

10. Add a calculated column:

    a. Clear the formats from the range H9:H49.

    b. Type **Net Profit** in cell H9.

    c. Type a formula in cell H10 that calculates the net profit, which is the cost of a sale minus any sales incentives.

11. Display only rows with a sales incentive. See Illustration A.

12. Adjust column widths as necessary.

13. Spell check the worksheet.

14. Print the worksheet.

15. Close the workbook, saving all changes.

Illustration A

Item #	Description	Product Type	Salesperson	Cost	SalesIncentive	Net Pro
41234	Dalmation puppy	Dog	Alice Harper	356	3.56	352.44
48795	Siamese kitten	Cat	Bob Cook	485.75	4.86	480.89
41237	Scottie puppy	Dog	Bob Cook	315	3.15	311.85
41897	Golden Retriever puppy	Dog	Bob Cook	201.5	2.02	199.48
48552	Persian kitten	Cat	Alice Harper	185.75	1.86	183.89

Pete's Pets

Sales for Saturday, March 27, 2004

Sales Recap

Dogs sold	3	
Cats sold	2	
Fish sold	9	
Pet sales	$	1,696.37
Feed sales	$	200.71
Accessories	$	464.16

	Total Sales	Average Sales
Alice Harper	$ 1,059.37	$ 72.33
Bob Cook	$ 1,301.87	$ 48.15

	Total Fish Sales	Total Accessories Sales
Alice Harper	$ 135.15	$ 297.96
Bob Cook	$ 17.22	$ 166.20

	Average Fish Sales	Average Accessories Sales
Alice Harper	$ 22.53	$ 22.53

Skills Covered

- **Advanced Filtering**
- **Guidelines for Entering Criteria**
- **Examples of Advanced Criteria**

- **Remove an In-Place Advanced Filter**
- **Edit Extracted Records**

Software Skills   Although a regular filter allows you set up some custom criteria to control which records are displayed on the screen, it can't do all the things that an advanced filter can. With an advanced filter, you can extract the matching records and then format, sort, and make other changes to them without affecting the records in the list. This is handy when you want to print or format a subset of the list, or delete a few records from the subset that you don't want to use (even if they match the criteria). With this technique, you can create a custom list even if you can't specify the exact criteria for it. In addition, advanced filters let you create complex criteria using formulas, multiple conditions applied to a single field, and so on, to filter the list.

Application Skills   Next to the act of racing, and the pleasure of watching racing, the thing professional race instructors like to do most is look over statistics. You've been asked to create some additions to the racing results workbook for Giancarlo Franchetti's racing school to make it easier for Giancarlo and the other instructors to make sense of the results.

TERMS

Criteria range   Area of the worksheet in which you specify the criteria for selecting records from the list or table.

Extract   Copy records that match specified criteria to another place in the worksheet where they can be changed, sorted, formatted, printed, and so on.

Extract range   Area where Excel copies the list or table records that match the specified criteria.

NOTES

Advanced Filtering

- With an advanced filter, you can filter records in a list in one of two ways:
  - You can hide records that do not match the criteria you specify—in much the same way as with a regular filter.
  - You can **extract** (copy) records to another place in the worksheet.

- Although an advanced filter can hide records just like a regular filter, it's different in many ways.
  - An advanced filter allows you to enter more complex criteria than a regular filter.
  - Instead of selecting criteria from a drop-down list, you enter it in a special area in the workbook—perhaps a worksheet unto itself—set aside for that purpose.
  - In the marked cells of this **criteria range**, you enter the items you want to match from the list, or expressions that describe the type of comparison you wish to make.

- You then open a dialog box in which you specify the range where the list or table is contained, the range containing the criteria, and the range to which you want records copied/extracted (if applicable).

Advanced Filter dialog box

```
Advanced Filter              [?][X]
Action
  ○ Filter the list, in-place
  ◉ Copy to another location
List range:      $D$12:$I$105      [icon]
Criteria range:  $D$109:$J$110     [icon]
Copy to:         $D$113:$I$113     [icon]
☐ Unique records only
        [  OK  ]   [ Cancel ]
```

- To set up the criteria range, you simply copy the field names from the top of the list to another area of the worksheet, or to a separate worksheet in the same workbook.
  - The labels in the criteria range must exactly match the labels used in the list, which is why you should copy them rather than typing them.
  - After the criteria range is established, you type the criteria under the appropriate field name(s).
  - For example, to display only records belonging to Smith, you might type Smith under the Last Name field name in the criteria range you've established.

Guidelines for Entering Criteria

- You enter criteria in the criteria range, below the field names you copied.
  - The following examples are strictly for purposes of demonstration; the field names and contents of your list or table will likely differ from those shown here.
- If you want to establish an AND condition, where two or more criteria must be true for a record to match, then type the criteria under their proper field names in the same row.
  - For example, to display records where the quantity on hand is over 25 AND the cost is less than $10, type both criteria in the same row, each in their respective column.

- If you want to establish an OR condition, where any of two or more criteria will qualify a record as a match, then type the criteria under their proper field names, but in separate rows.
  - For example, to display records where the quantity on hand is over 25 OR the cost is less than $10, type the criteria in different rows.
- When you enter text, Excel looks for any match beginning with that text.
  - Typing *Sam* under the First Name label would match records such as *Sam*, *Samuel*, and *Samantha*.
- You can use wildcards when entering text criteria.
- A question mark (?) can be used to replace a single character in a specific position within the text.
  - For example, type *Sm?th* under the Last Name label to get *Smith* and *Smyth*.
- An asterisk (*) can be used to replace one or several characters within the text.
  - For example, type *Sm*th* under the Last Name label to get *Smith*, *Smyth*, *Smouth*, and *Smaningfith*.
- Because ? and * are assumed to be wildcards, if you want to find records that actually contain those characters, you must precede them with a tilde (~).
  - For example, type *RJ4~?S2* to get *RJ4?S2*.
- You can use operators to compare text, numbers, or dates.
  - Operators include < (less than), > (greater than), <= (less than or equal to), >= (greater than or equal to), <> (not equal to), and = (equal to).
  - For example, enter *>256000* under the *Annual Salary* label to get all records that contain an annual salary over $256,000.
  - You can use operators with dates as well. For example, enter *>=01/01/08* under the *Hire Date* label to get all records with a hire date on or after January 1, 2008.
  - You can also use operators with text, as in *<M*, which will display all records beginning with the letters *A* through *L*.

- You can use formulas to specify criteria.

  - For example, to display only records where the total sale (stored in column G) is greater than the average of column G, you could enter something like this for cell G5:

    =G5>AVERAGE($G$5:$G$21)

  - G5 in this example is the first cell in the list or table in column G.

  - You could also use the label cell (G4) or the label itself, as in this formula:

    ="Total Sales">AVERAGE($G$5:$G$21)

  - The comparison cell address uses relative cell addressing, while the rest of the formula must use absolute cell addresses (preceded by $).

  - To use a formula to specify criteria, type it in a cell that doesn't have a label above it.

  ✓ *For this reason, it's usually best to type a formula in the first column to the right of the criteria range you originally established.*

  - Be sure to redefine the criteria range to include the cell that contains the formula and the blank cell above it.

  - You can use more than one formula by typing the second formula in the next column, and adjusting the criteria range again.

  ✓ *If you need to use two formulas, and either one may be true in order to get a match, then type them in the same column in different rows.*

  ✓ *See examples in the next section for placement of formulas in the criteria range.*

Enter Criteria

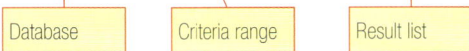

	A	B	C	D	E	F	G
1							
2	*Ace Computer Sales*						
3							
4							
5	**Name**	**Computer**	**Sale Amt.**				
6	Jones		>1300				
7							
8	**Name**	**Computer**	**Sale Amt.**		**Name**	**Computer**	**Sale Amt.**
9	Smith	Maxima	$ 1,230.00		Jones	Ultima	$ 1,495.00
10	Parker	Ultima	$ 1,505.00		Jones	Maxima	$ 1,340.00
11	Jones	Ultima	$ 1,495.00		Jones	Ultima	$ 1,580.00
12	Parker	Maxima	$ 1,280.00				
13	Smith	Maxima	$ 1,280.00				
14	Jones	Maxima	$ 1,340.00				
15	Parker	Ultima	$ 1,590.00				
16	Parker	Ultima	$ 1,620.00				
17	Smith	Maxima	$ 1,320.00				
18	Jones	Ultima	$ 1,580.00				
19							

Database   Criteria range   Result list

Examples of Advanced Criteria

- To display records for Smith and Jones from the sample shown here, type these criteria, in two rows, under the Name field.

Name	**Computer**	**Sale Amt.**
Smith		
Jones		

  ✓ *As on the preceding pages, the following examples show typical list or table field names. Be sure to copy the actual field names from your own list/table to the criteria range.*

- To display records for Smith where the total sale amount is over $1,200, type these criteria in one row under the appropriate field names:

Name	**Computer**	**Sale Amt.**
Smith		>1200

  ✓ *You could also display these records with the proper selections from two columns in filtered list or table.*

- To display Smith's sales records of Maxima computers with a total sales amount more than $1,250, type this in one row:

Name	**Computer**	**Sale Amt.**
Smith	Maxima	>1250

  ✓ *Again, you could display these records using a regular filter.*

- To display records for both Smith and Jones that have a sale amount over $1,250, type this in two rows:

Name	**Computer**	**Sale Amt.**
Smith		>1250
Jones		>1250

- To display records that have a sale amount over $1,250 or that involve Maxima computers (no matter what amount), type this in two rows:

Name	**Computer**	**Sale Amt.**
		>1250
	Maxima	

- To display records of sales of Maxima computers over $1,250, type this in one row:

Name	**Computer**	**Sale Amt.**
	Maxima	>1250

- To display records of sales of Maxima or Ultima computers over $1,250, type this in two rows:

Name	**Computer**	**Sale Amt.**
	Maxima	>1250
	Ultima	>1250

- To display records whose sale amount is greater than or equal to the average, type this in a cell without a label:

  Sale Amt.

  =C2>AVERAGE($C$2:$C$17)

  ✓ *Be sure to include the cell in which you type the formula and the blank cell above it, within the criteria range.*

  ✓ *The formula includes an expression of comparison, featuring the > operator, and which evaluates to TRUE or FALSE.*

- To display records whose sale amounts are between $1,250 and $2,000, type this in two cells without a label in the same row, but in different columns:

  Computer   Sale Amt.

  =C2>1250   =C2<2000

  ✓ *Don't type this in the cell below the Sale Amt. label—it won't work.*

- To display records whose total sale is greater than the average OR over $2,000, type this in two rows, but in the same column:

  Sale Amt.

  =C2>AVERAGE($C$2:$C$17)
  =C2>2000

Remove an In-Place Advanced Filter

- Unlike a regular filter, an advanced filter applied in-place to a list or table (rather than copied to another area of the worksheet) isn't easily detectable.

  - If the row numbers in the list or table are blue and the filter down-arrow buttons aren't visible, an advanced filter is in place.

- To remove an in-place advanced filter, click in the list/table and click the Clear button on the Data tab.

Edit Extracted Records

- If you elect to copy (extract) **extract range** records to another area of the worksheet (called the results list), you can edit them as needed.

- The results list must appear in the same worksheet as the source list from which its records were copied.

- You can change, format, print, sort, delete, and otherwise manipulate the extracted records as you like.

- Even if you alter the extracted records, it won't affect the original records in the list or table.

- This allows you to create a customized, professional-looking report with the extracted records.

- You can even delete some of the extracted records if you don't want to work with them; again, this does not affect the original data.

PROCEDURES

Set Up a Criteria Range

✓ *Prior to using Advanced Filter, you must first set up your criteria range.*

1. Select the field names for the table or list.
2. Click the **Copy** button 🔲 . . . . Ctrl + C
3. Click in the worksheet where you want to establish the criteria range.

✓ *Typically, you create a criteria range above or to the right of the list or table, separated from it by a few rows or columns, although you can create a separate Criteria worksheet if you like.*

4. Click the **Paste** button 🔲 . . . . Ctrl + V
5. Enter criteria in row(s) directly below the appropriate criteria labels.

✓ *Remember that formulas, if you use them, must be entered in cells that don't have a label above them.*

Set Up an Advanced Filter

1. Set up the criteria range as described in the earlier procedure.
2. Click in any cell within the list or table.
3. Click **Data** tab . . . . Alt , A

Sort & Filter Group

4. Click **Advanced** button 🔲 . . . . Q
5. If necessary, in the **List range** text box, type or select the range containing the list or table . . . . Alt + L
6. Click **Criteria Range** . . . . Alt + C
7. Type or select the criteria range.

✓ *Include the criteria label(s) with the criteria.*

✓ *If the criteria includes a formula, include the blank cell(s) above the cell(s) containing the formula.*

8. To hide the non-matching records, select **Filter the list, in-place**. . . . . `Alt`+`F`

OR

a. To copy matching records, select **Copy to another location** . . . . `Alt`+`O`

b. Click **Copy to** . . . . . . `Alt`+`T`

c. Type or select the range to which you want the results list copied.

OR

Enter the address of the upper-left cell of the range where you want the results list copied.

✓ *The destination range must be located in the same worksheet as the list or table.*

✓ *If you indicate a single cell as the Copy to range, Excel copies the filtered results to cells below and to the right of the cell, overwriting existing data without warning.*

9. If you don't want to display/extract duplicate records, select **Unique records only** . . . . `Alt`+`R`

10. Click **OK**. . . . . `Enter`

✓ *Any existing filter for the list or table is turned off, and drop-down arrows beside the field names are disabled.*

Show All Records in a Filtered List or Table

1. Click in any cell within the list or table.

2. Click **Data** tab . . . . `Alt`, `A`

   Sort & Filter Group

3. Click **Clear** button 🔣 . . . . `C`

Business Connection

Labor and Employment Laws

There are many laws and regulations that govern the relationship between employer and employees. Although it may seem that these laws have little impact on you and your everyday life, in fact they are very important. They cover topics ranging from the minimum wage to your rights regarding workplace discrimination and sexual harassment.

Law and Order

Working with a partner, research current labor and employment laws. Use Web sites such as the U.S. Department of Labor (http://www.dol.gov/) to look up information about compliance and the current employment law guide. Alternatively, use Boolean search strategies to locate information. For example, search for employment AND law to locate pages that include both phrases. Take note of the laws you feel might impact you or others in a typical workplace environment. Keep track of your sources so you can include a list of works cited or bibliography. When you have completed your research, create an Excel worksheet in which you can store information about the labor laws you feel are most important. List the name of the law, a brief summary, and a hyperlink to the Web page where you found information about the law. If you have time, create a Word document and write a scenario that illustrates a situation in which employment laws are not being followed, such as an employee being denied family leave, an office that is not handicap accessible, or an unsafe environment. Start a new page and write an explanation of how the law is being broken, what rights the employee has, and what action should be taken to solve the problem. To support your response, insert a hyperlink from the Word document to the Excel workbook.

EXERCISE DIRECTIONS

1. Start Excel, if necessary.
2. Open ⊙ **23Racers**.
3. Save the file as **23Racers_xx**.
4. Create a new worksheet, positioned after the July sheet, entitled **Criteria**.
5. Copy the field names from row 8 of either the June Race or July Race worksheet to row 8 of the Criteria worksheet.
6. Adjust column widths as necessary.
7. Use the Criteria worksheet to select records from the July Race worksheet, featuring only those racers who placed third or better in their qualifying heats, and copy those records to a separate range:

   a. In the Criteria worksheet, in the cell under Qualifying Heat, enter **<4**.

   b. Switch to the July Race worksheet, and click any cell in the list range.

   c. Click the Advanced button on the Data tab.

   ✓ *Under List range, the range $A$8:$H$44 should already appear.*

   d. Next to Criteria range, click the Collapse Dialog button.

   e. Switch to the Criteria worksheet, select the range A8:H9.

   ✓ *The criteria range should always include the entire field names row, plus as many rows beneath it that include criteria values or expressions, in their entirety.*

   f. Click the Restore Dialog button, then choose Copy to another location.

   g. Next to Copy to, click the Collapse Dialog button.

   h. In the July Race worksheet, click cell J8.

   i. Click the Restore Dialog button to return to the dialog box.

   j. Click OK.

   ✓ *Excel will copy all records that match the given criteria, including field names, and will format these records exactly as they appear in their original cells…except for their column width.*

   k. Adjust column widths as necessary.

8. Use the Criteria worksheet to filter records from the June Race worksheet to display only racers who qualified with a four-lap average of one minute or better:

   a. In the Criteria worksheet, clear the existing criteria.

   ✓ *This has no effect on the data that was copied to the July worksheet in step 7.*

   b. Under 4-Lap Qualifying Time, enter **<=12:01:00 AM**.

   ✓ *Excel stores all time values as relative to a point on the clock. So an elapsed time of one minute is stored as "12:01 AM," or one minute of elapsed time past midnight—which is Excel's "zero hour."*

   c. Switch to the June Race worksheet, and click any cell in the list range.

   d. Click the Advanced Filter button on the Data tab.

   e. Next to Criteria range, click the Collapse Dialog button.

   f. Switch to the Criteria worksheet, and select the range A8:H9.

   g. Click the Restore Dialog button.

   h. Click OK.

   ✓ *The list is now filtered in place.*

9. Use another portion of the Criteria worksheet to filter records from the July Race worksheet to display only racers whose qualifying time was above average:

   a. In the Criteria worksheet, copy the field name for 4-Lap Qualifying Time to cell J8.

   b. Adjust column widths as necessary.

   c. In cell K9, enter the formula **=D9<AVERAGE('July Race'!$D$9:$D$44)**.

   ✓ *Row 9 is the first row in the list, so your criteria formula should refer to that row.*

   d. Switch to the July Race worksheet, and click any cell in the original list range.

   e. Click the Advanced button on the Data tab.

   f. Choose Copy to another location.

   g. Next to Criteria range, click the Collapse Dialog button.

   h. Switch to the Criteria worksheet, and select the range J8:K9.

   ✓ *Note that cells J9 and K8 are blank.*

i. Click the Restore Dialog button.

j. Click OK.

k. Adjust column widths as needed.

✓ *The list now appears as shown in Illustration A.*

10. Use another portion of the Criteria worksheet to have the June Race worksheet show only racers whose July qualifying times were faster than their June times:

a. In the Criteria worksheet, copy the field names from columns A through H to row 13.

b. In cell I14, enter a formula that contains an expression that compares whether the time value in cell D9 of July Race is less than the time value in cell D9 of June Race.

✓ *Notice all the cells below the field name row are left blank, and that the formula appears in the first column in the range where no field name appears.*

✓ *If you entered the formula correctly, cell I14 should read FALSE.*

c. Switch to the June Race worksheet, and click any cell in the list range.

d. Click the Advanced Filter button on the Data tab.

e. Next to Criteria range, click the Collapse Dialog button.

f. Switch to the Criteria worksheet, and select the range A13:I14.

g. Click the Restore Dialog button, and then choose Copy to another location.

h. Next to the Copy to box, click the Collapse Dialog button.

i. In the June Race worksheet, click cell J8.

j. Click the Restore Dialog button.

k. Click OK.

✓ *Notice that the newly created range contains records that are not showing in the original range to the left. The filter for that range remains active.*

l. Adjust column widths as necessary.

11. Spell check each worksheet.

12. Print each worksheet.

13. Close the workbook, saving all changes.

Illustration A

Racer Last Name	Racer First Name	Racer Number	4-Lap Qualifying Time	Qualifying Heat	Heat Result	Race Result	Pts. Towards Championship
Allan	Carl	5	00:58.61	2	3	8	19
Alvarez	Martin	92	00:58.59	1	2	1	37
Cannon	Doug	16	01:00.12	3	3	9	15
Cannon	Joshua	9	00:57.14	1	4		2
Cordes	Jorg	65	01:00.13	1	3	5	24
Farmer	Bob	3	01:03.88	3	4		5
Farmer	Rita	89	00:59.17	3	9		0
Gallegos	Mario	11	01:01.34	2	10		0
Gallegos	Rodrigo	4	00:58.14	3	1	7	23
Hu	Joi	71	01:04.36	4	1	10	15
Janese	Jay	98	01:00.79	4	4		6
Jasti	Pardha	8	01:01.64	1	1	2	35
Jefferson	Antwon	39	01:03.90	2	1	3	36
Kanai	Saburo	44	01:04.25	2	8		2
Loving	Greg	17	01:05.67	2	2	4	32
Miller	Thomas	56	00:59.31	3	6		3
Moreno	Jorge	77	01:00.53	4	8		2
Sechrest	Art	1	00:59.34	4	7		3
Wilson	Thomas	46	01:03.60	4	2	6	26

ON YOUR OWN

1. Start Excel, if necessary.
2. Open 💿 **23PetInventory**.
3. Save the file as **OXL23_xx**.
4. Use an advanced filter to create a separate (extracted) list of items that need to be reordered.

   ✓ *An item needs to be reordered if its current inventory is at or below the Reorder When value. Use a formula containing an expression that determines this.*

5. After extracting the matching records, make some modifications to them, so you can use the extraction range as an order form:

   a. First, add a column called **On Order**.

   b. Order 10 cases of each pet food product (bonies are not considered a pet food product in this instance).

   c. Order 2 cases each of the larger items, like dog beds and scratching posts.

   d. Order 4 cases of the smaller items, like bones, leashes, and toys.

6. Compute the total cost of the order:

   a. First, calculate the cost per item by multiplying the cases ordered by the price per case.

   b. Total the cost of the order. See Illustration A.

   c. Add in extra costs like tax (8.75%) and the $100 delivery fee.

7. Format the order form however you like:

   a. Make sure you include the company name (Pete's Pets) and its address (214 North Place Street, Cumberland, Ohio 43732) on the order form.

   b. Add formatting to make the order form look professional.

8. Adjust column widths as necessary.
9. Spell check the order form.
10. Print the order form.
11. Save and close the workbook.
12. Exit Excel.

Illustration A

SOXL23 - Microsoft Excel

Pete's Pets
214 North Place Street, Cumberland, Ohio 43732

Product #	Description	Price	Current Inventory	Reorder When	Number per Case	My Cost	Price per Case	On Order	Order Cost
34897	Sm. Bonie	$2.00	22	25	100	$ 0.50	$ 50.00	4	$ 200.00
34898	Med. Bonie	$2.75	18	25	100	$ 0.53	$ 53.00	4	$ 212.00
34899	Lg. Bonie	$3.50	6	25	100	$ 0.64	$ 64.00	4	$ 256.00
44212	Sm. Training Leash	$13.75	9	10	25	$ 7.60	$ 190.00	4	$ 760.00
44213	Lg. Training Leash	$15.25	6	10	25	$ 9.80	$ 245.00	4	$ 980.00
55123	2 Tier Scratch Post	$22.50	3	5	5	$ 11.75	$ 58.75	2	$ 117.50
34897	Chew Toys, asst.	$3.25	27	30	25	$ 0.75	$ 18.75	4	$ 75.00
77898	Med. Cedar Chip Bed	$23.50	4	5	5	$ 14.80	$ 74.00	2	$ 148.00
83122	Gourmet Delight - Turkey	$2.25	27	30	14	$ 1.80	$ 25.20	10	$ 252.00
83123	Gourmet Delight - Chicken	$2.25	24	30	14	$ 1.90	$ 26.60	10	$ 266.00
83144	Cat's Pride - Tuna	$3.75	16	18	36	$ 2.20	$ 79.20	10	$ 792.00
							Total		$ 4,058.50
							Tax		$ 355.12
							Delivery		$ 100.00
							Order Total		$ 4,513.62

Exercise | 24

Skills Covered

- **Sort Excel Items**
- **Rules for Sorting**
- **Undo a Sort**
- **Restore Original Record Order**

Software Skills   Entering data in random order makes the job a bit easier, since you don't have to organize the information first. But trying to find information in a disorganized database is time consuming. So, after entering data into a list, the first order of business is ordering (sorting) the data.

Application Skills   When you add a new patient to the list of cats and dogs in the Wood Hills Animal Clinic patients list, it appears at the end of that list, which ruins the alphabetical order. You've seen other Excel users insert new rows in the middle of lists, by judging for themselves where those new entries belong. But (surprise!) Excel can sort entries for you extremely easily and quickly.

TERMS

Ascending order   An arrangement of items in alphabetical order (A to Z) or numerical order (1, 2, 3, and so on). Dates are arranged from oldest to most recent.

Descending order   An arrangement of items in reverse alphabetical order (Z to A) or reverse numerical order (10, 9, 8, and so on). Dates are arranged from most recent to oldest.

Key   One level within a sort. For example, you might sort a list by last name (one key) and then sort duplicate last names by first name (another key).

NOTES

Sort Excel Items

- After entering data into an Excel list or table, you can arrange the items however you wish.

- You might want to sort a list in alphabetical order (for example, a list of names), or numerical order (a price list), or date order (a list of employees and their hire dates).

- Lists can be sorted in **ascending order** or **descending order**.
  - Ascending order will arrange labels alphabetically (A to Z), numbers from smallest to largest, and dates from oldest to most recent.
  - Descending order is simply the reverse of ascending order.

- You can sort any contiguous data in the worksheet; it doesn't have to be a list or table. For example, you might want to sort an expense report to list all the expenses in order by account number.

- Data can be sorted using more than one **key**.
  - A key is a single sort level.
  - In the following example, an employee listing has been sorted by ZIP code. Employees with duplicate ZIP codes are then sorted by surname (last name), and those with duplicate surnames are sorted by given name (first name) for a total of three keys.

Sort sample

  - You can sort a list, using a maximum of three keys, in a single sort command.
- You can sort data by using the sort buttons on the Data tab, with the Sort dialog box, or with the down-arrow button that appears beside the field names in the top row of an Excel table.
  - The sort buttons change names depending on the type of data you're trying to sort.
  - If you're sorting text, the buttons are called Sort A to Z and Sort Z to A.
  - If you're sorting numbers, the buttons are called Sort Smallest to Largest and Sort Largest to Smallest.
  - If you're sorting dates, the buttons are called Sort Oldest to Newest and Sort Newest to Oldest.

Sort buttons

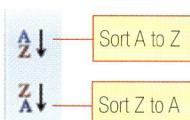

Sort dialog box

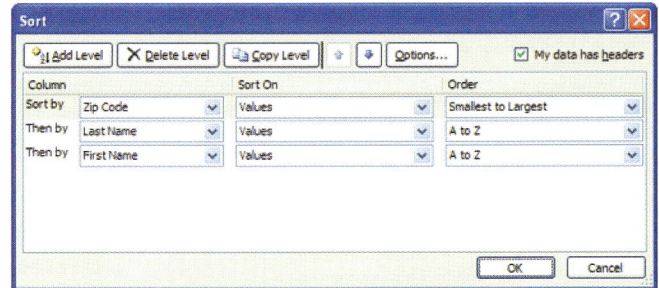

Rules for Sorting

- Excel sorts data based on the actual cell content, not the displayed results.
- If you choose to sort in ascending order, items are arranged as follows:
  - *Numeric sort*—Numbers are sorted from the largest negative number to the largest positive number.

    For example, -3, -2, -1, 0, 1, 2, and so on.
  - *Alphanumeric sort*—Labels (text or text/number combinations) are sorted first by symbols, then by letters.

    Symbols are arranged in this order:
    (space) ! " # $ % & ( ) * , . / : ; ? @ [\ ] ^ _
    ` { | } ~ + < = >

    Letters are arranged alphabetically, A to Z.
  - Hyphens (-) and apostrophes (') are ignored in alphanumeric sorts, except when sorting cells whose contents are identical apart from a hyphen or apostrophe. In those situations, the cell containing the symbol is placed last.
  - If names in the list contain spaces (*de Lancie*), the sort results may differ from what you expect. Because spaces sort to the top of the list, *de Lancie* lands above *Dean* and *Debrazzi*.
  - Alphanumeric sorts on number/text combination may also surprise you. Combinations like 1Q through 11Q, for example, sort like this *10Q, 11Q, 1Q, 2Q, 3Q*, and so on.
  - Dates are sorted chronologically.

    For example, 1/10/09 would come before 2/12/09.
  - If a cell in the sort column is blank, that record is placed at the end of the list.

  ✓ *This is true whether the sort is ascending or descending.*

■ As an example of sorted records, consider this list:

Jay's Grill	1256 Adams Ave.
CompuTrain	12 Brown Street
Central Perk	
Carriage Club	Carriage Center
Giving Tree	? Mark Building

■ If the list is sorted by address (ascending order), you'll end up with:

CompuTrain	12 Brown Street
Jay's Grill	1256 Adams Ave.
Giving Tree	? Mark Building
Carriage Club	Carriage Center
Central Perk	

■ Notice that the record that doesn't contain an address is placed last.

■ Using the Sort Option dialog box, you can sort left to right (across a row) rather than top to bottom (down a column). This option is useful if your list is organized with a horizontal rather than a vertical orientation.

■ You also can sort with case sensitivity. In a case-sensitive sort, capital letters are sorted after lower-case letters, so *kit* appears above *Kit*.

■ If conditional formatting has been applied to the table or list, you can sort by cell and/or font color, or cell icon.

Undo a Sort

■ You can undo a sort if you click the Undo button immediately after completing the sort.

■ If you don't undo a sort immediately, the original sort order is lost.

■ To protect your data, always save the workbook prior to sorting.

✓ *If something goes wrong, simply close the workbook without saving changes, and open the saved version from disk.*

Restore Original Record Order

■ If you want to keep your original sort order as well as the new, sorted list, copy the original list to another sheet in the workbook and then sort.

■ Another way to restore the original record order at any time is to include a unique field in every record.

• For example, you could include a field called *Record Number*, and fill in unique numbers for each record. (Make sure all numbers are the same length.)

• To restore the original order, simply sort by the Record Number column.

PROCEDURES

Sort a List in Ascending or Descending Order

1. Select cell in the column you want to sort by.
2. Click **Data** tab . . . . [Alt], [A]

   Sort & Filter Group

3. Click **Sort A to Z, Sort Smallest to Largest, Sort Oldest to Newest** button [↓] . . . . [A]

   OR

   Click **Sort Z to A, Sort Largest to Smallest, Sort Newest to Oldest** button [↓] . . . . [D]

Sort in a Table in Ascending or Descending Order

1. Click arrow next to field name for column you want to sort by.
2. Click **Sort A to Z, Sort Smallest to Largest, Sort Oldest to Newest** . . . . [S]

   OR

   Click **Sort Z to A, Sort Largest to Smallest, Sort Newest to Oldest** . . . . [O]

Sort in a Table by Conditional Formatting

1. Click arrow next to field name for a conditional column you want to sort by.
2. Click **Sort by Color** . . . . [T]
3. Choose a cell or font color from the list . . . . [↑]/[↓], [Enter]

   OR

   a. Click **More Cell Colors** . . . . [↑]/[↓], [Enter]
   b. Select a color from the palette that appears . . . [→]/[←]/[↑]/[↓]
   c. Click **OK** . . . . [Enter]

   OR

   ■ Click **Automatic** to sort by the automatic font color.

Create a Custom Sort

1. Select any cell in list or table.
2. Click **Data** tab . . . . [Alt], [A]

   Sort & Filter Group

3. Click **Sort** button [↓↑] . . . . [S]
4. Select a column from the **Sort by** list. . . . . [↑]/[↓], [Enter]
5. Select a data type to **Sort On** . . . . [⇄],[↑]/[↓], [Enter]

   ✓ *For example, you can sort on the cell value, or its conditional formatting.*

6. Select a sort **Order** . . . . [↑]/[↓], [Enter]

   ✓ *You can sort in ascending or descending order, or create a custom sort by entering a list of sort values in the worksheet and selecting that Custom List.*

7. Add additional sort keys as desired:

   a. Click **Add Level** . . . . . `Alt`+`A`

   ✓ *You can click Copy Level to copy the current sort level, and then quickly modify the copy to add a new level.*

   ✓ *Click Delete Level to remove a sort level.*

   b. Select a column from the **Then by** list. . . . . `↑`/`↓`, `Enter`

   c. Repeat steps 5–7.

8. Set sort options:

   a. Click **Options** . . . . `Alt`+`O`

   b. To sort by upper- and lowercase, select **Case sensitive** . . . . `C`

   c. Sort by columns by selecting **Sort top to bottom** . . . . `T`

   OR

   Sort by rows by selecting **Sort left to right** . . . . `L`

9. Click **OK**. . . . . `Enter`

Undo a Sort

✓ *It's best to undo a sort immediately.*

■ Click the **Undo** button 🔄 on the Quick Access Toolbar.

EXERCISE DIRECTIONS

1. Start Excel, if necessary.

2. Open 💿 **24Patients**.

3. Save the file as **24Patients_*xx***.

4. Sort the table alphabetically by breed:

   a. Click the down-arrow beside the Breed field name.

   b. From the list, choose Sort A to Z.

5. Adjust column widths as needed, spell check, and print the worksheet.

6. Divide cats from dogs by sorting:

   a. Click cell B6.

   b. Click Data tab

   c. Click Sort A to Z

   ✓ *Notice that the cat breeds and the dog breeds are still sorted alphabetically as well, by virtue of the sort you performed earlier.*

7. Print the worksheet.

8. Sort the table by cat or dog, then sex (males first), then breed (see Illustration A):

   a. Click anywhere inside the table.

   b. Click Data tab

   c. Click Sort button

   d. Select Cat or Dog? from the Sort by list.

   e. Select Values from the Sort On list.

   f. Select A to Z from the Order list.

   g. Click Add Level.

   h. Select Sex from the Then by list.

   i. Select Values from the Sort On list.

   j. Select Z to A from the Order list.

   k. Click Add Level.

   l. Select Breed from the Then by list.

   m. Select Values from the Sort On list.

   n. Select A to Z from the Order list.

   o. Click OK.

9. Print the worksheet.

10. Close the workbook, saving all changes.

Illustration A

S24Patients - Microsoft Excel

	Patient Name	Cat or Dog?	Breed	Sex	Owner Last Name	Owner First Name
6	K'ao Kung	Cat	Balinese	N	Whitaker	Verna
7	Figaro	Cat	Abyssian	M	Damir	Rafiquil
8	Foz Cat	Cat	American Bobtail - Longhair	M	Echols	Jyoti
9	Bogart	Cat	British SH	M	Scott	Kate
10	Hamlet	Cat	British SH	M	Turner	Teresa
11	Basil	Cat	Devon Rex	M	Lee	Wu
12	Kwanzaa	Cat	DSH	M	Whitaker	Shamir
13	Pyewackett	Cat	DSH	M	Woo	Kum
14	Mai Tai	Cat	Himalayan	M	Thorton	Vanessa
15	Maiimoto	Cat	Korat	M	Ryan	Meghan
16	Marshall	Cat	Maine Coon	M	Sweeney	Dyan
17	Rahjah	Cat	Persian	M	Willard	Mima
18	Mayhem	Cat	American Bobtail - Longhair	F	Thompson	Doug
19	Lee Ling	Cat	Cornish Rex	F	Yamaguchi	She Wu
20	Harlow	Cat	DSH	F	Wasserman	Jay
21	Hazel	Cat	DSH	F	Whitney	Antonia
22	Maddie	Cat	DSH	F	Askren	Mollica
23	Nikki	Cat	DSH	F	Arzate	Lisa
24	Bon Chat	Cat	Himalayan	F	Russell	Melissa
25	Jazz	Cat	Ocicat	F	Ryan	Shakur
26	Kahlua	Cat	Russian Blue	F	Sventeck	Robert
27	Kayto	Cat	Siamese	F	Waters	Alyce
28	Sagwa	Cat	Siamese	F	Wilson	Shale
29	Spice Cat	Cat	Siamese	F	Flynn	Katerina
30	Akemi	Dog	Akita Inu	M	Woo	Daniel
31	Barney	Dog	Beagle	M	Nuniez	Juan
32	Snowball	Dog	Bichon Frise	M	Rwizi	Jorita
33	Carlos	Dog	Chihuahua	M	Leaminson	Carl
34	Sherlock	Dog	German Shepherd	M	Alvarez	Rita
35	Blacky	Dog	Labrador Retriever	M	Hassan	Eram
36	Shamrock	Dog	Labrador Retriever	M	Nguyen	Chu Ci

Patient List

ON YOUR OWN

1. Start Excel, if necessary.

2. Design a list to track homes for sale in your area.

   ✓ *Pretend that you're thinking about putting your own house up for sale, and you want to check out the competition. Include columns for the asking price, address, neighborhood or association, square footage, number of bedrooms, and extras, like a family room, study, basement, fenced yard, and so on.*

3. Save the file as **OXL24_*xx***.

4. Format the worksheet attractively, adding a title, some clip art, and some color. You can format your data as a table if you want.

5. Connect to the Internet to find data for your list/table:

   a. Enter at least 15 homes into the list.

   ✓ *If you don't have Internet access, you can get house listings from your local newspaper.*

   b. Use the real estate listings online to make your list realistic.

   ✓ *Be sure to add your own home to the list as well, along with what you think your asking price will be. (If you don't own a home, make one up!) To make your home easier to spot in the list, type an asterisk (*) at the end of its address. Sort the list by neighborhood (level 1), and then by asking price (level 2).*

6. Answer some key questions using the information in your list/table:

   a. Which house is the most expensive in each neighborhood?

   b. Which house is the least expensive?

   c. Which neighborhood has the highest number of houses for sale?

7. Sort the list by square footage:

   a. Which house has the most square footage? What is its asking price?

   b. Which house has the least? What is its asking price?

8. Sort the list by the number of bedrooms (level 1) and by square footage (level 2):

   a. Which houses have the same number of bedrooms as yours? What are their asking prices?

   b. Which house has square footage closest to the amount in your own home? What is its asking price?

   c. Do the houses that are similar to yours have features that yours doesn't?

9. Now that you have more information, adjust the asking price of your own house, if necessary.

   ✓ *How close was your original asking price to reality?*

10. Adjust column widths as necessary.

11. Spell check the worksheet.

12. Print the worksheet.

13. Close the workbook, saving all changes.

Skills Covered

- **Add Subtotals**
- **Create Nested Subtotals**
- **Remove a Subtotal**
- **Hide/Display Details**
- **Manually Outline and Add Subtotals**

Software Skills With the Subtotals feature, you can create automatic totals within the records of a database to help you perform more complex analyses. For example, if the database contains sales records for various stores, you can create totals for each store or each salesperson. If the database lists employee information, you can create totals for weekly and annual salaries at each location. With the Subtotals feature, you can total numeric data instantly without having to insert rows, create formulas, and copy data. Instead, it all happens with a few simple clicks.

Application Skills August has come and gone, and the usage statistics for Giant Frog Supermarkets' leased network space have been added to Intellidata's ongoing usage logs. With so much new data to keep track of, the workbook now needs to be reorganized so managers can view meaningful summaries of the data.

TERMS

Database function A specialized type of function for databases/lists. For example, the DSUM() function totals the values in a given range, but only for the database records that match criteria you supply.

Function A preprogrammed calculation. For example, the SUM() function totals the values in a specified range.

NOTES

Add Subtotals

- With the Subtotal feature, you can quickly insert subtotals between similar rows in an Excel list without having to create custom functions.

  ✓ *You cannot use the Subtotal feature with an Excel table.*

  - Instead of entering DSUM() formulas to total a field for particular rows, you can use the Subtotal feature.
  - For example, you can subtotal a sales list to compute the amount sold by each salesperson on a given day.

- You can also use the Subtotal feature to insert other **database functions**, such as DCOUNT(), DAVERAGE(), and so on.

  ✓ *To learn more about using database functions, see Exercise 26.*

- The Subtotal feature does the following:
  - Calculates subtotals for all rows that contain the same entry in one column.
  - For example, if you select the field Salesperson, Excel will create subtotals for each salesperson.
  - Inserts the totals in a row just below that group of data.
  - Calculates a grand total.
  - Inserts a label for each group totaled/subtotaled.

- Displays the outline controls.

  ✓ *The outline controls, shown in the figure, allow you to control the level of detail displayed.*

Subtotals allow you to control the level of detail

- For the Subtotal feature to work, all records containing values that contribute to that subtotal (or other calculation) must be sorted together.

  - Before applying the subtotal feature, sort the list so that all records that are to be calculated together, are grouped together. This way, all the "Sacramento" entries will be in a group.

  - Excel inserts a subtotal line whenever it detects a change in the value of the chosen field—for instance, a change from "Sacramento" to "San Francisco."

  - Also, if the subtotal line is to show the average pledge amount for all callers to the Sacramento office, then each pledge must contain "Sacramento" in one column—preferably one with a meaningful field name, such as "Office."

- When click the Subtotal button on the Data tab, a dialog box displays, from which you can make several choices:

  - *At each change in*—Select the field name by which you want to total.

  - *Use function*—Select a database function.

  - *Add subtotal to*—Select one or more fields to use with the database function you selected.

  - *Replace current subtotals*—Select this option to create a new subtotal within a database, removing any current subtotals. Deselect this option to retain current subtotals.

- *Page break between groups*—Places each subtotaled group on its own page.
- *Summary below data*—Inserts the subtotals/grand total below each group, rather than above it.
- *Remove All*—Removes all subtotals.

Subtotals dialog box

- Subtotals act just like any other formula; if you change the data, the total will recalculate automatically.

- You can use the Subtotal feature on a filtered list.

  - The totals are calculated based only on the displayed data.

  ✓ *To learn more about filtering a list, see Exercise 22.*

- As mentioned previously, you cannot use the Subtotals feature on an Excel table.

  - To enable a table to use subtotals, first convert it back to a list.

Create Nested Subtotals

- You can create subtotals within subtotals (nested subtotals).

- For example, you could create a subtotal for each salesperson and for each store (including the entire sales staff for that store).

- To create nested subtotals:

  - Sort the list by both of the fields you wish to total.

  - For example, sort by Store (key 1) and then by Salesperson (key 2).

  - Create the first subtotal using Store as the field.

  - Create the second subtotal using Salesperson as the field, but this time turn off the option to replace the current subtotals (thus keeping the subtotals for the Store field intact).

✓ *See Exercise 24 for help in sorting.*

Remove a Subtotal

- You can remove the subtotals from a list by clicking the Remove All button in the Subtotal dialog box.

- You can also remove subtotals by creating new subtotals that replace old ones.

- If you just created the subtotals and you don't like the results, click the Undo button on the Quick Access Toolbar to remove the subtotals, and then start over.

Hide/Display Details

- The Subtotal feature displays the outline controls around the worksheet frame.

- With the outline controls, you can hide or display the records within any given group.

  - For example, you could hide the details of each salesperson's individual sales, and show only his or her subtotal.

  - You could also show details for some salespeople while hiding the details for others.

- The first subtotal added to a worksheet subdivides it into *three* levels of data.

  - The highest detail number always represents the view with *all* the data.

  - Detail level 1 always represents grand totals only.

  - Intermediate detail levels represent summaries of detail levels.

  - Each subtotal added to a worksheet that already contains subtotals, adds one detail level.

Manually Outline and Add Subtotals

- The Subtotal feature creates subtotals in a list automatically.

  - The Subtotal feature also creates an outline you can use to expand or collapse detail rows.

- Even with the Subtotal feature, you might still want to manually outline (group) a list.

  - For example, you might use the Group feature to manually group particular rows together.

  - Using Group, you can also create a list that contains totals for *multiple fields in the same row*.

  - Group also allows you to manually group columns together, in a situation where your data is arranged mainly in rows (rather than mainly in columns).

- Another reason to use the Group feature is to add subtotals to an Excel table.

  - You can also use the Group feature to add the outlining controls to an Excel table.

PROCEDURES

Subtotal a List

1. Sort list by the column(s) you want to subtotal.

   ✓ *Items you want to subtotal should be grouped together.*

2. Select any cell in list.

3. Click **Data** tab . . . . ⌐Alt⌐, ⌐A⌐

   Outline Group

3. Click **Subtotal** button ▦ . . . . . ⌐B⌐

4. Click **At each change in** . . . . ⌐Alt⌐+⌐A⌐

5. Select the column by which you wish to subtotal . . . . ⌐↑⌐/⌐↓⌐, ⌐Enter⌐

   ✓ *A new subtotal will be calculated at each change within the column you choose here.*

6. Click **Use function** . . . . . . ⌐Alt⌐+⌐U⌐

7. Select desired function . . . . ⌐↑⌐/⌐↓⌐, ⌐Enter⌐

8. Select **Add subtotal to** . . . ⌐Alt⌐+⌐D⌐

9. Click columns(s) containing the values to calculate . . . . ⌐↑⌐/⌐↓⌐, Space

To replace current subtotals:

- Select **Replace current subtotals** . . . . ⌐Alt⌐+⌐C⌐

To insert page breaks between subtotaled groups:

- Select **Page break between groups** . . . . ⌐Alt⌐+⌐P⌐

To place subtotals and grand totals above data:

- Deselect **Summary below data** . . . . ⌐Alt⌐+⌐S⌐

10. Click **OK** . . . . ⌐Enter⌐

Remove Automatic Subtotals

1. Sort list by the column(s) you want to subtotal.

   ✓ *Items you want to subtotal should be grouped together.*

2. Select any cell in list.
3. Click **Data** tab . . . . `Alt`, `A`

   Outline Group

4. Click **Subtotal** button ▦ . . . . `B`
5. Click **Remove All**. . . . . . `Alt`+`R`
6. Click **OK**. . . . . `Enter`

Create Nested Subtotals

1. Sort list by the column(s) you want to subtotal.

   ✓ *Items you want to subtotal should be grouped together.*

2. Subtotal the first group in database.
3. Select any cell in list.
4. Click **Data** tab . . . . `Alt`, `A`

   Outline Group

5. Click **Subtotal** button ▦ . . . . `B`
6. Click **At each change in**. . . . . `Alt`+`A`
7. Select the column by which you wish to subtotal . . . . `↑`/`↓`, `Enter`

   ✓ *A new subtotal will be calculated at each change within the column you choose here.*

8. Click **Use function** . . . . . . `Alt`+`U`
9. Select desired function . . . . `↑`/`↓`, `Enter`
10. Select **Add subtotal to** . . . `Alt`+`D`
11. Deselect **Replace current subtotals** . . . . `Alt`+`C`
12. Set other options as desired:

To insert page breaks between subtotaled groups:

- Select **Page break between groups** . . . . `Alt`+`P`

To place subtotals and grand totals above data:

- Deselect **Summary below data** . . . . `Alt`+`S`
13. Click **OK**. . . . . `Enter`

Expand Outline Levels

1. Click in the subtotal row whose total you wish to expand.
2. Click **Data** tab . . . . `Alt`, `A`

   Outline Group

3. Click **Show Detail** button ▦ . . . . `J`

   OR

   Click the **Show Detail** button ⊞ for the group you want to expand.

   OR

   Click the **row level** button `1` for the lowest level you want to show.

   ✓ *Lower numbers show less detail.*

Collapse Outline Levels

1. Click in the subtotal row whose total you wish to collapse.
2. Click **Data** tab . . . . `Alt`, `A`

   Outline Group

3. Click **Hide Detail** button ▦ . . . . `H`

   OR

   Click the **Hide Detail** button ⊟ for the group you want to collapse.

Manually Outline a List

   ✓ *Use this procedure to manually group selected rows or columns for an outline.*

   ✓ *Prior to grouping columns, you must insert blank columns and manually enter subtotal formulas between the groups you want to create.*

1. Select the rows or columns you wish to group within the outline.
2. Click **Data** tab . . . . `Alt`, `A`

   Outline Group

3. Click **Group** button ▦ . . . . `G`

EXERCISE DIRECTIONS

1. Start Excel, if necessary.
2. Open ⊙ **25UsageStats**.
3. Save the file as **25UsageStats_xx**.
4. Change to the Usage statistics 0804 worksheet
5. Create subtotals for each Sunday that begins a measurement period:
   a. Select the range A5:G140.
   b. Click the Subtotal button on the Data tab.
   c. From the At each change in list, choose Date.
   d. From the Use function list, choose Sum.
   e. From the Add subtotal to list, select Avg. Bandwidth, Data In, Data Out, and Transactions.
   f. Clear the Replace current subtotals check box.
   g. Clear the Page break between groups.
   h. Select the Summary below data check box.
   i. Click OK.

   ✓ *There are now three levels of detail. Level 3 shows all the data; level 2 shows just the subtotals for each week; and level 1 shows only the grand totals.*

6. Adjust column widths as necessary.
7. Calculate the average bandwidth for each department:
   a. With the range still selected, click the Subtotal button again.
   b. From the At each change in list, choose Department.
   c. From the Use function list, choose Average.
   d. From the Add subtotal to list, select Avg. Bandwidth. Clear Data In, Data Out, and Transactions.
   e. Click OK.

   ✓ *There are now four levels of detail. Level 1 is the grand total (plus the "grand average" bandwidth). Level 2 summarizes each week, and level 3 summarizes each department. Level 4 contains the complete data.*

8. Create subtotals for each department:
   a. With the range still selected, click the Subtotal button again.
   b. From the At each change in list, choose Department.
   c. From the Use function list, choose Sum.
   d. From the Add subtotal to list, select Avg. Bandwidth, Data In, Data Out, and Transactions.
   e. Click OK.

   ✓ *There are now five levels of detail.*

9. Click outline level button 3 to display only the department averages, weekly totals, and grand totals.
10. Spell check the worksheet.
11. Print the worksheet.
12. Display the detail rows for the Accounting department for the week of August 22.
13. Print the worksheet.
14. Click outline level button 2 to display just weekly totals.
15. Expand the outline to show all the department averages for the week of August 29.
16. Expand the outline to show the Point of sale department's detail for that week, as shown in Illustration A.
17. Manually add a new group:
    a. Insert a new row above row 236.
    b. Type **POS North and South Total** in cell C236.
    c. Apply bold, right alignment to cell C236.
    d. In cell D236, insert a formula that totals the average bandwidths for Point of sale North and Point of sale South.
    e. Select rows 234 to 236, then click the Group button on the Data tab to group the three rows. See Illustration A.
18. Print the worksheet.
19. Close the workbook, saving all changes.

	Date	Department	Region	Avg. Bandwidth Kb/sec	Data In Mb	Data Out Mb	Transactions
31	7/4/2008 Total			1404.9	23093	133364	579502
57	7/11/2008 Total			1339.5	22300	125960	555785
83	7/18/2008 Total			1377.7	23944	129681	566206
109	7/25/2008 Total			1464.4	25935	139778	586438
135	8/1/2008 Total			1439.5	24978	142019	578358
161	8/8/2008 Total			1400.8	23830	139363	572934
187	8/15/2008 Total			1406.2	24204	139935	487461
213	8/22/2008 Total			1410.9	27659	149379	577563
218		Merchandising Average		51.9			
223		Purchasing Average		82.8			
228		Distribution Average		17.66666667			
233		Accounting Average		171.0333333			
234	8/29/2008	Point of sale	North	203.3	6115	28024	89135
235	8/29/2008	Point of sale	South	155.8	1732	15331	62357
236		POS North and South Total		179.55			
237	8/29/2008	Point of sale	Central	104.3	1900	15367	62654
238		Point of sale Total		642.95	9747	58722	214146
239		Point of sale Average		160.7375			
240	8/29/2008 Total			1613.15	28952	158298	605427
241		Grand Total					
242		Grand Average		94.53713235			
243	Grand Total			12857.05	224895	1257777	5109674
244							

ON YOUR OWN

1. Start Excel, if necessary.
2. Open 💿 **25ApplianceSales**.
3. Save the file as **OXL25_xx**.
4. Create subtotals for each state and each store.

   ✓ *Hint: Sort the database first, using State as key 1 and Store as key 2.*

   ✓ *After sorting, use the Subtotal feature to create each subtotal. Use the Sum function and the Price field. After subtotaling the states, create subtotals for the stores. Remember to deselect the Replace current subtotals option so you don't lose the state subtotals.*

5. Display only the subtotals.

   ✓ *If necessary, widen the columns so you can see all the numbers.*

6. Spell check the worksheet.
7. Print the worksheet.

8. Clear all subtotals.
9. Create new subtotals for each store, totaling the dollar volume and count for each appliance:

   a. Sort the database by Store and Appliance.

   b. Create a subtotal for each store showing the dollar volume.

   c. Create another subtotal for each appliance type displaying the number of appliances sold. (Retain the dollar subtotals as well.)

10. Print the worksheet.
11. Clear all subtotals.
12. Sort the list again, creating subtotals of your own choice, such as subtotals for each sales person and each store (see Illustration A).
13. Adjust column widths as necessary.
14. Print the worksheet.
15. Close the workbook, saving all changes.

Illustration A

	State	Store	Salesperson	Appliance	Price
8	Indiana	Blakely Square	Alice Poole	Dryer	$ 430.00
9	Indiana	Blakely Square	Alice Poole	Refrigerator	$ 1,488.00
10	Indiana	Blakely Square	Alice Poole	Stove	$ 435.00
11	Indiana	Blakely Square	Alice Poole	Television	$ 1,295.00
12	Indiana	Blakely Square	Alice Poole	Washer	$ 440.00
13			**Alice Poole Total**		$ 4,088.00
14	Indiana	Blakely Square	Bill Whiner	Stove	$ 425.00
15	Indiana	Blakely Square	Bill Whiner	Television	$ 650.00
16			**Bill Whiner Total**		$ 1,075.00
17		**Blakely Square Total**			$ 5,163.00
18	Indiana	Brown Street	Jack Smithe	Dishwasher	$ 345.00
19	Indiana	Brown Street	Jack Smithe	Refrigerator	$ 898.00
20	Indiana	Brown Street	Jack Smithe	Stove	$ 425.00
21	Indiana	Brown Street	Jack Smithe	Television	$ 895.00
22	Indiana	Brown Street	Jack Smithe	Television	$ 1,295.00
23			**Jack Smithe Total**		$ 3,858.00
24	Indiana	Brown Street	Joe Cooper	Dryer	$ 440.00
25	Indiana	Brown Street	Joe Cooper	Refrigerator	$ 1,488.00
26	Indiana	Brown Street	Joe Cooper	Refrigerator	$ 1,295.00
27	Indiana	Brown Street	Joe Cooper	Television	$ 399.00
28	Indiana	Brown Street	Joe Cooper	Washer	$ 430.00
29			**Joe Cooper Total**		$ 4,052.00
30	Indiana	Brown Street	Sally Peters	Dishwasher	$ 355.00
31	Indiana	Brown Street	Sally Peters	Dryer	$ 425.00
32	Indiana	Brown Street	Sally Peters	Stove	$ 358.00
33	Indiana	Brown Street	Sally Peters	Stove	$ 435.00
34	Indiana	Brown Street	Sally Peters	Television	$ 1,295.00
35	Indiana	Brown Street	Sally Peters	Washer	$ 425.00
36			**Sally Peters Total**		$ 3,293.00
37		**Brown Street Total**			$ 11,203.00
38	**Indiana Total**				$ 16,366.00
39	Illinois	Harper Ave.	Marta Allerges	Dishwasher	$ 345.00

Skills Covered

- **Use Database Functions**
- **Excel's Database Functions**

Software Skills   Functions can perform many automatic calculations, such as totaling a range of cells or finding the minimum value. With a list or table, you may wish to perform these same functions on selected rows that meet specific criteria, such as totaling the sales amounts for all the rows with the name Bill Barker in the Salesperson field. With database functions, you can perform all sorts of calculations and analyses on your data.

Application Skills   Your boss at Wood Hills Animal Clinic has asked you to create a report that answers specific questions about some points of concern regarding the monthly inventory. You've decided that the easiest way to do that is to utilize Excel's database functions, which you've just learned about.

TERMS

Argument   The parameters for a particular function. All database functions use three arguments: the list range, a field from the list, and the criteria you want to use to qualify the function.

Criteria range   The range that contains the criteria.

Database   An organized collection of data. Database data is commonly organized by rows (sometimes known as records) and columns (fields).

Database range   The range that includes all the list detail rows and the field name (column labels) row.

Field   A single column in a database.

Function   A preprogrammed calculation. You give a function a particular set of parameters, such as a range of cells, and it calculates the result for you.

Record   A single row in a database.

NOTES

Use Database Functions

- Excel provides several **functions** specifically designed to be used with a table or a list.

- A table or list is essentially a **database**.

- With one of these functions, you can perform a calculation on **records** in your table or list that meet particular criteria.

  ✓ *For example, you could use the DSUM function to total the sales records for Bobby Brown.*

- You enter the criteria you want to use with the database function by typing the criteria in the worksheet, just as you do with advanced filters.

  ✓ *For information on how to enter criteria, see Exercise 23.*

- All database functions have three **arguments**:

  - The **database range** is the range in the table or list that includes all the records and the field name row.

  - The **field** is the name of the column you wish to use in the function. Instead of the field name, you can also specify a number that represents the field's database column (not the worksheet column).

  - The **criteria range** is the range that contains the criteria.

- Each database function follows this syntax:

  =dfunction(database range, field, criteria range)

  - For example:

    =DSUM(B3:G16,F3,B20:G20)

  - This function totals the values in column F that meet the criteria in the range B20:G20.

  - As with other functions, the simplest way to enter a database function is to use Formula AutoComplete or the Insert Function dialog box.

- You can use named ranges in your functions.

  - For example, you can name the database and the criteria range.

  - This saves you the trouble of typing the range(s) manually.

  - It also provides a margin of safety if you copy the functions to other places in the workbook.

- After you enter a database function, a result is displayed immediately.

  - If you change the criteria in the criteria range, the result of the function will also change—immediately.

  - If you don't want to change the original result but you want to reference the same field in a new function, just make a copy of the field label for your criteria range.

- When you don't require explicit criteria, you can specify the database range again as the function's third argument.

  - For example, if you need the DAVERAGE function to average everything in one field of the database range, copying the entire contents of that field into a separate criteria range would be redundant.

  - But you can't specify *nothing* as the third argument, so you pass the database range (more conveniently, by name) and let that serve as the function's criteria.

Excel's Database Functions

- Excel has many functions that are designed specifically to be used with a database.

- Many of these functions are similar in purpose to functions you've seen before, such as SUM, AVERAGE, and so on.

Excel's database functions

DAVERAGE   Finds the average value in the selected field for records meeting the criteria.

DCOUNT   Counts the cells containing numbers in the selected field for records meeting the criteria.

DCOUNTA   Counts only nonblank cells in the selected field for records meeting the criteria.

DGET   Returns the value in the selected field for the single record meeting the criteria. Displays the error message #NUM! if more than one record meets the criteria.

DMAX   Finds the maximum value in the selected field for records meeting the criteria.

DMIN   Finds the minimum value in the selected field for records meeting the criteria.

DPRODUCT   Multiplies the values in a field times the values in the field used in the criteria.

DSTDEV   Estimates the standard deviation of a sample of the values in the selected field for records meeting the criteria.

DSTDEVP   Calculates the standard deviation for all the values in the selected field for records meeting the criteria.

DSUM   Finds the sum of values in the selected field for records meeting the criteria.

DVAR   Estimates variance based on a sample of the values in the selected field for records meeting the criteria.

DVARP   Calculates variance based on all the values in the selected field for records meeting the criteria.

PROCEDURES

Enter a Database Function Manually Using AutoComplete

1. Set up the criteria range in the worksheet.

   ✓ *Follow the steps in Exercise 23 in the procedure "Set Up a Criteria Range."*

2. Click cell where result should display . . . . ⬆/⬇/⬅/➡

3. Type =

4. Type the first letters of function name.

5. Double-click function in AutoComplete list . . . . ⬆/⬇, ⬅

   ✓ *Notice that AutoComplete enters the left parenthesis for you, and prompts you for the proper arguments.*

6. Type or select the **Database** range.

7. Type ,

8. Type or select the field name you want to use in the function.

9. Type ,

10. Type or select the criteria range.

11. Complete the function . . . . . . ⬅

Insert a Database Function

1. Set up the criteria range in the worksheet.

   ✓ *Follow the steps in Exercise 23 in the procedure "Set Up a Criteria Range."*

2. Click cell where result should display . . . . ➡/⬅/⬆/⬇

3. Click **Insert Function** button *ƒx*.

   OR

   a. Click **Formulas** tab. . . Alt , M

   b. Click **Insert Function** button *ƒx* . . . . F

4. Select **Database** from **Or select a category** list . . . . Alt +C, ⬇/⬆, Enter

5. Select function from **Select a function** list . . . . Alt +N, ⬆/⬇

6. Click **OK** . . . . Enter

   ✓ *The Function Arguments dialog box appears.*

7. Type or select the **Database** range.

8. Click in the **Field** box . . . . . . ⬅

9. Type or select the field name you want to use in the function.

10. Click in the **Criteria** box . . . . . ⬅

11. Type or select the criteria range.

12. Click **OK** . . . . Enter

   ✓ *If you prefer, you can type the database function directly into the cell, rather than using the Insert Function dialog box.*

EXERCISE DIRECTIONS

1. Start Excel, if necessary.

2. Open 💿 **26AugDrugSales**.

3. Save the file as **26AugDrugSales_xx**.

4. In the August Sales worksheet, sort the list by drug name.

5. Name the entire list range **Sales_August**.

6. In the Aug Sales Analysis worksheet, enter a calculation that identifies the "Highest grossing item":

   a. In cell C3, enter this formula, which finds the maximum total sales value matching the criteria:

      =DMAX(Sales_August,"Total Sales", Sales_August)

   ✓ *Here, **Sales_August** can serve as the criteria range, because we're searching for the highest dollar sales among all items.*

   ✓ *Note that the solution is a value, not the name of the item itself.*

   ✓ *There's one problem with this function, which we can't solve in this context: If two items happened to have sales totaling the same amount, this function would have returned an error.*

   b. In cell N3, enter **=C3**.

   ✓ *This sets up the criteria range for the database function that will retrieve the name of the drug.*

   c. In cell B3, enter this formula, which searches the database range for a match to the value in the criteria range:

      =DGET(Sales_August,"Drug",N2:N3)

7. Enter a calculation that finds the "Best selling flea medication":

   a. In the criteria range for this formula (E5:E6), under For use on, enter **Flea***.

   ✓ *The asterisk wildcard means the function will account for records that contain both **Flea** and **Flea and Tick**.*

   b. In cell C6, enter this formula, which finds the maximum total sales value matching the criteria:

      =DMAX(Sales_August,"Total Sales",E5:E6)

   ✓ *Notice the use of the single column criteria. We want to be able to use the entire criteria range for the next function.*

c. In cell N6, enter **=C6**.

d. In cell B6, enter this formula, which searches the database range for a match to the value in the criteria range:

=DGET(Sales_August,"Drug",N5:N6)

8. Enter a formula in cell C9 that calculates the "Average on hand":

   a. Use the DAVERAGE database function.

   b. Use the Items on Hand column as the field and the list itself as the function's criteria.

9. Create a list of "Items stocked in above average quantity":

   ✓ *What we really want to know here is what item sells the least among those items we order the most. But first, we have to apply an advanced filter as explained in Exercise 23.*

   a. In cell B11, type **Items on Hand**.

   b. In cell C12, enter a formula containing an expression comparing whether the uppermost entry under "Items on Hand" in the Sales_August list (cell G7) is greater than the value in cell C9 on the Aug Sales Analysis sheet.

   c. Have the advanced filter copy its results to a range in the August Sales worksheet, beginning at cell M6.

10. Enter a formula in cell B15 that displays the "Lowest seller among highly ordered items":

    a. First, enter a formula in cell C15 that uses the DMIN function to determine what the lowest selling amount is.

    ✓ *Use the **No. Sold** column in the newly extracted range as the range, and use the range itself as the function's criteria range.*

b. Copy the result (44) to the appropriate column in the criteria range to the right (cell L15).

c. Next, enter a formula in cell B15 that uses DGET to retrieve the name of the drug that sold so few units.

✓ *If more than one drug had sold this many items, the DGET function would return the first name it encountered of the drugs meeting the criteria. In a sorted list, this first name would be the one closest to "Aa."*

11. Enter a formula in cell C18 that uses DSUM to calculate the "Total feline item sales".

    ✓ *Since felines include both cats and kittens, enter criteria (in cells F18 and F19) so that both cats and kittens are counted.*

    ✓ *You need to account for entries that include Cat, Dog or Cat, Cat or Kitten, or Puppy or Kitten, which you can do with just two criteria: *Cat and *Kitten.*

12. Enter a formula in cell C22 that uses DSUM to calculate the "Total sales from Drontal Allwormer for dogs".

    ✓ *You'll only need one row for the criteria range, since this function must account for **both** possibilities (Drontal and Dog) simultaneously.*

13. Format all cells appropriately.

    ✓ *Results of database functions that happen to deal with currencies need to be formatted with Accounting format, 2 decimal places.*

14. Adjust column widths as necessary.

15. Spell check the worksheet.

16. Print the worksheet.

17. Close the workbook, saving all changes.

ON YOUR OWN

1. Start Excel, if necessary.
2. Open 🄾 **26CateringSupplies**.
3. Save the file as **OXL26_xx**.
4. Add a column called **Total Weight**, before the *Total Cost* column.
5. For the *Total Weight* column, compute the total weight of each case ordered.
6. Create a new worksheet entitled **Supplies totals**, and place it after the Supplies list worksheet.
7. Prepare the criteria range:
   a. Copy the Vendor label (cell B7 in Supplies list) to the range B4:G4 in the Supplies totals worksheet.
   b. Copy the name of each vendor beneath a label.

8. Create an area below the criteria range, formatted as you like, and use database functions to compute the following for each vendor (see Illustration A):
   a. Number of cases ordered.
   b. Average cost per case.
   c. Total weight.
   d. Cost of the order.
   e. To find the Shipping charge, calculate $20 for every 50 lbs. of weight.
   f. To find the Total cost, add the cost of the order plus the shipping cost.
9. Adjust column widths as necessary.
10. Spell check the workbook.
11. Print the workbook.
12. Close the workbook, saving all changes.

Illustration A

	A	B	C	D	E	F	G
1							
2							
3							
4		Vendor	Vendor	Vendor	Vendor	Vendor	Vendor
5		Clarksville Food Supply	JC Foods	Emily's Herbs	Town Bakery	Mike's Meat Supply	Clarksville Fishery
6	No. of cases ordered	40	61	25	30	27	22
7	Average cost per case	$ 16.45	$ 15.74	$ 16.19	$ 22.73	$ 35.25	$ 37.63
8	Total weight	$ 597.00	$ 707.00	$ 95.75	$ 396.00	$ 1,350.00	$ 660.00
9	Cost of order	$ 729.25	$ 939.55	$ 417.65	$ 676.90	$ 934.25	$ 844.25
10	Shipping charge	$ 238.80	$ 282.80	$ 38.30	$ 158.40	$ 540.00	$ 264.00
11	Total cost	$ 968.05	$ 1,222.35	$ 455.95	$ 835.30	$ 1,474.25	$ 1,108.25
12							

Skills Covered

- **Find and Replace**
- **Find Cells That Match Particular Criteria**

Software Skills   Using the Find and Replace feature, you can locate data within a worksheet and quickly replace it with something else. This is especially useful when making changes to a large worksheet.

Application Skills   As the manager of Giancarlo Franchetti's Go-Cart Speedrome, you're getting more comfortable with Excel, and as a result, you have quite a collection of workbooks. Recent changes in your operations, however, have created errors in many of the workbooks. But with the help of Find and Replace, you'll quickly have things in order again.

TERMS

Find   A command that helps you locate specific data in a worksheet.

Replace   A command that works with Find to replace specific data with something else.

NOTES

Find and Replace

- With **Find**, you can locate text or numbers in a worksheet.

  ✓ *You might do this to locate an area of the worksheet you need to change or view. For example, you could search for a particular employee, or a particular sales office.*

- Using **Replace**, you can replace what you find with something else.

  ✓ *You could use this technique to quickly replace outdated information in a worksheet.*

- You can confirm each replacement, or simply replace all occurrences without confirmation.

  ✓ *Don't use Replace All without verifying each instance unless you're absolutely sure that you won't accidentally replace the wrong data. Using Replace All to change Jan to Feb throughout a worksheet, for example, will accidentally change Janice Smith to Febice Smith and Tom Jansen to Tom Febsen.*

- You can search the current worksheet or an entire workbook.

- Using the options in the Find/Replace dialog box, you can customize the search in other ways as well:

  - You can search by rows or columns, whichever you feel will produce the quickest results.

  - You can search only cells with formulas, values, or comments.

  - You can search for cells containing particular formats, or formats plus some kind of data.

  - You can search for cells whose entire contents match the search criteria, rather than cells that contain additional data. For example, you can search for "Sales" and exclude "Sales Total" and "Sales Department."

- You can search for text that matches not only your search criteria, but its case as well. For example, you can search for "Sales" and exclude "sales."

Set search options

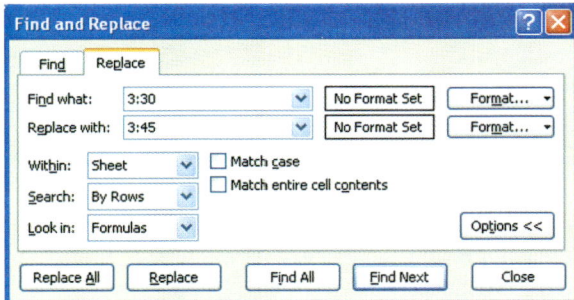

Find Cells That Match Particular Criteria

- If your goal is not to locate data, but to find particular kinds of cells quickly and then select them, then you need a different kind of Find command—Go To Special.
- Using Go To Special, you can locate cells that contain:
  - Comments
  - Constants
  - Formulas
  - Row differences, Column differences
  - Precedents, Dependents
  - Blanks
  - Conditional formats
  - Data validation
- You can also locate:
  - Cells in the current region
  - Cells in the current array
  - Objects
  - The last cell with data
  - Visible (non-hidden) cells
- Some of these commands are accessible from the Find & Select menu on the Home tab; others are accessed through the Go To Special dialog box.

Go To Special dialog box

PROCEDURES

Find (Ctrl+F)

1. Select any cell to search entire worksheet.

   OR

   Select cells to search.

   OR

   Select sheet(s) to search.

2. Click **Home** tab . . . . [Alt], [H]

   Editing Group

3. Click **Find & Select** button 🔍 . . . . [F], [D]

4. Click **Find** . . . . [F]

5. Click in **Find what** text box . . . . [Alt]+[N]

6. Type character(s) to find.

   ✓ You can use wildcard characters (* and ?) to represent any character (?) or group of characters (*) in a search. To find data containing a question mark (?) or asterisk (*), you must type a tilde (~) before the character (~? or ~*).

7. Click **Options**, then set options as desired . . . . [Alt]+[T]

To set a format to find:

a. Click **Format** . . . . [Alt]+[M]

b. Click appropriate tab . . . . [Alt]+[←]

c. Select desired format(s) to find.

d. Click **OK** . . . . [Enter]

OR

a. Click arrow on **Format** button.

b. Click **Choose Format From Cell** . . . . [C]

c. Click cell that contains the format(s) you wish to find.

To set where to search:

a. Click **Within** . . . . [Alt]+[H]

b. Click desired search area . . . . [↑]/[↓], [Enter]

To set a search direction:

a. Click **Search** . . . . [Alt]+[S]

b. Click desired search direction. . . . . [↑]/[↓], [Enter]

To search formula results or comments:

a. Click **Look in** . . . . `Alt`+`L`

b. Click desired search
type . . . . `↑`/`↓`, `Enter`

To make search case sensitive:

■ Select **Match case** . . . `Alt`+`C`

To find cells that match exactly:

■ Select **Match entire cell
contents** . . . . `Alt`+`O`

8. Click **Find Next** . . . . . . `Alt`+`F`

✓ *Excel highlights the first cell meeting
the search criteria.*

9. Perform one of the following:

To find next match:

■ Click **Find Next** . . . . . `Alt`+`F`

OR

To find all occurrences:

■ Click **Find All** . . . . `Alt`+`I`

✓ *This produces a list of cells matching
your criteria. You can click an item in
this list to select that cell.*

To close the dialog box and discontinue the search:

■ Click **Close** . . . . `Esc`

Replace *(Ctrl+H)*

1. Select any cell to search entire
worksheet.

OR

Select cells to search.

OR

Select sheet(s) to search.

2. Click **Home** tab . . . . `Alt`, `H`

Editing Group

3. Click **Find & Select**
button ⟨🔍⟩ . . . . `F`, `D`

4. Click **Replace** . . . . `R`

5. Click in **Find what** text
box . . . . `Alt`+`N`

6. Type character(s) to find.

✓ *You can use wildcard characters (* and
?) to represent any character (?) or
group of characters (*) in a search. To
find data containing a question mark
(?) or asterisk (*), you must type a tilde
(~) before the character (~? or ~*).*

7. Click **Options**, then set options
as desired . . . . `Alt`+`T`

To set a format to find:

a. Click **Format** . . . . `Alt`+`M`

b. Click appropriate
tab . . . . `Alt`+`⇥`

c. Select desired format(s) to
find.

d. Click **OK** . . . . `Enter`

OR

a. Click arrow on **Format** button

b. Click **Choose Format From
Cell** . . . . `C`

c. Click cell that contains the
format(s) you wish to find.

To set where to search:

a. Click **Within** . . . . `Alt`+`H`

b. Click desired search
area . . . . `↑`/`↓`, `Enter`

To set a search direction:

a. Click **Search** . . . . `Alt`+`S`

b. Click desired search
direction . . . . `↑`/`↓`, `Enter`

To search formula results or comments:

a. Click **Look in** . . . . `Alt`+`L`

b. Click desired search
type . . . . `↑`/`↓`, `Enter`

To make search case sensitive:

■ Select **Match case** . . . `Alt`+`C`

To find cells that match exactly:

■ Select **Match entire cell
contents** . . . . `Alt`+`O`

8. Click **Replace** tab . . . . `Alt`+`P`

9. Click in the **Replace with** text
box . . . . `Alt`+`E`

10. Type the character(s) you want to
use as a replacement.

11. Set replacement format if desired:

a. Click **Format** . . . . `Alt`+`M`

b. Click appropriate
tab . . . . `Ctrl`+`⇥`

c. Select desired format(s) to use
as replacements.

d. Click **OK** . . . . `Enter`

OR

a. Click arrow on **Format** button.

b. Click **Choose Format From
Cell** . . . . `C`

c. Click cell that contains the
format(s) you wish to use as
replacements.

12. Click **Find Next** . . . . `Alt`+`F`

✓ *Excel selects first cell meeting the
search criteria.*

13. Perform one of the following:

To globally replace matching cells:

■ Click **Replace All** . . . . `Alt`+`A`

OR

To replace active cell and find the next match:

■ Click **Replace** . . . . . . `Alt`+`R`

OR

To find all occurrences:

■ Click **Find All** . . . . `Alt`+`I`

✓ *This produces a list of cells matching
your criteria. You can click an item in
this list to move the cursor to that cell.*

OR

To retain contents of active cell and find next match:

■ Click **Find Next** . . . . . `Alt`+`F`

OR

To close the dialog box and discontinue the search:

■ Click **Close** . . . . `Esc`

Use Go To Special

1. Select any cell to search entire worksheet.

   OR

   Select cells to search.

   OR

   Select sheet(s) to search.

2. Click **Home** tab . . . . ⌨Alt , ⌨H

3. Click **Find & Select** button 🔍 . . . . ⌨F , ⌨D

4. Click **Go to Special** . . . . ⌨S

5. Select the type of cell to search for:

   a. **Formulas** . . . . ⌨F

   b. Select formula result type:
      - **Numbers** . . . . ⌨U
      - **Text** . . . . ⌨X
      - **Logicals** . . . . ⌨G
      - **Errors** . . . . ⌨E

   OR

   a. **Dependents** . . . . ⌨D

   b. Select dependent type:
      - **Direct only** . . . . ⌨I
      - **All levels** . . . . ⌨L

   OR

   a. **Data validation** . . . . ⌨V

   b. Select validation type:
      - **All** . . . . ⌨L
      - **Same** . . . . ⌨E

   OR

   - **Comments** . . . . ⌨C
   - **Constants** . . . . ⌨O
   - **Blanks** . . . . ⌨K
   - **Current region** . . . . ⌨R
   - **Current array** . . . . ⌨A
   - **Objects** . . . . ⌨B
   - **Row differences** . . . . ⌨W
   - **Column differences** . . . . . ⌨M
   - **Last cell** . . . . ⌨S
   - **Visible cells only** . . . . . . ⌨Y
   - **Conditional formats** . . . . . ⌨T

6. Click **OK** . . . . ⌨Enter

   ✓ *Matching cells are selected.*

Select Matching Data Quickly

1. Select any cell to search entire worksheet.

   OR

   Select cells to search.

   OR

   Select sheet(s) to search.

2. Click **Home** tab . . . . ⌨Alt , ⌨H

3. Click **Find & Select** button 🔍 . . . . ⌨F , ⌨D

4. Select the type of cell to search for:
   - **Formulas** . . . . ⌨U
   - **Comments** . . . . ⌨M
   - **Conditional Formatting** . . . ⌨C
   - **Constants** . . . . ⌨N
   - **Data Validation** . . . . ⌨V
   - **Select Objects** . . . . ⌨O

   ✓ *Matching cells are selected.*

EXERCISE DIRECTIONS

1. Start Excel, if necessary.
2. Open 💿 **27MonthlyAdmissions**.
3. Save the workbook as **27MonthlyAdmissions_xx**.
4. Search and replace data:

   a. Click the Find & Select button on the Home tab and choose Replace.

   b. In the Find what box, type **3:30**.

   c. In the Replace with box, type **3:45**.

   d. Click Find Next.

   e. Cell A11 becomes active.

   f. Click Replace.

   g. Cell A12 becomes active.

   h. Click Replace All to change all occurrences. See Illustration A.

   ✓ *Excel tells you how many occurrences have been changed.*

   i. Click OK.

5. Replace more data:
   a. In the Find what box, type **5:30**.
   b. In the Replace with box, type **5:45**.
   c. Click Find Next.
   d. Cell A13 becomes active.
   e. Click Replace to change the closing time for that session.
   f. Cell A11 becomes active again.
   g. Click Find Next.
   h. Cell A12 becomes active again.
   i. Click Replace to change the closing time for that session.
   j. Cell A11 becomes active again.
   k. Click Close to end the Find and Replace procedure.

6. Find and select all the formulas:
   a. Click cell B9.
   b. Click the Find & Select button on the Home tab.
   c. Click Formulas.

   ✓ *All the cells that contain formulas are selected.*

7. Select your data using the Go To Special command:
   a. Click cell B9.
   b. Click the Find & Select button on the Home tab.
   c. Click Go to Special.
   d. Click Current region and click OK.

   ✓ *The range A8:E23 is selected.*

   e. Deselect the range by clicking cell B9 again.

8. Widen columns as needed.
9. Spell check the worksheet.
10. Print the worksheet.
11. Close the workbook, saving all changes.

Illustration A

	A	B	C	D	E	F
1						
2						
3		*Giancarlo Franchetti's Go-Cart Speedrome*				
4						
5		**Admission Tracker**				
6		**Month:**	**August**			
7						
8		**Adult**	**Child**	**Team Racers**	**Total Racers**	
9	*Sunday 12:30-2:30*	417	663	89	1,169	
10	*Sunday 3:15 - 5:15*	493	719	60	1,272	
11	*Wednesday 3:45 - 5:30*	210	322	34	566	
12	*Thursday 3:45 - 5:45*	636	485	29	1,151	
13	*Friday 3:45 - 5:45*	414	419	100	933	
14	*Friday 6:00 - 8:00*	717	916	140	1,773	
15	*Friday 8:30 - 10:30*	811	251	138	1,200	
16	*Saturday 11:30 - 1:30*	591	46	239	875	
17	*Saturday 1:45 - 3:45*	758	705	128	1,591	
18	*Saturday 4:00 - 6:00*	484	734	80	1,298	
19	*Saturday 6:15 - 8:15*	665	989	162	1,815	
20	*Saturday 8:30 - 10:30*	863	565	168	1,596	
21	**Total Admissions**	7,058	6,813	1,366	15,238	
22	*Admission Price*	$ 10.00	$ 7.00	$ 5.00		
23	**Total Receipts**	$ 70,584.20	$ 47,690.79	$ 6,831.30	$125,106.29	
24						
25	**Grand Total Receipts**	$125,106.29				
26						

S27MonthlyAdmissions - Microsoft Excel

ON YOUR OWN

1. Start Excel, if necessary.
2. Use Basic Search to help you list the soccer team cookie workbooks.
3. Open ⌨ **OXL26_xx**, created in the On Your Own section of Exercise 26, or 💿 **27CateringSupplies**.
4. Save the file as **OXL27_xx**.
5. You now get your sugar, flour, and salt from a different vendor.
   a. Find cells that display the vendor Clarksville Food Supply.
   b. Replace the vendor for descriptions containing flour, sugar, and salt with Scott's Organic Food Supply, the name of the new vendor.
6. Scott's Organic Food Supply charges $14.70 on the same foods that cost $14.95 from the previous vendor. Use Find and Replace to make this change. See Illustration A.
7. Use Go To Special to select all the cells with number formulas.
8. Apply Aqua, Accent 5, Lighter 80% to the selection.
9. Widen columns as needed.
10. Spell check the worksheet.
11. Print the worksheet.
12. Close the workbook, saving all changes.

Illustration A

SOXL27 - Microsoft Excel

Kat's Catering

Description	Vendor	Cost per Case	Case Weight in Lbs.	Cases Ordered	Total Weight	Total Cost
32 oz Tomato Sauce	Clarksville Food Supply	$22.95	6.50	4	26.00	$91.80
12 oz Tomato Paste	Clarksville Food Supply	$14.75	4.25	6	25.50	$88.50
Tomatoes	JC Foods	$21.95	25.50	6	153.00	$131.70
25 lb. Flour	Scott's Organic Food Supply	$13.75	25.00	3	75.00	$41.25
25 lb. Sugar	Scott's Organic Food Supply	$14.70	25.00	4	100.00	$58.80
10 lb. Confectioners Sugar	Scott's Organic Food Supply	$11.95	20.00	3	60.00	$35.85
22 oz Kosher Salt	Scott's Organic Food Supply	$13.50	15.75	2	31.50	$27.00
25 lb. Wheat Flour	Scott's Organic Food Supply	$14.70	25.00	4	100.00	$58.80
32 oz, Chicken Stock	Clarksville Food Supply	$11.50	7.00	5	35.00	$57.50
Green Peppers	JC Foods	$14.95	11.25	8	90.00	$119.60
White Onions	JC Foods	$15.75	15.75	9	141.75	$141.75
Yellow Onions	JC Foods	$15.75	15.75	10	157.50	$157.50
Button Mushrooms	JC Foods	$13.50	7.25	11	79.75	$148.50
Shitake Mushrooms	Emily's Herbs	$18.95	7.25	7	50.75	$132.65
Basil	Emily's Herbs	$16.50	2.25	6	13.50	$99.00
Oregano	Emily's Herbs	$16.50	2.25	5	11.25	$82.50
Green Onions	Emily's Herbs	$12.50	3.75	3	11.25	$37.50
Sage	Emily's Herbs	$16.50	2.25	4	9.00	$66.00
Dinner Rolls - Wheat	Town Bakery	$26.75	11.50	11	126.50	$294.25
Dinner Rolls - White	Town Bakery	$22.95	11.50	7	80.50	$160.65
4 lb. Butter	Clarksville Food Supply	$29.75	16.00	9	144.00	$267.75
French Bread	Town Bakery	$18.50	15.75	12	189.00	$222.00
Beef Tenderloins	Mike's Meat Supply	$38.75	50.00	11	550.00	$426.25
Salmon	Clarksville Fishery	$41.75	30.00	13	390.00	$542.75
Trout	Clarksville Fishery	$33.50	30.00	9	270.00	$301.50
Chicken	Mike's Meat Supply	$31.75	50.00	16	800.00	$508.00
Mozzarella	JC Foods	$13.75	5.00	8	40.00	$110.00
Parmesan	JC Foods	$14.50	5.00	9	45.00	$130.50

Exercise | 28

Skills Covered

- **Find Exact Matches with VLOOKUP and HLOOKUP**
- **Logical Functions**

Software Skills   With the VLOOKUP and HLOOKUP functions, you can look up information in a table based on a known value. For example, you could look up the phone number for a particular client. At the same time, you could look up that client's address and phone number. VLOOKUP and HLOOKUP, however, normally locate either an exact match to the value you're searching for, or the next lesser value. But you can make these functions find only exact matches when needed.

Application Skills   The employee listing for PhotoTown is pretty useful, but you had an incident lately where it was necessary to call an employee's emergency contact after an employee fell sick. Even though the listing isn't large, it still took a few minutes to find the information because you were so nervous. You've decided to add a special section to the worksheet to make it easy to locate contact information quickly, so you don't waste precious minutes the next time you have an emergency.

TERMS

Argument   A variable used in a function. An argument can be a number, text, formula, or a cell reference. A comma separates each argument in a function.

Excel table   Data arranged in columns and specially formatted with column headers that contain commands that allow you to sort, filter, and perform other functions on the table.

Expression   A sort of equation (such as B6>25) that returns a value, such as TRUE or FALSE. Excel uses expressions to identify cells to include in certain formulas such as IF and IFERROR.

Function   A preprogrammed Excel formula for a complex calculation.

List   A range of Excel data organized primarily by columns.

Range name   Name given to a set of adjacent cells. You might name a range in order to make it more convenient to reference that range in a formula or a function, such as VLOOKUP.

NOTES

Finding Exact Matches with VLOOKUP and HLOOKUP

- You can lookup values in a **list** or **Excel table** using the **functions** VLOOKUP and HLOOKUP.
  - VLOOKUP looks up values vertically, in a particular column.
  - HLOOKUP looks up values horizontally, in a particular row.

- Normally, VLOOKUP and HLOOKUP locate either the exact value you specify, or if that value isn't in the specified column/row, the next lesser value is found.

  ✓ *This assumes that the values in the lookup column/row are sorted. If they are not sorted, then VLOOKUP will return the first value it finds that's either a match or less than the match value.*

- You can tell VLOOKUP and HLOOKUP to find an exact match only. In such a case, if a match is not found, the function returns the error #NA.

- To specify that an exact match is required, set the range_lookup **argument** to FALSE:

  =VLOOKUP(lookup_value,table-array, col_index_num,range_lookup)

  =HLOOKUP(lookup_value,table-array, row_index_num,range_lookup)

  - *lookup_value* is text or a value that you're looking for.

  ✓ *VLOOKUP looks for this value in the first column of the specified range; HLOOKUP looks for this value in the first row of the specified range.*

  - *table-array* is the range reference or **range name** of the list or table.

  ✓ *This range does not include the column labels (if using VLOOKUP) or row labels (if using HLOOKUP).*

  - *col_index_num* or *row_index_num* is the column or row number in the table/list from which the matching value should be returned.

  ✓ *Once VLOOKUP or HLOOKUP finds a match for the lookup_value, it marks the row or column in which that match was found. Next, the function moves over to the row or column number you've indicated, and returns the value found there.*

  - *range_lookup* is set to TRUE by default. To require exact matches only, set this argument to FALSE.

  ✓ *Again, keep in mind that for TRUE to work properly, the lookup column/row must be sorted from smallest to largest. To use FALSE however, the values do not need to be sorted at all.*

Logical Functions

- IF is a logical function of which you are already familiar; the IF function can be used to compare two values, and if they match, perform a specific calculation.

- If the values don't match, then the IF function tells Excel to perform some other calculation.

- You use logical functions to test for particular conditions.

- Use the IFERROR function to alert you if a particular formula finds an error.
  - The syntax of the IFERROR function is =IFERROR(*value,value_if_error*).
  - value is an **expression** that results in either a value or an error.
  - Excel first evaluates the *value* expression. If this results in an error, such as #DIV/0 (dividing by zero), then Excel displays the *value_if_error* amount.
  - For example, IFERROR(A1/B1,"No divisor") displays the text *No divisor, if B1 is zero or blank*.

- Use the AND function to test whether certain conditions are true.
  - The syntax of the AND function is =AND(*logical1,logica2*,etc.)
  - The argument, *logical1*, is an expression that compares two values. The expression is either TRUE or FALSE.
  - For example, you might use the expression, A1>B1 to compare the two values like this: =AND(A1>B1)
  - If A1 is indeed greater than B1, then the test evaluates to TRUE. Otherwise, the test is FALSE.
  - You can combine AND with IF to test for multiple conditions before a particular formula is performed.
  - For example, =IF(AND(A1>B1,A1>1000),A1*.05,A1*.02) says that, if A1 is greater than B1 *and* greater than 1000, then multiply A1 times 5%, otherwise, multiply A1 by only 2%.

- Use the OR function in a manner similar to AND, to test whether certain conditions are true.
  - The syntax of the OR function is =OR(*logical1,logical2*,etc.)

- The argument, *logical1*, is an expression that compares two values. The expression is either TRUE or FALSE.
- For example, you might use the expression A1>B1 to compare the two values like this: =OR(A1>B1)
- If A1 is indeed greater than B1, then the test evaluates to TRUE. Otherwise, the test is FALSE.
- With only one argument, the OR function seems pretty similar to AND. However, if you use more than one argument, you'll see a difference. For example, =OR(A1>B1,A1>1000) will equal TRUE if A1 is greater than B1 or A1 is greater than 1000.
- You can combine OR with IF to test for multiple conditions before a particular formula is performed.
- For example, =IF(OR(A1>B1,A1>1000),A1*.05,A1*.02) says that, if A1 is greater than B1 *or* greater than 1000, then multiply A1 times 5%, otherwise, multiply A1 by only 2%.
- Unlike AND, either condition could be true for the OR function to return the TRUE value.

■ Use the NOT function to test whether a certain condition is *not* true.
- The syntax of the NOT function is =NOT(*logical*).
- The argument *logical*, is an expression that compares two values. The expression is either TRUE or FALSE.
- For example, you might use the expression A1>B1 to compare the two values like this: =NOT(A1>B1)
- If A1 is greater than B1, then the test evaluates to TRUE, but the NOT function returns FALSE.
- You can combine NOT with other logical functions to perform a calculation only if something isn't TRUE.
- For example, =IF(AND(A1>B1,NOT(A1=1000)),A1*.05,A1*.02) says that, if A1 is greater than B1 and A1 is *not* equal to 1000, then multiply A1 times 5%, otherwise, multiply A1 by only 2%.
- Unlike AND, either condition could be true for the OR function to return the TRUE value.

PROCEDURES

Insert a VLOOKUP or HLOOKUP Function

1. Click cell where result should display . . . . ⬛/⬛/⬛/⬛
2. Click **Formulas** tab . . . . . [Alt], [M]

   Function Library Group

3. Click **Lookup & Reference** button 🔲 . . . . [O]
4. Select **VLOOKUP** or **HLOOKUP** . . . . [↑]/[↓], [Enter]
5. Click in the **Lookup_value** box.
6. Type the item to lookup.

   ✓ *Item can be an actual item or a reference to a cell containing the item.*

   ✓ *You can click a cell in the worksheet to insert a cell reference.*

7. Click in the **Table_array** box . . . . [⬛]
8. Type the table range.

   ✓ *You can select a range in the worksheet to insert cell references.*

9. Click in the **Row_index_num** or **Col_index_num** box . . . . [⬛]
10. Type the row or column number to search for lookup value.
11. Click in the **Range_lookup** box . . . . [⬛]
12. Type approximate match value:
    - To find a match or the next closest match, type **TRUE**.
    - To find only an exact match, type **FALSE**.
13. Click **OK**. . . . . [Enter]

Enter Logical Function

1. Click cell where result should display. . . . . ⬛/⬛/⬛/⬛
2. Click **Formulas** tab . . . . . [Alt], [M]

   Function Library Group

3. Click **Logical** button 🔲 . . . . . . [L]
4. Click function to use . . . . [↑]/[↓], [Enter]

   ✓ *The Function Arguments dialog box appears.*

5. Enter arguments.
6. Click **OK**. . . . . [Enter]

EXERCISE DIRECTIONS

1. Start Excel, if necessary.
2. Open 🔵 **28PhotoTownEEListing**.
3. Save the file as **28PhotoTownEEListing_xx**.
4. Enter a formula in cell L5 to lookup a phone number based on an employee's ID number:
   a. Use the VLOOKUP function.
   b. The lookup value, the ID number, will be entered in cell L4.
   c. The table array should include the column labels, so use the range A7:H37.
   d. The data you want VLOOKUP to return is located in the Emergency Phone column, which is column number 8 of the table.
   e. You only want VLOOKUP to find an exact match, so use the FALSE argument for *range_lookup*.
5. What happens if someone enters an invalid employee ID? You can use IFERROR to fix that:
   a. Edit the formula in cell L5: between the = sign and VLOOKUP, type **IFERROR(**
   b. Press End to move to the end of the formula.
   c. Type a comma **,**.
   d. Type the message you want to appear if there's an error, which there will be if someone enters an ID number that isn't in the table: **"Invalid ID"**.
   e. Type a closing parenthesis **)** and press Enter to complete the formula. See Illustration A.
6. Enter a similar formula in cell I5, to lookup a phone number if someone types in their name:
   a. You also want to display a message if someone enters a name that's not in the list, so you'll just start out the formula that way. Type **=IFERROR(**
   b. Type **VLOOKUP(**
   c. The lookup value, the employee name, will be entered in cell I4.

   d. The table array we used before was the range A7:H37, but VLOOKUP only looks for a match in the first column of the range, so we'll fool it by using C7:H37 as our range.
   e. The data you want VLOOKUP to return is located in the Emergency Phone column, which is column number 6 of the specified range.
   f. You only want VLOOKUP to find an exact match, so use the FALSE argument for *range_lookup*.
   g. Type a parenthesis **)** to close the VLOOKUP function.
   h. Type a comma **,**.
   i. Type the message you want to appear if there's an error (if someone enters an incorrect name): **"Invalid Name"**.
   j. Type a closing parenthesis **)** and press Enter to complete the formula.
7. Test out your new formulas:
   a. Type **Corrine Walters** in cell I5 and press Enter. The phone number, 842-4510, should appear in cell I6.
   b. Now try typing an incorrect name (yours) in cell I5. Assuming your name doesn't happen to be in the list, you should see the error message, "Invalid Name."

   ✓ *If your name is in the list, just type another name.*

   c. Let's test out the ID lookup. Type **31524** in cell L4 and press Enter. The phone number, 251-4796, should appear in cell L5.
8. Adjust column widths as necessary.
9. Spell check the workbook.
10. Print the workbook.
11. Close the workbook, saving all changes.

Illustration A

S28PhotoTownEEListing - Microsoft Excel

PhotoTown Employee Listing

Miller Rd

Unit #2166

Find an emergency phone number

Enter Employee Name   **OR**   Employee ID number

| Name | Corrine Walters | ID # | 31524 |
| Phone Number | 842-4510 | Phone Number | 251-4796 |

Employee ID Number	Title	Name	Department Number	Department Name	Rate	Soc Sec No.	Emergency Phone Number
14558	Mr.	Akira Ota	911748qc	Quality Control	$7.25	285-68-9853	853-1277
17564	Mr.	Juan Nuniez	914522in	Inker	$7.00	208-65-4932	849-1515
18946	Mr.	Shakur Brown	482178ca	Cashier	$7.00	505-43-9587	291-2510
20965	Mrs.	Rafiquil Damir	911748qc	Quality Control	$6.15	102-33-5656	542-0021
22415	Mr.	Jairo Campos	914522in	Inker	$7.20	110-56-2897	975-0909
23151	Ms.	Jewel Vidito	911748qc	Quality Control	$6.55	885-63-7158	875-5267
25448	Mr.	Jyoti Shaw	911748qc	Quality Control	$6.50	389-24-6567	846-3563
27995	Mrs.	Maria Navarro	910412pr	Processing	$6.30	302-42-8465	297-1894
28499	Mr.	Chu Gi Nguyen	911748qc	Quality Control	$6.85	823-55-6487	873-9664
28645	Mr.	Wu Lee	918796so	Special Orders	$7.00	255-41-9784	257-1253
30388	Mrs.	Lucy Fan	910412pr	Processing	$6.55	334-25-6959	722-1043
31022	Mrs.	Meghan Ryan	910412pr	Processing	$7.00	421-85-6452	575-1818
31524	Mrs.	Jan Borough	911748qc	Quality Control	$6.50	727-25-6981	251-4796
31885	Ms.	Kere Freed	910412pr	Processing	$7.10	222-15-9484	255-1133
32151	Mr.	Tony Navarro	271858kc	Kiosk Control	$6.35	401-78-9855	547-7430
32152	Ms.	Katerina Flynn	271858kc	Kiosk Control	$7.10	107-45-9111	846-9812
33785	Mr.	Eram Hassan	271858kc	Kiosk Control	$6.85	203-25-6984	299-6136
36684	Mrs.	Shiree Wilson	482178ca	Cashier	$7.10	415-65-6658	873-5253
37785	Mrs.	Corrine Walters	918796so	Special Orders	$6.65	622-34-8891	842-4510
41885	Mrs.	Kate Scott	482178ca	Cashier	$6.85	489-55-4862	255-6751
44185	Mrs.	Jennifer Flynn	482178ca	Cashier	$7.00	221-32-9585	849-3557
55412	Mrs.	Su Yamaguchi	910412pr	Processing	$6.30	324-75-8021	291-1897
55648	Mr.	Tyrell Johnson	218975am	Asst. Manager	$6.50	468-25-9684	251-6539
57445	Mr.	Shale Wilson	482178ca	Cashier	$7.00	375-86-3425	297-8090
58945	Mrs.	Antonia Whitney	271858kc	Kiosk Control	$6.75	312-86-7141	290-1334
60219	Ms.	Verna Latinz	911748qc	Quality Control	$6.30	705-85-6352	844-4333
63778	Mr.	Carlos Altare	910412pr	Processing	$6.30	504-12-3131	251-9052
64121	Mrs.	Diana Dogwood	918796so	Special Orders	$6.20	821-55-3262	722-1487
67415	Mr.	Shamir Lewis	910412pr	Processing	$7.10	112-42-7897	975-0484
71335	Mr.	Taneed Black	218975am	Asst. Manager	$7.00	775-15-1315	255-6479

Payroll

ON YOUR OWN

1. Start Excel, if necessary.

2. Open ⌨ OXL14_xx, created in the On Your Own section of Exercise 14, or open 💿 28Earnings.

3. Save the file as OXL28_xx.

4. Delete the range A10:B10.

   ✓ You've decided to calculate bonuses on a graduating scale.

5. The commissions are being recalculated:
   a. Commissions will only be given to employees with sales over $35,000, and above the average sales.
   b. For those who qualify, the commission will still be calculated at 6% of sales.
   c. Use IF, AND, and AVERAGE to enter the formula in cell C13.
   d. Be sure to use absolute references where applicable, and then copy the formula down column C.

6. Create a table of bonus amounts:
   a. Bonuses begin at $35,000 in sales and increase for every $2,500 worth of additional sales.
   b. The bonus at $35,000 is $100. Bonuses increase by $100 for each sales tier, up to a maximum of $1,000 bonus ($57,500 in sales).
   c. Name the range **Bonus**.

   ✓ When naming the range, do not include any column headings in your selected range.

7. Use VLOOKUP:
   a. In cell D13, enter a formula using VLOOKUP to look up the appropriate bonus amount for the first salesperson. See Illustration A.
   b. Use IFERROR to display 0 in the Bonus column if someone's sales amount is under the $35,000 minimum needed to qualify for a bonus.

8. Adjust column widths as necessary.

9. Spell check the worksheet.

10. Print the worksheet.

11. Close the workbook, saving all changes.

Illustration A

Old Southern Furniture

Biweekly Earnings Review
1/1/2009

Commission Rate   6%

Salesperson	Sales	Comm.	Bonus	Total Earnings		Sales Amt	Bonus
Carl Jackson	$ 44,202.00	$ 2,652.12	$ 400.00	$ 3,052.12		$ 35,000	$ 100.00
Ni Li Yung	$ 41,524.00	$ 2,491.44	$ 300.00	$ 2,791.44		$ 37,500	$ 200.00
Tom Wilson	$ 43,574.00	$ 2,614.44	$ 400.00	$ 3,014.44		$ 40,000	$ 300.00
Jill Palmer	$ 39,612.00	$ 2,376.72	$ 200.00	$ 2,576.72		$ 42,500	$ 400.00
Rita Nuez	$ 39,061.00	$ -	$ 200.00	$ 200.00		$ 45,000	$ 500.00
Maureen Baker	$ 38,893.00	$ -	$ 200.00	$ 200.00		$ 47,500	$ 600.00
Kim Cheng	$ 31,120.00	$ -	$ -	$ -		$ 50,000	$ 700.00
Lloyd Hamilton	$ 41,922.00	$ 2,515.32	$ 300.00	$ 2,815.32		$ 52,500	$ 800.00
Ed Fulton	$ 45,609.00	$ 2,736.54	$ 500.00	$ 3,236.54		$ 55,000	$ 900.00
Maria Alvarez	$ 30,952.00	$ -	$ -	$ -		$ 57,500	$ 1,000.00
Katie Wilson	$ 31,472.00	$ -	$ -	$ -			
Tim Brown	$ 44,783.00	$ 2,686.98	$ 400.00	$ 3,086.98			

Skills Covered

- **Create Scenarios**

Software Skills   With scenarios, you can create and save several versions of a worksheet based on "what-if" data. For example, you can create a best case, probable case, and worst case scenario for your company's annual sales. After you create your scenarios, you can use Report Manager to print the various versions of your data quickly.

Application Skills   A customer of Breakaway Bike Shop is in a dilemma about some bike work he would like to have done. Some work is needed right away, while other parts that are showing wear could conceivably be put off until after the holidays. The only problem is that your labor charge is going up in January, so the customer needs help deciding between several scenarios—doing some of the work now and putting the rest of indefinitely, doing all of the work now, or waiting until after Christmas to do the work. Using scenarios, you will quickly create the reports he needs to compare the costs and make his decision.

TERMS

Scenario   A what-if analysis tool you can use to create several versions of a worksheet, based on changing variables.

Variable   An input value that changes depending on the desired outcome.

NOTES

Create Scenarios

- To help you deal with the outcome of an unpredictable future, you can create and save versions of your worksheet data based on changing **variables**.

- With **scenarios**, you can plug in the most likely values for several possible situations, and save the scenarios with the resulting worksheet data.
  - You can print and compare scenarios.
  - You can also create a summary worksheet to compare scenarios.

- After you save scenarios, you can switch between them easily.
  - When you switch to a particular scenario, Excel plugs the saved values into the appropriate cells in your worksheet, and then adjusts formula results as needed.

- You change from one scenario to another by using the Scenario Manager dialog box.
  - You can also create, summarize, delete, and merge scenarios with this dialog box.

Scenario Manager dialog box

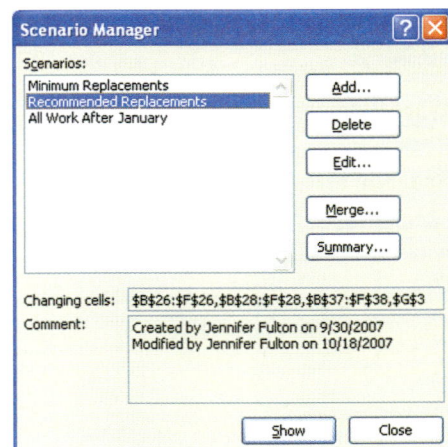

- Merging scenarios is a process that copies the scenarios from one worksheet to the current worksheet.

- When you create a summary of your scenarios, a new worksheet is inserted, and each scenario, its variables, and the affected cells you select are all listed in a regular or PivotTable report (your choice).

PROCEDURES

Create a Scenario

1. Click **Data** tab . . . . `Alt`, `A`

   Data Tools Group

2. Click **What-if Analysis** button 📊 . . . . `W`
3. Click **Scenario Manager** . . . . . `S`
4. Click **Add** . . . . `Alt`+`A`
5. In **Scenario name** box, enter a name for the scenario. . . . . `Alt`+`N`
6. In **Changing cells** box, select or enter cell reference(s). . . . . `Alt`+`C`
7. Select the protection options you want:
   - **Prevent changes** . . . . `Alt`+`P`
   - **Hide**. . . . . `Alt`+`D`
8. Click **OK**. . . . . `Enter`
9. In **Scenario Values** dialog box, enter values for changing cell(s).
10. Click **OK**. . . . . `Enter`

   ✓ If you click Add instead of OK, the Add Scenario dialog box is redisplayed so you can add yet another scenario.

11. Click **Close**.

Delete a Scenario

1. Click **Data** tab . . . . `Alt`, `A`

   Data Tools Group

2. Click **What-if Analysis** button 📊 . . . . `W`
3. Click **Scenario Manager** . . . . . `S`
4. In the **Scenarios** list, click the scenario you want to delete. . . . . `Alt`+`C`, `↑`/`↓`

5. Click **Delete**. . . . . `Alt`+`D`

   ✓ Note that Excel doesn't require confirmation when deleting a scenario. Be sure that you want to do this before clicking the Delete button; deletions can't be undone.

6. Click **Close** . . . . `Enter`

Edit a Scenario

1. Click **Data** tab . . . . `Alt`, `A`

   Data Tools Group

2. Click **What-if Analysis** button 📊 . . . . `W`
3. Click **Scenario Manager** . . . . . `S`
4. In the **Scenarios** list, click the scenario you want to edit . . . . `Alt`+`C`, `↑`/`↓`
5. Click **Edit** . . . . `Alt`+`E`
6. Make changes to the scenario's parameters as needed.
7. Click **OK**. . . . . `Enter`
8. Make changes to the scenario's values as needed.
9. Click **OK** again . . . . `Enter`
10. Click **Close** . . . . `Enter`

View a Scenario

1. Click **Data** tab . . . . `Alt`, `A`

   Data Tools Group

2. Click **What-if Analysis** button 📊 . . . . `W`
3. Click **Scenario Manager** . . . . . `S`
4. Select a scenario. . . . . `⇥`, `↑`/`↓`

5. Click **Show** . . . . `Alt`+`S`

   ✓ The values associated with the scenario you selected are displayed in the worksheet, but the dialog box remains open so you can switch to another scenario.

6. Click **Close** . . . . `Enter`

Create a Scenario Summary

1. Click **Data** tab . . . . `Alt`, `A`

   Data Tools Group

2. Click **What-if Analysis** button 📊 . . . . `W`
3. Click **Scenario Manager** . . . . . `S`
4. Click **Summary** . . . . `Alt`+`U`
5. Click **Scenario summary**. . . . . `Alt`+`S`

   OR

   Click **Scenario PivotTable report** . . . . `Alt`+`P`
6. Select the range of result cells.
7. Click **OK**. . . . . `Enter`

Merge Scenarios

1. Click **Data** tab . . . . `Alt`, `A`

   Data Tools Group

2. Click **What-if Analysis** button 📊 . . . . `W`
3. Click **Scenario Manager** . . . . . `S`
4. Click **Merge**. . . . . `Alt`+`M`
5. Open **Book** list and select the workbook that contains the scenarios you want to merge . . . . `Alt`+`B`, `↑`/`↓`
6. Select **Sheet** that contains the scenarios to merge . . . . `Alt`+`S`, `↑`/`↓`
7. Click **OK**. . . . . `Enter`

EXERCISE DIRECTIONS

1. Start Excel, if necessary.
2. Open ⊙ **29PartsReplacement**.
3. Save the workbook as **29PartsReplacement_xx**.
4. Create a scenario called **Minimum Replacements** in which the values in the following ranges are saved as they currently appear:
   - B26:F26
   - B28:F28
   - B37:F38
   - G3

   ✓ *When prompted to enter the range of changing cells, simply select each range with the mouse and press comma to enter the next range. When prompted to enter values, click OK to accept the current ones.*

5. Create another scenario called **Recommended Replacements** in which these values change:
   - B26   RPL
   - C26   2
   - D26   Aurens BR321
   - E26   1
   - F26   39.25
   - B28   RPL
   - C28   2
   - D28   Aurens BL321
   - E28   .10
   - F28   4.95
   - B37   RPL
   - C37   1
   - D37   Road Warrior 18F
   - E37   .15
   - F37   25.75
   - B38   RPL
   - C38   1
   - D38   Road Warrior 18R
   - E38   .25
   - F38   28.95

6. Create another scenario called **All Work After January** in which the values of the cells listed in step 5 change as described in that step and the value in cell G3 changes to 50.00:
   a. The simplest way to accomplish this is to first display the changed values in the worksheet—so use the Scenario Manager to display the values associated with the Recommended Replacements scenario.
   b. Click Add, type the scenario name, **All Work After January**, and click OK.
   c. You can review each value, but they should be the same as those you entered in step 5. Scroll down to the last value and change cell G3 to 50.00. Click OK.
7. Create a summary report:
   a. Choose the Scenario summary.
   b. Enter G3 as the result cell and click OK.
8. Adjust column widths as needed.
9. Spell check the workbook.
10. Print the workbook.
11. Save the workbook and exit Excel.

ON YOUR OWN

1. Start Excel, if necessary.
2. Open ⊙ 29Theater.
3. Save the workbook as OXL29_xx.
4. On the *Glass Menagerie* worksheet, create a scenario with the existing data and name it **Scenario 1**. Use cells C6:C11, E5, and G6:G7 as the changing cells.

   ✓ *You'll get a message telling you that one of the cells will be converted from a formula to its result. Click OK.*

5. Create a scenario named **Scenario 2** where tickets are priced at $9.00 with only 85% of the seats sold (theater capacity is 1420), while still reaching the profit goal of $1,200.

6. You won't be able to reach these goals without changing some of the estimated costs of the project—shown in the range C6:C11. Think about the following as you make decisions on what to change:

   ■ Certain costs are fixed and can't be reduced—theater rental, royalty fee, and the union electrician.

   ■ You know of a printer that will print the playbills at a lesser cost ($4.10) but they are of much lower quality. Do you want to make that sacrifice?

   ■ Do you dare print fewer playbills than the capacity of the theater? How many less could you get away with?

   ■ Can you skimp a little on costumes and scenery? How much on each?

   ✓ *You can enter new values manually, if you like, or use Solver to change the values you want to adjust until you meet the profit goal.*

7. After adjusting values to meet the profit goal, change cell E5 to read, **If the play is 85% sold out:** before saving the scenario.
8. Change to the *Music Man* worksheet.
9. Use the Scenario Manager to merge (copy) the scenarios from the *Glass Menagerie* worksheet over to the *Music Man* worksheet:

   a. Edit Scenario 1, changing the value of cell C6 to **1225**, C7 to **1300**, and C10 to **325**.

   b. Delete Scenario 2.

   c. In the worksheet, change cell E5 to **If the play is 85% sold out:**.

   d. Change cell G6 to **1207**.

   e. Use Solver to help you adjust the values so you still show a profit of $1200:

   • You can probably charge more for admission to this play, up to about $9.50, since it is very popular.

   • You can maybe save some money on the scenery and reuse some materials created for the *Our Town* play you did last year, but you can't sacrifice anything on the costumes.

   • You can use the less expensive playbills to save money.

   f. After adjusting the values, save them as a new scenario called **Scenario 2**.

10. Adjust column widths as needed.
11. Spell check both worksheets.
12. For both worksheets, display each scenario and print it.
13. Save the workbook and exit Excel.

Skills Covered

- **Data Consolidation**
- **Create Consolidation Tables**

Software Skills   Excel's data consolidation feature allows you to consolidate the data from similar worksheets into a single worksheet. For example, you may have a workbook that contains separate worksheets for three months' worth of sales. After consolidation, you have a single worksheet that contains the totals for the three-month period. Of course, you can use other database functions, too; for example, you could consolidate the three sales worksheets to find the average sales per month.

Application Skills   It's the end of the quarter, and it's time to draw some conclusions about product sales for Holy Habañero, which sells its hot sauces through eight different sales channels. Since the details for each month are stored on separate worksheets, you've decided to use the Consolidate command to bring the data together.

TERMS

Consolidation by category   Consolidating data from worksheets that are designed similarly into a single worksheet.

Consolidation by position   Consolidating similar data from worksheets that aren't organized exactly the same.

Consolidation table   The table of consolidated data that results from using the Consolidate command.

NOTES

Data Consolidation

- With Excel's Consolidate feature, you can consolidate data from separate ranges into a single worksheet.

  ✓ *You can also consolidate data using 3-D formulas.*

  - The data can come from the same worksheet, separate worksheets, and even separate workbooks.

  - You can consolidate similarly structured databases using the **consolidate by position** option.

  - Consolidate data organized in different ways using the **consolidate by category** option.

Consolidation dalog box

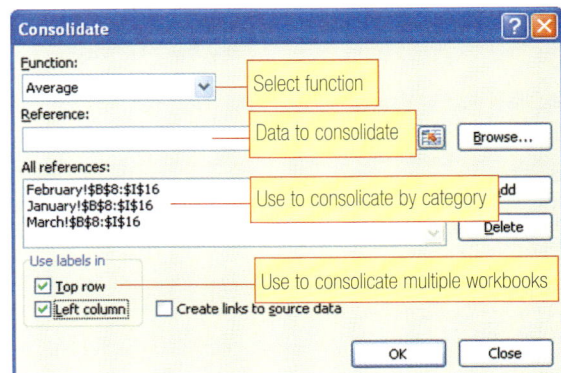

369

- When you consolidate data by position, you're telling Excel to consolidate the data in the exact same cells on several worksheets.
- When you consolidate data by category, you're telling Excel to consolidate data based on the row and column labels you're using.
  - For example, Excel will add data from cell C3 on one worksheet, with cell D4 on another, if they are both identified by row and column labels such as "July Red Shirt Sales."
- Regardless of whether you consolidate data by position or category, you can tell Excel to update the data automatically when changes occur.

Create Consolidation Tables

- Follow these general guidelines when making choices in the Consolidate dialog box to create your **consolidation table**:
  - Select the function you want to use, such as SUM, AVERAGE, COUNT, and so on.
  - Add as many ranges as needed to the All references list.
  - Copy the column and row labels from the database with the options in the Use labels in area of the dialog box.
  - If the data you want to consolidate is located in different workbooks, use the Create links to source data option to have Excel update the table automatically whenever the source data changes.

PROCEDURES

Consolidate Data

1. If data comes from separate workbooks, open and arrange the workbooks on the screen.
2. Change to the destination worksheet.
3. Click in the upper-left cell of the range in which you want the consolidated data to appear.
4. Click **Data** tab . . . . Alt, A

   Data Tools Group

5. Click **Consolidate** button . . . . N
6. Open **Function** list . . . . . . Alt+F

7. Select function you want to use . . . . $\uparrow$/$\downarrow$, $Enter$
8. Click in **Reference** box . . Alt+R
9. Select or type the first range you want to consolidate.
10. Click **Add** . . . . Alt+A

    ✓ The range is added to the **All references** list.

11. Repeat steps 8 through 10 for each range you wish to consolidate.
12. To create a link to the source data, select **Create links to source data** . . . . Alt+S

    ✓ You can't link the data if the destination range and the source data are on the same worksheet.

13. If your consolidated ranges include labels, select either or both of the following:

    ✓ You can select these options if you're consolidating by position as well, if you want Excel to copy the row and column labels for you.

    - **Top row** . . . . Alt+T
    - **Left column** . . . . Alt+L
14. Click **OK** . . . . $Enter$

EXERCISE DIRECTIONS

1. Start Excel, if necessary.
2. Open 💿 **30HHQtr1Breakdown**.
3. Save the file as **30HHQtr1Breakdown_xx**.
4. Make a copy of the March worksheet for use as a template for the consolidated figures:
   a. Place the copied worksheet at the end of the sheet tabs.
   b. Change the new worksheet's tab to Totals.
   c. Clear the input figures in the Unit Sales portion of the copied worksheet: B8:I16.
   d. Change cell B4 to read Q1 2008 Totals.
5. Total the unit sales for the last three months:
   a. In the Totals worksheet, click cell B8.
   b. Click the Consolidate button on the Data tab.
   c. Choose Sum from the Function list.
   d. Click in the Reference box, and then select the range B8:I16 on the January worksheet.
   e. Click Add.
   f. Repeat steps d and e, adding the same range on the February and March worksheets.

   ✓ *You shouldn't have to reselect the same range again even in the different worksheets, since consolidation expects you to use the same range address with each worksheet you address.*

   ✓ *Do not select any of the **Use labels in** options.*

   g. Check Create links to source data.
   h. Click OK.

   ✓ *Excel inserts hidden rows that contain links to the selected data. To view these hidden rows, click the plus sign next to any agency name.*

6. Test the automatic updating process by changing cell H12 in the January worksheet to **960**.

   ✓ *Cell J27 in the Totals worksheet should change from 13,339 to 13,371.*

7. Make another copy of the March worksheet:
   a. Place the copied sheet behind the Totals sheet.
   b. Change the new worksheet's tab to **Averages**.
   c. Clear that copy's Unit Sales inputs (B8:I16) as well.
   d. Change cell B4 to read **Q1 2008 Averages**.

8. Average the bookings for the last three months:
   a. On the Averages worksheet, click cell B8.
   b. Click the Consolidate button on the Data tab.
   c. Choose Average from the Function list.
   d. Select range B8:I16 for the January, February, and March worksheets.
   e. Do not select the Create links to source data option.
   f. Click OK.

   ✓ *Notice that this time, no hidden rows are created. If you make a change to the data, however, that change will not be reflected in the averages shown. Instead, you can simply follow these steps again to update the data manually.*

9. Test updating once more by changing cell D15 on the February worksheet to **90**.

   ✓ *Cell J39 in the Totals worksheet should change from 4,353 to 4,363. See Illustration A.*

   ✓ *Meanwhile, the entire row 15 in the Averages worksheet remains as it was.*

10. Update the averages:
    a. On the Averages worksheet, click cell B8.
    b. Click the Consolidate button on the Data tab.
    c. Make sure that correct ranges are selected and that Average has been chosen in the Function list.
    d. Click OK.

    ✓ *Notice now that cell J15 in Averages has changed from 1,451 to 1,454.*

11. Adjust column widths as needed.
12. Spell check the Totals and Averages sheets.
13. Print the Totals and Averages sheets.
14. Close the workbook, saving all changes.

S30HHQtr1Breakdown - Microsoft Excel

Holy Habañero!

Monthly Sales Breakdown
Q1 2008 Totals

Unit sales

	Retail				Wholesale				Total
	Direct mail catalog	Fundraising catalog	Online	Trade exhibits	Non-profit resellers	For-profit retailers (unit)	For-profit retailers (bulk)	Restaurants (bulk)	
Belly of the Beast	249	182	305	356	323	647	1,632	1,488	5,182
Magma Core	339	173	110	581	295	418	1,760	1,648	5,324
Typhoon Warning	278	155	579	971	891	1,721	3,328	2,528	10,451
Uranium 235	1,564	1,885	1,985	2,744	602	2,474	3,808	3,536	18,598
Szechuan Singe	1,067	1,164	1,240	1,575	1,623	2,142	2,816	1,744	13,371
Wasabi Fusion	282	450	783	1,362	1,983	2,442	3,936	2,736	13,974
Sorrento Serrano	236	350	477	233	447	1,073	1,088	272	4,176
Yucatan Bomb	255	224	280	186	228	1,334	1,472	384	4,363
Toast Jammer	185	379	113	143	336	831	-	-	1,987

Gross sales

	Direct mail catalog	Fundraising catalog	Online	Trade exhibits	Non-profit resellers	For-profit retailers (unit)	For-profit retailers (bulk)	Restaurants (bulk)	
Belly of the Beast	$ 1,730.55	$ 1,264.90	$ 2,424.75	$ 2,830.20	$ 1,130.50	$ 3,073.25	$ 6,936.00	$ 5,952.00	$ 25,342.15
Magma Core	$ 2,356.05	$ 1,202.35	$ 874.50	$ 4,618.95	$ 1,032.50	$ 1,985.50	$ 7,480.00	$ 6,592.00	$ 26,141.85
Typhoon Warning	$ 1,932.10	$ 1,077.25	$ 4,603.05	$ 7,719.45	$ 3,118.50	$ 8,174.75	$14,144.00	$10,112.00	$ 50,881.10
Uranium 235	$10,869.80	$13,100.75	$15,780.75	$21,814.80	$ 2,107.00	$11,751.50	$16,184.00	$14,144.00	$ 105,752.60
Szechuan Singe	$ 9,549.65	$10,417.80	$12,338.00	$15,671.25	$ 7,709.25	$11,245.50	$14,784.00	$ 8,720.00	$ 90,435.45
Wasabi Fusion	$ 2,523.90	$ 4,027.50	$ 7,790.85	$13,551.90	$ 9,419.25	$12,820.50	$20,664.00	$13,680.00	$ 84,477.90
Sorrento Serrano	$ 2,112.20	$ 3,132.50	$ 4,746.15	$ 2,318.35	$ 2,123.25	$ 5,633.25	$ 5,712.00	$ 1,360.00	$ 27,137.70
Yucatan Bomb	$ 1,517.25	$ 1,332.80	$ 1,946.00	$ 1,292.70	$ 672.60	$ 4,335.50	$ 5,520.00	$ 1,152.00	$ 17,768.85
Toast Jammer	$ 1,100.75	$ 2,255.05	$ 785.35	$ 993.85	$ 991.20	$ 2,700.75	$ -	$ -	$ 8,826.95

		$ 436,764.55
	Taxes paid	$ 8,753.95
	Sales after taxes	$ 428,010.60

Unit prices | January | February | March | **Totals** | Averages

ON YOUR OWN

1. Start Excel, if necessary.
2. Open ⊙ **30ApplianceDailySales**.
3. Save the file as **OXL30_xx**.
4. Consolidate the sales data from Monday to Sunday into a single table:
   a. Use the SUM function.
   b. Copy the row and column labels.
   c. Do not create a link to the source data.
   d. Place the consolidated table on the Summary worksheet.
   e. Format the table however you like.

5. Below the first table, create a second consolidation table to show the average sales per day (see Illustration A):
   a. Use the same ranges.
   b. Choose the AVERAGE function.
   c. Copy the row and column labels.
   d. Do not create a link to the source data.
   e. Format the table however you like.
6. Adjust column widths as necessary.
7. Spell check the Summary worksheet.
8. Print the Summary worksheet.
9. Close the workbook, saving all changes.

Illustration A

JJ Fulton Appliances

Brown Street Store
Summary of Sales, Week of August 12th

Totals for the Week

	Dishwasher	Oven	Refrigerator	Television	Washer	Dryer	Total Sales	Commission
Jack Smithe	9	8	9	7	8	7	$ 28,214.47	$ 2,045.55
Joe Cooper	7	3	6	9	5	6	$ 22,050.09	$ 1,598.63
Sally Peters	3	6	9	16	6	4	$ 31,646.51	$ 2,294.37
Peter Carter	7	4	3	13	2	2	$ 20,325.26	$ 1,473.58

Averages for the Week

	Dishwasher	Oven	Refrigerator	Television	Washer	Dryer	Total Sales	Commission
Jack Smithe	1.80	1.60	1.50	2.33	1.60	1.75	$ 4,030.64	$ 292.22
Joe Cooper	1.75	1.50	2.00	1.80	1.67	1.20	$ 3,150.01	$ 228.38
Sally Peters	1.00	1.20	2.25	2.67	1.50	1.33	$ 4,520.93	$ 327.77
Peter Carter	1.40	1.33	1.00	2.17	1.00	1.00	$ 2,903.61	$ 210.51

Exercise | 31

Critical Thinking

Application Skills You are the bookkeeper at the Miller Road location of PhotoTown. You've just learned that the bookkeeping functions of your own store and those of the Cermak Road location are going to be merged—which means, from now on, your payroll worksheets will need to account for both sets of employees simultaneously, while maintaining the distinction between the two.

EXERCISE DIRECTIONS

1. Start Excel, if necessary.
2. Open 31PhotoTownPayroll_1109.
3. Save the file as 31PhotoTownPayroll_1109_*xx*.
4. Use VLOOKUP to lookup the medical cost for each employee:
   a. Enter the formula in cell N8.
   b. The value to lookup is in cell M8.
   c. The table range is U8:V10.

   ✓ *Be sure to use an absolute reference so you can copy the formula.*

   d. The matching cost is in the second column of the table.
   e. You're looking for an exact match.
5. Copy the formula to down the column.

   ✓ *There's a problem when someone opted for no medical coverage.*

6. Edit the formula in cell N8, and use IFERROR to display 0 if the VLOOKUP formula returns an error.
7. Copy the formula down the column again.
8. Sort the employees by last name, then first name, in ascending order.

9. Sort the list in ascending order by Location, Last Name, and First Name.
10. Add subtotals that display the total amounts paid to employees (gross pay) at the two locations, and the total amounts withheld from their paychecks (net pay). (See Illustration A.)
11. Adjust column widths as needed.
12. Spell check the worksheet.
13. Print the worksheet.
14. Remove the subtotals.
15. Use a filter to display only the highest paid (above average net pay) Miller Rd. employees.
16. Print the worksheet.
17. Remove the filter.
18. Use an advanced filter to create a list of everyone making $8.00 or less, with Family medical coverage:
    a. Set up a criteria range by copying the column labels to the range beginning in cell X7.
    b. Enter the criteria under the proper column heading.
    c. Extract the records that match the criteria, and place them a few rows below the criteria range.

19. Calculate some information based on the extracted data:

   a. Type **Location** in cells Z19 and AA19.

   b. Type **Miller Rd.** in cell Z20, and **Cermak Rd.** in cell AA20. See Illustration B.

   c. Type **Avg. Rate** in cell Y21.

   d. In cells Z21 and AA21, use a database function to determine the average wages among low wage earners at the Miller Rd. store, and at the Cermak Rd. store.

   e. Format the results with Currency Style, 2 decimal places. Format the labels as you like.

20. Adjust column widths again, check spelling, and print the worksheet again.

21. Open 💿 **31PhotoTownPayroll_1116**:

   a. Copy the payroll worksheet in the November 16th workbook.

   b. Paste the copy onto a blank worksheet in the **31PhotoTownPayroll_1109_***xx*.

   c. Rename this new sheet **Nov 16**.

   d. Rename the Payroll sheet **Nov 9**.

   e. Add another new sheet to the end, and call it **Nov Totals**.

22. Use the Consolidate command to add the Nov 9 and Nov 16 totals:

   a. Add the range A7:R42 in the Nov 9 worksheet.

   b. Add the range A7:R42 in the Nov 16 worksheet.

   c. Use the Top row labels.

   d. Do not create links to source data.

   e. Consolidate added the Rate field, so recopy it from one of the November worksheets.

   f. Copy the other missing data from one of the November worksheets. See Illustration C.

23. Adjust the column widths.

24. Spell check the worksheet.

25. Print the worksheet.

26. Close all files, saving all changes.

Illustration A

Illustration B

S31PhotoTownPayroll_1109 - Microsoft Excel

	Check #	Location	EE ID No	Title	First Name	Last Name	Hours Wkd <=8.00	Rate	Gross Pay	Fed	SS	State	Medical Family	Med Cost	401-K %	401-K	LTD	Net Pay
7																		
8																		
9																		
10																		
11																		
12	Check #	Location	EE ID No	Title	First Name	Last Name	Hours Wkd	Rate	Gross Pay	Fed	SS	State	Medical	Med Cost	401-K %	401-K	LTD	Net Pay
13	65935	Cermak Rd.	22785	Mr.	Mika	Gritada	40.00	$8.00	$320.00	$60.80	$24.80	$19.20	Family	$5.95	4%	$25.60	$4.69	$178.96
14	65934	Cermak Rd.	22854	Mr.	Abe	Rittenhouse	40.00	$7.80	$312.00	$59.28	$24.18	$18.72	Family	$5.95	3%	$18.72	$6.01	$179.14
15	65952	Miller Rd.	28645	Mr.	Wu	Lee	40.00	$7.00	$280.00	$53.20	$21.70	$16.80	Family	$5.95	2%	$5.60	$0.00	$176.75
16	65954	Miller Rd.	27995	Mrs.	Maria	Navarro	22.00	$6.30	$138.60	$26.33	$10.74	$8.32	Family	$5.95	2%	$2.77	$0.00	$84.49
17	65965	Miller Rd.	36684	Mrs.	Shiree	Wilson	40.00	$7.10	$284.00	$53.96	$22.01	$17.04	Family	$5.95	0%	$0.00	$0.00	$185.04

		Location Miller Rd.	Location Cermak
19			
20		Location Miller Rd.	Location Cermak
21	Avg. Rate	$6.80	$7.90

Illustration C

S31PhotoTownPayroll_1109 - Microsoft Excel

	A	B	C	D	E	F	G	H	I	J	K	L	M	N	O	P	Q
1	Check #	Location	EE ID No	Title	First Name	Last Name	Hours Wkd	Rate	Gross Pay	Fed	SS	State	Medical	Med Cost	401-K %	401-K	LTD
2	131878	Cermak Rd.	38448	Ms.	Carol	Chen	61.00	$9.25	$564.25	$107.21	$43.73	$33.86	Single Plus 1	$9.50	6%	$44.40	$4.
3	131880	Cermak Rd.	21544	Ms.	Eileen	Costello	80.00	$9.75	$780.00	$148.20	$60.45	$46.80	Family	$11.90	6%	$46.80	$2.
4	131876	Cermak Rd.	61522	Mr.	Marty	Gonzales	80.00	$9.15	$732.00	$139.08	$56.73	$43.92	Family	$11.90	6%	$43.92	$5.
5	131870	Cermak Rd.	22785	Mr.	Mika	Gritada	78.00	$8.00	$624.00	$118.56	$48.36	$37.44	Family	$11.90	8%	$51.20	$9.
6	131872	Cermak Rd.	38514	Mr.	Randall	Lohr	80.00	$8.35	$668.00	$126.92	$51.77	$40.08	Single	$6.50	8%	$53.44	$10.
7	131866	Cermak Rd.	37855	Mr.	Nathan	Monroe	68.00	$7.50	$510.00	$96.90	$39.53	$30.60		$0.00	0%	$0.00	$0.
8	131874	Cermak Rd.	34789	Ms.	Maria	Nachez	76.00	$8.50	$646.00	$122.74	$50.07	$38.76	Family	$11.90	6%	$40.80	$8.
9	131868	Cermak Rd.	22854	Mr.	Abe	Rittenhouse	72.00	$7.80	$561.60	$106.70	$43.52	$33.70	Family	$11.90	6%	$37.44	$12.
10	131882	Cermak Rd.	38748	Mr.	Anthony	Splendoria	56.00	$10.50	$588.00	$111.72	$45.57	$35.28		$0.00	8%	$67.20	$1.
11	131864	Cermak Rd.	37745	Mr.	Kim	Woo	40.00	$7.25	$290.00	$55.10	$22.48	$17.40		$0.00	0%	$0.00	$0.
12	131884	Miller Rd.	63778	Mr.	Carlos	Altare	52.00	$9.75	$507.00	$96.33	$39.29	$30.42		$0.00	4%	$10.14	$0.
13	131886	Miller Rd.	31524	Mrs.	Jan	Borough	44.00	$6.75	$297.00	$56.43	$23.02	$17.82	Single Plus 1	$9.50	6%	$8.91	$0.
14	131888	Miller Rd.	18946	Mr.	Shakur	Brown	80.00	$7.00	$560.00	$106.40	$43.40	$33.60	Single	$6.50	4%	$11.20	$9.
15	131890	Miller Rd.	37895	Ms.	Janine	Carroll	50.00	$6.50	$325.00	$61.75	$25.19	$19.50		$0.00	4%	$6.50	$5.
16	131892	Miller Rd.	20965	Mr.	Rafiquil	Damir	77.00	$6.15	$473.55	$89.97	$36.70	$28.41	Single	$6.50	4%	$9.47	$9.
17	131894	Miller Rd.	30388	Mrs.	Lucy	Fan	25.50	$6.55	$167.03	$31.73	$12.94	$10.02	Single Plus 1	$9.50	0%	$0.00	$0.
18	131896	Miller Rd.	44185	Mrs.	Jennifer	Flynn	28.50	$8.35	$237.98	$45.22	$18.44	$14.28		$0.00	8%	$9.52	$10.
19	131898	Miller Rd.	32152	Ms.	Katerina	Flynn	51.00	$7.25	$369.75	$70.25	$28.66	$22.19	Single	$6.50	4%	$7.40	$0.
20	131900	Miller Rd.	33785	Mr.	Eram	Hassan	48.75	$6.85	$333.94	$63.45	$25.88	$20.04	Single Plus 1	$9.50	0%	$0.00	$12.
21	131902	Miller Rd.	60219	Ms.	Verna	Latinz	63.50	$6.30	$400.05	$76.01	$31.00	$24.00	Single	$6.50	6%	$12.00	$10.
22	131904	Miller Rd.	28645	Mr.	Wu	Lee	67.00	$7.00	$469.00	$89.11	$36.35	$28.14	Family	$11.90	4%	$9.38	$0.
23	131906	Miller Rd.	67415	Mr.	Shamir	Lewis	64.00	$7.25	$464.00	$88.16	$35.96	$27.84	Single	$6.50	8%	$18.56	$0.
24	131908	Miller Rd.	27995	Mrs.	Maria	Navarro	38.00	$6.30	$239.40	$45.49	$18.55	$14.36	Family	$11.90	4%	$4.79	$0.
25	131910	Miller Rd.	32151	Mr.	Tony	Navarro	28.50	$6.35	$180.98	$34.39	$14.03	$10.86		$0.00	0%	$0.00	$1.
26	131912	Miller Rd.	28499	Mr.	Chu Gi	Nguyen	24.00	$6.85	$164.40	$31.24	$12.74	$9.86	Single	$6.50	6%	$4.93	$0.
27	131914	Miller Rd.	17564	Mr.	Juan	Nuniez	40.00	$7.10	$284.00	$53.96	$22.01	$17.04	Single Plus 1	$9.50	0%	$0.00	$0.
28	131916	Miller Rd.	31022	Mrs.	Meghan	Ryan	30.50	$7.00	$213.50	$40.57	$16.55	$12.81		$0.00	4%	$4.27	$0.
29	131918	Miller Rd.	41885	Mrs.	Kate	Scott	34.75	$10.00	$347.50	$66.03	$26.93	$20.85	Single Plus 1	$9.50	0%	$0.00	$0.
30	131920	Miller Rd.	60435	Mr.	Wallace	Van Croy	36.00	$6.50	$234.00	$44.46	$18.14	$14.04	Single Plus 1	$9.50	0%	$0.00	$10.
31	131922	Miller Rd.	23151	Ms.	Jewel	Vidito	42.00	$6.75	$283.50	$53.87	$21.97	$17.01	Single	$6.50	0%	$0.00	$0.
32	131924	Miller Rd.	37785	Mrs.	Corrine	Walters	53.75	$9.75	$524.06	$99.57	$40.61	$31.44	Family	$11.90	6%	$15.72	$5.
33	131926	Miller Rd.	58945	Mrs.	Antonia	Whitney	33.75	$6.75	$227.81	$43.28	$17.63	$13.67		$0.00	4%	$4.56	$0.
34	131928	Miller Rd.	57445	Mr.	Shale	Wilson	68.50	$7.10	$486.35	$92.41	$37.69	$29.18	Single	$6.50	8%	$19.45	$0.
35	131930	Miller Rd.	36684	Mrs.	Shiree	Wilson	72.00	$7.10	$511.20	$97.13	$39.62	$30.67	Family	$11.90	0%	$0.00	$0.
36	131932	Miller Rd.	55412	Mrs.	Su	Yamaguchi	57.00	$8.35	$475.95	$90.43	$36.89	$28.56	Single	$6.50	8%	$19.04	$0.

Nov 9 / Nov 16 / Nov Totals

Curriculum Integration

Application Skills   In American History, your class is studying the Titanic. Questions have been raised as to whether the rule of the sea, "women and children first," was followed. You and your classmates hope to analyze the data and come up with an analysis of who was most likely to survive.

EXERCISE DIRECTIONS

Start Excel, if necessary, and open 🔘 **32TitanicData**. Save the file as **32TitanicData_xx**.

First thing you've noticed is that the data is not as readable as it might be. For example, in the Survived column, a 1 represents Yes, and a 0 represents No. Use Find & Replace to replace the numbers with text: Yes and No. You'll find that the Match entire cell contents option is especially helpful.

Next, sort the database into two groups—those who survived and those who did not. Within each group, sort by class, and within class, sex, and then age. Sort the Survived column in Z to A order, so those who survived appear first.

Add subtotals that count the survivors (or non-survivors) for each class. Add a page break between groups. Add a nested subtotal that calculates the average age for each class. Do not add additional page breaks. Add another nested subtotal that counts the number of survivors (or non-survivors) by sex.

Use the outline controls to display only the totals, then adjust column widths as needed to display data. Check spelling in the workbook. Print the worksheet. Redisplay all data and remove the subtotals.

Now you'll do some further analysis on the survivors. Set up a criteria area, and use DCOUNT to total the female survivors, male survivors, and child survivors. For female and male survivors, count only people older than 18. You'll need to set up two criteria ranges for females, and subtract those people 18 and under from the total number of females. Repeat this process for male passengers. For children, count people 18 and younger (male or female).

Create a similar area to calculate the total non-survivors. See Illustration A. Adjust column widths as needed to display data and check spelling in the workbook. Print the worksheet.

Close the workbook.

Illustration A

S32TitanicData - Microsoft Excel

Name Box: A6   fx: 50

	H	I	J	K	...	N	O	P	Q	R	S	T	U	V	W
5	Room	Ticket #	Boat	Sex		Order	Class	Survived?	Name	Age	Embarked	Destinati	Room	Ticket #	Boat
6			4	female				Yes		<=18					
7	B-5	24160 L221	2	female		Order	Class	Survived?	Name	Age	Embarked	Destinati	Room	Ticket #	Boat
8	B-18	111361 L57 19s 7d	4	female				Yes							
9			9	female		Order	Class	Survived?	Name	Age	Embarked	Destinati	Room	Ticket #	Boat
10			3	female				Yes		<=18					
11			8	female		Order	Class	Survived?	Name	Age	Embarked	Destinati	Room	Ticket #	Boat
12		17608 L262 7s 6d	4	female				Yes							
13			6	female											
14			8	female		Order	Class	Survived?	Name	Age	Embarked	Destinati	Room	Ticket #	Boat
15		17754 L224 10s 6d	4	female				Yes		<=18					
16	B-49		7	female											
17	C-125	17582 L153 9s 3d	3	female				Total	% of Survivors	% of Total					
18			5	female		Male survivors		119	26.50%	9.06%					
19				female		Female survivors		267	59.47%	20.34%					
20			5	female		Child survivors		63	14.03%	4.80%					
21	D-?	13502 L77	10	female				449							
22		17608 L262 7s 6d	4	female											
23			6	female											
24			5	female											
25			7	female		Order	Class	Survived?	Name	Age	Embarked	Destinati	Room	Ticket #	Boat
26			5	female				No		<=18					
27			7	female		Order	Class	Survived?	Name	Age	Embarked	Destinati	Room	Ticket #	Boat
28			10	female				No							
29			6	female		Order	Class	Survived?	Name	Age	Embarked	Destinati	Room	Ticket #	Boat
30			7	female				No		<=18					
31			10	female		Order	Class	Survived?	Name	Age	Embarked	Destinati	Room	Ticket #	Boat
32			7	female				No							
33	C-87		4	female											
34			3	female		Order	Class	Survived?	Name	Age	Embarked	Destinati	Room	Ticket #	Boat
35			6	female				No		<=18					
36			8	female											
37			10	female				Total	% of Non-Survivors	% of Total					

Sheet1   Sheet2   Sheet3

Ready   80%

Lesson | 4
Protect and Share Worksheets and Create Special Charts

Skills Covered

- **Add or Remove Data in a Chart**
- **Set Data Label Options**
- **Set Data Table Options**
- **Format a Data Series**

Software Skills A chart presents complex numerical data in a graphical format. Because a chart tells its story visually, you must make the most of the way your chart looks. There are many ways in which you can enhance a chart; for example, you can add color or pattern to the chart background, and format the value and category axes so that the numbers are easier to understand.

Application Skills You're keeping the books for Midwest Technical, and you've been asked to produce a few charts to go into a budget report and a presentation for the owner. He really loves pie charts and column charts, so you're going to give him both.

TERMS

Categories For most charts, a category is information in a worksheet row. If you select multiple rows of data for a chart, you'll create multiple categories, and these categories will be listed along the x-axis.

Data series For most charts, a data series is the information in a worksheet column. If you select multiple columns of data for a chart, you'll create multiple data series. Each data series is then represented by its own color bar, line, or column.

Data table This optional table looks like a small worksheet, and displays the data used to create the chart.

Legend key A color that identifies each of the data series in a chart.

NOTES

Add or Remove Data in a Chart

- After creating a chart, you can change the initial data range to add data to the chart.
- For example, you might add a **data series** to the chart for an additional store, salesperson, product, and so on.
- You can remove data from a chart as well.
- When a chart is selected, the current data range is surrounded by colored Range Finder borders, as shown here.
  - You can drag the colored border to another range to select that range instead.
  - You can also use the drag handle on the Range Finder border to expand or contract the data range used by the chart.

- If the data and the chart are on different worksheets, you can use the Copy and Paste commands to add data to a chart.

Change the data range

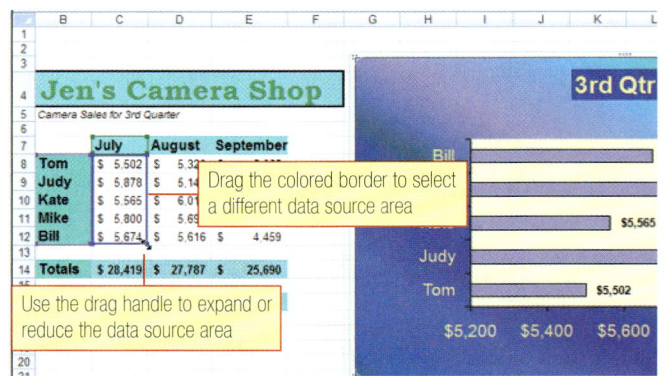

- If the data for a chart is stored on a different worksheet, you may find the Select Data Source dialog box easier to use when adjusting data ranges used by a chart.
- Using the dialog box, you can:
  - Select a new data range for the chart.
  - Select a different data range for an individual series.
  - Switch between displaying data by rows or by columns.
  - Change the order in which data series appear on the chart.
  - Change the data series names (the names that appear in the chart legend).
  - Change the range that contains the data labels.

Select Data Source dialog box

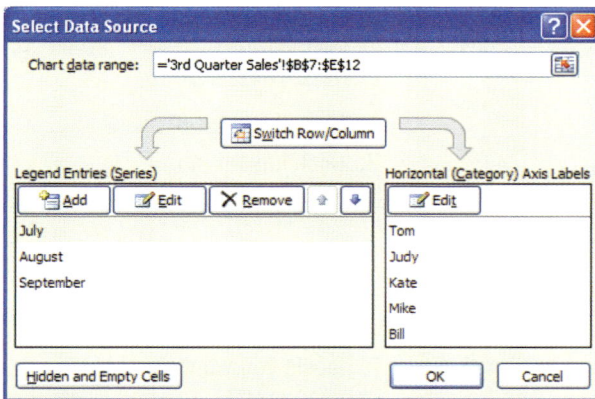

Set Data Label Options

- You can add data labels to a chart by simply choosing where you want the labels placed.
- For example, you might choose to center each data label over the corresponding data point.
- You can also choose exactly what to display in the data label, such as the:
  - Data series name
  - **Category** name
  - Data value and/or percentage
  - **Legend key**

Set Data Table Options

- You can add a data table to a chart.
- Adding a **data table** to a chart allows a viewer to easily understand the values plotted on the chart.

- Data tables have only a few basic options beyond normal formatting such as the fill and border color:
  - You can add a border around the cells in the data table—horizontally, vertically, or around the table's outline.
  - You can also choose whether or not to display the legend keys as part of the table.

Format a Data Series

- When you create a chart, Excel automatically assigns a color to each series in the chart.
  - You may want to change the color of a particular data series to improve the look of a chart, or simply because you don't like the color.
  - Even if you're printing the chart in black and white, you may want to change the color of a data series to better distinguish it from other colors in the chart that translate to a similar gray tone.

✓ *You can format various chart elements such as the chart title, legend, axis titles, data labels, and data table. After you learn how to select an individual data series in this exercise, you'll be able to apply those same formats to a particular data series.*

- In certain chart types such as bar and column charts, you can adjust the amount of space between each series in a group by changing the Series Options.
  - You can also change the width of bars and columns.
- In line charts, you can change the type and look of the markers used to plot each data point.
- In pie charts, you can change the position of the first slice within the pie, and the amount of separation between slices.

Format Data Series

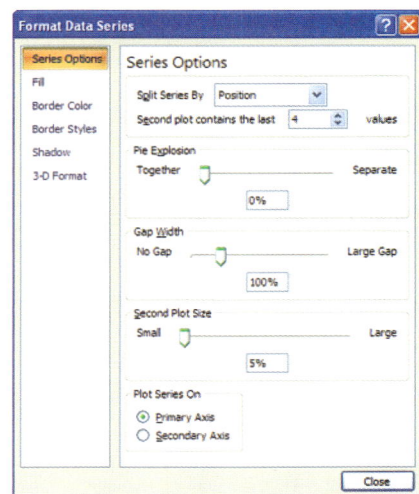

PROCEDURES

Add Data to a Chart

To add data with Copy and Paste:

1. Select the chart data you wish to add, including appropriate row and column labels.
2. Click **Home** tab . . . . `Alt`, `H`

   Clipboard Group

3. Click **Copy** button 🔲 . . . . `C`
4. Click the chart to select it.
5. Click **Home** tab . . . . `Alt`, `H`

   Clipboard Group

6. Click **Paste** button 🔲 . . . `V`, `P`

To add data by using the Range Finder:

■ Drag the handle on a selection to expand it to include more data.

   OR

■ Drag the outline of the selection to move it to another range.

Remove Chart Data

To remove an entire data series:

1. Click an item in the data series you wish to remove.
2. Press **Delete** . . . . `Delete`

To delete data by using the Range Finder:

■ Drag the handle on a selection to reduce its size and remove selected data.

Change Chart Data

1. Click the chart to select it.
2. Click **Design** tab . . . `Alt`, `J`, `C`

   Data Group

3. Click **Select Data** button 🔲 . . . . `E`

To change data range:

a. Click in **Chart data range** box . . . . `Alt`+`D`
b. Type or select new data range.

To switch between data by rows and data by columns:

■ Click **Switch Row/Column** . . . . `Alt`+`W`

To change a data series:

a. Select **Legend Entries (Series)** to change . . . . `Alt`+`S`, `→`/`←`/`↑`/`↓`
b. Click **Edit** . . . . `Alt`+`E`
c. To change series label, click in **Series name** box and select or type address of cell with label. . . . . `Alt`+`N`
d. To change series data range, click in **Series values** box and select or type new range. . . . . `Alt`+`V`
e. Click **OK** . . . . `Enter`

To add a data series:

a. Click **Add** . . . . `Alt`+`A`
b. click in **Series name** box and select or type address of cell with label. . . . . `Alt`+`N`
c. Click in **Series values** box and select or type new range. . . . . `Alt`+`V`
d. Click **OK** . . . . `Enter`

To change the order of the data series:

a. Select **Legend Entries (Series)** to change . . . . `Alt`+`S`, `→`/`←`/`↑`/`↓`
b. To move the series up in the list, click 🔼.

   OR

   To move the series down in the list, click 🔽.

To remove a data series:

a. Select **Legend Entries (Series)** to change . . . . `Alt`+`S`, `→`/`←`/`↑`/`↓`
b. Click **Remove** . . . . . . `Alt`+`R`

To change category labels:

a. Select **Horizontal (Category) Axis Label** to change . . . . `Alt`+`C`, `→`/`←`/`↑`/`↓`
b. Click **Edit** . . . . `Alt`+`T`
c. Click in **Axis label range** box and select or type new label. . . . . `Alt`+`A`
d. Click **OK** . . . . `Enter`

Set Data Label Options

1. Click the chart to select it.
2. Click **Layout** tab . . . . `Alt`, `J`, `A`

   Current Selection Group

3. Click arrow on the **Chart Elements** list `Chart Area ▼` . . . . `E`
4. Select the series of data labels you want to change. . . . . `↑`/`↓`, `Enter`

   Current Selection Group

5. Click **Format Selection** button 🔲 . . . . . `Alt`, `J`, `A`, `M`
6. Select data to display on the labels:

   ✓ *Options will vary, based on chart type.*

   ■ **Series Name** . . . . `Alt`+`S`
   ■ **Category Name** . . . . . `Alt`+`G`
   ■ **Value** . . . . `Alt`+`V`
   ■ **X Value** . . . . `Alt`+`X`
   ■ **Y Value** . . . . `Alt`+`Y`
   ■ **Percentage** . . . . `Alt`+`P`
   ■ **Show Leader Lines** . . `Alt`+`S`
   ■ **Bubble size** . . . . `Alt`+`B`

7. Select data label position:

✓ *Options will vary, based on chart type.*

- **C**enter . . . . `Alt`+`C`
- **Inside End** . . . . `Alt`+`I`
- **Inside Base** . . . . `Alt`+`D`
- **O**utside End . . . . `Alt`+`O`
- Best **F**it . . . . `Alt`+`F`
- Le**f**t . . . . `Alt`+`F`
- **R**ight . . . . `Alt`+`R`
- Abo**v**e . . . . `Alt`+`V`
- Belo**w** . . . . `Alt`+`W`

8. To display the legend key, click **Include legend key in label** . . . . `Alt`+`L`

9. If you selected multiple data to display, select a **Separator** to use between each data item in the label. . . . . `Alt`+`E`

10. Click **Close** . . . . `Enter`

Set Data Table Options

1. Click the chart to select it.

2. Click **Layout** tab. . . . `Alt`, `J`, `A`

   Labels Group

3. Click **Data Table** . . . . `D`

4. Click **Show Data Table** . . `↓`, `Enter`

   Current Selection Group

5. Click arrow on the **Chart Elements** list `Chart Area` . . . . `E`

6. Select **Data Table** . . . `↑`/`↓`, `Enter`

   Current Selection Group

7. Click **Format Selection** button . . . . . `Alt`, `J`, `A`, `M`

8. Select data table borders:

- **H**orizontal . . . . `Alt`+`H`
- **V**ertical . . . . `Alt`+`V`
- **O**utline. . . . . `Alt`+`O`

9. To include the legend keys in the data table, click **Show legend keys**. . . . . `Alt`+`S`

10. Click **Close** . . . . `Enter`

Format a Single Data Series

1. Click the data series you want to select.

   OR

  a. Click the chart to select it.

  b. Click **Layout** tab . . `Alt`, `J`, `A`

   Current Selection Group

  c. Click arrow on the **Chart Elements** list

   `Chart Area` . . . . `E`

  d. Select the data series you want to work with . . . . `↑`/`↓`, `Enter`

   Current Selection Group

2. Click **Format Selection** button . . . . . `Alt`, `J`, `A`, `M`

3. Select formatting options, clicking a category in the left list to display options as needed.

4. Click **Close** . . . . `Enter`

Set Data Series Options

1. Click chart to select it.

2. Click **Layout** tab. . . . `Alt`, `J`, `A`

   Current Selection Group

3. Click arrow on the **Chart Elements** list `Chart Area` . . . . `E`

4. Select any data series from the list.

✓ *Since these options apply to all data series, it doesn't matter which one you choose.*

   Current Selection Group

5. Click **Format Selection** button . . . . . `Alt`, `J`, `A`, `M`

✓ *Leave Series Options selected in the list at left. The Series Options that appear vary by chart type.*

In a 3-D line chart:

- Adjust the spacing between each series in a 3-D chart by adjusting the **Gap Depth** slider . . . . `Alt`+`D`, `↑`/`↓`

In a column or bar chart:

- Adjust the spacing between the data series in each category group by adjusting **Series Overlap** . . . . . `Alt`+`O`, `↑`/`↓`
- Adjust the spacing between categories by adjusting **Gap Width**. . . . . . . `Alt`+`W`, `↑`/`↓`
- Adjust the spacing between each series in a 3-D chart by adjusting the **Gap Depth**. . . . . . . `Alt`+`D`, `↑`/`↓`

In a pie or doughnut chart:

- Change the location of the first slice within the pie by dragging the **Angle of first slice** slider . . `Alt`+`A`, `↑`/`↓`
- Adjust the separation between pie slices by dragging the **Pie Explosion** slider . . . . `Alt`+`X`, `↑`/`↓`
- Adjust the separation between selected data points and the doughnut center by dragging the **Doughnut Explosion** slider.
- Adjust the size of the doughnut hole by dragging the **Doughnut Hole Size** slider . . . . `Alt`+`D`, `↑`/`↓`

In a pie of pie or bar of pie chart:

✓ *The lines that connect the primary chart with the secondary chart are listed as another series in the Chart Elements list. To change the color, style, and format of these lines, select them from the Chart Elements list and then the click Format Selection button .*

a. Select which slices appear in the secondary chart by selecting an option from the **Split Series By** list (Position, Value, Percentage Value, or Custom). . . . . `Alt`+`P`, `↑`/`↓`, `Enter`

b. Set the number of values that appear in the secondary chart by typing a value in the text box that appears . . . . ⌨Alt+⌨E, ##

✓ *If you choose Custom in step a, then click the chart to select a point then choosing an option from the Point Belongs to list.*

c. Explode (separate) a slice from its pie by clicking on it and dragging the **Pie Explosion** slider . . . .⌨Alt+⌨X, ⌨↑/⌨↓

d. Adjust the distance between slices by dragging the **Gap Width** slider . . . .⌨Alt+⌨W, ⌨↑/⌨↓

e. Control the size of the secondary chart relative to the first chart by dragging the **Second Plot Size** slider . . . .⌨Alt+⌨S, ⌨↑/⌨↓

In a bubble chart:

a. Select what determines the size of the bubbles
- Data affect the entire **Area of bubbles**. . . . . . .⌨Alt+⌨A
- Data affects only the **Width of bubbles**. . . . . . .⌨Alt+⌨W

b. To adjust the scale of the bubbles in relation to the data, drag the **Scale bubble size to** slider . . . .⌨Alt+⌨S, ##

c. To include a series even if contains nothing but negative values, select **Show negative bubbles** . . . .⌨Alt+⌨N

In a radar chart:

- Remove category labels by deselecting **Category labels** . . . .⌨Alt+⌨C

6. Select the axis you want to plot each series:
- **Primary Axis** . . . .⌨Alt+⌨P
- **Secondary Axis** . . . . .⌨Alt+⌨S

7. Click **Close** . . . .⌨Enter

EXERCISE DIRECTIONS

1. Start Excel, if necessary.
2. Open 🔘 **33MWTFirstQuarterBudget**.
3. Save the workbook as **33MWTFirstQuarterBudget_xx**.
4. Create a Pie in 3D chart that includes only the Sales & Marketing budget (A6:B12):
   a. Using the Chart Title button on the Layout tab, entitle the chart with a centered, overlay title, Sales & Marketing Budget.
   b. Remove the legend.
   c. Label each wedge with the category name, dollar value, and percentage of total, and position the data labels outside end.
   d. Include the leader lines.

e. Relocate and expand the chart so that it occupies the range A16:F41.

✓ *Although this chart type is called "3-D Pie Chart," it's not technically a 3D chart, because it doesn't use three axes. You'll see how a real 3D chart works in Lesson 36.*

5. Format the chart area:
   a. Click the chart area or select it from the Chart Elements list.
   b. Click the Format Selection button.
   c. On the Fill page, click the Gradient fill option and choose Fog from the Preset colors list.
   d. Choose a linear Type and set the Angle to 315.

6. Reduce the plot area and move the chart title as shown in Illustration A.

7. Since you can't do anything to change what you'll be spending on wages, benefits, and insurance, remove those amounts from the chart:

   a. Click the chart.

   b. Click the Select Data button on the Design tab.

   c. Select or type the range A7:B10 and A12:B12 in the Chart data range box.

   d. Click OK.

8. Rotate the pie so that the largest wedge is in the back:

   a. Change to the Layout tab, and choose Series 1 from the Chart Elements list.

   b. Click the Format Selection button.

   c. On the Series Options page, set Angle of first slice to 275 degrees.

   d. Click Close.

9. Drag the data labels outside the pie area as shown in Illustration A, so that they are easier to read.

10. Create a new chart that compares the Sales & Marketing and the Research & Development budgets:

    a. Create 3-D Cone chart with the above chart title **Budget Comparison**.

    b. Remove the legend and add a data table with legend keys.

    c. Remove the horizontal table border on the data table.

    d. Resize the chart to fit the range H16:P41.

11. Change the font used in the chart's data table to 8 pt.

12. Format the chart area:

    a. Select Chart Area from the Chart Elements list, and click the Format Selection button.

    b. On the Fill page, click the Gradient fill option, select Fog from the Preset colors list, choose the linear Type, set the Angle to 45 degrees, and click Close.

13. Format the plot area:

    a. Select Plot Area from the Chart Elements list, and click the Format Selection button.

    b. On the Fill page, click the Picture or texture fill option, select the Recycled paper texture, set Transparency to 50%, and click Close.

    c. Click the Format tab, click the Shape Effects button, point to Soft Edges, and select 2.5 Point.

14. Format the data series:

    a. Select Series:"Sales & Marketing" from the Charts Elements list, and click the Format Selection button.

    b. On the Series Options page, change the Gap Width to 65%.

    c. Set the Gap Depth to 35%.

    d. Click Close.

15. Adjust the axes (see Illustration B):

    a. Remove the labels on the Depth (Series) Axis by selecting it from the Chart Elements list.

    b. Click the Format Selection button on the Layout tab.

    c. Select None from the Axis labels list.

    d. Change the text along the Vertical (Value) Axis and the Horizontal (Category) Axis to 8 pt. by selecting each axis in turn, and choosing 8 from the Font Size list on the Home tab.

    e. Reduce the decimal points on the Vertical (Value) Axis to zero by selecting it from the Chart Elements list, clicking the Format Selection button on the Layout tab, and setting the Decimal places on the Number page to zero.

16. Spell check the worksheet.

17. Print the worksheet.

18. Close the workbook, saving all changes.

Illustration A

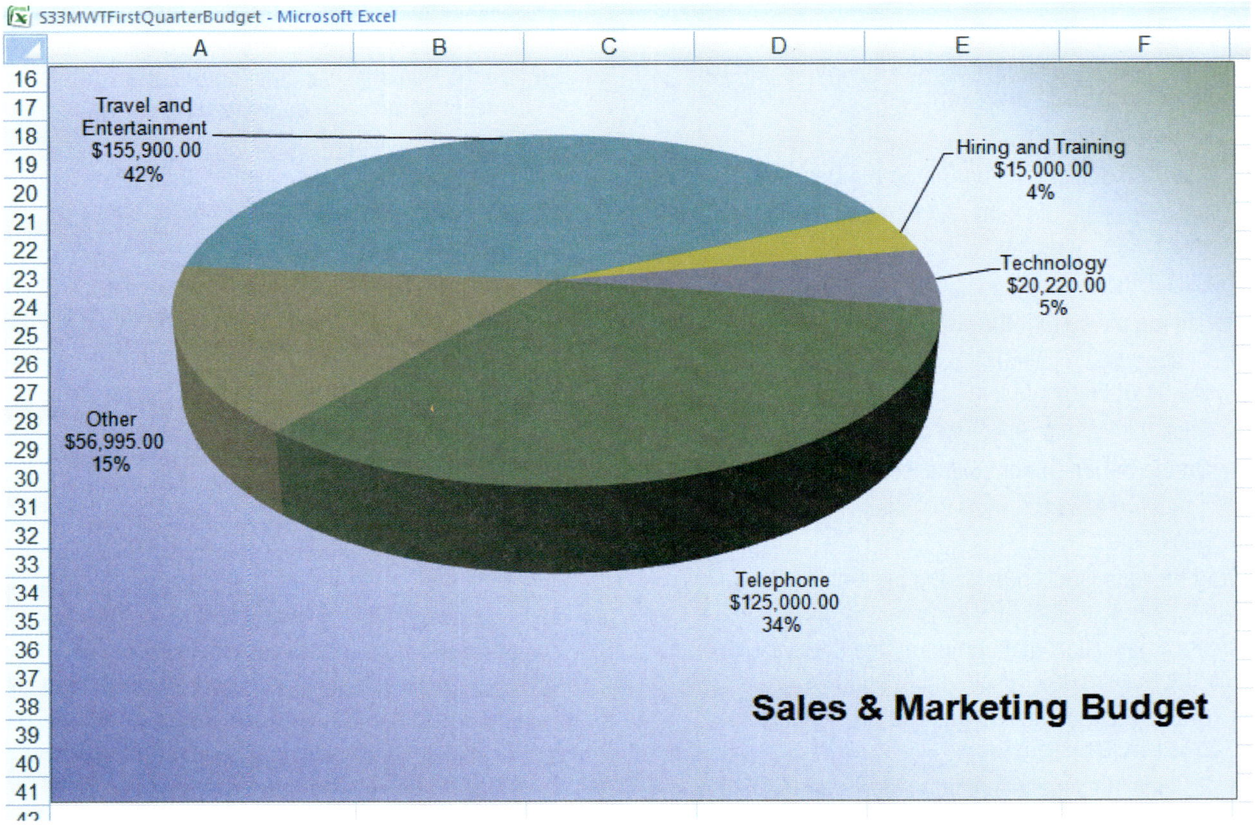

Travel and
Entertainment
$155,900.00
42%

Hiring and Training
$15,000.00
4%

Technology
$20,220.00
5%

Other
$56,995.00
15%

Telephone
$125,000.00
34%

Sales & Marketing Budget

Illustration B

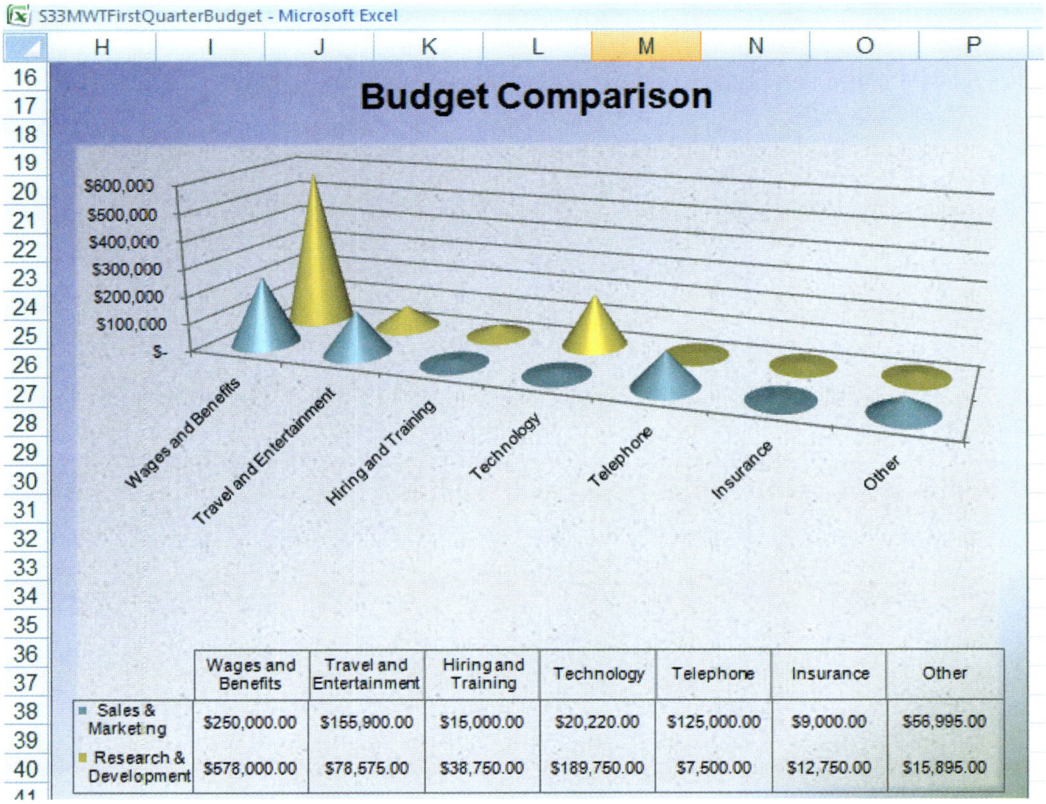

Budget Comparison

	Wages and Benefits	Travel and Entertainment	Hiring and Training	Technology	Telephone	Insurance	Other
Sales & Marketing	$250,000.00	$155,900.00	$15,000.00	$20,220.00	$125,000.00	$9,000.00	$56,995.00
Research & Development	$578,000.00	$78,575.00	$38,750.00	$189,750.00	$7,500.00	$12,750.00	$15,895.00

ON YOUR OWN

1. Start Excel, if necessary.
2. Open 💿 **33AntiquesSales3Q**.
3. Save the workbook as **OXL33_*xx***.
4. Select the range D8:E14, and create a clustered column chart:
   a. Add a centered overlay title **July Revenues**.
   b. Remove the legend.
   c. Add a data table with legend keys, but remove the table outline border.
   d. Place the chart on the Sheet1 worksheet, in the range A21:N35.
5. Add the August and September data to the chart and change the chart title to **3rd Qtr Revenues**.

6. Format the chart as you like, but format each data series separately:
   a. Add a texture to one data series.
   b. Add a two-color gradient fill to a different data series.
   c. Set the Series Overlap to -75%.
   d. Set the Gap Width to 60%.
7. Remove the data for end tables and chairs from the chart. See Illustration A.
8. Spell check the worksheet.
9. Print the worksheet.
10. Close the workbook, saving all changes.

Illustration A

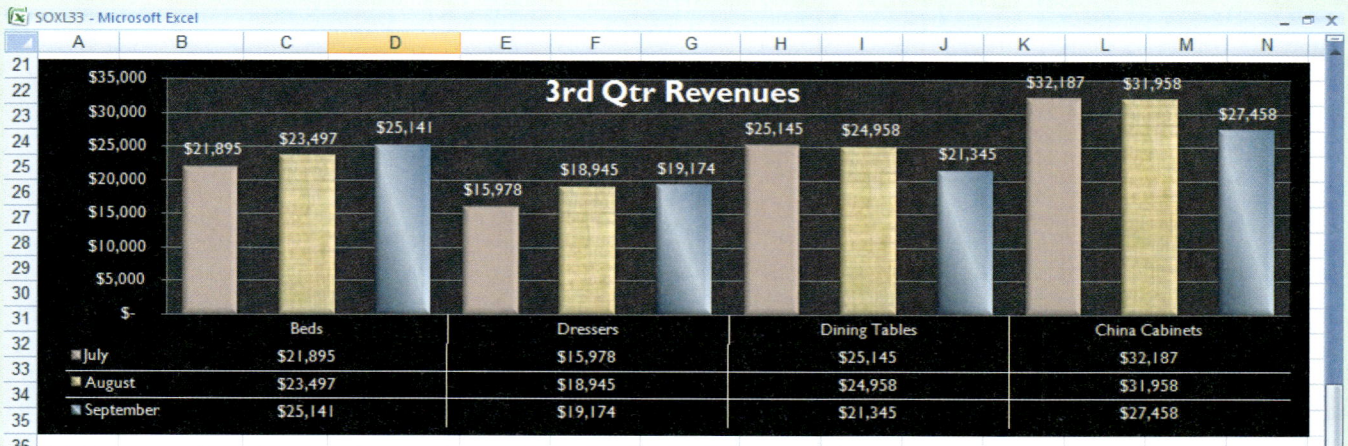

Exercise | 34

Skills Covered

■ **Create a Stock Chart**
■ **Add a Secondary Value Axis to a Chart**

■ **Change Data Marker Format**

Software Skills   Because Excel is used every day by thousands of investors—many of whom invest as a profession—it has to be capable of producing charts specifically tailored to the needs and expectations of those users. A stock chart is no ordinary graphical rendering, since it often has to show several related values (such as opening and closing values) on a single chart.

Application Skills   You're tracking the performance of a handful of major stocks for your own personal portfolio. Your broker gives you occasional advice, but you're the one making your own investment decisions, so you need some graphical data to help you make better sense of the ups and downs of a particular stock you're interested in—Midwest Technical.

TERMS

Data marker   A symbol that appears on a stock chart to mark a particular type of data, such as the stock close value.

NOTES

Create a Stock Chart

■ Charting stock data requires a special type of chart designed to handle standard stock information.

■ Excel offers four different kinds of stock charts:
  - High-Low-Close
  - Open-High-Low-Close
  - Volume-High-Low-Close
  - Volume-Open-High-Low-Close

■ Each chart handles a different set of data taken from this standard set of stock information:
  - Volume—the number of shares of a particular stock traded during the market day.
  - Open—the value of the stock at the time when the market opened for the day.
  - High—the highest value at which the stock was traded that day.

  - Low—the lowest value at which the stock was traded that day.
  - Close—the value of the stock when the market closed for the day.

■ To create a stock chart, you must enter the data in columns (or rows) in the order specified by the type of stock chart you want.

  ✓ *For example, if you select the Open-High-Low-Close chart, you must enter the data in four columns (or rows) in this order: Open, High, Low, and Close.*

  - As row (or column) labels, you can use the stock symbol or name (if you're going to track more than one type of stock), or the date (if you're tracking one stock's trading pattern over several days).

■ A stock chart is also ideal for charting certain kinds of scientific data, such as temperature changes throughout the day.

Sample stock chart with temperatures

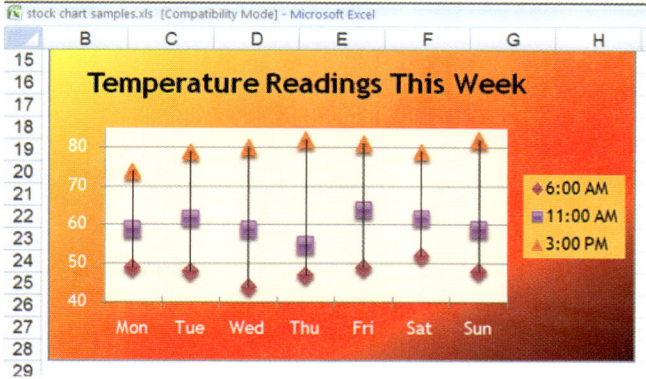

Add a Secondary Value Axis to a Chart

■ To track two related but different values, use two value axes in the chart.

■ The value axes appear on opposite sides of the chart.

■ For example, Excel uses two value axes for a stock chart that includes both the volume of stock trading and the value of the stock.

  ● One axis plots the stock's trading volume.

  ● The other axis plots the stock's value at open, close, high, and low points in the day.

■ Secondary value axes are most common on stock charts and will appear automatically when Excel determines that two value axes are needed, but you can manually add a secondary axis to other types of charts as well.

Chart with two value axes

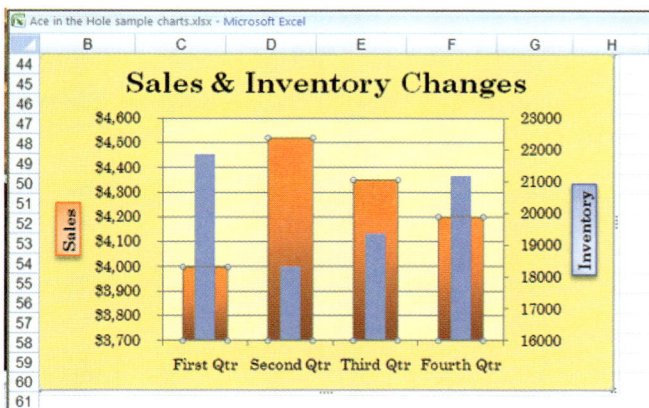

Change Data Marker Format

■ When you create a stock chart, Excel uses a series of standard **data markers** for the open, close, high-low, volume, close up, and close down values.

■ Some of these markers may be too small, too dark, or too light to appear clearly on a printout.

■ To improve the appearance of your chart, you may want to adjust the data markers used by Excel.

■ You do that by selecting a series to change, and using the Format Data Series dialog box.

Format Data Markers dialog box

■ You can change the fill color, size, shape, outline color, and outline style of each data marker used in a stock chart.

■ You can also change the data markers used in line, xy (scatter), and radar charts.

PROCEDURES

Create a Stock Chart

1. Select data to chart.
2. Click **Insert** tab . . . . [Alt], [N]

   Charts group

3. Click arrow on the **Other Charts** button [⬤] . . . . [O]
4. Select the stock chart that matches your data . . . . [→]/[←]/[↑]/[↓], [Enter]

Add a Secondary Value Axis

1. Click stock, line, scatter, or radar chart to select it.
2. Click **Layout** tab. . . . [Alt], [J], [A]

   Current Selection Group

3. Click arrow on the **Chart Elements** list [Chart Area ▾] . . . . [E]
4. Select the data series you want to chart on a secondary axis.

   Current Selection Group

5. Click **Format Selection** button [🖾] . . . . . [Alt], [J], [A], [M]
6. Click **Secondary Axis** . . . [Alt]+[S]
7. Click **Close** . . . . [Enter]

Format Data Markers

1. Click the chart to select it.
2. Click **Layout** tab. . . . [Alt], [J], [A]

   Current Selection Group

3. Click arrow on the **Chart Elements** list [Chart Area ▾] . . . . [E]
4. Select the data series whose markers you want to change.

   Current Selection Group

5. Click **Format Selection** button [🖾] . . . . . [Alt], [J], [A], [M]
6. Click **Marker Options** . . . . [↑]/[↓]

---

7. Select Marker Type:
   - ■ Click **A̲utomatic** . . . . . [Alt]+[U]

   OR

   - ■ Click **N̲one** . . . . [Alt]+[O]

   OR

   a. Click **Built-In** . . . . [⇥], [↓]
   b. Select a marker **Type** . . . . [⇥], [↑]/[↓]
   c. Select marker **Size** . . . . [⇥], [↑]/[↓]

8. Click **Marker Fill** . . . . [⇥], [↑]/[↓]
   - ■ Select **N̲o fill** . . . . [Alt]+[N]

   OR

To fill marker with color:

   a. Select **S̲olid fill** . . . . . [Alt]+[S]
   b. Select a solid **C̲olor** . . . . [Alt]+[C], [→]/[←]/[↑]/[↓], [Enter]
   c. Set **T̲ransparency** . . . . [Alt]+[T], [↑]/[↓]

   OR

   a. Select **G̲radient fill**. . . [Alt]+[G]
   b. Select from the **Preset colors** . . . . [Alt]+[R], [→]/[←]/[↑]/[↓], [Enter]
   c. Set gradient **Type** . . . . [Alt]+[Y], [↓], [Enter]
   d. Set gradient **Direction** . . . . [Alt]+[D], [←]/[→], [Enter]
   d. Set gradient **Angle** . . . . [Alt]+[E], [↑]/[↓]

   ✓ *You can create a custom gradient by setting gradient stops or colors through which the gradient slowly changes. For example, you might set three stops: blue, red, and green, and let the gradient change gradually from one color to the next. Each stop can be set anywhere along the gradient line (its Stop position), with a particular Color, and Transparency.*

To fill marker with texture:

   a. Select **P̲icture or texture fill** . . . . [Alt]+[P]
   b. Select a **Texture** . . . . . [Alt]+[U], [→]/[←]/[↑]/[↓], [Enter]

To fill marker with picture:

   a. Select **P̲icture or texture fill** . . . . [Alt]+[P]
   b. Click **F̲ile** . . . . [Alt]+[F]
   c. Select desired drive and folder from **Look i̲n** drop-down list . . . . [Alt]+[I]
   d. Double-click graphic file.

   OR

   a. Select **P̲icture or texture fill** . . . . [Alt]+[P]
   b. Click **Clip Art** . . . . [Alt]+[R]
   c. Type **Search te̲xt** . . . . [Alt]+[T]
   d. If desired, select **Include content from O̲ffice Online** . . . . [Alt]+[O]
   e. Click **G̲o** . . . . [Alt]+[G]
   f. Select clip art image . . . . [→]/[←]/[↑]/[↓]
   g. Click **OK** . . . . [Enter]

   ✓ *You can offset either a picture or a clip art image so that it doesn't fill the entire chart or plot area. You can also adjust the Transparency to make it possible to see through the background.*

To use the default color:

   - ■ Select **A̲utomatic** to apply normal background color (usually white) . . . . [Alt]+[U]

9. Click **Marker Line Color** . . [↑]/[↓]
   - ■ Select **N̲o fill** . . . . [Alt]+[N]

   OR

To fill marker outline with color:

a. Select **Solid line** . . . . [Alt]+[S]

b. Select a solid **Color** . . . . . . [C], [→]/[←]/[↑]/[↓], [Enter]

c. Set **Transparency**. . . . [Alt]+[T], [↑]/[↓]

OR

a. Select **Gradient line** . . . . [Alt]+[G]

b. Select a **Preset colors** . . . . [Alt]+[R], [→]/[←]/[↑]/[↓], [Enter]

c. Set gradient **Type** . . . . [Alt]+[Y], [↓], [Enter]

d. Set gradient **Direction** . . . . [Alt]+[D], [←]/[→], [Enter]

e. Set gradient **Angle** . . . . [Alt]+[E], [↑]/[↓]

✓ *You can create a custom gradient by setting gradient stops, or colors through which the gradient slowly changes. For example, you might set three stops: blue, red, and green, and let the gradient change gradually from one color to the next. Each stop can be set anywhere along the gradient line (its Stop position), with a particular Color, and Transparency.*

OR

■ Select **Automatic** to apply normal line color (usually black) . . . . [Alt]+[U]

10. Click **Marker Line Style** . . . [↑]/[↓]

a. Select **Width** . . . . [Alt]+[W], [↑]/[↓]

b. Select **Compound type** . . . . [Alt]+[C], [↑]/[↓], [Enter]

c. Select **Dash type** . . . . [Alt]+[D], [↑]/[↓], [Enter]

d. Select **Cap type** . . . . . [Alt]+[A], [↑]/[↓], [Enter]

e. Select **Join type** . . . . . [Alt]+[J], [↑]/[↓], [Enter]

f. If applicable, change the arrow settings:

• Set **Begin type** . . [Alt]+[B], [↑]/[↓], [Enter]

• Set **End type** . . . . [Alt]+[E], [↑]/[↓], [Enter]

• Set **Begin size** . . . [Alt]+[S], [↑]/[↓], [Enter]

• Set **End size** . . . . [Alt]+[N], [↑]/[↓], [Enter]

g. To smooth the appearance of the line, click **Smoothed Line** . . . . [Alt]+[M]

11. Click **Close** . . . . [Enter]

EXERCISE DIRECTIONS

1. Start Excel, if necessary.
2. Start Excel and open ⊙ **34MWTStock2008**.
3. Save the workbook **34MWTStock2008_xx**.

   ✓ *You received this data from Midwest Technical's accountant, but in order to generate a stock chart, its data must be put in a specific columnar order.*

4. Rearrange the worksheet as follows:

   a. Move the *Volume* column inbetween the *Date* and *Open* columns by cutting the column and using the Insert button on the Home tab to insert the cut cells.

   b. Sort the rows in ascending date order.

5. Select the range A5:F5.
6. Press Ctrl and select the additional range A28:F48.
7. Create a Volume-Open-High-Low-Close stock chart:

   a. Click the Insert tab and click the Other Charts button.

   b. Choose the chart sub-type, Volume-Open-High-Low-Close, from the Stock section.

   c. Move the chart to its own sheet named **Feb Stock Chart**. See Illustration A.

   d. Add a centered, overlap title **Midwest Technical NYSE Daily Trades February 2008**.

   e. Add a primary vertical axis title, rotated, **Volume (millions)**.

   f. Add a secondary vertical axis title, rotated, **Value ($)**.

8. There are gaps along the Category axis where Excel insists on plotting non-existing dates:

   a. To fix this problem, from the Chart Elements list on the Layout tab, select Horizontal (Category) Axis.

   b. Click the Format Selection button.

   c. Change the Axis Type to Text axis and click Close.

9. Format the chart as follows:

   a. Select the Style 4 chart style.

   b. Apply a Gold gradient fill to the chart area, with a Radial type and the last Direction choice.

   c. Apply an Aqua, Accent 1, Darker 25% solid fill to the plot area, and adjust the Transparency to 65%.

   d. Change the scale of the Vertical (Value) Axis so that it uses Millions as its display unit. Don't show the units label.

   e. Format the Secondary Vertical (Value) Axis with Currency format, zero decimal places, $ symbol.

   f. Format the Horizontal (Category) Axis using the number (date) format, 3/14.

10. Change the data markers as indicated:

    a. Change the Open series marker to the filled square (the first option), 7 points in size.

    ✓ *Hint: Select Series "Open" in the Chart Elements list on the Layout tab, and then click the Format Selection button.*

    b. Change the High series marker to a triangle (the third option), 7 pt., with a solid marker fill color of Aqua, Accent 1, Lighter 40%, and a solid marker line color of Gold, Accent 2, Lighter 40%.

    c. Change the Low series marker to a plus sign (second to last option), 8 pt., with a marker line style width of 1.5 pt.

    d. Change the Close series marker to an asterisk (fifth option), 7 pt., with a solid marker line color of Olive Green, Accent 4, Darker 25%, and a marker line style width of 1.5 pt.

    e. Change the Up-Bars 2 series to solid fill Gold, Accent 2, Lighter 60%.

    ✓ *Here's how to read the chart: For each day of trading, the vertical line represents the value range between the highest and lowest transaction prices of the day.*

    ✓ *The light yellow bars show up-trends between the opening price for the day and the closing price. Notice how each opening price is not the same as yesterday's closing price. The dark green bars show down-trends between opening and closing prices.*

    ✓ *The day's trading data is superimposed over the trading volume, which is measured against a different Y-axis on the right side of the chart. When high trading volume pushes a stock value lower or higher, it's generally on account of major news.*

11. Display the legend at the bottom of the chart.
12. Spell check the workbook.
13. Print the workbook.
14. Close the workbook, saving all changes.

Illustration A

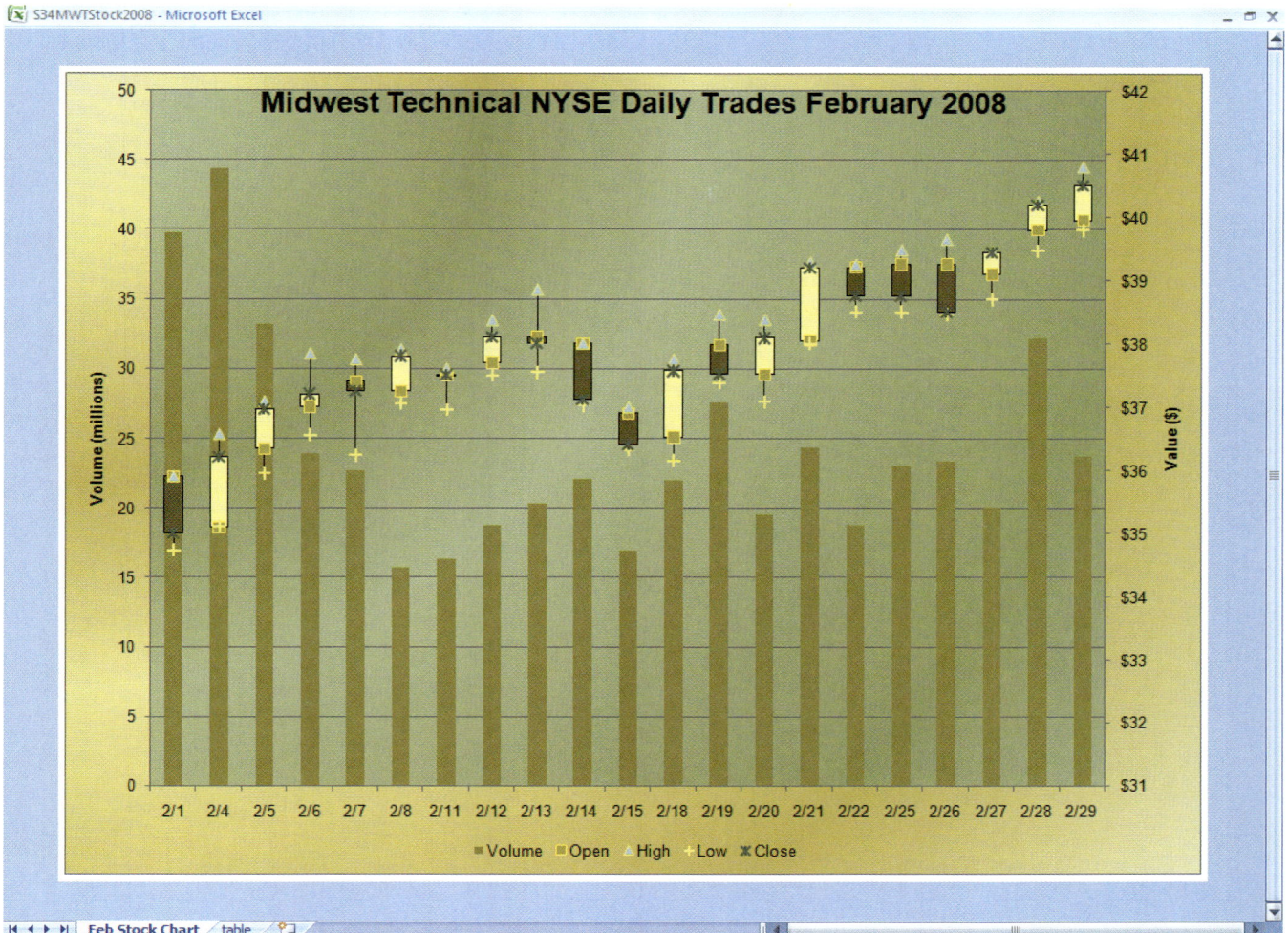

Business Connection

Job Application Forms

Most employers have job application forms that prospective employees fill out the first time they visit. Job application forms vary, but usually include fields for entering your name, address, and contact information, employment history—including dates and locations, education, and references. Some forms may be filled out on a computer or online, but most are manually filled out using paper and a pen. It is a good idea to familiarize yourself with the type of information usually required on a job application form, and even to bring a sample form filled out with your information with you when you visit an employer. That way, you can copy the information from the sample to the actual form, so that you are certain you have the information correct.

Comparing Job Application Forms

Collect sample job application forms from local businesses, your career center, or by looking for applications online. Use Excel to record information about each form you collect, such as the name of the employer, the position that is open, and the date on which you received the form. You can catalog the forms by writing a small ID number in a corner, and then including that number in your worksheet. Compare the printed forms to see how they are the same, and how they are different. Practice filling out one or more of the forms, being sure to include all of the information, and making sure the information is correct. Use a black or blue pen to write on paper forms, and be sure your handwriting is legible so anyone can read it. Check your spelling carefully. If you are missing any information, track it down and fill it in. That way, you will be prepared when it is time to fill out a job application form for a job you really want.

ON YOUR OWN

1. Start Excel, if necessary.
2. Open ⊙ **34WeeklyTemps**.
3. Save the workbook as **OXL34_xx**.
4. Create a High-Low-Close stock chart using the temperature data, and save it on its own sheet (see Illustration A).
5. Format the data markers to produce an attractive chart that is easy to understand.
6. Add formatting to the chart background, plot area, legend, value axis, and category axis as desired.
7. Spell check the chart.
8. Print the chart.
9. Close the workbook, saving all changes.

Illustration A

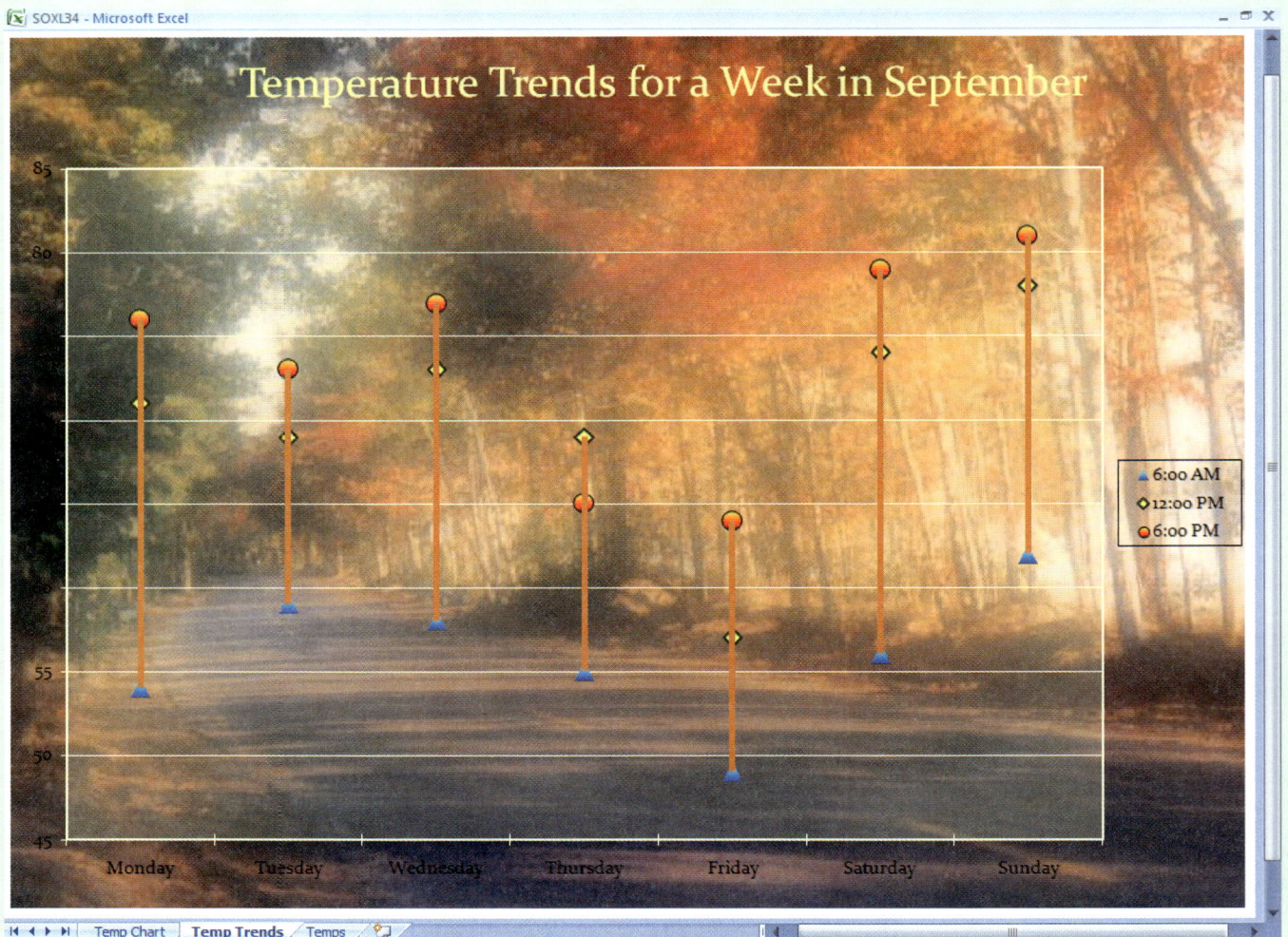

Exercise | 35

Skills Covered

- Create an Exploded Pie Chart
- Size the Plot Area or Legend in a Chart
- Create a Stacked Area Chart

Software Skills   Although a pie chart may be a great chart type for emphasizing your data, an exploded pie chart may be better. In an exploded pie chart, one or more pieces are "pulled away" from the pie in order to better emphasize them. When creating an exploded pie chart, you may wish to resize the plot area to provide more room in which to explode a pie piece or two. In addition, you may want to reduce the size of the legend to provide a larger area in which to plot data. If an exploded pie chart isn't right for your data, a stacked area chart, which emphasizes the difference between data series, may be a better choice.

Application Skills   You've been asked by the administrative head of Wood Hills Animal Clinic to produce some charts that better illustrate its monthly expenses, in order for her to decide where she may be able to cut costs.

TERMS

Exploded pie chart   A chart in which one or more pieces are separated from the rest of the pie for emphasis.

Legend   An optional part of a chart, the legend displays a description of each data series included in the chart.

Plot area   The area within a chart in which the data is plotted.

Stacked area chart   A special type of area chart in which the values for each data series are stacked on one another, creating one large area.

NOTES

Create an Exploded Pie Chart

- If an ordinary pie chart doesn't tell the entire story about your data, you can use an **exploded pie chart**.

- In an exploded pie chart, one or more pieces of the pie are separated from the rest of the pie, enabling you to emphasize certain data.

- Excel offers two different exploded pie types, one 2-D and the other 3-D.

  - In both chart types, all pieces of the pie are exploded (separated from each other).

- You can create a customized exploded pie by dragging one or more pieces of a regular pie chart outward (or parts of an exploded pie inward).

- In a pie of pie chart, which is similar to an exploded pie chart, a data series is taken from the first pie and illustrated in a second, smaller pie.

  - You might use this type of chart to better illustrate a small series of values in the larger pie.

- After creating the pie of pie chart, you can adjust the values displayed in the second pie as needed.

  - Another way to illustrate a subgroup is a *bar of pie* chart which uses a vertical bar chart instead of a second pie chart to illustrate the data.

Exploded pie and pie of pie

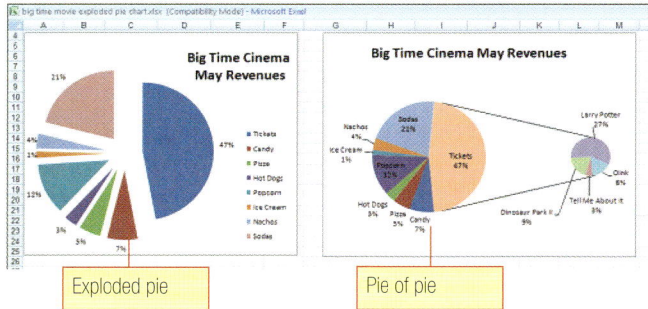

Exploded pie

Pie of pie

Size the Plot Area or Legend in a Chart

- Often, when creating an exploded pie chart, you may need to resize the **plot area** to create a larger space in which to work.

- To expand the plot area, you may need to reduce or resize the **legend**.

- You resize the plot area or legend as you might any other object, by dragging one of its sizing handles.

Resizing the plot area

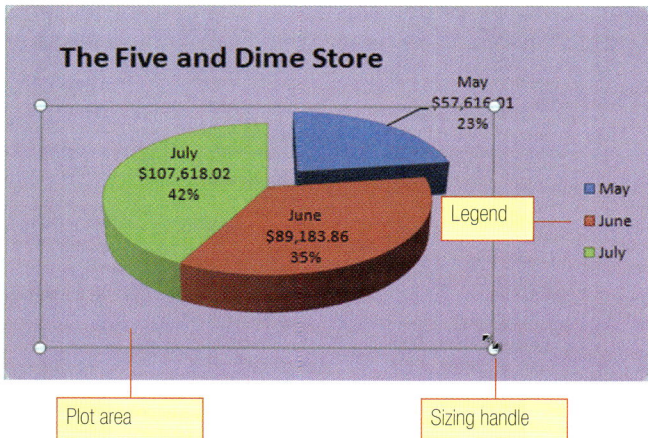

Plot area

Sizing handle

Create a Stacked Area Chart

- In a **stacked area chart**, the values in each data series are stacked on top of each another, creating a larger area.

  - Whereas a line chart would show the relative positions of multiple series compared to one another, a stacked area chart shows their cumulative positions.

  - Each entry is stacked on top of the previous one, forming a peak that represents the sum of all series' entries together.

- Use a stacked area chart to emphasize the difference in values between two data series, while also illustrating the total of the two.

- In a 100% stacked area chart, for each category, all of the series combine to consume the entire height of the chart.

Stacked area chart

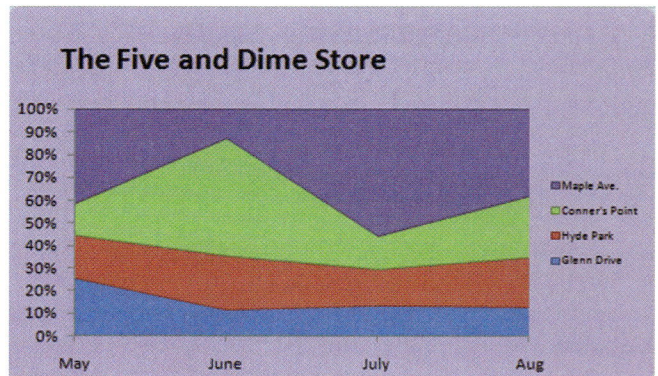

✓ *The point of this chart is to track the relative contribution of each series to the cumulative total.*

- Both stacked area and 100% stacked area charts come in 2-D and 3-D versions.

PROCEDURES

Create an Exploded Chart

1. Select data to chart.
2. Click **Insert** tab . . . . `Alt`, `N`

   Charts group

3. Click arrow on the **Pie** button 🥧 . . . . `E`
4. Select the **Exploded Pie** or **Exploded pie in 3-D** chart . . . . `→`/`←`/`↑`/`↓`, `Enter`

Explode a Pie Section Manually

1. Select the pie chart you wish to change.
2. Click a pie section to select it.

   ✓ *You may need to click the section twice (not a double-click) to select a single pie slice instead of the entire pie.*

3. Drag the pie slice to the desired position.

   ✓ *This same basic process can be used to drag a piece of an exploded pie inward, so that it is no longer "exploded."*

Explode a Pie Section

1. Click the chart to select it.
2. Click **Layout** tab. . . . `Alt`, `J`, `A`

   Current Selection Group

3. Click arrow on the **Chart Elements** list | Chart Area ▼ | . . . . `E`
4. Select the data series.

   ✓ *Do not select the Series Lines 1, which is used to format the lines that connect the two charts.*

   Current Selection Group

5. Click **Format Selection** button 🔧 . . . . . `Alt`, `J`, `A`, `M`
6. On the Series Options page, explode (separate) a slice from its pie by clicking on it and dragging the **Pie Explosion** slider . . . . `Alt`+`X`, `↑`/`↓`

---

7. Adjust the distance between slices by dragging the **Gap Width** slider . . . . `Alt`+`W`, `↑`/`↓`
8. Click **Close** . . . . `Enter`

Create a Pie of Pie or Bar of Pie Chart

1. Select data to chart.
2. Click **Insert** tab . . . . `Alt`, `N`

   Charts group

3. Click arrow on the **Pie** button 🥧 . . . . `E`
4. Select the **Pie of Pie** or **Bar of Pie** chart . . . . `→`/`←`/`↑`/`↓`, `Enter`

   ✓ *Excel automatically decides which data should appear in the secondary pie (or bar) chart, and which belongs in the primary pie. If necessary, adjust the grouping by continuing to step 5.*

5. Drag and drop the pie slices as needed between the pie (or pie and bar) charts.

Select the Values to Display in Secondary Pie of Pie or Bar of Pie Chart

1. Click the chart to select it.
2. Click **Layout** tab. . . . `Alt`, `J`, `A`

   Current Selection Group

3. Click arrow on the **Chart Elements** list | Chart Area ▼ | . . . . `E`
4. Select the data series.

   ✓ *Do not select the Series Lines 1, which is used to format the lines that connect the two charts.*

   Current Selection Group

5. Click **Format Selection** button 🔧 . . . . . `Alt`, `J`, `A`, `M`
6. On the Series Options page, open the **Split Series By** list . . . . `Alt`+`P`

---

7. Select how you want to split values between the two charts . . . . `↑`/`↓`, `Enter`

   ✓ *You can choose among Position, Value, Percentage value, or Custom.*

8. Set appropriate option:
   - If you chose Position in step 7, select or type a number in the **Second plot contains the last: xx values** box . . . . . . `Alt`+`E`, `→`/`←`/`↑`/`↓`

   OR
   - If you chose Value or Percentage value in step 7, select or type a number in the **Second plot contains all values less than** box . . . . `Alt`+`E`, `→`/`←`/`↑`/`↓`

   OR
   a. If you chose Custom in step 7, click a pie or bar slice you want to move to a different chart.

   ✓ *The Format Data Point dialog box appears.*

   b. Choose the chart (plot) in which you want to include the data point from the **Point Belongs to** list.
9. Click **Close** . . . . `Enter`

Adjust the Size of the Secondary Pie in a Pie of Pie or Bar of Pie Chart

1. Click the chart to select it.
2. Click **Layout** tab. . . . `Alt`, `J`, `A`

   Current Selection Group

3. Click arrow on the **Chart Elements** list | Chart Area ▼ | . . . . `E`
4. Select the data series.

   ✓ *Do not select the Series Lines 1, which is used to format the lines that connect the two charts.*

5. Click **Format Selection**
   button [icon] . . . . . [Alt], [J], [A], [M]

6. On the Series Options page, adjust the size of the secondary chart relative to the first chart by dragging the **Second Plot Size** slider . . . . [Alt]+[S], [↑]/[↓]

7. Adjust the distance between the first pie and the second by dragging the **Gap Width** slider. . . . . [Alt]+[W], [↑]/[↓]

8. Click **Close** . . . . [Enter]

Manually Resize Plot Area or Legend

1. Select the chart or display the chart sheet you wish to change.

2. Select plot area or legend.

   ✓ *Handles appear on border of the object.*

3. Point to handle on side or corner of object to resize.

   ✓ *Use a corner handle to resize the object proportionally.*

4. Drag object's outline to size.

5. Release mouse button when object is desired size.

   ✓ *Text associated with the object—such as data labels or legend text—is automatically resized as well.*

Create a Stacked Area Chart

1. Select data to chart.

2. Click **Insert** tab . . . . [Alt], [N]

3. Click arrow on the **Area** button [icon] . . . . [A]

4. Select the **100% Stacked Area** or **100% Stacked Area in 3-D** chart . . . . [→]/[←]/[↑]/[↓], [Enter]

EXERCISE DIRECTIONS

1. Start Excel, if necessary.
2. Open [icon] **35BalSheetP&L**.
3. Save the workbook as **35BalSheetP&L_xx**.
4. Create pie of pie chart:
   a. Select the ranges B45:B55 and D45:D55 on the P&L sheet.
   b. Click the Pie button on the Insert tab and choose Pie of Pie.
   c. Move the chart to a new sheet called **General & Admin**.
   d. Move the chart sheet so it's after the P&L sheet in the sheet tabs.
   e. Apply chart style #26.
   f. Add an above chart title **General & Administrative Costs** set at 36 pt.
   g. Apply the Peacock gradient, set at 135° angle.
5. Adjust the chart so that the breakdown pie on the right is larger than the main pie on the left, and contains every data point *except* payroll taxes:
   a. Click on the chart and then select Series 1 from the Chart Elements list on the Layout tab.
   b. Click the Format Selection button.
   c. In the Split Series By list, select Percentage Value.
   d. Set Second plot contains all the values less than to 40%.
   e. Set the Second Plot Size to 135.
   f. Set Gap Width to 150.
   g. Click Close.

6. Remove the legend.
7. Add data labels that include the category and the value, and use the Outside End option to position them.
8. The data labels are still a bit hard to see, but resizing the plot area should help. Resize and position it as shown in Illustration A.
9. Click within the Payroll taxes data label just after the comma and press Enter to create two lines of text as shown in Illustration A.
10. Explode the "Other" pie slice on the first pie by dragging it outward.
11. Spell check the chart.
12. Print the chart.
13. Create a stacked area chart based on data in the Patient care breakdown worksheet:
    a. Select the range A9:G18.
    b. Click the Area button on the Insert tab and choose 100% Stacked Area.
    c. Move the chart to a new sheet called **Patient Care Chart**, and move it after the Patient care breakdown sheet.
    d. Apply chart style #44.
    e. Add a chart title **Patient Care Costs** in 40 pt. Drag the chart title to the left as shown in Illustration B.
    f. Move the legend to the left.
    g. Click the Switch Row/Column button on the Design tab to display the months as categories.

h. Move the Vertical (Value) Axis labels to the right of the plot area by selecting them from the Chart Elements list, clicking the Format Selection button, and choosing High from the Axis Labels list.

i. Resize the plot area as shown in Illustration B.

14. Spell check the sheet.

15. Print the chart.

16. Close the workbook, saving all changes.

Illustration A

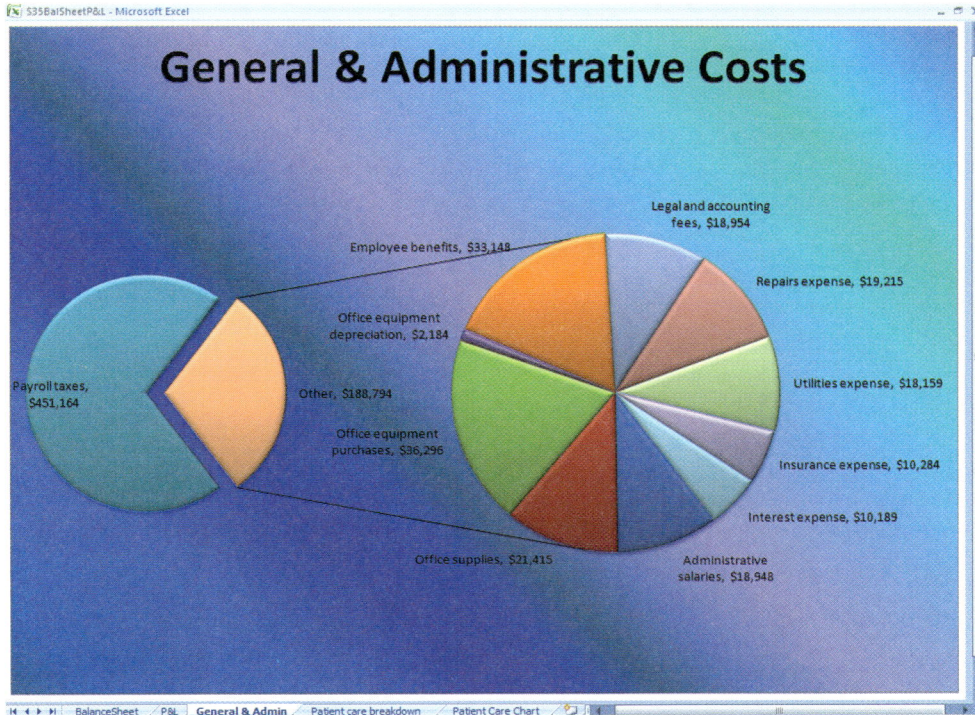

Illustration B

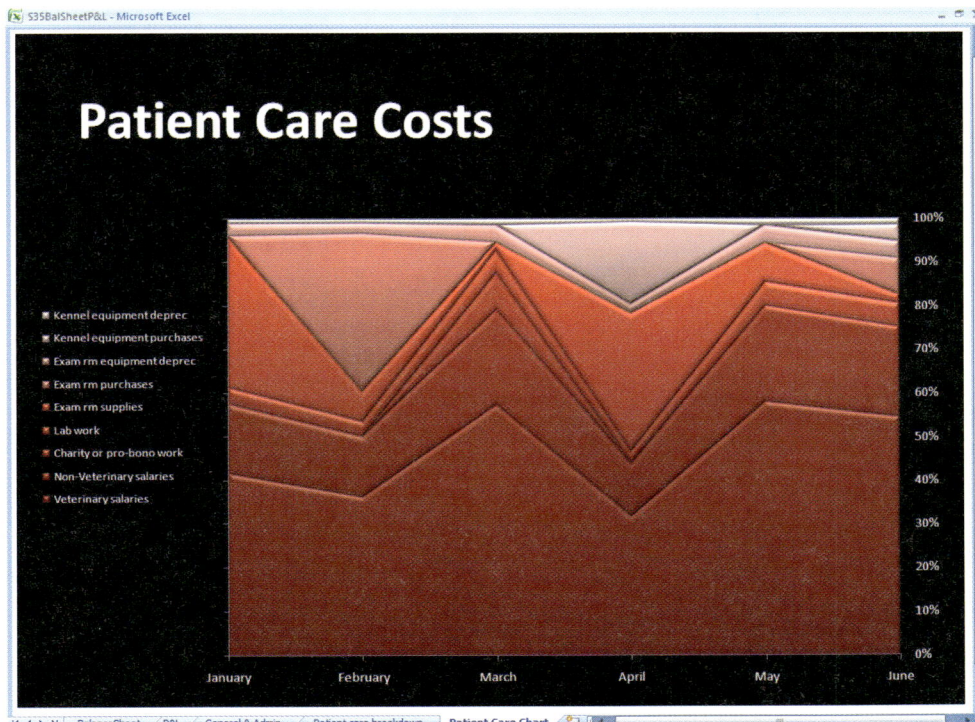

ON YOUR OWN

1. Start Excel, if necessary.
2. Open ⊙ **35Catering**.
3. Save the workbook as **OXL35_xx**.
4. Create a Bar of pie chart with the ranges C5:H5 and C11:H11:
   a. Move the chart to a sheet entitled **July Income**.
   b. Add a chart title called **Income from July Parties**.
   c. Format the chart as you like, adding data labels and removing the legend if desired.
   d. Resize the plot area to create as large a chart as possible.
   e. Place Labor, Setup, and Delivery in the secondary chart (see Illustration A).
   f. Explode the Food pie slice.

5. Create a stacked area chart with the range B5:H9:
   a. Move the chart to its own sheet called **July Breakdown**.
   b. Add a chart title **Breakdown of July Revenue**.
6. Format the chart as you like, but make these changes as well:
   a. Format the chart background.
   b. Format each series in the chart with a fill effect instead of a solid color.
7. Spell check both charts.
8. Print both charts.
9. Save the workbook and exit Excel.

Illustration A

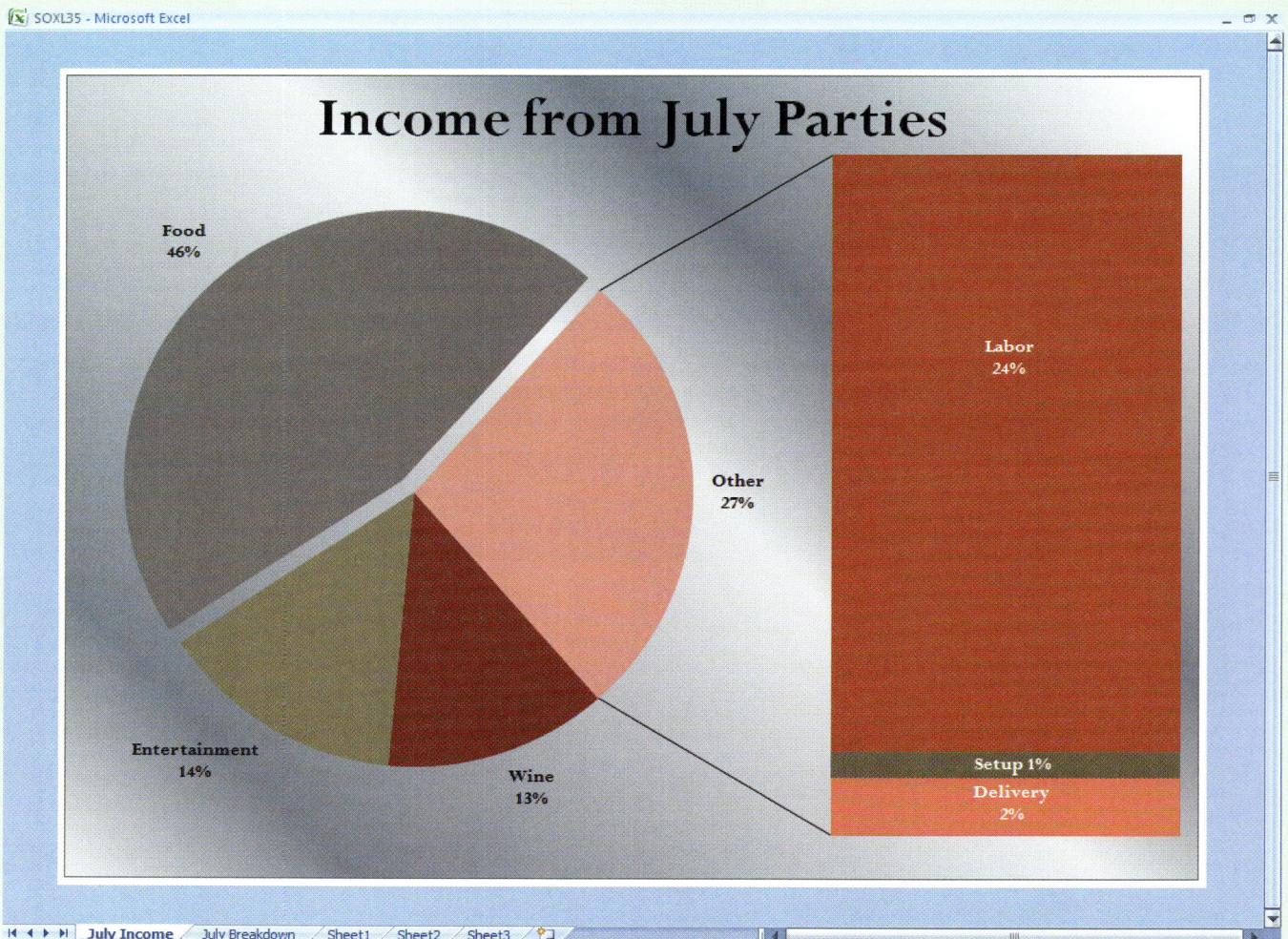

Exercise | 36

Skills Covered

- **Create a 3-D Chart**
- **Change the View of a 3-D Chart**

- **Display or Hide Chart Gridlines**

Software Skills   When you're creating a chart for a big presentation or printed report, you want that chart to look as good as possible. Sometimes, changing from a flat 2-D chart to a 3-D chart is all you need to do. Using a 3-D chart adds a high-tech look to an otherwise ordinary presentation of the facts. When creating a 3-D chart, you may want to change its perspective to enhance the presentation of data. You also may want to display or hide gridlines and/or data labels to make the values easier to understand.

Application Skills   You work for Intellidata, and you need a stunning demonstration to convince your client, Giant Frog Supermarkets, to upgrade its service level agreements for its Point of Sale division to save it some money, and save Intellidata's data center managers some headaches. It's time for Giant Frog to take a trip into the third dimension—3-D charts, that is.

TERMS

3-D chart   A chart in which the data is presented in three dimensions: width, height, and depth.

Gridlines   Horizontal lines that appear on a chart, extending from the value axis. You can also display vertical gridlines from the category axis, although that's less common. Gridlines come in two varieties: major gridlines and minor gridlines (which fall between major gridlines).

Z-axis   An axis that appears on 3-D charts. In a two-dimensional chart, the x-axis represents the category (usually horizontal or width) axis, and the y-axis represents the value (usually vertical or height) axis. In a 3-D chart, the z-axis becomes the value axis, and, where applicable, the y-axis becomes the series (depth) axis.

NOTES

Create a 3-D Chart

- Excel provides a 3-D version of nearly every category of chart: bar, column, line, pie, and so on.
- 3-D charts have an additional axis, called the series or depth axis.
  - In a 2-D chart, each series appears only in the legend (assuming a legend is displayed).

- A series is typically created from each column of data in the selected data range for a chart.
- When you use a 3-D chart, each series in your chart is plotted along the **z-axis** (the series or depth axis).

- Some charts, while listed as 3-D charts, aren't truly three-dimensional, but are simply 2-D charts with some perspective added.
  - A true 3-D chart has three axes: x, y, and z.
  - A 2-D chart with perspective added has only two axes, x and y.

Two different types of 3-D charts

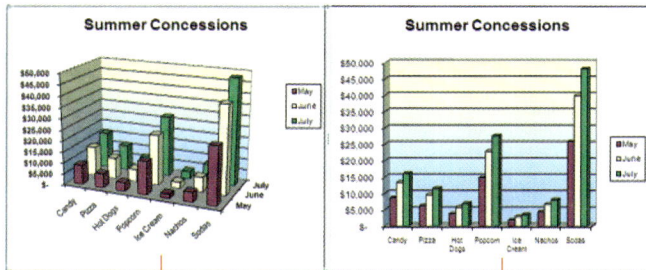

A true 3-D chart has three axes

2-D chart with perspective

Change the View of a 3-D Chart

- After creating a 3-D chart (or a 2-D chart with perspective), you may wish to change that perspective or view.
- You can tilt the floor of the chart up or down.
- You can rotate the chart floor left or right.

- If you choose not to lock the axes at right angles, you can change the chart's 3-D perspective.
  - ✓ You cannot tilt the floor of the chart left or right, which is why you can't change the rotation of the z-axis of a 3-D chart.

Changing the 3-D view

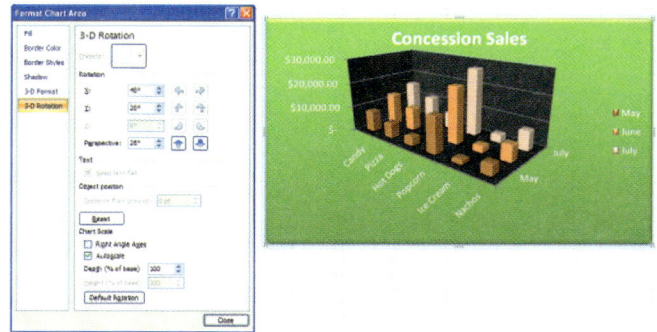

- You can change the depth of the chart, and make the chart floor narrower (shallower).

Display or Hide Chart Gridlines

- On a 3-D chart, **gridlines** become a bit more important than on a 2-D chart, since they help to guide the eye along the axis.
  - ✓ You can add or remove gridlines for any chart type.
  - You can increase the number of major gridlines by changing the point at which the gridlines recur.
  - You can also display minor gridlines.

PROCEDURES

Change the View of a 3-D Chart

1. Click the chart to select it.
2. Click **Layout** tab. . . . Alt , J , A

3. Click **3-D Rotation**
   button □ . . . . #3
4. Set 3-D options:

To tilt the floor up or down (rotate along the y-axis):

a. Click in **Y** box . . . . . . Alt + Y
b. Type rotation amount in box.

To rotate the chart floor left or right (rotate along the x-axis):

a. Click in **X** box . . . . . . Alt + X
b. Type rotation amount in box.

To change perspective (field of view):

✓ *This option is not available if **Right Angle Axes** is selected.*

a. Click in **Perspective**
   box. . . . . Alt + E
b. Type rotation amount in box.

OR

a. Click perspective button ⬆
   or ⬇.
b. Repeat step a, click and
   hold down the button,
   or press **Spacebar** until
   you reach desired
   perspective . . . . Spacebar

To lock axes at right angles:

■ Click **Right angle
   axes**. . . . . Alt + X

✓ *This eliminates the illusion of perspective, in favor of an orthographic view.
In a perspective view, objects that are
further away are smaller; in an orthographic view, objects that are further
away are still the same size. So if you
display a column with the Right angle
axes option turned on (orthographic
view), the side furthest away from you
is shown in the same size as the front
side of the column, even though it's
further away. If you apply perspective,
the side of the column furthest away
from you will appear smaller.*

To scale the chart automatically:

■ Select **Autoscale** . . . . Alt + S

To set the depth and height as a percentage of base of chart:

a. Click in **Depth (& of base)**
   box. . . . . Alt + T
b. Type a value between 0 and
   2000.
c. Click **Height % of base** text
   box. . . . . Alt + H

✓ *This option is not available if Autoscale
is selected.*

d. Type number between 0 and
   500.

To return to default settings:

■ Click **Default
   Rotation**. . . . . Alt + O

5. Click **Close** . . . . Enter

Display or Hide Gridlines

1. Select chart.
2. Click **Layout** tab. . . . Alt + J , A

3. Click **Gridlines** button ▦ . . . . G

4. Choose which gridlines to display
   or hide:

   ■ **Primary Horizontal
      Gridlines** . . . . H
   ■ **Primary Vertical
      Gridlines** V

5. Choose the type of gridlines
   you want . . . . ↑ / ↓ , Enter

   ■ **None**
   ■ **Major Gridlines**
   ■ **Minor Gridlines**
   ■ **Major & Minor Gridlines**

Change the Frequency of Gridlines

1. Click the chart to select it.
2. Click **Layout** tab. . . . Alt , J , A

3. Click arrow on the **Chart Elements**
   list [Chart Area ▼] . . . . E
4. Select the Value axis.

✓ *Although you can display gridlines
along the other axes as well, you can
only change the frequency of the
gridlines along the Value axis.*

5. Click **Format Selection**
   button 🗝 . . . . . Alt , J , A , M
6. Set the frequency of major gridlines:

   a. Click **Major unit Fixed**
      option . . . . Alt + X
   b. Type a value in the text box
      that represents the frequency
      at which you want the major
      gridlines to appear

7. Set the frequency of minor gridlines:

   a. Click **Minor unit Fixed**
      option . . . . Alt + E
   b. Type a value in the text box
      that represents the frequency
      at which you want the minor
      gridlines to appear

8. Click **Close** . . . . Enter

EXERCISE DIRECTIONS

1. Start Excel, if necessary.
2. Open ⌨ **25UsageStats_xx** or 💿 **36UsageStats**.
3. Save the workbook as **36UsageStats_xx**.
4. On the Forecasts worksheet, type the dates **7/4/2008**, **7/11/2008**, **7/18/2008**, and **7/25/2008** in the cells D1:G1.
5. On the Forecasts worksheet, create a 3-D Cone chart using the range B1:G7
   a. Move the chart to its own sheet, called **July Forecast**.
   b. Add the centered overlay chart title **July Forecast: Merchandising & Purchasing**.
   c. Remove the legend.
   d. Apply chart style #34.
   e. Apply a solid color fill, Olive Green, Accent 3, Lighter 60%, to the chart area.
   f. Create a Primary Vertical Axis rotated title **Kb/sec**.
6. Display the major and minor gridlines on the horizontal axis:
   a. Click the Gridlines button on the Layout tab.
   b. Point to Primary Horizontal Gridlines.
   c. Click Major & Minor Gridlines.
   d. Select Vertical (Value) Axis from the Charts Elements list on the Layout tab.
   e. Click the Format Selection button.
   f. On the Axis Options page, set the Maximum to Fixed, 130.
   g. Set the Minor unit to Fixed, 5.
   h. Click Close.
7. Adjust the three-dimensional view:
   a. Click the 3-D Rotation button on the Layout tab.
   b. Set the X rotation to 40°.
   c. Set the Y rotation to 20°.
   d. Change the Perspective to 25°.
   e. Change the Depth (% of Base) to 80.
   f. Click Close.
8. Change the chart title to two lines, and drag it downward, positioning it on the chart sheet as shown in Illustration A.
9. Spell check the worksheet.
10. Print the chart.
11. Close the workbook, saving all changes.

Illustration A

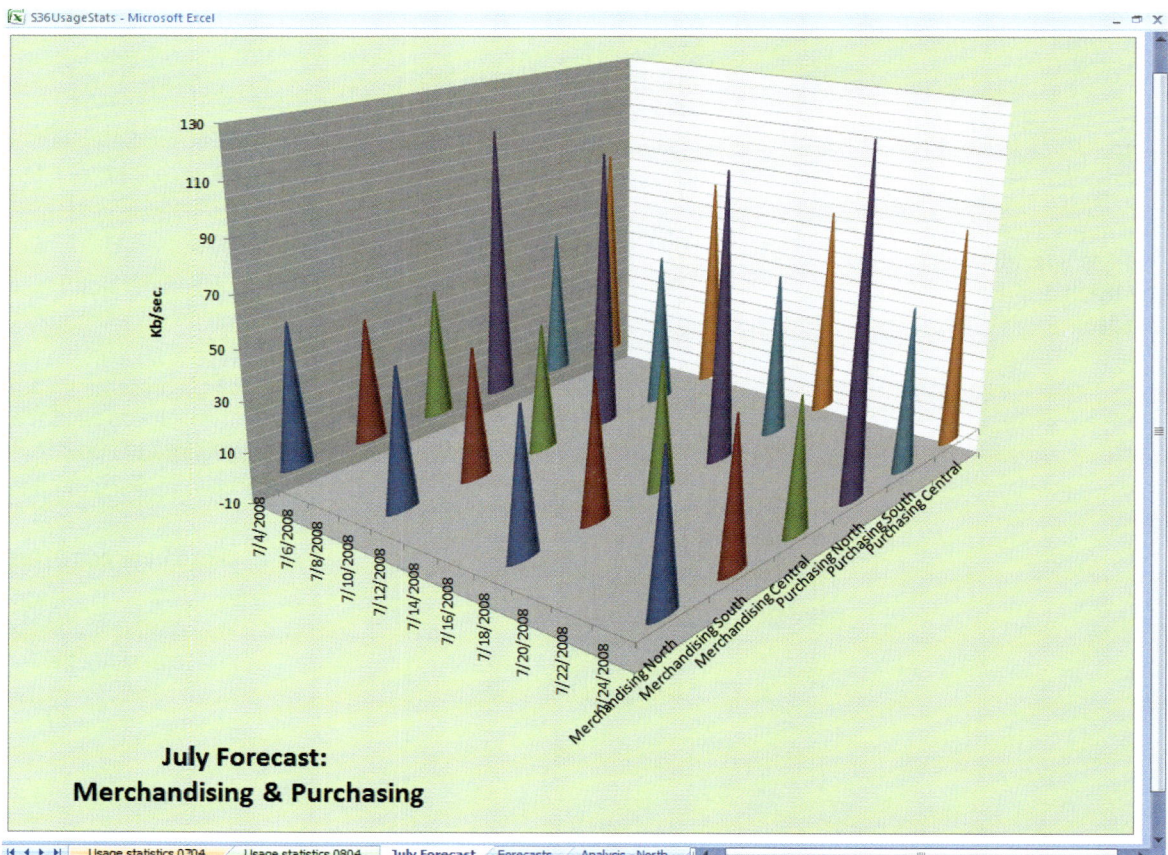

July Forecast:
Merchandising & Purchasing

ON YOUR OWN

1. Start Excel, if necessary, and open 🔘 **36BoxOffice**.

2. Save the file as **OXL36_xx**.

3. Create a Clustered Bar in 3-D chart with the range A6:F7 (see Illustration A):

   a. Display minor gridlines for the value (Z) axis.

   b. Display your choice of data labels.

   c. Add a chart title **Tickets Sold**.

4. Format the chart as you wish, but include these changes:

   a. Format the minor gridlines using a style you like.

   b. Change the 3-D perspective.

   c. Increase the distance (gap) between bars.

5. Spell check the worksheet.

6. Print the chart.

7. Create a Pie in 3-D chart using the ranges B6:F6 and B9:F9:

   a. Display your choice of data labels.

   b. Add a chart title **Total Receipts**.

8. Format the chart as you wish, but include these changes:

   a. Change the 3-D perspective.

   b. Explode the pie piece representing the production of *Romeo and Juliet*.

9. Print the chart.

10. Create a 3-D Column chart using the range A6:F7 and A9:F9.

11. Format the chart as you wish, but include these changes:

    a. Change the 3-D perspective.

    b. Apply the cylinder shape to the Tickets Sold data series.

    ✓ *To change the shape of bars and columns in 3-D charts, select the data series to change, open the Format Data Series dialog box, change to the Shape page, and select the shape you want.*

    c. Apply a fill effect to the walls of the chart.

    d. Add a chart title **Tickets Sold**.

12. Print the chart.

13. Close the workbook, saving all changes.

Illustration A

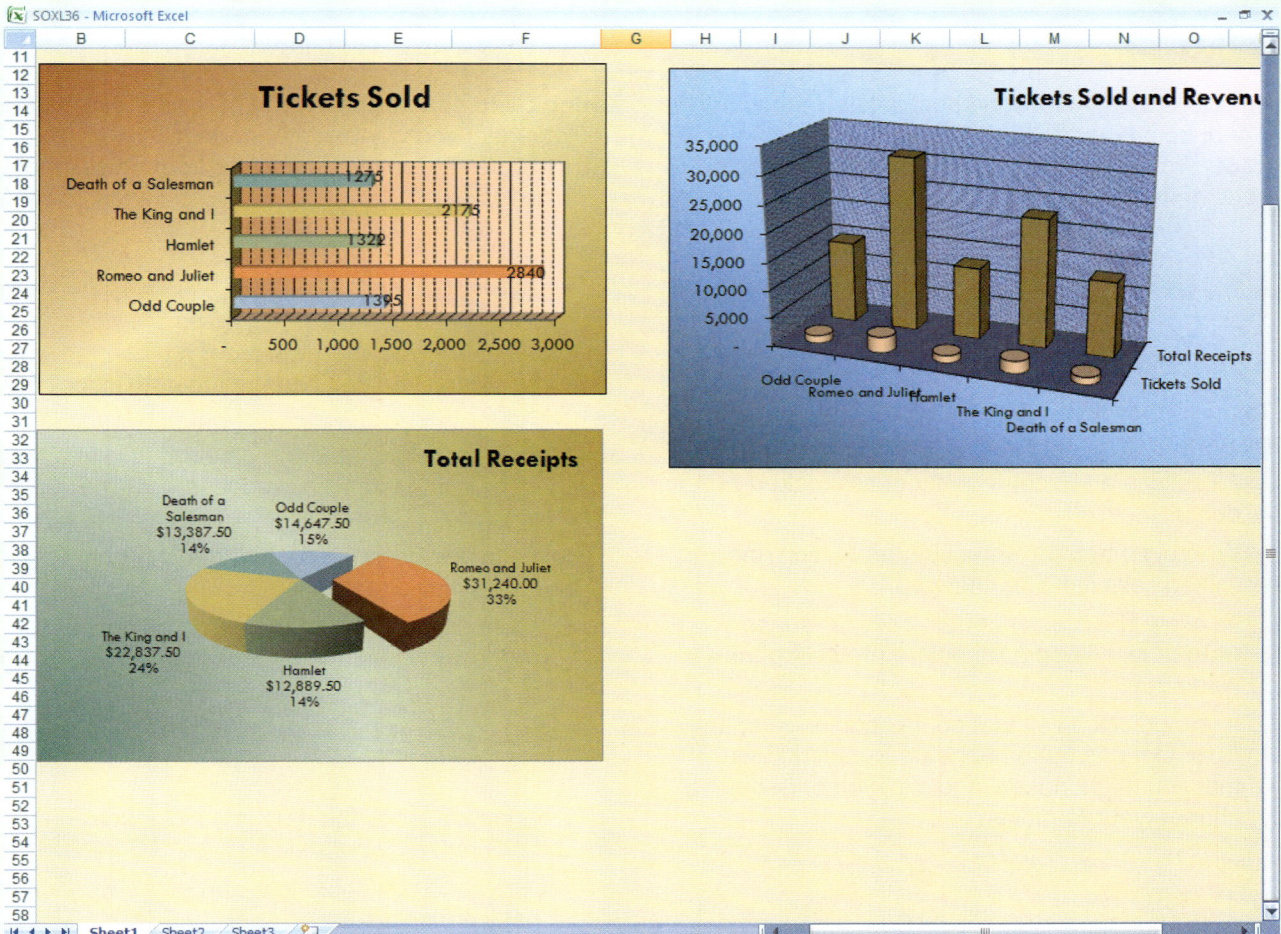

Skills Covered

- **Lock/Unlock Cells in a Worksheet**
- **Protect a Range**
- **Protect a Worksheet**
- **Protect Workbooks**

Software Skills   If you design worksheets for others to use, or if you share a lot of workbooks, you may wish to protect certain areas of a worksheet from changes. You can protect any cell you want to prevent it from accepting new data or changes. You can also protect an entire worksheet or workbook so that others may only view its contents.

Application Skills   The specialty end of your business is growing at Photo-Town, and so you've created an order form that customers can use when ordering t-shirts, mugs, calendars, and cards emblazoned with a photo. The order form will be available for use through computers set up in a self-serve area. To prevent customers from changing the prices or ordering something that's no longer available, you want to protect certain areas of the worksheet while still allowing you and your assistant full access.

TERMS

Lock   Cells that, if the worksheet is later protected, cannot be changed.

Protect   To prevent changes to locked or protected areas or items.

Unlock   To enable changes in particular cells of a worksheet you want to later protect.

Unprotect   To remove protection from a worksheet or workbook.

NOTES

Lock/Unlock Cells in a Worksheet

- To prevent changes to selected cells or ranges in a worksheet, you can **protect** the worksheet.
  - All cells in an Excel worksheet are **locked** by default.
  - When you turn on worksheet protection, the locked cells can't be changed.
  - To allow changes in certain cells or ranges, **unlock** just those cells before protecting the worksheet.
  - If you unlock a cell that contains a formula, an Error Options button appears to remind you that you might not want to allow other people to change your formulas.

  ✓ *You can ignore these errors when they appear, or tell Excel to lock the cell again.*

- If necessary, you can **unprotect** a protected worksheet so that you can change the data in locked cells.
- You can protect charts and other objects in a worksheet by using this same process.
- If someone tries to make a change to a protected cell, a message indicates that the cell is protected and considered read-only.
  - Users move between the unlocked cells of a protected worksheet by pressing Tab.

  ✓ *However, if ranges were locked using the Allow Users to Edit Ranges dialog box as explained in the next section, the Tab key does not work.*

  - Users can copy the data in a locked cell, but they can't move or delete it.
  - Data can't be copied to a part of the worksheet that's protected.

Protect a Range

- When you unlock cells to allow changes, you can tell Excel to allow changes from anyone, or just selected individuals.

- To unlock cells for everyone, remove the Lock Cell protection format.

- To allow changes to selected individuals, use the Allow Users to Edit Ranges dialog box.

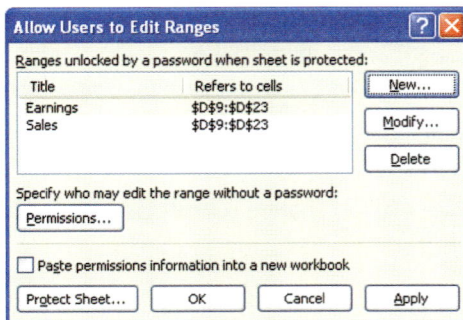

- When protecting ranges within a worksheet, you can tell Excel to create a workbook with the details of the permissions you've granted—the range addresses and passwords you've specified.

Allow Users to Edit Ranges dialog box

Protect a Worksheet

- When you activate worksheet protection, the cells you have unlocked are not protected.
  - Changes can be made to these cells.

- You can also prevent changes to objects in the worksheet (such as clip art or drawn images), hyperlinks, PivotTables, and scenarios (stored variations of a worksheet).

- When protecting a sheet, you can prevent certain actions, such as formatting, inserting columns and rows, deleting columns and rows, sorting, and filtering.

Protect Sheet dialog box

- You can password-protect the sheet so that no one can unprotect the worksheet accidentally.
  - If you forget the password, you won't be able to unprotect the worksheet later on.
  - However, you can copy the data to another, unprotected worksheet.
  - Passwords are case sensitive.

Protect Workbooks

- You can protect an entire workbook against certain kinds of changes.

- By applying this protection, you can prevent worksheets from being added, moved, hidden, unhidden, renamed, or deleted.

- You can also prevent a workbook's window from being resized or repositioned.

- If you add a password, you can prevent users from changing the protection level of a workbook.

Protect Structure and Windows dialog box

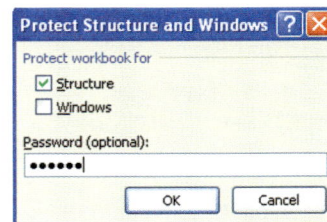

- If you want to share a workbook with others, and track the changes they make, you can still protect the workbook so that they can't erase the change history.

- You'll learn how to track changes to a workbook in the next exercise.

PROCEDURES

Lock/Unlock Cells in a Worksheet

✓ *Locks or unlocks specific cells. By default, all cells in a worksheet are locked. This procedure allows anyone to make changes to unlocked cells.*

1. If necessary, unprotect worksheet as explained in this section.

   ✓ *You can't lock or unlock cells if the worksheet is protected.*

2. Select cell(s) to unlock or lock.
3. Click **Home** tab . . . . `Alt`, `H`

   Cells Group

3. Click **Format** button 📑 . . . . . . `O`
4. Deselect or select **Lock Cell** . . . . `L`
5. Repeat steps for each cell or range to lock or unlock.
6. Protect worksheet.

Lock/Unlock Objects in a Worksheet

✓ *Locks or unlocks objects such as embedded charts, clip art, or drawn objects such as text boxes. By default, all objects in a worksheet are locked when a worksheet is protected.*

1. If necessary, unprotect worksheet.

   ✓ *You can't lock or unlock cells if the worksheet is protected.*

2. Click object to unlock or lock.
3. Click **Format** tab . . . `Alt`, `J`, `D`

   Size Group

4. Click **Size** dialog box launcher button 🔲 . . . . `S`, `Z`
5. Click **Properties** tab . . . . `Ctrl`+`⇥`
6. Deselect or select **Locked** . . . . `Alt`+`L`

---

7. Click **Close** . . . . `Enter`
8. Repeat steps for each object to lock or unlock.
9. Protect worksheet.

Protect a Range

✓ *This procedure unlocks a range only to individual users.*

1. If necessary, unprotect worksheet.

   ✓ *You can't lock or unlock cells if the worksheet is protected.*

2. Click **Review** tab . . . . `Alt`, `R`

   Changes Group

3. Click **Allow Users to Edit Ranges** button 🗐 . . . . `U`
4. Click **New** . . . . `Alt`+`N`
5. Click in the **Title** box . . . . `Alt`+`T`
6. Type a name for the protected range.
7. Click in the **Refers to cells** box . . . . `Alt`+`R`
8. Type or select a range to protect.
9. Click in the **Range password** box . . . . `Alt`+`P`
10. Type a password.

    ✓ *Give this password only to those users you wish to be able to make changes to this range.*

11. Click **OK**. . . . . `Enter`
12. Type the password again.
13. Click **OK** to confirm . . . . `Enter`
14. Repeat steps 4 to 13 to allow changes to other ranges.
15. Click **Protect Sheet** to protect the worksheet now. . . . . `Alt`+`O`

    OR

    Click **OK** to protect the worksheet later.

    ✓ *Follow the steps given in the Protect a Sheet procedure to protect the worksheet.*

Unprotect a Range

1. Unprotect the sheet.

   ✓ *You can't unlock a range if the worksheet is protected.*

2. Click **Review** tab . . . . `Alt`, `R`

   Changes Group

3. Click **Allow Users to Edit Ranges** button 🗐 . . . . `U`
4. Select the range you wish to unprotect.
5. Click **Delete**. . . . . `Alt`+`D`
6. Click **OK**. . . . . `Enter`
7. If you wish to protect other selected ranges, turn on sheet protection again.

Change a Protected Range

1. Unprotect the sheet.

   ✓ *You can't unlock a range if the worksheet is protected.*

2. Click **Review** tab . . . . `Alt`, `R`

   Changes Group

3. Click **Allow Users to Edit Ranges** button 🗐 . . . . `U`
4. Select the range you wish to change.
5. Click **Modify** . . . . `Alt`+`M`
5. If you like, in the **Title** box, type a new name for the protected range . . . . `Alt`+`T`
6. If you like, in the **Refers to cells** box, type or select a new range to protect. . . . . `Alt`+`R`
7. To change the password protecting the range:
   a. Click **Password** . . . . . `Alt`+`P`
   b. Type new password in the **New password** box . . . . . . `Alt`+`N`
   c. Type the password again in the **Confirm new password** box. . . . . `Alt`+`C`
   d. Click **OK**.

8. Click **OK**.
9. Protect the sheet again by clicking **Protect Sheet** . . . . `Alt`+`O`

Protect a Sheet

1. Lock or unlock cells, ranges, and objects as desired.

   ✓ *By default, all cells and objects in a worksheet are locked.*

2. Click **Review** tab . . . . . . `Alt`, `R`

   Changes Group

3. Click **Protect Sheet** button . . . . `P`, `S`
4. If needed, click the **Protect worksheet and contents of locked cells** option to turn it on . . . . `Alt`+`C`
5. To prevent someone from turning off worksheet protection, type a password in **Password to unprotect sheet** text box. . . . . . `Alt`+`P`
6. Select options from **Allow all users of this worksheet to** list box. . . . . . `Alt`+`O`, `↑`/`↓`, `Spacebar`
7. Click **OK**. . . . . `Enter`
8. If a password was typed, retype password in text box.
9. Click **OK**. . . . . `Enter`

Unprotect a Sheet

1. Click **Review** tab . . . . `Alt`, `R`

   Changes Group

2. Click **Unprotect Sheet** button . . . . `P`, `S`
3. If sheet is password-protected, type password in **Password** text box.
4. Click **OK**. . . . . `Enter`

Protect a Workbook

1. Click **Review** tab . . . . `Alt`, `R`

   Changes Group

2. Click **Protect Workbook** button . . . . `P`, `W`
3. Click **Protect Structure and Windows** . . . . `W`

To protect structure of worksheets:

■ Select **Structure** . . . . . `Alt`+`S`

To protect windows:

■ Select **Windows** . . . . . `Alt`+`W`

To password-protect workbook:

■ Type a password in **Password (optional)** text box. . . `Alt`+`P`

4. Click **OK**. . . . . `Enter`
5. If a password was typed, retype password in text box.
6. Click **OK**. . . . . `Enter`

Unprotect a Workbook

1. Click **Review** tab . . . . `Alt`, `R`

   Changes Group

2. Click **Protect Workbook** button . . . . `P`, `W`
3. If workbook is password-protected, type password in **Password** text box.
4. Click **OK**. . . . . `Enter`

EXERCISE DIRECTIONS

1. Start Excel, if necessary.
2. Open 🔵 **37PhotoOrderForm**.
3. Save the workbook as **37PhotoOrderForm_xx**.
4. In the Order Form worksheet, unlock the areas into which data may be typed:
   a. Select the range B8:B9.
   b. Click the Format button on the Home tab.
   c. Click the Lock Cell command.
   d. Repeat these steps to unlock cells E9, G9, I9, B12:B28, G12:G28, B35:B49, D35:D49, B53, and G36.
5. Lock the worksheet:
   a. Click the Review tab and click Protect Sheet button.
   b. Type **mysecret** in the Password to unprotect sheet box.

   c. Make sure that the Select unlocked cells option is the only one turned on in the *Allow all users of this worksheet to* section, then click OK.
   d. Confirm the password by typing **mysecret** again and click OK.
6. Protect the Product Listing worksheet so that only you can make changes:
   a. Change to the Product Listing worksheet.
   b. Select the range name Products from the Name box.
   c. Click the Allow Users to Edit Ranges button on the Review tab.
   d. Click New.
   e. In the Title box type **Product Listing**.
   f. In the Range Password box, type **supersecret**. Click OK.
   g. Type **supersecret** again to confirm it, and click OK.

h. Click Protect Sheet.

i. Type **secretsheet** in the Password to unprotect sheet box.

j. Turn on the Select locked cells, Select unlocked cells, Insert rows, and Sort options and click OK.

k. Confirm the password and click OK.

7. Save the workbook, and then resave it as **37AJuarez_*xx***.

8. Enter the invoice data in the Order Form worksheet shown in Illustration A.

✓ *Press Tab to move from field to field. Notice that the cursor only moves to the cells in which you are allowed to add data.*

9. Try to click in cell A2. Again, notice that you cannot select an invalid cell.

10. Change to the Product Listing worksheet.

11. Change cell E15 to 25.00:

a. Click cell E15 and type **2**.

✓ *A notice appears, telling you that the cell is protected and that to make a change, you need to type in the password.*

b. Type the password **supersecret** and click OK.

c. Type **25** in cell E15 and press Enter.

✓ *You'll be able to continue to make changes to the sheet until you close the workbook.*

12. Print the Order Form worksheet.

13. Close the workbook, saving all changes.

Illustration A

S37AJuarez - Microsoft Excel

PhotoTown

Customer Photo Product Order Form

Date   8/10/2008

| Customer Name | Allison Juarez | | | | | | | |
| Address | 3121 Oakland Ave. | | City | Chicago | State | Illinois | Zip | 60621 |

Item #	Description	Size	Color	Qty	Price per Item	Total
CA46B	Calendar card featuring 4" x 6" photo	4" x 10"	Light beige	4	$ 9.50	$ 38.00
PB4610	A customized album of your favorite photos	4" x 6"	Up to 10 photos	2	$ 8.50	$ 17.00
TS101W	100% all cotton t-shirt, with photo of your choice	Child's S (2-4)	White	1	$ 12.50	$ 12.50
TS103W	100% all cotton t-shirt, with photo of your choice	Child's L (7-8)	White	1	$ 15.75	$ 15.75
GC050	Photo card featuring a favorite 4" x 6" photo	50 cards and envelopes	White	1	$ 14.00	$ 14.00

	Total items ordered	9
	Subtotal	$ 97.25
	Tax	$ 5.84
	Grand total	$ 103.09

Special Instructions
If you're ordering greeting cards, please select icon to use

We're married!	Baby's first birthday	Greeting card text (optional charge)
Our wedding day	Thank you!	
Look here's here (baby)	Many thanks	
Just arrived (baby)	Sending you lots of love	
The newest edition (baby)	Merry Christmas and a Happy New Year	
Our family just got bigger (baby)	Greetings from our home to yours	

Order Form / Product Listing

ON YOUR OWN

1. Start Excel, if necessary.
2. Open ⊙ **37MarcusFurniture**.
3. Save the workbook as **OXL37_*xx***.
4. On the Feb Earnings worksheet, unlock cell A5 and all the cells in the Sales column.
5. Protect the worksheet, but don't enter a password.
6. Bill Mergenthal's base salary was raised to $850 and Mary Williams replaced Pat Kawalski at a base salary of $750. Try to make those changes on the worksheet.
7. Unprotect the worksheet and make the changes in step 6. See Illustration A.
8. Protect the worksheet again; this time turn off the "Select locked cells" option.
9. Enter fictional sales amounts from $6,000 to $15,000 in column D. Vary the amounts to create a nice variety.
10. Copy the Feb Earnings worksheet, place it before the Comm-Bonus worksheet, and name it **Mar Earnings**.
11. Change the text in cell A5 to **March Earnings Report**.
12. Try to make an entry in any cell in the table other than in the Sales column to see if the cells are still locked.
13. Make an entry in the Sales column to see if the cells are unlocked, and then delete all the entries in the Sales column.
14. Protect the entire workbook's structure (not the windows), with the password **marcus**.
15. Try making a copy of the Mar Earnings worksheet.
16. Spell check the Feb Earnings worksheet.
17. Print the Feb Earnings worksheet.
18. Close the workbook, saving all changes.

Illustration A

SOXL37 - Microsoft Excel

Marcus Furniture

February Earnings Report

ASSOCIATE	BASE SALARY	SALES	COMM. RATE	COMM. AMT.	BONUS	TOTAL EARNINGS
Bob Walraven	$1,000.00	$14,978.00	11%	$1,647.58	$450.00	$3,097.58
Mike Davis	$1,000.00	$10,254.00	8%	$820.32	$300.00	$2,120.32
Bill Mergenthal	$850.00	$7,521.00	5%	$376.05	$0.00	$1,226.05
Pete Sanger	$850.00	$9,874.00	7%	$691.18	$250.00	$1,791.18
Dorothy Bishop	$750.00	$6,023.00	4%	$240.92	$0.00	$990.92
Mary La Rue	$1,100.00	$13,458.00	11%	$1,480.38	$450.00	$3,030.38
Ernest Dedmon	$1,000.00	$9,141.00	7%	$639.87	$250.00	$1,889.87
Karen Frisch	$750.00	$10,394.00	8%	$831.52	$300.00	$1,881.52
Mary Williams	$750.00	$7,889.00	5%	$394.45	$0.00	$1,144.45
Mike McCutcheon	$750.00	$6,574.00	4%	$262.96	$0.00	$1,012.96
Lorna Myers	$900.00	$10,974.00	8%	$877.92	$300.00	$2,077.92
James Neely	$950.00	$14,958.00	11%	$1,645.38	$450.00	$3,045.38
Scott Gratten	$850.00	$13,425.00	11%	$1,476.75	$450.00	$2,776.75
Betty Miller	$925.00	$10,957.00	8%	$876.56	$300.00	$2,101.56
Fillard Willmore	$1,000.00	$14,958.00	11%	$1,645.38	$450.00	$3,095.38

Skills Covered

- **Share Workbooks**
- **Work with a Shared Workbook**
- **Track Changes**
- **Merge Changes**

Software Skills If you create a workbook with data that's maintained by several people, you can use Excel to help you keep track of the simultaneous changes being made and to automatically resolve them. For example, you may have a customer database that all your salespeople maintain. In other cases, you may want to track the changes made to a file passed around for review and then later merge these changes into a single final version of the file. When sharing a file, you can protect it as well, to prevent changes from unauthorized people.

Application Skills Two different sales associates at Breakaway Bike Shop have looked up separate values for replacement parts that come from different catalogs, and neither of their figures matched what the repairperson recorded. Your job is to reconcile the figures by merging changes from the latest version of the worksheet over changes made to earlier versions.

TERMS

Shared workbook A workbook to which several people can make changes at the same time. Such a workbook is typically placed in a central directory on a company network, where the users can access it.

Track Changes A feature that records changes made to a file; you can review and accept or reject these changes.

NOTES

Share Workbooks

- When you share a workbook, you make it possible for multiple users to make changes to the workbook simultaneously.

  ✓ *For example, you might wish to share a client database, project worksheet, inventory database, or department budget.*

- Typically, **shared workbooks** are located on a network, accessible to the people who need to use the workbook(s).

  - Although you must share a workbook (allow simultaneous access) in order to track its changes, you can still protect that workbook with a password if you want to prevent others from turning off track changes and/or modifying areas of the workbook you've protected (as discussed in Exercise 37).

- Workbooks that contain Excel tables or XML data cannot be shared.

  ✓ *You can always convert an Excel table to regular data, or remove XML data if you want to still share a workbook.*

- There are certain tasks you can't perform on a shared workbook:
  - Delete worksheets.
  - Delete chart sheets.
  - Insert or delete a range of cells.

  ✓ *You can insert or delete entire rows and columns, however.*

  - Merge or split merged cells.
  - Add or change conditional formats. (You'll see any existing conditional formats.)
  - Set up or change data validation, passwords, or worksheet/workbook protection.

- Create or modify charts, clip art, shapes, hyperlinks, and other objects.
- Create or modify scenarios, outlines, and PivotTables.
- Group or outline data, add subtotals, create or modify data tables. (You can view existing data and subtotals, however.)
- Create, modify, assign, or view macros stored in the workbook.
- Modify or remove array formulas.

- When you share a workbook, those changes are not highlighted on-screen, although they are tracked.
  - Use the **Track Changes** feature to highlight cells in which changes are made.

Work with a Shared Workbook

- After a workbook is shared, you are prompted each time you save it.
  - At that point, you're prompted with the changes made by other users since the last time you saved the workbook.
  - Excel can update you periodically with these changes if you like.
- When you save changes to a workbook that's been shared, you can designate how you want Excel to handle simultaneous changes to the same cell.

Track Changes

- With the Track Changes feature, you can keep track of the changes made to a workbook by a group of people.
  - When you turn on the Track Changes option, the workbook is automatically shared, which means that multiple people can make changes to it at the same time.
  - However, this doesn't mean that you must allow users simultaneous access to the workbook in order for them to make changes to it.
  - You can route the workbook to people sequentially, allowing each person to make their changes individually.
  - You can also send the workbook to several people simultaneously, and later merge their changes to the workbook.

- When you turn Track Changes on, you share the workbook and turn on change highlighting.
  - However, if you share a workbook using only the Track Changes feature, the workbook is shared using the Share Workbook defaults.
  - Thus, the history is kept for only 30 days, changes are saved only when the workbook is saved, you'll be asked how to resolve conflicting changes, and print/filter settings are tracked.
  - If you wish to modify the Share Workbook options, then use that command to make changes after you turn on the Track Changes option.
  - To protect your shared workbook, you must use the Protect and Share Workbook command *before* you turn on Track Changes.
- Because the workbook is shared, you won't be able to make certain types of changes to it (see the previous section for more information).
- Each person's changes are highlighted in the workbook using a different color, so the author of the change is easy to determine.
- Some changes aren't tracked, including the following:
  - Formatting changes
  - Rows or columns that have been hidden or unhidden
  - Worksheets that have been inserted or deleted (new sheet names are tracked, but not highlighted)
  - New or changed comments
  - Cells whose values change because of a change made to another cell
  - Unsaved changes
- After changes are made to a workbook, you can easily review them, accept the ones you wish to make permanent, and reject the ones you wish to ignore.
- Changes are only tracked within a workbook for 30 days, although you can change this interval if you wish when you turn Track Changes on.

Merge Changes

- You can distribute a shared workbook with Track Changes to multiple people via e-mail, allowing them to review the workbook in their own time.

- When you receive the copies of the workbook via e-mail, you can merge the changes in these multiple copies into a single workbook.
  - Save each copy of the workbook you receive with a different file name, such as Share1, Share2, and so on.
  - These copies can then be merged into a single workbook.

- The history of changes made to the workbooks is used to create a single, final copy of the workbook.
  - This history is created because you turned the Track Changes option on, prior to routing the workbook to several people.

- Data is merged into the starting workbook from the other workbooks you select to merge.
  - Changes are made in the order in which the workbooks appear in the Select Files to Merge into Current Document dialog box.

PROCEDURES

Share a Workbook without a Password

1. Click **Review** tab . . . . ⎰Alt⎱, ⎰R⎱

   Changes Group

2. Click **Share Workbook** button ⎰⎱ . . . . ⎰W⎱

3. Select **Allow changes by more than one user at the same time** . . . . ⎰Alt⎱+⎰A⎱

4. Click the **Advanced** tab . . . . ⎰Ctrl⎱+⎰⇥⎱

5. If you want, change the amount of time for which changes are tracked:

   ✓ *You must allow enough time to track changes and merge the workbooks later if you plan to do that.*

   a. Click **Keep change history for** box . . . . ⎰Alt⎱+⎰K⎱

   b. Enter the length of time for which you want changes tracked in the **days** box . . . . ⎰Alt⎱+⎰Y⎱, ##

   OR

   - Click **Don't keep change history** . . . . ⎰Alt⎱+⎰D⎱

6. Specify when changes are updated to the shared file:

   - Click **When file is saved** . . . . ⎰Alt⎱+ ⎰W⎱

   OR

   a. Click **Automatically every** . . . . ⎰Alt⎱+⎰A⎱

   b. Change the time period at which changes are saved in the **minutes** box . . . . ⎰Alt⎱+⎰I⎱, ##

   c. Select an option:

   - **Save my changes and see others' changes** . . . . ⎰Alt⎱+⎰C⎱

   OR

   - **Just see other users' changes** . . . . ⎰Alt⎱+⎰J⎱

7. Indicate how you want conflicting changes handled:

   - Click **Ask me which changes win** . . . . ⎰Alt⎱+⎰S⎱

   OR

   - Click **The changes being saved win** . . . . ⎰Alt⎱+⎰T⎱

8. Select any additional settings you want saved:

   - **Print settings** . . . . ⎰Alt⎱+⎰P⎱
   - **Filter settings** . . . . . . ⎰Alt⎱+⎰F⎱

9. Click **OK** . . . . ⎰Enter⎱

10. When prompted, click **OK** again to save the workbook . . . . ⎰Enter⎱

    ✓ *[Shared] appears in the title bar of the workbook to remind you that the file is now in shared mode.*

Share a Workbook with a Password

1. Click **Review** tab . . . . ⎰Alt⎱, ⎰R⎱

   Changes Group

2. Click **Protect and Share Workbook** button ⎰⎱ . . . . ⎰O⎱

3. Select **Sharing with track changes** . . . . ⎰Alt⎱+⎰S⎱

4. Type a **Password** . . . . . . ⎰Alt⎱+⎰P⎱

5. Click **OK** . . . . ⎰Enter⎱

6. Type the password again to confirm.

7. Click **OK** . . . . ⎰Enter⎱

8. Click **OK** to resave the workbook . . . . ⎰Enter⎱

Remove a User from a Shared Workbook

1. Click **Review** tab . . . . ⎰Alt⎱, ⎰R⎱

   Changes Group

2. Click **Share Workbook** button ⎰⎱ . . . . ⎰W⎱

3. Click **Editing** tab . . . . . . ⎰Ctrl⎱+⎰⇥⎱

4. Select a name from the **Who has this workbook open now** list . . . . ⎰Alt⎱+⎰W⎱, ⎰→⎱/⎰←⎱/⎰↑⎱/⎰↓⎱, ⎰Enter⎱

5. Click **Remove User** . . . . . ⎰Alt⎱+⎰R⎱

   ✓ *This removes the user from the open workbook, but they can access it again whenever they like. To permanently prevent access, the workbook should be shared with a password.*

Resolving Conflicts in a Shared Workbook

✓ *Use this procedure to resolve conflicts that occur when two users make changes to the same cell in an un-saved workbook.*

1. Read the description of the first conflicting change that appears in the Resolve Conflicts dialog box when you attempt to save a shared workbook with conflicting changes.
2. Decide how to resolve the conflict:
   - Click **Accept Mine**.
   OR
   - Click **Accept Other**.
3. Repeat steps 1 and 2 to resolve additional conflicts.

✓ *You can click Accept All Mine or Accept All Others to accept all further conflicts without viewing them.*

Unshare an Unprotected Workbook

1. Click **Review** tab . . . . `Alt`, `R`

   Changes Group
2. Click **Share Workbook** button 🖼 . . . . `W`
3. Select **Allow changes by more than one user at the same time** . . . . `Alt`+`A`

   ✓ *This action turns the option off.*
4. Click **OK**. . . . . `Enter`
5. To confirm, click **Yes** . . . . `Enter`

Unprotect a Shared Workbook

1. Click **Review** tab . . . . `Alt`, `R`

   Changes Group
2. Click **Unprotect Shared Workbook** . . . . `O`
3. Type a **Password** . . . . `Alt`+`P`
4. Click **OK**. . . . . `Enter`
5. Click **Yes** . . . . `Y`

Track Changes Only

1. Click **Review** tab . . . . `Alt`, `R`

   Changes Group
2. Click **Track Changes** . . . . `G`
3. Click **Highlight Changes** . . . . . `H`
4. Click **Track changes while editing** . . . . `Alt`+`T`

   ✓ *If the workbook is already shared, this option is unavailable. You need to unshare first.*
5. To mark cells with changes, select **Highlight changes on screen** . . . . `Alt`+`S`
6. Click **OK**. . . . . `Enter`
7. Click **OK** to confirm . . . . `Enter`

List Track Changes on a Separate Sheet

1. Click **Review** tab . . . . `Alt`, `R`

   Changes Group
2. Click **Track Changes** . . . . `G`
3. Click **Highlight Changes** . . . . . `H`
4. Select All from the **When** list . . . . `Alt`+`N`, `→`/`←`/`↑`/`↓`, `Enter`
5. Select **List changes on a new sheet** . . . . `Alt`+`L`

   ✓ *For the above option to be active, you have to turn on track changes, track one change, and save the workbook.*
6. Click **OK**. . . . . `Enter`

Accept or Reject Changes

1. Click **Review** tab . . . . `Alt`, `R`

   Changes Group
2. Click **Track Changes** . . . . `G`
3. Click **Accept or Reject Changes** . . . . `C`
4. If prompted to save the workbook, click **OK** . . . . `Enter`
5. Select which changes you want to review:
   a. Choose the timeframe for the changes to review from the **When** list . . . . `Alt`+`N`, `↑`/`↓`, `Enter`
   b. Choose whose changes you wish to review from the **Who** list . . . . . `Alt`+`O`, `↑`/`↓`, `Enter`
   c. Type or select the range for the part of the worksheet you wish to review in the **Where** box . . . . . `Alt`+`R`, `↑`/`↓`, `Enter`
6. Click **OK**. . . . . `Enter`
7. When a change is highlighted, select an option:
   - **Accept** the change . . . `Alt`+`A`
   - **Reject** the change . . . `Alt`+`R`
   - **Accept All** of the remaining changes without reviewing them . . . . `Alt`+`C`
   - **Reject All** of the remaining changes without reviewing them . . . . `Alt`+`J`

Merge Changes

1. Open the workbook into which you want to merge the changes.

   ✓ *If needed, add the Compare and Merge Workbooks button to the Quick Access Toolbar before proceeding. To do that, click the Customize Quick Access Toolbar button and then click More Commands. Choose All Commands from the Choose commands from list, select Compare and Merge Workbooks, and click Add to add the button to the Quick Access Toolbar. Click OK.*
2. Click **Compare and Merge Workbooks** button 🔵 on the Quick Access Toolbar.
3. If prompted, click **OK** to save the workbook . . . . `Enter`
4. Select the workbooks you wish to merge into the current workbook.
5. Click **OK**. . . . . `Enter`

   ✓ *Data from the workbooks you selected is used to change the data in the current workbook.*

   ✓ *Only the data from the last workbook merged appears in the final, merged workbook. To review the changes made when the workbooks were merged, follow the steps in the procedure "Accept or Reject Changes." If multiple changes are shown for a particular cell in the Accept or Reject Changes dialog box, you must select one of the changes before clicking Accept or Reject.*

EXERCISE DIRECTIONS

1. Start Excel, if necessary.

2. Open ⌨ **29PartsReplacement_xx** or 💿 **38PartsReplacement**.

3. Save the workbook as **38PartsReplacement_xx**.

4. Protect the shared workbook with the password Jan2Ullrich:

   a. Click the Protect and Share Workbook button on the Review tab.

   b. Turn on the option Sharing with track changes.

   c. Click the Password box, type the password **Jan2Ullrich**, then click OK.

   d. Retype the password and click OK to confirm.

   e. Click OK to continue.

5. Change cell E11 to **.75**.

   ✓ *Notice that the change is not highlighted, although Excel is tracking it.*

6. Unshare and unprotect the workbook:

   a. Click the Unprotect Shared Workbook button on the Review tab.

   b. Type the password **Jan2Ullrich**, and click OK.

   c. Click Yes to continue.

7. Share the workbook without a password:

   a. Click the Share Workbook button on the Review tab.

   b. Turn on the option Allow changes by more than one user.

   c. Click the Advanced tab.

   d. Change the change history to 365 days (1 year).

   e. Click OK.

   f. Click OK to resave the workbook.

8. Make an additional copy of the workbook, saved with the file name **38PartsReplacement_2_xx**.

9. Turn on Track Changes to highlight changes on-screen:

   a. Click the Track Changes button on the Review tab.

   b. Click Highlight Changes.

   c. Click OK.

   ✓ *You'll see an error message, but just click OK to ignore it.*

10. Make the following changes:

    a. Change cell F11 to **$37.50**.

    b. Change cell F21 to **$1.75**.

    c. Change cell F22 to **$9.95**.

11. Spell check the worksheet.

12. Print the worksheet.

13. Close the workbook, saving all changes.

14. Reopen **38PartsReplacement_xx**, and make the following changes:

    a. Change cell F12 to **$44.95**.

    b. Change cell F22 to **$8.95**.

15. Spell check the worksheet.

16. Adjust column widths as needed.

17. Print the worksheet.

18. Save the workbook.

19. List the changes on a separate worksheet:

    a. Click the Track Changes button on the Review tab.

    b. Click Highlight Changes.

    c. Select All from the When list.

    d. Select the List changes on a new sheet check box, and click OK.

    e. Print the History worksheet.

    f. Save the workbook again.

    ✓ *Notice that the History worksheet is removed.*

20. Merge the data from **38PartsReplacement_xx** into the **38PartsReplacement_2_xx** workbook (see Illustration A):

    a. Change to the Detail tab so you can see the changes after they are merged.

    b. Click the Compare and Merge Workbooks button on the Quick Access Toolbar.

    ✓ *If the button is not on the toolbar, add it before continuing.*

    c. Select the **38PartsReplacement_2_xx** workbook and click OK.

    ✓ *Notice cell F22 reads $9.95. This is the change that was made to worksheet version 2, and the one that was kept when it was merged with the original worksheet version.*

21. Spell check the worksheet

22. Adjust column widths as needed.

23. Print the worksheet.

24. Close the workbook, saving all changes.

Illustration A

	A	B	C	D	E	F	G
	S38PartsReplacement [Shared] - Microsoft Excel						
1				Parts Replacement Detail			
2							
3		Customer #:	2814		Labor per hour rate:		$40.00
4		Customer name:	Kai Yu		Work scheduled to begin:		11/22/2008
5		Daytime phone:	(303) 257-1919				
6		Bike model:	2003 Giadormo Outback				
7		Condition	Quantity	Manufacturer	Labor (hrs.)	Part price	Charge
8	Headset	Good					-
9	Bottom bracket	Good					-
10	Crankset	Good					-
11	Front derailleur	RPL	1	Giadormo DX50	0.75	$37.50	$67.50
12	Rear derailleur	RPL	1	Giadormo DX50B	0.75	$44.95	$74.95
13	Front fork	Good					-
14	Rear suspension fork	N/A					-
15	Top tube	Good					-
16	Head tube	Good					-
17	Down tube	Good					-
18	Seatstay	Good					-
19	Seat	Good					-
20	Chainstay	RPL	1	Giadormo CH410	0.10	$5.25	$9.25
21	Chainring	RPL	1	Giadormo CH412	0.10	$1.75	$5.75
22	Chain	RPL	1	Chain Rigger DLX 22147	0.25	$9.95	$19.95
23	Coaster brake	N/A					-
24	Rim brake	N/A					-
25	Rotor brake	N/A					-
26	Caliper brake	RPL	2	Aurens BR321	1.00	$39.25	$118.50
27	Disc brake	N/A					-
28	Brake lever	RPL	2	Aurens BL321	10.00	$4.95	$409.90
29	Quick release	N/A					-
30	Front hub	Good					-
31	Rear hub	Good					-
32	Lockring	Good					-
33	Sprocket	Good					-
34	Cable	Good					-
35	Left pedal	Good					-
36	Right pedal	Good					-
37	Front tire	RPL	1	Road Warrior 18F	15.00	$25.75	$625.75
38	Rear tire	RPL	1	Road Warrior 18R	25.00	$28.95	$1,028.95
39	Front wheel	RPL	1	Giadormo FWC1014			-

Scenario Summary | **Detail**

ON YOUR OWN

1. Start Excel, if necessary.
2. Open ⊙ **38EvergreenSales**.
3. Save the workbook as **OXL38_xx**.
4. Turn on Track Changes.
5. Make the following changes:
   a. For store 123, change Trees to **$2,145.00**.
   b. For store 123, change Flowers to **$458.00**.
   c. For store 123, change Herbs to **$225.00**.
   d. For store 214, change Flowers to **$1,055.00**.
   e. For store 214, change Herbs to **$256.00**.
   f. For store 218, change Trees to **$2,087.00**.
   g. For store 218, change Shrubs to **$955.00**.
   h. For store 218, change Herbs to **$135.00**.

6. Save the workbook.
7. Create a history of the changes and print it.
8. Review each of the changes, and accept only the following ones (see Illustration A):
   a. For store 123, change Trees to $2,145.00.
   b. For store 123, change Herbs to $225.00.
   c. For store 214, change Herbs to $256.00.
   d. For store 218, change Trees to $2,087.00.
   e. For store 218, change Herbs to $135.00.
9. Adjust column widths as necessary.
10. Spell check the worksheet.
11. Print the worksheet.
12. Close the workbook, saving all changes.

Illustration A

	Trees	Shrubs	Flowers	Herbs	Total Sales
Evergreen Nursery					
Store 123	$ 2,145.00	$ 1,855.00	$ 398.00	$ 225.00	$ 4,623.00
Store 214	$ 3,015.00	$ 1,035.00	$ 587.00	$ 256.00	$ 4,893.00
Store 218	$ 2,087.00	$ 975.00	$ 210.00	$ 135.00	$ 3,407.00
Totals by Item	$ 7,247.00	$ 3,865.00	$ 1,195.00	$ 616.00	$ 12,923.00

SOXL38 [Shared] - Microsoft Excel

Skills Covered

- **Control Data Entry**
- **Copy and Paste Validation Rules**
- **Circle Invalid Data**
- **Remove Duplicate Data**

Software Skills   After creating a database and adding, changing, and deleting records, you soon realize just how easy it is to enter incorrect information. This is especially true when several people maintain a database. Since the accuracy of your data is often critical—especially if the data tells you what to charge for a product or what to pay someone—controlling the validity of the data is paramount.

Application Skills   As one of the many store employees of PhotoTown's location outside the University of Illinois at Chicago, one of your countless jobs this week is to make the photo product order form easier to use. You've already gone a long way toward updating the worksheet, but the boss also wants all the empty space to be sewn up whenever an order contains only a few items, and he also wants all forms to contain only information that matches up with the inventory and product listings.

TERMS

Input message   A message that appears when a user clicks in a cell providing information on how to enter valid data.

Paste Special   A variation of the Paste command that allows you to copy part of the data relating to a cell—in this case, the validity rules associated with that cell—and not the data in the cell itself.

Validation   A process that enables you to maintain the accuracy of a database by specifying acceptable entries for a particular field.

NOTES

Control Data Entry

- With data **validation**, you can control the accuracy of the data entered into a worksheet.

- By specifying the type of entries that are acceptable, you can prevent invalid data from being entered.

  ✓ *For example, you could create a list of valid department numbers, and prevent someone from entering a department number that wasn't on the list.*

- You can set other rules as well, such as whole numbers only; numbers less than or greater than some value; or data of a specific length, such as five characters only.

- With the Custom option, you can enter a formula that compares the entry value with a value in another column.

- For example, you could set up a rule that if the Rented column contains the word YES, then the Number of Occupants field must have a value greater than zero.

- If you restrict entries to a specified list, a down-arrow button appears when the cell is selected. Clicking the button displays a drop-down list of the acceptable entries, from which you can select.

Data Validation dialog box

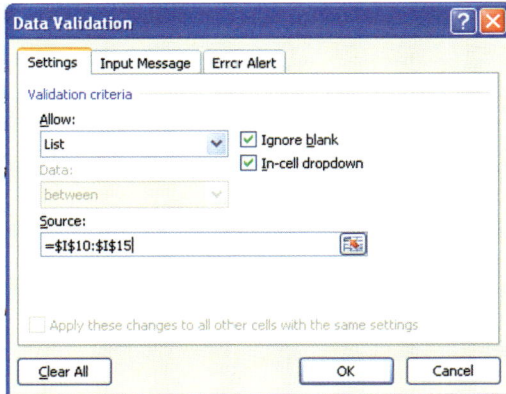

- Entries in a restricted list are case-sensitive.
  - If the list specifies *Yes* and the user instead types *yes*, for example, Excel will reject the entry. Whenever possible, use lowercase letters for list entries to prevent case-sensitivity problems and speed up data entry.
- The downside to using data validation is that it is designed to check against data entered directly into cells in the worksheet.
- Data validation doesn't apply if the cell entry is the result of:
  - Data copied there using the fill handle.
  - Data pasted or moved from another location.
  - Data that is the result of a formula.
- However, you can find invalid entries created by these methods with the Circle Invalid Data command (see below).
- Excel's AutoComplete feature can complicate data entry in an Excel worksheet, because AutoComplete can alter the case of an entry or complete an entry in a manner the user doesn't intend.
  - For example, if a previous entry in the field is Westlane and the user is entering only West, AutoComplete will nonetheless fill in Westlane.
  - To turn off the AutoComplete feature, click the Office Button, click Excel Options, click Advanced, and deselect the Enable AutoComplete for cell values option.

- Data validation can prevent incorrect entries and speed up data entry, but other methods can be faster for entering some types of data.
  - To enter data for a set of new parts at a particular warehouse, for example, enter only the unique data for each part. Then fill in all the cells in the Warehouse field at once—select the cells, type the entry, and press Ctrl+Enter.
  - Or type the entry in the first cell and use the fill handle to complete the remaining cells.
- After entering the criteria for what constitutes a valid entry, you can also specify a particular error message to appear when an incorrect entry is typed.

Error message

- In addition, you can create an **input message** that displays when a user clicks a cell to help that user enter the right type of data.

Input message

Copy and Paste Validation Rules

- After creating rules that limit the valid entries for a cell, use the **Paste Special** command to copy the rules to the other cells in the same column. This allows you to create one set of rules for an entire column.

- Another way to apply the same validation rule to an entire column is to select the column before creating the validation rule. The new rule applies to all cells in the selection.

- If the same rule will apply to multiple columns, select all those columns before creating the rule.

Circle Invalid Data

- With the Circle Invalid Data command, data that violates specified validation rules is identified quickly with a red circle.

- By using the Circle Invalid Data command, you can identify invalid data that was entered by copying and pasting, using the fill handle, or as the result of a formula—all methods that bypass Excel's validation rules.

- As you correct the data, the circle in that cell automatically disappears.

- You can remove any remaining circles (for errors you want to ignore) with the Clear Validation Circles command.

- Invalid data appears in a red circle.

Remove Duplicate Data

- Another type of invalid data that might be entered into a worksheet is a duplicate entry.

- Sometimes, duplicates are valid. For example, if two people happen to make $12.35 an hour, that might be perfectly normal.

- However, if the worksheet contains a database, such as a list of employees or customers, duplicates may indicate an error.

- To remove duplicate entries from a range, use the Remove Duplicates command.

- When you remove duplicate entries this way, Excel identifies what it considers duplicates, and automatically removes them for you.

  ✓ *You can also isolate duplicate entries by copying only unique records to another range using Advanced Filter. See Exercise 23.*

  ✓ *In addition, you can conditionally format a range using Highlight Cell Rules to identify duplicate entries, then manually remove them. See Exercise 7.*

- You cannot remove duplicates from data that is outlined or subtotaled.

- To remove duplicates, remove the outlining/subtotaling.

  ✓ *See Exercise 25.*

PROCEDURES

Set Data Validation for a Cell

1. Select the cell(s) to receive validation settings.
2. Click **Data** tab . . . . [Alt], [A]

   Data Tools Group

3. Click **Data Validation** button 📋 . . . . [V]
4. Click **Data Validation** . . . . [V]
5. Click **Settings** tab . . . . [S]

To restrict entries to a number:

a. Select **Whole number** or **Decimal** in the **Allow** list . . . . . [Alt]+[A], [↑]/[↓], [Enter]
b. Select a **Data** operator . . . . [Alt]+[D], [↑]/[↓], [Enter]
c. Specify the **Minimum** acceptable value . . . . [Alt]+[M]
d. Specify the **Maximum** acceptable value . . . . [Alt]+[X]

To restrict entries to a date or time:

a. Select **Date** or **Time** in the **Allow** list . . . . [Alt]+[A], [↑]/[↓], [Enter]
b. Select a **Data** operator . . . . [Alt]+[D], [↑]/[↓], [Enter]
c. Specify acceptable **Start date** or **Start time** . . . . [Alt]+[S]
d. Specify acceptable **End date** or **End time** settings . . . . [Alt]+[N]

To restrict text entries to a certain length:

a. Select **Text length** in the **Allow** list . . . . `Alt`+`A`, `↑`/`↓`, `Enter`

b. Select a **Data** operator . . . . `Alt`+`D`, `↑`/`↓`, `Enter`

c. Specify the **Minimum** acceptable value . . . . `Alt`+`M`

d. Specify the **Maximum** acceptable value . . . . `Alt`+`X`

To display a drop-down list of acceptable entries in the cell:

a. Select **List** in the **Allow** list . . . . `Alt`+`A`, `↑`/`↓`, `Enter`

b. Click in the **Source** box and type a list of acceptable entries, separated by commas . . . . `Alt`+`S`

✓ *For example, type* Living Room, Kitchen, Office/Den, Bedroom.

OR

Click the **Collapse Dialog** button and type or select the cell or range in the worksheet that contains the entry list. (Use an absolute reference.)

✓ *The entry list can be a range of cells with one item per cell or a single cell with a list of items separated by commas. If you've given the list range a name, type the name preceded by an equals sign like this: =SalesList.*

c. Select **In-cell dropdown** . . . . `Alt`+`I`

To create a custom restriction based on a formula:

a. Select **Custom** in the **Allow** list . . . . `Alt`+`A`, `↑`/`↓`, `Enter`

b. Click in the **Formula** box and type a formula, using appropriate absolute, mixed, and relative references . . . `Alt`+`F`

✓ *Formulas must evaluate to TRUE or FALSE.*

OR

Click the **Collapse Dialog** button and select a cell in the worksheet that contains the formula. (Use an absolute reference.)

OR

Type = (equal sign) followed by the address of the cell containing the formula.

6. Add an input message if desired:

a. Click **Input Message** tab . . . . `Ctrl`+`⇥`

b. Click **Show input message when cell is selected** . . . . `Alt`+`S`

c. Enter message **Title** . . . . `Alt`+`T`

d. Enter **Input message** . . . . `Alt`+`I`

7. Add an error message if desired:

a. Click **Error Alert** . . . . `Ctrl`+`⇥`

b. Click **Show error alert after invalid data is entered** . . . . `Alt`+`S`

c. Select alert **Style** . . . . `Alt`+`Y`, `↑`/`↓`, `Enter`

✓ *A stop alert refuses the entry. A warning alert asks whether the reader wants to proceed with the entry despite the validation rule. An information alert presents the error message.*

d. Enter **Title** . . . . `Alt`+`T`

e. Enter **Error message** . . . . `Alt`+`E`

8. Click **OK** . . . . `Enter`

Copy Validation Rules

1. Select cell(s) whose validation rules you wish to copy.

2. Click **Home** tab . . . . `Alt`, `H`

Clipboard Group

3. Click **Copy** button . . . . `C`

4. Select the destination range.

5. Click **Home** tab . . . . `Alt`, `H`

Clipboard Group

6. Click arrow on **Paste** button . . . . `V`

7. Click **Paste Special** . . . . `S`

8. Select **Validation** . . . . `N`

9. Click **OK** . . . . `Enter`

Find Cells with Validation Rules

1. Click **Home** tab . . . . `Alt`, `H`

Editing Group

2. Click **Find & Select** button . . . . `F`, `D`

3. Click **Go To** . . . . `G`

4. Click **Special** . . . . `Alt`+`S`

5. Select **Data validation** . . . `Alt`+`V`

6. To highlight all cells with data validation rules, click **All** . . . . `Alt`+`E`

OR

To highlight cells with the same validation rules as the current cell, click **Same** . . . . `Alt`+`E`

7. Click **OK** . . . . `Enter`

Circle Invalid Data

1. Click **Data** tab . . . . `Alt`, `A`

Data Tools Group

2. Click **Data Validation** button . . . . `V`

3. Click the **Circle Invalid Data** . . `I`

✓ *Excel displays red circles around all data that doesn't meet the specified validation rules. Cells without validation rules are ignored.*

Correct Invalid Data

1. Display validation circles.
2. Select a cell containing a validation circle.
3. Correct the entry in the cell so that it is now valid.

   ✓ *The red circle is automatically removed.*

Clear Validation Circles

1. Click **Data** tab . . . . ⌊Alt⌋, ⌊A⌋

   Data Tools Group

2. Click **Data Validation** button ▣ . . . . ⌊V⌋
3. Click the **Clear Validation Circles**. . . . . ⌊R⌋

   ✓ *All validation circles disappear.*

Remove Duplicate Data

1. Click within the list or table.
2. Click **Data** tab . . . . ⌊Alt⌋, ⌊A⌋

   Data Tools Group

3. Click **Remove Duplicates** button ▣ . . . . ⌊M⌋
4. Select the columns you want Excel to check for duplicate entries.
5. Click **OK**. . . . . ⌊Enter⌋

   ✓ *Excel removes duplicate entries and displays a message telling you how many.*

6. Click **OK**. . . . . ⌊Enter⌋

EXERCISE DIRECTIONS

1. Start Excel, if necessary.
2. Open 💿 **39PhotoOrderForm**.
3. Save the file as **39PhotoOrderForm_*xx***.
4. Test the new, list-based order form:
   a. Click cell A16.
   b. Type **PZ101** and press Tab.

   ✓ *The Description field should read Photo puzzle.*

   c. Under Qty, enter **1**.
5. Add a validation rule for the Item # field:
   a. Click cell A16.
   b. Click the Data Validation button on the Data tab.
   c. On the Settings tab, under Allow, choose List.
   d. Under Source, type **=Index**.

   ✓ *Here, **Index** is a hidden range that contains a copy of the Item # field in the Product Listing worksheet.*

   ✓ *This range was copied here because data validation rules for any cell can only refer to other cells in the same worksheet.*

   e. Click OK.
6. Add a validation rule for the Qty field:
   a. Click cell F16 and click the Data Validation button on the Data tab.
   b. On the Settings tab, under Allow, choose Whole Number.
   c. Under Data, choose greater than.
   d. Under Minimum, type **0**.
   e. Clear the Ignore blank check box.
   f. On the Error Alert tab, under Style, choose Information.

   g. In the Title box, type **Quantity**.
   h. In the Error message box, type **Quantity must be greater than zero.**
   i. Click OK.
7. Test the validation rules:
   a. Click cell H16 and press Tab to add a new row to the table.

   ✓ *A drop-down arrow will appear beside the cell A17.*

   b. From the list, choose BL101.
   c. Under the Qty field, type **0**.
   d. Press Tab. When you receive your own warning, click OK.
   e. On the Data tab, click the Data Validation arrow and then click Circle Invalid Data.

   ✓ *A red circle should appear around cell F17.*

   f. On the Data tab, click the Data Validation arrow and then click Clear Validation Circles.
   g. Delete this new row.
   h. Clear row 16 by deleting the contents of cells A16 and F16.
   i. Click outside the list.

   ✓ *The list should retract itself to one empty row.*

8. Add a validation rule for the Greeting card text cell:
   a. Click the big, merged cell at location D3, and click the Data Validation button on the Data tab.
   b. On the Settings tab, under Allow, choose Text length.
   c. Under Data, choose less than or equal to.
   d. In the Maximum box, type **180**.

e. On the Input Message tab, in the Title box, type **Greeting card text**.

f. In the Input message field, type **Message should be no greater than 180 characters**.

g. On the Error Alert tab, in the Title box, type **Greeting card text**.

h. In the Error message field, type **Message is too long for the space provided.**

i. Click OK.

9. Test this new validation rule:

  a. Click outside cell D3, then click it again.

✓ *You should see your own popup window outside the cell.*

  b. Type the following:

✓ *Press Alt+Enter to type text on the next line.*

Wheaten's Glenn Apple Orchard

First Annual Harvest Festival
September 12th to 28th
10:00 A.M. to 6:00 P.M.

Hay rides, apple picking, cider tasting, corn maze, and more!
Take NC-7 to R.R. 12, west 10 miles.

  c. Press Enter.

  d. Respond to the warning by clicking Retry.

e. Edit the entry to fit:

Wheaten's Glenn Apple Orchard
Harvest Festival
Sept. 12th to 28th
10 A.M. to 6 P.M.

Hay rides, apple picking, cider tasting, corn maze, and more!
NC-7 to R.R. 12, west 10 m.

✓ *Make row 7 taller so the text message displays fully.*

10. Enter the data shown in Illustration A.

11. They ordered a lot of items. Better check for duplicate entries before you print:

  a. Click cell A16.

  b. Click the Remove Duplicates button on the Data tab.

✓ *The range of items is selected.*

  c. Click OK. You'll see a message telling you that one item has been removed. Click OK.

12. Widen columns as necessary.

13. Spell check the worksheet.

14. Print the worksheet.

15. Close the workbook, saving all changes.

Illustration A

ON YOUR OWN

1. Start Excel, if necessary.
2. Open 🔘 **39Raises**.
3. Save the file as **OXL39_xx**.
4. Add a new column called **Raise Begins**:

   ✓ *Insert the new column between the existing columns F and G.*

   a. Create a formula in cell G8 that computes the date when the raise will begin, which occurs annually from the date of hire.

   ✓ *You could take the date of hire plus 365 (or 365.25 if you prefer), and then format the cell so that it displays only the month and day. The formula would look like this:*

   =C8+365

   ✓ *To show the complete date with the current year, you could use this formula:*

   =DATE(YEAR(TODAY()),MONTH(C8),DAY(C8))

   ✓ *Using the YEAR function, you get the current year from today's date; using the MONTH function, you get 2 from the hire date in cell C8; and using the DAY function, you get 12 from the hire date in cell C8. Put them all together using the DATE function, and assuming 2004 is the current year, you get (2004, 2, 12) which is displayed in the cell as 2/12/2004.*

   b. Copy the formula to the other cells in column G (G9:G12).

5. Add data validation to column E questioning any raises above the average of 5%.

   ✓ *Use Custom, with a formula such as =H8<D8+(D8*.06).*

   ✓ *Issue a warning alert, not a stop alert. For example, you might ask, "This score is above the normal 5%. Is that correct?" A user could then change the score if it was entered incorrectly, or ignore the error and continue.*

6. Add an input message that instructs the user to enter a whole number between 1 and 10.

7. In column F, add a formula that computes the raise percent:

   a. A person receiving a score of 5 gets a 5% raise; a score of 7 gets a 7% raise, and so on.

   ✓ *To compute the raise percent, take the review score divided by 100. For example, if the first person got a review score of 10, the formula would take 10/100, which is 10%.*

   b. Format column F with Percent Style, 0 decimal places.

8. In column H, add a formula that computes the new rate:

   ✓ *Multiply the old rate by (1 plus the rate percent).*

9. Format column H with Currency Style, 2 decimal places.

10. Give everyone a raise rating; be sure to try some numbers that will trigger the error message. Accept some of the incorrect entries.

11. Use the Circle Invalid Data command to locate invalid entries.

12. Lower the scores on the circled entries, or, if the scores are correct, clear the validation circles.

13. Adjust column widths as necessary.

14. Spell check the worksheet.

15. Print the worksheet.

16. Close the workbook, saving all changes.

Skills Covered

- **Use Document Inspector to Remove Private Information from Workbooks**
- **Restrict Access to Workbooks with IRM**
- **Identify Workbooks Using Keywords**
- **Add Digital Signatures**
- **Mark Workbooks as Final**

Software Skills   To make it easier for you to locate a saved file later on, you may want to change the workbook properties.

Application Skills   The First Quarter budget is complete and ready for distribution. You have only a few minor additions to make, and then you'll be ready to prepare the workbook for sharing by removing private information, restricting access, and marking the workbook as the final version.

TERMS

Digital signature   Also known as a certificate, a digital signature is a special file you can attach to a macro to let other people know it came from you.

Information Rights Management   Also known as IRM, a system of access rights stored within a file.

Macro   A small recorded program created in Excel's Visual Basic programming language to automate repetitive actions.

Metadata   Data that describes the data in a file.

Trusted publisher   You can designate which macro publishers (designers) you trust, and together they form a list of "trusted publishers" for your computer.

Virus   A computer program that can alter or damage other files when executed.

NOTES

Use Document Inspector to Remove Private Information from Workbooks

- There are many steps you might go through to prepare a document for sharing with your colleagues and clients, including of course, proofreading it for errors.

- Another step you might want to take is to remove hidden personal information (**metadata**) that's included in the workbook file.

- Here's a list of some of the items a workbook contain that you might not want to share:

  - *Track changes* and the data that goes with a workbook collaboration, such as back and forth comments (including the names of the people who made them), and earlier versions of worksheet data.

  - *Workbook properties*, which include your name and your company's name (which were entered when Excel was installed), and other data you may have entered yourself in order to make it easier to identify a workbook more easily than simply using its filename. Workbook properties may include e-mail addresses and file paths, depending on the Excel features you have used while working on the workbook.

- *Headers, footers, and watermarks* may contain information that you would prefer be kept private and not shared with the general public, such as your name or your company's name.
- *Hidden data* is data that exists in a worksheet, but hidden—such as hidden rows, columns, and worksheets. You might also have hidden objects such as shapes that are formatted as invisible. Custom XML data might also be included with the workbook, but hidden.

■ To remove such data, you can use the Document Inspector.
- Although the Document Inspector warns you before it removes anything, you should still be careful because you may not be able to undo its results.
- You should make a copy of your workbook first, and use the Document Inspector on the copy.
- You can pick and choose the type of information you want the Document Inspector to remove.

Decide which private data to remove

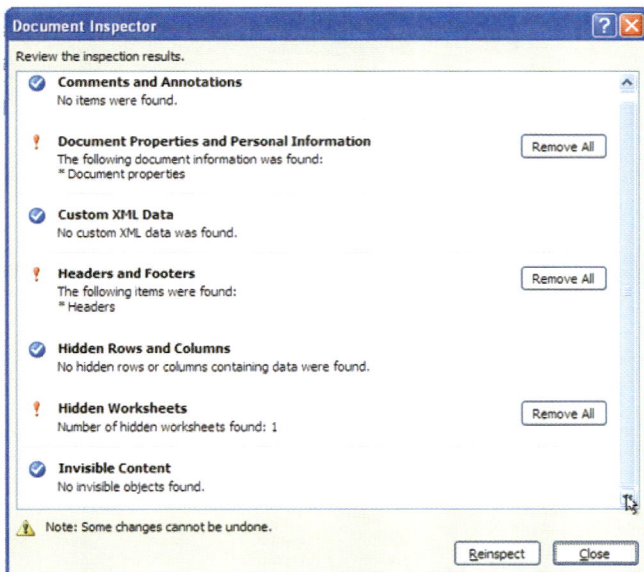

Restrict Access to Workbooks with IRM

■ You can restrict access to the data in a document no matter where is located, using **Information Rights Management**.

■ Unlike network security, where a file's access level changes if it is copied from the network, IRM access levels stay with a file because they are a part of it.

■ You can use Information Rights Management on workbooks, macro-enabled workbooks, templates, and macro-enabled templates.

■ You grant permission to a workbook using the Permission dialog box.

Permission dialog box

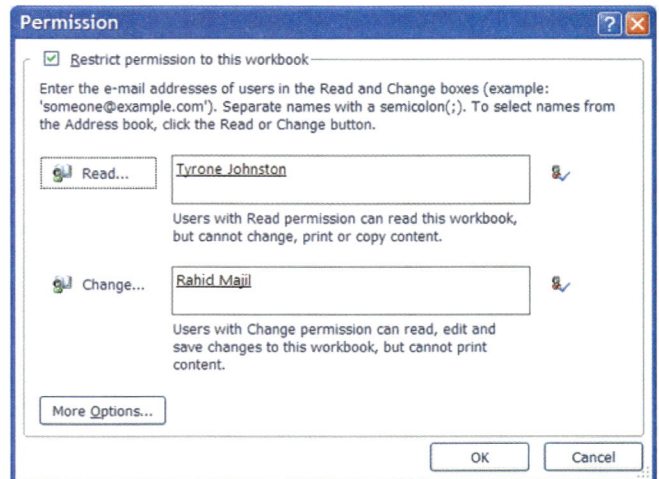

■ With IRM, you can:
- Provide access to a workbook while preventing a recipient from printing, forwarding, copying, modifying, faxing or pasting its data.
- Prevent data from being captured by Print Screen.
- Restrict certain data regardless of where the workbook is sent.
- Prevent a user from viewing data after a certain date.

- Using IRM, you can restrict access to all documents for a particular user, or restrict access to a particular document.

  ✓ *You can also restrict access to a certain group of people, you need to use Microsoft Active Directory services.*

Enable additional restrictions using a second Permissions dialog box

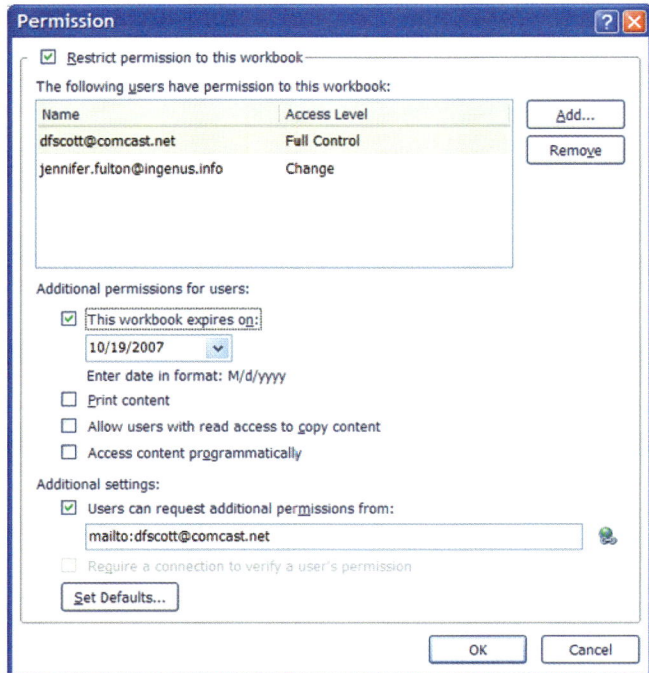

- Information Rights Management isn't perfect, however. You can't prevent access if someone is especially determined. Using IRM, you can't prevent:
  - Damage caused by viruses.
  - Data captured by malicious programs.
  - Data from being copied through a screen capture program—not Print Screen.
  - Data from being copied by hand, retyped in another document, or captured using a camera.
- Prior to using Information Rights Management, you must install the Windows Rights Management Services Client.

  ✓ *The Windows Rights Management Services Client is available for download from Microsoft's Web site. If you use Windows Vista, the client should be already installed.*

- The first time you try to open a workbook that uses IRM to restrict access, Excel sends your e-mail address and other identifying information (such as your permission levels) to a licensing server.
  - After the licensing server verifies your identity, you'll be given a user license.
  - After obtaining a user license for an IRM file, you can open it.

Identify Workbooks Using Keywords

- The workbook properties contain information that you can search for later, when trying to locate the file you wish to open.

  ✓ *You can see some of these properties by simply pointing to a file name in the Open dialog box.*

Workbook Properties pane

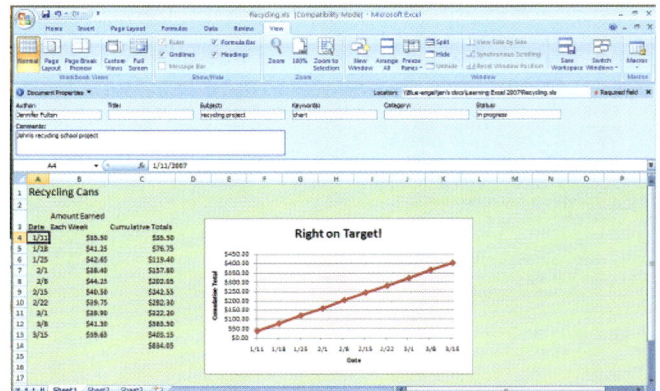

- By default, the workbook properties contain the author's name (in this case, your name) and your company name, both of which were entered when you installed Microsoft Excel.

  ✓ *On a school computer, general school information was probably entered.*

- In addition, you can add other information that might make it easier for you to locate the file later on, such as the workbook title and subject.
- When modifying workbook properties, you can also save a preview picture of the worksheet.
  - This option saves page one of the workbook so you can view it in the Open dialog box.
  - Saving a preview will allow you to quickly identify a workbook, because you can see it before you open it.
  - However, saving a preview increases the size of your file on disk.

Add Digital Signatures

- Excel can check your workbooks before you open them for the presence of potential macro viruses.

- A **virus**, hidden in a **macro**, could perform actions that might damage your workbook, corrupt your data, and disable your system.

- When you open a workbook that contains macros, Excel typically disables them and displays a warning message to remind you of the possible dangers of using foreign macros.

- Some macros come from a trusted source, and therefore shouldn't be summarily disabled by Excel. So Excel examines each workbook and decides what to do:

  - Excel checks each macro in the workbook to see if it is **digitally signed** by the person who created it.

  - Next, Excel checks if the signature is valid (the signature is registered with an online digital certification database and has not expired.)

  - Finally, Excel checks to see if the person who signed the macro is a **trusted publisher**.

- If a workbook with macros fails these three tests, Excel displays its warning message.

- When the warning message is displayed, you can choose to enable or disable the macros in the file.

A warning tells you that macros have been disabled

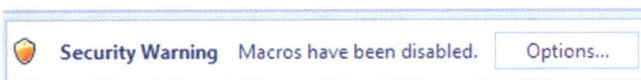

- You purchase a digital signature from a third party, who then independently verifies your identity to other people, such as colleagues with whom you share files.

Mark Workbooks as Final

- One problem with sharing a workbook is preventing someone from changing your formulas or data.

  - If someone unfamiliar with a worksheet makes a change, the data or the results may be rendered invalid or incorrect.

  - You can prevent changes to data by protecting a range, worksheet, or workbook.

  ✓ *See Exercise 37.*

- Another way to prevent changes to data is to mark a workbook as the "final" version.

  - When you mark a workbook as final, the workbook is changed to read-only access.

  - Typing, editing, and proofing data is prevented in a read-only workbook.

  - In the workbook's prosperities, the Status is changed to Final.

- However, if you mark a workbook as final and save it in an early version of Excel, the result will only be considered read-only if opened in Excel 2007.

  - If the workbook is opened in an earlier version of Excel, it will not be read-only anymore and the user will be able to make changes.

- When a workbook is marked as final, an icon appears on the status bar.

Mark a workbook as final to prevent changes

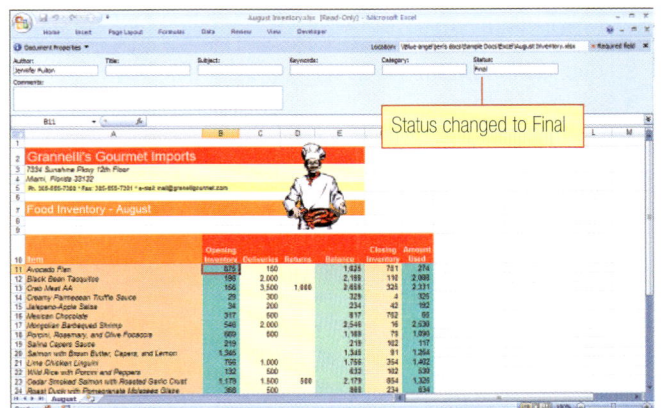

PROCEDURES

Use Document Inspector

1. Make a copy of your workbook.
2. Click **Office Button** 🗔 . . . Alt , F
3. Point to **Pre**pare . . . . E
4. Click **I**nspect Document I
5. Select the items you want the Document Inspector to look for.
6. Click **Inspect** . . . . Enter

   ✓ *If prompted to save changes to the file, click Yes.*

7. In the results list that appears, review any data that was found and click **Remove All** in that section to remove that data type.

   ✓ *If you want, you can click Reinspect and change the settings you choose in step 5, and have the Document Inspector look for these new items.*

8. When you're through removing any data you do not wish to share, click **Close**.

Restrict Access to a Workbook with IRM

1. Save your workbook first, before proceeding.
2. Click **Office Button** 🗔 . . . Alt , F
3. Point to **Pre**pare . . . . E
4. Click **R**estrict Permission . . . . R
5. Click **R**estricted Access . . . . . R
6. Click **R**estrict permission to this workbook . . . . Alt + R
7. Grant permission to read and/or change the contents of the document only:
   a. Click **Read**.
   b. Choose the e-mail address of the person you wish to grant permission to.
   c. Click **Read**.

      OR

      Click **Change**.
   d. Click **OK**.

8. To set other options, click **More Options** . . . . Alt + O
   a. To set an expiration date for permission, click **This workbook expires on** and select a date . . . . Alt + N , ↑ / ↓ , Enter
   b. To allow a user to print the workbook, click **Print content** . . . . Alt + P
   c. To allow a user with read-only access to copy information, click **Allow users with read access to copy content** . . . . Alt + C
   d. To allow a user to access information through some kind of third-party software, click **Access content programmatically** . . . . Alt + O
   e. To change the e-mail address you want permission requests sent to, enable the **Users can request additional permissions from** option, and type an address in the box . . . . Alt + M , *e-mail_address*
   f. To require that a user's permission be checked regularly, click **Require a connection to verify a user's permission** . . . . Alt + Q
9. Click **OK** . . . . Enter

   ✓ *A message appears above the worksheet, telling you that permission to access this workbook has been restricted.*

Change Workbook Properties

1. Click **Office Button** 🗔 . . . Alt , F
2. Point to **Pre**pare . . . . E
3. Click **P**roperties . . . . P
4. Enter whatever properties you wish:
   a. Change the **Author** if desired.
   b. Enter the workbook **Title**.
   c. Enter a **Subject**.
   d. Enter some **Keywords** you can search for later.
   e. Enter a **Category** for the workbook data.
   f. Enter the workbook **Status**.
   g. Enter any **Comments** about the workbook.
5. Save a preview of your workbook for later display:

   ✓ *To view page one of a workbook you've saved with a preview, click the Views button in the Open dialog box and choose Preview. Then click the file you wish to view. In Windows Vista, use the Preview Pane in Explorer to preview files.*

   a. Click the **Document Properties** button 🛈 Document Properties ▼ .
   b. Click **Advanced Properties**.
   c. Click **Summary** tab . . . . Ctrl + ⇥
   d. Click **Save preview picture**.

   ✓ *In Windows Vista, click Save Thumbnails for All Excel Documents instead.*

   e. Click **OK** . . . . Enter
6. Close the Properties pane.

Attach a Digital Signature to a Macro

✓ *Digital signatures are removed if you change a macro, so only sign macros that you've tested and finalized. You must use a choice in the Popular category of the Excel Options dialog box to display the Developer tab.*

1. Click **Developer** tab . . . . . ⌨Alt⌨, ⌨L⌨

   Code Group

2. Click **Visual Basic** button 🖼 . . . . ⌨V⌨

3. Select the macro you wish to sign from those listed in the Project pane on the left.

4. Click **Tools** . . . . ⌨Alt⌨+⌨T⌨

5. Click **Digital Signature** . . . . . . ⌨D⌨

6. If needed, select your digital certificate:

   a. Click **Choose** . . . . ⌨Alt⌨+⌨C⌨

   b. Choose a certificate from those listed . . . . ⌨↑⌨/⌨↓⌨

   c. Click **OK** . . . . ⌨Enter⌨

7. Click **OK** . . . . ⌨Enter⌨

Mark as Final

1. Click **Office Button** 🖼 . . . ⌨Alt⌨, ⌨F⌨

2. Point to **Prepare** . . . . ⌨E⌨

3. Click **Mark as Final** . . . . ⌨F⌨

   ✓ *A message appears to let you know that the workbook will be marked as final and then saved.*

4. Click **OK** . . . . ⌨Enter⌨

5. If an informative message appears explaining that changes will not be allowed, click **OK** again . . . . . . ⌨Enter⌨

Unmark a Workbook Marked as Final

1. Click **Office Button** 🖼 . . . ⌨Alt⌨, ⌨F⌨

2. Point to **Prepare** . . . . ⌨E⌨

3. Click **Mark as Final** . . . . ⌨F⌨

EXERCISE DIRECTIONS

1. Start Excel, if necessary.

2. Open 💿 **40MWTFirstQuarterBudget_Final**.

3. Save the file as **40MWTFirstQuarterBudget_Final_xx**.

4. Add some workbook properties to help you identify this workbook later on:

   a. Click the Office Button and point to Prepare.

   b. Click Properties.

   c. Replace the name in the Author box with your name.

   d. Type **First Quarter Budget** in the Subject box.

   e. Type **budget first quarter** in the Keywords box.

   f. Type **budget company** in the Category box.

   g. Close the Properties pane.

5. Mark your copy of the workbook as a final copy:

   a. Click the Office Button and point to Prepare.

   b. Click Mark as Final.

   c. Click OK.

   d. Click OK again.

6. Save this final version for distribution, using the file name **40MWTFirstQuarterBudget_Final_For_Distribution_xx**.

7. Remove the Mark as Final notation so you can prepare the workbook for distribution:

   a. Click the Office Button and point to Prepare.

   b. Click Mark as Final.

8. Now, use Document Inspector to remove private information before you distribute this final version of the budget:

   a. Save the workbook.

   b. Click the Office Button and point to Prepare.

   c. Click Inspect Document.

   d. You want to look for any private or hidden info, so leave everything selected and click Inspect.

   e. Click Remove All next to all categories but Headers and Footers.

   f. Click Close.

   g. Click the View tab, then click the Page Layout button to view the header so you can see if it contains any private info.

   h. Click in the box on the left and remove the filename and path.

   i. Edit the text in the middle box to remove the version number.

9. Adjust column widths as necessary.

10. Spell check the worksheet.

11. Print the worksheet.

12. Mark this distribution copy as final again:

   a. Click the Office Button and point to Prepare.

   b. Click Mark as Final.

   c. Click OK.

   d. Click OK again.

13. Close the workbook, saving all changes.

ON YOUR OWN

1. Start Excel, if necessary.

2. Open the file 🖮 **OXL29_xx**, created in the On Your Own section of Exercise 29, or open 💿 **40Theater**.

3. Save the file as **OXL40_xx**.

4. Use the stored scenarios to display the final estimates:
   a. For the *Glass Menagerie*, show the scenario if the play is sold out. See Illustration A.
   b. For the *Music Man*, show the scenario if the play is sold out completely

5. Use Document Inspector to remove private information.

6. Adjust column widths as necessary.

7. Spell check the workbook.

8. Print the workbook.

9. Mark the workbook as final.

10. Close the workbook, saving all changes.

Illustration A

SOXL40 - Microsoft Excel

	A	B	C	D	E	F	G	H
1								
2			**The Back Street Players Presents**					
3		*The Glass Menagerie*						
4								
5					*If the play is a sellout:*			
6		Costumes	$ 750.00		Tickets Sold		1420	
7		Scenery	$1,025.00		Ticket Price	$	8.75	
8		Theater Rental	$1,500.00		Revenue	$ 12,425.00		
9		Electrician	$ 225.00					
10		Royalty fee	$1,350.00		Expenses	$ 11,027.00		
11		Playbills	$6,177.00		Profit	$ 1,398.00		
12								
13								
14	No. of Playbills Printed		1207					
15	Cost each to print		$ 4.10					
16								
17								

Critical Thinking

Application Skills You are the founder of a public relations firm called Jones PR. You are looking for additional capital from angel investors and other local seed capital sources, and will need to make presentations to investors soon. One important set of data you need to present is a Cash Flow Projection. The cash flow project will forecast your company's future performance based on data you have captured from past performance. You need to embellish the raw data you'll present with some charts that show comparisons and trends. You also need to add validation to a cell to make sure your projections meet your minimum requirements and protect the workbook against unwanted changes.

EXERCISE DIRECTIONS

1. Start Excel, if necessary.
2. Open the workbook ⊙ **41JonesPRCashFlow**.
3. Save the file as **41JonesPRCashFlow_xx**.
4. Adjust worksheet formatting as you prefer.
5. Apply validation to cell B4 to ensure entries make there are a whole number greater than 15,000.
6. Attempt to enter 1000 in cell B4. Click Cancel when the validation warning appears.
7. Enter 16000 in cell B4. Notice that previously applied conditional formatting rules make the entries in cells B7:C7 turn red.
8. Select the range A12:N12 and insert a Line with Markers chart.
9. Move the chart to its own sheet called Comparison.
10. Return to the Cash Flow worksheet, and select and copy the range A38:N38.
11. Return to the Comparison worksheet and paste the copied data into the chart.
12. Add Receipts vs. Cash Out as a centered overlay title for the chart.
13. Edit the chart series so that the ranges C12:N12 and C38:N38 on the Cash Flow sheet are charted, omitting the blank cells in column B.
14. Specify the range C6:N6 on the Cash Flow sheet for the axis labels. The resulting chart should resemble Illustration A.

15. Return to the Cash Flow worksheet.
16. Select the range A38:N38 again and insert a Scattered Only with Markers Chart.
17. Move the chart to its own sheet called Trend.
18. Edit the chart series so that the range C38:N38 on the Cash Flow sheet is charted, omitting the blank cell in column B.
19. Specify the range C6:N6 on the Cash Flow sheet for the X axis labels, making sure that cell A6 is specified as the series name, and hide the Y axis label.
20. Add Cash Out Trend as a centered overlay title for the chart.
21. Make sure that data labels appear to the right of the data points on the chart.
22. Add a Linear trendline to the chart to show the trend for cash out over time. The finished chart should look like Illustration B.

   ✓ Use the Trendline button drop-down list in the Analysis group of the (Chart Tools) Layout tab to add predefined trendlines in a chart.

23. Lock all cells on the Cash Flow sheet.
24. Protect the Cash Flow worksheet, preventing the selection of locked cells, with the password trend.
25. Print the two charts from the workbook.
26. Close the workbook, saving all changes.

Illustration A

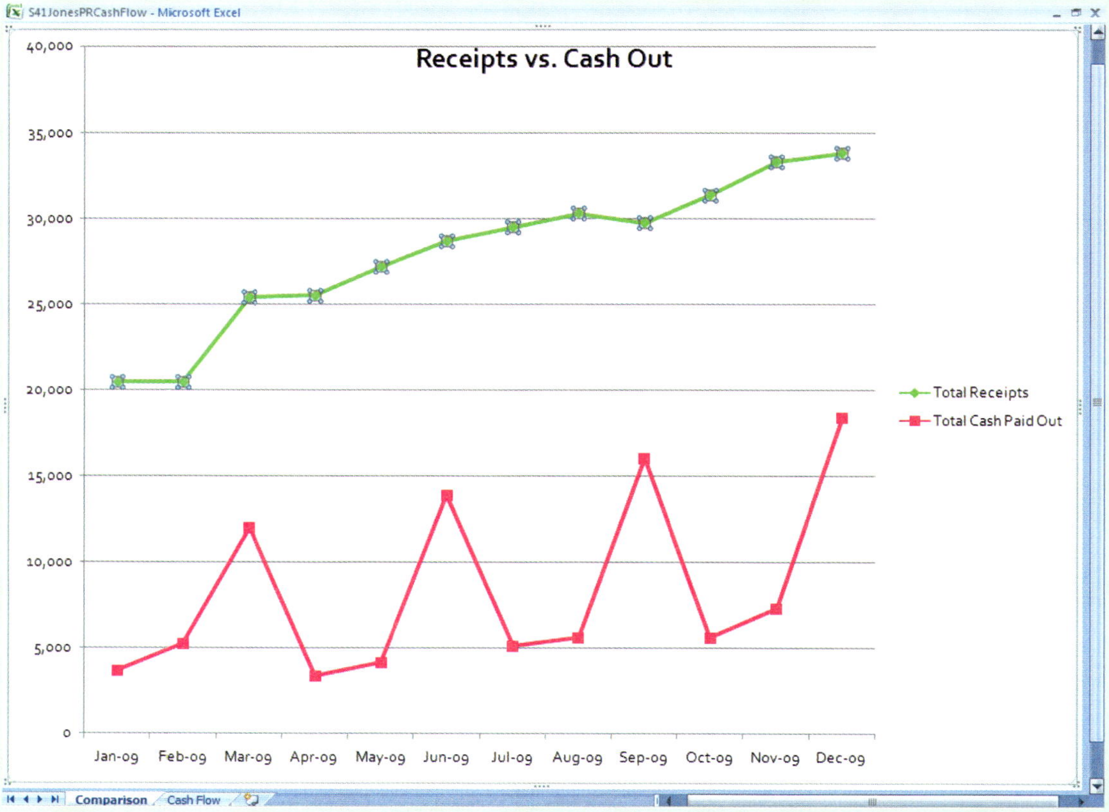
S41JonesPRCashFlow - Microsoft Excel
Receipts vs. Cash Out
40,000
35,000
30,000
25,000
20,000
15,000
10,000
5,000
0
Jan-09
Feb-09
Mar-09
Apr-09
May-09
Jun-09
Jul-09
Aug-09
Sep-09
Oct-09
Nov-09
Dec-09
Total Receipts
Total Cash Paid Out
Comparison
Cash Flow

Illustration B

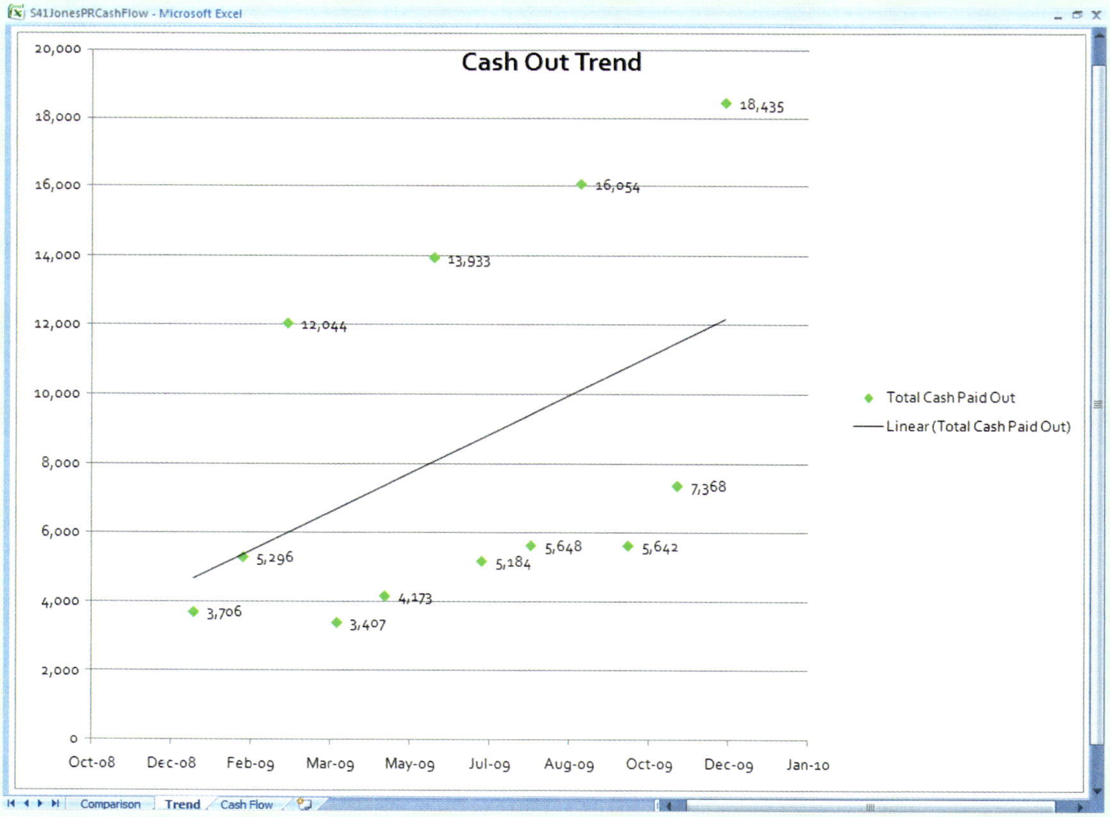
S41JonesPRCashFlow - Microsoft Excel
Cash Out Trend
20,000
18,000
16,000
14,000
12,000
10,000
8,000
6,000
4,000
2,000
0
18,435
16,054
13,933
12,044
7,368
5,296
5,648
5,642
5,184
3,706
4,173
3,407
Oct-08
Dec-08
Feb-09
Mar-09
May-09
Jul-09
Aug-09
Oct-09
Dec-09
Jan-10
Total Cash Paid Out
Linear (Total Cash Paid Out)
Comparison
Trend
Cash Flow

Exercise | 42

Curriculum Integration

Application Skills   In social studies, your class is currently studying inventions and their impact on American culture. You've decided to focus on television and its possible relationship to obesity, poor academic performance, and health issues such as heart disease and diabetes. The easiest way to make sense of all the data you'll be gathering is charts, so you plan on creating a few. Since this is a team project, you'll want to put some safeguards in the workbook to prevent invalid data and unauthorized changes. (If the team cannot find actual data, developing sample data is OK.)

EXERCISE DIRECTIONS

Start Excel, if necessary, and begin a new, blank workbook. Save the file with an appropriate file name, such as **42TVWatching_xx**.

Add an appropriate title for the first worksheet, such as **TV Watching Habits**. Use column and row labels appropriate for your data, such as Age, Hours Spent Watching, and Percentage of the Day Spent Watching. Create other sheets as needed to gather data about health-related issues such as Diabetes, Heart Disease, and Obesity; TV watching by education level, or other issues uncovered in your research. Add some data validation rules to issue warnings when data may be incorrect, such as entering more than 10 hours a day spent watching TV (which would be pretty unusual to say the least). Adjust column widths as necessary. Spell check the workbook. Print the workbook.

Create applicable charts and format them. Use 3-D charts, exploded pie charts, and charts with two value axes where applicable. Once you feel satisfied with the structure of the workbook, protect all the sheets in the workbook, assigning the password **TVSTATS**. Enable track changes as well if you want to track which members of your team made specific changes, and you'd like a chance to accept or reject such changes.

Add properties to the workbook that describe it fully and make it easier for your teammates to locate on the school's network. Save and close the workbook.

Lesson | 1

Managing Tables and Data

Skills Covered

- **Plan Table Structure**
- **Normalize Table Structure**
- **Split a Table Using the Table Analyzer**
- **Copy a Table**
- **Delete a Table**
- **Rename a Table**

Software Skills Access works best when the tables you create conform to certain logical organizational standards called normalization. You can learn to normalize your tables manually based on applying the rules of normalization; you can also get help from the Table Analyzer feature in Access to do so.

Application Skills Ace Learning, an academic tutoring company, has hired you to help them develop a database for their business. They have a database already created, but some of the tables in it are not normalized. You will help them normalize their tables in this exercise.

TERMS

1NF (First Normal Form) A normalization standard that dictates that the table must contain no duplicate records.

2NF (Second Normal Form) A normalization standard that dictates that all other fields must be fully dependent on the primary key.

3NF (Third Normal Form) A normalization standard that dictates that every field must be directly dependent on the primary or composite key fields, not just indirectly dependent.

Composite key A primary key that consists of two or more fields, the unique combination of which forms the primary key.

Normalized A table that has been structured so that it conforms to 1NF, 2NF, and 3NF.

Primary key The unique identifying field for each record, such as an ID number.

NOTES

Plan Table Structure

- The choices you make as you design Access tables play a big part in the database's usability and effectiveness.
- In an effective database, tables will:
  - Calculate values when more appropriate than storing the raw data.
  - Link to external sources when required.
  - Use the appropriate field types and formats.
- An effective database should also apply data normalization rules to all tables.

Deciding What Data to Calculate

- Not all data needs to be stored in the database. Some data is better off being calculated when you run a report or query.
- For example, suppose you want to be able to add sales tax to invoices generated in Access. One way would be to set up a field in the Items table that lists the amount of sales tax to charge on that item.

Sales tax for each item is hard-coded as data

Item #	Description	Price	Sales Tax
1	Coffee, 5 lb, dark roast	$40.00	$2.80
2	Coffee, 2 lb, dark roast	$20.00	$1.40
3	Coffee, 5 lb, medium roast	$39.00	$2.73
4	Coffee, 2 lb, medium roast	$19.00	$1.33

- But what if the sales tax rate changes? Then you would have to manually go through the whole table and reenter the sales tax amounts. Similarly, what if a price changes? You would also have to recalculate and reenter the sales tax for that item.

- It is better to allow Access to calculate the sales tax on each item. You can do this by adding a calculated field to a query or report. For example, in the following figure, a 7% sales tax field is calculated in Query Design view. Calculated fields in queries are covered in Exercise 22.

The sales tax is more appropriate as a calculated field in a query

Field:	Item #	Description	Price	Sales Tax: [Price]*0.07
Table:	Items	Items	Items	
Sort:				
Show:	☑	☑	☑	☑
Criteria:				
or:				

- If you had different levels of sales tax, you could set up a more complex query that pulled sales tax amounts from a Sales Tax table depending on the item.

Summarize Data by Adding a Total Row

- If you do not need to perform any operations on the calculation, but simply want to see it onscreen, one attractive option is to add a Total row to a table or query datasheet. You can see any of several common calculations at the bottom of a column, and you do not have to set up any calculations in queries or other objects.

- To turn on/off the Total row, while displaying the table datasheet, click the Totals button on the Home tab. The Total row appears below the last record.

- Then open the drop-down list for a particular field in the Total row and select the calculation you want to appear. Your choices are None, Sum, Average, Count, Maximum, Minimum, Standard Deviation, and Variance.

Decide What Data to Link

- Some data that you need to use in your database may be permanently housed somewhere else, such as in a spreadsheet on a co-worker's PC or on a server in some other database format.

- You must decide on a case-by-case basis whether data is better off being imported into your own Access database or linked from the original.

Display the Total row and select a calculation for a field

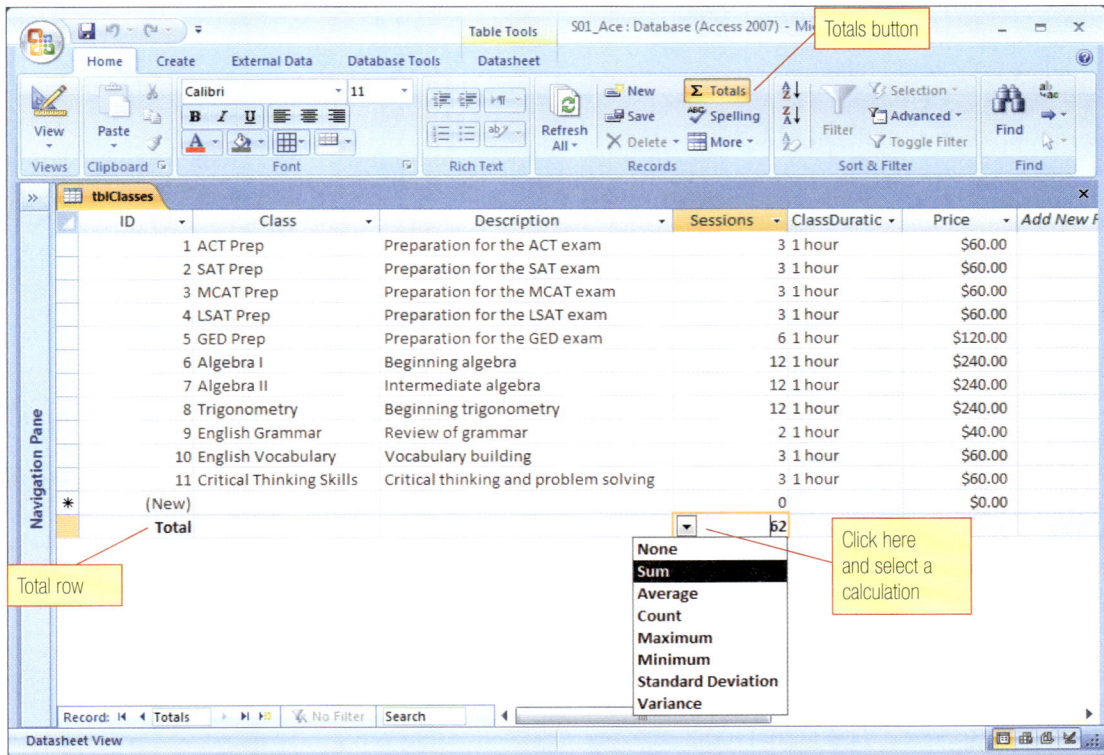

- If you import the data into Access, it loses its connection to the original. Any changes made to the original source will not be reflected in Access.

- If you link to the original source, changes will be reflected in Access as they are made in the original.

- Linking to a data source can slow the speed at which the database opens, closes, and is accessed, so you should not link to a data source unless 1) the data source is likely to change, and 2) you need those changes to be shown in Access.

- You will learn more about linking data in Exercise 4.

Identify Appropriate Field Types

- Choosing an appropriate type for each field can help reduce data entry errors and make the data easier to understand. For example:
  - Use logical (Yes/No) fields when the only possible values for the field are Yes/No, On/Off, or True/False.
  - Use a lookup (created with the Lookup Wizard) when there is a closed set of valid values for a field (such as Team A/Team B/Team C).
  - Use a Currency data type when a number represents currency, or use a regular Number data type and then choose the Currency format for it.
  - Use a Memo field type when you need a very large field size that may fluctuate greatly between records. Memo fields cannot be indexed and have some other limitations as well, so use Memo fields only when necessary.
  - Use a multivalue field when it is possible for a single record to have multiple values for a field. Multivalue fields are new to Access 2007; if you use multivalue fields, you will be unable to save the database to a previous Access version.

Normalize Table Structure

- A database is said to be **normalized** if it follows certain structural rules for avoiding repeated and redundant data.

- Normalization addresses problems such as:
  - Logical inconsistencies from the same information appearing differently in multiple records (such as a customer's address being different in two different orders).
  - Deletion of important data that should be retained when all records of a certain type are deleted (such as tax ID information about an instructor being removed if he is no longer actively teaching).

- Database designers rely on three main criteria for determining a table's degree of vulnerability to logical inconsistencies and abnormalities: **1NF (First Normal Form)**, **2NF (Second Normal Form)**, and **3NF (Third Normal Form)**.

- A table is in 1NF if it does not allow duplicate rows or null values. A table with a unique **primary key** or **composite key** (which by definition prevents two records from being complete duplicates of one another) and without any null values is in 1NF.

- A table is in 2NF if it is in 1NF and if all of the other fields are fully dependent on the primary key.
  - For example, suppose you have a table with the following fields: Employee ID, Employee Name, Employee Address, and Skill.

This table is not in 2NF

Employee ID	Employee Name	Employee Address	Skill
1	Bob Smith	123 Main Street	Typing
1	Bob Smith	123 Main Street	Filing
2	Sharon Jones	370 East Warren	Typing
2	Sharon Jones	370 East Warren	Spreadsheets

  - The combination of Employee ID and Skill is the composite key (that is, each record has a unique combination of those two values, but individual records might have the same value as one or the other of those fields).
  - This table is NOT in 2NF because there is the possibility for the same employee ID to have two different addresses in this table, which would be in error.
  - To normalize this table, you would need to create two separate tables: one with Employee ID and Skill in it, and another with Employee ID, Employee Name, and Employee Address in it.

Splitting the information into two tables puts it in 2NF

Employee ID	Employee Name	Employee Address
1	Bob Smith	123 Main Street
2	Sharon Jones	370 East Warren

Employee ID	Skill
1	Typing
1	Filing
2	Typing
2	Spreadsheets

- A table is in 3NF if it is in 2NF and if every field is directly dependent on the primary or composite key fields, not just indirectly dependent.
  - For example, suppose you want to keep track of departments and their managers. Each department has only one manager, and each manager has only one department.
  - You have a Departments table with these fields: Department, Manager, and Hire Date.

This table is not in 3NF

Department	Manager	Hire Date
Sales	Bruce Duncan	12/7/2007
Operations	Jan Roth	5/15/2008
Accounting	Judy Braswell	8/1/2005
Marketing	Riley O'Malley	2/16/2002

  - The Department field is the primary key. The Hire Date is only indirectly related to the Department field. It is directly related to the Manager field. The manager's hire date is irrelevant to the department.
  - In this example, the manager's hire date and the department name should not be in the same table. You should have separate tables for Managers and Departments.

Splitting the information into two tables puts it in 3NF

Department	Manager
Sales	Bruce Duncan
Operations	Jan Roth
Accounting	Judy Braswell
Marketing	Riley O'Malley

Manager	Hire Date
Bruce Duncan	12/7/2007
Jan Roth	5/15/2008
Judy Braswell	8/1/2005
Riley O'Malley	2/16/2002

- Whenever possible, you should try to use ID numbers for primary keys rather than text, even if it means adding another field to the table. It is much easier to make typos when typing text, so relying on the accuracy of text-based fields to be the primary key can be risky.
- The Managers and Departments tables can further be improved by adding Department and Manager ID fields.

Use ID fields for the primary key whenever possible

Department ID	Department	Manager
D01	Sales	M01
D02	Operations	M02
D03	Accounting	M03
D04	Marketing	M04

Manager ID	Manager	Hire Date
M01	Bruce Duncan	12/7/2007
M02	Jan Roth	5/15/2008
M03	Judy Braswell	8/1/2005
M04	Riley O'Malley	2/16/2002

A Normalization Example

- Now let's take a look at an example, to further reinforce the concepts you just learned.
- The example table at the bottom of this page is not normalized.
- This table could be problematic to use in the following ways:
  - What if a position is described differently for the same person? For example, what if Edith's title is entered as Executive Secretary in some records?
  - What if a person gets promoted into another position?
  - What if there are data entry errors because of the unnecessary retyping of certain data, such as entries in the Position, Dept. Name, and Training fields?
  - What if an employee quits and you delete his entries, but he was the only person to have taken a particular training class? Does that class's information get deleted from the system entirely?

Example table

Employee ID	First	Last	Position	Dept. ID	Dept. Name	Training	Date
1	John	Bell	Accountant	D1	Accounting	Orientation	4/15/09
1	John	Bell	Accountant	D1	Accounting	Time Cards	4/16/09
1	John	Bell	Accountant	D1	Accounting	Supervision	4/20/09
2	Edith	O'Reilly	Secretary	D2	Operations	Orientation	6/1/10
2	Edith	O'Reilly	Secretary	D2	Operations	Time Cards	6/2/10

- To normalize the table to 3NF, it needs to be split up into four separate tables, as shown below. The primary key fields are shown in italics here. Notice that the Training Completed table has a composite key consisting of a unique combination of Class ID and Employee ID.

Employees
Employee ID
First
Last
Position
Department

Departments
Department ID
Department Name

Training Completed
Class ID
Employee ID
Date

Training Classes
Class ID
Class Name

- You would then need to create relationships between the tables, as in the following illustration:

Employees
Employee ID
First
Last
Position
Department

Departments
Department ID
Department Name

Training Completed
Class ID
Employee ID
Date

Training Classes
Class ID
Class Name

Split a Table Using the Table Analyzer

- The Table Analyzer offers a point-and-click interface that looks for normalization problems in your tables. If you are having trouble seeing the normalization issues intuitively, you may find this tool helpful.

- The Table Analyzer works by looking at the table to identify repeated data, which could indicate 1NF or 2NF issues, and splitting the table to solve the problem. It creates new tables; the original is left alone. You can then delete the original if desired.

- To use the Table Analyzer, click Analyze Table on the Database Tools tab, and then work through the wizard step-by-step, reading the information that appears.

- The first two screens are for information only. You can click the links to see examples if desired; otherwise just click Next to move through them.

- Then you are asked to select the table to analyze. Make your selection and click Next.

Select the table to analyze

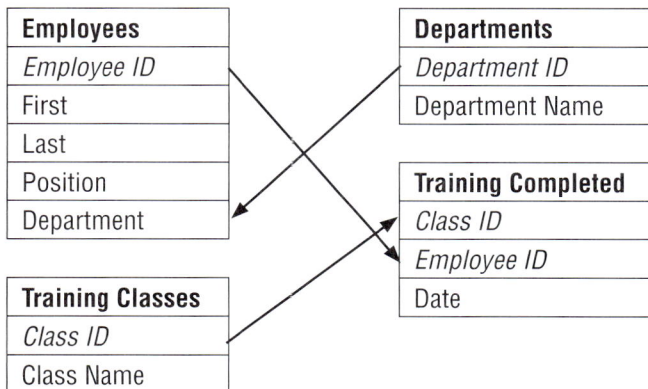

- Next, you are asked whether you want the wizard to decide which fields go in which tables. This is usually a good idea, unless you are very comfortable with your understanding of normalization rules and want a specific result.

- The wizard will then show you a diagram of the groupings it proposes. You can accept its groupings, or you can drag-and-drop fields to move them around. You can also edit the table names. The default table names are generic (Table1, Table2, and so on).

Modify the field groupings if desired, and name the tables

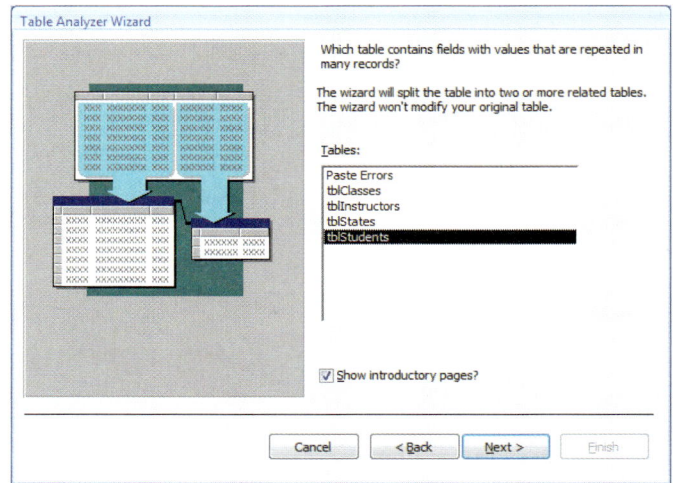

- Next, it asks whether the bold fields uniquely identify each record. You can set the primary key for each table if they are not correct.

- Finally, the wizard asks if you want to create a query that looks like the original table.

- If you choose not to let the wizard decide which fields go where, it presents you with a single table, and you must split them out into other tables on your own.

Copy a Table

- When you need additional tables that are very similar in structure to an existing one, you can save yourself some time by copying the existing table and then making any changes to it that are needed.

- To copy a table, first close it. Then from the navigation pane, select it and press Ctrl+C, or right-click it and choose Copy from the shortcut menu. Then press Ctrl+V to paste it, or right-click a blank area and choose Paste.

- You have a choice of pasting the structure only, pasting the structure and data, or appending the data to an existing table.

Paste Table As dialog box

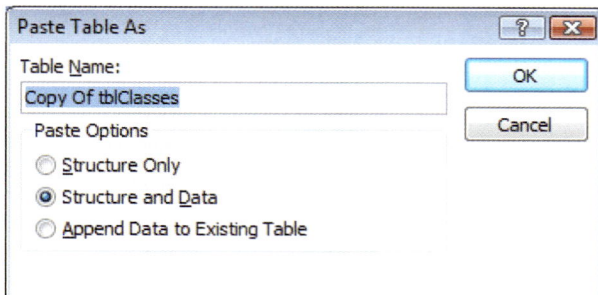

Delete a Table

- You might want to delete a table if the situation changes such that the data it contains is no longer useful, or if you realize you made a mistake in creating it.

- To delete a table, first close it. Then from the navigation pane, right-click the table and choose Delete, or select it and then press the Delete key on the keyboard. If prompted to confirm, click Yes.

- WARNING: Deleting a table permanently deletes all the data in it.

Rename a Table

- As you fine-tune your database's table designs, you may decide that you need to rename a certain table. To do so, first make sure the table is closed. Then right-click it in the Navigation Pane, click Rename, and type the new name.

- When you rename a table, all instances of that table name are automatically changed (for example, in relationships, and in queries, forms, and reports). However, any labels within those objects that reported the table's name do not change. For example, if the report's title had the old name in it, the old name will continue to appear until you manually edit it in Design view.

Renaming a table

PROCEDURES

Split a Table Using the Table Analyzer

1. Click **Database Tools** tab . . . . `Alt`+`A`

   Analyze Group

2. Click **Analyze Table** button

   `🖳 Analyze Table` . . . . `B`

   ✓ *The Table Analyzer Wizard runs.*

3. Read the information and click **Next** . . . . `Alt`+`N`

4. Read more information and click **Next** . . . . `Alt`+`N`

5. Select the table to analyze.

6. Click **Next** . . . . `Enter`

7. Click **Yes, let the wizard decide** . . . . `Alt`+`Y`

8. Drag fields among the suggested tables as needed.

9. Rename each table by doing the following:

   a. Double-click the generic name (Table1, for example).

   b. Type the new name.

   c. Click **OK** . . . . `Enter`

10. Click **Next** . . . . `Alt`+`N`

11. If the primary keys are not correct in one or more tables:

    a. Click the field that should be the primary key.

    b. Click the **Primary Key** button

       `🔑` .

    ✓ *The ScreenTip for the Primary Key button is Set Unique Identifier.*

12. Click **Next** . . . . `Alt`+`N`

    ✓ *If similar values are identified in one or more fields, a Correcting Typographical Errors screen appears.*

13. If prompted to correct typographical errors:

    a. Scan the list of possible errors.

    b. If any should change, open the **Correction** drop-down list and select record to copy from.

    c. When finished, click **Next** . . . . `Alt`+`N`

    ✓ *Next, you can create a query that duplicates the old version of the table if desired.*

14. Click **Yes, create the query** . . . . `Alt`+`Y`

    OR

    Click **No, don't create the query** . . . . `Alt`+`O`

15. Click **Finish** . . . . `Alt`+`F`

Copy a Table

1. Click table in navigation pane.

2. Press `Ctrl`+`C`.

   ✓ *You can right-click the table and choose Copy instead of steps 1–2 if desired.*

3. Press `Ctrl`+`V`.

4. In the **Table Name** box, edit the name if desired.

5. Click a paste option:

   - **Structure Only** . . . . . . `Alt`+`S`
   - **Structure and Data** . . `Alt`+`D`
   - **Append Data to Existing Table** . . . . `Alt`+`A`

6. Click **OK** . . . . `Enter`

Delete a Table

1. Right-click table in navigation pane.

2. Click **Delete** . . . . `L`, `L`, `Enter`

3. Click **Yes** . . . . `Alt`+`Y`

   OR

1. Click table in navigation pane.

2. Press `Delete`.

3. Click **Yes** . . . . `Alt`+`Y`

Rename a Table

1. Right-click table in navigation pane.

2. Click **Rename.**

3. Type the new name.

4. Press `Enter`.

   OR

1. Click the table in navigation pane.

2. Press `F2`.

3. Type the new name.

4. Press `Enter`.

EXERCISE DIRECTIONS

1. Start Access, if necessary.

2. Open 🔵 **01ACE** and save a copy of it as **01ACE_xx**.

3. Split tblClasses into two tables manually by doing the following:

   a. Copy tblClasses (structure and data) and name the copy **tblClassOfferings**.

   b. Open tblClassOfferings in Design view.

   c. Change the primary key field to Session.

   d. Delete the following fields. If prompted to delete one or more indexes, choose Yes.

      ClassName

      Description

      NumberOfSessions

      ClassDuration

      Price

   e. Move the Session field to the top of the list of fields in tblClassOfferings.

   f. Change the field type of the ClassID field to Number.

   g. Change the caption for the ClassID field to Class.

   h. Switch to Datasheet view, saving your design changes.

   i. Change the class values as follows, and then close the datasheet:

Session	Class
111	**1**
112	**2**
113	**3**
114	**4**
115	**5**
116	**6**
117	**7**
118	**8**
119	**9**
120	**10**
121	**11**

   j. Open tblClasses in Datasheet view and delete records with IDs 13 through 23.

   k. Switch to Design view and delete the following fields:

      Session

      SizeLimit

      Instructor

      StartDate

      StartTime

4. Split tblStudents using the Table Analyzer tool:

   a. Start the Table Analyzer, click Next twice to move through the descriptive text, and then select tblStudents and click Next.

   b. Click Yes, let the wizard decide. The Wizard proposes four tables.

   c. Drag the bottom borders of each table window down so you can see all the fields in each one.

   d. Drag the City and State fields from Table4 to the bottom of Table2.

   e. Drag the ZIP field from Table3 to the bottom of Table2. There should now be two tables, as shown in Illustration A.

   f. Double-click Table1, and change the name to **tblEnrollment**.

   g. Double-click Table2, and change the name to **tblStudentContactInfo**.

   h. Click Next to move on. When asked about the primary key fields, leave them as-is for now and click Next.

   i. Click Next to skip correcting typographical errors.

   j. Click Yes, create the query.

   k. Click Finish.

5. Close the tblStudents query, which is open in Datasheet view.

6. Delete tblStudents_OLD, which is the original table that Access renamed.

7. Open tblStudentContactInfo in Design view and move the ID field up to the top of the field list. Then close it, saving your changes.

8. Open tblEnrollment in Design view and do the following to clean it up:

   a. Remove the primary key from the ID field and delete that field.

   b. Rename the tblStudentContactInfo_ID field to **StudentID**. In the Caption property for that field, change the caption to Student ID.

   c. Move the StudentID field to the top of the list.

   d. On the Lookup tab of the StudentID field's properties, change the Display Control setting to Text Box.

   e. Make both fields a composite key (that is, make them both primary key fields).

   ✓ *Hint: To do this, select both fields and then click the Primary Key button on the ribbon.*

9. Close the table, saving your changes.

10. Delete the tblStudents query.

11. Exit Access.

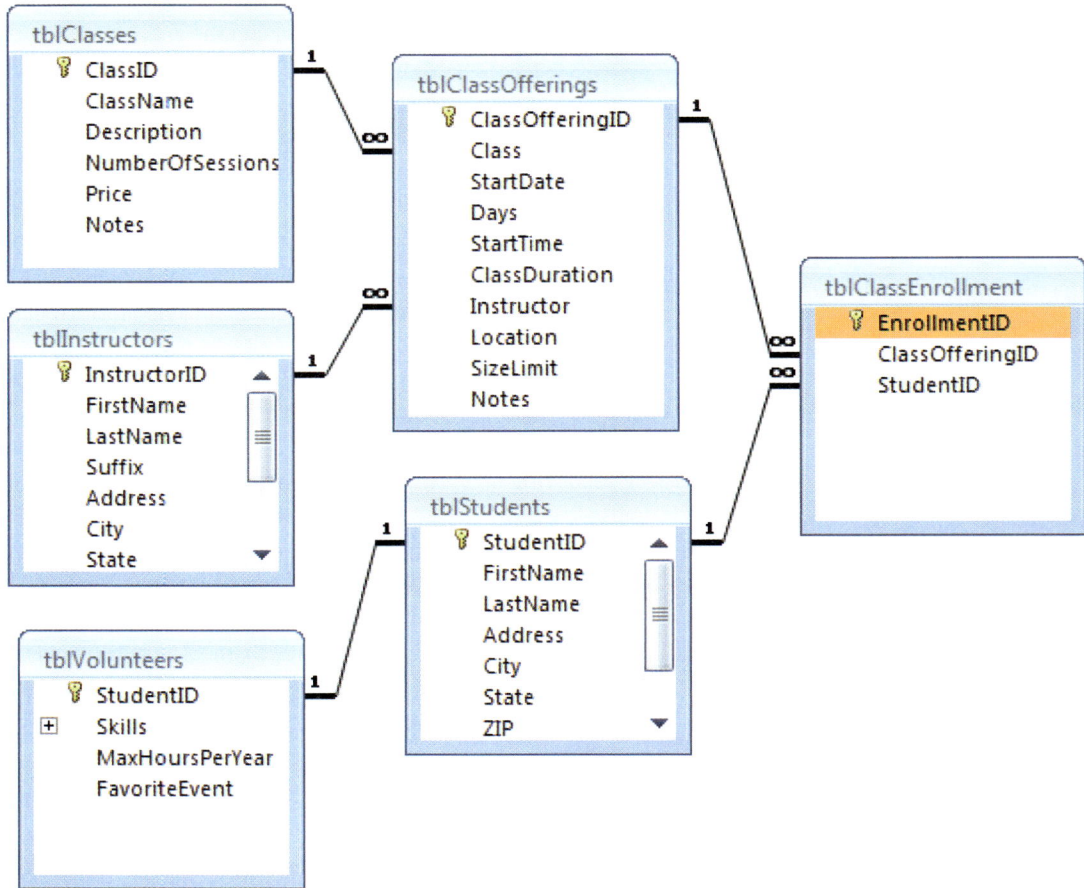

ON YOUR OWN

You have been asked to create a database for Sycamore Knoll, a small bed and breakfast. The owners wish to store the following types of information:

- Guest contact information
- Information about each of the five guest rooms
- Booking data showing which guest has booked which room for which night

1. Using a paper and pencil, design the tables and fields you will need for this database. Make sure the table structures are fully normalized to 3NF. Make sure each table has a primary key or a composite key.

2. Start Access and create the tables needed for this database in a new database file. Name the file **OAC01_xx**.

3. Save your changes, and exit Access.

Business Connection

Personal Characteristics

Personal characteristics are the attributes that define your personality and make you unique. They affect the way you react to different situations and people, and the way other people react to you. Your personal characteristics also impact your success at work. Employers appreciate employees who exhibit positive characteristics, such as a positive attitude, friendliness, an ability to compromise, leadership skills, responsibility, and an ethical nature. They do not appreciate laziness, greed, dishonesty, or a negative attitude. Identifying your own personal characteristics can help you achieve a positive relationship with your employer and co-workers.

Catalog Characteristics

Create a database of personal characteristics. Include fields for whether the characteristic is positive or negative, a description of the characteristic, and how the characteristic affects a person. You might even provide a field for someone who exhibits the characteristic, such as George Washington for Leadership. When the database is complete, create queries for positive and negative characteristics.

Skills Covered

- **Create a One-to-Many Relationship**
- **Enforce Referential Integrity**
- **Create a One-to-One Relationship**
- **Print a Relationship Report**
- **Work with Join Types**

Software Skills   Normalizing a database, as you learned in the previous exercise, often requires splitting tables. To ensure that the data is connected when it exists in different tables, you must create relationships between those tables.

Application Skills   Ace Learning likes the table structure you proposed in Exercise 1 and has only minor changes to the tables. They would now like your help in creating relationships between the tables.

TERMS

Cascade delete   A feature that automatically deletes the matching records in a related table when a record in the original table is deleted.

Cascade update   A feature that automatically updates the value in a related table when a value in the original table changes.

Inner join   A join that includes only records that have corresponding matches in a related table.

One-to-many relationship   A relationship between the primary key in one table and the equivalent non–primary-key field in another table.

One-to-one relationship   A relationship between the primary key fields in two tables, or between fields that contain unique values for each record.

Outer join   A join that includes all the records in one table, but only the records in a related table that have a corresponding record in the original table.

Referential integrity   An assurance that data in one table matches up with valid data in the related table.

NOTES

Create a One-to-Many Relationship

- Most of the relationships in a database are **one-to-many**. On the "one" side is the primary key field of one of the tables. Each record has a unique value for this field. On the "many" side is a non–primary-key, non-unique field in another table.

- For example, in a veterinary practice, a single owner might have multiple pets. If you have an Owners table and a Pets table, both might contain an OwnerID field. In the Owners table, each record has a unique value for OwnerID. That is the "one" side. In the Pets table, many records can have the same value for the OwnerID field. That is the "many" side.

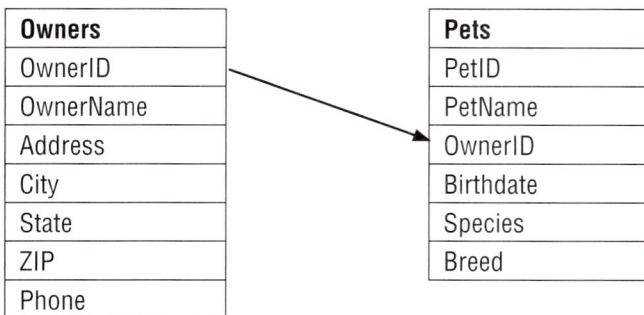

Owners		Pets
OwnerID		PetID
OwnerName		PetName
Address		OwnerID
City		Birthdate
State		Species
ZIP		Breed
Phone		

- To create a one-to-many relationship, open the Relationships window and drag the primary key from the "one" table to the corresponding non–primary-key field in the "many" table.

Enforce Referential Integrity

- When you create a relationship, you have the option of enforcing **referential integrity**. If you do, Access will make sure that there are no entries in the table that is serving as the "many" side that do not have a valid corresponding entry on the "one" side. For example, it will not let you enter an OwnerID in the Pets table that is not a match to a valid OwnerID from the Owners table. This is useful in preventing data entry errors and avoiding orphaned records.

- Two options are available if you enforce referential integrity: **cascade update** and **cascade delete**.

- Cascade update automatically changes the entries on the "many" side if the data changes on the "one" side. For example, if you change the OwnerID for a particular person in the Owner's table, the OwnerID for all the pets that person owns will be automatically updated in the Pets table.

- Cascade delete automatically deletes records from the table on the "many" side if the record is deleted in the table on the "one" side. For example, if you delete one of the records from the Owners table, the records for all of that owner's pets will automatically be deleted from the Pets table.

Create a One-to-One Relationship

- In a **one-to-one relationship**, the primary keys in two tables are joined to one another. The overall effect is that you have two tables that are part of a single logical unit.

- In a one-to-one relationship situation, logically it makes just as much sense to have all the fields in a single table. There is no normalization reason to split them.

- For practical reasons, however, you might want some fields split out into a separate table. For example, if some fields are not commonly used, or used only for certain projects, you might prefer to store them in a separate table. When you need to include those fields, you can run a query that joins the field lists from the two tables into a single datasheet.

- Suppose, for example, that some employees are also volunteers at a United Way charity event that is sponsored by your company. You might put information about volunteering in a separate table from the Employees table, with a one-to-one relationship between the EmployeeID fields in the two tables.

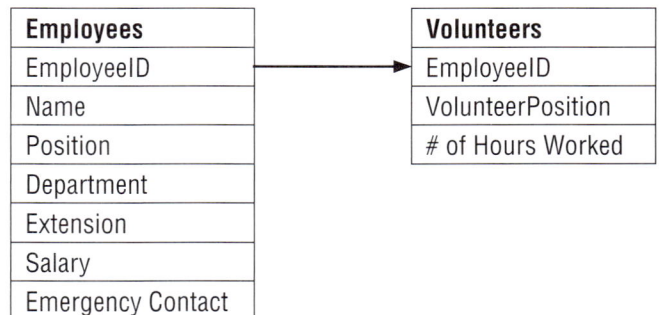

Employees		Volunteers
EmployeeID		EmployeeID
Name		VolunteerPosition
Position		# of Hours Worked
Department		
Extension		
Salary		
Emergency Contact		

Print a Relationship Report

■ You may sometimes find it useful to print a report that shows the relationships of all tables in your database. To do this, use the Relationship Report button (on the Relationship Tools Design tab when the Relationships window is open).

■ Clicking the Relationship Report button generates a report that shows the relationships very much as they appear in the Relationships window. You can click Print to print the report or modify it in any of the ways you would modify any other report (such as setting margins, page headers/footers, and so on).

Work with Join Types

■ When you create queries that pull fields from multiple related tables, join type becomes important. Join type determines which records will be included when compiling a list of records by pulling information from both tables.

■ For example, you might want to allow entries in the Volunteers table only for employees who have a valid corresponding record in the Employees table.

■ If you create a one-to-one relationship between the primary key fields in each table (EmployeeID in each table), and you enforce referential integrity, you have a choice of join types:

  • You can force each table to contain only records for which there is a corresponding record in the other table. This is called an **inner join**.

  • You can allow the Volunteers table to contain records for which there is no match in the Employees table, but not vice-versa. This is called an **outer join**.

  • You can allow the Employees table to contain records for which there is no match in the Volunteers table, but not vice-versa. (This is the one we want for our example, since not all employees are volunteers, but all volunteers are employees.) This is also an outer join.

■ You can set a join type in the Relationships window, which will apply to all queries created based on the affected tables, or you can set a join type on-the-fly in Query Design view for a specific query.

Choose a Join Type in the Relationships Window

■ To select a join type from the Relationships window, first display the Relationships window from the Database Tools tab.

■ Double-click the relationship line between the two tables. (Create the relationship first if it does not already exist.) Then click the Join Type button, and then the desired join type.

Select a join type from the Relationships window

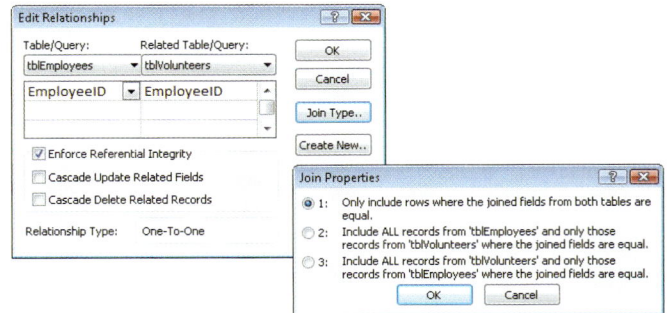

Choose a Join Type in Query Design View

■ You can also select the join type from Query Design view. The setting applies only to that query.

■ First, add the tables to the query design if needed. If no relationship exists yet between the desired fields, drag to create it. If a relationship is created within Query Design view, it is not called a relationship; it is called a join. It applies only to this query.

■ Then double-click the relationship line to display the Join Properties dialog box. You can then specify the join type you want in that dialog box.

Select a join type from Query Design view

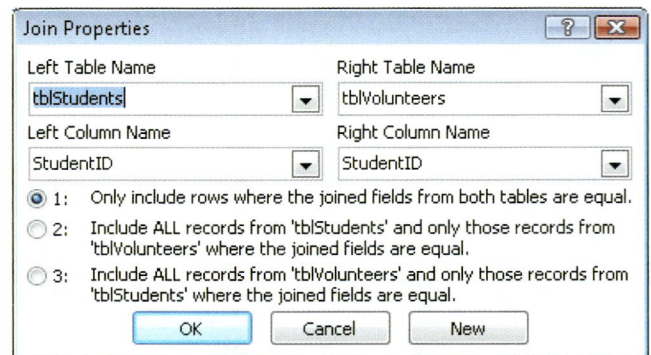

PROCEDURES

Display the Relationships Window

1. Click **Database Tools**
   tab . . . . `Alt`+`A`

   ### Show/Hide Group

2. Click **Relationships** button
   Relationships . . . . `E`

   ✓ *The Relationships window opens. If there are no tables in the layout yet, the Show Table dialog box appears.*

3. If the Show Table dialog box appears, do one of the following:
   - To add tables to the layout, see the following procedure (starting with step 2).
   - To *not* add tables now, click **Close** . . . . `Alt`+`C`

Add More Tables to the Relationships Window Layout

In the Relationships window:

Relationships Group

1. Click **Show Table**
   button . . . . `S`, `T`
2. Add any tables to the layout as needed:
   a. Click table you want to include.
   b. Click **Add** . . . . `Alt`+`A`
   c. Repeat steps a and b to add other tables as needed.
3. Click **Close** . . . . `Alt`+`C`

Remove a Table from the Relationships Window Layout

In the Relationships window:
1. Click the title bar of the table.
2. Press `Delete`.

Close the Relationships Window

- Click the **Close** button `Close` on the Relationship Tools Design tab.

Create a Relationship

In the Relationships window:

1. Drag from a field in one table to the equivalent field in another table:
   - For a one-to-many relationship, drag from the primary key field in one table to a non–primary-key field in another table that contains the same information.
   - For a one-to-one relationship, drag from the primary key field in one table (or a field that contains unique values) to the primary key field (or again, a field that contains unique values) in another table that contains the same information.

   ✓ *The Edit Relationships dialog box opens.*

2. (Optional) To enforce referential integrity:
   a. Click **Enforce Referential Integrity** . . . . `Alt`+`E`
   b. (Optional) Click **Cascade Update Related Fields** . . . . `Alt`+`U`
   c. (Optional) Click **Cascade Delete Related Records** . . . . `Alt`+`D`

3. (Optional) To change the join type:
   a. Click **Join Type** . . . . . `Alt`+`J`
   b. Click one of the join options:
      - **Only include rows where the joined fields from both tables are equal** . . . . `Alt`+`1`
      - **Include ALL records from '(first table)' and only those records from '(second table)' where the joined fields are equal** . . . . `Alt`+`2`
      - **Include ALL records from '(second table)' and only those records from '(first table)' where the joined fields are equal** . . . . `Alt`+`3`
   c. Click **OK** . . . . `Enter`

4. Click **Create** . . . . `Alt`+`C`

Edit a Relationship

In the Relationships window:

1. Double-click the relationship line between two tables.

   ✓ *The Edit Relationships dialog box opens.*

2. Mark or clear the **Enforce Referential Integrity** check box . . . . `Alt`+`E`

3. If Enforce Referential Integrity is marked:
   a. Mark or clear **Cascade Update Related Fields** . . . . `Alt`+`U`
   b. Mark or clear **Cascade Delete Related Records** . . . . `Alt`+`D`

4. (Optional) Change the join type:
   a. Click **Join Type** . . . . . `Alt`+`J`
   b. Click one of the join options:
      - **Only include rows where the joined fields from both tables are equal** . . . . `Alt`+`1`
      - **Include ALL records from '(first table)' and only those records from '(second table)' where the joined fields are equal** . . . . `Alt`+`2`
      - **Include ALL records from '(second table)' and only those records from '(first table)' where the joined fields are equal** . . . . `Alt`+`3`
   c. Click **OK** . . . . `Enter`

5. Click **OK** . . . . `Enter`

Delete a Relationship

In the Relationships window:

1. Click the relationship line between two tables.
2. Press [Delete].
3. Click **Yes** . . . . [Alt]+[Y]

Print a Relationship Report

In the Relationships window:

Tools Group

1. Click **Relationship Report** button

   Relationship Report . . . . [R]

   ✓ *The Print Preview tab displays.*

Print Group

2. Click **Print** button

   . . . . [Alt]+[P], [P], [D]
3. Click **OK** . . . . [Enter]

Create a Join in Query Design View

In Query Design view:

1. Drag from a field in one table to the matching field in another table.
2. Double-click the line between the two tables.

   ✓ *The Join Properties dialog box opens.*

3. Confirm that the table and field names are correct.
4. Select a join option:
   - **Only include rows where the joined fields from both tables are equal** . . . . [Alt]+[1]
   - **Include ALL records from '(first table)' and only those records from '(second table)' where the joined fields are equal** . . . . [Alt]+[@ / 2]

- **Include ALL records from '(second table)' and only those records from '(first table)' where the joined fields are equal** . . . . [Alt]+[# / 3]

5. Click **OK** . . . . [Enter]

Remove a Join in Query Design View

In Query Design view:

1. Click the line between the two tables to select it.
2. Press [Delete].

EXERCISE DIRECTIONS

1. Start Access, if necessary.
2. Open 💿 **02ACE** and save a copy of it as **02ACE_xx**.
3. Display the Relationships window, and add all of the tables except tblStates to the layout.
4. Create the following relationships. When you have finished, your relationships should look similar to those shown in Illustration A.

Between...	...and	Enforce Referential Integrity?	Cascade Update?	Cascade Delete?
InstructorID field in tblInstructors	Instructor field in tblClassOfferings	Yes	Yes	No
ClassID field in tblClasses	Class field in tblClassOfferings	Yes	Yes	Yes
ClassOfferingID field in tblClassOfferings	ClassOfferingID field in tblClassEnrollment	Yes	Yes	Yes
StudentID field in tblStudents	StudentID field in tblClassEnrollment	Yes	Yes	Yes
StudentID field in tblStudents	StudentID field in tblVolunteers	Yes	Yes	No

Illustration A

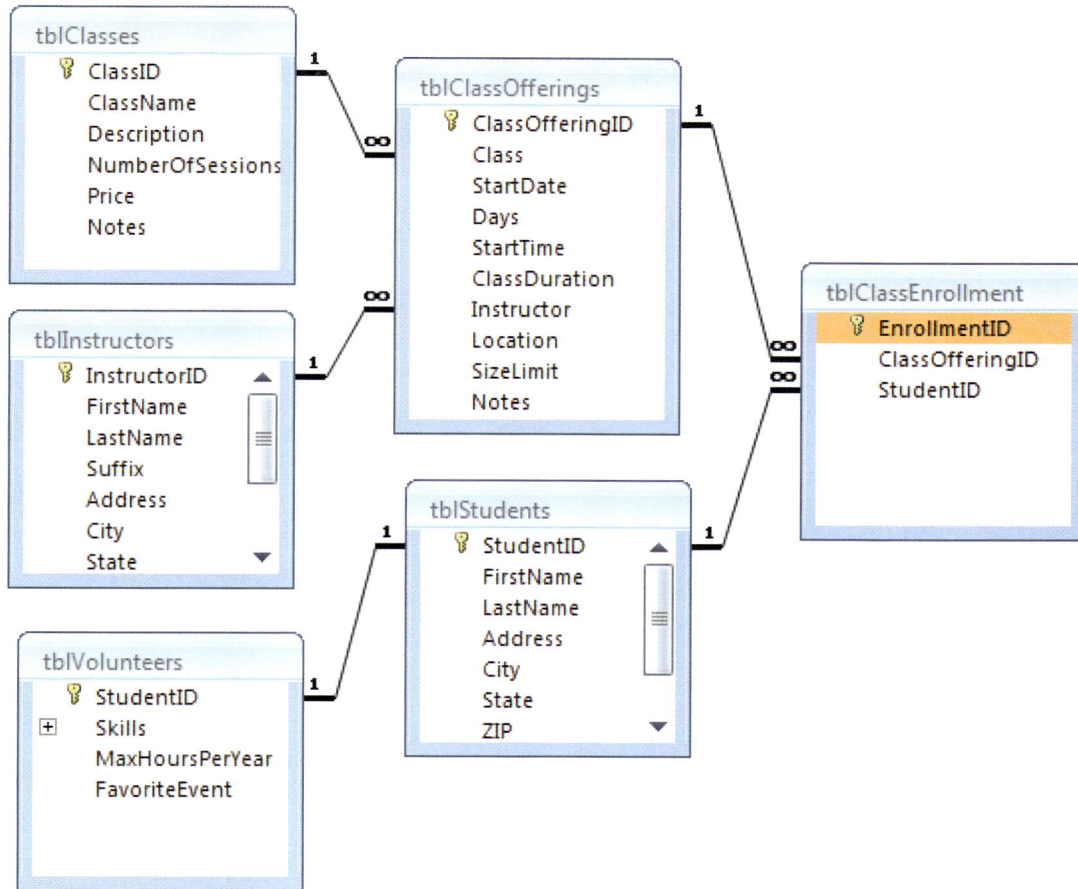

tblClasses
- 🔑 ClassID
- ClassName
- Description
- NumberOfSessions
- Price
- Notes

tblClassOfferings
- 🔑 ClassOfferingID
- Class
- StartDate
- Days
- StartTime
- ClassDuration
- Instructor
- Location
- SizeLimit
- Notes

tblInstructors
- 🔑 InstructorID
- FirstName
- LastName
- Suffix
- Address
- City
- State

tblClassEnrollment
- 🔑 EnrollmentID
- ClassOfferingID
- StudentID

tblStudents
- 🔑 StudentID
- FirstName
- LastName
- Address
- City
- State
- ZIP

tblVolunteers
- 🔑 StudentID
- ⊞ Skills
- MaxHoursPerYear
- FavoriteEvent

5. Close the Relationships window, saving changes to the layout.

6. Start a new query in *Query Design* view, and add tblStudents and tblVolunteers to it. To do this:
   a. On the Create tab, click Query Design.
   b. In the Show Table dialog box, double-click *tblStudents* and *tblVolunteers*.
   c. Click Close.

   ✓ *Notice that the relationship appears automatically because you set it up earlier.*

7. Edit the join type for the relationship so that only students who appear in tblVolunteers will appear in the query results.

8. Drag the following fields to the grid at the bottom of Query Design view:
   - From tblStudents: FirstName, LastName
   - From tblVolunteers: Skills, MaxHoursPerYear.

9. Run the query. The results should resemble Illustration B.

10. Save the query as **qryStudentVolunteers**.

11. Exit Access.

Illustration B

First	Last	Skills	MaxHoursPerYear
Marilyn	Feinberg	Manual labor, Peer support	20
Sherry	Addams	Manual labor, Office skills, Peer support	20
Simi	Anderson	Manual labor	10
Amy	Burrow	In-class assistance, Public relations	10

ON YOUR OWN

1. Start Access and open the ⊙ **02FOSTER** database. Save a copy of it as **OAC02_xx**. This database is for a dog rescue organization. These are the tables it contains:

   - **tblVolunteers:** Contact information for everyone who helps with the organization, including both people who foster dogs in their homes and people who have other duties.

   - **tblDogs:** Information about the dogs that are in foster homes, waiting to be adopted.

   - **tblFosterMatchups:** The assignments of dogs to foster homes.

   - **tblFosterHomes:** The information about the volunteers who foster dogs in their homes, including details about the foster home situation. All of the foster home providers are volunteers (in tblVolunteers), but not all volunteers are foster home providers.

2. In the Relationships window, establish appropriate relationships between the tables in this database. Enforce referential integrity wherever you think it may be useful in maintaining the database. Think about the following when deciding what settings to use:

   - What if a volunteer quits? Should their foster home information in tblFosterHomes be deleted? Should their matchups in tblFosterMatchups be deleted?

   - What if a dog gets adopted and therefore removed from tblDogs? Should their entry in tblFosterMatchups be deleted?

   - What if a volunteer's ID changes? Should that change be automatically made in tblFosterHomes and tblFosterMatchups as well?

3. Print the relationships using a Relationship Report (on the Design tab) and submit the report for grading.

4. Close the database and exit Access.

Skills Covered

- **Require an Entry and Allow Zero-Length Entries**
- **Index a Field**
- **Work with Memo Fields**
- **Create and Use Attachment Fields**
- **Work with Table Properties**

Software Skills After defining the table structures for your database and creating the relationships between them, you may want to tweak the internal properties of one or more tables, including setting up special field types such as Memo and Attachment and setting options for the table as a whole.

Application Skills The database you have been creating for Ace Learning still needs some work. Managers would like to be able to attach data files to the records in tblInstructors, and they would like to have memo fields in some of the tables where history is tracked.

TERMS

Allow Zero Length A property for a text, hyperlink, or memo field that enables that field to be non-blank but still contain zero characters.

Attachment field A field type that enables the user to insert and store data files from other programs in the database. The attachments can then be saved to disk outside the database whenever needed, or opened in their native applications.

Index A feature of Access that allows you to speed up searches and sorts and can require that a field contain unique values for each record.

Required A property for a field (except AutoNumber type) that, when set to Yes, forces the user to make an entry in the field for each record.

Rich text formatting A widely accepted type of text formatting that includes font, font size, font color, attributes such as bold and italics, and indentation.

NOTES

Require an Entry and Allow Zero-Length Entries

- Two field properties determine whether or not a field must contain data: **Required** and **Allow Zero Length**. They are different in these ways:
  - Required can be set for all field types except AutoNumber (because AutoNumber is by definition a required field). This property is set to No by default. If you set Yes for the Required property and then try to save a record that contains no entry for that field, an error message appears.
  - Allow Zero Length is set specifically for text, hyperlink, or memo fields. This property allows you to enter an empty text string—that is, a text string that is zero characters in length, to indicate that the field does not apply to that record, such as a middle initial entry for someone who has no middle initial.
- Access allows these two field properties to be set independently, so the possibility exists for having a field that is required and yet that allows zero length. If both of those conditions exist, Access stores a zero-length text string instead of a null value in the field when you leave it blank.

Set the Required and Allow Zero Length properties for a field

General	Lookup	
Field Size	50	
Format		
Input Mask		
Caption		
Default Value		
Validation Rule		
Validation Text		
Required	No	
Allow Zero Length	Yes	
Indexed	No	
Unicode Compression	Yes	
IME Mode	No Control	
IME Sentence Mode	None	
Smart Tags		

Index a Field

- An **index** makes searching, sorting, and grouping go faster. The speed improves when you use the Find and Sort commands in tables, queries, and forms; the sort and criteria rows in queries; and the sorting and grouping options in reports.
- A minor drawback of indexing comes when you add or delete records. If you are adding one record at a time, you won't see a difference. However, appending many records at once may take longer if you have many indexes.
- When you create a primary key, the field is automatically indexed. You can index other fields by changing the Indexed property of the field to Yes (No Duplicates) or Yes (Duplicates OK).
- Index as many fields as you need, but you cannot index memo, OLE object, attachment, or hyperlink fields.
- To see a list of all indexes, click the Indexes button on the Table Tools Design tab in Table Design view.

Indexes window

Indexes: tblInstructors

	Index Name	Field Name	Sort Order
	PrimaryKey	InstructorID	Ascending
	ZIP	ZIP	Ascending

Index Properties

Primary	No	
Unique	No	The name for this index. Each index can use up to 10 fields.
Ignore Nulls	No	

- Each index has a name, a field (or fields) that makes up the index, a sort order, and three properties:
  - Primary: This identifies which index is the primary key. You can set this by assigning a primary key in Table Design view. Only one index can be the primary index.
  - Unique: When you set the Indexed property to Yes (No Duplicates), this property changes to Yes.
  - Ignore Nulls: If you expect to have lots of blanks, change this to Yes to exclude null values from the index and speed up the searches.

Work with Memo Fields

- On the surface, a memo field might appear to be simply a text field with a larger size limit. A memo field can contain up to 65,536 characters (whereas a Text field is limited to 255 characters).

- However, the Memo field type has some other differences as well. For example, you can't index on a memo field.

- New in Access 2007, you can apply **rich text formatting** to the text in a memo field. For example, you can make certain text bold or underlined, and you can apply different fonts and colors.

- To apply rich text formatting to text in a memo field, you must first set the Text Format property for that field to Rich Text. By default it is Plain Text.

  ✓ *The Font group and Rich Text group on the Home tab contain buttons for formatting text. If you apply formatting to text in a field that has a type other than Memo, or if you have not yet set the Text Format property for that memo field to Rich Text, the formatting applies to the entire datasheet.*

Properties for a memo field include Text Format and Append Only

General	Lookup	
Caption		
Default Value		
Validation Rule		
Validation Text		
Required	No	
Allow Zero Length	Yes	
Indexed	No	
Unicode Compression	Yes	
IME Mode	No Control	
IME Sentence Mode	None	
Smart Tags		
Text Format	Rich Text	
Text Align	General	
Append Only	No	

- Another feature of the Memo field type is the ability to set a memo field to Append Only. This is one of the field's properties; when it is set to Yes, history will be collected on this field. This enables the memo field to be used for ongoing note-taking for records, without worrying that an untrained or careless worker will accidentally delete something that should be retained.

- The property name "Append Only" is somewhat misleading, in that the property does not prevent you from deleting or changing the content of the field. Instead, it makes a Show column history command available for that field when you right-click the field. When you choose that command, a History dialog box opens that contains the versions of the field's content over time.

View the History for a memo field when it is set to Append Only

History for Notes	
History of changes for:	
Column name: Notes	
Table name: tblStudents	

[Version: 7/1/2008 11:31:14 AM] Nominated for Student of the Year   12/1/08 Dean's List

OK

- If you want to clear the history for the field, you must set Append Only to No in the field properties in Table Design view, and then save the table. This clears the history from all records. You can then reset Append Only to Yes if desired.

Create and Use Attachment Fields

- **Attachment fields** are new in Access 2007. You can attach data files from word processing programs, spreadsheets, graphics editing programs, and so on. Attachments cannot be edited directly from within Access; the native application launches to edit them.

- Create an attachment field in Table Design view by setting the field type to Attachment. You cannot change a field's type to Attachment; you can only select the Attachment type when you first create the field.

- When you double-click the paper clip icon for an attachment field in a datasheet or form, the Attachments dialog box opens. From here you can:

  - Click Add to select a file to add as an attachment.

  - Click an attachment and click Remove to detach the attachment from the record.

  - Click Open to open the selected attachment in its native program.

  - Click Save As to save the attachment file as a separate file to your hard disk.

  - Click Save All to save all the attachment files as separate files to your hard disk.

Manage a record's attachments in the Attachments dialog box

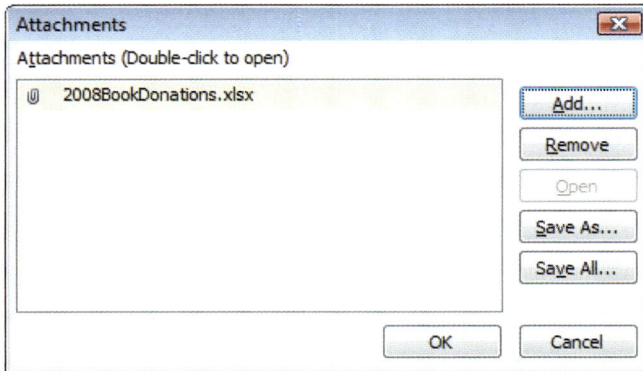

Work with Table Properties

- Just as each field in a table has field properties, the table itself has table properties. These apply to the entire table.

- To display the Property Sheet for the table, open the table in Design view and then click the Property Sheet button on the Table Tools Design tab.

- Here are the properties you can set for a table:

  - Display Views on SharePoint Site: Specifies whether views that are based on the table can be displayed on a SharePoint site.

- Subdatasheet Expanded: Specifies whether or not any subdatasheets appear expanded by default when the table opens. If the subdatasheet is not expanded, a plus sign appears next to each record, and you can click that plus sign to manually expand the subdatasheet for a particular record.

Example of a subdatasheet

- Subdatasheet Height: If the subdatasheet is set to be expanded, this setting controls how large it will be.

- Orientation: Set the view orientation for left-to-right or right-to-left, depending on your language. (English is left-to-right.)

- Description: Text you enter here will appear in ToolTips for the table.

Display a table's Property Sheet

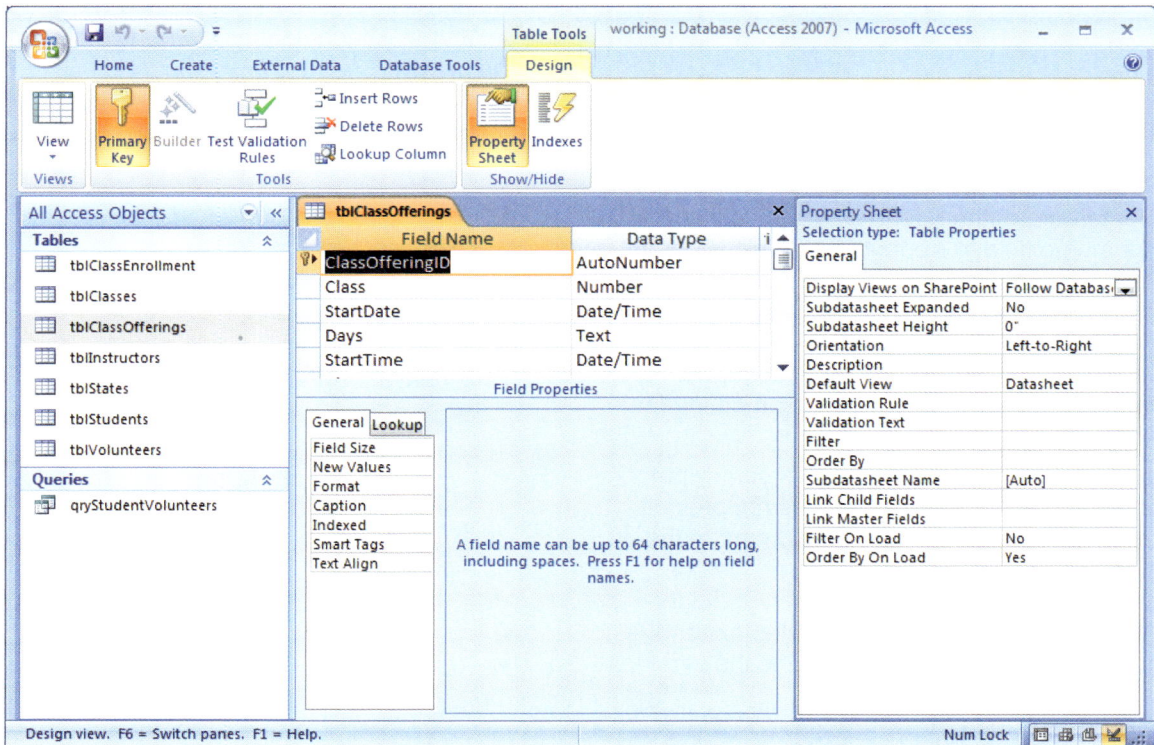

- Default View: Set Datasheet, PivotTable, or PivotChart as the default view when the table is opened.

- Validation Rule: You can enter an expression here that must be true whenever you add or change a record. You can also add validation rules to individual fields, of course; this box is mainly for multifield validation rules, such as for setting up conditions where one field's value must be greater than another's (for example, end time must come after start time).

- Validation Text: If you create a validation rule (see above), this specifies the message that is displayed when a record violates the rule.

- Filter: Here you can define criteria so that only rows matching the criteria will appear in the datasheet—like creating a query that filters records without actually creating the query.

- Order By: You can select one or more fields by which the data should be sorted by default.

- Subdatasheet Name: Here you can choose which subdatasheet should appear (if any). This is useful if the table has relationships with more than one other table and the wrong one is showing in the subdatasheet.

- Link Child Fields: This lists the fields in the table that are used for the subdatasheet that match the Link Master Fields property (see below).

- Link Master Fields: This lists the fields in the table that match the Link Child Fields property (see above).

- Filter On Load: If you defined criteria in the Filter field, you can set that criteria to be applied or not when the table opens. This is useful to temporarily turn the filtering off without erasing what you have put in the Filter field.

- Order By On Load: If you entered anything in the Order By field, you can turn it on or off here, so that the sort order is applied or not applied when the table opens.

- ■ To get more space to enter or edit a property, click in the property and press Shift + F2.

PROCEDURES

Set a Field's Required Property

1. Open the table to modify.
2. Click **Home** tab . . . . Alt + H

   Views Group

3. Click **View** button drop-down arrow View . . . . W
4. Click **Design view** . . . . D
5. Select field.
6. Click in **Required** property.
7. Click drop-down arrow and click **Yes**.

   OR

   Click **No**.

Set a Field's All Zero Length Property

In Table Design view:

1. Select field.
2. Click in **Allow Zero Length** property.
3. Click drop-down arrow and click **Yes**.

   OR

   Click **No**.

Set a Field's Index Property

In Table Design view:

1. Select field.
2. Click in **Indexed** property.
3. Click drop-down arrow and click **Yes (Duplicates OK)**.

   OR

   Click **Yes (No Duplicates)**.

View the Indexed Field List

In Table Design view:

   Show/Hide Group

1. Click **Indexes** Indexes .
2. View the indexes.
3. If desired, make changes to an index:
   a. Click row representing the index to change.
   b. Change the Primary, Unique, and/or Ignore Nulls values.
4. Close the Indexes window.

Set a Memo Field to Use Rich Text

In Table Design view:

1. Select field.
2. Click in **Text Format** property.
3. Click drop-down arrow and click **Rich Text**.

Enter Formatted Text in a Memo Field

In Datasheet view:

1. Type text in a memo field.
2. Select the text to be formatted.
3. Click button(s) on Home tab in Font and Rich Text groups to format text.

Set a Memo Field for Append Only

In Table Design view:

1. Select field.
2. Click in **Append Only** property.
3. Click drop-down arrow and click **Yes**.

View the History for an Append-Only Memo Field

In Datasheet view:

1. Right-click the field.
2. Click **Show column history** . . . H
3. Read history.
4. Click **OK**. . . . . Enter

Add an Attachment to a Record

In a datasheet or form:

1. Double-click the paperclip icon ⬀(0) in an attachment field.
2. Click **Add** . . . . Alt +A
3. Select the file to attach.
4. Click **Open** . . . . Alt +O
5. Click **OK**.

Detach an Attachment from a Record

In a datasheet or form:

1. Double-click the paperclip icon ⬀(1) in an attachment field.
2. Click the attachment.
3. Click **Remove** . . . . Alt +R
4. Click **OK**.

Open an Attachment

In a datasheet or form:

1. Double-click the paperclip icon ⬀(1) in an attachment field.
2. Click the attachment.
3. Click **Open** . . . . Alt +O
4. Edit the attachment in its native application.
5. Save your work and close the attachment.
6. In Attachments dialog box, click **OK**.
7. If prompted to save updates to the database, click **Yes** . . . . . Alt +Y

Save an Attachment Outside of Access

In a datasheet or form:

1. Double-click the paperclip icon ⬀(1) in an attachment field.
2. Click the attachment.
3. Click **Save As** . . . . Alt +S
4. Navigate to the location in which to save.
5. Click **Save** . . . . Alt +S
6. In Attachments dialog box, click **OK**.

Save All Attachments

In a datasheet or form:

1. Double-click the paperclip icon ⬀(1) in an attachment field.
2. Click the attachment.
3. Click **Save All** . . . . Alt +V
4. Navigate to the location in which to save.
5. Click **Select** . . . . Alt +S

Display and Edit Table Properties

In Table Design view:

    Show/Hide Group

1. Click **Property Sheet** button . . . . H , P
2. Make any changes desired to the table's properties.
3. Click **Property Sheet** button to close sheet. . . . H , P

EXERCISE DIRECTIONS

1. Start Access, if necessary.
2. Open 🅞 **03ACE** and save a copy of it as **03ACE_xx**.
3. Open tblInstructors in Table Design view and add an attachment field called Documentation.
4. Display the Property Sheet for the table, and set Order By to **LastName**. Make sure Order By On Load is set to Yes.
5. Save the changes and switch to Datasheet view. Confirm that the instructors are sorted by last name.
6. In Windows, copy the file 🅞 **03REYNOLDS.txt** from the data files to the location where you are storing your finished work.
7. For the entry for instructor Wendy Reynolds, attach the file 🅞 **03REYNOLDS** to the Documentation field. Attach the copy you made in the location where you are storing your finished work, not the original file.
8. Open the attachment, and change the year of her degree from 1990 to 1991. Close the file, saving your changes.
9. Use Save As to save the attachment **03REYNOLDS** to your hard disk as **03TEXT_xx**.
10. Open tblStudents in Table Design view.
11. Add a memo field called Notes, and set its Append Only property to Yes.
12. Set the Notes field's Text Format property to Rich Text.
13. Save the changes and switch to Datasheet view.
14. In the record for Sean Gartner, enter the following note into the Notes field:

    10/1/08: Nominated for Student of the Year

15. Format the words Student of the Year in bold and italics.
16. Edit the entry to read:

    10/1/08: Nominated for Student of the Year
    12/1/08 Dean's List

17. View the field's history.
18. Save all changes and close the database. Exit Access.

ON YOUR OWN

1. Start Access and open the ⊙ **03FOSTER** database. Save a copy of it as **OAC03_xx**.

2. Add a memo type field to tblDogs. Name the field **Notes**, and set it to Append Only. Set its Text Format property to Rich Text.

3. Add an attachment type field to tblDogs. Name the field **Photos**.

4. Index the Breed and Age fields with Duplicates OK.

5. Enter the following record into tblDogs in Datasheet view:

   Call Name: **Duncan**

   Breed: **Shetland Sheepdog**

   Purebred? **Yes**

   Age: **3**

   Sex: **Male**

   ReadyForAdoption? **Yes**

   Neutered? **Yes**

   Temperament: **Excellent**

   GoodWithKids? **Yes**

   GoodWithCats? **No**

   GoodWithOtherDogs? **Yes**

   SpecialMedicalNeeds: **None**

   SpecialLifestyleNeeds: **Fenced yard**

   Notes: **High-energy**

6. Make the words *High-energy* bright red.

7. Attach the file ⊙ **03DUNCAN** to the Photos field for this record.

8. Close the database and exit Access.

Skills Covered

- **Set Up Excel Data to Be Imported into Access**
- **Get External Data from an Excel Workbook**
- **Link to an Excel Worksheet**

- **Import or Link to a Table in Another Database**
- **Remove a Linked Table**
- **Refresh or Update a Link**

Software Skills Excel and Access are both components of Microsoft Office, and as such they have a very close relationship. So close, in fact, that an Excel worksheet can function as a table in Access. It can either be imported into an Access database as a table, or linked to a database as a sort of "virtual table" that retains its identity as an Excel worksheet.

Application Skills Ace Learning has just informed you that they have some data in Excel that they would like imported into the new database you are creating for them. One of the spreadsheets should be permanently imported, but the other will need to be linked so that the original is maintained as well.

TERMS

Import To take data from one file and place the information in another file.

Link To create a path in one file to data in another file.

NOTES

Set Up Excel Data to Be Imported into Access

- You can **import** Excel data into an existing Access table or create a new table to hold the imported data.

- The Excel data needs to be organized in database format—that is, with each column as a field and each row as a record, just like Datasheet view in Access.

- Field names should appear in the first row of the table, and there should be no blank rows above or within the data area, nor blank columns.

- If you plan to import the data into an existing Access table, the field names must be exactly the same in Excel as in Access; otherwise you'll get an error when you attempt the import.

  ✓ *Access can be very picky about importing into an existing table. Unless you have a good reason to append data to an existing table, it's usually better to place incoming data in a new table.*

Get External Data from an Excel Workbook

- When you choose to import from an Excel workbook, the Import Spreadsheet Wizard walks you through the process.

- The wizard will first ask what file to import from and how you want it imported: as a new table, appended to an existing table, or linked to the Excel file so that future changes are reflected in both locations. (If you want it linked, see the *Link to an Excel Worksheet* section.)

First select the file from which to import and how to place it in the database

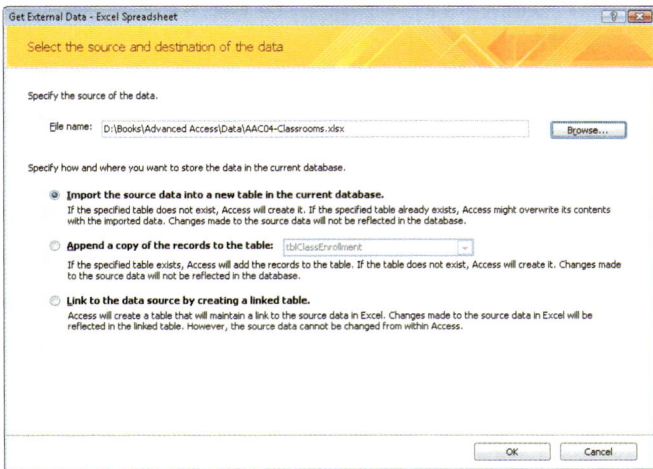

- Next, it asks what worksheet to import from. All the sheets in the selected workbook appear to choose from.

- The wizard then asks whether the first row contains the column headings. If you mark the check box for this, Access will use whatever it finds in the first row as the field names.

- Next, you have the opportunity to change the options for each of the fields. You can specify a different field name, data type, and indexing property, or you can choose to skip a field altogether (that is, not import it).

Choose how to handle each field being imported

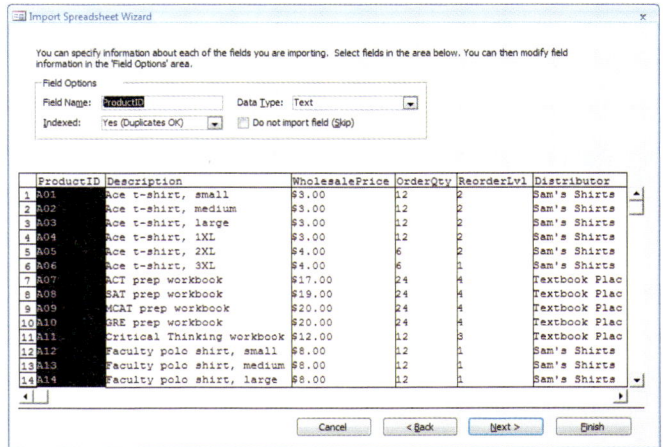

- Next, the wizard asks about the primary key. If you choose to let Access add the primary key, a new field is created for it. If you choose your own primary key, you can specify one of the existing fields. You can also choose not to have a primary key at all, although this is not recommended in most cases.

- Finally, you specify a name for the table and click Finish.

- You have the option of saving the import steps if desired. This might be useful if you frequently import or reimport the same data from the same location. If you mark the Save import steps check box, extra options appear in the last step of the wizard, in which you can specify a name for the saved specifications and/or create an Outlook task to remind you to do the import.

Import steps can be saved for later reuse

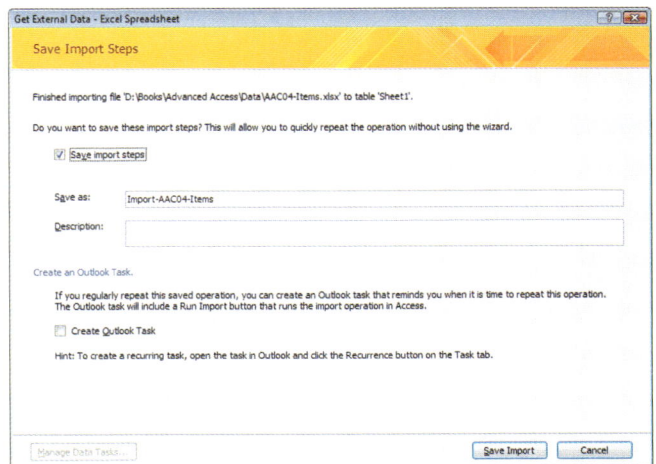

Link to an Excel Worksheet

- The process for setting up a **link** to an Excel worksheet is virtually identical to that for importing from one. With a link, you are not prompted for field properties or a primary key, so it is a simpler procedure, but otherwise the same.

- You cannot save the import steps when creating a link. That's because there is no need to do so; a link is dynamic and automatically updates from the source, so you would not need to re-link.

- Once you have linked a worksheet, it becomes a linked table in the Navigation Pane of the database. Its icon looks like an Excel icon, as a reminder that it is not a real Access table, but rather a link to Excel.

**A linked table has an icon
different from the other tables**

- You can use a linked table just like any other table in Access. The only thing you cannot do is modify fields (add, remove, change field names, or change data types or properties). You must do that in the original Excel data file, not within Access.

Import or Link to a Table in Another Database

- You can also import or link to objects from other Access databases.

- You can import a table from one database to another as a quick way of copying data from one location to another. You can also import queries, forms, reports, macros, and modules. For these objects to work, however, they must refer to tables that have valid equivalents in the database into which they are being imported. For example, a query that refers to tblEmployees will work only if there is also a tblEmployees in the destination database.

- You can link to a table in another database as well, just as you link to data in Excel. Changes you make in one place will be reflected in the other, and vice-versa. This allows two or more database files to make use of the same data source and have it always be up-to-date.

- To import or link from Access, click Access in the Import group on the External Data tab. Then follow the prompts in the wizard that appears.

- The wizard displays an Import Objects dialog box, in which you can select objects by type. For example, the tables appear on the Tables tab. For more options, such as choosing whether to import relationships between imported tables and choosing whether to import the data along with the table definitions, click the Options button.

You can choose to import objects other than tables

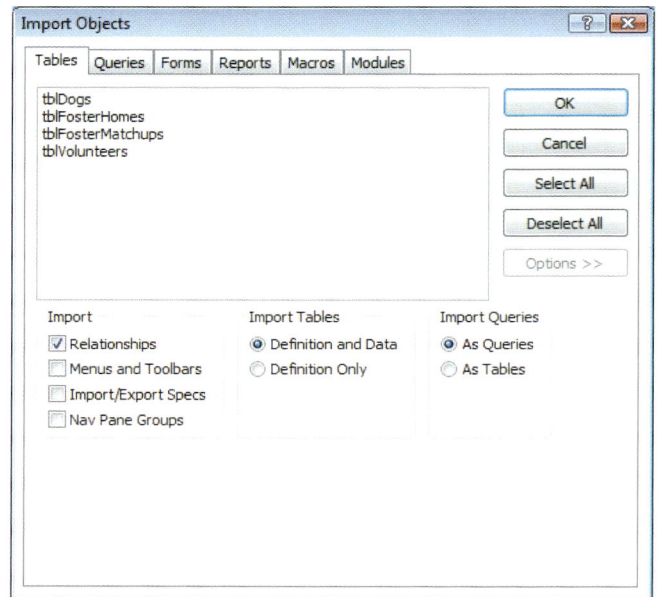

- If you are linking, the Link Tables dialog box appears instead. It is the same as the Import Objects dialog box except it has only one tab—Tables—and it lacks the Options button.

Remove a Linked Table

- To remove a linked table, right-click it and choose Delete, just as for any other table.

- Removing a linked table deletes the link but does not affect the original data source. You can recreate the link any time you want it.

- If you decide you want the data imported rather than linked, the easiest way is to delete the link and then import the data from scratch, as you would from any other Excel or Access data source. There is no command for converting a link to an import.

Refresh or Update a Link

■ If the location of the source data file changes, you might need to update the link. You can check your links and update them if needed by opening up the Linked Table Manager. To do that, right-click any linked table and choose Linked Table Manager.

■ In the Linked Table Manager dialog box, place a check mark next to each link to update, and then click OK. If any data sources are not in their expected locations, you are prompted to re-select them.

■ You can also force Access to prompt for a new location by marking the Always prompt for new location check box. When this check box is marked, all links are prompted for a location when you click OK, not just the ones that are found to be broken.

Update links via the Linked Table Manager

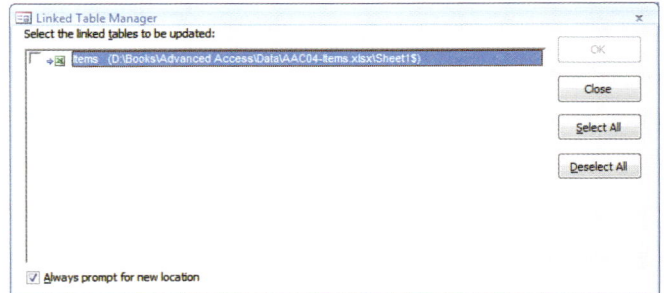

PROCEDURES

Import Data from an Excel Worksheet to a New Table

1. Click **External Data** tab . . . . `Alt`+`X`

   Import Group

2. Click **Excel** button Excel . . . `C`
3. Click **Browse** button . . . . `Alt`+`R`
4. Select the file from which to import.
5. Click **Open** . . . . `Alt`+`O`
6. Select **Import the source data into existing new table in the current database** . . . . `Alt`+`I`
7. Click **OK** . . . . `Enter`
8. Click the worksheet to import.
9. Click **Next** . . . . `Alt`+`N`
10. If the first row contains field names, click **First Row Contains Column Headings** . . . . `Alt`+`I`
11. Click **Next** . . . . `Alt`+`N`

12. If desired, change any field options for each field:
    - **Field Name** . . . . `Alt`+`M`
    - **Data Type** . . . . `Alt`+`T`
    - **Indexed** . . . . `Alt`+`I`

    ✓ *You can skip any fields that you don't want to import by clicking the Do not import field (Skip) check box when that field is selected.*

13. Click **Next** . . . . `Alt`+`N`
14. Choose how you want to handle the primary key:
    - **Let Access add primary key** . . . . `Alt`+`A`
    - **Choose my own primary key** . . . . `Alt`+`C`
    - **No primary key** . . . . . `Alt`+`O`
15. If you selected *Choose my own primary key* in step 14, select the field to use.
16. Click **Next** . . . . `Alt`+`N`
17. In the Import to Table box, type the name for the new table.
18. Click **Finish** . . . . `Alt`+`F`

    ✓ *If you want to save the import steps, see the Save Import Steps procedure.*

19. Click **Close** . . . . `Alt`+`C`

Append Data from an Excel Worksheet to an Existing Table

1. Ensure you have a table in Access with the same fields as the data source.
2. Click **External Data** tab . . . . `Alt`+`X`

   Import Group

3. Click **Excel** button Excel . . . `C`
4. Click **Browse** button . . . . `Alt`+`R`
5. Select the file from which to import.
6. Click **Open** . . . . `Alt`+`O`
7. Select **Append a copy of the records to the table** . . . . `Alt`+`A`
8. Select the table to use.
9. Click **OK**.
10. Click the worksheet from which to import.
11. Click **Next** . . . . `Alt`+`N`
12. Click **Next** . . . . `Alt`+`N`
13. Click **Finish** . . . . `Alt`+`F`

    ✓ *If you want to save the import steps, see the Save Import Steps procedure.*

14. Click **Close** . . . . `Alt`+`C`

Save Import Steps

After clicking Finish when importing data:

1. Select the **Save import steps** check box . . . . `Alt`+`S`
2. Click **Save as** box . . . . . . `Alt`+`A` and type a name for the saved steps.
3. (Optional) Click **Description** box and type a description of the saved procedure . . . . `Alt`+`D`
4. (Optional) If you regularly repeat the operation click **Create Outlook Task**. . . . . `Alt`+`O`
5. Click **Save Import** . . . . . . `Alt`+`S`
6. If you chose to create an Outlook task, click **Save & Close** in Outlook to confirm the task.

Re-Run Saved Import Steps

1. Click **External Data** tab . . . . `Alt`+`X`

   Import Group

2. Click **Saved Imports** button . . . . `V`
3. Click the import to re-run.
4. Click **Run** . . . . `Alt`+`R`
5. Click **OK** . . . . `Enter`
6. Click **Close** . . . . `Alt`+`C`

Link Data from an Excel Worksheet

1. Click **External Data** tab . . . . `Alt`+`X`

   Import Group

2. Click **Excel** button . . . . `C`
3. Click **Browse** button . . . . `Alt`+`R`
4. Select the file from which to import.
5. Click **Open** . . . . `Alt`+`O`
6. Select **Link to the data source by creating a linked table** . . . . `Alt`+`L`
7. Click **OK** . . . . `Enter`

8. Click the worksheet to which to link.
9. Click **Next** . . . . `Alt`+`N`
10. If the first row contains field names, click **First Row Contains Column Headings** . . . . `Alt`+`I`
11. Click **Next** . . . . `Alt`+`N`
12. In the **Linked Table Name** box, type the name for the new table.
13. Click **Finish** . . . . `Alt`+`F`
14. Click **OK**. . . . . `Enter`

Remove a Linked Table

In the Navigation Pane:

1. Right-click the linked table.
2. Click **Delete** . . . . `L`, `L`, `Enter`
3. Click **Yes** . . . . `Alt`+`Y`

Import from Another Access Database

1. Click **External Data** tab . . . . `Alt`+`X`

   Import Group

2. Click **Access** button
   Access . . . . `A`
3. Click **Browse** button . . . . `Alt`+`R`
4. Select the file from which to import.
5. Click **Open** . . . . `Alt`+`O`
6. Select **Import tables, queries, forms, reports, macros, and modules into the current database** . . . . `Alt`+`I`
7. Click **OK**.

   ✓ The Import Objects dialog box appears.

8. Click each table you want to import.

   ✓ If you accidentally click a table you do not want, click it again to deselect it.

9. (Optional) To import other object types, click the tab for that type and then click the object(s) to import.

10. (Optional) Set import options:
    a. Click **Options** button . . . . `Alt`+`O`
    b. Mark any of the Import check boxes as needed:
       - **Relationships** . . . `Alt`+`R`
       - **Menus and Toolbars** . . . . `Alt`+`M`
       - **Import/Export Specs** . . . . `Alt`+`S`
       - **Nav Pane Groups** . . . . `Alt`+`N`
    c. Choose whether to import the data or not:
       - **Definition and Data** . . . . `Alt`+`D`
       - **Definition Only** . . . `Alt`+`F`
    d. Choose how to import queries:
       - **As Queries** . . . . . `Alt`+`Q`
       - **As Tables** . . . . . . `Alt`+`B`
11. Click **OK**. . . . . `Enter`
12. Click **Close** . . . . `Alt`+`C`

    ✓ If you want to save the import steps, see the Save Import Steps procedure.

Link Data from Another Access Database

1. Click **External Data** tab . . . . `Alt`+`X`

   Import Group

2. Click **Access** button
   Access . . . . `A`
3. Click **Browse** button . . . . `Alt`+`R`
4. Select the file with which to link.
5. Click **Open** . . . . `Alt`+`O`
6. Select **Link to the data source by creating a linked table** . . . . `Alt`+`L`
7. Click **OK**. . . . . `Enter`

   ✓ The Link Tables dialog box appears.

8. Click each table you want to link.

   ✓ If you accidentally click a table you do not want, click it again to deselect it.

9. Click **OK**. . . . . `Enter`

Refresh Linked Tables

1. Right-click any linked table.
2. Click **Linked Table Manager** . . . . K
3. Click to place check mark next to each table to refresh.
4. Click **OK** . . . . Enter
5. Click **OK** . . . . Enter
6. If prompted, reselect the data source(s).
7. Click **Close**.

Change the Location of a Linked Table

1. Right-click any linked table.
2. Click **Linked Table Manager** . . . . K
3. Click to place check mark next to table to change.
4. Mark **Always prompt for new location** check box . . . . . Alt +A
5. Click **OK** . . . . Enter

6. Re-select data source.
7. Click **Open** . . . . Alt +O
8. Click **OK** . . . . Enter
9. Click **Close**.

EXERCISE DIRECTIONS

1. Start Access, if necessary.
2. Open 04ACE and save a copy of it as 04ACE_*xx*.
3. Import the data from the Excel file 04CLASSROOMS, from Sheet1, into a new table called **tblClassrooms**.
   - The first row contains the field names.
   - Choose your own primary key, and choose the Location field.
   - Do not save the import steps.
4. Copy the file 04ITEMS from the data files to the location where you are saving your finished work.
5. Create a link from the Excel file 04ITEMS (Sheet1). Use the copy you just placed in your finished work location, not the original. Use these settings:
   - The first row contains the field names.
   - Name the linked table **tblItems**.

6. Import the query qryClassesAndInstructors from the Access file 04EXTRA.
7. Run the query to confirm that it works.
8. In Windows, move the file 04ITEMS into a different location, such as the folder where you are storing your solution files.
9. Use the Linked Table Manager to update its location in Access.
10. Save all changes and close the database. Exit Access.

ON YOUR OWN

1. Start Access and open the 🔵 **04FOSTER** database. Save a copy of it as **OAC04_xx**.

2. Import the data from the file 🔵 **04DOGS** into tblDogs, appending it to the current data. The first row contains field names. You will get some errors; that is okay.

   ✓ *Note: this is a comma-separated values (csv) file, not an Excel file. The import process is almost identical except on the External Data tab, in the Import group, choose Text File rather than Excel.*

3. Open the table 04DOGS_ImportErrors and view its content. When import errors occur, they are presented to you in this format. All the entries refer to the Photos field, which did not have any data in the source document anyway.

4. Delete the table 04DOGS_ImportErrors.

5. Save all changes and close the database. Exit Access.

Exercise | 5

Skills Covered

- **Export Data to Other Formats**
- **Save and Run Export Specifications**
- **Publish in PDF or XPS Format**

Software Skills If you need to analyze your Access data, Excel may be a better tool because of its additional functions and analytical commands. In some cases, you may also need to convert Access data to a table in Word or export to a plain text file for use in some proprietary database system.

Application Skills Ace Learning would like to send copies of some of its data tables to an outside consultant who uses a third-party, proprietary database system. They are not sure what data format would be best to receive data in, so Ace has asked you to export the data in a variety of formats so the consultant can experiment with his system and choose which data format works best.

TERMS

Delimited Separated by a consistently used character. For example, a delimited data source might separate each field with commas and each record with paragraph breaks.

Export To save data or an object so that it is accessible from outside of its native program.

Fixed width A data source type in which each field is represented by a fixed number of characters. If a particular record does not use all the allotted characters, spaces are inserted to make up the total.

NOTES

Export Data to Other Formats

- You can **export** tables from Access in a variety of formats, one table at a time. (You cannot save the entire Access database in a different format.)

- If you export to Excel or Word, you can export a much wider variety of objects, not just tables. Excel will accept tables, queries, or forms; Word will accept all those objects and also reports.

- You can also export to plain text files, to HTML (Web) pages, and to several other formats of spreadsheet and database applications.

Export to Excel

- One of the most common formats to which to export is Excel. To do this, click the Excel button in the Export group of the External Data tab. (Do not confuse this with the Excel button in the Import group.)

- An Export – Excel Spreadsheet wizard runs. The file name is filled in automatically using a default name based on whatever object was selected when you clicked the button. Change the file name and/or location if desired.

- You can optionally export data with formatting and layout.

■ You can optionally save the export steps for later reuse. This might be useful if you frequently need to update your exported copy, for example. Saving export steps works just like saving import steps, which you learned about in Exercise 4.

Export to a Text File

■ The process for exporting to a text file is similar to that for an Excel file except you start with the Text File button in the Export group.

■ Exporting to a text file results in one of two file types:

  ● A **delimited** file, in which fields are separated by characters such as commas and records are separated by paragraph breaks.

  ● A **fixed width** file, in which fields are aligned in columns with spaces occupying any extra space resulting from differing lengths of entries.

■ You are prompted to choose whether you want Delimited or Fixed Width as part of the Export Text Wizard.

Select the type of separation between fields

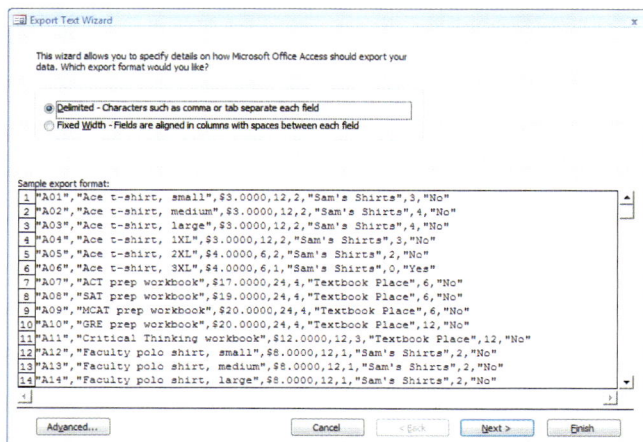

■ If you choose delimited, you are then prompted to choose the delimiter character (for example, tab, semicolon, or comma).

■ If you choose Fixed Width, you are prompted to signify where the field breaks occur. Drag the vertical line on the sample to move it as needed.

  ✓ *The widths shown by default are based on the field sizes you set up in Table Design view. If you see only one field, scroll to the right; the others are there. You just need to drag the line to the left to decrease the width.*

Drag the divider line between fields

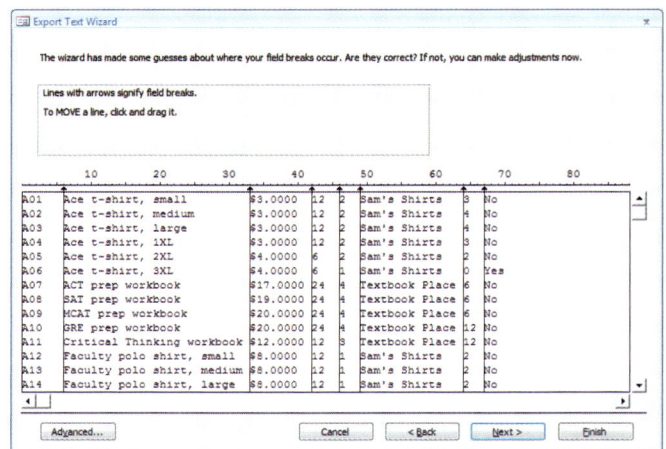

Export to Word

■ Exporting to Word is the same as to Excel except you start with the Word button in the Export group. The selected object is actually exported as a Rich Text Format (RTF) file. RTF is a generic word processing format suitable for use in Word or in most other word processing programs.

Export to Another Access Database

■ You can export any object type to another Access database. The command for this is buried beneath the More button in the Export group. Click More, and then click Access Database.

■ Select the database to which to export the object, and click OK. An Export dialog box appears asking for the name that the exported object will have in the destination database. By default it is the same name as it had originally but you can change this (for example, to avoid a problem with duplicate names).

■ If you are exporting a table, you further have a choice of exporting both the definition and the data, or just the definition (that is, the fields and their properties).

Rename the exported object if desired

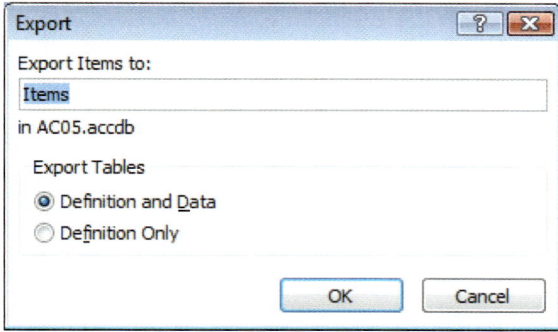

Save and Run Export Specifications

■ The last step of most export operations offers to let you save your export specifications. If you mark the Save export steps check box, additional options appear where you can specify a file name and description. You can also create an Outlook task. This all works exactly as it did with import specifications in Exercise 4.

Save export specifications

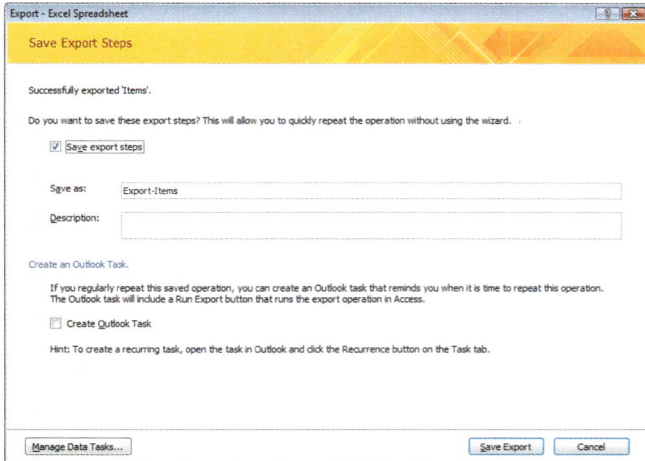

■ To run a saved export specification, click Saved Exports in the Export group on the External Data tab, select the saved export to run, and click Run.

Publish in PDF or XPS Format

■ PDF is a page description language, as is XPS. The main difference is that PDF is owned by Adobe, whereas XPS is owned by Microsoft.

■ If you have Windows Vista, you have all the software needed to create and view XPS files already. If you have Windows XP, you will be prompted to download .NET Framework and the needed add-in to support the XPS format.

■ Access 2007 offers the ability to export objects to either of those formats, producing an uneditable page that can be printed and shared, like a report.

■ To export to one of these formats, click the PDF or XPS button in the Export group on the External Data tab.

■ In the Publish as PDF or XPS dialog box, select the format from the Save as type list.

■ You can choose Standard or Minimum size for the quality level.

Export to PDF or XPS format

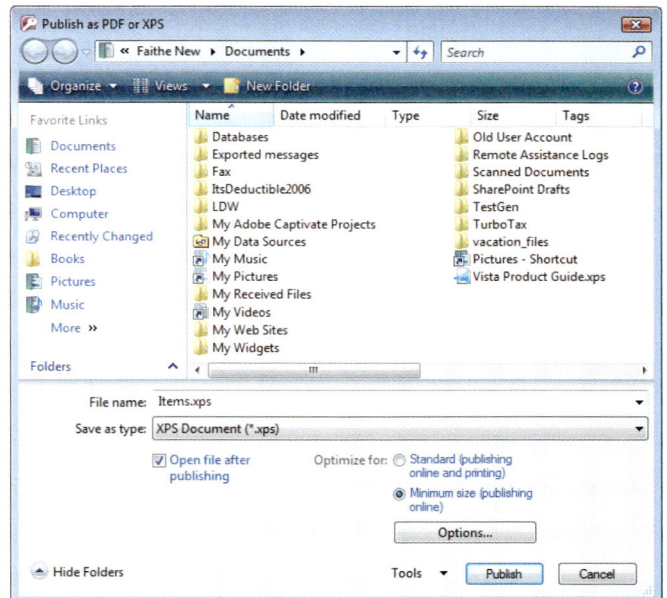

- For additional options, click the Options button. From the Options dialog box, you can select a range to export, and you can set options specific to the format you chose.
- After publishing, an XPS file opens automatically in Internet Explorer, for previewing the result.
- If you have Adobe Reader or Adobe Acrobat, or some other program that displays PDF files, the published PDF file opens in that program.

Set export options if desired

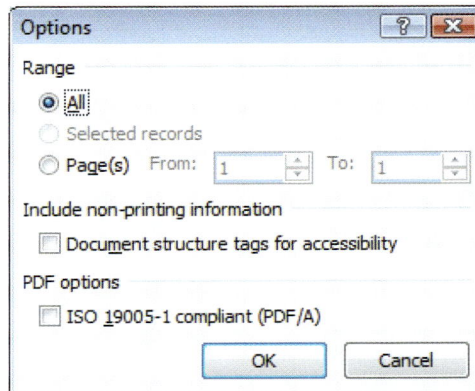

PROCEDURES

Export to Excel

1. Open the table, query, or other object to be exported in Datasheet view. or select it in the navigation pane
2. Click **External Data** tab . . . . `Alt`+`X`

   Export Group

3. Click **Excel** button . . . . . . `X`
4. Confirm the file name and location. If incorrect:
   a. Click **B**rowse . . . . `Alt`+`R`
   b. Select the desired location.
   c. Click **File name** box . . . . `Alt`+`F` and type the desired name.
   d. Click **Save** . . . . `Alt`+`S`
5. Confirm the file format. If incorrect:
   a. Click **File format** drop-down arrow . . . . `Alt`+`T`
   b. Select Excel format desired.

   ✓ *Use Microsoft Excel 97 – Excel 2003 Workbook for backward compatibility with most earlier versions of Excel. Use Microsoft Excel 5.0/5 Workbook for backward compatibility with very old versions, or if you are not sure what version you need compatibility with.*

6. (Optional) To export any formatting, mark the **Export data with formatting and layout** check box . . . . `Alt`+`W`
7. Click **OK** . . . . `Enter`

   ✓ *If you want to save export steps, see Save Export Steps below.*

8. Click **Close** . . . . `Alt`+`C`

Save Export Steps

After clicking OK to complete an export:

1. Mark the **Save export steps** check box . . . . `Alt`+`V`
2. Click **Save as** and change the name if desired . . . . `Alt`+`A`
3. (Optional) Click **Description** box and type a description of the saved procedure . . . . `Alt`+`D`
4. (Optional) Click **Create Outlook Task** . . . . `Alt`+`O`
5. Click **Save Export** . . . . . . `Alt`+`S`
6. If you chose to create an Outlook task, click **Save & Close** in Outlook to confirm the task.

Run Saved Export Steps

1. Click **External Data** tab . . . . `Alt`+`X`

   Export Group

2. Click **Saved Exports** button . . . . `P`
3. Click the export to re-run.
4. Click **Run** . . . . `Alt`+`R`
5. Click **OK** . . . . `Enter`
6. Click **Close** . . . . `Alt`+`C`

Export to a Delimited Text File

1. Open the table to be exported in Datasheet view.
2. Click **External Data** tab . . . . `Alt`+`X`

   Export Group

3. Click **Text File** button

   Text File . . . . `T`

4. Confirm the file name and location. If incorrect:
   a. Click **B**rowse . . . . `Alt`+`R`
   b. Select the desired location.
   c. Click **File name** box and type the desired name . . . . `Alt`+`F`
   d. Click **Save** . . . . `Alt`+`S`

5. Click **OK**. . . . . `Enter`
6. Click **D**elimited . . . . `Alt`+`D`
7. Click **N**ext . . . . `Alt`+`N`
8. Click the desired delimiter character.
9. (Optional) Mark **Include Field Names on First Row** . . . . `Alt`+`I`
10. Click **N**ext . . . . `Alt`+`N`
11. Confirm the path and file name.
12. Click **F**inish . . . . `Alt`+`F`
13. Click **C**lose . . . . `Alt`+`C`

✓ *If you want to save export steps, see* Save Export Steps *after step 12.*

Export to a Fixed Width Text File

1. Open the table to be exported in Datasheet view.
2. Click **External Data** tab. . . . . `Alt`+`X`

   Export Group

3. Click **Text File** button
   Text File
   . . . . `T`
4. Confirm the file name and location. If incorrect:
   a. Click **B**rowse. . . . . . . `Alt`+`R`
   b. Select the desired location.
   c. Click **File name** box and type the desired name . . . . `Alt`+`F`
   d. Click **S**ave. . . . . `Alt`+`S`
5. Click **OK**. . . . . `Enter`
6. Click Fixed **W**idth . . . . . . `Alt`+`W`
7. Click **N**ext . . . . `Alt`+`N`
8. Drag the dividers between fields as needed.
9. Click **N**ext . . . . `Alt`+`N`
10. Confirm the path and file name.
11. Click **F**inish . . . . `Alt`+`F`
12. Click **C**lose . . . . `Alt`+`C`

✓ *If you want to save export steps, see* Save Export Steps *after step 11.*

Export to Word

1. Open the table, query, or other object to be exported in Datasheet view.
2. Click **External Data** tab. . . . . `Alt`+`X`

   Export Group

3. Click **Word** button 🗇 Word . . . `W`
4. Confirm the file name and location. If incorrect:
   a. Click **B**rowse. . . . . . . `Alt`+`R`
   b. Select the desired location.
   c. Click **File name** box and type the desired name . . . . `Alt`+`F`
   d. Click **S**ave. . . . . `Alt`+`S`
5. (Optional) Mark the **Open destination file after the export operation is complete** check box . . . . `Alt`+`A`
6. Click **OK**. . . . . `Enter`
7. If you marked the check box in step 4, return to Access and click **C**lose. . . . . `Alt`+`C`

✓ *If you want to save export steps, see* Save Export Steps *after step 6.*

Export to Another Access Database

1. Open the table, query, or other object to be exported in Datasheet view.
2. Click **External Data** tab. . . . . `Alt`+`X`

   Export Group

3. Click **More** button
   🖳 More ▾ . . . . `G`
4. Click **A**ccess database . . . . . . `A`
5. Click **B**rowse . . . . `Alt`+`R`
6. Select the database into which the object should be imported.
7. Click **S**ave . . . . `Alt`+`S`
8. Click **OK**.

✓ *The Export dialog box opens.*

9. Confirm the name to use for the exported copy. Change if needed.
10. Choose how to export, if a table:
    ■ **Definition and D**ata . . `Alt`+`D`
    ■ **Definition Only** . . . . . `Alt`+`F`
11. Click **OK**.
12. Click **C**lose . . . . `Alt`+`C`

✓ *If you want to save export steps, see* Save Export Steps *after step 11.*

Export to PDF or XPS Format

You must install an Add-In from Microsoft to have access to the PDF or XPS command on the External Data tab.

1. Open the table, query, or other object to be exported in Datasheet view.
2. (Optional) If you want to export only certain records, select them.
3. Click **External Data** tab. . . . . `Alt`+`X`

   Export Group

4. Click **PDF or XPS** button . . . . `F`

✓ *The Publish as PDF or XPS dialog box opens.*

5. Confirm the file name and location; change if needed.
6. Click **Save as type** list and select **PDF** or **XPS Document** . . . . `Alt`+`T`
7. Choose how to optimize the file:
   ■ **St**andard . . . . `Alt`+`A`
   ■ **M**inimum size . . . . . . `Alt`+`M`
8. (Optional) Click **Options** and then do the following. . . . . `Alt`+`O`
   a. Select an export range:
      ■ **All** . . . . `Alt`+`A`
      ■ **Selected records** . . . . `Alt`+`R`
      ■ **Page(s)** . . . . `G`
   b. Mark or clear check boxes for format-specific settings.
   c. Click **OK** . . . . `Enter`
9. Click **Publi**s**h** . . . . `Alt`+`S`

EXERCISE DIRECTIONS

1. Start Access, if necessary. Open 💿 **05ACE** and save a copy of it as **05ACE_xx**.

2. Export tblItems to a tab-delimited text file called **05ITEMS_TXT_xx**. Include the field names in the first row.

3. Export tblItems to a Word document called **05ITEMS_RTF_xx**.

4. Export tblItems to an Excel 97/2003 format workbook called **05ITEMS_XLS_xx**.

5. Publish tblItems as an XPS file called **05ITEMS_XPS_xx**. Optimize for printing (Standard size). Save the export steps. Call the saved steps **Items in XPS**.

   ✓ Note: If you are running Windows XP and you do not have an XPS add-in installed, either install it or use PDF format instead.

6. Re-publish as an XPS file by re-running your saved export. Overwrite the file you created in step 5.

7. Save all changes and close the database. Exit Access.

ON YOUR OWN

1. Start Access. Create a new blank database and call it **OAC05-1_xx**.

2. Open the 💿 **05FOSTER** database and export a copy of all its objects to **OAC05-1_xx**.

3. Open **OAC05-1_xx**.

   ✓ If you see a message about selecting Tables and Related Views and asking if you want to continue, click OK.

4. Re-sort the Navigation Pane by object type.

   ✓ To do this, open the drop-down list for the Navigation Pane and click Object Type.

5. Open the Relationships window and establish the needed relationships between the tables. Enforce referential integrity for all relationships.

   ✓ Try to figure them out on your own logically. If you need help, reopen **05FOSTER** and look at the relationships there.

6. Export qryFosterHomesInfo to an Excel file. Name the file **OAC05-2_xx**.

7. Close the database. Exit Access.

Skills Covered

- **Convert to a Different Access Format**
- **Compact and Repair a Database**
- **Split a Database**
- **Configure Database Options**
- **Set Database Properties**

Software Skills Sometimes the database file itself may need some modification, either because it is not in the right format or because it lacks the right properties or options. In this exercise, you will learn how to modify, configure, and split an Access database file to make it more effective.

Application Skills Ace Learning has informed you that the database you have been creating for them will eventually be shared on a network where not all users have Access 2007. Because of the database's multivalued fields, converting it to 2002/2003 format may be a challenge, but you have agreed to try, and also to create a split version of the database for them to test on their network.

TERMS

Back end In a split database, the file containing the tables, stored in a central location such as a server.

Compact To remove temporary structures that are no longer needed in the database and rearrange data so items are organized efficiently on the hard disk.

Front end In a split database, the file containing all objects except the tables, stored on individual user hard drives.

Properties Attributes that describe an object. In the case of a database, properties can include key-words, categories, and author name.

NOTES

Convert to a Different Access Format

- Access 2007 supports several database formats: Access 2000, Access 2002/2003, and the default, Access 2007.

- However, not all features are available unless you use Access 2007 format. For example, you cannot use multivalued fields in earlier-version files, nor attachments, offline data, or links to external files that are not supported by earlier versions.

- In most cases, you will want to use Access 2007 format. However, sometimes you might need backward-compatibility, for example if you want to share the database with others who use an earlier version of Access.

- To convert a database to another format, use options on the Office button menu's Save As submenu. For example, to convert to 2002/2003 format, open the Office menu, point to Save As, and then click Access 2002 - 2003 Database.

Choose another Access format

- If the database has 2007-specific features, an error message will appear, letting you know that the file cannot be saved in an earlier format.

- A database stored in an earlier Access format can also be upgraded to 2007 format. To do this, click the Office button, click Convert, and follow the prompts.

Compact and Repair a Database

- As you build the database, Access places data on the hard drive in available spots. When you add records to a table, create a form, delete a report, and then add more records, the parts of the table are scattered throughout the hard drive.

- When you delete forms, queries, records, or other parts of the database, Access leaves a "hole" in the database.

- **Compacting** the database removes the holes and organizes like data in adjacent spots on the hard drive, significantly reducing the size of the database and improving performance.

- With the database open, click the Office button, point to Manage, and click Compact and Repair Database. No prompt appears; there are no options for the command.

- You can set the database so that every time it closes, it will automatically compact. Open the Office menu, click Access Options, and click Current Database. Then mark the Compact on Close check box.

Split a Database

- If you are the only user on the database, it will run faster if Access and the database are on your local hard drive instead of a network drive.

- If multiple users are using the database via a shared network location, however, the database will run faster if it is split in two. One database file contains the tables and remains on the network drive. The other database contains the other objects and is copied to each user's hard drive.

- The tables database is called the **back end**. The other database is called the **front end**. In the front end, the tables are linked to the back end.

Comparison of objects in front end vs. back end

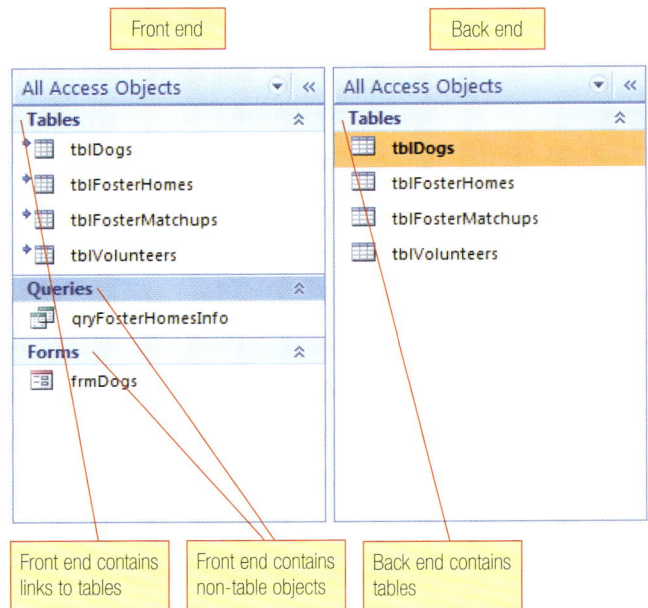

- In addition to improving speed, splitting the database is useful to developers who can make design changes with a copy of the front end not attached to the live data.

- Then when the design changes are completed, the front end can be copied to the users' computers.

- You can also overcome size restrictions by splitting the database. If the full database file is larger than you can easily transfer, e-mail, or save, splitting it can alleviate the problem.

- To split the database into a front and back end, click Access Database on the Database Tools tab and follow the prompts.

Database Splitter dialog box

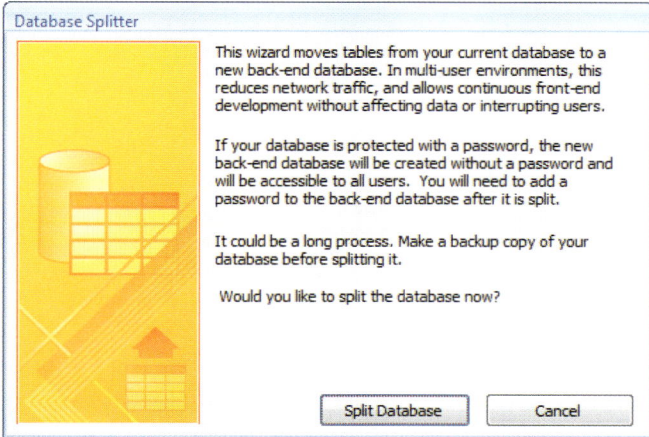

Database Splitter

This wizard moves tables from your current database to a new back-end database. In multi-user environments, this reduces network traffic, and allows continuous front-end development without affecting data or interrupting users.

If your database is protected with a password, the new back-end database will be created without a password and will be accessible to all users. You will need to add a password to the back-end database after it is split.

It could be a long process. Make a backup copy of your database before splitting it.

Would you like to split the database now?

[Split Database] [Cancel]

- If you move the back end database, you will need to update the links in the front end.
- Open the front end database file and then click Linked Table Manager on the Database Tools tab.
- The tables in the back end are listed in the Linked Table Manager dialog box. Select them, click OK, and when prompted, identify the new location.

Linked Table Manager

Linked Table Manager

Select the linked tables to be updated:

- tblDogs (D:\Books\Advanced Access\working_be.accdb)
- tblFosterHomes (D:\Books\Advanced Access\working_be.accdb)
- tblFosterMatchups (D:\Books\Advanced Access\working_be.accdb)
- tblVolunteers (D:\Books\Advanced Access\working_be.accdb)

[OK] [Cancel] [Select All] [Deselect All]

☐ Always prompt for new location

Configure Database Options

- You can customize a variety of settings in Access 2007 that determine how the program behaves and looks in both subtle and not-so-subtle ways. All these options are accessed by opening the Office menu and clicking Access Options.
- The Access Options dialog box has categories listed along the left side. Click a category to see a page of options. Some of the option pages are so long that they don't display all at once; you might need to scroll down to see additional options in a category.

Set database options

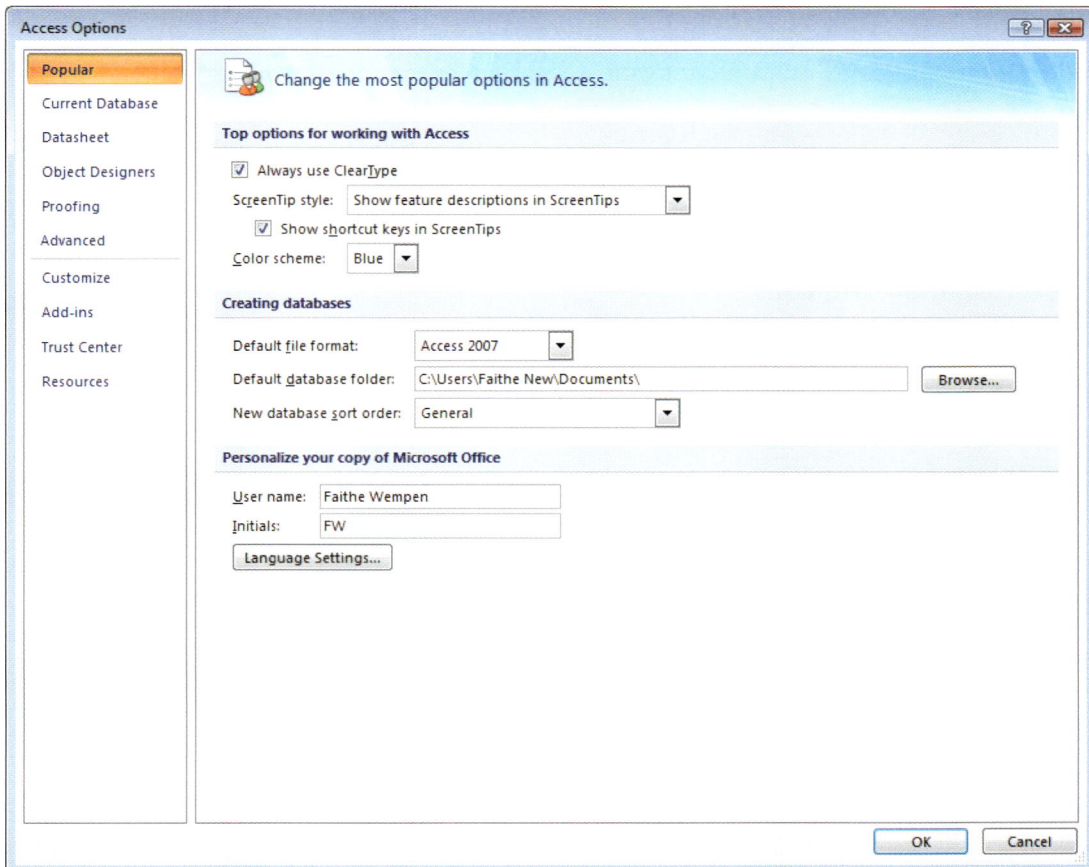

Access Options

| Popular |
| Current Database |
| Datasheet |
| Object Designers |
| Proofing |
| Advanced |
| Customize |
| Add-ins |
| Trust Center |
| Resources |

Change the most popular options in Access.

Top options for working with Access

☑ Always use ClearType

ScreenTip style: Show feature descriptions in ScreenTips

☑ Show shortcut keys in ScreenTips

Color scheme: Blue

Creating databases

Default file format: Access 2007

Default database folder: C:\Users\Faithe New\Documents\   [Browse...]

New database sort order: General

Personalize your copy of Microsoft Office

User name: Faithe Wempen

Initials: FW

[Language Settings...]

[OK] [Cancel]

- The categories include:
  - Popular: A few of the most commonly set options, with no particular theme.
  - Current Database: Options that apply only to the open database.
  - Datasheet: Options that apply to the way datasheets are displayed (colors, fonts, etc.).
  - Object Designers: Options that apply to working in Layout and Design views, such as when designing forms and reports.
  - Proofing: Options that control spell checking and automatic corrections.
  - Advanced: Less-common options.
  - Customize: A system that enables you to customize the Quick Access Toolbar.
  - Add-ins: A management tool for add-ins you can use with Access.
  - Trust Center: A management area for setting up and controlling trusted locations and security.
  - Resource: A series of links to online and offline sources of more information about Access.
- Here are a few important options you should know how to set.

Error Checking

- When you are working in Form or Report Design view, you can optionally have messages pop up to identify potential errors. To turn this feature on/off, display the Object Designers category, and in the Error checking section, mark or clear the Enable error checking check box. You can also turn on/off specific types of error checking within that section, and change the color of the error indicator.

Error checking options

Navigation Pane Behavior

- For the current database, you can specify whether or not the Navigation Pane appears. In most cases you want it to appear, because it's your entry into the object list from which you work. However, if you are trying to make a database as idiot-proof as possible after its design work has been completed, you might want to hide it so users are not tempted to experiment with the database's objects.
- To hide or display the Navigation Pane, display the Current Database category, and in the Navigation group, mark or clear the Display Navigation Pane check box.

Choose to show or hide the Navigation Pane

✓ You can also click the Navigation Options button below the check box to determine what groups will appear on the Navigation Pane.

Choose a Startup Form

- Another way to force users to stay away from object design and focus on the data is to present them with a startup form. You will learn in Lesson 2 how to design navigation forms that serve as menu systems.
- To specify a form to load when the database opens, on the Current Database category, under the Application Options heading, select a form from the Display Form drop-down list.

Choose to use a form at startup if desired

Format Datasheets

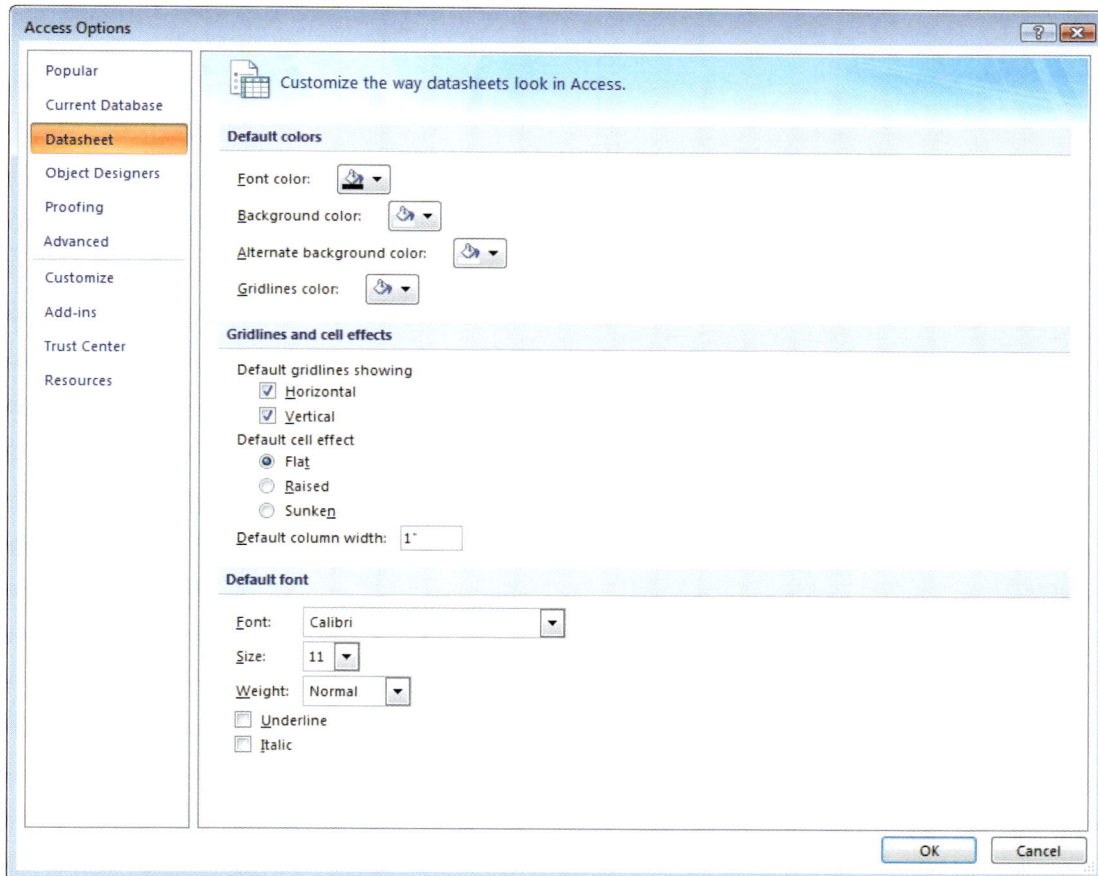

- If you find the text on datasheets difficult to read, you might want to increase the font size or change to a different typeface (font). To do this, display the Datasheet category and then use the controls provided to change colors, gridlines, cell effects, and font choices.

Set Database Properties

- Database files have **properties**, just as do other Office application files. Examples of properties include the database's title, subject, author, company, category, keywords, and comments. You can use these properties to search for a database file and to organize a library of database files on a server or on your local hard disk.

- Both built-in and custom properties are available. To work with the built-in properties for the current database's file, click the Office button, point to Manage, and click Database Properties. The properties dialog box for the file opens with the Summary tab showing.

- To populate (fill in) a property, click in its text box and type an entry.

- You can also create custom properties, for situations where there is no built-in property that expresses what you want. For example, you might want to record information about which of several office locations a database references. You might create a new custom property called Location for this.

Format datasheets

Access Options

Popular	Customize the way datasheets look in Access.
Current Database	
Datasheet	**Default colors**
Object Designers	_F_ont color:
Proofing	_B_ackground color:
Advanced	_A_lternate background color:
Customize	_G_ridlines color:
Add-ins	
Trust Center	**Gridlines and cell effects**
Resources	Default gridlines showing
	☑ _H_orizontal
	☑ _V_ertical
	Default cell effect
	⦿ _F_lat
	○ _R_aised
	○ Sunk_e_n
	_D_efault column width: 1"
	Default font
	_F_ont: Calibri
	_S_ize: 11
	_W_eight: Normal
	☐ _U_nderline
	☐ _I_talic

OK   Cancel

- On the Custom tab in the properties box is a list of predefined custom properties you can choose from, if any of them meet your needs. For our example, perhaps the Office custom property would be suitable to track locations. (You could still create a custom property called Locations if you preferred to do so.)

Set up properties for the database file to make it easier to find later

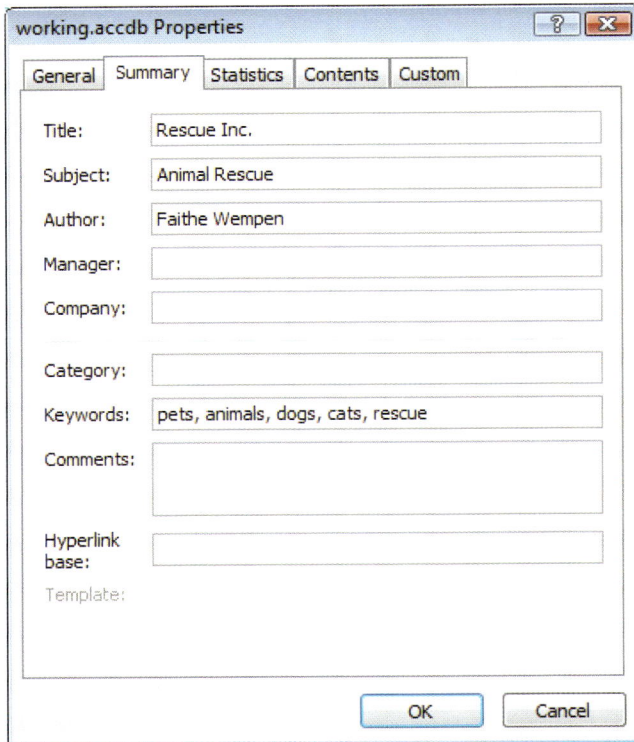

- For a custom property, specify the name and type and then enter the value for that property in the Value box.

Create custom properties if desired

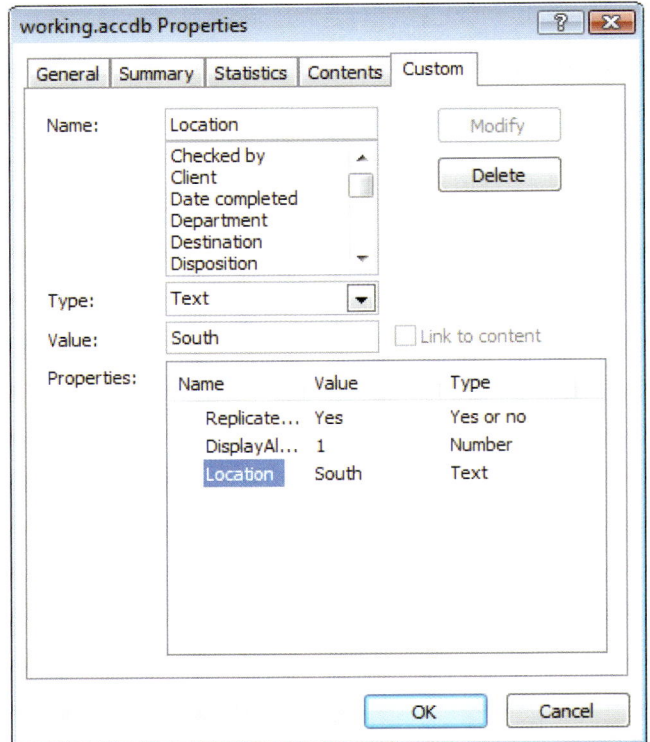

PROCEDURES

Convert to Access 2002/2003 Format

1. Open the database, but close all objects within it.
2. Click **Office Button** ⊞ ... Alt , F
3. Point to **Save As** .... F

   ✓ *If Save As is not available, select an object in the Navigation Pane and try again.*

4. Click **Access 2002 - 2003 Database**.................. @2
5. Click **File name** box .... Alt + N and type a name for the converted database.
6. Click **Save** .... Alt + S

Convert to Access 2007 Format

1. Open the database, but close all objects within it.
2. Click **Office Button** ⊞ ... Alt , F
3. Click **Convert** V
4. Click **File name** box .... Alt + N and type a name for the converted database.
5. Click **Save** .... Alt + S
6. Click **OK** .... Enter

Compact and Repair a Database

1. Click **Office Button** ⊞ ... Alt , F
2. Point to **Manage** .... M
3. Click **Compact and Repair Database**.............. C

Set a Database to Automatically Compact When Closed

1. Click **Office Button** ⊞ ... Alt , F
2. Click **Access Options**........ I
3. Click **Current Database**.
4. Mark the **Compact on Close** check box .... Alt + C
5. Click **OK**.................. Enter
6. Click **OK**.................. Enter

   ✓ *Close and reopen the database for the setting to take effect.*

Split the Database

1. Open database to split.
2. Click **Database Tools** tab . . . . `Alt`+`A`

   Move Data Group

3. Click **Access Database** button . . . . `S`
4. Click **Split Database** . . . . `Enter`
5. (Optional) Change the name or location of the back end database file.
6. Click **Split** . . . . `Alt`+`S`
7. Click **OK** . . . . `Enter`

Update Location of Back End

With front end database open:

1. Click **Database Tools** tab . . . . `Alt`+`A`

   Database Tools Group

2. Click **Linked Table Manager** button . . . . `L`
3. Click **Select All** . . . . `Alt`+`S`
4. Click **OK** . . . . `Enter`
5. Browse to locate back end file and select it.
6. Click **Open** . . . . `Alt`+`O`
7. Click **OK** . . . . `Enter`
8. Click **Close**.

Configure Database Options

1. Open the database to which options should apply.

   ✓ *Some options apply only to the current database. If you are not going to be changing one of those settings, it does not matter which database is open.*

2. Click **Office Button** . . . `Alt`, `F`
3. Click **Access Options** . . . . `I`
4. Click the desired category at left.
5. Change the desired option(s).
6. Click **OK** . . . . `Enter`

   ✓ *See the following for specific settings.*

To turn error checking on or off:

1. Click **Office Button** . . . `Alt`, `F`
2. Click **Access Options** . . . . `I`
3. Click **Object Designers**.
4. Mark or clear **Enable error checking** check box . . . . `Alt`+`C`, `C`, `Spacebar`
5. (Optional) Mark or clear check boxes for individual types of errors.
6. (Optional) Click **Error indicator color** button and choose another color.
7. Click **OK** . . . . `Enter`

To turn Navigation Pane on or off:

1. Open the database to which options should apply.
2. Click **Office Button** . . . `Alt`, `F`
3. Click **Access Options** . . . . `I`
4. Click **Current Database**.
5. Mark or clear **Display Navigation Pane** check box . . . . `Alt`+`N`
6. Click **OK** . . . . `Enter`

To choose startup form:

1. Open the database to which options should apply.
2. Click **Office Button** . . . `Alt`, `F`
3. Click **Access Options** . . . . `I`
4. Click **Current Database**.
5. Open **Display Form** list and choose a form . . . . `Alt`+`D`, `↓`
6. Click **OK** . . . . `Enter`

To set datasheet default formatting:

1. Click **Office Button** . . . `Alt`, `F`
2. Click **Access Options** . . . . `I`
3. Click **Datasheet**.
4. Set database formatting options.
5. Click **OK** . . . . `Enter`

Populate Preset Database Properties

1. Click **Office Button** . . . `Alt`, `F`
2. Point to **Manage** . . . . `M`
3. Click **Database Properties** . . . `T`
4. Click **Summary** tab.
5. Type values for any property.
6. Click **OK** . . . . `Enter`

Create Custom Database Properties

1. Click **Office Button** . . . `Alt`, `F`
2. Point to **Manage** . . . . `M`
3. Click **Database Properties** . . . `T`
4. Click **Custom** tab.
5. Click a custom property on the **Name** list.

   OR

   Type a new property name.
6. Select property type from **Type** list.
7. Type value in **Value** box.
8. Click **Add** button . . . . `Alt`+`A`
9. Click **OK** . . . . `Enter`

EXERCISE DIRECTIONS

1. Start Access, if necessary.

2. Open ⊙ **06ACE** and try to save a copy of it in Access 2002/2003 format.

   ✓ *A warning appears that it can't be done because the database uses features that require the current file format.*

3. Save a copy in Access 2007 format as **06ACE_2007_xx**.

4. Go through the database and strip out all fields that make it incompatible with the 2002/2003 format:

   ■ In tblInstructors, delete the Documentation field.

   ■ In tblVolunteers, delete the Skills field.

   ■ Delete the link to tblItems.

   ■ In the tblStudents table, set the Notes field to plain text and turn off Append Only.

5. Save the database in 2002/2003 format as **06ACE_2003_xx**. (Access will provide a different extension automatically when you choose the earlier format.)

   ✓ *After the save to the new format, the Navigation Pane might change to show only the queries in the database. You can fix this by opening its drop-down menu and choosing All Access Items.*

6. Split the database. Call the back end file **06ACE_2003_be_xx** and save it in the same location as your other solution files.

7. In Windows, move **06ACE_2003_be_xx** to another location, such as on a network drive. (Your instructor may tell you where to move it.)

8. Update the links to the tables, using the Linked Table Manager, to reflect the new location of the back end.

9. Open the back-end database file.

10. Open the Properties for the file, and type the Keyword **backend**.

11. In the Access Options for the file, set the Navigation Pane to not appear.

12. Close and reopen the file to confirm that the Navigation Pane does not appear.

13. Exit Access.

ON YOUR OWN

1. Start Access.

2. Open the ⊙ **06FOSTER** database. Save it in Access 2002/2003 format as **OAC06_1_xx**.

   ✓ *You will need to figure out why it won't save in that format, and make changes to the properties of the fields that are preventing it. If you can't change a field's properties, you must delete the field entirely. As a reminder, the reasons why a conversion might fail include multi-valued lookup fields, Memo fields that have Append Only set to Yes, and attachment fields.*

3. Convert it back to Access 2007 format, and save it as **OAC06_2_xx**.

4. Close the database. Exit Access.

Skills Covered

- **Identify Object Dependencies**
- **Print Database Information with the Database Documenter**

Software Skills   As you create more and more complex databases, it can become difficult to remember which objects depend on which others. For example, one query might be based on another query, which in turn might be based on a table. In this exercise you will learn how to identify object dependencies, and how to create a thorough report of the database's structure.

Application Skills   You will soon be turning over the Ace Learning database to another consultant, and you want to document your work on it thus far. You will review the dependencies in the database, and then create a report with the Database Documenter.

TERMS

Object dependencies   Relationships between objects, such that one object depends on the data or structure of the other.

NOTES

Identify Object Dependencies

- Because Access is a relational database system with relationships between objects, many times the changes you make in one object affect another object.
- This is true not only between related tables, but also between tables and the forms, reports, and queries that are based on them. For example, if you change the name of a field in a table design, you might need to manually edit the label for that field on a report.

- In a complex database, it can be difficult to recall what objects rely on what others. The Object Dependencies task pane can help a user keep track of how objects depend on each other.
- When the **Object Dependencies** task pane is open, you can select an object from the Navigation Pane and see its dependencies. The Object Dependencies task pane has two buttons: Objects that depend on me, and Objects that I depend on. Click one or the other to see the forward or backward dependencies.
- If you select a different object in the Navigation Pane, the Object Dependencies task pane does not immediately update. Click its Refresh button to make it update.

View object dependencies

Print Database Information with the Database Documenter

■ Documenting a database involves creating a detailed report of its structure, dependencies, properties for every object and every field, and so on. A complete documentation of a database can be used to rebuild it in the event of loss or corruption of the data file.

■ To document a database, click the Database Documenter button on the Database Tools tab. Then in the Documenter dialog box, place check marks next to the objects you want to document. To document all the objects of the type shown on the active tab, click Select All. To document all objects of all types, click the All Object Types tab and then click Select All.

■ When you click OK, Access generates a report called Object Definition. You can print this report as a full documentation of your database and keep it in a safe location.

Choose which objects to document

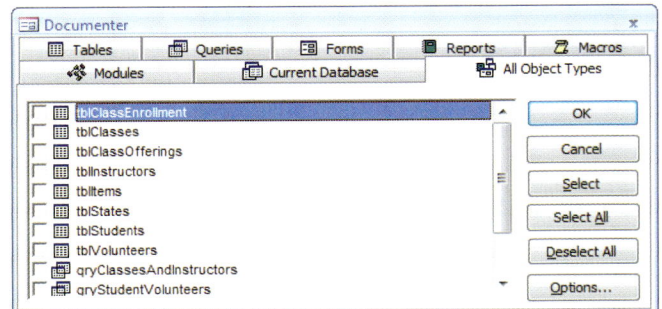

■ You cannot save the report in the database as you would a regular report; the Save command is unavailable.

■ However, you can export it in any of a variety of formats, including Word, plain text, PDF, or XPS. The export buttons are found in the Data group in Print Preview.

Print or save the report

PROCEDURES

Identify Object Dependencies

1. Click **Database Tools** tab . . . . Alt + A

   Show/Hide Group

2. Click **Object Dependencies** button

   Object Dependencies . . . . O

3. If a warning appears about enabling name AutoCorrect, click **OK** . . . . Enter

4. Select an object in the Navigation Pane.

5. Click **Refresh** in the Object Dependencies pane.

6. Click **Objects that depend on me** in the Object Dependencies pane.

7. View the list of objects that depend on the selected one.

8. Click **Objects that I depend on** in the Object Dependencies pane.

9. View the list of objects that the selected object depends on.

10. Repeat steps 4–9 as needed.

11. Click **Object Dependencies** button

    Object Dependencies

    to close the pane . . . . O

Document a Database

1. Click **Database Tools** tab . . . . Alt + A

   Analyze Group

2. Click **Database Documenter** button

   Database Documenter . . . . . U

3. Mark check boxes for items to document.

   OR

   a. Click **All Object Types** tab.

   b. Click **Select All** . . . . . Alt + A

4. Click **OK**. . . . . Enter

   ✓ *The report displays in Print Preview.*

Print a Documentation Report

With the report displayed in Print Preview:

1. Click **Office Button** 🔘 . . . Alt , F

2. Click **Print** . . . . P

3. Set any print options desired.

4. Click **OK**. . . . . Enter

Export a Documentation Report to Microsoft Word

With the report displayed in Print Preview:

Data Group

1. Click **Word** button

   Word . . . . Alt + P , W

2. (Optional) Change file name if desired.

3. Click **OK**. . . . . Enter

4. Click **Close** . . . . Alt + C

Export a Documentation Report to PDF or XPS

With the report displayed in Print Preview:

Data Group

1. Click **PDF or XPS** button . . . . Alt + P , F

2. Choose file type from **Save as type** list . . . . Alt + T

3. Accept default file name.

   OR

   Change file name in **File name** box . . . . Alt + N

4. Click **Publish** . . . . Alt + S

485

EXERCISE DIRECTIONS

1. Start Access, if necessary. Open 07ACE and save it as **07ACE_xx**.

2. Document the entire database and export the report to an XPS file called **07EXPORT_XPS_xx**.

   ✓ Note: If your PC does not save in XPS, use PDF format instead.

3. Use the Object Dependencies task pane to determine what tables the qryClassesAndInstructors query depends on, and write it here or write it on a separate piece of paper to turn in:

   _____

   _____

4. Determine what objects depend on tblVolunteers, and write them here, or on a separate piece of paper:

   _____

   _____

5. Exit Access.

ON YOUR OWN

1. Start Access. Open the 07FOSTER database. Save it as **OAC07-1_xx**.

2. In Microsoft Word, create a new document, and make a list of all the objects in the database.

3. Use the Object Dependencies task pane to determine what objects depend on each object, and what objects each one depends on, and write this information in Word.

4. Save your work in Word as **OAC07-2_xx**.

5. Document the database and export it as a plain text file named **OAC07-3_xx**. Use Unicode encoding.

6. Exit Access.

Exercise | 8

Critical Thinking

Application Skills Because of your experience with databases for Ace Learning, you have been hired to create a database for Green Thumb Gardening, a landscaping company. The owner has provided you with some notes about what kind of data he wants to track; now it is up to you to build and document the database.

EXERCISE DIRECTIONS

1. Start a new blank database and name it **08GREEN_xx**.
2. Using the notes from Illustration A, create tables for the database. You can add fields other than the ones mentioned if you think they will be helpful. Use what you know of database normalization to structure the tables.
3. Set field properties, types, and lookups within each table as appropriate to ease data entry. For example, you could use lookups, input masks, captions, make certain fields required, and so on.
4. Create relationships as appropriate between the tables. Enforce referential integrity where it is helpful to do so.
5. Document the database, and save the report as a PDF file called **08REPORT_xx**.
6. Close the database. Exit Access.

Illustration A

Notes from Meeting with Owner

Customers: Contact information (mailing address, phone number, e-mail), services they have signed up for

Services: Name, description, cost billed to customer, time interval between treatments, number of treatments (or ongoing)

Employees: Badge number, name, contact information, pay rate, social security number, job title, hire date, which company vehicle is assigned to the person, if they have one

Schedule of customers signed up for service

Status of whether or not a particular service has been performed for a customer yet

Information about which employee performed the service and on what date

Company vehicles: Make, model, year, color, notes on any problems with it, which employee it is assigned to

Exercise | 9

Curriculum Integration

Application Skills   In Business class, you have been talking about how businesses encourage customer loyalty by using various promotions and mailings. In this exercise, you will design a database that will be used to track the effectiveness of various business promotions in terms of number of customers responding to the promotion compared to the number of customers contacted.

EXERCISE DIRECTIONS

Marketing Concepts, Inc. tracks the following information about each of the promotions it runs:

- Customer data (contact information, etc.)
- Information about the promotion itself (media type, description, cost to produce, amount billed to customer)
- Information about the release of the promotion (number of ads placed, phone calls made, e-mails sent, or whatever medium was used)
- Information about the return rate of the promotion

They will then use this data to analyze which promotions are the most effective for their customers to run in terms of cost per customer, and which promotions are the most profitable for Marketing Concepts to sell to customers.

Plan the tables for a database that will track all this information effectively. Use what you know of data normalization rules, field types, and so on to make it as clear and well organized as possible.

Create a new database called **09MARKETING_xx** and then create the tables you planned.

Create the needed relationships between tables in the Relationships window.

Display the Relationships window and enlarge the boxes for each of the tables so that all fields are completely visible.

Print a report showing the Relationships window layout.

Close the database and exit Access.

Lesson | 2

Improving Forms and Reports

Skills Covered

■ **About Layout View**

■ **Change the Report Layout**

■ **Change the Page Setup**

■ **Create a New Report in Layout View**

Software Skills   The default reports that Access creates are fine for some circumstances, but in many cases you can improve them with a few simple tweaks. For example, you can control the print layout and change the margins, or change the page orientation.

Application Skills   Michigan Avenue Athletic Club would like you to improve on a report in their database of members and fitness class offerings. You will set up a print layout for this report that makes it as attractive as possible. You will also create a new report that shows each instructor's teaching assignments.

TERMS

Print layout   The placement of fields on a report page.

Stacked report   A report that arranges data in rows, with each field for each record on a separate row.

Tabular report   A report that arranges data in columns, with each column representing a field.

NOTES

About Layout View

■ **Print layout** refers to the placement of fields on a report page. It can include margin settings, field sizes, spaces between fields, placement of text labels, page orientation, and more.

■ You can change the print layout either in Design view or in Layout view. Layout view is new in Access 2007. It enables you to move, resize, and arrange fields in a what-you-see-is-what-you-get environment where the actual data appears in the fields as you are changing the layout, unlike in Design view. This exercise focuses on Layout view.

■ To view a report in Layout view, right-click it on the Navigation Pane and click Layout View. Alternatively, if the report is already open in Print Preview, you can click the View button on the Home tab to enter Layout view.

■ When you are working in Layout view, three additional tabs appear on the ribbon: Report Layout Tools Format, Arrange, and Page Setup:

● Report Layout Tools Format: Contains buttons and commands for formatting and grouping controls and for adding more controls to the report. You will learn more about these options in Exercise 11.

● Report Layout Tools Arrange: Enables you to quickly change the overall layout of the report fields and the positioning of individual objects.

● Report Layout Tools Page Setup: Offers commands to control the page size and orientation, margins, and number of columns.

Change the Report Layout

■ Use the Report Layout Tools Arrange tab to control the layout and arrangement of the fields on the report.

■ Each field and its data appear in separate tabular cells on the layout. Each of these cells can have its margins and paddings set individually.

■ The Control Margins drop-down list on the Arrange tab refers to the internal margins within the cells of the layout, not to the margins for the entire page. The margin setting here determines how much blank space there will be between the inner edge of a cell and the text within it.

■ The Control Padding drop-down list sets the space between the outer edge of a cell and the outer edge of an adjacent cell in the layout grid.

A layout has margins within each cell and padding outside each cell

Margin		Padding		
TTh			12/15/2009	4:00 PM

Switch Between Layout Types

■ A report can be laid out either in Tabular or Stacked mode.

■ A **tabular report** arranges data in columns, with each column representing a field.

Tabular layout

Class	Start	Instructor
Low Impact Aerobics	12/14/2009	Reynolds
Aerobic Kickboxing	12/15/2009	Stevens
Water aerobics	12/14/2009	Reynolds
Beginning Yoga	12/15/2009	Landis
Beginning Yoga	12/14/2009	Landis
Intermediate Yoga	12/14/2009	Landis
Advanced Yoga	12/14/2009	Landis

■ A **stacked report** arranges data in rows, with each field for each record in a separate row.

Stacked layout

Class	Low Impact Aerobics
Start	12/14/2009
Instructor	Reynolds
Class	Aerobic Kickboxing
Start	12/15/2009
Instructor	Stevens
Class	Water aerobics
Start	12/14/2009
Instructor	Reynolds
Class	Beginning Yoga
Start	12/15/2009
Instructor	Landis
Class	Beginning Yoga
Start	12/14/2009
Instructor	Landis

■ To switch between the two modes, select all the fields to affect and then use the Tabular or Stacked button on the Arrange tab.

■ You can select all the fields at once by clicking the Select All icon (with the four-headed arrow) in the upper-left corner of the layout grid.

Select all fields in the grid by clicking here

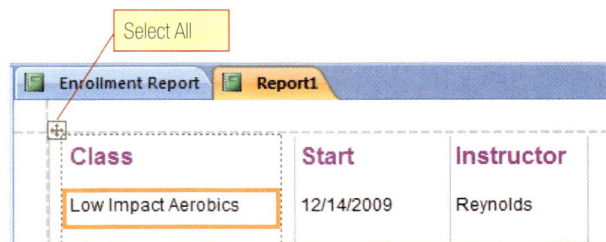

Select All

Enrollment Report	Report1

Class	Start	Instructor
Low Impact Aerobics	12/14/2009	Reynolds

■ The reason you must select fields to affect before changing the layout is that it is possible to have a combination report, using tabular layout for some fields and stacked layout for others.

■ The Remove button takes a field out of the layout grid, making it a free-floating object on the report. This might be useful to position a field in a precise location, for example.

Change a Column Width

- If a column is not wide enough to accommodate the widest entry in it, you might want to widen the column.

- To do so, position the mouse pointer at the right edge of the column and drag to the right.

Reorder Fields

- You can change the order of the fields by dragging the field to the left or right (in a tabular layout) or up or down (in a stacked layout).

Delete Fields

- To remove a field from the layout, select it and press ⌫. Any fields to its right or below it move to close up the hole.

Add Fields

- To add a field to the layout, on the Report Layout Tools Format tab, click Add Existing Fields. A Field List task pane appears. From there you can expand a list of fields in the available tables and drag-and-drop a field onto the layout grid.

Insert a Title

- If the report does not already have a label at the top that functions as a title, you can add one by clicking the Title button on the Report Layout Tools Format tab.

Add a title placeholder to the report, if desired, and then fill in the desired title

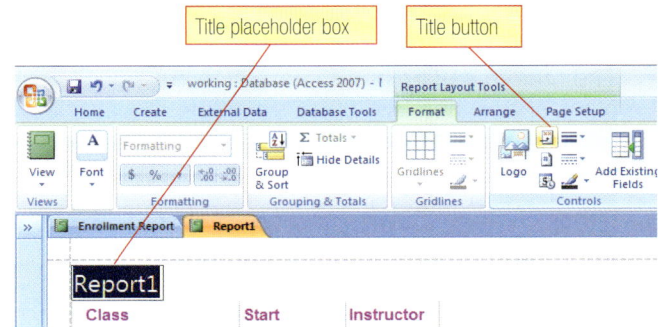

Drag fields onto the layout to add them

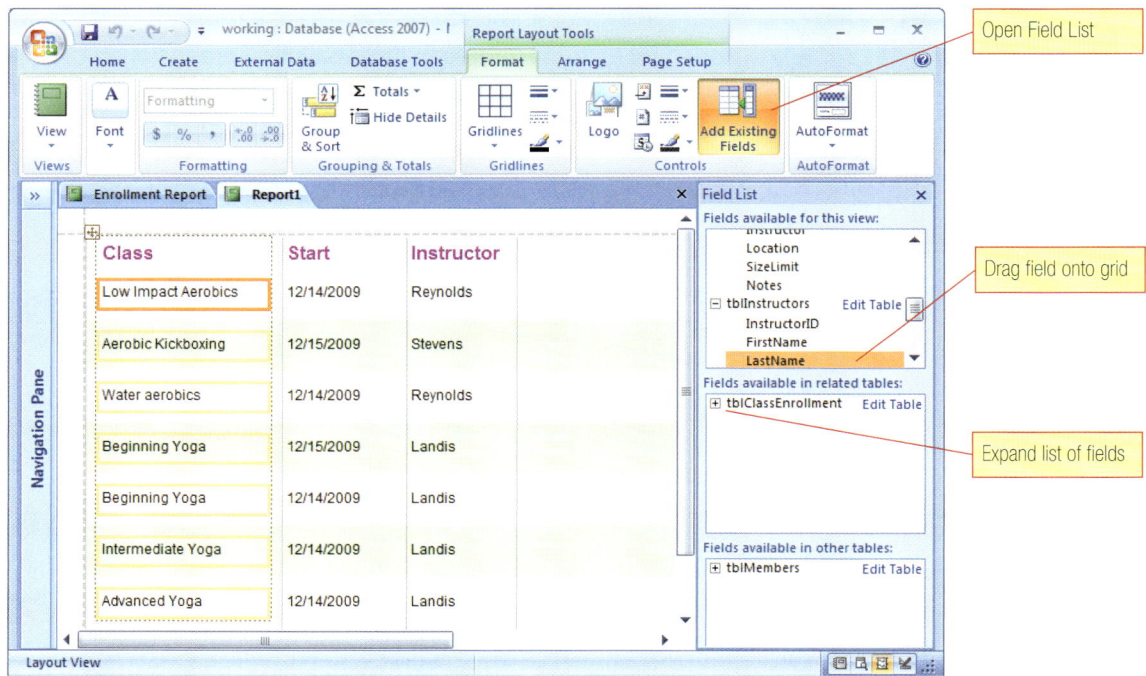

Change the Page Setup

- Page setup includes the paper size, page orientation, page margins, and number of columns. All of these are controlled from the Page Layout group.

The Report layout tools

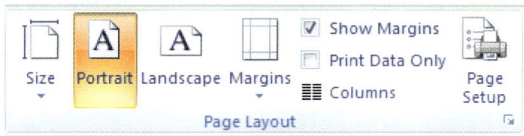

- On the Page Layout group, you can:
  - Select a paper size from the Size button's list.
  - Click Portrait or Landscape to change page orientation.
  - Select a margin preset from the Margins button's list.
  - Mark or clear the Show Margins check box to show or hide margins in Layout view.
  - Mark or clear the Print Data Only check box to print data only or not. You might do this, for example, if filling out a pre-printed form. You would want to see the pre-printed labels and headings onscreen but not on the hard copy.
  - Select a number of columns from the Columns button's list.
  - Click Page Setup to open a Page Setup dialog box in which you have greater control over many of these settings, such as the ability to specify exact margin amounts.

Page Setup dialog box

Create a New Report in Layout View

- To start a new report in Layout view, click Blank Report on the Create tab. The Field List task pane opens automatically, showing the fields available in all tables.

- From here you can drag-and-drop fields onto the layout. You can also insert logos, title boxes, and other placeholders as needed, as you would when editing an existing report.

  ✓ *For best results, choose the report layout (tabular or stacked) immediately after placing the first field in the report, so you can see what you are doing as you go.*

Start a new blank report in Layout view

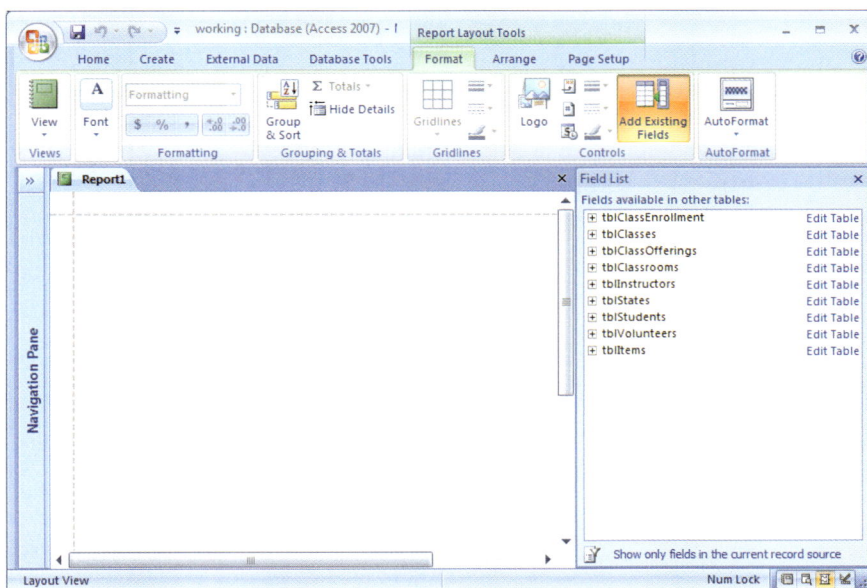

PROCEDURES

Open a Report in Layout View

1. Right-click the report in the Navigation Pane.

   OR

   If the report is already open in some other view, right-click its tab.

2. Click **Layout View** . . . . Ⓨ

Change Internal Margins in Cells

In Layout view:

1. Select the cell(s) to affect.

   ✓ *Hold down Shift as you click on additional cells after clicking the first one, or press Ctrl+A to select the entire layout.*

2. Click **Report Layout Tools Arrange** tab . . . . [Alt]+Ⓝ

   Control Layout Group

3. Click **Control Margins** [A] Control Margins ▾ button . . . . Ⓜ

4. Click a preset:
   - **None** . . . . Ⓝ
   - **Narrow** . . . . Ⓐ
   - **Medium** . . . . Ⓜ
   - **Wide** . . . . Ⓦ

Change Padding for Cells

In Layout view:

1. Select the cell(s) to affect.

   ✓ *Hold down Shift as you click on additional cells after clicking the first one, or press Ctrl+A to select the entire layout.*

2. Click **Report Layout Tools Arrange** tab . . . . [Alt]+Ⓝ

   Control Layout Group

3. Click **Control Padding** Control Padding ▾ button . . . . Ⓟ

4. Click a preset:
   - **None** . . . . Ⓝ
   - **Narrow** . . . . Ⓐ
   - **Medium** . . . . Ⓜ
   - **Wide** . . . . Ⓦ

Switch Between Layout Types

In Layout view:

1. Select the cell(s) to affect.

   ✓ *Hold down Shift as you click on additional cells after clicking the first one, or press Ctrl+A to select the entire layout.*

2. Click **Report Layout Tools Arrange** tab . . . . [Alt]+Ⓝ

   Control Layout Group

3. Click **Tabular** Tabular button . . . . Ⓢ, Ⓤ

   OR

   Click **Stacked** Stacked button . . . . Ⓞ

Change a Column Width

In Layout view:

1. Select the cell(s) to affect.

   ✓ *The entire column is resized, no matter which cell in it you select.*

2. Position the mouse pointer at the right edge of the cell.

   ✓ *The pointer becomes a double-headed horizontal arrow* ↔ .

3. Hold down the left mouse button and drag to the right or left.

4. Release the mouse button.

Reorder Fields

In Layout view:

1. Select the field to affect.

   ✓ *In a tabular report, the field labels are in the first row, at the top of each column. In a stacked report, the field labels are in the first column, to the left of the data. In a stacked report there may be more than one copy of a field's label; moving any of them moves all of them in all copies.*

2. Position the mouse pointer in the middle of the cell.

   ✓ *The pointer shows a four-headed arrow* .

3. Drag the field to a new position.

Delete a Field

In Layout view:

1. Select the field to affect.

2. Press Delete.

Add a Field

In Layout view:

1. Click **Report Layout Tools Format** tab . . . . [Alt]+Ⓜ

   Controls Group

2. Click **Add Existing Fields** Add Existing Fields button . . . . Ⓧ

3. If needed, click plus sign icon ⊞ to expand the field list for a table.

4. Drag field onto report layout grid.

   OR

   Double-click the field to add it to the right or below the last field.

Insert a Title

In Layout view:

1. Click **Report Layout Tools Format** tab . . . . Alt +M

   Controls Group

2. Click **Title** button 🔲 . . . . . . T
3. Type the title and click outside the control.

Change the Paper Size

In Layout view:

1. Click **Report Layout Tools Page Setup** tab . . . . Alt +S

   Page Layout Group

2. Click **Size** button Size . . . S , Z
3. Click the desired paper size.

Change the Page Orientation

In Layout view:

1. Click **Report Layout Tools Page Setup** tab . . . . Alt +S

   Page Layout Group

2. Click **Portrait** Portrait button . . . . R

   OR

   Click **Landscape** Landscape button L

Apply a Page Margin Preset

In Layout view:

1. Click **Report Layout Tools Page Setup** tab . . . . Alt +S

   Page Layout Group

2. Click **Margins** Margins button . . . M
3. Click a margin preset:
   - **Normal**
   - **Wide**
   - **Narrow**

Set Custom Page Margins

In Layout view:

1. Click **Report Layout Tools Page Setup** tab . . . . Alt +S

   Page Layout Group

2. Click **Page Setup** Page Setup button . . . . S , P
3. Click **Print Options** tab.
4. Enter values in boxes for Margins settings:
   - **Top** . . . . Alt +T
   - **Bottom** . . . . Alt +B
   - **Left** . . . . Alt +F
   - **Right** . . . . Alt +G
5. Click **OK** . . . . Enter

Create a New Report in Layout View

1. Click **Report Layout Tools Create** tab . . . . Alt +C

   Reports Group

2. Click **Blank Report** Page Setup button . . . . R , B
3. If needed, click plus sign icon ⊞ to expand the field list for a table.
4. Drag field onto report layout grid.

EXERCISE DIRECTIONS

1. Start Access, if necessary.
2. Open ⊙ **10MICHIGAN** and save a copy of it as **10MICHIGAN_xx**.
3. Open rptEnrollment in Layout view.
4. Widen the Classes column so that all entries in it fit.
5. Narrow the other columns so that they are no wider than they need to be in order for their data to fit.
6. Drag the left edge of the Class field to the left so it aligns with the dotted outline margin guide.
7. Add the ClassDuration field to the layout, between Start Time and Taught By.
8. Use the Align Text Left button on the Report Layout Tools Format tab to make the contents of all fields, and their headings, left-aligned.
9. Move the Taught By field immediately to the right of the Class field.
10. Set the Padding for the entire report to Medium.
11. Change the page orientation to Portrait.
12. Change the page margins to Normal.
13. View the report in Print Preview. Then save and close the report.
14. Start a new blank report.
15. Add the Class field to the report from tblClassOfferings.
16. Add the ClassName field to the report from tblClasses and widen it so that all class names fit on one line each.
17. Add the FirstName and LastName fields to the report from tblInstructors.
18. Remove the Class field that you added in step 15 (the one that shows the classes as numbers, not names).
19. Add a title of **Teaching Assignments** to the report.
20. Switch the report to a Stacked layout.
21. Save the report as **rptAssignments** and close it.
22. Close the database and exit Access.

ON YOUR OWN

1. Start Access and open the 🔵 **10FOSTER** database. Save a copy of it as **OAC10_xx**.

2. Use the Report Wizard to create a report that contains the following fields:

   from tblDogs: Call Name

   from qryFosterHomesInfo: FirstName, LastName, City, State

3. Set up the report to view the data by the fields from the query. Do not add any sorting or additional grouping. Use the Stepped layout and Portrait orientation. Use the None style. Name the report **rptFosterHomes**.

4. In Layout view, make the following changes to the report:

   a. Edit the report title to read **Foster Homes**

   b. Tighten up the columns so there is not a lot of extra space between them.

   c. Change to a Stacked layout for all fields.

   d. Set the Padding for the Call Names to Wide.

   e. Move the Call Name field to the left so that it left-aligns with the second column, as in Illustration A.

   ✓ *You can do this by dragging the left border of the Call Name field label to the left, then dragging the right border to the left. Alternatively you can remove that field from the layout with the Remove button on the Arrange tab and then drag it over.*

   f. Remove the date and page number from the bottom of the report.

   ✓ *Hint: Select them and press Delete, just as you would when removing a field.*

5. Save and close the report.

6. Close the database and exit Access.

Illustration A

Foster Homes

FirstName	Kathy
LastName	Buchanan
City	Indianapolis
State	IN
Call Name	Duncan
FirstName	Margaret
LastName	Hermstead
City	Noblesville
State	IN
Call Name	Emma

Skills Covered

- **Format Controls on Forms and Reports**
- **Use Conditional Formatting**

- **Bind and Unbind Fields to Controls**
- **Concatenate Fields**

Software Skills   Forms and reports are very similar in terms of the formatting you can apply to them. Both enable you to position fields and labels for optimal viewing; the main difference is that a form is designed for onscreen use whereas a report is designed to be printed. In this exercise, you will learn some tips and tricks for formatting, binding, and concatenating fields on forms and reports.

Application Skills   Michigan Avenue Athletic Club would like the Teaching Assignments report in their database to show the instructors' full names on a single line, rather than a separate line for first and last names. You will make this change by creating a concatenated control in that report. You will also modify a form that shows class offerings such that if a particular class is on sale, the sale price is shown onscreen and is marked with special formatting.

TERMS

Bound control   A control that displays its content from a table or query field.

Concatenate   To comine two or more text strings.

Conditional formatting   Formatting that is applied only when a condition is met.

Control   Any object on a form or report, including fields, text labels, pictures, and so on.

Expression   A logical condition including comparison operators such as greater than (>), less than (<), or equals (=).

Unbound control   A control that has no connection to a field from a table or query.

NOTES

Format Controls on Forms and Reports

- You can apply the same types of formatting to **controls** on forms and reports that you would apply in any word processing program. For example, you can change the font, size, color, font attributes such as bold and italic, and text alignment (left, right, center).

- You can also apply a background fill to the control, which applies color behind the text in that control's frame.

- All these formatting features are found in the Font group on the Format tab when the form or report is in Layout view, or on the Design tab when in Design view.

Text formatting controls

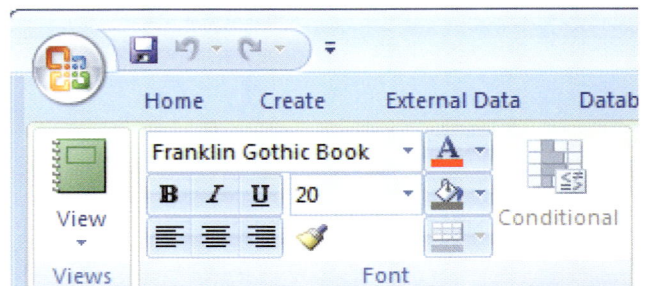

- There are some minor differences in the use of the formatting commands between Layout and Design view. One of these is that in Layout view, when you change the font size, the control's frame expands as needed to accommodate the new text. In Design view it does not; you must manually resize the control.

- To copy formatting between controls, use Format Painter. Select the control that is already formatted correctly, and click the Format Painter button. Then click the control to receive the formatting.

  ✓ *To paint the formatting onto multiple destinations without having to re-select the source each time, double-click instead of single-click the Format Painter button.*

- In Report Layout view, you can use Alternate Fill/Back Color to shade every other row in the data list for easier reading.

- The easiest way to change the formatting on a form or report is with AutoFormat. Open the AutoFormat drop-down list on the Format tab (in Layout view) or the Arrange tab (in Design view) and select the desired format.

- You can start with an AutoFormat and then adjust it manually as needed.

- AutoFormats in Access share the same themes as in other Office applications, so you can coordinate the work you create in the various programs.

Apply an AutoFormat for quick formatting

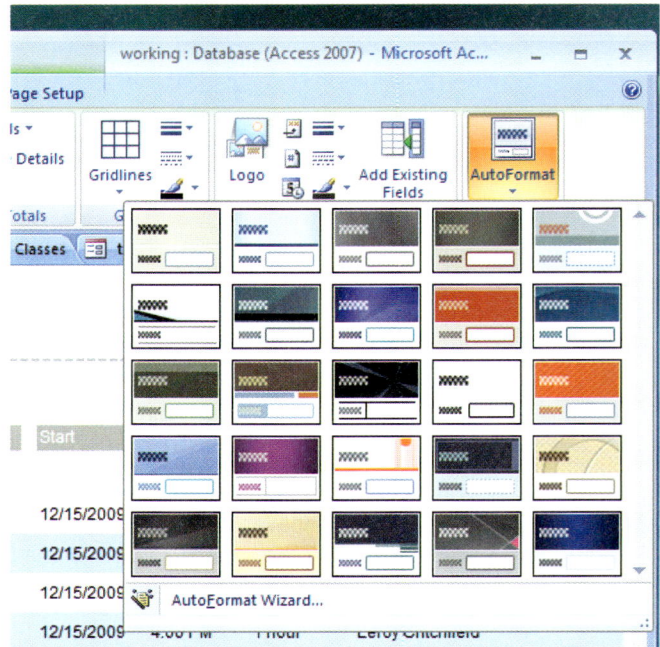

Alternate the fill color in the data rows on a report

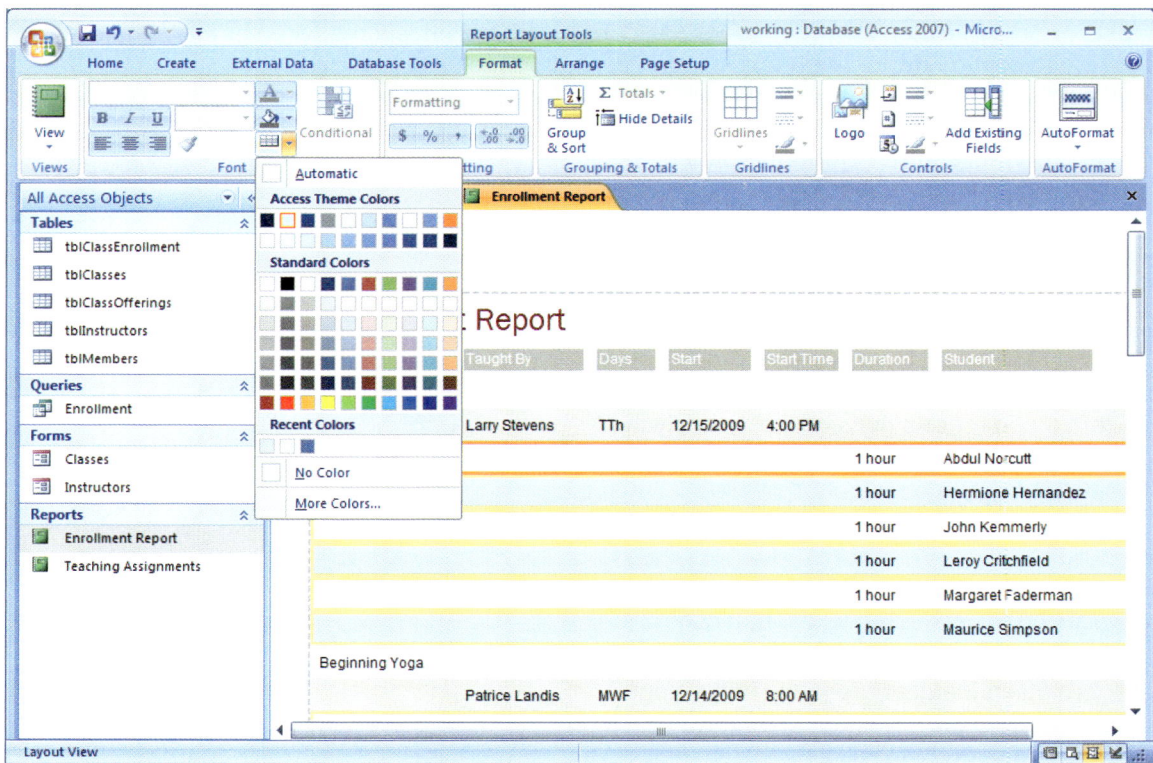

Use Conditional Formatting

- **Conditional formatting** sets up special formatting conditions that should apply if the value in a field or other control meets certain criteria.

- Some examples: You could color items with low sales (under a certain dollar amount) in red to indicate a problem, or you could underline the names of students who have not yet paid for a class.

- Conditional formatting can be applied to both forms and reports, in both Design and Layout views.

- Select the control and click the Conditional button. In Design view, from the button is on the Design tab; in Layout view, the button is on the Format tab.

- In the Conditional Formatting dialog box, set up the desired formatting. The default formatting appears automatically based on how you have formatted the control already. You can change it here if desired.

- The Condition 1 area contains the same kinds of formatting buttons, and also a place where you can set up a logical condition to be met. If the condition is met, the formatting you specify here overrides the default formatting.

- You can set up multiple conditions by clicking the Add button to get additional sets of buttons. Use the Delete button to remove a formatting condition.

Set up conditional formatting

- Conditional formatting conditions can be set either by the field's value or by an **expression**. An expression is a formula. It can reference field names (enclosed in square brackets).

- For example: [Quantity] * [Unit Price] > 1000 is an example of an expression. In this case the conditional formatting would apply if multiplying the values from the Quantity and Unit Price fields resulted in a value of less than 1000.

- You must use an expression if you want to format a control (or multiple controls) based on the value of another control, or based on the result of a calculation.

- You must also use an expression to apply conditional formatting to an unbound control (that is, a control that is not connected to a field in an underlying table, query, or SQL statement). The date in a report's footer is an example of an unbound control.

- You can use almost all of the functions from Microsoft Office Excel in expressions in Access. You do not have to type an equals sign at the beginning of a function in the Conditional Formatting dialog box.

- For example, suppose you want the date at the bottom of the report to print in bold if the report is being printed on a Monday, because it is the first report of the week.

- Excel has a WEEKDAY function that converts a date to a number representing the day of the week (starting with Sunday as 1). Excel also has a NOW function that returns today's date and time. You can combine these to make an expression for conditional formatting: WEEKDAY(NOW)=2.

Bind and Unbind Fields to Controls

- A control on a form or report can be either bound or unbound. A **bound control** has a control source of a field from a table or query in your database. The fields you place on your form or report are bound controls. An **unbound control** does not. The page number and date codes at the bottom of a report are unbound controls, as are titles and other labels.

- To change a control's binding, view its properties. In Layout or Design view, right-click the field and choose Properties. Then, in the Property Sheet that appears, in the Control Source box, change the field name. The Control Source box can be found on both the Data and the All tabs.

A bound control's data source is in the Control Source box

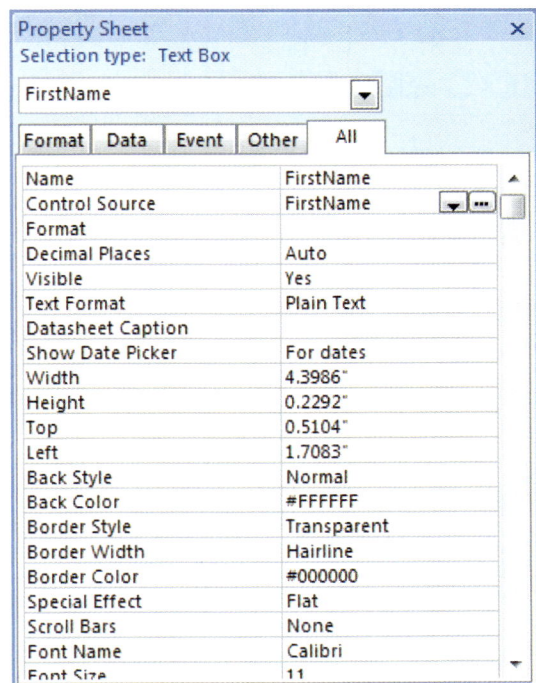

- When you click in the Control Source box, a drop-down list appears of the fields in the currently selected data source (table or query). You can select one of these to avoid potential typing errors in manually typing the field name.

- Alternatively, you can click the Build (…) button to open the Expression Builder. From here you can pick fields from other data sources or create more complex expressions.

- For example, you can pick a field from a query or table that is not the primary data source for this form or report (provided it is at least related to the primary data source).

You can select a record source from the Expression Builder

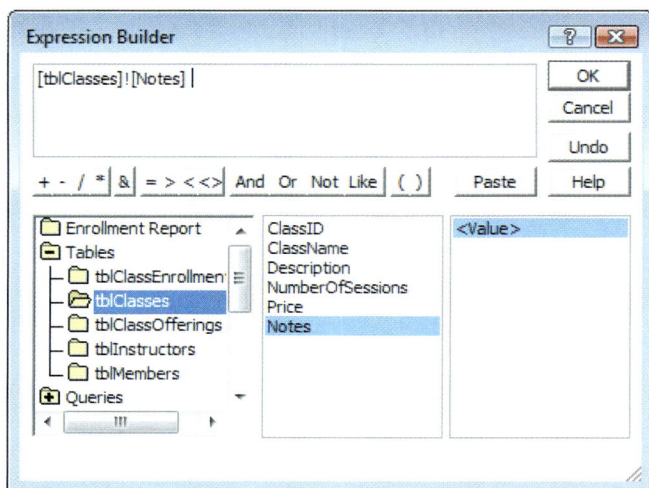

- In the left pane of the Expression Builder, double-click the type of source, and then double-click the table or query that contains the field. Finally, double-click the field name from the center pane.

  ✓ *If you know the exact names of the table and field you want to reference in the control, you can manually type them in as an expression; you do not have to go through the Expression Builder. For example, to reference the Notes field in the Employees table you would type =[Employees]![Notes].*

- To unbind a control from the data source, clear the value in the Control Source box.

Concatenate Fields

- On some reports, it may look better if multiple fields are combined in a single control, such as first and last name.

- To **concatenate** (combine) fields, first delete their original individual fields from the report. Then add a new text box with the Text Box tool in Design view. (You cannot do this from Layout view.)

- In the next text box, type an expression that begins with an equals sign and then contains the field names, in square brackets, separated by amper-sand signs (&).

- To include spaces or fixed text or punctuation between the fields, enclose it in quotation marks.

- For example, to combine FirstName and LastName fields:
  =[FirstName]&" "&[LastName]

- To combine City, State, and ZIP fields:
  =[City]&", "&[State]&" "&[ZIP]

PROCEDURES

Format Controls on Forms and Reports

1. Open the form or report in Layout or Design view.

2. Select the control(s) to format.

   ✓ *To select multiple controls, hold down Ctrl as you click each one.*

3. If in Layout view, click **Format** tab:

   Forms . . . . [Alt]+[G]
   Reports . . . . [Alt]+[M]

OR
If in Design view, click **Design** tab:

Forms . . . . [Alt]+[G]
Reports . . . . [Alt]+[M]

4. Perform one or more of the following formatting actions.

To change the font:

Font Group

1. Open **Font** drop-down list:

   Forms . . . . . [Alt]+[G], [F], [F], [↓]
   Reports . . . . [Alt]+[M], [F], [F], [↓]

2. Click the desired font. . . . . [↑]/[↓]

To change the font size:

Font Group

1. Open **Font Size** drop-down list:

   Forms . . . . . [Alt]+[G], [F], [S], [↓]
   Reports . . . . [Alt]+[M], [F], [S], [↓]

2. Click the desired font size . . . . [↑]/[↓]

To change the font color:

Font Group

1. Open **Font Color** drop-down list:

   Forms . . . . `Alt`+`G`, `F`, `C`

   Reports . . . . `Alt`+`M`, `F`, `C`

2. Click the desired font color.

   OR

   Click **Automatic** . . . . `A`

   OR

   a. Click **More Colors** . . . . . . `M`

   b. Click the desired color.

   c. Click **OK** . . . . `Enter`

To change the background color:

Font Group

1. Open **Fill/Back Color** drop-down list:

   Forms . . . . `Alt`+`G`, `F`, `B`

   Reports . . . . `Alt`+`M`, `F`, `B`

2. Click the desired background color.

   OR

   Click **Automatic** . . . . `A`

   OR

   a. Click **More Colors** . . . . . . `M`

   b. Click the desired color.

   c. Click **OK** . . . . `Enter`

To apply text attributes:

Font Group

- Click Bold button **B** :

  Forms . . . . `Alt`+`G`, `!`

  Reports . . . . `Alt`+`M`, `!`

- Click Italic button *I* :

  Forms . . . . `Alt`+`G`, `@`

  Reports . . . . `Alt`+`M`, `@`

- Click Underline button **U** :

  Forms . . . . `Alt`+`G`, `#`

  Reports . . . . `Alt`+`M`, `#`

Change the Horizontal Alignment

Font Group

- Click Left button ≡ :

  Forms . . . . `Alt`+`G`, `A`, `L`

  Reports . . . . `Alt`+`M`, `A`, `L`

- Click Center button ≡ :

  Forms . . . . `Alt`+`G`, `A`, `C`

  Reports . . . . `Alt`+`M`, `A`, `C`

- Click Right button ≡ :

  Forms . . . . `Alt`+`G`, `A`, `R`

  Reports . . . . `Alt`+`M`, `A`, `R`

Alternate Fill Colors for Rows of Data

In Layout view, in a tabular report:

1. Select a row of data.

2. Click **Format** tab . . . . `Alt`+`M`

Font Group

3. Click **Alternate Fill/Back Color** button arrow

   . . . . `F`, `A`

4. Click the desired color to alternate.

   OR

   Click **Automatic** . . . . `A`

   OR

   a. Click **More Colors** . . . . . . `M`

   b. Click the desired color.

   c. Click **OK** . . . . `Enter`

   OR

   Click **No Color** . . . . `N`

Copy Formatting Between Controls

In Layout or Design view on a form or report:

1. Select a control from which to copy formatting.

2. If in Layout view, click **Format** tab:

   Forms . . . . `Alt`+`G`

   Reports . . . . `Alt`+`M`

   OR

   If in Design view, click **Design** tab:

   Forms . . . . `Alt`+`G`

   Reports . . . . `Alt`+`M`

Font Group

3. Click **Format Painter** button

   . . . . `F`, `P`

   ✓ Double-click to toggle Format Painter on until you turn it off, to format multiple controls.

4. Click the control to format.

   ✓ If you double-clicked in step 3, click additional controls to format, or press Esc to cancel the operation.

Conditionally Format a Field

In Layout or Design View:

1. Select the field control to conditionally format.

   ✓ It must be a control that is bound to a field. If you want to format some other control, see Use Conditional Formatting with an Expression.

2. If in Layout view, click **Format** tab:

   Forms . . . . `Alt`+`G`

   Reports . . . . `Alt`+`M`

   OR

   If in Design view, click **Design** tab:

   Forms . . . . `Alt`+`G`

   Reports . . . . `Alt`+`M`

Font Group

3. Click **Conditional** button . . . . `O`

4. Confirm the default formatting for the control in the Default Formatting section.

5. Set up the condition:

   a. Set the first drop-down list to **Field Value Is**.

   b. Set the second drop-down list to the desired operator.

   c. Enter an expression in the text box(es) to describe the condition.

   ✓ If you choose between in step b, two text boxes appear; otherwise one text box appears.

6. Click the buttons to set the desired formatting if the condition is true:

- **Bold** **B**
- **Italic** *I*
- **Underline** U̲
- **Fill Color** 🎨 ▾
- **Font Color** **A** ▾

7. (Optional) Click **Add** and repeat steps 5–6 as needed.

8. Click **OK**. . . . . `Enter`

Use Conditional Formatting with an Expression

In Layout or Design View:

1. Select the control to conditionally format.

2. If in Layout view, click **Format** tab:

Forms . . . . `Alt`+`G`
Reports . . . . `Alt`+`M`

OR

If in Design view, click **Design** tab:

Forms . . . . `Alt`+`G`
Reports . . . . `Alt`+`M`

Font Group

3. Click **Conditional** button . . . . `O`

4. Confirm the default formatting for the control in the Default Formatting section.

5. Set up the condition:

a. Set the first drop-down list to **Expression Is**.

b. Enter an expression in the text box to describe the condition.

6. Click the buttons to set up the desired formatting if the condition is true:

- **Bold** **B**
- **Italic** *I*
- **Underline** U̲
- **Fill Color** 🎨 ▾
- **Font Color** **A** ▾

7. (Optional) Click **Add** and repeat steps 5–6 as needed.

8. Click **OK**. . . . . `Enter`

Change Field Bound to Control

In Design or Layout view:

1. Right-click a control.

2. Click **Properties**. . . . . `P`

✓ The Property Sheet appears for that control.

3. Click **Control Source**.

4. Open drop-down list and click field to bind to control.

OR

a. Click **Build** button ⌄.

b. Double-click **Tables** or **Queries** in left pane.

c. Double-click desired table or query.

d. Double-click desired field.

e. Click **OK**.

Bind Field to Unbound Control

In Design view:

1. Create an unbound text box, if needed:

a. Click **Design** tab . . . . . `Alt`+`G` or `Alt`+`M`

Controls Group

b. Click **Text Box** button **ab|** . . . . `C`, `X`

c. Drag on form or report to create text box.

2. Select the new text box.

3. Click **Property Sheet** button . . . . `H`, `P`

OR

a. Right-click the text box.

b. Click **Properties** . . . . `P`

4. Click **Control Source**.

5. Open drop-down list and select a field.

OR

a. Click **Build** button ⌄.

b. Double-click **Tables** or **Queries** in left pane.

c. Double-click desired table or query.

d. Double-click desired field.

e. Click **OK**.

Unbind Field from Bound Control

In Design or Layout view:

1. Right-click a control.

2. Click **Properties**. . . . . `P`

✓ The Property Sheet appears for that control.

3. Select text in Control Source box.

4. Press `Delete`.

Concatenate Fields

In Design view:

1. Create an unbound text box:

a. Click **Design** tab . . . . . `Alt`+`G` or `Alt`+`M`

Controls Group

b. Click **Text Box** button **ab|** . . . . `C`, `X`

c. Drag on form or report to create text box.

2. Click inside new text box and type an equals sign . . . . `+ =`

3. Type first field name enclosed in square brackets.

4. Type `&`

5. (Optional) Type punctuation or spaces enclosed in quotation marks.

6. Type `&` and then type next field name enclosed in square brackets.

7. Repeat steps 4–6 as needed.

8. (Optional) Delete label associated with new text box.

9. (Optional) Delete any individual fields that the new text box is replacing.

✓ To delete a label or field, click it so that selection handles appear around it and then press Delete.

EXERCISE DIRECTIONS

1. Start Access, if necessary.
2. Open ⊙ **11MICHIGAN** and save a copy of it as **11MICHIGAN_***xx*.
3. Open rptAssignments in Design view.
4. Delete the FirstName and LastName fields, and replace them with a single unbound text box.
5. Change the unbound text box's label to **Name**.
6. Format the Name and Class labels as bright blue and bold.
7. Right-align, size, and position the Class and Name labels as shown in Illustration A.

Illustration A

8. In the unbound text box, concatenate the values from the FirstName and LastName fields, with a single space between them.
9. Convert both the Class and Name fields to a Tabular layout. Left-align the labels in the Page Header section.
10. Tighten up the vertical size of the Detail section so there is no blank space between the field and the Page Footer.
11. View the report in Print Preview. The report should look like illustration B.

Illustration B

12. Close the Teaching Assignments report, saving your changes.
13. Open the tblClassOfferings table in Datasheet view and place a check mark in the Sale column for records 1, 3, and 6. Then close the datasheet.
14. Open frmClassOfferings in Layout view.
15. Left-align the Sessions and Price fields.
16. Switch to Design view.
17. Delete the Price and Sale fields.
18. Add an unbound text box, and change its label to **Price**. Align and size the Price label and the unbound text box to match the other labels and text boxes on the form.
19. Enter the following in the unbound text box:

    =IIf([Sale]=Yes,[Price]/2,[Price])

20. Switch to Form view to check your work; then switch back to Design view.
21. Display the Property Sheet for the unbound field and set its format to Currency. Left-align its content.
22. Set up conditional formatting for the unbound text box such that if Sale=Yes, the price shows as bold and bright red.
23. Switch to Form view and move through the records, making sure that the Price field appears in bold and red for records 1, 3, and 6, as in Illustration C.

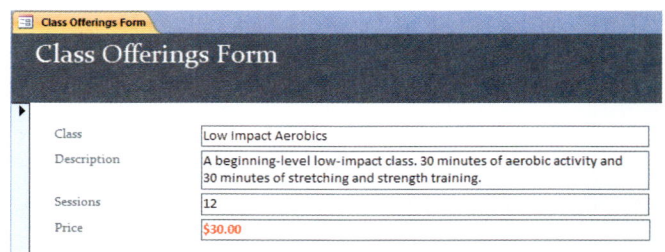

Illustration C

24. Close all open objects, saving your changes, and exit Access.

ON YOUR OWN

1. Start Access and open the ⊙ **11FOSTER** database. Save a copy of it as **OAC11_xx**.

2. Format the rptFosterAssignments report attractively, using any methods you learned in this exercise.

3. Replace the separate FirstName and LastName fields on the report with a single concatenated field.

   ✓ *If you want to move a label from the VolunteerID Header section to the Page Header section, select it, press Ctrl+X to cut it, then select the Page Header section and press Ctrl+V to paste it there. You cannot drag-and-drop between sections of a report or form.*

4. Close the report, saving your changes.

5. Set up conditional formatting in frmDogs for the Sex field so that if the value is Male, it appears in blue, and if it is female, it appears in pink.

6. Save your work and close Access.

Business Connection

Career Clusters

Career Clusters are groups of careers organized to help link education with business. There are 16 career clusters, and each cluster includes pathways to specific careers. For example, the Health Science career cluster includes such pathways as nursing, pharmacology, and radiology. Using career clusters can help you identify the area you are most interested in, and can help you focus your education so you can achieve a job in your selected field.

Reporting on Career Clusters

Working alone or in teams, spend some time researching the 16 career clusters and the pathways in each cluster. You might find information from your classroom instructor, the career center, or on the Internet at a site such as careerclusters.org. When you have completed your research, create a database of the clusters and the pathways. Include fields for information such as types of occupations in each pathway, employers in each pathway, education required, skills required, and even starting salaries. When the database is complete, generate a report about one of the career clusters. Deliver an impromptu presentation about the cluster to your classmates.

Skills Covered

- **Use Datasheet Forms**
- **Use Multi-Item Forms**
- **Use Split Forms**

- **PivotTable Basics**
- **Create a PivotTable Form**
- **Filter a PivotTable View**

Software Skills   Access 2007 offers a variety of form views. In this exercise, you will try your hand at using several types of form views that differ from the traditional default layout, and you will learn how to create PivotTables and use a form in PivotTable view.

Application Skills   You have been asked by a friend who works at Sycamore Knoll Bed and Breakfast for suggestions on improving their database. You will set up their database's forms to use various views that demonstrate the power of forms in Access 2007, and you will show them how to use a PivotTable form to analyze their data.

TERMS

Multi-item form   A form that shows more than one record at a time.

PivotTable   A tabular structure into which you can place fields from a table or query to help summarize and analyze the data.

Split form   A form view that shows Datasheet view in half the window and Form view fields in the other half.

View   A formatting filter through which an object can be seen. Different views arrange fields and records differently onscreen without changing the underlying structure.

NOTES

Use Datasheet Forms

- A datasheet form is not an actual type of form, but rather a **view** of a form. Rather than viewing the form in Form view (the default), you view it in Datasheet view.

  ✓ *Datasheet view is especially handy for subforms, which you will learn about in Exercise 14.*

- To view any existing form as a datasheet, open the form normally (in Form view) and then right-click its tab and choose Datasheet View.

Switch to Datasheet view

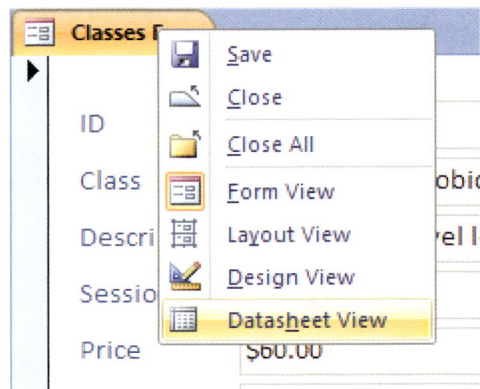

505

- You can force a form to always open in Datasheet view by default. To do this, open the form's Property Sheet (from Layout or Design view) and set the Default View property to Datasheet.

Set the form to open in Datasheet view by default

✓ *Also in the Property Sheet you can prevent certain views from being accessed for the form. Notice the settings for Allow Form View, Allow Datasheet View, Allow PivotTable View, and so on. If Datasheet view is not available for a form, check its properties on the Properties Sheet and make sure that Allow Datasheet View is set to Yes.*

- You can also create a new form that is automatically set to a default Datasheet view. To do this, select the table, query, or form on which you want to base the new form, click More Forms on the Create tab, and then click Datasheet. This creates an ordinary stacked form, but sets its default view to Datasheet.

- When you base a form on another form, it takes its fields and other settings from that form, like making a copy of it, and applies whatever new view you have chosen.

Use Multi-Item Forms

- Like the datasheet form, a **multi-item form** is also not actually a form type, but rather a view of a form (Continuous Forms view). In this view, multiple records are displayed at once. The form can use any arrangement (tabular or stacked).

A form in Continuous Forms view

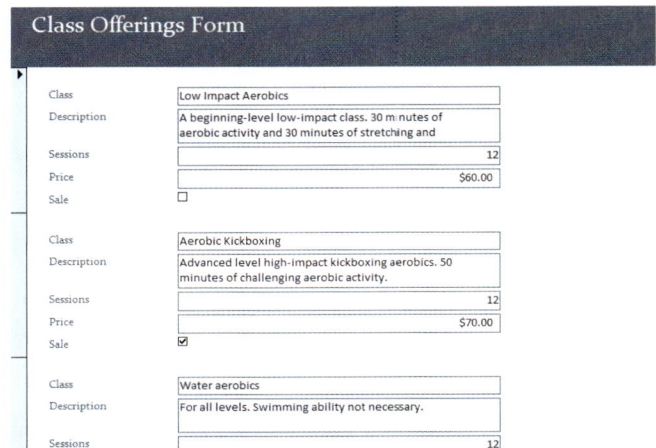

- You can set any existing form to display as multi-item. In Design view, open its Property Sheet and set the Default View to Continuous Forms. Then close and reopen the form.

- You can also create a new multi-item form from any table, query, or form. This results in a tabular layout form. To do this, select a table or query and then click Multiple Items on the Create tab.

Use Split Forms

- A **split form** is one that displays a Datasheet view on half the screen and Form view on the other half. It is useful in cases where you want to browse the data records easily, as with a datasheet, but you also want the ease of data entry that Form view provides.

- As with the other views discussed so far in this exercise, Split view is just a view, not an actual type of form. Any form can be viewed as a Split form by setting its Default View to Split Form (in Design view) and then closing and reopening the form.

- You can also create a new split form from any table, query, or form. Select it and then click the Split Form button on the Create tab.

A form in Split view

PivotTable Basics

- The PivotTable feature originated in Excel and is included in Access because it can help tremendously in analyzing data.

- A **PivotTable** is essentially an empty grid, into which you drag-and-drop field names.

- You display the PivotTable grid for a table or query by right-clicking the tab of an open table or query in Datasheet view and choosing PivotTable from the shortcut menu.

- The fields from the table or query appear in a field list. If the field list does not automatically appear, you can click the Field List button.

An empty PivotTable

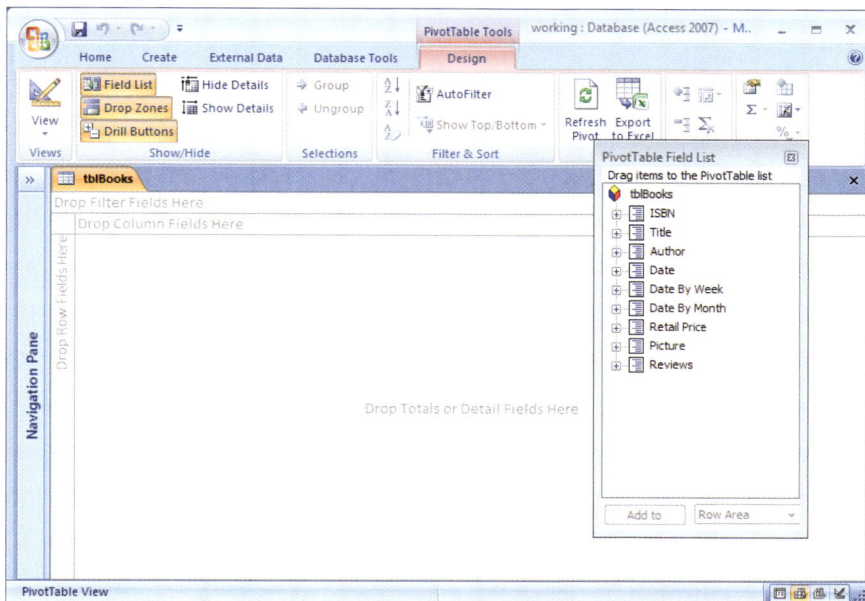

- To create the PivotTable, drag fields into the grid.
- Drag a field into the Drop Column Fields Here area and another one in the Drop Row Fields Here area. Then drag a third field into the Drop Totals or Detail Fields Here area.
- PivotTables are remarkably flexible. You can:
  - Click a plus sign to expand an area, or click a minus sign to collapse it.
  - Select a field and press [Delete] to remove it from the grid.
  - Drag other fields from the Field List to the grid to include them.
  - Filter to show only certain values (see the section *Filter a PivotTable View* below).

Create a PivotTable Form

- You can have only one PivotTable view for each table or query when you enter PivotTable view via the table or query datasheet.
- However, you can create PivotTable forms that are just like PivotTable views for tables or queries, and you can have as many different forms that refer to a specific table or query as you like.

- To create a PivotTable form for a query, table, or form, select it in the Navigation Pane, click More Forms on the Create tab, and then click PivotTable.
- A blank PivotTable grid appears, just as when displayed as a table or query view, except that by default the field list does not appear. (You can display it by clicking the Field List button, as you learned earlier.)

Filter a PivotTable View

- To filter the data so that it shows only certain values, click the down-pointing triangle next to one of the column names and clear the check boxes for the values you want to exclude.
- For example, to show only books that cost $24.99 or more in the preceding example, you would clear the check boxes for all prices of $24 or less as shown in the illustration on the following page.
- If you want to filter by a field that is not one of the column headings, drag the field to filter by to the Drop Filter Fields Here area.

A table in PivotTable view

Author	2007 Retail Price	2008 Retail Price	2009 Retail Price	Grand Total No Totals
Catherine Skintik		$30.00		
DDC Publishing		$16.00		
Ed Tittel			$89.00	
Faithe Wempen	$42.60	$30.00	$95.00	
J. Glenn Brookshear		$66.67		
James Kurose		$97.00		
Jennifer Fulton	$55.40			
Jennifer Fulton, Barbara Clemmons	$24.99			
Jennifer Fulton, Nancy Kaczmarczyk	$42.60			
John Truss		$85.00		
Katherine T. Pinard, Nancy Stevenson	$24.99			
Lisa Bucki, Eileen Ditmar		$30.00		
Lisa Friedrichsen		$25.99		
Matt Bishop	$74.99			

Filtering to exclude certain values

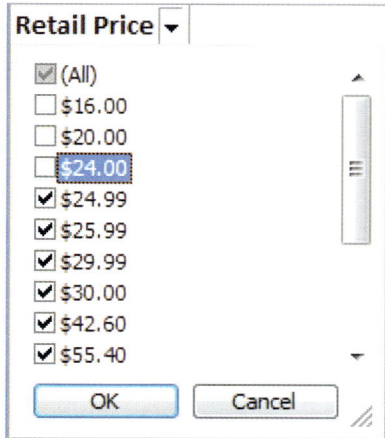

Retail Price ▼

- ☑ (All)
- ☐ $16.00
- ☐ $20.00
- ☐ $24.00
- ☑ $24.99
- ☑ $25.99
- ☑ $29.99
- ☑ $30.00
- ☑ $42.60
- ☑ $55.40

OK   Cancel

■ The presence of a field in the Drop Filter Fields Here area does not filter anything by default; you must then specify what criteria you want for the filter by opening its drop-down list and deselecting any values you don't want.

✓ *The down-pointing triangle turns blue when a filter is applied to remind you that the column is being filtered.*

■ You can quickly turn a filter on/off by clicking the AutoFilter button on the Design tab.

■ There is much more you can do with a PivotTable than can be covered here. Explore the commands on the PivotTable Tools tabs on the Ribbon on your own.

PROCEDURES

View a Form as a Datasheet

1. Open the form in Form view.
2. Right-click the form's tab.
3. Click **Datasheet View** . . . . ⒣

Set a Form to Open in a Specific View by Default

1. Open the form in Design view.
2. Click **Form Design Tools Design** tab . . . . ⒜⒧⒯+⒢

   Tools Group

3. Click **Property Sheet** button . . . . ⒣, ⒫
4. Open the **Default View** drop-down list.
5. Click the desired view:
   - **Single Form**
   - **Continuous Forms**
   - **Datasheet**
   - **PivotTable**
   - **PivotChart**
   - **Split Form**
6. Close the form, saving the changes.
7. Double-click the form in the Navigation Pane to open it in the chosen view.

Create a New Datasheet Form

1. Select a table, query, or form in Navigation Pane.
2. Click **Create** tab . . . . ⒜⒧⒯+⒞

   Forms Group

3. Click **More Forms** button

   More Forms ▼ . . . . ⒡, ⓜ
4. Click **Datasheet** . . . . ⒟

Create a New Multi-Item Form

1. Select a table, query, or form in Navigation Pane.
2. Click **Create** tab . . . . ⒜⒧⒯+⒞

   Forms Group

3. Click **Multiple Items** button . . . . ⓜ

Create a New Split Form

1. Select a table, query, or form in Navigation Pane.
2. Click **Create** tab . . . . ⒜⒧⒯+⒞

   Forms Group

3. Click **Split Form** button . . . . ⒫

Create a PivotTable Form

1. Select a table, query, or form in Navigation Pane.
2. Click **Create** tab . . . . ⒜⒧⒯+⒞

   Forms Group

3. Click **More Forms** button

   More Forms ▼ . . . . ⒡, ⓜ
4. Click **PivotTable** . . . . ⓣ

Enter PivotTable View for a Table or Query

1. Display the table or query in Datasheet view.
2. Right-click the tab.
3. Click **PivotTable View** . . . . ⓞ

Add Fields to PivotTable View

   Show/Hide Group

1. If the field list does not appear, click **Field List** button

   Field List . . . . ⒜⒧⒯+⒵, ⓣ, ⓛ
2. Click field in field list.
3. Drag field to PivotTable placeholder.

Delete Fields from PivotTable View

1. Click field on PivotTable.
2. Press [Delete].

Filter PivotTable Data

1. Click down arrow next to field name.
2. Deselect check boxes for each unwanted value.
3. Click **OK**. . . . . [Enter]

To add a filter field:

1. Drag a field to the **Drop Filter Fields Here** area.
2. Click down arrow next to field name there.
3. Deselect check boxes for each unwanted value.
4. Click **OK**. . . . . [Enter]

To turn off a filter:

■ Click **AutoFilter** button
  AutoFilter

EXERCISE DIRECTIONS

1. Start Access, if necessary.
2. Open 🔘 **12SYCAMORE** and save a copy of it as **12SYCAMORE_xx**.
3. Make a copy of frmReservations and name the copy **frmReservationsDatasheet**.
4. Set frmReservationsDatasheet to open by default in Datasheet view.
5. Create a new split form based on frmReservations and save it as **frmReservationsSplit**.
6. Create a new PivotTable form based on tblReservations.
7. Drag the Nights field to the Drop Row Fields Here area.

8. Click the plus sign by ReservationDate by Month in the Field List and drag Quarters to the Drop Column Fields Here area.
9. Drag the TotalDue field to the Drop Totals or Detail Fields Here area.
10. Drag the Suite field to the Drop Filter Fields Here area.
11. Exclude all suites except S1.
12. Save the form as **frmPivotS1**. The finished PivotTable should resemble Illustration A.
13. Close all open objects, saving your changes, and exit Access.

Illustration A

Suite ▾					
S1					

	Quarters ▾				
	⊞ Qtr3	⊞ Qtr4	⊞ Qtr1	⊞ Qtr4	Grand Total
	+ −	+ −	+ −	+ −	+ −
Nights ▾	TotalDue ▾	TotalDue ▾	TotalDue ▾	TotalDue ▾	No Totals
1	$95.00	$95.00	$95.00		
	$95.00				
	$95.00				
	$95.00				
2	$190.00			▸ $190.00	
Grand Total					

ON YOUR OWN

1. Start Access and open the ⊙ **12FOSTER** database. Save a copy of it as **OAC12_*xx*.**

2. Open frmVolunteers in Design view, and try to change its default view to Continuous Forms view. Notice the warning that appears.

3. Set the form's default view to Split Form. Then close and reopen the form in its default view.

> ✓ Notice that Split Form view shows two full instances of the same form: one in Datasheet view and one in Form view. It does not separate out the subform and the main form in separate split panes, as you might guess it would.

4. Close the form, saving your changes to it.

5. Create a new PivotTable form based on frmDogs.

6. Set up the PivotTable as shown in Illustration A.

7. Exclude all records in which GoodWithKids? is False.

8. Save the new form as **frmDogsGoodWithKids**.

9. Make a copy of frmDogsGoodWithKids and name the copy **frmGoodWithKidsDatasheet**.

10. Modify the properties of frmGoodWithKidsDatasheet so that it opens in Datasheet view by default.

11. Save your work and close Access.

Illustration A

Drop Filter Fields Here			
	GoodWithKids? ▾		
	FALSE	TRUE	Grand Total
	+ −	+ −	+ −
Sex ▾	Call Name ▾	Call Name ▾	No Totals
Female + −	Mac	Emma	
		Pokey	
Male + −		▸ Duncan	
		Sheldon	
		Smidgen	
Grand Total + −			

Skills Covered

- **About Report and Form Sections**
- **Turn Off or Hide Sections and Controls**
- **Sort and Group Report Data**

- **Move Controls Between Sections**
- **Add Report Statistics**
- **Filter Data Within Forms and Reports**

Software Skills   Forms and reports are organized into sections, with each section serving a specific purpose, such as to repeat column headings at the top of each page cr to group items that share the same value in a particular field. In this exercise, you will learn how to manage sections and how to create groupings and statistical summaries of each group.

Application Skills   In this exercise, you will continue improving the Sycamore Knoll database. You will add a date code to the footer of a form, but set the footer to be hidden by default, so you can show the change to the manager before it goes "live." You will also modify a Reservations report so that reservations are grouped by date and a count of the number of reservations per week is included.

TERMS

Footer   Sections that appear at the bottom of a report or form, below the detail area.

Header   Sections that appear at the top of a report or form, above the detail area.

Section   An area that specifies where on the page or form information is displayed, such as report header, report footer, group headers and footers, and the detail section.

Totals   Statistics that summarize report data, such as sum, count, or average.

NOTES

About Report and Form Sections

- Reports and forms both are divided into **sections**. Each section determines where the controls it contains will appear.

- At a minimum, a report or form contains the following sections:

  - Report or form **header**, which contains the title of the report or form. Sometimes you may wish to enhance the report or form header with a company logo or other graphic. Information in this header appears only on the first page.

  - Page header, which contains information repeated at the top of each report page. In a tabular report, the page header usually contains labels that identify the fields. In a stacked report, this section may be empty.

  - Detail, which contains the values for the fields. In a stacked report, the field names also usually appear in this section.

  - Page footer, which contains information that appears at the bottom of each report page, such as the page number and date.

  - Report or form **footer**, which contains information that appears at the bottom of the form, or only on the last page of the report, such as summary statistics.

- A report may also have sections for any groups you have created. You will learn about groups later in this exercise.

Report sections

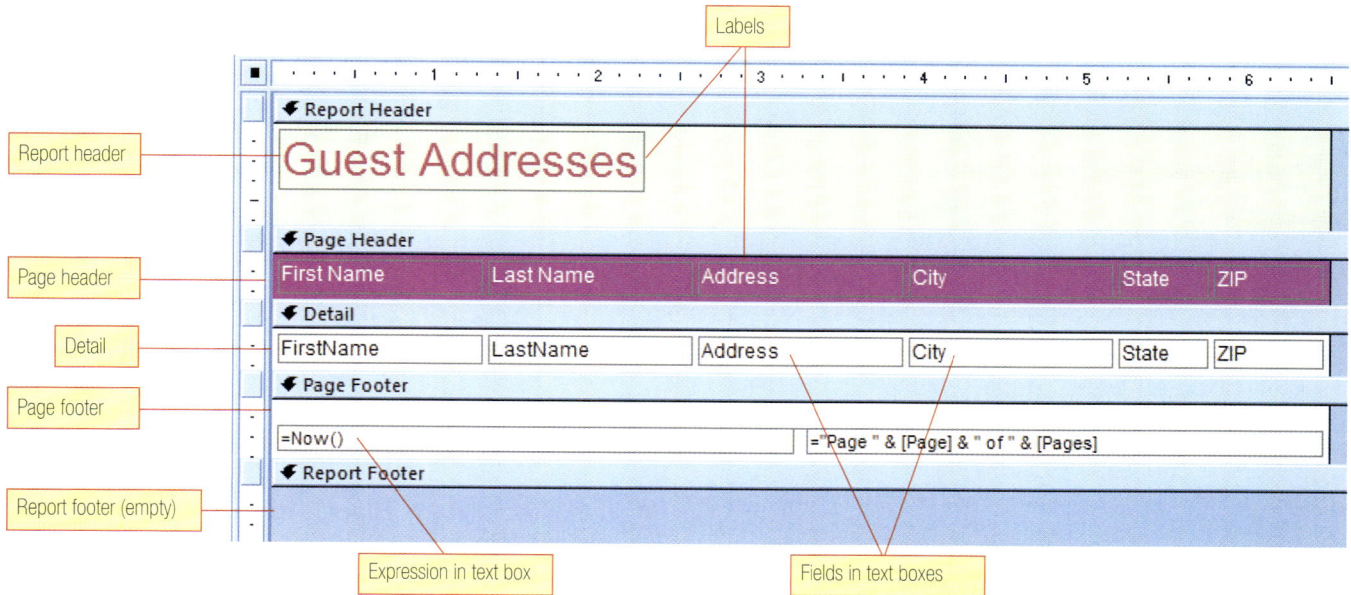

Labels

Report header

Guest Addresses

Page header

First Name	Last Name	Address	City	State	ZIP

Detail

FirstName	LastName	Address	City	State	ZIP

Page footer

=Now()   ="Page " & [Page] & " of " & [Pages]

Report footer (empty)

Expression in text box   Fields in text boxes

Change a Section's Size

- To change a section's size, first move, delete, or resize any controls if you want to make the section smaller. The section cannot be resized such that the controls in it don't fit anymore.

- Then move the mouse pointer to the bottom edge of the section. If it is not the lowermost section, the bottom edge of the section is the top edge of the bar containing the name of the next one. For example, the bottom of the Report Header section is the top of the Page Header section.

- When the mouse pointer becomes a double-headed arrow, drag the mouse pointer up or down to resize the section.

Resize a section by dragging

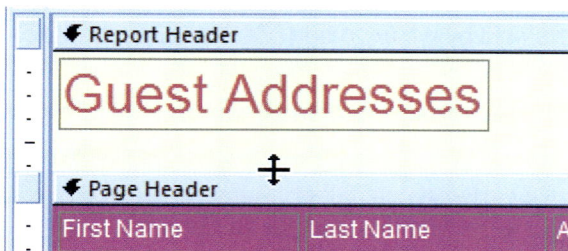

✦ Report Header

Guest Addresses

✦ Page Header

First Name	Last Name	A

Turn Off or Hide Sections and Controls

- If you turn off a section, any content in it is deleted. If you turn the section back on, it reappears, but it is blank, and you must reinsert controls into it.

- You can use buttons in Design view, on the Report Design Tools Arrange tab, to turn off the report, form, and page headers/footers.

  ✓ *A page header/footer does not appear onscreen for a form; it appears only if you print the form. Therefore, you should not use the page header/footer sections for anything that needs to appear onscreen.*

- As an alternative, you can hide any section by changing its Visible property (on the section's Property Sheet) to No. This turns the section display off without deleting its content.

  ✓ *To select a section, click its name in the layout in Design view. The bar with its name on it turns black, indicating it is selected.*

- You can also hide individual controls this same way; display the Property Sheet for the control and set Visible to No.

- Some of the sections are paired, such as report header/footer and page header/footer. They turn on/off as a pair. If you want one but not the other, delete any controls in the unwanted section and resize the section so it has no height, or hide the section as described above.

- If you hide the Detail section in a report that has groups with summary statistics (which are explained later in this exercise), only the group header and footer with summaries appear. This is how you would create a summary report.

Hide a form or report section or control by setting its Visible property to No

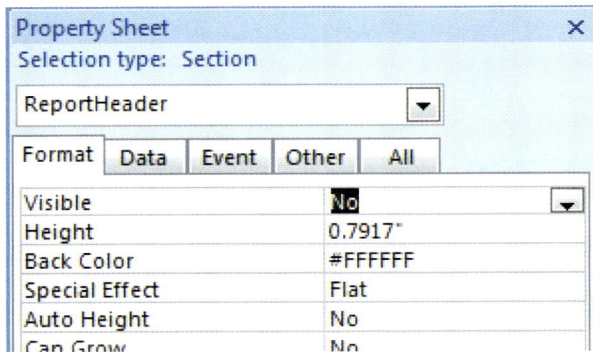

Property Sheet					×
Selection type: Section					

ReportHeader	▼

Format	Data	Event	Other	All

Visible	No	▼
Height	0.7917"	
Back Color	#FFFFFF	
Special Effect	Flat	
Auto Height	No	
Can Grow	No	

Sort and Group Report Data

- Sorting and grouping at the design level is done for reports only, not forms.

- To use sorting and grouping in a report, display the report in Design view, and then on the Report Design Tools Design tab, click the Group & Sort button. This turns on a Group, Sort, and Total pane at the bottom of the screen. By default it shows two buttons: Add a group and Add a sort.

The Group, Sort, and Total pane

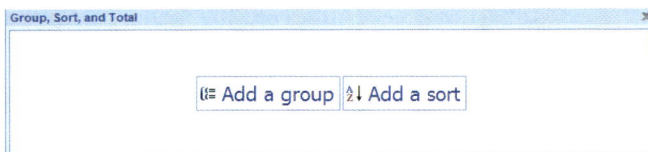

Group, Sort, and Total   ✕

       ⁞⁼ Add a group   ²↓ Add a sort

Group Records in a Report

- To group records, display the Group, Sort, and Total pane and then click Add a group.

- You are first prompted to select a field on which to group. Click the desired field.

- A grouping has a default sort order, which you can change from the group bar in the Group, Sort, and Total pane.

- When you select a field on which to group, a new header section is added to the report for it. However, the section is blank; Access does not automatically place (or move) the field into the section.

Choose the field by which to group

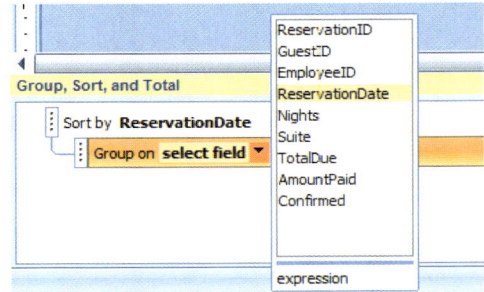

	ReservationID
	GuestID
	EmployeeID
Group, Sort, and Total	ReservationDate
	Nights
Sort by **ReservationDate**	Suite
Group on **select field** ▼	TotalDue
	AmountPaid
	Confirmed
	expression

- If the field already appears in the Detail area of the report (or in some other section), you can cut it to the Clipboard and then paste it into the new header section.

- If the field does not already appear on the report, you can add it, as you would add any field to a report layout. (Click Add Existing Fields and then drag the field onto the grid.)

- In a tabular report, you might want the field labels to be in the group header rather than the page header. You can select them and move them there with Cut and Paste.

- For more options to define the group operation, click the word *More* on the bar. The options will vary depending on the field type.

Sort Records in a Report

- Use sorting only if you just want to sort, not group. Grouping includes sorting.

- To sort the records in a report, click Add a sort in the Group, Sort, and Total pane. A gold sort bar appears, with a drop-down list from which to select the field by which to sort. Click the desired field.

Choose the field by which to sort

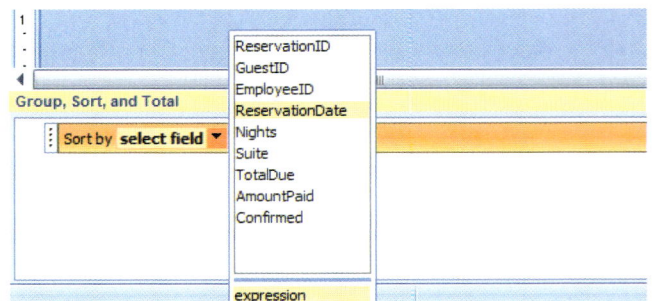

	ReservationID
	GuestID
	EmployeeID
Group, Sort, and Total	ReservationDate
	Nights
Sort by **select field** ▼	Suite
	TotalDue
	AmountPaid
	Confirmed
	expression

- The bar shows a default sort order that Access defines for you. The exact wording depends on the type of field. For example, for a date field, it might be "from oldest to newest." You can click this to select an alternate order if you prefer.

Change the sort order if desired

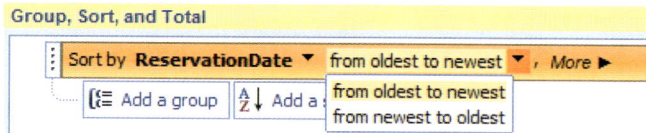

Group, Sort, and Total
Sort by **ReservationDate** ▼ from oldest to newest ▼ , More ►
〔≣ Add a group ᴬↆ Add a s〕 from oldest to newest / from newest to oldest

- In the event of a duplicate value in the sort field for two or more records, you might want to specify a second-level sort field. To do this, click Add a sort.

Keep a Group Together

- As mentioned earlier, you can click the word *More* for more options for the sorting or grouping in the Group, Sort, and Total pane.

- One of the options you can select there is whether or not to keep a group together on one page.

Keep a group together on a page

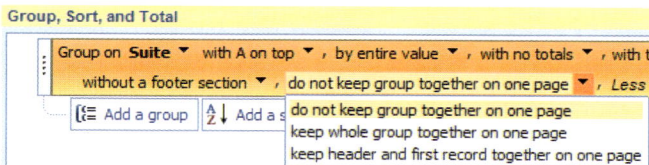

Group, Sort, and Total
Group on **Suite** ▼ with A on top ▼ , by entire value ▼ , with no totals ▼ , with ti
without a footer section ▼ , do not keep group together on one page ▼ , Less
〔≣ Add a group ᴬↆ Add a s〕 do not keep group together on one page / keep whole group together on one page / keep header and first record together on one page

Use a Group Footer

- By default, a report layout contains a header but not a footer section for each grouping you create. If you want a group footer section, you can click *More* and then click *with a footer section* or *without a footer section* to specify your preference.

Use a group footer or not

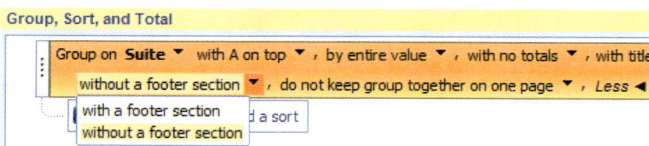

Group, Sort, and Total
Group on **Suite** ▼ with A on top ▼ , by entire value ▼ , with no totals ▼ , with title
without a footer section ▼ , do not keep group together on one page ▼ , Less ◄
with a footer section〕 d a sort / without a footer section

Move Controls Between Sections

- After turning on/off some headers or footers in the report or form, you might want to move some controls between sections.

- Some controls can be moved between sections with drag-and-drop. Others require you to use the Clipboard's Cut and Paste feature.

- To move a control, select it and cut it from its current location. Then select the section into which you want to move it and paste the control from the Clipboard. You might need to drag the control to reposition it within its new section.

Add Report Statistics

- Report statistics are called **totals** in Access.

- After clicking *More* for a grouping, you can click *with no totals* for a Totals box in which you can specify the statistics you want to display for each group. You can choose the field on which to total, the function to use (such as Sum or Average), whether or not to show grand totals, and whether to show totals in the group header or group footer.

Choose what statistics to display

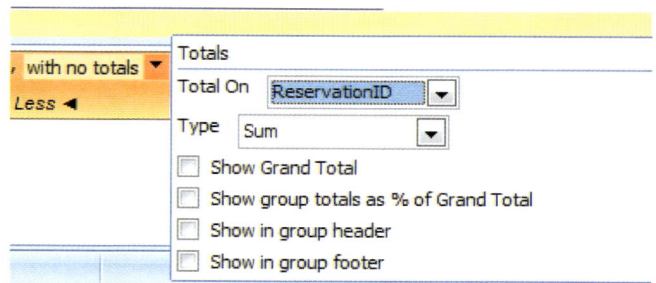

Totals	
, with no totals ▼	Total On ReservationID ▼
Less ◄	Type Sum ▼
	☐ Show Grand Total
	☐ Show group totals as % of Grand Total
	☐ Show in group header
	☐ Show in group footer

- When you specify totals, the expressions needed to create them are inserted automatically in the proper section(s).

- You can also manually enter your own expressions in text boxes you add in any section. Click the Text Box tool on the Design tab, and then click in a footer or header section and type any of the following:

  - =SUM([fieldname]) to total the values in the *fieldname* field.

  - =AVG([fieldname]) to average the values in the *fieldname* field.

  - =COUNT([fieldname]) to return the number of items in the *fieldname* field.

  - =MAX([fieldname]) to return the largest value in the *fieldname* field.

  - =MIN([fieldname]) to return the smallest value in the *fieldname* field.

✓ *If you just want to show the statistics and not the records themselves, click the Hide Details button on the Design tab.*

Filter Data Within Forms and Reports

- It is often just as easy to create a query that filters the data, and then base the form or report on that query, as it is to set up record filtering on the form or report layout itself.

- You can set up filtering for a form or report from Layout view. (It does not work in Design view.)

- To filter by example, right-click a field and then choose one of the filter commands on the shortcut menu. For example, in the following figure, the value of the right-clicked field was Johnson.

- You can also set up a custom filter. Point to the Filters command and open a submenu of additional filter choices. The exact name of the Filters command depends on the field type. For a text field, it is Text Filters; for a date field, it is Date Filters, and so on.

- This submenu provides Boolean options such as equals, does not equal, and so on.

- Then in the Custom Filter dialog box, type the desired value for the custom filter. You can use wildcard characters here such as * for any number of characters or ? for single characters.

Choose one of the simple example-based filters or choose a Boolean operator

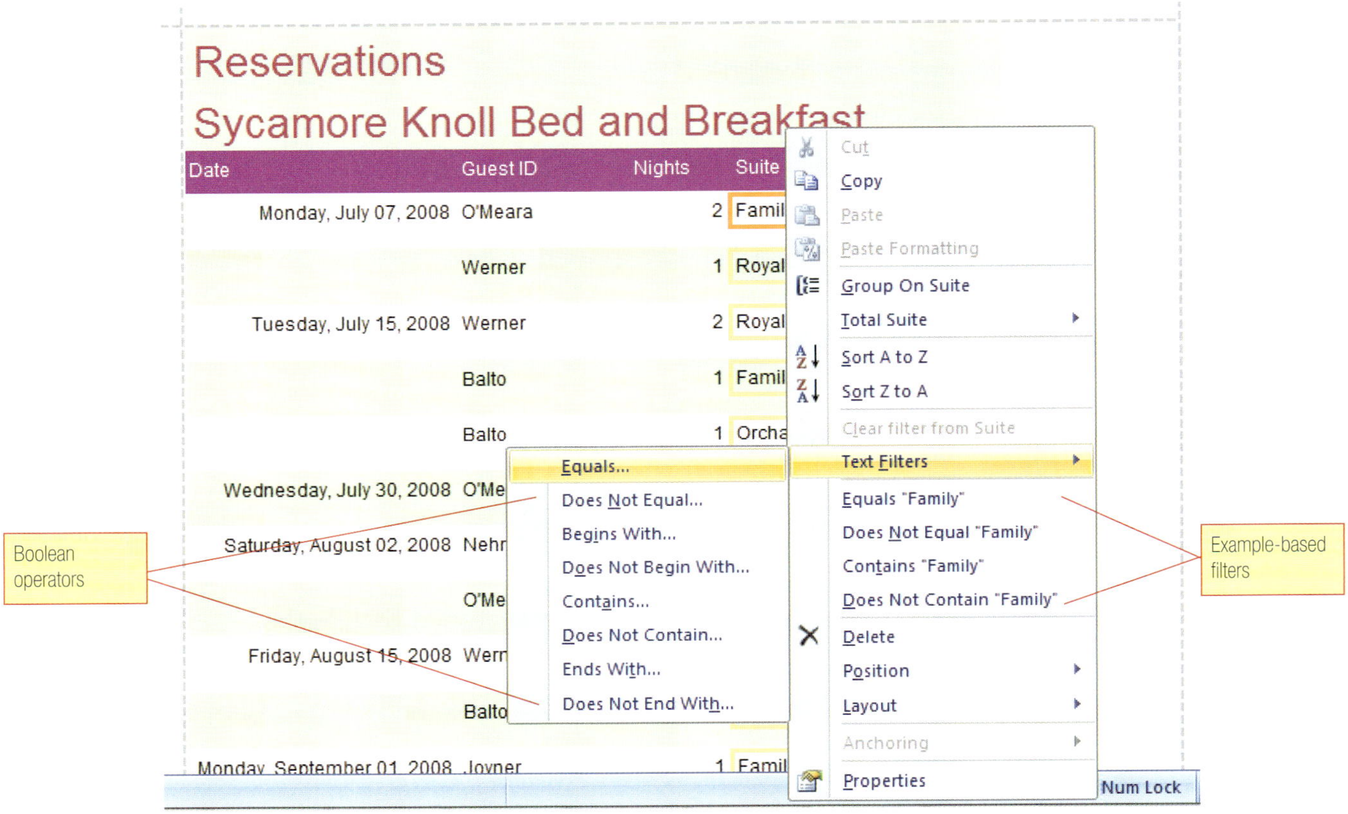

PROCEDURES

Change a Section's Size

In Design view:

1. If necessary, remove or resize controls within section.
2. Move mouse pointer to bottom edge of section.
3. Drag double-headed mouse pointer up or down.

Turn Sections On or Off

To turn on/off the Report or Form header and footer:

In Design view for a report or form:

1. Click **Arrange** tab:
   Reports . . . . `Alt`+`N`
   Forms . . . . `Alt`+`L`

   Show/Hide Group

2. Click **Report Header/Footer** button or **Form Header/Footer** button 📇 . . . . `J`

   ✓ *The Report Header/Footer and Form Header/Footer buttons are identical.*

To turn on/off the Page header and footer:

In Design view for a report:

1. Click **Arrange** tab:
   Reports . . . . `Alt`+`N`
   Forms . . . . `Alt`+`L`

   Show/Hide Group

2. Click **Page Header/Footer** button 📇 . . . . `H`

Hide or Display a Section or a Control

In Design view for a report or form:

1. Select the control or section.
2. Click **Design** tab:
   Reports . . . . `Alt`+`M`
   Forms . . . . `Alt`+`G`

Tools Group

3. Click **Property Sheet** button . . . . `H`, `P`
4. Click in the **Visible** box.
5. Click the down arrow.
6. Click **Yes** or **No**.

Display the Group, Sort, and Total Pane

In Design view for a report:

1. Click **Design** tab . . . . `Alt`+`M`

   Grouping & Totals Group

2. Click **Group & Sort** button
   Group & Sort . . . . `H`, `G`

Group Report Data

In the Group, Sort, and Total pane:

1. Click **Add a group**.
2. Click the field on which to group.

   ✓ *A grouping is sorted in ascending (A to Z) order by default.*

3. (Optional) Move controls and/or labels into group's header if desired.

   ✓ *See To move a control between sections.*

To sort a grouping in descending order:

In the Group, Sort, and Total pane:

1. Click down arrow to right of **with A on top** on bar representing grouping.
2. Click **with Z on top**.

To move a control between sections:

In Design view for a report:

1. Select control to move to a different section.
2. Press `Ctrl`+`X`.
3. Select section into which to move it.
4. Press `Ctrl`+`V`.
5. Drag control to reposition within the section as needed.

To enable the group footer:

In the Group, Sort, and Total pane:

1. If needed, click **More** on bar representing the grouping.
2. Click down arrow to right of **without a footer section**.
3. Click **with a footer section**.

To add group statistics:

In the Group, Sort, and Total pane:

1. If needed, click **More** on bar representing the grouping.
2. Click down arrow to right of **with no totals**.
3. Open **Total On** drop-down list and select field.
4. Open **Type** drop-down list and select statistic type.
5. Mark one or more check boxes to indicate location of statistic:
   - **Show Grand Total**
   - **Show group totals as % of Grand Total**
   - **Show in group header**
   - **Show in group footer**

To keep a group together:

In the Group, Sort, and Total pane:

1. If needed, click **More** on bar representing the grouping.
2. Click down arrow to right of **do not keep group together on one page**.
3. Click one of the following:
   - **Keep whole group together on one page**
   - **Keep header and first record together on one page**

Sort Report Data

In the Group, Sort, and Total pane:
1. Click **Add a sort**.
2. Click the field on which to sort.

   ✓ *A sort appears in ascending (A to Z) order by default.*

To change a sort to descending order:

In the Group, Sort, and Total pane:
1. Click down arrow to right of **with A on top** on bar representing sort.
2. Click **with Z on top**.

Delete a Sorting or Grouping

In the Group, Sort, and Total pane:
1. Click the bar representing the sorting or grouping.
2. Press Delete.

Apply a Basic Filter by Example to a Form or Report

1. Open the form or report in Layout view.
2. Right-click a field that contains the value to match.
3. Select one of the basic filtering options.

   ✓ *The option names depend on the field type, and include Equals and Does Not Equal.*

Apply a Custom Filter to a Form or Report

1. Open the form or report in Layout view.
2. Right-click any instance of the field on which you want to filter.
3. Point to the *type* **Filters** command, where *type* is the field type.

   ✓ *For example, for a text field, it would be Text Filters.*

4. Click the type of operator you want to use for the expression.
5. Fill in the parameters in the dialog box that appears.

   ✓ *The dialog box's name and its text boxes depend on the field type and the operator you chose.*

6. Click **OK**.

EXERCISE DIRECTIONS

1. Start Access, if necessary.
2. Open 🔵 **13SYCAMORE** and save a copy of it as **13SYCAMORE_xx**.
3. Open frmEmployees in Design view.
4. Insert a date code in the form footer:
   a. Drag the bottom of the Form Footer section down so that there is enough room for a text box, and then insert a new unbound text box. Size the text box to 2 inches wide.

   ✓ *Click the Ruler button on the Arrange tab (Show/Hide group) to turn on rulers so you can gauge how big 2 inches is.*

   b. In the unbound text box, type **=NOW()**.
   c. Delete the associated label for this text box and move the text box to the left side of the section.
5. Set the Form Footer to be hidden by changing its Visible property.
6. Close the form, saving your changes to it.

7. Open rptReservations in Design view.
8. Remove the current sort (by ReservationDate).
9. Group the report by ReservationDate, by week. (The default is by quarter.)
10. Move the ReservationDate field into the ReservationDateHeader section.
11. Turn on the display of a ReservationDate footer.
12. In the ReservationDate Footer section, add a Count Records statistic. Place it at the right side of the report, and add a label to its left that reads **Number of Reservations**. Make it right-aligned.

    ✓ *Use the Label tool on the Design tab. It is the one that looks like Aa. If you see a message that the label ought to be associated with a control, ignore it.*

13. View the report in Print Preview to check your work. It should resemble Illustration A.
14. Close all open objects, saving your changes, and exit Access.

Illustration A

Reservations
Sycamore Knoll Bed and Breakfast

Date	Guest ID	Nights	Suite	Confirmed
Monday, July 07, 2008				
	O'Meara	2	Family	True
	Werner	1	Royal	True
	Number of Reservations			2
Tuesday, July 15, 2008				
	Werner	2	Royal	True
	Balto	1	Family	True
	Balto	1	Orchard	True
	Number of Reservations			3
Saturday, August 02, 2008				
	Nehru	1	Hospitality	True
	O'Meara	3	Family	True
	O'Meara	2	Family	True
	Number of Reservations			3

ON YOUR OWN

1. Start Access and open the 13FOSTER database. Save a copy of it as **OAC13_xx**.

2. In rptFosterAssignments, add a count of the number of dogs in foster homes in the report footer, along with a **Number of dogs in foster homes** label.

3. Create a new report based on tblVolunteers using the Report button on the Create tab. Save the report as **rptVolunteers**.

4. In Layout view, remove the VolunteerID field and the page number code from the report.

5. Change the title in the Report Header section to **Volunteers by City**.

6. Group the report by city. Within each city group, sort records from A to Z by last name. Keep each group together on one page.

7. Set the Time code in the report header to be hidden.

8. Save your work and close Access.

Exercise | 14

Skills Covered

- **About Subforms and Subreports**
- **Create a Form or Subform with the Form Wizard**
- **Use the Subform or Subreport Wizard**
- **Create a Subreport or Subform with Drag-and-Drop**
- **Edit a Subform or Subreport**
- **Set Subform and Subreport Properties**

Software Skills When you have one set of records that is related to another, it is much easier to input new records when you can see the main record and the records that are related to it. For example, if you have an order record that could be related to one or more order detail items, the top half of the form might show the order information in general and the bottom half might show the items within the order.

Application Skills In this exercise, you will do some work for another company, The Textbook Exchange, which buys and sells used textbooks. You will set up a form with a subform that helps salespeople see at a glance the details of each book being offered for sale.

TERMS

Main form   In a form with a main form and subform, the part of the form that is the larger form into which the subform is embedded.

Subform   In a form with a main form and subform, the part of the form that is embedded within the main, larger form.

Subreport   Similar to a subform. A report can have a subreport that is embedded in the main report.

NOTES

About Subforms and Subreports

- **Subforms** and **subreports** allow you to see values related to a main record.
- You can go ten levels deep with a subform within a subform within the main form. However, one sub-form level deep is probably plenty in most circumstances; otherwise your forms get too complicated.

- A subform can be displayed in any view (Form view, Datasheet view, and so on). However, most subforms are displayed in Datasheet view by default because it is the most efficient view for packing a lot of information into a small space, and subforms are usually limited in the amount of space they occupy.

  ✓ *There must be a relationship between the table or query that comprises the main form and the one that comprises the sub-form. You must create that relationship before creating the form.*

- In a form with a subform, there are two sets of record-navigation controls. The subform has its own set, as does the main form.

A form with a subform

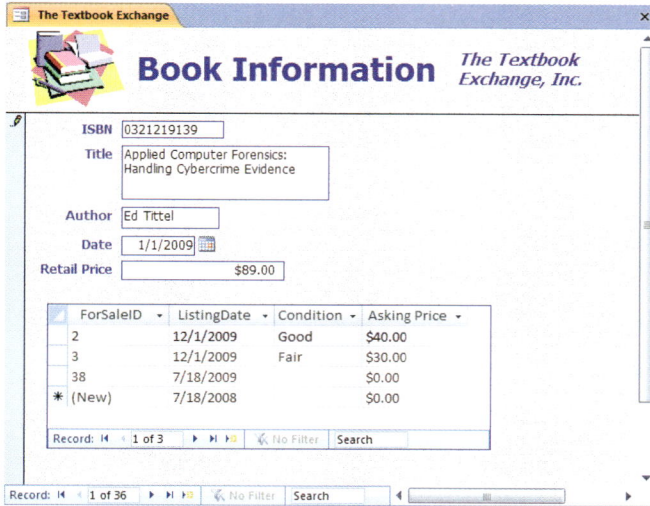

✓ *Once created, a subform also exists outside of the main form, as a separate form in the object list for your database. You can open it and use it as a separate form whenever you like. It is customary to include "subform" in the names you assign to subforms so you will remember what they were created for.*

- To create a subform, you can do any of the following:
  - Use the Form Wizard to create both the main form and the subform at the same time.
  - Create the main form and then use the Subform/Subreport button's wizard to build the subform.
  - Drag-and-drop another form onto an existing form in Design view to place it there as a subform.
- You will learn about each of these methods in this exercise.
- A subreport is much like a subform; the main difference is that it's on a report. The Report Wizard does not assist with creating a report/subreport combination, so you must set up a subreport via Design view.

Create a Form or Subform with the Form Wizard

- If you create the form and subform at the same time using the Form Wizard, Access does all the work for you.
- When you select fields from more than one table or query, the wizard automatically offers to set up the subform.

Choose fields from more than one table or query

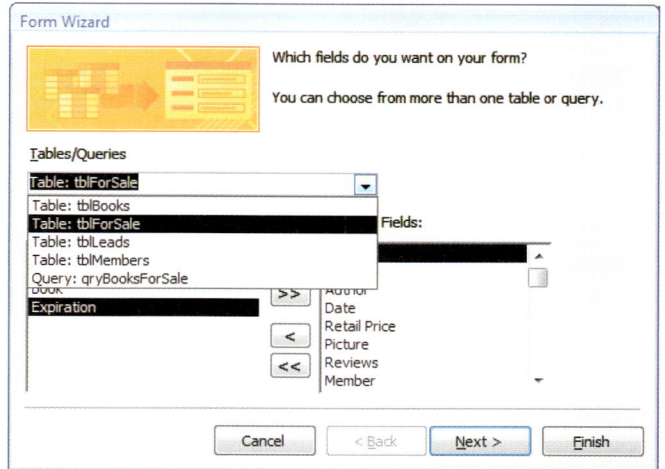

- In the second step of the Form Wizard, you choose to view your data by the main table or query. The wizard shows the main part of the form on top and the subform data on a box within the main form.
- The Linked forms option places a button on the main form instead of displaying the subform there. Users can click the button to open the subform separately.

Form Wizard—view by the main data

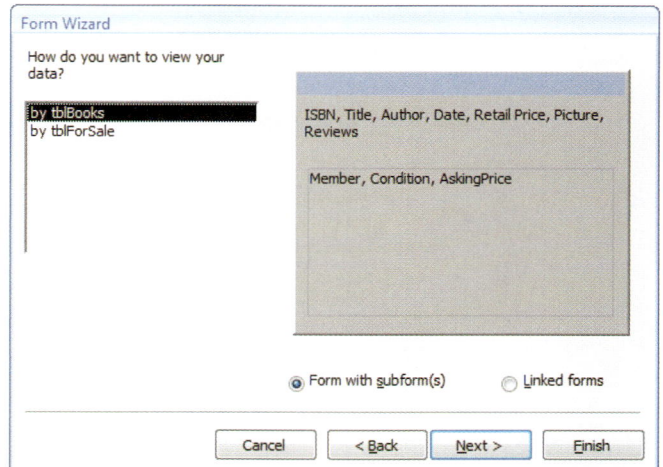

- Next, you are prompted to choose a layout for the subform. You can choose either tabular or datasheet.

- Next, you choose a style. It's just like choosing an AutoFormat style for a regular form.

- The last step asks for a title for the main form and subform. The main form title appears both in the form's tab and as the form name in the object list. The subform title appears on the subform object.

Use the Subform or Subreport Wizard

- The second way to create a subform or subreport is to add one to an existing form or report. You do this in Design view using the Subform/Subreport button in the Controls group.

- When you select this command and click on an existing form or report, a Subform or Subreport Wizard runs to guide you through the process.

Subform/Subreport button

✓ *Make sure the Use Control Wizards button is selected before you use the Subform/Subreport button.*

- Except for the name, the two wizards are nearly identical.

- The first step of the wizard asks you to select an existing table or query from which to create a new subform, or select an existing form to serve as a pre-made subform/subreport. (For a subreport, you can also select an existing report.)

Select a data source for a new subform, or an existing form to use

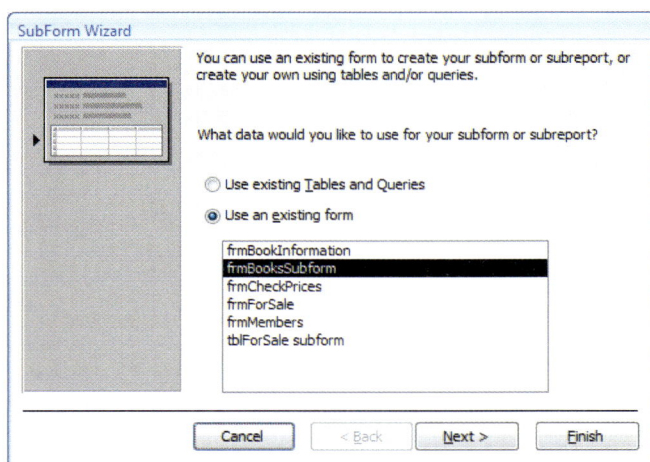

- If you choose to create a new subform or subreport based on existing tables and queries, you are prompted to select the fields to include, just as with the Form Wizard.

- You are next prompted to choose which fields link from the main form/report to the subform/subreport. Access makes a suggestion, but you can override it by selecting Define my own.

Choose how the form and the subform are related

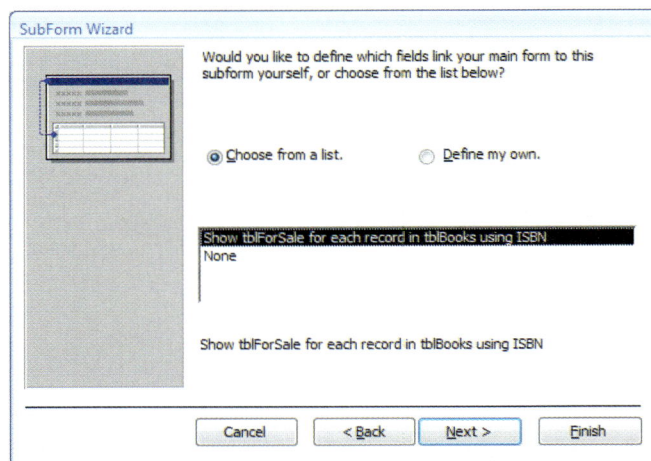

Create a Subreport or Subform with Drag-and-Drop

- The easiest way to create a subform on a form, or a subreport on a report, is if you have already created both of them separately. You can then drag the subform or subreport from the Navigation Pane onto the main one in Design view.

- You can also drag a table directly onto a form or report in Design view, and a wizard will ask you to verify the relationship.

Edit a Subform or Subreport

- You can change the size of the subform or subreport like any other object—by selecting it and then dragging its borders.

- When you save the form, both the main form and the subform (or the main report and subreport) are saved.

  ✓ *If you want to adjust the column widths on a Datasheet-view subform, it is easiest to do this in Layout view, where you can also see the data in the fields to gauge column width. In Design view, the subform appears in Form view, with the fields in a tabular arrangement, even though the subform will actually appear in Datasheet view.*

- When using a preexisting form or report as your subform or subreport, there may be fields that you do not want to be included on the subform. You can hide them from Layout view by right-clicking the unwanted field and choosing Hide Columns.

Set Subform and Subreport Properties

- With the Property Sheet open, you can set the subform's form (or subreport's report) or control properties.
- For example, to change the view of the subform, set the Default View property, as you learned earlier in this lesson.
- There are also some properties associated with the subform or subreport itself. Click the border surrounding the subform or subreport and the title of the Property Sheet will indicate the subform or subreport.

- Some of the important properties to look at are:

Property	Description
Can Grow	If there is more data than will fit, the subform or subreport can change size to accommodate all the data when printed. This property is on the Format tab.
Source Object	The name of the form or report that is the source. This property and the remaining properties described in this table can be found on the Data tab.
Link Child Fields	The name of the field in the Record Source of the subform or subreport that is related. Normally this is the many side of a one-to-many relationship.
Link Master Field	The name of the field in the Record Source of the main form or report that is related to the child field on the subform or subreport.
Enabled (subform only)	If you set this to No, the user cannot enter the subform.
Locked (subform only)	If you set this to Yes, the user cannot edit the data in the subform.

PROCEDURES

Create Main Form and Subform with Form Wizard

1. Click **Create** tab . . . . `Alt`+`C`

   Forms Group

2. Click **More Forms** button

   More Forms ▾ . . . . `F`, `M`

3. Click **Form Wizard** . . . . `W`
4. Select table or query for main form from **Tables/Queries** list.
5. Add fields from chosen table or query.
6. Select table or query for subform from **Tables/Queries** list.
7. Add fields from chosen table or query.

8. Click **Next** . . . . `Alt`+`N`
9. Choose which data source should be the main form.
10. Click **Next** . . . . `Alt`+`N`
11. Choose a view for the subform:

    Click **Tabular** . . . . `Alt`+`T`

    OR

    Click **Datasheet** . . . . `Alt`+`D`
12. Click **Next** . . . . `Alt`+`N`
13. Choose a style . . . . `↑`/`↓`
14. Click **Next** . . . . `Alt`+`N`
15. Type the names of your form and subform.

    OR

    Leave default names.
16. Click **Finish** . . . . `Alt`+`F`

Create New Subform or Subreport with Subform/Subreport Button

1. Open form or report in Design view.
2. Click **Design** tab:

   Forms . . . . `Alt`+`G`

   Reports . . . . `Alt`+`M`

   Controls Group

3. Make sure **Use Control Wizards** button ▯ is selected . . . . `P`
4. Click **Subform/Subreport** button

   ▦ . . . . `C`, `F`
5. Click on the form or report layout.
6. Click **Use Existing Tables and Queries**.

7. Click **Next** . . . . Alt+N
8. Choose table from Table/Queries drop-down list.
9. Select fields to include.
10. Click **Next** . . . . Alt+N
11. Choose from list of relationships.
    OR
    Click **Define my own** . . . . Alt+D and choose related fields.
12. Click **Next** . . . . Alt+N
13. Type name for subform or subreport.
14. Click **Finish** . . . . Alt+F

Add Existing Form or Report as a Subform or Subreport

Subform/Subreport Button Method:

1. Click **Design** tab:
   Forms . . . . Alt+G
   Reports . . . . Alt+M

2. Make sure **Use Control Wizards** button ⬚ is selected. . . . . . . P
3. Click **Subform/Subreport** button ▦ . . . . C, F
4. Click on the form or report layout.
5. Click **Use an existing report or form** . . . . Alt+E

   ✓ If working with a form/subform, the step 5 option will read **Use an existing form**.

6. Click the desired form or report.
7. Click **Next** . . . . Alt+N
8. Choose from list of relationships.
   OR
   Click **Define my own** . . . . Alt+D and choose related fields.
9. Click **Next** . . . . Alt+N
10. Type name for subform or subreport.
11. Click **Finish** . . . . Alt+F

Drag-and-Drop Method

1. Open form or report in Design view.
2. Drag table, query, form, or report (for a subreport only) from the Navigation Pane onto the layout.

   ✓ If you drag a table or query, complete the following steps:

3. Choose from list of relationships.
   OR
   Click **Define my own** and choose related fields.
4. Click **Next** . . . . Alt+N
5. Type name for subform or subreport.
6. Click **Finish** . . . . Alt+F

EXERCISE DIRECTIONS

1. Start Access, if necessary.
2. Open 💿 **14EXCHANGE** and save a copy of it as **14EXCHANGE_xx**.
3. Open frmMembers in Design view, and add frmForSale to it as a subform with drag-and-drop.
4. Switch to Form view.

   ✓ Notice that this does not look very good because of the large form header on the frmForSale form. It is clear that a new subform should be created, rather than trying to use an existing form as a subform.

5. Switch back to Design view and delete the subform.
6. In frmMembers, use the Subform Wizard to create a new subform based on tblForSale, containing only these fields: ListingDate, Book, Condition, AskingPrice. Use the default name for the subform.
7. Switch to Layout view and resize columns and the subform itself so that all data is visible in the subform. Delete the subform's label. See Illustration A.
8. Close the form, saving changes to both the form and the subform.
9. Open frmBookInformation in Design view and add a subform to it showing which members are selling each book.

   ✓ Use any method and settings you wish, but make sure that for each book, the user viewing the form will be able to see who is selling a copy (the seller's last name) and what the condition and asking price are.

10. Set up the subform to allow deletions but not edits or additions.

    ✓ To do this, open the subform as a separate form in Layout view, and view its Properties sheet. On the Data tab, set Allow Additions and Allow Edits to No.

11. Save and close all forms.
12. Use the Form Wizard to create a new form/subform combo called **frmMembers2**. The main form should use all the fields from tblMembers and the subform should show all fields from tblForSale and should open when you click a command button on the form (linked forms). For Style, use None. The subform should be named **frmForSaleSubform**.

13. Try out the button for the linked form in Form view. It doesn't work because the form title is covering it. Fix this problem in Design view by doing the following:

    a. Move the frmMembers2 label to the right to get it out of the way temporarily. Change that label's text to **Members**.

    b. Change the text on the button to **Member's Items**.

    c. Move the button into the Form Footer section using Cut and Paste.

    d. Drag the form title back to the left side of the Form Header section.

14. Test the button in Form view. It doesn't work, because moving it to another section has caused it to lose its event assignment.

15. Fix the problem by doing the following:

    a. Switch to Design view, and select the button.

    b. Open its Property Sheet.

    c. On the Event tab, click in the On Click box, and then open the drop-down list and choose [Event Procedure].

16. Test the button again in Form view. This time the sub-form opens.

17. Use Layout view to make any changes needed to the subform to make it more attractive by doing the following:

    a. Delete the ForSaleID and Member fields.

    b. Resize columns as needed

    c. Change the title to **Items for Sale**.

18. Use AutoFormat to apply the format of your choice for both the form and the subform.

    ✓ *When you apply the AutoFormat to the main form, a warning may appear that there is no style for a Toggle Button. Choose Update as a Command Button and click OK.*

19. Save your changes and close the database.

ON YOUR OWN

1. Start Access and open the ⊙ **14FOSTER** database. Save a copy of it as **OAC14_xx.**

2. Examine the two forms in this database: frmDogs and frmVolunteers. Determine what subform would be most beneficial for each of them, and then add the subform.

    ✓ *For example, when someone is viewing information about a particular dog, what information from another table or query besides its record source (tblDogs) would be valuable to see?*

3. Format the forms and subforms attractively.

4. Save your work and close Access.

Exercise | 15

Skills Covered

- **Open the Switchboard Manager**
- **Add or Delete a Switchboard Page**
- **Specify a Default Switchboard Page**
- **Edit a Switchboard Page's Content**
- **Format the Switchboard**
- **Activate or Deactivate the Switchboard**

Software Skills   All the powerful queries, reports, and other objects you create are perhaps a little intimidating for a beginning user. If you are going to allow other people to access the database, it might be a good idea to create a friendlier interface than the standard Navigation Pane. Access has a built-in system for this purpose called the Switchboard.

Application Skills   The Textbook Exchange has asked you to create a user-friendly interface from which employees can access the database objects. You will create a Switchboard system that does so.

TERMS

Switchboard   A set of system-generated forms that help less-experienced users access database objects.

NOTES

Open the Switchboard Manager

- The **Switchboard** is a set of forms that Access generates for navigation among database objects.

- The Switchboard is not just a single form, but a whole system of interconnected forms. The Forms Menu and Reports Menu buttons in the following figure open other forms, which are also part of the Switchboard.

- To create or modify the Switchboard, click Switchboard Manager on the Database Tools tab.

- If you have not yet created the Switchboard, a message appears that the Switchboard Manager was unable to find a valid Switchboard, and offering to create one. The Switchboard Manager lists each page of the switchboard. By default there is just one Main page, as shown in the following figure.

A typical Switchboard (main form)

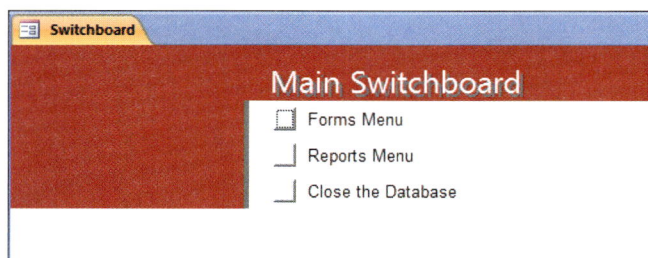

The Switchboard Manager lists the pages (forms) in the Switchboard

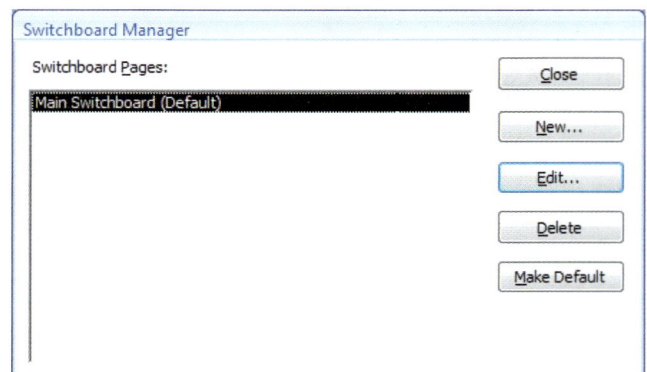

- The Main Switchboard page always exists; you cannot delete it. (You can change its content, however.)

- Each page appears as a separate form when you are working with the Switchboard, but you will see only a single form for the Switchboard in your list of forms in the Navigation Pane.

- That's because part of the benefit of the Switchboard system is that it keeps certain formatting features constant among all pages of the Switchboard. You can change formatting once—by modifying the Switchboard form in Design view—and the changes will apply to all pages.

- In contrast, if you manually create your own menu system with separate unbound forms, as you will learn in Exercise 16, you must apply formatting changes individually to each page.

Add or Delete a Switchboard Page

- Add a new Switchboard page if you want additional pages to be available from the Main page.

- To create a new page, click the New button in the Switchboard Manager window and follow the prompts. The new page displays in the Switchboard Manager's Switchboard Pages list.

- To delete a page, select it in the Switchboard Manager and click Delete.

Specify a Default Switchboard Page

- You can change which page appears first by clicking the desired page in the Switchboard Manager and then clicking Make Default.

Edit a Switchboard Page's Content

- To add entries to a new Switchboard page, or to edit an existing page, select the page from the Switchboard Manager's main window and then click the Edit button. The Edit Switchboard Page dialog box opens.

- By default, a new page is empty. You add entries that correspond to an action that the user will be able to select, such as opening a form or a report.

- To add an entry, click New and fill out the Edit Switchboard Item dialog box.

- In the Text box, enter the descriptive text that should appear for that menu item.

Edit an individual Switchboard item

- Open the Command drop-down list and select the action to perform.

  ✓ *When working with form-based commands, you have a choice of Open Form in Edit Mode or Open Form in Add Mode. Edit Mode starts on the first record, whereas Add Mode starts with a new blank record.*

- Next, select what object the command will apply to. The name of this bottommost list depends on what you chose in Command. For example, in the preceding figure, since a form command was chosen, the bottom drop-down list shows the available forms.

- To edit an existing entry, click it and then click Edit. The Edit Switchboard Item dialog box opens so you can make any desired changes to the text, command, or object.

Format the Switchboard

- You format the entire Switchboard as one unit; this keeps its formatting consistent across all pages.

- When at least one Switchboard page exists, a Switchboard form appears in the list of database forms in the Navigation Pane.

- You can open that form in Design or Layout view and edit it, much as you would edit any other form, including changing the background color.

- One thing that is very different, however, is that in Design view you will see blank placeholders with buttons next to them. These generically represent the text that will appear on each page.

- You can change the font used for the Switchboard text by formatting these blank placeholder boxes. You will not see the results of your formatting in Design view because there is no text to be shown there.

Activate or Deactivate the Switchboard

- To make the Switchboard load automatically when the database is opened, set it up as the default display form.

- To do this, set the Display Form value to Switchboard in the Current Database category in the Access Options dialog box.

- You might also want to hide the navigation pane so that users are limited to the commands provided on the Switchboard.

PROCEDURES

Open the Switchboard Manager

1. Click **Database Tools**
   tab . . . . `Alt`+`A`

   Database Tools Group

2. Click **Switchboard
   Manager** button

   Switchboard Manager . . . . . . `I`

3. If a message appears, click **Yes** to
   create switchboard . . . . `Y`

Create a Switchboard Page

In Switchboard Manager:

1. Click **New** . . . . `Alt`+`N`
2. Type page name.
3. Click **OK**. . . . . `Enter`

Delete a Switchboard Page

In Switchboard Manager:

1. Click page to delete.
2. Click **Delete**. . . . . `Alt`+`D`
3. Click **Yes** . . . . `Enter`

Change the Default Switchboard Page

In Switchboard Manager:

1. Click desired page.
2. Click **Make Default** . . . . . `Alt`+`M`

Add an Item to a Switchboard Page

In Switchboard Manager:

1. Click page on which item should
   appear.
2. Click **Edit** . . . . `Alt`+`E`
3. Click **New** . . . . `Alt`+`N`
4. Type name for item.
5. Click **Command** drop-down arrow
   and click desired command.

6. Click drop-down arrow for object
   list (name varies) and click desired
   object.
7. Click **OK**. . . . . `Enter`
8. Go back to step 3 to add another
   item.

   OR

   Click **Close** . . . . `Alt`+`C`
   to return to Switchboard Manager.

Delete an Item from a Switchboard Page

In Switchboard Manager:

1. Click page on which item appears.
2. Click **Edit**. . . . . `Alt`+`E`
3. Click item to delete.
4. Click **Delete**. . . . . `Alt`+`D`
5. Click **Yes** . . . . `Enter`
6. Go back to step 3 to delete
   another item.

   OR

   Click **Close** . . . . `Alt`+`C`
   to return to Switchboard Manager.

Edit an Item from a Switchboard Page

In Switchboard Manager:

1. Click page on which item appears.
2. Click **Edit**. . . . . `Alt`+`E`
3. Click item to edit.
4. Click **Edit**. . . . . `Alt`+`E`
5. Make changes to the Text, Com-
   mand, or object settings.
6. Click **OK**. . . . . `Enter`
7. Go back to step 3 to edit another
   item.

   OR

   Click **Close** to return to
   Switchboard Manager . . . `Alt`+`C`

Rearrange Items on a Switchboard Page

In Switchboard Manager:

1. Click page to be reordered.
2. Click **Edit** . . . . `Alt`+`E`
3. Click an item.
4. Click **Move Up** . . . . `Alt`+`U`

   OR

   Click **Move Down** . . . . . . `Alt`+`O`
5. Go back to step 3 to move another
   item.

   OR

   Click **Close** to return to
   Switchboard Manager . . . `Alt`+`C`

Format the Switchboard

1. Open the Switchboard form in
   Design or Layout view.
2. Format the form as you would any
   other form.

Show the Switchboard at Startup

1. Click **Office** button 🗔 . . . `Alt`+`F`
2. Click **Access Options**. . . . . . . `I`
3. Click **Current Database**.
4. Open the **Display Form**
   list . . . . `Alt`+`D`, `↓`
5. Click **Switchboard**.
6. Click **OK**. . . . . `Enter`
7. Click **OK**. . . . . `Enter`

EXERCISE DIRECTIONS

1. Start Access, if necessary.
2. Open 🔘 **15EXCHANGE** and save a copy of it as **15EXCHANGE_xx**.
3. Enable the switchboard.
4. Create two pages besides the main Switchboard page: Reports and Forms.
5. On the Reports page, create the following items:

Text	Command	Object
Books Report	Open Report	rptBooks
Customers Report	Open Report	rptCustomers
Return to Main Menu	Go to Switchboard	Main Switchboard

6. On the Forms page, create the following items:

Text	Command	Object
View Books	Open Form in Edit Mode	frmBooks
Add a New Book	Open Form in Add Mode	frmBooks
Place an Order	Open Form in Add Mode	frmOrders
Return to Main Menu	Go to Switchboard	Main Switchboard

7. On the Main Switchboard page, create the following items:

Text	Command	Object
Close the Database	Exit Application	(n/a)
Reports Menu	Go to Switchboard	Reports
Forms Menu	Go to Switchboard	Forms

8. Reorder the items on the Main switchboard in this order: Forms Menu, Reports Menu, Close the Database.
9. Close the Switchboard Manager and view the Switchboard form in Form view. Then close it.
10. Open the Switchboard Items table and change Main Switchboard to The Textbook Exchange. Then reopen the Switchboard form and confirm that the text you just typed appears.
11. Switch to Layout view and format the text next to the buttons as 10-point Arial.
12. Switch to Form view and check each button to make sure you can navigate between all three forms using the buttons, and that each form or report button opens the appropriate object.
13. Close the database.

ON YOUR OWN

1. Start Access and open the 🔘 **15CANDLES** database. Save it as **OAC15_xx**.
2. Create a switchboard system for this database with at least two other pages besides the Main Switchboard page.
3. Set up items on the pages so that every form (except the subform) and every report is accessible. Use meaningful text names for each item.
4. Add commands on each of the pages other than Main Switchboard that will return the user to the Main Switchboard.
5. Add a command on the Main Switchboard that will exit the database.
6. Arrange the items on each page in a logical order, with the commands to return to the Main Switchboard or close the database at the bottom.
7. Change the formatting of the Switchboard so that it has a plain white background (no colored rectangles) and uses black text for all labels including the top one. Move items around on the form as needed to create attractive spacing.
9. Set the Switchboard to load automatically when the database is opened. Close and reopen the database to confirm that the Switchboard opens.
10. Check your work; then close the database and exit Access.

Skills Covered

- **About Navigation Forms**
- **Create a Navigation Form**
- **Add Command Buttons to a Form**
- **Tie a Navigation Form into the Switchboard**
- **Set a Navigation Form to Load at Startup**

Software Skills   The Switchboard is the easiest way of creating user navigation forms, but there are some limitations. Each page of the Switchboard is formatted the same way, for example. Although it's a lot more work, you might want to create your own user navigation forms and tie them together into a Switchboard-like system that you develop yourself.

Application Skills   The Switchboard that you created for The Textbook Exchange in Exercise 15 is working well, but you wonder whether it would be better to have each page of the menu system appear in a different color background. Since this isn't possible with the Switchboard, you decide to try creating your own navigation forms.

TERMS

Command button   A button on a form that, when clicked, performs some action or command, such as opening a form or report.

Navigation form   An unbound form that exists to provide command buttons that move the user between other objects in a database.

Unbound form   A form that is not associated with any specific table or query.

NOTES

About Navigation Forms

- An **unbound form** is a form that has no data source (no table or query providing records to it). An unbound form can serve a variety of purposes, including creating your own dialog boxes and menus.

- A **navigation form** is a special type of unbound form that serves the same purpose as a Switchboard page. It displays various options for opening and editing data in forms and reports and contains command buttons for selecting those options.

- You can create your own navigation forms whenever the Switchboard's default offering does not meet your needs for some reason.

- You can create an entirely separate navigation system, or you can tie forms for specific pages into the Switchboard.

A sample navigation form

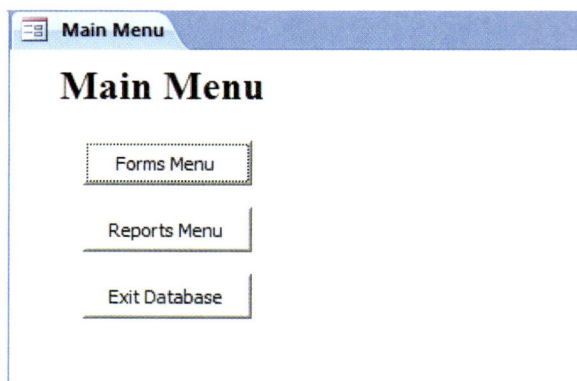

Create a Navigation Form

- To create a navigation form, start a new form without specifying a table or query on which it should be based.

- You can do this by clicking Blank Form on the Create tab.

Add Command Buttons to a Form

- The heart of a navigation form is a set of **command buttons**—buttons that the user will click to open objects.

- When you place a command button on a form in Design view, the Command Button Wizard runs, prompting you step by step to set up the button.

  ✓ *If you are creating a command button that will open another form, you must create that form before setting up that command button.*

- First, you choose a category and an action, as shown in the following illustration. Then you select the object to which that action applies (if applicable; not all actions require an object to act upon, such as closing the database).

Using the Command Button Wizard

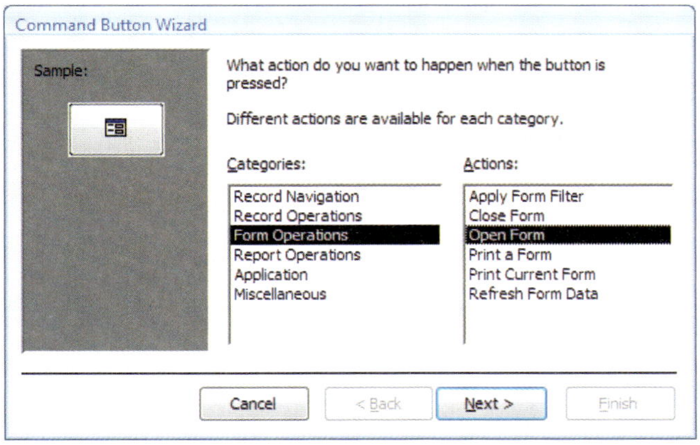

- You can also choose what text or picture the button face will display.

Selecting a button face (text or graphic)

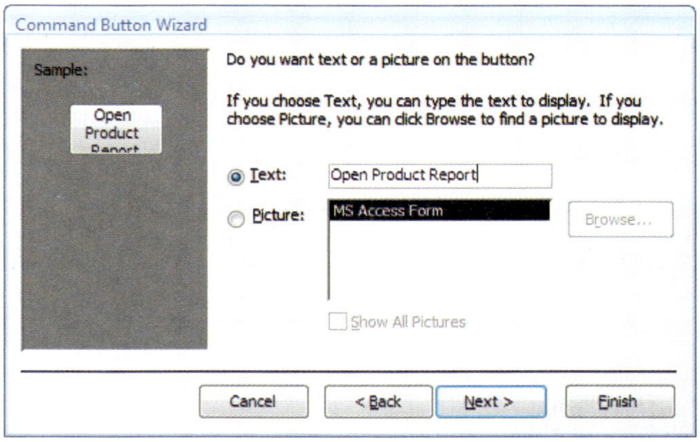

Tie a Navigation Form into the Switchboard

- You can use your own navigation forms as part of the Switchboard by creating an item on the Main Switchboard or any of the subordinate switchboards that opens the desired form.

- Set up the Switchboard item as if you were opening a form in Edit mode, and specify the navigation form's name as the form to open.

Tying a form into the Switchboard

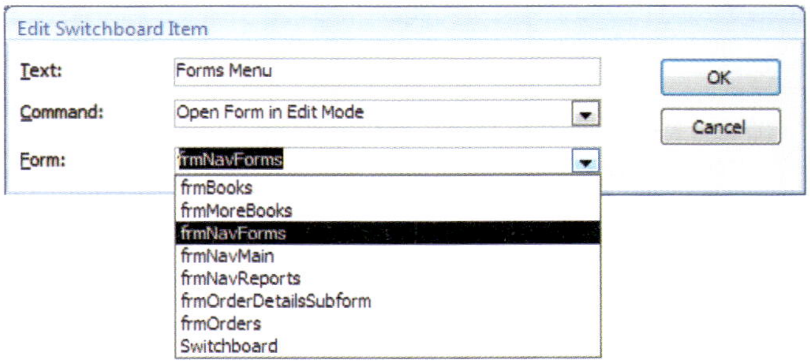

  ✓ *Make sure you include an item on your custom form that links back to the Switchboard so the user can return to it.*

Set a Navigation Form to Load at Startup

- If you want to use your own navigation form instead of the Switchboard, use the Display Form drop-down list in the Access Options dialog box to select your navigation form, just as you did with the Switchboard in Exercise 15.

PROCEDURES

Create an Unbound Form

1. Click **Create** tab . . . . `Alt`+`C`

   Forms Group

2. Click **Blank Form** button

   ☐ Blank Form . . . . `F`, `B`

3. Close the **Field List** pane.

4. Save the form with the desired name.

Add a Command Button to a Form

In Form Design view:

1. Click **Design** tab . . . . `Alt`+`G`

   Controls Group

2. Make sure **Use Control Wizards**

   button 🔲 is selected. . . . . . . `P`

3. Click **Command Button** tool

   ▬ . . . . `C`, `B`

4. Click the form.

   ✓ *The Command Button Wizard runs.*

5. Click the category of action that the button will represent.

6. Click the specific action that the button will represent.

7. Click **Next** . . . . `Alt`+`N`

8. Click the object on which to perform the chosen action.

9. Click **Next** . . . . `Alt`+`N`

10. Follow the prompts to specify other options if needed and click **Next** . . . . `Alt`+`N`

    ✓ *Additional options depend on the actions you chose in steps 8 and 9.*

11. Type caption for button.

    OR

    Choose picture for button.

12. Click **Next** . . . . `Alt`+`N`

13. Type a name for button.

14. Click **Finish** . . . . `Alt`+`F`

15. Save the form.

Add Link to Navigation Form to Switchboard

In Switchboard Manager:

1. Create a new Switchboard page if the page does not exist on which the link should be placed.

   ✓ *See Exercise 15 if needed.*

2. Click page on which link should appear.

3. Click **Edit** . . . . `Alt`+`E`

4. Click **New** . . . . `Alt`+`N`

5. Type name of form being linked to.

   ✓ *This does not have to be the exact name; make it a friendly name. For example, if linking to tblBooks, you might use Books Table.*

6. Click **Command** drop-down arrow and choose **Open Form in Edit Mode**.

7. Click **Form** drop-down arrow and click the desired form.

8. Click **OK**. . . . . `Enter`

9. Click **Close** to return to Switchboard Manager . . . `Alt`+`C`

10. Click **OK**. . . . . `Enter`

Set Navigation Form to Load at Startup

1. Click **Office Button** 🏢 . . . `Alt`+`F`

2. Click **Access Options**. . . . . . . `I`

3. Click **Current Database**.

4. Open **Display Form** drop-down list . . . . `Alt`+`D`

5. Click the desired form . . . . . . `↓`

6. Click **OK**.

EXERCISE DIRECTIONS

1. Start Access, if necessary.

2. Open ⊙ **16EXCHANGE** and save a copy of it as **16EXCHANGE_*xx***.

3. Create navigational forms that duplicate the functionality of the Forms and Reports pages in the Switchboard. Name them **frmNavForms** and **frmNavReports**.

   frmNavReports should have these buttons:

Books Report	opens rptBooks
Customers Report	opens rptCustomers
Main Menu	opens main Switchboard form

   frmNavForms should have these buttons:

View Books	opens frmBooks
Place an Order	opens frmOrders
Main Menu	opens main Switchboard form

4. Format your two new forms as desired. Make them identical in design.

5. Delete the Forms and Reports pages from the Switchboard, and edit the Main Switchboard so that your new navigation forms can be accessed from it.

6. Save your work, and try all the options in the Switchboard to make sure everything works.

7. Create a new navigation form, and call it **frmNavMain**. Format it the same as your other two navigation forms. frmNavMain should have these buttons:

Forms Menu	opens frmNavForms
Reports Menu	opens frmNavReports
Exit Database	closes the database file

   ✓ *To create a button that closes the database, choose Application as the category and Exit Application as the command.*

8. Set up the Startup properties for the database to load frmNavMain at startup.

9. Delete the Main Menu buttons on frmNavForms and frmNavReports and create them so that they open frmNavMain.

   ✓ *Or, for an extra challenge, manually edit the Click event procedure for the Main Menu buttons in the Property Sheet, changing "Switchboard" to "frmNavMain."*

10. Close the database and reopen it to confirm that frmNavMain opens automatically.

11. Try each button on each form to confirm that they all open the correct items.

12. Close the database.

ON YOUR OWN

1. Start Access and open the ⊙ **16CANDLES** database. Save it as **OAC16_*xx***.

2. Create a navigational form system that replaces the Switchboard, and set it to load at startup. Use whatever formatting and wording seems appropriate for the database. Make sure all forms (except the subform) and reports can be accessed from the system.

3. Check your work; then close the database and exit Access.

Exercise | 17

Skills Covered

- **Create a Chart Report**
- **Edit a Chart**

- **Change the Chart Type**

Software Skills Although Access is not known for its powerful charting capabilities the way Excel is, you can still produce attractive and useful charts using Access data.

Application Skills The manager of The Textbook Exchange has asked about charting in Access and would like to see some examples of what can be created. You will create a chart that summarizes the sales by salesperson to illustrate the value of charts.

TERMS

Legend A color-coded key that tells what each color in a chart represents.

Microsoft Graph A charting tool that creates embedded charts in applications such as Access.

NOTES

Create a Chart Report

- Access does not have its own native chart-creation capability; instead it uses another program, **Microsoft Graph**. The Microsoft Graph object is then embedded in a form or report. (Charts are most commonly placed on reports.)

- To create a chart report, first create a blank report using the Blank Report button on the Create tab. Then in Design view, use the Insert Chart button on the Design tab to start a new chart.

- The Chart Wizard runs, prompting you to select the table or query from which you want to pull data.

Base the chart on the data from a table or query

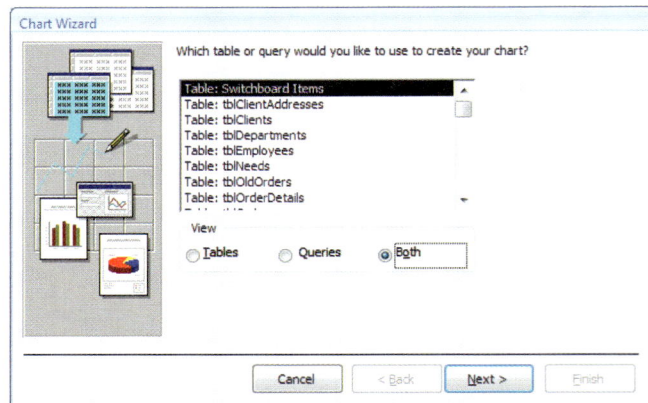

- Next, select the fields that contain the data you want for the chart.

- For a pie chart, select two fields: one containing the labels, and one containing numeric data. For example, to see each salesperson's sales, you might select Salesperson and Quantity.

- For a bar chart, select three fields: one containing the X-axis labels, one containing the Y-axis labels, and one containing the numeric data. For example, to see each salesperson's sales by month, you might select Salesperson, OrderDate, and Quantity.

- Next, select the chart type. The Chart Wizard does not offer as extensive a collection of chart types as Excel does, but there are enough for most basic uses.

Select a chart type

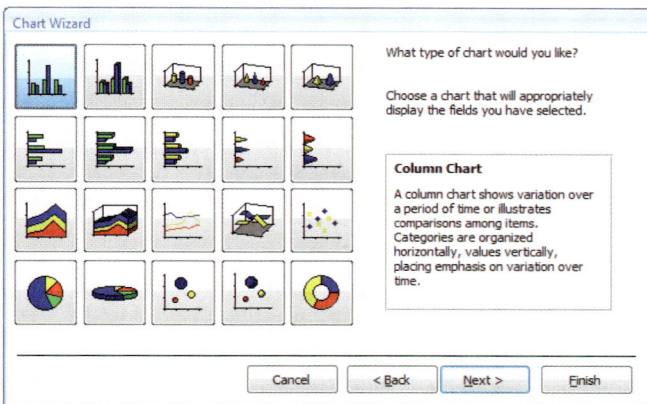

- Next, decide how you want to lay out the data in the chart. Drag the fields to/from the various placeholders as desired.

Lay out the chart

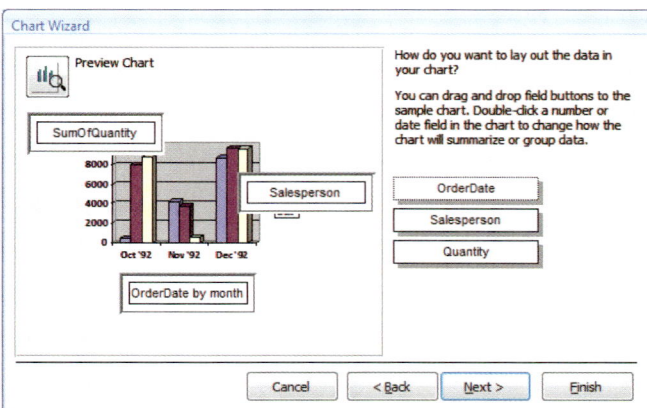

- Finally, name the chart (the name will appear as the chart's title in its own chart frame), and choose whether or not to display a legend.

- A **legend** is a color-coded key that tells what each color (or pattern) represents in the chart.

A legend explains the color coding

- Do not be alarmed if the chart does not show the data from your selected data source in Design view. This is one of the quirks of Microsoft Graph. Switch to Layout view or Report view to see your data.

Edit a Chart

- To edit the chart, you must return to Design view and double-click the chart. This opens Microsoft Graph. Notice that Microsoft Graph uses a traditional menu and toolbar system of navigation, unlike Office 2007.

- When you are working in Microsoft Graph, the chart displays dummy data, except for the chart title. You can format the labels, legend, axes, and so on, and those formatting settings will be passed on to the actual chart that is generated when you are in Layout or Report view.

- The small floating spreadsheet is called the datasheet. You can close it by clicking the View Datasheet button on the toolbar.

- Sometimes a chart can convey a different message if you display its data by row versus by column. To switch between the two, use the By Row and By Column buttons on the toolbar.

An embedded Microsoft Graph chart on a report

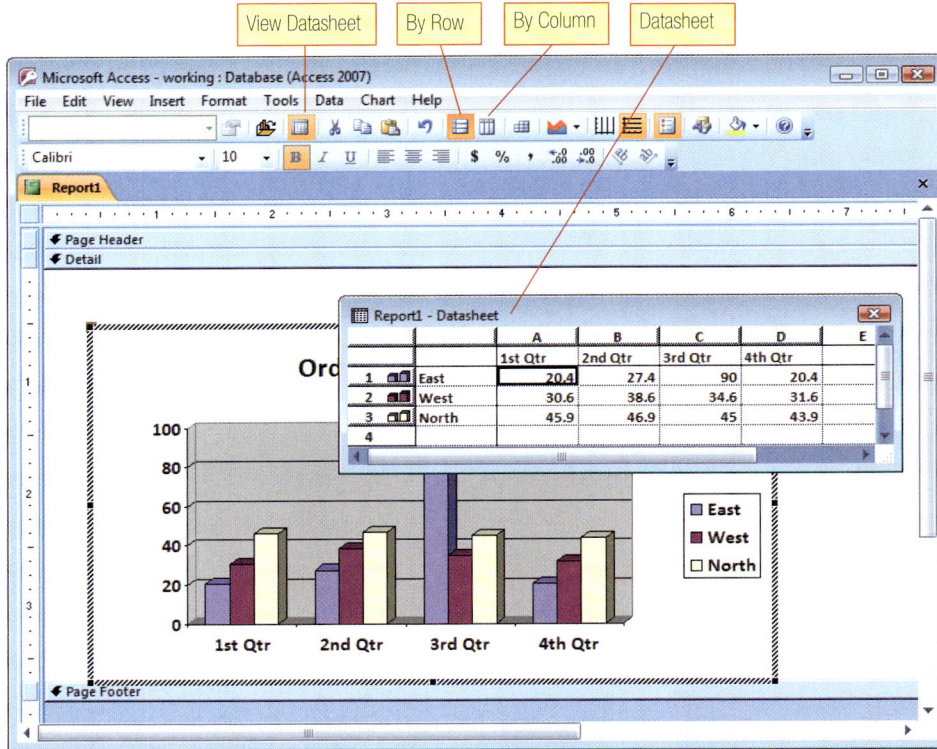

Set chart options

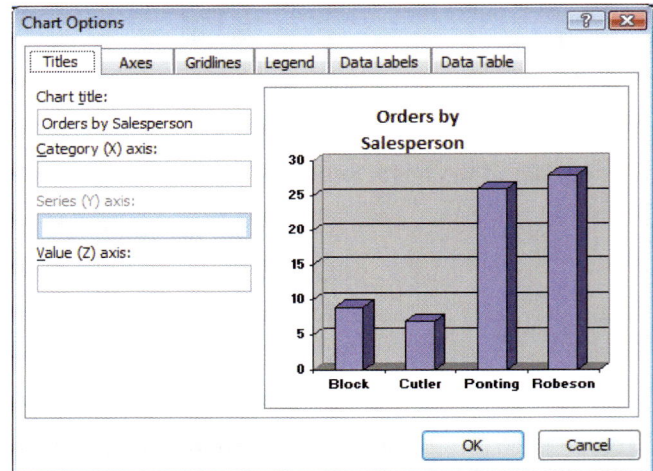

- You can toggle certain optional elements on/off on the chart by clicking the following buttons on the toolbar: **Data Table**, Category Axis Gridlines, Value Axis Gridlines, Legend.

- Many other chart features can be controlled from the Chart Options dialog box. Open the Chart menu and click Chart Options to display it. You can control the axis scale, legend, gridlines, titles, data labels, and data table from here.

Buttons for toggling on/off chart features

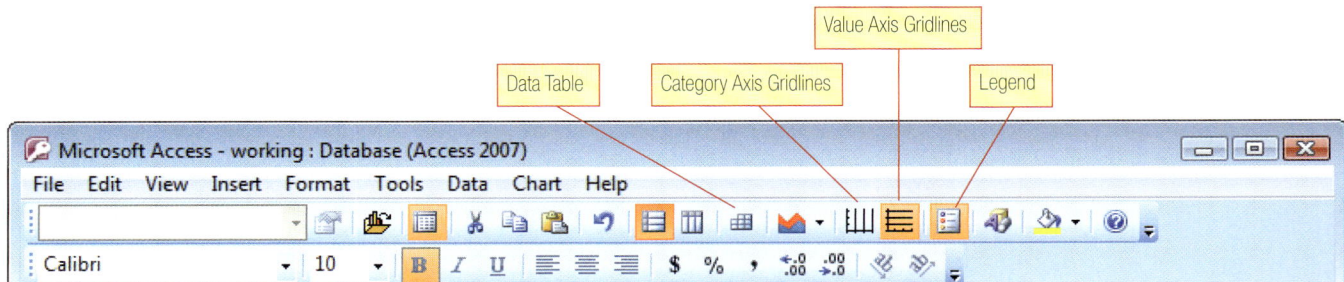

Buttons for applying character formatting

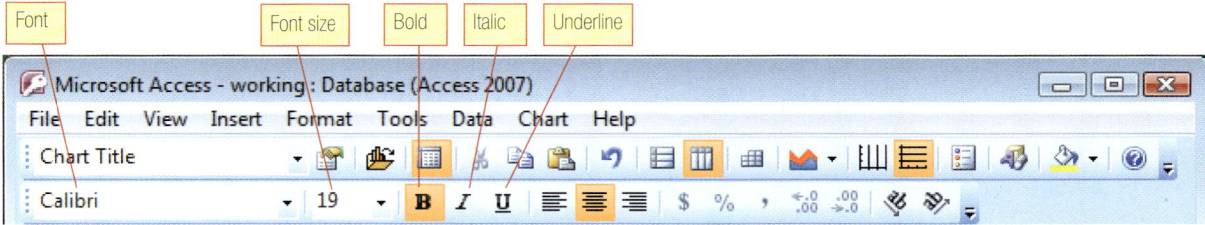

- You can use the character formatting buttons on the Formatting toolbar (the lower of the two toolbars, if they are on separate rows, or the rightmost one if they share a row) to format any of the text objects on the chart, such as the title, legend, and axes. Select any of these and then choose a different font, font size, attributes (such as bold and italic), and so on.

- There are also buttons on the Formatting toolbar for applying formatting to numbers, such as making numbers appear as currency or percentages and changing the number of decimal places.

- There are also buttons on the Formatting toolbar for aligning the text horizontally within its text box and slanting the text diagonally.

Buttons for formatting numbers

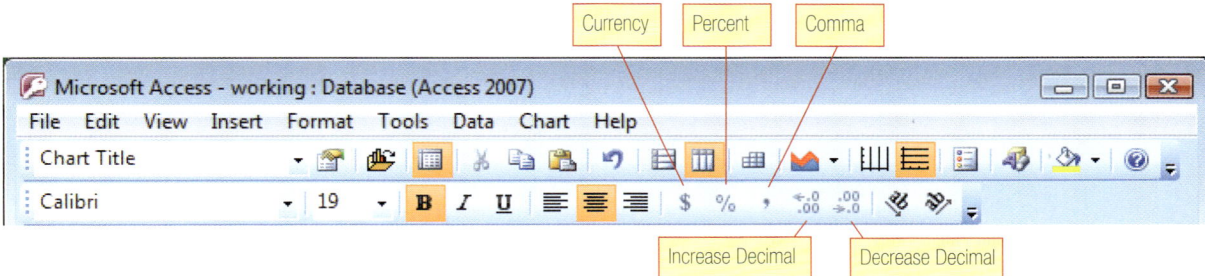

Buttons for aligning and slanting text

Change the Chart Type

- You can change the chart's type without having to recreate it entirely.

- To change the chart's type, open it in Microsoft Graph and then click the down arrow next to the Chart Type button. From the palette of types, click the one you want.

Select a different chart type

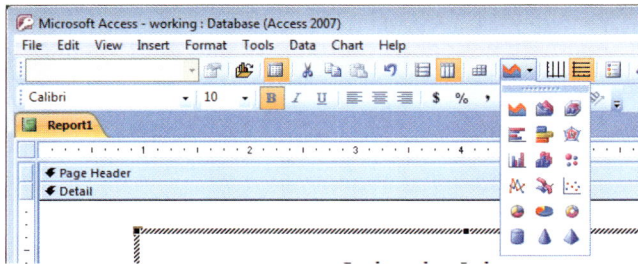

✓ *If you have a chart that uses three fields, such as a bar chart, and you switch to a chart that uses only two fields, such as the pie chart, only the first series will show (that is, the first color of bar from the legend).*

- For additional chart types, open the Chart menu and click Chart Type. From the Chart Type dialog box, you can select a type and a subtype. There is also a Custom Types tab that has some interesting preset formatting types on it.

Chart Type dialog box

PROCEDURES

Create a Blank Report

1. Click **Create** tab . . . . Alt + C

   Reports Group

2. Click **Blank Report** button

   ☐ Blank Report . . . . R , B

3. Close the **Field List** pane.

4. Save the report with the desired name.

Add a Chart to a Report

In Report Design view:

1. Click **Design** tab . . . . . . Alt + M

   Controls Group

2. Make sure **Use Control Wizards**

   button 🖪 is selected. . . . . . P

3. Click **Insert Chart** button

   📊 . . . . C , M

4. Click the Detail area of the report.

   ✓ *The Chart Wizard runs.*

5. Click the table or query from which to pull fields for the chart.

   ✓ *You can click the Tables, Queries, or Both button to choose how the list of objects is filtered.*

6. Click **Next** . . . . Alt + N

7. For each field to include:

   a. Click the field.

   b. Click the right arrow button

      > .

8. Click **Next** . . . . Alt + N

9. Click the chart type to use.

10. Click **Next** . . . . Alt + N

11. If needed, drag the fields to different placeholder areas.

    ✓ *For Date fields, Access decides on an interval by which to group, such as month. To change this, double-click the field in the layout to open a Group dialog box, and select a different interval.*

12. Click **Next** . . . . Alt + N

13. Change the title of the chart if desired.

14. Choose whether to display a legend:

    Click **Yes, display a legend** . . . . Alt + Y

    OR

    Click **No, don't display a legend** . . . . Alt + N

15. Click **Finish** . . . . Alt + F

Resize a Chart Object

1. Open the report or form that contains the chart in Design view.
2. Drag a selection handle on the chart's frame.

Open a Chart in Microsoft Graph

1. Open the report or form that contains the chart in Design view.
2. Double-click the chart.

Change the Chart Title

In Microsoft Graph:

1. Click in the chart title's text box.
2. Edit the text.

   OR

1. Click **Chart**. . . . . `Alt`+`C`
2. Click **Chart Options** . . . . `I`
3. Edit the text in the **Chart title** box.
4. Click **OK**. . . . . `Enter`

Add Category and Value Axis Titles

In Microsoft Graph:

1. Click **Chart**. . . . . `Alt`+`C`
2. Click **Chart Options** . . . . `I`
3. Click **Category (X) axis** box and type desired axis title . . . . `Alt`+`C`
4. Click **Value (Y) axis** box and type desired axis title . . . . `Alt`+`V`
5. Click **OK**. . . . . `Enter`

Turn Off Category or Value Axis Labels

In Microsoft Graph:

1. Click **Chart**. . . . . `Alt`+`C`
2. Click **Chart Options** . . . . `I`
3. Click **Axes** tab.
4. Clear **Category (X) axis** check box . . . . `Alt`+`G`

   AND/OR

   Clear **Value (Y) axis** check box . . . . `Alt`+`V`
5. Click **OK**. . . . . `Enter`

Display or Hide Gridlines

In Microsoft Graph:

   Click one of these buttons:

   - **Category Axis Gridlines** .
   - **Value Axis Gridlines** .

   OR

1. Click **Chart**. . . . . `Alt`+`C`
2. Click **Chart Options** . . . . `I`
3. Click **Gridlines** tab.
4. Mark or clear either of the following check boxes in the Category (X) axis section:
   - **Major gridlines** . . . . . `Alt`+`M`
   - **Minor gridlines** . . . . . `Alt`+`I`
5. Mark or clear either of the following check boxes in the Value (Y) axis section:
   - **Major gridlines** . . . . . `Alt`+`O`
   - **Minor gridlines** . . . . . `Alt`+`G`

   ✓ *If working with a 3-D chart, there will also be a Z axis. Set the gridlines for it the same way as for X and Y axes.*

6. Click **OK**. . . . . `Enter`

Display or Hide the Legend

In Microsoft Graph:

   - Click the **Legend** button .

   OR

1. Click **Chart**. . . . . `Alt`+`C`
2. Click **Chart Options** . . . . `I`
3. Click **Legend** tab.
4. Mark or clear **Show Legend** check box . . . . `Alt`+`S`
5. Click **OK**. . . . . `Enter`

Change Legend Position

In Microsoft Graph:

1. Click **Chart**. . . . . `Alt`+`C`
2. Click **Chart Options** . . . . `I`
3. Click **Legend** tab.
4. Make sure **Show Legend** check box is marked . . . . `Alt`+`S`

5. Choose a placement option:
   - **Bottom** . . . . `Alt`+`M`
   - **Corner** . . . . `Alt`+`O`
   - **Top**. . . . . `Alt`+`T`
   - **Right** . . . . `Alt`+`R`
   - **Left** . . . . `Alt`+`L`
6. Click **OK**. . . . . `Enter`

Add Data Labels

In Microsoft Graph:

1. Click **Chart**. . . . . `Alt`+`C`
2. Click **Chart Options** . . . . `I`
3. Click **Data Labels** tab.
4. Mark check boxes for type of labels desired.
5. Click **OK**. . . . . `Enter`

Switch Between Plotting by Row or by Column

In Microsoft Graph:

   - **Click the By Row** button .

   OR

   - **Click the By Column** button .

Change Chart Type

In Microsoft Graph:

1. Click down arrow to right of **Chart Type** button .
2. Click desired type.

   OR

1. Click **Chart**. . . . . `Alt`+`C`
2. Click **Chart Type** . . . . `Y`
3. Click chart type from **Chart type** list.
4. Click subtype from **Chart sub-type** list.
5. Click **OK**. . . . . `Enter`

EXERCISE DIRECTIONS

1. Start Access, if necessary.
2. Open 🔘 **17EXCHANGE** and save a copy of it as **17EXCHANGE_xx**.
3. Create a new blank report and save it as **rptSalesChart**.
4. In Design view, place a chart in the Detail area of the report:
   a. Base it on qryOrdersWithDetails.
   b. Choose the Salesperson, OrderDate, and Total fields.
   c. Choose a Column chart (first chart in top row).
   d. Double-click OrderDate by Month and change the grouping to be by Day instead.
   e. Set the chart title to **Sales Data**.
   f. Enlarge the chart to fill most of the Detail area, so its details are clearly visible.

5. View the report in Report view to examine the chart; then switch back to Design view.
6. Make the following formatting changes to the chart:
   a. Change the title to **Sales by Salesperson** and format it as 14-point Times New Roman.
   b. Place the legend at the bottom of the chart.
   c. Apply Currency format to the axis containing the numeric values.
7. Change the chart type to a Bar chart with the Stacked Bar with 3-D Visual Effect subtype.
8. Make any other formatting adjustments that might be needed to make the chart attractive, such as changing font sizes for axes.
9. Save and close the report.
10. Exit the database.

ON YOUR OWN

1. Start Access and open the 🔘 **17CANDLES** database. Save it as **OAC17_xx**.
2. Create a new pie chart report showing the total amount that customers spent on each product. Name the report **rptProductSalesChart**. (Tip: Pull data from qryOrderInfo.)
3. Enlarge the chart frame to fill the Detail area.
4. Change the chart title to **Sales By Product**.

5. Turn data labels on for the Category name and hide the legend.
6. Change the data labels to 10-point Calibri font, not bold.
7. Switch the chart subtype to a pie with a 3-D visual effect.
8. Check your work in Report view. It should resemble Illustration A.
9. Save and close the report.
10. Exit the database.

Illustration A

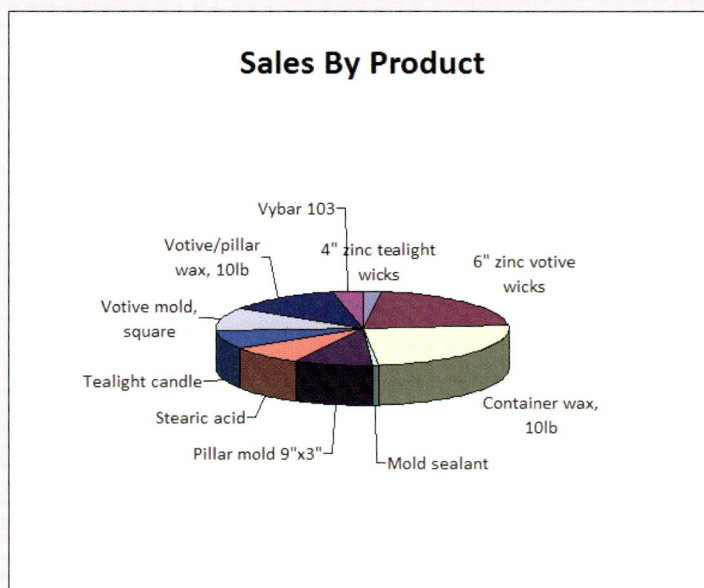

Sales By Product

Critical Thinking

Application Skills The Computers for Seniors donation program has a basic database in which donors and donations are being tracked. You will improve this database by adding some additional forms and reports to it, so that the organization's management can analyze and use the data more effectively.

EXERCISE DIRECTIONS

1. Open 💿 **18SENIORS** and save it as **18SENIORS_xx**.

2. Copy frmDonors, and name the copy **frmDonorsAndDonations**.

3. Place a newly created subform at the bottom of frmDonorsAndDonations that shows the individual donations, in Datasheet view. Name the new subform **frmDonationsSubform**.

4. Change the default view of the frmDonations form to Continuous Forms.

5. In frmDonations, set up conditional formatting so that if no thank-you note has been sent, the donor name appears in bright red.

    ✓ *Hint: Use the IsNull( ) function as an expression for the condition, with the field name in square brackets as the function's argument.*

6. Create a PivotTable form called **frmDonationsPivot** that uses Donation by Year as the column headings, DonorID as the row headings, and Donation Value as the detail data. Filter the data so that only donations where the ThankYouNote field is blank appear in the table.

7. Display the form footer for the frmDonors form and place a code there in an unbound text box that shows today's date.

    ✓ *Hint: Use the =NOW( ) function. In the Property Sheet for the unbound text box, set the Format to Short Date.*

8. Create a new query called **qryDonorsAndDonations** that combines all the fields from tblDonations and tblDonors.

9. Create a pie chart on a report called **rptDonationPieChart** that shows each donor's last name and the total value of what they have donated. Use the query you just created as the data source. Format the chart attractively, using whatever chart options you think are appropriate. Use data labels for category name and value, and do not use a legend. Format the numbers as currency.

10. Set up a Switchboard that accesses all forms and reports (except the subform and the Pivot Table), and set it to load at startup.

11. Close the database and exit Access.

Curriculum Integration

Application Skills   In Biology class, you are learning how to analyze data samples collected from field research. You have a database that contains a table of data collected about frog activity in Vermont from 2006 through 2008, and you will create some reports and charts that summarize the data.

EXERCISE DIRECTIONS

Open 19FROGS and save it as **19FROGS_xx**. In it, create a chart report that shows the overall trend of whether the frog activity is going up or down over time. Choose the best chart type to use for this. Name the chart report **Activity Trend**.

There are several data sources (tables/queries) from which to choose. Examine each one and select the best one for your needs.

Make the Frog Activity Report more attractive by applying formatting, adding a title, and adjusting column widths. Apply an AutoFormat to it if desired. Add grouping by year to the Frog Activity Report, and add an average of the Average Intensity field for each year group.

Use a PivotTable to examine the average intensities for each individual date and exclude dates where the Number of Visits is 1. Save it as **Multi-Visit Pivot**.

Close the database and exit Access.

Lesson | 3

Creating Advanced Queries

Exercise | 20

Skills Covered

- **Create Multi-Table Queries**
- **Remove Tables from Queries**
- **Identify Which Table to Draw a Field From**
- **Create Ad-Hoc Joins**

Software Skills   A query is a great way of tying multiple tables together for use as a single data source on which to base other objects such as forms or reports. In this exercise, you will learn how to connect multiple tables this way, by creating queries that include fields from multiple sources. You'll learn how to add tables to and remove tables from queries, and how to create ad-hoc joins between tables where no previous relationship existed.

Application Skills   The Textbook Exchange would like to have a report that includes information on customers and their ordering habits, but to do that, the report would need to be based upon multiple tables. To simplify this task, you will create a multi-table query that includes all the fields needed for that report, and then create the report based on that query.

TERMS

Ad-hoc join   A relationship between two tables that exists only within the query in which it is created.

NOTES

Create Multi-Table Queries

- You can include multiple tables in a query either from the Query Wizard or from Query Design view.
- When using the Simple Query Wizard to create the query, choose from more than one table (or query) before moving past the step in the wizard where you choose fields. After selecting fields from a table or query, reopen the Tables/Queries drop-down list and choose another table or query.
- When using Query Design view, select multiple tables or queries from the Show Table dialog box and click Add. If the Show Table dialog box does not automatically appear, click the Show Table button on the Query Tools Design tab.

Select from multiple data sources when creating the query with the Simple Query Wizard

Select multiple tables or queries to appear in the query design

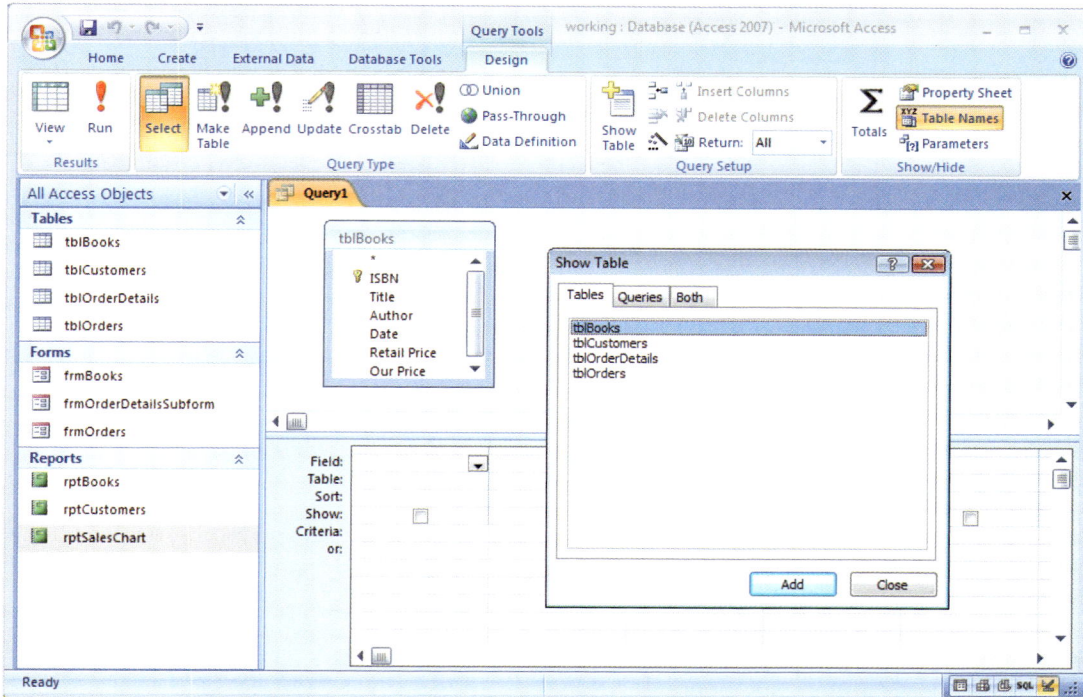

- The selected tables and/or queries appear as field lists in the top part of the Query Design window. You can drag the fields into the query design grid to place them in the query.
- If you add to a query design a table or query to the query design grid that is already included in the query, a second copy of it appears in the upper portion of the query design workspace. The name is the same except it is followed by a _1. It works the same as the original, but it does not show any join lines between it and other tables.

Remove Tables from Queries

- If you end up with tables or queries in the query design workspace that you are not pulling fields from in the grid, you can leave them there, or you can delete them from the query.
- To delete a table/query from the query, select it and press [Delete]. Alternatively, you can right-click it and choose Remove Table.
- When you do so, any fields that were being pulled from that table/query disappear from the query design grid.

Query design grid

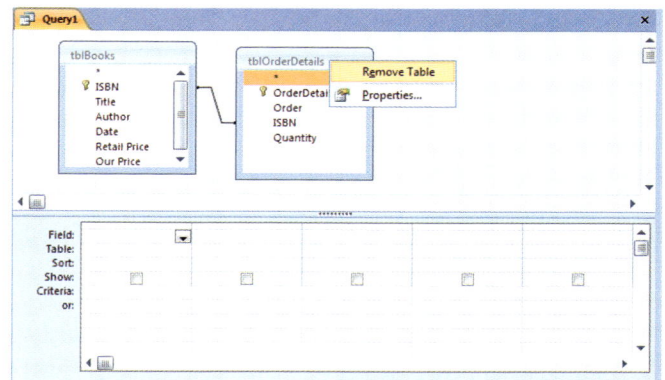

Identify Which Table to Draw a Field From

- In some cases, the same field name may appear in more than one table/query. You can specify which table/query to draw that field from by using the Table row in the query design grid.
- When you place a field into the grid by dragging it from one of the tables/queries, or by double-clicking a field in one of the tables/queries, the correct table/query name is automatically filled in on the Table row.

Choose which table/query the field should be drawn from

Field:	ISBN
Table:	tblOrderDetails ▼
Sort:	tblBooks
Show:	tblOrderDetails
Criteria:	
or:	

✓ *If the Table row does not appear in the query design grid, make sure the Table Names button is selected on the Query Tools Design tab.*

Create Ad-Hoc Joins

■ An **ad-hoc join** is a connection between two tables that exists only within the query in which you create it. Access provides an opportunity for you to create temporary, informal relationships between data sources for the purpose of building the query without those relationships persisting outside.

■ To create an ad-hoc join, drag from a field in one field list (in the query design workspace) to the equivalent field in another table's field list.

■ Unlike in the Relationships window, you cannot enforce referential integrity in an ad-hoc join.

■ After creating the join, you can change its type by double-clicking the join line. The Join Properties dialog box opens. Select the description that best matches what you want the join to accomplish in the query and click OK.

✓ *You learned about the types of joins, such as outer and inner joins, in Exercise 2. Review that material now if needed.*

Define the join type

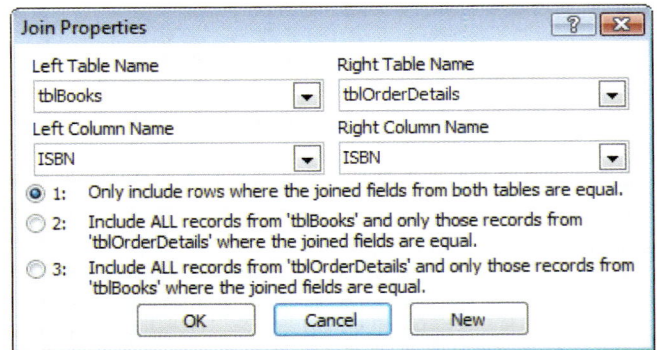

Join Properties

Left Table Name	Right Table Name
tblBooks ▼	tblOrderDetails ▼
Left Column Name	Right Column Name
ISBN ▼	ISBN ▼

- ◉ 1: Only include rows where the joined fields from both tables are equal.
- ○ 2: Include ALL records from 'tblBooks' and only those records from 'tblOrderDetails' where the joined fields are equal.
- ○ 3: Include ALL records from 'tblOrderDetails' and only those records from 'tblBooks' where the joined fields are equal.

[OK] [Cancel] [New]

■ To remove an ad-hoc join, select the line and press [Delete].

PROCEDURES

Create a Multi-Table Query with the Simple Query Wizard

1. Click **Create** tab . . . . [Alt]+[C]

   Other Group

2. Click **Query Wizard** button . . . . [Q], [W]
3. Click **OK** . . . . [Enter]
4. Select table or query from the Tables/Queries list.
5. Select field(s) to use from this table or query.
6. Repeat steps 4–5 as needed to select from multiple tables or queries.
7. Click **Next** . . . . [Alt]+[N]
8. If prompted to create a Detail or Summary query, leave Detail selected and click **Next** . . . . [Alt]+[N]
8. Type a name for the query.
9. Click **Finish** . . . . [Alt]+[F]

Create a Multi-Table Query in Query Design View

1. Click **Create** tab . . . . [Alt]+[C]

   Other Group

2. Click **Query Design** button . . . . [Q], [D]
3. Click a table or query to include.

   ✓ *Click the Tables, Queries, or Both tab to see lists of only tables, only queries, or both in one list.*

4. Click **Add** . . . . [Alt]+[A]
5. Repeat steps 3–4 as needed to choose multiple tables or queries.
6. Click **Close** . . . . [Alt]+[C]
7. Add fields to the query and save it as you normally would.

Add More Tables to a Query

In Query Design view:

1. Click **Query Tools Design**
   tab . . . . `Alt`+`R`

   Query Setup Group

2. Click **Show Table**
   button . . . . `S`, `T`

3. Click a table or query to include.

   ✓ *Click the Tables, Queries, or Both tab to see lists of only tables, only queries, or both in one list.*

4. Click **Add** . . . . `Alt`+`A`

5. Repeat steps 3–4 as needed to choose multiple tables or queries.

6. Click **Close** . . . . `Alt`+`C`

Remove a Table from a Query

In Query Design view:

1. Click the table to remove.

2. Press `Delete`.

   OR

1. Right-click table to remove.

2. Click **Remove Table** . . . . `E`

Change the Table from Which a Field Is Drawn

In Query Design view:

1. Open **Table** drop-down list for desired field.

2. Click different table/query source.

Create an Ad-Hoc Join

In Query Design view:

1. Click field in table's field list in query design workspace.

2. Drag field to equivalent field in other table's field list.

Change Join Properties

In Query Design view:

1. Double-click join line between two tables.

2. Select desired join type.

3. Click **OK** . . . . `Enter`

EXERCISE DIRECTIONS

1. Start Access, if necessary.

2. Open 🔘 **20EXCHANGE** and save a copy of it as **20EXCHANGE_xx**.

3. Start a new query in Query Design view, and add the tblCustomers and tblOrders tables to it.

4. Reopen the Show Table dialog box, and add tblOrderDetails and tblBooks.

5. Remove tblBooks from the query design.

6. Add the following fields to the query:

   From tblCustomers: First, Last

   From tblOrderDetails: ISBN, Quantity

   ✓ *Notice that we did not include any fields from tblOrders. It is nevertheless necessary to include this table in the query design because it functions as the connector between the other two tables.*

7. Edit the properties of the join between tblCustomers and tblOrders so that it includes all records from tblOrders and only the records in tblCustomers where the joined fields are equal.

8. Save the query as **qryWhatCustomersOrder**.

9. View the query in Datasheet view. Notice that the ISBN field does not actually show the ISBN number of the book, but you need it to.

10. Switch back to Design view. Add the tblBooks table to the query.

11. Change the ISBN field in the query design grid so that it comes from tblBooks.

12. View the query in Datasheet view and verify that the ISBN number appears in the ISBN field.

13. Save your work and close the query. Close the database file.

ON YOUR OWN

1. Start Access and open the 🔘 **20CANDLES** database. Save a copy of it as **OAC20_xx**.

2. Start a new query in Query Design view that includes the following tables: tblCustomers, tblOrders, tblOrderDetails, tblProducts, and tblEmployees.

3. Add the following fields to the query:

   From tblCustomers: FirstName, LastName

   From tblOrders: OrderDate (sorted in Ascending order), Salesperson

   From tblProducts: ProductName, PricePerUnit

   From tblOrderDetails: Quantity

4. Remove tblEmployees from the query design.

5. Save the query as **qryOrderInfo** and check your work in Datasheet view.

6. Close the database.

Exercise | 21

Skills Covered

Software Skills   Sometimes it can be difficult to see the meaning in data if there's too much of it shown in too much detail. It is often helpful to create summary queries that help you pull statistics out of a large pool of data.

Application Skills   Sycamore Knoll Bed and Breakfast has been using the database you helped them create in Lesson 2 to store reservation information, and quite a bit of data has been collected. The office manager would now like to gather some statistics from the data to help plan future pricing and marketing. You will create some summary queries that will help her make sense of the data.

TERMS

Aggregate function   Functions that summarize grouped data. These functions include sum, count, average, minimum, maximum, and other functions.

Top values   Property of a query that shows a set number of records in a query. When sorted descending, the query shows the top values in the list. When sorted ascending, the query shows the bottom values in the list.

NOTES

Understand Summary Queries

- A summary query is very different in purpose from a detail (normal) query. A summary query usually does not contain very many fields—only the fields that you are interested in either grouping by or calculating.

- Whereas a detail query shows every record that matches the query criteria, a summary query shows just a statistical summary. This can be very useful when trying to make strategic business decisions.

A sample summary query

ReservationDate By Month	Sum Of TotalDue
April 2009	$365.00
August 2008	$690.00
December 2009	$190.00
February 2009	$190.00
January 2009	$285.00
July 2008	$1,175.00
June 2009	$190.00
March 2009	$95.00
May 2009	$405.00
October 2008	$365.00
September 2008	$1,610.00

qryRevenue

Summarize with the Simple Query Wizard

■ When you create a query that includes numeric data fields, the Simple Query Wizard gives you the option of either a detail or a summary query.

■ When you choose Summary, the Summary Options button becomes available. Click it and then choose one or more **aggregate functions** for the query.

Options in the Simple Query Wizard for summarizing data

■ Using the Simple Query Wizard to create a summary query has many advantages, including the ability to group data in chunks (such as for a whole month of dates together rather than each individual date separately) without having to manually write the complex code required to show the data in groups.

■ Therefore, the best way to create a summary query is to use the wizard and then edit the query as needed in Query Design view.

Summarize Data in Query Design View

■ You can also create a summary query manually in Query Design view.

■ To create a summary query in Query Design view, click the Totals button on the Query Tools Design tab. This adds a new row, Total, to the query design grid.

■ The default value for each field in the Total row is Group By. The summary will be grouped by each of the fields with this setting.

✓ *Include only the essential fields in a summary query. A field should not be present in the query unless it is being used as a criterion, calculated, or grouped by.*

■ You can open the drop-down list for the Total row and choose an aggregate function for the field on which you want to calculate.

Select an aggregate function

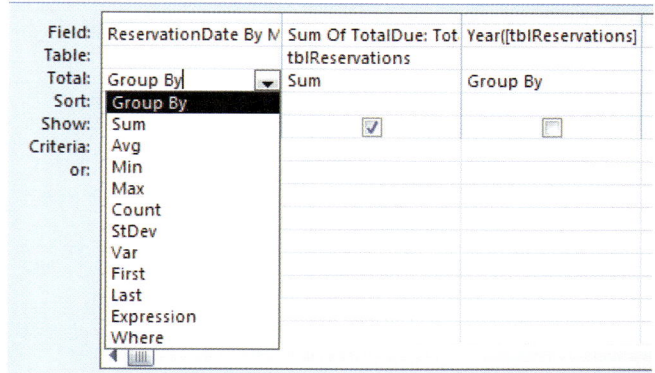

✓ *Some of the aggregate functions require the data to be numeric, such as Sum; others, such as Count, will work on any data type.*

■ If you want to just show the calculation(s) for the entire table, do not use any Group By fields.

■ Here are the aggregate functions you can choose from:

Use	To . . .
Sum	Total numeric values by each Group By field.
Avg	Total numeric values and divide by the number of records in each Group By field.
Min	Find the lowest value in each Group By field. If the Min field is text, the function finds the first alphabetical value. If the field is a number, the function finds the lowest number. If the field is a date, the function finds the earliest date.
Max	Find the highest value in each Group By field. If the Max field is text, the function finds the last alphabetical value. If the field is a number, the function finds the largest number. If the field is a date, the function finds the latest date.
Count	Find the number of records in each Group By field.
StDev	Calculate the standard deviation of the number by each Group By field. This is used to see how close all the values are to the average.

Var	Calculate the variance of the number by each Group By field. This is another measure of how close the values are to the average.
First	Find the field's first record input for each Group By field.
Last	Find the field's last record input for each Group By field.
Expression	If you have a calculated field (e.g., Quantity*Price), you can choose Expression in the Total row and put a formula such as Sum([Quantity]*[Price]) in the Field row.
Where	Refer the query to the Criteria row. This enables you to include fields in the query purely for criteria purposes without grouping or calculating by that field.

Show Top Values

■ The **top values** property of a query allows you to see the top (or bottom) values of your list.

■ You can use top values in conjunction with a summary query to see a summary of the highest categories, or use it without Totals turned on to see the individual records with the lowest or highest values.

■ If you want to see the highest values, first sort the field descending. If you want to see the lowest values, first sort the field ascending.

■ Choose a value in the Top Values box or type a value or percent in the Property Sheet for the query.

Top Values box

Property Sheet	×
Selection type: Query Properties	

General	
Description	
Default View	Datasheet
Output All Fields	No
Top Values	All
Unique Values	5
Unique Records	25
Source Database	100
Source Connect Str	5%
Record Locks	25%
Recordset Type	All
ODBC Timeout	60

■ If you choose or type a percent, the number of values depends on the total number of records. If there are 50 records, 10% will show 5 records.

■ If there is a tie on the last record, the query will show all ties. For example, if the 10th, 11th, and 12th records had the same value, you would see all 12 records even though 10 was input in Top Values.

■ You can also set the desired values from the Return drop-down list on the Design tab.

PROCEDURES

Use the Simple Query Wizard to Create a Summary Query

1. Click **Create** tab . . . . [Alt]+[C]

   Other Group

2. Click **Query Wizard** button . . . . [Q], [W]
3. Click **OK** . . . . [Enter]
4. Select table or query from the Tables/Queries list.
5. Select field(s) to use from this table or query.

6. Repeat steps 4–5 as needed to select from multiple tables or queries.
7. Click **Next** . . . . [Alt]+[N]
8. Click **Summary** . . . . [Alt]+[S]
9. Click **Summary Options** . . . . [Alt]+[O]
10. Check boxes for each field and summary value desired.
11. If desired, click **Count records** . . . . [Alt]+[C]
12. Click **OK** . . . . [Enter]

13. Click **Next** . . . . [Alt]+[N]
14. If prompted, choose how you want the values grouped, and then click **Next** . . . . [Alt]+[N]

   ✓ The above step appears only if you have chosen a field with a groupable type, such as date (which can be grouped into Month, Year, and so on).

15. Type a title for the query in the provided text box.
16. Choose to **Open the query to view information** . . . . [Alt]+[O]
17. Click **Finish** . . . . [Alt]+[F]

Summarize Data in Query Design view

To show or hide the Total row:

1. Open the query in Design view.
2. Click **Query Tools Design**
   tab . . . . Alt + R

   Show/Hide Group

3. Click **Totals** button Σ Totals . . S , O

   ✓ The default setting for each field in the Totals row is Group By. Change it to an aggregate function (see below) for the fields to calculate.

To select an aggregate function:

1. Click down arrow in **Total** row.
2. Click an aggregate function.

To show top values:

1. Click **Sort** down arrow and choose Descending or Ascending for desired field.
2. Display the Property Sheet for the query if it does not already appear.

2. Click down arrow on **Top Values** box in the Property Sheet and choose number or percent.

   OR

   Type number or percent in **Top Values** box.

   ✓ You can also choose a top values amount from the Return drop-down list on the Design tab in Query Design view.

EXERCISE DIRECTIONS

1. Start Access, if necessary.
2. Open 🔵 **21SYCAMORE** and save a copy of it as **21SYCAMORE_xx**.
3. Using the Simple Query Wizard, create a summary query based on tblReservations that sums the TotalDue field by month. Name it **qryRevenue**.

   ✓ You need only two fields: ReservationDate and TotalDue.

4. Open the new query in Query Design view and examine the entries in the Field row for each field. Then close the query.

   ✓ Notice that each is a complex formula. Also notice that there is a non-displaying field that calculates the year. The wizard sets up these things for you. This is one advantage of using the wizard.

5. In Query Design view, create a summary query based on tblReservations that groups by the Suite name and sums the number of reserved nights for each suite.. Save the new query as **qrySuitePopularity** and close the query.

6. Use the Simple Query Wizard to create a summary query:

   a. Include LastName from tblGuests.
   b. Include ReservationDate and Nights from tblReservations.
   c. Sum by the Nights field.
   d. Group dates by Year
   e. Name it **qryBestCustomers**.
   f. Open it in Query Design view after creating it.

7. Set a criterion for the ReservationDate field that shows only reservations in 2008, and set that field to not display in the query results.

   Tip: For the criterion, simply enter 2008. Because the date is shown by year in this field, only the year is needed.

8. Sort the results by the LastName field in Ascending order.

9. Use the Top Values option to limit the query result to only the top five guests. Check your work in Datasheet view. Notice that it lists the first five guests alphabetically.

10. Remove the sort by LastName and instead sort in descending order by Sum Of Nights. Check your work again in Datasheet view.

11. Save your work and close the database.

ON YOUR OWN

1. Start Access and open the 21MUSIC database. Save a copy of it as **OAC21_xx**.

2. Open qrySummaryByCategory in Design view and examine the expression used in the Quantity field.

   ✓ *This query represents one way of performing a summary. It is not the way you learned in this exercise, however. It uses an expression.*

3. Close qrySummaryByCategory.

4. Create a new query in Query Design view called **qryNewSummaryByCategory** that does the same thing that qrySummaryByCategory does, but uses a Count aggregate function in the Total row rather than an expression.

   ✓ *Hint: You need only one table: tblRecordings. Group by MusicCategoryID and count by RecordingID.*

5. Create a new query in Query Design view that tells the average number of tracks on each category of recordings. Call it **qryAvgTracksByCategory**.

6. Create a new query using the Simple Query Wizard that shows how much money was spent buying recordings per month and the number of recordings purchased in each month. Call it **qryMonthlyExpenditure**. Limit its results to the top 25% of months in terms of amount spent. (This should result in two months of data showing.)

7. Save your work and close Access.

Skills Covered

- **Change Field Format in a Query Design**
- **Change Field Names in a Query Design**
- **Add Calculations to a Query**

Software Skills   Sometimes a field in a query does not look the way you would like it to. If you need certain data in the query to appear in a specific format, you can format it just as in a datasheet. You can also change the column heading for a field in the query results. Your queries can also contain the results of calculations performed on one or more fields.

Application Skills   The summary queries you created in Exercise 21 have proved very useful to Sycamore Knoll, but the manager would like them to be more attractive and have different headings on some columns. You will make these improvements. She has also requested that you create a new query that calculates the amount that each guest still owes on his or her account.

TERMS

No new terms in this exercise.

NOTES

Change Field Format in a Query Design

- By default, most of the table properties of a field stay the same when you use that field in a query.
- You can change the way a field looks in a query, however, by changing its field properties there.
- To open its field properties, do either of the following in Query Design view:
  - Right-click on a field and choose Properties.
  - Click in the field and click the Property Sheet button on the Query Tools Design tab.
- In the Property Sheet, the Format property displays options in the drop-down list depending on the data type.

A field's Property Sheet

Property Sheet		✕
Selection type: Field Properties		
General Lookup		

Description		
Format	Currency	▼
Decimal Places	General Number	3456.789
Input Mask	Currency	$3,456.79
Caption	Euro	€3,456.79
Smart Tags	Fixed	3456.79
	Standard	3,456.79
	Percent	123.00%
	Scientific	3.46E+03

- You can also type a custom format in the Format property, such as m/d/yyyy to display the four-digit year along with the month and day. For more details on custom formats, click in the Format property and press F1.
- Text fields do not have any drop-down choices in the Format property.
- Type > (greater than) in the Format property to force a text field to be all uppercase or < (less than) to force the field to display in lowercase.
- The result of your format choice appears in Datasheet view.
- The Description property allows you to add a note to help you remember what the field does. The description will appear on the status bar in Datasheet and Form views when you are in the field.
- The Input Mask property validates each character as you type it in the field and displays parentheses, dashes, or other characters. Click the Build button to the right of the field and choose a build option in the Input Mask Wizard, just as you do when working in a table's Design view.
- By default, Yes/No fields appear as check boxes. If you want them to display Yes or No, click on the Lookup tab in the Property Sheet and change the Display Control property from Check Box to Text Box.

Change Field Names in a Query Design

- You have two ways of changing field names that appear at the tops of the columns in Datasheet view.
- In Query Design view you can click to the left of the field name in the Field row, type the new name, and type a colon (:) before the contents.
- You can also open the Property Sheet and type the new name in the Caption property.

- Query field name changes do not affect table design, but any new reports or forms based on this query will show the new name as the caption.

Type a new name for a field

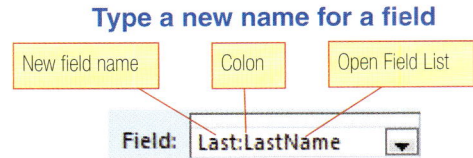

- New field name — Colon — Open Field List
- Field: Last:LastName

Add Calculations to a Query

- If you want to do a calculation on one or more fields, type the formula in a blank field cell in Query Design view.
- First type a new field name in the Field row, and a colon (:).
- Then type the calculation, enclosing each field name in square brackets. For example:
  - Amount: [Quantity]*[Price]
  - Sale Price: [Price]-[Discount]
  - Name: [FirstName]&" "&[LastName]
- The latter example uses concatenation, which you learned about in Exercise 11. The quotation marks around the space indicate the space is text to be added in the Name field. If you wanted to add a comma and a space, you would type ", ".
- Some of the more common operator symbols are:

Symbol	Meaning
+ (plus)	Addition
- (dash)	Subtraction
* (asterisk)	Multiplication
/ (slash)	Division
&	Concatenate text together

- If you have more than one table in the query with the same field name in it, references to it must show the table name, then a period, then the field name, like this:

  [tblClients.FirstName]&" "&[tblClients.LastName]

- By default, multiplication and division occur before addition and subtraction even if they occur to the right. To override this order, include parentheses. For example, 2+5*2 = 12, but (2+5)*2 = 14.

PROCEDURES

Change Field Format in a Query Design

In Query Design view:
1. Select field to change.
2. Click **Query Tools Design** tab . . . . Alt + R

3. Click **Property Sheet** button . . . . H, P
4. Make a choice in the Format box's drop-down list.

   OR

   Type a custom format into the Format box.

Change Field Names in a Query

In Query Design view:
1. Place cursor before field name to be changed. (Do not highlight.)
2. Type new field name followed by a colon.
3. Press Enter.

   ✓ *If there is already a name and colon preceding the field name, replace the text before the colon instead of these steps.*

Alternate Method:
1. Select field to change.
2. Click **Query Tools Design** tab . . . . Alt + R

3. Click **Property Sheet** button . . . . H, P
4. Type new field name in Caption property.

Add Calculations to a Query

In Query Design view:
1. Place cursor in a new Field cell.
2. Type new field name followed by a colon.
3. Type a formula, enclosing field names in square brackets.
4. Press Enter.

EXERCISE DIRECTIONS

1. Start Access, if necessary.
2. Open **22SYCAMORE** and save a copy of it as **22SYCAMORE_xx**.
3. Open qryBestCustomers in Query Design view and make the following changes:
   a. Replace the LastName column with a single column called **Name** that concatenates the FirstName and LastName fields.
   b. Rename the SumOfNights column to **Nights**.
4. Close the query, saving your changes.
5. Open qryRevenue in Query Design view and make the following changes:
   a. Using the Property Sheet, rename the first two columns Month and Revenue, respectively.
   b. Set the number of decimal places for the Revenue column to 0.
6. Close the query, saving your changes.
7. Open qrySuitePopularity in Query Design view.
8. Add the TotalDue field to the query using Revenue as the column name and apply the Sum aggregate function to it.
9. Close the query, saving your changes.
10. Copy qryRevenue and name the copy **qryAccountsReceivable**.
11. Add a calculated field to qryAccountsReceivable that shows the difference between TotalDue and AmountPaid. Call the new column **Receivable**.
12. Format the new column as Currency with 0 decimal places.
13. Set the Year field (the nondisplaying field) to be sorted in Ascending order.
14. View the query in a datasheet. Illustration A shows an example.

    ✓ *The Year column contains a formula that calculates the actual numeric value of each month/year combination, so that's the column you must sort by. If you sort by the column that actually displays the month/year, it will be an alphabetical sort by month name.*

15. Save the query and close the database.

qryAccountsReceivable		
Month	Revenue	Receivable
July 2008	$1,175	$0.00
August 2008	$690	$0.00
September 2008	$1,150	$0.00
September 2008	$270	$135.00
September 2008	$190	$190.00
October 2008	$95	$0.00
October 2008	$270	$135.00
January 2009	$95	$0.00
January 2009	$190	$190.00
February 2009	$190	$0.00
March 2009	$95	$95.00
April 2009	$95	$95.00
April 2009	$270	$270.00
May 2009	$405	$0.00
June 2009	$190	$95.00
December 2009	$190	$95.00

ON YOUR OWN

1. Start Access and open the 22MUSIC database. Save a copy of it as OAC22_xx.

2. In qryAvgTracksByCategory, change column headings to Category and Average Tracks.

   ✓ Use the Property Sheet for a field to change its caption if typing a caption and colon in front of the field name does not work. It usually works, but not always.

3. Set the Average Tracks column to use Fixed format and zero (0) decimal places.

4. In qryMonthlyExpenditure, change the column headings to Month, Amount, and Number, respectively.

5. Add a new column called **Average Recording** and use it to show the average cost per recording for each month.

   ✓ Use the Avg aggregate function on the PurchasePrice field.

6. Remove the Top Values filter so that this query shows data from the entire table.

7. Display and print the query results.

8. Close the database, saving all changes.

Skills Covered

- **About Parameter Queries**
- **Create Criteria-Based Prompts**
- **Create a Field Prompt**
- **Show All Records If No Parameter Is Entered**

Software Skills   Instead of creating many similar queries, you can create one query that will prompt you for different possibilities. For example, if you use the same query to look up addresses in different states and you have a version of the query for each state, you can create a single query that prompts you for the state each time you run it.

Application Skills   In creating mailings and reports for The Textbook Exchange, you want to be able to target people and books in the database that have specific properties, but the desired properties may change each time you run the query. For example, you might want to see all the people in a certain state or city. In this exercise, you will create parameter queries that will prompt you to include criteria values.

TERMS

Parameter   A value that is required to run a query (or other object). The parameter is entered in a dialog box.

SQL (Structured Query Language)   A computer language common to database programs that is generally used for selecting or managing data.

NOTES

About Parameter Queries

- **Parameter** queries allow you to use the same query to extract data that meets different criteria.

- For example, suppose you want one query to show all customers in a specific city and another to show customers in a different city. You can place a parameter in the Criteria row of the City field in the query design. When you run the query, you are prompted to enter the desired city.

- You can run parameter queries as a select query or change the query type to an action query. (See Exercise 24.) For example, you could prompt the user for which records to delete every month.

- A parameter query can also be the source for a report or form. For example, you could request a date range for a report or choose a state for printing mailing labels.

- The parameter can be in a stand-alone query or can be part of the **SQL** statement in a form or report's Record Source property.

- You can have multiple prompts in one query, or even in one box within one query.

- For example, for an invoice date field, you could type Between [Enter Start Date] and [Enter End Date] to create two prompts to give you a date range to select specific invoices.

Create Criteria-Based Prompts

■ Perhaps the most common type of parameter occurs in the Criteria row of a query's design.

■ Place the message you want for the prompt in square brackets. In the following figure, the criteria box shows [Which State?].

Query Design view with criteria parameter

Field:	FirstName	Address	City	State	ZIP
Table:	tblGuests	tblGuests	tblGuests	tblGuests	tblGuests
Sort:					
Show:	☑	☑	☑	☑	☑
Criteria:				[Which state?]	
or:					

■ When you run the query, a dialog box displays with the message and a text box for your input.

Dialog box from criteria parameter

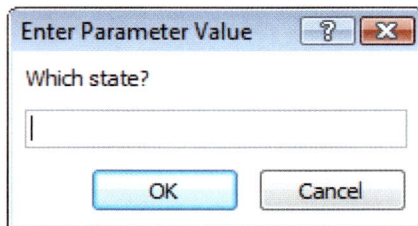

Enter Parameter Value

Which state?

[   ]

OK   Cancel

■ Access takes the value typed in the message box and places it in the Criteria row in place of the prompt to select the records.

■ If you want to rerun the prompt from Datasheet view without returning to Design view, press [Shift] + [F9].

■ The prompt can be combined with other criteria to permit a variety of responses. Suppose, for example, you were prompting for a particular state:

Entry in Criteria	Permissible Responses
[Which State?]	Entire state abbreviation.
Like [Which State?]	Entire state abbreviation.
	Any portion of field contents with a wildcard; for example, c* displays CA, CO, CN. *A displays CA, IA, PA, WA.
Like [Which State?] or Is Not Null	Entire state abbreviation. Any portion of field contents with a wildcard. Nothing (press Enter or click OK) displays all records.

Like [Which State?] & "*"	Same as above except wildcard displays all entries with the letter in any position. For example, *A displays AR, CA, and so on.

Create a Field Prompt

■ You can also place a parameter in the Field row of the query design.

■ Generally, the purpose of a field parameter is to create a calculation using the same value in every record.

■ For example, you may want to see the value of a variable price decrease for every record:

New Price: [AskingPrice]-([AskingPrice]*[Percentage Decrease?]/100)

✓ Note that this calculation does not actually change the prices in the database; to do that you would need to run an action query, as described in Exercise 24.

■ Here's an explanation of that example:
  ● [Asking Price] is a field name. For example, suppose a record's asking price were $30.
  ● The rest of the expression is in parentheses, indicating that it should be performed first, before being subtracted from the [AskingPrice] amount.
  ● [Percentage Decrease?] is a prompt, not a field name.
  ● [Percentage Decrease?] is divided by 100 to create a percentage (such as 0.10) when a whole number is entered (such as 10). If you wanted to make that clearer, to avoid entry errors, you could include a more verbose instruction, such as:

New Price: [AskingPrice]-([AskingPrice]*[Enter the desired percentage of decrease as a whole number]/100)

Show All Records If No Parameter Is Entered

■ One minor issue with parameter queries is that if the user does not enter anything for the parameter, no records will show.

■ In fact, however, what you probably want is for all records to show if the user enters no parameter.

■ To accomplish this, tack on & "*" at the end of the parameter. This allows all records to show if the parameter returns a null value.

PROCEDURES

Insert Prompt in Query Criteria

1. Open query in Query Design view.
2. Move to field.
3. Click in Criteria row.
4. Type prompt in square brackets.

Insert Prompt in Query Field Calculation

1. Open query in Query Design view.
2. Move to field.
3. Click in Field row or Update To row.
4. Type prompt in square brackets within an expression.

EXERCISE DIRECTIONS

The first part of this exercise uses a relational operator (>=) along with a specific entered value. It also converts user input as a whole number to a percentage (as stored in the field) by dividing by 100.

1. Start Access, if necessary.
2. Open 🔵 **23EXCHANGE** and save a copy of it as **23EXCHANGE_xx**.
3. Copy qryBooksForSale and give it the name **qryBooksByDiscount**.
4. In qryBooksByDiscount, enter a prompt as a criterion for the Discount field that will enable the user to enter a whole number for the minimum percentage of discount to show.

   ✓ *For example, >=([Show books that are discounted by at least what percentage?]/100).*

5. Test the query using 60 as the parameter value.
6. Print one copy of the resulting recordset in Landscape orientation, adjusting the field widths if needed so it will fit on a single sheet.
7. Change the query's parameter criterion so that leaving the parameter value empty will display all records.

   ✓ *Add &"*" to the end of the parameter statement.*

8. Test the query by pressing ⌨ when the parameter value box appears.
9. Print one copy of the result in Landscape orientation.
10. Save and close the query.

The following part of this exercise creates a query that allows the user to specify the beginning of a string in a field, not necessarily the entire content of the field. This allows a range of values to display.

1. Create a query based on tblBooks (all fields) that will show only the books that begin with a certain string of numbers in their ISBN. Name it **qryBooksByISBN**.

   ✓ *For example, for the criteria for the ISBN field, you might use Like [ISBN begins with:]&"*".*

2. Test the query: Use 1 as the parameter value. Print one copy of the result in Landscape orientation.
3. Test ((Shift)+(F9)) the query using 02 as the parameter value.
4. Test the query using nothing (null) as the parameter value.

   ✓ *The result should display all records. The use of the wildcard accepts null as the parameter value.*

5. Save the query.

The following part of the exercise uses two parameters, for City and State. This allows the user to filter by either or both, depending on his needs.

1. Create a new query called **qryCustomerByLocation** that uses all the fields in tblCustomers.
2. Create parameter criteria for both the City and State fields that prompt the user to enter the desired city or state. For example, for the city, you might use Like [What city?]&"*".

   ✓ *Don't forget to add &"*" at the end of the formula so that if the user enters nothing, all records will be included.*

3. Run the query, specifying **Macon** as the city name and not entering a state name.
4. Print one copy of the resulting recordset in Landscape orientation.
5. Save the query.
6. Close the database.

ON YOUR OWN

1. Start Access and open the 🔵 **23CANDLES** database. Save a copy of it as **OAC23_*xx*.**

2. Add a parameter prompt to qryCustomerPhone that prompts the user to input the desired area code for the phone number, and displays all records if nothing is input.

3. Run the query to show only area codes of 317, and print the results.

4. For qryEmployeeList, set up parameters that will first ask for the employee's ID (if known), and then for the employee's last name. If neither is entered, all records will display.

5. Create a copy of qryOrderInfo and give it the name **qryOrderDiscount**. Create a parameter field called Discount Price (that is, a new calculated field that includes a parameter) that shows new totals at an entered amount of discount. Format the new column as Currency with two decimal places.

✓ *Make sure that if the user does not enter any discount percentage, the Discount Price column will show the same values as in the Total column. There are various ways of achieving this. One way (not necessarily the simplest way) is to use the IIF( ) function, like this:*

✓ *Discount Price: IIf([PricePerUnit]-([PricePerUnit]*[Discount percentage, as a whole number:]*0.01)<[PricePerUnit], [PricePerUnit]-([PricePerUnit]*[Discount percentage, as a whole number:]*0.01),[PricePerUnit])*

6. Print the query results when shown with a 15% discount.

7. Save your work and close Access.

Business Connection

Who Are You?

Understanding yourself can help you choose a career that you will find fulfilling and satisfying. It means taking a good look inside yourself, and making an honest appraisal of what you see. You must take into consideration your personality, your values, your interests, your skills, and your abilities. It can be difficult to appraise oneself, because not only is it difficult to recognize unfavorable qualities, but it can also be difficult to recognize positive qualities. An honest self-assessment, however, can be a valuable tool during a career search.

Catalog Yourself

Working in teams, use research to learn more about the self-assessment process. Your instructor might have an evaluation form you can look at, or you might be able to find one online. Look into the types of things it is important to identify during such an assessment. When you are ready, make a database in which you can store information about yourselves. You might want to include fields for personality traits, interests, and abilities, as well as professional and personal priorities, values, and goals. When the database is complete, create a form that you can use to enter the information. Have each team member fill out a form for him or herself. Use the information to identify careers you might find interesting.

Exercise | 24

Skills Covered

- **About Action Queries**
- **Back Up a Table**
- **Create a Make Table Query**

- **Create an Update Query**
- **Create an Append Query**
- **Create a Delete Query**

Software Skills Action queries can save a significant amount of time if you need to change a number of records at once. You may want to delete or update records based on criteria. You can also create a new table or add records to an existing table.

Application Skills The owners of The Textbook Exchange have decided to start a new spin-off company called The Textbook Place that will sell only new books, but will sell them at 20% off retail prices. They have started a new database file with some of the old data plus some new data. You will use action queries to further prepare this data for use.

TERMS

Action query A query that changes the value of one or more records.

Append query A query that adds records to another table.

Delete query A query that removes records from a table.

Make table query A query that creates a new table using records from another table.

Update query A query that changes the entry in one or more fields in multiple records at once.

NOTES

About Action Queries

- **Action queries** modify records based on criteria you add.

- A good starting point for an action query is to begin with a regular query and view the datasheet to make sure the selection is what you want to change. Then modify the query in Query Design view to apply the action functionality.

- Be careful with action queries. Each time you run them, they make permanent changes to the table.

- There are four kinds of action queries: **make table query**, **update query**, **append query**, and **delete query**.

- Any of these queries can have parameters in the Criteria, Field or Update To rows (see Exercise 23).

Back Up a Table

- Before running an action query, you should back up the original table, especially if you have not run that query before and are not certain what it will do.

- In the Navigation Pane, select the table and copy it. Then paste the table, type a name for the new copy, and choose Structure and Data to make sure that all of the table is backed up, not just its structure.

Paste Table As dialog box

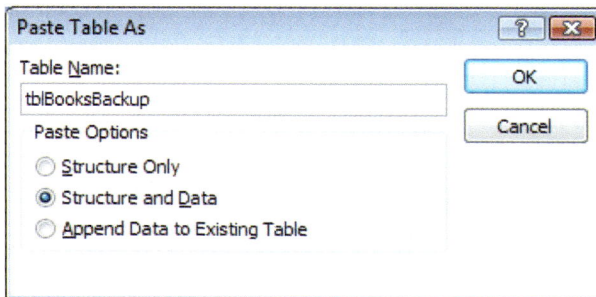

Create a Make Table Query

- Whereas the backup procedure you just learned makes a copy of the entire table, a make table query makes a copy of only specific fields or records you specify.

- Create a select query first, and display the results in Datasheet view to make sure you have the right fields and records.

  ✓ *If you are just making a list of items for the table (to create a combo box or list box, for example), open the Property Sheet for the query and change the Unique Values property to Yes.*

- Then click the Make Table button on the Query Tools Design tab. The Make Table dialog box appears.

- In the dialog box, type the table name and specify whether you want the table to reside in the current database or in another database. If you choose another database, type the file name for it.

Make Table dialog box

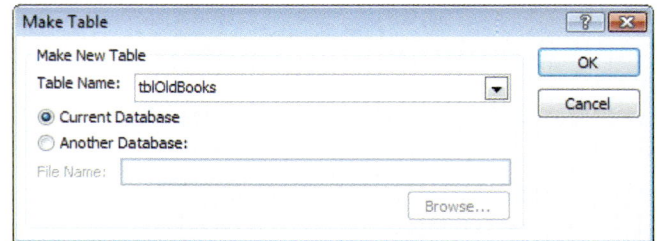

- After clicking OK in the Make Table dialog box, you return to the query design. To run the query, click the Run button on the Query Tools Design tab.

  ✓ *For select queries, clicking the Run button and switching to Datasheet view do the same thing. For action queries, however, they do not. The Run button performs the action; switching to Datasheet view does not.*

Create an Update Query

- An update query enables you to change the value of one or more fields in the records you select.

- Create a select query first, and display it in Datasheet view to make sure you have the fields and records you want.

- Then in Query Design view, click the Update button on the Query Tools Design tab. The query design grid changes to add a new row: Update To.

- In the Update To row for the field, type the expression that describes the updated data. For example, for the AskingPrice field, you might enter [Retail Price]*0.8, which will make the value in the Asking-Price field 80% of the value in the Retail Price field.

Query design for an update query

Field:	Condition	Retail Price	AskingPrice	Last
Table:	qryBooksForSale	qryBooksForSale	qryBooksForSale	qryBooksForSale
Update To:			[RetailPrice]*0.8	
Criteria:				
or:				

- To view the records to be changed by the update, switch to Datasheet view. The records display, but they do not show the update values. You can switch to Datasheet view for any action query to review results without changing the database objects.

■ To update the records, click the Run button on the Query Tools Design tab.

■ Access will let you know how many records will be updated. Click Yes to change the records (you can't undo this action) or No to cancel the update.

Create an Append Query

■ An append query will take records from one table and add them to another table.

■ You might use an append query to import records from one table into another.

> ✓ *To move records from one table to another, you might use an append query to copy certain records into another table and then use a delete query to remove them from the original table.*

■ Before you start, make sure you have another table prepared with the fields you want to add to. If necessary, use a make table query to make the table first.

■ Create a select query with the fields you want to add to the other table, and then display the result in Datasheet view to make sure you have the right data.

■ Then in Query Design view, click Append on the Query Tools Design tab. The Append dialog box opens, asking for the table name in this or another database (similar to the Make Table dialog box).

■ After you choose OK, the query design grid changes to add a new row, Append To. Choose the fields from the other table in this Append To row.

■ If the field names match, they will automatically appear in the Append To row. If the field names in the second table do not match, you will have to choose them.

Query design for an append query

Field:	ISBN	Title	Author	Date	Retail Price
Table:	tblBooks	tblBooks	tblBooks	tblBooks	tblBooks
Sort:					
Append To:	ISBN	Title	Author	Date	Retail Price
Criteria:					
or:					

■ Click the Run button to append. Access will let you know how many records will append. Click Yes to add the records or No to cancel.

Create a Delete Query

■ An append query and a delete query are often run together. For example, first you append old records to an archive table for storage, and then you delete them from the current table.

■ Create a select query with the records you want to delete. Then in Query Design view, click Delete. After you choose the query type, the query design grid shows a new row, Delete. Enter any criteria on that row as needed.

■ To run the query, click the Run button. Access will let you know how many records it will delete. Click Yes to remove the records or No to cancel the deletion.

PROCEDURES

Back Up a Table

In the Navigation Pane:

1. Click the table to copy.
2. Press Ctrl + C.

   > ✓ *You can also right-click the table and click Copy, or click the Copy button on the Home tab (Clipboard group).*

3. Press Ctrl + V.

   > ✓ *You can also right-click an empty area of the Navigation Pane and click Paste, or click the Paste button on the Home tab (Clipboard group).*

4. Type name of new table.

5. Keep the default choice, **Structure and Data**, to make a complete backup of the table.

   OR

   Choose **Structure Only** to create a copy of the table's structure (fields and properties).

6. Click **OK** . . . . Enter

Create a Make Table Query

1. Create or open a select query in Query Design view.
2. Click **Query Tools Design** tab . . . . Alt + R

3. Click **Make Table** button . . . . M
4. Type name for new table.
5. Keep the default choice, **Current Database** . . . . Alt + C

   OR

   a. Click **Another Database** . . . . Alt + A

   b. Type database in **File Name** text box . . . . . Alt + F

6. Click **OK** . . . . Enter

7. Click **Run** Run
   button . . . . [Alt]+[R], [G]
8. Click **Yes** . . . . [Alt]+[Y]

Create Update Query

1. Create or open a select query in Query Design view.
2. Click **Query Tools Design** tab . . . . [Alt]+[R]

   Query Type Group

3. Click **Update** Update
   button . . . . [D]
4. Type update expression in Update To row.

   Results Group

5. Click **Run** Run
   button . . . . [Alt]+[R], [G]
6. Click **Yes** . . . . [Alt]+[Y]

Create Append Query

1. If necessary, create target table first by copying only the structure of an existing table. See Back Up a Table.
2. In Design view for new table, remove all default values, validation rules, and validation text entries.
3. In Design view for new table, delete and add fields if you are planning to append only some of the fields from the source table.
4. Create or open a select query in Query Design view based on the original table.

   Query Type Group

5. Click **Append** Append
   button . . . . [P]
6. Type name for new table.
7. Keep the default choice, **Current Database**. . . . . [Alt]+[C]

   OR

   a. Click **Another Database** . . . . [Alt]+[A]
   b. Type database in **File Name** text box . . . . . [Alt]+[F]
8. Click **OK**. . . . . [Enter]

9. Click **Run** Run
   button . . . . [Alt]+[R], [G]
10. Click **Yes** . . . . [Alt]+[Y]

Create Delete Query

1. Create or open a select query in Query Design view.
2. Click **Query Tools Design** tab . . . . [Alt]+[R]

   Query Type Group

3. Click **Delete** Delete
   button . . . . [X]
4. Type any criteria expressions in Delete row to define records to delete.

   Results Group

5. Click **Run** Run
   button . . . . [Alt]+[R], [G]
6. Click **Yes** . . . . [Alt]+[Y]

EXERCISE DIRECTIONS

1. Start Access, if necessary.
2. Open ◎ **24EXCHANGE** and save a copy of it as **24EXCHANGE_xx**.
3. Make a copy of tblBooks called **tblBooksBackup** that contains both the structure and the data.

Append Query

1. Start a select query based on tblMoreBooks in Query Design view, using all fields except OutOfPrint. Turn it into an append query that appends tblMoreBooks to tblBooks. Run the query to do the append operation.

   ✓ *Not all field names are exactly the same. You will need to specify the match-up for Retail Price. In addition, the Out of Print field does not appear in the original tblBooks, so you will not be able to append it.*

2. Save the append query as **qryAppendMoreBooks** and close it.

Make Table Query

1. Start a select query based on tblBooks, using all fields.
2. Enter criteria that will include only books that were published prior to 01/01/2007.
3. Test the query by running it; then return to Query Design view. The results should contain 9 records.
4. Change the query to a make table query that creates a new table called **tblOldBooks** based on the select query's criteria. Run the query.
5. Save the query as **qryPre2007** and close it.
6. Open tblOldBooks in Datasheet view to confirm that it contains 9 records; then close it.

Delete Query

1. Create a new query in Design view that contains just the ISBN and Date fields from tblBooks.

2. Change it to a Delete query and set up criteria so that records that have dates before 01/01/2007 will be deleted.

3. Run the query. An error appears that Access can't delete 3 of the records due to key violations. Click Yes to delete the others.

4. Save the query as qryDeletePre2007 and close it.

   ✓ *The reason those records cannot be deleted is that there have been orders placed for them. You will need to modify the relationship between tblBooks so that cascade delete is in effect.*

5. Open the Relationships window and open the Edit Relationships dialog box for the relationship between tblBooks and tblOrderDetails. Turn on Cascade Delete Related Records.

6. Exit from the Relationships window and re-run qryDeletePre2007. This time it deletes the remaining 3 records.

Update Query

1. Create a select query based on tblBooks. Include only the ISBN, Retail Price, and Our Price fields.

2. Change the query to an update query that will set the value in the Our Price field to 60% of the Retail Price field's value.

3. Run the query and save it as **qryOurPrice**.

4. Open tblBooks in Datasheet view to confirm that the Our Price field is now appropriately populated with 40% off retail prices.

5. Reopen qryOurPrice in Design view, and in the Update To row, add a parameter that will prompt the user to enter the percentage of discount between Retail Price and Our Price:

   [Retail Price]*[Enter a discount percentage as a whole number]/100

6. Rerun the query and enter 20 as the parameter amount.

7. View tblBooks in Datasheet view to confirm that Our Price is now 20% off retail prices.

8. Close the database.

ON YOUR OWN

1. Start Access and open the ⊙ 24CANDLES database. Save a copy of it as OAC24_xx.

2. Use a make table query to copy all the records from tblOrders to a new table called **tblOldOrders** where the order date is earlier than 01/01/2008. Save the query as **qryCopyOldOrders**.

3. Make a copy of tblProducts, and call the copy tblProductsBackup.

4. Increase all the prices in tblProducts by 20% if the current price is under $1.99; otherwise increase the price by 15%.

   ✓ *Create two separate queries for step 3. Name them qrySmallUpdate and qryLargeUpdate. Don't use a dollar sign in the criteria.*

4. Make a new table from the data in tblProducts that contains only tealight candles. (Do not include tealight wicks.) Name the table **tblTealightCandles**. Do not save the query.

5. Close the database, and exit Access.

Skills Covered

- **Use the Crosstab Query Wizard**
- **Show Row Headers**
- **Show Column Headers**
- **Choose Value Field**
- **Use Crosstab Query Design View**

Software Skills   Crosstab queries are a rather "special purpose" item. Instead of presenting just summary data, or just detail data, they allow you to combine summary and detail in specific ways to deliver information you need. In this way, they are somewhat like PivotTables.

Application Skills   The Textbook Exchange has had such success with their business that they have spun off yet another division, called The Bookseller Source, that will offer large quantities of textbooks to bookstores at 50% off retail prices. They have already set up the database for this business and have three days' worth of sales data entered. Now the owners would like to look at the data for these first few days to evaluate what items are selling well and which salespeople are performing the best. You will use crosstab queries to produce this data.

TERMS

Column heading   The field that provides labels for the columns in a crosstab query.

Crosstab Query   A query that summarizes one field by two or more other category fields. The category fields display in row and column headings. At the intersection of each row and column is a summary (sum, average, count) of the value.

Row heading   One or more fields that label each row of a crosstab query.

Value   The field that provides the data to summarize for the intersection of each column and row of a crosstab query.

NOTES

Use the Crosstab Query Wizard

- Crosstab queries are a special type of query that combines summary and detail data, much like a PivotTable does.

- The **Crosstab Query** Wizard leads you through the steps to create a query that summarizes a data field by a row category field and a column category field.

- If the fields that you want to summarize are in more than one table, create a query first that joins those tables before you use the Crosstab Query Wizard, and base the crosstab query on that query.

The results of a crosstab query

| qrySaleValuePerDay-Crosstab | | | | |
Salesperson	Total All Days	1/15/2009	1/16/2009	1/17/2009
Christine Cutler	$12,338.00	$7,498.50		$4,839.50
Julie Burrow	$80,291.38	$61,109.00	$14,184.38	$4,998.00
Marjorie Hopper	$109,952.00	$75,220.00	$30,107.50	$4,624.50
Melissa Louks	$66,745.50	$34,748.00		$31,997.50

- To start the Crosstab Query Wizard, click the Query Wizard button on the Create tab, and then in the New Query dialog box, click Crosstab Query Wizard and click OK.

- The first step of the Crosstab Query Wizard asks you to choose the source for your data. It can be a table or another query.

Choose source for crosstab query

Crosstab Query Wizard

Which table or query contains the fields you want for the crosstab query results?

Query: qryDeletePre2000
Query: qryOrdersWithDetails

> Choose table or query

To include fields from more than one table, create a query containing all the fields you need and then use this query to make the crosstab query.

View

○ Tables ● Queries ○ Both

> You can list tables, queries, or both

Sample:

	Header1	Header2	Header3
	TOTAL		

Cancel   < Back   Next >   Finish

Show Row Headers

- The second step of the Crosstab Query Wizard asks you to choose which field will be the source for **row headings** in the left column of the query.

- All like values from the row heading field are grouped together, and each unique value in the row heading field becomes a heading for each row of the query.

- You can choose up to three fields for row headings.

Choose row heading

Crosstab Query Wizard

Which fields' values do you want as row headings?

You can select up to three fields.

Select fields in the order you want information sorted. For example, you could sort and group values by Country and then Region.

Available Fields:

First
Last
OrderDate
ISBN
Quantity
Our Price
Total

Selected Fields:

Salesperson

> Choose field for row heading

>   >>   <   <<

Sample:

Salesperson	Header1	Header2	Header3
Salesperson1	TOTAL		
Salesperson2			
Salesperson3			
Salesperson4			

> Each value in the field becomes a heading for each row of the query

Cancel   < Back   Next >   Finish

Show Column Headers

- The third step of the wizard asks you to choose which field will be the source for **column headings**, along the top of the query.

- All like values from the column heading field are grouped together, and each unique value in the column heading field becomes a heading for the data columns of the query.

- You can choose only one field for a column heading.

- If you choose a field that is a Date data type for a row or column heading, you will be asked how you want to group the dates on the next step of the wizard. You can choose Year, Month, or another date category.

Choose Value Field

- The next step of the wizard allows you to choose a **value** field to summarize. Generally this field is a number that you can sum. Sometimes this field is a text or other type of field that you may want to count.

- You choose both the field and the function you want to perform on it.

- Use the following functions. (This list of functions changes depending on whether the value data field is a number or other data type.)

Use	To . . .
Avg	Total (numeric only) values and divide by the number in the intersection of each row and column field.
Count	Find the number of records in the intersection of each row and column field.
First	Find the field's first record input for the intersection of each row and column.
Last	Find the field's last record input for the intersection of each row and column.
Max	Find the highest value in the intersection of each row and column field. If the Max field is text, the function finds the last alphabetical value. If the field is a number, the function finds the largest number. If the field is a date, the function finds the latest date.
Min	Find the lowest value in the intersection of each row and column field. If the Min field is text, the function finds the first alphabetical value. If the field is a number, the function finds the lowest number. If the field is a date, the function finds the earliest date.
StDev	Calculate the standard deviation of the number in the intersection of each row and column. This is used to see how close all the values are to the average (number fields only).

Choose column heading

568

Choose value field and function

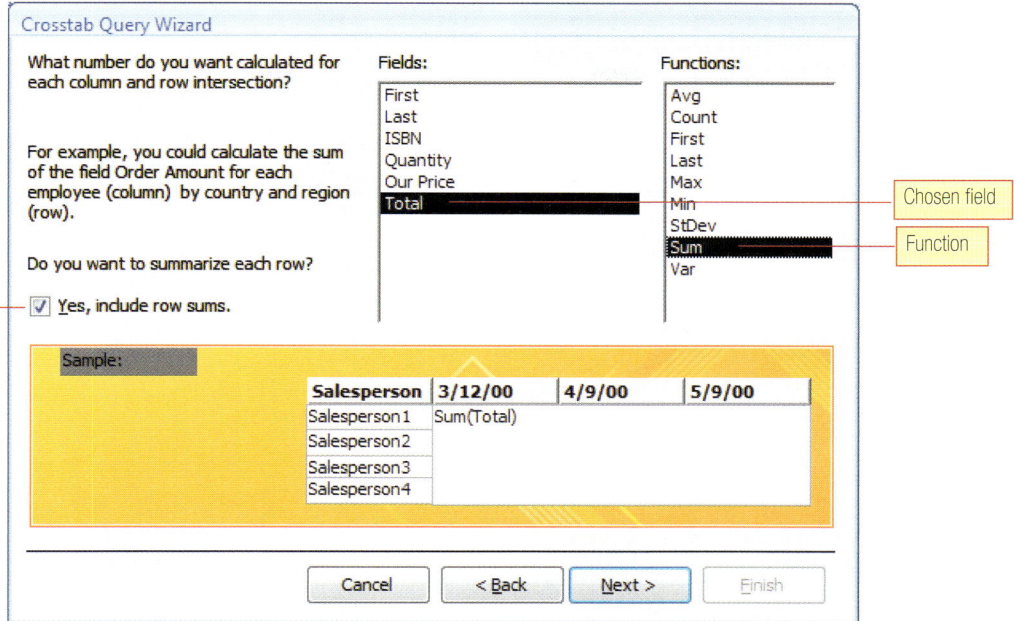

Sum	Total (numeric only) values by the intersection of each row and column field.
Var	Calculate the variance of the number in the intersection of each row and column. This is another measure of how close the values are to the average (number fields only).

- In this step of the wizard, you can also choose if you want a total for each row. (This will total all column values for each row.)

- The last step of the wizard prompts you for a name for the query and asks if you want to open it in Design view or Datasheet view.

Use Crosstab Query Design View

- In a crosstab query, a Crosstab row appears in the query design grid. You can make any query into a crosstab query by clicking the Crosstab button on the Query Tools Design tab, just like you did for other action queries in Exercise 24.

- The choices in the Crosstab row are Row Heading, Column Heading, and Value. You must have at least one of each.

- You can have more than one Row Heading field, but not more than one Column Heading or Value field.

- The Total row for the Row Heading and Column Heading fields says Group By.

- If you choose to display row totals, the Crosstab row also says Row Heading, but the Total row shows the Sum (or other) function.

- The Total row for the Value field shows the function you want to apply, such as Sum.

- Choose Where in the Total row to select only certain records, and type values in the Criteria rows.

- Switch to Datasheet view or click the Run button to see the results of the crosstab query.

Crosstab query in Query Design view

	Row field (note "Row Heading" in Crosstab row)	Format function added for date field	Column field (note "Column Heading" in Crosstab row)	This sum appears at the intersection of row and column	This represents the column for each row's grand total
Field:	[Salesperson]	Format([OrderDate],"Short Date")		[Total]	Total Of Total: [Total]
Table:	qryOrdersWithDetails			qryOrdersWithDetails	qryOrdersWithDetails
Total:	Group By	Group By		Sum	Sum
Crosstab:	Row Heading	Column Heading		Value	Row Heading
Sort:					
Criteria:					
or:					

PROCEDURES

Use the Crosstab Query Wizard

1. Click **Create** tab . . . . `Alt`+`C`

2. Click **Query Wizard** button . . . . `Q`, `W`
3. Click **Crosstab Query Wizard** . . . . `↓`
4. Click **OK** . . . . `Enter`
5. Click an option to display objects:
   - **Tables** . . . . `Alt`+`T`
   - **Queries**
   - **Both** . . . . `Alt`+`O`
6. Click desired table or query.
7. Click **Next** . . . . `Alt`+`N`
8. Double-click the row field.
9. Repeat step 7 if necessary.
10. Click **Next** . . . . `Alt`+`N`
11. Click column field.
12. Click **Next** . . . . `Alt`+`N`
13. If you chose a date field, choose a date interval, and then click **Next** . . . . `Alt`+`N`
14. Click the value field in **Fields** list.
15. Click the function in the **Functions** list.
16. If desired, choose **Yes, include row sums** . . . . `Alt`+`Y`
17. Click **Next** . . . . `Alt`+`N`
18. Give the query a title in the provided text box.
19. Choose to view the query or modify the design.
20. Click **Finish** . . . . `Alt`+`F`

Convert a Query to a Crosstab Query

1. Open the query in Query Design view.
2. Click **Query Tools Design** tab . . . . `Alt`+`R`

3. Click **Crosstab** button . . . . `O`
4. Remove any fields that are not appropriate to the crosstab query.
5. Choose either **Group By** or a function in the Total row for each field.
6. Choose **Row Heading, Column Heading**, or **Value** in the Crosstab row for each field.

   ✓ *You must have at least one of each.*

7. Click **Run** button to run the query . . . . `Alt`+`R`, `G`

EXERCISE DIRECTIONS

1. Start Access, if necessary.
2. Open **25BOOKSELLER** and save a copy of it as **25BOOKSELLER_xx**.
3. Use the Crosstab Query Wizard to create the query based on qryOrdersWithDetails as follows:
   a. Use Salesperson for the rows.
   b. Use OrderDate for the columns.
   c. Use Date as the interval.
   d. Use Total as the calculated field.
   e. Use Sum as the function.
   f. Include row sums.
   g. Name the query **qrySalesValuePerDay-Crosstab**.
4. Open the query in Query Design view and change the column name of the Total Of Total column to **Total All Days**.
5. Run the query. Save it and close it.
6. Make a copy of the query, and name the copy **qrySalesQuantityPerDay-Crosstab**.
7. Open qrySalesQuantityPerDay-Crosstab in Query Design view.
8. Edit the query so that it shows the total number of books sold, rather than the value of the books sold, per salesperson per day. See Illustration A. Save and close the query.
9. Start a new query in Query Design view based on qryOrdersWithDetails.
10. Choose Crosstab query as the query type.
11. Enter the appropriate fields and settings to produce the results shown in Illustration B:
    a. The dates are the row headings.
    b. The salespeople are the column headings.
    c. The average price of the books sold (Our Price field) is the value.
12. Save the new query as **qryAvgPricePerDay-Crosstab**.
13. Close all open objects and close the database.

Illustration A

Salesperson	Total Quantity All Days	1/15/2009	1/16/2009	1/17/2009
Christine Cutler	600	300		300
Julie Burrow	2675	1600	675	400
Marjorie Hopper	2875	2050	675	150
Melissa Louks	2000	1000		1000

Illustration B

Order Date	Christine Cutler	Julie Burrow	Marjorie Hopper	Melissa Louks
1/15/2009	$27.50	$36.71	$32.92	$20.00
1/16/2009		$18.50	$31.93	
1/17/2009	$17.10	$12.50	$35.00	$32.00

ON YOUR OWN

1. Start Access and open the ⊙ **25CANDLES** database. Save it as **OAC25_*xx***.

2. Using the Crosstab Query Wizard, create a new crosstab query based on qryOrderInfo as follows:
   a. Use ProductName and PricePerUnit as the row headings.
   b. Use LastName as the column headings.
   c. Use Quantity as the value.
   d. Use Sum as the function.
   e. Name the query **qryQtyByCustomer-Crosstab**.

3. Save a copy of the query under a different name: **qryQtyBySalesperson-Crosstab**.

4. Modify the query so that Salesperson rather than Name is used for column headings.

5. Modify the query to sort the results in Ascending order by PricePerUnit.

6. Save and close the query.

7. Open qryOrderInfo in Design view and add a Total calculated field that multiples the quantity by the price per unit. Then save and close the query.

7. Use the Crosstab Query Wizard to create a new Crosstab query based on qryOrderInfo that shows the total dollar value of products ordered by each customer (by last name) per month:
   a. Do not show row sums.
   b. Format the amounts as currency with two decimal places.
   c. Name it **qryValueByCustomer-Crosstab**.

8. Close the database and exit Access.

Exercise | 26

Skills Covered

- **Use the Find Unmatched Query Wizard**
- **Use the Find Duplicates Query Wizard**

Software Skills   The Find Unmatched Query Wizard and the Find Duplicates Query Wizard are two special-purpose query types for specific tasks. They do just what their names indicate. The Find Unmatched Query Wizard compares two tables and reports records from one that do not have a corresponding entry in the other. The Find Duplicates query lists records that have the same value for one or more specified fields.

Application Skills   You want to clean up the tables in The Textbook Source database to make sure that all the details in tblOrderDetails have valid entries in tblOrders and to make sure that there are no duplicate entries for the bookstores with different contact people entered. You will use queries to track down this information.

TERMS

Duplicate   Two or more records that contain the same data in a field that ought to be unique for each record.

Unmatched   Records that should have a corresponding reference in another table but do not.

NOTES

Use the Find Unmatched Query Wizard

- The Find Unmatched Query Wizard leads you through the steps to create a query that will show records which do not match up with corresponding values in another table.

- Suppose, for example, that you have separate tables for Orders and OrderDetails. Every record in OrderDetails should refer to a valid order number in the Orders table. If there are detail records that do not, they are **unmatched**.

  ✓ *This type of error would not occur if you were enforcing referential integrity in the relationship between the two tables. This illustrates the importance of referential integrity, covered in Exercise 2.*

- To run this wizard, click the Query Wizard button on the Create tab, and then click Find Unmatched Query Wizard in the New Query dialog box.

- The first step of the wizard asks you to identify the table or query containing the records you want in the results. For our example with orders and details, the appropriate choice here would be tblOrderDetails.

Select the table or query containing the records

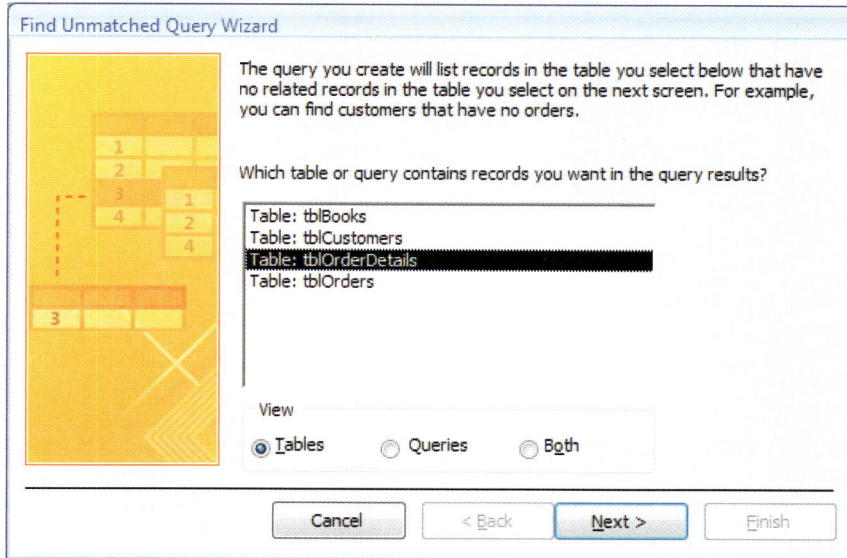

- Next, the wizard asks which table or query is related to it. Choose from the list.
- You are then asked to pick the fields on which the two chosen tables or queries are related. If there is an existing relationship between them, it appears as the default.

- Next, the wizard asks which fields you want to see in the results. In many cases, you will not need the entire set of fields because you are running this query mainly for reference in helping you track down errors.
- In the last step of the wizard, you specify a name for the query.

Specify how the two are related

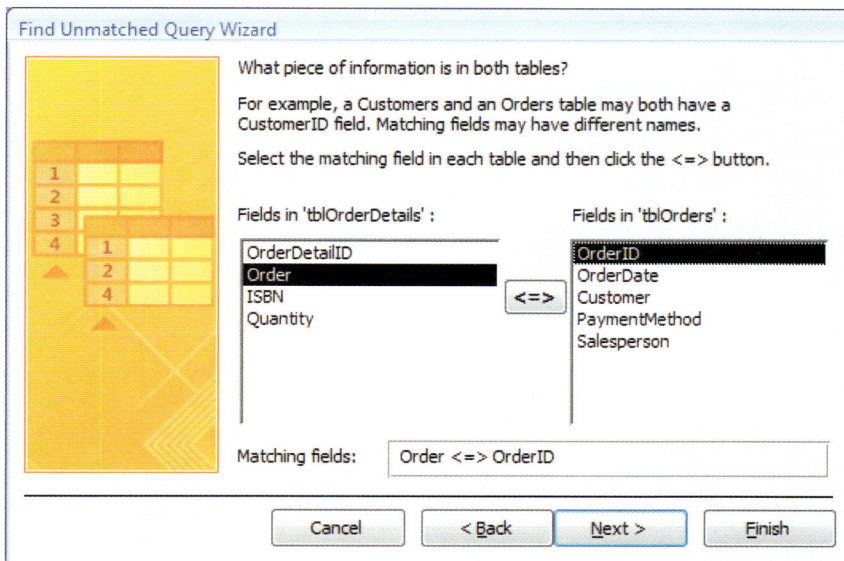

Results showing order details with no valid associated order number

OrderDetaill ▾	Order ▾	ISBN ▾	Quantity ▾
12	7	Computer Networks, 4th Edition	650
13	7	Computer Science: An Overview 7th Edition	700
32	19	The Web Wizard's Guide to Freeware and Shareware	200
33	19	Authentication: From Passwords to Public Keys	100
34	19	Internet Visual Reference Basics	100
*	(New)		

- The results appear in a datasheet, just like a select query. You can print it to use as a reference when fixing the problems.

Use the Find Duplicates Query Wizard

- The Find Duplicates Query Wizard is like a super "search" that helps ferret out duplication in your data.

- For example, suppose you want a single record in your Customers table for each business, but you have ended up with some businesses entered multiple times with different contact people in each record. You could find the **duplicates** with the Find Duplicates Query Wizard.

  ✓ *This error would not occur if you set up the business name field to not allow duplicates. Setting its Indexed setting to Yes (No Duplicates) would prevent the problem from happening in the future.*

- Running the Find Duplicates Query Wizard starts by clicking the Query Wizard button, just as with other query wizards. Select the desired wizard and click OK to run it.

- First, you specify the table or query in which you want to search for duplicates.

- Next, you pick the field(s) that should be unique for each record. You do not need to include the primary key field or any field that is set to require unique values because those fields can be assumed to be unique already.

- Next, choose what additional fields you want to appear in the query results. These additional fields may be helpful in identifying the records so you can fix them.

- Finally, give the query a name and finish the wizard. The results appear in a datasheet.

Pick the fields for which you want to identify duplicate values

Find Duplicates Query Wizard

Which fields might contain duplicate information?

For example, if you are looking for cities with more than one customer, you would choose City and Region fields here.

Available fields:

ID
First
Last
Address
City
State
ZIP

> | >> | < | <<

Duplicate-value fields:

Store
Phone

Cancel | < Back | Next > | Finish

PROCEDURES

Run a Find Unmatched Query

1. Click **Create** tab . . . . `Alt`+`C`

   Other Group

2. Click **Query Wizard** button . . . . `Q`, `W`
3. Click **Find Unmatched Query Wizard**.
4. Click **OK** . . . . `Enter`
5. Click an option to display objects:
   - **T**ables . . . . `Alt`+`T`
   - **Q**ueries
   - B**o**th . . . . `Alt`+`O`
6. Click desired table or query.
7. Click **Next** . . . . `Alt`+`N`
8. Click an option to display objects:
   - **T**ables . . . . `Alt`+`T`
   - **Q**ueries
   - B**o**th . . . . `Alt`+`O`
9. Click table or query with which you want to compare the one you selected in step 6.
10. Click **Next** . . . . `Alt`+`N`

11. Check corresponding fields. If incorrect fields are selected:
    a. Click the field on the left side.
    b. Click corresponding field on the right side.
    c. Click `<=>` button.
12. Click **Next** . . . . `Alt`+`N`
13. (Optional) Add more fields to the query results:
    a. Click an additional field that you want in the query results.
    b. Click `>` button.
    c. Repeat a and b as needed.
14. Click **Next** . . . . `Alt`+`N`
15. Type a name for the query.
16. Click **F**inish . . . . `Alt`+`F`

Run a Find Duplicates Query

1. Click **Create** tab . . . . `Alt`+`C`

   Other Group

2. Click **Query Wizard** button . . . . `Q`, `W`

3. Click **Find Duplicates Query Wizard**.
4. Click **OK** . . . . `Enter`
5. Click an option to display objects:
   - **T**ables . . . . `Alt`+`T`
   - **Q**ueries
   - B**o**th . . . . `Alt`+`O`
6. Click desired table or query.
7. Click **Next** . . . . `Alt`+`N`
8. Click a field for which you want to identify duplicates.
9. Click `>` button.
10. Repeat steps 7–8 as needed.
11. Click **Next** . . . . `Alt`+`N`
12. (Optional) Click an additional field that you want in the query results.
13. Click `>` button.
14. Repeat steps 12–13 as needed.
15. Click **Next** . . . . `Alt`+`N`
16. Type a name for the query.
17. Click **F**inish . . . . `Alt`+`F`

EXERCISE DIRECTIONS

1. Start Access, if necessary.
2. Open **26SOURCE** and save a copy of it as **26SOURCE_xx**.
3. Use the Find Duplicates Query Wizard to find all the records in tblCustomers with a duplicate value in either Store or Phone. Show all fields.
4. Save the query as **qryFindDuplicateCustomers**.
5. Fix the records in the table so that each store exists only once. You can delete either of the duplicate records to achieve this.
6. Rerun qryFindDuplicateCustomers to confirm that all duplicates have been fixed. If you have caught them all, you will have an empty recordset.

7. Open tblCustomers in Design view and set the Store and Phone fields' Indexed properties to Yes (No Duplicates) so the problem will not happen again.
8. Use the Find Unmatched Query Wizard to find all the records in tblOrderDetails with no corresponding order number in tblOrders.
9. Save the query as **qryFindOrphanDetails**.
10. Delete all the records that the query finds.
11. Open the Relationships window and enforce referential integrity between tblOrders and tblOrderDetails so the problem will not happen again.
12. Close the database.

ON YOUR OWN

1. Start Access and open the 26CANDLES database. Save it as **OAC26_xx**.

2. Create a Find Duplicates query called **qryProduct-Duplicates** that finds all products in tblProducts that have the same ProductName and lists their part numbers, descriptions, and prices per unit.

3. Run and print the query; then close it. Do not modify or delete any records.

4. Create a Find Unmatched query called **qryUnmatched-OrderDetails** that finds order details that do not have an associated order, if any.

5. Create a Find Unmatched query called **qryUnused-PaymentMethods** that displays all payment records from tblPaymentMethods that are not used in any order in tblOrders.

6. Close the database and exit Access.

Critical Thinking

Application Skills   Now that you know more about advanced queries, you have the skills to develop some queries that will provide meaningful data analysis for a client. Your client in this exercise is a company called Clown-n-Around, a non-profit organization. You will develop some queries for them that include parameters, actions, and finding unmatched and duplicate records.

EXERCISE DIRECTIONS

1. Open 27CLOWN and save it as 27CLOWN_xx.
2. Create a query called **qryInStock** that shows products from tblLogoItems (all fields) and prompts the user with a parameter to enter an item category as the criterion. If the user does not enter a category, it should show all items.
3. Use a make table query to make a new table called **tblNonMembers** based on tblMailingList that contains only people who are non-members. Save the query as **qryMakeTableNonMembers**.
4. Use a delete query to delete the non-members from tblMailingList. Save the query as **qryDeleteNonMembers**.
5. Open the Relationships window and remove Enforce Referential Integrity from these relationships:

    Between tblMembershipType and tblMailingList

    Between tblMemberOrders and tblLogoItems
6. Use an Update query to change the name of the Over 65 membership category to Senior in tblMailingList. Save the query as **qryChangeCategoryName**.
7. Open tblMembershipType and change Over 65 to **Senior**.
8. Reestablish referential integrity between tblMailingList and tblMembershipType.
9. Delete record 8 (the Tote Bag) from tblLogoItems.
10. Use a Find Unmatched query to locate any member orders for the tote bag. Do not modify the found records. Save the query as **qryOrdersDeletedItems**.
11. Create a crosstab query called **qryMemberTotalOrders-Crosstab** based on qryMemberOrderDiscounts that shows each member who has placed an order as the rows, the date by month as the column headers, and the sum of the member's order amounts (with discount) as the data.
12. Format the data as Currency with two decimal places. Change the title for the Total Of Total with Discount column to **Discounted Total**. Illustration A shows the query results.
13. Close the database and exit Access.

Illustration A

qryMemberTotalOrders-Crosstab					
Member	Discounted Total	Jan	Feb	Mar	Apr
Avery	$36.00			$36.00	
Brown	$32.40			$32.40	
Ireland	$38.00				$38.00
Marsh	$22.50				$22.50

Exercise | 28

Curriculum Integration

Application Skills   In Business class, you are analyzing some databases to determine what products are most profitable and are selling the best. You will analyze two databases in Access and use the data that you glean from them to develop a PowerPoint presentation that presents your recommendations and findings.

EXERCISE DIRECTIONS

Examine the sales data in **28SALTY** and **28SWEET**. Create and run queries as needed to determine the answers to the following questions:

- What were the best-selling and second-best-selling salty items in terms of quantity?
- What were the best-selling and second-best-selling sweet items in terms of quantity?
- In overall profit (retail minus wholesale cost), which was the most successful sweet item, and how much profit was made on it? What was the most successful salty item, and how much profit?
- Which customer had the highest total sales for salty items, and how much was that sales amount? For sweet items?
- Which customer provided the most profit for salty items, and how much profit was that? For sweet items?
- Which is the most profitable item to sell, in terms of amount of profit made per unit?

Develop an attractive PowerPoint presentation that conveys all this information. Name it **28SALES_*xx***.

Lesson | 1

Advanced Text and Master Features

Skills Covered

- **Use the Outline Tab to Create Slide Content**
- **Apply More Than One Theme**
- **Replace Fonts Throughout a Presentation**
- **Work with WordArt Styles**
- **Add Presentation Properties**

Software Skills Creating presentation content in the Outline tab allows you to concentrate on text. Apply more than one theme to increase formatting options. If you do not like a theme font, you can replace it throughout a presentation using Replace Fonts or Slide Master view. Add visual interest to slides by changing WordArt styles and applying WordArt styles to existing text. Add properties to a presentation to identify information about the presentation.

Application Skills Planet Earth, a local environmental action group, has asked you to prepare a presentation that can be shown at your civic garden center to encourage city residents to "go green." In this exercise, you begin the presentation, apply themes, replace fonts, work with WordArt styles, and add presentation properties.

TERMS

Properties Details about a presentation (or any document) that describe or identify the file.

NOTES

Use the Outline Tab to Create Slide Content

- The Outline tab, behind the Slides tab in the Slides/Outline pane, lets you view all slide content in outline format.
- Many PowerPoint users prefer to create presentation text in the Outline tab because they can concentrate on the text and move quickly from slide to slide.
- To begin a new presentation in the Outline tab, click next to the first slide icon and type the text that will become the slide title. As you type the text in the Outline tab, it appears on the current slide in the Slide pane.
- Press ⌨[Enter] to start a new slide in the Outline pane. If you do not want a new slide but want to insert a subtitle or bulleted content, press ⌨[→] to "back up" to the previous slide and insert the subordinate text. You can then press ⌨[Shift]+⌨[←] to return to the first level of the outline and create the next slide title.

The Outline tab shows slide content in outline form

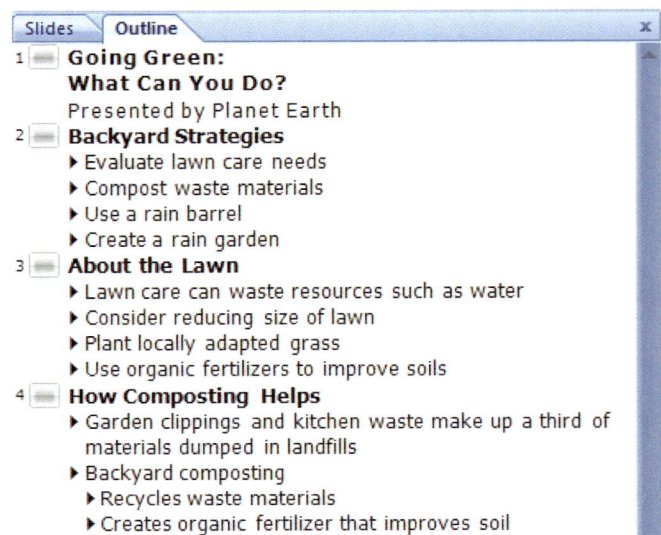

Slides	Outline	x

1. **Going Green:**
   What Can You Do?
   Presented by Planet Earth
2. **Backyard Strategies**
   - Evaluate lawn care needs
   - Compost waste materials
   - Use a rain barrel
   - Create a rain garden
3. **About the Lawn**
   - Lawn care can waste resources such as water
   - Consider reducing size of lawn
   - Plant locally adapted grass
   - Use organic fertilizers to improve soils
4. **How Composting Helps**
   - Garden clippings and kitchen waste make up a third of materials dumped in landfills
   - Backyard composting
     - Recycles waste materials
     - Creates organic fertilizer that improves soil

Apply More Than One Theme

- PowerPoint's themes allow you to quickly format all slides in a presentation with colors, fonts, effects, and layouts.

- You may sometimes wish to apply more than one theme to a presentation to have access to additional formatting options. For example, you may want to use the Picture with Caption layout of one theme and format the remaining slides with a complementary theme.

- Another way to make more than one theme available in a presentation is to add a slide master in Slide Master view. This subject is covered in Exercise 4 of this lesson.

Replace Fonts Throughout a Presentation

- You know already that PowerPoint themes include a set of designated fonts that you can easily change by simply applying a new set of theme fonts.

- In some cases, however, you may want to replace only one of the theme's fonts, or you may want to modify all the heading fonts by changing the font style. If you have applied more than one theme to a presentation, for example, you may want to "blend" the themes by making sure the heading styles are the same for both themes.

- Although you can change fonts manually on each slide, this is not an efficient practice. You have two options for replacing fonts that are faster and safer than making manual changes on a series of slides.

- The first option is to use the Replace Fonts command, located on the Replace menu in the Editing group on the Home tab.

- Selecting this command opens the Replace Font dialog box.

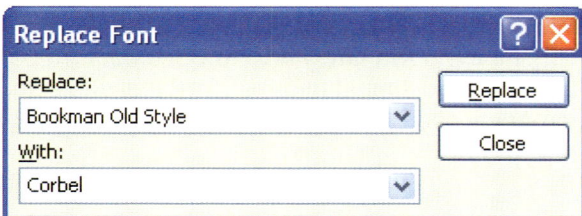

Replace Font dialog box

- Use this dialog box to select one of the fonts in the current presentation and choose a different font to replace it with.

- This feature can be a great savings of time if you know you want to change every instance of a font throughout a presentation.

- If you need to change more than one font, however, or change font formatting for all slides, it is more efficient to adjust fonts using the slide master.

- Change fonts in the slide master by clicking in the text to which you want to apply new font formatting. Apply the formats using the commands in the Font group on the Home tab.

- The following illustration shows a default slide master in which the slide title font has been changed to Cambria from the default Calibri. Shadow font style has been applied, and the text has also been left aligned.

Change font formatting in Slide Master view

- All slides based on this master will display the new font formatting for the slide title text. The changed font formatting also applies to any new slides based on this layout.

Work with WordArt Styles

- WordArt graphics offer a visual punch for text on a slide. Options in the WordArt Styles group on the Drawing Tools Format tab allow you to modify a WordArt graphic in a number of ways: You can change text fill color, text outline formats, or text effects.

- You can also apply Quick Styles to the WordArt graphic to change the graphic's appearance. The WordArt gallery allows you to apply Quick Styles that format all text in the WordArt graphic or format only selected text.

Apply a Quick Style to all text or selected text in the graphic

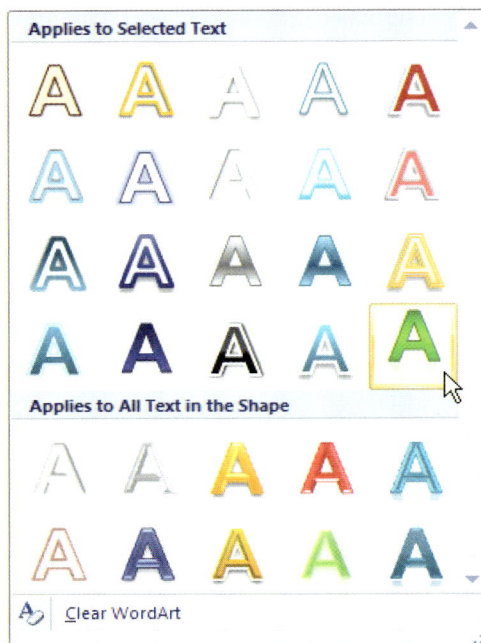

- You have another option for using WordArt styles in a presentation: You can apply the styles to any text in the presentation for a special visual effect.

- Use the WordArt Styles gallery on the Drawing Tools Format tab to apply a WordArt style to text. The text maintains its original size but takes on the WordArt style.

- The following illustration shows a presentation title and subtitle that have been formatted with WordArt styles.

Existing text formatted with WordArt styles

- WordArt styles can make a heading stand out on a slide, but use caution in applying WordArt styles to multiple lines of text.

Add Presentation Properties

- When you create a presentation, you can store information about the presentation called **properties**. Properties can include the author of the presentation, its title, and keywords to help you quickly identify the presentation.

- You add properties using the Document Information Panel.

- The Document Information Panel shows information that PowerPoint collects for you, such as the file location, as well as standard properties you supply yourself, such as the author, title, status, and any comments you want to add.

- Document properties, which are sometimes referred to as *metadata*, not only allow you to provide information about a presentation but also make it easy to organize and locate files that have the same kinds of information. When searching for files, for example, you can use document properties as criteria in the search.

- You can see more properties for a document by clicking the down arrow next to Document Properties in the Document Information Panel and selecting Advanced Properties to open the Properties dialog box.

- The tabs in the Properties dialog box allow you to view general file information, a summary of current properties, statistics about the presentation, such as when it was created and how many slides it has, and the contents of all slides in the presentation. You can use the Custom tab to create your own categories of properties.

- You can view or edit properties at any time by displaying the Document Information Panel or the Properties dialog box.

- After you have added properties to a presentation, you can view them when you save or open the file by changing the View in the Save As or Open dialog box.

Document Information Panel

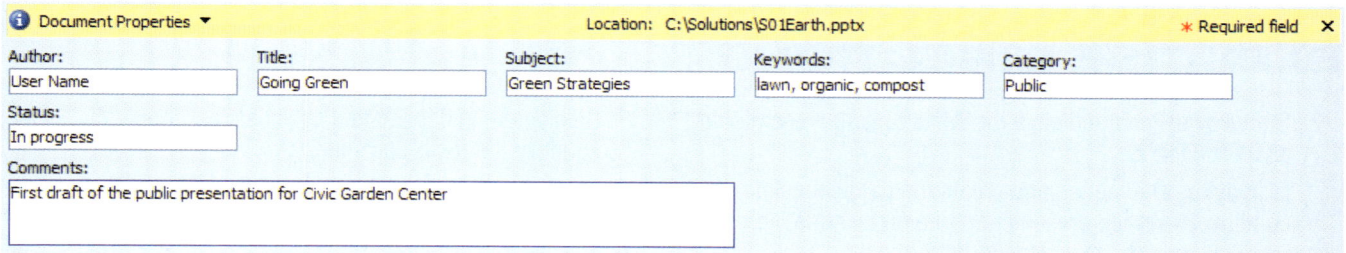

Document Properties ▼		Location: C:\Solutions\S01Earth.pptx		✳ Required field ✕

Author:	Title:	Subject:	Keywords:	Category:
User Name	Going Green	Green Strategies	lawn, organic, compost	Public

Status:
In progress

Comments:
First draft of the public presentation for Civic Garden Center

PROCEDURES

Use the Outline Tab to Create Slide Content

1. Click **Outline** tab in the Slides/Outline pane.
2. In a new presentation, click to the right of the slide 1 symbol and type the presentation title.
3. Press (Enter), press (⇆), and then type the presentation subtitle.
4. Press (Enter), press (Shift)+(⇆) to start a new slide, and then type the slide title.
5. Press (Enter), press (⇆), and then type the first bullet item.

   ✓ *Press Tab again to create a second-level bullet item. Return to the first bullet level by pressing Shift+Tab.*

Apply More Than One Theme

1. Select slide(s) to which you want to apply the first theme.
2. Click **Design** tab .... (Alt)+(G)

   Themes Group

3. Right-click the desired theme.
4. Click **Apply to Selected Slides** .... (S), (Enter)
5. Repeat steps 1–4 to apply additional themes to slides in the presentation.

Replace Fonts Throughout a Presentation

To use Replace Fonts command:

1. Click **Home** tab .... (Alt)+(H)

   Editing Group

2. Click **Replace** button ⁿ⁺ₐᵇ꜀ .... (R)
3. Click **Replace Fonts** .... (O)
4. Click **Replace** down arrow................ (P), (↓) and select the font to be replaced.
5. Click **With** down arrow............ (Alt)+(W), (↓) and select the replacement font.
6. Click **Replace** .... (Alt)+(R)
7. Repeat steps 4–6 to replace additional fonts if desired.
8. Click **Close** .... (Enter)

To change fonts in Slide Master view:

1. Click **View** tab .... (Alt)+(W)

   Presentation Views Group

2. Click **Slide Master** button ▭ .... (M)
3. Click in the text to modify and use Font tools on the Home tab to make changes.

Apply WordArt Styles to Existing Graphic or Text

1. Select existing WordArt or text to which you want to apply WordArt styles.
2. Click **Drawing Tools Format** tab .... (Alt)+(J), (D)

   WordArt Styles Group

3. Select any of the WordArt formatting tools to apply to selected text.

   - Click **More** button ▾ to select a Quick Style from the WordArt gallery .... (K)
   - Click **Text Fill** button 🅰 down arrow to apply a fill. .... (T), (I)
   - Click **Text Outline** button 🖊 down arrow to choose outline formats .... (T), (O)
   - Click **Text Effects** button 🅰 down arrow to choose a category of effects .... (T), (X)

Add Document Properties

1. Click **Office Button** 🗒 . . . Alt + F
2. Point to **Prepare** . . . . E
3. Click **Properties**. . . . . P

4. Type properties in supplied text boxes.
5. Click ✕ to close the Document Information Panel.

To view advanced properties:

1. Click down arrow to right of Document Properties heading in Document Information Panel.
2. Click Advanced Properties.
3. Click Properties dialog box close button ❌ when finished viewing properties.

EXERCISE DIRECTIONS

1. Start PowerPoint and save the default blank presentation as **01EARTH_*xx***.

2. Display the Outline tab and create the following slide content. To set the presentation title on two lines, press Shift + Enter after the first two words of the title.

Slide 1

Going Green:
What Can You Do?
Presented by Planet Earth

Slide 2

Backyard Strategies
- **Evaluate lawn care needs**
- **Compost waste materials**
- **Use a rain barrel**
- **Create a rain garden**

Slide 3

About the Lawn
- **Lawn care can waste resources such as water**
- **Consider reducing size of lawn**
- **Plant locally adapted grass**
- **Use organic fertilizers to improve soils**

Slide 4

How Composting Helps
- **Garden clippings and kitchen waste make up a third of materials dumped in landfills**
- **Backyard composting**
  - **Recycles waste materials**
  - **Creates organic fertilizer that improves soil**

3. Display the Slides tab and select slide 1. Apply the Foundry theme to this slide.

4. Select slides 2–4 and apply the Origin theme to these slides.

5. Add a new slide at the end of the presentation that uses the Foundry Picture with Caption layout.

6. In the picture area of slide 5, insert the picture file ◉ **01COMPOST**. Then insert the following title and text in the appropriate placeholders.

Composting Helps!

A compost pile can be used to recycle kitchen wastes, grass clippings, autumn leaves, and other plant materials

7. Use Replace Fonts to replace the Rockwell font throughout the presentation with Bookman Old Style.

8. Display slide 2 and go to Slide Master view. The Origin slide master should be at the top of the slide thumbnail pane. Change the font of all bulleted text to Corbel.

9. Display slide 1 and apply the Fill - Text 2, Outline - Background 2 WordArt style to both the title and subtitle. Your slide should look similar to Illustration A.

10. Open the Document Information Panel and add the following properties to the presentation:

Author: **Your name**

Title: **Going Green**

Subject: **Green strategies**

Keywords: **lawn, organic, composting**

Category: **Public presentations**

Status: **In progress**

Comments: **First draft of the public presentation for the Civic Garden Center**

11. Close the Document Information Panel.

12. Save your changes, close the presentation, and exit PowerPoint.

Illustration A

ON YOUR OWN

"Going green" is currently providing some interesting new business opportunities. In this exercise, identify several green business trends, create and conduct a survey to gather information on how "green" your friends and neighbors are, and then begin a presentation that you might show to fellow investors in green technology.

1. Using the Internet, identify some of the most common "green" business opportunities, such as investment in solar or wind power generating equipment, organic products and agriculture, recycling, hybrid vehicles, and so on.

2. Create a survey to gather information on how often your respondents actually use green technology and what additional green options they might support in your city or town.

   ✓ See Exercise 28 in the Microsoft Word unit of this book for information on creating forms and surveys. You may want to create a form to use when conducting your survey.

3. Conduct the survey and analyze the results to identify the top three green trends your respondents currently support or would strongly support if available.

4. Start PowerPoint and save the blank presentation as **OPP01_*xx***.

5. Use the Outline tab to create a title slide, a slide that lists common green business trends, a slide that lists the green technologies included in your survey, and a slide that lists the results of your analysis.

6. Add a slide with the Blank layout and insert a WordArt graphic with a slogan of a few words that supports green technology. Illustration A shows one option.

7. Apply one or more themes to the presentation and modify fonts as necessary using Replace Fonts or Slide Master view.

8. After applying the theme(s), change the WordArt Quick Style to modify the look of the WordArt graphic, and apply WordArt styles to other text as desired.

9. Add appropriate properties to the presentation if desired.

10. Assess the completed presentation and decide whether you want to add it to your employment portfolio as an example of your achievement. If you do, print the slides as a handout for the portfolio.

11. Save your changes, close the presentation, and exit PowerPoint.

Illustration A

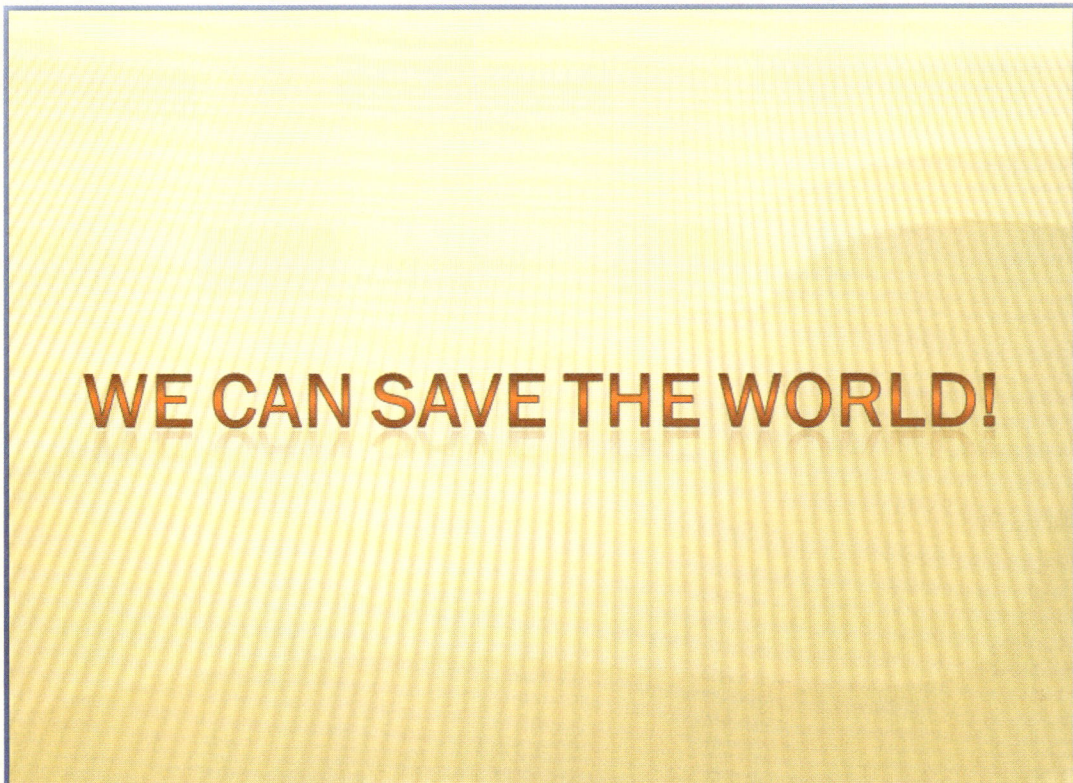

WE CAN SAVE THE WORLD!

Skills Covered

- **Adjust Paragraph Indents**
- **Set Tab Stops**
- **Work with Placeholders and Text Boxes**

- **Use Text Alignment and Direction Options**

Software Skills To fine-tune text on a slide, you can adjust the paragraph indent. Use tabs to align one or more lines of text on a slide. Both placeholders and text boxes can be moved, resized, formatted, or deleted from a slide. You can apply horizontal or vertical alignment options to text, or you can change text direction to achieve special effects.

Application Skills In this exercise, you begin work on a presentation for Yesterday's Playthings, a shop specializing in antique and collectible toys and games. You will adjust indents to improve the appearance of text on slides and use tabs to format a simple table of information. You will add several text boxes and adjust text alignment and direction.

TERMS

Hanging indent An indent in which the first line is not indented but all subsequent lines are indented.

Indent The amount of space a paragraph is set from the left edge of the placeholder.

Tab stops Incremental indents set for text so that each time you press the Tab key, the text indents to a set point.

NOTES

Adjust Paragraph Indents

- An **indent** controls the amount of space between text and the left edge of the text's placeholder. You can adjust paragraph indents in PowerPoint just as you do in a word processing program such as Microsoft Word.

- An indent may apply to an entire paragraph, to only the first line of the paragraph, or to all lines except the first line of the paragraph.

- By default, bulleted text on a PowerPoint slide has a **hanging indent**. The first line is not indented, and subsequent lines indent and align under the first word of the paragraph.

- If you turn off bullet formatting, the first line of the paragraph extends to the left margin of the placeholder and subsequent lines are indented.

Hanging indent applied to bulleted paragraphs

- A hanging indent has a first line that is not indented; subsequent lines are aligned on the first word of the paragraph

  If the bullet formatting is turned off, the first line of the paragraph extends to the left margin of the placeholder

- If you want to turn off bullet formatting to emphasize a paragraph of text (for example, to set a quotation by itself on a slide), you should remove the hanging indent to give your text a more professional appearance.

- You have other indent options to choose from besides the default hanging indent.
  - Apply a left indent to move an entire paragraph toward the right of the slide. You can use this indent in conjunction with a hanging indent to move a paragraph right and still maintain the hanging indent.
  - Apply a first-line indent to indent only the first line of a paragraph. You generally apply this type of indent to a paragraph that does not have bullet formatting.

Left and first-line indents

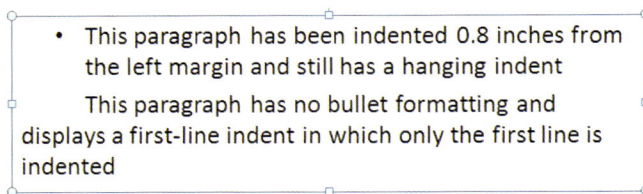

- This paragraph has been indented 0.8 inches from the left margin and still has a hanging indent

  This paragraph has no bullet formatting and displays a first-line indent in which only the first line is indented

- You have two options for adjusting indents: You can drag indent markers on the ruler, or you can specify the desired indent in the Paragraph dialog box.
- The ruler displays indent markers for the currently selected paragraph.

Indent markers for a first-level bullet paragraph

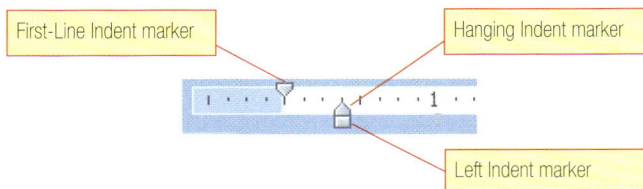

First-Line Indent marker

Hanging Indent marker

Left Indent marker

- As you would expect, the First-Line Indent marker controls the indent of the first line of the paragraph. If it is to the left of the other indent markers, you have a hanging indent. If it is to the right of the other markers, you have a first-line indent.
- The Hanging Indent marker (the upward-pointing marker) controls the indent of all lines of text following the first line.
- The Left Indent marker (the rectangular marker below the Hanging Indent marker) controls both the First-Line Indent and the Hanging Indent markers. Dragging this marker will move the other two markers at the same time, maintaining their relative positions.
- To adjust indents using the indent markers, simply drag them to the desired position on the ruler.

- To adjust the indent of a single paragraph, click in the paragraph to position the insertion point and then make the adjustment. To adjust more than one paragraph, select the paragraphs and then adjust the indent.
- The positions of the indent markers on the ruler are determined by the bullet level. Second-level bullet markers appear further to the right on the ruler.
- Using the ruler to set indents allows you to "eyeball" the indent positions. If you know the exact measurements you want to use for an indent, you can set them in the Paragraph dialog box.
- Use the Indentation Before text and Special boxes in the Paragraph dialog box to set the amount of space before (to the left of) the first line and the indent type, such as First line or Hanging.

Specify an indent in the Paragraph dialog box

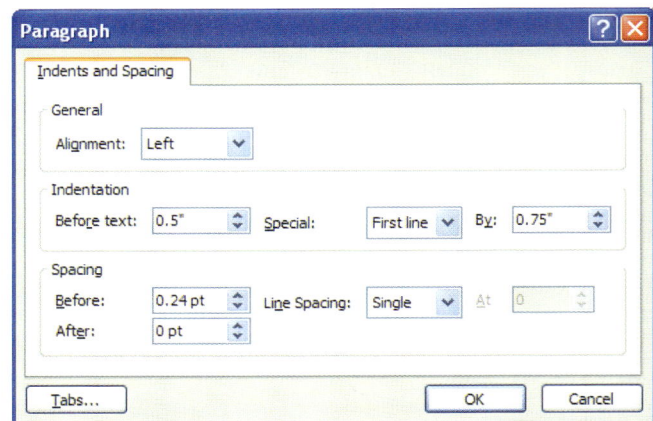

- If you select a first-line or hanging indent, you must specify the amount of the indent in the By box. Choose (none) in the Special list if you want only a left indent.

Set Tab Stops

- You can set **tab stops** in a placeholder to control text position just as you would in a word processing document.
- Tab stops can be used to align text at the left, center, right, or on a decimal.
- By default, PowerPoint sets tab stops at 1 inch increments on the ruler. You can add tab stops where you need them by selecting a tab type from the tab selector and then clicking on the ruler.
- Clear a tab by dragging the tab marker off of the ruler. Move a tab stop by dragging the marker to a new position.

■ Use tabs when you have only a few columns to organize. If you need to set up a number of columns and rows, however, you will find it easier to use a PowerPoint table.

Work with Placeholders and Text Boxes

■ You can work with placeholders and text boxes in a number of ways to set text on a slide. You can adjust position, size, or rotation of any placeholder or text box. You can also remove any placeholder or text box if you no longer need it on the slide.

■ To move a placeholder or text box, position the mouse pointer on the outside border to display a four-headed arrow. Then click and drag the object to its new position.

Select a placeholder to move it

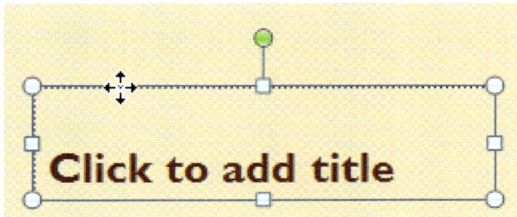

■ To resize a placeholder or text box, position the mouse pointer on a sizing handle to display a two-headed arrow and then drag inward or outward to reduce or enlarge the object.

Drag a sizing handle to resize an object

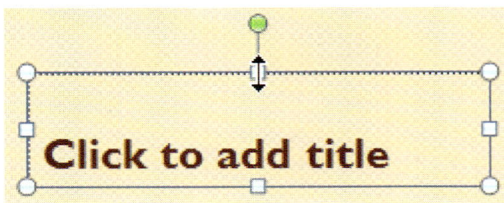

■ To rotate a placeholder or text box, position the mouse pointer on the green rotate handle at the top of the object and drag to the left or right to rotate the object.

Rotate an object

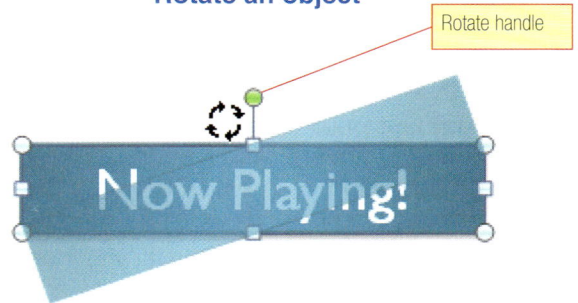

■ To remove any placeholder or text box, click its outside border to select the object and then press `Delete`.

Use Text Alignment and Direction Options

■ Text alignment controls the position of text within a placeholder. PowerPoint allows you to specify both horizontal and vertical alignment.

■ Themes control the default alignment of text in placeholders, but you can modify both horizontal and vertical alignment using buttons in the Paragraph group on the Home tab.

■ The following illustration shows alignment options available in PowerPoint.

Horizontal and vertical alignment options

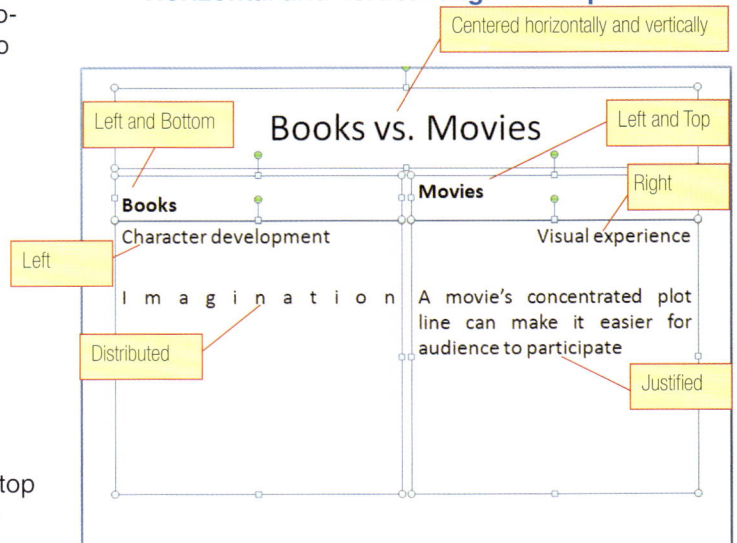

- Horizontal alignment options will be familiar to you from word processing applications. You can left-align, center, right-align, or justify text in any placeholder to add interest or enhance text appearance.

- Common horizontal alignments can be applied using buttons on the Home tab or the Mini toolbar. Distributed alignment is available only in the Paragraph dialog box's Alignment list.

- Vertical alignment options are available from the Align Text button's menu.

Align Text options

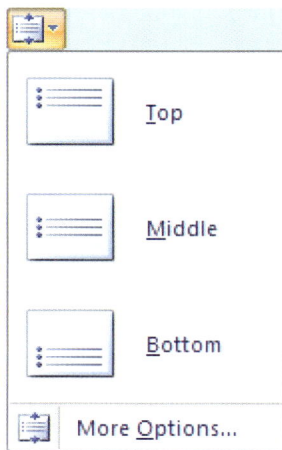

- Clicking the More Options command on this menu opens the Format Text Effects dialog box, where you can select from alignments as well as other special text effects.

- If you change vertical alignment in any placeholder, all text within that placeholder changes to the selected alignment.

- You can also adjust the orientation or direction of text in a text box so that text reads from the bottom up or the top down. The following illustration shows options for changing text direction.

Text direction options

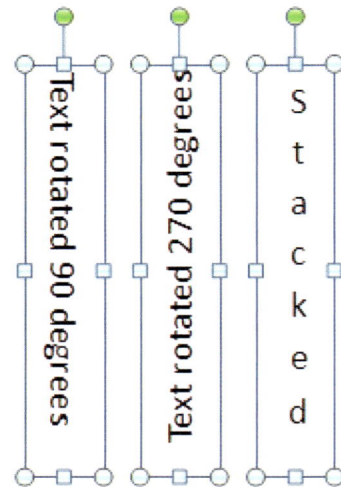

- You use the Text Direction button in the Paragraph group on the Home tab to change text direction.

- While you can actually change text direction in any placeholder, it is easier to control the size and position of text with a vertical orientation if you enclose it in a text box.

PROCEDURES

Adjust Paragraph Indents

To adjust indent using the ruler:

1. Display the ruler and click in the paragraph to adjust or select multiple paragraphs.
2. Click and drag the appropriate indent marker on the ruler.

To adjust indent using the Paragraph dialog box:

1. Click in the paragraph to adjust or select multiple paragraphs.
2. Click **Home** tab . . . . Alt +H

   Paragraph Group

3. Click **Paragraph** dialog box launcher ⌐ . . . . P , G
4. Click **Before text** and type measurement or click increment arrow. . . . . Alt +R
5. Click **Special** . . . . Alt +S
6. Select from **Special** list . . . . ↑ / ↓ , Enter
7. Click **By** if necessary and type measurement or click increment arrow. . . . . Alt +Y
8. Click **OK**. . . . . Enter

Set Tab Stops

1. Click in the paragraph for which you want to set tab stops, or select multiple paragraphs.
2. Display the ruler if necessary.
3. Click **tab selector** ⌐ to the left of the ruler until the type of tab stop you want displays in the tab selector.
   - **Left tab** ⌐
   - **Center tab** ⊥
   - **Right tab** ⌐
   - **Decimal tab** ⊥
4. Click on ruler where tab stop should be positioned.

To delete a tab stop:
- Drag the tab stop marker off the ruler.

To adjust the position of the tab stop:
- Drag the tab stop marker on the ruler.

Work with Placeholders and Text Boxes

To move an object:
1. Click on outside border of object to display four-headed pointer.
2. Click and drag the object to the desired location.

To resize an object:
1. Click an object to display sizing handles.
2. Click on a sizing handle to display two-headed pointer.
3. Click and drag inward or outward to reduce or enlarge object.

To rotate an object:
1. Click object to select it and display rotation handle.
2. Position pointer over rotation handle to display circular pointer ↻ .
3. Click and drag left or right to rotate object.
4. Release mouse button when desired rotation has been achieved.

Change Horizontal and Vertical Alignment (*Ctrl+L, Ctrl+E, Ctrl+R, Ctrl+J*)

To change horizontal alignment:
1. Select text or placeholder, or click to place insertion point in any paragraph you want to align.
2. Click **Home** tab . . . . Alt +H

   Paragraph Group

3. Select desired alignment button:
   - **Align Text Left** ≡ . . . . A , L
   - **Center** ≡ . . . . A , C
   - **Align Text Right** ≡ . . A , R
   - **Justify** ≡ . . . . A , J

   OR
- Use same alignment options on Mini toolbar.

   ✓ *Justify button is not shown on the Mini toolbar.*

To change vertical alignment:
1. Click **Home** tab . . . . Alt +H

   Paragraph Group

2. Click **Align Text** button ⌐ . . . . A , T
3. Select a vertical alignment:
   - **Top**. . . . . T
   - **Middle**. . . . . M
   - **Bottom**. . . . . B

Set Text Direction

1. Select the text box by clicking its outside border.
2. Click **Home** tab . . . . Alt +H

   Paragraph Group

3. Click the **Text Direction** button ‖ê- . . . . A , X
4. Select a text direction:
   - **Horizontal** . . . . H
   - **Rotate all text 90°**. . . . . . . R
   - **Rotate all text 270°**. . . . . . O
   - **Stacked** . . . . S

EXERCISE DIRECTIONS

1. Start PowerPoint and open 🔘 **02TOYS**. Save the presentation as **02TOYS_xx**.

2. On slide 1, change horizontal alignment of both the title and subtitle to left. Change the vertical alignment of the subtitle to Middle and the vertical alignment of the title to Top.

3. Display slide 2. Note that the title on this slide uses Middle alignment. Change this vertical alignment to Bottom on all slides by changing the alignment on the slide master in Slide Master view.

4. On slide 2, insert a text box and type the text **Goldie Bear, 1915**. Change the text to 14-point Corbel, rotate it 270 degrees, and resize the text box so that the text fits on a single line. Position the text box to the right of the bear illustration. Align the box at the bottom of the bear.

5. Display slide 4. Apply Justify alignment to all three paragraphs. Adjust indents as follows:

   a. Turn off bullet formatting for all three bullet items in the content placeholder. Remove the hanging indent for all three paragraphs.

   b. Set a left indent of 1 inch for the second paragraph and a left indent of 2 inches for the third paragraph.

6. Display slide 5. Set Bottom alignment for the two subheadings (AT HOME and ON THE ROAD). Remove the bullet formatting for all content items. Remove the hanging indent for the address information, but leave the hanging indent for the ON THE ROAD entries.

7. Still on slide 5, delete the text box below the illustration. Insert a new text box about 2.5 inches wide with the text **Show Cancelled!** Change the text to Corbel bold and apply a Quick Style format of your choice to the text box. Rotate it to the left slightly and then move it to cover the last show in the ON THE ROAD column.

8. Display slide 6. In the content placeholder, turn off bullet formatting and remove the hanging indent. Using tabs, insert the following tabular material.

Item	Originally	Sale Price
Keepsake marbles	**$12.95**	**$8.95**
Duncan yoyos	**$15.50**	**$11.50**
Vintage golf clubs	**$35.00–$75.00**	**$18.50–$30.00**

9. Set appropriate tabs to space the information attractively on the slide. Modify text formats of the table if desired. (You may want to choose a different color for the column header items.)

10. Shorten the table placeholder so you can add a text box at the bottom of the slide. Insert the text **And Much, Much More!** and format as desired. Your table should look similar to Illustration A.

11. Save your changes, close the presentation, and exit PowerPoint.

Illustration A

592

ON YOUR OWN

1. Start PowerPoint and open ⊙ **02GIVING**. Save the presentation as **OPP02_xx**.

2. On slide 1, apply Bottom alignment to the title. Move the subtitle placeholder to align at the left with the title placeholder. Apply the Stacked text direction to the DRAFT text and adjust the text box size to allow the text to stack properly.

3. Display slide 2. Delete the empty title placeholder. Remove bullet formatting from both paragraphs and adjust paragraph indent. Delete the text box at the bottom of the slide.

4. Display slide 3. The process of applying a new theme to this presentation has resulted in incorrect hanging indents for bullet items. Adjust paragraph indents on the slide master to solve this problem:

   a. Adjust indentation for first-level bullet items to 0.38 inches before text with a hanging indent of 0.38 inches.

   b. Adjust indentation for second-level bullet items to 0.75 inches before text with a hanging indent of 0.38 inches.

   c. Display slide 6 and click the Reset button to apply the new master settings.

5. Display slide 7. Using tabs, create a simple table that lists some sample goods you could contribute to a homeless or women's shelter. Illustration A shows a sample slide.

6. On slide 8, right-align the title and caption and adjust the caption placeholder width to avoid having one word on the last line.

7. Save your changes, close the presentation, and exit PowerPoint.

Illustration A

Sample Contributions

For homeless shelters	Personal products
	Playing cards
	Paper goods
	Good used clothing
For women's shelters	Personal products
	Small toys/games
	Diapers
	Children's clothing

6/23/2008   The Power of Giving   7

Skills Covered

- **Find and Replace Text**
- **Use the Reference Tools**
- **View Slides in Grayscale or Black and White**

- **Send Presentation Materials to Microsoft Word**

Software Skills The Find and Replace features allow you to quickly locate and change text throughout a presentation. Use PowerPoint's reference tools to find synonyms, translate text, or locate online resources. You can view slides in grayscale or black and white to see how they will look if printed on a non-color printer. Send presentation materials to Microsoft Word to take advantage of Word's formatting options.

Application Skills You continue working on the presentation for Yesterday's Playthings. In this exercise, you replace text and use the Thesaurus to finalize your presentation text. You display the slides in grayscale and send them to Microsoft Word.

TERMS

No new terms in this exercise.

NOTES

Find and Replace Text

- In a slide show that consists of only a few slides, you may have no difficulty locating specific text. If your presentation has many slides, finding text can be time consuming.

- If you intend to replace the text you have found, you risk missing instances of the text if you simply scroll through the slides.

- You can make the process of finding and replacing text more foolproof by using the Find and Replace options in the Editing group on the Home tab.

- To simply find instances of a word or phrase, use the Find button to open the Find dialog box.

- This feature functions the same way it does in a word processing program such as Microsoft Word: Type the text you want to find and then click the Find Next button.

- PowerPoint searches the presentation and highlights the first instance that matches your text string.

Finding text using the Find dialog box

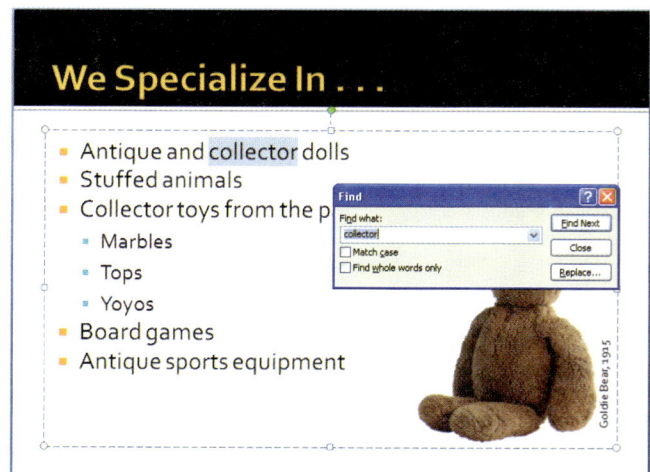

We Specialize In . . .

- Antique and collector dolls
- Stuffed animals
- Collector toys from the p
  - Marbles
  - Tops
  - Yoyos
- Board games
- Antique sports equipment

- You can save yourself some searching time by selecting options in the Find dialog box. Select Match case to have PowerPoint search for instances that match the exact capitalization of your search string. Select Find whole words only to have PowerPoint find only complete words, not parts of words.

- If you want to replace the text you have found, you can click the Replace button in the Find dialog box to open the Replace dialog box, or click the Replace button on the Home tab if the Find dialog box is not already open.

- Specify the text to find, if necessary, and the replacement text, and then click the Find Next button to start the process.

- You have the same options in this dialog box for matching case and finding whole words. You can choose to replace an instance or replace all instances.

  ✓ *Replacing all instances can be risky unless you know your content well.*

- You can use Find and Replace in either the Slide pane or in the Outline tab of the Slides/Outline pane.

Use the Reference Tools

- The Proofing group on PowerPoint's Review tab contains a number of reference tools that can help you finalize a presentation.

  - The Spelling checker searches for words that do not appear in the dictionary.

  - The Research tool allows you to search for a word or phrase in a thesaurus, dictionary, or online reference site.

  - The Thesaurus lets you find synonyms and antonyms for a selected word.

  - Translate allows you to translate a selected word or phrase into any of 14 languages.

  - Use Language to specify the default language for the presentation. If a spelling dictionary is available for the chosen language, the presentation can be spell checked in that language.

- Of these tools, you may find the Thesaurus most useful. A thesaurus can help you replace overworked words with more interesting or specific ones.

- To use the Thesaurus, select a word in the presentation and then start the Thesaurus. It opens in a task pane as shown in the following illustration.

Thesaurus displays in the Research task pane

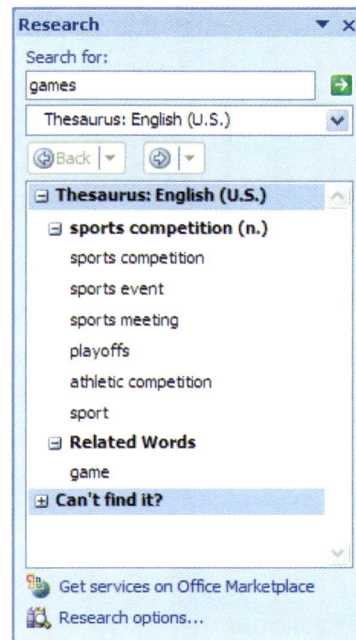

- To choose one of the suggested synonyms, point to one of the suggestions to display a down arrow at the right side of the pane and click Insert on the drop-down list.

- You can also choose to look up one of the suggestions by simply clicking it in the list. You then see synonyms for that word or phrase. Moving from word to word in this way, you can very often find a word or phrase that's exactly what you need.

View Slides in Grayscale or Black and White

- You can view a color presentation in grayscale or in black and white.

- When you view or print a presentation in grayscale, the colors change to varying tones of gray. When you view a presentation from the pure black and white view, most colors are converted to either black or white.

  ✓ *If a presentation has a black background area, that area may display in gray in both grayscale and pure black and white view.*

Presentation displayed in grayscale

- Switching to grayscale or black and white view allows you to concentrate on the slide's text and layout rather than its color design elements. If you intend to print your slide materials in grayscale or black and white, this view can show you how your printed materials will look.

- Use the settings in the Color/Grayscale group on the View tab to switch to Grayscale or Pure Black and White view.

- Selecting one of these options displays the presentation in the chosen view, with options for the view on a tab such as the Grayscale tab in the previous illustration.

- Options in the Change Selected Object group may be dimmed until you select an object on the slide.

- Applying a grayscale or pure black and white view does not change the presentation permanently to that view. You can return to color view at any time by clicking the Back to Color View button.

Send Presentation Materials to Microsoft Word

- The most common way to output presentation materials is to print them. You have another option for outputting presentation materials, however: You can export the presentation to Microsoft Word as handouts or as an outline.

- Exporting a presentation to Microsoft Word gives you the option of using Word's tools to format the handouts.

- Use the Create Handouts in Microsoft Office Word command on the Office Button menu's Publish submenu to begin the process of sending materials to Word.

- The Send To Microsoft Office Word dialog box opens to allow you to select an export option.

Send To Microsoft Office Word dialog box

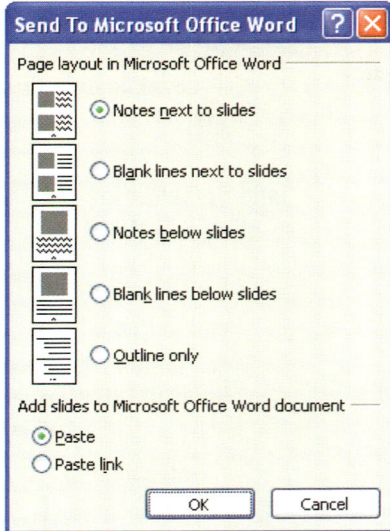

- You have two options for positioning slide notes relative to the slide pictures and two options for placing blank lines that your audience can use to take their own notes. You can also choose to send only the outline. The exported outline retains the font used in the presentation and displays at a large point size.

- One advantage to sending the outline to Word over simply printing the outline from PowerPoint is that you can easily format the outline in Word using styles.

- Note that you can choose either to paste the presentation materials in a Word document or paste link them. When you choose the Paste link option, you create a link between the Word document and the PowerPoint presentation. Any changes you save to the slides in PowerPoint will appear in the Word document.

  ✓ *You do not have the paste/paste link options when exporting an outline.*

- Exported slides may display in a Word table similar to the one shown in the following illustration.

Slides display in a Microsoft Word table

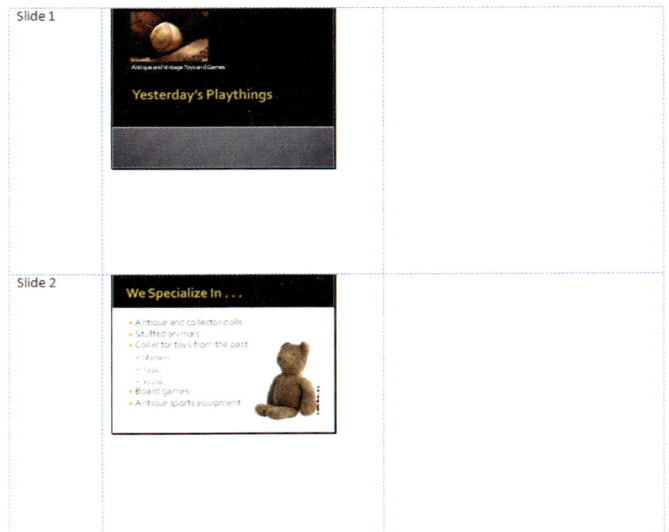

- You can modify the size of the slide images, format text, and add new text as desired to customize your handouts.

PROCEDURES

Find and Replace Text

To find text:

1. Click **Home** tab . . . . ⎡Alt⎤+⎡H⎤

   Editing Group

2. Click **Find** button 🔍 . . . ⎡F⎤, ⎡D⎤
3. Click in **Find what** box. . . ⎡Alt⎤+⎡N⎤ and type search string.
   - Click **Match case** if desired to match capitalization of search string exactly . . . . ⎡Alt⎤+⎡C⎤
   - Click **Find whole words only** if desired to find only whole words . . . . ⎡Alt⎤+⎡W⎤
4. Click **Find Next** . . . . ⎡Alt⎤+⎡F⎤ to find first instance.
5. Continue clicking **Find Next** to find additional instances.
6. Click **Close** to end process.

To replace text:

1. Click **Home** tab . . . . ⎡Alt⎤+⎡H⎤

   Editing Group

2. Click **Replace** button ᵃᵇ⁄ₐ꜀ . . . . ⎡R⎤
3. Click **Replace** . . . . ⎡R⎤

   OR

   Click **Replace** in Find dialog box . . . . ⎡Alt⎤+⎡R⎤
4. Click in **Find what** box and type search string . . . . ⎡Alt⎤+⎡N⎤
5. Click in **Replace with** box and type replacement string. . . . . ⎡Alt⎤+⎡P⎤
   - Click **Match case** if desired to match capitalization of search string exactly . . . . ⎡Alt⎤+⎡C⎤
   - Click **Find whole words only** if desired to find only whole words . . . . ⎡Alt⎤+⎡W⎤

6. Click **Find Next** to find first instance. . . . . ⎡Alt⎤+⎡F⎤
7. Click **Replace** to replace instance. . . . . ⎡Alt⎤+⎡R⎤

   OR

   Click **Replace All** to replace all instances . . . . ⎡Alt⎤+⎡A⎤
8. Click **Close** to end process.

Use the Thesaurus

1. Select word for which you want to find a synonym.
2. Click **Review** tab . . . . ⎡Alt⎤+⎡R⎤

   Proofing Group

3. Click **Thesaurus** button
   📖 . . . . ⎡E⎤
4. Point to a word in the task pane you want to use as a synonym to display list arrow.
5. Click **Insert** . . . . ⎡I⎤

To research a different word in the task pane:

- Click any word in the task pane results to see synonyms for that word.

View Slides in Grayscale or Black and White

1. Click **View** tab . . . . ⎡Alt⎤+⎡W⎤

   Color/Grayscale Group

2. Click **Grayscale** button
   ⬛ . . . . ⎡O⎤

   OR

   Click **Pure Black and White** button ⬛ . . . . ⎡B⎤
3. Click an element on any slide to activate buttons on the Change Selected Object group.

To return to color view:

- Click **Back to Color View** button 🔲 . . . . ⎡Alt⎤+⎡W⎤, ⎡C⎤

Send Presentation Materials to Microsoft Word

1. Click **Office Button** 🔵 . . . ⎡Alt⎤+⎡F⎤
2. Point to **Publish** . . . . ⎡U⎤
3. Click **Create Handouts in Microsoft Office Word** . . . . ⎡H⎤
4. Select a page layout option:
   - **Notes next to slides** . . . . ⎡Alt⎤+⎡N⎤
   - **Blank lines next to slides** . . . . ⎡Alt⎤+⎡A⎤
   - **Notes below slides** . . ⎡Alt⎤+⎡B⎤
   - **Blank lines below slides** . . . . ⎡Alt⎤+⎡K⎤
   - **Outline only** . . . . ⎡Alt⎤+⎡O⎤
5. Select an option for adding slides to a Word document:
   - **Paste** . . . . ⎡Alt⎤+⎡P⎤
   - **Paste link** . . . . ⎡Alt⎤+⎡I⎤
6. Click **OK** . . . . ⎡Enter⎤

EXERCISE DIRECTIONS

1. Start PowerPoint and open 📟 **02TOYS_xx** or open 💿 **03TOYS**. Save the presentation as **03TOYS_xx**.

2. Find the first instance of the word *collector* in the presentation.

3. Choose to replace this word with the word **collectible**.

4. Replace each instance of *collector* with *collectible*, then close the Replace dialog box. Capitalize the word *collectible* that was replaced at the beginning of the third bullet on slide 2.

5. Display slide 3 and select the word *appreciated* in the second paragraph. Start the Thesaurus and replace the selected word with a more appropriate word.

6. Display the presentation in grayscale.

7. Send the presentation to Word, choosing the Notes next to slides and the Paste link options. Apply the Module theme to the Word document and format the table with a table Quick Style of your choice. Illustration A shows one option. Save the Word document as **03TOYS_ HANDOUTS_xx**.

8. In PowerPoint, restore color view, save the presentation, and exit PowerPoint.

9. Return to the Word document and notice that the linked document now displays the slides in color. Save your changes, close the document, and exit Word.

Illustration A

ON YOUR OWN

1. Start PowerPoint and open ⌨ **OPP02_xx** or open ⊙ **03GIVING**. Save the presentation as **OPP03_xx**.

2. Review the presentation to see if you can modify language in any way to make your meanings clearer.
   - You may want to replace some words throughout the presentation, such as *homeless* or *giving*. Illustration A shows a sample slide with the word *homeless* replaced by a synonym.
   - Use the Thesaurus to find more meaningful words for some words in the presentation.

3. Send the presentation to Word with notes under the slides. You do not need to link. Save the document as **OPP03_HANDOUTS_xx**. Close the document, and exit Word.

4. Save your changes, close the presentation, and exit PowerPoint.

Illustration A

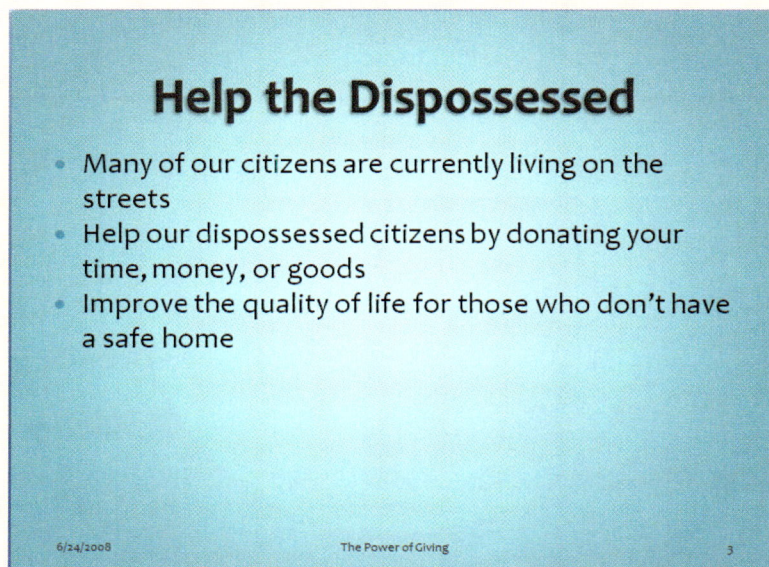

Help the Dispossessed

- Many of our citizens are currently living on the streets
- Help our dispossessed citizens by donating your time, money, or goods
- Improve the quality of life for those who don't have a safe home

6/24/2008   The Power of Giving   3

Skills Covered

■ **Use Advanced Slide Master Features**   ■ **Use Advanced Notes and Handout Master Formats**

Software Skills Another way to apply more than one theme in a presentation is to add a slide master in Slide Master view. Use the Master Layout dialog box to restore master elements that have been removed. Use formatting features such as backgrounds and Quick Styles to improve slide master appearance.

Application Skills You continue working on the presentation for Yesterday's Playthings. In this exercise, you add and customize a new slide master and apply custom formats to the handout master.

TERMS

No new terms in this exercise.

NOTES

Use Advanced Slide Master Features

■ You learned in Exercise 1 of this lesson that you can work with multiple themes in a presentation. In that exercise, you added themes to a presentation by applying different themes to selected slides.

■ You can also add themes to a presentation by adding slide masters in Slide Master view.

■ Clicking Insert Slide Master in the Edit Master group on the Slide Master tab adds a new slide master in the slide thumbnail pane.

■ The new master displays the default Office theme and is designated as 2, indicating it is the second master in the presentation. The new master includes all the standard layouts below the slide master. You can use the Rename command to give the new slide master a more meaningful name.

Add a slide master in Slide Master view

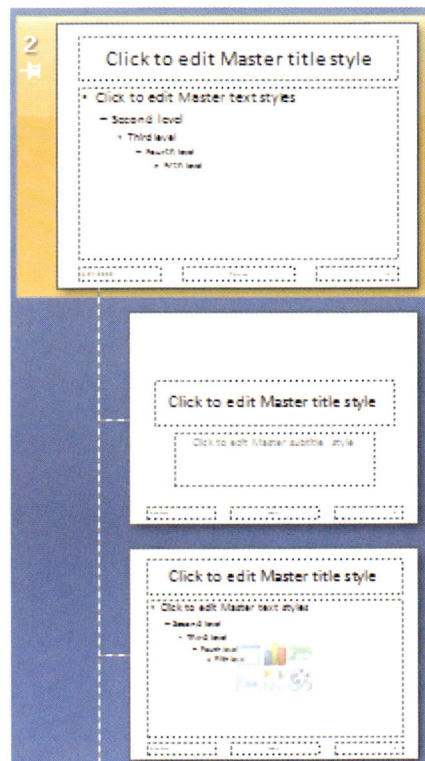

- Note also the pushpin symbol below the number 2 in the previous illustration. This symbol indicates the master is being preserved for use even though no slides currently use any of these master layouts. If a slide master that you add does not automatically display this symbol, you can click the Preserve button in the Edit Master group to preserve the master.

- You can also add a new slide master with a theme other than the Office theme using the Themes button in the Edit Themes group.

- You can add as many masters as you want, but keep in mind that using many themes in a presentation will compromise your presentation's visual consistency.

- When adding multiple slide masters to a presentation, you can add completely distinct themes, as you did in Exercise 1, or you can add another instance of the same theme. Using multiple versions of the same theme allows you to apply different background or color formatting to slides while maintaining the same fonts and layouts for a consistent appearance.

- The Master Layout group of the Slide Master tab contains several commands that help you work more efficiently with slide masters.

- With a slide layout selected (rather than the slide master), the Title and Footers check boxes are active. Deselect either or both to remove the title or the date, footer, and slide number placeholders from the master. Display these placeholders again by selecting the appropriate check box.

- You can also select and delete any default placeholder on a master. If you decide you want to restore a deleted placeholder, you can do so using the Master Layout dialog box. This command is active when the slide master is selected.

- By default, the dialog box shows all placeholders selected and unavailable for change. If any of the default placeholders have been removed from a master, that placeholder is active in the Master Layout dialog box so that you can select it to restore it.

- In the following illustration, for example, the Date and Footer placeholders have been deleted from the slide master. Selecting the check boxes for these items restores the placeholders.

Use Master Layout to restore a default placeholder

Use Advanced Notes and Handout Master Formats

- You can customize both the notes and handout masters to improve visual appearance when notes pages or handouts are printed.

- For example, you can apply graphic formats such as Quick Styles or fills, borders, and effects to any placeholder on the notes or handout master. You can also add content to the master, such as a new text box or a graphic that will then display on all pages.

- When adding content such as a text box to the handout master, consider that your added content must be positioned so it doesn't interfere with the slide image placeholders for layouts other than the one you are currently working with.

- If you insert a text box above the slide image on the one-slide-per-page layout, for example, it will obscure the slide images for other handout layouts.

- Note that even though the Themes button appears on the Notes Master tab and the Handout Master tab, you cannot use it to apply a theme. You can, however, use the Colors, Fonts, and Effects buttons to apply theme formatting to your masters.

- By default, the notes and handout masters use the Office theme colors, fonts, and effects, no matter what theme is applied to the slides in the presentation. Changing fonts and colors to match the current theme can give your notes pages consistency with the slides.

- Use the Background Styles option in the Background group to apply a background that will fill the entire notes page or handout. Background colors are controlled by the theme colors you have applied to the master.

PROCEDURES

Insert a New Slide Master

1. Click **View** tab . . . . [Alt]+[W]

   Presentation Views Group

2. Click **Slide Master** button
   . . . . [M]

3. Click **Insert Slide Master** button
   . . . . [N]

   OR

   - Click **Themes** button
     . . . . [H]

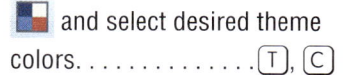

   - Right-click the theme you want to use for the new master.

   - Click **Add as New Slide Master** . . . . [N]

Restore Master Layout Placeholders

1. Select the slide master in Slide Master view.

2. Click **Master Layout** button
   . . . . [L]

3. Select check boxes of placeholders to restore.

4. Click **OK**. . . . . [Enter]

Apply Notes Master and Handout Master Formats

1. Click **View** tab . . . . [Alt]+[W]

   Presentation Views Group

2. Click **Notes Master** button
   . . . . [K]

   OR

   Click **Handout Master** button
   . . . . [H]

3. Apply formats as desired:

   - Click **Theme Colors** button and select desired theme colors. . . . . [T], [C]

   - Click **Theme Fonts** button and select desired theme fonts . . . . [T], [F]

   - Click **Background Styles** button and select a page background · · · · · · · · · · · [B]

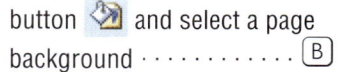

   - Add a shape or text box to the master and format as desired.

Business Connection

First Impressions

A first impression is the opinion someone forms about you the first time you meet. A job interview is usually when you make a first impression on a potential employer. You can take steps to insure your first impression is a good one by being on time, being prepared, and by dressing appropriately. You only get one chance to make a first impression, so do your best to make it positive!

Dressing for the Occasion

Working alone or in teams, research the appropriate attire for a job interview in a variety of workplace environments. Assign each member of the team a different responsibility, and set goals and deadlines for completing the project. Use your career center, the library, or the Internet to find out whether it is necessary to wear a suit, a dress, or if casual clothing is fine. Consider grooming as well, such as whether hair should be neat and clean, if shaving is necessary, and whether it is acceptable to wear jewelry or makeup. When you have completed your research, create a presentation about how to dress appropriately for a job interview. Include graphics, animations, and transitions to make the presentation interesting. Explain why is it important to dress appropriately, and show examples of both proper and improper attire. Proofread and preview the presentation and make corrections as necessary. Prepare handouts, and practice delivering the presentation to an audience. When you are ready, deliver the presentation to the class.

EXERCISE DIRECTIONS

1. Start PowerPoint and open 📟 03TOYS_xx or open 💿 04TOYS. Save the presentation as 04TOYS_xx.

2. Add a new slide master in Slide Master view using the Module theme (the same theme that is currently applied to the presentation). You will customize this master to create a different look that can be blended with the original Module theme slides.

3. Rename the new master **Light Module** (click Rename in the Edit Master group). Make the following changes on the Light Module slide master:

   a. Select the black shape at the top of the slide behind the title placeholder. Apply the Intense Effect - Accent 2 Quick Style to this shape.

   b. Select the thin white horizontal shape below the shape you just reformatted and apply a fill of Rose, Accent 3, Darker 25%.

   c. Change the title font color to White, Background 1.

   d. Change the size of first-level bulleted text to 28 and second-level bulleted text to 25.

4. Click the title slide layout below the Light Module slide master and make the following changes:

   a. Change the background style to Style 1.

   b. Select the black shape that takes up the top two-thirds of the slide and apply the Moderate Effect - Accent 2 Quick Style.

   c. Select the thin white horizontal shape below the shape you just reformatted and apply a fill of Gold, Accent 1.

   d. Change the title font color to Black, Text 1, Lighter 25%.

5. Close Slide Master view. Display slide 6 and apply the Light Module Title and Content layout. Your slide should look similar to Illustration A.

6. Save your changes, close the presentation, and exit PowerPoint.

Illustration A

Item	Originally	Sale Price
Keepsake marbles	$12.95	$8.95
Duncan yoyos	$15.50	$11.50
Vintage golf clubs	$35.00 - $75.00	$18.50 - $30.00

Summer Show Specials . . .

And Much, Much More!

ON YOUR OWN

1. Start PowerPoint and open 🔲**OPP02_*xx*** or open 💿 **04GIVING**. Save the presentation as **OPP04_*xx***.

2. Display the notes page master and make the following changes to the master:

   a. Apply different theme colors and theme fonts that complement the presentation's appearance.

   ✓ *You may want to download the Human theme that is used for the presentation: Display the Themes gallery and click More Themes on Microsoft Office Online. Scroll down to find the Human theme and download it as directed. After downloading, you will have access to the theme's fonts and colors.*

   b. Change the background style to Style 2.

   c. Insert a Rectangle shape at the top of the page the same height as the header and date placeholders. Apply a Quick Style of your choice to the shape and send it to the back.

   d. Change the size of the header and date text to 14 point, apply bold, and change the color if desired to contrast better with the shape behind the text.

3. Close Notes Page Master view and switch to Notes Page view. Illustration A shows a sample of one of the presentation's slides in this view.

4. Save your changes, close the presentation, and exit PowerPoint.

Illustration A

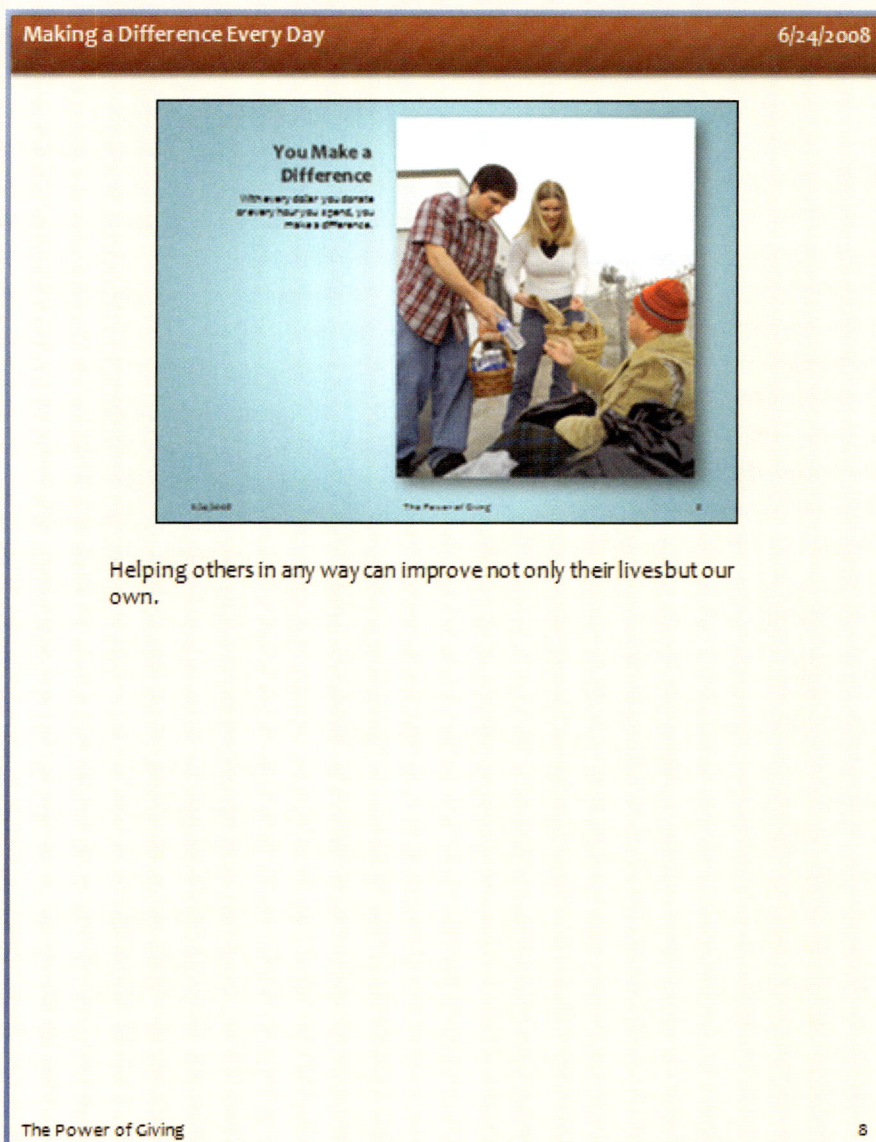

Helping others in any way can improve not only their lives but our own.

Critical Thinking

Application Skills   Peterson Home Health Care has asked you to create a presentation that can be used at local health fairs to give viewers information about the company's home health care options. You will start work on that presentation in this exercise.

EXERCISE DIRECTIONS

1. Start PowerPoint and open 🔵 **05PETERSON**. Save the presentation as **05PETERSON_xx**.

2. Replace the Bookman Old Style font with Calibri. Then in Slide Master view:
   a. Change all headings to Corbel and all body text to Calibri.
   b. Change the color of headings to Black, Text 1.
   c. Change vertical alignment of headings to Bottom and horizontal alignment to center.

3. Make the following changes on slide 1:
   a. Move the subtitle placeholder to the right to align at the right side with the title placeholder.
   b. Change the alignment of both the title and subtitle to right alignment.
   c. Adjust the height of the title placeholder so the text does not have to be AutoFit in the placeholder and then apply Middle alignment.
   d. Apply a Quick Style format of your choice to the title placeholder.
   e. Apply a WordArt style to the title text.

4. A slide is missing from the presentation. Using the Outline tab, insert the following material after slide 1:

   Our Reputation
   - **Quality home health care**
   - **Excellent client service**
   - **Excellent nursing staff**

5. Make the following changes to slide 2:
   a. Remove bullet formatting from the three paragraphs in the content placeholder.
   b. Remove the hanging indent on these three paragraphs and center them.
   c. Change the font size to 32 and the line spacing to 1.5.

6. On slide 4, insert a text box as follows:
   a. Click to the left of the picture to insert the text box.
   b. Change the text direction to rotate it 270 degrees.
   c. Type the text **Gentle, professional home care**. Change the font to Calibri.
   d. Adjust the position of the text box to leave room between it and the picture, and to be as tall as the picture. Apply a Quick Style of your choice and increase the font size so the text takes up more room in the text box. Your slide should look similar to Illustration A.

7. Copy the text box on slide 4 and paste it on slide 5. Delete the content placeholder behind the picture on the right side of slide 5. Change the text in the text box to read **Experienced nurses and helpers**.

8. On slide 6, turn off bullet and hanging indent formatting in the content placeholder and insert the following material, using tabs to space the columns of text:

	Hourly	Daily	Holidays
LPN	$18.50	$140.00	+$5.00/hour
RN	$25.00	$190.00	+$5.50/hour
Home helper	$9.50	$70.00	+$3.50/hour

9. Reduce the height of the content placeholder to free up some space below the table. Create a text box that is about 6.5 inches wide below the table and type the following content:

   Fees listed above are sample rates that apply in many situations. Fees may vary according to personnel assigned, level of care required, amount of advance notice, and other circumstances. Please call to discuss your situation and we will provide you with a firm quote.

10. Format the text in the text box as follows:

    a. Change the font to Calibri 18 point italic and center the text.

    b. Apply a fill, outline, and effect of your choice to the text box.

11. Add a new slide with the Blank layout after slide 7 and insert a WordArt graphic using the text **Quality Home Care**.

12. Format the WordArt as desired by changing shape, fill, outline, and effect.

13. Find all instances of *prn* and replace them with **as needed**.

14. Use the Thesaurus to find a replacement for the word *Excellent* in the third paragraph on slide 2.

15. Send the outline of the presentation to Word and format it using Word's Title, Subtitle, and headings styles from the Styles gallery. Remove the line break in the title. Save the outline document as **05PETERSON_OUTLINE_xx**.

16. Save your changes, close all documents, and exit PowerPoint and Word.

Illustration A

Curriculum Integration

Application Skills   For a global perspectives class, you have been asked to create a presentation giving information about a country in Europe. Your presentation should include statistics such as current population, largest cities, climate and terrain, currency, form of government, and so on. Before you begin this exercise, locate the following information:

■   A profile of a chosen country (*The CIA World Factbook 2009* is a good place to start).

EXERCISE DIRECTIONS

Begin a new blank presentation and save it with an appropriate name, such as **06FRANCE_*xx***. Apply a theme of your choice. Insert a title and subtitle and apply WordArt formatting of your choice to both objects.

Add a slide with a Blank layout and insert one or more text boxes in which you give a brief history of your country. Use first-line indents to set off paragraphs of text. Format the text box(es) as desired. Add a vertical text box to the left of the history text box that includes the stacked text **HISTORY**. Adjust alignment, character spacing, and text box formats to make the stacked text look attractive. Illustration A shows an example.

Using the Outline tab, add a slide to summarize the climate and terrain of your country. Use several levels of bullets as necessary to describe the country's features.

Add a slide to summarize information on your country's people. Insert the following information on the slide and then set a tab to right align the number for each statistic at the right side of the placeholder.

■   Population

■   Median age

■   Population growth rate

■   Life expectancy (you may express this as total population or male and female, or all three)

Add a slide that lists in numeric order the five largest cities in your country, with their populations. Use number formatting for the list, and separate the city names from the populations using tabs. Shorten the placeholder so you can add a text box that indicates if the population figure is for the city only or the city and suburbs. Format the text box as desired.

Add a slide to summarize the country's government. Include the type of government, the branches of government, and any important information about each branch. Boldface each branch of the government.

Add a slide to summarize the country's economy. Include on this slide the currency, with its symbol, the chief exports and imports, and the gross domestic product (GDP) per capita.

In Slide Master view, add another slide master with the same format you used for the presentation. Rename and modify the new slide master to give you a variation of the default theme. Make any other changes to text formats that you wish to improve the look of the slides. Apply your new slide master to at least one of the slides.

Send the presentation to Microsoft Word using a format of your choice. Save the Word document with an appropriate name such as **06FRANCE_HANDOUTS_xx**. Close the document, and exit Word.

Save changes to the presentation and close it. Exit PowerPoint.

Illustration A

Lesson | 2

Advanced Graphic Features

Exercise | 7

Skills Covered

- **Customize Slide Backgrounds**
- **Create a Color or Gradient Background**
- **Create a Picture or Texture Background**

Software Skills Though themes provide you with interesting backgrounds, you can also customize your own backgrounds using color, a gradient, a texture, or a picture.

Application Skills You work for Thorn Hill Gardens, a park on the site of a former grand estate that is open for tours and conducts seasonal workshops in horticulture. You have been asked to prepare a presentation that can be shown to garden clubs and horticulture classes at nearby colleges. You will begin the presentation by customizing some backgrounds for the slides.

TERMS

Gradient Gradations of color usually from a light color to a darker color, although gradients can consist of more than two colors.

NOTES

Customize Slide Backgrounds

- You should by now be familiar with a number of PowerPoint's theme backgrounds. You may find yourself wishing as you apply a particular theme that you could change the background to create a different visual statement or to more closely meet your needs.

- You can use the Format Background dialog box to create a number of background effects that will ensure your presentation is one of a kind.

- Select from a solid, gradient, or picture or texture fill. The choices available in the lower portion of the dialog box change depending which fill option you choose.

- You will learn how to create these background fills in the following sections.

Format Background dialog box

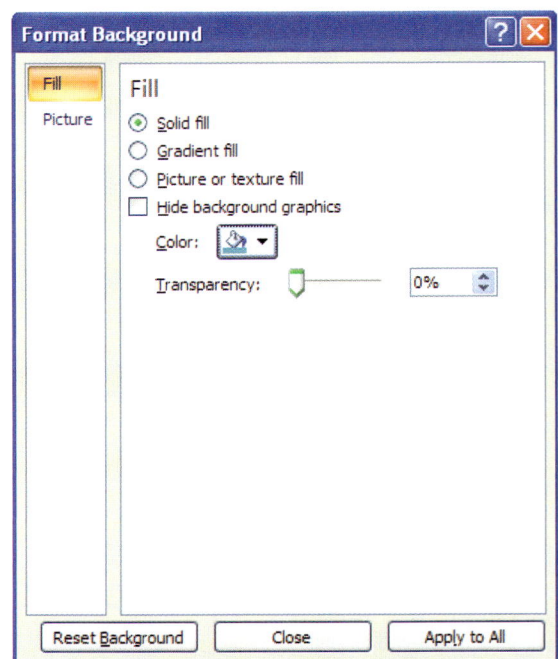

■ You can use the Apply to All button to apply your new background to all slides in the presentation. If you don't click this button, the background applies only to the current slide.

■ If you find that you don't like the changes you have made, you can click the Reset Background button to restore the default background.

■ Note that the fill options available in the Format Background dialog box are also available for any object that can be filled, such as a text box, a shape, a table cell, a chart background, and so on. You can access the fill options by right-clicking the object and selecting a command with a name such as Format Shape.

Create a Color or Gradient Background

■ The easiest background fill to create is a solid color background. After you click the Solid fill option, the dialog box displays a Color button to open a theme color palette and a Transparency slider to adjust the opacity of the color.

■ You can choose any color from the Color palette or one of the Standard colors at the bottom of the palette. Or, click More Colors to open the Colors dialog box so you can pick a color.

■ As you drag the Transparency slider to the right, your chosen color is mixed with increasing amounts of white so that it lightens or fades.

   ✓ *Keep in mind that a background color should not overwhelm the type on a slide, so adjusting transparency is often a good way to keep the background under control.*

■ A **gradient** is a color fill that shades from one color to another. Gradient fills give an object a more interesting look than a plain color fill because of the variation in color tone.

■ Clicking the Gradient fill option in the Format Background dialog box displays the settings shown in the following illustration.

Gradient fill options in the Format Background dialog box

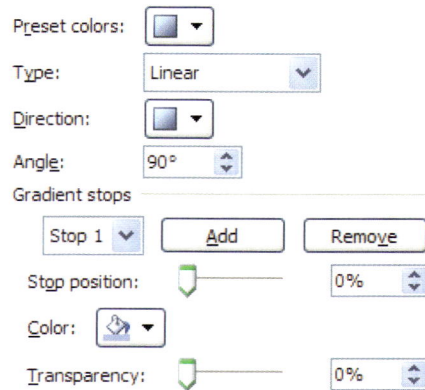

■ Click the Preset colors box to see a gallery of gradients that have already been created for you.

■ The Type list lets you choose how the gradient displays: Linear, for example, goes from one side of a slide to another, while Radial radiates out from the center of the slide.

■ After you choose a type, you can fine-tune the gradient appearance by selecting a direction that the gradient will flow. Directions for linear gradients, for instance, include Linear Diagonal, Linear Down, and Linear Left.

■ Use the Angle setting to adjust the direction in which the gradient flows.

■ Use the options in the Gradient stops area of the dialog box to choose the colors for the gradient. A gradient stop is the location at which the color changes. You can choose a color for each stop, and drag the Stop position slider to determine how much of the object will be filled with that color.

   ✓ *Or, set the position more precisely by typing a percentage.*

■ Add a stop if you want to add another color to the gradient. Remove a stop to create a less complex gradient.

■ Use the Transparency slider to soften the gradient by making the colors more transparent.

Create a Picture or Texture Background

■ When you click the Picture or texture fill option, the controls below the option button become active, allowing you to select a texture or insert a picture from a file or the Clip Organizer.

Picture or texture background options

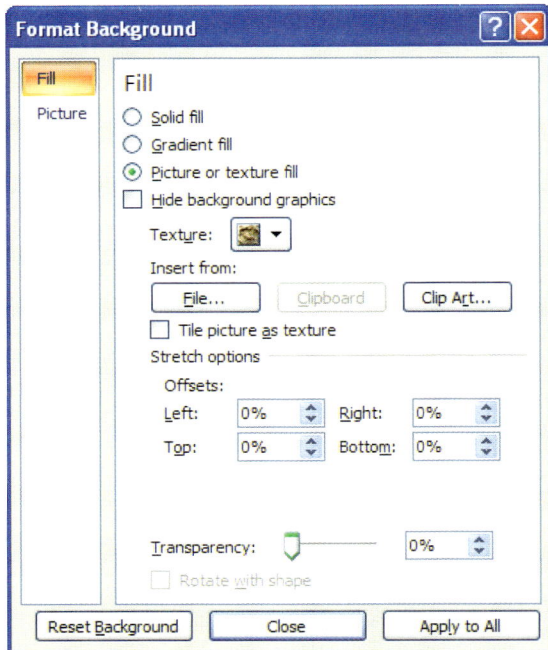

```
┌─────────────────────────────────────────────┐
│ Format Background                      [?][X]│
├─────────────────────────────────────────────┤
│ ┌──────┐  Fill                               │
│ │ Fill │   ○ Solid fill                      │
│ ├──────┤   ○ Gradient fill                   │
│ │Picture│  ● Picture or texture fill         │
│ └──────┘   □ Hide background graphics        │
│                                              │
│            Texture:  [🖼][▼]                  │
│                                              │
│            Insert from:                      │
│            [ File... ] [Clipboard] [Clip Art...]│
│            □ Tile picture as texture         │
│            Stretch options                   │
│            Offsets:                          │
│            Left:  [0%][↕]  Right:  [0%][↕]   │
│            Top:   [0%][↕]  Bottom: [0%][↕]   │
│                                              │
│            Transparency: [▽────] [0%][↕]     │
│            □ Rotate with shape               │
├─────────────────────────────────────────────┤
│ [Reset Background] [  Close  ] [Apply to All]│
└─────────────────────────────────────────────┘
```

■ By default, Tile picture as texture is not selected when you choose to insert a picture, so the picture covers the entire slide. You use the Stretch options to control how the image covers the slide. If you want the picture to appear multiple times on the slide, select Tile picture as texture and then use the Tiling options to adjust scale and offset (vertical or horizontal position on the slide).

■ The Transparency option is very important for picture backgrounds. Washing out the picture by increasing its transparency can make it much easier to read type on the slide.

■ You can make other changes to picture formats by clicking the Picture category in the Format Background dialog box.

✓ *You learn more about picture formatting in Exercise 12 in this lesson.*

■ Clicking the Texture button displays a gallery of standard Office textures. These textures have been available in a number of previous PowerPoint versions, so they may look familiar to you.

■ Click any texture in the gallery to apply it immediately to the current slide. Textures are usually tiled to cover the background. You can change the scale of the tiles to create a different effect or adjust the offset.

■ As for a picture, you may want to adjust transparency to avoid overwhelming the type on your slide with the sometimes strongly colored textures. You can also choose to change font color to contrast well with the darker textures.

PROCEDURES

Customize a Slide Background

1. Click **Design** tab . . . . [Alt]+[G]

   Background Group

2. Click **Background Styles** button
   [🖼] . . . . [B]

3. Click **Format Background** . . . . [B]

4. Choose one of the option buttons to create a solid, gradient, picture, or texture fill.

   ✓ *Specific instructions for type of fill are given below.*

5. Click **Close** to apply background to current slide only . . . . [Enter]

OR

Click **Apply to All** to apply to all slides in presentation . . . . [Alt]+[L]

Restore Default Slide Background

Restore background in Normal view:

1. Click **Design** tab . . . . [Alt]+[G]

   Background Group

2. Click **Background Styles** button
   [🖼] . . . . [B]

3. Click **Reset Slide Background** . . . . [R]

Restore background while in Format Background dialog box:

■ Click **Reset Background** . . . . [Alt]+[B]

Create a Color Background

In Format Background dialog box:

1. Click **Solid fill** . . . . [Alt]+[S]

2. Click **Color** button to display theme color palette . . . . . [Alt]+[C]

3. Select theme color or Standard color . . . . . . [↓], [↑], [←], [→], [Enter]

   OR

a. Click **More Colors**....... $\boxed{\text{M}}$

b. Select a color in the Colors dialog box.

c. Click **OK** .... $\boxed{\text{Enter}}$

4. Drag **Transparency** slider if desired to adjust opacity of color .... $\boxed{\text{Alt}}$+$\boxed{\text{T}}$, $\boxed{\rightarrow}$, $\boxed{\leftarrow}$

Create a Gradient Background

In Format Background dialog box:

1. Click **Gradient fill** ...... $\boxed{\text{Alt}}$+$\boxed{\text{G}}$

   ✓ *A gradient fill immediately fills background using shades of most recently created gradient.*

2. Click **Preset colors** ..... $\boxed{\text{Alt}}$+$\boxed{\text{R}}$

3. Select a preset gradient. .... $\boxed{\downarrow}$, $\boxed{\uparrow}$, $\boxed{\leftarrow}$, $\boxed{\rightarrow}$, $\boxed{\text{Enter}}$

   OR

   Create a custom gradient.

To create a custom gradient:

1. With **Stop 1** displayed in Gradient stops area, click **Color** button and select a color from the theme color palette or any other color palette .... $\boxed{\text{Alt}}$+$\boxed{\text{C}}$

2. Drag **Stop position** slider if desired to specify percentage of background used by selected color .... $\boxed{\text{Alt}}$+$\boxed{\text{O}}$, $\boxed{\leftarrow}$, $\boxed{\rightarrow}$

3. Click **Stop 1** list arrow to display list of stops and select **Stop 2**.

4. Click **Color** button and select a color from the theme color palette or any other color palette .... $\boxed{\text{Alt}}$+$\boxed{\text{C}}$

5. Adjust Stop position if desired as directed in step 2.

6. Continue to select gradient stops and select colors until gradient is adjusted.

To choose type of gradient:

1. Click **Type** .... $\boxed{\text{Alt}}$+$\boxed{\text{Y}}$

2. Select from list of gradient types .... $\boxed{\downarrow}$, $\boxed{\uparrow}$, $\boxed{\text{Enter}}$

To change direction and angle of gradient:

1. Click **Direction**........ $\boxed{\text{Alt}}$+$\boxed{\text{D}}$

2. Select from gallery of preset directions... $\boxed{\downarrow}$, $\boxed{\uparrow}$, $\boxed{\leftarrow}$, $\boxed{\rightarrow}$, $\boxed{\text{Enter}}$

3. Click **Angle** .... $\boxed{\text{Alt}}$+$\boxed{\text{E}}$

4. Type desired angle.

   OR

   Click increment arrows to increase/reduce angle by 10 degree increments.

To add a stop to a gradient:

1. Display stop in gradient stop list that will be before new stop.

2. Click **Add** .... $\boxed{\text{Alt}}$+$\boxed{\text{A}}$

3. Select a color and stop position for the new gradient stop.

To remove a stop from a gradient:

1. Display the gradient stop list.

2. Select gradient stop to remove.

3. Click **Remove** .... $\boxed{\text{Alt}}$+$\boxed{\text{V}}$

Create a Picture Background

In Format Background dialog box:

1. Click **Picture or texture fill** .... $\boxed{\text{Alt}}$+$\boxed{\text{P}}$

   ✓ *A texture may immediately fill the slide background.*

2. Click **File** .... $\boxed{\text{Alt}}$+$\boxed{\text{F}}$

3. Navigate to location of picture and select picture.

4. Click **Insert** .... $\boxed{\text{Alt}}$+$\boxed{\text{S}}$

5. Adjust Offset measurements to position picture on slide.

6. Drag **Transparency** slider if desired to adjust opacity of image .... $\boxed{\text{Alt}}$+$\boxed{\text{T}}$, $\boxed{\rightarrow}$, $\boxed{\leftarrow}$

Create a Texture Background

In Format Background dialog box:

1. Click **Picture or texture fill** .... $\boxed{\text{Alt}}$+$\boxed{\text{P}}$

   ✓ *A texture may immediately fill the slide background.*

2. Click **Texture** .... $\boxed{\text{Alt}}$+$\boxed{\text{U}}$

3. Select texture from gallery ..... $\boxed{\downarrow}$, $\boxed{\uparrow}$, $\boxed{\leftarrow}$, $\boxed{\rightarrow}$, $\boxed{\text{Enter}}$

4. Drag **Transparency** slider if desired to adjust opacity of image .... $\boxed{\text{Alt}}$+$\boxed{\text{T}}$, $\boxed{\rightarrow}$, $\boxed{\leftarrow}$

EXERCISE DIRECTIONS

1. Start PowerPoint to open a new, blank presentation and apply the Civic theme. Save the presentation as **07THORN_*xx***.

2. Type the title **Thorn Hill Gardens** and the subtitle **FOUR SEASONS OF COLOR**.

3. Begin by applying a picture background to the title slide to represent the spring season:

   a. Choose a picture background and insert the ⊙ **07SPRING** picture from the data files.

   b. Adjust transparency to 60% and close the Format Background dialog box.

   c. In Slide Master view, change the color of slide titles and the title slide's subtitle to Black to provide a slightly better contrast with the backgrounds you are creating. Remove the green shape at the bottoms of all slides. Your slide should look similar to Illustration A.

4. Add a new slide with the Title and Content layout. Create a solid color background for the summer season as follows:

   a. Choose a green color from the theme colors and then adjust transparency as desired to make a fresh green background.

   b. Insert the title text **Summer Events**.

5. Add a new slide with the Title and Content layout. Create a custom gradient background for the fall season as follows:

   a. With the Linear gradient type selected, choose the first option on the Direction palette, Linear Diagonal.

   b. With Stop 1 displayed in the Gradient stops area, choose the Dark Yellow, Accent 2, Lighter 40% color from the theme colors palette. Move the Stop position slider to 20%.

   c. Select Stop 2 and specify Orange from the Standard colors. Move the Stop position slider to 35%.

   d. Select Stop 3 and specify the Red, Accent 1, Darker 25% color. Move the Stop position slider to 100%.

   e. Remove any other gradient stops in the list and close the dialog box.

   f. Insert the title text **Fall Fun**.

6. Add a new slide with the Title and Content layout. Create a texture background for the winter season as follows:

   a. Select the White marble texture and adjust transparency to 70%.

   b. Insert the title text **Winter Wonderland**.

7. Save your changes, close the presentation, and exit PowerPoint.

Illustration A

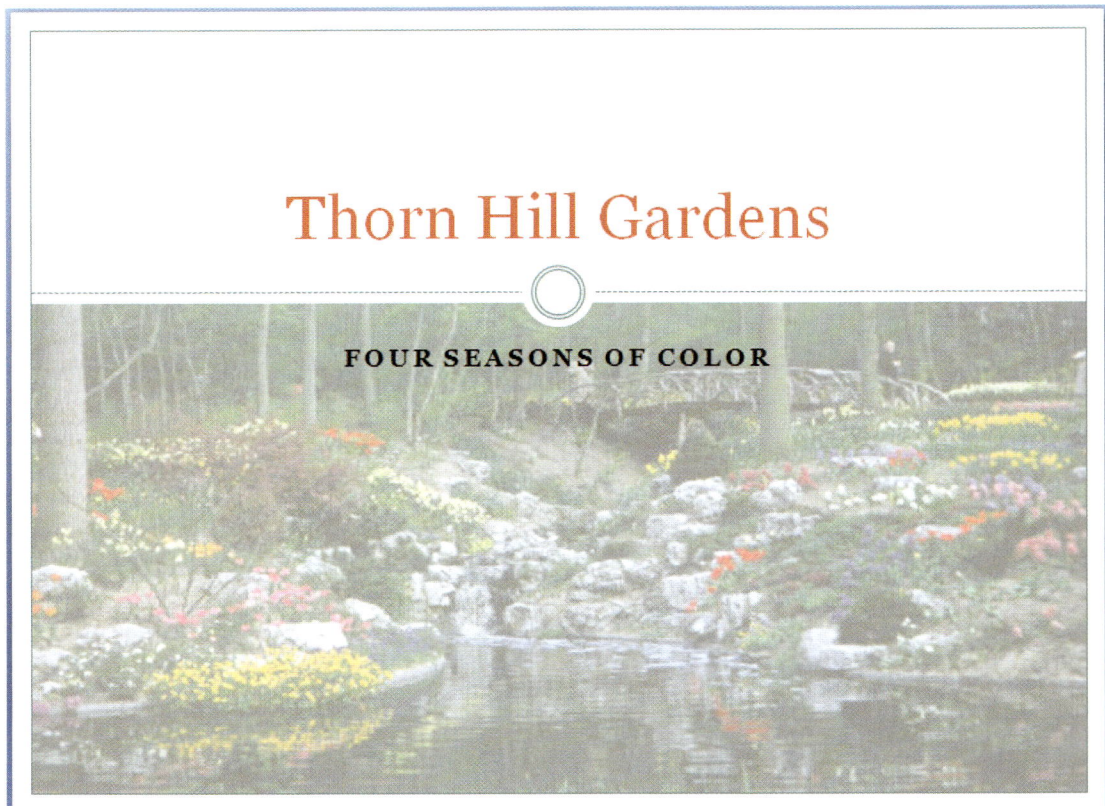

ON YOUR OWN

1. Open 07GIVING. Save the presentation as OPP07_xx.

2. On the slide master for the presentation, adjust the radial gradient by adding a new color to give the gradient more depth. You may make the new color lighter or darker than the two current gradient stops.

3. On slide 1, add a picture background, using a clip art image (try a keyword such as *giving* or *helping*). Adjust the appearance of the picture as desired. Illustration A shows one option.

4. On slide 8, create a new background using a color, a gradient, or a texture.

5. Save your changes, close the presentation, and exit PowerPoint.

Illustration A

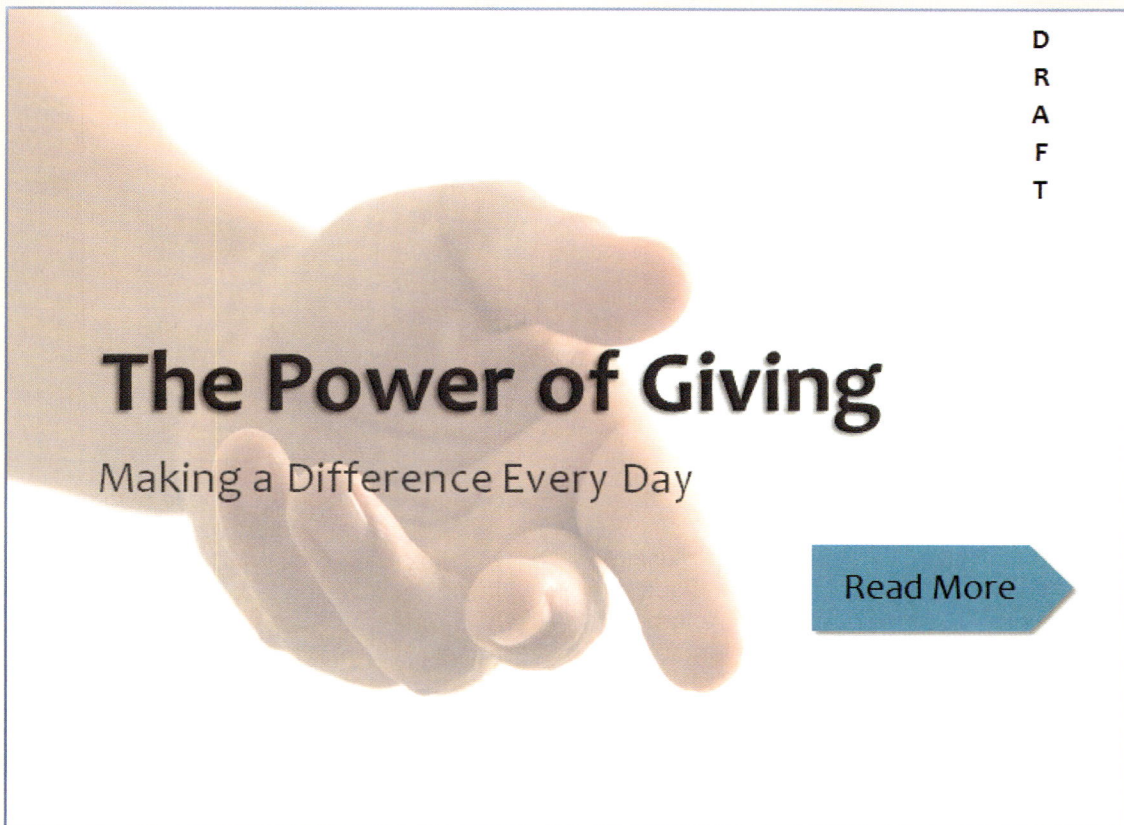

Exercise | 8

Skills Covered

- **Draw a Table**
- **Advanced Table Formatting**

- **Add an Image to a Table**

Software Skills Use the Draw Table feature to insert a table outline and the desired rows and columns. Table formats enhance visual interest and also contribute to readability. For additional interest, add an image to a table.

Application Skills In this exercise, you work on a presentation announcing the Michigan Avenue Athletic Club's new yoga classes. You draw a table and then format the new table and an existing table in a variety of ways.

TERMS

No new terms in this exercise.

NOTES

Draw a Table

- Though you can easily add a table to a slide using the Insert Table icon in any content placeholder, you may on occasion want to use the Draw Table feature. This feature is especially useful for tables that do not have regular arrangements of rows and columns.

- Click the Draw Table command on the Table menu and draw the table outline on a slide.

Draw a table outline with the Draw Table pointer

- When you release the mouse pointer, a table container displays. To draw row and column borders, you must then click the Draw Table button on the Table Tools Design tab.

- Use the Pen Style, Pen Weight, and Pen Color tools to specify border formats before you draw the table structure. You can also specify these formats after a table is created and use the Draw Table pointer to draw the formats on top of existing formats to change them.

- When drawing row and column borders, as shown in the following illustration, you must not touch the table container, or the pointer will create a new table container rather than a column or row.

Add rows and columns to a table

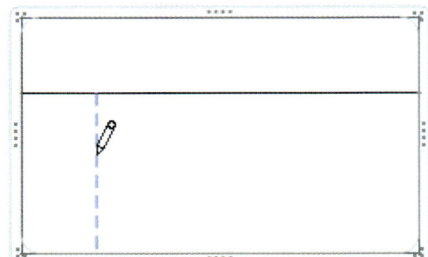

■ If you insert a border incorrectly, you can click the border with the Eraser tool to remove it.

Advanced Table Formatting

■ PowerPoint provides a number of tools on the Table Tools Design and Table Tools Layout tabs to help you format a table. Sophisticated table formats not only improve appearance but also can improve readability.

Adjust Cell and Table Size

■ Use the tools in the Cell Size group on the Table Tools Layout tab to specify exact height and width for a selected cell. The Distribute Rows and Distribute Columns buttons allow you to make all selected rows the same height or all selected columns the same width.

■ Use the Table Size group tools to specify an exact height and width for the table. If you select the Lock Aspect Ratio check box, any change you make to one dimension will resize the other dimension proportionally.

Change Text Alignment and Direction

■ The Alignment group on the Table Tools Layout tab provides a number of alignment options.

• You can align cell content both horizontally and vertically. Note that when a table's column headings run to more than one line, best practice is to align all headings at the bottom of the cell as shown in the following illustration.

• You can change the text direction to rotate or stack it, the same way you applied text direction in text boxes.

• Specify cell margins such as Narrow and Wide that adjust the amount of space around content in a cell.

Advanced table formats

	Class Name	Continuing Class	New Class
Classes	Pilates	X	
	Hot Yoga		X
	Fitness Fun	X	

Modify Cell Fill, Borders, and Effects

■ You already know that you can use a Quick Style from the Table Styles gallery to instantly apply sophisticated fill and border formats to a table.

■ The styles available in the Table Styles gallery depend on the options selected in the Table Style Options group. The check boxes in the Table Style Options group let you select parts of a table to receive special emphasis.

■ Clicking the Header Row check box, for example, ensures that the first row of the table will have a fill and other formatting that make the row stand out. The Banded Rows and Banded Columns options supply alternate fill colors for rows or columns to make it easy to differentiate content by row or column.

■ As you select or deselect table style options, the Quick Styles in the Table Style gallery change to show the formatting options you have selected.

■ If you want to control styles yourself, you can use the Shading, Borders, and Effects buttons in the Table Styles group.

• The Shading button allows you to select a color, picture, gradient, or texture fill for selected cells, or supply a background color or picture to fill the entire table.

• The Borders button lets you select borders for any or all sides of a cell or table, including diagonal borders to split cells on the diagonal.

• Use the Effects button to display categories of familiar effects such as Bevel, Shadow, and Reflection. Bevel effects can be applied to individual cells, but the Shadow and Reflection effects can be applied only to the entire table. The previous illustration shows a bevel effect applied to cells and a shadow effect applied to the entire table.

Add an Image to a Table

■ You have several options for adding an image to a table: You can use the image as a background for a selected cell or cells, or you can use the image as the background for the entire table.

■ To insert an image as the background for one or more selected cells, you can use the Picture command on the Shading palette to navigate to the image you want to insert. However, if you have selected more than one cell, the image is inserted into each cell, as shown in the following illustration.

Image inserted into selected cells

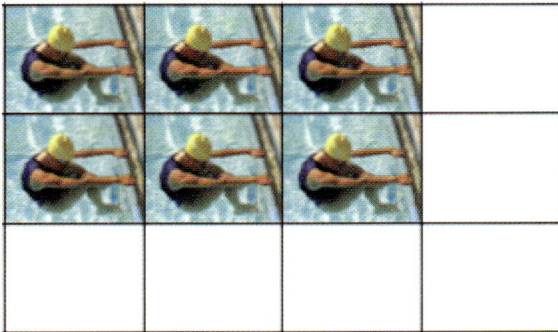

- This result is probably not what you have in mind, unless you wish to have multiple copies of an image in a table for a special effect.
- For better control over the process of adding an image to selected cells, use the Format Shape dialog box. Note that the settings in the Fill category of this dialog box are almost identical to those in the Format Background dialog box you worked with in Exercise 7.

Format Shape dialog box

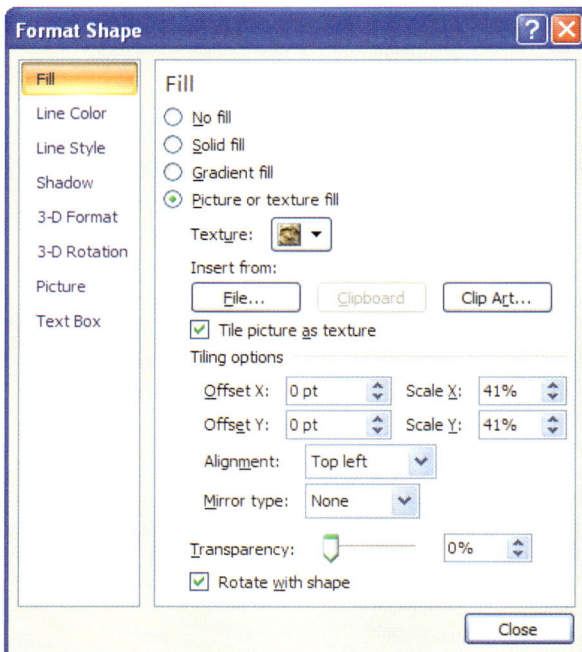

- When adding a picture to table cells, you will usually want to select the Tile picture as texture check box. You can then specify how the image is positioned in the selection area and adjust the size of the image to better fit the area. The tiling options shown in the previous illustration result in the image shown in the following illustration.

Image stretched over selected cells

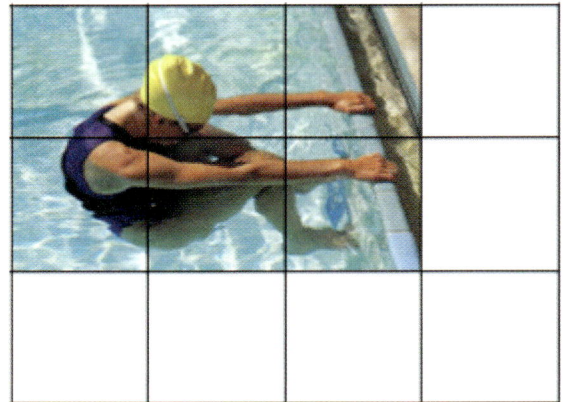

- If you want to use an image as a background for table cells, you can adjust transparency so that text can easily be read on top of the image background.
- You have the same general options when using an image as the background for an entire table. If you use the Table Background option on the Shading palette to insert a picture background, the image is spread out over all cells in the table, but you have no options for changing the position or transparency of the image.
- For best control of a table background image, select the cells in the table and use the Format Shape dialog box to insert and format the image.
- It can take some tweaking to get an image to fit the way you want in a table or table cells. You may need to adjust position and size and the table itself to keep from seeing multiple images tiled over the table. But the visual effect is worth the effort.

PROCEDURES

Draw a Table

1. Click **Insert** tab . . . . [Alt]+[N]

   Tables Group

2. Click **Table** button 🔲 . . . . . . [T]
3. Click **Draw Table** . . . . [D]
4. Drag Draw Table pointer to create table outline.

   Draw Borders Group

5. Click **Draw Table** button
   📝 . . . . [Alt]+[J], [T], [D]
6. Drag Draw Table pointer within outside border to create rows and columns.

   ✓ To format borders with style, weight, or color, make these selections in the Draw Borders group before drawing borders.

7. To remove a border, click **Eraser** 📝 button and click with the Eraser pointer on the border to remove . . . . [Alt]+[J], [T], [E]

Modify Table Layout

1. Click the table to select it.
2. Click **Table Tools Layout** tab . . . . [Alt]+[J], [L]

To change table size:

1. Click anywhere in the table to size.

   Table Size Group

2. Click **Table Height** box 📐 and type new value or use spin arrow to set value . . . . . . [T], [H]

   OR

   Click **Table Width** box 📐 and type new value or use spin arrow to set value . . . . . . [T], [W]

   ✓ If Lock Aspect Ratio is selected, changing one dimension will automatically change the other a corresponding amount.

To change column width or row height:

1. Click in a row or column to size.

   Cell Size Group

2. Click **Table Row Height** box 📐 and type new value or use spin arrow to set value . . . . [H]

   OR

   Click **Table Column Width** box 📐 and type new value or use spin arrow to set value . . . . . . [W]

To distribute rows evenly:

1. Select a series of rows to distribute.

   Cell Size Group

2. Click **Distribute Rows** button 📐 . . . . [U], [R]

To distribute columns evenly:

1. Select a series of columns to distribute.

   Cell Size Group

2. Click **Distribute Columns** button 📐 . . . . [U], [C]

To change horizontal alignment:

1. Select text to align.

   Alignment Group

2. Select desired alignment button:

   ■ **Align Text Left** 📄 . . . [A], [L]
   ■ **Center** 📄 . . . . [A], [C]
   ■ **Align Text Right**
     📄 . . . . [A], [R]

To change vertical alignment:

1. Select text to align.

   Alignment Group

2. Select desired alignment button:

   ■ **Align Top** 📄 . . . . [O]
   ■ **Center Vertically** 📄 . . . . [C]
   ■ **Align Bottom** 📄 . . . . [B]

To change text direction:

1. Select table text to align.

   Alignment Group

2. Click **Text Direction** button 📐 . . . . [A], [X]
3. Select a text direction:

   ■ **Horizontal** . . . . [H]
   ■ **Rotate all text 90°** . . . . . . [R]
   ■ **Rotate all text 270°** . . . . . [O]
   ■ **Stacked** . . . . [S]

To change cell margins:

1. Select table cell or cells.

   Alignment Group

2. Click **Cell Margins** button 📐 . . . . [N]
3. Select a margin option:

   ■ **Normal**
   ■ **None**
   ■ **Narrow**
   ■ **Wide**

Apply Table Formats

1. Click the table to select it.
2. Click **Table Tools Design** tab . . . . [Alt]+[J], [T]

To choose table style options:

1. Click in the table.

Table Style Options Group

2. Click check boxes to select por-
   tions of the table to receive special
   emphasis:
   - **Header Row** . . . . O
   - **Total Row** . . . . J
   - **Banded Rows** . . . . R
   - **First Column** . . . . M
   - **Last Column** . . . . N
   - **Banded Columns** . . . . U

To apply formats to selected cells:

- Click **Shading** button 🖌 and
  select a color, picture, gradient, or
  texture to fill table cells . . . . . . H

- Click **Borders** button ⊞ down
  arrow and select the desired
  border to apply to the current
  cell. B

- Click **Effects** button ⬭ and
  select from bevel, shadow,
  or reflection effects for the
  table . . . . F

Add an Image to a Table

To add an image to selected cells:

1. Select cells that will contain
   image.
2. Click **Table Tools Design**
   tab . . . . Alt +J, T

Table Styles Group

3. Click **Shading** button 🖌 . . . . H
4. Click **Picture** . . . . P
5. Navigate to location of picture
   and select picture.
6. Click **Insert** . . . . Alt +S

OR

1. Select cells that will contain
   image.
2. Click **Home** tab . . . . Alt +H

Drawing Group

3. Click **Drawing** dialog box launcher
   ⬓ . . . . O
4. Click **Picture or texture
   fill** . . . . Alt +P
5. Click **File** . . . . Alt +F
6. Navigate to location of picture and
   select picture.
7. Click **Insert** . . . . Alt +S
8. Adjust the image position:
   - Click **Tile picture as
     texture** to spread the
     picture over all selected
     cells . . . . Alt +A
   - Adjust Offset measurements
     to move image horizontally or
     vertically from chosen align-
     ment point.
   - Adjust Scale measurements
     to reduce image horizontally
     or vertically by a specified
     percentage from original size.
   - Choose an Alignment option to
     set the point at which the im-
     age aligns in the selected cells.
   - Drag the Transparency slider
     to make image increasingly
     transparent.
9. Click **Close** . . . . Enter

To add an image as a background for the entire table:

1. Select the table by clicking
   anywhere in it.
2. Click **Table Tools Design**
   tab . . . . Alt +J, T

Table Styles Group

3. Click **Shading** button 🖌 . . . . H
4. Click **Table Background** . . . . . B
5. Click **Picture** . . . . P
6. Navigate to location of picture and
   select picture.
7. Click **Insert** . . . . Alt +S

OR

1. Select all cells in the table.
2. Click **Home** tab . . . . Alt +H

Drawing Group

3. Click **Drawing** dialog box launcher
   ⬓ . . . . O
4. Click **Picture or texture
   fill** . . . . Alt +P
5. Click **File** . . . . Alt +F
6. Navigate to location of picture and
   select picture.
7. Click **Insert** . . . . Alt +S
8. Adjust the image position:
   - Click **Tile picture as
     texture** to spread the
     picture over all selected
     cells . . . . Alt +A
   - Adjust Offset measurements
     to move image horizontally or
     vertically from chosen align-
     ment point.
   - Adjust Scale measurements
     to reduce image horizontally
     or vertically by a specified
     percentage from original size.
   - Choose an Alignment option to
     set the point at which the im-
     age aligns in the selected cells.
   - Drag the Transparency slider
     to make image increasingly
     transparent.
9. Click **Close** . . . . Enter

EXERCISE DIRECTIONS

1. Start PowerPoint and open ⊙ **08YOGA**. Save the presentation as **08YOGA_xx**. Begin your work by formatting the existing table.

2. Display slide 3 and format the table as follows:

   a. Select the following table style options: Header Row, Banded Rows, and First Column. Deselect any other selected options, and then apply the Medium Style 2 - Accent 3 table style.

   b. Specify a column width of about 2.1 inches for the first column, and then distribute the remaining columns equally, making sure all the times stay on one line. Make sure the table width is about 8.5 inches

   c. Center the entries in all columns except the first.

   d. Select the column heading cells and apply the Angle Bevel effect, and then remove all borders from the selected column heading cells.

3. The table could use a little more visual appeal. Add an image to the first column as follows:

   a. Select all cells in the first column except the column heading *Day*.

   b. Open the Format Shape dialog box and choose to insert a picture fill.

   c. Navigate to the data files and select ⊙ **08PICTURE**.

   d. Choose to tile the picture. Set both Scale values to 40%, change the Offset X value to -10 pt, and change the Y Offset value to 40 pt. The image should now fit neatly in the selected cell area.

   e. Change transparency to 50%.

   f. Change text color in the selected cells to black and remove bold font style. Your table should look like Illustration A.

4. Display slide 4. In the right content placeholder, draw the table shown in Illustration B and then format it as shown.

   a. The table should be about 4.4 inches wide. After drawing the borders, distribute rows and columns as necessary to make them the same size.

   b. Use middle alignment for the cells in the body of the table.

   c. Apply shading and 1½ point black borders as shown.

   d. Apply a shadow effect to the entire table. Delete the content placeholder.

5. Save your changes, close the presentation, and exit PowerPoint.

Illustration A

Yoga Classes at MAAC

Day	Ashtanga	Anusara	Vinyasa	Beginner
Monday	9:00 – 10:30 6:00 – 7:20	7:30 – 9:00		
Tuesday	9:00 – 10:30	11:30 – 1:00	6:00 – 7:20	
Wednesday	9:00 – 10:30			7:30 – 9:00
Thursday	4:30 – 5:20		6:00 – 7:20	
Friday	9:00 – 10:30 4:30 – 5:30			7:30 – 9:00
Saturday	12:00 – 1:20	1:30 – 2:50	9:30 – 10:50	

		Member	
		Yes	No
Payment Options	5 class pass	$55	$75
	10 class pass	$100	$120
	20 class pass	$180	$210
	Beginner course	$95	$115

ON YOUR OWN

In today's workplace, it is more important than ever before to understand the value of an entire employment package—not merely the yearly salary but also the health, retirement, and other compensation options that are on the table. In this exercise, research some common employment benefits and evaluate the offerings of several companies you would like to work for.

1. Using the Internet, locate definitions for these employment package options: cafeteria plan, individual retirement account (IRA), tax-sheltered annuity, retirement fund, commission, benefits, and transportation assistance.

2. Contact three businesses locally that you would like to work for, or peruse online employment pages for those or other companies. Identify which of the employment package options you researched are offered by your selected companies.

3. Start PowerPoint and create a new presentation. Save the presentation as **OPP08_xx**.

4. Apply a theme of your choice. Add appropriate text to the title slide. Add a slide and use it to list the options you researched in step 1 along with a brief definition of each. You may need to use more than one slide for these definitions.

5. On a new slide, insert a table that lists the employment options and the three companies you analyzed. Use Xs to indicate which companies offer which benefits.

6. Format the table as desired. You may want to locate an appropriate clip art image to use as a background for part or all of the table, as shown in Illustration A.

7. Assess the completed presentation and decide whether you want to add it to your employment portfolio as an example of your achievement. If you do, print the slides as a handout for the portfolio.

8. Save your changes, close the presentation, and exit PowerPoint.

Illustration A

Benefits Packages for My Prospects

Options	Blue Hill Coffee	Fifth Avenue Clothiers	Four Flags Park
Cafeteria plan	X	X	
Individual retirement account (IRA)			X
Tax-sheltered annuity		X	
Retirement (pension)			
Commission		X	
Benefits	X	X	X
Transportation assistance			X

Skills Covered

- **Create an Excel Worksheet on a Slide**
- **Add Existing Microsoft Office Objects to Slides**
- **Use Paste Special to Embed or Link Data**
- **Copy Objects from Slide to Slide**

Software Skills   Tables are one way to organize information on a slide. Another way to organize data is to create an Excel worksheet right on a slide or link worksheet data from Excel. You can paste, embed, or link other materials from other Office applications to add content to slides. If you have an object in one presentation that you want to use in another, you can use Copy and Paste to add the object to the current presentation and then decide how to apply theme formatting to the pasted object.

Application Skills   Planet Earth has developed a pilot program to sell eco-friendly products in urban neighborhoods, and you have been asked to create a presentation for the board to show the results of the program. In this exercise, you embed a Word table and link Excel worksheet data in the presentation. You will also copy the Planet Earth logo from an archive presentation and paste it in the current presentation.

TERMS

Destination   The location or application in which you place an element that was originally in another location or application.

Source   The original location or application of an element you intend to place in another location or application.

NOTES

Create an Excel Worksheet on a Slide

- If you want to show data that may need to be calculated or otherwise manipulated, you can create an Excel worksheet object on a PowerPoint slide. You have two options for creating a worksheet on a slide: the Excel Spreadsheet command on the Table menu and the Insert Object dialog box.

- Use the Excel Spreadsheet option on the Table menu to create a new worksheet object on a slide. This option displays a blank Excel worksheet as shown in the following illustration.

New Excel worksheet on a slide

- The worksheet object displays a diagonal-line (hatched) border that indicates the object is embedded on the slide.

- The Insert Object button on the Insert tab opens the Insert Object dialog box. You can use this dialog box to select from a list of objects you might want to create on a slide, including an Excel Worksheet.

Insert Object dialog box

Add Existing Microsoft Office Objects to Slides

- If the data you want to display on the slide already exists as a file, you can insert the file on the slide using the Insert Object dialog box's Create from file option. This option displays the dialog box shown in the following illustration. Use the Browse button to navigate to the file you want to insert on the slide.

Browse for an existing file

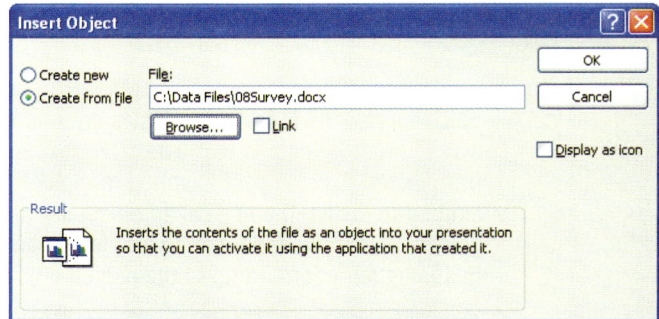

- The worksheet object inserted with the Excel Spreadsheet command is quite small, containing only four visible cells. If you use the Insert Object dialog box to insert a worksheet, you have many more rows and columns to work with.

- You can drag a sizing handle to display more worksheet cells or hide cells you don't need. The following illustration shows how to drag to reveal more cells in the worksheet.

Drag a handle to display more cells in the worksheet

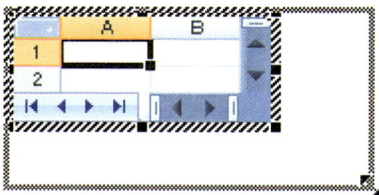

- When you enter text in an Excel worksheet you have inserted using either of these methods, you are actually working in Excel, so you can use all of Excel's features to calculate, manipulate, and format data.

- When you have finished working with the worksheet, click outside it on the slide to close the object. To modify data in the worksheet, double-click on the object to open it for editing in Excel.

- Clicking outside the worksheet displays a heavy light-blue container border such as the one that surrounds any PowerPoint table. You can resize the embedded object by dragging a corner handle of this border.

- Inserting data this way embeds the file on the slide so that you can work with the data using the tools from the file's original application. The embedded data is surrounded by a heavy blue container border on the slide. To edit the object in its original application, double-click the object.

- Note that this feature inserts the entire file, or, in the case of Excel, an entire worksheet, on your slide. If you want only a portion of the data, you should use the Paste Special option discussed in the next section.

- You can also choose to link a file you insert using the Insert Object dialog box by clicking the Link check box in the dialog box.

- A linked file maintains a relationship between the inserted object and the original so that when the original file is modified, the object on the slide shows the same changes.

- If you double-click a linked object to edit it, the original file opens in its source application. You make all edits in the original file, rather than on the PowerPoint slide.

Use Paste Special to Embed or Link Data

- If you do not want to insert an entire file on a slide, you can use the Copy and Paste Special commands to embed or link only a selection of data from another application.

- After you copy the data in another application—for example, Word, Excel, or even Access in the Office 2007 suite—you use the Paste Special command on the Paste menu.

Use the Paste Special dialog box to embed or link data

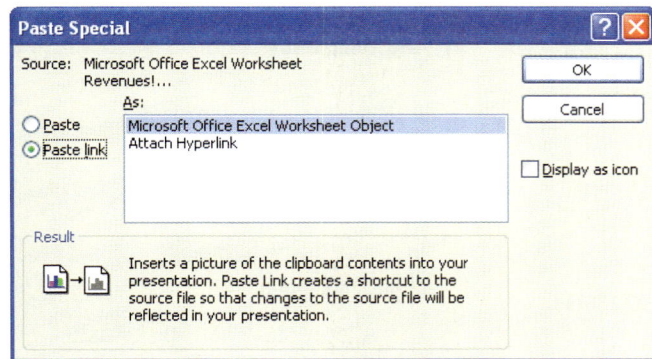

- If you choose the Paste option, the copied data is embedded on the slide and you can edit it using the tools of the original application.

- If you choose the Paste link option, the data is linked to the original file. Any change you make to the original data will also appear on the slide.

- The Paste Special dialog box offers different ways to paste data depending on the application in which the data was copied.

- You can also use the Paste Special dialog box when pasting text you have cut or copied in PowerPoint. Besides pasting the object in several text formats, you can choose to paste in one of several picture formats, such as PNG, GIF, or JPG. A benefit to pasting text in any of the Picture formats is that you can then treat the pasted text as a picture and apply interesting effects to it.

Copy Objects from Slide to Slide

- You can copy any element from an existing presentation to paste in your current presentation. This makes it easy to reuse charts, graphics, pictures, diagrams, or other material, saving time and ensuring consistency.

- You can also copy elements from one slide to another within a presentation.

- The easiest way to transfer an element from one presentation or slide to another is to use the Copy and Paste commands.

- When pasting or linking material from slide to slide, presentation to presentation, or application to application, it is helpful to use the terms **source** and **destination**.

- The source is the original location of material you are going to paste. The destination is the location where you paste that material.

- A source can be a slide in a presentation, another presentation, or another application.

- When you copy an object from one presentation or slide to another, it pastes in the same location on the destination slide that it occupied on the source slide.

- If an element that uses theme colors (such as a graphic created from shapes) is copied from one presentation to another, it will by default adjust to use colors of the destination presentation.

- If you wish to maintain the colors of the source presentation, click the Paste Options button that displays after the paste and select Keep Source Formatting.

Paste Options choices

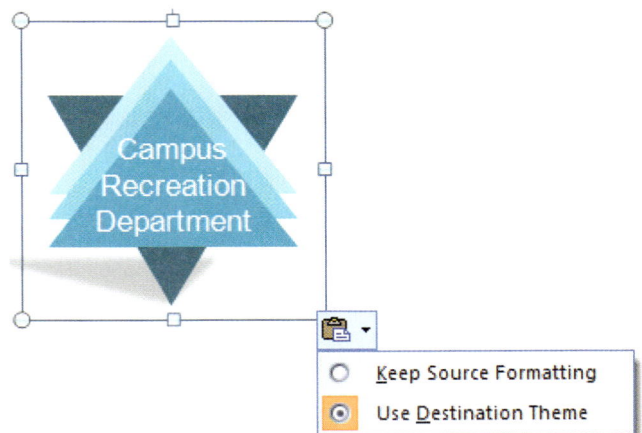

- The Paste Options button also displays if you copy other objects from one presentation to another, such as a text placeholder.

- You can choose whether to keep the original (source) formatting for text or adjust it to match the theme fonts of the destination presentation.

PROCEDURES

Insert an Excel Worksheet

To insert a blank worksheet:

1. Click **Insert** tab . . . . Alt + N

   #### Tables Group

2. Click **Table** button 🔳 . . . . . . T
3. Click **E̲xcel Spreadsheet** X

To insert an existing file:

1. Click **Insert** tab . . . . Alt + N

   #### Text Group

2. Click **Object** button 🖼️ . . . . . J
3. Click **Create from f̲ile** . . . Alt + F
4. Click **B̲rowse** . . . . Alt + B
5. Navigate to the location of the file and select it.
6. Click **OK**. . . . . Enter
7. Click **OK**. . . . . Enter

Resize a Worksheet

To crop unnecessary blank cells:

1. Double-click worksheet object if necessary to display diagonal line border.
2. Click on handle in bottom center of border and drag upward to crop any blank cells below data.
3. Click on handle in center of right border and drag to the left to crop any blank cells to the right of data.
4. Click outside the worksheet.

To resize the worksheet object:

1. Click once on the worksheet object to display the thick light blue container border.
2. Click on the lower-right corner and drag to resize the entire container without distorting text in worksheet.

Insert or Edit Data in a Worksheet

1. Double-click the worksheet object to display the diagonal line border and the Excel Ribbon.
2. Type or edit text as you would in Excel.

Use Paste Special to Embed or Link Data

1. In the source application, select the data you want to paste or paste link.
2. Click **Home** tab . . . . Alt + H

   #### Clipboard Group

3. Click **Copy** button 📋 C
4. In PowerPoint, display the slide where the copied data will appear.
5. Click **Home** tab . . . . Alt + H

   #### Clipboard Group

6. Click **Paste** button 📋 down arrow. V
7. Click **Paste S̲pecial** . . . . S
8. Click **P̲aste** . . . . Alt + P

   OR

   Click **Paste l̲ink** . . . . Alt + L
9. Select format for pasted data . . . . Alt + A , ↑ , ↓
10. Click **OK**. . . . . Enter

Copy Objects from Slide to Slide

1. Display the slide that contains the element you want to copy.

   ✓ *The slide can be in the current presentation or in a different presentation.*

2. Click the object you want to copy to select it.
3. Click **Home** tab . . . . Alt + H

   #### Clipboard Group

4. Click **Copy** button 📋 C
5. Display the slide on which you want to paste the element.
6. Click **Paste** button 📋 . . . . Alt + H , V

To specify theme formatting of pasted element:

1. After paste action, click **Paste Options** button 📋.
2. Select an option:
   - Click **K̲eep Source Formatting** to maintain color, font, or other formatting from original. . . . . K
   - Click **Use D̲estination Theme** to allow formats to adjust to theme on destination slide. . . . . D

EXERCISE DIRECTIONS

1. Start PowerPoint and open ⊙ **09EARTH**. Save the presentation as **09EARTH_xx**.

2. In Word, open ⊙ **09SURVEY** and save the file as **09SURVEY_xx** in the same location that you saved the presentation file. In Excel, open ⊙ **09RESULTS** and save it as **09RESULTS_xx** in the same location that you saved the presentation file. Close both files and their applications.

3. In PowerPoint, display slide 1 if necessary. Add to this presentation the Planet Earth logo from an archive presentation.

   a. Open ⊙ **09EARTH_ARCHIVE** and copy the graphic in the upper-right corner of the title slide. (The graphic is grouped; click outside the objects to select the entire group.)

   b. Paste the copied graphic on slide 1 of **09EARTH_xx**. Notice that the colors and the font adjust to the current theme automatically. You want to maintain the original colors, so click the Paste Options button and select Keep Source Formatting.

   c. Copy the logo graphic you just pasted and paste it on slide 6. Note that because you are pasting the graphic within the presentation, the Paste Options button does not appear.

   d. Move the graphic to the bottom center of slide 6.

4. Display slide 3. Insert the existing Word file **09SURVEY_xx** on the slide. Open the document for editing and make the following changes:

   a. Align all column heads at the bottom and center all percent values.

   b. Apply a white shading to all cells but the column headings.

   c. Sort the table by the Very Likely column in descending order to show which products respondents are mostly likely to use.

   ✓ *Click the Sort button on the Table Tools Layout tab to initiate the sort.*

5. Click outside the embedded document to deselect it.

   ✓ *The text may look somewhat "fuzzy" on the slide, but it should look clear when viewed in Slide Show view.*

6. Display slide 5. Open **09RESULTS_xx** in Excel, display the Expenses worksheet if necessary, and copy the cells in the range A3:D10.

7. Use Paste Special to paste the copied data on the PowerPoint slide. Double-click the embedded worksheet for editing and apply white fill to the cells that are not currently filled. Position the worksheet data attractively on the slide.

8. Display slide 7. In Excel, display the Revenues worksheet and copy the cells in the range A3:I15.

9. Use Paste Special to paste link the copied data on the PowerPoint slide. Notice that the sales figures for June are not yet in and the project is losing money. Position the pasted object attractively on the slide.

10. You now have the June sales figures. Switch to Excel and enter the following amounts in the Excel worksheet: beehive compost bin, **6**; wire compost bin, **7**; urn rain barrel, **5**; English rain barrel, **11**; pagoda solar light, **18**; lantern solar light, **10**.

11. Note the results of an IF function and conditional formatting in the Status column. Save and close the Excel worksheet. You should see the updated figures on the slide in PowerPoint, as shown in Illustration A.

12. Save your changes, close all presentations, and exit PowerPoint and Excel.

Eco-Sales Revenues

Item	Price	April	May	June	Sold	Revenue	Status
Compost bin, beehive	$175	10	5	6	21	$3,675	
Compost bin, wire bin	$30	25	18	7	50	1,500	Sold Out
				Compost Total		**$5,175**	
Rain barrel, urn	$175	9	10	5	24	$4,200	
Rain barrel, English	$130	15	9	11	35	4,550	Sold Out
				Rain Barrel Total		**$8,750**	
Solar lights, pagoda	$60	12	20	18	50	$3,000	Sold Out
Solar lights, lantern	$45	18	22	10	50	2,250	Sold Out
				Solar Lights Total		**$5,250**	
				Total Revenue		**$19,175**	
				Total Expenses		**$15,750**	
				Profit/Loss		**$3,425**	

ON YOUR OWN

1. Start PowerPoint and open 09CAMPUS. Save the presentation as OPP09_xx.

2. Display slide 2. Use the Excel Spreadsheet command on the Table button on the Insert tab to insert a new worksheet on the slide.

3. Enlarge the worksheet to show columns A through G and rows 1 through 10. Enter the data shown in Illustration A in the worksheet.

4. In the Total Revenue column, create a formula that sums the new memberships for all four quarters and multiplies the sum times the appropriate fee. (For example, you might use =SUM(B3:E3)*F3.)

Illustration A

	New Memberships					Total Revenue
	Qtr 1	Qtr 2	Qtr 3	Qtr 4	Fee	
Part-time/graduates	56	48	36	45	$200	
Faculty	24	21	18	23	$440	
Employees	37	31	15	28	$440	
Alumni	21	19	14	18	$560	
Community	15	13	10	14	$680	
Total						
Average						

5. In the Total and Average rows, insert functions to total and average the new memberships for each quarter. (For example, in cell B9, insert the formula =SUM(B3:B7); in cell B10, insert the formula =AVERAGE(B3:B7); copy formulas for the remaining quarters.) Total the revenue for all types of memberships in cell G9.

6. Apply the Flow theme so the data in the worksheet matches the font of the presentation.

7. Adjust the font size to be as large as possible and then format the worksheet attractively with cell styles, fills, and border options as desired. Illustration B shows one formatting option.

8. Display slide 1. Select the text in the subtitle and cut it, then delete the subtitle placeholder.

9. Use Paste Special to paste the cut text as a PNG picture. Then apply an interesting effect to the picture.

10. Save your changes, close the presentation, and exit PowerPoint.

Illustration B

Annual Memberships

| | New Memberships | | | | | Total |
	Qtr 1	Qtr 2	Qtr 3	Qtr 4	Fee	Revenue
Parttime/graduates	56	48	36	45	$200	$37,000
Faculty	24	21	18	23	$440	$37,840
Employees	37	31	15	28	$440	$48,840
Alumni	21	19	14	18	$560	$40,320
Community	15	13	10	14	$680	$35,360
Total	153	132	93	128		$199,360
Average	30.6	26.4	18.6	25.6		

Skills Covered

- **Advanced Chart Formatting**

Software Skills   PowerPoint offers a number of advanced charting options that help you create sophisticated-looking charts on slides. Insert shapes or text boxes to point out trends or add information. Select specific parts of the chart for in-depth formatting. Control chart formats such as titles, labels, and gridlines from the Chart Tools Layout tab.

Application Skills   In this exercise, you work on a presentation for the Michigan Avenue Athletic Club's year-end review. You add several charts to show revenues and trends in food purchases at the club's café and then format the charts using advanced techniques.

TERMS

No new terms in this exercise.

NOTES

Advanced Chart Formatting

- Because of the formatting built in to default charts, any new chart you insert on a slide has a pleasing appearance. You can make a chart more useful and visually appealing, however, by making full use of the charting capabilities included in PowerPoint.

- Options on the three Chart Tools contextual tabs give you many options for improving your charts.

Select a New Data Source

- When you insert a chart, PowerPoint assumes you wish to enter the data for the chart and displays an Excel worksheet with default data that you can replace.

- You may on occasion want to use the data from an existing worksheet, rather than re-enter the data in the default chart worksheet. You have two options for selecting data from an existing worksheet to create a chart.

- You can simply copy the data from the existing worksheet and then paste it into the chart work-sheet. Make sure the blue chart range border surrounds the pasted data. The PowerPoint default chart instantly updates to show the new data.

- You can also use the Select Data feature to specify a data range for the chart. To select the data from the existing worksheet, click the Collapse Dialog button in the Select Data Source dialog box, switch to the existing worksheet, and select the data range for the chart.

- The dialog box then shows the data range that will be used for the chart, as well as the legend and horizontal axis labels. Clicking OK closes the dialog box and updates the PowerPoint chart with the new data.

- Note that some editing may be required to display legend and axis labels correctly. In the following illustration, the legend entries need to be edited to display the correct data. To do so, click the Edit button, collapse the dialog box, and select the appropriate data from the worksheet.

Select data from an existing worksheet

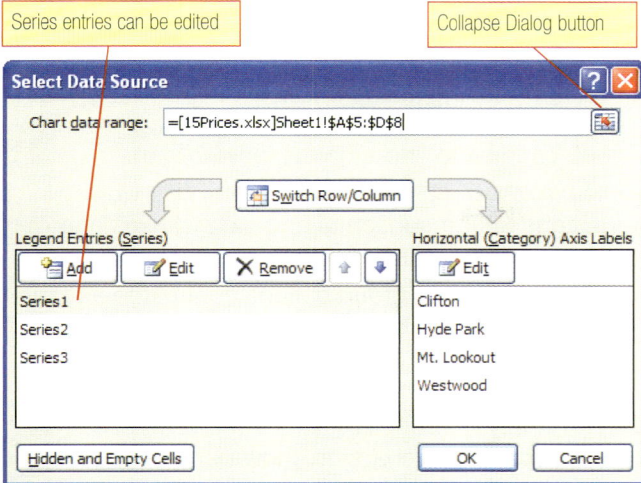

Series entries can be edited

Collapse Dialog button

Select Data Source

Chart data range: =[15Prices.xlsx]Sheet1!$A$5:$D$8

Switch Row/Column

Legend Entries (Series)

Add | Edit | ✕ Remove | ⬆ | ⬇

Series1
Series2
Series3

Horizontal (Category) Axis Labels

Edit

Clifton
Hyde Park
Mt. Lookout
Westwood

Hidden and Empty Cells | OK | Cancel

■ Using the Select Data Source dialog box can require some effort, as you will have to select the existing worksheet each time you want to edit the data in some way, but this dialog box also allows you considerable control over how your data appears. Besides editing the legend and axis labels, for example, you can add or remove series to display only the data you want to see.

Insert Shapes and Text Boxes on a Chart

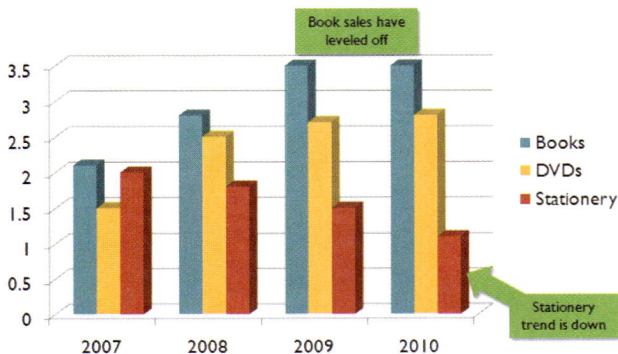

■ You may sometimes wish to add information to a chart in the form of a shape or text box to point out a trend or explain a data point. The Insert group on the Chart Tools Layout tab includes Picture, Shapes, and Text Box buttons that make it easy for you to add such information.

■ The following illustration shows two text boxes and a shape added to point out trends in sales. Shapes and text boxes may be formatted with fills, outlines, and effects to add visual interest.

Insert shapes and text boxes on a chart

Select and Format Parts of a Chart

■ Use the tools in the Current Selection group on either the Chart Tools Layout or Chart Tools Format tab to select a specific chart element and then format that element.

■ The Chart Elements drop-down list allows you to select a specific chart element, such as the plot area or the legend.

■ The Format Selection button opens a dialog box where you can find options for formatting the current selection, such as the vertical axis of a column chart shown in the following illustration.

Format Axis dialog box

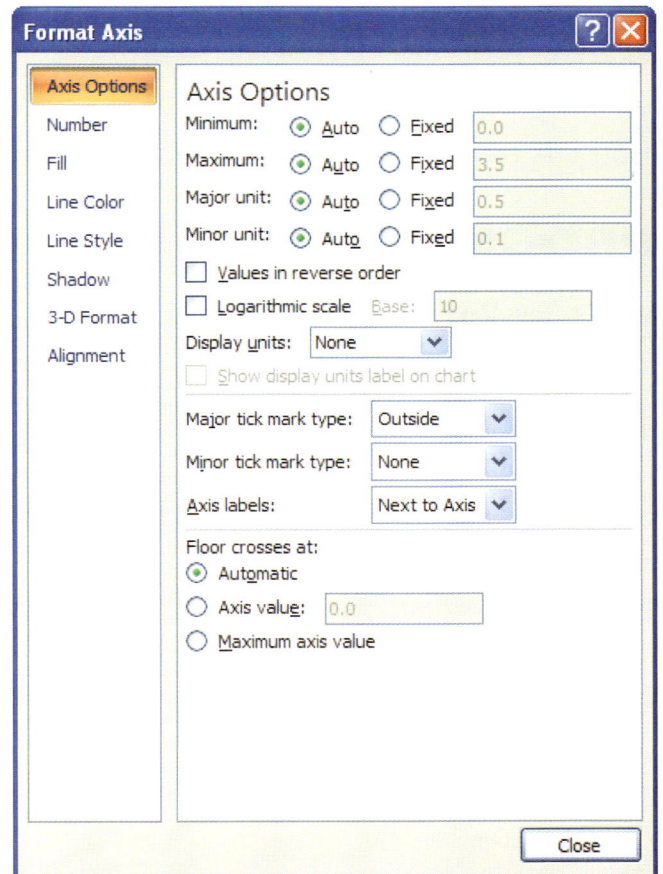

Format Axis

Axis Options
Number
Fill
Line Color
Line Style
Shadow
3-D Format
Alignment

Axis Options

Minimum: ⦿ Auto ◯ Fixed 0.0

Maximum: ⦿ Auto ◯ Fixed 3.5

Major unit: ⦿ Auto ◯ Fixed 0.5

Minor unit: ⦿ Auto ◯ Fixed 0.1

☐ Values in reverse order

☐ Logarithmic scale Base: 10

Display units: None

☐ Show display units label on chart

Major tick mark type: Outside

Minor tick mark type: None

Axis labels: Next to Axis

Floor crosses at:
⦿ Automatic
◯ Axis value: 0.0
◯ Maximum axis value

Close

■ Options in Format dialog boxes vary according to what part of the chart is currently selected. Many of these formatting options will be familiar from other features. You can apply a gradient to a chart element, for example, using the same skills you learned to create a gradient background.

■ You can also simply click an element to select it. If you are selecting a data series marker, the first click selects all markers for that series, and a second click selects only that marker.

- You can then apply a Quick Style; apply fill, outline, or effect options; apply WordArt styles to selected text; change the arrangement of objects in the chart; or resize the chart precisely.

- The formatting options on the Chart Tools Format tab work the same way as when you apply them to text boxes or table elements.

- You can also use text formatting options on the Home tab to modify font, font size, font style, or font color and paragraph formatting options to adjust alignment.

- You can select text in a chart by clicking to display the text box. Clicking some items, such as data labels, will select all labels for that data series.

Use the Chart Tools Layout Tab

- Groups on the Chart Tools Layout tab allow you to control many chart elements.

- The Labels group provides buttons for chart elements that act as labels, such as the chart title or the axis titles. Clicking any of these buttons displays a menu of options for turning on or off the label and positioning it. The menu usually also includes a More Options command that opens a dialog box you can use to fine-tune the label format.

- The Axes group buttons let you choose view options for the horizontal and vertical axes and choose how to display the chart's gridlines.

- The Background group buttons control the appearance of the area behind the data series markers. These options vary according to whether the chart is 2-D or 3-D.

- The Analysis group contains buttons that control lines you add to charts to show trends and other lines and bars that help you to analyze plotted data. These options are not available in a 3-D chart.

- As you adjust the chart layout using the buttons on this tab, the chart immediately changes to reflect options you have turned on or off.

PROCEDURES

Select a New Data Source

To copy data from an existing worksheet:

1. Click the chart to select it and display the default Excel chart worksheet.

2. Open the existing worksheet in Excel and select the data to be used for the chart.

   #### Clipboard Group

3. Click **Copy** button
   🗐 . . . . Alt+H, C

4. Display the default chart worksheet and click in cell A1.

5. Click **Paste** button 📋 .

To use Select Data:

1. In Excel, open the workbook from which you want to select data.

2. Click the chart in PowerPoint to select it.

3. Click **Chart Tools Design**
   tab . . . . Alt+J, C

Data Group

4. Click **Select Data** button
   📊 to open the Select Data
   Source dialog box . . . . E

5. Click Collapse Dialog button in Select Data Source dialog box.

6. Display the worksheet from which you want to select data and then select the desired data range.

7. Click the Expand Dialog button to restore the dialog box.

   ✓ *Edit the legend and axis labels if necessary.*

8. Click **OK**. . . . . Enter

Select and Format Parts of a Chart

1. Click the chart to select it.

2. Click **Chart Tools Layout**
   tab . . . . Alt+J, A

   #### Current Selection Group

3. Click **Chart Elements** down arrow and select the chart element to format . . . . E, ↓

4. Click **Format Selection** button
   🖌 . . . . M

5. Click categories at the left side of the dialog box and make selections in the main pane of the dialog box to select formatting options.

6. Click **OK**. . . . . Enter

   OR

1. Click an element on the chart to select it.

2. Click **Chart Tools Format**
   tab . . . . Alt+J, O

   #### Shape Styles Group

3. Use the Shape Styles and WordArt Styles buttons to apply fills, outlines, effects, and text styles.

Control Chart Elements Using the Chart Tools Layout Tab

1. Click the chart to select it.

2. Click **Chart Tools Layout**
   tab . . . . Alt+J, A

3. Click the desired button to add or format a chart element, and then make the desired selection from the button's menu.

EXERCISE DIRECTIONS

1. Start PowerPoint and open ⊙ **10CAFE**. Save the presentation as **10CAFE_xx**.

2. Display slide 3 and insert the following chart data for a 3-D Clustered Column chart:

	Muffin	Bagel	Fruit
Winter	14	16	12
Spring	24	18	8
Summer	28	17	10
Fall	33	21	7

3. Select the chart area and open the Format Chart Area dialog box. Make the following changes to the chart area:

   a. Choose the Picture or texture fill option and insert the picture file ⊙ **10BAGELS**. Change transparency to 30%.

   b. Apply a rounded-corner solid line border, using the color Orange, Accent 6, Darker 50%. Change the line width to 3 pt.

4. Select the Walls element and apply a solid fill of Tan, Background 2. Then select the Floor element and apply the same fill color.

5. Select the legend and apply Tan, Background 2 fill and a shadow effect.

6. Select the vertical axis and format the numbers as currency with 0 decimal places. Add a rotated vertical axis title that reads **In Thousands**.

7. Add a text box near the Fall muffin column that reads **Muffin sales increase after switch to Great Grains**. Format the text box as desired.

8. Display slide 4 and choose to insert a Line with Markers chart that uses the following data:

	Breads	Salads/ Fruits	Hot Foods	Sandwiches
Winter	110	145	195	165
Spring	95	151	174	154
Summer	85	178	105	158
Fall	92	149	134	170

9. Add the chart title **Trends in Food Choices** using the Above Chart option on the Chart Title menu. Then use what you have learned in this exercise to format the chart as desired. You may want to apply an interesting fill such as a picture, texture, or gradient to the chart area; modify the line formats; add a border; adjust the appearance and location of the legend; and so on. Illustration A shows an example of formats you might apply.

10. Analyze the trends in this chart to see what kinds of foods are most popular at particular times of the year. From what you observe, what time of year would be the best time to add cold pasta salads to the café menu? Insert a text box and a line shape on the chart that point out the best time to add these salads.

11. Save your changes, close the presentation, and exit PowerPoint.

Illustration A

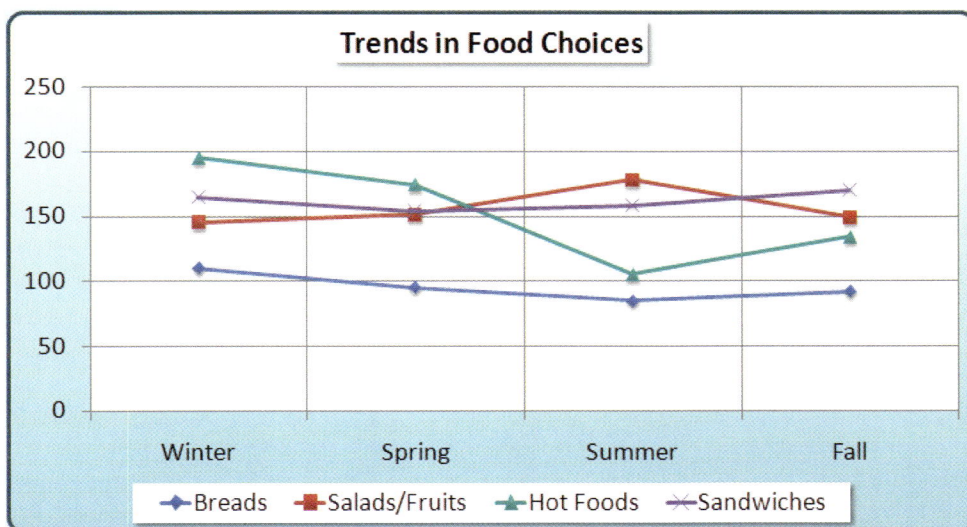

ON YOUR OWN

1. Start PowerPoint and open ⌨️**09EARTH_xx** or open 💿**10EARTH**. Save the presentation as **OPP10_xx**.

2. Add a new slide at the end of the presentation with the Title and Content layout. Insert the title **Revenue by Component**.

3. Choose to insert a 3-D pie chart. After the chart worksheet displays, open the **09RESULTS_xx** Excel worksheet you used in Exercise 9, or open 💿**10RESULTS**. Display the Revenues worksheet.

4. Use Select Data to open the Select Data Source dialog box. Select the range G6:H6. Hold down Ctrl and select the range G9:H9, and then G12:H12. Expand the dialog box if necessary and click OK to update the PowerPoint chart. Close both Excel worksheets.

5. Add data labels to the chart. Format the chart as desired to improve its appearance. Illustration A shows some formatting options. Add a shape or text box that points out some feature of the data.

6. Save your changes, close the presentation, and exit PowerPoint.

Illustration A

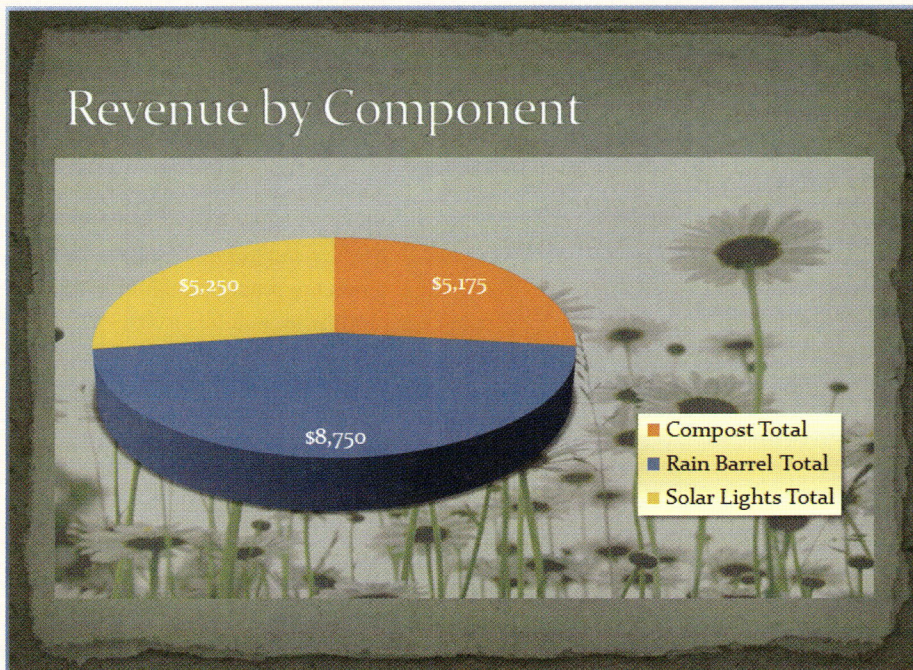

Revenue by Component

- Compost Total
- Rain Barrel Total
- Solar Lights Total

$5,250 · $5,175 · $8,750

Skills Covered

- **Create SmartArt from a Bulleted List**
- **Change Diagram Layout or Category**
- **Modify SmartArt Design and Format**

Software Skills You can create a SmartArt diagram from any bulleted list. Once you have created the diagram, you can change to a different SmartArt category or a different layout in the same category. You can modify design by changing orientation and layout, promoting and demoting shapes, adding bullets to shapes, and even adjusting shape size.

Application Skills In this exercise, you work on a presentation for Thorn Hill Gardens. Thorn Hill wishes to add one or more features to the Gardens to enhance visitor experience. You will prepare two SmartArt diagrams to help the directors identify a decision-making process and set up a team to choose the first new feature for the Gardens.

TERMS

No new terms in this exercise

NOTES

Create SmartArt from a Bulleted List

- If you have created a content slide with bullet items that you think would have more impact as a SmartArt graphic, you do not have to re-enter the text in a new graphic. You can instead simply convert the bulleted items to a graphic.

- Use the Convert to SmartArt Graphic button on the Home tab to display a gallery of graphic layouts you can choose among.

- As you rest your pointer on a layout in this gallery, the bulleted items in your placeholder display in that layout.

- If you do not find a layout you like, click the More SmartArt Graphics command at the bottom of the gallery to open the Choose a SmartArt Graphic dialog box where you have many more choices.

Convert a bulleted list to a graphic

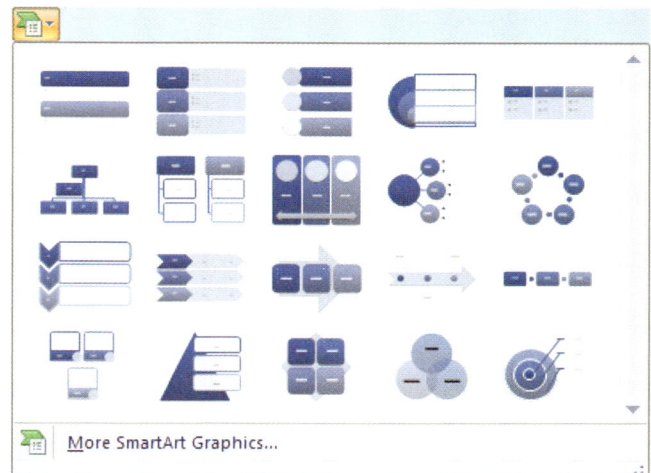

More SmartArt Graphics...

Change Diagram Layout or Category

- SmartArt diagrams are organized according to type: List, Process, Cycle, Hierarchy, Relationship, Matrix, Pyramid.

- Each diagram category offers many different layouts.

- You can easily change a diagram to a different layout of the same category by choosing an option from the Layouts group on the SmartArt Tools Design tab. Making such a change usually does not require any further editing to display the original text in the new layout.

- You can also change a SmartArt diagram from one category to another. When you make this kind of change, text that displayed in one type of diagram may not display correctly in another type. The illustration at the bottom of the page shows what happens when you change a cycle diagram to a relationship diagram.

- The diagram shows only the first shape, and other text is marked with a red X in the Text pane. You can display this text and correct the diagram by demoting any text marked with a red X.

  ✓ *Read more about promoting and demoting in the next section.*

Modify SmartArt Design and Format

- The SmartArt Tools Design and Format tabs provide you with a number of options for fine-tuning a SmartArt diagram.

- The Create Graphic group on the SmartArt Tools Design tab supplies tools for changing the structure of the current graphic.

- Use the Add Shape button to insert another shape in the graphic. Depending on the graphic layout, you have options to add a shape above, below, to the left, or to the right, or add an assistant if you are working with an organization chart.

- The Add Bullet button lets you add a bullet item to an existing bullet list or to a shape that does not ordinarily include a bullet item.

- Use the Right to Left button to change the orientation of the graphic so that objects flip horizontally from one side of the graphic to the other.

- The Layout button is active only for organization charts and allows you to specify how subordinate levels align under higher-level shapes.

- The Promote and Demote buttons let you change the display level of shapes and bullet items.

  - When you demote a shape, it becomes a bullet item.

  - When you demote a bullet item, it is indented to become a second-level bullet item.

  - When you promote a bullet item, it becomes a shape.

  - You usually cannot promote shape items, unless you are working with an organization chart. In an organization chart, you can promote any shape (except the top-level shape) to move it to the next higher organizational level.

- The Shapes group on the SmartArt Tools Format tab gives you additional options for changing the look of a SmartArt diagram.

- Use the Edit in 2-D option to edit a shape in a two-dimensional view (available only if you have applied a three-dimensional style to a graphic).

- Use Change Shape to replace the currently selected shape with a different one from the Shapes gallery.

- Use Larger or Smaller to adjust the size of the selected shape. Be careful when using these options, as you may end up distorting the relationships between shapes in the diagram.

Change one diagram type to another

Type your text here   ✕

- Identify problem
- ✕ Brainstorm solution
- ✕ Try solution 1
- ✕ If not resolved, try next option

Radial Cycle
Anything above marked with a red X will not appear in this SmartArt graphic and will not be saved.
Learn more

Identify problem

PROCEDURES

Create SmartArt from a Bulleted List

1. Select placeholder that contains bulleted items to be used for list.
2. Click **Home** tab . . . . [Alt]+[H]

   Paragraph Group

3. Click **Convert to SmartArt Graphic** button [icon] . . . . [M]
4. Select a layout from the gallery.

   OR

   a. Click **More SmartArt Graphics**. . . . . [M]
   b. Select the desired SmartArt type and layout.
   c. Click **OK** . . . . [Enter]

Change SmartArt Diagram Layout or Category

To change the SmartArt diagram layout:

1. Click the SmartArt graphic to select it.
2. Click **SmartArt Tools Design** tab. . . . . [Alt]+[J], [S]

   Layouts Group

3. Click **More** button [icon] to view all SmartArt layouts for the current category . . . . [L]
4. Select a layout . . . . . [↓], [↑], [←], [→], [Enter]

To change the SmartArt diagram category:

1. Click the SmartArt graphic to select it.
2. Click **SmartArt Tools Design** tab. . . . . [Alt]+[J], [S]

Layouts Group

3. Click **More** button [icon] . . . . [L]
4. Click **More layouts** . . . . [M]
5. Select the desired diagram type, and then select a layout for that type.
6. Click **OK**. . . . . [Enter]

Modify SmartArt Graphic Design and Format

To add a shape:

1. Select a shape near where you want to add the new shape.
2. Click **SmartArt Tools Design** tab. . . . . [Alt]+[J], [S]

   Create Graphic Group

3. Click **Add Shape** button [icon] down arrow . . . . [O]
4. Click one of the choices for adding a shape after, before, above, below, or other option specific to the type of SmartArt graphic.

To delete a shape:

1. Click the shape to delete to select it.
2. Press [Delete].

To add a bullet to a shape:

1. Select a shape that should contain the bullet item.
2. Click **SmartArt Tools Design** tab. . . . . [Alt]+[J], [S]

   Create Graphic Group

3. Click **Add Bullet** button [icon] . . . . [B]

To change diagram orientation:

1. Click in the diagram to select it.
2. Click **SmartArt Tools Design** tab . . . . [Alt]+[J], [S]

   Create Graphic Group

3. Click **Right to Left** button [icon] . . . . [R]

To change layout of organization chart:

1. Click on a higher-level shape.
2. Click **SmartArt Tools Design** tab . . . . [Alt]+[J], [S]

   Create Graphic Group

3. Click **Layout** button [icon] . . . . . . [G]
4. Select the desired layout option:
   - **Standard** . . . . [S]
   - **Both**. . . . . [B]
   - **Left Hanging** . . . . [L]
   - **Right Hanging**. . . . . [R]

To promote or demote a shape or bullet item:

1. Select a shape or click in a bullet item.
2. Click **SmartArt Tools Design** tab. . . . . [Alt]+[J], [S]

   Create Graphic Group

3. Click **Promote** button [icon] . . . . [P]

   OR

   Click **Demote** button [icon] . . . . [D]

To adjust shape size:

1. Click the shape to select it.
2. Click **SmartArt Tools Format** tab. . . . . [Alt]+[J], [O]

   Shapes Group

3. Click **Smaller** button [icon] to reduce size of shape . . . . [D]

   OR

   Click **Larger** button [icon] to increase size of shape . . . . [N]

EXERCISE DIRECTIONS

1. Start PowerPoint and open ◎ **11THORN**. Save the presentation as **11THORN_xx**.

2. Display slide 3 and convert the bulleted list to a Basic Cycle SmartArt diagram. This isn't quite the look you want, so change the layout to Continuous Cycle.

3. Modify the diagram as follows:

   a. Demote the *How much support for new feature?* item so it becomes a bullet on the previous shape, where it belongs.

   b. Add a bullet to the *Vote on* option shape and insert the text **Full Board plus staff**.

   c. Add a new shape after the *Vote on* option shape and insert the text **If no consensus, repeat process**.

   d. Apply a new color scheme (use the Change Colors gallery) and Quick Style of your choice.

4. Add a slide with the Title and Content layout and insert the title **Decision-Making Team**.

5. Insert the Organization Chart SmartArt diagram shown in Illustration A. Then make the following changes:

   a. Promote the Callie Bishop shape.

   b. Change the orientation from right to left.

   c. Select the Ellen Beres shape and then change the layout to Both.

   d. Apply a new color scheme and Quick Style of your choice.

6. Save your changes, close the presentation, and exit PowerPoint.

Illustration A

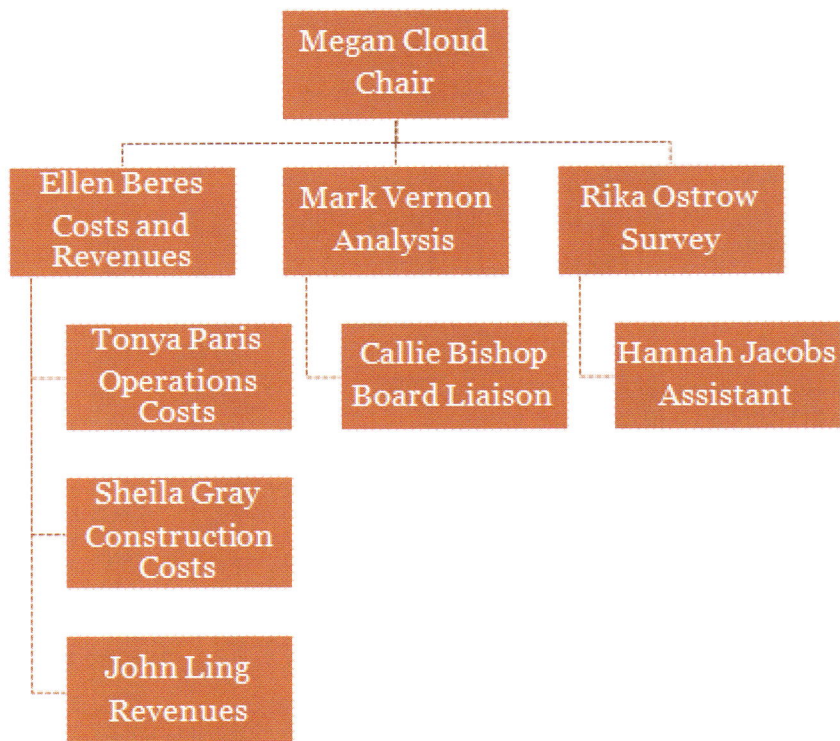

ON YOUR OWN

1. Start PowerPoint and open 🔘 **11PETERSON**. Save the presentation as **OPP11_xx**.

2. Display slide 3 and convert the bulleted list to the Continuous Block Process diagram.

3. This SmartArt type isn't exactly what you want. Make the following changes:

   a. Change the diagram to the Opposing Arrows layout in the Relationship category.

   b. Adjust the text in the Text pane by demoting *Processor speed*, *Built-in security*, and *Networking*. Then demote the three entries below *Down side*.

   c. Select each arrow and click the Smaller button one time to slightly reduce the arrow sizes.

   d. Modify the diagram colors and style as desired. Illustration A shows one option.

4. Convert the bulleted list on slide 4 to the Alternating Flow layout in the Process category. Modify the diagram as follows:

   a. You have forgotten one of the stages: Add a shape after Stage 1 and enter the following text in the Text pane:

      Stage 2

      Hire a contractor

      Work out budget and timeline

   b. Adjust the numbers in the other stages.

   c. Reduce the size of the Stage shapes by clicking the Smaller button twice for each shape.

   d. Modify the diagram colors and style as desired.

5. Save your changes, close the presentation, and exit PowerPoint.

Illustration A

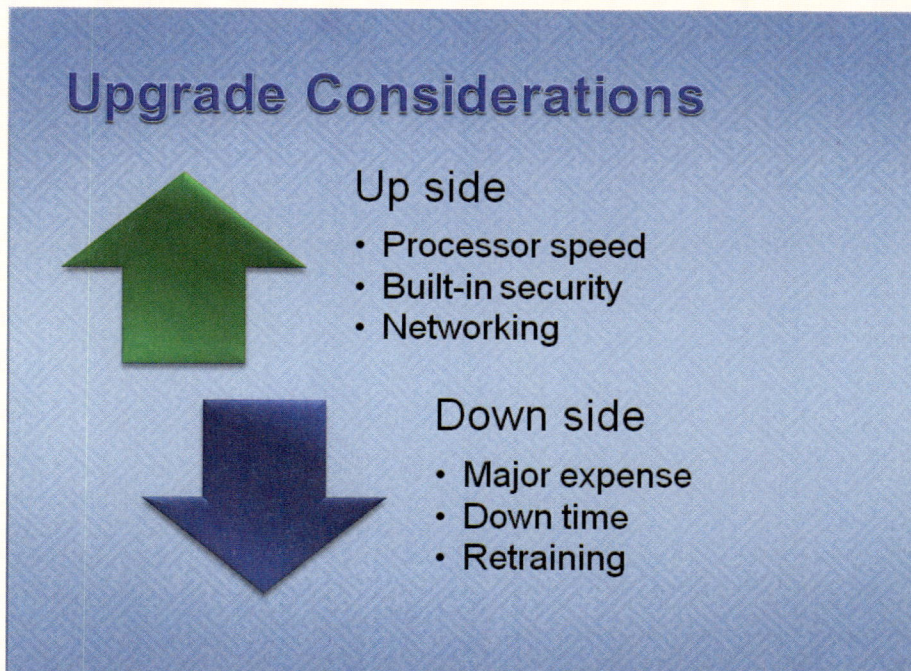

Skills Covered

- **About Picture Formats**
- **Advanced Picture Formatting**
- **Save a Slide as a Picture**

Software Skills Understanding picture formats helps you select an appropriate file type for your presentation. Advanced formatting options such as brightness and contrast adjustments and recoloring options allow you to create sophisticated picture effects. You can save any slide as a picture to use it as an illustration in another Office 2007 application.

Application Skills Thorn Hill Gardens wants to run a presentation on a kiosk at the main entrance advertising the annual Butterfly Show. In this exercise, you add several pictures to a presentation and format pictures according to file type.

TERMS

Bitmap image Graphic created from arrangements of small squares called pixels. Also called raster images.

Lossless compression Compression accomplished without loss of data.

Lossy compression Compression in which part of a file's data is discarded to reduce file size.

Pixel Term that stands for *picture element*, a single point on a computer monitor screen.

Vector image Drawings made up of lines and curves defined by *vectors*, which describe an object mathematically according to its geometric characteristics.

NOTES

About Picture Formats

- PowerPoint 2007 can accept a number of picture formats, including both **bitmap** and **vector** images.
- The table on the following page lists some of the more common formats that PowerPoint supports, with their file extensions.

- Understanding the advantages and disadvantages of these common graphic file formats can help you choose pictures for your presentations.
- For small graphics with a limited number of colors, for example, a picture in GIF or PNG format will be perfectly adequate. Photographs, on the other hand, should be saved in JPG or TIFF format.

Format	Extension	Characteristics
WMF	.wmf	Windows Metafile. Contains both bitmap and vector information and is optimized for use in Windows applications.
PNG	.png	Portable Network Graphics. A bitmap format that supports **lossless compression** and allows transparency; no color limitations.
BMP	.bmp	Windows Bitmap. Does not support file compression so files may be large; widely compatible with Windows programs.
GIF	.gif	Graphics Interchange Format. A widely supported bitmap format that uses lossless compression; maximum of 256 colors; allows transparency.
JPEG	.jpg	Joint Photographic Experts Group. A bitmap format that allows a tradeoff of **lossy compression** and quality; best option for photographs and used by most digital cameras.
TIFF	.tif	Tagged Image File Format. Can be compressed or uncompressed; uncompressed file sizes may be very large. Most widely used format for print publishing; not supported by Web browsers.

- When selecting pictures, you may also want to consider all the ways your presentation might be used. If you plan on displaying it only on a screen or a computer monitor, file formats such as GIF and JPG will provide a good-quality appearance. If you plan to print your slide materials, you may want to use TIFF images for better-quality printed appearance.

- Another consideration when choosing pictures is file size. The higher the picture quality, the larger the presentation's file size. You can modify file size by compressing pictures you have inserted in the presentation. You learn about compressing pictures in Exercise 14.

Advanced Picture Formatting

- The Quick Styles on the Picture Tools Format tab are the easiest way to change the appearance of a picture on a slide.

- Other options on this tab allow you to create interesting and unusual picture effects as well as specify a precise size.

- Use the tools in the Adjust group to modify the appearance of the image. Some of these tools provide menus of preset adjustments so you can quickly apply an adjustment; you may also have the option of opening a dialog box for more control over the adjustment.

- Use the Brightness menu to adjust the lightness of the image. You can choose a brightness from the menu or use the Picture Corrections Options command to open the Format Picture dialog box, discussed later in this section.

- Use the Contrast menu to adjust the difference between light and dark areas of an image. Select from preset options or open the Format Picture dialog box for more control over contrast.

- The Recolor tool allows you to apply current theme colors to the selected image to create a special effect. Select a color in the Recolor gallery to use in the recoloring process.

- You can also select the Set Transparent Color command on this gallery to make one of the image's colors transparent.

- When you click this command, a paintbrush icon attaches to the pointer. Click on the color you want to make transparent, as shown at left in the following illustration. All pixels of that color are removed to allow the background to show through, as shown at the right. You can make only one color transparent in a graphic.

Click a color to make transparent (left) and the background shows through (right)

- Use the Compress Pictures option to reduce the file size of pictures embedded in a presentation. You will learn more about this option in Exercise 14.

- The Change Picture option reopens the Insert Picture dialog box so you can replace the currently selected picture with a different one.

- Use the Reset Picture option to restore a picture's original settings. Clicking this button reverses any changes you have made to size, brightness, contrast, or color.

- The Picture Correction Options command on the Brightness and Contrast menus opens the Format Picture dialog box.

Format Picture dialog box

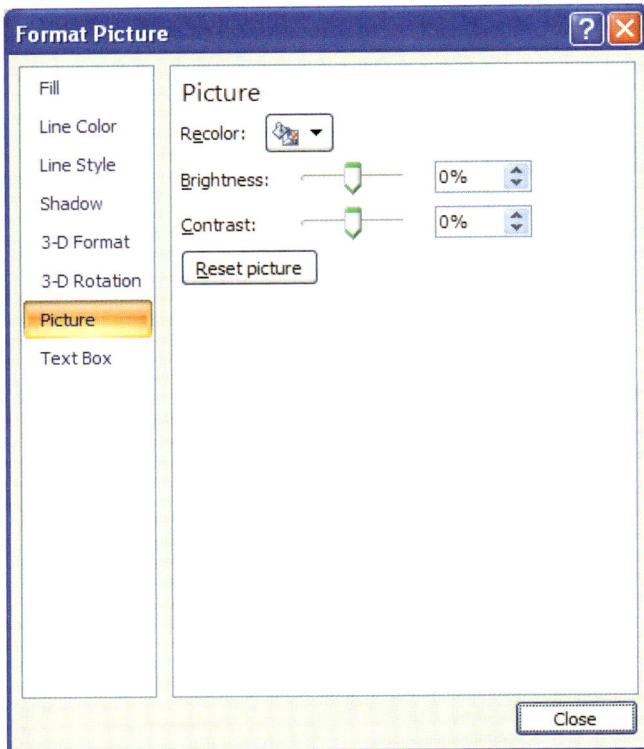

- You can use this dialog box to make a number of adjustments at one time to brightness, contrast, and color, or you can reset the picture to its original appearance.

- Note that this dialog box gives you a number of other options as well for modifying fill, border, and effects such as shadow and three-dimensional rotation.

Save a Slide as a Picture

- PowerPoint slides are generally graphically interesting, with sophisticated layouts and colors. You can save a single slide or an entire presentation in a graphic file format that allows you to insert the slides as pictures in other applications, such as Word documents.

- Use the Save As dialog box to select the format in which you want to save the slide(s), as shown in the following illustration.

Save slides as pictures

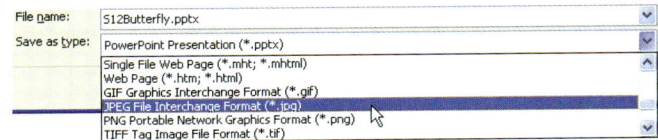

- You can choose among seven picture file formats. Once you have provided a name for the new file, selected a format, and issued the Save command, PowerPoint displays a dialog box to ask if you want to save only the current slide or every slide in the current presentation.

- The resulting files can be used just like any other picture file.

PROCEDURES

Advanced Picture Formatting

To adjust brightness and contrast:

1. Click the picture to select it.
2. Click **Picture Tools Format** tab . . . . `Alt`+`J`, `P`

   Adjust Group

3. Click **Brightness** button

   ☼ . . . . `B`

   OR

   Click **Contrast** button

   ◑ . . . . `N`

4. Select a preset brightness or contrast option . . . . `↓`, `Enter`

   OR

   a. Click **Picture Corrections Options**. . . . . `C`
   b. Drag the Brightness or Contrast slider, or use spin arrows to adjust the percentage of change.
   c. Click **Close** . . . . `Enter`

To recolor a picture:

1. Click the picture to select it.
2. Click **Picture Tools Format** tab . . . . `Alt`+`J`, `P`

Adjust Group

3. Click **Recolor** button

   . . . . `E`

4. Select from the Color Modes, Dark Variations, or Light Variations options . . . . `↓`, `↑`, `←`, `→`

   OR

   a. Click **More Variations**. . . . `M`
   b. Select a theme color or color from Standard Colors palette, or click More Colors to select a color from Colors dialog box.
5. Press `Enter`.

To set transparent color:

1. Click the picture to select it.
2. Click **Picture Tools Format** tab. . . . . `Alt`+`J`, `P`

   Adjust Group

3. Click **Recolor** button

   . . . . `E`

4. Click **Set Transparent Color** . . . . `S`
5. Click on the color on the image to make transparent.

To reset a picture to its original appearance:

1. Click the picture to select it.
2. Click **Picture Tools Format** tab . . . . `Alt`+`J`, `P`

   Adjust Group

3. Click **Reset Picture** button

   . . . . `Q`

Save a Slide as a Picture

1. Display the slide to save, if desired.
2. Click **Office Button** . . . `Alt`+`F`
3. Click **Save As** . . . . `A`
4. Type a name for the saved slide(s).
5. Click **Save as type** . . . . . . `Alt`+`T`
6. Select the desired picture format . . . . `↓`
7. Click **Save** . . . . `Alt`+`S`

Business Connection

Interviewing Skills

A job interview may only last 15 to 20 minutes, but it might be the only chance you get to convince the employer that you are right for the job. There are ways you can prepare for an interview so that you are ready to make the most of your face to face opportunity. You can learn about the company so you can speak knowledgably and ask appropriate questions. You can prepare and bring documents such as your resume, a cover letter, your portfolio, and examples of your achievement. And, you can practice interviewing so that you can feel comfortable when you are in the real situation.

The Art of the Interview

Imagine you are a career counselor advising people on how to identify and obtain a job. One thing you can do is teach them how to prepare for a job interview, and how to conduct themselves during the interview. Create a presentation that you could show to your clients, describing skills that they should cultivate in order to succeed at an interview. Include information about what to expect at the interview, how to prepare for an interview, and how to act during the interview. Proofread and preview the presentation and make corrections as necessary. Prepare handouts, and practice delivering the presentation to an audience. When you are ready, deliver the presentation to the class. At the end of the presentation, select someone from the audience and act out an impromptu job interview using the information you included in your presentation.

EXERCISE DIRECTIONS

1. Start PowerPoint and open ⊚ **12BUTTERFLY**. Save the presentation as **12BUTTERFLY_xx**.

2. On slide 1, insert the JPEG data file ⊚ **12BUTTERFLY1**. Format the picture as follows.
   a. Crop 1.5 inches from the left side of the picture so that it is 4.5 by 4.5 inches square.
   b. Scale the picture to 75% and then apply the Soft Edge Oval picture style. Center the picture below the subtitle.
   c. Recolor the picture using the Accent color 3 Light option.

3. Display slide 2 and recolor the clip art picture using Accent color 1 Light.

4. The resulting clip isn't very exciting. Reset the picture to its original appearance, then make the bright orange color transparent. Reapply the Accent color 1 Light color for a more subtle effect.

5. Display slide 3, and insert the JPEG picture file ⊚ **12BUTTERFLY2** in the content placeholder.

6. Format the picture as follows:
   a. Adjust brightness to make the picture 10% brighter. Adjust contrast to +30%.
   b. Apply the Drop Shadow Rectangle picture style. Your slide should look similar to Illustration A.

7. Display slide 4, and insert the JPEG picture file ⊚ **12BUTTERFLY3** in the content placeholder. Adjust contrast to +25%. Apply the Drop Shadow Rectangle picture style.

8. Save slide 3 as a picture with the JPG format and name it **12SLIDE3_xx**.

9. Save your changes, close the presentation, and exit PowerPoint.

Illustration A

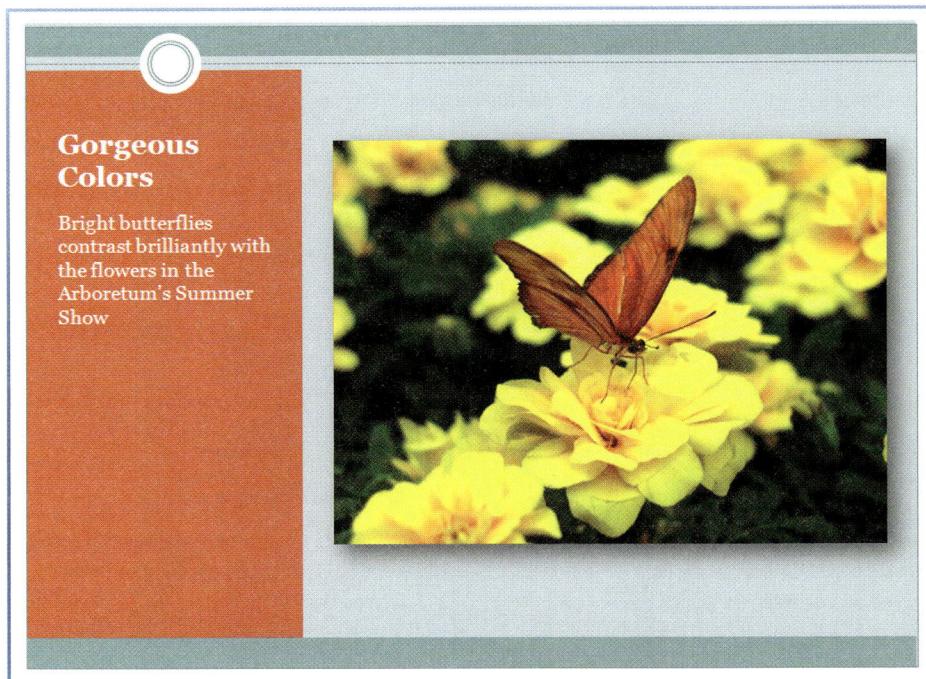

646

ON YOUR OWN

1. Open ⌨ **OPP11_xx** or 💿 **12PETERSON**. Save the presentation as **OPP12_xx**.

2. Insert a clip art on slide 1 and make one of the colors in the clip transparent to integrate the picture better on the slide.

3. Select a picture to appear on slide 2. You may use clip art files, your own picture files, or free pictures on line. Consider the graphic file format of the picture you choose to make sure it will display the picture well.

4. Modify the picture as necessary: you may adjust brightness and contrast for a special effect or recolor the picture. If desired, apply a picture style to the picture. Illustration A shows one option.

5. Save your changes, close the presentation, and exit PowerPoint.

Illustration A

Skills Covered

- **About Multimedia Presentations**
- **Advanced Movie Options**
- **Advanced Sound Options**

Software Skills   To make a presentation "come alive," use multimedia content such as animation, movies, and sounds. Media clips can add considerable impact to a presentation as well as convey information in ways that other graphic objects cannot.

Application Skills   Voyager Adventure Travel is beginning the task of adding a new hiking package to their list of adventures. The decision-making process requires consideration of both pros and cons for each suggested venue, and you have been asked to prepare a slide show to present the information. In this exercise, you will begin work on the presentation with pros and cons for Glacier National Park.

TERMS

Multimedia   Presentation of information using a variety of media such as text, still images, animation, video, and audio.

NOTES

About Multimedia Presentations

- **Multimedia** presentations display information in a variety of media, including text, pictures, movies, animations, and sounds.

- Multimedia content not only adds visual and audio interest to slides but also presents information in ways that plain text cannot. A simple picture can convey an image that would take many words to describe; likewise, a movie can show a process or sequence of events that might take many pictures to convey.

- You can choose how much or how little multimedia content to include in a presentation. A simple style might use only still pictures and PowerPoint animations in addition to text to add multimedia interest. A more complex style might include text, pictures, movies, and sounds that you control using custom animation options.

  ✓ *You learn more about custom animation options in Lesson 3.*

- When deciding on multimedia options for a presentation, you must consider the trade-off between multimedia impact and the presentation's file size. Multimedia files such as videos and sounds can be quite large.

- You also need appropriate computer resources, such as speakers and video or sound cards to play media files successfully.

- Use good research standards when locating multimedia content. Always request permission to use materials you may find on the Internet, or follow directives for crediting persons or agencies. When creating a presentation for personal use, you can use CD music tracks for background sound, but you should not use such copyrighted materials if you plan to sell your presentation or publish it on the Web.

- If you decide to include multimedia content in a presentation, you will find that PowerPoint offers a number of options for playing both movies and sounds.

Advanced Movie Options

- In PowerPoint, a *movie* can mean one of two things: an animated clip art graphic or an existing movie file saved in a standard video format.

- Use one of these options to insert a movie on a slide:
  - Click the Insert Media Clip icon in any content placeholder to insert an existing movie file.
  - Click the Movie button on the Insert tab to insert a movie file.
  - Click the Movie button's down arrow to display a menu and choose either Movie from File or Movie from Clip Organizer.

- Choosing the Movie from Clip Organizer option opens the Clip Art task pane with available animated graphic movie files displayed in the results area and Movies already selected as the media type.

- You can search for movies using keywords just as when searching for other types of clip art. A search for movies related to the keyword *butterfly* returns the files shown in the illustration at right.

- Note the small star symbol at the lower-right corner of each thumbnail. This symbol signifies the file is animated.

- Insert an animated graphic movie the same way as any other clip art object, by clicking it in the task pane. Most animated graphic movies are fairly small and some cannot be enlarged without loss of quality.

- To see the animation in motion, display the slide in Slide Show view.

- If you choose to insert an existing movie file, the Insert Movie dialog box opens to allow you to navigate to the location of the file.

Locate an animated graphic movie in the Clip Art task pane

- The following table lists some of the common video formats PowerPoint can handle.

- You need to understand video formats to determine the quality of video clips you intend to insert. A file in MPEG1 format, for example, is not likely to display with the same quality as an MPEG2 file, but it will be smaller in size.

- Likewise, you need to know that PowerPoint does not support some popular video formats, such as QuickTime or RealMedia files.

- Once you have selected and inserted a video clip, you can use the tools on the Movie Tools Options tab to work with a movie. (See the illustration on the following page.)

Format	Extension	Characteristics
ASF	.asf	Advanced Streaming Format. Microsoft's streaming format that can contain video, audio, slide shows, and other synchronized content.
AVI	.avi	Audio/Video Interleave. A file format that stores alternating (interleaved) sections of audio and video content: widely used for playing video with sound on Windows systems; AVI is a container (a format that stores different types of data), not a form of compression.
MPEG	.mpg, .mpeg	Moving Picture Experts Group. A standard format for lossy audio and visual compression that comes in several formats, such as MPEG1 (CD quality) and MPEG2 (DVD quality).
WMV	.wmv	Windows Media Video. Microsoft's lossy compression format for motion video; it results in files that take up little room on a system.

- Use the Preview button in the Play group to preview the movie while in Normal view.
- The Movie Options group gives you more control over how the movie plays during the presentation.
  - Use the Slide Show Volume option to control the movie's volume if it includes sound.
  - Change the play setting using the Play Movie list. You can play the movie automatically, when clicked, or set the movie to continue playing as you continue to display later slides.
  - You can choose to hide the movie during the show, play it at full screen size, loop it (play it over and over) until you stop it by pressing Esc, or return the movie to its first frame after it has finished playing.
- Use the Arrange tools to adjust the order or alignment of the movie object relative to other objects on the slide.
- Use the Size controls to adjust the height and width of the movie object. Be careful when doing so that you don't distort the movie images.
- The Picture Tools Format tab is also active when a movie object is selected. You can apply picture formats such as borders and effects to a movie object to further enhance it.
- When you insert a movie file on a slide, you establish a link from the file to the presentation. For this reason, you should store movie files in the same folder as the presentation and insert the file from that folder so PowerPoint will know where to find the file during the presentation.

  ✓ *If you find that a movie will not play or does not appear on a slide during a presentation, the link has probably been broken by moving the presentation or the movie file from its previous location. To reestablish it, reinsert the movie object from a known file location.*

Advanced Sound Options

- Use the Sound button on the Insert tab to choose what kind of sound to insert:
  - Sound from File allows you to select an existing sound file using the Insert Sound dialog box. This process is similar to inserting an existing movie file.

- Sound from Clip Organizer opens the Clip Art task pane with all available sound files displayed and the Sounds media type selected. You can search for a sound by keyword just as you search for clip art or movies.
- Play CD Audio Track lets you play one or more tracks from a CD in your computer's CD or DVD drive. Choosing this option opens the Insert CD Audio dialog box, where you can choose the track to start and end with and set the amount of time to play the track. You can also choose to loop the audio, adjust its volume, and hide the sound icon if desired.

Insert CD Audio dialog box

- Use the Record Sound option to record your own sound or music for the slide.
- The sound file can be in any of a number of standard sound formats. The following table shows some of the common sound formats PowerPoint can handle.

Format	Extension	Characteristics
AU	.au	Unix Audio. A format frequently used for sound clips on the Internet; can play on Windows, Mac, and other operating systems.
MIDI	.mid	Musical Instrument Digital Interface. MIDI files contain commands that instruct synthesizers to recreate passages of music.
MP3	.mp3	MPEG Audio Layer 3. Most popular format for storing music using a lossy compression.
WAV	.wav	Wave Form. Standard format for storing high-quality uncompressed sounds; because they are not compressed, these files can be very large.
WMA	.wma	Windows Media Audio. Microsoft format used to distribute sound files, typically music, on the Internet.

■ Choosing a sound file requires some knowledge of these common formats. For example, when you see the .mid file extension, you should understand that the file will play synthesized music.

■ When selecting a sound file, you should also consider that sound files may be either embedded on the slide or linked to the slide. Only WAV files smaller than the maximum sound file size (100 KB by default) will be embedded on the slide. All other file formats, and WAV files larger than the maximum file size, will be linked to the slide. This means you will have to make sure that the sound file you insert is stored in the same folder with the presentation.

✓ *To reestablish a link to a sound file, move the sound file to the same folder with the presentation and reinsert the sound file from that location.*

■ Note that the sound files that display in the Clip Art task pane are all WAV files, and some are considerably larger than the 100 KB maximum for embedding.

■ To make sure these files continue to play correctly no matter where the presentation is viewed, you can copy the file to your Clip Organizer. It will then be available to copy to the folder that contains your presentation.

■ Use the Sound Tools Options tab to control sound options.

■ Many of these options look similar to those on the Movie Tools Options tab and operate in the same way. You can use Preview to listen to the sound in Normal view, for example, and use the Sound Options group tools to hide the sound icon, loop the sound, or adjust the play setting.

■ The Max Sound File Size setting in the Sound Options group determines whether a sound file will be embedded or linked to the slide. You can adjust the maximum file size, but be aware that if you allow for larger WAV files to be added to the presentation, you may increase its file size significantly.

■ If you choose to play a CD track on a slide, you use the CD Audio Tools Options tab to control how the track plays. You can have the track play across a series of slides, for example, rather than on a single slide.

Sound Tools Options tab

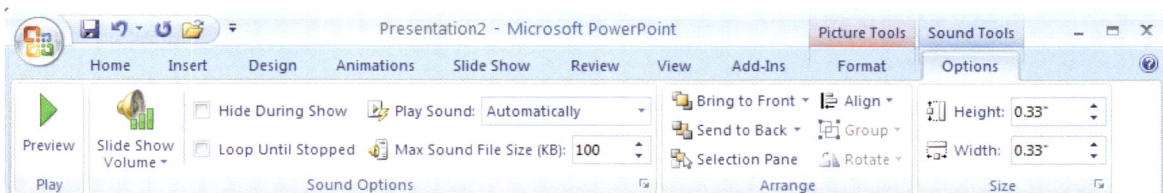

PROCEDURES

Insert a Movie

To insert an animated graphic movie:

1. Click **Insert** tab . . . . Alt + N

   Media Clips Group

2. Click **Movie** button 🎞 V
3. Click **Movie from Clip Organizer** . . . . M
4. In the Clip Art task pane, type a keyword in the Search for box.
5. Click the Search in down arrow and select collections to search.
6. Click **Go** to begin search . . . . Enter
7. Click animated graphic file from the search results to insert the movie on the slide.

To insert an existing movie file:

1. Click **Insert Media Clip** button 🎞 in any content placeholder.

   OR

   a. Click **Insert** tab . . . . . Alt + N

      Media Clips Group

   b. Click **Movie** button 🎞 . . . V
   c. Click **Movie from File** . . . . F
2. Navigate to the location where the file is stored and select the file.
3. Click **OK** . . . . Enter
4. Choose how to play the movie:
   - Click **Automatically** to start the movie when the slide displays . . . . A
   - Click **When Clicked** to start the movie when you click it C

To control movie options:

1. Click the movie object to select it.
2. Click **Movie Tools Options** tab . . . . Alt + J, N
3. Select options on this tab to control the movie as desired.

Insert Sounds and Music

To insert a sound from the Clip Organizer:

1. Click **Insert** tab . . . . Alt + N

   Media Clips Group

2. Click **Sound** button 🔊 . . . . . . O
3. Click **Sound from the Clip Organizer** . . . . S
4. In the Clip Art task pane, type a keyword in the Search for box.
5. Click the Search in down arrow and select collections to search.
6. Click **Go** to begin search . . . . . Enter
7. Click sound file from the search results to insert the sound icon on the slide.
8. Choose how to play the sound:
   - Click **Automatically** to play the sound when the slide displays . . . . A
   - Click **When Clicked** to play the sound when you click the sound icon C

To insert an existing sound file:

1. Click **Insert** tab . . . . Alt + N

   Media Clips Group

2. Click **Sound** button 🔊 . . . . . . O
3. Click **Sound from File** . . . . F
4. Navigate to the location where the file is stored and select the file.
5. Click **OK** . . . . Enter

6. Choose how to play the sound:
   - Click **Automatically** to start the sound when the slide displays . . . . A
   - Click **When Clicked** to start the sound when you click it C

To make a clip art sound file available offline:

1. Right-click the sound thumbnail in the Clip Art task pane.
2. Click **Copy to Collection** . . . . . Y

   OR

   Click **Make Available Offline** . . . . A
3. Select the folder in the Clip Organizer where you want to store the sound clip.
4. Click **OK** . . . . Enter
5. Click **Organize clips** in the Clip Art task pane.
6. Select the folder that you specified in step 3.
7. Right-click on the sound clip and select **Copy** C
8. Navigate to the folder that contains your presentation.
9. Right-click in the folder and select **Paste**.

   ✓ After saving a sound clip to a specific folder, use the Sound from File option to insert the clip on the slide.

To control sound options:

1. Click sound object to select it.
2. Click **Sound Tools Options** tab . . . . Alt + J, N
3. Select options on this tab to control the sound as desired.

EXERCISE DIRECTIONS

1. Start PowerPoint and open ⊚ **13VOYAGER**. Save the presentation as **13VOYAGER_xx**.

2. On slide 3, insert the JPEG file ⊚ **13GOAT**. Format as follows:
   a. Crop the picture to show only the mountain goat and part of the background around it. Then resize the picture to be about 2.1 inches high.
   b. Flip the image horizontally and recolor using the Accent color 1 Light option.
   c. Move the image to the upper-right corner of the slide.

3. Display slide 5. Save the MPEG movie file ⊚ **13FIRE1** to your solutions folder, and then insert it from that location in the content placeholder on slide 5. Choose to play the movie automatically.

4. Format the movie as follows:
   a. Move the movie up slightly to insert more space between the bottom of the movie and the credit information.
   b. Choose to play the movie at full screen size.
   c. Apply a picture format of your choice to the movie. Illustration A shows one option.

5. Display slide 6 and insert the JPEG file ⊚ **13FIRE2**. Move the picture above the caption and then format the picture as desired.

6. Add a sound clip to slide 6 as follows:
   a. Choose to insert a sound from the Clip Organizer.
   b. Search using the keyword *helicopter* to locate the sound of a helicopter flyover. Rest the mouse pointer on each thumbnail to see file sizes, and then right-click a file that is larger than 100 KB in size.
   c. Make the sound file available offline and copy it to your solutions folder. Rename it appropriately, such as **13HELICOPTER_xx**.
   d. Insert the sound file on slide 6, and choose to have it play automatically.
   e. Move the sound icon off the slide so it will not display when you show the slides. Set the sound file to play across slides, so it will play from slide 6 to slide 7.

7. Display slide 7 and insert the JPEG file ⊚ **13FIRE3**. Format the picture to match other images in the presentation.

8. View the slides in Slide Show view to see the movie and hear the sound.

9. Save your changes, close the presentation, and exit PowerPoint.

Illustration A

2003 Fires in Glacier

Credit: NASA/Goddard Space Flight Center
Scientific Visualization Studio, Jeff Schmaltz, Jacques Descloitres

ON YOUR OWN

1. Open 12BUTTERFLY_xx or 13BUTTERFLY. Save the presentation as OPP13_xx.

2. Locate a sound or music file that complements the information in your presentation. You may use a sound effect or a music file. If you choose a music file, decide whether you want the music to play on a single slide or across multiple slides. If the sound file is large, copy it to your solutions folder.

3. Locate clip art animated graphics of butterflies and add several to the slides throughout the presentation. Illustration A shows a butterfly animated graphic added to the title slide.

4. View your slides in Slide Show view to check sound and movie settings.

5. Save your changes, close the presentation, and exit PowerPoint.

Illustration A

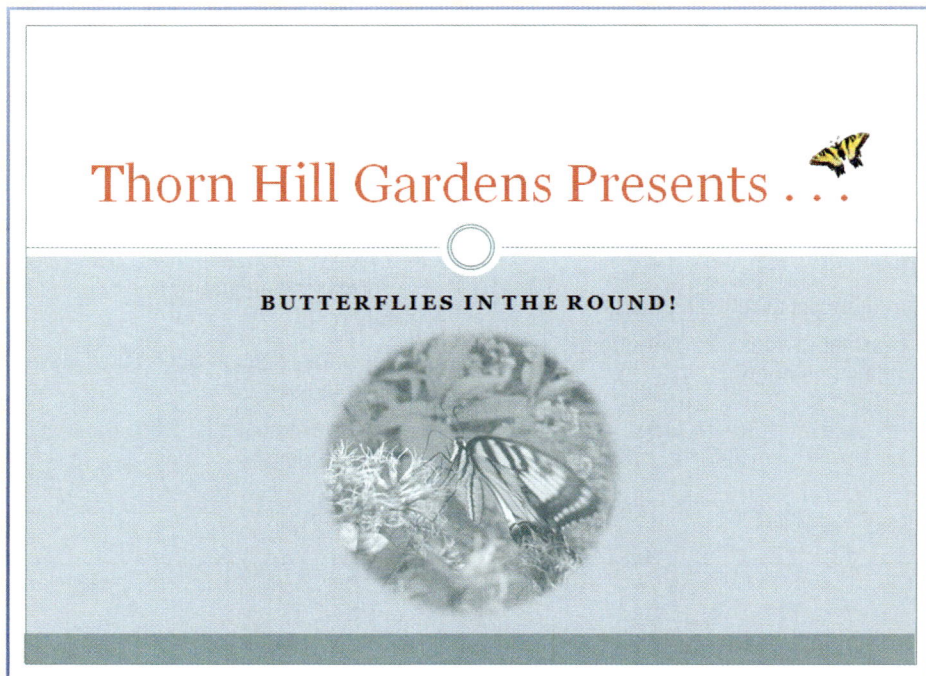

Thorn Hill Gardens Presents . . .

BUTTERFLIES IN THE ROUND!

Skills Covered

- **Create a Photo Album**
- **Compress Pictures**

Software Skills   PowerPoint's Photo Album feature makes it easy to create a presentation that consists of illustrations and their captions. You can arrange the photos in a number of layouts and apply enhancements such as frames and other effects. To reduce file size of a presentation, you can compress pictures.

Application Skills   Voyager Adventure Travel has decided to approve the Glacier National Park hiking adventure and wants you to create a photo album of Glacier Park images to present at a travel show.

TERMS

Resolution   The number of dots or pixels per linear unit of output. For example, a computer monitor's resolution is usually 72 pixels per inch.

NOTES

Create a Photo Album

- PowerPoint's Photo Album feature allows you to collect pictures and then create a new presentation to display those pictures as an album.

- A PowerPoint photo album is just like a physical photo album in that it is designed primarily to showcase images. You can add text in the form of captions or text boxes, but the focus of a photo album is on the pictures.

- Use the Photo Album button on the Insert tab to begin creating a new photo album.

- The Photo Album dialog box is where you choose pictures for the album and select settings for the way the pictures will display.

Photo Album dialog box

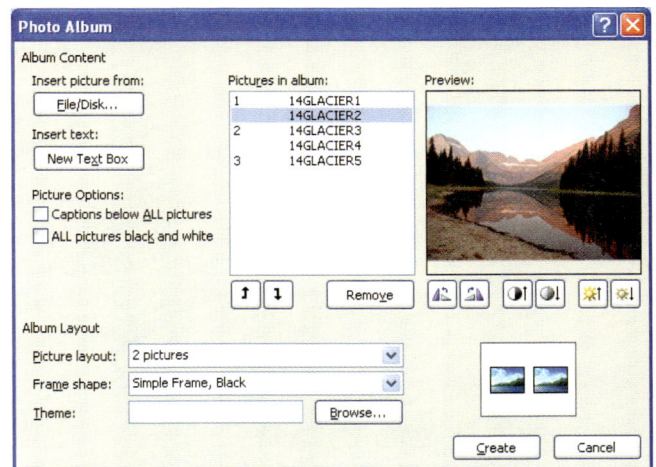

- Selected picture file names display in the Pictures in album list in the center of the dialog box. The currently selected picture displays in the Preview area.

- You can choose to add a text box to the list of pictures. Text boxes display according to the current picture layout, at the same size as the pictures. If you have chosen to lay out the album with two pictures per page, for example, you can insert a text box in the place of one of those images so that you have a picture and a text box on the same slide.

- You can adjust the order of pictures or remove a selected picture. Use the buttons below the preview to flip the picture horizontally or vertically, adjust its contrast, or adjust its brightness.

- The Picture Options check boxes allow you to add a caption to each picture or transform all pictures to black and white. By default, the captions that display use the picture's file name, but you can replace these captions with more descriptive ones on the slides.

- The Album Layout area gives you a number of options for formatting the album.
  - Select from seven different picture layout options, including the Fit to slide option that displays each picture the full size of the slide; options to display one, two, and four pictures per slide; and options to display varying numbers of pictures with slide titles. As you select one of these layout options, the small preview at the right shows your choice.
  - Choose from seven different frame options, from a simple black frame to shadow and soft edge effects.
  - Select one of PowerPoint's default themes, or another available theme, to format the album.

- Once you are satisfied with the list of pictures and the settings, you create the album. PowerPoint places the chosen pictures in a new presentation that includes a title slide with a default title and the current user name in the subtitle.

- You save the photo album like any other Power-Point presentation.

- The following illustration shows how a new photo album looks in Slide Sorter view.

A photo album in Slide Sorter view

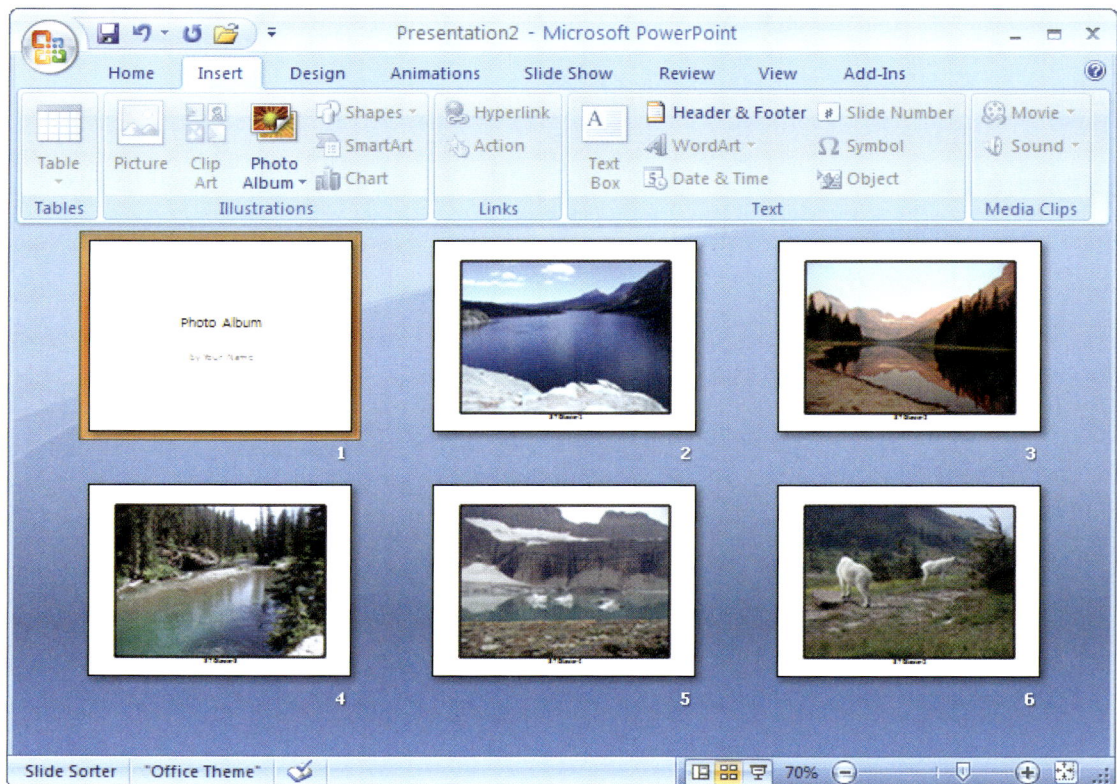

- You can edit an existing photo album by displaying it in Normal view and then clicking the down arrow on the Photo Album button. Choosing Edit Photo Album opens the Photo Album dialog box. After you make changes, click the Update button to apply your changes to the album.

- If you did not choose a theme in the Photo Album dialog box, you can apply one at any time to the presentation.

Compress Pictures

- A photo album—or any presentation that contains pictures, movies, or sounds—can turn into a large file that may be a challenge to store or take extra time to open.

- To streamline a presentation's file size, use the Compress Pictures option on the Picture Tools Format tab.

- Clicking this button opens the Compress Pictures dialog box.

Compress Pictures dialog box

- By default, PowerPoint will compress all pictures in the presentation. If you want to compress only a selected picture or pictures, click the Apply to selected pictures only check box.

- For more control over the compression settings, click the Options button to display the Compression Settings dialog box.

Compression Settings dialog box

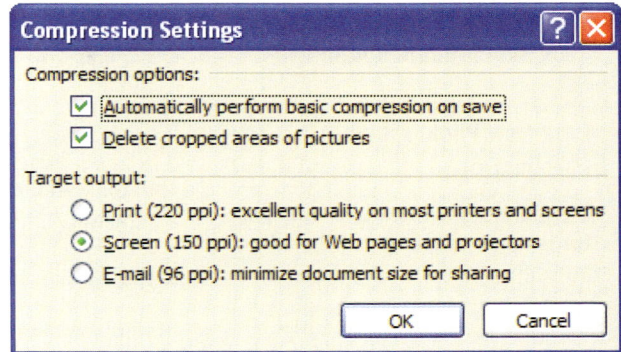

- Note that by default PowerPoint compresses pictures automatically when the file is saved.

- If you have cropped pictures to hide areas you don't want to see, you can choose to delete the cropped portions of the pictures. Once you do this, of course, you cannot go back and uncrop a picture.

- The Target output settings allow you to choose a **resolution** appropriate for the way the pictures will be viewed. Measurements for the resolution are given in ppi, pixels per inch.

- If the slides will eventually be printed, use the Print setting for the best quality. Slides that will be viewed on a screen will look fine at the Screen setting. Use the E-mail setting to reduce file size so a presentation will transmit quickly.

PROCEDURES

Create a Photo Album

1. Click **Insert** tab . . . . `Alt`+`N`

   Illustrations Group

2. Click **Photo Album** button

   . . . . `A`

3. Click **New Photo Album** . . . . . `A`

4. Click **File/Disk** . . . . `Alt`+`F`

5. Navigate to the location of the pictures you want to use in the album and select one or more pictures.

6. Click **Insert** . . . . `Alt`+`S`

   ✓ *Repeat step 6 until all pictures are inserted.*

7. Click **Create** . . . . `Alt`+`C`

To change the order of pictures in the album:

In Photo Album or Edit Photo Album dialog box:

1. Select a picture in the **Pictures in album** list . . . `Alt`+`R`, `↓` or `↑`

2. Click `↑` to move picture up in the list.

   OR

   Click `↓` to move picture down in the list.

To remove a picture from the album list:

In Photo Album Edit Photo Album dialog box:

1. Select a picture in the **Pictures in album** list . . . `Alt`+`R`, `↓` or `↑`

2. Click **Remove** . . . . `Alt`+`V`

To specify picture options:

In Photo Album or Edit Photo Album dialog box:

- Click **Captions below ALL pictures** check box . . . . `Alt`+`A`

   ✓ *This option is not available for the Fit to slide picture layout.*

- Click **ALL pictures black and white** . . . . `Alt`+`K`

To specify a layout for the album:

In Photo Album or Edit Photo Album dialog box:

1. Click **Picture layout** down arrow . . . . `Alt`+`P`, `↓`

2. Select the desired layout . . . . `↓`, `Enter`

To specify frame options:

In Photo Album or Edit Photo Album dialog box:

1. Click **Frame shape** down arrow . . . . `Alt`+`M`, `↓`

2. Select the desired frame option . . . . `↓`, `Enter`

To specify a theme:

In Photo Album or Edit Photo Album dialog box

1. Click **Browse** . . . . `Alt`+`B`

2. Choose a theme . . . . `↓`, `↑`, `←`, `→`

3. Click **Select** . . . . `Enter`

Edit a Photo Album

1. Click **Insert** tab . . . . `Alt`+`N`

   Illustrations Group

2. Click **Photo Album** button

   . . . . `A`

3. Click **Edit Photo Album** . . . . . . `E`

4. Modify settings in Photo Album dialog box as desired.

5. Click **Update** . . . . `Alt`+`U`

Compress Pictures

1. Select any picture in a presentation, or select only the pictures you want to compress.

2. Click **Picture Tools Format** tab . . . . `Alt`+`J`, `P`

   Adjust Group

3. Click **Compress Pictures** button

   . . . . `M`

4. Click **OK** . . . . `Enter`
   to compress all pictures in the presentation.

   OR

   a. Click **Apply to selected pictures only** . . . . . . `Alt`+`A`

   b. Click **OK** . . . . `Enter`

To specify compression settings:

In Compress Pictures dialog box:

1. Click **Options** . . . . `Alt`+`O`

2. Select compression options:

   - **Automatically perform basic compression on save** . . . . `Alt`+`A`

   - **Delete cropped areas of pictures** . . . . `Alt`+`D`

3. Select target output settings:

   - **Print (300 ppi)** for slides that will printed . . . . `Alt`+`P`

   - **Screen (150 ppi)** for slides that will be viewed on a monitor or other screen . . . . `Alt`+`S`

   - **E-mail (96 ppi)** for slides that will be sent via e-mail . . . . `Alt`+`E`

4. Click **OK** . . . . `Enter`

5. Click **OK** . . . . `Enter`

EXERCISE DIRECTIONS

1. Start PowerPoint and choose to begin a new photo album.

2. Select the following JPEG files for the album:
   ◉ **14GLACIER1**, ◉ **14GLACIER2**, ◉ **14GLACIER3**, ◉ **14GLACIER4**, and ◉ **14GLACIER5**.

3. Make the following changes in the dialog box:
   a. Make sure the pictures are listed from 1 to 5, and then move **14GLACIER2** below **14GLACIER3** in the picture list.
   b. Choose the 1 picture layout.
   c. Choose any frame option.
   d. Choose to set captions below all pictures.

4. Create the album.

5. On the title slide, change the title to **Voyager Travel Adventures Presents**. Change the subtitle to **Glacier National Park**.

6. View the slides in Slide Show view to see the pictures in the album.

7. The captions do not add much to the album. Choose to edit the album and turn off captions for all slides. Then select the Center Shadow Rectangle frame option and update the photo album.

8. Apply the Concourse theme to the title slide only.

9. View your album again in Slide Show view to check your final settings. Your first picture slide should look similar to Illustration A.

10. Compress all pictures in the presentation for screen output.

11. Save the presentation as **14GLACIER_xx**, close the presentation, and exit PowerPoint.

Illustration A

ON YOUR OWN

Create a photo album of places in your city, town, or neighborhood. Before you begin this exercise, take pictures using a digital camera, scan existing pictures, or locate pictures on the Internet that you can save to your computer. Try to find or create at least five pictures.

1. Start PowerPoint and begin a new photo album.
2. Insert your pictures in the album and arrange them in an attractive way.
3. Select the number of pictures per slide and decide whether or not to add captions. You may also want to add text boxes to allow you to insert explanatory text.
4. View the completed album and change captions if desired.
5. Edit the photo album to choose a different frame style.
6. Edit the title slide to use your name and an appropriate title. Apply a theme if desired. Illustration A shows a sample layout for one slide.
7. Save the presentation as **OPP14_xx**.
8. View your slides in Slide Show view to check your pictures.
9. Save your changes, close the presentation, and exit PowerPoint.

Illustration A

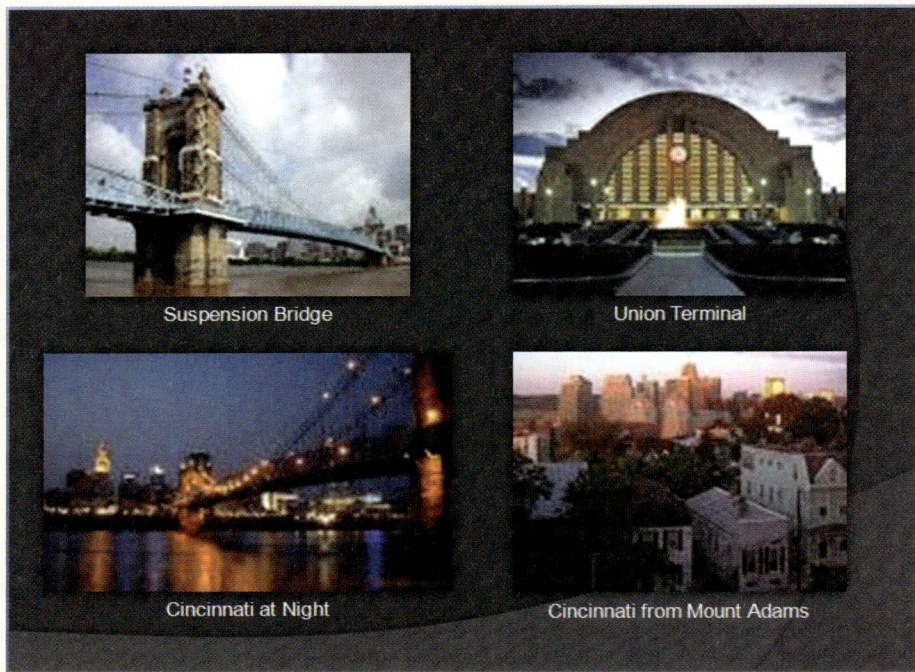

Suspension Bridge

Union Terminal

Cincinnati at Night

Cincinnati from Mount Adams

Exercise | 15

Critical Thinking

Application Skills   Restoration Architecture has reserved a booth at a regional home and garden show and wants to show a presentation that details work on a Victorian house in an urban neighborhood. You have been asked to begin work on this presentation, which will include pictures, a table, a SmartArt diagram, and a chart.

EXERCISE DIRECTIONS

1. Start PowerPoint and open ⊙ **15RESTORATION**. Save the presentation as **15RESTORATION_xx**.

2. On slide 1, customize the background as follows: Insert the JPEG file ⊙ **15BACKGROUND**, adjust the left and right offsets slightly so the picture covers the entire slide, and change transparency to 65%.

3. Display slide 2 and Slide Master view. Then open the ⊙ **15ARCHIVE** presentation and copy the Restoration Architecture logo from slide 2. Close **15ARCHIVE**. Paste the logo on the slide master and choose to use the destination theme.

4. Close Slide Master view. Still on slide 2, insert the JPEG file ⊙ **15BEFORE**. Adjust brightness to 30% and contrast to 60% and apply a picture style of your choice.

5. On slide 3, format the slide background as follows:
   - Choose a picture background and then locate a clip art file of new construction (use the keyword *house*) or another suitable picture.
   - Adjust transparency so the picture doesn't obscure the text, and then recolor the picture as desired to create a pleasing effect.

6. On slide 4, insert a 3-D column chart that uses data from the range A4:D8 of the ⊙ **15PRICES** data file. You may if desired copy this data to the chart worksheet. If you do not copy the data, you will need to do some editing of the legend entries and the category axis labels to display the chart data correctly.

7. Format the chart as follows:
   a. Add the chart title **Average Sales by Year**. Add the vertical axis title **In Thousands**.
   b. Move the legend to the bottom of the chart and format as desired.
   c. Add a text box above the Westwood columns that reads **Sales in Westwood slow to recover**. Format the text box as desired.
   d. Apply a gradient fill and a border to the chart area, using colors of your choice.

8. On slide 5, draw the table shown in Illustration A and add the text as shown. Adjust cell alignments as desired and apply a Quick Style. Then select the three Year columns and add the background JPEG image ⊙ **15PAINT**. Use the Format Shape dialog box (click the Drawing group dialog box launcher on the Home tab) and tile the picture as a texture. Adjust the size and position of the picture as necessary to fill the cells completely, and change transparency so type is easily readable.

9. On slide 6, in the left placeholder, convert the bulleted list to a Basic Cycle SmartArt diagram.

10. The Basic Cycle layout isn't quite what you want. Modify the diagram as follows:
   a. Change the diagram to the Staggered Process layout in the Process category.
   b. Change orientation from right to left. Add a bullet to the third shape that reads **See picture at right**.
   c. Reduce the size of each downward-pointing arrow, and then format the diagram as desired.

11. Still on slide 6, insert the JPEG file 🔘 **15GUTTER**, and format the picture with the same style you used for the picture on slide 2.

12. Open the data file 🔘 **15ROOFING** in Excel. On slide 7, use Paste Special to embed the data in the range A1:C9. Then adjust the embedded object as follows:

    a. Delete the content placeholder on the slide.

    b. Open the embedded worksheet for editing and delete row 5.

    c. Use the SUM function to total the values in columns B and C, and then format the Total row as desired.

    d. Increase the size of the worksheet container so that its width is about 8.2 inches.

13. On slide 8, insert the JPEG file 🔘 **15FINAL**. Adjust brightness and contrast as desired to improve the picture's appearance and apply the same picture style used for other pictures.

14. Compress all pictures in the presentation to Screen resolution.

15. Locate an appropriate music clip in Clip Art files and insert the clip on slide 1. Set it to play across slides.

16. Save your changes, close the presentation and all other files, and exit PowerPoint and Excel.

Illustration A

Scope of Work

Restoration Architecture

		Year 1	Year 2	Year 3
Critical Tasks	Lead abatement – interior and exterior	X		
	Roofing repairs	X		
	Removal of decrepit garage	X		
	Exterior repair and paint	X	X	
	Interior plaster and paint	X	X	X
	Floor refinishing		X	X
	HVAC and plumbing	X		X
	Landscaping		X	X

Curriculum Integration

Application Skills Many of us have heard of the theory of relativity, but not so many of us can explain what it means or why it is important. You have been asked to prepare a presentation to explain Einstein's theories of relativity and explore the concept of light speed. Before you begin this exercise, do some research to locate:

- One or more pictures of Albert Einstein that you can download and save to your computer.

- Explanations (simple!) of both the special theory of relativity and the general theory of relativity. (Wikipedia has a good explanation.)

- A video clip in an appropriate video file format that relates to the solar system, the sun, or the universe in some way. You can find excellent video clips of this type at the Scientific Visualization Studio on the Goddard Space Flight Center Web site.

EXERCISE DIRECTIONS

Begin a new presentation. You may use a blank presentation or use one of PowerPoint's online presentation templates. Save the presentation with an appropriate name, such as **16RELATIVITY_xx**. Insert an appropriate title and subtitle on the first slide.

Modify the slide masters if desired to customize backgrounds, fonts, and colors. You may also want to customize bullets.

Add a slide to explain the basics of special relativity. Use one of the pictures of Einstein you downloaded and modify and format the picture as required to improve its appearance.

Add a slide that explains the consequences of special relativity, one of which is the mass-energy equivalence (the famous equation $e = mc^2$).

Add a slide to explain the basics of general relativity. Insert a second picture of Einstein if you have one and format it attractively.

Add a slide that spells out the meaning of the famous equation. On this slide, insert the video clip you downloaded. You may want to customize the slide background to blend the clip into the slide. Be sure to add a credit for the site from which you downloaded the clip.

Add a slide on which you draw a table that shows speeds of various fast things, such as a human runner over 100 meters, the fastest land animal, the fastest bird, the speed of sound, and the speed of light. Include several measuring systems in the table, such as miles per hour and meters per second, and convert speeds when practical. Illustration A shows an example. Customize the table by adding a picture or texture.

Save changes to the presentation and close it. Exit PowerPoint.

Relative Speeds

		Miles/hour	Miles/sec	Meters/sec
A S O F 2 0 0 8	Fastest human runner, 100 m	23.1	0.006	10.32
	Fastest bird — Flying (merganser)	80	0.022	36
	Fastest bird — Diving (peregrine)	217	0.060	97
	Fastest animal (cheetah)	70	0.019	31
	Fastest commercial aircraft currently flying (Boeing 747)	567	0.157	253
	Sound through air	770	0.214	344
	Light through a vacuum		186,282	299,792,458

Relativity and All That

Lesson | 3

Advanced Presentation Features

Skills Covered

- **Advanced Animation Options**
- **Change or Remove an Animation**

Software Skills Animating slides is another way to add multimedia interest to a presentation. Using custom animation options, you can add entrance, emphasis, and exit effects, as well as move an object along a path. Use advanced features to trigger animations and delay effects. Change or remove an animation at any time.

Application Skills Natural Light has asked you to add animations to a presentation that will be available in the showroom for visitors to browse. In this exercise, you work with a number of custom animation options.

TERMS

Path A line or shape on a slide that an object will follow when a Motion Path animation is applied to the object.

NOTES

Advanced Animation Options

- PowerPoint makes it easy to animate objects using built-in animations from the Animate list on the Animations tab. For advanced animation effects, however, you use the Custom Animation task pane.

- Options in the Custom Animation task pane allow you to select individual parts of an object to animate, to apply special effects such as hiding an object after animating it, to adjust timing so that an effect occurs just when you want it to, and to set an animation so that it occurs when you click on another object on the slide.

Work with the Animation List

- Each type of animation effect has its own symbol, such as the green star for entrance effects and the red star for exit effects. These symbols help you identify in the animation list what kinds of effects are applied to objects.

- This can be especially helpful if you assign more than one kind of effect to an object. In the following illustration, for example, an entrance, emphasis, and exit effect have been applied to one WordArt placeholder. The symbols make it easy to check that the effects are in the correct order.

Multiple effects applied to one object

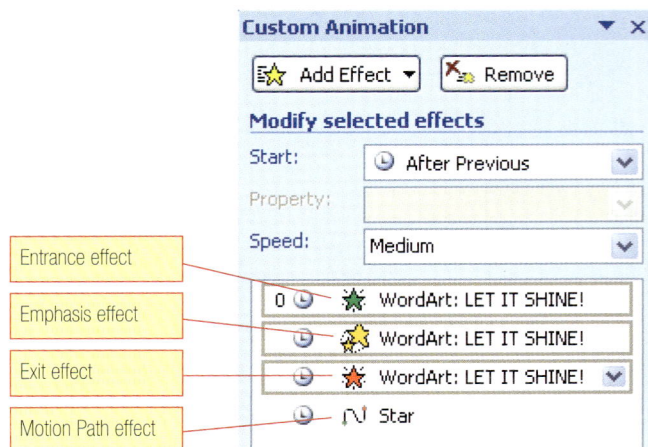

■ If the object you are animating has more than one line or part, such as a text content placeholder or a chart or diagram, a bar displays below the effect with a Click to expand contents arrow, as shown at left in the following illustration. Clicking the arrow displays all the parts of the object, as shown at the right. You can then select each part of the object to apply custom animation settings.

Expand an effect to see all parts

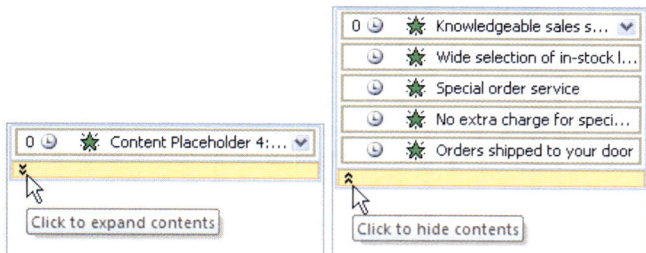

■ When you have finished animating the parts, use the Click to hide contents arrow to collapse the effect and save room in the animation list.

Create a Motion Path Animation

■ Motion path animation allows you to specify a **path** along which an object will travel.

■ The path may be one of a number of straight lines, such as Diagonal Down Right, Left, or Up, or you can draw a custom path using the Line, Freeform, Curve, or Scribble tool.

■ You can also click More Motion Paths on the Motion Paths submenu to open a dialog box where you can select from many shape options, such as stars, arcs, loops, and spirals.

Motion path options

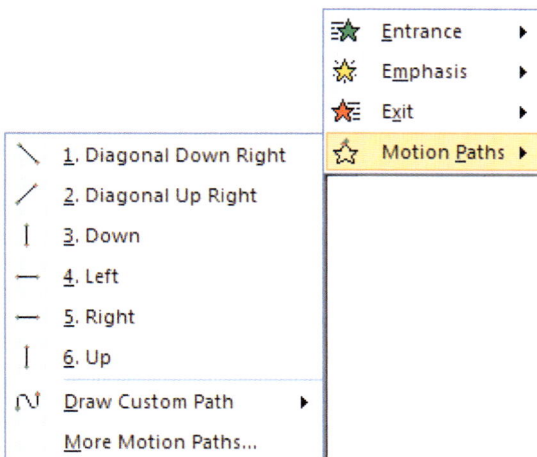

■ After you choose the motion path, the object and the path display as shown in the illustration below. The dotted line represents the path, and the red arrow and line represent the end of the path, the point at which animation stops.

■ You can adjust the motion path if it is not in the right position or the right duration.

● Move the mouse pointer on top of the red arrow to display a four-headed mouse pointer, then drag to move the path. It will maintain its direction or shape as you move it.

● Click on the path to display handles at each end of the path. You can then click on a handle to adjust the position of the red arrow. Use this method to move one end of the path while leaving the other in place, or to shorten or lengthen the path.

Motion path for an object

Advanced Effect Options

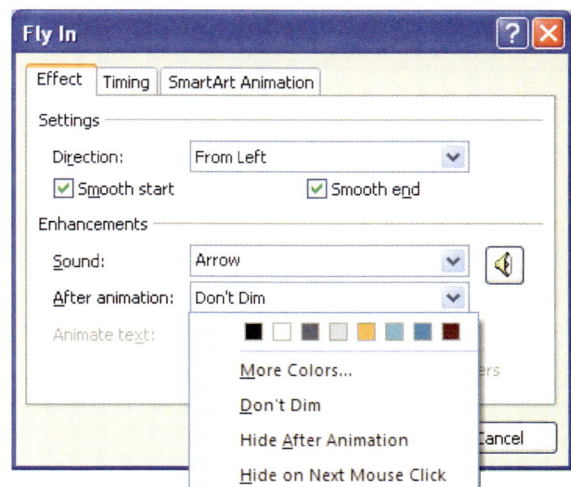

■ The Effect tab in the Effect Options dialog box for an animation offers a number of special effects you can apply to an object. The effects available depend on the type of object being animated. The following illustration shows effects available when animating a shape.

Advanced effects

- You can adjust the direction of the animation and choose Smooth start and Smooth end to control how the object starts and stops during the animation.

- All animation types allow you to select a sound effect from the Sound list to accompany the effect.

  ✓ *Use sound effects sparingly; it can be distracting to hear the same sound effect over and over when multiple parts of an object are animated.*

- The After animation palette shown in the previous illustration gives you a number of options for emphasizing or deemphasizing an object after the animation ends. You can hide the object after the animation, hide it the next time you click the mouse, or change its color.

- If the animated object contains text, the Animate text settings become active, allowing you to animate the text all at once, by word, or by letter, and set the delay between words or letters.

Advanced Timing Options

- All Effect Options dialog boxes include a Timing tab such as the one shown in the following illustration.

Timing options

- Use the Delay setting to specify an amount of time that must elapse before the animation begins. This feature allows you to control exactly when an animation takes place.

- You can also adjust the speed and apply a repeat setting to replay the animation a specific number of times or until the next click or the next slide displays.

- Use the Rewind when done playing option to return the object to its original position or state. If you have a picture fade into view, for example, the Rewind setting will remove it from the slide after the animation finishes.

- You can also specify a trigger for an animation—an object on the slide that you click to start the animation. In the previous illustration, the object is set to animate when the slide title is clicked.

- Using triggers is one way to make a slide show interactive. In the next exercise, you will learn another way to create an interactive presentation using links and action settings.

Display the Timeline

- Refining animation timings can require some effort, especially if you need to keep displaying the Timing dialog box to adjust delays and effect durations.

- PowerPoint offers another option to help you control timing of effects. The Show Advanced Timeline command on the effect menu displays a timeline like the one in the following illustration.

Advanced timeline

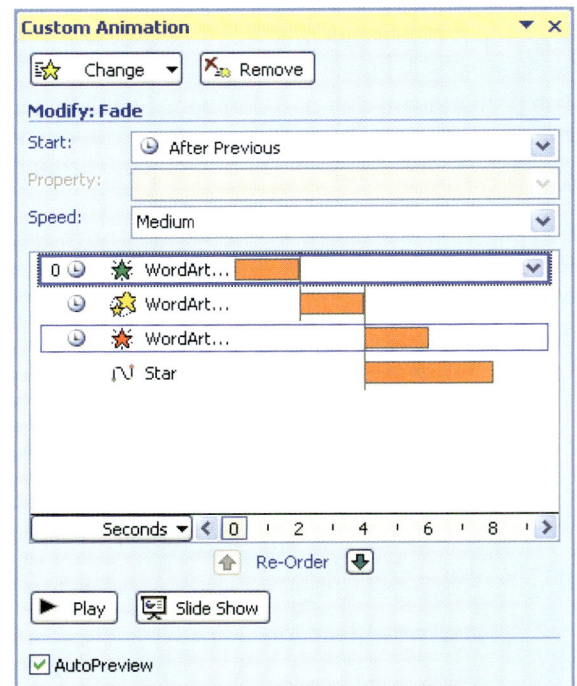

- The orange bars indicate the duration of each effect and when it starts relative to other effects. In the previous illustration, for example, the emphasis effect starts after the entrance effect and the exit effect starts after the emphasis effect, so there is no overlap. The motion path effect applied to the Star object starts at the same time as the exit effect because it uses the With Previous start option.

■ The timeline includes a seconds gauge at the bottom of the task pane. You can use this gauge to see the duration of each effect as well as the overall duration of all animations on the slide.

■ You can use the timeline to set a delay or adjust the length of an effect or double-click an orange bar to open the Timing dialog box for further adjustments. When you are finished with the timeline, you can hide it again.

Change or Remove an Animation

■ You may find that a particular animation option isn't giving you the effect you want. You can use the Change button on the Custom Animation task pane to display the list of effect types just as when you use the Add Effect button to start a custom animation.

■ You can also click the Remove button to delete the effect entirely.

PROCEDURES

Animate Separate Parts of an Object

1. Click effect in animation list in the Custom Animation task pane to select it.
2. Click **Click to expand contents** ⊗.
3. Select each effect in the list and apply custom animation settings as desired.
4. Click **Click to hide contents** ⊗ to hide contents.

Create a Motion Path Animation

1. Select the object to which to apply the animation.
2. Click **Add Effect** in the Custom Animation task pane.
3. Click **Motion Paths** . . . . [P]
4. Select a motion path from the submenu.

   OR

   a. Click **Draw Custom Path**. . [D]
   b. Select a drawing tool option:
      ■ **Line** . . . . [L]
      ■ **Curve** . . . . [C]
      ■ **Freeform** . . . . [F]
      ■ **Scribble** . . . . [S]
   c. Draw the desired path.

   OR

   a. Click **More Motion Paths** . . . . [M]
   b. Select a motion path shape.
   c. Click **OK** . . . . [Enter]

To adjust a motion path:

■ Click the motion path to select it and drag the path to a new position.

   OR

1. Click the motion path to select it.
2. Position the mouse pointer over one of the path's sizing handles and drag to adjust the position of the sizing handle.

Apply Advanced Effect Options

1. In the Custom Animation task pane, click the down arrow of an effect in the effects list.
2. Click **Effect Options** . . . . [E]
3. Choose any of the effects on the Effect tab listed below, then click **OK** . . . . [Enter]

To add a sound to an effect:

In the Effect dialog box:

1. Click **Sound** list arrow . . . . [Alt]+[S], [↓]
2. Select the desired sound . . . . . [Enter]

To apply an effect after animation ends:

In the Effect dialog box:

1. Click **After animation** list arrow . . . . [Alt]+[A], [↓]
2. Choose any of the options on the palette:
   ■ Select a color to apply to the object after animation.
   ■ Click **Hide After Animation** . . . . [A]
   ■ Click **Hide on Next Mouse Click** . . . . [H]

To animate text:

In the Effect dialog box:

1. Click **Animate text** list arrow . . . . [Alt]+[X], [↓]
2. Choose any of the options on the palette . . . . [Enter]
   ■ **All at once**
   ■ **By word**
   ■ **By letter**
3. For By word or By letter, set a value for the percent delay between word or letters.

Apply Advanced Timing Options

1. In the Custom Animation task pane, click the down arrow of an effect in the effects list.
2. Click **Timing** . . . . [T]
3. Choose any of the options listed below, then click **OK** . . . . [Enter]

To choose a start option:

1. Click **Start** list arrow . . . . [Alt]+[S], [↓]
2. Select the desired start option . . . . [↑], [↓], [Enter]

To set a delay:

1. Click **Delay** . . . . [Alt]+[D]
2. Type a delay value.

   OR

   Use spin arrows to set delay in 0.5 second intervals.

To set a speed:

1. Click **Speed** list
   arrow . . . . [Alt]+[E], [↓]
2. Select the desired speed
   option . . . . [↑], [↓], [Enter]

To set a repeat:

1. Click **Repeat** list
   arrow . . . . [Alt]+[R], [↓]
2. Select the desired repeat
   interval . . . . [↑], [↓], [Enter]

To rewind after animation:

- Click **Rewind when done
  playing** . . . . [Alt]+[W]

To set a trigger:

1. Click **Triggers** . . . . [Alt]+[T]
2. Select the desired trigger option:
   - **Animate as part of click
     sequence** . . . . [Alt]+[A]
   - **Start effect on click
     of** and then click down arrow
     and select object that will act
     as trigger . . . . [Alt]+[C]

Work with the Advanced Timeline

To display the timeline:

1. In the Custom Animation task
   pane, click the down arrow of an
   effect in the effects list.
2. Click **Show Advanced
   Timeline** . . . . [S]

To adjust duration of effect:

- Position the mouse pointer on the
  right edge of an orange bar and
  drag left or right.

To set a delay:

- Position the mouse pointer on
  the left edge of an orange bar and
  drag to the right.

  OR

- Click on an orange bar and drag
  the entire bar to the right.

Change or Remove an Animation

To change an animation effect:

1. Select effect to be changed in effects list.
2. In the Custom Animation task
   pane, click **Change**.
3. Select a new effect and adjust it as
   desired.

To remove an animation effect:

1. Select text or object from which to
   remove animation.
2. In the Custom Animation task
   pane, click **Remove**.

EXERCISE DIRECTIONS

1. Start PowerPoint and open 🔵 **17LIGHT**. Save the
   presentation as **17LIGHT_xx**.

2. On slide 1, select the Star object. Apply the Flicker
   emphasis effect (you may need to use More Effects
   to locate this effect). Change the start option to After
   Previous and the Color to the lighter blue in the palette.
   Choose to repeat the effect until the next mouse click.

3. Still on slide 1, apply a Dissolve In entrance effect to
   the title and subtitle. Use With Previous for the title to
   animate it along with the star. Use After Previous for the
   subtitle. Change the color of the title to black after the
   animation.

4. Display slide 4 and apply animation effects as follows:
   a. Set the Sales placeholder to fly in from the left, After
      Previous, Fast, with a smooth end.
   b. Expand the placeholder effect, select the Sales text
      object, and change the effect to a Fade entrance ef-
      fect, After Previous.
   c. Select the content placeholder below the Sales object
      and fade the text into view After Previous.
   d. Apply the same settings to the Service placeholder
      that you applied to the Sales placeholder, but fly the
      shape in from the right.
   e. Apply the same settings to the content placeholder
      below Service as to the other content placeholder.
   f. Delay the start of the Service placeholder by 1.5
      seconds.

5. Display slide 5 and apply a Fly In entrance animation to the SmartArt graphic, After Previous, Fast, From Left. Then modify the animation effects as follows:

   a. Change the SmartArt Animation option in the Effect Options dialog box to One by one, and then expand the effect to see all the shapes that make up the diagram.

   b. Using the timeline, adjust duration and delay of each shape so that a viewer has time to read the Step 1 shape before the first bulleted shape appears, read the text in this shape before the Step 2 shape appears, and so on. Use the Play button and Slide Show button to test your delays until you are satisfied with the results.

6. On slide 6, set a trigger to animate the picture with a Wipe entrance effect, from Top, Fast, when the slide title is clicked. Then animate the picture description with a Fade effect so it displays after the picture.

7. On slide 7, apply to the WordArt object the Fade entrance effect, the Grow/Shrink emphasis effect, and the Fade exit effect, with settings of your choice.

8. Optional: Create a motion path effect for the Star object so that the star moves to the center of the slide after the WordArt object exits.

9. Run the presentation to check all effects, and then adjust them as necessary.

10. You're not certain the effects applied to the presentation title are working. Remove the animation effects from both the title and subtitle.

11. Save your changes, close the presentation, and exit PowerPoint.

ON YOUR OWN

1. Open 🔘 **17EARTH**. Save the presentation as **OPP17_xx**.

2. On slide 1, add a motion path animation to the logo to bring it down above the center of the title. Adjust timing as necessary to make the movement smooth.

3. Also on slide 1, apply a Fade entrance effect to the title and choose to animate the text by word with a 20% delay between words. Animate the subtitle as desired.

4. On slides 3 and 5, apply entrance or emphasis effects to the tables.

5. On slide 5, select the orange outline object that surrounds the Total Expenses amount. Animate the shape with an entrance effect (you may want to set a delay before this animation to allow the audience to understand the worksheet), and then apply the Blink emphasis effect. Repeat the Blink effect several times to draw attention to the total expenses.

6. On slide 6, apply an Ease Out exit effect to the logo and an Ease In entrance effect to the photo. Adjust the effects so that they are taking place at the same time, with the photo coming into view as the logo moves off the slide.

7. On slide 7, animate the chart with an entrance effect that displays each month as a group. Expand the effect. Animate each monthly values text box and move these animations to follow the appearance of the month's data series, so that the monthly total displays immediately after the month's columns.

8. Apply entrance and emphasis effects to the Profit text box to draw attention to it. You may also want to add a sound effect such as Applause.

9. Animate the chart on slide 8 as desired.

10. Save your changes, close the presentation, and exit PowerPoint.

Skills Covered

- **Advanced Hyperlink Options**
- **Work with Action Settings**

Software Skills   Hyperlinks and action settings can be used to create interactive presentations that allow viewers to jump to different locations in the presentation, open other presentations or Web sites, send an e-mail message, run programs, or interact with objects on the slide.

Application Skills   Peterson Home Health Care is starting the process of training employees on Microsoft Office 2007 after the installation of the new network and workstations. In this exercise, you will begin work on a presentation that employees can access from their own computers to learn more about Microsoft Office 2007. You will create links and action items to make it easy for employees to interact with the training materials.

TERMS

Action   A setting that performs a specific action, such as running an application or jumping to a specific slide.

Target   The slide, show, file, or page that will display when you click a link on a slide.

NOTES

Advanced Hyperlink Options

- Adding links to slides can make a presentation more interactive. Use a link to jump instantly from one slide to another, to a custom show in the current presentation, or to a different presentation.

- You can use links to move from a presentation to another application to view data in that application. This is an easy way to view Microsoft Excel data during a presentation, for example, if you do not want to insert the Excel data on a slide.

- If the computer on which you are presenting the slides has an active Internet connection, you can also use a link to jump from a slide to any site on the Web.

- You can set up a link using text from a text placeholder or any object on the slide, such as a shape or picture. After you select the object for the link, you use the Hyperlink button on the Insert tab to open the Insert Hyperlink dialog box.

- The Insert Hyperlink dialog box allows you to select the **target** of the link—the slide, show, file, or page that will display or the page that will open when the link is clicked.

Choose the target of the link

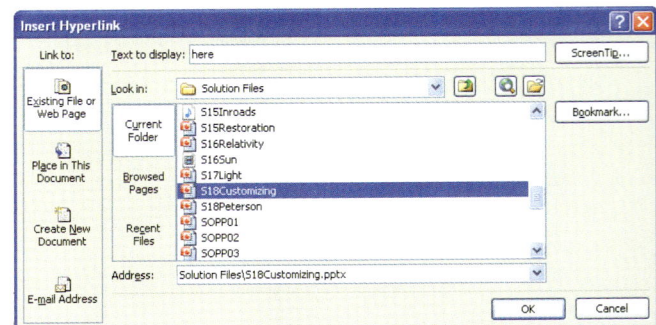

- You have four target options to choose from.

- Existing File or Web Page lets you locate a file on your system or network. After you select the file, its path displays in the Address box near the bottom of the dialog box, as shown in the previous illustration.

- You can also use the Browse the Web button to open your browser. After you navigate to the page you want to use as your target, return to PowerPoint. The Web page address will automatically appear in the Address box.

- Place in This Document lets you select a slide or custom show from the current presentation. As you click a slide for the target, it displays in the Slide preview area.

- Create New Document allows you to specify the name of a new document and link to it at the same time. PowerPoint creates the document according to the file extension you use when you specify the file name. If you create a file with the name Results.xlsx, for example, Excel opens so you can enter data in the Results workbook.

- The E-mail Address option lets you link to an e-mail address. You might use this option when setting up a presentation to be viewed by an individual on his or her own computer. Clicking the link opens the default e-mail program to send a message to the specified e-mail address.

- If you want to provide a little extra help to a viewer about what will happen when a link is clicked, you can provide a ScreenTip.

Specify a ScreenTip for a link

- Microsoft Office 2007 programs are very security conscious. When you link to a target outside the current presentation, PowerPoint may display a security warning dialog box to ask if you want to open the target. If you trust the target, you can answer yes to this warning.

Work with Action Settings

- Another way to control what happens during a presentation is to create **actions** that perform specific chores.

- Like links, actions allow you to link to a slide in the current presentation, a custom show, another presentation, a Web page URL, or another file.

- Actions are most commonly associated with action buttons, shapes you select from the Shapes gallery and draw on a slide to perform specific chores. You can insert an action button designed to display the first or last slide of a presentation when clicked, for example.

- You have a number of other options for applying actions, however.

  - You can use an action to run a program or macro. For instance, you can attach an action to a shape so that when you click the shape, a program such as Excel starts.

  ✓ *You may have to respond to a security warning the first time you run a program.*

  - You can use an action to control an object you have inserted on the slide. The object must be inserted using the Insert Object dialog box; you can create a new object or use an existing file. If you use an existing file, you can choose in the Insert Object dialog box to display the object as an icon on the slide.

  - You can use an action setting to play a sound effect or sound file.

- Click the Action button in the Links group on the Insert tab to open the Action Settings dialog box.

Action Settings dialog box

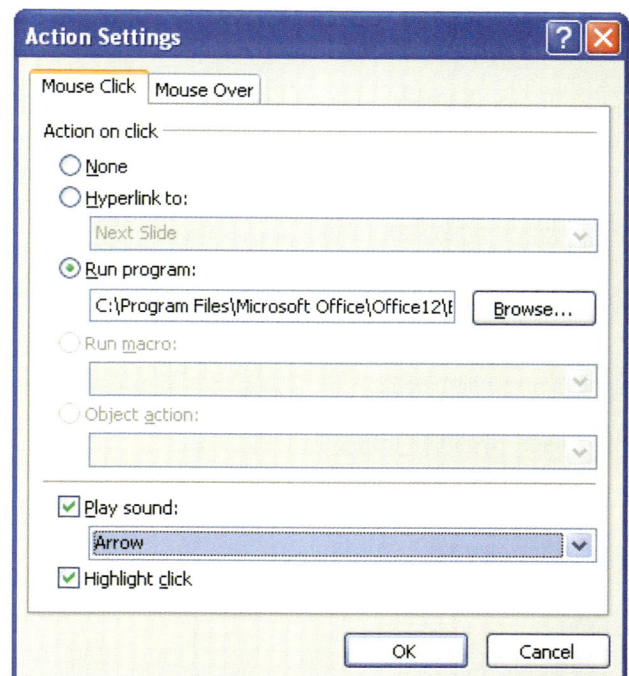

- Click the action option, such as Hyperlink to, Run program, or Play sound. You can then provide additional information to carry out the action, such as what target to link to or what sound file to play.
- Note the Highlight click check box in the Action Settings dialog box. When this option is selected, the shape or text to which you are applying the action setting will change size as you click it.
- The Action Settings dialog box contains two tabs, Mouse Click and Mouse Over. By default, you set actions on the Mouse Click tab, which means that the action takes place when you click on the action object during the presentation.
- The Mouse Over tab contains the same options as the Mouse Click tab. Actions you set on this tab will take place when you hover the mouse pointer over the action object.

PROCEDURES

Insert a Link on a Slide

1. Select the text or object that will become the link.
2. Click **Insert** tab . . . . `Alt`+`N`

   Links Group

3. Click **Hyperlink** button 🌐 . . `I`
4. Choose what to link to:
   - **Existing File or Web Page** . . . . `Alt`+`X`
   - **Place in This Document** . . . . `Alt`+`A`

   ✓ *Use this option to see slides and custom shows in the current presentation.*

   - **Create New Document** . . . . `Alt`+`N`

   ✓ *To set up a link to a new document, see To link to a new document.*

   - **E-mail Address** . . . . . `Alt`+`M`

   ✓ *To set up a link to an e-mail address, see To link to an e-mail address.*

5. Navigate to the page, slide, custom show, or other target of the link and select it.
6. Click **OK** . . . . `Enter`

To link to a new document:

In the Insert Hyperlink dialog box:

1. Click **Create New Document** . . . . `Alt`+`N`
2. Type name of new document, including the extension appropriate for the file type.

3. Check the current Full Path and if necessary, specify a location for the new file:
   a. Click **Change** . . . . . . `Alt`+`C`
   b. Navigate to the location where the new file will be stored.
   c. Click **OK** . . . . `Enter`
4. Choose when to edit the new file:
   - Click **Edit the new document later** . . . . `Alt`+`L`
   - Click **Edit the new document now** . . . . `Alt`+`N`
5. Click **OK** . . . . `Enter`

To link to an e-mail address:

In the Insert Hyperlink dialog box:

1. Click **E-mail Address** . . . . `Alt`+`M`
2. Type desired e-mail address.

   OR
   a. Click **Recently used e-mail addresses** . . . . `Alt`+`C`
   b. Select the desired e-mail address . . . . `↓`, `↑`
3. Click **Subject** . . . . `Alt`+`U`
4. Type subject.
4. Click **OK** . . . . `Enter`

Work with Action Settings

1. Select the text or object to which you want to apply the action setting.
2. Click **Insert** tab . . . . `Alt`+`N`

   Links Group

3. Click **Action** button 🔲 . . . . . . `K`
4. Select the setting option as described below.
5. Click **OK** . . . . `Enter`

To link to a slide, URL, or presentation:

1. Click **Hyperlink to** . . . . `Alt`+`H`, `↓`
2. Select the target of the link and, if necessary, supply additional information, such as the desired URL or file name.

To run a program:

1. Click **Run program** . . . . . `Alt`+`R`
2. Type the path to the program.

   OR
   a. Click **Browse** . . . . `Alt`+`B`
   b. Navigate to the desired program and select it.
   c. Click **OK** . . . . `Enter`

To set an action for an object:

1. Click **Object action** . . . . `Alt`+`A`, `↓`
2. Select **Edit** or **Open**.

   ✓ *Note that the object to which the action setting is applied must have been inserted on the slide using the Object command on the Insert tab.*

To play a sound:

1. Click **Play sound** . . . `Alt`+`P`, `↓`
2. Select the desired sound.

To highlight click:

- Click **Highlight click** . . . . `Alt`+`C`

EXERCISE DIRECTIONS

1. Start PowerPoint and open ⊙ **18PETERSON**. Save the presentation as **18PETERSON_xx**. Also open ⊙ **18TEST** and save in the solution folder as **18TEST_xx**. Then open ⊙ **18CUSTOMIZING** and save in the solution folder as **18CUSTOMIZING_xx**.

2. In **18PETERSON_xx**, display slide 2 and link each item in the content area to the correct slide in the presentation so viewers can click a link to start a new section of the tutorial.

3. Open Slide Master view. On the Title and Content layout (*not* the slide master), insert two text boxes at the bottom of the slide to the right of the footer, the same height as the footer placeholder. Insert in the first text box the text **Questions?** and in the second text box **More info . . . .** . Format the text boxes with a Quick Style of your choice and set up links as follows:

    a. Select the *Questions* text box and create a link to an e-mail address. Insert the address **jpeterson@ petersonhomehealth.com**.

    ✓ *This e-mail address is a dummy for setup purposes only.*

    b. Select the *More info* box and create a link to the Office Online home page at **http://office.microsoft. com/en-us/default.aspx**.

    c. Add the following ScreenTip to the *More info* link: **Visit Microsoft Office Online**.

4. Insert a Custom action button from the Shapes gallery to the right of the *More info* box and link the button to slide 2. Select the Highlight click option in the Action Settings dialog box. Type **Contents** on the action button, and format the button with the same Quick Style as the text boxes but a different color, as shown in Illustration A.

5. Make sure all three boxes are the same height. Align top and distribute the three boxes horizontally. Then select the boxes, copy them, and paste them on all slide layouts except the title and section header layout and the picture layouts. Exit Slide Master view.

6. Display slide 4 and select the *Open Word* shape. Apply an action setting that will run Microsoft Word: Browse to C:\Program Files\Microsoft Office\Office12\WINWORD.

    ✓ *You may need to display hidden files to have access to the program files directory; consult your instructor if necessary.*

7. Select the *Open Excel* shape and browse to the same location, but select EXCEL in the Office12 folder.

8. Display slide 6. Choose to insert an object from an existing file, browse to the solution files, and select **18TEST_xx**. In the Insert Object dialog box, select Display as icon, click Change Icon, and then change the caption to **Test 1**. Position the object below the *Test Your Knowledge* text box. Apply the Object action setting, choosing the Open option.

9. Display slide 8 and select the word *here* in the last bullet item. Link this word to **18CUSTOMIZING_xx**. Then open **18CUSTOMIZING_xx**, select the shape at the top of the first slide, and link it to **18PETERSON_xx**. Close the **18CUSTOMIZING_xx** presentation.

10. You are ready to test your interactive presentation. Follow these steps in Slide Show view:

    a. On slide 2, test each of the links to slides, using the Contents action button to return each time to slide 2.

    b. Test the Questions and More info buttons. Close the e-mail message window without creating a message, and close the Web page after you are done viewing it.

    c. On slide 4, click the Open Word shape, and then click Enable when alerted to the potential security risk. Close Word, then click the Open Excel shape, Enable if necessary, and close Excel.

    d. On slide 6, click the Test 1 object to open a Word document with three questions. For extra credit, answer the questions and then save the document with a new name such as **18ANSWERS_xx**. Close the document to return to the presentation.

    e. On slide 8, click the link that takes you to **18CUSTOMIZING_xx**. Use the link to navigate to the information on customizing the Quick Access Toolbar, then use the action button to return to the first slide and the button to return to **18PETERSON_xx**.

11. Save your changes, close both presentations, and exit PowerPoint.

Contents

2

- Introduction
- Ribbon Interface
- Office Button Menu
- Quick Access Toolbar
- Mini Toolbar

7/10/2008   Learning Office 2007

Questions?   More info . .   Contents

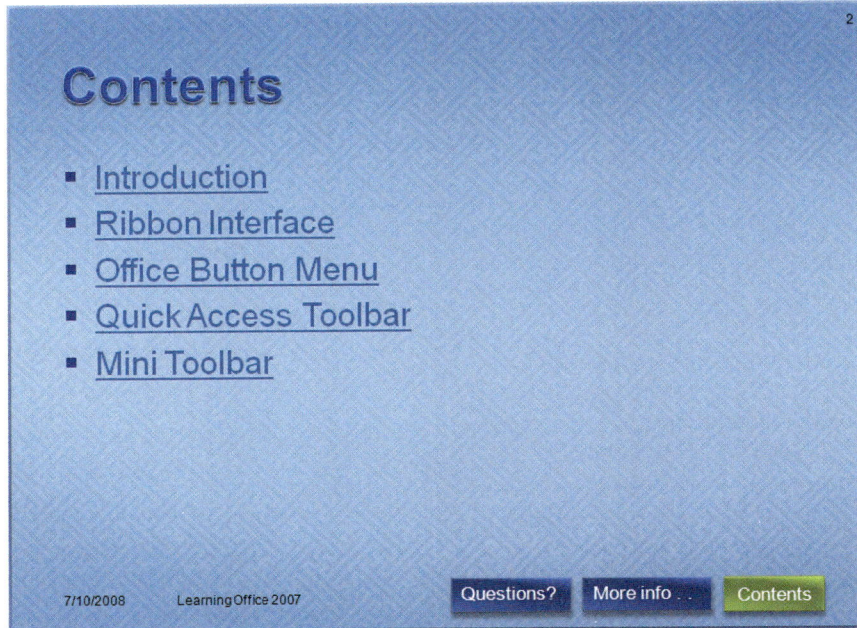

Business Connection

Management Decisions

We all make decisions every day. Decisions help us solve problems, achieve goals, and resolve conflicts. Some are basic, such as what to eat for lunch, but some are important, and should be considered carefully, such as what to do after high school. In business, managers make decisions that affect the business and the employees. Knowing how to use the steps in the decision-making process can help you make decisions that are right for you—and for other people around you.

Presenting the Decision-Making Process

Working alone or in a team, research the steps in the decision-making process. Find out what resources people use to make decisions, and how they can use the decision-making process to solve problems and achieve specific goals. Then, create a presentation that illustrates the decision-making process. Include information about why people make decisions, and the types of decisions they might make. Set up slides for each step in the process, and use graphics and animations to bring the slides to life. Explain each step, and provide examples of how the step might be used. When the presentation is complete, check the spelling and grammar and preview the slide show. Make corrections as necessary and then present it to your class.

ON YOUR OWN

More employees than ever before spend their working days sitting at a computer workstation. Principles of ergonomics can help to ensure that employees who work with computers are productive and free from physical stresses.

1. Using the Internet, locate information on requirements of an ergonomically sound work environment; specifically, look for information on how to adjust components of a computer workstation. Sites such as OSHA publish checklists that employees and management can follow to avoid workplace stresses. Identify several sites that contain useful information so that you can link to these sites in your presentation.

2. Start PowerPoint and create a new presentation. Save the presentation as **OPP18_***xx*. Apply a theme of your choice. Add appropriate text to the title slide.

3. Present the information you have researched in an organized way over a series of slides. For example, you may have a slide that presents information on how to adjust the position of a computer monitor, another slide that discusses how wrists and arms should be positioned, and so on. Illustration A shows an example of an introductory slide.

4. If possible, save pictures from your Web sites to illustrate your presentation. Give proper credit for the site where you located the picture.

5. Use only one slide for each requirement. Insert links on slides to direct readers to additional information about a particular subject.

6. Set up a contents slide that gives easy access to each topic using links, with an action button to return viewers to the contents slide.

7. Assess the completed presentation and decide whether you want to add it to your employment portfolio as an example of your achievement. If you do, print the slides as a handout for the portfolio.

8. Save your changes, close the presentation, and exit PowerPoint.

Illustration A

Introduction

- Improper workstation setup can lead to a number of physical problems
  - Eyestrain
  - Neck, shoulder, arm, and wrist strain
  - Numbness and tingling in fingers
  - Lower back and leg pain
- Ergonomic principles can reduce these problems and increase productivity

Contents

Skills Covered

- **Add Narration**
- **Advanced Slide Show Setup Options**

- **Save a Presentation as a PowerPoint Show**

Software Skills You can add narration to a presentation so that you don't have to be present to get your main points across. Explore all options in the Set Up Show dialog box to present your slides in the most effective way. Save the presentation as a Show so that it opens directly in Slide Show view.

Application Skills In this exercise, you will configure the Peterson Office 2007 tutorial presentation to be browsed by an individual. You will add narration and then save the presentation as a PowerPoint Show.

TERMS

Narration A recording of your voice that describes or enhances the message in each slide.

NOTES

Add Narration to a Presentation

- You might want to record voice **narration** for a self-running slide show to explain or emphasize your points to the audience.

  ✓ *To do so, your computer must have a microphone, speakers, and sound card.*

- You can record voice or sound for one slide or for all slides. Narration takes precedence over all other sounds on a slide.

- To record narration, use the Record Narration button on the Slide Show tab to open the Record Narration dialog box, shown in the following illustration.

Record Narration dialog box

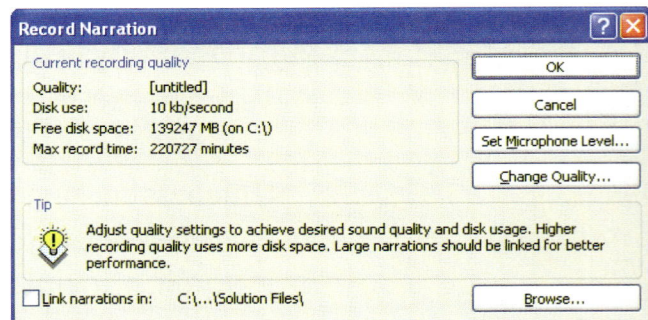

- Before you begin adding narration to slides, you can use the options in this dialog box to specify settings that will optimize your narration sound.

  - Use the Set Microphone Level option to make sure your microphone is working correctly.

- Use the Change Quality option to open the Sound Selection dialog box, shown in the following illustration. You can choose from three quality settings: CD Quality, Radio Quality, or Telephone Quality. The Attributes list allows you to select further sound quality settings. Keep in mind that the better the quality of the recording, the more disk space the recording takes.

Sound Selection dialog box

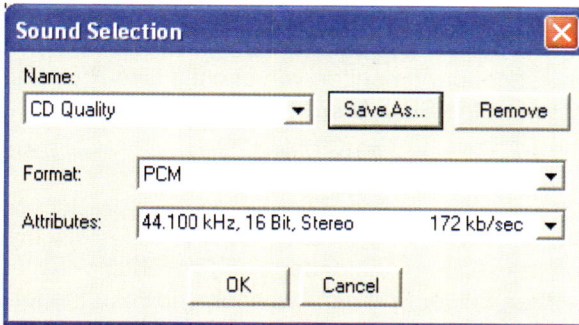

- The Tip in the Record Narration dialog box suggests linking a narration file to the presentation if you are using best sound quality and recording a large amount of narration. You can browse to the location where you want to save the linked sound file, which should be in the same folder as the presentation.

- When you have finished specifying settings, clicking the OK button displays the following dialog box if you do not already have the first slide displayed. As indicated, you can start on the current slide or the first slide. Once you make a choice here, the presentation displays in Slide Show view so you can match your narration to each slide.

Choose the first slide to narrate

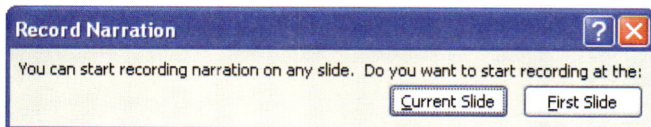

- When you have finished your narration, PowerPoint lets you know the narration has been stored and gives you the option of saving your slide timings.

- In Normal view, you will see that each slide to which you added narration has a sound icon displayed in the lower-right corner. Viewers can click the icons to hear your narration, or you can use the Sound Tools Options tab to specify that the narration will play automatically.

Advanced Slide Show Setup Options

- The Set Up Show dialog box contains a number of features that can be used to fine-tune presentation options.

- Many users assume that all slide shows are shown to an audience and controlled by a speaker, but PowerPoint actually offers three show type options, as shown in the following illustration.

Show type options

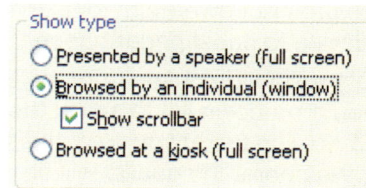

- Use *Presented by a speaker (full screen)* if your presentation will be delivered by a moderator to a live audience. Slides are displayed at full screen size, the way they are when you view them in Slide Show view.

- Select *Browsed by an individual (window)* if you intend for the presentation to be viewed by an individual on his or her own computer. Slides display within a window that includes a title bar and window sizing controls, as shown in the following illustration. If you select the Show scrollbar check box, a vertical scrollbar displays to make it easy for the viewer to navigate the presentation.

Browsed by an individual (window) slide show option

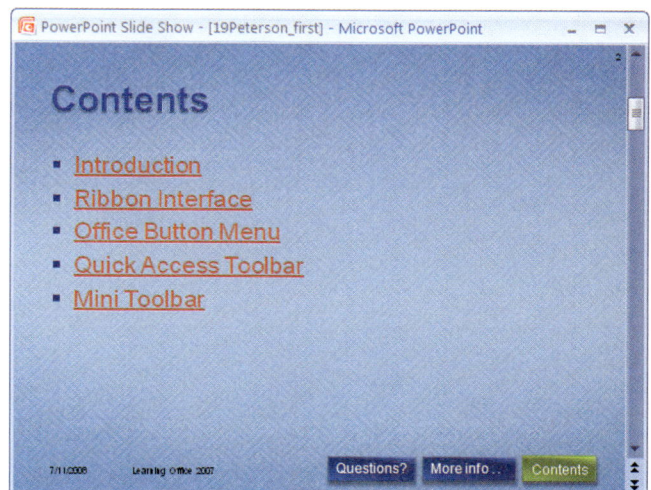

- Choose *Browsed at a kiosk (full screen)* when you want the presentation to run unattended, without a speaker to introduce the slides. This option is typically used when you prepare a presentation to run at a show where the slides loop over and over so that viewers can watch as much of the presentation as they want.

■ Use options in the Performance area of the dialog box to control your system's performance.

- If your system has a video graphics accelerator, select the Use hardware graphics acceleration option to prompt PowerPoint to take advantage of this device to boost performance.

- Choose a resolution option from the Slide show resolution drop-down list to adjust the speed/quality ratio. The faster you want the slides to display, the poorer the quality will be, and vice versa.

✓ *You can also select a resolution from the Resolution drop-down list in the Monitors group on the Slide Show tab.*

■ Presenter View is an advanced feature that simplifies the process of presenting slides to an audience. Using Presenter View, you can display the presentation for the audience on one monitor while you view the presentation on another monitor.

■ To use Presenter View, you must have a computer or projection device that allows you to attach multiple monitors. PowerPoint supports the use of two monitors only, even if your system allows you to connect more than two monitors.

■ After you specify which of the monitors is the primary monitor and extend the Windows desktop to the secondary monitor, you choose Use Presenter View on the Slide Show tab.

✓ *For further information on attaching and configuring multiple monitors, see Windows Help.*

■ When Presenter View is active, the slides display on the secondary monitor. The Presenter View screen on your primary monitor, shown in the following illustration, makes it easy to control slides and see your notes. As well, you can access information on your system without having to interrupt the presentation.

Presenter View

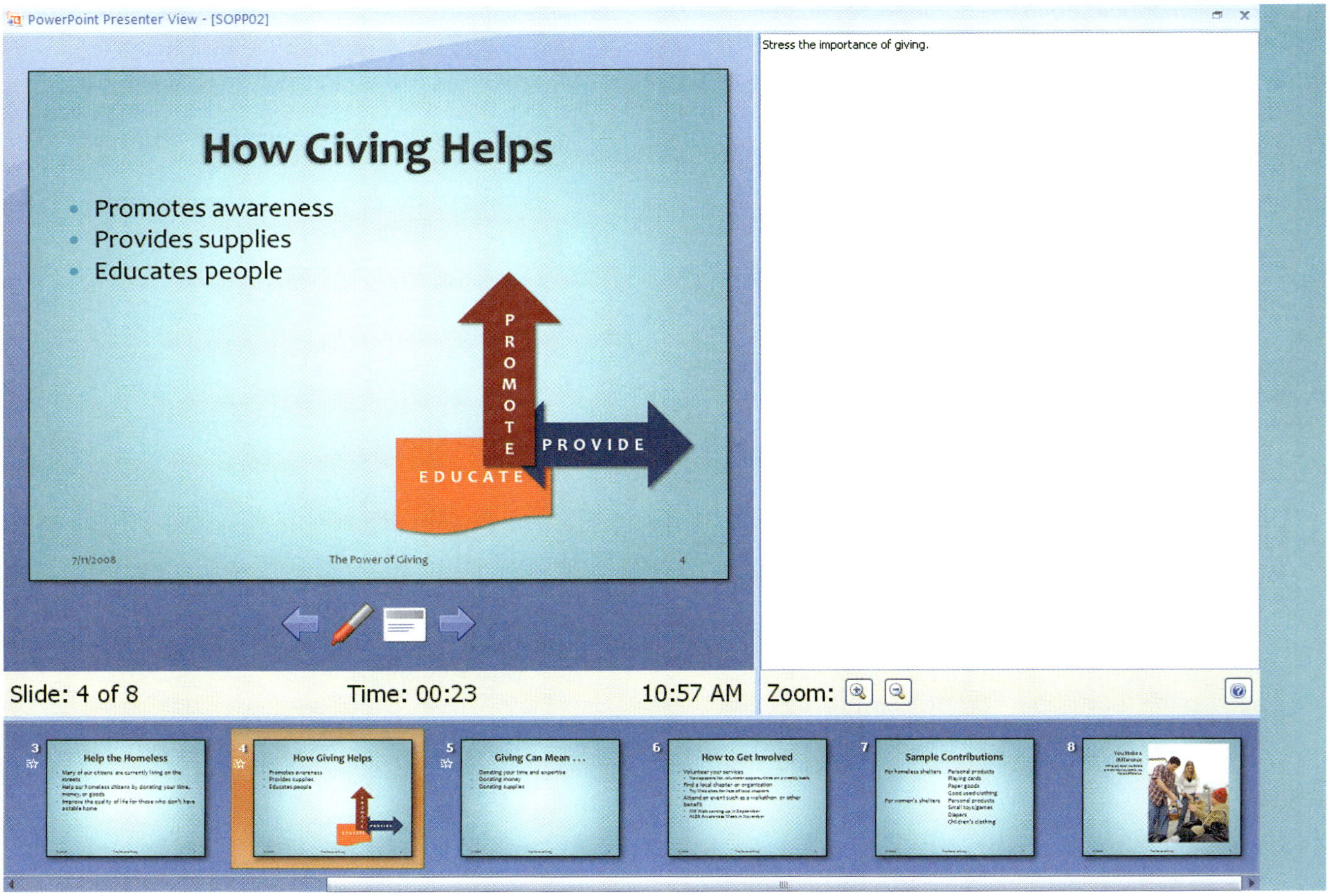

- The Slide pane at the left shows a large version of the current slide, with the usual presentation tools beneath. As you work with these controls, the slide on the secondary monitor displays the effects. If you annotate (add notes) in Presenter View, for example, the annotations appear both your monitor and on the secondary monitor.

- A Notes pane shows any notes you have added for the slide. You can use the Zoom button to enlarge the notes for easy reading.

- The Slide Sorter pane at the bottom of the screen allows you to easily choose the next slide to present.

Save a Presentation as a PowerPoint Show

- If you know that a presenter will not want to spend any time editing a slide show in PowerPoint before presenting it, you can save the presentation as a PowerPoint Show.

- A file saved as a PowerPoint Show has an extension of .ppsx rather than the standard PowerPoint 2007 .pptx extension. The file icon will also look slightly different from the icon used for regular PowerPoint presentations.

- The PowerPoint Show format opens a presentation automatically in Slide Show view, so that the presenter does not have to first start PowerPoint, then open the presentation, then launch Slide Show view.

PROCEDURES

Add Narration to a Presentation

1. Click **Slide Show** tab . . . . [Alt]+[S]

   Set Up Group

2. Click **Record Narration** button . . . . [N]

3. Check microphone:
   a. Click **Set Microphone Level** . . . . [Alt]+[M]
   b. Speak into the microphone to record levels.
   c. Click **OK** . . . . [Enter]

4. Specify sound quality:
   a. Click **Change Quality** . . . . [Alt]+[C]
   b. In the **Name** drop-down box, choose one of the following:
      - **CD Quality**
      - **Radio Quality**
      - **Telephone Quality**
   c. Click **OK** . . . . [Enter]

5. Specify a location to save linked sound files:
   a. Click **Link narrations in** check box . . . . [Alt]+[L]

   b. Click **Browse** and navigate to the location where you want to save the file . . . . . [Alt]+[B]
   c. Click **Select** . . . . [Alt]+[E]

6. Click **OK** . . . . [Enter]

7. Choose the slide to begin narration on:
   - Click **Current Slide** to start the narration with the current slide . . . . [Alt]+[C]
   - Click **First Slide** to start narration on the first slide . . . . [Alt]+[F]

   ✓ These options are available only if a slide other than slide 1 is displayed in Normal view.

8. Speak into the microphone to record as you view a slide, and advance each slide as needed.

9. When you have finished going through the slide show:
   - Click **Save** to save the timings with the narration . . . . [S]

   OR

   - Click **Don't Save** to discard slide timings . . . . [D]

Set Slide Show Options

1. Click **Slide Show** tab . . . . [Alt]+[S]

   Set Up Group

2. Click **Set Up Slide Show** button . . . . [S]

3. Select options to set up the show as indicated below.

4. Click **OK** . . . . [Enter]

To choose show type:

1. Choose one of the following show types:
   - **Presented by a speaker** . . . . [Alt]+[P]
   - **Browsed by an individual** . . . . [Alt]+[B]
   - **Browsed at a kiosk** . . . [Alt]+[K]

   ✓ If you choose Browsed by an individual, click Show scrollbar to display the scroll bar that allows you to move easily from slide to slide.

To set performance options:

1. Choose from the following options:
   - Click **Use hardware graphics acceleration** if you have a video graphics accelerator . . . . $\boxed{\text{Alt}}$+$\boxed{\text{G}}$
   - Click **Slide show resolution** and select a resolution . . . . . . $\boxed{\text{Alt}}$+$\boxed{\text{R}}$, $\boxed{\downarrow}$

Use Presenter View

1. Attach a second monitor to your computer or projection device and configure it as directed in Windows Help.
2. With both monitors active, click **Slide Show** tab . . . . $\boxed{\text{Alt}}$+$\boxed{\text{S}}$

3. Click **Use Presenter View** check box . . . . $\boxed{\text{V}}$
4. Click **Show Presentation On** and select the monitor that will display the slides (usually the secondary monitor) . . . . $\boxed{\text{O}}$

   ✓ *You can also select the display monitor in the Set Up Show dialog box.*

5. Start Slide Show view as you usually would. Presenter View opens on the primary monitor and the first slide displays on the secondary monitor.
6. Control the slide show from Presenter View. End the show as you usually would.

Save a Presentation as a Show

1. Open the presentation to save as a show.
2. Click **Office Button** 🔘 . . . $\boxed{\text{Alt}}$+$\boxed{\text{F}}$
3. Point to **Save As** right-pointing arrow . . . . $\boxed{\text{F}}$
4. Click **PowerPoint Show** . . . . . . $\boxed{\text{S}}$
5. Type a different name for the file if desired.
6. Click **Save** . . . . $\boxed{\text{Alt}}$+$\boxed{\text{S}}$

EXERCISE DIRECTIONS

1. Start PowerPoint and open ⌨ **18PETERSON_xx** or open 💿 **19PETERSON**. Save the presentation as **19PETERSON_xx**.
2. If you have a microphone attached to your computer, record the following narration on slide 1: **Welcome to Learning Office 2007**.
3. Set the show to be browsed by an individual, and choose to show the scrollbar.
4. Run the show and browse through it using the scrollbar.
5. Save the presentation as a PowerPoint Show with the name **19PETERSONSHOW_xx**. Close the file.
6. Start the show from My Computer or Windows Explorer to see how it opens directly in Slide Show view.
7. Save your changes, close the presentation, and exit PowerPoint.

ON YOUR OWN

1. Start PowerPoint and open 💿 **19EARTH**. Save the presentation as **OPP19_xx**.
2. If you have the capability, record narration for some of the slides to point out important issues.
3. If you have the capability to use multiple monitors, set up the presentation to use Presenter View.
4. Choose to use hardware acceleration and change the resolution to a different value. For smoother animations, you may want to change some effects to start On Click rather than automatically.
5. Deliver the presentation to your class, controlling the presentation from your computer. Use the presentation tools to move from slide to slide and control the animations.
6. When you have finished delivering the presentation, exit Presenter View.
7. Save your changes, close the presentation, and exit PowerPoint.

Skills Covered

- **Protect a Presentation**
- **Work with Comments and Markup**
- **Run the Compatibility Checker**
- **Use the Document Inspector**

Software Skills   If you need to share a presentation with others, you can take steps to make sure the presentation will not be altered by anyone unauthorized to edit the slides. Use comments to share information or request changes and control the display of comments by showing or hiding markup on the slides. Use the Compatibility Checker and Document Inspector to check and prepare a presentation for its final use.

Application Skills   In this exercise, you learn how to protect a presentation you created for Restoration Architecture by setting permissions and applying a digital signature and passwords. You also work with markup and run the Compatibility Checker and Document Inspector.

TERMS

Digital signature   A feature that provides a way to authenticate a presentation's author and ensure that the presentation has not been changed.

Encryption   The process of transforming data into a form that cannot be read or decoded without a key (password).

Information Rights Management (IRM)   A feature that lets an author or administrator control who has permission to use a file.

Permissions   Rights to read or modify a file.

NOTES

Protect a Presentation

- If you regularly share presentations with others, such as team members or other colleagues, you need to know how to protect your work so that it is not changed without your permission.

- PowerPoint 2007 offers more security features than previous versions of the program, reflecting the heightened awareness in the work world of the damage that can be done by hackers or those in the workplace who might tamper with your files.

- You can set passwords, **encrypt** a presentation, apply a **digital signature**, or set **permissions** for a presentation. These options are discussed in depth in the following sections.

Apply Passwords to a Presentation

- Passwords are familiar security devices that require a user to enter a word or phrase specified by the author of a file before that file can be opened or edited.

- In PowerPoint 2007, you can set passwords when saving a presentation. In the Save As dialog box, click the Tools button and select General Options.

- Note that you can set two different passwords in this dialog box: one that is required to open the file and another that is required if you want to modify the file.

General Options dialog box

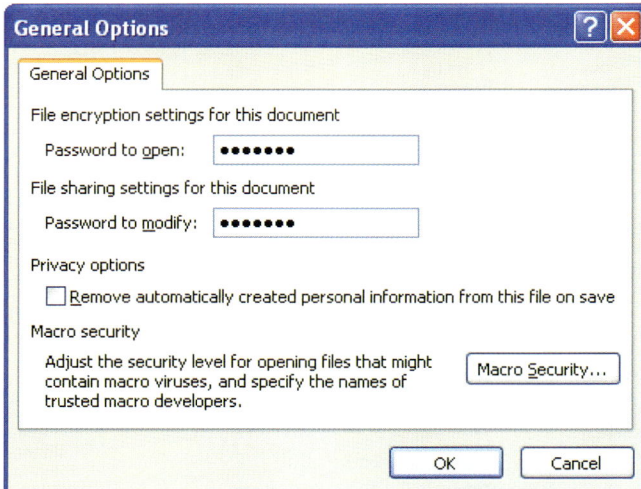

General Options

General Options

File encryption settings for this document

Password to open: ••••••••

File sharing settings for this document

Password to modify: ••••••••

Privacy options

☐ Remove automatically created personal information from this file on save

Macro security

Adjust the security level for opening files that might contain macro viruses, and specify the names of trusted macro developers.   [Macro Security...]

[OK] [Cancel]

- When you open a presentation to which a password has been applied, a dialog box displays to allow you to enter the password. If you have requested passwords for both opening and modifying, you must supply both before you can work with the presentation.

- If a password has been specified for opening a presentation, you must have it to display the slides. If a password has been specified for modifying a presentation, you do not need it to display the slides. You can choose to open a Read Only copy of the presentation that you can review but not change.

- Remove password protection by displaying the General Options dialog box and clearing the passwords you entered.

Encrypt a Presentation

- Another way to protect a presentation is to apply encryption. When you encrypt any document, you convert it into a form that cannot be read. Decoding an encrypted file requires a *key*, or password.

- To encrypt a presentation, point to the Prepare command on the Office Button menu and then select Encrypt Document on the submenu.

- PowerPoint requires you to enter a password. You must then confirm the password.

- Encrypt Document actually provides the same level of protection as specifying a password to open a file in the General Options dialog box, and you can use either method to apply encryption. Use the Save As method when you are saving the file; use the Encrypt Document method at any time while working with the presentation.

Encrypt Document dialog box

Encrypt Document

Encrypt the contents of this file

Password:

••••••••

Caution: If you lose or forget the password, it cannot be recovered. It is advisable to keep a list of passwords and their corresponding document names in a safe place. (Remember that passwords are case-sensitive.)

[OK] [Cancel]

- Remove encryption as discussed above for removing passwords, or display the Encrypt Document dialog box again and clear the password from it.

Add a Digital Signature

- A digital signature provides a different form of security for a presentation. Rather than preventing someone from tampering with the file, it provides the assurance that the file was created by a specific person and has not been changed since that person applied the signature.

- A digital signature requires an author to acquire a certificate that is issued by some trusted authority. A person who receives a presentation with a digital signature knows that the author's identity has been confirmed by that trusted authority and the file is safe to open.

- Commercial certificates can cost quite a bit of money, but you can create one for the purposes of testing this feature using Microsoft Office tools.

- You become your own "trusted authority," so such a digital signature is not worth much as a form of security, but it can give you an idea how digital signatures work.

- You apply a digital signature using the Add a Digital Signature command on the Office Button menu's Prepare submenu. If you have a signature "on file" on your computer, the Sign dialog box displays.

Sign dialog box

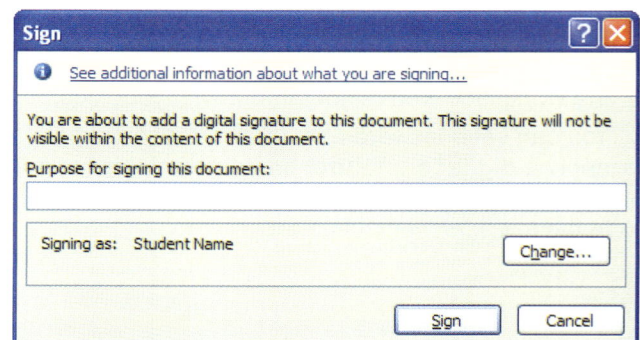

Sign

ⓘ See additional information about what you are signing...

You are about to add a digital signature to this document. This signature will not be visible within the content of this document.

Purpose for signing this document:

Signing as: Student Name   [Change...]

[Sign] [Cancel]

Presentation file after a digital signature has been applied

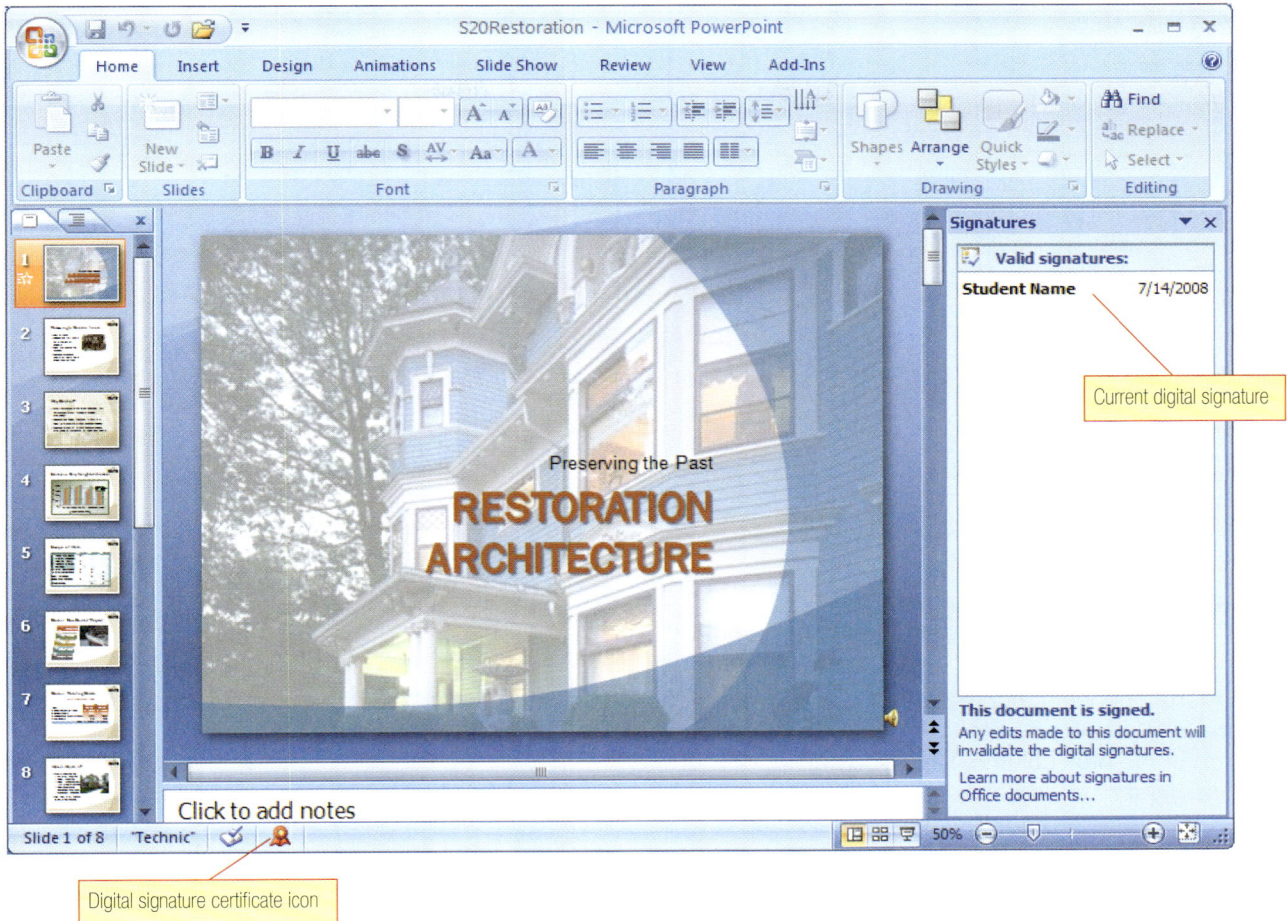

Current digital signature

Digital signature certificate icon

- You can supply a purpose for the signature, or simply click the Sign button to apply the signature. After informing you that the presentation has been signed, PowerPoint displays the Signatures task pane and a certificate icon.

- A presentation to which a digital signature has been applied is "locked" so that you cannot edit it, because editing would invalidate the signature.

- Some commands on the Office Button menu are still active, however, and if you issue one of these commands, you are informed that it will invalidate the current signature. An invalid signature displays in red.

Invalid digital signature

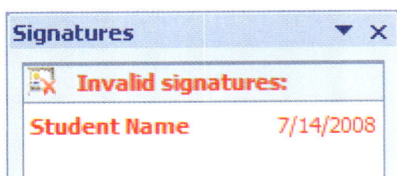

- You can revalidate the signature by pointing to the signature to display a down arrow and then selecting Sign Again.

- You can also use this list menu to remove a signature so that you can continue to edit a presentation.

Restrict Permission Using Information Rights Management

- The final security option you can apply to prevent unauthorized persons from opening or changing your presentations is to set permissions using **Information Rights Management (IRM)**.

- Information Rights Management (IRM) is a feature that allows an author or administrator to control who has access to a file.

- You use the Protect Presentation button on the Review tab or the Restrict Permission command on the Office Button menu's Prepare submenu to start the process of specifying permissions. If you have a valid IRM certificate, you will then see a Permission dialog box.

Permission dialog box

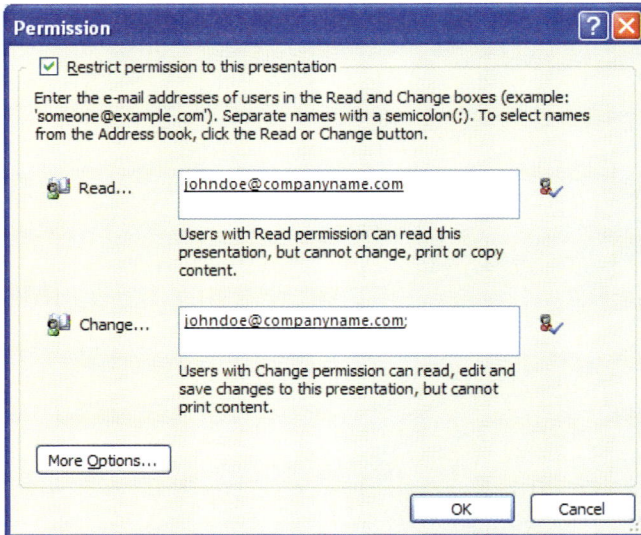

Additional permission options

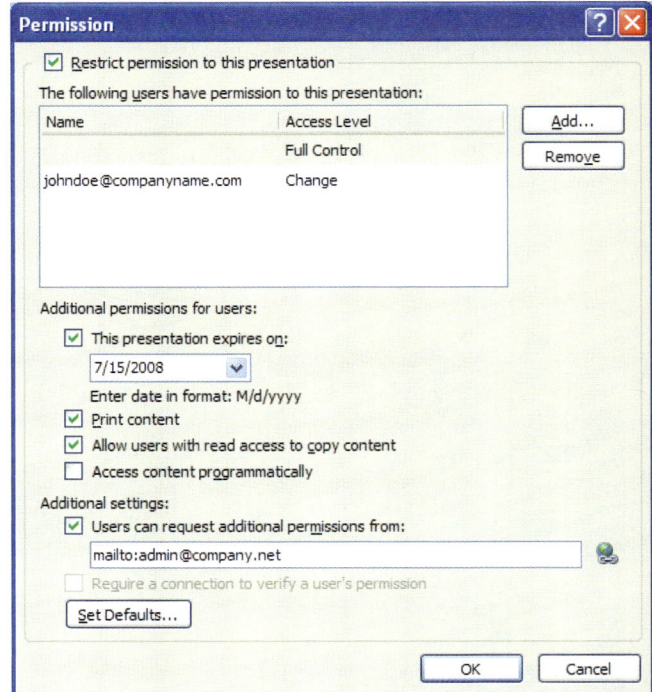

- To permit users to read or change a presentation, you insert their e-mail addresses in the appropriate boxes.

- The More Options button opens the version of the Permission dialog box shown in the illustration at the top of the next column. Here you can work with the list of users to add or remove a user; specify a date on which a permission expires; select additional permissions for a user, such as the right to copy or print material; and provide an e-mail address so a user can request further information about permissions.

- After you have set permissions, a message bar displays below the Ribbon to indicate that permission has been restricted for this presentation. You can change permission options by clicking the Change Permission button. Deselecting the Restrict permission to this presentation check box removes the protection.

- Information Rights Management is a robust form of security because the permissions travel with the file as you send it to others. If a recipient is not on the list of permitted users, he or she cannot read or change the file.

- If a user who is not on the list tries to open a file with permissions set, he or she will receive a message indicating that the file is restricted and that he or she does not have the credentials to open the file. The user can click a button to get credentials by downloading the IRM service.

- Because this is a higher-level security feature, it is not available for all Microsoft Office packages. If you have Microsoft Office 2007 Professional Plus, Enterprise, or Ultimate, you can download a trial version of the IRM certificate. If you have another Office package, you may not be able to use this feature.

Restricted Access message

Work with Comments and Markup

- As you work with a presentation, you may want to insert notes for yourself about information you need to add or work that needs to be done on a slide. If you have been asked to review a presentation, you might want to give the author your views on specific points.

- It is inappropriate to use the Notes pane for such information. Instead, you can use comments to supply information for yourself or someone else.

- You can add a comment to an entire slide or to selected text or other selected object. If you do not select any object, the comment displays in the upper-left corner of the slide.

Comment inserted on a slide

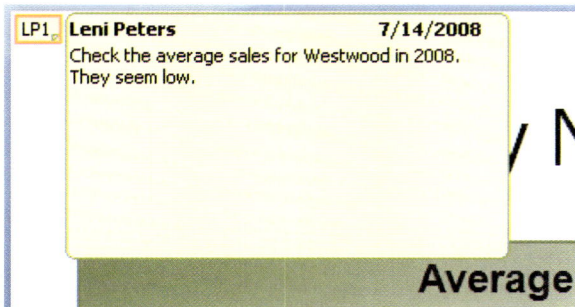

- The name and initials that display on each comment are those of the current user. The date displayed is the current date.

- When you are done creating a comment, click outside the comment box to close the comment box. The comment marker remains in view on the slide. To read a comment that is not open, point to the comment marker to open the comment box.

- You use the Comments group on the Review tab to work with comments and markup.

Comments group options

- Use the New Comment button to insert a comment. The Edit Comment button opens a selected comment so you can modify it. The Delete button allows you to remove a single comment, all comments on a slide, or all comments throughout a presentation.

- If you have a number of comments in a presentation, the Previous and Next buttons allow you to move quickly from comment to comment, opening each so you can read it.

- When you open a presentation that contains comments, the comment markers display on the slides by default, and the Show Markup button is active on the Review tab.

- If you want to hide comments as you review a presentation, click the Show Markup button to deactivate it. The comment markers then disappear from the slides.

Run the Compatibility Checker

- The Compatibility Checker is a tool designed to flag features in your current presentation that are not supported in previous PowerPoint versions.

- It is especially important to use this feature before saving to an earlier version of PowerPoint, because some of PowerPoint 2007's effects cannot be edited in previous versions of the program.

- When you click Run Compatibility Checker from the Prepare submenu, the Compatibility Checker reviews each slide for compatibility issues and then displays a report.

Compatibility Checker report

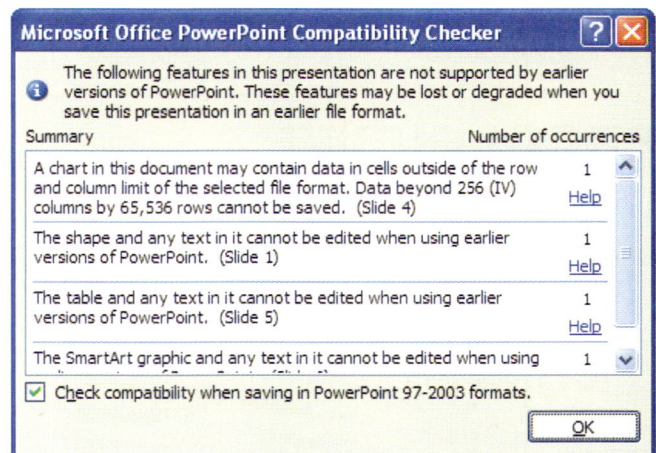

- The Summary tells you the compatibility issue, such as a SmartArt graphic that cannot be edited in earlier versions of PowerPoint, lets you know how many times the issue occurs, and offers a Help link that provides more information about the issue.

- In most cases, the compatibility issues will not compromise the look of the slides when they are shown in other versions of PowerPoint. Though you will not be able to edit a SmartArt graphic, for example, its components are saved as pictures that will display the same way they do in PowerPoint 2007.

- The help files offer advice on how to modify PowerPoint 2007 features if you want to maintain some edibility. For example, you can convert a SmartArt graphic to separate shapes so that you can edit them in any version of PowerPoint.

Use the Document Inspector

- Companies and organizations are increasingly careful about sharing files that contain properties such as those you added to a presentation earlier in the course. Properties can reveal a lot about a file, including who wrote it or reviewed it, when the file was created or edited, and so on.

- The Inspect Document option searches for personal information you may not want to accompany a presentation when you send it to someone else.

- After you issue the Inspect Document command, PowerPoint displays a dialog box to tell you what kinds of hidden and personal information the Document Inspector can locate.

What the Document Inspector looks for

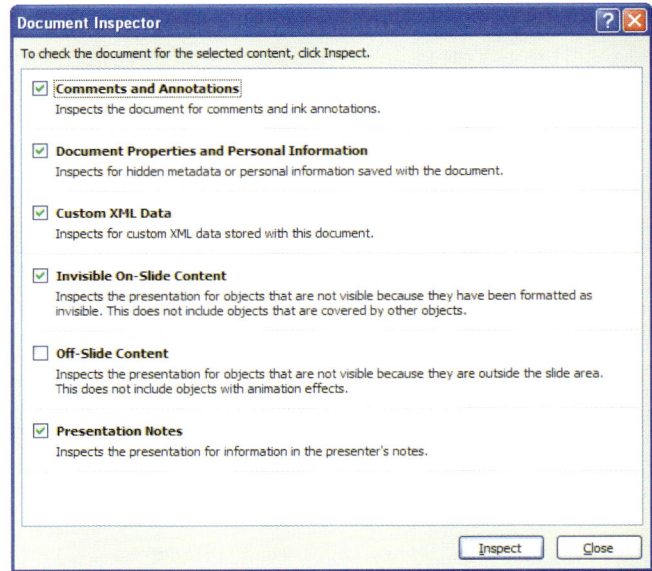

- After you choose the types of content that the Document Inspector will look for, you inspect the presentation.

- The Document Inspector creates a report that shows the types of information the Document Inspector found. Buttons give you the option of removing all sensitive data so that it will not be included with the presentation if you send it elsewhere.

- You can reinspect the presentation after removing inspection results if desired.

PROCEDURES

Apply Passwords to a Presentation

1. Click **Office Button** 🏁 . . . `Alt`+`F`
2. Click **Save As** . . . . `A`
3. Click **Tools** . . . . `Alt`+`L`, `↓`
4. Click **General Options** . . . . `G`
5. Click **Password to open** . . . . `Alt`+`O`
6. Type password to be used to open file.
7. Click **Password to modify** . . . . `Alt`+`M`
8. Type password to be used to modify file.
9. Click **OK** . . . . `Enter`
10. Confirm password to open by reentering the password.

11. Click **OK** . . . . `Enter`
12. Confirm password to modify by reentering the password.
13. Click **OK** . . . . `Enter`
14. Click **Save** . . . . `Alt`+`S`

To remove a password:

1. Click **Office Button** 🏁 . . . `Alt`+`F`
2. Click **Save As** . . . . `A`
3. Click **Tools** . . . . `Alt`+`L`, `↓`
4. Click **General Options** . . . . `G`
5. Click **Password to open** . . . . `Alt`+`O`
6. Delete the password in the box.
7. Click **Password to modify** . . . . `Alt`+`M`

8. Delete the password in the box.
9. Click **OK** . . . . `Enter`
10. Click **Save** . . . . `Alt`+`S`

Encrypt a Presentation

1. Click **Office Button** 🏁 . . . `Alt`+`F`
2. Point to **Prepare** . . . . `E`
3. Click **Encrypt Document** . . . . . `E`
4. Click **Password** . . . . `Alt`+`R`
5. Type the desired password.
6. Click **OK** . . . . `Enter`
7. Confirm password to open by reentering the password.
8. Click **OK** . . . . `Enter`

To remove encryption:

1. Click **Office Button** 🔘 . . . Alt + F
2. Point to **Pr̲epare** . . . . E
3. Click **E̲ncrypt Document** . . . . . E
4. Click **Passwor̲d** . . . . Alt + R
5. Delete the password from the box.
6. Click **OK**. . . . . Enter

Create a Digital Signature

Use the instructions below to create a self-signing digital signature you can use to test this feature.

1. Click Windows **Start** button
   🏁 start / 🔘 . . . . . Ctrl + Esc
2. Point to **All P̲rograms**.
3. Point to **Microsoft Office**.
4. Point to **Microsoft Office Tools**.
5. Click **Digital Certificate for VBA Projects**.
6. Click **Y̲our certificate's name** . . . . Alt + Y
7. Type the name you want to use on your certificate.
8. Click **OK**. . . . . Enter
9. Click **OK** again . . . . Enter

Apply a Digital Signature

1. Click **Office Button** 🔘 . . . Alt + F
2. Point to **Pr̲epare** . . . . E
3. Click **Add a Digital Signature** . . . . S
4. Click **OK**.
5. Type a purpose for the signature if desired.
6. If the signature is not the one you created:
   a. Click **C̲hange** . . . . . . Alt + H
   b. Click your signature.
   c. Click **OK** . . . . Enter
7. Click **S̲ign** . . . . Alt + S
8. Click **OK**. . . . . Enter

To remove a digital signature:

1. Click 🎖 in status bar if necessary to display Signatures task pane.
2. Point to signature you want to remove in Signatures task pane.
3. Click down arrow at right side of signature.
4. Click **Remove Sig̲nature** . . . . . N
5. Click **Y̲es** to remove signature . . . . Alt + Y
   OR
   Click **N̲o** to retain the signature . . . . Alt + N
6. If you clicked **Yes**, click **OK** to complete the process.

Set Permissions Using Information Rights Management

Instructions below assume you have an IRM certificate installed. If you do not, see your instructor for further help.

1. Click **Office Button** 🔘 . . . Alt + F
2. Point to **Pr̲epare** . . . . E
3. Point to **R̲estrict Permission** . . . . R
4. Click **R̲estricted Access** . . . . . R
   OR
1. Click **Review** tab . . . . Alt + R

   Protect Group

2. Click **Protect Presentation** button
   📄 . . . . P
3. Click **R̲estricted Access** . . . . . R

To specify permitted users:

In the Permission dialog box:

1. Click **R̲estrict permission to this presentation** . . . . Alt + R
2. Click in **Read** box and type e-mail address(es) of permitted user(s).
3. Click in **Change** box and type e-mail address(es) of permitted user(s).
4. Click **OK**. . . . . Enter

To remove permissions:

1. Display Permission dialog box.
2. Click **Restrict permission to this presentation** . . . . Alt + R

Work with Comments and Markup

Insert a comment:

1. Display the slide on which you want to comment, or select text or an object to which the comment should be attached.
2. Click **Review** tab . . . . Alt + R

   Comments Group

3. Click **New Comment** button
   📁 C
4. Type the comment text in the comment box.
5. Click outside the box to close the comment box.

View a comment:

■ Point to the comment marker to open the comment box.

Modify a comment:

1. Click a comment marker to select it.
2. Click **Review** tab . . . . Alt + R

   Comments Group

3. Click **Edit Comment** button
   📝 . . . . T
4. Modify the comment text as desired.

Delete a comment:

1. Display the slide on which the comment appears.
2. Click **Review** tab . . . . Alt + R

   Comments Group

3. Click **Delete** button ✉ . . . . . D

   OR

   a. Click **Delete** button down arrow.
   b. Choose what to delete:
      - Click **Delete** . . . . D to remove a single or selected comment.
      - Click **Delete All Markup on the Current Slide** . . A
      - Click **Delete All Markup in this Presentation** . . . . P

To show or hide markup:

1. Click **Review** tab . . . . Alt + R

   Comments Group

2. Click **Show Markup** button ✎ to show or hide markup . . . . H

Run the Compatibility Checker

1. Click **Office Button** 🔘 . . . Alt + F
2. Point to **Pr epare** . . . . E
3. Click **Run Compatibility Checker**. C
4. Read the report on compatibility issues.
5. Click **OK**. . . . . Enter

Use the Document Inspector

1. Click **Office Button** 🔘 . . . Alt + F
2. Point to **Pr epare** . . . . E
3. Click **Inspect Document** I
4. Select content that Document Inspector will inspect.
5. Click **Inspect** . . . . Alt + I
6. Review results and if desired click **Remove All** to remove information.
7. Click **Close** . . . . Alt + C

EXERCISE DIRECTIONS

1. Start PowerPoint and open 💿 **20RESTORATION**. Save the presentation as **20RESTORATION_xx**.
2. On slide 1, insert a comment to remind yourself to check that the sound file is stored in the same folder with the presentation.
3. On slide 7, insert a comment to suggest that the final figures for the two areas of roofing repair be totaled to give an overall sum.
4. Save the presentation, then apply encryption with the password **restore**. Send the presentation to your instructor if you have e-mail capability to confirm that you have inserted the two comments as instructed.

5. Save your changes and close the presentation. While it is closed, confirm that the sound file used on slide 1 of the presentation is stored in the same folder as the presentation.
6. Open the presentation and supply the correct password. Then remove encryption.
7. Delete the comment on slide 1.
8. Run the Compatibility Checker to see what issues might arise if you have to save this presentation in 97-2003 format.
9. Run the Document Inspector. You have decided not to act on the comment on slide 7, so remove all comments and personal information.
10. Save your changes, close the presentation, and exit PowerPoint.

ON YOUR OWN

1. Start PowerPoint and open 🔘 **20BUTTERFLY**. Save the presentation as **OPP20_xx**.

2. Add a comment on slide 1 to Callie Bishop indicating that this first draft of the presentation is ready for her review.

3. If you have the ability to protect the presentation using information rights management, set permissions for your instructor or a classmate to read the presentation only.

4. If you have a digital signature available, sign the presentation with your signature.

5. Try editing the comment you inserted. You should not be able to make any changes in the presentation, though you can read all slides.

6. E-mail the presentation to your instructor. Click OK when you are informed the action will invalidate the digital signature.

7. If you were able to set permissions, remove the permission at this point, and then remove the digital signature.

8. Run the Compatibility Checker and the Document Inspector. Remove all of the items the Document Inspector identifies.

9. Re-sign the presentation.

10. Save and close the presentation, and exit PowerPoint.

Skills Covered

- **Save as a Web Site**
- **Set Publishing Options**
- **View a Web Presentation**

Software Skills   Save your presentation as a Web site and publish it to the Web so that a larger audience can view it. You might, for example, already have a Web site established for customers to view your products or services. Add a presentation to the site to interest more customers and provide an additional resource.

Application Skills   In this exercise, you will save the Thorn Hill Gardens butterfly show presentation as Web pages so that it can be added to Thorn Hill's Web site.

TERMS

HTML (Hypertext Markup Language)   A formatting language used to create Web pages. Web browsers can read the HTML language over the Internet.

Publish   Set options to make the presentation more suitable for viewing on the Web by specific browsers.

Web site   A collection of Web pages; a site usually contains information about a specific topic.

NOTES

Save a Presentation as a Web Site

- Save a presentation as a **Web site** so you can **publish** it to the World Wide Web or an intranet at a company, organization, or school.

- PowerPoint lets you save a presentation in **HTML (Hypertext Markup Language)** format so that you can open it in a Web browser such as Internet Explorer.

- In a presentation Web site, each slide becomes a separate page in the site. The title slide is the home page of the site.

- You have two options when saving a presentation for Web use.

  - Use the Single File Web Page file type in the Save As dialog box to save the presentation as one file using the MHT file format.

  - Use the Web Page file type to save the presentation in HTM format.

Save as Web page options in Save As dialog box

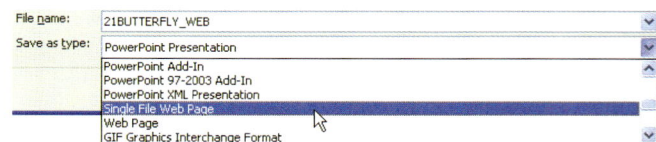

- When you save in MHT format, everything the browser needs to display the Web site is included in one file. Although this is convenient, not all browsers can use the MHT format.

- When you save in HTM format, PowerPoint creates the Web file and also creates a folder with the same name to hold supporting files, such as buttons, images, backgrounds, and so on. You must be sure to upload both the presentation file and the supporting files folder to the Web server that will host your site.

- Links on your presentation Web pages work just as when you show the presentation in Slide Show view. Action buttons may not work quite as well, depending on your browser, and multimedia files such as sounds and movies may not display or play correctly.

  ✓ *Be sure to test your Web site in a number of browsers. For best results, specify Internet Explorer 6.0 or later as the browser of choice.*

Set Publishing Options

- After you select a Web page file format, the Save As dialog box changes to show other files saved in that format (if any) in the current folder.

- The default page title is shown below the Save as type box. The page title displays in the browser's title bar (or tab, if you are using a browser that supports tabbed browsing).

- You can change the page title using the Change Title button.

- You can click Save to convert the presentation to a Web site using all slides and default publishing settings.

- For more control over the publishing settings, click the Publish button to open the Publish as Web Page dialog box.

Publish as Web Page dialog box

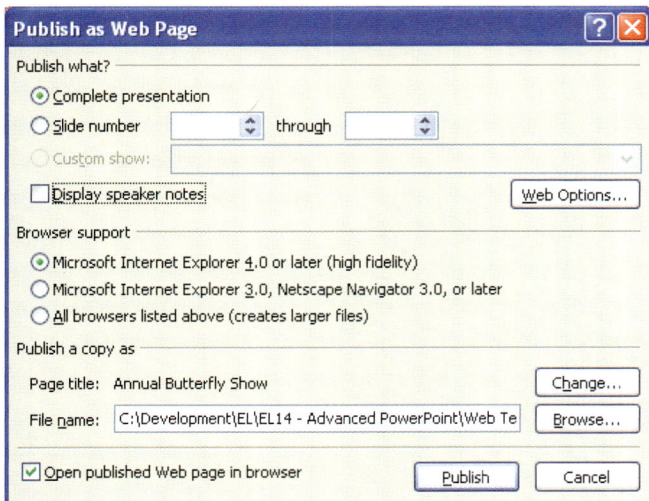

- In the Publish what? area, you can choose a range of slides to publish or a custom show. You can also choose whether to display any speaker notes your presentation includes.

- The Browser support area allows you to choose browser versions you want your Web site to support.

- In the Publish a copy as section of the dialog box, you once again have the option to change the page title, and you can check the path for the Web site.

- To save time, select the Open published Web page in browser check box. As soon as you click the Publish button, the presentation is converted and opens in your default browser.

- To further customize a presentation, click the Web Options button in the Publish as Web Page dialog box.

- The Web Options dialog box has six tabs of options you can select. On the General tab, for example, choose to add navigation controls, specify a color scheme for the outline that accompanies the slides in the Web site, control slide animation, and resize graphics to fit the browser window.

Web Options dialog box

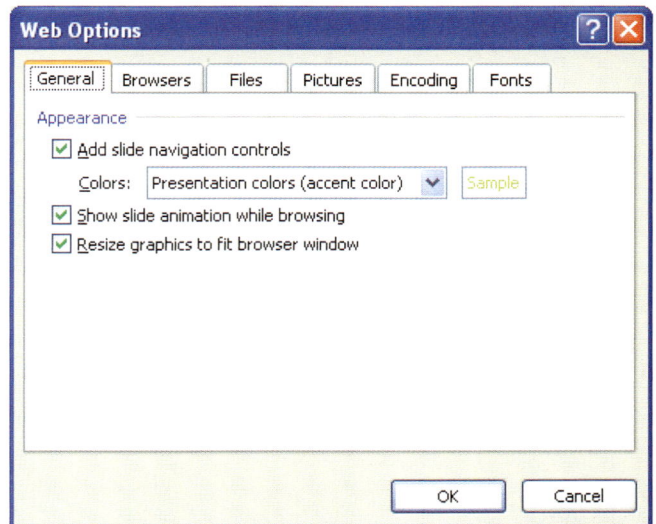

- Other tabs in this dialog box offer additional settings you may need to adjust:

  - On the Browsers tab, you can select the browser and browser version you want to target. If you have Internet Explorer 6.0 or later, you should specify that target browser for best results in testing Web pages. Select other options that relate to the target browser, such as whether PNG graphics are supported.

  - The Files tab allows you to specify how files are organized and named and whether Web pages created in Office applications can be edited in those applications.

  - Use the Pictures tab to set a default screen size for pictures that will work for most site visitors.

  - The Encoding and Fonts tabs define settings for use in the United States. You generally do not need to change these settings.

- When you have adjusted settings as desired, you can close this dialog box and publish the presentation.

- If your ultimate goal in creating a presentation is to publish it as a Web site, you should keep the following tips in mind when creating content:
  - Add action buttons and hyperlinks for easier navigation. You want your audience to access your Web pages easily.
  - Use small graphics and pictures to cut downloading time. If a visitor to your site has to wait a long time for a picture to download, that person will likely move on instead of wait.
  - Use one major heading on each page to let readers know where they are. Don't squeeze too much text on one page.
  - As a general rule, use the GIF image format for clip art graphics or other pictures with few colors; use JPEG format for photographs; use PNG format for buttons, bullets, and small images.

View a Web Presentation

- You view your presentation on the Web as you would any Web page; simply enter your URL in the Address box of the browser or use the Open command on the browser's File menu to open the presentation.

  ✓ You may need to authorize active content in your browser before the Web page will display.

- A Web presentation generally looks similar to the one shown in the following illustration.

- When you publish your presentation to the Web, the presentation automatically includes a navigation frame, a slide frame, controls for showing or hiding frames, and a full-screen viewing option.

- Click in a slide title in the navigation frame to display that slide, or use the previous slide and next slide arrows to navigate.

- You can hide the slide titles by clicking the Outline button at the bottom of the navigation frame, or expand the outline to show all text on each slide.

- Click the Full Screen Slide Show button to see each slide in the full screen.

A Web presentation in a browser

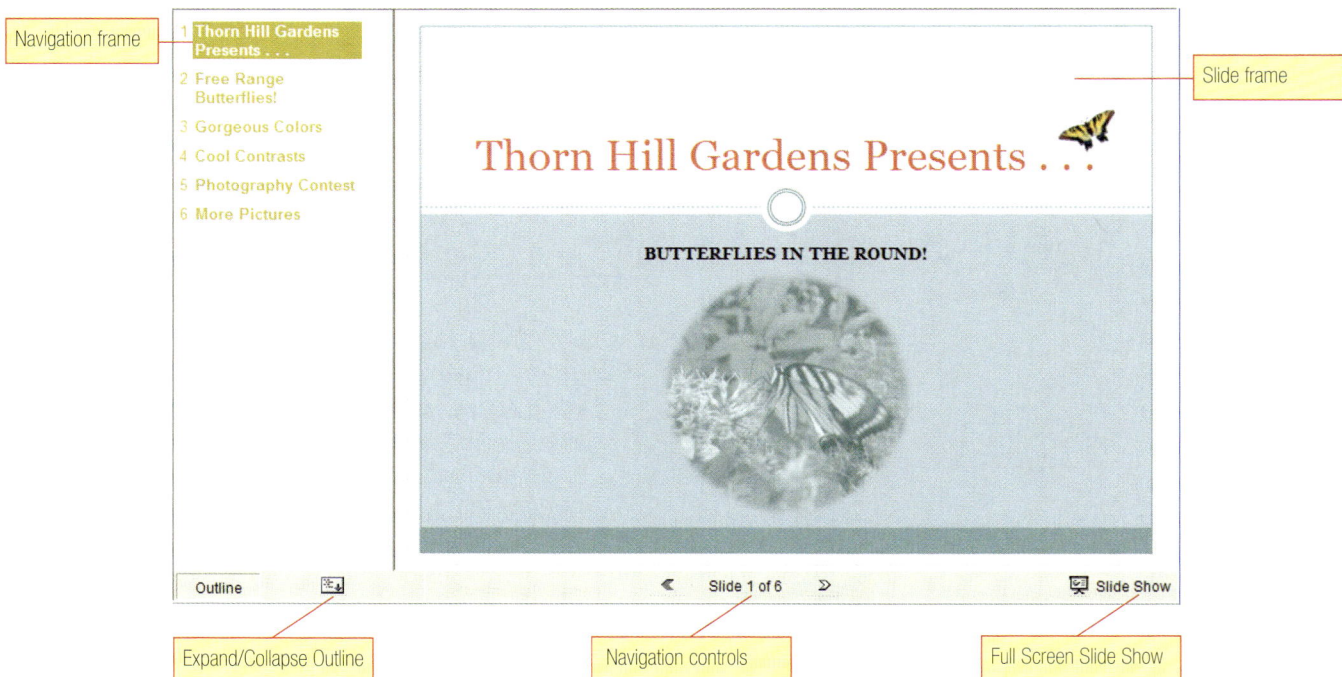

Navigation frame

1 Thorn Hill Gardens Presents . . .
2 Free Range Butterflies!
3 Gorgeous Colors
4 Cool Contrasts
5 Photography Contest
6 More Pictures

Slide frame

Thorn Hill Gardens Presents . . .

BUTTERFLIES IN THE ROUND!

Outline

Expand/Collapse Outline

Slide 1 of 6

Navigation controls

Slide Show

Full Screen Slide Show

PROCEDURES

Save a Presentation as a Web Site

1. Open the presentation to save as a Web site.
2. Click **Office Button** 🪟 . . . Alt + F
3. Click **Save As** . . . . A
4. Type a different name for the file if desired.
5. Click **Save as type** . . . . . . Alt + T
6. Select **Single File Web Page (*.mht; *.mhtml)** or **Web Page (*.htm; *.html)** . . . . ↓ , Enter
7. Change page title if desired:
   a. Click **Change Title** . . Alt + C
   b. Type new page title.
   c. Click **OK** . . . . Enter
8. Click **Save** . . . . Alt + S

Specify Publishing Options

1. Follow steps 1–7 in previous procedure.
2. Click **Publish** . . . . Alt + P
3. Select desired options in the Publish as Web Page dialog box.
4. Specify additional options:
   a. Click **Web Options** . . . . Alt + W
   b. Click each tab in Web Options dialog box to select options.
   c. Click **OK** . . . . Enter
5. Click **Publish** . . . . Alt + P

View a Web Presentation

1. Open the presentation in your browser.
2. Click a slide title in the navigation frame to advance to that slide.

   OR

   Click the **Next Slide** or **Previous Slide** button below the slide frame.
3. Click the **Outline** button to show or hide the navigation frame.
4. Click the **Collapse/Expand Outline** button 📑 to show or hide bullet items below each slide title in the outline.
5. Click the **Full Screen Slide Show** button 📽️ to display the slides in the full browser screen.

EXERCISE DIRECTIONS

1. Start PowerPoint and open 💿 **21BUTTERFLY**. Save the presentation as **21BUTTERFLY_xx**.
2. In reviewing the slides before publishing, you notice that slides 3 and 4 are out of place. Select and cut the slides and then paste them at the end of the presentation.
3. Apply animation effects of your choice to the pictures on slides 5 and 6 and the action button on slide 5.
4. Save the presentation as a Web Page in the location where you are saving other PowerPoint presentations with the name **21BUTTERFLY_WEB_xx**. Change the title to **Annual Butterfly Show**. Click Publish in the Save As dialog box to set the following publishing options:
   a. Click the Web Options button and display the General tab. In the Colors list, select Presentation colors (accent color). Choose to show slide animation while browsing.
   b. Click the Browsers tab. On the *People who view this web page will be using* list, choose Microsoft Internet Explorer 6 or later.
   c. Click OK, and then choose to open the published page in the browser.
5. Click the Publish button to convert the file and open it in your browser.
6. If necessary, right-click the message bar in Internet Explorer and click Allow Blocked Content. Click Yes to confirm. Your presentation should look similar to Illustration A when it opens.
7. Navigate through the slides using the outline or navigation buttons, checking the link and the action button.
8. Expand the outline, then hide the outline. Restore the outline and collapse it.
9. View the presentation in the full browser window. Right-click any slide and click End Show to stop the full-screen version.
10. Close the Web site and your browser.
11. Save and close the **21BUTTERFLY_xx** presentation and exit PowerPoint.

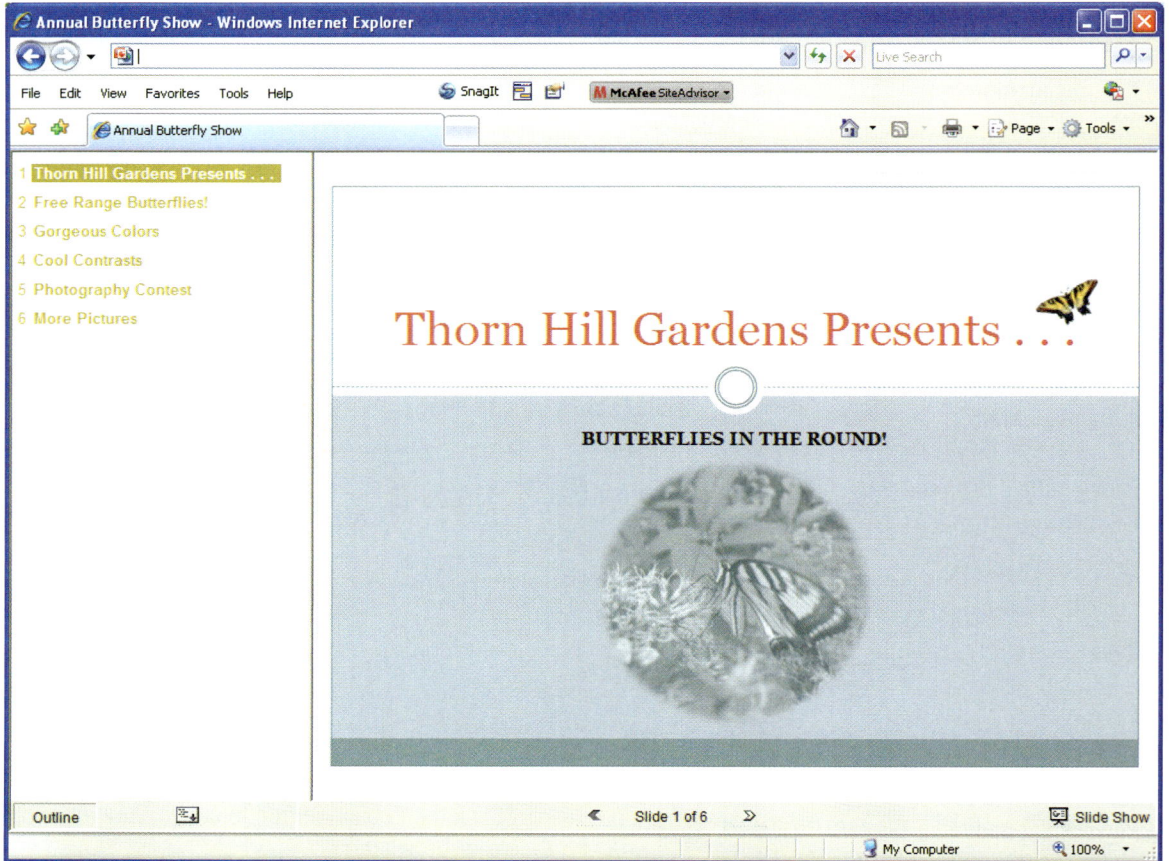

ON YOUR OWN

This exercise challenges you to do some troubleshooting and problem-solving. When you first view the Web site created in step 2, you will probably see effects you do not like. Modify the presentation and resave the Web presentation until you achieve good-looking results. The steps below will give you some hints.

1. Start PowerPoint and open ⊙ **21EARTH**. Save the presentation as **OPP21_xx**.

2. Save the presentation as a Web Page with the name **OPP21_WEB_xx**, supplying an appropriate page title and using other publishing options of your choice. Illustration A shows one option for Web display settings.

   ✓ *Don't worry if your slide titles do not display in the contents frame.*

3. Publish the presentation. View the presentation and make a list of problems you see. You may consider these changes:

   a. On slide 1, if you see a heavy border around text in the slide title, it might be caused by the animation effect.

   b. On slide 6, the heavy shadow behind the logo might be caused by the current animation effect; consider trying another effect. You may also want to remove the shadow effect from the picture in the right content placeholder.

   c. On slide 7, the text boxes containing the monthly totals may look better with no transparency applied and unanimated.

   d. On slide 8, the pointing arrow may look better without a shadow effect and animation applied.

4. Make any other changes to animation settings you think will improve the presentation. You can use the File > Edit with Microsoft Office PowerPoint command in your browser to open the presentation in PowerPoint for editing.

5. When you are happy with the look of the Web presentation, close the Web site and the browser.

6. Save any changes you have made to **OPP21_xx** and exit PowerPoint.

Illustration A

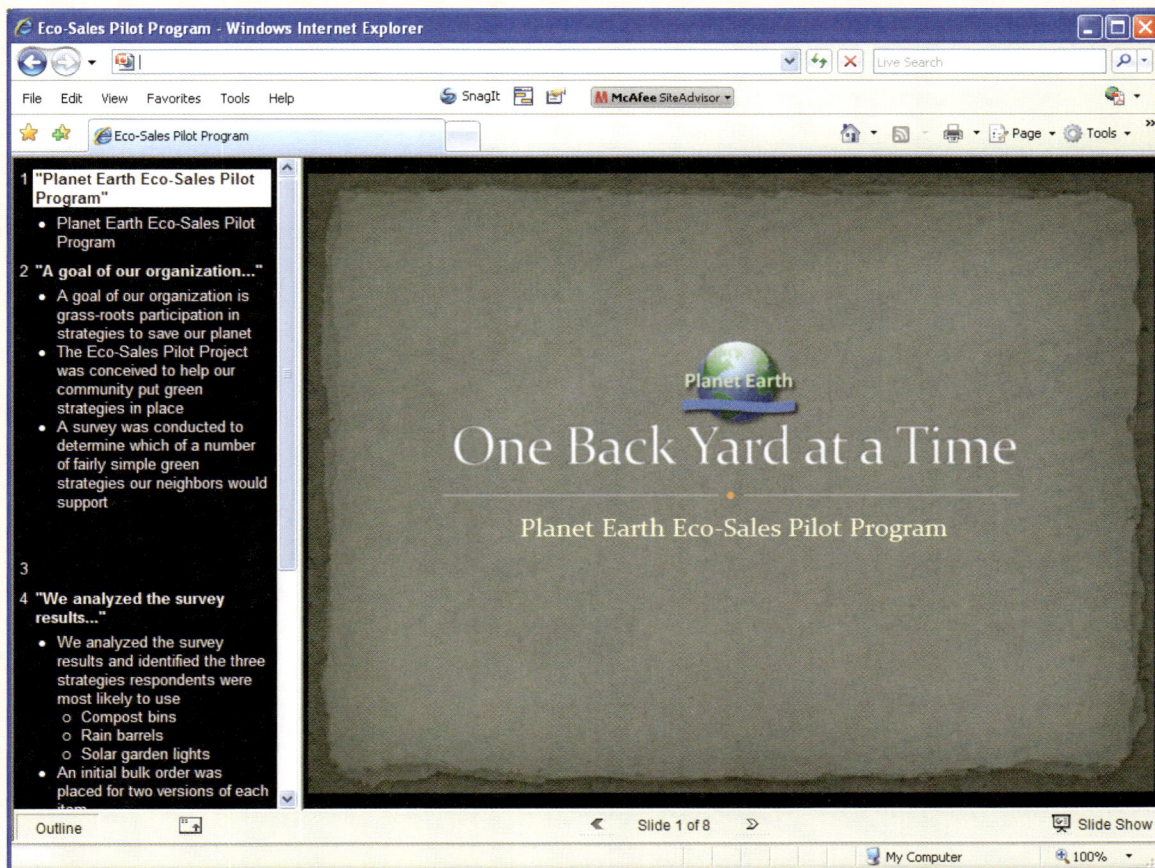

Critical Thinking

Application Skills   Voyager Travel Adventures is preparing a presentation on their newest adventure location, Glacier National Park. In this exercise, you complete some final tasks on the presentation, including creating animations, inserting links, adding action buttons, adding comments, making final checks of document content, and adding security options.

EXERCISE DIRECTIONS

1. Start PowerPoint and open 💿 **22VOYAGER**. Save the presentation as **22VOYAGER_xx**. Then open the presentation 💿 **22GLACIER_ALBUM** and the Word document 💿 **22GLACIER_PACKAGES** and save both files in your solutions folder as **22GLACIER_ALBUM_xx** and **22GLACIER_PACKAGES_xx**, respectively.

2. On slide 1 of **22VOYAGER_xx**, add a comment to your supervisor, Jan Weeks, letting her know the presentation is a draft that you will finalize when all information is in. Change the properties of the presentation to insert your name as the author.

3. Display slide 2 and create a link from the phrase *Web cams* in the last bullet item to **http://www.nps.gov/glac/photosmultimedia/webcams.htm**.

4. Still on slide 2, insert actions as follows:

   a. Create a text box in the lower-right corner with the text **A brief look at . . .** Add an action setting to the text box that links to the **22GLACIER_PACKAGES_xx** file in your solution folder.

   b. Draw a Custom action button about the same size as the text box and use the Mouse Over tab in the Action Settings dialog box to link to the **22GLACIER_ALBUM_xx** presentation.

   c. Format the text button and action button as desired, and position the action button behind and slightly below the text box, so that you can easily rest the mouse pointer on it during the presentation.

5. On slide 3, apply an entrance animation effect of your choice to the SmartArt diagram. Use the timeline to create delays as necessary to adjust the appearance of each element.

6. On slide 4, insert a sound file from the Clip Organizer of a train. Set the sound to play across slides if it is fairly long.

7. On slide 6, insert all of the 💿 **22FLORA** images from the data files. Adjust sizes and apply a picture format as desired, and then create a pleasing layout for the images. Illustration A shows one option. Animate the pictures so they appear one by one in a random order.

   ✓ You may crop images as desired to change their shape.

8. On slide 7, choose at least five of the 💿 **22FAUNA** images from the data files. Adjust sizes and apply a picture format as desired. Stack the images so they are centered on each other in the middle of the slide, and then use motion path settings to move each picture to a new location on the slide.

   ✓ Use the Selection pane to hide each image after you apply its motion path so you can work with the next image in the stack. To open the Selection pane, with an image selected, click the Picture Tools Format tab and then click Selection Pane in the Arrange group. You may want to give each picture a name in the Selection Pane by double-clicking the default Picture name and keying a new name.

9. On slide 8, apply emphasis or exit animation to the text.

10. Run the presentation to test your animations and links. Close the browser after testing the Web cams link; close Word after viewing the packages document; play the album slide show all the way through and then end it to return to your main presentation.

11. Apply the password **glacier1** to the presentation and then send the presentation to your instructor.

12. Choose to use hardware graphics acceleration and adjust the resolution as desired so the presentation is good quality without being too slow.

13. You may need to save this presentation in an earlier format. Run the Compatibility Checker and take notes on what formats you might have to change before saving in 97-2003 format.

14. Compress all pictures in the presentation to Screen resolution. Then run the Document Inspector to remove all comments and personal information. Remove the password.

15. Save the presentation as a PowerPoint Show with the name **22VOYAGERSHOW_xx**.

16. Close the presentation and exit PowerPoint.

Illustration A

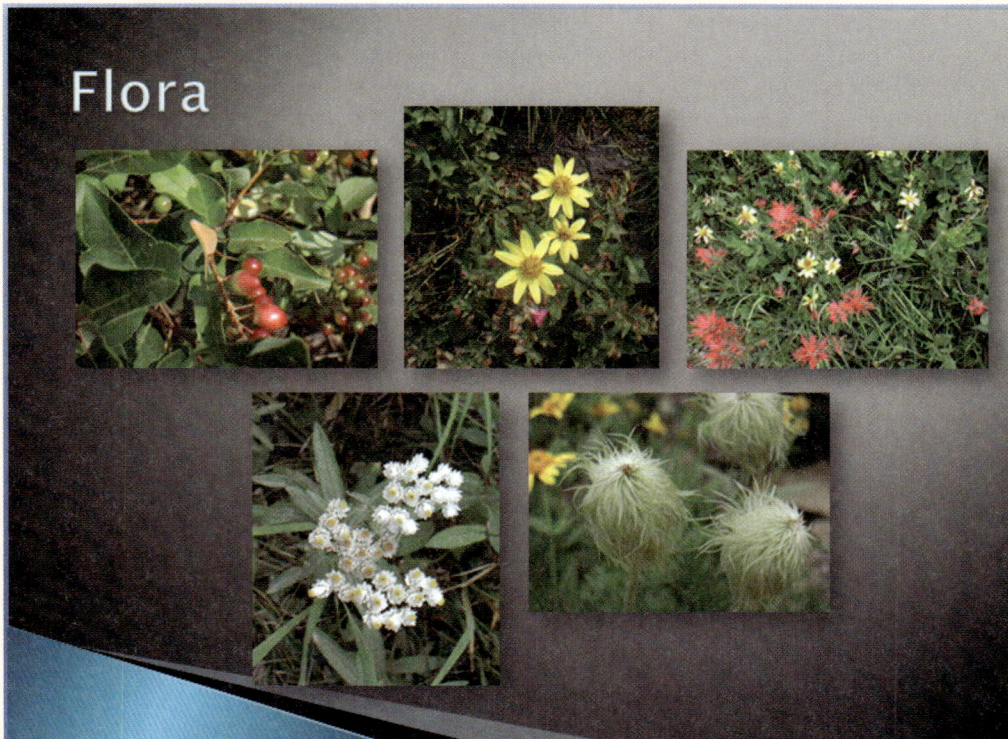

Curriculum Integration

Application Skills   Your English Literature class is about to begin a unit on Shakespeare's plays. To get the class in the mood, your instructor has asked you to prepare a presentation that lists some famous quotes and common sayings that can be found in Shakespeare's plays. To add interest, you will create the presentation in the form of a quiz to challenge students to guess which plays the quotes come from. Before you begin, locate:

■ A picture of Shakespeare that you can download and save to your computer.

■ A good dictionary of quotations.

■ Information on Shakespeare's contributions to the English language, if desired.

EXERCISE DIRECTIONS

Begin a new presentation. You may use a blank presentation or use one of PowerPoint's online presentation templates. Save the presentation with an appropriate name, such as **23SHAKESPEARE_xx**. Insert an appropriate title and subtitle on the first slide.

Create an introductory slide that gives some information on Shakespeare's contributions to English language and literature. Place the picture of Shakespeare on this page and format as desired.

Use the dictionary of quotations to identify a number of quotes that are familiar to you, or familiar sayings. Divide the quotations by the type of play: histories, comedies, and tragedies. If necessary, look up how Shakespeare's plays are assigned to these categories online or in a volume of Shakespeare's plays.

Modify the slide masters if desired to set up a main frame that will contain the quote, allowing room on the right for the names of plays and on the left for buttons you will use as triggers to identify the correct play. Illustration A shows one arrangement.

Place your quotes on three slides, one each for history, comedy, and tragedy. Add answer buttons for each quote and text boxes that contain the names of the plays from which the quotes are taken, arranged in alphabetical order. Align and distribute the quotes, buttons, and text boxes to space them evenly on the slides.

Set up animations so that when a viewer clicks the answer button to the left of the quote, the text box containing the correct play title blinks three times.

If you have the capability to add narration, use narration to explain on slide 3 how to use the answer buttons to trigger the correct answer. Test the presentation to check your triggers.

Set up the presentation to be browsed by an individual, and show the scrollbar. Then save the presentation as **23SHAKESPEARE_WEB_xx** and publish it with appropriate settings. Make any changes to the Web presentation necessary to improve its appearance in the browser.

Save changes to the presentation and close it. Exit PowerPoint.

Illustration A

Challenge Exercises

Exercise 1

- Link a Worksheet into a Word Document
- Locate Data on the Internet
- Edit an Excel Worksheet
- Update a Linked Object in a Word Document

Exercise 2

- Save a Word Document as a Web Page
- Insert Graphics on a Web Page
- Link Excel Data with a Web Page
- Update Linked Data

Exercise 3

- Use an Access Database as a Merge Data Source
- Change the Data Source for a Merge

Exercise 4

- Locate Data on the Internet
- Copy Data from a Web Page to a Word Document
- Send a Word Document as an E-Mail Attachment
- Create a Presentation
- Create Presentation Handouts
- Deliver a Presentation

Exercise 5

- Create a PowerPoint Presentation from a Word Outline
- Generate Presentation Handouts with Word

Exercise 6

- Use a Resume Template
- Create an Access Database
- Merge an Access Database with Word to Create a Directory

Exercise 7

- Plan a Team Project
- Write a Research Report
- Prepare a Presentation
- Create Presentation Handouts
- Deliver a Presentation

Exercise 8

- Use Smart Tags to Locate Financial Data on the Internet
- Copy Data from the Internet into an Excel Worksheet
- Use Excel Worksheet Data to Create a Word Table
- Attach a Word Document to an E-Mail Message

Exercise 9

- Import Data from Excel into Word
- Import Data from Access into Word

Exercise 10

- Use Newsletter Formatting
- Insert and Format Clip Art
- Insert and Format Text Boxes
- Insert and Format WordArt
- Insert and Format a Chart
- Copy Excel Data to a Word Document
- Format a Table

Skills Covered

Application Skills   You have been asked to organize a four-day trip to the Botanical Gardens in Montreal, Canada, for the Horticultural Shop Owners Association. You have an Excel worksheet listing lodging costs in Canadian dollars. In this exercise, you will link the worksheet to a Word memo, use the Research tool to locate current exchange rates on the Web, and then edit the Excel worksheet to convert the costs to U.S. dollars. Finally, you will update the link to the Word document and format the data in Word.

If you do not have a live connection to the Internet, a Web page file with a currency exchange table is provided for use in this exercise.

EXERCISE DIRECTIONS

1. Start Word, if necessary, open 🔘 **01TRIP**, and save the file as **01TRIP_xx**.

2. Start Excel, open the workbook 🔘 **01COSTS**, and save the file as **01COSTS_xx**.

3. Copy the range A1:D10 to the Clipboard.

4. Switch back to Word and link the worksheet object on to the last line of the **01TRIP_xx** document.

5. Set the link for manual updating.

6. Use the Research tool to search for Web site pages with current currency exchange rates (such as www.x-rates.com). Alternatively, open the Web page file 🔘 **01EXCHANGE** in Internet Explorer.

7. Locate the exchange rate for the number of Canadian dollars per one U.S dollar, and copy it to the Clipboard.

   ✓ *Be careful to copy only the exchange rate with no additional spaces before it or after it. If you copy additional spaces, you may see an error in the Excel worksheet when you paste the data. If so, delete the data from the cell and try again.*

8. Switch to the **01COSTS_xx** worksheet in Excel.

9. Paste the data from the Clipboard into cell C5, then copy it to cells C6:C8.

10. Disconnect from the Internet, if necessary.

11. In the **01COSTS_xx** worksheet, create a formula in cell D5 to calculate the current cost in U.S. dollars of lodging in a four-star hotel.

    ✓ *Hint: Divide the cost in Canadian dollars by the exchange rate.*

12. Copy the formula to cells D6:D8.

13. Apply the Accent2 cell style to cells A1:D2 and the 20% Accent2 cell style to cells A3:D10.

14. Save the changes to the Excel workbook.

15. Switch to the **01TRIP_xx** document in Word and update the link.

16. Center the object horizontally.

17. Check the spelling and grammar in the document.

18. Preview the document. If should look similar to Illustration A.

19. Save and close all open documents and exit all open applications.

Illustration A

MEMORANDUM

To: Ms. Knowlton
From: Your Name
Date: Today's Date
Re: Current Lodging Costs in Montreal

I received the lodging costs from the travel official in Montreal, but they were in Canadian dollars. I converted them to U.S. dollars based on today's rates. Of course there's no guarantee that the exchange rate will be the same in June. I'll update the worksheet information on a regular basis, which will keep the information in this memo up to date, too.

Lodging Packages; Four Days, Three Nights* Montreal, Canada			
Accommodations	Cost (CAD)	Exchange Rate	Cost (USD)
Four Star	$ 575.00	0.978473	$ 587.65
Three Star	$ 515.00	0.978473	$ 526.33
Economy	$ 465.00	0.978473	$ 475.23
Budget	$ 350.00	0.978473	$ 357.70

*Rates Based on Double Occupancy

Skills Covered

- **Save a Word Document as a Web Page**
- **Insert Graphics on a Web Page**
- **Link Excel Data with a Web Page**
- **Update Linked Data**

Application Skills   The president of the Horticultural Shop Owners Association wants you to make information about the trip to the botanical gardens in Montreal, Canada, available on the organization's Web site. In this exercise, you will create a Word document about the trip and save it as a Web page. You will locate clip art and insert it on the Web page. You will also link worksheet information about lodging costs to the Web document, so if the conversion rate changes, the information on the Web site will remain current.

EXERCISE DIRECTIONS

1. Start Word, if necessary, open 💿 **02TRIP**, and save the document as a single-file Web page with the title **Botanical Gardens Tour** and the file name **02TRIP_xx**.

2. Apply the Trek theme to the Web page, and apply the Light Yellow, Background 2 color to the page background.

3. Use the Clip Art task pane to locate a suitable clip art image and photo and insert them into the **02TRIP_xx** Web page document. Suitable images might include flowers, plants, gardens, travel, or Montreal.

   ✓ Alternatively, insert the graphics files 💿 **02CITY** and 💿 **02GARDEN** provided with this book.

4. Set the text wrap around both graphics to Square.

5. Resize and position the objects so that in Print Preview the document looks similar to Illustration A. For example, set the alignment for the picture to Top Left, and right-align the photo so it displays to the right of the bulleted list.

6. Save the changes.

7. Start Excel and open the workbook ⌨️ **01COSTS_xx** that you used in Challenge Exercise 1, or open 💿 **02COSTS**. Save the file as **02COSTS_xx**.

8. Apply the Trek theme to the worksheet.

9. Copy the range A1:D10 to the Clipboard.

10. Switch back to the **02TRIP_xx** Web page in Word and link the worksheet object on the last line of the document.

11. Switch back to the **02COSTS_xx** file in Excel.

12. Change the exchange rate in cells C5:C8 to .965.

13. Increase the font size in cells A1:D10 to 14 points, and then adjust the widths of columns B, C, and D as necessary.

14. Switch back to the Web page in Word, and update the link, if necessary.

15. Center the object horizontally on the Web page.

16. Check the spelling and grammar.

17. Preview the Web page document. It should look similar to Illustration A. (Note that in Print Preview, the background page color may not display. If you preview the document in your browser, the background color will display, but the document will not have the same page layout.)

18. Print the document.

19. Save and close all open documents, and exit all open applications.

Illustration A

Tour Montreal's Botanical Gardens

Join members of the Horticultural Shop Owners Association on an exciting trip to beautiful Montreal, Canada!

Please contact Ms. Knowlton at the association for more information.

Highlights include:

- Four days/three nights including transportation and lodging
- Knowledgeable tour guides
- Fine dining
- Magnificent gardens
- Optional sightseeing

Exchange rates are changing daily. The current cost of lodging is listed below:

Lodging Packages; Four Days, Three Nights* Montreal, Canada			
Accommodations	Cost (CAD)	Exchange Rate	Cost (USD)
Four Star	$ 575.00	0.965	$ 595.85
Three Star	$ 515.00	0.965	$ 533.68
Economy	$ 465.00	0.965	$ 481.87
Budget	$ 350.00	0.965	$ 362.69

*Rates Based on Double Occupancy

Exercise | 3

Skills Covered

■ **Use an Access Database as a Merge Data Source**

■ **Change the Data Source for a Merge**

Application Skills You are a store manager for Liberty Blooms. You want to send out mailings to your customers about upcoming sales and events, but you want to customize the mailings for those you know are interested in cut flowers and for those you know are interested in gardening. You have all of the mailing information stored in an Access database. In this exercise, you will create queries in the database that filter out the two groups. You will create a form letter document in Word, and then merge it first with one query and then with the other query. You will use all names in the database to generate envelopes.

EXERCISE DIRECTIONS

1. Open the 💿 **03DATA** Access database, and save a copy of it as **03DATA_xx**.

2. Open the **03DATA_xx** database in Access and create a query named **Cut Flowers** that filters the Addresses table to display only the customers interested in cut flowers.

3. Create a second query named **Gardening** that filters the Addresses table to display only the customers interested in gardening. Exit Access, saving all changes.

4. Start Word, if necessary, create a new blank document, and save it as **03CUTS_xx**.

5. Use Mail Merge to create a form letter that uses the Cut Flowers query in the **03DATA_xx** database as the data source.

6. Type the letter shown in Illustration A, inserting merge fields and merge blocks as necessary. Use a serif font, such as Times New Roman. If necessary, set the line spacing to single and the spacing after paragraphs to 0 points (or use the No Spacing style).

7. Merge all of the letters to a new document and save it as **03CUTLETS_xx**.

8. Check the spelling and grammar in the document, and then print the first letter only.

9. Save the changes to the **03CUTS_xx** document, and then save it as a new document with the name **03GARDEN_xx**.

10. Change the recipient list to use the Gardening query in the **03DATA_xx** database.

11. Merge all of the letters to a new document and save it as **03GARDENLETS_xx**.

12. Check the spelling and grammar in the document, and then print the first letter only.

13. Close all open Word documents, saving all changes.

14. Create a new blank document and save it as **03MAIL_xx**.

15. Use Mail Merge to create envelopes for all of the letters, using the Addresses table in the **03DATA_xx** database as the data source.

    ✓ *You may type your own return address if you want.*

16. Merge the envelopes to a new document, and save it as **03ENV_xx**.

17. Print the first page of the **03ENV_xx** document.

18. Close all open documents, saving all changes.

Illustration A

Today's Date

«AddressBlock»

«GreetingLine»

Great news from Liberty Blooms!

I know how much you love «Interest», so I want to make sure you know about the AMAZING SALE starting next Monday. All of the plants, equipment, and accessories that you need are going to be marked down. There will be bargains like you've never seen before!

So, «FirstName», I expect to see you bright and early next Monday. I know you wouldn't want to miss out on such stupendous savings!

Best regards,

Your Name
Store Manager

P.S. Because I share your enthusiasm for «Interest», bring in this letter and I'll give you an extra 10% off your entire purchase.

Exercise | 4

Skills Covered

- **Locate Data on the Internet**
- **Copy Data from a Web Page to a Word Document**
- **Send a Word Document as an E-Mail Attachment**
- **Create a Presentation**
- **Create Presentation Handouts**
- **Deliver a Presentation**

Application Skills Executive Recruitment Resources, a job search and placement agency, is growing quickly. Until now, employees have worked on standalone desktop computers or on notebook systems that they can take away from the office. You have been asked to research methods of connecting computers into a network, present the options, and make a recommendation for which option would be best. You will use the Internet and other resources to learn about different types of networks. You will use the information you find to write a report describing the options, which you will send as an e-mail attachment. You will then create and deliver a presentation in which you recommend one option.

The solution files for this project are samples, as each student will end up with a different result.

EXERCISE DIRECTIONS

Research the Topic

1. Start Word, create a new document, and save it as **06NETWORK_*xx***.

2. Select a theme and a style set.

3. At the top of the page, enter the title **Computer Networks**.

4. Create a header with your name flush left and the date flush right, and a footer with the page number centered.

5. Start your research by looking up the definition of the term network online or in a library. You can use the Research task pane or a search engine in your browser to search research sites for the keyword network, or use a dictionary or encyclopedia.

   ✓ *Hint: Use the Microsoft Encarta or Webopedia Web site.*

6. Select a reliable Web site with a clear and concise definition, and then copy the definition to the Word document. If there are pictures or illustrations, you may want to copy them as well. Insert citations, or enter the source information in the Source Manager to use to generate a bibliography.

7. Continue your research by locating definitions and/or descriptions of common types of computer networks. Copy the information to your Word document, along with source information. Try to include at least three of the following:

   - Local-area networks (LANs)
   - Wide-area networks (WANs)
   - Campus-area networks (CANs)
   - Metropolitan-area networks (MANs)
   - Home-area networks (HANs)

8. Look up the definition of network topology. Copy the information to your Word document, along with source information. Try to include examples of at least three types of topology, such as bus, star, and ring.

9. Look up the difference between a wired network and a wireless network, and copy the information to your Word document, along with source information.

10. Save the Word document.

Prepare the Report and Send It Via E-Mail

1. Read the information you have in the document. Edit and format the document to create a report that provides information about different types of computer networks in a clear and concise manner. Use complete sentences, proper grammar, and correct spelling. Organize the report into paragraphs. Use bulleted lists or indented paragraphs to identify key points. Include graphics and illustrations if appropriate. Include citations, and insert a bibliography or list of works cited, if necessary.

2. Check the spelling and grammar in the report and make corrections. Ask a classmate to read the report and offer suggestions for improvement. Make the changes and save the document.

3. Display the document in Print Preview. (A sample is shown in Illustration A.) Print the document.

4. Send the document as an attachment to an e-mail message addressed to **mail@exrr.net**.

   ✓ *This is a fictitious e-mail address. Your instructor may ask you to use a different address.*

5. Type the subject **Network Report**, and type the following message: **I have attached a report summarizing my research on the different types of computer networks that are available. Let's set up a time when I can deliver a presentation with a recommendation.** Remember to use proper telecommunications ethics and etiquette.

Create and Deliver a Presentation

1. Use PowerPoint to create a presentation named **04PRES_*xx***. In the presentation, explain your recommendation for the network best suited for Executive Recruitment Resources. Include information from your report. Make the presentation visually appealing by using colors, graphics, transitions, and animations. Keep in mind that you want to use the presentation to convince viewers that your recommendation is correct.

2. Check the spelling and grammar in the presentation and make corrections.

3. Ask a classmate to preview the presentation and offer suggestions. Incorporate the suggestions into the presentation.

4. Practice delivering the presentation to an audience. You might want to prepare speaker's notes to use during the presentation.

5. Make handouts to accompany the presentation.

6. On the day you are to display the presentation, dress appropriately. Conduct yourself in a professional manner. Keep in mind the importance of exhibiting a professional attitude.

7. Deliver your presentation to the class.

8. Watch your classmates' presentations politely. Pay attention so that you can ask them questions.

Business Connection

Teamwork

Teamwork is when two or more people work together to solve a problem or achieve a goal. It involves cooperation, communication, trust, friendliness, and a sense of humor. In business, effective teamwork is essential for success, and someone who cannot function as a member of a team is not likely to be kept around for long. Within each team there is usually a leader who helps direct the team members toward success. The leader may change, depending on the task at hand. Leaders must know how to encourage others, but must also work together with the team.

The Qualities of a Good Team

Select one aspect of teamwork, and write a personal essay about why you think it is important. Set up the document using proper formatting for a one-page report. Include a title, thesis statement, and at least two paragraphs supporting your opinion. When you have completed the report, ask a classmate to read it and offer feedback. Remember to check and correct spelling and grammatical mistakes. Write the topic you selected on a slip of paper and pass it to a classmate. Take a slip from a different classmate. Deliver an impromptu presentation to the class about the topic on the slip of paper you received.

Student's Name

Today's Date

Computer Networks

A computer network is a system used to link two or more computers for the purpose of sharing resources such as files and printers; sending electronic messages; and running programs on other computers. (Scott F. Midkiff 2008) The two most common types of networks are local area networks (LANs) and Wide Area Networks (WANs).

LAN: A network that covers a small area. LANs are typically used in offices, homes, or university campuses. (B. E. Scott F. Midkiff 2008)

WAN: A network that is meant to cover a wide geographic area, usually over telephone lines, as compared to a local area network that operates in a single company or institution. The Internet is an example of a WAN. (Microsoft Corp. 2008)

Home Area Network (HAN): A network contained within a user's home that connects a person's digital devices, from multiple computers and their peripheral devices to telephones, VCRs, televisions, video games, home security systems, "smart" appliances, fax machines and other digital devices. (Jupitermedia Corp. 2008)

Network topology is the actual geometric arrangement of a computer system. (Jupitermedia Corp. 2008). Some common types of LAN topology include ring, token ring, bus, and star.

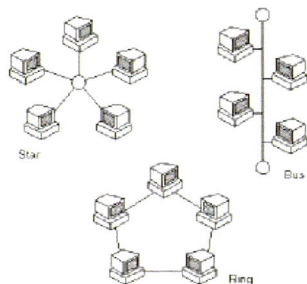

Figure A: Common LAN Topology

Ring Network. A local area network in which devices (nodes) are connected in a closed loop, or ring. (Microsoft Corp. 2008)

Token Ring Network. A local area network formed in a ring (closed loop) topology that uses token passing as a means of regulating traffic on the line. (Microsoft Corp. 2008)

Bus Network. A local area network in which all nodes are connected to a main communications line (bus). (Microsoft Corp. 2008)

Star Network. A local area network in which each node is connected to a central computer in a star-shaped configuration; commonly, a network consisting of a central computer (the hub) surrounded by terminals. (Microsoft Corp. 2008)

A wired network uses wires such as Ethernet cables to connect devices. Wireless networks use radio waves and/or microwaves to create the connections. Many of the same network protocols, like TCP/IP, work in both wired and wireless networks. Some advantages of wireless include mobility and elimination of unsightly cables. Disadvantages of wireless include the potential for radio interference due to weather, other wireless devices, or obstructions like walls. (Mitchell 2008)

A virtual private network (VPN) is a form of WAN that enables remote access to a LAN. A key feature of a VPN is its ability to work over both private networks as well as public networks like the Internet. VPN technology includes various security mechanisms to protect the virtual, private connections. Two benefits of using a VPN are cost savings and ease of use. (Mitchell 2008)

1

Skills Covered

- **Create a PowerPoint Presentation from a Word Outline**
- **Generate Presentation Handouts with Word**

Application Skills   The Horticultural Shop Owners Association wants you to create a presentation to use at an informational meeting about the trip to the botanical gardens in Montreal. You will start with a Word outline. You will also use Word to create handouts for the meeting. You will deliver the presentation to your class.

EXERCISE DIRECTIONS

1. Start Word, if necessary, open the file 💿 **05OUT**, and save the document as **05OUT_xx**.

2. Start PowerPoint and save the new blank presentation file as **05PRES_xx**.

3. Use the **05OUT_xx** document to create slides.
   a. On the Home tab in PowerPoint, click the New Slide button.
   b. Click Slides from Outline.
   c. Locate and select the **05OUT_xx** document.
   d. Click Insert.

4. Delete the blank title slide and apply the Title Slide layout to the new slide 1.

5. Apply the Trek theme to the presentation. Reset the slides to display the theme fonts.

6. Apply the Split Horizontal In slide transition at slow speed to all slides in the presentation, set to advance on a mouse click or automatically after 10 seconds.

7. Preview the slide show from the beginning, make corrections or adjustments as necessary, and then save all changes.

8. Publish the presentation as handouts in Word. Select options to paste the slides into the document, and use the layout that displays blank lines to the right of the slides.

9. Save the new Word document as **05HAND_xx**, and apply the Trek theme, to coordinate the handouts with the presentation.

10. Move the insertion point to the beginning of the document and insert a next page section break.

11. On the new first page, type the following lines of text in the Title style, centered horizontally and vertically (substitute your own name for the sample text *Your Name*):

    Horticultural Shop Owners Association
    Annual Garden Tour Presentation Handout
    Draft 1
    Prepared by
    Your Name

12. To improve the appearance of the slide images in the handout, select the middle column of the table and adjust paragraph spacing to leave 6 pts. of space before each paragraph.

13. Create a footer on each page in the document with the page number flush left and today's date flush right.

14. Check the spelling and grammar in the document.

15. Preview the document, two pages at a time; it should look similar to Illustrations A and B.

16. Print the handouts. Close all open documents, saving all changes.

17. On the day you are to display the presentation, dress as if you are attending the informational meeting as a presenter. Conduct yourself in a professional manner as you distribute the handouts and display the presentation.

18. At the conclusion of the presentation discuss with your classmates the importance of exhibiting a professional appearance and a professional attitude.

Illustration A

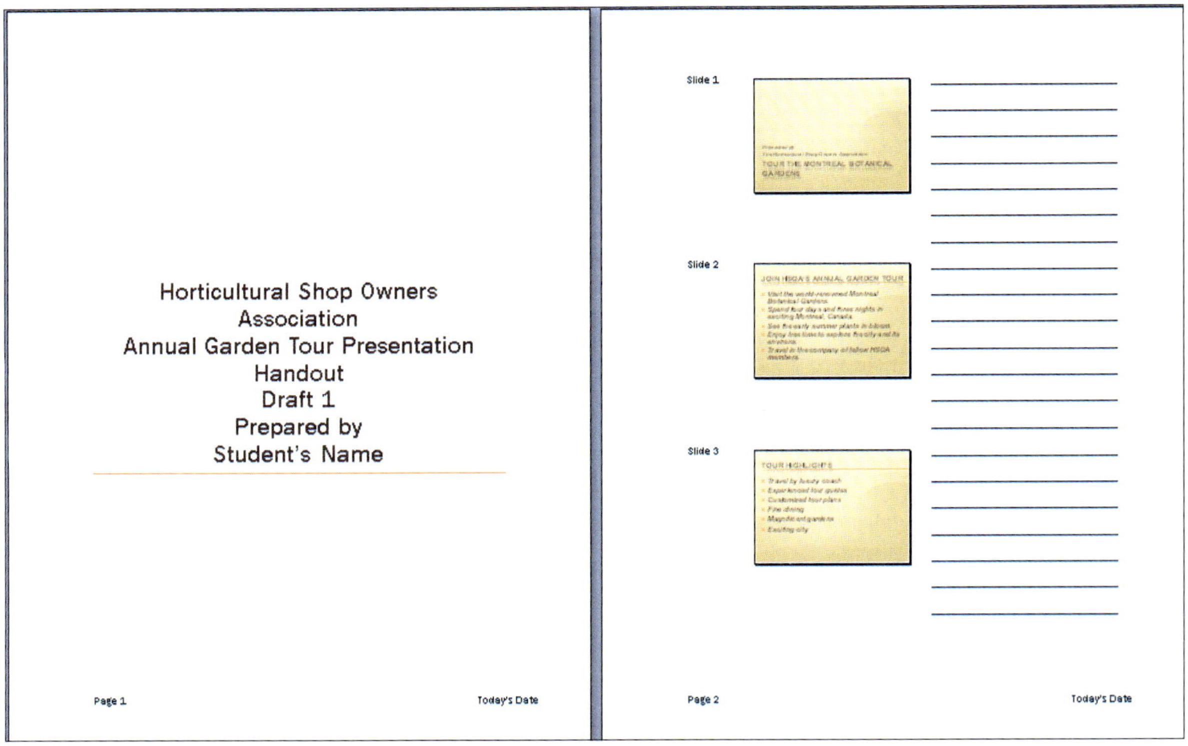

Illustration B

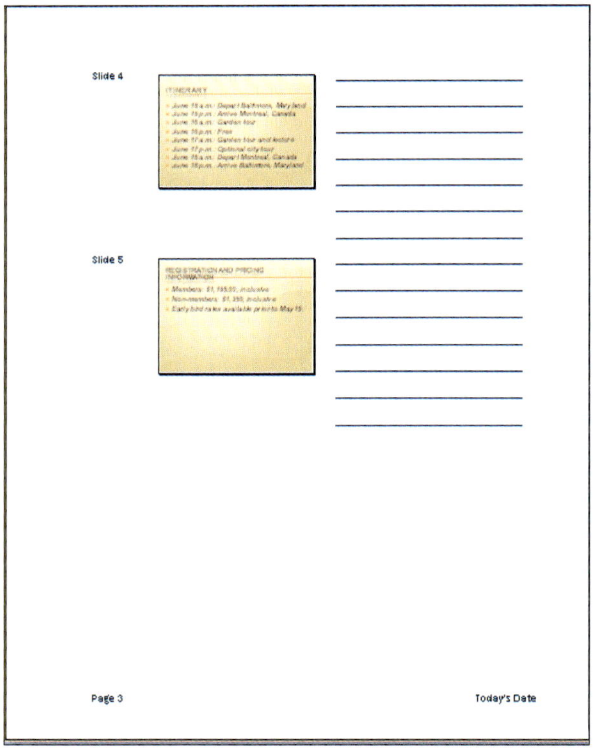

Skills Covered

- **Use a Resume Template**
- **Create an Access Database**

- **Merge an Access Database with Word to Create a Directory**

Application Skills   Your supervisor at Executive Recruitment Resources has been promoted, leaving her position vacant. You would like to apply for the job. You need to update your resume and compile a list of references to submit with your application. In this exercise, you will use a Word template to create a resume. You will enter reference information in an Access database file, and then merge the database with a Word document to create a directory list. To complete this exercise, you will use your own experience and references so that you can add the documents to your employment portfolio.

The solution files for this exercise are samples, as each student will create personalized documents.

EXERCISE DIRECTIONS

Create a Resume Based on a Template

1. Start Word, if necessary, and create a new document based on a basic resume template. You may select any template you like. Alternatively, if you have an existing resume document, open that document. Save the file as **06RESUME_xx**.

   ✓ *In the New Document dialog box, select Resumes and CVs under Microsoft Office Online, and then click Basic to display the available templates. If you cannot access the templates online, use the ⊙ **06RESUME** template file supplied with the data files for this book.*

2. Fill in the data to complete the resume document. Be as accurate as possible, including dates and company names where appropriate. Add or delete bullet items, as necessary. Include volunteer activities as well as any awards or special achievements. You may even want to change the headings to suit your own accomplishments. Delete any placeholders that you do not use.

3. When you have filled in the resume, check the spelling and grammar and make corrections.

4. Display the document in Print Preview. (A sample is shown in Illustration A.) It is best if the document fits on a single page. Make adjustments in spacing and font size, if necessary.

5. Ask a classmate to review the resume and to offer comments and suggestions. Incorporate the suggestions into the document.

6. Check the spelling and grammar again, display the document in Print Preview, and then print the resume.

Compile a Database of References

1. Think about the people you would like to use as references. A reference is usually someone who knows your work ethics, attitude toward responsibility, and personality. Some might be employers or supervisors, some might be teachers, instructors, or school administrators, and some might be personal acquaintances.

2. Start Access and create a new database file named **06REFER_xx**.

3. Create a table named **Contacts.**

4. Create fields and enter records for at least five references. Include the first and last name of the reference, the company name, the phone number, the e-mail address, and the mailing address for each employer reference. Also include a field where you can identify the type of reference, such as employer, friend, teacher, or counselor. You may have multiple references from the same company.

5. Check the spelling in the table.

6. Exit Access.

Use Merge to Create a List of References

1. Start Word, if necessary, create a new blank document, and save it as 06LIST_*xx*.

2. Insert a header with your name flush left and today's date flush right.

3. Use Merge to set up a directory, using the Contacts table in the 06REFER_*xx* database as the data source.

4. In the directory, include the title, first name, last name, company, phone, and e-mail information for each reference.

5. Format the information in the directory so it is easy to read.

6. Merge the directory to a new document, including all records. Save the document as 06DIRECTORY_*xx*.

7. At the top of the document enter the title **Reference Sheet**.

8. Display the document in Print Preview. (A sample is shown in Illustration B.) Print the document.

9. Close all documents, saving all changes, and exit all open programs.

10. Add the resume document and the list of references to your employment portfolio.

Illustration A

Student's Name

Sample Street, Sample City, State 00000. 555-555-5555. sname@mail.net

Objective
To obtain a position of responsibility in which I can use my communications skills.

Experience
Assistant
10/08 – present Executive Recruitment Resources, Inc., Phoenix, AZ
- Create documents with Microsoft Office Word 2007
- Create spreadsheets with Microsoft Office Excel 2007
- Create presentations with Microsoft Office PowerPoint 2007
- Create database files with Microsoft Office Access 2007

Intern
7/08 – 10/08 Executive Recruitment Resources, Inc., Phoenix, AZ
- Copy documents
- Back up files
- Answer phones

Volunteer
2/08 – present Humane Society, Phoenix, AZ
- Walk dogs
- Clean litter boxes
- Answer phones

News carrier
6/05 – 7/08 Daily News, Phoenix, AZ
- Delivered daily newspapers
- Maintained customer list
- Collected payments

Education
State University, Phoenix, AZ
8/06 – present
- Marketing Major/History Minor
- GPA: 3.42
- Dean's List

Interests
- Member of Business Association
- Member of Business Team
- Accomplished user of Microsoft Office 2007 suite of programs
- Skiing, hiking, running, reading, traveling

References
References are available on request.

Illustration B

Student's Name   Today's Date

Reference Sheet

Name: Mr. James Shepherdson
Company: Executive Recruitment Resources, Inc.
Phone: 602-555-6325
E-Mail: jjshep@errinc.net

Name: Ms. Marie Aucoin
Company: High School
Phone: 602-555-5555
E-Mail: maucoin@school.net

Name: Mr. Antoine Shields
Company: Executive Recruitment Resources, Inc
Phone: 602-555-6325
E-Mail: ashields@errinc.net

Name: Mr. Bernard Baker
Company: Humane Society
Phone: 602-555-5555
E-Mail: bbaker@azspca.net

Name: Ms. Lynne Denning
Company: Business Association
Phone: 602-555-5551
E-Mail: ldening@unicollege.net

Skills Covered

- **Plan a Team Project**
- **Write a Research Report**
- **Prepare a Presentation**
- **Create Presentation Handouts**
- **Deliver a Presentation**

Application Skills   Liberty Blooms Flower Shop has asked you to be part of a team that is researching ways that the shop could use the Internet to improve business. In this exercise, you will work in a group to learn about how retail stores such as flower shops can benefit from using the World Wide Web. You will also learn about potential pitfalls. You will store your information in spreadsheets, database files, and documents. You will use the information you have gathered to write a report that presents and supports a recommendation for the business. You will include illustrations such as charts, tables, and pictures. You will create a presentation to accompany your report, which you will deliver to your class.

There are no sample solution files for this project, as each team will end up with a different result.

EXERCISE DIRECTIONS

The Planning Stage

1. Meet as a group to discuss the project and decide the approach you want to take. Keep in mind that the goal of the project is to find ways to use the Web to improve business.

2. Agree on a main thesis. Some ideas to consider include:
   - What makes an effective Web site?
   - Should online shopping be used in place of or in addition to in-store shopping?
   - How can a retailer advertise on the Web?

3. Decide what sources you will use to gather the information you need. You might use the Internet or a library, or you might contact retailers directly to ask them about their experiences.

4. Set goals for the team as a whole.

5. Set individual goals so each team member understands his or her responsibility. You must decide how the work will be divided. For example, will all team members be involved in research? If so, one member might be responsible for research on the Internet, and another might be responsible for research at the library. Or, one might look for information about benefits of the Internet, and another might look for pitfalls. Another approach is to have each team member responsible for a different aspect of the project. For example, one might be responsible for managing and organizing the project, two might handle the research, and someone else might type the report.

6. Create a schedule, including deadlines for each important milestone, such as when all research must be complete and when a draft of the typed report must be complete. Include meeting dates when you can all get together to review your progress and discuss your findings.

7. Agree on the way to record source information so you have it available to include in the one-page report.

8. When the planning and organization are complete, begin the project.

Research and Write the Report

1. Work together to complete the research, and meet regularly to discuss your results.

2. Organize the information that you gather into files, using descriptive file names. For example, store data in an Excel workbook or Access database and store text notes in Word documents. If you find multimedia files such as pictures, sounds, or video, store them in a folder or on a removable storage device so that you can use them when you create your presentation. You may want to log information about each file in an Access database.

3. When you feel that as a group you have enough information to begin a report, use Word to create the document, using the file name 07REPORT_*xx*. You may want to start with an outline. Format the report correctly, including margins, headings, headers or footers, and footnotes or endnotes, or citations as necessary. Include information explaining what you have learned, including how other businesses use the Web. Present your recommendation and the facts to support it. Include illustrations such as charts and tables that you create using the data you have gathered and stored in files.

4. When the report is complete, check the spelling and grammar.

5. Ask someone in a different group to proofread the document and offer suggestions for ways to improve it.

6. Make changes and corrections as necessary.

7. Display the document in Print Preview, and then print it.

The Presentation

1. Use PowerPoint to create a presentation named 07PRES_*xx* that supports your report. Make the presentation visually appealing by using colors, graphics, transitions, and animations. Keep in mind that you want to use the presentation to convince viewers that your recommendation is correct. Preview the presentation and make corrections and adjustments as necessary.

2. Discuss as a team how you will deliver the presentation. Agree on who will be responsible for the technical aspects, such as setting up and showing the presentation, and who will be responsible for speaking. Prepare to answer questions that the class might have.

3. Practice delivering the presentation to an audience. Prepare speaker's notes to use during the presentation.

4. Make handouts to accompany the presentation.

5. On the day you are to display the presentation, dress appropriately. Conduct yourself in a professional manner. Keep in mind the importance of exhibiting a professional attitude.

6. Deliver your presentation to the other teams.

7. Watch the other teams' presentations politely. Pay attention so that you can ask them questions.

Exercise | 8

Skills Covered

- **Use Smart Tags to Locate Financial Data on the Internet**
- **Copy Data from the Internet into an Excel Worksheet**
- **Use Excel Worksheet Data to Create a Word Table**
- **Attach a Word Document to an E-Mail Message**

Application Skills   A group of employees at Long Shot, Inc. has formed an investment club. As the club treasurer, you have been tracking the portfolio. You believe it is time to sell some stock in order to spread the investments into other market segments. In this exercise, you will use smart tags to access the Internet to look up the current trading prices of the stocks. You will copy the information into an Excel worksheet you have already prepared, then copy the entire worksheet into a Word document. Finally, you will attach the Word document to an e-mail message and send it to the club president.

If you use a live connection, the links and data may not be quite the same as those used in the exercise steps, as the information changes frequently. The e-mail address supplied in this exercise is fictitious. If you try to send the message, it will come back as undeliverable. If you have an Internet connection and a mail service provider, your instructor may want you to substitute a real e-mail address.

EXERCISE DIRECTIONS

Collect Data from the Internet

1. Start Microsoft Excel, open the workbook ◉ **08STOCKS**, and save the file as **08STOCKS_xx**.

2. Replace the sample text *Today's Date* with the current date.

3. Enable smart tags, if necessary.

4. Move the mouse pointer over the ticker symbol for Amazon.com.

   ✓ *If smart tags are not displayed in the worksheet, make sure the Label data with smart tags option is selected on the Smart Tags tab of the AutoCorrect Options dialog box, and that all recognizers are selected.*

5. Click the Smart Tag Actions button, and then click Financial symbol on the drop-down menu.

6. On the Actions menu, click Stock quote on MSN MoneyCentral.

7. Sign in to your Internet Service Provider if prompted.

8. On the MoneyCentral stock quote page that is displayed, select the current trading stock price and copy it to the Clipboard.

   ✓ *Be careful to copy only the stock price with no additional spaces before it or after it. If you copy additional spaces, you may see an error in the Excel worksheet when you paste the data. If so, delete the data from the cell and try again.*

9. Switch to the Excel worksheet and paste it into cell F6. If necessary, adjust column widths to display all data.

   ✓ *The worksheet is set up to calculate the current value and the return on investment, and display the results in the appropriate cells.*

10. Repeat steps 4 through 9 to get stock quotes for each company using the ticker symbols in cells B7, B8, and B9, and then copy and paste the data into the appropriate cells in column F.

11. When you have collected all of the data and pasted it into the worksheet, close all open tabs in your browser and close your browser. Save the Excel workbook.

Copy Excel Data to Word

1. Start Word, if necessary, open the document 🔘 **08INVEST**, and save it as **08INVEST_xx**.

2. In the **08STOCKS_xx** worksheet, copy the range A1:H9 to the Clipboard.

3. Close the Excel file, saving all changes, and exit Excel.

4. Switch to the **08INVEST_xx** Word document, and paste the worksheet on the last line of the memo.

5. Apply the Table List 1 style to the table in the Word document.

6. Delete all unnecessary space(s) in the table, such as those before and after the dollar signs in the Original Investment, Value, and Return columns.

7. Adjust column widths as necessary so the data wraps correctly and is easy to read. If necessary, change the font size to 10 points.

8. Merge and center the data in the first two rows, and center the entire table horizontally on the page.

9. Check the spelling and grammar in the document.

10. Preview the Word document. It should look similar to Illustration A.

   ✓ *The current prices will vary.*

11. Print the document.

Send a Word Document as an E-Mail Attachment

1. Send the document as an attachment to an e mail message addressed to **mail@longshotinc.net**.

   ✓ *This is a fictitious e mail address. Your instructor may ask you to use a different address.*

2. Type the subject **Stock Prices**, and type the following message: **Here's the information I promised. Get back to me ASAP – these stocks are volatile and we have to act fast**. Remember to use proper telecommunications ethics and etiquette.

3. Close the **08INVEST_xx** file, saving all changes.

4. Exit all open programs.

Illustration A

MEMORANDUM

To:	Investment Club President
From:	Student's Name
Date:	Today's Date
Subject:	Current Portfolio Value

I have prepared an analysis of our current portfolio. We are holding our own, which is great considering the current market. I suggest taking a loss on the pharmaceuticals, if necessary, and looking into some biotech or agricultural companies. Let me know what you think. There's still time to act before the market closes today. Also, you can use the smart tags in the Ticker Symbol column to check the current stock prices if you want.

Long Shot, Inc.							
Investment Club							
Date:	Today's Date						
Company	Ticker Symbol	Shares Owned	Purchase Price	Original Investment	Last Trade	Value	Return
Amazon.com	AMZN	100	31.45	$3,145.00	**77.57**	$7,757.00	$4,612.00
Cisco Systems, Inc.	CSCO	100	22.33	$2,233.00	**22.38**	$2,238.00	$5.00
Eli Lilly and Company	LLY	100	51.48	$5,148.00	**48.17**	$4,817.00	$(331.00)
Intel Corp	INTC	100	34.48	$3,448.00	**22.13**	$2,213.00	$(1,235.00)

Exercise | 9

Skills Covered

■ **Import Data from Excel into Word**　　　■ **Import Data from Access into Word**

Application Skills　As the Director of Training at Long Shot, Inc., you want to send a memo to the Director of Human Resources with information about three new instructors you would like to hire. You already have their names and addresses stored in an Access database file, and you have information about the courses they will teach in an Excel worksheet file. In this exercise, you import the information from the Excel file and the Access file into a Word memo document.

EXERCISE DIRECTIONS

1. Start Word and Access, if necessary.

2. Open the Access database file ⊙ **09HIRES**. and save a copy as **09HIRES_xx.** Open the New Hires table.

3. Select the three records in the table and copy them to the Clipboard. Close the **09HIRES_xx** database file.

4. Open the Word document ⊙ **09MEMO** and save it as **09MEMO_xx.**

5. Replace the sample text *Your Name* with your own name, and the sample date *Today's date* with the current date.

6. Position the insertion point on the last line of the document.

7. Paste the Access data from the Clipboard into the Word memo.

8. In the **09MEMO_xx** document, delete the first row in the table (New Hires).

9. Delete the three blank columns from the table (Company Name, Address Line 2, and Country).

10. Move the insertion point to the end of the document and insert a blank line.

11. Save the changes to the **09MEMO_xx** document.

12. Open the Excel workbook file ⊙ **09COURSES** and save the file as **09COURSES_xx.**

13. Select the range A2:C8 and copy the selection to the Clipboard.

14. Switch to the **09MEMO_xx** document.

15. Paste the Excel data from the Clipboard on to the last line of the **09MEMO_xx** document.

16. Center the table horizontally on the page.

17. Display the document in Print Preview. It should look similar to Illustration A.

18. Print the document.

19. Close all open programs and documents, saving all changes.

Long Shot, Inc.

INTERDEPARTMENT MEMORANDUM

To: Director of Human Resources
From: Student's Name
Date: Today's date
Re: Training Department Expenses

I have made a decision regarding the hiring of three new instructors for the training department. Below you will find their contact information as well as a schedule detailing the courses I would like them to teach. Please tender their offers as soon as possible. Please give me a call if you have any questions. Thanks.

Title	First Name	Last Name	Address Line 1	City	State	ZIP Code	Home Phone	Work Phone	E-mail Address
Mr.	George	Kaplan	980 Main Street	Ithaca	NY	14850	607-555-1234	607-555-4321	gkaplan@mail.com
Ms.	Patricia	Boyd	65 Blueberry Lane	Ithaca	NY	14850	607-555-5678	607-555-8765	pboyd@mail.com
Mrs.	Hannah	Thompson	3232 Chestnut Street	Ithaca	NY	14850	607-555-9012	607-555-2109	hthomspon@mail.com

COURSE NAME	SESSIONS OFFERED	INSTRUCTOR
Word Processing 1	Fall	H. Thompson
Word Processing 2	Fall	G. Kaplan
Word Processing 3	Winter	G. Kaplan
Using the Internet	Spring	P. Boyd
Database Management	Winter	P. Boyd
Spreadsheet Basics	Spring	H. Thompson

Skills Covered

- **Use Newsletter Formatting**
- **Insert and Format Clip Art**
- **Insert and Format Text Boxes**
- **Insert and Format WordArt**
- **Insert and Format a Chart**
- **Copy Excel Data to a Word Document**
- **Format a Table**

Application Skills Fresh Food Fair has asked you to create a brochure providing information about the new home delivery service. In this exercise, you will create a two-page document that can be printed as a double-sided, three-fold brochure. To set up the document you will use columns, sections, text boxes, and clip art.

You can complete this exercise using Word or a digital design program such as Publisher. If you use a digital design program, you may need to adjust formatting such as font size and spacing to fit the content within the columns.

EXERCISE DIRECTIONS

Set Up the Brochure Document

1. Before creating the document, create a mock-up using a blank piece of paper. Hold the paper in "landscape orientation" with the long side at the top, and fold it in thirds. This creates six panels—three on one side of the page and three on the other side of the page. Unfold the paper and label the top of each panel, from left to right as: inside left, inside middle, and inside right. Flip the paper over horizontally and label the top of each panel from left to right as: front, back, and unmarked. When the page is folded correctly, these labels will help you lay out the content in your Word document.

2. Start Word or your digital design program, if necessary, create a new blank document, and save the document as **10BROCHURE_xx**.

   ✓ You may want to use a template for a 3-fold brochure.

3. Change the orientation to landscape.

4. Insert a blank line, and then insert a next page section break. This creates a document with two pages with a blank line on each page. Page 1 will be the outside of the brochure and page 2 will be the inside.

5. Divide both sections into three columns of equal of width.

6. Display text boundaries so you can see the margins for each column. (On the Advanced tab of the Word Options dialog box, select the Show text boundaries check box under Show document content.)

Enter Content for Page 1

1. The left column on page 1 corresponds to the unmarked panel on your mock-up. In this panel, you will enter information about the history of Fresh Food Fair.

   a. In the Heading 1 style, type **History of Fresh Food Fair.**

   b. Press [Enter], increase the font size to 12 points, add 6 points of space before the paragraph, and apply a first-line indent.

   c. Type the following paragraphs:

   Back in 1992, Kimberly and Jack Thompson were looking for a way to deliver the fresh, home-grown produce from their family farm to people living in less rural areas. They brought their merchandise to established grocery stores and discussed distribution, but the only store that was interested was a small, neighborhood market called Food Fair. Food Fair started selling the fresh food in a special section.
   After three successful years, the owner of Food Fair wanted to retire. He offered to sell the market to the Thompsons. In 1996, the market reopened as the first Fresh Food Fair grocery store. The rest, as they say, is history. There are now seven Fresh Food Fair retail outlets and an online store, as well.

   d. Insert a column break.

2. The middle column on page 1 corresponds to the back panel on your mock-up. In this panel you will insert a picture and a text box, in which you will type the store's address information.

a. Use the Clip Art task pane to locate an appropriate photo or drawing, such as a farm or fresh produce, and insert it in the document.

b. Leave the text wrapping set to In Line with text, and size the picture to fit within the text boundaries of the column.

c. Below the picture, insert a text box approximately 1 inch high by 2.5 inches wide and enter the following lines of text, using the No Spacing style:

Fresh Food Fair

"Fresh from Us to You"

Route 117, Bolton, MA 01740

www.freshfoodfair.net

d. Change the first line to 14 point bold. Change the second line to 12 point italic, and center all four lines in the text box.

e. Apply the Compound Outline - Accent 1 Quick Style to the text box.

f. Position the text box in the bottom center with Square text wrapping.

3. Position the insertion point to the left of the page break mark and insert a column break to move the insertion point to the top of the right column. This column corresponds to the front panel on your mock-up. In this panel, you will create two WordArt objects and insert a text box to create the front of the brochure.

a. Create a new WordArt object using the WordArt style 23 style. Enter the text **Fresh Food Fair** using the default font settings.

b. Change the Shape Fill pattern background color to standard Light Green.

c. Change the Shape to Inflate Top.

d. Position the object in the top right keeping the wrapping set to In Line withText.

e. Insert a second WordArt object using the WordArt style 2 style. Enter the text **"Fresh from Us to You"** in 36-point Cambria.

f. Change the fill color to standard Yellow and change the shape to Deflate Top.

g. Leave the text wrapping set to In Line with Text, and make sure the object is positioned below the first WordArt object.

h. Insert a text box approximately 3.75 inches high by 2.5 inches wide below the WordArt and enter the following lines of text, using the No Spacing style:

Introducing

Home

Delivery

Service

A convenient way for you to enjoy the very best we have to offer!

i. Change the font size for the first line and the last paragraph to 20 points. Change the second, third, and fourth lines to 36 points. Center all of the text in the text box.

j. Apply the Diagonal Gradient - Accent 3 Quick Style to the text box.

k. Align the text box vertically with the bottom margin. Position it horizontally 6.5 inches to the right of the margin.

4. Check the spelling and grammar in the document and then save it. Display it in Print Preview. Page 1 should look similar to Illustration A.

Enter Content for Page 2

1. Move the insertion point to the top of page 2. The left column on page 2 corresponds to the inside left panel on your mock-up. In this panel, you will enter information about the home delivery service.

a. In the Heading 1 style, type **Introducing Home Delivery**.

b. Press `Enter`, increase the font size to 12 points, add 6 points of space before the paragraph, and apply a first-line indent.

c. Type the following paragraphs:

Imagine that you no longer have to make multiple trips to the grocery store in order to enjoy fresh, wholesome food every day.
Imagine that you can have groceries delivered to your door without having to load the kids in the minivan, or trek through bad weather.
Imagine not only having the groceries delivered, but having someone carry them directly into your kitchen for you.
Imagine no more! The reality is here! Fresh Food Fair is pleased to announce our new home delivery service, designed to make life easier for the busy 21st century family.
Take a test drive today to find out how wonderful home delivery can be.

d. Insert a column break.

2. The middle column on page 2 corresponds to the inside middle panel on your mock-up. In this panel, you will insert a pie chart showing the results of a survey asking whether customers wanted home delivery service.

   a. Insert a pie chart and enter the following data in the chart worksheet. Delete the content you do not need, and resize the chart data range to fit the entered data only. Minimize the worksheet.

	No	Maybe	Yes	Don't Know
Responses	10	16	71	3

   b. Switch the rows and columns to properly display the chart. Edit the chart title to **Would You Use Home Delivery?** and change the font size to 11 points.

   c. Insert a new line after the chart. In the Heading 1 style, type **You Spoke. We Listened**, and center it horizontally.

   d. Press [Enter], increase the font size to 12 points, add 6 points of space before the paragraph, and apply a first-line indent.

   e. Type the following paragraphs:

   You—our valued customers—overwhelmingly responded to our survey with a resounding Yes! You would use home delivery if it was available. A whopping 71% of you said you would use home delivery, and a mere 10% said you were not interested at all. We listened, and home delivery is here. We hope you like it as much as we think you will.

   f. Press [Enter] and then insert a column break.

3. The right column on page 2 corresponds to the inside right panel on your mock-up. In this panel, you will insert ordering information already stored in an Excel workbook.

   a. In the Heading 1 style, type **Ordering Informa-tion**, and center it horizontally. Apply formatting to leave 24 pts. of space after the paragraph, then press [Enter] to start a new line.

   b. Start Excel, open the workbook 🔵 **10ORDERS**, and save the file as **10ORDERS_xx**.

   c. Copy cells A4:B10 to the Clipboard, and then exit Excel.

   d. Paste the data onto the last line in the right column of the **10BROCHURE_xx** document.

   e. Apply the Medium Grid 1 - Accent 3 style to the table.

   f. Apply an Olive Green Accent 3, 1 point border around the outside of the table.

   g. Adjust the size of the table and the column widths so that the table fits within the text boundaries of the column.

4. Check the spelling and grammar in the document and then save it. Display it in Print Preview. Page 2 should look similar to Illustration A.

Complete and Print the Brochure

1. If you have a printer that can make double-sided copies, print the brochure with page 1 on one side of the sheet and page 2 on the other.

2. If your printer cannot make double-sided copies, print page 1 of the document.

3. Reload the printed document in the printer so that you can print on the other side.

   ✓ *Ask your instructor for information on loading paper into the printer for double-sided printing. On some printers, you insert the printed side down, top first. On other printers, you insert the printed side up. You may want to print a test page using a document containing text only. You can mark the top, bottom, left, and right of the page so you know how to insert it for double-sided printing.*

4. Print page 2 of the document.

5. Fold the sheet of paper in thirds, so the document looks like a three-fold brochure.

6. Ask a classmate to review the brochure and offer comments and suggestions. Incorporate the suggestions into the document, and save the changes.

7. Print and fold a new copy of the brochure.

8. Close all open documents, saving all changes.

Illustration A

History of Fresh Food Fair

Back in 1992, Kimberly and Jack Thompson were looking for a way to deliver the fresh, home-grown produce from their family farm to people living in less rural areas. They brought their merchandise to established grocery stores and discussed distribution, but the only store that was interested was a small, neighborhood market called Food Fair. Food Fair started selling the fresh food in a special section.

After three successful years, the owner of Food Fair wanted to retire. He offered to sell the market to the Thompsons. In 1996, the market reopened as the first Fresh Food Fair grocery store. The rest, as they say, is history. There are now seven Fresh Food Fair retail outlets and an online store, as well.

Fresh Food Fair
"Fresh from Us to You"
Route 117, Bolton, MA 01740
www.freshfoodfair.net

Fresh Food Fair
"Fresh from Us to You"

Introducing
Home Delivery Service
A convenient way for you to enjoy the very best we have to offer!

Illustration B

Introducing Home Delivery

Imagine that you no longer have to make multiple trips to the grocery store in order to enjoy fresh, wholesome food every day.

Imagine that you can have groceries delivered to your door without having to load the kids in the minivan, or trek through bad weather.

Imagine not only having the groceries delivered, but having someone carry them directly into your kitchen for you.

Imagine no more! The reality is here! Fresh Food Fair is pleased to announce our new home delivery service, designed to make life easier for the busy 21st century family.

Take a test drive today to find out how wonderful home delivery can be.

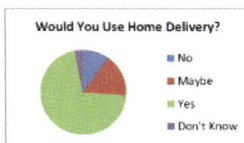

Would You Use Home Delivery?

- No
- Maybe
- Yes
- Don't Know

You Spoke. We Listened.

You—our valued customers—overwhelmingly responded to our survey with a resounding Yes! You would use home delivery if it was available.

A whopping 71% of you said you would use home delivery, and a mere 10% said you were not interested at all. We listened, and home delivery is here. We hope you like it as much as we think you will.

Ordering Information

Cost of products:	As marked
Cost of delivery:	$35.00
Service available:	Monday through Saturday
Hours for ordering:	7:30 a.m. until 5:00 p.m.
Orders placed before 3:00 p.m. will be delivered the same day.	
Orders placed after 3:00 p.m. will be delivered by noon on the following day.	
Products available for home delivery include fresh fruits and vegetables, packaged goods, and dairy. Delivery of meats (including fish and chicken) will be available in the future.	

Index

M

macros. *See also* Excel
  PowerPoint, actions running macros in, 673
margins
  in Access reports, 493
  Excel, setting in, 256, 257
  Word objects, adding to, 99, 100
Mark Citations dialog box, Word, 48
Mark Index Entry dialog box, Word, 39
Master Layout dialog box, PowerPoint, 602
Matrix category, SmartArt, 178
Max function. *See* Access
merging Word document with Access database, 192–193
Microsoft Graph, 534–538
Microsoft Office 2007. *See also* Access; Excel; PowerPoint;
      Word
  multiple programs, running, 159
  multiple windows, arranging, 159–160
  screen elements of, 159
  as software suite, 159
  switching between programs, 161
Microsoft Office Publisher 2007, 3
Microsoft Outlook, 159
MIDI format, 651
Min function. *See* Access
MLA style bibliographies, 46, 48
mouse settings in PowerPoint, 674
movies with PowerPoint, 649–650
MPEG format, 649
MP3 format, 651
multimedia presentations. *See* PowerPoint
multiplication operation in Access, 554

N

Name box, Excel, 208
naming/renaming. *See also* Access; PowerPoint
  Excel folders, 250
narration to PowerPoint presentation, 678–679
Navigation Pane, Access, 478
normalized tables. *See* Access
notes. *See* PowerPoint
NOT function, Excel, 361
numbers. *See* Excel

O

objects. *See* Access; Excel; integration; PowerPoint
Office Clipboard. *See* Clipboard
OneNote, 159
order. *See* Excel
OR function, Excel, 360–361
organization charts, Word, 177, 178
orientation. *See* Access
orphans, Word handling, 2, 4
outlines. *See also* PowerPoint
  Excel, outlines for subtotals in, 343
  Word, outlines around graphics in, 89, 90

P

Page Setup dialog box
  in Access, 493
  Excel, Margins tab in, 257
  Word, Paper tab in, 3
paper size
  in Access, 493
  in Word, 2, 3
Paragraph dialog box
  in PowerPoint, 588
  Word, Line and Page Breaks tab, 4
parameter queries. *See* Access
passim, 46, 48
passwords. *See also* Word
  Excel worksheets, protecting, 407
  for PowerPoint presentations, 683–684
Paste Special command. *See also* Word
  in Excel, 421
Paste Special dialog box
  in PowerPoint, 627
  in Word, 166–167
patterns for Excel cells, 240–241
PDF format
  Access data, exporting, 471–472
  Excel workbook as PDF file, saving, 249–250
pensions, employment packages offering, 20
Permission dialog box
  in Excel, 427–428
  in PowerPoint, 686
permissions. *See* PowerPoint
phishing, Word security tools and, 134, 135
Photo Album dialog box, PowerPoint, 655–657
photo albums. *See* PowerPoint
Picture Corrections Options command, PowerPoint, 643–644
pie charts. *See also* Excel
  Access, creating in, 535
  in Word, 179
PivotTables. *See also* Access
  Excel, preventing changes in, 407
placeholders. *See* PowerPoint
plagiarism, 61, 62
PNG format, 642–643, 693
PowerPoint. *See also* integration; Word
  action buttons, 673
    for Web publishing, 694
  actions, creating, 672, 673–674
  Action Settings dialog box, 673–674
  alignment, 589–590
    of movie objects, 650
    tables, text alignment in, 619
  Analysis group, Chart Tools Layout tab, 634
  animations
    advanced options, 666
    deleting, 669
    editing, 669
    effect options for, 667–668